W9-BJD-510

Rick Steves'

BEST OF EUROPE

2002

Europe

AVALON
TRAVEL

Other ATP travel guidebooks by Rick Steves
Rick Steves' Europe Through the Back Door
Rick Steves' Europe 101: History and Art for the Traveler (with Gene Openshaw)
Rick Steves' Mona Winks: Self-Guided Tours of Europe's Top Museums
   (with Gene Openshaw)
Rick Steves' Postcards from Europe
Rick Steves' France, Belgium & the Netherlands (with Steve Smith)
Rick Steves' Germany, Austria & Switzerland
Rick Steves' Great Britain
Rick Steves' Ireland (with Pat O'Connor)
Rick Steves' Italy
Rick Steves' Scandinavia
Rick Steves' Spain & Portugal
Rick Steves' Florence (with Gene Openshaw)
Rick Steves' London (with Gene Openshaw)
Rick Steves' Paris (with Steve Smith and Gene Openshaw)
Rick Steves' Rome (with Gene Openshaw)
Rick Steves' Venice (with Gene Openshaw)
Rick Steves' Phrase Books: German, French, Italian, Spanish/Portuguese,
   and French/Italian/German

Avalon Travel Publishing, 5855 Beaudry Street, Emeryville, CA 94608

Text copyright © 2002, 2001, 2000, 1999, 1998, 1997, 1996 by Rick Steves
Cover copyright © 2002, 2001 by Avalon Travel Publishing, Inc.
All rights reserved.
Maps copyright © 2002 by Europe Through the Back Door

Printed in the United States of America by R.R. Donnelley
First printing January 2002

For the latest on Rick Steves' lectures, guidebooks, tours, and public
television series, contact Europe Through the Back Door, Box 2009,
Edmonds, WA 98020, tel. 425/771-8303, fax 425/771-0833,
www.ricksteves.com, or e-mail: rick@ricksteves.com.

ISBN: 1-56691-352-7
ISSN: 1096-7702

Europe Through the Back Door Editors: Risa Laib, Jacquie Maupin,
   and Lauren Mills
Avalon Travel Publishing Editor: Kate Willis
Research Assistance: Norman Bell, Carlos Galvin, Cameron Hewitt,
   Richard Karpen, Risa Laib, Jacquie Maupin, and Steve Smith
Production & Typesetting: Kathleen Sparkes, White Hart Design
Design: Linda Braun
Cover Design: Janine Lehmann
Maps: David C. Hoerlein
Cover Photo: Il Duomo (cathedral and temple), Siena, Italy;
   Leo de Wys Inc./Jacobs

Distributed to the book trade by Publishers Group West, Berkeley, California

CONTENTS

Europe's Best Destinations

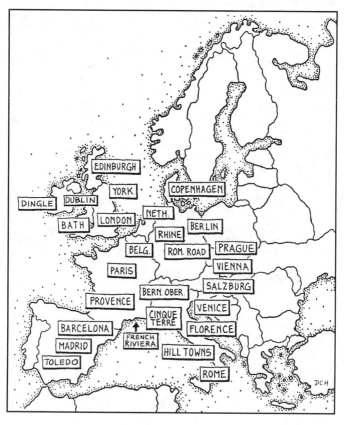

INTRODUCTION

This book breaks Europe into its top big-city, small-town, and rural destinations. It then gives you all the information and opinions necessary to wring the maximum value out of your limited time and money in each of them. If you plan to stay for two months or less in Europe, this lean and mean book is all you need.

Experiencing Europe's culture, people, and natural wonders economically and hassle-free has been my goal for more than 25 years of traveling, tour guiding, and travel writing. With this book, I pass on to you the lessons I've learned, updated for 2002.

Rick Steves' Best of Europe is the crème de la crème of places featured in my Country Guides. This book is balanced to include a comfortable mix of exciting big cities and cozy small towns: from Paris, London, and Rome to traffic-free Italian Riviera ports, alpine villages, and mom-and-pop châteaus. It covers the predictable biggies and mixes in a healthy dose of Back Door intimacy. Along with Leonardo in the Louvre, you'll enjoy Caterina in her Cantina. I've been selective. For example, rather than listing countless castles and hill towns, I recommend the best three or four of each.

The best is, of course, only my opinion. But after more than two decades of travel research, I've developed a sixth sense for what tickles the traveler's fancy.

This Information Is Accurate and Up-to-Date

This book is updated every year. Most publishers of guidebooks that cover Europe from top to bottom can afford an update only every two or three years (and even then, it's often by letter). Since this book covers only my favorite places, my research partners and I are able to update it in person each year. Even with an annual update, things change. But if you're traveling with the current edition of this book, I guarantee you're using the most up-to-date information available (for the latest, visit www.ricksteves.com /update). If you're packing an old book, you'll learn the seriousness of your mistake...in Europe. Your trip costs at least $10 per waking hour. Your time is valuable. This guidebook saves lots of time.

Planning Your Trip

This book is organized by destinations. Each destination is covered as a mini-vacation on its own, filled with exciting sights and homey, affordable places to stay. In each chapter, you'll find the following:

Planning Your Time contains a suggested schedule, with thoughts on how to best use your limited time.

Orientation includes tourist information, city transportation, and an easy-to-read map designed to make the text clear and your arrival smooth.

Sights are rated: ▲▲▲—Don't miss; ▲▲—Try hard to see; ▲—Worthwhile if you can make it; No rating—Worth knowing about.

Sleeping and Eating, includes addresses and phone numbers of my favorite budget hotels and restaurants.

Transportation Connections covers how to reach nearby destinations by train or bus.

The **appendix** is a traveler's tool kit, with telephone tips, a climate chart, and a list of national tourist offices.

Browse through this book, choose your favorite destinations, and link them up. Then have a great trip! You'll travel like a temporary local, getting the most out of every mile, minute, and dollar.

You won't waste time on mediocre sights because this guidebook, unlike others, covers only the best. Since your major financial pitfalls are lousy, expensive hotels, I've worked hard to assemble good-value accommodations for each stop. And as you travel the route I know and love, I'm happy you'll be meeting some of my favorite Europeans.

Trip Costs

Five components make up your trip cost: airfare, surface transportation, room and board, sightseeing/entertainment, and shopping/miscellany.

Airfare: Don't try to sort through the mess yourself. Get and use a good travel agent. A basic round-trip U.S.A.-to-Europe flight should cost $600 to $1,000 (even cheaper in winter), depending on where you fly from and when. Always consider saving time and money in Europe by flying "open-jaw" (flying into one city and out of another, such as flying into London and out of Rome).

Surface Transportation: Your best mode depends upon the time you have and the scope of your trip. For many it's a Eurailpass (3 weeks-$740; 1 month-$918; 2 months-$1,298; 15 days in 2 months-$888). Train passes are normally available only outside of Europe. You may save money by simply buying tickets as you go (see "Transportation," below).

Drivers can figure $200 per person per week (based on 2 people splitting the cost of the car, tolls, gas, and insurance). Car rental is cheapest to arrange from the U.S.A. Leasing, for trips over three weeks, is even cheaper.

Room and Board: You can thrive in Europe in 2002 on an overall average of $80 a day per person for room and board (less for the smaller cities). A $80 a day budget allows $10 for lunch, $5 for snacks, $15 for dinner, and $50 for lodging (based on 2 people splitting the cost of a $100 double room that includes breakfast). That's doable. Students and tightwads will do it on $35 or $40 ($15–20 per bed, $20 for meals and snacks). But budget sleeping and eating

Exchange Rates

I've priced things in local currencies throughout this book. Most countries in this book have adopted the euro currency: Austria, Belgium, France, Germany, Ireland, Italy, the Netherlands, and Spain.

1 euro (€) = about 90 cents, and €1.10 = about $1.

One euro is broken down into 100 cents. You'll find coins ranging from 1 cent to 2 euros, and bills from 5 euros to 500 euros. To convert prices in euros into dollars, take 10 percent off the price in euros: €10 = $9, €25 = $22.50, and €140 = $126. For information on the euro, see the European Central Bank's Web site: www.euro.ecb.int.

Britain, Denmark, Switzerland, and the Czech Republic have kept their traditional currencies:

1 British pound (£) = about $1.50, and £0.70 = about $1.

1 Danish kroner (kr) = about 11 cents, and 9 kr = about $1.

1 Swiss franc (SF) = about 60 cents, and 1.70 SF = about $1.

1 Czech koruna (kč) = about 3 cents, and 40 kč = about $1.

To convert British prices into dollars, add 50 percent: £6 is about $9, £3 is about $4.50, and 80p is about $1.20. To roughly translate Danish prices into dollars, divide by ten (90 kr = about $9, actually around $10). To do a quick-and-dirty conversion of Swiss francs into dollars, divide in half (60 SF = $30, actually $36) or, more precisely, multiply by six and drop the last digit (60 SF: 60 x 6 = 360, or $36). To convert Czech prices into dollars, drop the last digit and divide by three (2,000 kč = about $67).

require the skills and information covered below (or much more extensively in *Rick Steves' Europe Through the Back Door*).

Sightseeing and Entertainment: In big cities, figure $5 to $10 per major sight, $2 for minor ones, and $25 for splurge experiences (e.g., tours, concerts, gelato binges). An overall average of $15 a day works for most. Don't skimp here. After all, this category directly powers most of the experiences all the other expenses are designed to make possible.

Shopping and Miscellany: Figure $1 per postcard and $2 per coffee, beer, and ice-cream cone. Shopping can vary in cost from nearly nothing to a small fortune. Good budget travelers find that this category has little to do with assembling a trip full of lifelong and wonderful memories.

Prices, Times, and Discounts

The prices in this book, as well as the hours and telephone numbers, are accurate as of late 2001. Europe is always changing, and I know you'll understand that this, like any other guidebook, starts to yellow even before it's printed—especially this transition year of 2002, with the materialization of the euro currency. Because it's possible that hoteliers might adjust prices a bit in 2002, depending on the latest exchange rate, the prices in this book are approximate.

In Europe—and in this book—you'll be using the 24-hour clock. After 12:00 noon, keep going—13:00, 14:00, and so on. For anything over 12, subtract 12 and add p.m. (14:00 is 2 p.m.).

While discounts for sights and transportation are not listed in this book, seniors (60 and over), students (with International Student Identity Cards), and youths (under 18) may snare discounts—but only by asking. Some discounts (particularly for sights) are granted only to European residents.

When to Go

May, June, September, and October are the best travel months. Peak season (July and August) offers the sunniest weather and the most exciting slate of activities—but the worst crowds. During this busy time, it's best to reserve rooms well in advance, particularly for the big cities (see "Making Reservations," below).

Off-season, October through April, expect generally shorter hours at attractions, more lunchtime breaks, fewer activities, and fewer guided tours in English. If you're traveling off-season, be careful to confirm opening times.

As a general rule of thumb any time of year, the climate north of the Alps is mild (like Seattle), and south of the Alps it's like Arizona. For specifics, check the Climate Chart in the appendix. If you wilt in the heat, avoid the Mediterranean in summer. If you want blue skies in the Alps, Britain, and Scandinavia, travel in the height of summer. Plan your itinerary to beat the heat (for a spring trip, start in the south and work north) but also to moderate culture shock (start in mild Britain and work south and east) and minimize crowds. Touristy places in the core of Europe (Germany, the Alps, France, Italy, and Greece) suffer most from crowds.

Sightseeing Priorities

Depending on the length of your trip, here are my recommended priorities. Assuming you're traveling by train, I've taken geographical proximity into account.

5 days:	London, Paris
7 days, add:	Amsterdam, Haarlem
10 days, add:	Rhine, Rothenburg

Europe's Best 70 Days

14 days, add: Salzburg, Swiss Alps
17 days, add: Venice, Florence
21 days, add: Rome, Cinque Terre
24 days, add: Siena, Bavarian sights
30 days, add: Arles (Provence), Barcelona, Madrid
36 days, add: Vienna, Prague, Berlin
40 days, add: Copenhagen, Bath
70 days: See Europe's Best 70 Days map on this page.

Red Tape, News, and Banking

Red Tape: You currently need a passport but no visa and no shots to travel in Europe. Crossing borders is easy. Sometimes you won't even realize it's happened. When you do change countries, however, you change phone cards, postage stamps, gas prices, ways to flush a toilet, words for "hello," figurehead monarchs, and breakfast breads. Plan ahead for these changes.

Twelve European countries have adopted the euro currency, but some haven't, including Denmark, Britain, Switzerland, and the Czech Republic. If you're about to cross a border with spare coins you won't be able to use anywhere else, spend them on candy, souvenirs, gas, or a telephone call home.

The Best of Europe in Three Weeks

Day 01	Arrive in Amsterdam, stay in Haarlem
Day 02	Amsterdam
Day 03	To Rhine, Bacharach
Day 04	Cruise Rhine, tour Rheinfels Castle
Day 05	Rothenburg
Day 06	Munich
Day 07	Castle Day in Bavaria and Tirol, Reutte
Day 08	To Venice
Day 09	Venice
Day 10	Florence
Day 11	Siena, Florence
Day 12	Rome
Day 13	Rome
Day 14	Civita di Bagnoregio
Day 15	Italian Riviera, Cinque Terre, Vernazza
Day 16	Beach time or hiking Riviera trails
Day 17	To the Alps, Gimmelwald
Day 18	Alps Appreciation Day
Day 19	To Beaune in Burgundy
Day 20	Versailles, drop car
Day 21	Paris
Day 22	Paris

While this itinerary is designed to be done by car, with a few small modifications, it works great by train. Stay in Füssen in Bavaria rather than Reutte in Tirol. The hill town of Orvieto is easier to reach than Civita. Consider skipping Beaune if you'd prefer to take an overnight train from Switzerland to Paris. Do Versailles as an easy daytrip from Paris.

News: Americans keep in touch with the *International Herald Tribune* (published almost daily via satellite throughout Europe). Every Tuesday, the European editions of *Time* and *Newsweek* hit the stands with articles of particular interest to European travelers. Sports addicts can get their fix from *USA Today*. News in English will only be sold where there's enough demand: in big cities and tourist centers. If you're concerned about how some event might affect your safety as an American traveling abroad, call the U.S. consulate or embassy in the nearest big city for advice.

Banking: Bring plastic (ATM, credit, or debit cards) along with some traveler's checks in dollars as a backup.

To withdraw cash from a bank machine, you'll need a four-digit PIN (numbers only, no letters) and your bank card. Before you go, verify with your bank that your card will work, then

Europe's Best Three Weeks

use it whenever possible (bring 2 cards in case one gets demagnetized or eaten by a machine). If you plan on getting cash advances with your regular credit card, be sure to ask the card company about fees before you leave.

Visa and MasterCard are more commonly accepted than American Express. Just like at home, credit or debit cards work easily at larger hotels, restaurants, and shops, but smaller businesses prefer payment in local currency.

Regular banks have the best rates for cashing traveler's checks. For a large exchange, it pays to compare rates and fees. Post offices and train stations usually change money if you can't get to a bank.

You should use a money belt. Thieves target tourists. A money belt (call 425/771-8303 for our free newsletter/catalog) provides peace of mind. You can carry lots of cash safely in a money belt.

Don't be petty about changing money. You don't need to waste time every few days returning to a bank or tracking down a cash machine. Change a week's worth of money, get big bills, stuff it in your money belt, and travel!

Travel Smart

Upon arrival in a new town, lay the groundwork for a smooth departure. Reread this book as you travel and visit local tourist information offices. Buy a phone card and use it for reservations, reconfirmations, and double-checking hours. Enjoy the friendliness of the local people. Ask questions. Most locals are eager to point you in their idea of the right direction. Wear your money belt, learn the local currency, and develop a simple formula to quickly estimate rough prices in dollars. Keep a notepad in your pocket for organizing your thoughts. Those who expect to travel smart, do.

As you read this book, note the days of markets and festivals and when sights are closed. Anticipate problem days: Mondays are bad in Florence, Tuesdays are bad in Paris. Museums and sights, especially large ones, usually stop admitting people 30 to 60 minutes before closing time.

Sundays have the same pros and cons as they do for travelers in the United States. Sightseeing attractions are generally open, shops and banks are closed, and city traffic is light. Rowdy evenings are rare on Sundays. Saturdays in Europe are virtually weekdays with earlier closing hours. Hotels in tourist areas are most crowded on Fridays and Saturdays.

Plan ahead for banking, laundry, post office chores, and picnics. Mix intense and relaxed periods. Every trip (and every traveler) needs at least a few slack days. Pace yourself. Assume you will return.

Tourist Information

The tourist information office is your best first stop in any new city. Try to arrive, or at least telephone, before it closes. In this book, I'll refer to a tourist information office as a TI. Throughout Europe, you'll find TIs are usually well organized and English speaking.

As national budgets tighten, many TIs have been privatized. This means they become sales agents for big tours and hotels, and their "information" becomes unavoidably colored. While the TI has listings of all the rooms and is eager to book you one, use their room-finding service only as a last resort. Across Europe, room-finding services are charging commissions from hotels, taking fees from travelers, blacklisting establishments that buck their materialistic rules, and are unable to give hard opinions on the relative value of one place over another. The accommodations stakes are too high to go potluck through the TI. By using the listings in this book, you can avoid that kind of "help."

Tourist Offices, U.S.A. Addresses: Each country has a national tourist office in the U.S.A. (see the appendix for addresses). Before your trip, you can ask for the free general information packet and for specific information (such as city maps and schedules of upcoming festivals).

Recommended Guidebooks

You may want some supplemental information, especially if you'll be traveling beyond my recommended destinations. When you consider the improvements they'll make in your $3,000 vacation, $25 or $35 for extra maps and books is money well spent. Especially for several people traveling by car, the weight and expense are negligible.

The Lonely Planet guides to various European countries are thorough, well researched (though not updated annually), and packed with good maps and hotel recommendations for low- to moderate-budget travelers. The hip, insightful Rough Guide series (by British researchers, not updated annually) and the highly opinionated Let's Go series (annually updated by Harvard students) are great for students and vagabonds. If you're a back-packer with a train pass and interested in the youth and night scene, get Let's Go. The popular, skinny green Michelin guides (covering most southern countries and French regions) are excel-lent, especially if you're driving. They're known for their city and sightseeing maps, dry but concise and helpful information on all major sights, and good cultural and historical background. English editions are sold locally at tourist shops and gas stations.

Rick Steves' Books and Videos

Rick Steves' Europe Through the Back Door 2002 gives you budget travel tips on minimizing jet lag, packing light, planning your itinerary, traveling by car or train, finding budget beds without reservations, changing money, avoiding rip-offs, outsmarting thieves, hurdling the language barrier, staying healthy, taking great photographs, using your bidet, and much more. The book also includes chapters on my 35 favorite "Back Doors."

Rick Steves Country Guides are a series of eight guide-books—including this one—covering Britain; Ireland; France/Belgium/Netherlands; Italy; Spain/Portugal; Scandinavia; and Germany/Austria/Switzerland. These are updated annually and come out in December (except for this guidebook, which is available in January). If you wish this book covered more of any particular country, my Country Guides are for you.

My **City Guides** cover London, Paris, and Rome, and—new for 2002—Venice and Florence. For more thorough coverage of Europe's greatest cities, complete with self-guided, illustrated tours through the grandest museums, consider these handy, easy-to-pack guidebooks (updated annually, available in January, except for Venice and Florence, which come out in March).

Rick Steves' Europe 101: History and Art for the Traveler (with Gene Openshaw, 2000) gives you the story of Europe's people, history, and art. Written for smart people who were sleep-ing in their history and art classes before they knew they were going to Europe, *101* helps Europe's sights come alive.

Rick Steves' Mona Winks (with Gene Openshaw, 2001) gives you fun, easy-to-follow self-guided tours of the major museums and historic highlights in cities covered in this book, including **Amsterdam** (Rijksmuseum and Van Gogh Museum), **London** (British Museum, British Library, National Gallery, Tate Britain, Westminster Abbey, and a Westminster Walk), **Venice** (St. Mark's, Doge's Palace, and Accademia Gallery), **Florence** (Uffizi Gallery, Bargello, Michelangelo's *David*, and a Renaissance Walk), **Rome** (Colosseum, Forum, Pantheon, National Museum of Rome, Borghese Gallery, Vatican Museum, and St. Peter's Basilica), **Madrid** (Prado), and **Paris** (Louvre, Orsay Museum, Rodin Museum, Notre-Dame, Sainte-Chapelle, and a tour of Europe's greatest palace, Versailles). If you're planning on touring these sights, *Mona* will be a valued friend.

Rick Steves' Phrase Books: After more than 25 years as an English-only traveler struggling with other phrase books, I've designed a series of practical, fun, and budget-oriented phrase books to help you ask the *gelato* man for a free little taste and the hotel receptionist for a room with no street noise. If you want to chat with your cabbie and make hotel reservations over the phone, my pocket-sized Rick Steves' Phrase Books (for French; German; Italian; combined French/Italian/German; and Spanish/Portuguese, 1999) will come in handy.

My new public television series, *Rick Steves' Europe*, begins airing 13 new shows in the fall of 2002. My new series and my first series, *Travels in Europe with Rick Steves*, feature 68 half-hour episodes on Europe. The shows run throughout the United States on public television and the Travel Channel. They're also available as information-packed videotapes, along with my two-hour slideshow lectures (call 425/771-8303 for free newsletter/catalog).

Rick Steves' Postcards from Europe (1999), my autobiographical book, packs 25 years of travel anecdotes and insights into the ultimate 3,000-mile European adventure. Through my guidebooks, I share my favorite European discoveries with you. *Postcards* introduces you to my favorite European friends.

All of my books are published by Avalon Travel Publishing (www.travelmatters.com).

Maps

The maps in this book, drawn by Dave Hoerlein, are concise and simple. Dave, who is well-traveled in Europe, has designed the maps to help you locate recommended places and get to the tourist offices, where you can pick up a more in-depth map (usually free) of the city or region.

For an overall map of Europe, consider my new Rick Steves' Europe Planning Map—geared to travelers' needs—with sightseeing destinations listed prominently (for our free newsletter/catalog, contact us at 425/771-8303 or www.ricksteves.com).

European bookstores, especially in tourist areas, have good selections of maps. For drivers, I'd recommend a 1:200,000 or 1:300,000 scale map for each country. Train travelers can usually manage fine with the freebies they get with their train pass and at the local tourist offices.

Tours of Europe

Travel agents will tell you about typical tours of Europe, but they won't tell you about ours. At Europe Through the Back Door, we run 21-day tours of Europe featuring most of the highlights in this book (departures April-October, 26 people on a big roomy bus with 2 great guides). We also offer regional tours of Britain, Ireland, France, Spain/Portugal, Italy, Germany/Austria/Switzerland, Scandinavia, Turkey, and Eastern Europe. And we lead week-long getaways in winter and spring to London, Paris, and Rome. For details, call us at 425/771-8303 or visit www.ricksteves.com.

Transportation in Europe

By Car or Train?

Each has pros and cons. Cars are an expensive headache in big cities but give you more control for delving deep into the countryside. Groups of three or more go cheaper by car. If you're packing heavy (with kids), go by car. Trains are best for city-to-city travel and give you the convenience of doing long stretches overnight. By train, I arrive relaxed and well rested—not so by car. A rail 'n' drive pass allows you to mix train and car travel. When thoughtfully used, this pass economically gives you the best of both transportation worlds.

Traveling by Train

A major mistake Americans make is relating public transportation in Europe to the pathetic public transportation they're used to at home. By rail you'll have the Continent by the tail. While many simply buy tickets as they go ("point to point"), the various train passes give you the simplicity of ticket-free, unlimited travel, and depending on how much traveling you do, often offer a tremendous savings over regular point-to-point tickets. The Eurailpass gives you several options (explained in the box on page 13).

For a free 40-page Railpass Guide analyzing the railpass and point-to-point ticket deals available in both the U.S.A. and in Europe, call my office at 425/771-8303 (or find it at www.ricksteves.com). This booklet is updated each January. Regardless of where you get your train pass, this information will help you know you're getting the right one for your trip. To study train schedules in advance on the Web, check www .reiseauskunft.bahn.de/bin/query.exe/en.

Europe by Rail: Time and Cost

This map can help you determine if a railpass is right for you. Add up the ticket prices for your route. If your total is about the same or more than the cost of a pass, buy the pass (unless you like waiting in lines at train stations).

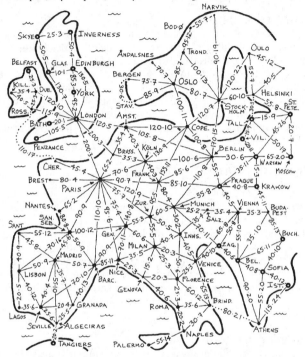

The **first number** between cities = **cost** in $US for a one-way, second-class ticket. The **second number** = number of **hours** the trip takes.

- ● = Cities served by Eurailpass
- ○ = Cities not served by Eurailpass (for example, if you want to go from Berlin to Prague, you'll need to pay extra for the portion through the Czech Republic)
- ••• = Boat Crossings

Important: These fares and times are based on the Eurail Tariff Guide. Actual prices may vary due to currency fluctuations and local promotions. Local competition can cut the actual price of some boat crossings (from Italy to Greece, for example) by 50 percent or more. For approximate first-class rail prices, multiply the prices shown by 1.5. In some cases, faster trains (like the TGV in France) are available, cutting the hours indicated on the map. Travelers under age 26 can receive up to 1/3 off the second-class fares shown. Eurailpasses are not honored in the United Kingdom, Turkey, or Eastern Europe (except for Hungary).

Prices listed are for 2002. My free *Rick Steves' Guide to European Railpasses* has more details. To get the railpass guide, call us at 425/771-8303 or visit www.ricksteves.com/rail. Prices subject to change.

EURAILPASSES

These passes cover all 17 Eurail countries: Austria, Belgium, Denmark, Finland, France, Germany, Greece, Hungary, Ireland, Italy, Luxembourg, Netherlands, Norway, Portugal, Spain, Sweden, and Switzerland.

	1st class	1st class Saver	2nd class Youth
10 days in 2 months flexi	$674	$574	$473
15 days in 2 months flexi	888	756	622
15 consecutive days	572	486	401
21 consecutive days	740	630	518
1 month consec. days	918	780	644
2 months consec. days	1298	1106	910
3 months consec. days	1606	1366	1126

EUROPASSES

All Europasses include France, Germany, Italy, Spain and Switzerland. Up to two of the following extra-cost "zones" may be added: Austria/Hungary; Belgium/Netherlands/Luxembourg; Portugal; Greece (includes the Brindisi, Italy to Patras, Greece boat).

	1st class	1st class Saver	2nd class Youth
5 days in 2 months	$360	$306	$253
6 days in 2 months	400	340	282
8 days in 2 months	474	404	332
10 days in 2 months	544	464	382
15 days in 2 months	710	604	497
With one add-on zone	+62	+54	+43
With two add-on zones	+102	+88	+72

SELECTPASSES

This pass covers travel in three adjacent countries. For details, visit www.ricksteves.com/rail or see *Rick Steves' Guide to European Railpasses.*

	1st class Selectpass	1st class Saverpass	2nd class Youthpass
5 days in 2 months	$346	$294	$243
6 days in 2 months	380	322	266
8 days in 2 months	444	378	310
10 days in 2 months	502	428	352

Saverpass prices are per person for 2 or more people traveling together at all times. Prices subject to change.

Youthpasses: Under age 26 only.

Kids 4-11 pay half adult fare; under 4: free.

FIRST CLASS EURAILDRIVE PASSES

4 first class rail days and 2 car days in a 2 month period.

Car categories	2 adults	1 adult	Extra car day	Extra rail day
Economy	$370	$420	$50	$43
Compact	384	448	64	43
Intermediate	396	472	76	43
Small Automatic	414	508	94	43

Prices are per person. Third and fourth persons sharing car get a 4-day out of 2-month railpass for approx. $320 (kids 4-11 $160). You can add rail days (max. 5) and car days (no limit). Rail travel in all 17 Eurail countries, car available in most (not Scandinavia).

FIRST CLASS EUROPASS DRIVE

3 first class rail days and 2 car days in a 2-month period. To order Rail 'n Drive passes, call Rail Europe at 800/438-7245 or DER at 800/549-3737. Prices are subject to change.

Car categories	2 adults	1 adult	Extra car day	Extra rail day
Economy	$286	$334	$48	$36
Compact	300	362	62	36
Intermediate	314	390	76	36
Small Automatic	328	418	90	36

Prices are per person. You can add rail days (max. 7) and car days (no limit). Rail travel and car rental in France, Germany, Italy, Switzerland, and Spain only.

FIRST CLASS SELECTPASS DRIVE

Any 3 days of rail travel + 2 days of Hertz or Avis car rental in 2 months within 3 adjoining countries.

Car Categories	2 adults	1 adult	Extra car day	Extra rail day
Economy	$280	$330	$50	$33
Compact	294	358	64	33
Intermediate	306	382	76	33
Small Automatic	324	418	94	33

Prices are per person. You can add rail days (max. 7) and car days (no limit). Rail travel and car rental in three connecting Eurail countries (no car in Scandinavia).

Eurailpass/Selectpass diagram key:

*Every **Eurailpass** includes travel in every country shown above. A **Selectpass** can be designed to connect a "chain" of any three countries in this diagram linked by direct lines. (Examples that qualify: Norway-Sweden-Germany; Spain-France-Italy; Austria-Italy-Greece.) "Benelux" is considered one country.*

Eurailpass, Europass, and Eurail Selectpass

The granddaddy of European railpasses, Eurail, gives you unlimited rail travel on the national trains of 17 European countries. That's 160,000 kilometers of track through all of western Europe, including Ireland, Greece, and Hungary (but excluding Great Britain and most of eastern Europe). The pass includes many bonuses, such as free boat rides on the Rhine, Mosel, Danube, and lakes of Switzerland; several international ferries (Sweden–Finland and Italy–Greece, plus a 50 percent discount on the Ireland–France route); and a 60 percent discount on the Romantic Road bus tour through Germany.

The Europass is more focused (and cheaper) than the Eurailpass, covering five countries (France, Germany, Switzerland, Italy, and Spain), with an extra-cost option to add adjacent countries.

The Eurail Selectpass, which covers any three Eurail countries connected by rail or ferry (such as Austria, Italy, and Greece) is fine for a focused trip, but to see the Best of Europe, you'd do best with a Eurailpass. All of these passes give a 15 percent Saverpass discount to two or more companions traveling together.

Eurail Analysis

Break-even point? For an at-a-glance break-even point, remember that a one-month Eurailpass pays for itself if your route is Amsterdam–Rome–Madrid–Paris on first class or Copenhagen–Rome–Madrid–Copenhagen on second class. A one-month Eurail Youthpass saves you money if you're traveling from Amsterdam to Rome to Madrid and back to Amsterdam. Passes pay for themselves quicker in the north, where the cost per kilometer is higher. Check the "Europe by Rail: Time and Cost" map, on page 12 to see if your planned travels merit the purchase of a train pass. If it's about even, go with the pass for the convenience of not having to wait in line to buy tickets and for the fun and freedom to travel "free."

Using one Eurailpass versus a series of country passes: While nearly every country has its own mini-version of the Eurailpass, trips covering several countries are usually cheapest with the budget whirlwind traveler's old standby, the Eurailpass, or its budget cousins, the Europass and Eurail Selectpass. This is because the more rail days included in a pass, the cheaper your per-day cost is. A group of country passes with a few rail days apiece will have a high per-day cost, while a Eurailpass with a longer life span offers a better deal overall. However, if you're traveling in a single country, an individual country railpass (such as Francerail or Germanrail) is often a better value than any of the Eurail passes.

EurailDrive Pass: The EurailDrive Pass is for those who want to combine train travel with the freedom of having a car a day here and a day there. Great areas for a day of joyriding include the Dutch countryside; Germany's Rhine, Mosel, or

Bavaria; France's Provence; Italy's Tuscany and Umbria; or "car hiking" in the Alps. When comparing prices, remember that each day of car rental comes with about $30 of extra expenses (CDW insurance, gas, parking), which you'll divide among the people in your party.

Car Rental

It's cheaper to arrange European car rentals in the United States, so check rates with your travel agent or directly with the companies. Rent by the week with unlimited mileage. If you'll be renting for three weeks or more, ask your agent about leasing, which is a scheme to save on insurance and taxes. I normally rent the smallest, least expensive model. Explore your drop-off options (and costs).

For peace of mind, I spring for the Collision Damage Waiver insurance (CDW, about $10–15 per day), which has a zero-deductible rather than the standard value-of-the-car "deductible." Ask your travel agent about money-saving alternatives to CDW. A few gold credit cards cover CDW insurance; quiz your credit card company on the worst-case scenario. Or consider Travel Guard, which offers CDW insurance for $6 a day (U.S. tel. 800/826-1300, www.travelguard.com); it'll cover you throughout Europe but not in Scotland, Ireland, and Italy.

Note that if you'll be driving in Italy, theft insurance (separate from CDW insurance) is mandatory. The insurance usually costs about $10 to $15 a day, payable when you pick up the car.

If you plan to drive your rental car into the Czech Republic, keep these tips in mind: State your travel plans up front to the rental company. Some won't allow any of their rental cars to enter eastern European countries due to the high theft rate. Some won't allow certain types of cars: BMWs, Mercedes, and convertibles. Ask about extra fees—some companies automatically tack on theft and collision coverage for a Czech excursion. To avoid hassles at the Czech border, ask the rental agent to mark your contract with the company's permission to cross.

Driving

For much of Europe, all you need is your valid U.S. driver's license and a car. Confirm with your rental company if an international license is required in the countries you plan to visit. Those traveling in Austria, Germany, Italy, Portugal, Spain, and eastern Europe should probably get an international driver's license (at your local AAA office—$10 plus the cost of two passport-type photos).

While gas is expensive, if you keep an eye on the big picture, paying $4 per gallon is more a psychological trauma than a financial one. I use the freeways whenever possible. They are free in the Netherlands and Germany. You'll pay a one-time road fee of

Standard European Road Signs

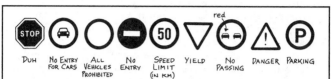

about $25 as you enter Switzerland and about $7 for Austria. The Italian autostradas and French autoroutes are punctuated by toll booths (charging about $1 for every 10 minutes). The alternative to these superfreeways often is being marooned in rural traffic. The autostrada/autoroute usually saves enough time, gas, and nausea to justify its expense. Mix scenic country-road rambling with high-speed autobahning, but don't forget that in Europe, the shortest distance between two points is the autobahn.

Metric: Outside of Britain, get used to metric. A liter is about a quart, four to a gallon. A kilometer is six-tenths of a mile. I figure kilometers to miles by cutting them in half and adding back 10 percent of the original (120 km: 60 + 12 = 72 miles, 300 km: 150 + 30 = 180 miles).

Parking: Parking is a costly headache in big cities. You'll pay about $20 a day to park safely. Ask at your hotel for advice. I keep a pile of coins in my ashtray for parking meters, public phones, Laundromats, and wishing wells.

Telephones, Mail, and E-mail

Smart travelers learn the phone system and use it daily to reserve or reconfirm rooms, find out tourist information, or phone home. Many European phone booths take **phone cards** rather than coins. Each country sells phone cards good for use in that country's phones. (For example, you can use a Swiss phone card to make local and international calls from Switzerland, but it won't do a thing for you in France.) Buy a phone card from post offices, newsstands, or tobacco shops. Insert the card into the phone and make your call, and the value is automatically deducted from your card. If you use coins instead, have a bunch handy.

The new **PIN cards** allow you to dial from any phone, even your hotel room. After you buy the card (at exchange bureaus, newsstands, or mini-marts), just follow the instructions. You'll end up dialing lots more numbers (whether it's a local or international call), but you'll save money per minute, especially on overseas calls. There's no one brand name; just ask for an international calling card. Get a low denomination in case it's a dud.

Avoid using **hotel room phones**, which are rip-offs for anything other than local calls, PIN card calls (see above), or calling-card calls (see below). You'll sometimes find easy-to-use "talk now, pay later" **metered phones** at post offices in major cities.

Making Calls within a European Country: You'll save money by dialing direct. You just need to learn to break the codes. About half of all European countries—including Britain—use area codes; the other half uses a direct-dial system without area codes.

In countries that use area codes (such as Austria, Britain, the Czech Republic, Finland, Germany, Ireland, the Netherlands, and Sweden), you dial the local number when calling within a city, and you add the area code if calling long-distance within the country. For example, Berlin's area code is 030, and the number of one of my recommended Berlin hotels is 3150-3944. To call it from Frankfurt, dial 030/3150-3944.

To make calls within a country that uses a direct-dial system (Belgium, Denmark, France, Italy, Portugal, Norway, Spain, and Switzerland), you dial the same number whether you're calling across the country or across the street.

Making International Calls: You always start with the international access code (011 if you're calling from America or Canada, or 00 from Europe), then dial the country code of the country you're calling (see chart in appendix).

What you dial next depends on the phone system of the country you're calling. If the country uses area codes, drop the initial zero of the area code, then dial the rest of the number. To call the Berlin hotel from Copenhagen, dial 00, 49 (Germany's country code), 30/3150-3944 (omitting the initial zero in the area code).

Countries that use direct-dial systems (no area codes) vary in how they're accessed internationally by phone. For instance, if you're making an international call to Denmark, Italy, Norway, Portugal, or Spain, simply dial the international access code, country code, and phone number. But if you're calling Belgium, France, or Switzerland, drop the initial zero of the phone number. Example: To call a Paris hotel (tel. 01 47 05 49 15) from London, dial 00, 33 (France's country code), then 1 47 05 49 15 (phone number without the initial zero).

To call my office from Europe, I dial 00 (Europe's international access code), 1 (U.S.A.'s country code), 425 (Edmonds' area code), and 771-8303.

European time is six/nine hours ahead of the east/west coast of the U.S.A.

USA Direct Services: Calling home from Europe is easy with AT&T, MCI, or Sprint calling cards, but these are no longer a good value since direct-dial rates have dropped. It's cheaper to call direct. But if you prefer to use a calling card, here's the scoop: Each card company has a toll-free number in each European country (see appendix for list of AT&T, MCI, and

Sprint numbers) that puts you in touch with an English-speaking operator who takes your card number and the number you want to call, puts you through, and bills your home phone number for the call. Sprint is the priciest, costing $3 for the first minute with a $4.50 connection fee; if you get an answering machine, it'll cost you $7.50 to say "Sorry I missed you." For less than 25 cents, call first with a coin or European phone card to see if the answering machine is off or if the right person's at home. It's outrageously expensive to use your calling card to make calls between European countries; it's much cheaper to call direct using a phone card, PIN card, or coins.

Mail: To arrange for mail delivery, reserve a few hotels along your route in advance and give their addresses to friends or use American Express Company's mail services (available to anyone who has at least one AmEx traveler's check). Allow 10 days for a letter to arrive. Federal Express makes two-day deliveries—for a price. Phoning is so easy that I've dispensed with mail stops all together.

E-mail: More and more hoteliers have e-mail addresses and Web sites (listed in this book). Note that mom-and-pop pensions, which can get deluged by e-mail, are not always able to respond immediately to an e-mail you've sent.

Cybercafés are available in most cities, giving you reasonably inexpensive and easy Internet access. Look for the cybercafés listed in this book, or ask at the local TI, computer store, or your hotel.

Sleeping

In the interest of smart use of your time, I favor hotels and restaurants handy to your sightseeing activities. Rather than list hotels scattered throughout a city, I describe my favorite two or three neighborhoods and recommend the best accommodations values in each, from $10 bunks to $150 doubles.

Now that hotels are so expensive and tourist information offices' room-finding services are so greedy, it's more important than ever for budget travelers to have a good listing of rooms and call directly to make reservations. This book gives you a wide range of budget accommodations to choose from: hostels, bed-and-breakfasts, guest houses, pensions, small hotels, and splurges. I like places that are quiet, clean, small, central, traditional, friendly, and not listed in other guidebooks. Most places I list are a good value, having at least five of these seven virtues.

Rooms with private bathrooms are often bigger and renovated, while the cheaper rooms without bathrooms often will be on the top floor or not yet refurbished. Any room without a bathroom has access to a bathroom in the corridor (free unless otherwise noted). Rooms with tubs often cost more than rooms with showers. All rooms have a sink. Unless I note a difference,

Sleep Code

To give maximum information in a minimum of space, I use this code to describe accommodations listed in this book. Prices listed are per room, not per person. When there is a range of prices in one category, the price will fluctuate with the season, size of room, or length of stay.

S = Single room (or price for one person in a double).

D = Double or Twin. Double beds are usually big enough for non-romantic couples.

T = Triple (often a double bed with a single bed moved in).

Q = Quad (an extra child's bed is usually less).

b = Private bathroom with toilet and shower or tub.

s = Private shower or tub only (the toilet is down the hall).

CC = Accepts credit cards.

no CC = Does not accept credit cards; you'll need to pay with the local currency.

SE = Speaks English. This code is used only when it seems predictable that you'll encounter English-speaking staff.

NSE = Does not speak English. Used only when it's unlikely you'll encounter English-speaking staff.

According to this code, a couple staying at a "Db-€90, CC, SE" hotel in Spain would pay a total of 90 euros (about $81) for a double room with a private bathroom. The hotel accepts credit cards or euros in payment, and the staff speaks English.

the cost of a room includes a continental breakfast. When breakfast is not included, the price is usually posted in your hotel room.

Before accepting a room, confirm your understanding of the complete price. The only tip my recommended hotels would like is a friendly, easygoing guest. I appreciate feedback on your hotel experiences.

Hotels

While most hotels listed in this book cluster around $60 to $80 per double, they range from $25 (very simple, toilet and shower down the hall) to $190 (maximum plumbing and more) per double. The cost is higher in big cities and heavily touristed cities and lower off the beaten track. Three or four people can save money by requesting one big room. Traveling alone can get expensive: A single room is often only 20 percent cheaper than a double. If you'll accept a room with twin beds and you ask for a double, you may be turned away. Ask for "a room for two people" if you'll take a twin or a double.

Rooms are generally safe, but don't leave valuables lying around. More (or different) pillows and blankets are usually in the closet or available on request. Remember, in Europe towels and linen aren't always replaced every day. Drip-dry and conserve.

A very simple continental breakfast is almost always included. (Breakfasts in Europe, like towels and people, get smaller as you go south.) If you like juice and protein for breakfast, supply it yourself. I enjoy a box of juice in my hotel room and often supplement the skimpy breakfast with a piece of fruit and cheese.

Pay your bill the evening before you leave to avoid the time-wasting crowd at the reception desk in the morning.

Making Reservations

It's possible to travel at any time of year without reservations (especially if you arrive early in the day), but given the high stakes, erratic accommodations values, and the quality of the gems I've found for this book, I'd highly recommend calling for rooms at least a day or two in advance as you travel (your fluent receptionist will likely help you call your next hotel if you pay for the call). Even if a hotel clerk says the hotel is fully booked, you can try calling between 09:00 and 10:00 on the day you plan to arrive. That's when the hotel clerk knows who'll be checking out and just which rooms will be available. I've taken great pains to list telephone numbers with long-distance instructions (see "Telephones," above and the appendix). Use the telephone and the convenient phone cards. Most hotels listed are accustomed to English-only speakers. A hotel receptionist will trust you and hold a room until 16:00 (4:00 p.m.) without a deposit, though some will ask for a credit card number. Honor (or cancel by phone) your reservations. Long distance is cheap and easy from public phone booths. Don't let these people down—I promised you'd call and cancel if for some reason you won't show up. Don't needlessly confirm rooms through the tourist office; they'll take a commission.

If you know exactly which dates you need and really want a particular place, reserve a room well in advance before you leave home. To reserve from home, call, e-mail, fax, or write the hotel. Phone and fax costs are reasonable, e-mail is a steal, and simple English is usually fine. To fax, use the form in the appendix (or find it online at www.ricksteves.com/reservation). If you're writing, add the zip code and confirm the need and method for a deposit. A two-night stay in August would be "two nights, 16/8/02 to 18/8/02" (Europeans write the date in this order—

day/month/year—and hotel jargon counts your stay from your
day of arrival through your day of departure).

If you send a reservation request and receive a response
with rates stating that rooms are available, this is not a confirmation. You must confirm that the rates are fine and that indeed
you want the room. You'll often receive a response requesting
one night's deposit. A credit card number and expiration date
will usually work. If you use your credit card for the deposit,
you can pay with your card or cash when you arrive; if you don't
show up, you'll be billed for one night. Reconfirm your reservations several days in advance for safety.

Bed-and-Breakfasts
You can stay in private homes throughout Europe and enjoy
double the cultural intimacy for about half the cost of hotels.
You'll find them mainly in smaller towns and in the countryside
(so they are most handy for those with a car). In Germany, look
for *Zimmer* signs. For Italian *affitta camere* and French *chambre
d'hôte* (CH), ask at local tourist offices. Doubles cost about $50,
and you'll often share a bathroom with the family. While your
European hosts will rarely speak English (except in Switzerland,
the Netherlands, Belgium, and Scandinavia), they will almost
always be enthusiastic, delightful hosts.

Hostels
For $10 to $20 a night, you can stay at one of Europe's 2,000
youth hostels. While most hostels admit nonmembers for an
extra fee, it's best to join the club and buy a youth hostel card
before you go (call Hostelling International at 202/783-6161
or order online at www.hiayh.org). Except in Bavaria (where
you must be under 27 to stay in a hostel), travelers of any age
are welcome as long as they don't mind dorm-style accommodations and making lots of traveling friends. Cheap meals are
sometimes available, and kitchen facilities are usually provided
for do-it-yourselfers. Expect crowds in the summer, snoring,
and lots of youth groups giggling and making rude noises
while you try to sleep. Family rooms and doubles are often
available on request, but it's basically boys' dorms and girls'
dorms. Many hostels are locked up from about 10:00 until
17:00, and a 23:00 curfew is often enforced. Hosteling is ideal
for those traveling single: prices are per bed, not per room,
and you'll have an instant circle of friends. More and more
hostels are getting their business acts together, taking credit
card reservations over the phone and leaving sign-in forms
on the door for each available room. If you're serious about
traveling cheaply, get a card, carry your own sheets, and
cook in the members' kitchens.

Camping

For $5 to $10 per person per night, you can camp your way
through Europe. "Camping" is an international word, and
you'll see signs everywhere. All you need is a tent and a sleeping
bag. Good campground guides are published, and camping
information is also readily available at local tourist information
offices. Europeans love to holiday camp. It's a social rather
than a nature experience and a great way for traveling Americans
to make local friends. Camping is ideal for families traveling
by car on a tight budget.

Eating European

Europeans are masters at the art of fine living. That means eating
long and eating well. Two-hour lunches, three-hour dinners, and
endless hours sitting in outdoor cafés are the norm. Americans eat
on their way to an evening event and complain if the check is slow
in coming. For Europeans, the meal is an end in itself, and only
rude waiters rush you.

Even those of us who liked dorm food will find that the
local cafés, cuisine, and wines become a highlight of our European
adventure. This is sightseeing for your palate, and even if the
rest of you is sleeping in cheap hotels, your taste buds will want
an occasional first-class splurge. You can eat well without going
broke. But be careful: You're just as likely to blow a small fortune
on a mediocre meal as you are to dine wonderfully for $15.

Restaurants

When restaurant hunting, choose a place filled with locals, not
the place with the big neon signs boasting "We Speak English
and Accept Credit Cards." Look for menus posted outside; if
you don't see one, move along.

For a no-stress meal in France and Italy, look for set-price
menus (called the tourist menu, *menu del giorno*, *prix-fixe*, or
simply *le menu*) that give you several choices of courses. At some
restaurants, the *menu* is cheaper at lunch than dinner. Combination plates (*le plat* in France, *plato combinado* in Spain) provide
house specialties at reasonable prices.

Galloping gourmets bring a menu translator. The *Marling
Menu Master*, available in French, Italian, and German editions,
is excellent.

These days, tipping is included in the bill in most cafés and
restaurants. If it's not, the menu will tell you. Still, even if the
service is included, it's polite to leave the change (up to 5 percent)
if the service was good.

When you're in the mood for something halfway between
a restaurant and a picnic meal, look for take-out food stands,
bakeries (with sandwiches and small pizzas to go), delis with

stools or a table, a department store cafeteria, or simple little
eateries for fast and easy sit-down restaurant food.

Picnics
So that I can afford the occasional splurge in a nice restaurant,
I like to picnic. In addition to the savings, picnicking is a great
way to sample local specialties. And, in the process of assembling
your meal, you get to plunge into local markets like a European.

Gather supplies early. Many shops close for a lunch break.
While it's fun to visit the small specialty shops, a *supermarché* gives
you more efficiency with less color for less cost.

When driving, I organize a backseat pantry in a cardboard
box: plastic cups, paper towels, a water bottle (the standard dispos-
able European half liter plastic mineral water bottle works fine),
a damp cloth in a Zip-loc baggie, a Swiss army knife, and a petite
tablecloth. To take care of juice once and for all, stow a rack of
liter boxes of orange juice in the trunk. (Look for "100%" on the
label or you'll get a sickly sweet orange drink.)

Picnics (especially French ones) can be an adventure in high
cuisine. Be daring: Try the smelly cheeses, midget pickles, ugly
pâtés, and minuscule yogurts. Local shopkeepers sell small quantities of produce and even slice and stuff a sandwich for you.

A typical picnic for two might be fresh bread (half loaves on
request), two tomatoes, three carrots, 100 grams of cheese (about a
quarter-pound, called an *etto* in Italy), 100 grams of meat, two apples,
a liter box of orange juice, and yogurt. Total cost for two: about $8.

Stranger in a Strange Land
We travel all the way to Europe to enjoy differences—to become
temporary locals. You'll experience frustrations. Certain truths
that we find "God-given" or "self-evident," like cold beer, ice
in drinks, bottomless cups of coffee, hot showers, body odor
smelling bad, and bigger being better, are suddenly not so true.
One of the benefits of travel is the eye-opening realization that
there are logical, civil, and even better alternatives. A willingness
to go local ensures that you'll enjoy a full dose of local hospitality.

If there is a negative aspect to the European image of
Americans, we can appear loud, aggressive, impolite, rich, and
a bit naive. While Europeans look bemusedly at some of our
Yankee excesses—and worriedly at others—they nearly always
afford us individual travelers all the warmth we deserve.

Back Door Manners
While updating this book, I heard over and over again that my
readers are considerate and fun to have as guests. Thank you
for traveling as temporary locals who are sensitive to the culture.
It's fun to follow you in my travels.

Send Me a Postcard, Drop Me a Line

If you enjoy a successful trip with the help of this book and would like to share your discoveries, please fill out the survey at the end of this book (or find it online at www.ricksteves.com/feedback) and send it to me at Europe Through the Back Door, Box 2009, Edmonds, WA 98020. I personally read and value all feedback.

For our latest travel information, tap into our Web site: www.ricksteves.com. To check on updates for this book, visit www.ricksteves.com/update. My e-mail address is rick @ricksteves.com. Anyone is welcome to request a free issue of our *Back Door* quarterly newsletter.

Judging from all the positive feedback I receive from travelers who have used this book, it's safe to assume you'll enjoy a great, affordable vacation—with the finesse of an experienced, independent traveler. Thanks, and happy travels!

BACK DOOR TRAVEL PHILOSOPHY
As taught in *Rick Steves' Europe Through the Back Door*

Travel is intensified living—maximum thrills per minute and one of the last great sources of legal adventure. Travel is freedom. It's recess, and we need it.

Experiencing the real Europe requires catching it by surprise, going casual..."Through the Back Door."

Affording travel is a matter of priorities. (Make do with the old car.) You can travel—simply, safely, and comfortably—anywhere in Europe for $80 a day plus transportation costs. In many ways, spending more money only builds a thicker wall between you and what you came to see. Europe is a cultural carnival and, time after time, you'll find that its best acts are free and the best seats are the cheap ones.

A tight budget forces you to travel close to the ground, meeting and communicating with the people, not relying on service with a purchased smile. Never sacrifice sleep, nutrition, safety, or cleanliness in the name of budget. Simply enjoy the local-style alternatives to expensive hotels and restaurants.

Extroverts have more fun. If your trip is low on magic moments, kick yourself and make things happen. If you don't enjoy a place, maybe you don't know enough about it. Seek the truth. Recognize tourist traps. Give a culture the benefit of your open mind. See things as different but not better or worse. Any culture has much to share.

Of course, travel, like the world, is a series of hills and valleys. Be fanatically positive and militantly optimistic. If something's not to your liking, change your liking. Travel is addicting. It can make you a happier American as well as a citizen of the world. Our Earth is home to 6 billion equally important people. It's humbling to travel and find that people don't envy Americans. They like us, but with all due respect, they wouldn't trade passports.

Globetrotting destroys ethnocentricity. It helps you understand and appreciate different cultures. Travel changes people. It broadens perspectives and teaches new ways to measure quality of life. Many travelers toss aside their hometown blinders. Their prized souvenirs are the strands of different cultures they decide to knit into their own character. The world is a cultural yarn shop. And Back Door Travelers are weaving the ultimate tapestry. Come on, join in!

VIENNA
(WIEN)

Vienna is a head without a body. For 640 years the capital of the once-grand Hapsburg Empire, she started and lost World War I and, with it, her far-flung holdings. Today you'll find an elegant capital of 1.6 million people (20 percent of Austria's population) ruling a small, relatively insignificant country. Culturally, historically, and from a sightseeing point of view, this city is the sum of its illustrious past. The city of Freud, Brahms, a gaggle of Strausses, Maria Theresa's many children, and a dynasty of Holy Roman Emperors is right up there with Paris, London, and Rome.

Vienna has always been the easternmost city of the West. In Roman times it was Vindobona, on the Danube facing the Germanic barbarians. In medieval times Vienna was Europe's bastion against the Ottoman Turks (a "horde" of 300,000 was repelled in 1683). While the ancient walls held out the Turks, World War II bombs destroyed nearly a quarter of the city's buildings. In modern times Vienna took a big bite out of the USSR's Warsaw Pact buffer zone.

The truly Viennese person is not Austrian but a second-generation Hapsburg cocktail, with grandparents from the distant corners of the old empire—Polish, Serbian, Hungarian, Romanian, Czech, or Italian. Vienna is the melting-pot capital of a now-collapsed empire that, in its heyday, consisted of 60 million—of which only 8 million were Austrian.

In 1900, Vienna's 2.2 million inhabitants made it the world's fifth-largest city (after New York, London, Paris, and Berlin). But the average Viennese mother today has 1.3 children, and the population is down to 1.6 million. (Dogs are the preferred "child.")

Some ad agency has convinced Vienna to make Elisabeth, wife of Emperor Franz Josef, with her narcissism and difficulties with

Vienna Overview

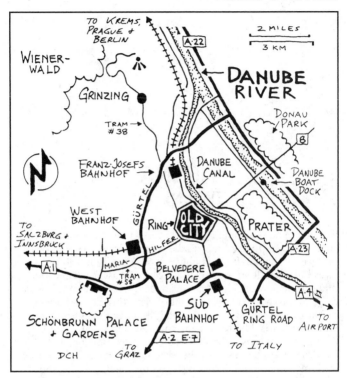

royal life, the darling of the local tourist scene. You'll see "Sissy" all over town. But stay focused on the Hapsburgs who mattered.

Of the Hapsburgs who ruled Austria from 1273 to 1918, Maria Theresa (ruled 1740–1765) and Franz Josef (ruled 1848–1916) are the most famous. People are quick to remember Maria Theresa as the mother of 16 children (12 survived). This was actually no big deal back then (one of her daughters had 18 kids, and a son fathered 16). Maria Theresa's reign followed the Austrian defeat of the Turks, when Europe recognized Austria as a great power. She was a strong and effective queen. (Her rival, the Prussian emperor, said, "When at last the Hapsburgs get a great man, it's a woman.")

Maria Theresa was a great social reformer. During her reign she avoided wars and expanded her empire by skillfully marrying her children into the right families. With daughter Marie Antoinette's marriage into the French Bourbon family (to Louis XVI), for instance, a country that had been an enemy became an ally.

(Unfortunately for Marie, she arrived in time for the Revolution, and she lost her head.)

In tune with her age and as a great reformer, Maria Theresa's "Robin Hood" policies helped Austria glide through the "age of revolution" without turmoil. She taxed the church and the nobility and provided six years of obligatory education to all children and free health care to all in her realm. And she welcomed the boy genius Mozart into her court.

As far back as the 12th century, Vienna was a mecca for musicians—both sacred and secular (troubadours). The Hapsburg emperors of the 17th and 18th centuries were not only generous supporters of music but fine musicians and composers themselves. (Maria Theresa played a mean double bass.) Composers like Haydn, Mozart, Beethoven, Schubert, Brahms, and Mahler gravitated to this music-friendly environment. They taught each other, jammed together, and spent a lot of time in Hapsburg palaces. Beethoven was a famous figure, walking—lost in musical thought—through Vienna's woods.

After the defeat of Napoleon and the Congress of Vienna in 1815 (which shaped 19th-century Europe), Vienna enjoyed its violin-filled belle epoque, which shaped our romantic image of the city—fine wine, chocolates, cafés, and waltzes. "Waltz King" Johann Strauss and his brothers kept Vienna's 300 ballrooms spinning.

This musical tradition continues into modern times, leaving some prestigious Viennese institutions for today's tourists to enjoy: the Opera, the Boys' Choir, and the great Baroque halls and churches, all busy with classical and waltz concerts.

Planning Your Time

For a big city, Vienna is pleasant and laid-back. Vienna is worth two days and two nights on the speediest trip. Not only is it packed with great sights, but it's also a joy to simply spend time in. It seems like Vienna was designed to help people just meander through a day. To be grand-tour efficient, you could sleep in and sleep out on the train (Berlin, Venice, Rome, the Swiss Alps, Paris, and the Rhine are each handy night trains away). For the best Austrian experience, I'd come in from Salzburg via Hallstatt, and spend two days this way:

Day 1: 09:00-Circle the "Ring" by tram, following the self-guided tour (see "Do-It-Yourself Bus Orientation Tour," below), 10:00-Tour Opera (take care of any TI and ticket needs), 11:00-Horse lovers tour the Lipizzaner Museum and see the horses practicing (not July–Aug); art fans can visit the Academy of Fine Arts; people watchers and picnic gatherers wander Naschmarkt, 12:00-Lunch at Buffet Trzesniewski or Rosenberger Markt Restaurant, 13:00-Tour Hofburg, visiting royal apartments, treasury, and Kaisergruft, 16:30-Stroll Kärntner Strasse, tour

St. Stephan's cathedral, and stroll Graben and Kohlmarkt, 19:00-Choose classical music (concert or opera), House of Music museum, or *Heurige* wine garden.

Day 2: 09:00-Schönbrunn Palace , 13:00-Kunsthistorisches Museum after lunch, 15:00-Your choice of the many sights left to see in Vienna, Evening-See Day 1 evening options.

Orientation (area code: 01)

Vienna, or Wien (veen) in German, is bordered on three sides by the Vienna Woods (Wienerwald) and on one side by the Danube (Donau). To the southeast is industrial sprawl. The Alps, which arc across Europe from Marseilles, end at Vienna's wooded hills. These provide a popular playground for walking and new-wine drinking. This greenery's momentum carries on into the city. You'll notice more than half of Vienna is parkland, filled with ponds, gardens, trees, and statue memories of Austria's glory days.

Think of the city map as a target. The bull's-eye is the cathedral, the first circle is the Ring, and the second is the Gürtel. The old town snuggles around towering St. Stephan's Cathedral south of the Donau, and is bound tightly by the Ringstrasse. The Ring, marking what was the city wall, circles the first district (or *Bezirk*). The Gürtel, a broader ring road, contains the rest of downtown (*Bezirkes* 2–9).

Addresses start with the *Bezirk*, followed by street and building number. Any address higher than the ninth *Bezirk* is beyond the Gürtel, far from the center. The middle two digits of Vienna's postal codes show the district, or *Bezirk*. The address "7, Lindengasse 4" is in the seventh district, #4 on Linden Street. Its postal code would be 1070. Nearly all your sightseeing will be done in the core first district or along the Ringstrasse. As a tourist, concern yourself only with this compact old center. When you do, sprawling Vienna suddenly becomes manageable.

Tourist Information

Vienna has one real tourist office (near the Opera in the old center). Hotel and ticket booking agencies answer questions and give out maps and brochures at the train stations and airport.

The main Vienna tourist office is at a slick and spacious location a block behind the Opera House at Albertinaplatz (daily 09:00–19:00, tel. 01/211-14222, www.info.wien.at). Confirm your sightseeing plans and pick up the free and essential city map with a list of museums and hours (also available at most hotels), the monthly program of concerts (called "Programm"), and the youth guide (*Ten Good Reasons For Vienna*).

Consider the TI's handy €3.75 *Vienna from A to Z* booklet. Every important building sports a numbered flag banner that keys into this guidebook. A to Z numbers are keyed into the TI's city map. When lost, find one of the "famous-building flags" and match its number to your map. If you're at a "famous building," check the map to see what other key numbers are nearby, then check the A to Z book description to see if you want to go in. This system is especially helpful for those just wandering aimlessly among Vienna's historic charms.

Skip the much promoted €15 "Vienna Card." It gives you a 72-hour transit pass (worth €11) and insignificant discounts at museums on the push list.

Arrival in Vienna

By Train at the West Station (Westbahnhof): Train travelers arriving from Munich, Salzburg, and Melk land at the Westbahnhof. The Reisebüro am Bahnhof books hotels (for a fee), has free maps, and answers questions (daily 07:00–22:00). To get to the city center (and most likely, your hotel), catch the U-3 metro (buy the €4.50 24-hr pass from a *Tabak* shop in the station or from a machine—good on all city transit). U-3 signs lead down to the metro tracks. If your hotel is along Mariahilfer Strasse, your stop is on this line (direction: Simmering; see "Sleeping," below). If you're sleeping in the center or just sightseeing, ride five stops to Stephansplatz, escalate in the exit direction "Stephansplatz," and you'll hit the cathedral. The TI is a five-minute stroll down the busy Kärntner Strasse pedestrian street.

The Westbahnhof has a grocery store (daily 05:30–23:00), ATMs, change offices (station ticket windows offer better rates and shorter lines than change offices), storage facilities, and rental bikes (see "Getting around Vienna," below). Airport buses and taxis wait in front of the station.

By Train at the South Station (Südbahnhof): Those arriving from Italy and Prague land here. The Südbahnhof has all the services, including bike rental, left luggage, and a TI (daily 09:00–19:00). To reach Vienna's center, follow the "S" (*Schnellbahn*) signs to the right and down the stairs, and take any train in the direction "Floridsdorf"; transfer in two stops (at Landsstrasse/Wien Mitte) to the U-3 (yellow) line, direction "Ottakring," which goes directly to Stephansplatz and Mariahilfer Strasse hotels. Also, tram D goes to the Ring, and bus #13A goes to Mariahilfer Strasse.

By Train at Franz Josef Station: If you're coming from Krems (in Danube Valley), you'll arrive at Vienna's Franz Josef station. From here, take tram D into town. But even better, get off at Spittelau (the stop before Franz Josef) because it has a U-Bahn station.

By Plane: The airport (16km/10 miles from town, tel. 01/7007-22233) is connected by €5 shuttle buses (2/hr) to either the Westbahnhof (35 min) or the City Air Terminal (20 min; next to Hilton and Wien-Mitte station—with easy metro connections,

near river in old center). There is also an hourly train from the
airport to the Südbahnhof. Taxis into town cost about €35. Hotels
arrange for fixed-rate car service to the airport (€30, 30-min ride).

Getting around Vienna

By Bus, Tram, and Metro: Take full advantage of Vienna's simple, cheap, and superefficient transit system. Buses, trams, and the
metro all use the same tickets. Buy your tickets from *Tabak* shops,
station machines, or Vorverkauf offices in the station. You have
lots of choices:

- single tickets (€1.40, €1.60 if bought on tram—exact
  change only, good for 1 journey with necessary transfers)
- 24-hour pass (€4.50)
- 72-hour pass (€11)
- 7-day pass (€11.50, Mon–Sun)
- 8 *Tage Umwelt Streifennetzkarte*: eight all-day trips for
  €22 (can be shared, e.g., 4 people for 2 days each). Per-
  person cost: €2.75/day (compared to €4.50/day for a
  24-hour pass—a big savings for groups).

Take a moment to study the eye-friendly city center map on
metro station walls to internalize how the metro and tram system
can help you (metro routes are signed by the end-of-the-line stop).
I use the tram mostly to zip along the Ring (tram #1 or #2), and
take the metro to more outlying sights or hotels. The €1.50
transit map is overkill. All necessary routes are listed on the free
tourist city map. Numbered lines (e.g., #38) are trams, numbers
followed by an "A" (e.g., #38A) are buses. Lines that begin with
"U" (e.g., U-3) are subways, or *Unterbahnen*.

Stamp a time on your ticket or transit pass as you enter
the system or tram (stiff €44 fine if caught without a validated
ticket—then they make you buy a ticket). Rookies miss stops
because they fail to open the door. Push buttons, pull latches—
do whatever it takes. Study your street map before you exit the
metro. Choosing the right exit—signposted from the moment
you step off the train—saves lots of walking (for information
call 01/790-9105).

By Taxi: Vienna's comfortable, civilized, and easy-to-flag-
down taxis start at €2. You'll pay €7.25 to €11 to go from the
Opera to the South or West Train Station, depending on traffic.

By Bike: Good as the city's transit system is, you may want
to rent a bike and follow one of the routes recommended in the
TI's biking brochure. Bikes are available at any train station (daily
07:45–22:00, €9/day with railpass or train ticket, €13 without;
rent early in morning before supply runs out, tel. 01/5800-32985).
Pedal Power offers rental bikes (€24/half day, €32/24 hrs,
includes delivery and pickup from your hotel) and 3.5-hour,
two-language city tours (€23, includes bike, daily at 10:00,

Austellungsstrasse 3, U-1 to Praterstern and 5-min walk, tel. 01/729-7234, www.pedalpower.at).

By Buggy: Rich romantics get around by traditional horse and buggy. You'll see the horse buggies, called *Fiakers*, clip-clopping tourists on tours lasting 20 minutes (€37), 40 minutes (€58), or one hour (€95).

Helpful Hints

Bank Alert: Abundant ATMs are the smart way to change money. Banking is expensive in Vienna. Save three percent by comparing rates. (Warning: "Rieger Bank" is an expensive exchange bureau in disguise.) Banks are open weekdays roughly from 08:00 to 15:00 and until 17:30 on Tuesday and Thursday. After-hours you can change money at train stations, the airport, or post offices. Commissions of €7.50 are sadly normal (American Express charges no commissions on its checks, Mon–Fri 09:00–17:30, Sat 09:00–12:00, closed Sun, Kärntner Strasse 21-23, tel. 01/5154-0456).

Post Offices: Choose from the main post office (Postgasse in center, open 24 hrs daily, handy metered phones), West and South Train Stations (open 06:00–23:00), and one near the Opera (Mon–Fri 07:00–19:00, closed Sat–Sun, Krugerstrasse 13).

English Bookstores: Consider the British Bookshop (Mon–Fri 09:30–18:30, Sat 09:30–17:00, closed Sun, at the corner of Weihburggasse and Seilerstätte, tel. 01/512-1945; same hrs at Mariahilferstrasse 4, tel. 01/522-6730) or Shakespeare & Co. (Mon–Sat 09:00–19:00, closed Sun, north of Höher Markt square, Sterngasse 2, tel. 01/535-5053).

Internet Access: The TI has an updated list. Amadeus on the fifth floor of the Steffl mall is central and free (Mon–Fri 09:30–19:00, Sat 9:30–17:00, closed Sun, Kärntner Strasse 19, tel. 01/513-1450). Internet Aktiv is near the Mariahilfer Strasse hotels (Zieglergasse 29, tel. 01/526-7389). Coffeeshop Company, a Starbucks-like place, gives 10 free minutes of Internet access to customers (Mon–Sat 07:00–23:00, Sun 08:00–20:00, just off Kärntner Strasse at Krugerstrasse 6, tel. 01/513-0844). For more time online and less coffee, try Surfland Internet Café down the street (daily 10:00–23:00, Krugerstrasse 10, tel. 01/512-7701).

City Tours

Walks—The *Walks in Vienna* brochure at the TI describes Vienna's guided walks in English (basic 90-min intro, €11, daily at 14:15 from TI and other locations, tel. 01/894-5363, www.wienguide.at).

To learn more about Vienna's classical music all-stars, take the new Music Mile walk (due to be completed by summer 2002). Commemorative "walk of fame" plaques embedded in the sidewalk follow a route that stretches from Theater an der Wien outside the Ring, then past the Opera to Stephansplatz. You can connect the stars on your own, but you'll get more information by renting an audioguide—either follow the narrated route or plot your own course, homing in on your favorite composers (€5 for 3 hrs, €1.50 for each additional hr, visit ticket pavilion at Opera or info point at Linke Wienzeile 6, both offices open daily 11:00–19:00).

For a more personal touch, Monika Tentschert, a local teacher and private guide who knows her stuff, charges €142 for a half-day tour (tel. 01/212-0640).

Bus Tours—Vienna Line offers hop-on hop-off tours covering the 14 predictable sightseeing stops. Given Vienna's excellent public transportation and this outfit's meager one-to-two-bus-per-hour frequency, I'd take this not to hop on and off, but only to get the narrated orientation drive through town (in German and English, €18, ticket good for 2 days, or €10 if you stay on for 1 ride). The basic Vienna city sights tour includes a visit to the Schönbrunn Palace and a bus tour around town (€29, 2–3/day, 3.5 hrs; to book this or get info on other tours call 01/712-46830).

Do-It-Yourself Bus Orientation Tour

▲▲**Ringstrasse Tram #2 Tour**—In the 1860s, Emperor Franz Josef had the city's ingrown medieval wall torn down and replaced with a grand boulevard 60 meters (190 feet) wide. The road, arc-ing nearly five kilometers (3 miles) around the city's core, predates all the buildings that line it. So what you'll see is neo-Gothic, neoclassical, and neo-Renaissance. One of Europe's great streets, it's lined with many of the city's top sights. Trams #1 and #2 and a great bike path circle the whole route and so should you.

This self-service tram tour gives you a fun orientation and a ridiculously quick glimpse of the major sights as you glide by (€1.40, 30-min circular tour). For an actual look at these sights, consider biking or hiking most of the route. Tram #1 goes clock-wise; tram #2, counterclockwise. Most sights are on the outside, so tram #2 is better (sit on the right—ideally in the front of the front car). Start at the Opera House. You can jump on and off as you go—trams come every five minutes. Read ahead and pay attention, these sights can fly by. Let's go:

☛ Immediately on the left: The city's main pedestrian drag, Kärntner Strasse, leads to the zigzag roof of **St. Stephan's Cathedral**. This tram tour makes a 360-degree circle around the cathedral, staying about this same distance from it.

☛ At first bend (before first stop): Look right toward the tall fountain and the guy on a horse. Schwartzenberg Platz shows off its **equestrian statue** of Prince Charles Schwartzenberg, who fought Napoleon. Behind that is the Russian monument (behind the fountain), which was built in 1945 as a forced thanks to the Soviets for liberating Austria from the Nazis. Formerly a sore point, now it's just ignored.

Vienna

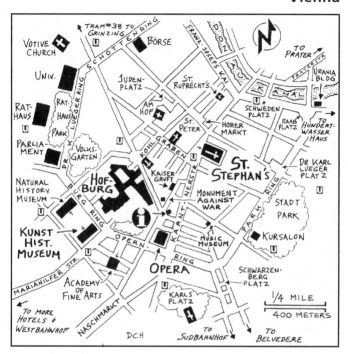

☛ Going down Schubertring, you reach the huge *Stadtpark* (city park) on the right, which honors 20 great Viennese musicians and composers with statues. At the beginning of the park, the white-and-yellow concert hall behind the trees is the **Kursalon**, opened in 1867 by the Strauss brothers, who directed many waltzes here.

☛ Immediately after next stop: In the same park, the gilded statue of Waltz King **Johann Strauss** holds his violin as he did when he conducted his orchestra.

☛ While at next stop at end of park: On the left, a green statue of Dr. Karl Lueger honors the popular man who was mayor of Vienna until 1910.

☛ At next bend: On the right, the quaint white building with military helmets decorating the windows was the Austrian ministry of war—back when that was a serious operation. Field Marshal Radetzky, a military big shot in the 19th century under Franz Josef, still sits on his high horse. He's pointing towards the post office, the only Art Nouveau building on the Ring. Locals call the architecture along the Ring "**historicism**" because it's all neo-this and neo-that—generally fitting the purpose of the particular building (for example, farther along the Ring, we'll see a neo-Gothic city hall—recalling when medieval burghers ran the city government in Gothic days, a neoclassical parliament building—celebrating ancient Greek notions of democracy, and a neo-Renaissance opera house—venerating the high culture filling it).

☛ At next corner: The white-domed building over your right shoulder as you turn is the Urania, Franz Josef's 1910 **observatory**. Lean forward and look behind it for a peek at the huge red cars of the giant 100-year-old Ferris wheel in Vienna's Prater Park (fun for families, described in "Top People-Watching and Strolling Sights," below).

☛ Now you're rolling along the **Danube Canal**. This "Baby Danube" is one of the many small arms of the river that once made up the Danube at this location. The rest have been gathered together in a mightier modern-day Danube, farther away. This was the site of the original Roman town, Vindobona. In three long blocks, on the left (opposite BP station, be ready—it passes fast), you'll see the ivy-covered walls and round Romanesque arches of St. Ruprechts, the oldest church in Vienna (built in the 11th century on a bit of Roman ruins). By about 1200, Vienna had grown to fill the area within this ring road.

☛ Leaving the canal, turning up Schottenring, at first stop: On the left, the orange-and-white, neo-Renaissance temple of money, the **Börse**, is Vienna's stock exchange.

☛ Next stop, at corner: The huge, frilly, neo-Gothic church on the right is a "votive church," built as a thanks to God when an 1853 assassination attempt on Emperor Franz Josef failed. Ahead on the right (in front of tram stop) is the Vienna University building (established in 1365, it has no real campus as the buildings are scattered around town). It faces (on the left, behind gilded angel) a chunk of the old city wall.

☛ At next stop on right: The neo-Gothic city hall, flying the flag of Europe, towers over **Rathaus Platz**, a festive site in summer with a huge screen showing outdoor movies, opera, and concerts. Immediately across the street (on left) is the **Hofburg Theater**, Austria's national theater.

☛ At next stop on right: The neo-Greek temple of democracy houses the **Austrian Parliament**. The lady with the golden helmet is Athena, goddess of wisdom. Across the street (on left) is the royal park called the *Volksgarten*.

☛ After the next stop on the right is the **Natural History Museum**, the first of Vienna's huge twin museums. It faces the **Kunsthistorisches Museum**, containing the city's greatest collection of paintings. A hefty statue of Empress Maria Theresa sits between the museums, facing the grand gate to the **Hofburg**, the emperor's palace (on left). Of the five arches, only the center one was used by the emperor.

☛ Fifty meters (165 feet) after the next stop, on the left through a gate in the black iron fence, is the statue of Mozart. It's one of many charms in the **Burggarten**, which until 1880 was the private garden of the emperor. Vienna had more than its share of intellectual and creative geniuses. A hundred meters farther (on left, just out of the park), Goethe sits in a big, thought-provoking chair playing trivia with Schiller (across the street on your right). Behind the statue of Schiller is the Academy of Fine Arts.

☛ Hey, there's the **Opera** again. Jump off the bus and see the rest of the city.

Sights—Vienna's Old Center

Sights are listed in a logical walking order.

▲▲▲**Opera (Staatsoper)**—The Opera, facing the Ring and near the TI, is a central point for any visitor. While the critical reception of the building 130 years ago led the architect to commit suicide, and though it's been rebuilt since the WWII bombings, it's still a dazzling place (€4.35, by guided 35-min tour only, daily in English, July–Aug at 11:00, 13:00, 14:00, 15:00, and often at 10:00 and 16:00; Sept–June open fewer days and only in the afternoon). Tours are often canceled for rehearsals and shows, so check the posted schedule or call 01/514-442-613 or 01/514-442-421.

The Vienna State Opera is one of the world's top opera houses, even though the Vienna Philharmonic Orchestra doesn't perform here. Instead its farm team plays in the pit (you can't get into the best orchestra in town without doing time here first). There are 300 performances a year—nearly nightly, except in July and August when the singers rest their voices. Expensive seats are normally sold out.

Tickets for seats: For ticket information call 01/513-1513 (phone answered daily 10:00–21:00, www.culturall.com or www.wiener-staatsoper.at). Last-minute tickets are sold for €29 from 09:00 to 14:00 the day before.

Standing room: Unless Pavarotti is in town, it's easy to get one of 567 *Stehplatz* (standing-room spots, €2.20–3.65 at the very top or—better—downstairs). The *Stehplatz* ticket window in the front lobby opens 80 minutes before each performance (tel. 01/5144-42419). If fewer than 567 people are in line, there's no need to line up early. You can even buy standing-room tickets after the show has started—in case you only want a little taste of opera (see "Rick's crude tip," below): enter through the door on Operngasse closest to the fountain and knock on the door marked "Revisionsdienst" to see if they have any *Stehplätze* left. Dress is casual (but do your best) at the standing-room bar. The "no shorts" rule is enforced only by sticklers. Locals who are in the know wear scarves to the opera. It's an unwritten rule that you can save your spot along the rail by tying your scarf to it. Don't try to sneak your way into marked territory—you're liable to get hissed at.

Rick's crude tip: For me, three hours is a lot of opera. But just to see and hear the Opera House in action for half an hour is a treat. You can buy a standing-room spot intending to just drop in for part of the show. Ushers don't mind letting tourists with standing-room tickets in for a short look. Ending time is posted in the lobby—you could drop in for just the finale. If you go for the start or finish you'll see Vienna dressed up. With all the time you save, consider stopping by...

Sacher Café, home of every chocoholic's fantasy, the *Sacher-torte*, faces the rear of the Opera. While locals complain that the cakes have gone downhill, a coffee and slice of cake here is €7.50 well invested (daily 08:00–23:30, Philharmoniker Strasse 4, tel. 01/595-477-621).

▲**Monument against War and Fascism**—A powerful four-part statue stands behind the Opera House on Albertinaplatz. The split white statue, *The Gates of Violence*, remembers the victims of the 1938 to 1945 Nazi rule of Austria. A montage of wartime images—clubs and gas masks, a dying woman birthing a future soldier, slave laborers—sits on a pedestal of granite cut from the infamous quarry at Mauthausen, a nearby concentration camp. The hunched-over figure on the ground behind is a Jew forced to wash anti-Nazi graffiti off a street with a toothbrush. The statue with its head buried in the stone reminds Austrians of the consequences of not keeping their government on track. The 1945 declaration of Austria's second republic is cut into the stone behind that. The monument stands over the spot where a hundred people were buried alive while hiding in the cellar of a fancy building, demolished in a WWII bombing attack.

Austria was pulled into World War II by Germany, who annexed the country in 1938, saying Austrians were wannabe Germans anyway. But Austrians are not Germans—never were, never will be. They're quick to tell you that while Austria was founded in 976, Germany wasn't born until 1870. For seven years during World War II (1938–1945), there was no Austria. In 1955, after 10 years of joint occupation by the victorious Allies, Austria regained her independence.

▲**Kärntner Strasse**—This grand mall-like street (traffic free since 1974) is the people-watching delight of this in-love-with-life city. It points south in the direction of the southern Austrian state of Kärnten (for which it's named). Starting from the Opera, you'll find lots of action—shops, street music, the city casino (at #41), American Express (#21-23), and then, finally, the cathedral.

▲▲**Haus der Musik**—Vienna's newest museum is long overdue—the House of Music. While it has a floor devoted to the Vienna Philharmonic and fine audiovisual exhibits on each of the famous hometown boys (Haydn, Mozart, Beethoven, Strauss, and Mahler), this museum is unique for its effective use of interactive touch-screen computers and headphones to literally put you in the musical driving seat. You can twist, dissect, and bend sounds to make your own musical language, merging your voice with a duck's quack or a city's traffic roar. Wander through the "sonosphere" and marvel at the amazing acoustics—I could actually hear what I thought only a piano tuner can hear. Pick up a virtual baton to conduct the Vienna Philharmonic Orchestra (each time you screw up, the orchestra stops and ridicules you). Really seeing the place takes time. It's open late and makes a good evening activity (€8, €5 for Vienna Philharmonic museum in same building, €9.50-combo ticket for both, daily 10:00–22:00, 2 blocks from Opera at Seilerstatte 30, tel. 01/51648, www.hdm.at).

▲▲**St. Stephan's Cathedral**—Stephansdom is the Gothic needle around which Vienna spins. It's survived Vienna's many wars and symbolizes the city's freedom (Mon–Sat 06:00–22:00, Sun 07:00–22:00, entertaining English tours daily April–Oct at 15:45, information board inside entry has tour schedules and time of impressive daily 50-min Mass).

This is the third church to stand on this spot. (In fact, an older Romanesque chapel—the Virgilkapelle—is on display in the adjacent metro station.) The last bit of the 11th-century Romanesque church, the portal and the round windows of the towers, can be seen on the west end (above the entry). The church survived the bombs of World War II, but, in the last days of the war, fires from the street fighting between Russian and Nazi troops leapt to the rooftop; the original timbered Gothic rooftop burned, and the cathedral's huge bell crashed to the ground. With a financial outpouring of civic pride, the roof of this symbol of Austria was rebuilt in its original splendor by 1952. The ceramic tiles are purely decorative (locals each "own" one for the many small post-war donations made to finance the rebuilding).

Inside, find the Gothic sandstone **pulpit** in the middle of the nave (on left). A spiral stairway winds up to the lectern, surrounded and supported by the four Latin Church fathers: Saints Ambrose, Jerome, Gregory, and Augustine. The railing leading up swarms with symbolism: lizards (animals of light), battle toads (animals of darkness), and the "Dog of the Lord" standing at the top to be sure none of those toads pollute the sermon. Below the toads, wheels with three parts (the Trinity) roll up while wheels with four parts (standing for the four seasons, symbolizing mortal life) roll down. This work, by Anton Pilgram, has all the elements of flamboyant Gothic in miniature. But this was around 1500, and the Italian Renaissance was going strong in Italy. While Gothic persisted in the north, the Renaissance spirit had already arrived. Pilgram included a rare self-portrait bust in his work (the guy

with sculptor's tools, looking out a window under the stairs).
Gothic art was done for the glory of God. Artists were anonymous. In the more humanist Renaissance, man was allowed to
shine—and artists became famous.

St. Stephan's is draped in history—carved in its walls and
buried in its **crypt** (left transept, €3, Mon–Sat 10:00–11:30,
13:30–16:30, Sun 13:30–16:30, entry only with occasional tours
that may occur 2–4/hr, tel. 01/5155-23526). You can ascend both
towers, the north (via crowded elevator inside on the left) and the
south (outside right transept, by spiral staircase). The north shows
you a big **bell** (the 21-ton Pummerin, cast from the cannon captured from the Turks in 1683, supposedly the second biggest bell
in the world that rings by swinging) but a mediocre view (€3.75,
daily 09:00–18:00). The 135-meter-high (450-foot) **south tower**,
called St. Stephan's Tower, offers a great view—343 tightly wound
steps up the spiral staircase (€2.75, daily 09:00–17:30, this hike
burns about 1 *Sachertorte* of calories). From the top, use your
Vienna from A to Z to locate the famous sights.

The peaceful **Cathedral Museum** (Dom Museum, outside
left transept past horses) gives a close-up look at piles of religious
paintings, statues, and a treasury (€5, Tue–Sat 10:00–17:00, closed
Sun–Mon, Stephansplatz 6).

After your visit to St. Stephan's, consider stopping by the
popular **Zanoni & Zanoni** for gelato (daily 07:00–24:00, turn
right as you exit cathedral and go up Rotenturmstrasse 1 block to
Lugeck 7, tel. 01/512-7979).

▲▲**Stephansplatz, Graben, and Kohlmarkt**—The atmosphere
of the church square, Stephansplatz, is colorful and lively. At
nearby Graben Street (which was once a *Graben* or "ditch"),
top-notch street entertainment dances around an exotic **plague
monument** (at Brauner Strass). In medieval times, people did not
understand the causes of plagues and figured they were a punishment from God. It was common for survivors to thank God with
a monument like this one from the 1600s. Find Emperor Leopold,
who ruled during the plague and made this statue in gratitude.
(Hint: The typical inbreeding of royal families left him with a
gaping underbite.) Below Leopold, "Faith" (with the help of a
disgusting little cupid) tosses old naked women—symbolizing the
plague—into the abyss.

Just beyond the monument is a fine set of public toilets
(€0.50). **St. Peter's Church** faces the toilets. Step into this festival of Baroque (from 1708) and check out the jeweled skeletons
(flanking the altar)—anonymous martyrs donated by the pope.

At the end of Graben, turn left on **Kohlmarkt**, Vienna's most
elegant shopping street (except for "American Catalog Shopping,"
at #5, second floor). Kohlmarkt leads to the palace. En route, day-
dream about the edible window displays at Demel (Kohlmarkt 14).

Then drool through the interior (coffee and cake for €7.50). Shops like this boast "K. u. K." This means a shop considered good enough for the *König und Kaiser* (king and emperor—same guy).

Kohlmarkt ends at Michaelerplatz. The stables of the Spanish Riding School face this square a block to the left. Notice the Roman excavation in the center. Enter the Hofburg Palace by walking through the gate, under the dome, and into the first square (In der Burg).

Sights—Vienna's Hofburg Palace

▲▲**Hofburg**—The complex, confusing, and imposing Imperial Palace, with 640 years of architecture, demands your attention. This first Hapsburg residence grew with the family empire from the 13th century until 1913, when the new wing was opened. The winter residence of the Hapsburg rulers until 1918, it's still the home of the Spanish Riding School, the Vienna Boys' Choir, the Austrian president's office, 5,000 government workers, and several important museums.

Rather than lose yourself in its myriad halls and courtyards, focus on three things: the Imperial Apartments, Treasury, and Neue Burg (New Palace).

Orient from **In der Burg Square**. The statue is of Emperor Franz II, grandson of Maria Theresa, grandfather of Franz Josef, and father-in-law of Napoleon. Behind him is a tower with three kinds of clocks (the yellow disk shows the stage of the moon tonight). On the right, a door leads to the Imperial Apartments and Hofburg model. Franz II faces the oldest part of the palace. The colorful gate, which used to have a drawbridge, leads to the 13th-century Swiss Court (named for the Swiss mercenary guards once stationed here), the Schatzkammer (treasury), and the Hofburgkappelle (palace chapel, where the Boys' Choir sings the Mass). For the Hero's Square and the New Palace, continue opposite the way you entered In der Burg, passing through the left-most tunnel (with a tiny but handy sandwich bar— Hofburg Stüberl).

Tour the Imperial Apartments first.

▲▲**Imperial Apartments (Kaiserappartements)**—These lavish, Versailles-type "wish-I-were-God" royal rooms are a small, down-town version of the grander Schönbrunn Palace. If rushed and you have time for only one, these suffice (€7, daily 09:00–17:00, last entry 16:30, from courtyard through St. Michael's Gate, just off Michaelerplatz, tel. 01/533-7570). Study the great Hofburg model outside near the ticket line. Palace visits are a one-way romp through 20 rooms. You'll find some helpful English infor-mation within, and, together with the following description, you won't need the €7 Hofburg guidebook. The €3.50 audioguide is only worthwhile for the Hapsburg history buff. Tickets include

Vienna's Hofburg Palace

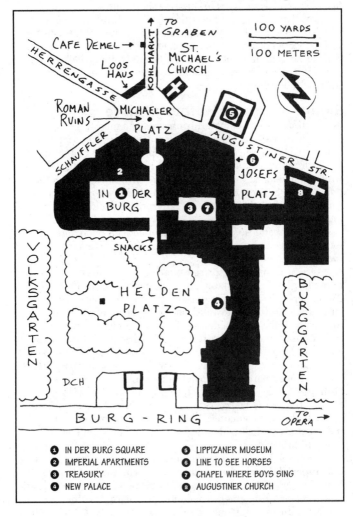

❶ IN DER BURG SQUARE	❺ LIPPIZANER MUSEUM
❷ IMPERIAL APARTMENTS	❻ LINE TO SEE HORSES
❸ TREASURY	❼ CHAPEL WHERE BOYS SING
❹ NEW PALACE	❽ AUGUSTINER CHURCH

the royal silver and porcelain collection (*Silberkammer*) near the turnstile.

Get your ticket and climb two flights. The first two rooms give an overview (in English) of Empress Elisabeth's assortment of luxury homes, including the Hofburg. Throughout the tour, look for the banners—hanging in front of windows—that contain descriptions in English of royal life.

Amble through the first several furnished rooms to the...

Waiting room for the audience room: Every citizen had the right to meet privately with the emperor. Three huge paintings would entertain guests while they waited. They were propaganda, showing crowds of commoners enthusiastic about their Hapsburg royalty. On the right: The emperor returning to Vienna celebrating news that Napoleon had begun his retreat in 1809. Left: The return of the emperor from the 1814 Peace of Paris, the treaty that ended the Napoleonic wars. (The 1815 Congress of Vienna that followed was the greatest assembly of diplomats in European history. Its goal: to establish peace through a "balance of power" among nations. While rulers ignored nationalism in favor of continued dynastic rule, this worked for about 100 years, when a colossal war—World War I—wiped out Europe's royal families.) Center: Less important, the emperor makes his first public appearance to adoring crowds after recovering from a life-threatening illness (1826). The chandelier—considered the best in the palace—is Baroque of Bohemian crystal.

Audience room: Suddenly you were face-to-face with the emp. The portrait on the easel shows Franz Josef (who gets my vote for the greatest Hapsburg emperor) in 1915 when he was over 80 years old. Famously energetic, he lived a spartan life dedicated to duty. He'd stand at the high table here to meet with commoners who came to show gratitude or make a request. (Standing kept things moving.) On the table you see a partial list of 56 appointments he had on January 3, 1910.

Conference room: The emperor presided here over the equivalent of cabinet meetings. Remember, after 1867 he ruled the Austro-Hungarian Empire and Hungarians sat at these meetings. The paintings on the wall show the military defeat of a popular Hungarian uprising...subtle.

Emperor Franz Josef's study: The desk was originally between the windows. Franz Josef could look up from his work and see his lovely empress Elisabeth's reflection in the mirror. Notice the trompe l'oeil paintings above each door giving the believable illusion of marble relief.

The walls between the rooms are wide enough to hide servants' corridors (the door to his valet's room is in the back left corner, behind the desk). The emperor lived with a personal staff of 14: three valets, four lackeys, two doormen, two manservants, and three chambermaids.

Emperor's bedroom: This features his famous spartan iron bed and portable washstand (necessary until 1880 when the palace got running water). A small painted porcelain portrait of the newlywed royal couple sits on the dresser. Franz Josef lived here after his estrangement from Sissy. An etching shows the empress—an avid hunter—riding sidesaddle while jumping a hedge. The big

Sissy

Empress Elisabeth, Emperor Franz Joseph's mysterious, narcissistic, and beautiful wife, is in vogue. She was mostly silent, worked out frantically to maintain her Barbie Doll figure, and spent hours each day tending to her ankle-length hair. Sissy's main purpose in life seemed to be to preserve her reputation as a beautiful empress and maintain her fairy-tale hair. In spite of severe dieting and fanatic exercise, age took its toll. After turning 30, she allowed no more portraits painted and was seen in public generally with a delicate fan covering her face. Complex and influential, she was adored by Franz Joseph whom she respected. Her personal mission and political cause was promoting Hungary's bid for nationalism. Her personal tragedy was the death of her son Rudolf, the crown prince, by suicide. Disliking Vienna and the confines of the court, she traveled more and more frequently. Over the years, the restless Sissy and her hardworking husband became estranged. In 1898, while visiting Geneva, Switzerland, she was murdered by an Italian anarchist. Sissy has been compared to Princess Diana because of her beauty, bittersweet life, and tragic death.

ornate stove in the corner was fed from behind. Through the 19th century, this was a standard form of heating.

Great salon: See the paintings of the emperor and empress in grand gala ballroom outfits from 1865.

Small salon/smoking room: This is dedicated to the memory of the assassinated Emperor Maximillian of Mexico (bearded portrait, Franz Josef's brother, killed in 1867). A smoking room was necessary in the early 19th century, when smoking was newly fashionable but only for men and then not in the presence of women.

Empress' bedroom and drawing room: This was Sissy's, refurbished neo-rococo in 1854. She lived here—the bed was rolled in and out daily—until her death in 1898.

Sissy's dressing/gymnastic room: This was the marital bedroom of the newlywed couple. The open bathroom door shows her huge copper tub. Servants worked two hours a day on Sissy's famous hair here. She'd exercise on the wooden structure. While she had a tough time with people, she did fine with animals. Her favorite circus horses, Flick and Flock, prance on the wall.

Empress' great salon: The room is painted with Mediterranean escapes, the 19th-century equivalent of travel posters. The statue is of Elisa, Napoleon's oldest sister (by the neoclassical master Canova). At the end of the hall, admire the Empress' hard-earned thin waist. Turn the corner and pass through the anterooms of Alexander's apartments.

Red salon: The Gobelin wall hangings were a 1776 gift from Marie Antoinette and Louis XVI in Paris to their Viennese counterparts.

Dining room: It's dinnertime, and Franz Josef has called his large family together. The settings are modest...just silver. Gold was saved for formal state dinners. Next to each name card was a menu with the chef responsible for each dish. (Talk about pressure.) While the Hofburg had tableware for 4,000, feeding 3,000 was a typical day. The cellar was stocked with 60,000 bottles of wine. The kitchen was huge—50 birds could be roasted on the hand-driven spits at once.

Successors room: The last room is dedicated to Franz Josef's first two heirs: Rudolf (his troubled son, who committed suicide in 1889) and Franz Ferdinand (his liberal nephew, assassinated in Sarajevo in 1914). Back on the street, two quick lefts take you back to the palace square (In der Burg) and the treasury.

▲▲▲**Treasury (Weltliche und Geistliche Schatzkammer)**—This Secular and Religious Treasure Room contains the best jewels on the Continent. Slip through the vault doors and reflect on the glitter of 21 rooms filled with scepters, swords, crowns, orbs, weighty robes, double-headed eagles, gowns, gem-studded bangles, and a 2.5-meter-tall, 500-year-old unicorn horn (or maybe the tusk of a narwhal)—which was incredibly powerful in the old days, giving its owner the grace of God. Remember that these were owned by the Holy Roman Emperor—a divine monarch (€7, Wed–Mon 10:00–18:00, closed Tue, follow *Schatzkammer* signs through the black, red, and gold arch leading from the main courtyard into Schweizerhof, tel. 01/533-6046). Take advantage of the ingenious and extremely helpful Art-Guide mini-video (free). Point this infrared computer at display cases to get information.

Room 2: The personal crown of Rudolf II survived since 1602 because it was considered too well crafted to cannibalize for other crowns. This crown is a big deal because it's the adopted crown of the Austrian Empire, established in 1806 after Napoleon dissolved the Holy Roman Empire (so named because it had tried to be the grand continuation of the Roman Empire). Pressured by Napoleon, the Austrian Francis II—who'd been Holy Roman Emperor—became Francis I, Emperor of Austria. Francis I/II (the stern guy on the wall) ruled from 1792 to 1835. Look at the crown. Its design merges the typical medieval king's crown and a bishop's miter.

Rooms 3 and 4: These contain some of the coronation vestments and regalia needed for the new Austrian emperor.

Room 5: Ponder the Throne Cradle. Napoleon's son was born in 1811 and made king of Rome. The little eagle at the foot is symbolically not yet able to fly but glory bound. Glory is symbolized by the star with dad's big "N" raised high.

Room 11: The collection's highlight is the 10th-century crown of the Holy Roman Emperor. The imperial crown swirls with symbolism "proving" that the emperor is both holy and Roman. The jeweled arch over the top is reminiscent of the parade helmet of ancient Roman emperors whose successors the HRE claimed to be. The cross on top says that the HRE rules as Christ's representative on earth. King Solomon's portrait (right of cross) is Old Testament proof that kings can be wise and good. King David (next panel) is similar proof that they can be just. The crown's eight sides represent the celestial city of Jerusalem's eight gates. The jewels on the front panel symbolize the Twelve Apostles. The nearby 11th-century Imperial Cross preceded the emperor in ceremonies. Crusted with jewels, it carried a substantial chunk of *the* cross (see it below).

Two cases in this room have jewels from the reign of Karl der Grosse (Charlemagne), the greatest ruler of medieval Europe. Notice Charlemagne modeling the crown in the tall painting adjacent.

Room 12: This features a painting of the coronation of Josef II in 1764, wearing the crown and royal garb you've just seen.

Room 16: Most tourists walk right by perhaps the most exquisite workmanship in the entire treasury, the royal vestments (15th century). Look closely—they are painted with gold and silver threads.

▲**Hero's Square and the New Palace (Heldenplatz and the Neue Burg)**—This last grand addition to the palace, from just before World War I, was built for Franz Ferdinand but never used. (It was tradition for rulers not to move into their predecessor's quarters.) Its grand facade arches around Heldenplatz, or Hero's Square. Notice statues of the two great Austrian heroes on horseback: Prince Eugene of Savoy (who saved the city from the Turks) and Archduke Charles (first to beat Napoleon in a battle, breaking Nappy's image of invincibility and heralding the end of the Napoleonic age). The frilly spires of Vienna's neo-Gothic city hall break the horizon and a line of horse-drawn carriages await their customers.

▲**New Palace Museums: Armor, Music, and Ancient Greek Statues**—The Neue Burg—labeled "Kunsthistorisches Museum" because it contains one wing from the main museum across the way—houses three small but fine museums (same ticket): an armory, historical musical instruments, and classical statuary from ancient Ephesus. The musical instruments are particularly entertaining. Free radio headsets—when they work—play appropriate music in each room. Wait for the brief German description to finish, and you might hear the instruments you're seeing. Stay tuned in, as graceful period music accompanies your wander through the neighboring halls of medieval weaponry—a killer collection of crossbows, swords, and armor. An added bonus is the chance to wander all alone among those royal Hapsburg halls, stairways, and painted ceilings (€7, Wed–Mon 10:00–18:00, closed Tue, almost no tourists, not a word of English—and proud of it).

More Hofburg Sights

These sights are near—and associated with—the palace.

▲**Lipizzaner Museum**—A must for horse lovers, this tidy museum in the Renaissance Stallburg Palace shows (and tells in English) the 400-year history of the famous riding school. Videos show the horses in action on TVs throughout the museum. The 45-minute movie in the basement theater also has great horse footage (showings alternate in German and English).

A highlight for many is the opportunity to view the stable from a museum window and actually see the famous white horses just sitting there looking common (€5, daily 09:00–18:00, Reitschulgasse 2 between Josefsplatz and Michaelerplatz, tel. 01/533-7811). Part of the exhibit explains how, at the end of World War II, U.S. General Patton—knowing that the Soviets were about to take control of Vienna—ordered a raid on the stable to save the horses and insure the survival of their fine old bloodlines.

Seeing the Lipizzaner Stallions: Seats for performances by Vienna's prestigious Spanish Riding School book up long in advance, but standing room is usually available the same day (tickets-€21.80–65.40, standing room-€18, May–June and Sept–Oct Sun at 10:45, sometimes also Wed at 19:00). Lucky for the masses, training sessions in a chandeliered Baroque hall are open to the public (€7.25 at the door, roughly Feb–June and Sept–Oct, Tue–Fri 10:00–12:00; occasional rehearsals with music on Sat are more entertaining than the generally low-energy training sessions; check first to be sure the horses are in town, tel. 01/533-9031, www.spanische-reitschule.com). Tourists line up early at Josefsplatz, gate 2. Save money and avoid the wait by buying the €10 combo ticket covering both the museum and the training session. Or, better yet, simply show up late. Tourists line up for hours to get in at 10:00, but almost no one stays for the full two hours—except for the horses. As people leave, new tickets are printed continuously, so you can just waltz in with no wait at all after 11:00.

▲**Augustinian Church**—Step into the nearby Augustinerkirche (on Josefsplatz), the Gothic and neo-Gothic church where the Hapsburgs latched, then buried, their hearts (weddings took place here and the royal hearts are in the vault). Don't miss the exquisite Canova tomb (neoclassical, 1805) of Maria Theresa's favorite daughter, Maria Christina, with its incredibly sad white-marble

procession. The church's 11:00 Sunday Mass is a hit with music
lovers (pipe organ and choral, especially outside of summer).
▲▲**Kaisergruft, the Remains of the Hapsburgs**—Visiting the
imperial remains is not as easy as you might imagine. These original organ donors left their bodies—147 in all—in the Kaisergruft
(Capuchin Crypt), their hearts in the Augustinian Church (church
open daily, but to see the goods you'll have to talk to a priest;
Augustinerstrasse 3), and their entrails in the crypt below St.
Stephan's Cathedral. Don't tripe.

Upon entering the Kaisergruft (€3.75, daily 09:30–16:00, last
entry 15:40, behind Opera on Neuer Markt), see the Capuchin
brother at the door and buy the €0.35 map with a Hapsburg family
tree and a chart locating each coffin. The double coffin of Maria
Theresa and her husband is worth a close look for its artwork.
Don't miss the tombs of Franz Josef, Sissy (always with fresh flowers), and—the latest addition—Empress Zita, buried in 1989. Her
burial procession was probably the last such Old Regime event in
European history. The monarchy died hard in Austria. Take a whiff.
The crypt smells funny and will probably be closed sometime in
the near future for restoration and freshening up.

Rather than chasing down all these body parts, remember that
the magnificence of this city is the real remains of the Hapsburgs.
Pan up. Watch the clouds glide by the ornate gables of Vienna.

Sights—Schönbrunn Palace

▲▲▲**Schönbrunn Palace**—Among Europe's palaces, only
Schloss Schönbrunn rivals Versailles. Located six kilometers
(4 miles) from the center, it was the Hapsburgs' summer residence. It's big—1,441 rooms—but don't worry, only 40 rooms
are shown to the public. (The families of 260 civil servants
actually rent simple apartments in the rest of the palace.)

While the exterior is Baroque, the interior was finished under
Maria Theresa in let-them-eat-cake rococo. The chandeliers are
either of hand-carved wood with gold-leaf gilding or of Bohemian
crystal. Thick walls hid the servants as they ran around stoking the
ceramic stoves from the back, and so on. Most of the public rooms
are decorated in neo-Baroque as they were under Franz Josef
(ruled 1848–1916). When World War II bombs rained on the city
and the palace grounds, the palace itself took only one direct hit.
Thankfully, that bomb, which crashed through three floors,
including the sumptuous central ballroom, was a dud.

Reservations and Hours: Schönbrunn suffers from crowds.
To avoid the long delays, make a reservation by telephone (tel.
01/8111-3239, answered daily 08:00–17:00). You'll get an appointment time and ticket number. Check in at least 30 minutes early.
Upon arrival, go to the second desk, give your number, pick
up your ticket, and jump in ahead of the masses. If you show up

without calling first, you deserve the frustration. Wait in line, buy your ticket, and wait until the listed time to enter (which could be tomorrow). Kill time in the gardens or coach museum (palace open April–Oct daily 08:30–17:00, July–Aug maybe until 19:00, Nov–March daily 08:30–16:30). Crowds are worst from 09:30 to 11:30 and on weekends; it's least crowded from 12:00 to 14:00 and after 16:00.

Cost and Tours: The admission price is the price of the tour you select. Choose among two recorded audioguide tours (Imperial Tour or the bigger Grand Tour) or a live tour. The audioguided Imperial Tour covers 22 rooms (€8, 60 min, Grand Palace rooms plus apartments of Franz Josef and Elisabeth). I'd recommend the Grand Tour, which covers those 22 rooms plus 18 more (€10, 75 min, adds apartments of Maria Theresa). While there are occasional live guided tours doing all 40 rooms (Grand Tour entrance plus €2.50, call day before your visit to ask if English tour is scheduled), I prefer the headphones.

Getting to Palace: Take tram #58 from Westbahnhof directly to the palace or ride U-4 to Schönbrunn and walk 300 meters (900 feet). The main entrance is in the left side of the palace (as you face it).

Coach Museum Wagenburg—The Schönbrunn coach museum is a 19th-century traffic jam of 50 impressive royal carriages and sleighs. Highlights include silly sedan chairs, the death-black hearse carriage (used for Franz Josef in 1916 and most recently for Empress Zita in 1989), and an extravagantly gilded imperial carriage pulled by eight Cinderella horses (€4.50, April–Oct daily 09:00–18:00, Nov–March 10:00–16:00, last entry 30 min before closing time, closed Mon in winter, 200 meters/650 feet from palace, walk through right arch as you face palace, tel. 01/877-3244).

Palace Gardens—After strolling through all the Hapsburgs tucked neatly into their crypts, a stroll through the emperor's garden with countless commoners is a celebration of the natural (and necessary) evolution of civilization from autocracy into real democracy. As a civilization, we're doing well. The sculpted gardens (with a palm house, €3.50, May–Sept daily 09:30–18:00, Oct–April daily 09:30–17:00) lead past Europe's oldest zoo (*Tiergarten*, €9, combo ticket for zoo plus palm house costs €10.50, May–Sept daily 09:00–18:30, less off-season, built by Maria Theresa's husband for the entertainment and education of the court in 1752, tel. 01/877-9294) up to the Gloriette, a purely decorative monument celebrating an obscure Austrian military victory and offering a fine city view (and an expensive cup of coffee). The park is free (daily sunrise to dusk, entrance on either side of the palace).

Vienna's Other Top Sights
▲▲▲**Kunsthistorisches Museum**—This exciting museum across the Ring from the Hofburg Palace showcases the great Hapsburg

art collection—masterpieces by Dürer, Rubens, Titian, Raphael, and especially Brueghel. There's also a fine display of Egyptian, classical, and applied arts, including a divine golden salt bowl by Cellini. The paintings are hung on one glorious floor. Try the very helpful included audioguide (€7.50, higher depending on special exhibitions, Tue–Sun 10:00–18:00, Thu until 21:00, closed Mon except during some special exhibitions, tel. 01/525-240).

▲**Natural History Museum**—In the twin building facing the art museum, you'll find moon rocks, dinosaur stuff, and the fist-sized *Venus of Willendorf*—at 30,000 years old, the world's oldest sex symbol, found in the Danube Valley (€4, Wed–Mon 09:00–18:30, Wed until 21:00, closed Tue, tel. 01/521-770).

▲**Academy of Fine Arts**—This small but exciting collection includes works by Bosch, Botticelli, and Rubens; a Venice series by Guardi; and a self-portrait by 15-year-old Van Dyck (€3.75, Tue–Sun 10:00–16:00, closed Mon, 3 blocks from Opera at Schillerplatz 3, tel. 01/5881-6225). As you wander the halls of this academy, ponder how history might have been different if Hitler—who applied to study architecture here but was rejected—would have been accepted.

KunstHausWien—This "make yourself at home" modern-art museum is a hit with lovers of modern art. It features the work of local painter/environmentalist Hundertwasser (€7, combo ticket for €11.75 includes special exhibitions, half price on Mon, daily 10:00–19:00, U-3: Landstrasse, Weissgerberstrasse 13, tel. 01/712-0491).

Nearby, the one-with-nature **Hundertwasserhaus** (at Löwengasse and Kegelgasse) is a complex of 50 lived-in apartments. This was built in the 1980s as a breath of architectural fresh air in a city of boring blocky apartment complexes. It's not open to visitors but is worth visiting for its fun-loving and colorful patchwork exterior, the Hundertwasser festival of shops across the street, and for the pleasure of annoying its neighbors. People wait for years to get an apartment here.

▲**Belvedere Palace**—The elegant palace of Prince Eugene of Savoy (the still-much-appreciated conqueror of the Turks), and later home of Franz Ferdinand, houses the Austrian Gallery of 19th- and 20th-century art. Skip the lower palace and focus on the garden and the top floor of the upper palace (*Oberes Belvedere*) for a winning view of the city and a fine collection of Jugendstil art, Klimt, and Kokoschka (€7.50, Tue–Sun 10:00–18:00, Thu until 21:00, closed Mon, winter until 17:00, entrance at Prinz Eugen Strasse 27, tel. 01/7955-7134). Your ticket includes the Austrian Baroque and Gothic art in the Lower Palace.

Judenplatz Museum—This new museum offers a look into Vienna's 15th-century Jewish community, one of Europe's largest at the time. The museum incorporates in its basement the remains

Jugendstil

Vienna gave birth to its own curvaceous brand of Art Nouveau around the early 1900s: Jugendstil. The TI has a brochure laying out Vienna's 20th-century architecture. The best of Vienna's scattered Jugendstil sights: the Belvedere Palace collection, the clock on Höher Markt (which does a musical act at noon), and the Karlsplatz metro stop, where you'll find the gilded-cabbage-domed Secession gallery with the movement's slogan: "To each century its art and to art its liberty." Klimt, Wagner, and friends (who called themselves the Vienna Secession) first exhibited their "liberty style" art here in 1897.

of a medieval synagogue that were discovered during the construction of a new Holocaust memorial (the building made of books in the square in front of the museum). Walk through the ruins and watch a computer-generated film about what the synagogue and the surrounding ghetto looked like almost 600 years ago. The included audioguide explains everything. The museum also features a searchable database of the 65,000 Austrian Jews who were victims of the Holocaust (€3, or €7 combo ticket includes a synagogue and Jewish Museum of the City of Vienna, Sun–Thu 10:00–18:00, Fri 10:00–16:00, closed Sat, Judenplatz 8, tel. 01/535-0431).

Museums Quartier—This sprawling collection of blocky, modernistic museums is housed within the Baroque facade of the former imperial stables. The centerpiece is the **Leopold Museum**, which features modern Austrian art including a collection of works by Egon Schiele (€9, Wed–Mon 11:00–19:00, Fri 11:00–21:00, closed Tue, behind Kunsthistorisches Museum, U-2 or U-3: Volkstheater/Museumsplatz, Museumsplatz 1-5, tel. 01/524-4801).

Honorable Mention—There's much, much more. The city map lists everything. If you're into butterflies, Esperanto, undertakers, tobacco, clowns, fire fighting, Freud, or the homes of dead composers, you'll find them all in Vienna. Several good museums that try very hard but are submerged in the greatness of Vienna include: **Jewish Museum of the City of Vienna** (€5, or €8 combo ticket includes synagogue and new Judenplatz Museum—listed above, Sun–Fri 10:00–18:00, Thu 10:00–20:00, closed Sat, Dorotheergasse 11, tel. 01/5350431), **Historical Museum of the City of Vienna** (Tue–Sun 09:00–18:00, Karlsplatz), **Folkloric Museum of Austria** (Tue–Sun 10:00–17:00, Laudongasse 15, tel. 01/406-8905), and **Museum of Military History**, one of Europe's best if you like swords and shields (Heeresgeschichtliches

Museum, Sat–Thu 09:00–17:00, closed Fri, Arsenal district, Objekt 18, tel. 01/795-610). The **Albertina Museum**, with its superb collection of sketches and graphic art, is closed until 2003.

For a walk in the **Vienna Woods**, catch the U-4 metro to Heiligenstadt, then bus #38A to Kahlenberg, for great views and a café overlooking the city. From there it's a peaceful 45-minute downhill hike to the *Heurigen* of Nussdorf or Grinzing to enjoy some wine (see "Vienna's Wine Gardens," below).

Top People-Watching and Strolling Sights

▲**City Park**—Vienna's Stadtpark is a waltzing world of gardens, memorials to local musicians, ponds, peacocks, music in bandstands, and locals escaping the city. Notice the Jugendstil entry at the Stadtpark metro station. The Kursalon is where Strauss was the violin-toting master of waltzing ceremonies.

▲**Prater**—Vienna's sprawling amusement park tempts many visitors with its huge 65-meter-high (220 feet), famous, and lazy Ferris wheel (*Riesenrad*), roller coaster, bumper cars, Lilliputian railroad, and endless eateries. Especially if you're traveling with kids, this is a fun, goofy place to share the evening with thousands of Viennese (daily 09:00–24:00 in summer, U-1: Praterstern). For a local-style family dinner, eat at Schweizerhaus (good food, great beer) or Wieselburger Bierinsel.

Sunbathing—Like most Europeans, the Austrians worship the sun. Their lavish swimming centers are as much for tanning as for swimming. For the best man-made island beach, head for the "Danube Sea," Vienna's 30-kilometer (20-mile) beach along Danube Island (U-1: Donauinsel).

▲**Naschmarkt**—Vienna's ye olde produce market bustles daily, near the Opera along Wienzeile Street. It's likably seedy and surrounded by sausage stands, Turkish *döner kebab* stalls, cafés, and theaters. Each Saturday it's infested by a huge flea market where, in olden days, locals would come to hire a monkey to pick little critters out of their hair (Mon–Fri 07:00–18:00, Sat 06:00–13:00, U-4: Kettenbrückengasse). For a picnic park, walk a block down Schleifmühlgasse.

Summer Music Scene

Vienna is Europe's music capital. It's music *con brio* from October through June, reaching a symphonic climax during the Vienna Festival each May and June. Sadly, in July and August the Boys' Choir, the Opera, and many more music companies are—like you—on vacation. But Vienna hums year-round with live classical music. In the summer, you have these basic choices:

Touristy Mozart and Strauss Concerts—If the music comes to you, it's touristy—designed for flash-in-the-pan Mozart fans. Powdered-wig orchestra performances are given almost nightly in grand traditional settings (€30–50). Pesky wigged and powdered Mozarts peddle tickets in the streets with slick sales pitches about the magic of the venue and the quality of the musicians. Second-rate orchestras, clad in historic costumes, perform the greatest hits of Mozart and Strauss. While there's not a local person in the audience, the tourists generally enjoy the evening. To sort through all your options, check with the ticket office in the TI (same price as on the street but with all venues to choose from).

Strauss Concerts in the Kursalon—For years Strauss concerts have been held in the Kursalon, where the Waltz King himself directed wildly popular concerts 100 years ago (€29–44, daily July–Sept at about 20:00, tel. 01/718-9666; due to Kursalon renovation, concerts are sometimes held instead at the less exciting but still classy Palais Borse, at the north end of the Ring). Shows are a touristy mix of ballet, waltzes, 15-piece orchestra in wigs and old outfits, and a chance for anyone in the audience to get on the floor and waltz.

Serious Concerts—These events, including the Opera, are listed in the monthly *Programm* (available at TI). Tickets run from €22 to €73 (plus a stiff 22 percent booking fee when booked in advance or through a box office like the one at the TI). If you call a concert hall directly, they can advise you on the availability of (cheaper) tickets at the door. Vienna takes care of its starving artists (and tourists) by offering cheap standing-room tickets to top-notch music and opera (1 hour before show time).

Vienna's **Summer of Music Festival** assures that even from June through September you'll find lots of great concerts, choirs, and symphonies (special *Klang Bogen* brochure at TI; get tickets at Wien Ticket pavilion off Kärntner Strasse next to Opera House or go directly to location of particular event; Summer of Music tel. 01/42717).

Musicals—The Wien Ticket pavilion sells tickets to contemporary American and British musicals (e.g., *Hair*, *Cabaret*) and offers these tickets at half price at 14:00 the day of the show. Or you can reserve (full-price) tickets for the musicals by calling up to one day ahead (CC, call combined office of the 3 big theaters at tel. 01/58885).

▲▲**Vienna Boys' Choir**—The boys sing (heard but not seen, from a high balcony) at Mass in the Imperial Chapel (*Hofburgkapelle*) of the Hofburg (entrance at Schweizerhof) at 09:15 on Sundays, except in July and August. While seats must be reserved two months in advance (€5–28, tel. 01/533-9927, fax 011-431-533-992-775 from the U.S., or write Hofmusikkapelle, Hofburg-Schweizerhof, 1010 Wien), standing room inside is free and open to the first 60 who line up. Rather than line up early, you can simply swing by and stand in the narthex just outside, from where you can hear the boys and see the Mass on a TV monitor. Boys'

Choir concerts (on stage in the Konzerthaus) are also given Fridays at 15:30 in May, June, September, and October (€29–32, tel. 01/5880-4141). They're nice kids, but, for my taste, not worth all the commotion.

Vienna's Cafés

In Vienna the living room is down the street at the neighborhood coffeehouse. This tradition is just another example of the Viennese expertise in good living. Each of Vienna's many long-established (and sometimes even legendary) coffeehouses has its individual character (and characters). They offer newspapers, pastries, sofas, elegance, a smoky ambience, and a "take all the time you want" charm for the price of a cup of coffee. Order it *malange* (with a little milk) or *schwarzer* (black). Rather than buy the *Herald Tribune* ahead of time, buy a cup of coffee and read it for free Vienna-style.

My favorites are: **Café Hawelka**, with a dark, "brooding Trotsky" atmosphere, paintings on the walls by struggling artists who couldn't pay, a saloon-wood flavor, chalkboard menu, smoked velvet couches, an international selection of newspapers, and a phone that rings for regulars (Wed–Mon 08:00–02:00, Sun from 16:00, closed Tue, just off Graben, Dorotheergasse 6); **Café Central**, with Jugendstil decor and great *Apfelstrudel* (high prices and rude staff, Mon–Sat 08:00–20:00, closed Sun, Herrengasse 14, tel. 01/5333-76326); the **Café Sperl**, dating from 1880 with furnishings identical to the day it opened, from the coat tree to the chairs (Mon–Sat 07:00–23:00, Sun 11:00–20:00 except closed Sun in July–Aug, just off Naschmarkt near Mariahilfer Strasse, Gumpendorfer 11, tel. 01/586-4158); and the basic, untouristy **Café Ritter** (daily 07:30–23:30, Mariahilfer Strasse 73, U-3: Neubaugasse, near several recommended hotels, tel. 01/587-8237).

Vienna's Wine Gardens

The *Heurige* is a uniquely Viennese institution celebrating the *Heurige*, or new wine. When the Hapsburgs let Vienna's vintners sell their own wine tax free for 300 days a year, several hundred families opened *Heurigen* (wine-garden restaurants clustered around the edge of Vienna), and a tradition was born. Today they do their best to maintain their old-village atmosphere, serving the homemade new wine (the last vintage, until November 11, when a new vintage year begins) with light meals and strolling musicians. Most *Heurigen* are decorated with enormous antique presses from their vineyards. A *Heurige*'s schedule is based on when the wine is produced. Therefore, the wine gardens might be closed on any given day; always call ahead to confirm if you have your heart set on a particular place. (For a near-*Heurige* experience right downtown, drop by Gigerl Stadtheuriger; see "Eating," below.)

At any *Heurige*, fill your plate at a self-serve cold-cut buffet

(€6–9 for dinner). Dishes to look out for: *Stelze* (grilled knuckle of pork), *Fleischlaberln* (fried ground meat patties), *Schinkenfleckerln* (pasta with cheese and ham), *Schmalz* (a spread made with pig fat), *Blunzen* (black pudding...sausage made from blood), *Presskopf* (jellied brains and innards), *Liptauer* (spicy cheese spread), *Kornspitz* (wholemeal bread roll), and *Kummelbraten* (crispy roast pork with caraway). Waitresses will then take your wine order (€2.20 per quarter liter). Many locals claim it takes several years of practice to distinguish between *Heurige* and vinegar.

There are over 1,700 acres of vineyards within Vienna's city limits. For a *Heurige* evening, rather than go to a particular place, take a tram to the wine-garden district of your choice and wander around, choosing the place with the best ambience. Here are some options:

Grinzing: Of the many *Heurige* suburbs, Grinzing is the most famous, lively...and touristy. Many people precede their visit to Grinzing by riding bus #38A to its end, up to Kahlenberg for a grand Vienna view, and then ride 20 minutes back into the *Heurige* action. To go directly to the *Heurige*, take metro U-2 to Schottentor-Universität. Then hop on tram #38 to the end of the line (stop: Grinzing). Exit left from the tram station and follow Himmelgasse uphill towards the onion-top dome. You'll pass plenty of wine gardens—and tour buses—on your way up. Just past the dome you'll find the heart of the *Heurige*.

Here you can choose an inviting *Heurige*, or walk another 20 minutes up to **Weingut am Reisenberg** for a fantastic city view above the vineyards and away from the touristy commotion (Mon–Fri 16:00–24:00, Sat–Sun 11:00–24:00, Oct–Dec from 18:00, Oberer Reisenbergweg 15, tel. 01/320-9393). This classy, local place is easy to reach by bus (catch bus #38A at Grinzing tram station, ride it to Oberer Reisenbergweg stop, and walk up the alley from there; if you get lost, just follow the gussied-up locals). If you'd rather hike: Just past the onion-top dome, turn right onto Cobenzlgasse. Bear left at the next fork (Hohenstrasse) and continue uphill. Turn left on Oberer Reisenbergweg and walk up the alley 400 meters (vineyards on left). Head right at the first fork. The restaurant is another 150 meters uphill on your left.

Nussdorf: A less-touristy district—characteristic and popular with locals—Nussdorf has plenty of *Heurige* ambience. Right at the end of the route of tram D (from the center, catch it at U-2 or U-4: Schottenring), you'll find three fine places: **Heuriger Kierlinger** (daily 15:30–24:00, Kahlenbergstrasse 20, tel. 01/370-2264), **Steinschaden** (Mon–Fri 15:00–23:30, Sat 14:30–23:30, Sun 14:30–22:00, Kahlenbergerstrasse 18, tel. 01/370-1375), and **Schübel-Auer Heuriger** (Mon–Sat 16:00–24:00, closed Sun, Kahlengergerstrasse 22, tel. 01/370-2222). To get to Nussdorf from Grinzing, take bus #38A to the Grinzingerstrasse stop and hop on tram D (direction: Beethovengang).

As noted, bus #38A connects Grinzing and Nussdorf. Midway, Pfarrplatz features many decent spots including the famous and touristy **Beethovenhaus** (Mon–Sat 16:00–24:00, Sun 11:00–24:00, bus stop: Fernsprechamt/Heiligenstadt, 5-min walk from bus stop uphill on Dübling Nestelbachgasse to Pfarrplatz 2, tel. 01/370-3361). Beethoven lived—and composed his Sixth Symphony—here in 1817. (He hoped the local spa would cure his worsening deafness.)

Neustift am Walde: This neighborhood has lots of *Heurigen*, plenty of charm, and the fewest tourists of all (U-6: Nussdorfer-strasse, then bus #35A).

Gumpoldskirchen: This small medieval village farther outside of Vienna has more *Heurige* ambience than tourists. Ride the commuter train from the Opera to Gumpoldskirchen, and you'll find plenty of places to choose from.

Shopping
The best-value shopping street, with more than 2,000 shops, is Mariahilfer Strasse. For an aristocrat's flea market, drop by Austria's answer to Sotheby's, the **Dorotheum**—five floors of antique furniture and fancy knickknacks put up either for immediate sale or auction (often by people who inherited old things they don't have room for, Mon–Fri 10:00–18:00, Sat 09:00–17:00, closed Sun, between Graben and the Hofburg at Dorotheergasse 17, tel. 01/515-600).

Nightlife
If old music or new wine isn't your thing, Vienna has plenty of alternatives. For an up-to-date rundown on fun after dark, get the TI's free *Ten Reasons for Vienna* booklet. An area known as the "Bermuda Dreieck" (Triangle), north of the cathedral between Rotenturmstrasse and Judengasse, is the hot local nightspot, with lots of classy pubs, or *Beisl* (such as Krah Krah, Salzamt, Slammer, and Bermuda Brau), and music spots. The European Union has recently financed renovation of the Gürtel's red-light district (along Vienna's outer ring road, under the arches of the U-6 line) turning the neighborhood into a trendy hangout. On balmy summer evenings the liveliest scene is at Danube Island. If you just want a good movie, the English Cinema Haydn plays English-language movies nightly (Mariahilfer Strasse 57, tel. 01/587-2262).

Sleeping in Vienna
(€1.10 = about $1, country code: 43, area code: 01)
Sleep Code: **S** = Single, **D** = Double/Twin, **T** = Triple, **Q** = Quad, **b** = bathroom, **s** = shower only, **CC** = Credit Cards accepted, **no CC** = Credit Cards not accepted. English is spoken at each place.

Book accommodations by phone a few days in advance. Most places will hold a room without a deposit if you promise to arrive before 17:00. My recommendations stretch mainly from the center, and along the likeable Mariahilfer Strasse, to the Westbahnhof (West Station). Unless otherwise noted, prices include a continental breakfast. Postal code is 1XX0, with XX being the district. Even places with elevators often have a few stairs to climb, too.

Laundry: These are few and far between; ask at your hotel. Gottshalks will do your laundry in a day (€4/1 kilo, Mon–Fri 08:00–18:00, Sat 09:00–12:00, near St. Stephan's at Singerstrasse 22). Launderette, near Mariahilfer Strasse, is handy—when it's open (Mon–Wed 08:00–18:00, closed Thu–Sun, Siebensternstrasse 52, walk 4 blocks up Zollergasse from Mariahilfer Strasse).

Sleeping within the Ring, in the Old City Center

You'll pay extra to sleep in the old center. The first two places are in the shadow of St. Stephan's Cathedral, on or near the Graben, where the elegance of Old Vienna strums happily over the cobbles. The next two are near the Opera and TI, five minutes from the cathedral. If you can afford it, staying here gives you the best classy Vienna experience.

At **Pension Nossek** an elevator takes you above any street noise into Frau Bernad's and Frau Gundolf's world, where the children seem to be placed among the lace and flowers by an interior designer. Right on the wonderful Graben, this is a particularly good value (S-€44–51, Ss-€55, Sb-€62–65, Db-€98, €22 extra for sprawling suites, extra bed-€33, no CC, elevator, U-1 or U-3: Stephensplatz, Graben 17, tel. 01/5337-0410, fax 01/535-3646, e-mail: pension.nossek@faxvia.net).

Pension Pertschy circles an old courtyard and is bigger and more hotelesque than the others. The rooms are huge but musty. Those on the courtyard are quietest (Sb-€65–75, Db-€95–135 depending on size, cheaper off-season, extra person-€20–30 depending on season, CC, elevator, U-1 or U-3: Stephensplatz, Hapsburgergasse 5, tel. 01/534-490, fax 01/534-4949, www.pertschy.com, e-mail: pertschy@pertschy.com).

Baroque and doily as you'll find in this price range, **Pension Suzanne** is wonderfully located a few meters from the Opera. It's quiet and simple but run with the class of a bigger hotel (Sb-€69, Db-€84–105 depending on size, third person-€37, discounts in winter, CC, elevator, a block from Opera, U-1, U-2, or U-4: Karlsplatz, follow signs for Opera exit, Walfischgasse 4, 1010 Wien, tel. 01/513-2507, fax 01/513-2500, www.pension-suzanne .at, e-mail: info@pension-suzanne.at).

Hotel zur Wiener Staatsoper is quiet, rich, and hotelesque. Its rooms come with high ceilings, chandeliers, and fancy carpets on parquet floors—a good value for this locale and ideal for people

Hotels in Central Vienna

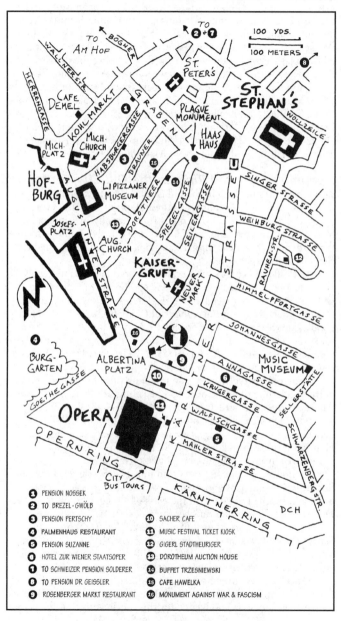

1 PENSION NOSSEK

2 TO BREZEL-GWÖLB

3 PENSION PERTSCHY

4 PALMENHAUS RESTAURANT

5 PENSION SUZANNE

6 HOTEL ZUR WIENER STAATSOPER

7 TO SCHWEIZER PENSION SOLDERER

8 TO PENSION DR GEISSLER

9 ROSENBERGER MARKT RESTAURANT

10 SACHER CAFE

11 MUSIC FESTIVAL TICKET KIOSK

12 GIGERL STADTHEURIGER

13 DOROTHEUM AUCTION HOUSE

14 BUFFET TRZESNIEWSKI

15 CAFE HAWELKA

16 MONUMENT AGAINST WAR & FASCISM

whose hotel tastes are a cut above mine (Sb-€76–84, Db-€102–123, Tb-€131–145, CC, prices depend on season, July–Aug and Dec–March are cheaper, extra bed-€22, elevator, U-1, U-2, or U-4: Karlsplatz, a block from Opera at Krugerstrasse 11, 1010 Wien, tel. 01/513-1274, fax 01/5131-27415, www.zurwienerstaatsoper.at, e-mail: office@zurwienerstaatsoper.at).

Schweizer Pension Solderer, family owned for three generations, is run by sisters Monica and Anita. It offers 11 homey rooms, parquet floors, and lots of tourist info, but too many house rules—such as not doing laundry in the sink—for some readers (S-€35–42, Ss-€51–55, Sb-€58–62, D-€55–62, Ds-€65-76, Db-€76-87, Tb-€97-100, Qb-€117-120, extra bed-€20, no CC, elevator, laundry-€11, nonsmoking rooms, U-2 and U-4: Schottenring, Heinrichsgasse 2, 1010 Wien, tel. 01/533-8156, fax 01/535-6469, http://members.chello.at/schweizer.pension, e-mail: schweizer.pension@chello.at).

Pension Dr. Geissler has comfortable rooms on the eighth floor of a modern building about 10 blocks northeast of St. Stephan's, just below the canal (S-€44, Ss-€58, Sb-€66, D-€58, Ds-€73, Db-€87, prices vary with season, CC, U-1 and U-4: Schwedenplatz, Postgasse 14, 1010 Wien, tel. 01/533-2803, fax 01/533-2635).

Hotels and Pensions along Mariahilfer Strasse

Lively Mariahilfer Strasse connects the West Station and the city center. The U-3 metro line, starting at the Westbahnhof, goes down Mariahilfer Strasse to the cathedral. This very Viennese street is a tourist-friendly and vibrant area filled with local shops and cafés. Most hotels are within a few steps of a metro stop, just one or two stops from the West Train Station (direction from the station: Simmering).

Pension Hargita has 19 generally small, bright, and tidy rooms (mostly twins) and Hungarian decor (S-€31, Ss-€35, D-€45, Ds-€53, Db-€60–66, Ts-€63, Tb-€69–77, Qb-€88, CC, breakfast-€3, U-3: Zieglergasse, corner of Mariahilfer Strasse and Andreasgasse, Andreasgasse 1, 1070 Wien, tel. 01/526-1928, fax 01/526-0492, www.hargita.at, e-mail: pension@hargita.at).

Pension Corvinus is bright, modern, and warmly run. Its comfortable rooms have small bathrooms (Sb-€58, Db-€91, Tb-€101, extra bed-€26, CC, elevator, air-con available, free Internet access, garage-€11/day, Mariahilfer Strasse 57-59, tel. 01/587-7239, fax 01/587-723-920, e-mail: hotel@corvinus.at). In the same building, **Haydn Hotel** is a big, hotelesque place with spacious rooms (Ss-€58–62, Sb-€58–69, Db-€72–100, suite-€109–218, apartment-€116–196, extra bed-€29, CC, elevator, air-con, garage-€11/day, Mariahilfer Strasse 57-59, tel. 01/587-4414, fax 01/586-1950, www.haydn-hotel.at, e-mail: info@haydn-hotel.at).

Pension Mariahilf is a four-star place offering a clean aristocratic air in an affordable and cozy pension package. Its 12 rooms are spacious and feel new, but with an Art Deco flair. With four stars, everything's done right. You'll find the latest American magazines and even free Mozart balls at the reception desk (Sb-€59–66, Db-€95–102, Tb-€124, no CC, elevator, U-3: Neubaugasse, Mariahilfer Strasse 49, tel. 01/586-1781, fax 01/586-178-122, e-mail: penma@atnet.at, warmly run by Frau and Herr Ender).

Astron Suite Hotel Wien consists of two stern business hotels a few blocks apart on Mariahilfer Strasse. Both rent ideal-for-families suites, each with a living room, two TVs, bathroom, desk, and kitchenette (Db suite-€144–173, apartment for 2–3 adults-€188–210, kids under 12 free, kids over 12-about €35 each, CC, elevator, nonsmoking rooms). One hotel is at Mariahilfer Strasse 78 (U-3: Zieglergasse, tel. 01/5245-6000, fax 01/524-560-015) and the other is at Mariahilfer Strasse 32 (U-3: Neubaugasse, tel. 01/521-720, fax 01/521-7215). Web site: www.astron-hotels.de.

Beyond its plain lobby, **Hotel Admiral** is a huge, quiet, family-run hotel that has large, comfortable rooms. Alexandra works hard to keep her guests happy, though others on the staff are less friendly (Sb-€63–66, Db-€73–91, breakfast extra, no CC, extra bed-€23, free parking, avoid their "taxi deal" to the airport if flying out of Vienna, U-2 or U-3: Volkstheater, a block off Mariahilfer Strasse at Karl Schweighofer Gasse 7, tel. 01/521-410, fax 01/521-4116, www.admiral.co.at, e-mail: hoteladmiralwien@aon.at).

At **K&T Boardinghouse** Tina and Fred Kaled rent four big, comfortable rooms (3 with full bathrooms) with the comforts you'd pay lots for in a hotel. This place—with the best cheap doubles in town—is homey with accommodating hosts who can help you make the most of your time in Vienna. The only drawback is that it's above (though not connected with) a sex shop, and you have to enter a door marked "Love Bird Erotic Markt" to get to the pension (S-€37–44, D-€51, Db-€58, Tb-€77, Qb-€95, no CC, no breakfast, free Internet access, laundry service, nonsmoking, 3 flights up, no elevator, Mariahilfer Strasse 72, tel. 01/523-2989, fax 01/522-0345, www.kaled.at, e-mail: kaled@chello.at).

Two women rent rooms out of their dark and homey apartments in the same building at Lindengasse 39 (1070 Wien, elevator). Each has high ceilings and Old World furnishings with two cavernous rooms sleeping two to four and a skinny twin room, all sharing one bathroom. These places are great if you're on a tight budget and wish you had a grandmother to visit in Vienna: **Maria Pribojszki** (S-€33, D-€48, T-€69, Q-€88, no CC, breakfast-€3.75, free laundry service for 4-night stays, apt. #7, tel. 01/523-9006, e-mail: e.boehm@xpoint.at) or **Budai Ildiko** (S-€29, D-€44, T-€64, Q-€82, no CC, no breakfast but free coffee,

Vienna: Hotels Outside the Ring

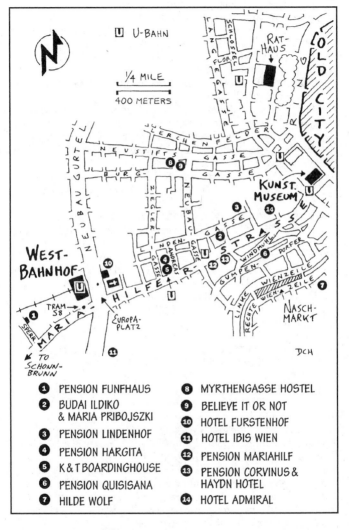

❶ PENSION FUNFHAUS	❽ MYRTHENGASSE HOSTEL
❷ BUDAI ILDIKO & MARIA PRIBOJSZKI	❾ BELIEVE IT OR NOT
	❿ HOTEL FURSTENHOF
❸ PENSION LINDENHOF	⓫ HOTEL IBIS WIEN
❹ PENSION HARGITA	⓬ PENSION MARIAHILF
❺ K & T BOARDINGHOUSE	⓭ PENSION CORVINUS & HAYDN HOTEL
❻ PENSION QUISISANA	
❼ HILDE WOLF	⓮ HOTEL ADMIRAL

laundry-€3.75, apt. #5, tel. 01/523-1058, tel. & fax 01/526-2595, e-mail: budai@hotmail.com).

Pension Quisisana—a tired but recently renovated time warp run by a charming old couple—is cheap and sleep worthy for vagabonds (S-€26, Ss-€29, D-€40, Ds-€45–48, Db-€53–56, third person-€19, no CC, Windmuhlgasse 6, 1060 Wien, tel. 01/587-7155, fax 01/587-715-633, www.quisisana-wien.co.at, e-mail: office@quisisana-wien.co.at).

Pension Lindenhof is worn but clean and filled with plants (S-€28, Sb-€35, D-€47, Db-€63, no CC, cheaper in winter, hall showers-€1.50, U-3: Neubaugasse, Linden-gasse 4, 1070 Wien, tel. 01/523-0498, fax 01/523-7362, e-mail: pensionlindenhof@yahoo.com).

Hilde Wolf shares her homey apartment with travelers (7 blocks off Mariahilfer Strasse and 3 blocks below Naschmarkt). Her four huge but stuffy rooms are like old libraries. Grandmotherly Hilde may do your laundry if you stay three nights. You need to keep your door ajar when possible to let the new air-conditioning circulate; if you need privacy, stay elsewhere (S-€33, D-€48, T-€70, Q-€89, reserve with CC but pay in cash, breakfast-€3.75, U-2: Karlsplatz, Schleifmühlgasse 7, 1040 Vienna, tel. 01/586-5103, fax 01/689-3505, www.schoolpool.at/bb, e-mail: santa.claus@aon.at).

Sleeping near the Westbahnhof Train Station

Hotel Ibis Wien, a modern high-rise hotel with American charm, is ideal for anyone tired of quaint old Europe. Its 340 cookie-cutter rooms are bright, comfortable, modern, and have all the conveniences (Sb-€64–69, Db-€79–84, Tb-€94–99, breakfast-€9, CC, elevator, smoke-free rooms, air-con, parking garage-€10/day, exit Westbahnhof to the right and walk 400 meters, Mariahilfer Gürtel 22-24, A-1060 Wien, tel. 01/59998, fax 01/597-9090, e-mail: H0796@accor-hotels.com).

Hotel Fürstenhof, right across from the station, charges top euro for its Old World, red-floral, spacious rooms and Internet access (S-€40, Sb-€63–88, D-€61, Db-€101, Tb-€104, Qb-€107, CC, Europlatz 4, tel. 01/523-3267, fax 01/523-326-726, www.hotel-fuerstenhof.com).

Pension Fünfhaus is big, clean, stark, and quiet. Although the neighborhood is run-down, this place is a good value (S-€29, Sb-€37, D-€44, Db-€50, T-€66, Tb-€72, apartments for 4 people-€88, no CC, closed mid-Nov–Feb, Sperrgasse 12, 1150 Wien, tel. 01/892-3545 or 01/892-0286, fax 01/892-0460, Frau Susi Tersch). Half the rooms are in the fine main building and half are in the annex, which has good rooms but is near the train tracks and a bit scary on the street at night. From the station, ride tram #52 or #58 two stops down Mariahilfer Strasse to Kranzgasse stop, backtrack two blocks to Sperrgasse.

Dorms and Hostels near Mariahilfer Strasse

Jugendherbergen Myrthengasse is a well-run youth hostel (beds-€15–17, nonmembers-€3 extra, no CC, includes sheets and breakfast, 3- to 6-bed rooms, some private rooms for couples and families, Myrthengasse 7, 1070 Wien, tel. 01/523-6316, fax

01/523-5849, e-mail: hostel@chello.at). Other hostels near
Mariahilfer Strasse are **Wombats City Hostel** (Grangasse 6, tel.
01/897-2336, e-mail: wombats@chello.at) and **Hostel Ruthen-
steiner** (Robert-Hamerling-Gasse 24, tel. 01/893-4202, e-mail:
info@hostelruthensteiner.com).

Believe It or Not is a friendly and basic place with two coed
rooms for up to 10 travelers under age 26. It's locked up from
10:00 to 12:30, has kitchen facilities, and no curfew (€12/bed,
€8 Nov–April, no CC, Myrthengasse 10, ring apt. #14, tel. 01/
526-4658, run by Gosha).

Eating in Vienna

The Viennese appreciate the fine points of life, and right up there
with waltzing is eating. The city has many atmospheric restaurants. As you ponder the Slavic and eastern European specialties
on menus, remember that Vienna's diverse empire may be gone,
but its flavor lingers.

While cuisines are routinely named for countries, Vienna
claims to be the only city with a cuisine of its own: Vienna soups
come with fillings (semolina dumpling, liver dumpling, or pancake
slices). *Gulasch* is a beef ragout of Hungarian origin (spiced with
onion and paprika). Of course, Vienna Schnitzel (*Wiener Schnitzel*)
is a breaded and fried veal cutlet. Another meat specialty is boiled
beef (*Tafelspitz*). While you're sure to have *Apfelstrudel*, try the
sweet cheese strudel, too (*Topfenstrudel*, wafer-thin strudel pastry
filled with sweet cheese and raisins).

On nearly every corner you can find a colorful *Beisl* (Viennese
tavern) filled with poetry teachers and their students, couples
loving without touching, housewives on their way home from
cello lessons, and waiters who enjoy serving hearty food and good
drink at an affordable price. Ask at your hotel for a good *Beisl*.

Wherever you're eating, some vocabulary will help. Try the
grüner Veltliner (dry white wine, any time), *Traubenmost* (a heavenly
grape juice on the verge of wine, sometimes just called *Most*, autumn
only), and *Sturm* (barely fermented *Most*, autumn only). The local
red wine (called *Portuguese*) is pretty good. Since the Austrian wine
is often very sweet, remember the word *Trocken* (dry). You can
order your wine by the *Viertel* (quarter liter) or *Achtel* (eighth liter).
Beer comes in a *Krugel* (half liter) or *Seidel* (0.3 liter).

Eating in the City Center

These eateries are within a five-minute walk of the cathedral:

Gigerl Stadtheuriger offers a near-*Heurige* experience (à la
Grinzing, see "Vienna's Wine Gardens," above) without leaving the
center. Just point to what looks good. Food is sold by the weight
(cheese and cold meats cost about €2.50–3.00/100 grams, salads
are about €1.10/100 grams; price sheet is posted, 10 *dag* equals

100 grams). They also have menu entrées, along with spinach strudel, quiche, *Apfelstrudel*, and, of course, casks of new and local wines. Meals run from €7.25 to €11 (daily 11:00–01:00, may open at 16:00 in 2002 due to construction next door, indoor/outdoor seating, behind cathedral, a block off Kärntner Strasse, a few cobbles off Rauhensteingasse on Blumenstock, tel. 01/513-4431).

The next five places are within a block of Am Hof square (U-3: Herrengasse). **Restaurant Ofenloch** serves good old-fashioned Viennese cuisine with friendly service both indoors and out. This 300-year-old eatery, with great traditional ambience, is central but not overrun with tourists (€15–22 meals, Mon–Fri 11:30–24:00, closed Sat–Sun, Kurrentgasse 8, tel. 01/533-8844). **Brezel-Gwölb**, a wonderfully atmospheric wine cellar with outdoor dining on a quiet square, serves delicious light meals, fine *Krautsuppe*, and old-fashioned local dishes. It's ideal for a romantic late-night glass of wine (daily 11:30–01:00, take Drahtgasse 20 meters off Am Hof, Ledererhof 9, tel. 01/533-8811). Around the corner, **Zum Scherer Sitz und Stehbeisl** is just as untouristy, with indoor or outdoor seating, a soothing woody atmosphere, intriguing decor, and local specialties (Mon–Sat 11:00–01:00, closed Sun, near Am Hof, Judenplatz 7, tel. 01/533-5164). Just below Am Hof, **Stadt-beisl** offers a good mix of value, local cuisine, and atmosphere (daily 10:00–24:00, Naglergasse 21, tel. 01/533-3507). Around the corner, the ancient and popular **Esterhazykeller** has traditional fare deep underground or outside on a delightful square (Mon–Fri 11:00–23:00, Sat–Sun 16:00–23:00, self-service buffet in lowest cellar or from menu, Haarhof 1, tel. 01/533-2614).

These wine cellars are fun and touristy but typical, in the old center of town, with reasonable prices and plenty of smoke: **Melker Stiftskeller**, less touristy, is a *Stadtheurige* in a deep and rustic cellar with hearty, inexpensive meals and new wine (Tue–Sat 17:00–24:00, closed Sun–Mon, between Am Hof and the Schotten-tor metro stop at Schottengasse 3, tel. 01/533-5530). **Zu den Drei Hacken** is famous for its local specialties (Mon–Sat 10:00–24:00, closed Sun, indoor/outdoor seating, CC, Singerstrasse 28).

Cafe Restaurant Palmenhaus, overlooking the palace gar-den (*Burggarten*), tucked away in a green and peaceful corner two blocks behind the Opera in the Hofburg's backyard, is a world apart. If you want to eat modern Austrian cuisine with palm trees rather than tourists, this is it. And at the edge of a huge park, it's great for families (€11 lunches, €15 dinners, daily 10:00–02:00, serious vegetarian dishes and good wine, indoors in greenhouse or outdoors, cool parkside outdoor pub just below, at Burggarten, tel. 01/533-1033).

Rosenberger Markt Restaurant is my favorite for a fast, light, and central lunch. Just a block toward the cathedral from the Opera, this place—while not cheap—is brilliant. Friendly and efficient, with special theme rooms for dining, it offers a fresh, smoke-free, and healthy cornucopia of food and drink (daily 10:30–23:00, lots of fruits, veggies, fresh-squeezed juices, addictive banana milk, ride the glass elevator downstairs, Maysedergasse 2, tel. 01/512-3458). You can stack a small salad or veggie plate into a tower of gobble for €2.50.

Buffet Trzesniewski is an institution—justly famous for its elegant and cheap finger sandwiches and small beers (€0.75 each). Three different sandwiches and a *kleines Bier* (*Pfiff*) make a fun, light lunch. Point to whichever delights look tasty and pay for them and a drink. Take your drink tokens to the lady on the right. Sit on the bench and scoot over to a tiny table when a spot opens up (Mon–Fri 08:30–19:30, Sat 09:00–17:00, closed Sun, 50 meters off Graben, nearly across from brooding Café Hawelka, on Dorotheergasse 2, tel. 01/512-3291).

Akakiko Sushi: If you're just schnitzeled out, this small chain of Japanese restaurants with an easy sushi menu may suit you (daily 10:00–24:00, next to downtown recommended eateries in the heart of old center at Heidenschuss 3 or at Mariahilfer Strasse 40, tel. 01/533-8514).

Eating near Mariahilfer Strasse

Mariahilfer Strasse is filled with reasonable cafés serving all types of cuisine. A few blocks away, on the romantic streets just north of Siebensterngasse (take Stiftgasse from Mariahilfer Strasse), several cobbled alleys open their sidewalks and courtyards to appreciative locals (ideal for dinner or a relaxing drink). Stroll Spitellberggasse, Schrankgasse, and Gutenberggassse and pick your favorite place. Check out the courtyard inside Spittelberggasse 3, and don't miss the vine-strewn wine garden inside Schrankgasse 1. For traditional Viennese cuisine, consider **Witwe Bolte** (daily 11:30–24:00, Gutenberggasse 13, tel. 01/523-1450).

Restaurant Beim Novak serves good local cuisine away from the modern rush (Mon–Sat 11:30–15:00, 18:00–24:00, closed Sun, a block down Andreasgasse from Mariahilfer Strasse at Richtergasse 12, tel. 01/523-3244).

Naschmarkt is Vienna's best Old World market, with plenty of fresh produce, cheap local-style eateries, cafés, and *döner kebab* and sausage stands (Mon–Fri 07:00–18:00, Sat until 12:00, closed Sun).

Transportation Connections—Vienna

Vienna has two main train stations: the Westbahnhof (West Train Station), serving Munich, Salzburg, Melk, and Budapest; and the Südbahnhof (South Train Station), serving Italy, Budapest, and Prague. A third station, Franz Josefs, serves Krems and the Danube Valley (but Melk is served by the Westbahnhof). Metro line U-3 connects the Westbahnhof with the center, tram D takes you from the Südbahnhof and the Franz Josefs station to downtown, and tram #18 connects West and South stations. Train info: tel. 051717 (wait through long German recording for operator).

By train to: Melk (hrly, 75 min, sometimes change in St. Pölten), **Krems** (hrly, 1 hr), **Salzburg** (hrly, 3 hrs), **Innsbruck** (every 2 hrs, 5.5 hrs), **Budapest** (6/day, 3 hrs), **Prague** (4/day, 4.5 hrs), **Munich** (hrly, 5.25 hrs, change in Salzburg, a few direct trains), **Berlin** (2/day, 10 hrs, longer on night train), **Zurich** (3/day, 9 hrs), **Rome** (1/day, 13.5 hrs), **Venice** (3/day, 7.5 hrs, longer on night train), **Frankfurt** (4/day, 7.5 hrs), **Amsterdam** (1/day, 14.5 hrs).

To Eastern Europe: Vienna is the springboard for a quick trip to Prague and Budapest—three hours by train from Budapest (€27, €54 round-trip, free with Eurail) and four hours from Prague (€35 one-way, €75 round-trip, €51.60 round-trip with Eurail). Americans don't need a visa to enter the Czech Republic, but Canadians do. Purchase tickets at most travel agencies. Eurail passholders bound for Prague must pay to ride the rails in the Czech Republic; for details, see "Transportation Connections" in the Berlin chapter.

SALZBURG, SALZKAMMERGUT, AND WEST AUSTRIA

Enjoy the sights, sounds, and splendor of Mozart's hometown, Salzburg, then commune with nature in the Salzkammergut, Austria's *Sound of Music* country. Amid hills alive with the Sound of Music, you'll find the tiny town of Hallstatt, as pretty as a postcard (and not much bigger). If you've ever yearned to yodel, do it here. Austria's Salzkammergut gives you plenty to yodel about.

SALZBURG

Salzburg is forever smiling to the tunes of Mozart and *The Sound of Music*. Thanks to its charmingly preserved old town, splendid gardens, Baroque churches, and Europe's largest intact medieval castle, Salzburg feels made for tourism.

But even without Mozart and the von Trapp family, Salzburg is steeped in history. In about A.D. 700, Bavaria gave Salzburg to Bishop Rupert for his promise to Christianize the area. Salzburg remained an independent state until Napoleon stormed in (around 1800). Salzburg managed to avoid the ravages of war for 1,200 years...until World War II. Half of the town was destroyed by WWII bombs, but the historic old town survived.

Eight million tourists crawl its cobbles each year. That's a lot of Mozart balls—and all that popularity has led to a glut of businesses hoping to catch the tourist dollar. Still, Salzburg makes for a pleasant visit.

Planning Your Time

While Vienna measures much higher on the Richter scale of sightseeing thrills, Salzburg is simply a touristy, stroller's delight. If you're going into the nearby Salzkammergut lake country, skip the *Sound of Music* tour—if not, allow half a day for it. The *S.O.M.*

Salzburg

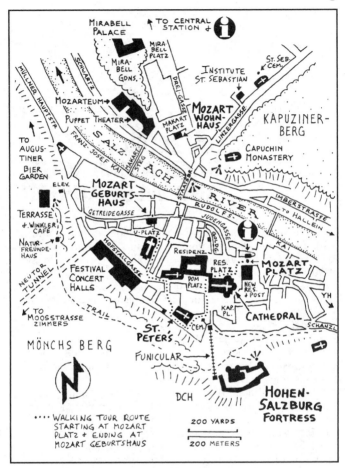

tour kills a nest of sightseeing birds with one ticket (city overview, *S.O.M.* sights, a luge ride, and a fine drive through the lakes).

You'll probably need two nights for Salzburg; nights are important for swilling beer in atmospheric local gardens and attending concerts in Baroque halls and chapels. Seriously consider one of Salzburg's many evening musical events (about €29–37). While the sights are mediocre, the town is an enjoyable Baroque museum of cobbled streets and elegant buildings. And to get away from it all, bike down the river or hike across the Mönchsberg.

Orientation (area code: 0662)

Salzburg, a city of 150,000 (Austria's fourth largest), is divided into old and new. The old town, sitting between the Salzach River and the 480-meter-high (1,600 feet) hill called Mönchsberg, holds nearly all the charm and most of the tourists.

Tourist Information: Salzburg's many TIs are helpful. There's one at the train station (April–Sept daily 08:45–19:45, Oct–March daily 08:45–19:00), on Mozartplatz in the old center (daily 09:00–19:00 in summer, closes at 18:00 off-season), on freeway exits, and at the airport (tel. 0662/8898-7330, www .salzburginfo.or.at). At any TI, you can pick up a city map (€0.75, free at most hotels), a list of sights with current hours, and a schedule of events. Book a concert upon arrival. The TIs also book rooms (€2.25 fee for up to 2 people, or €4.35 for 3 people or more).

Salzburg Card: The TI sells a Salzburg Card which covers all your public transportation (plus elevator and funicular) and admission to all the city sights (including Hellbrunn Palace), but it takes about three admissions to break even with the one-day card. If you like getting a card for the convenience, the two-day version is a better value (€20/24 hrs, €27/48 hrs; for about €10 extra per day you can get a "Salzburg Card Plus Light," which adds a dinner and 2 drinks per day at your choice of a list of restaurants, including the recommended Ährlich, Glockenspiel, Sternbräu, and Stiftskeller St. Peter; see "Eating in Salzburg," below).

Arrival in Salzburg

By Train: The little Salzburg station makes it easy. The TI is at track 2A. Downstairs, at street level, you'll find a place to store your luggage, rent bikes, buy tickets, and get train information. The bus station is across the street (where buses #1, #5, #6, #51, and #55 go to the old center; get off at the first stop after you cross the river for most sights and city center hotels, or just before the bridge for Linzergasse hotels). Figure €6.50 to €7.50 for a taxi to the center. To walk downtown (15 min), leave the station ticket hall to the left near the Bankomat cash machine and walk straight down Rainerstrasse, which leads under the tracks past Mirabellplatz, turning into Dreifaltigkeitsgasse. From here you can turn left onto Paris-Lodron Strasse or Linzergasse for many of the hotels listed in this book or cross the *Staatsbrücke* (bridge) for the old town (and more hotels). For a more dramatic approach, leave the station the same way but follow the tracks to the river, turn left, and walk the riverside path toward the castle.

By Car: Follow Zentrum signs to the center and park short-term on the street or longer under Mirabellplatz. Ask at your hotel for suggestions.

Getting around Salzburg

By Bus: Single-ride tickets are sold on the bus for €1.50. Daily passes called *Tageskarte* cost €3 (good for 1 calendar day only). Bus info: tel. 0662/4480-6262.

By Bike: Salzburg is bike friendly. The train station rents good bikes for €9; if you don't have a railpass or train ticket, you'll pay €13 (no deposit required, pay at counter #3, pick bike up at left-luggage counter, daily 06:00–22:00). Velo-Active rents bikes on Residenzplatz under the Glockenspiel in the old town (€4.50/hr, €14/24 hrs, €11/24 hrs with this book, mountain bikes €6/hr, €18/24 hrs, daily 09:00–19:00 but hours unreliable, less off-season and in bad weather, passport number for security, tel. 0662/435-5950 or 0676/435-5950).

By Funicular and Elevator: The old town is connected to Mönchsberg (and great views) via funicular and elevator. The **funicular** whisks you up to the imposing Hohensalzburg fortress (€6.50 round-trip includes fortress admission; funicular hours May–Sept daily 09:00–21:00, Oct–April daily 09:00–17:00, but lift goes later—until about 22:00—on summer nights when there is a concert in the fortress). You can't take the funicular up without paying for entrance to the fortress grounds—unless you have a concert ticket and it's within an hour before the performance (see "Music Scene," below).

The **elevator** on the east side of the old town propels you to the recommended Naturfreundehaus (see "Sleeping in the Old Town," below) and lots of wooded paths (€1.20 one-way, €2 round-trip).

By Taxi: Salzburg is a fine taxi town. Meters start at €2.40 (from train station to your hotel, allow about €6.50–7.50).

Helpful Hints

City View: For a painless, grand view, ride Hotel Stein's elevator to the seventh floor (free, mid-May–Sept only, near where Linzergasse meets the main bridge).

Internet Access: The Internet Café on Mozartplatz is fast and handy, right next to the TI (€1.50/10 min, €9/hr, daily 10:00–24:00, off-season until 23:00, 12 computers, Mozartplatz 5, second branch with shorter hours at Gstättengasse 3, tel. 0662/844-822).

Guide Association: Salzburg's many guides can give you a good three-hour walk through town for €120 (tel. 0662/840-406). Barbel Schalber packs in the information and enjoys leaving the touristy places (tel. 0662/632-225, e-mail: baxguide@utanet.at).

American Express: AmEx charges no commission to cash AmEx checks (Mon–Fri 09:00–17:30, Sat 09:00–12:00, Mozartplatz 5, A-5010 Salzburg, tel. 0662/8080).

Old Town Walking Tour

The two-language, one-hour guided walks of the old town are informative and worthwhile if you don't mind listening to a half hour of German (€7.50, daily at 12:15, not on winter Sun, start at TI on Mozartplatz, tel. 0662/8898-7330), but you can easily do it on your own.

Here's a basic old-town orientation walk (start on Mozartplatz in the old town):

Mozartplatz: This square features a statue of Mozart erected in 1842. Mozart spent most of his first 20 years (1756–1777) in Salzburg, the greatest Baroque city north of the Alps. But the city's much older. The Mozart statue actually sits on bits of Roman Salzburg. And the pink church of St. Michael overlooking the square is from A.D. 800. Surrounding you are Café Glockenspiel, an Internet café, the American Express office, and the tourist information office with a concert box office. Just around the corner is a pedestrian bridge leading over the Salzach River to the quiet, most medieval street in town, Steingasse (see "Sights—Across the River," below). Walk toward the cathedral into the big square with the huge fountain.

Residenz Platz: Salzburg's energetic Prince-Archbishop Wolf Dietrich (who ruled from 1587–1612) was raised in Rome, counted the Medicis as his buddies, and had grand Renaissance ambitions for Salzburg. After a convenient fire destroyed much of the old town, he set about building "the Rome of the North." This square, with his new cathedral and palace, was the centerpiece of his Baroque dream city. A series of interconnecting squares lead from here through the old town.

For centuries, Salzburg's leaders were both important church officials and princes of the Holy Roman Empire, hence their title—mixing sacred and secular authority. Wolf Dietrich abused his power and spent his last five years imprisoned in the Salzburg castle.

The fountain is as Italian as can be, with a Triton matching Bernini's famous Triton Fountain in Rome. As the north became aware of the exciting things going on in Italy, things Italian were respected. (You know, when a bumpkin in a faraway land "stuck a feather in his cap and called it macaroni.") Local architects even Italianized their names in order to raise their rates.

Near the fountain at Residenzplatz 6 is Julie Weger & Sohn, a picnic-friendly **grocery** (Mon–Fri 08:30–18:00, Sat 08:00–17:00, closed Sun).

Residenz: Dietrich's palace is connected to the cathedral by a skyway. A series of ornately decorated rooms and an art gallery are open to visitors with time to kill (€7.50 includes both palace and gallery with audioguide, €4.75 for picture gallery only, daily 10:00–17:00, tel. 0662/8042-2690).

Opposite the old Residenz is the new Residenz, which has long been a government administration building with the central post office and the Heimatwerk, a shop showing off all the best local handicrafts (Mon–Fri 09:00–18:00, Sat 09:00–13:00, closed Sun). Atop the new Residenz is the famous…

Glockenspiel: This bell tower has a carillon of 35 17th-century bells (cast in Antwerp) that chimes throughout the day and plays tunes (appropriate to the month) at 07:00, 11:00, and 18:00. There was a time when Salzburg could afford to take tourists to the top of the tower to actually see the big adjustable barrel turn…pulling the right bells in the right rhythm—a fascinating show. Notice the ornamental top: an upside-down heart in flames surrounding the solar system (symbolizing that God loves all).

Look back past Mozart's statue to the 1,266-meter-high (4,220 feet) Gaisberg—the forested hill with the television tower. A road leads to the top for a commanding view. It's a favorite destination for local bikers. Walking under the Prince-Archbishop's skyway, step into Domplatz, the cathedral square.

Salzburg Cathedral: Built in the 17th century, this was one of the first Baroque buildings north of the Alps (donation requested, May–Oct Mon–Sat 09:00–18:30, Sun 13:00–18:30, Nov–April Mon–Sat 10:00–17:00, Sun 13:00–17:00). The dates on the iron gates refer to milestones in the church's history: In 774 the previous church (long since destroyed) was founded by St. Virgil, to be replaced in 1628 by the church you see today. In 1959 the reconstruction was completed after a WWII bomb blew through the dome.

Wander inside. Built in just 14 years (1614–1628), the architecture is harmonious. When the pope visited in 1998, 5,000 people filled the cathedral (dimensions: 110 meters long, 70 meters tall). The baptismal font, left of the entry, is from the previous cathedral. Mozart was baptized here (Amadeus means "beloved by God"). Gape up. The interior is marvelous. Concert and Mass schedules are posted at the entrance; the Sunday Masses at 10:00 and 11:30 are famous for their music. Acoustics are best in pews immediately under the dome.

Under the skyway, a stairway leads down to the excavation site under the church with a few second-century Christian Roman mosaics and the foundation stones of the previous Romanesque and Gothic churches (€1.80, May–Oct Wed–Sun 09:00–17:00, July–Aug also open Mon–Tue, closed Nov–April, 0662/845-295). The Cathedral (or *Dom*) Museum has a rich collection of church art (entry at portico).

From Cathedral Square to St. Peter's: The cathedral square is surrounded by "ecclesiastical palaces." The statue of Mary (1771) is looking away from the church, but, if you stand in the rear of the square immediately under the middle arch, you'll see how she's positioned to be crowned by the two angels on the church facade.

From the arch, walk back across the square to the front of the cathedral and turn right (going past the underground public toilets) into the next square. Walk past the giant chessboard to the pond. This was a horse bath, the 18th-century equivalent of a car wash. Notice the puzzle above it—the artist wove the date of the structure into a phrase. It says, "Leopold the Ruler Built Me," using the letters LLDVICMXVXI, which totals 1732— the year it was built. A small road leads up to the castle (and castle lift). Leave the square through a gate on the right (past the souvenir stalls) which reads "St. Peter." It leads to a waterfall and St. Peter's Cemetery.

The waterfall is part of a canal system that has brought water into Salzburg from Berchtesgaden, 25 kilometers (16 miles) away, since 1150. The busy water used to flush out the streets (Saturday morning was flood-the-streets day) and power factories (over 100 firms as late as the 19th century). Drop into the traditional bakery at the waterfall (hard to beat their rocklike *Roggenbrot*, sold daily 07:00–17:30 except Sat mornings, closed Wed) and then step into the cemetery.

St. Peter's Cemetery: This collection of lovingly tended mini-gardens is butted up against the Mönchberg's rock wall (April–Sept daily 06:30–19:00, Oct–March daily 06:30–18:00). The graves are cared for by relatives. (In Austria, grave sites are rented not owned. Rent bills are sent out every 10 years. If no one cares enough to make the payment, you're gone.) Look up the cliff. Medieval hermit monks lived in the hillside. You can climb up to see their chapel (€1, May–Sept Tue–Sun 10:30–17:00, closed Mon, Oct–April Wed–Thu 10:30–15:30, Fri–Sun 10:30– 16:00, closed Mon–Tue). While the cemetery the von Trapp family hid out in was actually in Hollywood, it was inspired by this one. Walk through the cemetery (silence is requested) and out the opposite end. Drop into St. Peter's Church, a Romanesque basilica done up beautifully Baroque. Continue (through arch opposite hillside, left at church, take the second right, pass the public WC, another square, and church) to ...

Universitätsplatz: This square comes with a busy open-air produce market—Salzburg's liveliest (mornings Mon–Sat, best on Sat when the farmers are in town—60 percent of Austria's produce is now grown organically). You can see the market stall numbers in the pavement. Exit through the covered arcade at #10 to Getreidegasse. Several of these characteristic and nicely arcaded medieval tunnel passages connect Salzburg's streets.

Getreidegasse: This street was old Salzburg's busy, colorful main drag. (*Schmuck* means jewelry.) Famous for its old wrought-iron signs, the street still looks much as it did in Mozart's day.

(The Nordsee Restaurant was even more of a scandal than the coming of McDonald's—notice the medieval golden arches street sign.) Wolfgang was born on this street. Find his very gold house.

Mozart's Birthplace (Geburtshaus): Mozart was born here in 1756. It was in this building that he composed most of his boy-genius works. This is the most popular Mozart sight in town. Filled with scores of scores, portraits, old keyboard instruments and violins, and a furnished middle-class apartment from Mozart's time (all well described in English), it's almost a pilgrimage. If you're a fan, you'll have to check it out (€5.25, or €8 for combined ticket to Mozart's *Wohnhaus*—see "Sights—Across the River," below, July–Aug daily 09:00–19:00, Sept–June daily 09:00–18:00, last entry 30 min before closing time, Getreidegasse 9, tel. 0662/844-313). Note that Mozart's *Wohnhaus* provides a more informative visit than this more-visited site.

Sights—Above the Old Town

▲**Hohensalzburg Fortress**—Built on a rock 120 meters (400 feet) above the Salzach River, this castle is a testament to the importance of the salt trade. One of Europe's mightiest, it dominates Salzburg's skyline and offers incredible views. You can hike up or ride the *Festungsbahn* (funicular, €6.50 round-trip includes fortress courtyard, €6 one-way, pleasant to walk down). The castle visit has two parts—a relatively dull courtyard with some fine views (€3.75 or included in €6.50 funicular fare) and the palatial interior (worth the €3.75 extra admission). The included audioguide gives a 40-minute, room-by-room narration—good information but makes a short story long (feel free to skip rooms). The highlight is the commanding city view from the top of a tower. It ends at the museum showing the fortress through its battle-torn years including World War II (complex open daily year-round; mid-March–mid-June: grounds 09:00–18:00, interior 09:30–17:30; mid-June–mid Sept: grounds 08:30–20:00, interior 09:00–18:00; mid-Sept–mid-March: grounds 09:00–17:00, interior 09:30–17:00; last entry 30 min before closing time, tel. 0662/842-430).

Kids might enjoy the marionette exhibit in the fortress courtyard (adults-€2.50, kids-€1.50, July–Aug daily 09:30–18:00, mid-April–June and Sept–mid-Oct daily 10:00–17:00, closed Nov–March, tel. 0662/849-555).

▲**The Hills Are Alive Walk**—For a most enjoyable approach to the castle, consider riding the elevator from A. Neumayr Platz to the top (€1.25 one-way, €2 round-trip) and walking 20 minutes across Salzburg's little mountain, Mönchsberg. A trail goes through the woods high above the city to Festung Hohensalzburg (stay on the high paved paths, or you'll have a needless climb back up to the castle).

In 1669, a huge Mönchsberg landslide killed over 200

townspeople. Since then the cliffs have been carefully checked each spring and fall. Even today, you might see the crews of three on the cliff monitoring its stability.

Sights—Across the River

Salzach River—Cross the river (ideally on a pedestrian bridge—the one farthest upstream, built in 1903, is just a block off Mozartplatz). It's called "salt river" not because it's salty but because the important salt mines of Hallein are just 15 kilometers (9 miles) upstream. Salt could be transported from here all the way to the Danube and on to Russia. The riverbanks and roads were built in 1860. Before that, the Salzach was much wider and slower moving. Houses opposite the old town fronted the river with docks and garages for boats.

▲**Steingasse**—This street, a block in from the river, was the only street in the Middle Ages going south to Hallein. Today it's wonderfully peaceful and free of Salzburg's touristy crush. Wander down Steingasse (from Mozartplatz, cross the pedestrian bridge, go a block inland, and turn left).

There's a great castle viewpoint midway up Steingasse. Notice the oldest nunnery in the German-speaking world (established in 712) under the castle and to the left. Maria from *The Sound of Music* taught in this nunnery's school. In 1927, she and Herr von Trapp were married in the church you see here (not the church filmed in the movie). He was 47. She was 22. Hmmmm.

At #19 find the carvings on the old door. Look for the notices from beggars to the begging community (more numerous after the economic dislocation caused by the wars over religion following the Reformation) indicating whether the residents would give or not. The four ringers indicate four families lived at this address.

Across the street, the wall is gouged out. This was left even after the building was restored so locals could remember the American GI who tried to get a tank down this road during a visit to the Steingasse brothel.

At #9 a plaque shows where Joseph Mohr, who wrote the words to *Silent Night*, was born, poor and illegitimate, in 1792.

▲**St. Sebastian Cemetery**—Wander through this peaceful place—so Baroque and so Italian (free, April–Oct daily 09:00–19:00, Nov–March daily 9:00–16:00, Linzergasse 43). Mozart's father and most of his family are buried here (near entry on left). When Prince-Archbishop Wolf Dietrich had the cemetery moved from around the cathedral and put here, across the river, people didn't like it. To help popularize it, he had his mausoleum built as its centerpiece. Step into his dome, read the legalistic epitaph (posted in English), and look at the tomb through the grate in the floor. To get to the cemetery (Friedhof St. Sebastian), take Linzergasse, the best shopping street in Salzburg.

▲▲**Mozart's Wohnhaus**—This reconstruction of Mozart's second home (his family moved here when he was 17) is the most informative Mozart sight in town. The English-language audio-guides (free with admission, keep it carefully pointed at the transmitters and don't move while listening) provide a fascinating insight into Mozart's life and music. Along with the usual scores and old pianos, the highlight is an intriguing film (30 min, runs continuously, in English) that leaves you wanting to know more about Mozart and his remarkable family (€5, or €8 for combined ticket to birthplace, guidebook-€4.30, daily 09:00–18:00, July–Aug until 19:00, last tickets sold 30 min before closing, allow 1 hr for visit, across the river from the old town, Makartplatz 8, tel. 0662/8742-2740). The gift shop here sells CDs featuring Mozart's music performed on Mozart's piano.

▲**Mirabell Gardens and Palace (Schloss)**—The bubbly gardens, laid out in 1730, are always open and free. You may recognize the statues and the arbor featured in *The S.O.M.* A brass band plays free park concerts twice weekly (Sun 10:30, Wed 20:30). To properly enjoy the lavish Mirabell Palace—once Wolf Dietrich's summer palace and now the seat of the mayor—get a ticket to a *Schlosskonzert* (my favorite venue for a classical concert). Baroque music flying around a Baroque hall is a happy bird in the right cage. Tickets are around €26 to €31 (student-€14) and are rarely sold out (tel. 0662/848-586). The **Café Bazar**, a few blocks away (on Schwarzstrasse, towards Staatsbrücke) and overlooking the river, is a great place for a classy drink with an old town and castle view.

More Sights—Salzburg

▲▲**Riverside Bike Ride**—The Salzach River has smooth, flat, and scenic bike paths along each side. On a sunny day I can think of no more shout-worthy escape from the city. Hallein is a pleasant destination (with a salt mine tour, see "Sights—Near Salzburg," below, 15 km/9 miles away, the north or "new town" side of river is most scenic). Even a quickie ride from one end of town to the other is a great Salzburg experience. In the evening, the riverbanks are a hand-in-hand, floodlit-spires world.

▲▲*Sound of Music* **Tour**—I took this tour skeptically (as part of my research chores) and liked it. It includes a quick but good general city tour, stops for a luge ride (€3.75 extra, runs in summer in fair weather), hits some *S.O.M.* spots (including the stately home, gazebo, and wedding church), and shows you a lovely stretch of the Salzkammergut. The Salzburg Panorama Tours Company charges €30 for the four-hour, English-only tour (from Mirabellplatz daily at 09:30 and 14:00, ask for a reservation and a free hotel pickup; travelers with this book who buy their tickets with cash at the Mirabellplatz ticket booth get a 10 percent discount on this and any other tour they do; tel. 0662/874-029 or 0662/883-211,

Sound of Music Debunked

Rather than visit the real-life sights from the life of Maria von Trapp and family, most tourists want to see the places Hollywood chose to film this fanciful story. Local guides are happy not to burst any *S.O.M* pilgrim's bubble, but keep these points in mind:

- "Edelweiss" is not a cherished Austrian folk tune or national anthem. It was composed by Rodgers and Hammerstein for the movie.
- Maria was never a nun. She taught at the nunnery school.
- The colonel didn't run a tight domestic ship. In fact, his seven children were as unruly as most. He did use a whistle to call them. Each kid was trained to respond to a certain pitch.
- The family never escaped to Switzerland (which is a five-hour drive away). Rather, they went, legally, on a singing tour of the USA. The scene showing them climbing into Switzerland is actually near Berchtesgaden... home to Hitler's Eagle's Nest, and certainly not a smart place to flee.
- The actual von Trapp family house exists... but it's not the one you see in the film. In fact, the mansion in the movie is actually two different buildings (one used for the exterior and the other for the interior).
- Maria was given the choice: royalties or $8,000 for her story. She didn't think her story would sell so she traded all the rights for $8,000.

www.panoramatours.at). This is worthwhile for *S.O.M.* fans and those who won't otherwise be going into the Salzkammergut. Warning: Many think rolling through the Austrian countryside with 30 Americans singing "Doe, a deer" is pretty schmaltzy. Local Austrians don't understand all the commotion.

Several similar and very competitive tour companies offer every conceivable tour of and from Salzburg (Mozart sights, Berchtesgaden, salt mines, Salzkammergut lakes and mountains). Some hotels have their brochures and get a healthy commission. Bob's Special Tours uses a minibus (several different tours, Kaigasse 10, tel. 0662/849-511, www.bobstours.com).

▲**Hellbrunn Castle**—The attractions here are a garden full of clever trick fountains and the sadistic joy the tour guide gets from soaking tourists. The Baroque garden, one of the oldest in Europe, is pretty enough and now features *S.O.M.'s* "I am 16, going on 17" gazebo (€6.75 July–Aug, €6 Sept–June, includes 35-min tour,

Greater Salzburg

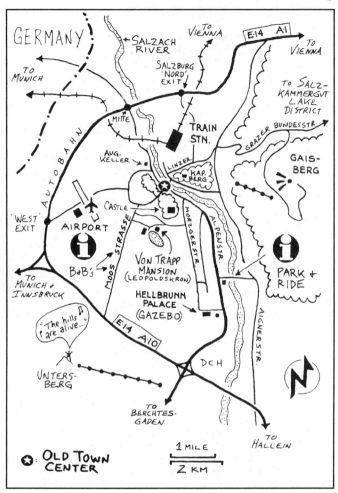

GERMANY

SALZACH RIVER

TO VIENNA

E14 A1

TO VIENNA

TO MUNICH

SALZBURG 'NORD' EXIT

TO SALZ-KAMMERGUT LAKE DISTRICT

MITTE

GRAZER BUNDESSTR.

TRAIN STN.

GAIS-BERG

AUG. KELLER

LINZER

KAP. BERG

A U T O B A H N

CASTLE

MOOS STRASSE

MORZGERSTR.

ALPENSTR.

'WEST' EXIT

AIRPORT

B&B's

VON TRAPP MANSION (LEOPOLDSKRON)

PARK + RIDE

TO MUNICH & INNSBRUCK

HELLBRUNN PALACE (GAZEBO)

AIGNERSTR.

E14 A10

"The hills are alive..."

DCH

UNTERS-BERG

TO BERCHTES-GADEN

TO HALLEIN

N

⊘ OLD TOWN CENTER

1 MILE

2 KM

covered by Salzburg Card, daily 09:00–17:30, July–Aug until 22:00, April and Oct until 16:30, closed Nov–March, tel. 0662/820-372). The archbishop's mediocre 17th-century palace, in the courtyard, is open by tour only (€3, 2/hr, 20 min; €7.50 combined ticket for water gardens and palace). Hellbrunn is almost five kilometers (3 miles) south of Salzburg (bus #55 from station or downtown, 2/hr, 20 min). It's most fun on a sunny day or with kids, but, for many, it's a lot of trouble for a few water tricks.

Music Scene

▲▲**Salzburg Festival**—Each summer, from late July to the end of August, Salzburg hosts its famous Salzburger Festspiele, founded in 1920 partly to employ Vienna's musicians in the summer. This fun and festive time is crowded, but there are plenty of beds (except for a few August weekends). Tickets are normally available the day of the concert unless it's a really big show (the ticket office on Mozartplatz, in the TI, prints a daily list of concerts). You can contact the Austrian National Tourist Office in the United States for specifics on this year's festival schedule and tickets (Box 1142, New York, NY 10108-1142, tel. 212/944-6880, fax 212/730-4568, www.experienceaustria.com, e-mail: info @oewnyc.com), but I've never planned in advance and have enjoyed great concerts with every visit.

▲▲**Musical Events outside of Festival Time**—Salzburg is busy throughout the year with 2,000 classical performances in its palaces and churches annually. Pick up the events calendar at the TI (free, comes out every other month). Whenever you visit, you'll have a number of concerts to choose from. There are nearly nightly concerts at the Mirabell Palace and up in the fortress (both with open seating and roughly €29–36 tickets, concerts at 19:30, 20:00, or 20:30, doors open 30 min early). The *Schlosskonzerte* at the Mirabell Palace offer a fine Baroque setting for your Mozart (tel. 0662/848-586). The fortress concerts, called *Festungskonzerte*, are held in the "prince's chamber" (usually chamber music, tel. 0662/825-858 to reserve, you can pick up tickets at the door). This medieval-feeling room atop the castle has windows overlooking the city, and the concert gives you a chance to enjoy a stroll through the castle courtyard and the grand city view (€6.50 round-trip for funicular; only €2.80 within an hour of the show if you have a concert ticket).

The almost daily "5:00 Concert" next to St. Peter's is cheaper, since it features young artists (€8.75, discount with Salzburg Card, July–Sept daily except Wed, 45 min, tel. 0662/8445-7619). While the series is named after the brother of Joseph Haydn, it features music from various masters.

Salzburg's impressive **Marionette Theater** performs operas with remarkable marionettes and recorded music (€22–35, nearly nightly May–Sept except Sun, tel. 0662/872-406, www .marionetten.at).

For those who'd like some classical music but would rather not sit through a concert, Stiftskeller St. Peter offers a **Mozart Dinner Concert** with a traditional candlelit three-course meal mixed with Mozart music performed by musicians in historic costumes in an elegant Baroque setting (€45, almost nightly at 20:00, see "Eating," below, call to reserve at 0662/828-6950).

The *S.O.M.* **musical** at the Sternbrau restaurant (see "Eating," below) gets good reviews from couples and families.

Sights—Near Salzburg

▲**Bad Dürnberg Salzbergwerke**—Like its salty neighbors, this salt mine tour and cable-car ride above the town of Hallein (15 km/9 miles from Salzburg) is a fun experience while wearing white overalls, sliding down the sleek wooden chutes, and crossing underground from Austria into Germany (€14.75, daily 09:00–17:00, English-speaking guides and information sheets, easy bus and train connections from Salzburg, tel. 06245/852-8515). A convenient "Salt Ticket" from Salzburg's train station covers admission, train, and cable-car fees for €21.

▲**Berchtesgaden**—This alpine resort just across the German border (20 km/12 miles from Salzburg) flaunts its attractions, and you may find yourself in a traffic jam of desperate tourists trying to turn their money into fun. During peak season, it's not worth the headaches for the speedy tourist. Berchtesgaden caters to long-term German guests.

From the station and TI (tel. 08652/967-150), buses go to the salt mines (a 15-min walk otherwise) and the idyllic Königsee (€13, 2-hr scenic cruises, 2/hr, stopovers anywhere, tel. 08652/963-618).

At the **salt mines**, you put on traditional miners' outfits, get on funny little trains, and zip deep into the mountain. For one hour you'll cruise subterranean lakes; slide speedily down two long, slick, wooden banisters; and learn how they mined salt so long ago. Call for crowd-avoidance advice. You can buy a ticket early and browse through the town until your appointed tour time (€11.50, May-mid–Oct daily 09:00–17:00, mid-Oct–April Mon–Sat 12:00–15:30, tel. 08652/60020).

Hitler's famous (but overrated) **Eagle's Nest** towers high above Obersalzberg near Berchtesgaden. The site is open to visitors, but little remains of the alpine retreat Hitler visited only five times. The bus ride up the private road and the lift to the top (a 600-meter/2,000-foot altitude gain) cost €15 from the station, €11.50 from the parking lot. If the weather's cloudy, as it often is, you'll Nazi a thing.

To get to Berchtesgaden from Salzburg, take the bus (2/hr, 30 min, bus station across street from Salzburg's train station); it's more scenic and direct than the train. Some travelers visit Berchtesgaden en route from Munich (hrly trains from Munich, 2.5 hrs, with 1 change).

Sleeping in Salzburg

**(€1.10 = about $1, country code: 43,
area code: 0662, zip code: 5020)**
Sleep Code: **S** = Single, **D** = Double/Twin, **T** = Triple, **Q** = Quad, **b** = bathroom, **s** = shower only, **CC** = Credit Cards accepted, **no CC** = Credit Cards not accepted, **SE** = Speaks English, **NSE** = No English.

Finding a room in Salzburg, even during the music festival, is usually easy. Unless otherwise noted, all my listings come with breakfast and at least some English is spoken. Rates rise significantly during the music festival (late July–Aug); these higher prices appear in the price ranges included in hotel listings below.

Laundromat: You'll find it near recommended Linzergasse hotels at the corner of Paris-Lodron Strasse and Wolf-Dietrich Strasse (Mon–Fri 07:30–18:00, Sat 08:00–12:00, self-serve or drop-off service, tel. 0662/876-381).

Sleeping on Linzergasse and Rupertgasse

These listings are between the train station and the old town in a pleasant neighborhood (with easy parking), a 15-minute walk from the train station (for directions, see "Arrival In Salzburg/By Train," above) and a 10- to 15-minute walk to the old town. If you're coming from the old town, simply cross the main bridge (Staatsbrücke) to nearly traffic-free Linzergasse. The first listings are on or very near Linzergasse, across the bridge from Mozartville. The last ones are farther out with easier parking.

Hotel Trumer Stube, a comfy little hotel-pension a few blocks from the river just off Linzergasse, has clean new rooms and a friendly can-do owner (Sb-€56–89, Db-€89–103, Tb-€89–103, Qb-€132–140, higher mid-July–Aug: Sb-€81–96, Db-€118–132, Tb-€132–146, Qb-€132–161, lower in winter, CC to reserve but pay cash, elevator, parking-€7.50, Bergstrasse 6, tel. 0662/874-776, fax 0662/874-326, www.trumer-stube.at, friendly Silvia SE).

Institute St. Sebastian—a somewhat sterile but very clean, historic building—has spacious public areas, a roof garden, and rents some of the best rooms and dorm beds in town for the money. The immaculate doubles come with modern baths and head-to-toe twin beds (Sb-€31, Db-€52, Tb-€68, CC, elevator, reception open July–Sept 07:30–12:00, 13:00–22:00, Oct–June 08:00–12:00, 16:00–21:00, Linzergasse 41, enter through arch at #37, tel. 0662/871-386, fax 0662/8713-8685). Students like the €17 bunks in 10-bed dorms (€2.25 less if you have sheets, no lockout time, lockers, free showers). Self-service kitchens on each floor (fridge space is free; just request a key). Ask about their washer and dryer.

Hotel Goldene Krone, about five blocks from the river, is big, quiet, and creaky-traditional but modern, with comforts rare in this price range (S-€22–33, Sb-€37–44, D-€55–58, Db-€62–73, Tb-€73–95, CC, elevator, Linzergasse 48, tel. 0662/872-300, fax 0662/8723-0066).

Pension zum Jungen Fuchs terrifies claustrophobes and turns on troglodytes. It's plain but clean and wonderfully located in a funky, dumpy old building (S-€24, D-€31, T-€41, no CC, no breakfast, just up from Hotel Krone at Linzergasse 54, tel. 0662/875-496).

Altstadthotel Wolf Dietrich, one block above Hotel zum Jungen Fuchs, around the corner on Wolf-Dietrich Strasse, is well located and a reasonable option if you want a formal hotel (29 rooms, Sb-€69–99, Db-€109–176; apartment for 2-€149–194, additional adult-€26–35, CC, garage, pool, sauna, Wolf-Dietrich Strasse 7, tel. 0662/871-275, fax 0662/882-320, www.salzburg-hotel.at).

Pensions on Rupertgasse: These two hotels are about five blocks farther from the river up Paris-Lodron Strasse to Rupertgasse, a breeze for drivers.

Pension Bergland is a charming, classy oasis of calm with rustic rooms and musical evenings (Sb-€45, Db-€74, Tb-€85, no CC, 2-night minimum for reservations, music room open 17:00–21:30, Internet access, bike rental, elevator, English library, Rupertgasse 15, tel. 0662/872-318, fax 0662/872-3188, www .berglandhotel.at).

The similar boutiquelike **Hotel Jedermann**, a few doors down, is tastefully done and comfortable with friendly owners, a cheery breakfast room, and a bird-chirping backyard garden (Sb-€50–58, Db-€65–87, Tb-€80–105, Qb-€102–134, CC, Internet access, Rupertgasse 25, tel. 0662/873-241, fax 0662/873-2419, www.hotel-jedermann.com).

Sleeping in (or above) the Old Town

Hotel Restaurant Weisses Kreuz is a classy, comfy, family-run place on a cobbled back street under the castle away from the crowds with a fine restaurant (Sb-€58–66, Db-€87, Tb-€116, CC, peaceful roof garden, garage, Bierjodlgasse 6, tel. 0662/845-641, fax 0662/845-6419, e-mail: weisses.kreuz@salzburginfo.or.at).

Gasthaus zur Goldenen Ente is in a 600-year-old building with medieval stone arches and narrow stairs. Located above a good restaurant, it's as central as you can be on a pedestrian street in old Salzburg. The 17 rooms are modern yet worn and the service is uneven—from friendly to brusque—depending on who's on duty (Sb-€53–60, Db-€79–93 with this book, extra person-€29, the higher prices occur July–Aug, buffet breakfast, CC, elevator, parking-€6/day, Goldgasse 10, tel. 0662/845-622, fax 0662/845-6229, www.ente.at, e-mail: ente@eunet.at, family Steinwender SE).

Naturfreundehaus, also called "Gasthaus Bürgerwehr," is a local version of a mountaineer's hut. It's a great budget alternative in a forest guarded by singing birds and snuggled in the remains of a 15th-century castle wall overlooking Salzburg, with magnificent town and mountain views (D-€20, €10/person in 4- to 6-bed dorms, cold water is free but a hot shower costs €0.75 for 4 min, breakfast-€2.75–3.50, dinner-€5–8.50, no CC, 01:00 curfew, open

May–Sept, 2 min from the top of the €2 round-trip Mönchsberg elevator, Mönchsberg 19, tel. 0662/841-729, fax 0662/425-503). High above the old town, it's the stone house to the left of the now-closed Café Winkler.

Zimmer

These are generally roomy and comfortable and come with a good breakfast, easy parking, tourist information, and do not accept credit cards unless specified. Off-season, competition softens prices. They are a bus ride from town, but, with a day pass and the frequent service, this shouldn't keep you away. Unsavory *Zimmer* skimmers lurk at the station. Ignore them.

Brigitte Lenglachner fills her big, traditional home with a warm welcome (S-€22, bunkbed D-€29, D-€37, Db-€44, T-€50, Tb-€64, Qb-€80, apartment with kitchen-Sb-€37, Db-€58, laundry service if you're staying at least 2 nights-€6 per load, Scheibenweg 8, tel. & fax 0662/438-044). It's a 10-minute walk northeast of the station (cross pedestrian Pioneer Bridge, turn right, walk along the river to the third street which is Scheibenweg, turn left, and it's halfway down on the right).

Trude Poppenberger's three pleasant rooms share a long mountain-view balcony (S-€24, D-€39, T-€57; if you stay 2 nights the prices go down and she'll do your laundry for €8; Wachtelgasse 9, tel. & fax 0662/430-094, e-mail: trudeshome @yline.com). She offers free pickup at the station. Or it's a 30-minute walk northwest of the station (cross pedestrian Pioneer Bridge, turn right, walk along river 300 meters, cross canal, left on Linke Glanzeile for 3 min, right onto Wachtelgasse).

Zimmers on Moosstrasse: The busy street called Moosstrasse, southwest of Mönchsberg, is lined with *Zimmers*. Those farther out are farmhouses. To get to any of these *Zimmers* from the train station, take bus #1, #5, #6, #51, or #55 to Makartplatz and then change to #60, or take bus #1 and change to bus #60 at the first stop after crossing the river (Hanuschplatz). If you are coming from the old town, catch bus #60 from Hanuschplatz, just downstream of the Staatsbrücke near the *Tabak* kiosk. Buy a €1.50 *Einzelkarte-Kernzone* ticket (for 1 trip) or a €3 *Tageskarte* (for the entire day) from the streetside machine and punch it when you get on the bus. If you're driving from the center, go through the tunnel, straight on Neutorstrasse, and take the fourth left onto Moosstrasse.

Maria Gassner rents 10 decent, comfortable rooms in her modern house (S-€22, Sb-€29, D-€33, Db-€37, big Db with balcony-€44, Tb-€66, Qb-€73, 10 percent more for 1-night stays, family deals, CC, €4.50 coin-op laundry, Moosstrasse 126-B, bus stop: Sendelweg, tel. 0662/824-990, fax 0662/822-075, e-mail: pension-maria.gassner@utanet.at).

Frau Ballwein offers cozy, charming rooms in a 160-year-old farmhouse that feels brand new (S-€18, Ss-€19, D-€31, Db-€37–44, Tb-€62, more for 1-night stays, family deals, ask about family apartment, farm-fresh breakfasts, Moosstrasse 69, bus stop: Gsengerweg, tel. & fax 0662/824-029, e-mail: haus .ballwein@gmx.net).

Haus Reichl also has good rooms (D/Db-€44, T/Tb-€66, Qb with balcony and view-€73, between Ballwein and Bankhammer B&Bs, 200 meters down Reiterweg to #52, bus stop: Gsengerweg, tel. & fax 0662/826-248, www.privatzimmer.at/haus -reichl, e-mail: haus.reichl@telering.at).

Helga Bankhammer rents pleasant rooms in a farmhouse with farm animals nearby (S/Sb-€26, D-€37–38, Db-€41, higher in July–Aug, CC, laundry, Moosstrasse 77, bus stop: Marienbad, tel. & fax 0662/830-067, www.privatzimmer.at/helga.bankhammer, e-mail: helga.bankhammer@telering.at).

Gästehaus Blobergerhof is rural and comfortable (Sb-€29–34, big, new Sb with balcony-€41–45, Db-€48–51, big, new Db with balcony-€69–79, extra bed-€15, ask about apartment, 10 percent more for 1-night stays, CC, breakfast buffet, free bike usage, laundry service, will pick up at station, Hammerauerstrasse 4, bus stop: Hammerauerstrasse, tel. 0662/830-227, fax 0662/827-061, www.blobergerhof.at, e-mail: keuschnigg@eunet.at).

Sleeping Elsewhere in Salzburg

Hotel am Nussdorferhof is a traditional, 31-room place, located about halfway between the old town and the *Zimmer*s on Moosstrasse. Run enthusiastically by Herbert and Ilse, the hotel has all the amenities, such as a sauna, whirlpool, and Internet access. It's a 15-minute walk, or short bus ride, from the old town (Sb-€64–79, Db-€93–130, Db suite-€180–209, includes breakfast buffet, CC, some waterbeds, some theme rooms, elevator, free bike rental, attached Italian restaurant, free parking, free shuttle to/from train station or airport, Moosstrasse 36, from station take bus #1, #5, #6, #51, or #55 to Makartplatz and then change to #60, bus stop: Nussdorferstrasse, tel. 0662/824-838, fax 0662/824-8389, www.nussdorferhof.at).

Sleeping near the Train Station

Pension Adlerhof, a plain and decent old place, is two blocks in front of the train station (left off Kaiserschutzenstrasse), but a 15-minute walk from the sightseeing action. It has a quirky staff and 35 well-maintained rooms (S-€29–37, Sb-€40–50, D-€51–58, Db-€65–80, Tb-€72–95, Qb-€80–116, Internet access, Elisabethstrasse 25, tel. 0662/875-236, fax 0662/873-6636, www.pension-adlerhof.com).

Gottfried's International Youth Hotel, a.k.a. the "Yo-Ho," is the most lively, handy, and American of Salzburg's many hostels (€12.50 in 6- to 8-bed dorms, D-€16/person, T or Q-€14/person, sheets included for €7.25 deposit, breakfast €2.25–3.50, CC, 6 blocks from station toward Linzergasse and 6 blocks from river at Paracelsusstrasse 9, tel. 0662/879-649, www.yoho.at). This easygoing place speaks English first; has cheap meals, 200 beds, lockers, Internet access, laundry, tour discounts, and no curfew; plays *The Sound of Music* free daily around noon; runs a lively bar; and welcomes anyone of any age. The noisy atmosphere and lack of a curfew can make it hard to sleep.

Eating in Salzburg

Salzburg boasts many inexpensive, fun, and atmospheric places to eat. I'm a sucker for big cellars with their smoky, Old World atmosphere, heavy medieval arches, time-darkened paintings, antlers, hearty meals, and plump patrons. These places, all centrally located in the old town, are famous with visitors but are also enjoyed by the locals. **Gasthaus zum Wilder Mann** is the place if the weather's bad and you're in the mood for Hofbräu atmosphere and a hearty, cheap meal at a shared table in one small, well-antlered room (Mon–Sat 11:00–21:00, closed Sun, open until 21:30 July–Aug, smoky, 2 min from Mozart's birthplace, enter from Getreidegasse 22 or Griesgasse 17, tel. 0662/841-787). For a quick lunch, get the *Bauernschmaus*, a mountain of dumplings, kraut, and peasant's meats.

Stiftskeller St. Peter has been in business for more than 1,000 years—it was mentioned in the biography of Charlemagne. It's classy (with strolling musicians), more central, and a good splurge for traditional Austrian cuisine in medieval sauce (meals €15–20, daily 11:00–24:00, indoor/outdoor seating, hosts Mozart Dinner Concert mentioned in "Music Scene," above: €45, nearly nightly at 20:00, call 0662/828-6950 to reserve, CC, next to St. Peter's church at foot of Mönchsberg, restaurant tel. 0662/841-268).

Gasthaus zur Goldenen Ente (see "Sleeping," above) serves great food in a classy, subdued hotel dining room. The chef, Robert, specializes in roast duck (*Ente*) and seafood, along with *Salzburger Nockerl*, the mountainous sweet soufflé served all over town. It's big enough for four (Mon–Fri 11:30–20:00, closed Sat–Sun, Goldgasse 10, tel. 0662/845-622).

Stieglkeller is a huge, atmospheric institution that has several rustic rooms and outdoor garden seating with a great rooftop view of the old town (May–Sept daily 10:00–23:00, closed Oct–April, 50 meters uphill from the lift to the castle, Festungsgasse 10, tel. 0662/842-681).

Sternbräu Inn is a sprawling complex of popular eateries (traditional and vegetarian). One elegant room hosts the *Sound of Music* dinner show. A piano player and a hard-working quartet of singers perform an entertaining mix of *Sound of Music* hits and traditional folk songs (€42 includes a schnitzel and crisp apple strudel dinner at 19:30, €27 for 20:30 show only, can sell out so reserve ahead, ideal for families, daily May–Sept, Griesgasse 23, tel. 0662/826-617, www.salzburginfo.at/soundofaustria).

Resch & Lieblich Bierhaus, wedged between the cliff side and the back of the big concert hall, is a rough and characteristic place popular with locals for salads, goulash, and light meals (daily 10:00–24:00, indoor/outdoor seating in rustic little cellar or under umbrellas on square, Toscaninihof, tel. 0662/843-675).

Café Glockenspiel, on Mozartplatz 2, is the place to see and be seen (July–Aug daily 09:00–24:00, less off-season, tel. 0662/841-403).

Nestled behind the cathedral and under the castle, **Restaurant Weisses Kreuz** serves fine Balkan cuisine in a pleasant dining room (Wed–Mon 11:30–14:45, 17:00–22:45, closed Tue, Bierjodlgasse 6, tel. 0662/845-641).

Restaurant Zipfer Bierhaus, facing Universitätsplatz, serves good salads and traditional meals at a decent price (Mon–Sat 10:00–24:00, closed Sun, tel. 0662/840-745).

Picnickers will appreciate the bustling morning **produce market** (daily except Sun) on Universitätsplatz, just behind Mozart's house.

Sausage stands serve the local fast food. The best places (such as the one on the side of the Collegiate Church just off Universitätsplatz) use the same boiling water all day, which fills the weenies with more flavor. Key weenie words: *bratwurst:* boiled white sausage, *bosna:* with onions and curry, *kas krainer:* with melted cheese inside, and *senf:* mustard (ask for sweet: *süss* or sharp: *scharf*). Only a tourist puts the sausage in a bun like a hot dog. Munch alternately between the meat and the bread (that's why you have two hands), and you'll look like a local.

Eating Away from the Center

These two places are on the old-town side of the river, about a 15-minute walk along the river (river on your right) from the Staatsbrücke bridge.

Krimplestätter employs 450 years of experience serving authentic old-Salzburger food in its authentic old-Austrian interior or its cheery garden (Tue–Sun 11:00–24:00, closed Mon all year and Sun Sept–April, Müllner Hauptstrasse 31, tel. 0662/432-274). For fine food with a wild finale, eat here and drink at the nearby Augustiner Bräustübl.

Augustiner Bräustübl, a monk-run brewery, is rustic and crude. On busy nights it's like a Munich beer hall with no music but the volume turned up. When it's cool, you'll enjoy a historic setting with beer-sloshed and smoke-stained halls. On balmy evenings it's a Monet painting with beer breath under chestnut trees in the garden. Local students mix with tourists eating hearty slabs of schnitzel with their fingers or cold meals from the self-serve picnic counter while children frolic on the playground kegs. Waiters only bring drinks. For food, go up the stairs, survey the hallway of deli counters, and assemble your meal (or, as long as you buy a drink, you can bring in your picnic, open daily 15:00–23:00, Augustinergasse 4, tel. 0662/431-246, head up Müllner Hauptstrasse northwest along the river, and ask for "Müllnerbräu," its local nickname). Don't be fooled by second-rate gardens serving the same beer nearby. Augustiner Bräustübl is a huge, 1,000-seat place within the Augustiner brewery. For your beer: Pick up a half-liter or full-liter mug ("*shank*" means self-serve price, "*bedienung*" is the price with waiter service), pay the lady, wash your mug, and give Mr. Keg your receipt and empty mug to be filled.

For dessert—after a visit to the strudel kiosk—enjoy the incomparable floodlit view of old Salzburg from the nearby Müllnersteg pedestrian bridge and a riverside stroll home.

Eating on or near Linzergasse

These cheaper places are near the recommended hotels on Linzergasse. **Frauenberger** is friendly, picnic ready, and inexpensive, with indoor or outdoor seating (Mon 08:00–14:00, Tue–Fri 08:00–14:00, 15:00–18:00, Sat 08:00–12:30, closed Sun, across from Linzergasse 16). **Spicy Spices** is a trippy vegetarian-Indian restaurant serving tasty curry and rice boxes, *samosas*, organic salads, vegan soups, and fresh juices (Mon–Sat 10:00–22:00, Sun 12:00–21:00, Wolf-Dietrich Strasse 1, tel. 0662/870-712). Nearby, **Restaurant Ährlich** offers a delicious variety of organic meals (Mon–Sat 18:00–22:00, also 12:00–14:00 July–Aug, closed Sun, Wolf-Dietrich Strasse 7, tel. 0662/8712-7539). Closer to the hotels on Rupertgasse and away from the tourists is the very local **Biergarten Weisse** (Mon–Sat 11:00–24:00, Sun 16:00–24:00, on Rupertgasse east of Bayerhamerstrasse, tel. 0662/872-246).

Transportation Connections—Salzburg

By train, Salzburg is the first stop over the German-Austrian border. Travelers using a Europass or a Eurail Selectpass that does not include Austria do not have to pay extra to get to Salzburg, provided they are going no farther into Austria. That means that if Salzburg is your only stop in the country, you won't have to add Austria to your pass or pay extra to get there.

By train to: Innsbruck (direct every 2 hrs, 2 hrs), **Vienna** (2/hr, 3.5 hrs), **Hallstatt** (hrly, 50 min to Attnang Puchheim, 20-min wait, 90 min to Hallstatt), **Reutte** (every 2 hrs, 4 hrs, transfer to a bus in Innsbruck), **Munich** (2/hr, 1.5–2 hrs). Train info: tel. 051717 (wait through long German recording for operator).

By car: To leave town driving west, go under the Mönchsberg tunnel and follow blue A1 signs to Munich. It's 90 minutes from Salzburg to Innsbruck.

SALZKAMMERGUT LAKE DISTRICT AND HALLSTATT

Commune with nature in Austria's Lake District. "The hills are alive," and you're surrounded by the loveliness that has turned on everyone from Emperor Franz Josef to Julie Andrews. This is *The Sound of Music* country. Idyllic and majestic, but not rugged, it's a gentle land of lakes, forested mountains, and storybook villages, rich in hiking opportunities and inexpensive lodging. Settle down in the postcard-pretty, lake-cuddling town of Hallstatt.

Planning Your Time

While there are plenty of lakes and charming villages, Hallstatt is really the only one that matters. One night and a few hours to browse are all you'll need to fall in love. To relax or take a hike in the surroundings, give it two nights and a day. It's a relaxing break between Salzburg and Vienna. My best Austrian week: the two big cities—Salzburg and Vienna, a bike ride along the Danube, and a stay in Hallstatt.

Orientation (area code: 06134)

Lovable Hallstatt is a tiny town bullied onto a ledge between a selfish mountain and a swan-ruled lake, with a waterfall ripping furiously through its middle. It can be toured on foot in about 15 minutes. The town is one of Europe's oldest, going back centuries before Christ. The symbol of Hallstatt, which you'll see all over town, is two spirals next to each other, a design based on jewelry from Bronze Age Celtic graves found high in the nearby mountains.

The charm of Hallstatt is the village and its lakeside setting. Go there to relax, nibble, wander, and paddle. While tourist crowds can trample much of Hallstatt's charm in August, the place is almost dead in the off-season. The lake is famous for its good fishing and pure water.

Tourist Information: The friendly and helpful TI, on the main drag, can explain hikes and excursions, arrange private tours of Hallstatt (€48), and find you a room (Mon–Fri 09:00–12:00, 14:00–17:00, in July–Aug also Sat–Sun 10:00–14:00, less off-season, a block from Marktplatz toward the lakefront parking, above post office, Seestrasse 169, tel. 06134/8208, www.hallstatt.net). Hallstatt gives anyone spending the night a "guest card" allowing free parking and discounts to local attractions (free, from your hotel, ask for it).

Hallstatt

NOT TO SCALE—
BUS STOP TO MARKTPLATZ
IS A 10 MINUTE WALK

SALT MINE

SMALL UPPER PARKING LOT #1 IN TUNNEL

CATHOLIC CHURCH

TO ECHERNTAL VALLEY

FUNICULAR

TUNNEL

TO BAD ISCHL & SALZBURG

MAIN ROAD

DR. MORTON WEG

MUSEUM

GROG ROAD

GOSAUMÜHL

MAIN RD.

BUS STOP W.C. + PARKING LOT #2

BOAT RENTAL

MARKT PLATZ

MARKT DOCK

BOAT RENTAL

TO OBERTRAUN

LAHN DOCK

PROT CHURCH

+ POST

HALLSTATTERSEE

TO HALLSTATT TRAIN STATION

❶ GASTHOF SIMONY	❹ PENSION SEETHALER	❼ PENSION SARSTEIN
❷ GASTHOF ZAUNER	❺ HELGA LENZ ZIMMER	❽ BRAUGASTHOF
❸ GASTHAUS ZUR MÜHLE	❻ FRAU ZIMMERMAN ZIMMER	❾ GAST. GRUNER ANGER

Arrival in Hallstatt

By Train: Hallstatt's train station is a wide spot on the tracks across the lake. *Stefanie* (a boat) meets you at the station and glides scenically across the lake into town (€1.80, meets each train until about 17:00—don't arrive after that). Last departing boat-train connection leaves Hallstatt around 17:00, and the first boat goes in the morning at 06:55 (10:00 on Sun). Walk left from the boat dock for the TI and most hotels. Since there's no train station in town, the TI can help you find schedule information.

By Car: The main road skirts Hallstatt via a long tunnel above the town. Parking is tight mid-June through mid-October. Hallstatt has several numbered parking areas outside the town center. Parking lot #1 is in the tunnel above the town (swing through to check for a spot, free with guest card). Otherwise several numbered lots are just after the tunnel. If you have a hotel reservation, the guard will let you drive into town to drop your bags (ask if your hotel has any in-town parking). It's a lovely 10- to 20-minute lakeside walk to the center of town from the lots. Without a guest card, you'll pay €4.35 per day for parking. Off-season parking in town is easy and free.

Helpful Hints

Bike Rental: Hotel Grüner Baum, facing the market square, rents bikes (€6/half day, €9/day).

Parks and Swimming: Green and peaceful lakeside parks line the south end of Lake Hallstatt. If you walk 10 minutes south of town to Hallstatt-Lahn, you'll find a grassy public park, playground, and swimming area with a fun man-made play island (*Badestrand* and *Bade-Insel*).

Views: For a great view over Hallstatt, hike above Helga Lenz's *Zimmer* as far as you like (see "Sleeping," below), or climb any path leading up the hill. The 40-minute steep hike down from the salt mine tour gives the best views (see "Sights," below).

Hallstatt Historic Town Walk

This short walk starts at the dock.

Boat Landing: There was a Hallstatt before there was a Rome. In fact, because of the importance of salt mining here, an entire epoch—the Hallstatt era from 800 to 400 B.C.—is named for this important spot. Through the centuries, salt was traded and people came and went by boat. You'll still see the traditional *Fuhr* boats, designed to carry heavy loads in shallow water.

Towering above the town is the Catholic church. Its faded St. Christopher—patron saint of travelers with his cane and baby Jesus on his shoulder—watched over those sailing in and out. Until 1875, the only way into town was by boat. Then came the train and the road. The good ship *Stefanie* shuttles travelers back and forth from here to the Hallstatt train station immediately across the lake. The *Bootverleih* sign advertises boat rentals (see "Lake Trip," below).

Notice the one-lane road out of town (with the waiting time, width, and height posted). Until 1966, when a bigger tunnel was built above Hallstatt, all the traffic crept single file right through the town.

Look down the shore at the huge homes. Housing several families back when Hallstatt's population was about double its present 1,000, many of these rent rooms to visitors today.

Parking is tight here in the tourist season. Locals and hotels have cards getting them into the prime town center lot. From October through May, the barricade is lifted and anyone can park here. Hallstatt is snowbound for about three months each winter. But the lake hasn't frozen over since 1981.

See any swans? They've patrolled the lake like they own it since the 1860s when Emperor Franz Josef and Empress Sissy—the Princess Di of her day—made this region their annual holiday retreat. Sissy loved swans, so locals made sure she'd see them here. During this period, the Romantics discovered Hallstatt, many top painters worked here, and the town got its first hotel.

Tiny Hallstatt has two big churches—Protestant (step into its cemetery, which is actually a grassy lakeside playground) and Catholic up above (described below with its fascinating bone chapel). After the Reformation, most of Hallstatt was Protestant. Then, under Hapsburg rule, it was mostly Catholic. Today, 60 percent of the town is Catholic. Walk over the town's stream, past the Protestant church one block to the...

Market Square: In 1750, a fire leveled this part of town. The buildings you see now are all late 18th century and built of stone rather than burnable wood. Take a close look at the two-dimensional, up-against-the-wall pear tree (it likes the sun-warmed wall). The statue features the Holy Trinity. At #58 study the painting of Hallstatt in 1750. Continue a block past Gasthof Simony to the pair of phone booths and step into the...

City Museum Square: Because 20th-century Hallstatt was of no industrial importance, it was untouched by World War II. But once upon a time its salt was worth defending. High above, peeking out of the trees, is Rudolf's Tower (*Rudolfsturm*). Originally a 13th-century watchtower protecting the salt mines and later the mansion of a salt-mine boss, today it's a restaurant with a great view. A zigzag trail connects the town with *Rudolfsturm* and the salt mines just beyond. The big white houses by the waterfall were water-powered mills that once ground Hallstatt's grain. If you hike up a few blocks, you'll see the river raging through town. Around you are the town's TI, post office, two museums, city hall, and the Janu Sport shop (with its prehistoric basement—described below). The statue on the square is of the mine manager who excavated prehistoric graves around 1850. Much of the *Schmuck* (jewelry) sold locally is inspired by the jewelry found in the area's Bronze Age tombs.

For thousands of years people have been leaching salt out of this mountain. A brine spring sprung here, attracting Bronze Age people around 1500 B.C. Later, they dug tunnels to mine the rock, which was 70 percent salt, dissolved it into a brine, and distilled out salt—precious for preserving meat (and making French fries so tasty). For a look at early salt-mining implements, visit the museum.

Sights—Hallstatt

Cultural Heritage Museum—Opening in mid-May of 2002, this newly renovated museum tells the story of how little Hallstatt was once a crucial salt-mining hub of a culture that spread from France to the Balkans during the "Hallstatt Period" (800–400 B.C.). Back then, Celtic tribes dug for precious salt, and Hallstatt was, as its name means, the "place of salt" (€6, April–Oct daily 10:00–18:00, Oct–April daily 10:00–16:00, Seestrasse 56, adjacent to TI, tel. 06134/8280). The Janu Sport shop across from the

TI dug into a prehistoric site, and now its basement is another small museum (free).

▲▲**Hallstatt's Catholic Church and Bone Chapel**—The Catholic church overlooks the town from above. From near the boat dock, hike up the covered wooden stairway and follow signs to *Kath. Kirche*. The lovely church has 500-year-old altars and frescoes dedicated to St. Barbara (patron of miners) and St. Catherine (patron of foresters—lots of wood was needed to fortify the many kilometers of tunnels and boil the brine to distill out the salt).

Behind the church, in the well-tended graveyard, is the 12th-century Chapel of St. Michael (even older than the church). Its bone chapel—or charnel house—contains over 600 painted skulls. Each skull has been lovingly named, dated, and decorated (skulls with dark, thick garlands are oldest—18th century, flowers indicate more recent—19th century). Space was so limited in this cemetery that bones had only 12 peaceful, buried years here before making way for the freshly dead. Many of the dug-up bones and skulls ended up in this chapel. They stopped this practice in the 1960s, about the same time the Catholic Church began permitting cremation (*Beinhaus*, €1, mid-May–Sept daily 10:00–18:00, Oct and Easter–mid-May 10:00–16:00 weather permitting, closed Nov–Easter).

▲**Lake Trip**—While there are full lake tours, you can ride *Stefanie* across the lake and back for €3.60. It stops at the tiny Hallstatt train station for 30 minutes giving you time to walk to a hanging bridge and enjoy the peaceful, deep part of the lake. Longer lake tours are also available from the same dock (€7/ 50 min, €8.50/75 min). Those into relaxation can rent a sleepy electric motorboat to enjoy town views from the water (€7/ 30 min, €10/60 min, until 19:00; boats have 2 speeds: slow and stop; spend an extra €1.50/30 min for faster 500-watt boats, rental place next to ferry dock, tel. 06134/8320).

▲▲**Salt Mine Tour**—If you have yet to do a salt mine, Hallstatt's—which claims to be the oldest in the world—is a good one. You'll ride a steep funicular high above the town (€7.75 round-trip, €4.75 one-way, May–Sept daily 09:00–18:00, Oct until 16:30, closed Nov–April, tel. 06134/8400), take a 10-minute hike, check your bag and put on old miners' clothes, hike 200 meters higher in your funny outfit to meet your guide, load onto the train, and ride into the mountain through a tunnel actually made by prehistoric miners. Inside, you'll listen to a great video (English headsets), slide down two banisters, and follow your guide. While the tour is mostly in German, the guide is required to speak English if you ask—so ask (€10.50, May–Sept daily 09:30–16:30, Oct daily 09:30–15:00, the 16:00 funicular departure catches the last tour at 16:30, no children

Salzkammergut Lakes

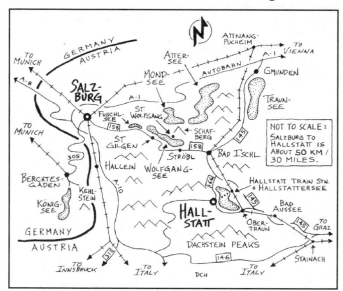

under age 4, rarely a long wait but arrive after 15:00 and you'll find no lines and a smaller group, tel. 06134/8400). The well-publicized ancient Celtic graveyard excavation sites nearby are really dead (precious little to see). If you skip the funicular, the scenic 40-minute hike back into town is (with strong knees) a joy.

At the base of the funicular, notice train tracks leading to the Erbstollen tunnel entrance. This lowest of the salt tunnels goes many kilometers into the mountain where a shaft connects it to the tunnels you just explored. Today the salty brine from these tunnels flows 40 kilometers (25 miles) through the world's oldest pipeline to the huge modern salt works (next to the highway) at Ebensee. You'll pass a stack of the original 120-year-old wooden pipes between the lift and the mine.

▲**Local Hikes**—Mountain lovers, hikers, and spelunkers keep busy for days using Hallstatt as their home base (ask the TI for ideas). Local hikes are well described in the TI's *Dachstein Hiking Guide* (€5.80, English). A good, short, and easy walk is the two-hour round-trip up the Echerntal Valley to the Waldbachstrub waterfall and back. With a car, consider hiking around nearby Altaussee (flat, 3-hour hike) or along Grundlsee to Tolpitzsee. Regular buses connect Hallstatt with Gosausee for a pleasant hour-long walk around that lake. The TI can recommend a great two-day hike with an overnight in a nearby mountain hut.

Sights—Near Hallstatt

▲▲**Dachstein Mountain Cable Car and Caves**—For a refreshing activity, ride a scenic cable car up a mountain to visit huge, chilly caves.

Dachstein Cable Car: From Obertraun, five kilometers beyond Hallstatt, a mighty gondola goes in three stages high up the Dachstein Plateau—crowned by Dachstein, the highest mountain in the Salzkammergut (over 2,700 meters/9,000 feet). The first segment stops at Schonbergalm (1,350 meters/4,500 feet) with a mountain restaurant and two huge caves (described below). The second segment goes to the summit of Krippenstein (1,980 meters/ 6,600 feet) with a classy hotel/restaurant and a rustic chalet restaurant. The third segment descends to Gjaidalm (1,740 meters/5,800 feet) from which several hikes begin. For a quick high-country experience, Krippenstein is better than Gjaidalm. From Krippenstein you'll survey a scrubby limestone "karst" landscape (which absorbs rainfall through its many cracks and ultimately carves all those caves) with 360-degree views of the surrounding mountains (cable-car ride to the caves–€12.50, to Krippenstein–€19, tel. 06134/8400).

Giant Ice Caves (Riesen-Eishohle, 1,350 meters/4,500 feet): These were discovered in 1910. Today, guides lead tours in German and English on an hour-long, one-kilometer (half-mile) hike through an eerie, icy, subterranean world, passing limestone canyons the size of subway stations. The limestone caverns, carved by rushing water, are named for scenes from Wagner operas— the favorite of the mountaineers who first came here. If you're nervous, note that the iron oxide covering the ceiling takes 5,000 years to form. Things are very stable.

At the lift station, report to the ticket window to get your cave appointment. While the temperature is just above freezing and the 600 steps help keep you warm, bring a sweater. Allow 90 minutes, including the 10-minute hike from the station (€7.25, or €11 combo ticket with Mammoth Caves, open mid-May– mid-Oct, hour-long tours from 09:00–16:00, stay in front and assert yourself for English information, tel. 06134/8400).

Drop by the little free museum near the lift station—in a local-style wood cabin designed to support 200 tons of snow— to see the huge cave system model, exhibits about its exploration, and info about life in the caves.

Mammoth Caves: While huge and well promoted, these are much less interesting than the Ice Caves and—for most— not worth the time. Of the 48-kilometer (30-mile) limestone labyrinth excavated so far, you'll walk a kilometer (half-mile) with a German-speaking guide (€7.25, or €11 combo ticket with Ice Caves, hour-long tours 10:00–15:00, open mid-May–mid-Oct, call a few days before to check on the schedule for an English guide, entrance a 10-min hike from lift station).

Luge Rides on the Hallstatt-Salzburg Road—If you're driving between Salzburg and Hallstatt, you'll pass two luge rides. Each is a ski lift which drags you backwards up the hill as you sit on your go-cart. At the top you ride the cart down the winding metal course. Operating the sled is simple. Push to go, pull to stop, take your hands off your stick and you get hurt.

Each course is just off the road with easy parking. The ride up and down takes about 15 minutes. Look for *Riesen-Rutschbahn* or *Sommerrodelbahn* signs. The one near Fuschlsee (closest to Salzburg) is half as long and half the price (€3.25/ride, €23.50/10 rides, 750 meters). The one near Wolfgangsee is a double course, more scenic with grand lake views (€5/ride, €35/10 rides, 1,300 meters, each track is the same speed). Courses are open Easter through October from 10:00 to 18:00 (July–Aug 09:30–20:00, tel. 06235/7297). These are fun, the concrete courses near Reutte are better.

Sleeping in Hallstatt
**(€1.10 = about $1, country code: 43,
area code: 06134, zip code: 4830)**
Sleep Code: **S** = Single, **D** = Double/Twin, **T** = Triple, **Q** = Quad, **b** = bathroom, **s** = shower only, **CC** = Credit Cards accepted, **no CC** = Credit Cards not accepted, **SE** = Speaks English, **NSE** = No English.

Hallstatt's TI can almost always find you a room (either in town or at B&Bs and small hotels outside of town—which are more likely to have rooms available and come with easy parking). Mid-July and August can be tight. Early August is worst. A bed in a private home costs about €20 with breakfast. It's hard to get a one-night advance reservation. But if you drop in and they have a spot, one-nighters are welcome. Prices include breakfast, lots of stairs, and a silent night. "*Zimmer mit Aussicht?*" means "Room with view?"—worth asking for. Only a few of my listings accept plastic, which goes for most businesses here.

Laundromat: A small full-service Laundromat is at the campground up from the island of Bade-Insel, just off the main road (€7.25 per load, based on weight). In the center, Hotel Grüner Baum does laundry for nonguests (€14.50 per load, facing market square).

Hotels
Gasthof Simony, my 500-year-old favorite, is right on the square with a lake view, balconies, creaky wood floors, slippery rag rugs, antique furniture, a lakefront garden, and a huge breakfast. Reserve in advance. For safety, reconfirm a day or two before you arrive and call again if arriving late (S-€28, Sb-€60, D-€40, Db-€75, third person-€26–33, no CC, Markt 105, tel. & fax 06134/8231, e-mail: susannescheutz@mulitkom.at, Susanne

Scheutz SE). Downstairs and in the lakefront garden, Frau Zopf runs a traditional Austrian restaurant—try her delicious home-made desserts. Grab a lakeside table.

Bräugasthof Hallstatt is another creaky old place—a former brewery—with eight mostly lake-view rooms near the town center (Sb-€38, Db-€66, Tb-€95, less off-season, CC, just past TI on the main drag at Seestrasse 120, tel. 06134/8221, fax 06134/82214, Lobisser family).

Gasthof Zauner, at the opposite end of the square from the Simony, is my second listing that accepts credit cards. It's a business machine offering 12 modern pine-flavored rooms with all the comforts on the main square, and a restaurant specializing in grilled meat and fish (Db-€90, CC, Marktplatz 51, tel. 06134/8246, fax 06134/82468, e-mail: zauner@hallstatt.at).

Away from the Center: Gasthof Pension Grüner Anger is a practical and modern 11-room place away from the medieval town center. It's big and quiet, a block from the base of the salt mine lift, and a 10-minute walk from the town center (Sb-€33, Db-€54, €57 in July–Aug, 1-night stays-€60, third person-€15, CC, parking lot, Lahn 10, tel. 06134/8397, fax 06134/83974, e-mail: anger@aon.at, Sulzbacher family).

Cheaper Options

Pension Seethaler is a homey old lodge with 45 beds and a breakfast room mossy with antlers, perched above the lake. The staff won't win any awards for congeniality, but it's a good, cheap, simple option (€16/person in S, D, T, or Q, €20/person in rooms with private bath, 3 nights or more-€1.50 less; coin-op showers downstairs-€0.50/8 min, Dr. Morton Weg 22, find the stairs to the left of Seestrasse 116, at the top of the stairs turn left, tel. 06134/8421, fax 06134/84214, e-mail: pension.seethaler @kronline.at, Frau Seethaler).

Helga Lenz is a five-minute climb above the Seethaler (look for the green *Zimmer* sign). This big, sprawling, woodsy house has a nifty garden perch, wins the best-view award, and is ideal for those who sleep well in tree houses (S only available April–June & Oct-€17, D-€30, Db-€35, T-€44, Tb-€51, 1-night stays-€2 per person extra, family room, closed Nov–March, Hallberg 17, tel. & fax 06134/8508, e-mail: haus-lenz@aon.at).

These two listings are 200 meters to the right of the ferry boat dock, with your back to the lake: **Frau Zimmermann** runs a three-room *Zimmer* (as her name implies) in a 500-year-old ram-shackle house with low beams, time-polished wood, and fine lake views (S-€16, D-€32, can be musty, Gosaumühlstrasse 69, tel. 06134/86853). She speaks little English, but you'll find yourself caught up in her charm and laughing together like old friends. A block away, **Pension Sarstein** has 25 beds in basic, dusty rooms with flower-bedecked, lake-view balconies, in a charming building run by friendly Frau Fischer. You can swim from her lakeside garden (D-€29, Ds-€41, Db-€47 with this book, 1-night stays-€1.50 per person extra, Gosaumühlstrasse 83, tel. 06134/8217, NSE).

Gasthaus zur Mühle Jugendherberge, below the waterfall with the best cheap beds in town, is popular for its great pizzas and cheap grub (bed in 3- to 20-bed coed dorms-€10, D-€22, sheets-€3 extra, family quads, breakfast-€3, big lockers with a €15 deposit, closed Nov, below tunnel car park, Kirchenweg 36, tel. & fax 06134/8318, e-mail: toeroe.f@magnet.at, run by Ferdinand Törö).

Eating in Hallstatt

You can enjoy good food inexpensively with delightful lakeside settings. While everyone cooks the typical Austrian fare, your best bet here is trout. *Reinanke* trout is from Lake Hallstatt. Restaurants in Hallstatt tend to have unreliable hours and close early on slow nights, so don't wait too long to get dinner.

Grab a front table at **Restaurant Simony's** lakeside garden (daily 11:00–21:00, closed Thu Oct–April, tel. 06134/8427, under Gasthof Simony, see "Sleeping," above). **Hotel Grüner Baum's** romantic restaurant is fancier and also good (May–Oct Sat–Thu 11:30–22:00, closed Friday and Nov–April, right on Market Square, tel. 06134/8263). Or feed the swans while your trout cooks at **Restaurant Bräugasthof** (May–Oct daily 10:00–21:00, closed Nov–April, fun menu, tel. 06134/20012, see "Sleeping," above). While it lacks a lakeside setting, **Gasthof Zauner's** classy restaurant is well respected for its grilled meat and fish, and the interior of its dining room is covered in real ivy that grows in through the windows (daily 11:30–14:30, 17:30–22:00, see "Sleeping," above). For the best pizza in town with a fun-loving local crowd, chow down cheap and hearty at **Gasthaus zur Mühle** (daily 11:00–14:00, 17:00–21:00, closed Tue in Oct–May, see "Sleeping," above). Locals like the smoky **Strand Café**, a 10-minute lakeside hike away, near the town beach (April–Oct Tue–Sun 11:30–14:00, 18:00–21:00, closed Mon and Nov–March, great garden setting on the lake, Seelande 102, tel. 06134/8234). For your late-night drink, savor the Market Square from the trendy little pub called **Ruth Zimmermann** (June–Oct daily 09:00–02:00, Nov–May daily 12:00–02:00, tel. 06134/8306).

Transportation Connections—Hallstatt

By train to: Salzburg (hrly, 90 min to Attnang Puchheim, short wait, 50 min to Salzburg), **Vienna** (hrly, 90 min to Attnang Puchheim, short wait, 2.5 hrs to Vienna). Daytrippers to Hallstatt can check bags at the Attnang Puchheim station. (Note: Connections there and back can be very fast—about 5 minutes. Have coins ready for the lockers at track 1.)

BRUGES
(BRUGGE)

With Renoir canals, pointy gilded architecture, time-tunnel art, and stay-awhile cafés, Bruges is a heavyweight sightseeing destination as well as a joy. Where else can you ride a bike along a canal, munch mussels, wash them down with the world's best beer, savor heavenly chocolate, and see Flemish Primitives and a Michelangelo, all within 300 meters of a bell tower that rings out "Don't worry, be happy" jingles every 15 minutes? And there's no language barrier.

The town is Brugge (broo-gha) in Flemish, Bruges (broozh) in French and English. Before it was Flemish or French, the name was a Viking word for "wharf" or "embarkment." Right from the start, Bruges was a trading center. In the 11th century, the city grew wealthy on the cloth trade. By the 14th century, Bruges' population was 40,000, as large as London, which was one of the biggest cities in the world. At the time, Bruges was the most important cloth market in northern Europe. In the 15th century, Bruges was the favored residence of the powerful Dukes of Burgundy. Commerce and the arts boomed. The artists Jan van Eyck and Hans Memling had studios here. But by the 16th century, the harbor had silted up and the economy collapsed. The Burgundian court left, Spain conquered Belgium in 1548, and Bruges' golden age abruptly ended. For generations, Bruges was known as a mysterious and dead city. In the 19th century, a new port, Zeebrugge, brought renewed vitality to the area. And 20th-century tourists discovered the town. Today Bruges prospers because of tourism: It's a uniquely well-preserved Gothic city and a handy gateway to Europe. It's no secret, but even with the crowds it's the kind of city where you don't mind being a tourist.

Bruges has been selected, along with Salamanca, Spain, to be a "Cultural Capital of Europe" in 2002 (www.brugge2002.be).

This means that the city will boast even more special events—and tourist crowds—than usual. There has been a flurry of renovation and new construction to prepare for the event, but the scaffolding and cranes disappear in 2002, when visitors enjoy sparkling new facades and landmarks: A pavilion in front of the Burg by Japanese architect Toyo Ito and a concert hall near t'Zand. The Groeninge Museum's collection will be traveling in Belgium (like you are) for most of the year to make way for a special exhibition of the works of Jan van Eyck (Jan–June).

Planning Your Time

Bruges needs at least two nights and a full, well-organized day. Even nonshoppers enjoy browsing here, and the Belgian love of life makes a hectic itinerary seem a little senseless. With one day, the speedy visitor could do this: 09:30-Climb the belfry, 10:00-Tour the Burg sights (visit the TI if necessary), 11:30-Take a boat tour, 12:15-Walk to the brewery, have lunch, and catch the 13:00 tour, 14:30-Walk through the Begijnhof, 15:00-Tour the Memling Museum (6 paintings), 15:45-See the Michelangelo in the church, 16:00-Tour the Groeninge Museum if you like Eyck (closes at 18:00, ideally buy tickets in advance, see "Groeninge Museum," listed under "Sights"). Rent a bike for an evening ride through the quiet backstreets (or take a €27.50 half-hour horse-and-buggy tour). Lose the tourists and find a dinner. (If this schedule seems insane, skip the belfry and the brewery—or stay another day.) Note that churches generally close from 12:00 to 14:00.

Orientation

The tourists' Bruges (you'll be sharing it) is contained within a one-kilometer-square canal, or moat. Nearly everything of interest and importance is within a cobbled and convenient swath between the train station and Market Square (a 15-min walk).

Tourist Information: The main office is on Burg Square (April–Sept Mon–Fri 09:30–18:30, Sat–Sun 10:00–12:00, 14:00–18:30, Oct–March Mon–Fri 09:30–17:00, Sat–Sun 09:30–13:00, 14:00–17:30, lockers and money-exchange desk, tel. 050-448-686, www.brugge.com, public WC in courtyard). The other TI is at the train station (April–Sept Mon–Sat 10:30–13:15, 14:00–18:30, Oct–March Mon–Sat 09:30–13:15, 14:00–17:30, closed Sun year-round). Both TIs sell a great €0.75 all-inclusive Bruges visitors guide with a map and listings of all of the sights and services. You can also pick up a bimonthly English program *events@brugge*, as well as a schedule of special events related to the "Brugge 2002" cultural capital celebration. Consider the TI's "combo" museum ticket, which may tie into the 2002 festivities. If you're fond of Flemish art and visiting before July, ask about the Jan van Eyck exhibition. The TIs also have train-schedule information and specifics on the various kinds of tours available. Bikers will want the *5X on the Bike around Bruges* map/guide, which sells for €1.25 and shows five routes through the countryside.

Internet Access: The relaxing Coffee Link, with mellow music and pleasant art, is located between the train station and the center of town (Mon–Sat 10:00–21:30, Sun 10:00–19:30, across from Church of Our Lady at Mariastraat 38, tel. 050-349-973).

Arrival in Bruges

By Train: From the train (and from TI near station), you'll see the square belfry tower marking the main square. Upon arrival, stop by the station TI (has lockers) to pick up the Bruges visitors guide (map in centerfold). There are no ATMs or exchange windows at the station, but you'll find both in the city center (15-min walk).

Buses marked *Centrum* speed to the Market Square, near most recommended hotels (€1 ticket, buy from driver, good for 1 hr). Buses #4 and #8 go farther, to the northeast part of town (to the windmills and a recommended B&B on Carmersstraat). The **taxi** fare to most hotels is around €6.

It's a 15-minute **walk** from the station to the center: Cross the busy street and canal in front of the station, head up Oostmeers, and turn right on Steenstraat to reach Market Square. You could rent a **bike** at the station for the duration of your stay (ticket window #3, daily 07:00–20:00, €9/day, €6.50/half day after 14:00, €12.50 deposit, tel. 050-302-421), but other bike-rental shops are closer to the center (see "Bruges Experiences," below).

By Car: Park at the train station for just €2.50 per day; show your parking receipt on the bus to get a free ride into town. The pricier underground parking garage at t'Zand costs €8.70 per day.

Helpful Hints

Shops are open from 09:00 to 18:00; a little later on Friday. Grocery stores are usually closed on Sunday. **Market days** are Wednesday morning (Market Square) and Saturday morning (t'Zand). On Saturday and Sunday afternoons, a flea market hops along Dijver in front of the Groeninge Museum.

The information number for all **museums** is 050-448-711. October through March is off-season (when some museums close on Tue).

The **post office** is on Market Square near the belfry (Mon–Fri 09:00–19:00, Sat 09:30–12:30, closed Sun, tel. 050-331-411).

Sights—Bruges

Bruges' sights are listed here in walking order, from Market Square to the Burg to the cluster of museums around the Church of Our Lady to the Begijnhof (10-min walk from beginning to end). Like Venice, the ultimate sight is the town itself, and the

Bruges

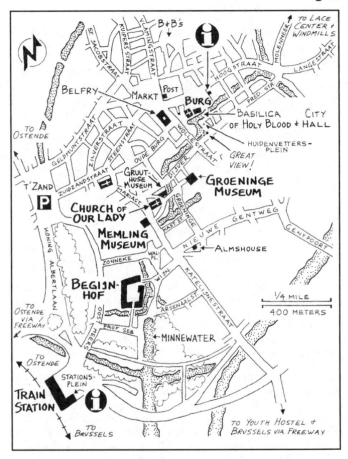

best way to enjoy that is to get lost on the backstreets, away from the lace shops and ice-cream stands.

Market Square (Markt)—Ringed by banks, the post office, lots of restaurant terraces, great old gabled buildings, and the belfry, this is the modern heart of the city. Most city buses go from here to the station. Under the belfry are two great Belgian French-fry stands, a quadrilingual Braille description of the old town, and a metal model of the tower. In Bruges' heyday as a trading center, a canal came right up to this square. **Geldmuntstraat**, just off the square, is a delightful street with many fun and practical shops and eateries.

▲▲**Belfry (Belfort)**—Most of this bell tower has stood over
Market Square since 1300. The octagonal lantern was added in
1486, making it 88 meters high—that's 366 steps (daily 09:30–
17:00, ticket window closes 45 min early, WC in courtyard).
The view is worth the climb and the €5. Survey the town. On
the horizon you can see the towns along the coast. Just before you
reach the top, peek into the carillon room. The 47 bells can be
played mechanically with the giant barrel and movable tabs (as
they do on each quarter hour) or with a manual keyboard (as it
does for regular concerts) with fists and feet rather than fingers.
Be there on the quarter hour, when things ring. It's *bellissimo* at
the top of the hour. Carillon concert times are listed at the base
of the belfry (year-round Sun at 14:15, also Oct–mid-June Wed
and Sat at 14:15). Back on the square, with your back to the belfry,
turn right onto pedestrian-only Breidelstraat and thread yourself
through the lace and *wafels* to Burg Square.

▲▲**Burg Square**—The opulent square called Burg is Bruges'
civic center, historically the birthplace of Bruges and the site of
the ninth-century castle of the first Count of Flanders. Today it's
the scene of outdoor concerts and home of the TI (with a €0.25
WC). It's surrounded by six centuries of architecture. Sweeping
counterclockwise 360 degrees, you'll go from **Romanesque** (the
round arches and thick walls of the brick basilica in the corner,
best seen inside the lower chapel) to the pointed **Gothic** arches of
the City Hall (with its "Gothic Room") to the well-proportioned
Renaissance windows of the Old Recorder's House (next door,
under the gilded statues) and past the TI and the park to the elaborate 17th-century **Baroque** of the Provost's House. Complete
your spin and walk to that corner.

▲**Basilica of the Holy Blood**—Originally the Chapel of Saint
Basil, it's famous for its relic of the blood of Christ which, according
to tradition, was brought to Bruges in 1150 after the Second
Crusade (and is displayed only during Friday worship services).
The lower chapel, accessed through the door labeled *Basiliek*,
is dark and solid—a fine example of Romanesque style (with some
beautiful statues). The upper chapel (separate entrance, climb the
stairs) is decorated Gothic and usually accompanied by appropriately
contemplative music. A €0.25 English flier tells about the relic,
art, and history. The small but sumptuous Basilica Museum (well
described in English) contains the gem-studded hexagonal reliquary
(c. 1600) that carries the relic on its yearly Ascension Day trip
through the streets of Bruges (museum is next to upper chapel,
€1.25, April–Sept daily 09:30–12:00, 14:00–18:00, Oct–March
Thu–Tue 10:00–12:00, 14:00–16:00, Wed 10:00–12:00 only).

▲**City Hall's Gothic Room**—Your ticket gives you a room full
of old town maps and paintings and a grand, beautifully restored
"Gothic Hall" from 1400. Its painted and carved wooden ceiling

features hanging arches (explained by an English flier). Notice the New Testament themes carved into the circular "vault keys." The wall murals are late-19th-century Romantic paintings of episodes from the city's history (described in the flier). The free ground-level lobby (closed on weekends) is a picture gallery of Belgium's colonial history, from the Spanish Bourbon king to Napoléon (€2.50, includes audioguide and admission to Renaissance Hall, daily 09:30–17:00, Burg 12).

Renaissance Hall (Brugse Vrije)—This is just one ornate room with an impressive Renaissance chimney. If you're into heraldry, the symbolism (explained in the free English flier) makes this worth a five-minute stop. If you're not, you'll wonder where the rest of the museum is (€3.75, includes admission to City Hall, daily 09:30–17:00, entry in the corner of the square at Burg 11a).

From Burg to Fish Market to View—From Burg, walk under the Goldfinger family down Blinde Ezelstraat. Just after you cross the bridge, the persistent little fish market (*Vismarkt*, fresh North Sea catch sold Tue–Sat 06:00–13:00) is on your left. Take an immediate right to Huidevettersplein, a tiny, picturesque, restaurant-filled square. Continue a few steps to Rozenhoedkaai Street, where you can get a great photo of the belfry reflected in the canal. Can you see its tilt? It leans about four feet. Down the canal (past a flea market on weekends) looms the huge spire of the Church of Our Lady (tallest brick spire in the Low Countries). Between you and the church are the next three museums.

▲▲▲**Groeninge Museum**—This museum usually houses a classy collection of mostly Flemish art, from Memling to Magritte. But for the first half of 2002, the building will be taken over by a special exhibition of the works of Flemish artist **Jan van Eyck** and his influence on the Mediterranean world (€10, daily 10:00–18:00, Wed until 21:00, reservations are recommended, same-day advance tickets available at TI, can book further in advance for an additional fee at tel. 070-223-302, in the U.S. call 1-800-669-8687).

After the Eyck exhibition ends on June 30, the Groeninge Museum will close to reshuffle art, then reopen probably in fall, starring its regular collection.

If you're visiting in fall: Rooms 1 through 18 take you from 1400 to 1945. While the museum has plenty of worthwhile modern art, the highlights are its vivid and pristine Flemish Primitives. ("Primitive" here means before the Renaissance.) Flemish art is shaped by its love of detail, its merchant patrons' egos, and the power of the Church. Lose yourself in the halls of Groeninge: Gaze across 15th-century canals, into the eyes of reassuring Marys, and through town squares littered with leotards, lace, and lopped-off heads (€6.20, daily 09:30–17:00, Oct–March closed Tue, Dijver 12, tel. 050-448-751).

The **Brangwyn Museum** (Arentshuis) next door is only interesting if you are into lace or the early-20th-century art of Brangwyn (€2, daily 09:30–17:00, Oct–March closed Tue, Dijver 16, tel. 050-448-763).

▲**Gruuthuse Museum**—A wealthy brewer's home, this is a sprawling smattering of everything from medieval bedpans to a guillotine (€5, daily 09:30–17:00, audioguides planned for 2002, Oct–March closed Tue, Dijver 17). Leaving the museum, contemplate the mountain of bricks towering 120 meters (394 feet) above as they have for 600 years.

▲▲**Church of Our Lady**—The church stands as a memorial to the power and wealth of Bruges in its heyday. A delicate *Madonna and Child* by Michelangelo is near the apse (to the right if you're facing the altar). It's said to be the only Michelangelo statue to leave Italy in his lifetime (thanks to the wealth generated by Bruges' cloth trade). If you like tombs and church art, pay to wander through the apse (€1.75, Michelangelo free, art-filled apse April–Sept Mon–Fri 10:00–12:00, 14:00–17:00, closes at 16:00 on Sat, Sun 14:00–16:00, Oct–March closes at 16:30, on Mariastraat).

▲▲**St. Jans Hospital/Memling Museum**—This medieval hospital (newly opened after 2 years of renovation) contains six much-loved paintings by the greatest of the Flemish Primitives, Hans Memling. His *Mystical Wedding of St. Catherine* triptych deserves a close look. Catherine and her "mystical groom," the baby Jesus, are flanked by a headless John the Baptist and a pensive John the Evangelist. The chairs are there so you can study it. If you understand the Book of Revelation, you'll understand St. John's wild and intricate vision. The St. Ursula Shrine, an ornate little mini-church in the same room, is filled with impressive detail (€7, daily 09:30–17:00, off-season closed Wed, across the street from the Church of Our Lady, Mariastraat 38).

▲▲**Straffe Hendrik Brewery Tour**—Belgians are Europe's beer connoisseurs. This fun and handy tour is a great way to pay your respects. The happy gang at this working family brewery gives entertaining and informative 45-minute, four-language tours (usually by friendly Inge, €3.75 including a beer, lots of very steep steps, great rooftop panorama, daily on the hour 11:00–16:00, 11:00 and 15:00 are your best times to avoid groups, Oct–March 11:00 and 15:00 only, 1 block past church and canal, take a right down skinny Stoofstraat to #26 on Walplein square, tel. 050-332-697). At Straffe Hendrik ("Strong Henry") they remind their drinkers: "The components of the beer are vitally necessary and contribute to a well-balanced life pattern. Nerves, muscles, visual sentience, and a healthy skin are stimulated by these in a positive manner. For longevity and lifelong equilibrium, drink Straffe Hendrik in moderation!"

Their bistro, where you'll be given your included-with-the-tour beer, serves a quick and hearty lunch plate (the €8.70 "meat selection and vegetables" is a beer-drinker's picnic for two; try some Belgian cheese or quiche, a house specialty). On sunny summer days, they offer a barbecue and salad bar for €10. You can eat indoors with the smell of hops or outdoors with the smell of hops. This is a great place to wait for your tour or to linger afterward. From here the lacy cuteness of Bruges crescendoes as you approach the Begijnhof.

▲▲**Begijnhof**—For military (and various other) reasons, there were more women than men in the medieval Low Countries. Towns provided Begijnhofs (buh-HINE-hofs), dignified places in which these *begijns* could live a life of piety and service (without having to take the same vows a nun would). You'll find Begijnhofs all over Belgium and Holland. Bruges' Begijnhof—now inhabited not by begijns but by Benedictine nuns—almost makes you want to don a habit and fold your hands as you walk under its wispy trees and whisper past its frugal little homes. For a good slice of Begijnhof life, walk through the simple museum (Begijn's House, left of entry gate, €1.50 with English explanations, daily 10:00–12:00, 13:45–17:30, off-season closes at 17:00).

Minnewater—Just south of the Begijnhof is Minnewater, an idyllic, clip-clop world of flower boxes, canals, swans, and tour boats packed like happy egg cartons.

Almshouses—Walking from the Begijnhof back to the center, you might detour along Nieuwe Gentweg to visit one of about 20 almshouses in the city. At #8, go through the door marked "Godshuis de Meulenaere 1613" (free) into the peaceful courtyard. This was a medieval form of housing for the poor. The rich would pay for someone's tiny room here in return for lots of prayers. The Diamond Museum (at the start of Nieuwe Gentweg) is less interesting than an encyclopedia (€5, daily 10:30–17:30).

Bruges Experiences

Chocolate—Bruggians are connoisseurs of fine chocolate. You'll be tempted by chocolate-filled display windows all over town. Godiva is the best big-factory/high-price/high-quality local brand, but there are plenty of smaller, family-run places in Bruges that offer good handmade chocolates.

You can find Bruges' smoothest, creamiest chocolate at **Dumon** (€1.60/100 grams). Stefaan makes the chocolate, his twin brother Christophe sells it near the Straffe Hendrik brewery (closed Mon, Walstraat 6, tel. 050-340-043), and their sister Nathalie runs a shop in a precious little gingerbread house just off Market Square (closed Wed, Eiermarkt 6, check out the basement display of old chocolate molds, tel. 050-346-282, www.chocolatierdumon.com).

Locals and tourists alike flock to **The Chocolate Line** (€3/100 grams), which feels more elegant and offers over 80 varieties. While you're sampling their ginger chocolate (shaped like a Buddha) or their saffron curry chocolate (a white elephant), you can watch them pouring chocolate into plastic molds in the back room (daily 09:30–18:30, Sun open at 10:30, Simon Stevinplein 19, between Church of Our Lady and Market Square, tel. 050-341-090).

The smaller **Sweertvaegher**, near Burg Square, features top-quality chocolate (€2.45/100 grams) made with fresh ingredients and no preservatives (Tue–Sun 09:30–18:15, closed Mon, Philipstockstraat 29, tel. 050-338-367).

Lace and Windmills by the Moat—A 10-minute walk from the center to the northeast end of town brings you to four windmills strung out along a pleasant grassy setting on the "big moat" canal (between Kruispoort and Dampoort, on Bruges side of the moat). One of the windmills (St. Janshuismolen) is open to visitors (€2, daily 09:30–12:30, 13:30–17:00, closed Oct–April, at the end of Carmersstraat).

To actually see lace being made, drop by the nearby **Lace Centre**, where ladies toss bobbins madly while their eyes go bad (€1.50 includes afternoon demonstrations and a small lace museum called Kantcentrum, as well as the adjacent Jerusalem Church; Mon–Fri 10:00–12:00, 14:00–18:00, until 17:00 on Sat, closed Sun, Peperstraat 3, tel. 050-448-764). The **Folklore Museum**, in the same neighborhood, is cute but forgettable (€2, daily 09:30–17:00, Oct–March closed Tue, Rolweg 40, tel. 050-330-044). To find either place, ask for the Jerusalem Church.

▲▲**Biking**—While the sights are close enough for easy walking, the town is a treat to bike through, and you can to get away from the tourist center. Consider a peaceful evening ride through the backstreets and around the outer canal. Rental shops have maps and ideas. The TI sells a handy *5X on the Bike around Bruges* map/guide for €1.25; it narrates five different bike routes (18–30 km) through the idyllic countryside nearby. The best trip is 30 minutes along the canal out to Damme and back. The Netherlands/Belgium border is a 40-minute pedal beyond Damme. Two shops rent bikes in the center of town (€2.50–2.75 for 1 hr, €5–5.60 for 4 hrs, or €8/day). Both offer free city maps and child seats. **Fietsen Popelier** doesn't require a deposit and sells a good map of the countryside for €1.85 (July–Sept daily 10:00–20:00, Oct–June Tue–Sun 10:00–18:00, closed Mon winter through Easter, 50 meters from Church of Our Lady at Mariastraat 26, tel. 050-343-262). 'T **Koffieboontje** asks for a €25 deposit, your passport, or a credit-card imprint (Hallestraat 4, closer to belfry, tel. 050-338-027). The less central **De Ketting** rents bikes for less (€5/day, daily 09:00–20:00, Gentpoortstraat 23, tel. 050-344-196).

Tours of Bruges

Bruges by Boat—The most relaxing and scenic (though not informative) way to see this city of canals is by boat, with the captain narrating. Boats leave from all over town (€5.50, 4/hr, 10:00–17:00, copycat 30-min rides). Boten Stael offers a €0.50 discount with this book (just over the canal from the Memling Museum at Katelijnestraat 4, tel. 050-332-771).

City Minibus Tours—"City Tour Bruges" gives 50-minute/ €9.50 rolling overviews of the town in an 18-seat, two-skylight minibus with dial-a-language headsets and video support. The tour leaves hourly (on the hr, 10:00–19:00 in summer, until 18:00 in spring and fall, less in winter) from Market Square. The narration, while clear, is slow-moving and boring. But the tour is a lazy way to cruise by virtually every sight in Bruges.

Walking Tours—Local guides walk small groups through the core of town daily in July and August and Saturday and Sunday in June and September (€3.75, depart from TI at 15:00). The tours, while earnest, are heavy on history and in two languages, so they may be less than peppy. Still, to propel you beyond the pretty gables and canal swans of Bruges, they are good medicine. A private guided tour costs €40 (reserve at least 3 days in advance through TI). Beginning in April 2002, special theme tours— including medieval Bruges, culinary Bruges, literary Bruges, and "twilight zone" Bruges—will celebrate the city's tenure as a cultural capital of Europe; ask for specifics at the TI or call ahead to reserve (tel. 050-448-685).

Bus Tours of Countryside—Quasimodo Tours offers those with extra time two excellent all-day tours through the rarely visited Flemish countryside. The "Flanders Fields" tour concentrates on World War I battlefields, trenches, memorials, and poppy-splattered fields (Sun, Tue, and Thu 09:00–16:30). The other is "Triple Treat": the port of Damme, a castle, a monastery, a brewery, and a chocolate factory, as well as a sampling of the treats—a waffle, chocolate, and beer (Mon, Wed, and Fri 09:00–16:00). Hardworking Lote leads all the tours himself, in English only (€45, €38 if under 26, CC, 29-seat nonsmoking bus, includes lunch, lots of walking, pickup at your hotel or the train station, tel. 050-370-470 to book, fax 050-374-960, www.quasimodo.be).

Bruges by Bike—The Backroad Bike Company, also run by Quasi-modo Tours, leads daily bike tours in and around Bruges (€13.50, 10:00 and 19:00, 8 km, 2 hrs) and through the nearby countryside to Damme (€16, 13:00, 25 km, 3–4 hrs, tel. 050-370-470).

Bus and Boat Tour—The Sightseeing Line offers a bus trip to Damme and a boat ride back (€16.50, April–Sept daily at 14:00, 2 hrs, leaves from Market Square).

Sights—Near Bruges

Dolfinarium—At Boudewijnpark, just outside of town, dol-phins make a splash several times a day (call for show times— tel. 050-383-838, €7.50 for 40-min show, Debaeckestraat 12,

www.boudewijnpark.be). The theme park's roller-skating rink
is open in the afternoon (and turns into an ice-skating rink off-
season). From Bruges, catch the "Sint Michiels" bus #7 or #17
from Kuipersstraat.

Flanders Fields—This World War I museum, 60 kilometers
southwest of Bruges, provides a moving look at the battles fought
near Ieper (Ypres in French). Use interactive computers to trace
the wartime lives of individual soldiers and citizens. Powerful
videos and ear-shattering audio complete the story (€10, March–
Nov special exhibition with expanded coverage and more computers, otherwise €7.50, April–Sept daily 10:00–18:00, Oct–March
Tue–Sun 10:00–17:00, ticket sales stop one hour before closing,
Grote Markt 34, Ieper, tel. 057-228-584, fax 057-228-589, www
.inflandersfields.be). From Bruges, catch a train to Ieper via Kortrijk (2 hrs). Drivers follow A17 to Kortrijk, then take A19 to Ieper.

Sleeping in Bruges
**(€1.10 = about $1, country code: 32, area code: 050,
zip code: 8000)**
Sleep Code: **S** = Single, **D** = Double/Twin, **T** = Triple, **Q** = Quad,
b = bathroom, **s** = shower only, **CC** = Credit Cards accepted,
no CC = Credit Cards not accepted. Everyone speaks English.

Most places are located between the train station and the old
center, with the most distant (and best) being a few blocks beyond
Market Square to the north and east. B&Bs offer the best value.
All include breakfast, are on quiet streets, and (with a few exceptions) keep the same prices throughout the year. Bruges is most
crowded Friday and Saturday evenings Easter through October—
with July and August weekends being worst. Since Bruges has been
designated a Cultural Capital of Europe in 2002, accommodations
will fill up more quickly than usual. Book in advance.

Bruges' most convenient place to do laundry is **Mr. Wash**
(self-service open daily until 22:00, just off Market Square at Sint
Jakobsstraat 33 in an arcade, tel. 050-335-902). A less central
Laundromat is at Gentportstraat 28 (daily 07:00–22:00).

Hotels
Hansa Hotel offers 24 rooms in a completely modernized old
building. It's tastefully decorated in elegant pastels and has all
the amenities. It's a great splurge (Sb-€115–195, Db-€125–205,
depending on room size, extra bed-€40, suites available, CC,
air-con, nonsmoking, elevator, free Internet access, sauna, tanning
bed, fitness room, bike rental for €6.20/half day, €11/day, Niklaas
Desparsstraat 11, a block north of Market Square, tel. 050-338-444,
fax 050-334-205, www.hansa.be, e-mail: information@hansa.be,
cheery and hardworking Johan and Isabelle).

Hotel Adornes is small, new, and classy—a great value.

It has 20 comfy rooms with full, modern bathrooms in a 17th-century canalside house, and offers free parking, free loaner bikes, and a cellar game and video lounge (Sb-€75–95, Db-€80–100 depending upon size, Tb-€115, Qb-€125, CC, elevator, near Van Nevel B&B, mentioned below, and Carmersstraat at St. Annarei 26, tel. 050-341-336, fax 050-342-085, e-mail: hotel .adornes@proximedia.be, Nathalie runs the family business).

Hotel Aarendshuis, an old merchant's mansion, is well-worn but comfortable. It's family-run and has 25 spacious rooms, dingy carpets, chandeliered public places, and a small garden (prices vary with size and luxury: Sb-€76, Db-€80–104, Tb-€112, Qb-€124, kids under 10 free, car park-€10, CC, elevator, 2 blocks off Burg Square at Hoogstraat 18, tel. 050-337-889, fax 050-330-816, e-mail: hotelaarendshuis@village.uunet.be). The owner, Danny, will take you on a one-hour sightseeing tour of Bruges in his turn-of-the-century "old-timer" car for the same price as a buggy ride (€25 for 2 people).

Hotel Cavalier, which has more stairs than character, serves a hearty buffet breakfast in a royal setting (Sb-€50–52, Db-€55–62, Tb-€70–75, Qb-€77–82, lofty "backpackers' doubles" on fourth floor-€40 or €45 with WC, CC, Kuipersstraat 25, tel. 050-330-207, fax 050-347-199, e-mail: hotel.cavalier@skynet.be, run by friendly Viviane De Clerck).

Hotel Egmond is quietly located in the middle of the placid Minnewater. Its 18th-century rooms have all the comforts (Sb-€82–102, Db-€112–120, Tb-€132–142, no CC, for longer stays ask about their apartments a few blocks away, Minnewater 15, tel. 050-341-445, fax 050-342-940, www.egmond.be).

Hotel Cordoeanier, a family-run place, rents 22 bright, simple, modern rooms on a quiet street two blocks off Market Square (Sb-€48–62, Db-€57–67, Tb-€72–80, Qb-€85, Quint/b-€97, higher prices are for weekends or luxury rooms, larger groups should ask about holiday house across the street, CC, nearly free Internet access, Cordoeanierstraat 16, tel. 050-339-051, fax 050-346-111, www.cordoeanier.be, Kris and Veerle).

Hotel Botaniek has three stars, nine small rooms, and a quiet location a block from Astrid Park (Sb-€65, Db-€75–85, Tb-€90, Qb-€100, CC, elevator, Waalsestraat 23, tel. 050-341-424, fax 050-345-939, e-mail: hotel.botaniek@pi.be).

Hotel De Pauw is tall, skinny, and family-run, with straightforward rooms on a quiet street across from a church (S-€40, Sb-€50, 2 top-floor D-€50, Db-€60–65, CC, free and easy street parking or pay garage, Sint Gilliskerkhof 8, tel. 050-337-118, fax 050-345-140, www.hoteldepauw.be, Philippe and Hilde).

Hotel Rembrandt-Rubens has 15 rooms in a creaky 500-year-old building with tipsy floors, a mysterious layout, tacky rooms, ancient dippy beds, elephant tusks, a gallery of creepy

Hotels in Bruges' Center

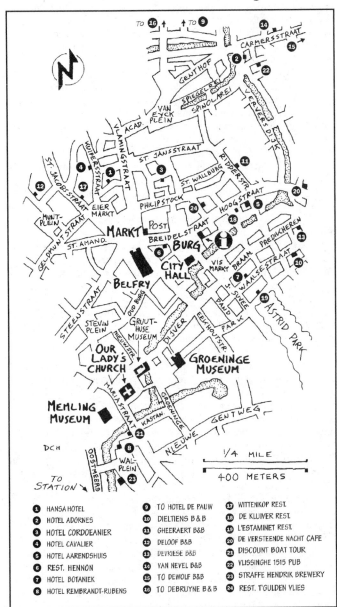

1 HANSA HOTEL	**9** TO HOTEL DE PAUW	**17** WITTENKOP REST.
2 HOTEL ADORNES	**10** DIELTIENS B & B	**18** DE KLUIVER REST.
3 HOTEL CORDOEANIER	**11** GHEERAERT B&B	**19** L'ESTAMINET REST.
4 HOTEL CAVALIER	**12** DELOOF B&B	**20** DE VERSTEENDE NACHT CAFE
5 HOTEL AARENDSHUIS	**13** DEVKIESE B&B	**21** DISCOUNT BOAT TOUR
6 REST. HENNON	**14** VAN NEVEL B&B	**22** VLISSINGHE 1515 PUB
7 HOTEL BOTANIEK	**15** TO DEWOLF B&B	**23** STRAFFE HENDRIK BREWERY
8 HOTEL REMBRANDT-RUBENS	**16** TO DEBRUYNE B & B	**24** REST. T'GULDEN VLIES

old paintings, and probably the Holy Grail in a drawer somewhere (S-€30, Ss-€40, one D-€40, Ds-€55, Db-€60, Tb-€75, Qb-€100, no CC, locked up from 24:00–7:30, on a quiet square between the Memlings and the brewery at Walplein 38, tel. 050-336-439, fax 050-677-780). The breakfast room (which must have been the knights' hall) overlooks a canal (while Rembrandt and Rubens overlook you from an ornately carved and tiled 1648 chimney). There's a little warmth behind Mrs. De Buyser's crankiness. The hotel has been in her family for 50 years.

Crowne Plaza Hotel Brugge is the most modern, comfortable, and central hotel option. Each of its 96 air-conditioned rooms comes with a magnifying mirror and trouser press (Db-€210–240, prices drop as low as €170 on weekdays and off-season, CC, elevator, pool, Burg 10, tel. 050-446-844, fax 050-446-868, www.crowneplaza.com).

Near Train Station: The **Hotel t'Keizershof** is a dollhouse of a hotel that lives by its motto, "Spend a night, not a fortune." It's simple and tidy, with seven small, cheery, old-time rooms split between two floors, a shower and toilet on each (S-€25, D-€36, T-€54, Q-€65, no CC, free and easy parking, laundry service-€7.50, Oostmeers 126, a block in front of train station, tel. 050-338-728, e-mail: hotel.keizershof@12move.be, Stefaan and Hilde).

Bed-and-Breakfasts

These places, run by people who enjoy their work, offer the best value. Each is central and offers lots of stairs and three or four doubles you'd pay €100 for in a hotel. Parking is generally easy on the street.

Koen and Annemie Dieltiens are a friendly couple who enjoy getting to know their guests and sharing a wealth of information on Bruges. You'll eat a hearty breakfast around a big table in their bright, comfortable, newly renovated house (Sb-€45, Db-€50, Tb-€70, Qb-€90, 1-night stays pay €5 extra per room, no CC, nonsmoking, Waalse Straat 40, 3 blocks southeast of Burg Square, tel. 050-334-294, fax 050-335-230, http://users.skynet.be/dieltiens, e-mail: koen.dieltiens@skynet.be). The Dieltiens also rent a cozy studio and apartment for two to six people in a nearby 17th-century house (2 people pay €350 per week for studio, €403 per week for apartment, prices higher for shorter stays and more people, cheaper off-season).

Debruyne B&B, run by Marie-Rose Debruyne and her architect husband Ronny D'Hespeel, offers artsy, original decor (check out the elephant-sized doors—Ronny's design) and genuine warmth (Sb-€45, Db-€50, Tb-€70, Qb-€90, 1-night stay-€5 extra per room, no CC, 5-min walk north of Market Square, look for Ronny's architect sign at Lange Raamstraat 18, tel. 050-347-606, fax 050-340-285, www.bedandbreakfastbruges.com).

Paul and Roos Gheeraert live on the first floor, while their guests take the second. This neoclassical mansion with big, bright, comfy rooms is another fine value (Sb-€45, Db-€50, Tb-€70, no CC, rooms have coffeemakers, TVs, and fridges, Ridderstraat 9, 4 blocks east of Market, tel. 050-335-627, fax 050-345-201, http://users.skynet.be/brugge-gheeraerte-mail: gheeraert.brugge @skynet.be,). They also rent three modern, fully equipped apartments and a large loft nearby (3-night minimum).

Chris Deloof's big, homey rooms are a good bet in the old center. Check out the fun, lofty A-frame room upstairs (Sb-€45, Ds/Db-€47–52, pleasant breakfast room, no CC, non-smoking, Geerwiynstraat 14, tel. & fax 050-340-544, www.sin.be /chrisdeloof, e-mail: chris.deloof@ping.be). Chris also rents a nearby apartment (Qb-€87) and a holiday house (Qb-€100), great for a family or group.

The **Van Nevel family** rents two attractive top-floor rooms with built-in beds in a 16th-century house (S-€33–40, D-€40–55, T-€63, includes breakfast, CC but cash preferred, nonsmoking, no sign but ring the bell at Carmersstraat 13, 10-min walk from Market Square, or bus #4 or #8 from train station or Market Square to Carmersbridge, tel. 050-346-860, fax 050-347-616, http://home.worldonline.be/~rvanneve, e-mail: Robert.VanNevel @advalvas.be). Robert enthusiastically shares the culture and history of Bruges with his guests.

Yvonne De Vriese rents three tidy B&B rooms on a corner overlooking two canals (S-€25, D-€37, Db-€44.65, third or fourth person-€12.40 extra, breakfast served in your room, CC, Predikherenstraat 40, 4 blocks east of Burg Square, take bus #6 or #16 from station and get off at the first stop on Predikheren Rei, tel. 050-334-224, fax 050-336-491, e-mail: ivonne.de.vriese @pandora.be).

Arnold Dewolf's B&B is in a stately, quiet neighborhood (S-€25, D-€35–37, T-€45, Q-€55, 5-bed-€60, no CC, family-friendly, near windmills, Oostproosse 9, tel. 050-338-366, www .ardewolf.be). From the train station, take bus #4 to Sasplein. Walk to the path behind the first windmill and turn left on Oostproosse.

Absoluut Verhulst is a modern-feeling B&B in a 400-year-old building (Sb-€50, Db-€75–93 depending on size of room, Tb-€115, Qb-€125, no CC, 5 min east of Market Square at Verbrand Nieuwland 1, tel. & fax 050-334-515, www.b-bverhulst .com, Frieda and Benno).

Hostels
Bruges has several good hostels offering beds for around €10 to €12 in two- to eight-bed rooms (singles go for around €15). Pick up the hostel info sheet at the station TI. The American-style **Charlie Rockets** bar and hostel is the liveliest and most central

(56 beds, €12.50 per bed, 2–6 per room, no CC, Hoogstraat 19, tel. 050-330-660, fax 050-343-630, www.charlierockets.com). These hostels are small, loose, and central: the dull **Snuffel Travelers Inn** (Ezelstraat 47, tel. 050-333-133), **Bauhaus International Party Hotel** (Langestraat 135, tel. 050-341-093, www.bauhaus.be), and the funky **Passage** (Dweerstraat 26, tel. 050-340-232; its hotel next door rents €35 doubles).

Eating in Bruges

Specialties include mussels cooked a variety of ways (one order can feed two), fish dishes, grilled meats, and French fries. Touristy places on the square come with great views and are affordable; candle-cool bistros flicker on backstreets. Don't eat before 19:30 unless you like eating alone. Tax and service are always included.

Bistro in den Wittenkop is very Flemish—a cluttered, laid-back, old-time place specializing in the beer-soaked equivalent of beef Bourguignon (€10–17 main courses, Tue–Sat 18:00–24:00, closed Sun–Mon, terrace in back, Sint Jakobsstraat 14, tel. 050-332-059).

De Kluiver is a pub serving hot snacks, light €10 meals, and great "sea snails in spiced bouillon" simmered in a whispering jazz ambience (Wed–Mon 18:00–24:00, closed Tue, Hoogstraat 12, tel. 050-338-927).

Pannekoekenhuisjje—the little pancake house—is a cute restaurant serving delicious, inexpensive pancake meals and homemade *wafels* (daily 10:00–22:00, just off Geldmuntstraat at Helmstraat 3, tel. 050-340-086). Enthusiastic chefs Mario and Rik have just opened **The Flemish Pot** next door at #5, offering vintage Flemish cuisine (same hours and tel. as above).

Lotus Vegetarisch Restaurant serves good veggie lunches only (€8 plates, Mon–Sat 11:45–13:45, closed Sun, just off Burg at Wapenmakersstraat 5, tel. 050-331-078).

Check out these two youthful, trendy, jazz-filled eateries: For hearty budget spaghetti (€6), head for **L'Estaminet**, on the northern border of peaceful Astrid Park (11:30–24:00, closed Mon afternoon and all day Thu, Park 5, tel. 050-330-916). Or try **De Versteende Nacht Jazzcafe** on Langestraat 11 (€12.50 meals, Tue–Thu 19:00–24:00, Fri–Sat 18:00–24:00, closed Sun–Mon, tel. 050-343-293).

Herberge Vlissinghe, the oldest pub in town (1515), serves hot snacks in a great atmosphere (open from 11:00 on, closed Mon–Tue, Blekersstraat 2). **Restaurant 't Gulden Vlies**, just off Burg, is good for a late dinner (€16 plates, Wed–Sun 19:00–03:00, closed Mon–Tue, Mallebergplaats 17, tel. 050-334-709).

Bistro de Eetkamer (the living room) offers stay-a-while elegance, fine service, and fine food (Thu–Mon 12:00–14:00, 18:30–23:00, Sat until 24:00, closed Tue–Wed, just south of

Markt, Eeekhout 6, tel. 050-337-886). Drop by **Bistro De Schaar** for good food and fun atmosphere (Fri–Wed 12:00–14:30, 18:00–23:00, Hooistraat 2, tel. 050-335-979).

The popular grill house **The Hobbit,** near two recommended bars (below), features an entertaining menu, including all-you-can-eat spareribs (daily 18:00–24:00, Kemelstraat 8-10, tel. 050-201-827).

Picnics and fast meals: Geldmuntstraat is a handy street when you're hungry. A block off Market Square, **Pickles Frituur** serves the best sit-down fries in town (ask about their deep-fried vegetarian food, Mon–Sat 11:00–24:00, sometimes later in summer, closed school days 14:00–16:30 and all day Sun, at the corner of Geldmuntstraat and Sint Jakobstraat, tel. 050-337-957). A block farther from Market Square on Geldmuntstraat, **Nopri Supermarket** is great for picnics (push-button produce pricer lets you buy as little as one mushroom, Mon–Sat 09:00–18:30, Fri until 19:00, closed Sun). The small **Delhaize grocery** is on Market Square opposite the belfry (Mon–Sat 08:00–12:00, 13:30–18:00, closed Sun). For midnight munchies, you'll find Indian-run corner grocery stores.

Frietjes: These local French fries are a treat. Proud and traditional *frituurs* serve tubs of fries and various local-style shish kebabs. Belgians dip their *frietjes* in mayonnaise, but ketchup is there for the Yankees (along with spicier sauces). For a quick, cheap, and scenic meal, hit a *frituur* and sit on the steps or benches overlooking Market Square, about 50 meters past the post office.

Beer: Belgium boasts more than 350 types of beer. Straffe Hendrik ("Strong Henry"), a potent and refreshing local brew, is, even to a Bud Lite kind of guy, obviously great beer. Among the more unusual to try: Dentergems (with coriander and orange peel) and Trappist (a dark, malty, monk-made beer). Non-beer drinkers enjoy Kriek (a cherry-flavored beer) and Frambozen Bier (raspberry-flavored beer). Each beer is served in its own unique glass. Any pub carries the basic beers, but for a selection of more than 300 types, including brews to suit any season, drink at **t'Brugs Beertje** (16:00–24:00, closed Wed, Kemelstraat 5, tel. 050-339-616). When you've finished those, step next door, where **Dreupel Huisje** serves more than 100 Belgian gins and liqueurs (Sun–Fri 18:00–24:00, Sat 18:00–02:00; if you're hungry, drop by The Hobbit, across the street). Another good place to gain an appreciation of the Belgian beer culture is **de Garre**. Rather than a noisy pub scene, it has a sit-down-and-focus-on-your-friend-and-the-fine-beer ambience (huge selection, off Breidelstraat, between Burg and Markt, on tiny Garre alley, daily 12:00–24:00, tel. 050-341-029).

Belgian Waffles: While Americans think of "Belgian" waffles for breakfast, the Belgians (who don't eat waffles or pancakes for breakfast) think of *wafels* as Liege style (dense, sweet, eaten plain and heated up, served take-away) and Brussels style (lighter, often with powdered sugar or whipped cream and fruit, served in tea-houses only in the afternoons from 14:00–18:00). For the best Liege-style *wafels* in town, stop by **Restaurant Hennon** for a *Luikse Wafel* (€1.50, May–Oct Tue–Sun 08:30–21:00, rest of year closes at 19:00, between Market Square and Burg at Breidelstraat 16, tel. 050-332-800). Rudy Hennon's extremely tasty *wafels*— and other dishes—are made with fresh ingredients.

Transportation Connections—Bruges
From nearby Brussels, an hour away by train, all of Europe is at your fingertips. Train info: tel. 050-302-424.

By train to: Brussels (2/hr, usually at :33 and :59, 1 hr), **Ghent** (4/hr, 40 min), **Ostende** (3/hr, 15 min), **Köln** (6/day, 4 hrs), **Paris** (hrly via Brussels, 2.5 hrs, must pay supplement of €10.50/second class, €21/first class, even with a railpass), **Amsterdam** (hrly, 3.5 hrs, transfer in Antwerp or Brussels).

Trains from England: Bruges is an ideal "welcome to Europe" stop after London. Take the Eurostar train from London to Brussels under the English Channel (10/day, 3 hrs), then transfer to Bruges (hrly, 1 hour). Or, if you'd prefer to cross the Channel by boat, catch the London-to-Dover train (2 hrs, from London's Victoria station), then the catamaran to Ostende (2 hrs; train station at Ostende catamaran terminal), then the Ostende-to-Bruges train (15 min). Five boats run daily (€37 one-way, same price for cheap five-day return ticket, reserve by phone with CC and pick up your ticket at the dock, tel. 059-559-955).

PRAGUE

It's amazing what 10 years of freedom can do. Prague has always been historic. Now it's fun, too. No place in Europe has become so popular so quickly. And for good reason: The capital of the Czech Republic—the only major city of central Europe to escape the bombs of the last century's wars—is one of Europe's best-preserved cities. It's slinky with sumptuous Art Nouveau facades, it offers tons of cheap Mozart and Vivaldi, and it brews the best beer in Europe. But more than the just the architecture and traditional culture, it's an explosion of pent-up entrepreneurial energy jumping for joy after 40 years of Communist rule. And its low prices will make your visit enjoyable and nearly stressless.

For a relaxing pause between the urban bustle of Vienna and Prague, visit the Czech town of Český Krumlov, the perfect big-city antidote, peaceful and happily hemmed in by its lazy river.

Planning Your Time

Two days (with 3 nights, or 2 nights and a night train) makes the long train ride in and out worthwhile and gives you time to get beyond the sightseeing and enjoy Prague's fun-loving ambience. Many wish they'd scheduled three days for Prague. From Munich, Berlin, and Vienna, it's about a six-hour train ride (during the day) or an overnight ride.

With two days in Prague, I'd spend a morning seeing the castle and a morning in the Jewish Quarter—the only two chunks of sightseeing that demand any brainpower. Spend your afternoons loitering around the Old Town, Charles Bridge, and the Little Quarter and your nights split between beer halls and live music. Keep in mind that Jewish sites close on Saturday.

Český Krumlov, 2.5 hours from Prague by train, could be a

Prague

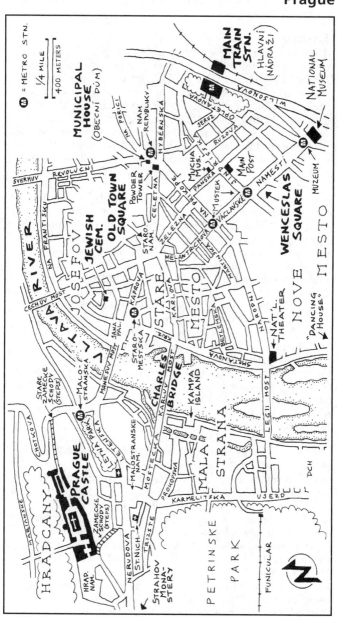

daytrip, but I'd spend the night (consider visiting Český on your way to or from Prague).

History

Medieval Prague: Prague's castle put it on the map in the ninth century. In the 10th century the region was incorporated into the German "Holy Roman" Empire. The 14th century was Prague's Golden Age, when Holy Roman Emperor Charles IV ruled from here, and Prague was one of Europe's largest and most highly cultured cities. During this period, Prague built St. Vitus Cathedral and Charles Bridge and established the first university in central Europe.

Emperor Charles IV: The greatest Czech ruler (14th century) was actually the Holy Roman Emperor back when Prague was bigger and more important than Vienna. The child of a Luxembourg nobleman and a Czech princess, he was a dynamic man on the cusp of the Renaissance. He spoke four languages, counted Petrarch as a friend, imported French architects to make Prague a grand capital, founded the first university north of the Alps, and invigorated the Czech national spirit. (He popularized the legend of the good king Wenceslas to give his people a near mythical King Arthur–type cultural standard bearer.) Much of Prague's architecture and history, from the Charles Bridge to the trouble caused by Jan Hus (below), can be traced to this man's rule. Under Charles IV, the Czech people gained esteem among Europeans.

Bucking the Pope and Germany: Jan Hus was a local preacher and professor who got in trouble with the Vatican a hundred years before Martin Luther. Like Luther, he preached in the people's language rather than Latin. To add insult to injury, he complained about church corruption. Tried for heresy and burned in 1415, Hus became both a religious and a national hero. While each age has defined Hus to its liking, the way he challenged authority while staying true to himself has always inspired and rallied the Czech people.

Religious Wars: The reformist times of Jan Hus (around 1400, when Czechs rebelled against both German and Roman Catholic control) led to a period of religious wars and ultimately loss of autonomy under Vienna. Prague stagnated under the Hapsburgs of Austria with the brief exception of Rudolf II's reign.

Under the late-16th-century rule of the Hapsburg King Rudolf II, Prague emerged again as a cultural and intellectual center. Astronomers Johannes Kepler, Tycho Brahe, and other scientists worked here. Much of Prague's great art can be attributed to this Hapsburg king who lived not in Vienna but in Prague.

The Thirty Years' War (1618–1648) began in Prague when locals (Czech nobles wanting religious and political autonomy) tossed two Catholic/Hapsburg officials out the window of the Prague Castle. Often called "the first world war" because it engulfed so many nations, these 30 years were particularly tough on Prague. During this period, its population dropped from 60,000 to 25,000. The result of this war was 300 years of Hapsburg rule. Prague became a backwater of Vienna.

Czech Nationalist Revival: The 19th century was a time of nationalism for people throughout Europe, including the Czechs, as the age of divine kings and ruling families was coming to a fitful end. Architecture and the arts (such as the completion of the cathedral, and Smetana's operas performed in the new National Theater) stirred the national spirit. With the end of World War I, the Hapsburgs were history, and in 1918 the independent country of Czechoslovakia was proclaimed with Prague as its capital.

Troubled 20th Century: Independence lasted only until 1939 when the Nazis swept in. Prague escaped the bombs of World War II but went almost directly from the Nazi frying pan into the Communist fire. Almost. A local uprising freed the city from the Nazis on May 8, 1945. The Russians "liberated" them again on May 9.

For centuries the Czechs were mostly rural folks with German merchants running the cities. Prague's cultural makeup comes from a rich mix of Czech, German, and Jewish people—historically about evenly divided. But after World War II only 5 percent of the Jewish population remained and virtually all the Germans were deported.

The Communist chapter (1948–1989) was grim. The "Prague Spring" revolt—initiated by a young generation of reform-minded Communists in 1968—was crushed. The charismatic leader Alexander Dubček was exiled (and made a forest ranger in the back woods), and the years after 1968 were particularly gray and disheartening. But eventually the Soviet empire crumbled. Czechoslovakia regained its freedom in the student- and artist-powered 1989 "Velvet Revolution" (so-called because there were no casualties). In 1993, the Czech and Slovak Republics agreed on the "Velvet Divorce" and became two separate countries.

Today, while not without its problems, the Czech Republic is enjoying a growing economy and a strong democracy. It is on track to be admitted in the European Union by 2005. Prague has emerged as one of the most popular tourist destinations in Europe.

Orientation (area code: 02)

Locals call their town "Praha." It's big, with 1.2 million people, but for a quick visit focus on its small old-town core. I will refer to the tourist landmarks in English (with the Czech name in parentheses). Study the map and learn these key places:

Main Train Station:	*Hlavní Nádraží*	(hlav-nee nah-dra-shzee)
Old Town:	*Staré Město*	(sta-rey mnyess-toh)
Old Town Square:	*Staroměstské Náměstí*	
	(starro-min-yes-ststi-keh nah-mnyess-tee)	

Prague's Four Towns

Until about 1800 the city was actually four distinct towns with four town squares separated by fortified walls.

Hradcany (**Castle Quarter**): Built regally on the hill, this was the home of the cathedral, monastery, castle, royal palace, and high nobility. Even today, you feel like clip-clopping through it in a fancy carriage. It has the high art and grand buildings, yet feels a bit sterile.

Malá Strana (**Little Quarter**): This Baroque town of fine homes and gardens was built by the aristocracy and merchant elite at the foot of the castle. The quarter burned in the 1500s and was rebuilt with the mansions of the generally domesticated European nobility who moved in to be near the king. The tradition remains as the successors of this power-brokering class—today's Parliament—now call this home.

Staré Město (**Old Town**): Charles Bridge connects the Little Quarter with the Old Town. A boom town in the 14th century, this has long been the busy commercial quarter filled with merchants, guilds, and natural supporters of Jan Hus (folks who wanted a Czech stamp on their religion). Trace the walls of this town in the modern road plan (with the Powder Tower being a remnant of a wall system that completed a fortified ring half provided by the river). The marshy area closest to the bend—least inhabitable and therefore allotted to the Jewish community—became the ghetto.

Nové Město (**New Town**): Nové Město rings the old town, cutting a swath from riverbank to riverbank, and is fortified with Prague's outer wall. In the 14th century, the king initiated the creation of this town, tripling the size of what would become Prague. Wenceslas Square was once the horse market of this busy working-class district. When you cross the moat (Na Príkope), which separates the old and new towns, you leave the tourists and enter the real work-a-day town.

New Town:	*Nové Město* (no-vay mnyess-toh)
Little Quarter:	*Malá Strana* (mah-lah strah-nah)
Jewish Quarter:	*Josefov* (yoo-zef-fohf)
Castle Area:	*Hradčany* (hrad-chah-nee)
Charles Bridge:	*Karluv Most* (kar-loov most)
Wenceslas Square:	*Václavske Náměstí* (vah-slawf-skeh nah-mnyess-tee)
The River:	*Vltava* (vul-tah-vah)

The Vltava River divides the west side (castle and Little Quarter) from the east side (train station, Old Town, New Town, and nearly all of the recommended hotels). Prague addresses come with a general zone. Praha 1 is in the old center on either side of the river. Praha 2 is in the new city south of Wenceslas Square. Praha 3 and higher indicates a location farther from the center.

Tourist Information

TIs are at four key locations: main train station, Old Town Square, below Wenceslas Square at Na Príkope 20, and the castle side of Charles Bridge (all locations open daily 09:00–19:00 except Charles Bridge which is open 10:00–18:00, tel. 02/2448-2202). They offer maps, phone cards, information on guided walks and bus tours, and bookings for concerts, hotel rooms, and rooms in private homes. Get the brochure listing all of Prague's museums and hours. *Prague This Month* is a free monthly listing of events. The English-language *Prague Post* is handy for entertainment listings and current events (sold at newsstands).

Helpful Hints

Formalities: Travel in Prague is like travel in Western Europe— 15 years ago and for half the price. Americans need no visa. (Because of a recent reciprocation flap, Canadians do need a visa.) Just flash your passport at the border. The U.S. embassy in Prague is near the Little Quarter Square, or Malostranske Námestí (Trziste 15, tel. 02/5753-0663). Since Eurailpasses don't cover the Czech Republic, you'll need to buy train tickets or a Prague Excursion pass for your travels to and from Prague (see "Transportation Connections—Prague," below).

Rip-offs: Prague's new freedom comes with new scams. There's no particular risk of violent crime, just green, rich tourists getting taken by con artists. Simply be on guard: on trains (thieves thrive on overnight trains and corrupt conductors intimidate Western tourists for bribes), changing money (tellers anywhere with bad arithmetic and inexplicable pauses while counting back your change), dealing with taxis (see "Getting around Prague," below), and in restaurants (see "Eating," below). Plainclothes policemen "looking for counterfeit money" are con artists. Don't show them your cash. Pickpockets—who can be little children or adults dressed as professionals or even as tourists— target Western tourists.

Telephoning: Czech phones work like any in Europe. For international calls, buy a phone card at a kiosk or your hotel (various prices). Calling the United States directly (dial 001, the area code, and the number) from a public phone booth with the local phone card, you'll get about three minutes for $1. To call Prague from abroad, dial the international code (00 in Europe or 011 in the U.S.), the Czech Republic code (420), then Prague's area code (dial 2; you drop the initial zero), followed by the local number.

Hotels often list phone numbers with the country and city codes
(420-2), numbers you don't need to dial when in Prague. For
cheap calls to America, buy an international PIN card (cards differ
wildly in cost per minute: for the same price of 500 kč, I-Call gives
you 40 minutes' worth of calls to the U.S., GlobalOne gives you
only 12 minutes).

Money: 40 koruna (kč) = about U.S. $1. There is no black
market. Assume anyone trying to sell money on the streets is
peddling obsolete currency. Buy and sell easily at the station
(5 percent fees), banks, or hotels. Change bureaus advertise no
commission and decent but deceptive rates. These rates are for
selling dollars. Their rates for buying your dollars are worse.
ATMs are everywhere and a much better value. Czech money
is tough to change in the West.

American Express: Václavske Náměstí 56, Praha 1 (foreign
exchange 09:00–19:00, travel service Mon–Fri 09:00–18:00, Sat
09:00–14:00, closed Sun, tel. 02/2221-1136) or Mosteka 12,
Praha 1 (open 09:00–19:30, tel. 02/5753-3247).

Internet Access: Internet cafés—which beg for business
all along Karlova Street on the city side of the bridge—are
commonplace.

Medical Help: For English-speaking help, contact the
American Medical Center (24 hours, Janovskeho 48, Praha 7,
tel. 02/8077-56). A 24-hour pharmacy is at Palackeho 5 (Praha 1,
tel. 02/2494-6982).

Local Help: Magic Praha is a tiny travel service run by hardworking, English-speaking Lida Steflova. A charming jill-of-all-
trades who takes her clients' needs seriously, she's particularly
helpful with accommodations, private tours, side trips to UNESCO-
protected towns, and airport or train station transfers anywhere
in the Czech Republic (Narodnil 7, Praha 1, 5th floor, tel. 02/2423-
2755, cellular 060-420-7225, e-mail: magicpraha@magicpraha.cz).

Best Views: Enjoy "the golden city of a hundred spires"
during the early evening when the light is warm and the colors are
rich. Good viewpoints include the restaurant terrace at the Strahov
Monastery (above the castle), the top of the east tower of Charles
Bridge, the Old Town Square clock tower, and the steps of the
National Museum overlooking Wenceslas Square.

Language: Czech, a Slavic language, has little resemblance
to Western European languages. These days English is "modern,"
and you'll find the language barrier minimal. If you speak German, it's helpful. An acute accent means you linger on that vowel.
The little smile above the c, s, or z makes it ch, sh, or zh.

Learn these key Czech words:

Hello/Goodbye (familiar)	*Ahoj* (ah-hoi)
Good day, Hello (formal)	*Dobrý den* (DOH-bree den)
Yes/No	*Ano* (AH-no)/*Ne* (neh)

Please	*Prosím* (proh-zeem)
Thank you	*Děkuji* (dyack-quee)
You're welcome	*Prosím* (proh-zeem)
Where is...?	*Kde je...?* (gday yeh)
Do you speak English?	*Mluvíte anglicky?*
	(MLOO-vit-eh ANG-litz-key)
krown (the money)	*koruna* (koh-roo-nah)

Arrival in Prague

Prague unnerves many travelers—it's relatively run-down, it's behind the former Iron Curtain, and you've heard stories of rip-offs and sky-high hotel prices. But, in reality, Prague is charming, safe, and ready to show you a good time.

By Train: Most travelers coming from and going to the West use the main station (Hlavní Nádraží) or the secondary station (Nádraží Holešovice). Trains to other points within the country use Masarykovo or Smíchov stations. Trains to/from Český Krumlov usually use Prague's main station, sometimes the Smíchov station. (For information on getting to Prague, see "Transportation Connections—Prague," below.)

Upon arrival, change money. The stations have ATMs (at the main station, a cash machine is near the subway entrance). Exchange bureau rates vary—compare by asking at two windows what you'll get for $100. Count carefully. At the same window, buy a city map (50 kč, with trams and metro lines marked and tiny sketches of the sights for ease in navigating). It's a mistake to try doing Prague without a good map—you'll refer to it constantly. Confirm your departure plans at the train information window. Consider arranging a room or tour at the TI or AVE travel agency (AVE has branches in both stations). The left-luggage counter is reportedly safer than the lockers.

At Prague's train stations, anyone arriving on an international train will be met at the tracks by room hustlers (snaring tourists for cheap rooms).

At Prague's main station, **Hlavní Nádraží**, the orange, low-ceilinged hall is a fascinating mix of travelers, kiosks, loitering teenagers, and older riffraff. The creepy station ambience is the work of Communist architects who took a classy building and made it just big. If you're killing time here (or for a glimpse of a more genteel age), go upstairs into the Art Nouveau hall. The station was originally named for Emperor Franz Josef, later named for President Woodrow Wilson (his promotion of self-determination led to the creation of the free state of Czechoslovakia in 1918), and then called simply the Main Station by the Communists (who weren't big fans of Wilson). Here under an elegant dome you can trace this history as you sip a coffee, enjoy music from the 1920s, and watch new arrivals spilling into the city.

From the main station, it's a 10-minute walk to Wenceslas Square (turn left out of the station and follow Washingtonova to the huge Narodni Museum and you're there). You can also catch trams #5, #9, or #26 (to find the stop, walk into park, head 2 min to right) or take the metro (inside station, look for the red "M" with 2 directions: Muzeum or Florenc; take Muzeum, then transfer to the green line—direction Dejvicka—and get off at either Můstek or Staroměstska; these stops straddle the Old Town). The courageous and savvy get a cabby to treat them fairly and get to their hotel fast and sweat free for no more than 150 kč (see "Getting around Prague," below; to avoid the train station taxi stand, go out the front door and downhill through the park to the first street for a rank of less criminal cabbies, or ride the metro a stop and catch one on the street). The park in front of the station— nicknamed Sherwood Forest—is filled with thieves at night.

The **Nádraží Holešovice** station is suburban mellow. The main hall has all the services of the main station in a compact area. Outside the first glass doors, the ATM is on the left, the metro is straight ahead (follow "Vstup" which means "entrance," take it 3 stops to the main station, 4 stops to the city center Muzeum stop), and taxis and trams are outside to the right (allow 200 kč for a cab to the center). Train info tel. 02/2422-4200.

By Plane: Your hotel can arrange for a shuttle minibus to take you economically to the airport. Taxis at the airport now take you into town at a fixed rate (without turning on the meter) of about 500 kč; establish the price before boarding. Airport info tel. 02/2011-3314.

Getting around Prague

You can walk nearly everywhere. But the metro is slick, the trams fun, and the taxis quick and easy once you're initiated.

Public Transport: The trams and metro work on the same cheap tickets. Buy from machines (press "enter" after the ticket type before inserting coins) at kiosks or purchase at hotels. For convenience, buy all the tickets you think you'll need: 15-minute ticket— 8 kč, 60-minute ticket—12 kč, 24-hour ticket—70 kč, three-day pass—180 kč. Cheaters, when caught, are fined 800 kč. The metro closes at midnight, but some trams keep running all night (identified with white numbers on blue backgrounds at tram stops).

City maps show the tram/bus/metro lines. The three-line metro system is handy and simple but doesn't serve many hotels and sights. Trams are also easy to use; track your route with your city map. They run every 5 to 10 minutes. Get used to hopping on and off. Be sure to always validate your ticket on the tram/bus/metro by sticking it in the machine (which stamps a time on it).

Taxis: Prague's taxis—notorious for meters that spin for tourists like pinwheels—are being tamed. Still, many cabbies are

Prague Metro

HOLEŠOVICKE
NADRAZI
TRAINS TO BERLIN, VIENNA & BUDAPEST

ČESKO-MORAVSKA

DEJVICÁ

VLTAVSKA

HRAD-KRANSKA

NAM REPUBLICKY

PALMOVKA

MALO-STRANSKA

FLORENC

PRAGUE CASTLE

INVALIDOVNA

STARO-MESTSKA

OLD TOWN SQ.

KRZIKOVA

MAIN TRAIN STATION
·HLAVNI NADRAZI·

TRAINS TO MUNICH, AMST & PARIS

CHARLES BRIDGE

WENC. SQ.

NAM. MIRU

MÚSTEK

PETŘÍN PARK

NARODNI TRIDA

MUZEUM

FLORA

I. P. PAVLOVO

JIRIHOZ PODĚBRAD

STRAŠ-NICKÁ

KARLOVO NAM.

VYŠEHRAD

SKALKA

ANDĚL

VYSEHRAD CASTLE

PRAŽSKÉHO

NOVÉ BUTOVICE

SMICH. NAM.

PANKRÁC

JINONICE

RADLICKÁ

BUDĚJOVICKA

KAČEROV

RIVER VLTAVA

ROZTYLY

CHODOV

HÁJE

OPATOV

---- LINE A (GREEN)
······ LINE B (YELLOW)
—— LINE C (RED)
〰〰 RIVER VLTAVA

NOT TO SCALE

DCH

no-neck mafia types who consider one sucker a good day's work. While most hotel receptionists and guidebooks advise avoiding taxis, I find Prague is a great taxi town and use them routinely. With the local rate, they're cheap (read the rates on the door: drop charge—30 kč, per-kilometer charge—22 kč, and wait time per min—5 kč). The key is the tiny *sazba* box on the magic meter showing the rate. If you have a cab called from a hotel or restaurant, you're likely to get a fair meter rate (which starts only when you take off). If a cabby tries to rip you off, simply pay 200 kč for a long ride. Let him follow you into the hotel if he insists you owe him more. (He won't.) The receptionist will defend you. Don't bother with any taxi parked in a touristy zone. Hailing a cab on the street (rather than at a taxi rank), you're most likely to be treated fairly. Before getting in ask "Do you use the meter?" by saying, "*Podle Taxa metru?*" (poh-dlah tax-ah met-roo).

Tours of Prague

Walking Tours—Prague Walks offers walking tours of the Old Town, the castle, and Jewish Quarter (250 kč, mostly 2 hrs, tel. 02/6121-4603, www.praguewalks.com, e-mail: pwalks@comp.cz). Consider their clever Good Morning Walk (8:00, before the crowds hit). Several decent companies give guided walks. For the latest, pick up the walking tour fliers at the TI. The TI has plenty of private guides available for hire on two-hour notice (3 hrs/1,200 kč, desk at Old Town Square TI, tel. 02/2448-2562).

Bus Tours—Cheap big-bus orientation tours provide an efficient once-over-lightly look at Prague and a convenient way to see the castle. Premiant City Tours offers 18 different tours including: quick city (350 kč, 2 hrs, 5/day), grand city (620 kč, 3.5 hrs, 2/day), Jewish Quarter (640 kč, 2 hrs), Prague by night, Bohemian glass, Terezín Concentration Camp memorial, Karlštejn Castle, Český Krumlov (1,690 kč, 8 hrs), and a river cruise. The tours feature live guides (in German and English) and depart from near the bottom of Wenceslas Square at Na Príkope 23. Get tickets at an AVE travel agency, hotel, on the bus, or at Na Príkope 23 (tel. 02/2494-6922, www.premiant.cz).

Tram Joyride—Tram #22 makes a fine joyride through town. Consider this as a scenic lead-up to touring the castle. Catch it at Metro: Náměstí Míru, roll through a bit of new town, the old town, across the river, and hop out just above the castle (at Pyramid Hotel and hike down the hill into castle area).

Self-Guided Walking Tour

The King's Walk (*Královská cesta*), the ancient way of coronation processions, is touristy but great. Pedestrian friendly and full of playful diversions, it connects the essential Prague sites. The king would be crowned in St. Vitus Cathedral in the Prague Castle, walk through the Little Quarter to the Church of St. Nicholas, cross Charles Bridge, and finish at the Old Town Square. If he hurried, he'd be done in 20 minutes. Like the main drag in Venice between St. Mark's and the Rialto bridge, this walk mesmerizes tourists. Use it as a spine, but venture off it—especially to eat.

While you could cover this route in the same direction as the king, he's long gone and it's a new morning in Prague. Here are Prague's essential sights in walking order, starting at Wenceslas Square, where modern independence was proclaimed, proceeding through the Old Town, across the bridge, and finishing at the castle. This walk laces together all the following recommended sights except the Jewish Quarter.

▲▲**Wenceslas Square (Václavske Náměstí)**—More a broad boulevard than a square (until recently trams rattled up and down its parklike median strip), it's named for the equestrian statue of King Wenceslas that stands at the top of the boulevard.

The square is a stage for modern Czech history: The Czech-oslovak state was proclaimed here in 1918. In 1968 the Soviets put down huge popular demonstrations here. Starting at the top (Metro: Muzeum), stroll down the square:

The **National Museum** (Národní Muzeum) stands grandly at the top. The only thing exciting about it is the view (80 kč, daily 10:00–18:00, halls of Czech fossils and animals).

The metro stop (Muzeum) is the cross point of two metro lines. From here you could roll a ball straight down the boulevard and through the heart of Prague to Charles Bridge.

Stand behind the statue facing the museum (uphill). The bullet marks left in the columns are from the Russian crackdown in 1968. Look left (about 10:00 on an imaginary clock) at the ugly Communist-era building—it housed the Parliament back when they voted with Moscow. A social-realism statue showing workers triumphing still stands at its base. It's now home to Radio Free Europe. After Communism fell, RFE lost its funding and could no longer afford its Munich headquarters. As gratitude for how its broadcasts kept their people in touch with real news, the current Czech government now rents the building to RFE for one koruna a year.

As you wander down this great square, notice the fun mix of **architectural styles**, all post-1850: Romantic neo-Gothic, neo-Renaissance, neo-Baroque from the 19th century, Art Nouveau from 1900, ugly functionalism from the mid-20th century (the "form follows function," "ornamentation is a crime" answer to Art Nouveau), Stalin Gothic from the 1950s "Communist epoch" (a good example is the Jalta building—a block downhill on the right), and glass-and-steel buildings of the 1970s.

St. Wenceslas (Václav), commemorated by the statue, is the "good king" of Christmas-carol fame. He was never really a king but the wise and benevolent 10th-century duke of Bohemia. A rare example of a well-educated and literate ruler, he was credited by his people for Christianizing his nation and lifting up the culture. Wenceslas astutely allied the Czechs with Saxony rather than Bavaria, giving the Czechs a vote when the Holy Roman Emperor was selected (and therefore more political importance). After being assassinated in 929, he became a symbol of Czech nationalism and statehood. Study the statue. Wenceslas is surrounded by the four other Czech patron saints. Notice the focus on books. As a small nation without great military power, national heroes are those who enrich the culture by thinking rather than fighting. Now this statue is a popular meeting point. Locals say, "I'll see you under the horse's tail."

Thirty meters below the big horse is a small, round garden with a low-key **memorial** "to the victims of Communism"—such as Jan Palach. In 1969, a group of patriots decided a self-immola-tion would stoke the fires of independence. They drew straws and

Prague

① PICK UP BUS TOUR AT #20
② BLACK LIGHT THEATER
③ NEAT PARK
④ HOTEL JULIAN
⑤ HOTEL CENTRAL
⑥ BETLEM CLUB
⑦ PENSION U MEDVIDKU
⑧ PENSION U KLENOTNIKA
⑨ HOTEL LUNIK
⑩ HOTEL UNION
⑪ HOTEL EUROPA
⑫ PENSION UNITAS
⑬ EXPRESS PENSION

Jan Palach got the short one. He set himself on fire for the cause of Czech independence and died on this place. Czechs are keen on anniversaries. On the 20th anniversary of Palach's death, demonstrations stoked the popular fire which 10 months later led to the overthrow of the Czech Communist government.

Walk a couple blocks downhill through the real people of Prague (not tourists) to the Grand Hotel Europa with its hard-to-miss dazzling Art Nouveau exterior and plush café interior.

In November 1989, this huge square was filled with hundreds of thousands of ecstatic Czechs believing freedom was at hand. Assembled on the balcony of the Melantrich building (opposite the Grand Hotel Europa, where you see the KNIHY sign) was a priest, a rock star (famous for his kick-ass-for-freedom lyrics), Alexander Dubček (hero of the 1968 revolt), and Vaclav Havel (the charismatic playwright, newly released from prison, and every freedom-loving Czech's Mandela). Using a sound system provided by the rock star, Havel's voice boomed over the gathered masses, announcing the resignation of the Czech politburo and saying the free Republic of Czechoslovakia was imminent. Picture the cold November evening with thousands of Czechs jingling their key chains for solidarity, chanting, "It's time to go now!" (While the revolt was stirring, government tanks could have given it the Tiananmen Square treatment—which spilled lots of patriotic blood in China just six months earlier. Locals figure Gorbachev must have made a phone call saying, "Let's not shed blood over this.")

Havel is still president and popular, although his popularity took a hit when he married for the second time to an actress 17 years his junior. (Some say his brain dropped about one meter.) His second (and last) five-year term ends in 2003.

Immediately opposite the Grand Hotel Europa is the **Lucerna Gallery**. This is a classic mall from the 1920s and '30s with shops, theaters, a ballroom in the basement, and the fine Lucerna café upstairs. Curiously, the place was built and is owned by the Havel family.

If you're ready for a coffee with a grand Wenceslas Square view, ride the elevator at the foot of Wenceslas Square (under cover near the top of the metro station, Na Príkope 9) to the **Blue Terrace** restaurant (described below).

▲**Na Príkope**—The bottom of Wenceslas Square meets a spacious pedestrian mall lined with stylish shops. Na Príkope (meaning "the moat") follows the line of the old town wall, leading from Wenceslas Square right to a former gate in that wall, the Powder Tower (Prasná Brána, not worth touring). While the tower area is probably not worth the detour on this walk, consider these reasons to explore it later: City tour buses leave from along this street. And, next to the Powder Tower, the dazzling **Municipal House** (Obecní Dum), with a great Art Nouveau facade, contains three recommended restaurants (see "Eating," below).

▲**Havelská Market**—Central Prague's best open-air flower and produce market scene is a block toward the Old Town Square from the bottom of Wenceslas Square. Laid out in the 13th century for the German trading community, it still keeps hungry locals and vagabonds fed cheaply. Since only those who produce their goods personally are allowed to have a stall, you'll be dealing with the actual farmer or craftsperson. (Knickknacks only on weekends.)

Czech Sex—The strip between the base of Wenceslas Square and the Market is notorious for its sex clubs filled mostly with Russian girls and German and Asian guys. Be warned, these routinely rip off naive tourists and can be dangerous.

▲▲▲**Old Town Square (Staroměstské Náměstí)**—The focal point for most visits, this has been a market square since the 11th century. It became the nucleus of a town (Staré Město) in the 13th century when its city hall was built. Today the old-time market stalls have been replaced by cafés, touristy horse buggies, and souvenir hawkers.

The **Hus Memorial**—erected in 1915, 500 years after his burning—marks the center of the square and symbolizes the long struggle for Czech freedom. Walk around the memorial. The Czech reformer Jan Hus stands tall between two groups of people: victorious Hussite patriots and Protestants defeated by the Hapsburgs. One of the patriots holds a cup—in the medieval Church, only priests could drink the wine at communion. Hussites fought for the right to take both the wine and the bread. Behind Hus, a mother with her children represents the ultimate rebirth of the Czech nation. Hus was excommunicated and burned in Germany a century before the age of Martin Luther.

Do a **spin tour** in the center of the square to get a look at architectural styles: Gothic, Renaissance, Baroque, rococo, and Art Nouveau.

Spin clockwise, starting with the green domes of the Baroque Church of St. Nicholas. A Hussite church, it's a popular venue for concerts. The Jewish Quarter (Josefov) is a few blocks behind it, down the uniquely tree-lined Paris Street (Parizska)—a cancan of mostly Art Nouveau facades. On the horizon, at the end of Paris Street, a giant metronome ticks where an imposing statue of Stalin once stood. Spin to the right past the Hus Memorial and the fine golden and mosaic Art Nouveau facade of the Ministry of the Economy. Notice the Gothic Tyn Church (described below) with its fanciful spires flanking a solid gold effigy of the Virgin Mary. Lining the uphill side of the square is an interesting row of pastel houses with Gothic, Renaissance, and Baroque facades. The pointed 75-meter-tall (246-foot) spire marks the 14th-century Old Town Hall, famous for its astronomical clock (described below). In front of the city hall, 27 white inlaid crosses mark the spot where 27 Protestant nobles, merchants, and intellectuals were beheaded in 1621 after rebelling against the Catholic Hapsburgs.

Tyn Church—The towering Tyn (pronounced "teen") Church facing the Old Town Square was rebuilt fancier than the original—but enjoy it. For 200 years after Hus' death, this was Prague's leading Hussite church.

The lane leading to the church from the Old Town Square has a public WC and the most convenient box office in town (see "Entertainment," below).

▲**Old Town Hall Astronomical Clock**—Join the gang—ignoring the ridiculous human sales racks—for the striking of the hour (daily 08:00–20:00) on the 15th-century town hall clock. As you wait, see if you can figure out how the clock works.

With revolving disks, celestial symbols, and sweeping hands, this clock keeps several versions of time. Two outer rings show the hour: Bohemian time (Gothic numbers, counts from sunset—find the zero, next to 23...supposedly the time of tonight's sunset) and modern time (24 Roman numerals, XII at the top being noon, XII at the bottom being midnight). Five hundred years ago, everything revolved around the earth (the fixed middle background).

To indicate the times of sunrise and sunset, arcing lines and moving spheres combine with the big hand (a sweeping golden sun) and the little hand (the moon showing various stages). Look for the orbits of the sun and moon as they rise through day (the blue zone) and night (the black zone).

If this seems complex today, it must have been a marvel 500 years ago. The circle below (added in the 19th century) shows the zodiac, scenes from the seasons of a rural peasant's life, and a ring of saints' names—one for each day of the year with a marker showing today's special saint (out of order).

Four statues flanking the clock represent 15th-century Prague's four biggest worries: invasion (a Turkish conqueror, his hedonism symbolized by a mandolin), death (a skeleton), greed (a miserly moneylender, which used to have "Jewish" features until after World War II, when anti-Semitism became politically incorrect), and vanity (enjoying the mirror). Another interpretation: earthly pleasures brought on by vanity, greed, and hedonism are fleeting because we are all mortal.

At the top of the hour (don't blink—the show is pretty quick): (1) Death tips his hourglass and pulls the cord ringing the bell; (2) the windows open and the Twelve Apostles parade by, acknowledging the gang of onlookers; (3) the rooster crows; and (4) the hour is rung. The hour is often off because of daylight saving time (completely senseless to 15th-century clockmakers). At the top of the next hour, stand under the tower—protected by a line of banner-wielding, powdered-wigged concert salespeople—and watch the tourists.

Left of the clock is the main TI, a local guides' desk, and an opportunity to pay three admissions: for the city hall (by tour only), a Gothic chapel (only interesting for a close-up of the Twelve Apostles and the clock mechanism well described in English), and the tower (long climb, fine view).

To reach the bridge, turn your back to the fancy Tyn Church and march with the crowds.

Karlova Street—This street winds through medieval old Prague from the City Hall Square to the Charles Bridge (it zigzags... just follow the crowds). This is a commercial gauntlet, and it's here that the touristy feeding frenzy of Prague is most ugly.

Hus and Luther

The word catholic means universal. The Roman Catholic church—in many ways the administrative ghost of the Roman Empire—is the only organization to survive from ancient times. For over a thousand years, it enforced its notion that the Vatican was the sole interpreter of God's word on earth, and the only legitimate way to be a Christian was as a Roman Catholic. Jan Hus lived and preached one hundred years before Martin Luther. Both were college professors as well as priests. Both drew huge public crowds as they preached in their university chapels. Both promoted a local religious autonomy. And both helped establish their national languages. (Hus gave the Czechs their unique accents to enable the letters to fit the sounds.) Both got in big trouble. While Hus was burnt, Luther survived. Living after Gutenberg, Luther was able to spread his message more cheaply and effectively thanks to the new printing press. Since Luther was high profile and German, killing him would have caused major political complications. While Hus may have loosened Rome's grip on Christianity, Luther orchestrated the Reformation that finally broke it. Today, both are revered as national heroes as well as religious reformers.

Street signs keep you on track, and *Karluv Most* signs point to the bridge. Obviously, you'll find great people watching but no good values on this drag.

Torture Museum—This gimmicky moneymaker is no different from any other European torture museum, but nevertheless interesting, showing 60 models of gruesome medieval tortures with well-written English descriptions (100 kč, daily 10:00–22:00, Karlova 2, just before the bridge, inside Colloredo-Mansfeld Palace).

Bethlehem Chapel (Betlémská Kaple)—Emperor Charles IV founded the first university north of the Alps, and this was its chapel. The room is plain with a focus on the pulpit and the message of the sermon. In around 1400, priest and professor Jan Hus preached his reformist ideas from this pulpit. While primarily meant for students and faculty, the Mass was open to the public. Soon huge crowds were drawn by Hus' empowering Lutherlike ideas: that people should be more involved in worship (e.g., actually drinking the wine at communion) and have better access to the word of God through services and scriptures written in the people's language rather than Latin. Standing-room-only crowds of over 3,000 were the norm as Hus preached. The stimulating and controversial ideas debated at the university spread throughout the city (30 kč, April–Oct daily 09:00–18:00, Nov–March daily 09:00–17:00, tel. 02/2448-2562).

▲▲▲**Charles Bridge (Karluv Most)**—This much-loved bridge, commissioned by the Holy Roman Emperor Charles IV in 1357, offers one of the most pleasant and entertaining 450-meter (500-yard) strolls in Europe. Until 1850, it was the only bridge crossing the river here. Be on the bridge when the sun is low for the best light, people watching, and photo opportunities.

Before crossing the bridge, step into the little square on the right with the statue of the Holy Roman Emperor Charles IV (Karlo Quatro). Charles ruled his vast empire from Prague in the 14th century. He's holding a contract establishing Prague's university—the first in central Europe. The women around his pedestal symbolize the university's four faculties: medicine, law, theology, and the arts. The statue was erected in 1848 to celebrate the university's 500th birthday. Enjoy the view across the river. The bridge tower—once a tollbooth—is considered one of the finest Gothic gates anywhere. Climb it for a fine view but nothing else (30 kč, daily 10:00–22:00).

Charles Bridge is famous for its statues. But most of those you see today are replicas—the originals are in city museums and out of the polluted air.

Two statues on the bridge are worth a comment: the crucifix (facing the castle, near the start on the right) is the spot where convicts would pause to pray on their way to execution on the Old Town Square. Farther on (midstream, on right) the statue of John Nepomuk—a saint of the Czech people—draws a crowd (look for the guy with the five golden stars and the shiny dog). Back in the 14th century, he was the priest to whom the queen confessed all her sins. The king wanted to know her secrets but Father John dutifully refused to tell. He was tortured, eventually killed, and tossed off the bridge. When he hit the water five stars appeared. The shiny spot on the base of the statue shows the heave-ho. Locals touch it to help wishes come true. The shiny dog killed the queen...but that's another story. From the end of the bridge (TI in tower on castle side), the street leads two blocks to the Little Quarter Square at the base of the huge St. Nicholas church.

Kampa Island and Lennon Wall—One hundred meters from the castle end of Charles Bridge, stairs lead down to the Kampa Island and its relaxing pub-lined square, breezy park, and river access.

From the square, a lane on the right leads past a water mill (many of which once lined the canal here) to the Lennon Wall (*Lennonova zed'*).

While the ideas of Lenin sat like a water-soaked trench coat upon the Czech people, the ideas of John Lennon gave many locals hope and a vision. When Lennon was killed in 1980, a memorial wall filled with graffiti spontaneously appeared. Night after night the police would paint over the "all you need is love" and "imagine" graffiti. And day after day it would reappear. Until independence came in 1989, travelers, freedom lovers, and local hippies gathered here. Even today, while the tension and danger associated with this wall is gone, the message stays fresh.

▲▲**Little Quarter (Malá Strana)**—This is the most characteristic, fun-to-wander old section of town. It's one of four medieval towns (along with Hradčany, Staré Město, and Nové Město) that united in the late 1700s to make modern Prague. It centers on the Little Quarter Square (Malostranské Náměstí) with the huge St. Nicholas church standing in the middle and a plague monument facing the church entry (uphill side).

Church of St. Nicholas (Kostel Sv. Mikuláše)—When the Jesuits came, they found the perfect piece of real estate for their church and associated school—the Little Quarter Square. Imagine this square without the big church in its middle—a real square. The Church of St. Nicholas is the best example of High Baroque in town. It's a Jesuit church, giddy with curves and illusions. The altar features a lavish gold-plated Nicholas flanked by the two top Jesuits: St. Ignatius Loyola and St. Francis Xavier (45 kč, April–Sept daily 09:00–16:00, built 1703–1760, 75-meter-high dome, tower climbable from outside right transept). From here, hike 10 minutes uphill to the castle.

Sights—Prague's Castle Area

▲▲**Prague Castle (Prazský Hrad)**—For over a thousand years, Czech rulers have ruled from the Prague Castle. It's huge (by some measures, the biggest castle on earth) and confusing—with plenty of sights not worth seeing. Rather than worry about rumors that you should spend all day here with long lists of museums to see, keep things simple. Five stops matter and are explained here: Castle Square, St. Vitus Cathedral, Old Royal Palace, Basilica of St. George, and the Golden Lane. One 120-kč ticket gets you into all these sights (April–Oct Tue–Sun 09:00–17:00, last entry at 16:00, closed Mon, closes one hour earlier Nov–March, tel. 02/2437-3368 or 02/2437-2434; the 145-kč audioguide is good but requires 2 hrs and, since you need to return it where you got it, makes it impossible to exit the castle area from the bottom).

Getting to the Castle: You can ride a taxi, catch a tram, or hike. Those hiking follow the main cobbled road from Charles Bridge through Malá Strana, the Little Quarter (the nearest subway stop is Malostranska). From the big church, hike uphill along Nerudova Street. After about 10 minutes, a steep lane on the right leads to the castle. (If you continue straight, Nerudova becomes Uvoz and heads past two recommended restaurants to the Strahov Monastery and Library.)

Prague's Castle Area

200 YARDS
200 METERS

TO TRAM #22 & #23
PRASNY MOST
TO MALOSTRANSKA METRO
RAMPART GARDENS
STARE ZAMECKE STEPS
ZAMECKE SCHODY STEPS
KE HRADU
UVOZ
NERUDOVA
THUNOVSKA
PCH
TO LITTLE QUARTER SQUARE & CHARLES BRIDGE

MALA STRANA

1. ARMORY MUSEUM
2. PLAGUE MONUMENT
3. NATIONAL GALLERY
4. GATE TO CASTLE
5. CAFE
6. INFO & TICKETS
7. ST. VITUS CATHEDRAL
8. OLD PALACE
9. ST. GEORGE'S BASILICA
10. GOLDEN LANE
11. TO DOMUS HENRICI HOTEL & STRAHOV MONASTERY
12. TO HOTEL SAX, USA EMBASSY
13. MALY BUDDHA TEA HOUSE
14. FORMER GARDENS OF COMMUNIST PRESIDENT

Trams #22 or #23 go from the National Theater or Malostranska to the castle. You have two options: Get off at the stop "Kralovsky Letohradek" for the castle or stay on farther to "Pohorelec" to see the Strahov Library and then hike down to the castle. Getting off the tram at Kralovsky Letohradek, you'll see the royal summer palace across the street. This love gift—a Czech Taj Mahal—from Emperor Ferdinand I, who really did love his Queen Anne, is the finest Renaissance building in town. Notice the fine reliefs, featuring classical rather than Christian stories. From here, walk through the park with fine views of the cathedral to the gate taking you over the moat and into the castle grounds. This garden—once the private grounds and residence (you'll see the building) of the Communist president—was opened to the public with the coming of freedom under Vaclav Havel.

Castle Square (Hradčanske Náměstí)—The big square facing the castle feels like the castle's entry, but it's actually the central square of the Castle Town. Enjoy the awesome city view and the two string quartets that play regularly at the gate (their CD is terrific; say hello to friendly, mustachioed Josef). A tranquil café hides a few steps down immediately to the right as you face the castle. From here stairs lead into the Little Quarter.

The Castle Square was a kind of Czech Pennsylvania Avenue. Look uphill from the gate. The Renaissance Schwarzenberg Palace (*Svarcenberskč palác*, on the left, with the fake big stones scratched on the wall) is now a museum of military history. A plague monument stands in the center. On the right find the archbishop's rococo yellow palace. From here a lane leads to the Sternberg Palace (*Sternberskč palác*), filled with the National Gallery's skippable collection of European paintings—mostly minor works by Dürer, Rubens, Rembrandt, and El Greco (90 kč, Tue–Sun 10:00–18:00, closed Mon).

Survey the castle from this square—the tip of a 500-meter-long series of courtyards, churches, and palaces. The guard changes on the hour (with the most ceremony at noon). Walk under the fighting giants, under an arch, into the second courtyard. The mod green awning (just past the ticket office) marks the offices of the Czech president, Vaclav Havel. You can walk through the castle and enter the cathedral without a ticket, but you'll need a ticket to see the castle properly (120-kč ticket covers cathedral apse and spire, Old Royal Palace, Basilica of St. George, and Powder Tower; hour-long, English tours depart from ticket office regularly but cover cathedral and Old Royal Palace only— 80 kč, reserve a few days in advance if you want a private guide— 400 kč, tel. 02/2437-3368). Huge throngs of tourists make the castle grounds one sea of people during peak times. Late afternoon is least crowded.

▲St. Vitus Cathedral (Katedrála Sv. Vita)—This Roman Catholic cathedral—containing the tombs and relics of the most important local saints and kings, including the first three Hapsburg kings—symbolizes the Czech spirit. What's up with the guys in suits carved into the facade below the big round window? They're the architects and builders who finished the church. Started in 1344, construction was stalled by wars and plagues. But, fueled by the 19th-century rise of Czech nationalism, Prague's top church was finished in 1929 for the 1,000th anniversary of the death of St. Wenceslas. It looks all Gothic, but it's two distinct halves: modern neo-Gothic and the original 14th-century Gothic. For 400 years, a temporary wall sealed off the unfinished cathedral.

On the left, the masterful 1931 Art Nouveau window is by Czech artist Alfons Mucha (if you like this, you'll love the Mucha museum downtown—described below under "Art Nouveau"). Notice Mucha's stirring nationalism: Methodious and Cyril top and center (leaders in Slavic-style Christianity). Cyril is baptizing the mythic, lanky, long-haired Czech man. Lower you'll see two

Czech flappers and the classic Czech patriarch in the lower right. Notice also Mucha's novel use of color: your eyes are drawn from blue (symbolizing the past) to the golden center (where the boy and the seer look into the future).

Show your ticket and circulate around the **apse** past a carved wood relief of Prague in 1630 (before Charles Bridge had any statues), lots of faded Gothic paintings, and tombs of local saints. A fancy roped-off chapel (right transept) houses the **tomb of Prince Wenceslas,** surrounded by precious 14th-century murals showing scenes of his life, and a locked door leading to the crown jewels. More kings are buried in the royal mausoleum in front of the high altar and in the crypt underneath. You can climb the **spire** for a fine view (20 kč, April–Oct daily except Sunday morning, 09:00–17:00, 287 steps).

Leaving the cathedral, turn left (past the public WC). The **obelisk** was erected in 1919—a single piece of granite celebrating the establishment of Czechoslovakia. (It was originally much taller but broke in transit—an inauspicious start for a nation destined to last only 70 years.) Find the 14th-century mosaic of the *Last Judgment* outside on the right transept. It was built Italian-style by the modern-and-cosmopolitan-for-his-era King Charles IV. Jesus oversees the action as some are going to heaven and some to hell. The Czech king and queen kneel directly below Jesus and the six patron saints. On coronation day, they would walk under this arch that would remind them (and their subjects) that even those holding great power are not above God's judgment. The royal crown and national jewels are kept in a chamber (see the grilled windows) above this entryway, which was the cathedral's main entry for centuries while the church was incomplete. Twenty meters to the right a door leads to the...

Old Royal Palace (Starý Kralovský Palác)—This was the seat of the Bohemian princes in the 12th century. While extensively rebuilt, the large hall is late Gothic. It was a multipurpose hall for the old nobility. It's big enough for jousts—even the staircase was designed to let a mounted soldier gallop in. It was filled with market stalls, giving nobles a chance to shop without actually going into town. In the 1400s, the nobility met here to elect their king. This tradition survives today as the parliament crowds into this room every five years to elect the Czech president. Look up at the impressive vaulted ceiling, look down on the chapel from the end, and go out on the balcony for a fine Prague view. Is that Paris in the distance? No, it's an observation tower built for an exhibition in 1891 (60 meters/197 feet tall; a quarter of the height of the Parisian big brother built in 1889). The spiral stairs on the left lead up to several rooms with painted coats of arms and no English explanations. There's nothing to see downstairs in the palace. Across from the palace exit is the basilica.

Basilica of St. George and Convent (Bazilika Sv. Jiří)—Step into the beautifully lit Basilica of St. George to see Prague's best-preserved Romanesque church. St. Ludmila was buried here in 973. This first Bohemian convent was established here near the palace. Today the convent (next door, separate admission) houses the Czech Gallery (best Czech paintings from Gothic, Renaissance, and Baroque periods). Continue walking downhill through the castle grounds. Turn left on the first street, which leads into a cute lane.

Golden Lane (Zlatá Ulička)—This street of old buildings, which originally housed goldsmiths, is now jammed with tourists and lined with expensive gift shops, boutiques, galleries, and cafés. The Czech writer Franz Kafka lived at #22. There's a deli/bistro at the top and a convenient public WC at the bottom. Beyond that, at the end of the castle, are fortifications beefed up in anticipation of the Turkish attack—the cause for most medieval arms buildups in Europe—and steps funneling the mobs of tourists back into town. At the bottom of the castle, continue down into the Little Quarter (Malá Strana) or follow the garden along the castle back to the castle square and on to the monastery.

Strahov Monastery and Library (Strahovský Kláster a Knihovna)—Twin Baroque domes standing high above the castle (a 10-min hike uphill) mark the Strahov Monastery. The church is Romanesque structure decorated in textbook Baroque (look through the window to see its interior). The adjacent library (50 kč, daily 09:00–11:45, 13:00–16:45) offers a peek at how enlightened thinkers in the 18th century impacted learning. Two rooms are filled with 17th-century books under ceilings decorated with appropriate themes. Because the Czechs were a rural people with almost no high culture at this time, there were few books in the Czech language. The theme of the first and bigger hall is philosophy, with the history of man's pursuit of knowledge painted on its ceiling. The other is theology. Notice the gilded locked case containing the "libri prohibiti" (prohibited books) at the end of the room. Only the abbot had the key, and you could read these books—like Copernicus, Jan Hus, even the French encyclopedia—only with the abbot's blessing. As the Age of Enlightenment took hold in Europe, monasteries still controlled the books. With the enlightenment, the hallway connecting these two library rooms was filled with cases illustrating the new practical approach to natural sciences. Find the baby dodo bird (which went extinct in the 17th century).

Sights—Prague's Jewish Quarter

▲▲▲**Jewish Quarter (Josefov)**—The Jewish people were dispersed by the Romans 2,000 years ago. Over the centuries, their culture survived in enclaves throughout the Western world: "The

Torah was their sanctuary which no army could destroy." Jews first came to Prague in the 10th century. The main intersection of Josefov (Maiselova and Siroka Streets) was the meeting point of two medieval trade routes.

When the Pope declared that Jews and Christians should not live together, Jews had to wear yellow badges, and their quarter was walled in so that it became a ghetto. In the 16th and 17th centuries, Prague had one of the biggest ghettos in Europe with 11,000 inhabitants. Within its six gates, Prague's Jewish Quarter was a gaggle of two hundred wooden buildings. Someone wrote: "Jews nested rather than dwelled."

The "outcasts" of Christianity relied mainly on profits from money lending (forbidden to Christians) and community solidarity to survive. While their money protected them, it was often also a curse. Throughout Europe, when times got tough and Christian debts to the Jewish community mounted, entire Jewish communities were evicted or killed.

In the 1780s Emperor Joseph II eased much of the discrimination against Jews. In 1848 the walls were torn down and the neighborhood, named Josefov in honor of the emperor who was less anti-Semitic than the norm, was incorporated as a district of Prague.

In 1897, ramshackle Josefov was razed and replaced with a new modern town—the original 31 streets and 220 buildings became 10 streets and 83 buildings. This is what you'll see today: an attractive neighborhood of fine, mostly Art Nouveau buildings, with a few surviving historic Jewish buildings. In the 1930s, some 50,000 Jews lived in Prague. Today only a couple of thousand remain.

As the Nazis decimated Jewish communities in the region, Prague's Jews were allowed to collect and archive their treasures in this museum. While the archivists ultimately died in concentration camps, their work survives. Seven sites scattered over a three-block area make up the tourists' Jewish Quarter. Six of the sites, called "the Museum," are treated as one admission. Your ticket comes with a map locating the sights and admission appointments: times you'll be let in if it's very crowded. (Without crowds, ignore the times.)

For all seven sights you'll pay 490 kč (290 kč for "the Museum" and 200 kč for the Old-New Synagogue, all sites open Sun–Fri 09:00–17:30, closed Sat—the Jewish Sabbath). There are occasional guided walks in English (often at 14:00, 40 kč, 2.5 hrs, start at Maisel Synagogue, tel. 02/2231-7191). Most stops are described in English. This museum is well presented and profoundly moving: It tells the story of the Jews of this region and, for me, is the most interesting Jewish site in Europe.

Maisel Synagogue (Maiselova Synagóga)—This shows a thousand years of Jewish history in Bohemia and Moravia. Exhibit topics include the origin of the Star of David, Jewish mysticism, discrimination, and the creation of Prague's ghetto.

Prague's Jewish Quarter

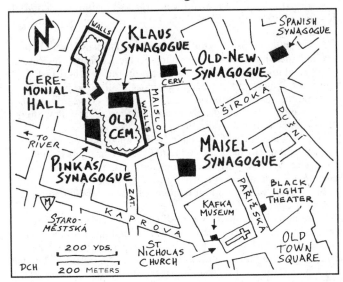

Spanish Synagogue (Španělská Synagóga)—This 19th-century, ornate, Moorish-style synagogue continues the history the Maisel Synagogue, covering the 18th, 19th, and tumultuous 20th centuries. The upstairs is particularly intriguing (with c. 1900 photos of Josefov).

Pinkas Synagogue (Pinkasova Synagóga)—A site of Jewish worship for 400 years, today this is a poignant memorial to the victims of the Nazis. Of the 120,000 Jews living in the area in 1939, only 15,000 lived to see liberation in 1945. The walls are covered with the handwritten names of 77,297 Czech Jews who were sent from here to the gas chambers of Auschwitz and other camps. Hometowns are in gold, family names are in red, followed by the individual's first name, birthday, and last date known to be alive in black. Notice that families generally perished together. Climb six steps into the women's gallery. The names near the ceiling in poor condition are from 1953. When the Communists moved in, they closed the synagogue and erased everything. With freedom, in 1989, the Pinkas Synagogue was reopened and all the names rewritten.

Upstairs is the **Terezín Children's Art Exhibit**. Terezín, near Prague, was a fortified town of 7,000 Czechs. The Nazis moved these people out and moved in 60,000 Jews, creating Theresienstadt, their model "Jewish town," a concentration camp dolled up for propaganda purposes. The town's medieval walls, originally to keep people from getting in, were used by Nazis to prevent people from getting out. Jewish culture seemed to thrive in Terezín as "citizens" put on plays and concerts, published a magazine, and raised their families in ways impressive to Red Cross inspectors. But virtually all of the Jews ended up dying at concentration camps in the East such as Auschwitz. The art of the children of Terezín survives as a striking testimony to the horror of the Holocaust. While the Communists kept the art away from the public, today it is well displayed and described in English.

Terezín is a powerful day trip from Prague for those interested in touring the concentration camp memorial/museum. You can either take a public bus (6/day, 60 min, leaves from Prague's Florenc bus station) or a tour bus (see "Tours of Prague," above).

Old Jewish Cemetery (Starý Zidovský Hřbitov)—As you wander among 12,000 evocative tombstones, remember that from 1439 until 1787 this was the only burial ground allowed for the Jews of Prague. With limited space and about 12,000 graves, tombs were piled atop each other. With its many layers, the cemetery became a small plateau. The Jewish word for cemetery means "House of Life"; like Christians, Jews believe that death is the gateway into the next world. Pebbles on the tombstones are "flowers of the desert," reminiscent of the old days when a rock was placed upon the sand gravesite to keep the body covered. Often a scrap of paper with a prayer on it is under a pebble.

Ceremonial Hall (Obradní Sín)—Leaving the cemetery you'll find a neo-Romanesque mortuary house built in 1911 for the purification of the dead (on left). It's filled with a worthwhile exhibition, described in English, on Jewish burial traditions with historic paintings of the cemetery.

Klaus Synagogue (Klauzová Synagóga)—This 17th-century synagogue (also at the exit of the cemetery) is the final wing of this museum, devoted to Jewish religious practices. On the ground floor, exhibits explain the festive Jewish calendar. Upstairs features the ritual stages of Jewish life.

Old-New Synagogue (Staronová Synagóga)—For over 700 years this has been the most important synagogue and central building in Josefov. Standing like a bomb-hardened bunker, it feels like it's survived plenty of hard times. Stairs take you down to the street level of the 13th century and into the Gothic interior. Built in 1270, it's the oldest synagogue in Europe. The Shrine of the Ark in front is the focus of worship. It holds the sacred scrolls of the Torah, the holiest place in the synagogue. The old rabbi's chair to the right remains empty out of respect. Twelve is a popular number (e.g., windows) because it symbolizes the 12 tribes of Israel. The slitlike windows on the left are an 18th-century addition allowing women to view the men-only services (separate 200 kč admission, Sun–Thu 09:30–18:00, Fri 09:30–17:00, closed Sat).

Art Nouveau

Prague is the best Art Nouveau town in Europe, with fun-loving facades gracing streets all over town. The streets of Josefov, the Mucha window in the St. Vitus Cathedral, and Hotel Europa, and its sisters on Wenceslas Square are just a few highlights. The top two places for Art Nouveau fans are the Mucha Museum and the Municipal House.

▲▲**Mucha Museum (Muchovo Muzeum)**—This is one of Europe's most enjoyable little museums. I find the art of Alfons Mucha (moo-kah, 1860–1939) insistently likeable. See the crucifixion scene he painted as an eight-year-old boy. Read how this popular Czech artist's posters, filled with Czech symbols and expressing his people's ideals and aspirations, were patriotic banners arousing the national spirit. And check out the photographs of his models. With the help of this abundant supply of slinky models, Mucha was a founding father of the Art Nouveau movement. Prague isn't much on museums, but, if you're into Art Nouveau, this one is great. Run by Mucha's grandson, it's two blocks off Wenceslas Square and wonderfully displayed on one comfortable floor (120 kč, daily 10:00–18:00, Panska 7, tel. 02/2423-3355, www.mucha.cz). While the exhibit is well described in English, the 30-kč English brochure on the art is a good supplement. The video is also worthwhile (30 min, hrly in English, ask upon entry).

Municipal House (Obecní Dum)—The Municipal House (built 1905–1911, near Powder Tower) features Prague's largest concert hall, a great Art Nouveau café with handy cyber access, and two other restaurants. Look for the *Homage to Prague* mosaic—with a goddesslike Praha presiding over a land of peace and high culture—on the building's striking facade; it stoked cultural pride and nationalist sentiment. Then choose your place for a meal or drink (see "Eating," below).

The Dancing House (Tancici Dum)—Prague also has some delightful modern architecture. If ever a building could get your toes tapping, check out the building nicknamed Fred and Ginger. This metallic samba was designed by Frank Gehry (who designed the equally striking Guggenheim Museum in Bilbao, Spain, and Seattle's Experience Music Project). It's easy to spot (two bridges down from the Charles Bridge where Jiraskuv bridge hits Nové Město, tram #17). A pleasant riverside walk from Charles Bridge to the Dancing House takes you by a famous riverside ballroom and the grand National Theater. Across the street from the theater is the venerable haunt of Prague's intelligentsia, **Kavarna Slavia**, a Vienna-style coffee house fine for a meal or drink with a view of the river.

Entertainment

Prague booms with live (and inexpensive) theater, classical, jazz, and pop entertainment. Everything's listed in Prague's monthly cultural events program (free at TI) and in the *Prague News*.

Black Light Theater, a kind of mime/modern dance variety show, has no language barrier and is, for many, more entertaining than a classical concert. Unique to Prague, this originated in the 1960s as a playful and almost mystifying theater of the absurd.

Six or eight classical "tourist" **concerts** daily fill delightful Old Town halls and churches with music of the crowd-pleasing sort: Vivaldi, Best of Mozart, Most Famous Arias, and works by local boy Anton Dvořák. Leafleteers are everywhere announcing the evening's events. Concerts typically cost 400 to 1,000 kč, start anywhere from 17:00 to 20:00, last one hour, and are usually quartets (e.g., flute, French horn, cello, violin).

Common venues are in the Little Quarter Square— Malostranské Náměstí (at the Church of St. Nicholas and the Prague Academy of Music in Liechtenstein Palace), at the city end of Charles Bridge (St. Francis Church), and on the Old Town Square (another St. Nicholas Church).

To really understand all your options (the street Mozarts are pushing only their concert), drop by the box office at the **Tyn Church**. The wall display clearly shows what's playing today and tomorrow (concerts, Black Light Theater, marionette shows, photos of each venue, and a map locating everything, daily 10:00–19:00, tel. 02/231-4936).

Young locals keep countless "music clubs" in business. A favorite with a handy locale and live music nightly is **Malostranska Beseda** (on the downhill side of the Little Quarter's main square). Many of the best local rock and jazz groups perform here (nightly from 20:30, generally about 100 kč cover).

Prague isn't great for a boat tour. Still, the hour-long **Vltava River cruises**, which leave from near the Malá Strana end of Charles Bridge about hourly (100 kč), are (while not very informative) scenic and relaxing.

Prague's top **sports** are soccer (that's "football" here, Feb– May and Aug–Nov) and hockey (they are a world power, routinely beating even Canada, Sept–April). Think about it: there are over a hundred Czech players in America's NHL. Tickets are normally easy to get (soccer—usually late Sat or Sun afternoon; hockey— weeknights; see *Prague News*). The two big Czech hockey rivals are Sparta and Slavia.

Shopping

The Czech malls are the galleries built in the 1920s, mothballed through the Communist era, and once again vibrant. You'll see these arcades leading off of Wenceslas Square and from the moat

(Na Příkope). The best—a classic arcade from a more elegant age—is the **Lucerna Gallery** on Wenceslas Square, immediately opposite Hotel Europa.

Sleeping in Prague
(40 kč = about $1, country code: 420, area code: 02)
Sleep Code: **S** = Single, **D** = Double/Twin, **T** = Triple, **Q** = Quad, **b** = bathroom, **s** = shower only, **CC** = Credit Cards accepted, **no CC** = Credit Cards not accepted.

Finding a bed in Prague worries Western tourists. It shouldn't. You have several options. Capitalism is working as Adam Smith promised: With a huge demand, the supply is increasing and the price is going up. Peak time is May, June, September, October, Christmas, and Easter. July and August are not too bad. Expect crowds on weekends. I've listed peak-time prices. If you're traveling in July or August, you'll save about 20 percent. English is generally spoken. Reserve by phone or e-mail. Generally, you simply promise to come and need no deposit.

To call Prague from outside the country, dial the international access code (00 if calling from Europe or 011 from U.S./Canada), Czech's country code (420), Prague's area code (2; you omit the initial zero), then the local number.

Room-Booking Services
Prague is awash with fancy rooms on the push list; private, small-time operators with rooms to rent in their apartments; and roving agents eager to book you a bed and earn a commission. You can save about 30 percent by showing up in Prague without a reservation and finding accommodations upon arrival. If driving, you'll see booking agencies as you enter town. Generally, book here and your host can come and lead you to their place.

AVE, at the main train station (**Hlavní Nádraží**), is a helpful and well-organized booking service (daily 06:00–23:00, tel. 02/5155-1011, fax 02/5155-5156, e-mail: ave@avetravel.cz). With the tracks at your back, walk down to the orange ceiling—their office is in the left corner by the exit to the rip-off taxis. Another AVE office is at Holešovice station. Their display board shows discounted hotels. They have a slew of private rooms and small pensions available ($50 pension doubles in the old center, $35 doubles a metro ride away). You can reserve by e-mail (using your credit card as a deposit) or just show up at the office and request a room.

Athos Travel, run by Filip Antos, is basically a Web site designed to set you up with budget beds in Prague (Na Strzi 5, Praha 4, tel. 02/4144-1695, fax 02/4144-1697, www.athos.cz, e-mail: info@athos.cz).

For a more personal touch, contact Lida at **Magic Praha**

for help with accommodations (tel. 02/2423-2755, e-mail:
magicpraha@magicpraha.cz, see "Helpful Hints," above).

Three-Star Hotels

Prague's three-star hotels—each plenty professional and comfortable—are often beholden to agencies that have a lock on rooms
(generally until 6 weeks in advance). Agencies get a 30 percent discount and can sell the rooms at whatever price they like between
that and the "rack rate." Consequently, Prague has a reputation of
being perpetually booked up. But as the agencies rarely use up
their allotment, the "crowds" are only an illusion. You need to
make reservations either long in advance, when the few rooms not
reserved for agencies are still available, or a few weeks in advance,
after the agencies have released their rooms.

Hotel Julian—an oasis of professional, predictable decency in
a quiet, untouristy neighborhood—is a five-minute taxi or tram
ride from the action on the castle side of the river. Its 29 spacious,
fresh, well-furnished rooms and big, homey, public spaces hide
behind a noble neoclassical facade. The staff is friendly and helpful
(Sb-3,080 kč, Db-3,380 kč, suite Db-4,180 kč, extra bed-900 kč,
family room, CC, 5 percent discount off best quoted rate with this
book, parking lot, elevator, Internet services, Elisky Peskove 11,
Praha 5, tel. 02/5731-1150, reception tel. 02/5731-1144, fax
02/5731-1149, www.julian.cz, e-mail: casjul@vol.cz). Free lockers
and a shower are available for those needing to check out early but
stay until late (e.g., for an overnight train). Mike's Chauffeur Service, based here, is reliable and affordable (see "Transportation
Connections," below).

Hotel Central is as likeable as an old horse. I stayed there in
the Communist days, and—while the rooms are modestly renovated—it hasn't changed a lot since. The 68 rooms are proletarian
plain, but the place is well run and the location, three blocks east of
the old square, is excellent (Sb-3,200 kč, Db-3,900 kč, Tb-4,400 kč,
low season 40 percent less, CC, elevator, Rybna 8, Praha 1, Metro:
Náměstí Republiky, tel. 02/2481-2041, fax 02/232-8404, e-mail:
what's that?). **Hotel Esprit**, next door, is also worth considering.

Betlem Club is a shiny jewel of comfort on a pleasant
medieval square in the heart of the Old Town across from the
Betlem Chapel where Jan Hus preached his trouble-making sermons. Its 22 modern and comfy rooms face a quiet inner courtyard, and breakfast is served in a Gothic cellar (Sb-2,500 kč,
Db-3,600 kč, extra bed-1,000 kč, prices flex with season, CC,
elevator, Betlémské Náměstí 9, Praha 1, tel. 02/2222-1575, fax
02/2222-0580, www.betlemclub.cz, e-mail: betlem.club@login.cz).

Hotel U Klenotnika, with 10 modern and comfortable
rooms in a plain building, is three blocks off the old square (Sb-
2,500 kč, Db-3,800 kč, Tb-4,500 kč, 10 percent off when booking

direct with this book, CC, no elevator, Rytirska 3, Praha 1, tel. 02/2421-1699, fax 02/2422-1025, info@uklenotnika.cz). They run a good restaurant.

Hotel Lunik, with 35 spacious rooms, is a stately but friendly no-nonsense place out of the medieval faux-rustic world and in a normal, pleasant business district. It's two metro stops from the main station (Metro: Pavlova) or a 10-minute walk from Wenceslas Square (Sb-1,790 kč, Db-2,500 kč, Tb-2,900 kč, CC, elevator, no reservations more than 6 weeks in advance, Londynska 50, Praha 2, tel. 02/2425-3974, fax 02/2425-3986, www.hotel-lunik.cz, e-mail: recepce@hotel-lunik.cz).

Hotel Union is a grand 1906 Art Nouveau building filling its street corner. Like Hotel Lunik, it's away from the touristy center in a more laid-back neighborhood a direct 10-minute ride to the station on tram #24 or to Charles Bridge on tram #18 (57 rooms, Sb-2,815 kč, Db-3,380 kč, Db deluxe-3,580 kč, extra bed-865 kč, CC, elevator, Nusle Ostrcilovo Náměstí 1, Praha 2, tel. 02/6121-4812, fax 02/6121-4820, e-mail: hotel.union@telecom.cz).

Hotel 16, a stately little place with an intriguing Art Nouveau facade, a garden, high ceilings, and a clean, sleek interior, rents 13 fine rooms (Sb-2,300 kč, Db-3,100 kč, Tb-3,500 kč, CC, elevator, a 10-min walk south of Wenceslas Square, Metro: Pavlova, Katerinska 16, 12800 Praha 2, tel. 02/2492-0636, fax 02/2492-0626, www.hotel16.cz, e-mail: hotel16@hotel16.cz).

Hotel Adria, with a prime Wenceslas Square location, cool Art Nouveau facade, 88 air-con rooms, and completely modern and business-class interior, is your big-time central splurge (Db-$185, CC, elevator, minibars...the works, Václavske Náměstí 26, tel. 02/2108-1111, fax 02/2108-1300, www.hoteladria.cz, e-mail: mailbox@hoteladria.cz).

Cloister Inn is a modern, three-star place with 70 rooms and more concrete than charm but plenty comfortable and well located (Sb-3,000–3,600 kč, Db-3,300–4,200 kč, Tb-3,800–5,000 kč, Konviktska 14, 11000 Praha 1, tel. 02/2421-1020, fax 02/2421-0800, www.cloister-inn.cz, e-mail: cloister@cloister-inn.cz).

Hotel Cerna Liska Praha is a small and modern-feeling three-star place with 12 comfortable rooms right on the Old Town Square (Sb-4,200 kč, Db-5,460 kč, 30 percent less Nov–March, CC, elevator, Mikulasska 2, tel. 02/2423-2250, fax 02/2423-2249, e-mail: cerna.liska@volny.cz).

Three-Star Hotels near the Castle in the Little Quarter (Malá Strana)

Hotel Sax, on a quiet corner a block below the action, will delight the artsy yuppie with its 22 rooms, airy atrium, and modern, stylish decor (Sb-4,000 kč, Db-4,800 kč, Db suite-5,600 kč, CC, elevator, near St. Nicholas church, 1 block below Nerudova at Jansky Vrsek 3, reserve long in advance, tel. 02/5753-1268, fax 02/5753-4101, e-mail: hotelsax@bon.cz).

Domus Henrici, just above the castle square, is a quiet retreat that charges—and gets—top dollar for its smartly appointed rooms, some of which include good views (Db-$150/$170/$195 depending on size, extra bed-$40, pleasant breakfast terrace, Loretanska 11, tel. 02/2051-1369, fax 02/2051-1502, www.domus-henrici.cz). This is a five-minute walk above the castle gate in a stately and quiet area.

Pensions and Cheaper Accommodations

With the rush of tourists into Prague, small 6- to 15-room pensions are popping up everywhere. Most have small, spartan rooms—often with no plumbing at all; sinks, showers, and toilets are down the hall. Breakfast is included in the price. Some of these places take bookings no more than a month in advance. All are in the Old Town, close to the Můstek metro station.

The **Laundromat** nearest most recommended hotels is at Karoliny Svetle 10 (200 kč/load, Mon–Sat 07:30–19:00, closed Sun, 200 meters from the bridge, on old town side).

Pension Unitas rents 34 small and tidy youth hostel–type rooms with plain, minimalist furnishings and no sinks (S-1,020 kč, D-1,200 kč, T-1,650 kč, Q-2,000 kč, T and Q are cramped with bunks in D-sized rooms, Bartolomejska 9, 11000 Praha 1, tel. 02/2232-7700, fax 02/2232-7709, www.cloister-inn.cz/unitas, e-mail: cloister@cloister-inn.cz).

Hotel Europa is in a class by itself. This landmark place, famous for its wonderful 1903 Art Nouveau facade, is the center-piece of Wenceslas Square. But someone pulled the plug on the hotel about 50 years ago, and it's a mess. It offers haunting beauty in all the public spaces with 90 dreary, ramshackle rooms and a weary staff (S-1,600 kč, Sb-3,000 kč, D-2,600 kč, Db-4,000 kč, T-3,100 kč, Tb-5,000 kč, CC, elevator, Václavské Náměstí 25, Praha 1, tel. 02/2422-8117, fax 02/2422-4544, e-mail: nyet).

Hotel Express rents 26 simple rooms and serves a lousy continental breakfast (Sb-2,600 kč, D-2,000 kč, Db-2,800 kč, Tb-3,200 kč, elevator, Skorepka 5, Praha 1, tel. 02/2421-1801, fax 02/2422-3309, e-mail: expres@zero.cz).

Pension U Medvidku has 22 comfortably renovated rooms in a big, rustic, medieval shell (Sb-2,265 kč, Db-3,000 kč, Tb-4,000 kč, CC, Na Perstyne 7, Praha 1, tel. 02/2421-1916, fax 02/2422-0930, www.umedvidku.cz, e-mail: info@umedvidku.cz). The pension runs a popular restaurant that has live music nightly until 23:00.

Guest House Lida, with homey and spacious rooms, fills a big house in a quiet residential area that's a 10-minute walk or five-minute tram ride from the center. Jan and Jiri Prouza, who run the place, are a wealth of information and know-how to make people feel at home (Db–$55, 10 percent off Nov–March, family rooms, Metro: Prazskeho Povstani, Lopatecka 26, 14700 Prague 4, tel. & fax 02/6121-4766, e-mail: lida@login.cz).

Eating in Prague

The beauty of Prague is wandering aimlessly through the winding old quarters marveling at the architecture, watching the people, and sniffing out fun restaurants. You can eat well for very little money. What you'd pay for a basic meal in Vienna or Munich will get you an elegant meal in Prague. Choose between traditional, dark Czech beerhall–type ambience, elegant *Jugendstil*/early 20th-century atmosphere, ethnic, or hip and modern.

Watch out for scams. Many restaurants put more care into ripping off green tourists (and even locals) than in their cooking. Tourists are routinely served cheaper meals than what they ordered, given a menu with a "personalized" price list, charged extra for things they didn't get, or shortchanged. Avoid any menu without clear and explicit prices. Understand each line on your bill (a 10 percent service is sometimes added—no need to tip beyond that) and deliberately count your change, parting with very large bills only if necessary. Never let your credit card out of your sight and check the numbers carefully. Make it a habit to get cash from an ATM to pay for your meals. Remember there are two parallel worlds in Prague: the tourist town and the real city. Generally if you walk two minutes away from the tourist flow, you'll find much better value, ambience, and service.

Art Nouveau Restaurants

The sumptuous Art Nouveau concert hall—**Municipal House**—has three special restaurants: a café, a French restaurant, and a beer cellar (Náměstí Republiky 5). The dressy café, **Kavarna Obecní Dům**, is drenched in chandeliered Art Nouveau elegance (light meals, 1 hot meal special daily—200 kč, live piano or jazz trio 17:00–21:00, cybercafé: 40 kč/10 min, tel. 02/2002-1001). **Francouzska Restaurace**, the fine and formal French restaurant, is in the next wing (500-kč meals). **Plzenska Restaurace**, downstairs, brags it's the most beautiful Art Nouveau pub in Europe (cheap meals, great atmosphere, daily 12:00–23:00).

Restaurant Mucha is touristy with decent Czech food in a formal Art Nouveau dining room (300-kč meals, daily until 24:00, Melantrichova 5).

Uniquely Czech Places near the Old Town Square

Prices go way down when you get away from the tourist areas. At least once, eat in a restaurant with no English menu.

Plzenska Restaurace U Dvou Kocek is a typical Czech pub with cheap, no-nonsense, hearty Czech food, great beer, and—

once upon a time—a local crowd (200 kč for 3 courses and beer, serving original Pilsner Urquell with accordion music nightly until 23:00, under an arcade, facing the tiny square between Perlova and Skorepka Streets).

Mlejnice is a fun little pub strewn with farm implements and happy eaters tucked away just out of the tourist crush two blocks from the Old Town Square (order carefully and understand your itemized bill, between Melantrichova and Železna at Kozna 14, reservations smart in evening, tel. 02/2422-8635).

Restaurant U Plebana is a quiet little place with good service, Czech cuisine, and a modern yet elegant setting (daily 12:00–23:00, Betlémské Náměstí 10, tel. 02/2222-1568).

Country Life Vegetarian Restaurant is a bright, easy, and smoke-free cafeteria that has a well-displayed buffet of salads and veggie hot dishes. It's midway between the Old Town Square and the bottom of Wenceslas Square. They are serious about their vegetarianism, serving only plant-based, unprocessed, and unre-fined food (Sun–Thu 11:00–20:30, Fri 11:00–18:00, closed Sat, through courtyard at Melantrichova 15/Michalska 18, tel. 02/2421-3366).

Czech Kitchen (Ceska Kuchyne) is a new blue-collar cafeteria serving steamy old Czech cuisine to a local clientele market. There's no English. Just pick up your tally sheet at the door, grab a tray, and point liberally to whatever you'd like. It's extremely cheap (daily 09:30–17:00, across from Havelská Market at Havelská 23).

Eating above the Castle

Ozivle Drevo, a stately yet traditional restaurant, feels like a country farmhouse and comes with perhaps the most commanding view terrace in all of Prague. It serves good quality traditional cuisine. Hiking up the Nerudova/Uvoz road, bypass the castle and carry on five minutes more to the Strahov Monastery (daily 11:00–23:00, Strahovske Nadvori 1, tel. 02/2051-7274).

Maly Buddha ("Little Buddha") serves delightful food—especially vegetarian—and takes its theme seriously. You'll step into a mellow, low-lit escape of bamboo and peace to be served by people with perfect complexions and almost no pulse. Ethnic eateries like this are trendy with young Czechs (Tue–Sun 13:00–22:30, closed Mon, smoke free, continue on road to castle, bypassing castle turnoff about 100 meters to Uvoz 46, tel. 02/2051-3894).

U Hrocha ("By The Hippo") is a very local little pub packed with beer drinkers and smoke. Just below the castle near Malá Strana's main square, it's actually the haunt of many members of Parliament—located just around the corner (daily 12:00–23:00, chalkboard lists daily meals, Thunovska 10).

Eating Elsewhere in Prague

Near the Jewish Quarter: **Kolkovna** is a big, new, woody yet modern place catering to locals and serving a fun mix of Czech and international cuisine (ribs, salads, cheese plates, great beer, across street from Spanish Synagogue at U Kolkovna 8, tel. 02/2481-9701). The **Franz Kafka Café** is pleasant for a snack or drink (on Siroka, a block from the cemetery).

With a view, at the base of Wenceslas Square: The **Modra Terasa (Blue Terrace) Restaurant** is a somewhat tired place serving good food uniquely perched for those wanting to survey Prague's grandest square while eating without a tourist in sight (smoky interior, fun terrace on sunny days, ride elevator at Na Mustku 9—from top of Metro station, tel. 02/2422-6288).

Czech Beer

For many, *pivo* (beer) is the top Czech tourist attraction. After all, the Czechs invented lager in nearby Pilsen. This is the famous Pilsner Urquell, a great lager on tap everywhere. Budvar is the local Budweiser, but it's not related to the American brew. Czechs are among the world's biggest beer drinkers—adults drink about 80 gallons a year. The big degree symbol on bottles and menus marks the beer's heaviness, not its alcohol content (12 degrees is darker, 10 degrees lighter). The smaller figure shows alcohol content. Order beer from the tap (*sudove pivo*) in either small (0.3 liter, *male pivo*) or large (0.5 liter, *pivo*). In many restaurants, a beer hits your table like a glass of water in the United States. *Pivo* for lunch has me sightseeing for the rest of the day on Czech knees. Be sure to venture beyond the Pilsner Urquell. There are plenty of other good Czech beers.

Tea Houses

Many Czech people prefer the mellow, smoke-free environs of a teahouse to the smoky traditional beer hall. While there are teahouses all over town, one fine example in a handy locale is **Dobra Cajovna** (Mon–Sat 10:00–21:30, Sun 15:00–21:30, near the base of Wenceslas Square at Vaclavske Náměstí 14). This teahouse, just a few steps off the bustle of the main square, takes you into a very peaceful world which elevates tea to an almost religious ritual. Ask for the English menu, which lovingly describes each tea (www.cajovna.com).

Transportation Connections—Prague

Getting to Prague: Those with railpasses need to purchase tickets to cover the portion of their journey from the border of the Czech Republic to Prague (buy at station before you board train for Prague). Or supplement your pass with a "Prague Excursion" pass, giving you passage from any Czech border station into

Prague and back to any border station within seven days. Ask about this pass (and get reservations) at the EurAide offices in Munich or Berlin (€46 first class, €36 second class, €26 for youths under 26, tel. 089/593-889). EurAide's U.S. office sells these passes for a bit less (U.S. tel. 941/480-1555, fax 941/480-1522). Direct trains leave Munich for Prague daily around 07:00, 14:00, and 23:00 (5–6 hr trip). Tickets cost about €52 from Munich or, if you have a railpass covering Germany, €16 from the border.

By train to: **Český Krumlov** (8/day, 4 hrs, verify departing station), **Berlin** (5/day, 5 hrs), **Munich** (3/day, 5 hrs), **Frankfurt** (3/day, 6 hrs), **Vienna** (3/day, 5 hrs), **Budapest** (6/day, 9 hrs). Train info: tel. 02/2422-4200. To purchase tickets, call Czech Rail Agency: tel. 02/800-805.

By bus to Český Krumlov (6/day, 3.5 hrs, 190 km/120 miles, take Metro to Florenc station; an easy direct bus leaves at about 09:00).

By car with a driver: Mike's Chauffeur Service is a reliable little company with fair and fixed rates around town and beyond (round-trip fares with waiting time included: Český Krumlov-3,500 kč, Terezín-1,700 kč, Karlštejn-1,500 kč, up to 4 people, tel. 02/5156-5161, e-mail: mike.chauffeur@cmail.cz). On the way to Český, Mike will stop at no extra charge at Hluboka Castle or Český Budijovice, where the original Bud beer is made.

Český Krumlov

Český Krumlov means "Czech bend in the river." Lassoed by its river and dominated by its castle, this simple, enchanting town (2.5 hr by train from Prague) feels lost in a time warp. It attracts a young, Bohemian crowd, drawn here for its beauty and cheap living. The town is best at night—save energy for a romantic post-dinner stroll.

The **TI** (closed Sun, tel. 0337/711-183), banks, ATMs, a few hotels, and taxis are on the main square. For Internet access, try South Bohemian University, just off the main square (Mon–Fri 09:00–18:00, Horni 155, tel. 0337/913-075).

If you stay the night, consider the comfortable **Hotel Zlaty Andel** on the main square (Sb-1,190 kč, Db-1,690-2,290 kč, Tb-2,690 kč, Qb-3,290 kč, CC, satellite TV, minibar, Náměstí Svornosti 10, tel. 0337/7123-1015, fax 0337/71235) or the near-elegant **Hotel Konvice** (Sb-1,150 kč, Db-1,400 kč, extra bed-500 kč, Qb apartment-2,600 kč, CC, Horni Ulice 144, tel. 0337/711-611, fax 0337/711-327).

For a good, reasonably priced meal with views over Český, try **Restaurant U Pisare Jana** (Horni 151, tel. 0337/712-401). **Na Louzi**, a block below the main square on Kajovska 66, is popular with locals and very cheap.

COPENHAGEN

Copenhagen (København), Denmark's capital, is the gateway to Scandinavia. And now, with the new bridge connecting Sweden and Denmark, Copenhagen is energized and ready to dethrone Stockholm as Scandinavia's powerhouse city. A busy day cruising the canals, wandering through the palace, and taking an old-town walk will give you your historical bearings. Then, after another day strolling the Strøget (Europe's greatest pedestrian shopping mall), biking the canals, and sampling the Danish good life, you'll feel right at home. Copenhagen is Scandinavia's cheapest and most fun-loving capital. So live it up.

Planning Your Time

A first visit deserves two days.

Day 1: Catch the 10:30 city walking tour (see "Tours of Copenhagen," below). After a Riz-Raz lunch, visit the Use It information center and catch the relaxing canal-boat tour out to *The Little Mermaid* and back. Enjoy the rest of the afternoon tracing Denmark's cultural roots in the National Museum and touring the Ny Carlsberg Glyptotek art gallery. Spend the evening strolling Strøget (follow "Heart and Soul" walk described below) or dipping into Christiania.

Day 2: At 10:00 explore the subterranean Christiansborg Castle ruins under today's palace or go neoclassical at Thorvaldsen's Museum. At 11:00 take the 50-minute guided tour of Denmark's royal Christiansborg Palace. After a *smørrebrød* lunch in a park, spend the afternoon seeing the Rosenborg Castle/crown jewels and the Nazi Resistance museum. Spend the evening at Tivoli Gardens.

With a third day, side-trip out to Roskilde and Frederiksborg.

Remember the efficiency of sleeping in and out by train. Most flights from the States arrive in the morning. After you arrive, head for Stockholm and Oslo (both are connected to Copenhagen by overnight trains). Kamikaze sightseers see Copenhagen as a Scandinavian bottleneck. They sleep in and out heading north and in and out heading south, with two days and no nights in Copenhagen. Considering the joy of Oslo and Stockholm, this isn't that crazy if you have limited time. You can check your bag at the station.

If you've yet to do so, consider setting yourself up in my top recommended rooms for your entire Scandinavian tour with a phone card and a quick trip to a pay phone.

Orientation

Nearly all of your sightseeing is in Copenhagen's compact old town. By doing things by bike or on foot you'll stumble into some charming bits of Copenhagen that many miss.

Study the map to understand the city: The medieval walls are now roads that define the center: Vestervoldgade (literally, "west rampart street"), Nørrevoldgade, and Østervoldgade. The fourth side is the harbor and the island of Slotsholmen where København ("merchants' harbor") was born in 1167. The next of the city's islands is Amager, where you'll find the local "Little Amsterdam" district of Christianshavn. What was Copenhagen's moat is now a string of pleasant lakes and parks, including Tivoli Gardens. You can still make out some of the zigzag pattern of the moats in the city's greenbelt. In 1850 Copenhagen's 120,000 residents all lived within this defensive system. Building in the "no man's land" outside the walls was only allowed with the understanding that in the event of an attack you'd burn your dwellings to clear the way for a good defense. Today, the buildings of historic importance lie within the *voldgade* ring. In the 17th century, King Christian IV extended the fortifications to the north, doubling the size of the city, adding a grid plan of streets and his Rosenborg Castle. This old "new town" has the Amalienborg Palace and *The Little Mermaid*.

For most visitors, the core of the town is the axis formed by the train station, Tivoli Gardens, Rådhus (City Hall) Square, and the Strøget pedestrian street. Bubbling with street life and colorful pedestrian zones, Copenhagen's great on foot. But be sure to get off the Strøget.

You need to remember one character in Copenhagen's history: Christian IV. Ruling from 1588 to 1648, he was Denmark's Renaissance king and royal party animal. The personal energy of this "Builder King" sparked a golden age when Copenhagen prospered and many of the city's grandest buildings were erected. Locals love to tell stories of everyone's favorite king, whose drinking was legendary.

Tourist Information

The tourist office is a for-profit company called "Wonderful Copenhagen." This colors the advice and information it provides. Drop by to get a city map and *Copenhagen This Week* (a free, handy, and misnamed monthly guide to the city, worth reading for its good maps, museum hours with telephone numbers, sightseeing tour ideas, shopping suggestions, and calendar of events, including free English tours and concerts; online at www.ctw.dk). Browse the TI's racks of brochures and get your questions answered (May–Sept Mon–Sat 10:00–16:00, July–Aug until 18:00 plus Sun 11:00–18:00, Oct–April Tue–Sat 10:00–16:00, across from train station on Bernstorffsgade, tel. 33 25 38 44, www.dt.dk, www.visitcopenhagen.dk).

To help with your sightseeing planning, take a peek at this week's entertainment program for Tivoli posted near the front door.

Use It (a 10-minute walk from the station) is a better information service. Government-sponsored and student-run, it caters to Copenhagen's young but welcomes travelers of any age. It's a friendly, driven-to-help, energetic, no-nonsense source of budget travel information, offering a free budget room-finding service, free Internet access, a jazz bar, a ride-finding board, free condoms, and free luggage lockers. Their free *Playtime* publication has Back Door–style articles on Copenhagen and the Danish culture, special budget tips, and self-guided tours for bikers, walkers, and those riding scenic bus #6. They have a list of private rooms (300-kr doubles). From the station, head down Strøget, then turn right on Rådhustræde for three blocks to #13 (mid-June–mid-Sept daily 09:00–19:00; otherwise Mon–Wed 11:00–16:00, Thu 11:00–18:00, Fri 11:00–14:00, closed Sat–Sun; tel. 33 73 06 20).

The two essential publications you need—a map and *Copenhagen This Week*—are free and available at the airport TI, the TI across from the station, Use It, and the lobby of the City Hall. Pick up a copy of each.

The **Copenhagen Card** covers the public transportation system and admissions to nearly all the sights in greater Copenhagen, which stretches from Helsingør to Roskilde. It includes virtually all the city sights, Tivoli, and the train from the airport. It's available at any TI (including the airport's): 24 hours for 175 kr; 48 hours for 295 kr; and 72 hours for 395 kr (www.woco.dk). It's hard to break even, unless you're planning to side-trip on the included (and otherwise expensive) rail service. It comes with a handy book explaining over 70 sights, such as: Christiansborg Palace (normally 40 kr), Christiansborg Castle ruins (20 kr), National Museum (40 kr), Ny Carlsberg Glyptotek (30 kr), Louisiana (60 kr), Tivoli (50 kr), Frederiksborg Castle (50 kr), and Roskilde Viking Ships (54 kr). It also includes round-trip train rides to Roskilde (70 kr) and Frederiksborg Castle (70 kr).

Arrival in Copenhagen

By Train: The main train station is called Hovedbanegården
(HOETH-ban-gorn; learn that word—you'll need to recognize it).
It's a temple of travel and a hive of travel-related activity, offering
lockers (35 kr/day), a *garderobe* (40 kr/day per rucksack), a post
office, a grocery store (daily 08:00–24:00), 24-hour thievery, and
bike rentals. The station has ATMs and a long-hour FOREX
exchange desk (daily 08:00–21:00, 10-kr fee per travelers check).
Showers (10 kr) are available at the public restrooms at the back
of the station (and under the bus terminal opposite City Hall).

While you're in the station, reserve your overnight train seat
or *couchette* out (at Rejse-bureau, Mon–Fri 10:00–17:00). International rides and all IC trains require reservations (usually 20 kr).
To get to Christianshavn B&Bs, catch bus #8 (4/hr, in front of
station on near side of Bernstorffsgade). Note the time the bus
departs, then stop by the TI (across the street) and pick up a free
Copenhagen city map that shows bus routes.

By Plane: Copenhagen's International Airport is a traveler's
dream, with a TI, bank (standard rates), post office, telephone
center, shopping mall, grocery store, and bakery. You can use U.S.
dollars at the airport and get change back in kroner (airport info
tel. 32 31 32 31 or 32 47 47 00, SAS info 32 32 00 00). Need to
kill a night at the airport? Try the **Transfer Hotel** located under
the Transit Hall. These fetal rest cabins, called *hvilekabiner*, are
especially handy for early flights (Sb-370 kr, Db-550 kr for 8 hrs,
prices vary for 4- to 16-hr periods, reception open 05:30–24:00,
easy telephone reservations, CC, sauna and showers available,
tel. 32 31 24 55, fax 32 31 31 09).

Getting Downtown from the Airport: Taxis are fast, civil,
accept credit cards, and, at about 150 kr to the town center, are
a good deal for foursomes. The Air Rail train (19.50 kr, 3/hr, 12
min) links the airport with the train station, Nørreport, and Østerport. City bus #250s gets you downtown (City Hall Square, TI)
in 20 minutes for 19.50 kr (6/hr, across the street and to the right
as you exit airport). If you're going from the airport to Christianshavn, ride #9 just past Christianshavn Torv and get off at Strandgade, the stop before crossing Knippelsbro.

Helpful Hints

Ferries: Book any ferries you plan to use in Scandinavia now.
Any travel agent can book the boat rides you plan to take later
on your trip, such as the Denmark–Norway ferry or Stockholm's
round-trip cruise to Helsinki–Stockholm (or call Silja Line's Danish office at 96 20 32 00, Mon-Thu 09:00-16:30, Fri 09:00–16:00).
With the new Øresund Bridge, you'll no longer need a ferry to
drive to Sweden, but the toll (230 kr) is the same as the Helsingør-
Helsingborg ferry, which still goes twice every hour.

Jazz Festival: The Copenhagen Jazz Festival—10 days starting the first Friday in July (July 5–14 in 2002)—puts the town in a rollicking slide-trombone mood. The Danes are Europe's jazz enthusiasts and this music festival fills the town with happiness. The TI prints up an extensive listing of each year's festival events. There's also an autumn version of the festival the first week of November.

Telephones: Use the telephone liberally. Everyone speaks English, and *This Week* and this book list phone numbers for everything you'll be doing. All telephone numbers in Denmark are eight digits, and there are no area codes. Calls anywhere in Denmark are cheap; calls to Norway and Sweden cost 6 kr per minute from a booth (half that from a private home). Get a phone card (at newsstands, starting at 30 kr).

Emergencies: Dial 112 and specify fire, police, or ambulance. Speak slowly and clearly and give your phone number and address. Emergency calls from public phones are free; no coins are needed.

Pharmacy: Steno Apotek is across from the train station (open 24 hrs daily, Vesterbrogade 6c, tel. 33 14 82 66).

U.S. Embassy: Dag Hammerskjolds Alle 24, tel. 35 55 31 44.

Getting around Copenhagen

By Bus and Subway: A fine bus and subway system called S-tog (Eurail valid on S-tog) makes getting around Copenhagen easy. A 13-kr two-zone ticket (pay as you board) gets you an hour's travel within the center. Consider the blue two-zone *klippekort* (80 kr for 10 one-hour "rides") and the 24-hour pass (70 kr, both sold at stations and the TI). Assume you'll be within the middle two zones. Drivers are patient, have change, and speak English. City maps list bus and subway routes. Locals are friendly and helpful. Copenhagen is a bit torn up as it puts together a slick new subway expansion that will open in a year or two.

By Bus Tour: Open Top Tour buses do a hop-on hop-off 60-minute circle connecting the city's top sights; for details, see "Tours of Copenhagen," below. Budget do-it-yourselfers simply ride city bus #6: from the Carlsberg Brewery, it stops at Tivoli, City Hall, National Museum, Royal Palace, Nyhavn, Amalienborg Castle, Kastellet, and *The Little Mermaid* (13 kr for a stop-and-go hour). The entire tour is described in Use It's *Playtime* magazine.

By Taxi: Taxis are plentiful and easy to call or flag down (22-kr drop charge, then 10 kr per km, CC). For a short ride, four people spend about the same by taxi as by bus (e.g., 50 kr from train station to Christianshavn B&Bs). Calling 35 35 35 35 will get you a taxi within minutes.

By Bike: Free! Copenhagen's radical "city bike" program is great for sightseers (though bikes can be hard to find at times). From May through November, 2,000 clunky but practical little bikes are scattered around the old-town center (basically the terrain covered in the Copenhagen map in this chapter). Simply locate one of the 150 racks, unlock a bike by popping a 20-kr coin into the handlebar, and pedal away. When you're done, plug your bike back into any other rack and your deposit coin will pop back out (if you can't find a rack, just abandon it and a bum will take it back and pocket your coin). These simple bikes come with "theft-proof" parts (unusable on regular bikes) and—they claim—computer tracer chips embedded in them so bike patrols can retrieve strays. These are funded by advertisements painted on the wheels and by a progressive electorate. Try this once and you'll find Copenhagen suddenly a lot smaller and easier.

For a serious bike tour, rent a more comfortable bike at Central or Østerport Stations' Cykelcenters (50 kr/day, Mon–Fri 08:00–18:00, Sat 09:00–13:00, summer Sun 10:00–13:00, closed Sun off-season, tel. 33 33 86 13). Bikers see more, save time and money, and really feel like temporary locals by doing everything by bike. Consider it.

Tours of Copenhagen

▲▲▲Walking Tours—Once upon a time, American **Richard Karpen** visited Copenhagen and fell in love with the city (and one of its women). His daily 90-minute tours wander in and out of buildings, courtyards, backstreets, and unusual parts of the "Old City." Along the way, he gives insightful and humorous background on the history and culture of Denmark, Copenhagen, and the Danes. Richard offers four entertaining tours: three city walks—each about two kilometers with breaks, covering different parts of the historic center—and a Rosenborg Castle tour (city tours depart from TI May–Sept Mon–Sat at 10:30, 50 kr, kids under 12 free; the Rosenborg Castle tour leaves from outside the castle ticket office at 13:30 Mon and Thu, 100 kr, which includes 50-kr castle admission; pick up schedule at TI or call Richard at 32 84 74 35). Richard has an infectious love of Copenhagen. His tours, while different, complement each other and are of equal "introduction" value.

Bus Tours—A variety of guided bus tours depart from City Hall Square in front of the Palace Hotel. **Copenhagen Excursions** runs both city tours and jaunts into the countryside, with themes such as Vikings, castles, and Hamlet. Their hop-on hop-off **Open Top Tours** do the basic 60-minute circle of the city sights—Tivoli, Royal Palace, National Museum, *The Little Mermaid*, Rosenborg Castle, Nyhavn, and more—with a taped narration (100 kr, 2/hr, April–Oct daily 09:30–17:00; you can get off, see a sight, and catch a later bus; bus departs City Hall below the *Lur Blowers* statue to the left of City Hall or at many other stops throughout city, pay driver, ticket good for 48 hrs, tel. 32 54 06 06, www.cex.dk). One of their

Copenhagen

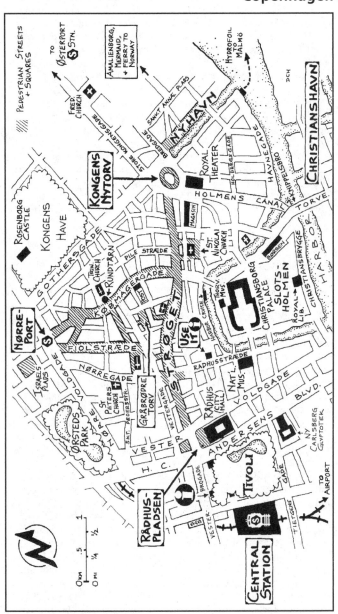

tours (offered on Sat only) goes to Sweden, giving you a chance to enjoy a trip over Europe's long Øresund Bridge from the windy open top of a double-decker bus, a brief stop in Malmo, and a few hours on your own in the charming university town of Lund (345 kr, June–Aug, Sat only at 11:15, 7 hrs, reservations required, needs 10 people to go, tel. 32 54 06 06).

▲▲**Harbor Cruise and Canal Tours**—Two companies offer essentially the same live, three-language, 50-minute tours through the city canals. Both boats leave at least twice an hour from near Christiansborg Palace, cruise around the palace and Christian-shavn area, and then proceed into the wide-open harbor. It's a relaxing way to see *The Little Mermaid* and munch a lazy picnic during the slow-moving narration. The low-overhead **Netto-Bådene** tour boats leave from Holmen's Bridge in front of the palace (20 kr, late April–Sept daily 10:00–17:00, later in July, sign at dock shows next departure, dress warmly—boats are open-top until Sept, tel. 32 54 41 02, www.havnerundfart.dk). The competition, **Canal Tours Copenhagen**, does the same tour for 50 kr (from Gammel Strand, 200 meters away; and from Nyhavn, April–Oct, daily 10:00–17:00). They also do a "water bus" hop-on hop-off version (30 kr, May–early Sept, 10:15-16:45, tel. 33 93 42 60). Go with Netto. There's no reason to pay double.

Bike Tours—**City Safari** offers 2.5-hour guided bike tours of Copenhagen (June–Aug daily 10:00 and 13:00, 150 kr includes bike, in English and Danish as needed, no reservation needed, show up 10 min in advance at the Danish Center for Archi-tecture, Gammel Dok Storehouse, Strandgade 27b, tel. 33 23 94 90, www.citysafari.dk, or ask at Use It; energetic Steen is a one-man show and speaks fine English).

Do-It-Yourself Orientation Walk: "Strøget and Copenhagen's Heart and Soul"

Start from **Rådhuspladsen** (City Hall Square), the bustling heart of Copenhagen, dominated by the spire of City Hall. This was Copen-hagen's fortified west end. In 1843, magazine publisher Georg Car-stensen convinced the king to let him build a pleasure garden outside the walls of crowded Copenhagen. The king quickly agreed, know-ing that people who are entertained forget about fighting for dem-ocracy. **Tivoli** became Europe's first great public amusement park. When the train lines came, the station was placed just beyond Tivoli.

Step inside the **City Hall** (Mon–Fri 07:45–17:00—described under "Sights," below). Old **Hans Christian Andersen** sits to the right of City Hall, almost begging to be in another photo (as he used to in real life). On a pedestal left of City Hall, note the *Lur Blowers* sculpture. The *lur* is a horn that was used 3,500 years ago. The ancient originals (which still play) are displayed in the National Museum. (City tour buses leave from below these horns.)

The **golden girls** high up on the tower (marked "Philips" in blue) opposite the Strøget's entrance tell the weather: on a bike (fair) or with an umbrella. These two have been called the only women in Copenhagen you can trust. Here in the traffic hub of this huge city you'll notice . . . not many cars. Denmark's 180 percent tax on car purchases makes the bus or bike a sweeter option.

The American trio of Burger King, 7-Eleven, and KFC marks the start of the otherwise charming **Strøget**. Copenhagen's 25-year-old experimental, tremendously successful, and most-copied pedestrian shopping mall is a string of lively (and individually named) streets and lovely squares that bunny-hop through the old town from City Hall to Nyhavn, which is a 15-minute stroll (or "*strøget*") away.

As you wander down this street, remember that the commercial focus of a historic street like Strøget drives up the land value, which generally trashes the charm and tears down the old buildings. Look above the street-level advertising to discover much of their 19th century character intact. While Strøget has become hamburgerized, historic bits and charming pieces of old Copenhagen are just off this commercial cancan.

After one block (at Kattesundet) make a side trip two blocks left into Copenhagen's colorful **university district**. Formerly the old brothel area, today this "Latin Quarter" is Soho chic. At Studiesstraede turn right and walk two blocks to the big neoclassical Cathedral of Our Lady (with John the Baptist up where the Greek mythological gods would normally be). Enter and find statues of Christ and the 12 apostles—masterpieces by the great Danish sculptor Thorvaldsen—all looking quite Greek. By standing on the corner across the street from the church, you can see why Golden Age Copenhagen (early 1800s) fancied itself a Nordic Athens. To the left is the university. And 300 meters to your right are the Greek Temple–like law courts.

Step into the university (up the middle steps of the big building) into a colorful lobby starring Athena and Apollo. The frescoes celebrate high thinking and themes such as the triumph of wisdom over barbarism. Notice how harmoniously the architecture, sculpture, and painting work together.

Rejoin Strøget (down where you see the law courts) at **Gammel Torv** and **Nytorv** (Old Square and New Square). This was the old town center. The Oriental-looking kiosk was one of the city's first community telephone centers before phones were privately owned—look at the reliefs ringing its top: an airplane with bird wings (c. 1900) and two women talking on the new-fangled phone. (It was thought business would popularize the telephone, but actually it was women . . . . Now, 100 years later, look at the cell phones.) The squirting woman and boy on the very old fountain in Gammel Torv were so offensive to people from the Victorian age that the pedestal was added, raising it—they hoped—out of view.

Walk down **Amagertorv** to the stately brick Holy Ghost church (note the fine spire, typical of old Danish churches). Under the step gable was a hospital run by monks. A block behind the church (walk down Valkendorfsgade and through a passage under a rust-colored building) is the leafy and caffeine-stained **Gråbrø-dretorv** (Grey Brothers' Square)—a popular place for an outdoor meal or drink in the summer—surrounded by fine old buildings. At the end of the square, the street Niels Hemmingsens Gade returns (past the Copenhagen Jazz House—good place for live music nightly) to Strøget. Continue down the pedestrian street to the next square with the stork fountain.

Amagertorv delights shoppers. Spin around and see Royal Copenhagen Porcelain (with demos), Holmegaard Glassware, George Jensen Jewelry and Silverware, and Illums Bolighus (modern design, Mon–Sat 10:00–18:00, Sun 12:00–17:00). Café Norden is a smoky but good place for a coffee with a view. From here you can see the imposing Parliament building, Christiansborg Palace and a horse statue of Bishop Absalon, the city's founder (canal boat tours leave nearby from Holmen's Bridge). A block toward the canal, running parallel to Strøget, starts Straedet, a second Strøget with cafés, antique shops, and no fast food. North of Amagertorv a broad pedestrian mall, Kobmagergade, leads past the Museum of Erotica to Christian IV's Round Tower.

The final stretch of Strøget leads past **Pistolstræde** (a cute lane of shops in restored 18th-century buildings leading off Strøget to the right from Østergade; wander way back into half-timbered section), McDonald's (good view from top floor), and major department stores (Illum and Magasin—see "Shopping," below) to Kongens Nytorv. **Kongens Nytorv** is the biggest square in town and is home to the Royal Theater, the French Embassy, and the venerable Hotel D'Angleterre. On the right, Hviids Vinstue, the town's oldest wine cellar (from 1723), is a colorful if smoky spot for an open-face sandwich and a beer (Kongens Nytorv 19). The statue in the middle celebrates Christian V who, in the 1670s, extended Copenhagen, adding this "King's New Square" (Kongens Nytorv). Across the square is the trendy harbor of Nyhavn.

Nyhavn, a recently gentrified sailors' quarter, is just opposite Kongens Nytorv. This formerly sleazy harbor is an interesting mix of tattoo parlors, taverns, and trendy cafés lining a canal filled with glamorous old sailboats of all sizes. Any historic sloop is welcome to moor here in Copenhagen's ever-changing boat museum. Hans Christian Andersen lived and wrote his first stories here (in the red double-gabled building on the right).

Continuing north along the harborside (from end of Nyhavn canal, turn left), you'll pass a huge ship that sails to Oslo every evening (at 17:00—see www.seaeurope.com). Follow the water-front to the modern fountain of Amaliehave Park.

The **Amalienborg Palace and Square** (a block inland, behind the fountain; described under "Sights," below) is a good example of orderly Baroque planning. Queen Margrethe II and her family live in the palace to your immediate left as you enter the square from the harbor side. Her son and heir to the throne, Crown Prince Frederik, recently moved into the palace directly opposite his mother's. While the guards change with royal fanfare at noon only when the queen is in residence, they shower every morning.

Leave the square on Amaliegade, heading north to Kastellet (Citadel) Park and past Denmark's World War II Resistance Museum. A short stroll past the Gefion fountain (showing the mythological story of the goddess who was given one night to carve a chunk out of Sweden to make into Denmark's main island, Zealand—which you're on) and a church built of flint brings you to the overrated, overfondled, and overphotographed symbol of Copenhagen, *Den Lille Havfrue—The Little Mermaid*.

You can get back downtown on foot, by taxi, or on bus #1, #6, or #9 from Store Kongensgade on the other side of Kastellet Park (a special bus may run from *The Little Mermaid* in summer).

Sights—Copenhagen

▲**City Hall (Rådhus)**—This city landmark, between the station/Tivoli/TI and Strøget pedestrian mall, offers private tours and trips up its 107-meter-tall (350 feet) tower. It's draped, inside and out, in Danish symbolism. Bishop Absalon (the city's founder) stands over the door. The polar bears climbing on the rooftop symbolize the giant Danish protectorate of Greenland. Step inside. The building is inspired by the city hall in Siena, Italy (with the necessary addition of a glass roof). Huge functions fill this grand hall (the iron grill in the center of the floor is an elevator for bringing up 1,200 chairs) while the busts of four illustrious local boys—the storyteller Hans Christian Andersen, the sculptor Bertel Thorvaldsen, the physicist Niels Bohr, and the building's architect Martin Nyrop—look on. Underneath the floor are national archives dating back to 1275—popular with Danes researching their family roots. The city hall is free and open to the public (Mon–Fri 09:30–16:00). You can wander throughout the building and into the peaceful garden out back. Guided tours (in English), which get you into more private, official rooms, are dry but interesting (30 kr, 45 min, year-round Mon–Fri at 15:00, Sat at 10:00 and 11:00). Tourists romp up the tower's 300 steps for the best aerial view of Copenhagen (20 kr, Mon–Fri 10:00, 12:00, and 14:00, Sat 12:00, off-season Mon–Sat 12:00, tel. 33 66 25 82). The lobby has racks of tourist information (city maps and *This Week*).

▲▲**Christiansborg Palace**—A complex of government buildings stands on the ruins of Copenhagen's original 12th-century castle: the Parliament, Supreme Court, Prime Minister's Office, the $65 million new Royal Library, several museums, and the Royal Stables.

While the current palace dates only from 1928 and the royal family moved out 200 years ago, it's the sixth to stand here in 800 years and is rich with tradition. The information-packed 50-minute English-language tours of the royal reception rooms are excellent. As you slip-slide on protect-the-floor slippers through 22 rooms, you'll gain a good feel for Danish history, royalty, and politics. (For instance, the family portrait of King Christian IX shows why he's nicknamed the father-in-law of Europe—with children eventually becoming or marrying royalty in Denmark, Russia, Greece, Britain, France, Germany and Norway.) The highlight is the dazzling set of tapestries—Danish-designed but Gobelin—made in Paris. This gift, given to the queen on her 60th birthday in 2000, celebrates 1,000 years of Danish history with wild wall-hangings from the Viking age to our chaotic age (admission by tour only, 40 kr, May–Sept daily 11:00, 13:00, and 15:00; Oct–April Tue, Thu, and Sat 11:00 and 15:00; from the equestrian statue in front, go through the wooden door, past the entrance to the Christiansborg Castle ruins, into the courtyard, and up the stairs on the right; tel. 33 92 64 92).

▲**Christiansborg Castle ruins**—An exhibit in the scant remains of the first castle built by Bishop Absalon—the 12th-century founder of Copenhagen—lies under the palace. There's precious little to see, but it's old and very well-described (20 kr, daily May–Sept 09:30–16:30, closed off-season Mon, Wed, and Sat, good 1-kr guide). Early birds note that this sight opens 30 minutes before other nearby sights.

▲**Thorvaldsen's Museum**—This museum tells the story and shows the monumental work of the great Danish neoclassical sculptor Bertel Thorvaldsen (1770–1844). Considered Canova's equal among neoclassical sculptors, Thorvaldsen spent 40 years in Rome. He was lured home to Copenhagen with the promise to showcase his work in a fine museum—which opened in the revolutionary year of 1848 as Denmark's first public art gallery (20 kr, Tue–Sun 10:00–17:00, closed Mon, free Wed, well-described, located in neoclassical building with colorful walls next to Christiansborg Palace, tel. 33 32 15 32).

Royal Library—Copenhagen's "Black Diamond" library is a striking black glass building leaning over the harbor at the edge of the palace complex. Wander through the old and new sections, read a magazine, and enjoy a classy—and pricey—lunch (restaurant open Mon–Sat 11:00–22:30, café 10:00–17:00, closed Sun; library hours: Mon–Fri 10:00–19:00, Sat 10:00–14:00, closed Sun, tel. 33 47 47 47).

▲▲▲**National Museum**—Focus on the excellent and curiously

enjoyable Danish collection, which traces this civilization from its ancient beginnings. Exhibits are laid out chronologically and described in English. Pick up the museum map. The free (with deposit) headsets describe the highlights but add nothing to the printed descriptions you'll find inside. Start with room #1 (opposite the entrance) and follow the numbers through the "prehistory" section on the ground floor—oak coffins with still-clothed and armed skeletons from 1300 B.C., ancient and still-playable *lur* horns, the 2,000-year old Gunderstrup Cauldron of art-textbook fame, lots of Viking stuff, and an excellent collection of well-translated rune stones. Then go upstairs, find room #101, and carry on—fascinating material on the Reformation, everyday town life in the 16th and 17th centuries, and, in room 126, a unique "cylinder perspective" of the royal family (from 1656) and two peep shows. The next floor takes you into modern times (40 kr, free Wed, Tue–Sun 10:00–17:00, closed Mon, mandatory bag check, cafeteria, enter at Ny Vestergade 10, tel. 33 13 44 11).

▲**Ny Carlsberg Glyptotek**—Scandinavia's top art gallery—with especially intoxicating Egyptian, Greek, and Etruscan collections; a fine sample of Danish Golden Age (early 19th century) painting; and a heady, if small, exhibit of 19th-century French paintings (in the new "French Wing," including Géricault, Delacroix, Manet, Impressionists, Gauguin before and after Tahiti)—is an impressive example of what beer money can do. Linger with marble gods under the palm leaves and glass dome of the very soothing winter garden. Designers, figuring Danes would be more interested in a lush garden than classical art, used this wonderful space as leafy bait to cleverly introduce locals to a few Greek and Roman statues. (It works for tourists, too.) One of the original Rodin *Thinker*s (wondering how to scale the Tivoli fence?) is in the museum's backyard. This collection is artfully displayed and thoughtfully described (30 kr, free Wed and Sun, Tue–Sun 10:00–16:00, closed Mon, 2-kr English brochure/guide, classy cafeteria under palms, behind Tivoli, Dantes Plads 7, tel. 33 41 81 41).

▲▲**Rosenborg Castle**—This finely furnished Dutch Renaissance–style castle was built by Christian IV in the early 1600s as a summer castle. Today it houses the Danish crown jewels and 500 years of royal knickknacks, including some great Christian IV memorabilia . . . like the shrapnel (removed from his eye and forehead after a naval battle) that he had made into earrings for his girlfriend. It would be fascinating if anything were explained in English. If you don't want to buy and read the palace guidebook or follow Richard Karpen's guided tour (offered Mon and Thu, see "Tours of Copenhagen," above), here are a few highlights:

In the Long Hall, the **throne** is made of unicorn horn (actually narwhal tusk from Greenland). Unicorn horn was believed to bring protection from evil and poison. The military themes decorating the room celebrate Danish victories over archenemy Sweden. The delightful **royal porcelain** display in a side room shows off the herbs and vegetables found in the realm.

The two **treasuries** (downstairs) will dazzle you. In the upper treasury, the two diamond and pearl-studded saddles were Christian IV's—the first for his coronation, the second for his son's wedding (constructed lavishly when the kingdom was nearly bankrupt to impress visiting dignitaries and bolster Denmark's credit rating). See if you can find the golden ring—a gift from a jealous king— with the hand of a promiscuous queen shaking hands with a penis. (Hint: It sits above a brooch of cupid complete with bow and arrow.) In the lower treasury, the tall, two-handed, 16th-century coronation sword was drawn by the new king who cut crosses into the air in four directions, symbolically promising to defend the realm from all attacks. Some consider Christian IV's coronation crown (from 1596, 7 pounds of gold and precious stones) the finest Renaissance crown in Europe. It radiates symbolism. Find: the symbols of justice (sword and scales); charity (a woman nursing— meaning the king will love God and his people as a mother loves her child); and fortitude (a woman on a lion with a sword). Climb the footstool to look inside. The shields of various Danish provinces remind the king that he's surrounded by his realms. The painting shows the coronation of Christian V at Fredericksburg in 1671 (50 kr, daily May–Sept 10:00–16:00, Oct 11:00–15:00, Nov–April 11:00–14:00, S-train: Nørreport, tel. 33 15 32 86).

▲**Rosenborg Gardens**—The Rosenborg Castle is surrounded by the royal pleasure gardens and, on sunny days, a minefield of sun-bathing Danish beauties and picnickers. When the royal family is in residence, there's a daily changing-of-the-guard mini-parade from the Royal Guard's barracks adjoining Rosenborg Castle (at 11:30) to Amalienborg Castle (at 12:00). The Queen's Rose Garden (across the moat from the palace) is a royal place for a picnic (cheap open-face sandwiches to go at Lorraine's, nearby at the corner of Borgergade and Dronningens Tværgade). The fine statue of Hans Christian Andersen in the park, actually erected in his lifetime (and approved by H. C. A.), is meant to symbolize how his stories had a message even for adults.

▲**Denmark's Resistance Museum (Frihedsmuseet)**—The fascinating story of Denmark's heroic Nazi resistance struggle (1940–1945) is well-explained in English. Stop in to gain a differ-ent perspective on World War II (30 kr, May–mid-Sept Tue– Sun 10:00–16:00, off-season Tue–Sun 11:00–15:00, closed Mon, on Churchillparken between the Queen's Palace and *The Little Mermaid*, bus #1, #6, #9, #19, or #29, tel. 33 13 77 14).

▲**Our Savior's (Vor Frelsers) Church**—The church's bright Baroque interior (1696), with the pipe organ supported by the royal elephants, is worth a look (free, helpful English flier,

April–Aug Mon-Sat 11:00–16:30, Sun 12:00-16:30, off-season closes 1 hr earlier, bus #2, #8, #9, #19, Sankt Annægade 29, tel. 32 57 27 98). The unique spiral spire that you'll admire from afar can be climbed for a great city view and a good aerial view of the Christiania commune below (20 kr, 400 steps, 95 meters/311 feet high, closed in bad weather and Nov–March).

Lille Mølle—This tiny, intimate museum shows off a 1916 Christianshavn house (40 kr, visits by guided tour only at 13:00, 14:00, 15:00, 16:00, closed Mon, just off south end of Torvegade at Christianshavn Voldgade, tel. 33 47 38 38). A fine café serves light lunches, dinners, and huge weekend brunches in its terrace garden.

Carlsberg Brewery—Denmark's beloved source of legal intoxicants, Carlsberg welcomes you to its Visitors Center with a free half-liter of beer (Tue-Sun 10:00–16:00, closed Mon, bus #6 or #18, enter at Gamle Carlsbergvej 11, around corner from brewery entrance, tel. 33 27 13 14).

Museum of Erotica—This museum's focus: The love life of *Homo sapiens*. Better than the Amsterdam equivalents, it offers a chance to visit a porno shop and call it a museum. It took some digging, but they've documented a history of sex from Pompeii to present day. Visitors get a peep into the world of 19th-century Copenhagen prostitutes and a chance to read up on the sex lives of Mussolini, Queen Elizabeth, Charlie Chaplin, and Casanova. After reviewing a lifetime of *Playboy* centerfolds and realizing how dull Marilyn Monroe's dress is without her in it, visitors sit down for the arguably artistic experience of watching the "electric *tabernakel*," a dozen silently slamming screens of porn (worth the 69 kr entry fee only if fascinated by sex, daily May–Sept 10:00–23:00, Oct–April 11:00–20:00, a block north of Strøget at Købmagergade 24, tel. 33 12 03 11). For a look at the real thing—unsanitized but free—wander Copenhagen's dreary little red-light district along Istedgade behind the train station.

Hovedbanegården—The great Copenhagen train station is a fascinating mesh of Scandinavian culture and transportation efficiency. Even if you're not a train traveler, check it out.

Nightlife—For the latest on Copenhagen's hopping jazz scene, inquire at the TI or pick up the "alternative" *Playtime* magazine at Use It. The **Copenhagen Jazz House** is a good bet for live jazz (around 90 kr, Tue–Thu and Sun at 20:30, Fri–Sat at 21:30, closed Mon, Niels Hemmingsensgade 10, tel. 33 15 47 00). For blues, try the **Mojo Blues Bar** (daily 20:00–05:00, Løngangsstræde 21 C, tel. 33 11 64 53).

If you'd rather dance, join Denmark's salsa-wave at **Sabor Latino Salsa Club**. Located one block south of the City Hall Square, it offers free salsa lessons in English. Salsa dancing is surprisingly easy to learn in this friendly environment and you'll get a chance to know the fun-loving Danes (20 kr on Thu, 40 kr Fri-Sat,

Thu-Sat at 21:00, free lesson 22:00–23:00, no reservation required, wear comfortable shoes, Vester Voldgade 85, tel. 33 11 97 66).

Tivoli

The world's grand old amusement park—over 150 years old— is 20 acres, 110,000 lanterns, and countless ice-cream cones of fun. You pay one admission price and find yourself lost in a Hans Christian Andersen wonderland of rides, restaurants, games, marching bands, roulette wheels, and funny mirrors. Tivoli is wonderfully Danish. It doesn't try to be Disney (50 kr, April–late Sept Sun–Thu 11:00–24:00, Fri–Sat 11:00–01:00, also open for "Christmas Market" mid-Nov–Dec daily 11:00–22:00—with ice skating on Tivoli Lake, tel. 33 15 10 01, www.tivoli.dk). Rides range in price from 10 to 50 kr (180 kr for all-day pass). All children's amusements are in full swing by 11:30; the rest of the amusements open by 14:00.

Entertainment in Tivoli: Upon arrival (through main entry, on right in shop), pick up a map and events schedule. Take a moment to sit down and plan your entertainment for the evening. Events are spread between 15:00 and 23:00; the 19:30 concert in the concert hall can be free or cost up to 500 kr, depending on the performer. If the Tivoli Symphony is playing, it's worth paying for. (Concert hall tickets include your Tivoli entry, so purchase before entering park—box office tel. 33 15 10 12). Free concerts, pantomime theater, ballet, acrobats, puppets, and other shows pop up all over the park, and a well-organized visitor can enjoy an exciting evening of entertainment without spending a single kroner. The children's theater, Valmuen, plays excellent traditional fairy tales daily at 12:00, 13:00, and 14:00 (13:00 show is in English in summer). Friday evenings feature a (usually free) rock or pop show at 22:00. On Wednesday and Saturday at 23:45, fireworks light up the sky. If you're catching an overnight train, Tivoli (across from the station) is the place to spend your last Copenhagen hours.

Eating at Tivoli: Generally, you'll pay amusement-park prices for amusement park–quality food inside. **Søcafeen**, by the lake, allows picnics if you buy a drink. The *pølse* (sausage) stands are cheap. **Færgekroen** is a good lakeside place for typical Danish food, beer, and an impromptu sing-along with a bunch of drunk Danes. The Croatian restaurant, **Hercegovina**, serves a 129-kr lunch buffet and a 159-kr dinner buffet. For a cake and coffee, consider the **Viften** café. **Georg**, to the left of the Concert Hall, has tasty 40-kr sandwiches and 100-kr dinners (dinner includes glass of wine).

Christiania

In 1971 the original 700 Christianians established squatters' rights in an abandoned military barracks just a 10-minute walk from the Danish parliament building. A generation later this "free city"—

an ultra-human mishmash of 1,000 idealists, anarchists, hippies, dope fiends, nonmaterialists, and people who dream only of being a Danish bicycle seat—not only survives, it thrives. This is a communal cornucopia of dogs, dirt, soft drugs, and dazed people, or a haven of peace, freedom, and no taboos, depending on your perspective. Locals will remind judgmental Americans that a society must make the choice: Allow for alternative lifestyles . . . or build more prisons.

For 25 years Christiania was a political hot potato; no one in the Danish establishment wanted it—or had the nerve to mash it. These days Christiania is connecting better with the rest of society—paying its utilities, taxes, and even offering daily walking tours (see below).

Passing under the city gate you'll find yourself on "Pusher Street" . . . the main drag. This is a line of stalls selling hash, pot, pipes, and souvenirs leading to the market square and a food circus beyond. Make a point of getting past this touristy side of Christiania. You'll find a fascinating ramshackle world of moats and earthen ramparts, alternative housing, unappetizing falafel stands, carpenter shops, hippie villas, children's playgrounds, and peaceful lanes. Be careful to distinguish between real Christianians and Christiania's uninvited guests—motley lowlife vagabonds from other countries who hang out here in the summer, skid row–type Greenlanders, and gawking tourists.

Soft Drugs: While hard drugs are out, hash and pot are sold openly (individual joints—30 kr, senior discounts) and smoked happily. While locals will assure you you're safe within Christiania, they'll remind you that it's risky to take pot out—Denmark is required by Uncle Sam to make a token effort to snare tourists leaving the "free city" with pot. Beefy marijuana plants stand on proud pedestals at the market square. Beyond that an open-air food circus (or the canal-view perch above it, on the earthen ramparts) creates just the right ambience to lose track of time.

Graffiti on the wall declares "a mind is a wonderful thing to waste." If you agree, buy a joint on Pusher Street, buy a drink and light up in a bar that allows smoking, then wander. Find the **Manefiskeren** (Moonfish) bar . . . Brueghel 2002. Cap your evening cruising through Tivoli with an ice-cream cone and singing, "Wonderful Wonderful Copenhagen."

Nitty-Gritty: Christiania is open all the time and visitors are welcome (down Prinsessegade behind Vor Frelsers' spiral church spire in Christianshavn). Photography is absolutely forbidden on Pusher Street (if you value your camera, don't even sneak a photo). Otherwise, you're welcome to snap photos, but ask residents before you photograph them. Guided tours are supposed to leave from the front entrance of Christiania at 15:00 (25 kr, 90 min, daily July–Aug, Sat–Sun rest of year, in English and Danish, tel. 32 57 96 70 to confirm). **Morgenstedet** is a good, cheap vegetarian place (left after Pusher Street). **Spiseloppen** is the classy, good-enough-for-Republicans restaurant (see "Eating," below).

More Sights—Copenhagen

The **National Art Museum** (Statens Museum for Kunst) fills an impressive building with Danish and European paintings from the 14th century until today. Of most interest is probably the Danish Golden Age of paintings—1800–1850 (40 kr, Tue–Sun 10:00–17:00, Wed until 20:00, closed Mon, Solvgade 48, tel. 33 74 84 94).

The noontime **changing of the guard** at the Amalienborg Palace is boring in the summer when the queen is not in residence—all they change is places.

Nyhavn, with its fine old ships, tattoo shops (pop into Tattoo Ole at #17—fun photos, very traditional), and jazz clubs, is a wonderful place to hang out.

The **Round Tower**, built in 1642 by Christian IV, connects a church, library, and observatory (the oldest functioning observatory in Europe) with a ramp that spirals up to a fine view of Copenhagen (15 kr, June–Aug Mon–Sat 10:00–20:00, Sun 12:00–20:00; Sept–May Mon–Sat 10:00–17:00, Sun 12:00–17:00; nothing to see inside but the ramp and the view, just off Strøget on Købmagergade).

Copenhagen's **Open Air Folk Museum (Frilandsmuseet)** is a park filled with traditional Danish architecture and folk culture (40 kr, free Wed, April–Sept Tue–Sun 10:00–17:00, closed Mon, shorter hours off-season, outside of town in the suburb of Lyngby, S-train to Sorgenfri or bus #184 or #194 to Kongevejen 100, Lyngby tel. 33 13 44 11).

Danes gather at Copenhagen's other great amusement park, **Bakken** (free, April–Aug daily 12:00–24:00, S-train: Klampenborg, then walk 10 min through the woods, tel. 39 63 73 00).

For a look at small-town Denmark, consider a trip a few minutes out of Copenhagen to the fishing village of **Dragør** (bus #250s from station 5 stops at Sundbyvesterplads, change to #350s).

Shopping

Copenhagen's colorful flea market is small but feisty and surprisingly cheap (summer Sat 08:00–14:00 at Israels Plads). An antique market enlivens Nybrogade (near Christiansborg Palace) every Friday and Saturday. For other street markets, ask at the TI.

Shops are generally open Monday through Friday from 10:00–19:00 and Saturday from 09:00–16:00. For a street's worth of shops selling "Scantiques," wander down Ravnsborggade from Nørrebrogade.

The city's top department stores (Illum at Østergade 52, tel. 33 14 40 02; and Magasin at Kongens Nytorv 13, tel. 33 11 44 33) offer a good, if expensive, look at today's Denmark. Both are on

Strøget and have fine cafeterias on their top floors. The department stores and the Politiken Bookstore on the Rådhus Square have a good selection of maps and English travel guides.

If you buy anything substantial from a shop displaying the Danish Tax-Free Shopping emblem, you can get back 70 percent of the 25 percent VAT (MOMS in Danish). If you have your purchase mailed, the tax can be deducted from your bill. For example: A 1,000-kr sweater includes 250 kr in MOMS tax, of which you can get 143 kr back. The shop gives you the receipt, you turn it in after customs at the airport, and pocket the cash—fast and simple. For details, call 32 52 55 66 (Mon–Fri 07:00–22:00), see *Copenhagen This Week*, or ask a merchant.

Sleeping in Copenhagen
(9 kr = about $1, country code: 45)

Sleep Code: **S** = Single, **D** = Double/Twin, **T** = Triple, **Q** = Quad, **b** = bathroom, **s** = shower only, **CC** = Credit Cards accepted, **no CC** = Credit Cards not accepted. Breakfast is generally included at hotels but not at private rooms or hostels.

I've listed cheap rooms in private homes in great neighborhoods an easy bus ride from the station, the best budget hotels in the center, and a few backpacker dorm options.

Sleeping in Rooms in Private Homes

Lots of travelers seem shy about rooms in private homes. Don't be. They are as private or social as you want them to be, offering great "at home in Denmark" experiences in good neighborhoods for a third the price of hotels. You'll get a key and come and go as you like. Always call ahead—they book in advance. Most are in apartments, run by single professional women supplementing their income. All speak English and afford a fine peek into Danish domestic life. Rooms generally have no sink. While they usually don't include breakfast, you'll have access to the kitchen. If their rooms are booked up, the women can often find you a place with a neighbor. You can trust the quality of their referrals. I almost always sleep in a private home.

Private Homes in Christianshavn

This area is a never-a-dull-moment hodgepodge of the chic, artistic, hippie, and hobo, with beer-drinking Greenlanders littering streets in the shadow of fancy government ministries. Colorful with lots of shops, cafés, and canals, it's an easy 10-minute walk to the center and has good bus connections to the airport and downtown. There's a **Laundromat** just off Christianshavn's main square at Dronningensgade 42. Take buses #8 or #28 to the central station (from just outside the 7-Eleven store); bus #2 to City Hall; and bus #9 to the airport.

Christianshavn

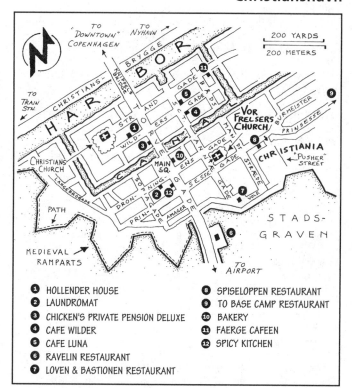

① HOLLENDER HOUSE
② LAUNDROMAT
③ CHICKEN'S PRIVATE PENSION DELUXE
④ CAFE WILDER
⑤ CAFE LUNA
⑥ RAVELIN RESTAURANT
⑦ LOVEN & BASTIONEN RESTAURANT
⑧ SPISELOPPEN RESTAURANT
⑨ TO BASE CAMP RESTAURANT
⑩ BAKERY
⑪ FAERGE CAFEEN
⑫ SPICY KITCHEN

Annette and Rudy Hollender enjoy sharing their 300-year-old home with my readers. Even with a long and skinny staircase, sinkless rooms, and two rooms sharing one toilet/shower, it's a comfortable and cheery place to call home (S-300 kr, D-400 kr, T-550 kr, no CC, half a block off Torvegade at Wildersgade 19, 1408 Copenhagen K, closed Nov–April, tel. 32 95 96 22, e-mail: hollender@adr.dk).

Chicken's Private Pension Deluxe, run by the laid-back Morten Frederiksen, rents five spacious rooms and two four-bed suites in a mod-funky-pleasant old house. The stairs are steep and the furniture is old-time rustic but elegant. It's a clean, comfy, good look at today's hip Danish lifestyle in a great location right on Christianshavn's main drag (S-250–300 kr, D-400 kr, T-550 kr, Q-700 kr, extra bed-100 kr, no CC, Torvegade 36, tel. 32 95 32 73, cellular 20 41 92 73, www.chickens.dk, e-mail: morten@chickens.dk).

South of Christianshavn, **Gitte Kongstad** rents two

apartments, each taking up an entire spacious floor in her flat.
You'll have a kitchenette, little garden, and your own bike (Db-
375 kr, extra bed-125 kr, no CC, family-friendly, bus #9 or #19
from airport, bus #12 or #13 from station, a 10-min pedal past
Christianshavn to Badensgade 2, 2300 Copenhagen, tel. & fax
32 97 71 97, e-mail: g.kongstad@post.tele.dk). While it's not
central, you'll feel at home here, and the bike ride into town (or
to the beach) is a snap.

Private Rooms a Block from Amalienborg Palace

Amaliegade is a stately cobbled street in a quiet neighborhood
(a 10-min walk north of Nyhavn and Strøget). You can look out
your window and see the palace guards changing. Many people
rent rooms to travelers here.

Puk (pook) and Line (lee-nuh) are artistic and professional
women who each rent out two rooms in their wonderfully mod
and Danish flats: **Puk De La Cour** (D-425 kr with breakfast,
no CC, kitchen/family room available, Amaliegade 34, 4th floor,
tel. 33 12 04 68, cellular 23 72 96 45, e-mail: holgerdelacour
@private.dk) and **Line Voutsinos** (May–Sept only, D-450 kr
with breakfast, extra bed-150 kr, no CC, Amaliegade 34, 3rd
floor, tel. & fax 33 14 71 42). Down the street, **Mrs. Thordahl**
also rents rooms (D-350 kr, no breakfast, no CC, Amaliegade 26,
tel. 33 12 05 78).

If you're unable to get a place at any of these homes, the
TI or Use It would love to send you to one from their stable of
locals renting out rooms.

Good Hotels in Central Copenhagen

These are listed in geographical order from the train station.
Prices include breakfast unless noted otherwise. All are big and
modern places with elevators and smoke-free rooms, and all
accept credit cards.

Hotel Nebo, a calm refuge with a friendly welcome and
comfy, spacious rooms, is half a block from the station at the
start of Copenhagen's sleazy street (S-510/450 kr, Sb-820/690 kr,
D-700/520 kr, older Db-920/740 kr, newly renovated Db-1,200/
870 kr, lower prices are for Oct–April, extra bed-250 kr, CC,
Istedgade 6, tel. 33 21 12 17, fax 33 23 47 74, www.nebo.dk,
e-mail: nebo@email.dk).

Hotel Excelsior is similar but with a little less warmth
and slightly higher prices (Sb-995 kr, Db-1,195 kr, CC, a block
from station and a block off busy Vesterbrogade at Colbjørnsens-
gade 6, DK-1652 Copenhagen, tel. 33 24 50 85, fax 33 24 50 87,
www.choicehotels.dk).

Webers Scandic Hotel, my classiest hotel by the train
station, faces busy Vesterbrogade but has a peaceful garden

Copenhagen Hotels

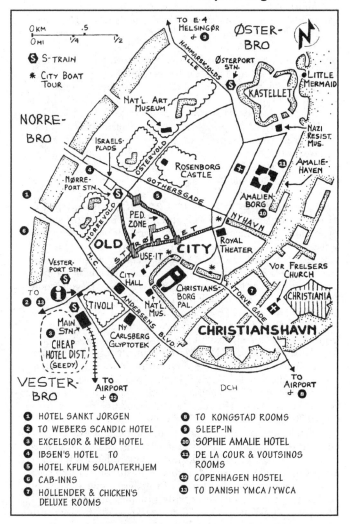

O KM .5
O MI ¼ ½

ⓈS-TRAIN

✳ CITY BOAT TOUR

TO E-4 HELSINGØR ✝ ❾

ØSTER-BRO

HAMMARSKJOLDS ALLE

ØSTERPORT STN.

Ⓢ

LITTLE MERMAID

KASTELLET

NAT'L. ART MUSEUM

NØRRE-BRO

ISRAELS-PLADS

ØSTERVOLD

ROSENBORG CASTLE

NAZI RESIST. MUS.

❶❶ AMALIE-HAVEN

❶

❹ NØRRE-PORT STN. Ⓢ

GOTHERSGADE

❺

AMALIEN-BORG ❶⓪

❻

NØRREVOLD

PED. ZONE

STRØGET

NYHAVN

✳

H.C.

OLD CITY

USE-IT

ROYAL THEATER

VOR FRELSERS CHURCH

VESTER-PORT STN. Ⓢ

CITY HALL

CHRISTIANS BORG PAL.

CHRISTIANIA

TO ❷ ❶❸

Ⓢ

TIVOLI

ANDERSENS BLVD.

NAT'L MUS.

TORVE GADE

❼

CHRISTIANSHAVN

❸ MAIN STN.

CHEAP HOTEL DIST. (SEEDY)

NY CARLSBERG GLYPTOTEK

VESTER-BRO

TO AIRPORT ✝ ❶❷

DCH

TO AIRPORT ✝ ❽

❶ HOTEL SANKT JORGEN
❷ TO WEBERS SCANDIC HOTEL
❸ EXCELSIOR & NEBO HOTEL
❹ IBSEN'S HOTEL TO
❺ HOTEL KFUM SOLDATERHJEM
❻ CAB-INNS
❼ HOLLENDER & CHICKEN'S DELUXE ROOMS

❽ TO KONGSTAD ROOMS
❾ SLEEP-IN
❶⓪ SOPHIE AMALIE HOTEL
❶❶ DE LA COUR & VOUTSINOS ROOMS
❶❷ COPENHAGEN HOSTEL
❶❸ TO DANISH YMCA / YWCA

courtyard (nice for breakfast). It has a modern, inviting interior (high-season rack rates: S-1,095, Sb-1,295–1,495 kr, Db-1,495–1,695 kr; but ask about weekend/summer rates late June–July and Fri–Sun all year, CC, sauna/exercise room, Vesterbrogade 11B, DK-1620 Copenhagen, tel. 33 31 14 32, fax 33 31 14 41, e-mail: webers@scandic-hotels.com).

Ibsens Hotel is an elegant 118-room hotel in a charming neighborhood away from the station commotion and a short walk from the old center (Sb-925–1,025 kr, Db-1,130–1,330 kr, higher prices for bigger rooms, they deal on slow days, third person-200 kr, CC, Vendersgade 23, DK-1363 Copenhagen, bus #14, #16, or #40 from the station, or S-train: Nørreport, tel. 33 13 19 13, fax 33 13 19 16, e-mail: hotel@ibsenshotel.dk).

Sophie Amalie Hotel is a classy and modern Danish-style hotel a block from the big cruise-ship harbor and a block from trendy Nyhavn (134 rooms, Sb-875/1,075/1,275 kr, Db-1,075/1,175/1,275 kr, prices vary with size of room from pretty tight to very spacious, prices include "environmental fee" of 22.50 kr, breakfast-95 kr, CC, but pay with cash and get 10 percent off, Sankt Annae Plads 21, tel. 33 13 34 00, fax 33 11 77 07, www.remmen.dk).

Special Cheaper Hotels in Central Copenhagen

Hotel Sankt Jørgen has 19 big, friendly-feeling rooms with plain old wooden furnishings. Brigitte and Mariane offer a warm welcome and a great value, though the rooms are musty from smokers (S-525 kr, D-625 kr, special prices promised with this book through 2002, third person-175 kr, 5-bed family rooms-1, 150 kr, 10 percent less in winter, breakfast served in your room, CC, elevator, a 12-min walk from station or catch bus #13 to first stop after lake, Julius Thomsensgade 22, DK-1632 Copenhagen V, tel. 35 37 15 11, fax 35 37 11 97, www.dkhotellist.dk/stjorgen/, e-mail: st.jorgen@teliamail.dk).

Hotel KFUM Soldaterhjem, originally for soldiers, rents eight singles and two doubles on the fifth floor, with a soldier-friendly game room (S-315 kr, 425 kr, D-480 kr, extra bed-110 kr, no breakfast, no CC, no elevator, Gothersgade 115, Copenhagen K, tel. 33 15 40 44). The reception is on the first floor up (Mon–Fri 10:00–23:00, Sat–Sun 15:00–23:00).

Cab-Inn is a radical innovation: identical, mostly collapsible, tiny but comfy, cruise ship–type staterooms, all bright, molded, and shiny with TV, coffeepot, shower, and toilet. Each room has a single bed that expands into a twin with one or two fold-down bunks on the walls. The staff will hardly give you the time of day, but it's tough to argue with this efficiency (Sb-510 kr, Db-630 kr, Tb-750 kr, Qb-870 kr, breakfast-50 kr, easy parking-50 kr, CC, www.cab-inn.dk). There are two virtually identical Cab-Inns in the same neighborhood (a 15-min walk northwest of the station): **Cab-Inn Copenhagen** (86 rooms, Danasvej 32-34, 1910 Frederiksberg C, tel. 33 21 04 00, fax 33 21 74 09) and **Cab-Inn Scandinavia** (201 rooms, its "Commodore" rooms have a real double bed for 100-kr extra, Vodroffsvej 55, tel. 35 36 11 11, fax 35 36 11 14).

Sleeping in Hostels

Copenhagen energetically accommodates the young vagabond on a shoestring. The Use It office is your best source of information. Each of these places charges about 100 kr per person for a bed and breakfast. Some don't allow sleeping bags, and if you don't have your own hostel bedsheet you'll normally have to rent one for around 30 kr. IYHF hostels normally sell noncardholders a "guest pass" for 25 kr.

The modern **Copenhagen Amager Hostel** (IYHF) is huge (528 beds), with 275-kr doubles, 390-kr triples, 460-kr quads, and five-bed dorms at 95 kr per bed (nonmembers fee-35 kr/night, sheets-35 kr, no curfew, excellent facilities, breakfast not included, cheap meals, Internet access, self-serve laundry). Unfortunately, it's on the edge of town (30 min from center by bus #250s with change to #100s, Vejlands Alle 200, 2300 Copenhagen S, tel. 32 52 29 08, fax 32 52 27 08, www.danhostel.dk).

The following two big, grungy, central crash pads are open in July and August only: **Danish YMCA/YWCA** (dorm bed-85 kr, 4- to 10-bed rooms, breakfast-35 kr, Valdemarsgade 15, 10-min walk from train station or bus #6, tel. 33 31 15 74) and **Sleep-In** (dorm bed 90 kr plus 20-kr deposit, sheets 30 kr plus 40-kr deposit, 4- or 6-bed cubicles in a huge 452-bed room, no curfew, breakfast-10 kr, lockers, always has room and free condoms, Blegdamsvej 132, bus #1, #6 or #14 to "Triangle" stop and look for sign, tel. 35 26 50 59, www.sleep-in.dk).

Sleep-in Green, the "ecological hostel," is very young and cool. It's open all year (100-kr bunks, sheets-30 kr, organic breakfast-30 kr, in a quiet spot a 15-min walk from the center, off Norrebrogade at Ravnsborggade 18, tel. 35 37 77 77).

Eating in Copenhagen

Picnics

Viktualiehandler (small delis) and bakeries, found on nearly every corner, sell fresh bread, tasty pastries (a *wienerbrød* is what we call a "Danish"), juice, milk, cheese, and yogurt (drinkable, in tall liter boxes). **Irma** (in arcade on Vesterbrogade next to Tivoli) and **Brugsen** are the two largest supermarket chains. **Netto** is a cut-rate outfit with the cheapest prices. The little grocery store in the central station is expensive but handy (daily 08:00–24:00).

Smørrebrød

Denmark's 300-year-old tradition of open-face sandwiches survives. Find a *smørrebrød* take-out shop and choose two or three that look good (around 15 kr each). You'll get them wrapped and ready for a park bench. With a cold drink, it makes for a fine, quick, and very Danish lunch. Tradition calls for three sandwich courses: herring first, then meat, then cheese. Downtown you'll find these handy local alternatives to Yankee fast-food chains: **Tria Cafe** (Mon–Fri 08:00–14:00, closed Sat–Sun, Gothersgade 12, near Kongens Nytorv); **Café Halvvejen** for sit-down *smørrebrød* (lunch only, on Krystalgade near the Round Tower); and, my favorite, **Domhusets Smørrebrød** (Mon–Fri 07:00–14:30, Kattesundet 18, tel. 33 15 98 98).

The Pølse

The famous Danish hot dog, sold in *pølsevogn* (sausage wagons) throughout the city, is another typically Danish institution that has resisted the onslaught of our global, Styrofoam-packaged, fast-food culture. Study the photo menu for variations of the Danish hot dog. These are fast, cheap, tasty, and—like their American cousins—almost worthless nutritionally. Even so, what the locals call the "dead man's finger" is the dog kids love to bite.

There's more to getting a *pølse* than simply ordering a hotdog. Employ these handy phrases: *rød* (red, the basic weenie); *medister* (spicy, better quality); *knæk* (short, stubby, tastier than *rød*); *ristet* (fried); *brød* (a bun, usually smaller than the sausage); *svøb* ("swaddled" in bacon); *Fransk* (French style, buried in a long skinny hole in the bun with sauce); and *flottenheimer* (a fat one with onions and sauce). *Sennep* is mustard and *ristet løg* are crispy, fried onions. Wash everything down with a *sodavand* (soda pop).

By hanging around a *pølsevogn* you can study this institution. Denmark's "cold feet cafés" are a form of social care: People who have difficulty finding jobs are licensed to run these wienermobiles. As they gain seniority they are promoted to work at more central locations. Danes like to gather here for munchies and *pølsesnak* ("sausage talk"), the local slang for empty chatter.

Inexpensive Restaurants near Strøget

Riz-Raz, around the corner from the canal boat rides at Kompagnistræde 20, serves a healthy all-you-can-eat 49-kr Mediterranean/vegetarian buffet lunch (daily 11:30–17:00) and an even bigger 59-kr dinner buffet (until 24:00, tel. 33 15 05 75). The dinner has to be the best deal in town. And they're happy to serve free water with your meal.

Det Lille Apotek, the "little pharmacy," is a reasonable, candlelit place that's been popular with locals for 200 years (sandwich lunches, traditional dinners for 100–150 kr nightly from 17:30, just off Strøget, between Frue Church and Round Tower at St. Kannikestræde 15, tel. 33 12 56 06). Their specialty is "Stone Beef," a big slab of tender, raw steak plopped down in front of you on a scalding-hot lava stone. Flip it over a few times and it's cooked within minutes.

Den Grimme Aelling is a practical place offering an inviting red meat and salad buffet for 115 kr (daily 12:00–15:00, 17:30–22:30, across from Det Lille Apotek at Store Kannikestraede 19, tel. 33 11 20 30).

Cafe Norden, smoky and very Danish with fine pastries, overlooks Amagertorv by the swan fountain. They have good light meals and salads and great people-watching from window seats on the second floor (order at the bar upstairs).

Grabrodretorv is perhaps the most popular square in the old center for a meal. It's a food circus—especially in good weather. Choose from Greek, Mexican, Danish, or a meal in the old streetcar #14.

At **El Porron**, you'll find good Spanish tapas (Vendersgade 10, a block from Ibsen's Hotel near Nørreport).

Department stores serving cheery, reasonable meals in their cafeterias include **Illum** (head to the elegant glass-domed top floor, Østergade 52) and **Magasin** (Kongens Nytorv 13).

Gammel Strand serves "Danish-inspired French" cuisine and is ideal for a dressy splurge in the old center (3-course *menu*-300 kr, Mon–Sat 17:30–22:00, closed Sun, reservations wise, across from the canal tour boats at Gammel Strand 42, tel. 33 91 21 21).

To explore your way through a world of traditional Danish food, try a Danish *koldt bord* (an all-you-can-eat buffet) at **Pilegaarden** (just off the walking street near Kongens Nytorv at Pilestraede 44, Tue-Sat 12:00-17:00, tel. 33 15 48 80). The central station's **Bistro Restaurant** is handy but touristy (150-kr dinner, served daily 11:30–22:00, tel. 33 69 21 12).

Eating in Christianshavn

This neighborhood is so cool, it's worth combining an evening wander with dinner even if you don't live here.

Faerge Cafeen is a fun-loving pub with a local following serving inexpensive traditional Danish specialties indoors or along the canal (daily specials about 70 kr, daily 17:00–21:00, Strandgade 50, tel. 32 54 46 24).

Twin cafés serve creative and hearty dinner salads by candlelight to a trendy local clientele: **Café Wilder** serves a three-salad plate (61 kr with bread) and a budget dinner plate for around 85 kr (tel. 32 54 71 83). Across the street, **Luna Café** is also good and serves a slower-paced meal. Each are open daily until 24:00 (reservations recommended, tel. 32 54 20 00) and located at the corner of Wildersgade and Skt. Annæ Gade, a block off Torvegade.

Ravelin Restaurant, on a tiny island on the big road just south of Christianshavn, serves good and traditional Danish-style food at reasonable prices to happy local crowds. Either dine indoors or on the lovely lakeside terrace (*smørrebrød* lunches 40–100 kr, dinners 100–170 kr, Torvegade 79, tel. 32 96 20 45).

Bastionen & Løven, at the little windmill (Lille Mølle), serves Scandinavian Nouveau cuisine on a Renoir terrace or in its Rembrandt interior (55-kr lunch specials, 130–200-kr dinners, 285 kr for 3-course *menu*, *menu* is small but fresh, daily 10:00–24:00, Voldgade 50, walk to the end of Torvegade and follow the ramparts up to the restaurant, at south end of Christianshavn, tel. 32 95 09 40).

Lagkagehuset, with a big selection of pastries and excellent fresh-baked bread and sandwiches, is a great place for breakfast (take-out coffee and pastries for 15 kr, Torvegade 45). **Spicy Kitchen** serves cheap and good Indian food (Torvegade 56).

In Christiania, the wonderfully classy **Spiseloppen** (meaning "the flea eats") serves great 120-kr vegetarian meals and 150-kr meaty ones by candlelight. Christiania is the free city/squatter town, located three blocks behind the spiral spire of Vor Frelser's church (restaurant open Tue–Sun 17:00–22:00, closed Mon, on top floor of old brick warehouse, turn right just inside Christiania's gate, reservations often necessary on weekends, tel. 32 57 95 58).

Base Camp lets you eat/drink/party in a military barracks converted into a sprawling restaurant with enough seating for you and 800 travel companions. Dance under an enormous disco ball inside, or settle a lounge chair into the sand at a grill table where you choose some tapas and a slab of raw meat or fish to cook (about 150 kr). Tucked away 400 meters past Christiania (go 400 meters out Prinsessegade, cross the hidden canal at Trangravsvej, look right), it's a great place to mingle with young, festive Danes (dinners from 18:00, closed Mon–Tue, disco usually Fri–Sat, occasionally closes for private parties, call ahead for evening's events, tel. 70 23 23 28).

Transportation Connections—Copenhagen

By train to: Hillerød/Frederiksborg (6/hr, 30 min), **Louisiana Museum** (Helsingør train to Humlebæk, 3/hr, 30 min), **Roskilde** (1–3/hr, 30 min), **Odense** (2/hr, 2 hrs), **Helsingør** (40/day, 50 min), **Stockholm** (5/day, 8 hrs), **Oslo** (4/day, 9 hrs), **Växjö** (10/day, 5 hrs, via Alvesta), **Kalmar** (10/day, 7 hrs, via Alvesta and Växjö), **Berlin** (4/day, 9 hrs, via Hamburg), **Amsterdam** (2/day, 11 hrs), and **Frankfurt/Rhine** (4/day, 8 hrs). Convenient overnight trains from Copenhagen run directly to Stockholm, Oslo, Amsterdam, and Frankfurt. National train info tel. 70 13 14 15. International train info tel. 70 13 14 16. Cheaper bus trips are listed at Use It.

PARIS

Paris offers sweeping boulevards, sleepy parks, world-class art galleries, chatty crêpe stands, Napoleon's body, sleek shopping malls, the Eiffel Tower, and people watching from outdoor cafés. Climb the Notre-Dame and the Eiffel Tower, cruise the Seine and the Champs-Elysées, and master the Louvre and Orsay Museums. Save some after-dark energy for one of the world's most romantic cities. Many people fall in love with Paris. Some see the essentials and flee, overwhelmed by the huge city. With the proper approach and a good orientation, you'll fall head over heels for Europe's capital city.

Planning Your Time
Paris in One, Two, or Three Days

Day 1
Morning: Follow "Historic Core of Paris" Walk (see "Sights," below), featuring Ile de la Cité, Notre-Dame, Latin Quarter, and Sainte-Chapelle (consider lunch at nearby Samaritaine view café).
Afternoon: Visit the Pompidou Center (at least from the outside), then walk to the Marais neighborhood: visit the place des Vosges and consider touring the Carnavalet Museum or the Jewish Art and History Museum nearby.
Evening: Cruise Seine River or take Paris by Night bus tour.

Day 2
Morning: Follow Champs-Elysées Walk from Arc de Triomphe down the grand Champs-Elysées boulevard to Tuileries Gardens.
Afternoon: Complete your walk through the Tuileries (several lunch cafés in the park), then tour the Louvre.
Evening: Enjoy Trocadero scene and twilight ride up Eiffel Tower.

Daily Reminder

Monday: The catacombs and these museums are closed today—Orsay, Rodin, Marmottan, Montmartre, Carnavalet, and Versailles; the Louvre is especially crowded, but the Richelieu wing stays open until 21:45. Some small stores don't open until 14:00. The rue Cler market is dead. Some restaurants and banks are closed. It's discount night at most cinemas.

Tuesday: Many museums are closed today, including the Louvre, Picasso, Cluny, and Pompidou Center. The Eiffel Tower, Orsay, and Versailles are particularly busy today.

Wednesday: All sights are open, the Louvre until 21:45. The weekly *Pariscope* magazine comes out today. School is out, so many child-related sights are open (and busy). Some cinemas offer discounts.

Thursday: All sights are open (except the Sewer Tour). The Orsay is open until 21:45. Department stores are open late.

Friday: All sights are open (except the Sewer Tour). Afternoon trains and roads leaving Paris are crowded; TGV reservation fees are higher.

Saturday: All sights are open (except the Jewish Art and History Museum). The fountains run at Versailles (July–Sept). Department stores are busy. The Jewish Quarter is quiet.

Sunday: Some museums are two-thirds price all day and/or free the first Sunday of the month, thus more crowded (e.g., Louvre, Orsay, Rodin, Cluny, Pompidou, and Picasso). The fountains run at Versailles (early April–early Oct). Most of Paris' stores are closed on Sunday, but shoppers will find relief in the lively Marais neighborhood—the Jewish Quarter—and in Bercy Village where many stores are open. Look for organ concerts at St. Sulpice and possibly other churches. The American Church usually offers a free evening concert at 18:00 (Sept–May). Most recommended restaurants in the rue Cler neighborhood are closed for dinner.

Day 3
Morning: Tour the Orsay Museum.
Afternoon: Either tour the Rodin Museum and Napoleon's Tomb or visit Versailles (take RER direct from Orsay).
Evening: Take Montmartre Walk, featuring Sacré-Coeur.

Orientation

Paris is split in half by the Seine River, divided into 20 *arrondissements* (proud and independent governmental jurisdictions), and circled by a ring-road freeway (the *périphérique*). You'll find Paris easier to navigate if you know which side of the river you're on, which *arrondissement* you're in, and which subway (Métro) stop you're closest to. If you're north of the river (the top half of any city map), you're on the Right Bank (*rive droite*). If you're south of it, you're on the Left Bank (*rive gauche*). Most of your sightseeing will take place within five blocks of the river.

Arrondissements are numbered, starting at Notre-Dame (ground zero) and moving in a clockwise spiral out to the ring road. The last two digits in a Parisian zip code are the *arrondissement* number. The notation for the Métro stop is "Mo." In Parisian jargon, Napoleon's tomb is on *la rive gauche* (the Left Bank) in the *7ème* (7th *arrondissement*), zip code 75007, Mo: Invalides. Paris Métro stops are used as a standard aid in giving directions, even for those not using the Métro. As you're tracking down addresses, these definitions will help: *place* (square), *rue* (road), and *pont* (bridge).

Tourist Information

Avoid the Paris tourist offices—long lines, short information, and a €0.75 charge for maps. This book, the *Pariscope* magazine (described below), and one of the freebie maps available at any hotel are all you need. The main TI is at 127 avenue des **Champs-Elysées** (daily 09:00–20:00, tel. 08 36 68 31 12—phone tree, or 01 49 52 53 10), but the other TIs are less crowded: at **Gare de Lyon** (daily 08:00–20:00, tel. 08 92 68 31 12, wait for English recording), at the **Eiffel Tower** (May–Sept daily 11:00–18:42, yes, 18:42, closed off-season, tel. 01 45 51 22 15), and at the **Louvre** (Wed–Mon 10:00–19:00, closed Tue). Both **airports** have handy TIs (called ADP) with long hours and short lines (see "Transportation Connections," below). For a complete list of museum hours and scheduled English-language museum tours, pick up the free *Musées, Monuments Historiques, et Expositions* booklet from any museum.

Pariscope: The *Pariscope* weekly magazine (or one of its clones, €0.50 at any newsstand) lists museum hours, art exhibits, concerts, music festivals, plays, movies, and nightclubs. Smart tour guides and sightseers rely on this for all the latest (www.pariscope.fr in French).

Web Sites: This short list is entertaining and at times useful: **www.bonjourparis.com** (a newsy site that claims to offer a virtual trip to Paris with interactive French lessons, tips on wine and food, and news on the latest Parisian trends), **www.paris-touristoffice.com** (the official site for Paris' TIs, offering practical information on hotels, special events, museums, children's activities, fashion, nightlife, and more), and **www.paris-anglo.com** (similar to bonjourparis.com with informative stories on visiting Paris, plus a directory of over 2,500 English-friendly businesses).

Maps: While Paris is littered with free maps, they don't

Paris Overview

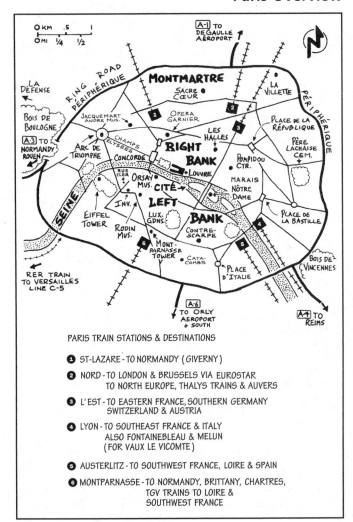

PARIS TRAIN STATIONS & DESTINATIONS

❶ ST-LAZARE - TO NORMANDY (GIVERNY)

❷ NORD - TO LONDON & BRUSSELS VIA EUROSTAR
TO NORTH EUROPE, THALYS TRAINS & AUVERS

❸ L'EST - TO EASTERN FRANCE, SOUTHERN GERMANY
SWITZERLAND & AUSTRIA

❹ LYON - TO SOUTHEAST FRANCE & ITALY
ALSO FONTAINEBLEAU & MELUN
(FOR VAUX LE VICOMTE)

❺ AUSTERLITZ - TO SOUTHWEST FRANCE, LOIRE & SPAIN

❻ MONTPARNASSE - TO NORMANDY, BRITTANY, CHARTRES,
TGV TRAINS TO LOIRE &
SOUTHWEST FRANCE

show all the streets. You may want the huge Michelin #10 map of
Paris. For an extended stay, I prefer the pocket-size, street-indexed
Paris Pratique (€6) with an easy-to-use Métro map.

Bookstores: There are many English-language bookstores
in Paris where you can pick up guidebooks (for nearly double
their American price), including: Shakespeare & Company (daily

12:00–24:00, some used travel books, 37 rue de la Boucherie, across river from Notre-Dame, tel. 01 43 26 96 50), W. H. Smith (248 rue de Rivoli, Mo: Concorde, tel. 01 44 77 88 99), and Brentanos (37 avenue de L'Opéra, Mo: Opéra, tel. 01 42 61 52 50).

American Church: The American Church is a nerve center for the American émigré community. It distributes a free, handy, and insightful monthly English-language newspaper called the *Paris Voice* (with useful reviews of concerts, plays, and current events; available at about 200 locations in Paris, www.parisvoice.com) and an advertisement paper called *France—U.S.A. Contacts* (full of useful information for those seeking work or long-term housing). The church faces the river between the Eiffel Tower and Orsay Museum (reception open Mon–Sat 09:30–22:30, Sun 09:00–19:30, 65 quai d'Orsay, Mo: Invalides, tel. 01 40 62 05 00).

Arrival in Paris

By Train: Paris has six train stations, all connected by Métro, bus, and taxi. All have ATMs, banks or change offices, information desks, telephones, cafés, lockers (*consigne automatique*), newsstands, and clever pickpockets. Hop the Métro to your hotel (see "Getting around Paris," below).

By Plane: For detailed information on getting from Paris' airports to downtown Paris (and vice versa), see "Transportation Connections" at the end of this chapter.

Helpful Hints

Theft Alert: Use your money belt and never carry a wallet in your back pocket or a purse over your shoulder. Thieves thrive in tourist areas and the Métro (at stations and in subway cars).

Museums: Most museums offer reduced prices on Sunday. Many sights stop admitting people 30 to 60 minutes before they close, and many begin closing rooms 45 minutes before the actual closing time. For the fewest crowds, visit very early, at lunch, or very late. Most museums have slightly shorter hours October through March. French holidays can really mess up your sightseeing plans (Jan 1, May 1, May 8, July 14, Nov 1, Nov 11, and Dec 25). See "Daily Reminder" in this chapter for other "closed" days. The best Impressionist art museums are the Orsay, Orangerie, and Marmottan.

Paris Museum Pass: In Paris there are two classes of sightseers: those with a museum pass and those who stand in line. Serious sightseers save time and money by getting this pass. Sold at museums, main Métro stations (including Ecole Militaire and Bastille stations), and TIs, it pays for itself in two admissions and gets you into most sights with no lining up (€13/1 day, €26/3 consecutive days, €39/5 consecutive days; no youth discounts). You can buy one on any day at any sight where it's valid (though supply can be limited at big sights like the Louvre, best to buy elsewhere). The pass is not activated until the first time you use it (you enter the date on the pass).

Included sights (and entry fee without the pass) you're likely to visit: Louvre (€7), Orsay (€7), Sainte-Chapelle (€5.50), Arc de Triomphe (€6), L'Orangerie (€6), Napoleon's Tomb and Les Invalides (€6), Carnavalet Museum (€5.50), Conciergerie (€5.50), Sewer Tour (€4), Cluny Museum (€6), Pompidou Center (€5), Notre-Dame towers (€5.50) and crypt (€3), Picasso Museum (€5), and Rodin Museum (€4). Outside Paris, the pass covers Versailles (€7) and its Trianons (€5), Château de Fontainebleau (€5.50), and Château Chantilly (€6). Notable sights not covered: Eiffel Tower, Montparnasse Tower, Marmottan Museum, Garnier Opéra, Jacquemart-André Museum, Jewish Art and History Museum, Grande Arche at La Défense, Jeu de Paume Exhibition Hall, Catacombs, new Paris story film, and the ladies of Pigalle.

Tally it up—but remember, an advantage of the pass is that you skip to the front of virtually all lines, saving hours of waiting, especially in summer (though everyone must pass through the slow-moving metal-detector lines, and some places can't accommodate a bypass lane, such as Notre-Dame's tower). With the pass, you'll pop painlessly into sights that you're walking by (even for a few minutes) that might otherwise not be worth the expense (e.g., Paris crypt, Conciergerie, Victor Hugo's House, Panthéon). Try to avoid buying your museum pass at a major museum, where supply can be spotty and lines long—remember they are sold at TIs, including those at the airports, and at key Métro stations. The free museum and monuments directory that comes with your pass lists the latest hours, phone numbers, and specifics on what kids pay. The cutoff age for free entry varies from 5 to 18. Most major art museums in Paris admit young people under 18 in for free.

Telephone Cards: Pick up the essential France *télécarte* at any *tabac* (tobacco shop), post office, newsstand, or TI (*une petite télécarte* is about €7; *une grande* is about €15). Smart travelers check things by telephone. Most public phones use *télécartes*. France's latest phone card, Kertel (pron: care-tel), allows you to dial from any phone, even from your hotel room (sold wherever *télécartes* are sold).

Useful Telephone Numbers: American Hospital—01 46 41 25 25, English-speaking pharmacy—01 45 62 02 41 (24 hrs, Mo: Georges V), Police—17, U.S. Embassy—01 43 12 22 22, Paris and France directory assistance—12, AT&T operator— 0800 99 00 11, MCI—0800 99 00 19, Sprint—0800 99 00 87.

Toilets: Carry small change for pay toilets, or walk into any sidewalk café like you own the place and find the toilet in the back. The toilets in museums are free and generally the best you'll find, and, if you have a museum pass, you can drop into almost any museum for the clean toilets. Modern, supersanitary, street-booth toilets provide both relief and a memory (coins required, don't leave small children inside unattended). Keep some toilet paper or tissues with you as some toilets are poorly supplied.

Getting around Paris

By Métro: Europe's best subway is divided into two systems— the Métro (for puddle-jumping everywhere in Paris) and the RER (which connects suburban destinations with a few stops in central Paris). You'll be using the Métro for almost all your trips (runs daily from 05:30–00:30). Occasionally you'll find the RER more convenient as it makes fewer stops (like an express bus).

In Paris you're never more than a 10-minute walk from a Métro station. One ticket takes you anywhere in the system with unlimited transfers. Save 40 percent by buying a *carnet* (car-nay) of 10 tickets for €9 at any Métro station (a single ticket is €1.30, kids 4–10 pay €4.75 for a *carnet*). Métro tickets work on city buses, though one ticket cannot be used as a transfer between subway and bus.

The new, overpriced, single or multiday *Paris Visite* Métro pass gives you free run of all Métro, RER, and bus routes in central Paris (and discounts at minor sights). You're better off buying *carnets* of 10 tickets (see above) and getting three days' use out of one *carnet* (most travelers use 3–4 tickets/day). The *Paris Visite* pass covers three progressively larger zones (zones 1–3, 1–5, and 1–8; sold at any Métro station, no photo required). Zones 1 through 3 include central Paris and virtually all tourist needs (1 day-€8.50 for adults/ €4.50 for kids under 12; 2 days-€13.75/€7; 3 days-€18.30/€9; and 5 days-€27/€13.75; no 4-day option). Zones 4 through 8 add suburban destinations, such as Versailles, Disneyland Paris, and the airports, for which you're better off buying individual tickets. The pass begins when you validate it (on bus or at Métro turnstile) and lasts for the consecutive number of days purchased. Note that tourists can no longer can buy the cheaper *Carte Orange* week- or month-long passes; these are now available only for French residents.

To get to your destination, determine the closest "Mo" stop and which line or lines will get you there. The lines have numbers, but they're best known by their direction or end-of-the-line stop. (For example, the La Défense/Château de Vincennes line runs between La Défense in the west and Vincennes in the east.)

Once in the Métro station, you'll see blue-and-white signs directing you to the train going in your direction (e.g., "direction: La Défense"). Insert your ticket in the automatic turnstile, pass through, and reclaim and keep your ticket until you exit the system. Fare inspectors regularly check for cheaters and accept absolutely no excuses from anyone. I repeat, keep that ticket until you leave the Métro system.

Transfers are free and can be made wherever lines cross.

Paris

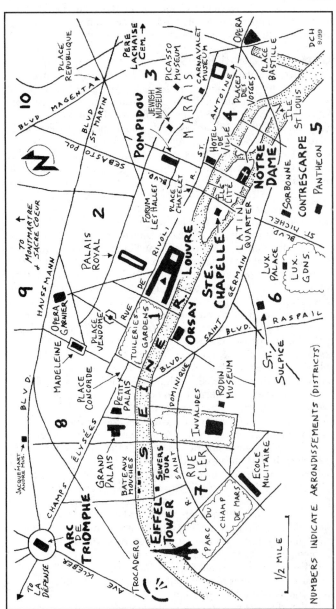

Key Words for the Métro and RER

- *direction* (dee-rek-see-ohn): direction
- *ligne* (leen-yuh): line
- *correspondance* (kor-res-pohn-dahns): transfer
- *sortie* (sor-tee): exit
- *carnet* (kar-nay): cheap set of 10 tickets
- *Pardon, madame/monsieur* (par-dohn, mah-dahm/mes-yur): Excuse me, lady/bud.
- *Je descend* (juh day-sahn): I'm getting off.
- *Donnez-moi mon porte-monnaie!*: Give me back my wallet!

Etiquette

- When waiting at the platform, get out of the way of those exiting their train. Board only once everyone is off.
- Avoid using the hinged seats when the car is jammed; they take up valuable standing space.
- In a crowded train, try not to block the exit. If you're blocking the door when the train stops, step out of the car and to the side, let others off, then get back on.
- Talk softly in the cars. Listen to how quietly Parisians can communicate and follow their lead.
- When leaving or entering a station, hold the door open for the person behind you.
- On escalators, stand on the right, pass on the left.

When you transfer, look for the orange *correspondance* (connections) signs when you exit your first train, then follow the proper direction sign.

Before you *sortie* (exit), check the helpful *plan du quartier* (map of the neighborhood) to get your bearings, locate your destination, and decide which *sortie* you want. At stops with several *sorties*, you can save lots of walking by choosing the best exit.

Thieves spend their days in the Métro. Be on guard. For example, if your pocket is picked as you pass through a turnstile, you end up stuck on the wrong side while the thief strolls away. Any jostle or commotion (especially when boarding or leaving trains) is likely the sign of a thief or team of thieves in action.

Paris has a huge homeless population and over 11 percent unemployment; expect a warm Métro welcome from panhandlers, musicians, and those selling magazines produced by the homeless community.

By RER: The RER (*Réseau Express Régionale*, pron. air-ay-air) is the suburban train system serving destinations such as Versailles, Disneyland Paris, and the airports. These routes are indicated by thick lines on your subway map and identified by letters A, B, C, and so on. The RER works like the Métro but can be speedier (if it serves your destination directly) because it makes only a few stops within the city. One Métro ticket is all you need for RER rides within central Paris. You can transfer between the Métro and RER systems with the same ticket. Unlike the Métro, you need to insert your ticket in a turnstile to exit the RER system, and, also unlike in the Métro, signage can vary between RER stations, meaning you have to pay attention and verify that you're heading the right direction (RER lines often split at the end of the line, leading to different signed *Destinations*—study your map and you'll do fine*).* To travel outside the city (to Versailles or the airport, for example), you'll need to buy a separate, more expensive ticket at the station window before boarding; make sure your stop is served by checking the signs over the train platform (not all trains serve all stops).

By City Bus: The trickier bus system is worth figuring out. Métro tickets are good on both bus and Métro, though you can't use the same ticket to transfer between the two systems. One ticket gets you anywhere in central Paris, but, if you leave the city center (shown as zone 1 on the diagram on board the bus), you must validate a second ticket. While the Métro shuts down about 00:30, some buses continue much later. Schedules are posted at bus stops. Handy bus-system maps (*plan des autobus*) are available in any Métro station and are provided in your *Paris Pratique* map book if you invest (€6).

Big system maps, posted at each bus and Métro stop, display the routes. Individual route diagrams show the exact routes of the lines serving that stop. Major stops are painted on the side of each bus. Enter through the front doors. Punch your Métro ticket in the machine behind the driver, or pay the higher cash fare. Get off the bus using the rear door. Even if you're not certain you've figured it out, do some joyriding (outside of rush hour). Lines #24, #63, and #69 are Paris' most scenic routes and make a great introduction to the city. Bus #69 is particularly handy, running between the Eiffel Tower, rue Cler (recommended hotels), Orsay, Louvre, Marais (recommended hotels), and Père Lachaise Cemetery. The handiest bus routes are listed for each hotel area recommended (see "Sleeping," below).

By Taxi: Parisian taxis are almost reasonable. A 10-minute ride costs about €8 *sans baggage* (versus €1 to get anywhere in town on the Métro). You can try waving one down (a glowing white light on the roof means it's free), but it's easier to ask your hotel to call for you or ask for the nearest taxi stand (*Où est une station de taxi?*; oo ay oon stah-see-ohn duh taxi). Taxi stands are indicated by a circled *T* on many city maps, including Michelin's #10 Paris. A typical taxi takes up to three people (maybe 4 if you're polite and pay €2 extra);

groups can use a *grand taxi*, which must be booked in advance (ask your hotel to call). If a taxi is summoned by phone, the meter starts as soon as the call is received. Higher rates are charged at night from 19:00 to 07:00, all day Sunday, and to either airport. There's a €1 charge for each piece of baggage. For a tip, round up to the nearest euro (minimum €0.50. Taxis are tough to find on Friday and Saturday nights, especially after the Métro closes (around 00:30). If you need to catch a train or flight early in the morning, consider booking a taxi the night before.

By Foot: Be careful! Parisian drivers are notorious for ignoring pedestrians. Never assume you have the right-of-way, even in a crosswalk. When crossing a street, keep your pace constant and don't stop suddenly. By law, drivers must miss pedestrians by one meter/three feet (1.5 meters/5 feet in the countryside). Drivers carefully calculate your speed and won't hit you, provided you don't alter your route or pace. Watch out for a lesser hazard: *merde*. Parisian dogs decorate the city's sidewalks with 16 tons of droppings a day. People get injured by slipping in it.

Organized Tours of Paris

Bus Tours: Paris Vision offers handy bus tours of Paris, day and night (advertised in hotel lobbies); its "Illuminated Paris" tour is much more interesting (see "Nightlife in Paris," below). Far better daytime bus tours are the hop-on hop-off double-decker bus services connecting Paris' main sights while providing running commentary (ideal in good weather when you can sit on top; see also Bâteau-Bus under "Boat Tours," below).

Two companies provide this service: **L'Open Tours** and **Les Cars Rouges** (pick up their brochures showing routes and stops from any TI or on their buses). The yellow buses of L'Open Tours provide more extensive coverage, with three different routes rolling by most of the important sights in Paris (the Paris Grand Tour offers the best introduction). Tickets are good for any route. Buy your tickets from the driver (€23/1-day ticket, €25/2-day ticket, kids 4–11 pay €11.50 for 1 or 2 days). Two or three buses depart hourly from about 10:00 to 18:00; expect to wait 10 to 20 minutes at each stop. You can hop off at any stop, then catch a later bus following the same circuit. You'll see these bright yellow, topless double-decker buses all over town—pick one up at the first important sight you visit, or start your tour at the Eiffel Tower stop (the first street on nonriver side of the tower, tel. 01 42 66 56 56). **Les Cars Rouges'** bright red buses offer largely the same service with fewer stops on a single, Grand Tour Route for less money (2-day tickets, €21-adult, €10-kids 4–12, tel. 01 53 95 39 53).

Boat Tours: Several companies offer one-hour boat cruises on the Seine (by far, best at night). The huge, mass-production **Bâteaux-Mouches** boats depart every 20 to 30 minutes from pont de l'Alma's right bank, the centrally located pont Neuf, and right in front of the Eiffel Tower, and are convenient to rue Cler hotels (€7, €4 for ages 4–12 and over 65, daily 10:00–22:30, useless taped explanations in 6 languages and tour groups by the dozens, tel. 01 42 25 96 10). The smaller and more intimate **Vedettes de pont Neuf** depart only once an hour from the center of the pont Neuf (twice an hour after dark), but they come with a live guide giving explanations in French and English and are convenient to Marais and Contrescarpe hotels (€8.50, €4 for ages 4–12 and over 65, tel. 01 46 33 98 38). From early April to early November, **Bâteau-Bus** operates boats on the Seine, connecting seven key stops about every 25 minutes: Eiffel Tower, Champs-Elysées, Orsay/place de la Concorde, Louvre, Notre-Dame, Hôtel de Ville, and St. Germain-des-Près. Pick up a schedule at any stop (or TI) and use the boats as a scenic alternative to the Métro. Tickets are available for one day (€10, €5.50 under 12) and two days (€12, €6 under 12). Boats run from 10:00 to 19:00, and until 21:00 June through September. **Paris Canal** departs twice daily for three-hour, one-way cruises between the Orsay and Parc de la Vilette. You'll cruise up the Seine, then along a quiet canal through nontouristy Paris, accompanied by English explanations (€15, €8.50 for kids 4–11, €11.50 for ages 12–25). One-way trips depart from near the Orsay at 09:30 from quai Anatole France, and from Parc de la Vilette (at Folie des Visites du Parc) at 14:30 (tel. 01 42 40 96 97).

Walking Tours: Paris Walking Tours offers a variety of excellent two-hour walks nearly daily for €10 (tel. 01 48 09 21 40 for recorded schedule in English, fax 01 42 43 75 51, www .pariswalkingtours.com). They focus on the Marais, Luxembourg Gardens, Garnier Opéra, Montmartre, and Hemingway's Paris. Ask about their family-friendly tours. Call ahead a day or two to learn their schedule and starting point. No reservations are required. These are thoughtfully prepared, humorous, and relaxing walking tours led by British or American guides. Don't hesitate to stand close to the guide to hear. For Lost Generation fans, **Paris Literary Promenades** takes you through areas once popular with literary giants, from Joyce to Beckett to Hemingway (€9, late May–mid-Oct, daily except Wed at 14:30 and 19:00, 2 hrs, tours depart from place de l'Odeon, tel. 01 48 07 80 72 or cellular 06 03 27 73 52). You can also hire a Parisian as your personal guide. Arnaud Servignat (tel. 06 72 77 94 50, e-mail: arnotour @noos.fr) and Marianne Siegler (tel. 01 42 52 32 51) are licensed local guides who freelance for individuals and families ($150/ 4 hrs, $250/day).

Bike Tours: Mike's Bullfrog Bike Tours—like a frat party on wheels—attracts a college crowd for its boisterous three- to four-hour rolls through Paris (€20, May–Nov daily at 11:00, also at 15:30 June–July, no CC, in English, no bikes or reservations needed, meet at south pillar of Eiffel Tower, cellular 06 09 98 08 60, www.mikesbiketours.com).

Excursion Tours: Many companies offer minivan and big-bus tours to regional sights (including all daytrips described below). **Paris Walking Tours** are the best, with informative and fun afternoon visits to the Impressionist artist retreats of Giverny and Auvers-sur-Oise (€47–56, includes admissions, see "Walking Tours," above). **Paris Vision** offers mass-produced, full-size bus and minivan tours to several popular regional destinations, including the Loire Valley, Champagne region, D-Day beaches, and Mont St. Michel. Their minivan tours are more expensive but more personal, in English, and offer pickup at your hotel (€130–200/person). Their full-size bus tours are multilingual and cost about half the price of a minivan tour—worth it for some simply for the ease of transportation to the sights (full-size buses depart from 214 rue de Rivoli, Mo: Tuileries, tel. 01 42 60 30 01, fax 01 42 86 95 36, www.parisvision.com).

Sights—The "Historic Core of Paris" Walk
(This information is distilled from the Historic Paris Walk chapter in *Rick Steves' Mona Winks*, by Gene Openshaw and Rick Steves.)

Allow four hours for this self-guided tour, including sightseeing. Start where the city did—on the Ile de la Cité. Face Notre-Dame and follow the dotted line on the "Core of Paris" map (within this chapter). To get to Notre-Dame, ride the Métro to Cité, Hôtel de Ville, or St. Michel and walk to the big square facing the...

▲▲**Notre-Dame Cathedral**—This 700-year-old cathedral is packed with history and tourists. Study its sculpture and windows, take in a Mass, eavesdrop on guides, and walk all around the outside (free, daily 08:00–18:45, €2.50 for treasury open daily 09:30–17:30—not covered by museum pass, free English tours normally Wed and Thu at 12:00 and Sat at 14:30, Sun Masses at 08:00, 08:45, 10:00, 11:30, 12:30, and 18:30, Mo: Cité, Hôtel de Ville, or St. Michel). Climb to the top for a great view of the city; you get 400 steps for only €5.50 (entrance outside, daily April–Sept 09:00–18:00, Oct–March 10:00–17:30). There are clean €0.50 toilets in front of the church near Charlemagne's statue.

The **cathedral facade** is worth a close look. The church is dedicated to "Our Lady" (Notre-Dame). Mary is center stage—cradling Jesus, surrounded by the halo of the rose window. Adam is on the left and Eve is on the right.

Below Mary and above the arches is a row of 28 statues known as the Kings of Judah. During the French Revolution, these Biblical kings were mistaken for the hated French kings. The citizens stormed the church, crying, "Off with their heads!" All were decapitated but have since been recapitated.

Speaking of decapitation, look at the carving above the

Core of Paris

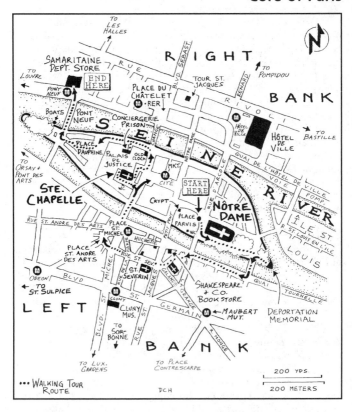

doorway on the left. The man with his head in his hands is
St. Denis. Back when there was a Roman temple on this spot,
Christianity began making converts. The fourth-century bishop
of Roman Paris, Denis, was beheaded. But these early Christians
were hard to keep down. The man who would become St. Denis
got up, tucked his head under his arm, and headed north until
he found just the right place to meet his maker: Montmartre.
(Athough the name "Montmartre" comes from the Roman
"Mount of Mars," later generations—thinking of their beheaded
patron St. Denis—preferred a less pagan version, "Mount of
Martyrs.") The Parisians were convinced of this miracle, Christianity gained ground, and a church soon replaced the pagan temple.

   Medieval art was OK if it embellished the house of God and
told Bible stories. For a fine example, move to the base of the
central column (at the foot of Mary, about where the head of

St. Denis could spit if he was real good). Working around from the left, find God telling a barely created Eve, "Have fun but no apples." Next, the sexiest serpent I've ever seen makes apples à la mode. Finally, Adam and Eve, now ashamed of their nakedness, are expelled by an angel. This is a tiny example in a church covered with meaning.

Now move to the right and study the carving above the **central portal**. It's the end of the world, and Christ sits on the throne of Judgment (just under the arches, holding his hands up). Below him an angel and a demon weigh souls in the balance. The "good" stand to the left, looking up to heaven. The "bad" ones to the right are chained up and led off to... Versailles on a Tuesday. The "ugly" ones must be the crazy sculpted demons to the right, at the base of the arch.

Wander through the interior. You'll be routed around the ambulatory, much as medieval pilgrims would have been. Don't miss the rose windows filling each of the transepts. Back outside, walk around the church through the park on the riverside for a close look at the flying buttresses.

The neo-Gothic 90-meter (300-foot) **spire** is a product of the 1860 reconstruction. Around its base are apostles and evangelists (the green men) as well as Viollet-le-Duc, the architect in charge of the work. Notice how the apostles look outward, blessing the city, while the architect (at top, seen from behind the church) looks up, admiring his spire.

The archaeological **crypt** is a worthwhile 15-minute stop with your museum pass (€3, Tue–Sun 10:00–17:30, closed Mon, enter 100 meters/325 feet in front of church). You'll see Roman ruins, trace the street plan of the medieval village, and see diagrams of how the earliest Paris grew and grew, all thoughtfully explained in English.

If you're hungry near Notre-Dame, the nearby Ile St. Louis has inexpensive *crêperies* and grocery stores open daily on its main drag. Plan a picnic for the quiet bench-filled park immediately behind the church (public WC).

Behind Notre-Dame, squeeze through the tourist buses, cross the street, and enter the iron gate into the park at the tip of the island. Look for the stairs and head down to reach...

▲▲**Deportation Memorial (Mémorial de la Déportation)**—This memorial to the 200,000 French victims of the Nazi concentration camps draws you into their experience. As you descend the steps, the city around you disappears. Surrounded by walls, you have become a prisoner. Your only freedom is your view of the sky and the tantalizing glimpse of the river below.

Enter the single-file chamber ahead. Inside, the circular plaque in the floor reads, "They descended into the mouth of the earth and they did not return." A hallway stretches in front of you, lined with 200,000 lighted crystals, one for each French citizen that died. Flickering at the far end is the eternal flame of hope. The tomb of the unknown deportee lies at your feet. Above, the inscription reads, "Dedicated to the living memory of the 200,000 French deportees sleeping in the night and the fog, exterminated in the Nazi concentration camps."

Above the exit as you leave is the message you'll find at all Nazi sights: "Forgive but never forget." (Free, April–Sept daily 10:00–12:00, 14:00–19:00, Oct–March daily 10:00–12:00, 14:00–17:00, east tip of island near Ile St. Louis, behind Notre-Dame, Mo: Cité.)

Ile St. Louis—Look across the river to the Ile St. Louis. If the Ile de la Cité is a tug laden with the history of Paris, it's towing this classy little residential dinghy laden only with boutiques, famous sorbet shops, and restaurants (see "Eating in Paris," below). This island wasn't developed until much later (18th century). What was a swampy mess is now harmonious Parisian architecture. The pedestrian bridge, pont Saint Louis, connects the two islands, leading right to rue Saint Louis en l'Ile. This spine of the island is lined with interesting shops. A short stroll takes you to the famous Berthillon ice-cream parlor (#31). Loop back to the pedestrian bridge along the parklike quays (walk north to the river and turn left). This walk is about as peaceful and romantic as Paris gets.

Before walking to the opposite end of the Ile de la Cité, loop through the Latin Quarter (as indicated on the map). From the Deportation Memorial, cross the bridge onto the Left Bank and enjoy the riverside view of the Notre-Dame and window shop among the green book stalls, browsing through used books, vintage posters, and souvenirs. At the little park and church (over the bridge from the front of Notre-Dame), venture inland a few blocks, basically arcing through the Latin Quarter and returning to the island two bridges down at place St. Michel.

▲**Latin Quarter**—This area, which gets its name from the language used here when it was an exclusive medieval university district, lies between Luxembourg Gardens and the Seine, centering around the Sorbonne University and boulevards St. Germain and St. Michel. This is the core of the Left Bank—it's crowded with international eateries, far-out bookshops, street singers, and jazz clubs. For colorful wandering and café sitting, afternoons and evenings are best (Mo: St. Michel).

Along rue Saint-Severin, you can still see the shadow of the medieval sewer system (the street slopes into a central channel of bricks). In the days before plumbing and toilets, when people still went to the river or neighborhood wells for their water, "flushing" meant throwing it out the window. Certain times of day were flushing times. Maids on the fourth floor would holler "*Garde de l'eau!*" ("Look out for the water!") and heave it into the streets, where it would eventually be washed down into the Seine.

Consider a visit to the Cluny Museum for its medieval art and unicorn tapestries (listed under "Sights—Southeast Paris," below).

Place St. Michel (facing the St. Michel bridge) is the traditional core of the Left Bank's artsy, liberal, hippie, Bohemian district of poets, philosophers, winos, and tourists. In less-commercial times, place St. Michel was a gathering point for the city's malcontents and misfits. Here, in 1871, the citizens took the streets from the government troops, set up barricades *Les Mis*–style, and established the Paris Commune. In World War II, the locals rose up against their Nazi oppressors (read the plaques by St. Michel fountain). And in the spring of 1968, a time of social upheaval all over the world, young students—battling riot batons and tear gas—took over the square and demanded change.

From place St. Michel, look across the river and find the spire of Sainte-Chapelle church and its weathervane angel (below). Cross the river on pont St. Michel and continue along boulevard du Palais. On your left you'll see the high-security doorway to Sainte-Chapelle. But first, carry on another 30 meters (100 feet) and turn right at a wide pedestrian street, the rue de Lutece.

Cité "Métropolitain" Stop—Of the 141 original turn-of-the-19th-century subway entrances, this is one of 17 survivors now preserved as a national art treasure. The curvy, plantlike ironwork is a textbook example of Art Nouveau, the style that rebelled against the erector-set squareness of the Industrial Age (e.g., Mr. Eiffel's tower).

The flower market right here on place Louis Lepine is a pleasant detour. On Sundays this square chirps with a busy bird market. And across the way is the Prefecture de Police, where Inspector Clouseau of *Pink Panther* fame used to work and where the local resistance fighters took the first building from the Nazis in August 1944, leading to the Allied liberation of Paris a week later.

Pause here to admire the view. Sainte-Chapelle is a pearl in an ugly architectural oyster, part of a complex of buildings that includes the Palace of Justice (to the right of Sainte-Chapelle, behind the fancy gates). Return to the entrance of Sainte-Chapelle. Everyone needs to pass through a metal detector to get in. Free toilets are ahead on the left. The line into the church may be long. (Museum-card holders can go directly in; pick up the excellent English info sheet.) Enter the humble ground floor of...

▲▲▲**Sainte-Chapelle**—This triumph of Gothic church architecture is a cathedral of glass like no other. It was speedily built from 1242 to 1248 for St. Louis IX (France's only canonized king) to house the supposed Crown of Thorns. Its architectural harmony is due to the fact that it was completed under the direction of one architect in only six years—unheard of in Gothic times. (Notre-Dame took more than 200 years to build.)

The design clearly shows an Old Regime approach to worship. The basement was for staff and other common folk. Royal Christians worshiped upstairs. The ground-floor paint job, a 19th-century restoration, is a reasonably accurate copy of the original.

Climb the spiral staircase to the **Chapelle Haute**. Fill the place with choral music, crank up the sunshine, face the top of the altar, and really believe that the Crown of Thorns was there, and this becomes one awesome space.

"Let there be light." In the Bible, it's clear: Light is divine. Light shining through stained glass was a symbol of God's grace shining down to earth. Gothic architects used their new technology to turn dark stone buildings into lanterns of light. The glory of Gothic shines brighter here than in any other church.

There are 15 separate panels of stained glass (6,500 square feet—two-thirds of it 13th-century original), with more than 1,100 different scenes, mostly from the Bible. In medieval times, scenes like these helped teach Bible stories to the illiterate.

The altar was raised up high to better display the relic—the Crown of Thorns—around which this chapel was built. The supposed crown cost King Louis three times as much as this church. Today it is kept in the Notre-Dame Treasury and shown only on Good Friday.

Louis' little private viewing window is in the wall to the right of the altar. Louis, both saintly and shy, liked to go to church without dealing with the rigors of public royal life. Here he could worship still dressed in his jammies.

Lay your camera on the ground and shoot the ceiling. Those ribs growing out of the slender columns are the essence of Gothic.

Books in the gift shop explain the stained glass in English. There are concerts (€15–23) almost every summer evening. (€5.50 entry, €8 combo-ticket with Conciergerie, daily April–Sept 09:30–18:30, Oct–March 10:00–17:00, Mo: Cité, tel. 01 48 01 91 35 for concert information.)

Palais du Justice—Back outside, as you walk around the church exterior, look down and notice how much Paris has risen in the 800 years since Sainte-Chapelle was built. You're in a huge complex of buildings that has housed the local government since ancient Roman times. It was the site of the original Gothic palace of the early kings of France. The only surviving medieval parts are the Sainte-Chapelle church and the Conciergerie prison.

Most of the site is now covered by the giant Palais de Justice, home of France's supreme court (built in 1776). "*Liberté, Egalité, Fraternité*" over the doors is a reminder that this was also the headquarters of the revolutionary government.

Now pass through the big iron gate to the noisy boulevard

du Palais and turn left (toward the Right Bank). On the corner is the site of the oldest public clock (built in 1334) in the city. While the present clock is said to be Baroque, it somehow still manages to keep accurate time.

Turn left onto quai de l'Horologe and walk along the river. The round medieval tower just ahead marks the entrance to the Conciergerie. Pop in to visit the courtyard and lobby (free). Step past the serious-looking guard into the courtyard.

Conciergerie—This former prison is a gloomy place. Kings used it to torture and execute failed assassins. The leaders of the Revolution put it to similar good use. The tower next to the entrance, called "the babbler," was named for the painful sounds that leaked from it.

Look at the stark lettering above the doorways. This was a no-nonsense revolutionary time. Everything, even lettering, was subjected to the test of reason. No frills or we chop 'em off.

Step inside; the lobby, with an English-language history display, is free. Marie Antoinette was imprisoned here. During a busy eight-month period in the Revolution, she was one of 2,600 prisoners kept here on the way to the guillotine. The interior, with its huge vaulted and pillared rooms, echoes with history but is pretty barren (€5.50, €8 with Sainte-Chapelle, daily April–Sept 09:30–18:30, Oct–March 10:00–17:00, good English descriptions, Mo: Cité). You can see Marie Antoinette's cell, housing a collection of her mementos. In another room, a list of those made "a foot shorter at the top" by the "national razor" includes ex-King Louis XVI, Charlotte Corday (who murdered Marat in his bathtub), and the chief revolutionary who got a taste of his own medicine, Maximilien Robespierre.

Back outside, wink at the flak-proof vested guard and turn left. Listen for babbles and continue your walk along the river. Across the river you can see the rooftop observatory—flags flapping—of the Samaritaine department store, where this walk will end. At the first corner, veer left past France's supreme-court building and into a sleepy triangular square called place Dauphine. Marvel at how such quaintness could be lodged in the midst of such greatness as you walk through the park to the end of the island. At the equestrian statue of Henry IV, turn right onto the bridge and take refuge in one of the nooks on the Eiffel Tower side.

Pont Neuf—This "new bridge" is now Paris' oldest. Built during Henry IV's reign (around 1600), its 12 arches span the widest part of the river. The fine view includes the park on the tip of the island (note Seine tour boats), the Orsay Museum, and the Louvre. These turrets were originally for vendors and street entertainers. In the days of Henry IV, who originated the promise of "a chicken in every pot," this would have been a lively scene.

Directly over the river, the first building you'll hit on the Right Bank is the venerable old department store, Samaritaine.

▲**Samaritaine Department Store Viewpoint**—Enter the store and go to the rooftop. Ride the glass elevator from near the pont Neuf entrance to the ninth floor (you'll be greeted by a WC—check out the sink). Pass the 10th-floor *terrasse* for the 11th-floor panorama (tight spiral staircase; watch your head). Quiz yourself. Working counterclockwise, find the Eiffel Tower, Invalides/Napoleon's Tomb, Montparnasse Tower, Henry IV statue on the tip of the island, Sorbonne University, the dome of the Panthéon, Sainte-Chapelle, Notre-Dame, Hôtel de Ville (city hall), Pompidou Center, Sacré-Coeur, Opéra, and Louvre. The Champs-Elysées leads to the Arc de Triomphe. Shadowing that—even bigger, while two times as distant—is the Grande Arche de la Défense. You'll find light, reasonably priced, and incredibly scenic meals on the breezy terrace, and a supermarket in the basement. (Rooftop view is free, daily 09:30–19:00, Mo: Pont Neuf, tel. 01 40 41 20 20.)

Sights—Paris' Museums near the Tuileries Gardens

The newly renovated Tuileries Gardens was once private property of kings and queens. Paris' grandest public park links these museums.

▲▲▲**Louvre**—This is Europe's oldest, biggest, greatest, and maybe most-crowded museum. There is no grander entry than through the pyramid, but metal detectors create a long line at times. To avoid the line, you have two choices: Museum-pass holders can use the group entrance in the pedestrian passageway between the pyramid and rue de Rivoli (facing the pyramid with your back to the Tuileries Gardens, go to your left, which is north; under the arches you'll find the entrance and escalator down). Or anyone can get into the Louvre from the slick underground Carrousel shopping mall that connects with the museum; enter the mall either at 99 rue de Rivoli at the door with the red awning or get off the Métro at the "Palais Royal/Musée du Louvre" stop and follow signs to "Musée du Louvre" (don't get off at the "Louvre Rivoli" Métro stop, which is farther away).

Pick up the free *Louvre Handbook* in English at the information desk under the pyramid as you enter. Don't try to cover the entire museum. The 90-minute English-language tours, which leave six times daily except Sunday, boil this overwhelming museum down to size (€5.50, tour tel. 01 40 20 52 09). Clever €5 digital audioguides (after ticket booths, at top of stairs) give you a receiver and a directory of about 130 masterpieces, allowing you to dial a (rather dull) commentary on included works as you stumble upon them. Rick Steves' and Gene Openshaw's museum guidebook, *Rick Steves' Mona Winks* (buy in United States), includes a self-guided tour of the Louvre.

Paris' Museums near the Tuileries Gardens

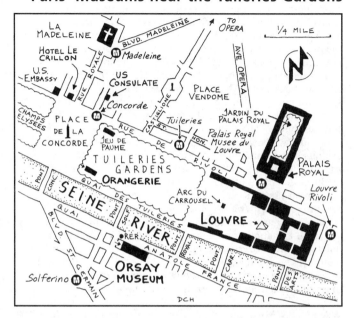

If you can't get a guide, start in the Denon wing and visit the **highlights**, in this order: Michelangelo's *Slaves*; Ancient Greek and Roman works (Parthenon frieze, *Venus de Milo*, Pompeii mosaics, Etruscan sarcophagi, Roman portrait busts, *Nike of Samothrace*); Apollo Gallery (jewels); French and Italian paintings in the Grande Galerie (a 400-meter hike and worth it); the *Mona Lisa* and her Italian Renaissance roommates; the nearby neoclassical collection (*Coronation of Napoléon*); and the Romantic collection, with works by Delacroix (*Liberty at the Barricades*) and Géricault (*Raft of the Medusa*).

Cost: €7, €5 after 15:00 and on Sunday, free on first Sunday of month and for those under 18, covered by museum pass. Tickets good all day. Reentry allowed.

Hours: Wednesday through Monday 09:00 to 18:00, closed Tuesday, all wings open Wednesday until 21:45, Richelieu Wing (only) open until 21:45 on Monday. Galleries start closing 30 minutes early. Closed January 1, Easter, May 1, November 1, and Christmas Day. Crowds are worst on Sunday, Monday, Wednesday, and mornings. Save money by visiting after 15:00. (You can enter the pyramid for free until 21:30. Go in at night and see it glow.) Tel. 01 40 20 51 51, recorded info tel. 01 40 20 53 17 (www.louvre.fr).

The newly renovated Richelieu wing and the underground shopping-mall extension add the finishing touches to Le Grand Louvre Project (which started in 1989 with the pyramid entrance). To explore this most recent extension of the Louvre, enter through the pyramid, walk toward the inverted pyramid, and uncover a post office, a handy TI and SNCF office, glittering boutiques and a dizzying assortment of good-value eateries (up the escalator), and the Palais-Royal Métro entrance. Stairs at the far end take you right into the Tuileries Gardens, a perfect antidote to the stuffy, crowded rooms of the Louvre.

Jeu de Paume—This one-time home to the Impressionist art collection (which is now located in the Orsay) hosts rotating exhibits of top contemporary artists (€6, not covered by museum pass, Tue 12:00–21:30, Wed–Fri 12:00–19:00, Sat–Sun 10:00–19:00, closed Mon, on place de la Concorde, just inside Tuileries Garden on rue de Rivoli side, Mo: Concorde).

L'Orangerie—After a two-year renovation, this museum of Impressionist art is due to reopen sometime in 2002. For specifics, ask at a TI or another museum (i.e., Louvre, Orsay). This small, quiet, and often-overlooked museum houses Monet's water lilies, many famous Renoirs, and a scattering of other great Impressionist works. The breezy round rooms of water lilies are two of the most enjoyable rooms in Paris (price and hours not set, located in Tuileries Garden near place de la Concorde, Mo: Concorde).

▲▲▲**Orsay Museum**—Paris' 19th-century art museum (actually, art from 1848–1914) includes Europe's greatest collection of Impressionist works. The museum is housed in a former train station (Gare d'Orsay) across the river and a lovely 15-minute walk downstream from the Louvre through the Tuileries Gardens. (The RER-C train line zips you right to "Musée d'Orsay"; the Métro stop Solferino is 3 blocks south of the Orsay.)

Until the summer of 2002, the main entry to the Orsay will be closed for renovation, and you will enter at a temporary entry facing the river.

Start on the ground floor. The "pretty" conservative-establishment art is in the south side. Then cross into the brutally truthful and, at that time, very shocking art of the realist rebels and Manet (north side of ground floor). Then ride the escalators at the far end (detouring at the top for a grand museum view) to the series of Impressionist rooms (Monet, Renoir, Dégas, et al).

Don't miss the Grand Ballroom (room 52, Arts et Decors de la IIIème République) and Art Nouveau on the mezzanine level. The restaurant Le Salon de Thé du Musée, near the ballroom, is worth a peek or even a lunch stop (affordable salad bar).

Cost and Hours: €7; €5 after 16:15, on Sunday, and for ages 18 to 25; free for youth under 18 and for anyone on the first Sunday of the month (June 20–Sept 20 Tue–Sun 09:00–18:00, Sept 21–June 19 Tue–Sat 10:00–18:00, Sun 09:00–18:00, Thu until 21:45 all year, closed Mon, last entrance 45 min before closing, galleries start closing 30 min early). Tickets are valid all day. The Orsay is covered by the museum pass. Pass holders can enter to the left of the main entrance (during the renovation, they can walk to the front of the line and show their passes). Ask for a free floor plan in English. English-language tours usually run daily except Sunday at 11:30, cost €5.50, take 90 minutes, and are also available on audioguide (€5). The Orsay is very crowded on Tuesday, when the Louvre is closed. Tel. 01 40 49 48 48.

Sights—Southwest Paris: The Eiffel Tower Neighborhood

▲▲▲**Eiffel Tower**—It's crowded and expensive but worth the trouble. Go early (by 08:45) or late in the day (after 20:00 in summer, otherwise 18:00) to avoid most crowds; weekends are worst. Pilier Nord (the north pillar) has the biggest elevator and, therefore, the fastest-moving line. It takes two elevators to get to the top (transfer at level 2), which means two lines and very long waits if you don't go early or late. A TI/ticket booth is between the Pilier Nord and Est (east pillar). The stairs (yes, you can walk up partway) are next to the Jules Verne restaurant entry. A sign in the jammed elevator tells you to beware of pickpockets.

The tower is 300 meters tall (1,000 feet), 15 centimeters (6 inches) taller in hot weather, covers 2.5 acres, and requires 50 tons of paint. Its 7,000 tons of metal are spread out so well at the base that it's no heavier per square inch than a linebacker on tiptoes. Visitors to Paris may find *Mona Lisa* to be less than expected, but the Eiffel Tower rarely disappoints, even in an era of skyscrapers.

Built a hundred years after the French Revolution (and in the midst of an Industrial one), the tower served no function but to impress. Bridge-builder Gustave Eiffel won the contest for the 1889 Centennial World's Fair by beating out such rival proposals as a giant guillotine. To a generation hooked on technology, the tower was the marvel of the age, a symbol of progress and of man's ingenuity. To others, it was a cloned-sheep monstrosity. The writer Maupassant routinely ate lunch in the tower just so he wouldn't have to look at it.

Delicate and graceful when seen from afar, it's massive—even a bit scary—from close up. You don't appreciate the size until you walk toward it; like a mountain, it seems so close but takes forever to reach. There are three observation platforms, at 60, 120, and 270 meters (200, 400, and 900 feet); the higher you go, the more you pay. Each requires a separate elevator (and a line), so plan on at least 90 minutes if you want to go to the top and back. The

Eiffel Tower to Invalides

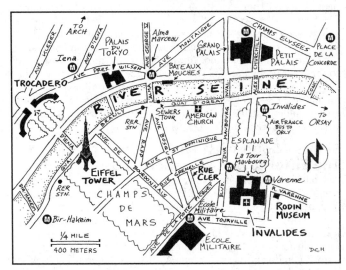

view from the 120-meter high (400 feet) second level is plenty. As you ascend through the metal beams, imagine being a worker, perched high above nothing, riveting this giant erector set together. On top, all of Paris lies before you, with a panorama guide. On a good day you can see for 65 kilometers (40 miles).

The first level has exhibits, a post office (daily 10:00–19:00, cancellation stamp will read Eiffel Tower), snack bar, WCs, and souvenirs. Read the informative signs (in English) describing the major monuments, see the entertaining free movie on the history of the tower, and don't miss a century of fireworks, including the entire millennium blast, on video. Then consider a drink or a sandwich overlooking all of Paris at the snack café (outdoor tables in summer) or at the city's best view bar/restaurant, **Altitude 95** (€15 lunches, €34–46 dinners, dinner seatings at 19:00 and 21:00, reserve well ahead for a view table; before you ascend to dine, drop by the booth between the north-*nord* and east-*est* pillars to pick up a pass that enables you to skip the line; tel. 01 45 55 20 04, fax 01 47 05 94 40).

The second level has the best views (walk up the stairway to get above the netting), a small cafeteria, WCs, and an Internet gimmick to have your photo at the Eiffel Tower sent into cyberspace (*La Gallerie des Visiteurs*).

It costs €4 to go to the first level, €7 to the second, and €10 to go all the way for the 270-meter view (900 feet, not covered by museum pass). On a budget? You can climb the stairs to the second level for only €3 (March–Sept daily 09:00–24:00, Oct–Feb 09:30–23:00, shorter lines at night, Mo: Trocadero, RER: Champ de Mars, tel. 01 44 11 23 23).

The best place to view the tower is from Trocadero Square to the north (a 10-min walk across the river, and a happening scene at night). Consider arriving at the Trocadero Métro stop, then walking toward the tower. Another great viewpoint is the long, grassy field, le Champ de Mars, to the south (after about 20:00 the *gendarmes* look the other way as Parisians stretch out or picnic on the grass). However impressive it may be by day, it's an awesome thing to see at twilight, when the tower becomes engorged with light and virile Paris lies back and lets night be on top.

▲**Paris Sewer Tour (Egouts)**—This quick and easy visit takes you along a few hundred meters of underground water tunnel lined with interesting displays, well-described in English, explaining the evolution of the world's longest sewer system. (If you lined up Paris' sewers, they would reach beyond Istanbul.) Don't miss the slide show, the fine WCs just beyond the gift shop, and the occasional tours in English (€4, covered by museum pass, Sat–Wed 11:00–17:00, closed Thu–Fri, where pont de l'Alma greets the Left Bank, Mo: Alma Marceau, RER Pont de l'Alma, tel. 01 47 05 10 29).

▲▲**Napoleon's Tomb and Army Museum (Les Invalides)**— The emperor lies majestically dead inside several coffins under a grand dome—a goose-bumping pilgrimage for historians. Napoleon is surrounded by the tombs of other French war heroes and a fine military museum in Hôtel des Invalides. Check out the interesting World War II wing. Follow signs to the "crypt" to find Roman Empire–style reliefs listing the accomplishments of Napoleon's administration. The restored dome glitters with 26 pounds of gold (€6, students and kids 12–17-€5, under 12 free, daily April–Sept 09:00–17:45, Oct–March 10:00–16:45, Napoleon's Tomb open June 15–Sept 15 until 18:45, Mo: La Tour Maubourg or Varennes, tel. 01 44 42 37 72).

▲▲**Rodin Museum**—This user-friendly museum is filled with passionate works by the greatest sculptor since Michelangelo. See *The Kiss*, *The Thinker*, *The Gates of Hell*, and many more. Don't miss the room full of work by Rodin's student and mistress, Camille Claudel (€4, €2.75 on Sun and for students, free for youth under 18 and for anyone first Sun of month; €0.75 for gardens only, which may be Paris' best deal as many works are well-displayed in the beautiful gardens; Tue–Sun 09:30–17:45, closed Mon and at 17:00 off-season; near Napoleon's Tomb, 77 rue de Varennes, Mo: Varennes, tel. 01 44 18 61 10). There's a good self-serve cafeteria as well as idyllic picnic spots in the family-friendly back garden.

▲▲**Marmottan**—In this private, intimate, less-visited museum, you'll find more than 100 paintings by Claude Monet (thanks to his son Michel), including the *Impressions of a Sunrise* painting that gave the movement its start—and name (€6, not covered by museum pass, Tue–Sun 10:00–17:30, closed Mon, 2 rue Louis Boilly, Mo: La Muette, follow museum signs 6 blocks through a delightful kid-filled park to museum, tel. 01 44 96 50 33). Combine this fine museum with a stroll down one of Paris' most pleasant shopping streets, the rue de Passy (from La Muette Métro stop).

Sights—Southeast Paris: The Latin Quarter

▲Latin Quarter—This Left Bank neighborhood, just opposite the Notre-Dame, is the Latin Quarter. (For more information and a walking tour, see "Historic Core of Paris" Walk, above.) This was the center of Roman Paris. But its touristic fame relates to the Latin Quarter's intriguing artsy, bohemian character. This was perhaps Europe's leading university district in the Middle Ages— home, since the 13th century, to the prestigious Sorbonne University. Back then, Latin was the language of higher education. And, since students here came from all over Europe, Latin served as their linguistic common denominator. Locals referred to the quarter by its language: Latin. In modern times this became the center of Paris' café culture. The neighborhood's main boulevards (St. Michel and St. Germain) are lined with cafés—once the haunts of great poets and philosophers, but now the hangouts of tired tourists. While still youthful and artsy, the area has become a tourist ghetto filled with cheap North African eateries.

▲▲Cluny Museum (Musée National du Moyen Age)—This treasure trove of medieval art fills the old Roman baths, offering close-up looks at stained glass, Notre-Dame carvings, fine gold-smithing and jewelry, and rooms of tapestries—the best of which is the exquisite *Lady with the Unicorn*. In five panels, a delicate-as-medieval-can-be noble lady introduces a delighted unicorn to the senses of taste, hearing, sight, smell, and touch (€6, €4 on Sun; Wed–Mon 09:15–17:45, closed Tue, near the corner of boulevards St. Michel and St. Germain, Mo: Cluny, tel. 01 53 73 78 00).

St. Germain des Prés—A church was first built on this site in A.D. 452. The church you see today was constructed in 1163. The area around the church hops at night with fire-eaters, mimes, and scads of artists (Mo: St. Germain-des-Près).

▲St. Sulpice Organ Concert—For pipe-organ enthusiasts, this is a delight. The Grand-Orgue at St. Sulpice has a rich history, with a line of 12 world-class organists (including Widor and Dupre) going back 300 years. Widor started the tradition of opening the loft to visitors after the 10:30 service on Sundays. Daniel Roth continues to welcome guests in three languages while playing five keyboards at once. The 10:30 Sunday Mass is followed by a high-powered 25-minute recital at 11:40. Then, just after noon, the small, unmarked door is opened (left of entry as you face the rear). Visitors scamper like 16th notes up spiral stairs, past the

Latin Quarter

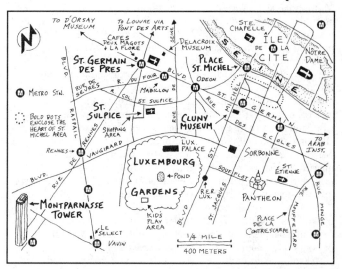

18th-century Stairmasters that were used to fill the billows, into a
world of 7,000 pipes, where they can watch the master performing
the next Mass. You'll generally have 30 minutes to kill (there's a
plush lounge) before the organ plays; visitors can leave at any time.
If late or rushed, show up around 12:30 and wait at the little door.
As someone leaves you can slip in (Mo: St. Sulpice or Mabillon).
The nearby St. Germain market is open Sundays and worth a stop.
▲▲**Luxembourg Gardens**—Paris' most beautiful, interesting, and
enjoyable garden/park/recreational area is a great place to watch
Parisians at rest and play. The brilliant flower plantings are completely changed three times a year, and the boxed trees are brought
out of the *orangerie* in May. Challenge the card and chess players
to a game (near the tennis courts), or find a free chair near the main
pond and take a breather. Notice any pigeons? A poor Ernest Hemingway used to hand hunt (read: strangle) them here. Paris Walking
Tours offers a good tour of the park (see "Organized Tours,"
above). The grand neoclassical domed Panthéon, now a mausoleum housing the tombs of several great Frenchmen, is a block
away and is only worth entering if you have a museum pass. The
park is open until dusk (Mo: Odéon, RER: Luxembourg). If you
enjoy the Luxembourg Gardens and want to see more, visit the
elegant Parc Monceau (Mo: Monceau) and the colorful Jardin des
Plantes (Mo: Jussieu or Gare d'Austerlitz, RER: Luxembourg).
Montparnasse Tower—This 59-floor superscraper—it's cheaper
and easier to get to the top than to that of the Eiffel Tower—

offers one of Paris' best views, since the Eiffel Tower is in it and Montparnasse Tower isn't. Buy the photo guide to the city, then go to the rooftop and orient yourself (€8, not covered by museum pass, daily in summer 09:30–23:30, off-season 10:00–22:00, disappointing after dark, entrance on rue l'Arrivé, Mo: Montparnasse). This is efficient when combined with a daytrip to Chartres, because trains to Chartres depart from the Montparnasse train station.

▲Catacombs—These underground tunnels contain the anonymous bones of six million permanent Parisians. In 1785 the Revolutionary government of Paris decided to make its congested city more spacious and sanitary by emptying the city cemeteries (which traditionally surrounded churches) into an official ossuary. The perfect locale was the many kilometers of underground tunnels from limestone quarries, which were, at that time, just outside the city. For decades, priests led ceremonial processions of black-veiled, bone-laden carts into the quarries where they were stacked into piles 1.5 meters high (5 feet) and as much as 24 meters deep (80 feet) behind neat walls of skull-studded tibia. Each transfer was completed with the placement of a plaque indicating the church and district where that pile of bones originated and the date they arrived.

From the entry of the Catacombs, a spiral staircase leads 18 meters down (60 feet). Then you begin a 1.5-kilometer-long (1 mile) subterranean walk. After several blocks of empty passageways, you ignore a sign announcing: "Halt, this is the empire of the dead." Along the way, plaques encourage visitors to reflect upon their destiny: "Happy is he who is forever faced with the hour of his death and prepares himself for the end every day." You emerge far from where you entered, with white limestone-covered toes, telling anyone in the know you've been underground gawking at bones. Note to wannabe Hamlets: An attendant checks your bag at the exit for stolen souvenirs (€5, not covered by museum pass, 1 place Denfert-Rochereau, Mo: Denfert-Rochereau, Tue–Fri 14:00–16:00, Sat–Sun 09:00–11:00, 14:00–16:00, closed Mon, tel. 01 43 22 47 63).

Sights—Northwest Paris

▲▲Place de la Concorde and the Champs-Elysées—This famous boulevard is Paris' backbone and greatest concentration of traffic. All of France seems to converge on the place de la Concorde, the city's largest square. It was here that the guillotine took the lives of thousands—including King Louis XVI and Marie Antoinette. Back then it was called the place de la Revolution.

Catherine de Médici wanted a place to drive her carriage, so she started draining the swamp that would become the Champs-Elysées. Napoleon put on the final touches, and it's been the place to be seen ever since. The Tour de France bicycle race ends here, as do all parades (French or foe) of any significance. While the boulevard has become a bit hamburgerized, a walk here is a must.

Take the Métro to the Arc de Triomphe (Mo: Etoile) and saunter down the Champs-Elysées (Métro stops every few blocks: FDR, George V, and Etoile).

▲▲▲**Arc de Triomphe**—Napoleon had the magnificent Arc de Triomphe commissioned to commemorate his victory at the Battle of Austerlitz. There's no triumphal arch bigger (50 meters/ 164 feet high, 40 meters/130 feet wide). And, with 12 converging boulevards, there's no traffic circle more thrilling to experience— either behind the wheel or on foot (take the underpass). An elevator or a spiral staircase leads to a cute museum about the arch and a grand view from the top, even after dark (€6, June–Sept daily 09:30–23:00, Oct–May daily 09:30–22:00, Mo: Etoile, use underpass to reach arch, tel. 01 43 80 31 31).

▲**Le Palais Garnier (a.k.a. "The Old Opera")**—This grand palace of the belle époque (late 19th century) was built for Napoleon III and finished in 1875. (After completing this project, Opéra architect Garnier went south to design the casino in Monte Carlo.) From the grand Avenue de l'Opéra—once lined with Paris' most fashionable haunts—the newly restored facade seems to say "all power to the wealthy." While huge, the actual theater seats only 2,000. The real show was before and after, when the elite of Paris— out to see and be seen—strutted their elegant stuff in the extravagant lobbies. Think of the grand marble stairway as a theater itself. As you wander the halls and gawk at the decor, imagine the place filled with the beautiful people of the day. The massive foundations straddle an underground lake (creating the mysterious world of the Phantom of the Opera). Tourists can peek from two boxes into the actual red velvet theater to see Marc Chagall's colorful ceiling (1964) playfully dancing around the eight-ton chandelier. Note the box seats next to the stage—the most expensive in the house with an obstructed view of the stage, but just right if you're there only to be seen. The elitism of this place prompted Mitterand to have a people's opera house built in the 1980s (symbolically on place de la Bastille, where the French Revolution began). This left the Garnier Opéra home only to a ballet and occasional concerts. While the library-museum is of interest to opera buffs, anyone will enjoy the second-floor grand foyer and Salon du Glacier, iced with decor typical of 1900 (€5, daily 10:00–17:00 except when in use for performance, English tours summers only, normally at 14:00, call to confirm; enter through the front off place de l'Opéra, Mo: Opéra, tel. 01 40 01 22 53). American Express and the *Paris Story* film are on the left side of the Opéra, and the venerable Galeries Lafayette department store is just behind.

Paris Story **Film**—This entertaining film gives a good and painless overview of Paris' turbulent, brilliant past, covering 2,000 years in 45 fast-moving minutes. Its cushy chairs make an ideal break from bad weather and sore feet and make it fun with kids

(€8, kids 6–18-€5, families with 2 kids and 2 parents-€21, not covered by the museum pass, shows are on the hour daily 09:00–18:00, next to Opéra at 11 rue Scribe, Mo: Opéra, tel. 01 42 66 62 06).

▲▲**Musée Jacquemart-André**—This thoroughly enjoyable museum showcases the lavish home of a wealthy, art-loving, 19th-century Parisian couple. After wandering the grand boulevards, you now get inside for an intimate look at the lifestyles of the Parisian rich and fabulous. Edouard André and his wife Nélie Jacquemart—who had no children—spent their lives and fortunes designing, building, and then decorating a sumptuous mansion. What makes this visit so rewarding is the fine audioguide tour (in English, free with admission). And to make it even more memorable, the place is strewn with paintings by Rembrandt, Botticelli, Uccello, Mantegna, Bellini, Boucher, Fragonard—enough to make a painting gallery famous. Plan on spending an hour with the audioguide (€8, not covered by museum pass, daily 10:00–18:00, elegant café, 158 boulevard Haussmann, Mo: Miromesnil, tel. 01 42 89 04 91).

▲**Grande Arche de La Défense**—The centerpiece of Paris' ambitious skyscraper complex (La Défense) is the Grande Arche. Built to celebrate the 200th anniversary of the 1789 French Revolution, the place is big—38 floors on more than 200 acres. It holds offices for 30,000 people. Notre-Dame Cathedral could fit under its arch. The La Défense complex is an interesting study in 1960s land-use planning. More than 100,000 workers commute here daily, directing lots of business and development away from downtown and allowing central Paris to retain its more elegant feel. This aspect makes sense to most Parisians, regardless of whatever else they feel about the controversial complex. You'll enjoy city views from the Arche elevator (€7, under €2.75–5, not covered by museum pass, daily 10:00–19:00, includes a film on its construction and art exhibits, RER or Mo: La Défense, follow signs to Grande Arche or get off 1 stop earlier at Esplanade de la Défense and walk through the interesting business complex, tel. 01 49 07 27 57).

Sights—North Paris: Montmartre

▲**Sacré-Coeur and Montmartre**—This Byzantine-looking church, while only 130 years old, is impressive. It was built as a "praise the Lord anyway" gesture after the French were humiliated by the Germans in a brief war in 1871. The church is open daily until 23:00. One block from the church, the place du Tertre was the haunt of Toulouse-Lautrec and the original Bohemians. Today it's mobbed by tourists and unoriginal bohemians but still fun (go early in the morning to beat the crowds). Wander down rue Lepic to the two remaining windmills (once there were 30). Rue des Saules leads to Paris' only vineyard. Métro: Anvers (an extra Métro ticket buys your way up the funicular and avoids the stairs) or the closer but less scenic Abbesses. A taxi to the top of the hill saves time and sweat.

Pigalle—Paris' red-light district, the infamous "Pig Alley," is at the foot of Butte Montmartre. *Ooh la la.* More shocking than dangerous. Walk from place Pigalle to place Blanche, teasing desperate barkers and fast-talking temptresses. In bars, a €150 bottle of cheap champagne comes with a friend. Stick to the bigger streets, hang on to your wallet, and exercise good judgment. Cancan can cost a fortune, as can con artists in topless bars. After dark, tour buses line the streets. Tour guides make big bucks by bringing their groups to touristic nightclubs like the Moulin Rouge (Mo: Pigalle and Abbesses).

Sights—Northeast Paris: Marais Neighborhood and More

The Marais neighborhood extends along the right bank of the Seine from the Pompidou Center to the Bastille. It contains more pre-Revolutionary lanes and buildings than anywhere else in town and is more atmospheric than touristy. It's medieval Paris. This is how much of the city looked until, in the mid-1800s, Napoleon III had Baron Haussmann blast out the narrow streets to construct broad boulevards (wide enough for the guns and ranks of the army, too wide for revolutionary barricades), creating modern Paris. Originally a swamp (*marais*) during the reign of Henry IV, this area became the hometown of the French aristocracy. In the 17th century, big shots built their private mansions (*hôtels*) close to Henry's place des Vosges. When strolling the Marais, stick to the west-east axis formed by rue Ste. Croix de la Bretonniere, rue des Rosiers (heart of Paris' Jewish community), and rue St. Antoine. On Sunday afternoons, this trendy area pulses with shoppers and café crowds.

▲**Place des Vosges**—Study the architecture in this grand square: nine pavilions per side. Some of the brickwork is real, some is fake. Walk to the center, where Louis XIII sits on a horse surrounded by locals enjoying their community park. Children frolic in the sandbox, lovers warm benches, and pigeons guard their fountains while trees shade this retreat from the glare of the big city. Henry IV built this centerpiece of the Marais in 1605. As hoped, this turned the Marais into Paris' most exclusive neighborhood. As the nobility flocked to Versailles in a later age, this, too, was a magnet for the rich and powerful of France. With the Revolution, the aristocratic elegance of this quarter became working-class, filled with gritty shops, artisans, immigrants, and Jews. **Victor Hugo** lived at #6, and you can visit his house (€3, Tue–Sun 10:00–17:40, closed Mon, 6 place des Vosges, tel. 01 42 72 10 16). Leave the place des Vosges through the doorway at southwest corner of the square (near the 3-star Michelin restaurant, l'Ambroisie) and pass through the elegant **Hotel de Sully** (great example of a Marais mansion) to rue St. Antoine.

▲▲**Pompidou Center**—Europe's greatest collection of far-out

Marais Neighborhood

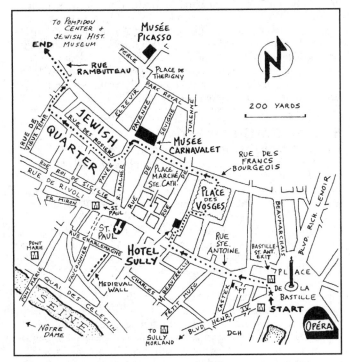

To Pompidou Center + Jewish Hist. Museum
END
MUSÉE PICASSO
PERLE
RUE RAMBUTEAU
PLACE DE THÉRIGNY
ELZEVIR
PARC ROYAL
PAYENNE
SÉVIGNÉ
TURENNE
200 YARDS
RUE DE VIEUX TEMP
JEWISH QUARTER
RUE DES ROSIERS
MUSÉE CARNAVALET
RUE DES FRANCS BOURGEOIS
RUE ROI DE SICILE
RUE DE RIVOLI
PAVÉE
R. MALHER
DE
PLACE MARCHÉ STE CATH.
PLACE DES VOSGES
BEAUMARCHAIS
BLVD. RICH. LENOIR
FR. MIRON
M ST. PAUL
RUE
RUE
ST. PAUL
RUE CHARLEMAGNE
HOTEL SULLY
RUE STE. ANTOINE
BASTILLE-ST. ANT. EXIT
PONT MARIE
M
TAVONNIER
MEDIEVAL WALL
CHARLES
BEAUVOIR
PETIT MUSC
CASTEX
PLACE DE LA BASTILLE
QUAI DES CÉLESTINS
M
M START
NÔTRE DAME
SEINE
TO M SULLY MORLAND
BLVD. HENRI IV
DCH
OPÉRA

modern art, the Musée National d'Art Moderne, is housed on the top floor of this newly renovated and colorful exoskeletal building. Once ahead of its time, this 20th-century art (remember that century?) has been waiting for the world to catch up with it. After so many Madonnas and Children, a piano smashed to bits and glued to the wall is refreshing (€5, audioguide-€4, Wed–Mon 11:00–21:00, closed Tue, to use escalator you need a ticket for the museum or a museum pass, good mezzanine-level café is cheaper than cafés outside, Mo: Rambuteau, tel. 01 44 78 12 33).

The Pompidou Center and its square are lively, with lots of people, street theater, and activity inside and out—a perpetual street fair. Kids of any age enjoy the fun, colorful fountain (called *Homage to Stravinsky*) on the square.

▲▲**Museum of Art and History of Judaism (Hôtel d'Aignan)**— This remarkable museum, located in a beautifully restored Marais mansion, tells the story of Judaism throughout Europe, from the Roman destruction of Jerusalem to the theft of famous artwork during World War II. Helpful audioguides and many English explanations make this an enjoyable history lesson. Move along at your own speed. The emphasis of the museum is to illustrate the cultural unity maintained by this continually dispersed population. You'll learn about the history of Jewish traditions, from bar mitzvahs to menorahs, and see exquisite traditional costumes and objects around which daily life revolved. Don't miss the explanation of the Dreyfus affair, a major event in early-1900 French politics. You'll also see photographs of and paintings by famous Jewish artists, including Chagall, Modigliani, and Soutine. The small section devoted to the deportation of Jews from Paris is very moving (€6, ages 18–25–€4, under 18 free, not covered by museum pass, Mon–Fri 11:00–18:00, Sun 10:00–18:00, closed Sat, 71 rue du Temple, Mo. Rambuteau or Hôtel de Ville, tel. 01 53 01 86 53).

▲**Picasso Museum (Hôtel Salé)**—This is the world's largest collection of Pablo Picasso's paintings, sculpture, sketches, and ceramics and includes his personal collection of Impressionist art. It's well-explained in English and worth ▲▲▲ if you're a fan (€5, Wed–Mon 09:30–18:00, closed Tue, 5 rue Thorigny, Mo: St. Paul or Chemin Vert, tel. 01 42 71 25 21).

▲▲**Carnavalet Museum**—The tumultuous history of Paris is well-displayed in this converted Marais mansion. Unfortunately, explanations are in French only, but many displays are fairly self-explanatory. You'll see paintings of Parisian scenes, French Revolution paraphernalia, old Parisian store signs, a small guillotine, a model of 16th-century Ile de la Cité (notice the bridge houses), and rooms full of 15th-century Parisian furniture (€5.50, Tue–Sun 10:00–17:40, closed Mon, 23 rue de Sévigné, Mo: St Paul, tel. 01 42 72 21 13).

Promenade Plantée Park—This three-kilometer (2-mile) narrow garden walk, once a train track and now a joy, runs from place de la Bastille (Mo: Bastille) along avenue Daumesnil to Saint-Mandé (Mo: Michel Bizot). Part of the park is elevated. At times you'll walk along the street until you pick up the next segment. From place de la Bastille, take avenue Daumesnil (past Opéra building) to the intersection with avenue Ledru Rollin. Walk up the stairs and through the gate (free, opens Mon–Fri at 08:00, Sat–Sun at 09:00, closes at sunset).

▲**Père Lachaise Cemetery**—Littered with the tombstones of many of the city's most illustrious dead, this is your best one-stop look at the fascinating, romantic world of permanent Parisians. The place is confusing, but maps will direct you to the graves of Chopin, Molière, Edith Piaf, Oscar Wilde, Gertrude Stein, Héloïse, and Abelard. In section 92, a series of statues memorializing the war makes the French war experience a bit more real (open until dusk, helpful €1.50 maps at flower store near entry, across street from Métro stop, Mo: Père Lachaise or bus #69).

Disappointments de Paris

Here are a few negatives to help you manage your limited time:

La Madeleine is a big, stark, neoclassical church with a postcard facade and a postbox interior. The famous aristocratic deli behind the church, Fauchon, is elegant, but so are many others handier to your hotel.

Paris' **Panthéon** (nothing like Rome's) is another stark neoclassical edifice, filled with mortal remains of great Frenchmen who mean little to the average American tourist.

The **Bastille** is Paris' most famous nonsight. The square is there, but confused tourists look everywhere and can't find the famous prison of Revolution fame. The building's gone and the square is good only as a jumping-off point for Promenade Plantée Park (see "Sights—Northeast Paris," above).

Finally, the **Latin Quarter** is a frail shadow of its characteristic self. It's more Tunisian, Greek, and Woolworth's than old-time Paris. The café life that turned on Hemingway and endeared boul' Miche and boulevard St. Germain to so many poets is also trampled by modern commercialism.

Best Shopping

Forum des Halles is a huge subterranean shopping center. It's fun, mod, and colorful but lacks a soul (Mo: Les Halles). The **Galeries Lafayette** behind the old Opéra Garnier is your best elegant, Old World, one-stop Parisian department store/shopping center (Mo: Opéra). Also visit the adjacent **Printemps** store and the historic (as well as handy) **Samaritaine** department store in several buildings near pont Neuf (Mo: Pont Neuf). Ritzy shops surround the Ritz Hotel at place Vendôme (Mo: Tuileries).

Palace of Versailles

Every king's dream, Versailles was the residence of the French king and the cultural heartbeat of Europe for about 100 years—until the Revolution of 1789 ended the notion that God deputized some people to rule for Him on earth. Louis XIV spent half a year's income of Europe's richest country turning his dad's hunting lodge into a palace fit for a divine monarch. Louis XV and Louis XVI spent much of the 18th century gilding Louis XIV's lily. In 1837, about 50 years after the royal family was evicted, King Louis Philippe opened the palace as a museum. Europe's next-best palaces are Versailles wanna-bes.

Information: A helpful TI is just past Sofitel Hôtel on your walk from the station to the palace (May–Sept daily 09:00–19:00, Oct–April daily 09:00–18:00, tel. 01 39 24 88 88, can order Versailles tickets online but they're easy to buy on-site, www.chateauversailles.fr). You'll also find information booths inside

Versailles

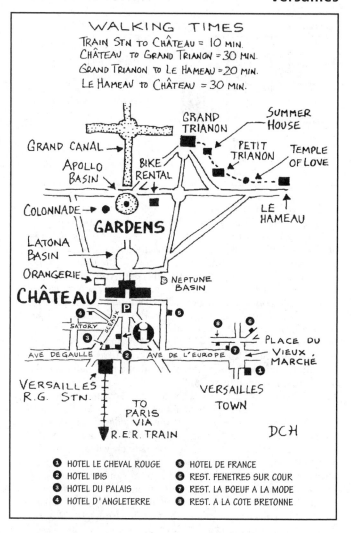

WALKING TIMES
TRAIN STN TO CHÂTEAU = 10 MIN.
CHÂTEAU TO GRAND TRIANON = 30 MIN.
GRAND TRIANON TO LE HAMEAU = 20 MIN.
LE HAMEAU TO CHÂTEAU = 30 MIN.

GRAND TRIANON
SUMMER HOUSE
GRAND CANAL
PETIT TRIANON
TEMPLE OF LOVE
APOLLO BASIN
BIKE RENTAL
COLONNADE
LE HAMEAU
GARDENS
LATONA BASIN
ORANGERIE
NEPTUNE BASIN
CHÂTEAU
SATORY
SCEAUX
AVE DE GAULLE
AVE DE L'EUROPE
PLACE DU VIEUX MARCHÉ
VERSAILLES R.G. STN.
VERSAILLES TOWN
TO PARIS VIA R.E.R. TRAIN
DCH

❶ HOTEL LE CHEVAL ROUGE
❷ HOTEL IBIS
❸ HOTEL DU PALAIS
❹ HOTEL D'ANGLETERRE
❺ HOTEL DE FRANCE
❻ REST. FENETRES SUR COUR
❼ REST. LA BOEUF A LA MODE
❽ REST. A LA COTE BRETONNE

the château (doors A, B-2, and C). The useful brochure, *Versailles Orientation Guide,* explains your sightseeing options.

   Ticket Options: The self-guided, one-way romp through the State Apartments, including the Hall of Mirrors, costs €7 (covered by museum pass; €5.50 after 15:30, on Sun, or for ages 18–25; under 18 free). The entry fee is payable at doors A, C,

Entrances to Versailles

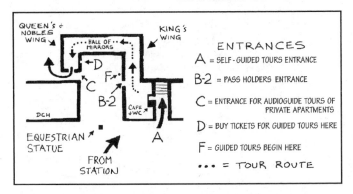

or D. If you want a guided tour through the other sections, you
need to pay the €7 base price, then pay extra for the tour.

Tours: Add €4 for a 60-minute guided tour of lesser-known
nobles' apartments (like those of the well-coiffed Madame Pom-
padour) or €6 for a 90-minute guided tour of the King's Private
Apartments (Louis XV, Louis XVI, and Marie Antoinette), the
chapel, and Opera House. Pay and get your tour appointment at
entrance D. Tour times are normally all allotted for the day by
13:00. Tours leave from door F (across the courtyard from door D).
Two informative but dry audioguide tours are available. Choose
between €4 for Louis XIV's Private Apartments at door C, or
€3.50 for the State Apartments and Hall of Mirrors at doors A or
B-2. Both audioguide tours are sold until one hour before closing.
Tours aren't covered by the museum pass. If you have extra time
before your tour, wander through the State Apartments or gardens.

Hours: May through September Tuesday through Sunday
09:00 to 18:30, October through April Tuesday through Sunday
09:00 to 17:30, closed Monday, last entry 30 minutes before
closing. In summer, Versailles is especially crowded around 10:00
and 13:00, and all day Tuesday and Sunday. To minimize crowds,
either arrive by 09:00 or after 15:30 (admission is cheaper after
15:30, but you'll miss the last guided tours of the day, which
generally depart around 15:00); tour the gardens after the palace
closes. The palace is great late. On my last visit, at 18:00, I was
the only tourist in the Hall of Mirrors...even on a Tuesday.

Time to Allow: Six hours round-trip from Paris (1 hour
each way in transit, 2 hours for palace, 2 for gardens).

Self-Guided Tour: For the basic self-guided tour, join the
line at entrance A if you need to pay admission. Those with a
museum pass are allowed in through entrance B-2 without a
wait. Enter the palace and take a one-way walk through the

State Apartments from the "King's Wing," through the magnificent Hall of Mirrors, and out via the "Queen's Wing."

The Hall of Mirrors was the ultimate hall of the day—75 meters long (250 feet), with 17 arched mirrors matching 17 windows with royal garden views, 24 gilded candelabra, eight busts of Roman emperors, and eight classical-style statues (7 are ancient originals). The ceiling is decorated with stories of Louis' triumphs. Imagine this place filled with silk gowns and powdered wigs, lit by thousands of candles. The mirrors—a luxurious rarity at the time—were a reflection of a time when aristocrats felt good about their looks and their fortunes. In another age altogether, this was the room in which the Treaty of Versailles was signed, ending World War I.

Before going downstairs at the end, take a stroll clockwise around the long room filled with the great battles of France murals. If you don't have *Rick Steves' Paris* or *Rick Steves' Mona Winks*, the guidebook called *The Châteaux, The Gardens, and Trianon* gives a room-by-room rundown.

Palace Gardens: The gardens offer a world of royal amusements. Outside the palace is L'Orangerie. Louis, the only one who could grow oranges in Paris, had an orange grove on wheels that could be wheeled in and out of his greenhouses according to the weather. A promenade leads from the palace to the Grand Canal, an artificial lake that, in Louis' day, was a mini-sea with nine ships, including a 32-cannon warship. France's royalty used to float up and down the canal in Venetian gondolas.

While Louis cleverly used palace life at Versailles to "domesticate" his nobility, turning otherwise meddlesome nobles into groveling socialites, all this pomp and ceremony hampered the royal family as well. For an escape from the public life at Versailles, they built more intimate palaces as retreats in their garden. Before the Revolution, there was plenty of space to retreat—the grounds were enclosed by a 40-kilometer-long fence.

The beautifully restored **Grand Trianon Palace** is as sumptuous as the main palace but much smaller. With its pastel-pink colonnade and more human scale, this is a place you'd like to call home. The nearby **Petit Trianon**, which has a fine neoclassical exterior with a skippable interior, was Marie Antoinette's favorite residence (€5 for both, €3 after 15:30, covered by museum pass, April–Oct Tue–Sun 12:00–18:00, closed Mon, Nov–March 12:00–17:00).

You can almost see princesses bobbing gaily in the branches as you walk through the enchanting forest, past the white marble temple of love (1778) to the queen's fake-peasant **Hamlet** (*Hameau*; interior not tourable). Palace life really got to Marie Antoinette. Sort of a back-to-basics queen, she retreated farther and farther from her blue-blooded reality. Her happiest days were at the hamlet, under a bonnet, tending her perfumed sheep and her manicured gardens in a thatch-happy wonderland.

Getting around the Gardens: It's a 30-minute hike from the palace, down the canal, past the two mini-palaces to the hamlet. You can rent bikes (€6/hr). The pokey tourist train runs between the canal and château (€5, 5/hr, 4 stops, you can hop on and off as you like, nearly worthless commentary).

Garden Hours: Except for fountain-filled weekends (see below), the gardens are free and open from 07:00 to sunset (as late as 21:30). There's a sandwich kiosk and a decent restaurant at the canal.

Fountain Spectacles: Classical music fills the king's backyard and the garden's fountains are in full squirt on Saturdays from July through September and on Sundays from early April through early October (schedule for both days: 11:00–12:00, 15:30–17:00, and 17:20–17:30). On these "spray days," the gardens cost €5 (ages 18–25-€3.50, free if under 18, not covered by museum pass, ask for map). Louis had his engineers literally reroute a river to fuel these fountains. Even by today's standards, they are impressive. For more information, pick up the map of the fountain show (*Les Grandes Eaux Musicales*) at any information booth. Also ask about the impressive *Les Fêtes de Nuit* nighttime spectacle (on some Sat, July–mid-Sept).

Getting There: Take the RER-C train (€5 round-trip, 30 min one-way) to Versailles R.G. or "Rive Gauche" (not Versailles C.H., which is farther from the palace). Trains named "Vick" leave about five times an hour for the palace from these RER stops: Invalides, Champ de Mars, Musée d'Orsay, St. Michel, Pont de l'Alma, and Gare d'Austerlitz. Any train named Vick goes to Versailles; don't board other trains. Get off at Versailles Rive Gauche (the end of the line), turn right out of the station, then left at the first boulevard. It's a 10-minute walk to the palace.

Your Eurailpass covers this inexpensive trip, but it uses up a valuable "flexi" day. Instead of using your pass, consider seeing Versailles on your way in or out of Paris. To get free passage, show your railpass at an SCNF ticket window (for example, at the Les Invalides or Musée d'Orsay RER stops) and get a *contremarque de passage*; keep this ticket to exit the system.

When returning from Versailles, look through the windows past the turnstiles for the departure board. Any train leaving Versailles goes as far as downtown Paris (they're marked "all stations until d'Austerlitz"). If you're uncertain, confirm with a local by asking, "*À Paris?*" ("To Paris?").

Allow €35 (each way) for a taxi from Paris to Versailles. To cut your park walking by 50 percent, consider having the taxi drop you at the Hamlet (*Hameau*).

Town of Versailles (zip code: 78000): After the palace closes and the tourists go, the prosperous, wholesome town of Versailles

Chartres

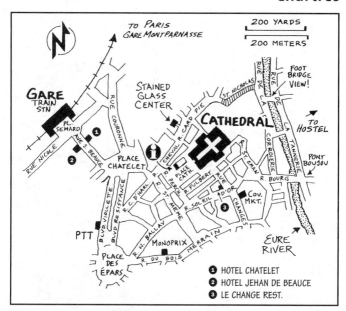

TO PARIS
GARE MONTPARNASSE

200 YARDS
200 METERS

N

GARE
TRAIN STN

STAINED
GLASS
CENTER

CATHEDRAL

FOOT
BRIDGE
VIEW!

RUE DE

ST. NICOLAS

RUE

TO
HOSTEL

PL.
SEMARD

RUE NICOLE

AVE 2 BEAUX

RUE COURONNE

R. CARD PIE

CHEVAL BLANC

i

PLACE
CHATELET

PONT
BOUJOU

CORROIERIE

R. TANNERIE

ST. ERMAN

R. D'OR

PLACE
CATH.

R. FULBERT

R. BOURG

R. PERCH

R. MEME

R. SOLEIL

R.C. D'HARL

BLVD VIOLLETTE

BLVD RESISTANCE

PTT

R. N. BALLAY

MONOPRIX

R. DU BOIS

MERRAIN

COV.
MKT.

R. CHANGES

EURE
RIVER

PLACE
DES
ÉPARS

❶ HOTEL CHATELET
❷ HOTEL JEHAN DE BEAUCE
❸ LE CHANGE REST.

feels a long way from Paris. The central market thrives on place du Marché on Sunday, Tuesday, and Friday until 13:00 (leaving the RER station, turn right and walk 10 min). Consider the wisdom of picking up or dropping your rental car in Versailles rather than in Paris. In Versailles, the Hertz and Avis offices are at Gare des Chantiers (Versailles C.H., served by Paris' Montparnasse station). Versailles makes a fine home base; see Versailles accommodations (and recommended restaurants) under "Sleeping," below.

More Day Trips from Paris

▲▲▲**Chartres**—In 1194, a terrible fire destroyed the church at Chartres that housed the much-venerated veil of Mary. With almost unbelievably good fortune, the monks found the veil miraculously preserved in the ashes. Money poured in for the building of a bigger and better cathedral—decorated with 2,000 carved figures and some of France's best stained glass. The cathedral feels too large for the city because it was designed to accommodate huge crowds of pilgrims. One of those pilgrims, an impressed Napoleon, declared after a visit in 1811: "Chartres is no place for an atheist." Rodin called it "the Acropolis of France." British Francophile Malcolm Miller or his assistant give great "Appreciation of Gothic" tours Monday through Saturday, usually at noon

Paris Daytrips

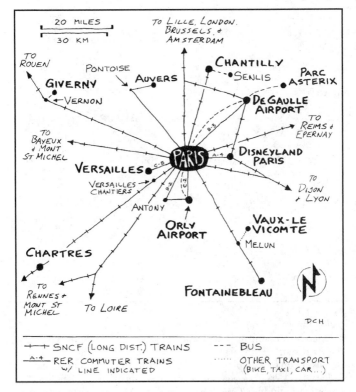

and 14:45 (verify times in advance, no tours off-season, call TI at 02 37 18 26 26). Each €6 tour is different; many people stay for both tours. Just show up at the church (daily 07:00–19:00).

Explore Chartres' pleasant city center and discover the picnic-friendly park behind the cathedral. The helpful **TI**, next to the cathedral, has a map with a self-guided tour of Chartres (Mon–Sat 09:00–19:00, Sun 09:00–17:30, tel. 02 37 18 26 26). Chartres is a one-hour train trip from the Gare Montparnasse (about €11 one-way, 10/day). To stay overnight, try the comfy **Hôtel Chatelet***** (Sb-€56–72, Db-€66, extra person-€9, streetside rooms cheaper, CC, 6 avenue Jehan de Beauce, tel. 02 37 21 78 00, fax 02 37 36 23 01, e-mail: hchatel@club-internet.fr) or the basic **Hôtel Jehan de Beauce**** (S-€24, D-€27, Ds-€31, Db-€37–47, Tb-€38, CC, 19 avenue Jehan de Beauce, tel. 02 37 21 01 41, fax 02 37 21 59 10).

▲**Giverny**—Monet spent 43 of his most creative years here (1883–1926). Monet's gardens and home are unfortunately split by a busy road and very popular with tourists. Buy your ticket, walk through the gardens, and take the underpass into the artist's famous lily-pad land. The path leads you over the Japanese Bridge, under weeping willows, and past countless scenes that leave artists aching for an easel. Back on the other side, stroll through his more robust, structured garden and his mildly interesting home. The jammed gift shop at the exit is Monet's actual skylit studio.

While lines may be long and tour groups may trample the flowers, true fans still find magic in those lily pads. Minimize crowds by arriving before 10:00 (get in line) or after 16:00 (€5.50, €4 for gardens only, April–Oct Tue–Sun 10:00–18:00, closed Mon and Nov–March, tel. 02 32 51 94 65).

Take the Rouen-bound train from Paris' Gare St. Lazare station to Vernon (about €21 round-trip, long gaps in service, know schedule before you go). From the Vernon train station to Monet's garden (4 kilometers/2.5 miles away), take the Vernon-Giverny bus (4/day, scheduled to meet most trains), hitch, taxi (€11 for up to 3, €12 for 4, tel. 07 76 08 50 78), or rent a bike at the bar opposite the station (€12, tel. 02 32 21 16 01, crummy ride on a busy road). Get return bus times from the ticket office in Giverny (note that driver sometimes skips last pickup), or ask them to call a taxi if you don't see one waiting at the bus stop (tel. 02 32 51 70 17 or 06 07 34 36 68). Bus stops are in the parking lot across from the entry to Monet's home and just beyond the American Impressionist Art Museum. Big tour companies do a Giverny daytrip from Paris for around $60.

The **American Impressionist Art Museum** (turn left when leaving Monet's place and walk 90 meters/300 feet) is devoted to American artists who followed Claude to Giverny. This bright, modern gallery has a good little Mary Cassatt section and gives us a rare chance to see French people appreciating our artists (same price and hours as Monet's home).

To sleep two blocks from Monet's home, try the adorable **Hôtel La Musardiere**** (Db-€46–69, Tb-€63–73, CC, 132 rue Claude Monet, 27620 Giverny, tel. 02 32 21 03 18, fax 02 32 21 60 00).

▲▲**Disneyland Paris**—Europe's Disneyland is basically a modern remake of California's, with most of the same rides and smiles. The main difference is that Mickey Mouse speaks French (and you can buy wine with your lunch). My kids went ducky. Locals love it. It's worth a day if Paris is handier than Florida or California. Crowds are a problem (tel. 01 64 74 30 00 for the latest). If possible, avoid Saturday, Sunday, Wednesday, school holidays, and July and August. After dinner, crowds are gone, and you'll walk right onto rides that had a 45-minute wait three hours earlier. To avoid lines at the five most popular rides, get a free FASTPASS at the entry (punch in machines at rides to reserve a ride). You'll also save time by buying your tickets ahead (at airport TIs, over 100 Métro stations, or along the Champs-Elysées at the TI, Disney Store, or Virgin Megastore). Food is fun but expensive. Smuggle in a picnic (€37, kids 3–11-€29, €18 for all ages from 17:00–23:00 in summer, kids under 3 always free, about 25 percent cheaper off-season, daily April–June 09:00–20:00; July–Aug 09:00–23:00; Sept–March Mon–Fri 10:00–20:00, Sat–Sun 09:00–20:00, tel. 01 60 30 60 30, fax 01 60 30 60 65, www.disneylandparis.com).

Disney brochures are in every Paris hotel. The RER (about €7 each way, direct from downtown Paris to Marne-la-Vallee in 30 min) drops you right into the park. The last train back to Paris leaves shortly after midnight.

To sleep reasonably at the huge Disney complex, try **Hôtel Sante Fe**** with shuttle service to the park every 12 minutes (Db-€214 includes breakfast and 2-day park pass, CC, tel. 01 60 30 60 30, fax 01 60 30 60 65).

Nightlife in Paris

Paris is brilliant after dark. Save energy from your day's sightseeing and get out at night. Whether it's a concert at Sainte-Chapelle, an elevator up the Arc de Triomphe, or a late-night café, experience the city of light lit. If a **Seine River cruise** appeals, see "Organized Tours of Paris," page 189.

The *Pariscope* magazine, in French, offers a complete weekly listing of music, cinema, theater, opera, and other special events (€0.50 at any newsstand, www.pariscope.fr). The *Paris Voice* newspaper, in English, has a monthly review of Paris entertainment (available at any English-language bookstore, French-American establishments, or the American Church, www.parisvoice.com).

Music
Jazz Clubs

With a lively mix of American, French, and international musicians, Paris has been an internationally acclaimed jazz capital since World War II. You'll pay from €6 to €24 to enter a jazz club (1 drink may be included; if not, expect to pay €5–9 per drink; beer is cheapest). See *Pariscope* magazine under "Musique" for listings, or, better, the American Church's *Paris Voice* paper for a good monthly review, or drop by the clubs to check out their calendars posted on the front door. Music starts after 22:00 in most clubs. Some offer dinner concerts from about 20:30 on. Here are a few good bets:

Caveau de la Huchette, a characteristic old jazz club for visitors, fills an ancient Latin Quarter cellar with live jazz and frenzied dancing every night (€9 weekday, €12 weekend admission, €5 drinks, Tue–Sun 21:30–02:30 or later, closed Mon, 5 rue de la Huchette, Mo: St. Michel, recorded info tel. 01 43 26 65 05).

For a hotbed of late-night activity and jazz, go to the

two-block-long rue des Lombards, at boulevard Sebastopol, midway between the river and Pompidou Center (Mo: Chatelet). **Au Duc des Lombards**, right at the corner, is one of the most popular and respected jazz clubs in Paris, with concerts generally at 21:00 (42 rue des Lombards, tel. 01 42 33 22 88). **Le Sunset** and **le Sunside** sit side by side a block west, offering more traditional jazz—Dixieland, big band—and fewer crowds, with concerts generally at 21:00 (60 rue des Lombards, Sunset tel. 01 40 26 46 60, Sunside tel. 01 40 26 21 25).

At the more down-to-earth and mellow **Le Cave du Franc Pinot**, you can enjoy a glass of chardonnay at the main-floor wine bar, then drop downstairs for a cool jazz scene (good dinner-and-jazz values as well, located on Ile St. Louis where Pont Marie meets the island, 1 quai de Bourbon, Mo: Pont Marie, tel. 01 46 33 60 64).

Classical Concerts

For classical music on any night, consult *Pariscope* magazine; the "Musique" section under "Concerts Classiques" lists concerts (free and fee). Look for posters at the churches. Churches that regularly host concerts include St. Sulpice, St. Germain-des-Près, Basilique de Madeleine, St. Eustache, St. Julien-le-Pauvre, and Sainte-Chapelle. It's worth the €15 to €23 entry for the pleasure of hearing Mozart surrounded by the stained glass of the tiny Sainte-Chapelle. Look also for daytime concerts in parks like the Luxembourg Gardens. Even the Galeries Lafayette department store offers concerts. Many are free (*entrée libre*), such as the Sunday atelier concert sponsored by the American Church (18:00, not every week, Sept–May, 65 quai d'Orsay, Mo: Invalides, RER: Pont de l'Alma, tel. 01 40 62 05 00).

Opera

Paris is home to two well-respected operas. The Opéra Garnier, Paris' first opera house, hosts opera and ballet performances. Come here for less expensive tickets and grand belle époque decor (Mo: Opéra, tel. 01 44 73 13 99). The Opéra de la Bastille is the massive modern opera house that dominates place de la Bastille. Come here for state-of-the-art special effects and modern interpretations of classic ballets and operas (Mo: Bastille, tel. 01 43 43 96 96). For tickets, call 01 44 73 13 00, go to the opera ticket offices (open 11:00–18:00), or, best, reserve on the Web at www.ticketavenue .com (for both operas).

Bus Tours

Paris Illumination Tours, run by Paris Vision, connect all the great illuminated sights of Paris with a 100-minute bus tour in 12 languages. Double-decker buses have huge windows, but customers continuing to the overrated Moulin Rouge get the most desirable front seats. You'll stampede on with a United Nations of tourists, get an audioguide, and listen to a tape-recorded spiel (interesting but occasionally hard to hear). Uninspired as it is, this provides an entertaining first-night overview of the city at its floodlit and scenic best (bring your city map to stay oriented as you go). Left-side seats are marginally better. Visibility is fine in the rain. You're entirely on the bus except for one five-minute cigarette break at the Eiffel Tower viewpoint (adult-€23, kids under 11 ride free, departures at 20:30 nightly all year, also 21:30 April–Oct only, departs from Paris Vision office at 214 rue de Rivoli, across the street from Mo: Tuileries). These trips are sold through your hotel (brochures in lobby) or direct at the address listed above. Look also for the same tour by minivan—pickup is at your hotel, the driver is a qualified guide, and there's a maximum of seven clients (€46/person, kids ages 4–11-€23, tel. for bus and minivans 01 42 60 30 01, fax 01 42 86 95 36, www.parisvision.com).

Sleeping in Paris
(€1.10 = about $1, country code: 33)

Sleep Code: **S** = Single, **D** = Double/Twin, **T** = Triple, **Q** = Quad, **b** = bathroom, **s** = shower only, **CC** = Credit Cards accepted, **no CC** = Credit Cards not accepted, * = French hotel rating system (0–4 stars).

I've focused on three safe, handy, and colorful neighborhoods: rue Cler, Marais, and Contrescarpe. For each, I list good hotels, helpful hints, and restaurants (see "Eating," below). Before reserving, read the descriptions of the three neighborhoods closely. Each offers different pros and cons, and your neighborhood is as important as your hotel for the success of your trip.

Reserve ahead for Paris, the sooner the better. Conventions clog Paris in September (worst), October, May, and June (very tough). In August, when Paris is quiet, some hotels offer lower rates to fill their rooms (if you're planning to visit Paris in the summer, the extra expense of an air-conditioned room can be money well spent). Most hotels accept telephone reservations, require prepayment with a credit-card number, and prefer a faxed follow-up to be sure everything is in order. For more information, see "Making Reservations" in this book's Introduction.

French hotels are rated by stars (indicated in this chapter by an *). One star is simple, two has most of the comforts, and three is generally a two-star with a mini-bar and fancier lobby (though I've tried to find three-star hotels that merit the expense; four stars offer more luxury than you have time to appreciate).

Old, characteristic, budget Parisian hotels have always been cramped. Retrofitted with elevators, toilets, and private showers (as most are today), they are even more cramped. Even three-star hotel rooms are small and often not worth the extra expense in

Paris. Some hotels include the hotel tax (*taxe du séjour*, about €0.60–0.90 per person per day), though most will add this to your bill. Two- and three-star hotels are required to have an English-speaking staff. Nearly all hotels listed will have someone who speaks English.

Recommended hotels have an elevator unless otherwise noted. Quad rooms usually have two double beds. Because rooms with double beds and showers are cheaper than rooms with twin beds and baths, room prices vary within each hotel.

You can save as much as €15 by finding the increasingly rare room without a private shower, though some hotels charge for down-the-hall showers. Singles (except for the rare closet-type rooms that fit only 1 twin bed) are simply doubles used by one person. They rent for only a little less than a double. Continental breakfasts average €6, buffet breakfasts (baked goods, cereal, yogurt, and fruit) cost €7.75 to €9.25. Café or picnic breakfasts are cheaper, but hotels usually give unlimited coffee.

Get advice from your hotel for safe parking (consider long-term parking at Orly Airport and taxi in). Meters are free in August. Garages are plentiful (€14–23/day, with special rates through some hotels). Self-serve Laundromats are common; ask your hotelier for the nearest one (*Où est un laverie automatique?*; ooh ay uh lah-vay-ree auto-mah-teek).

If you have any trouble finding a room using our listings, try one of these helpful Web sites: www.parishotel.com and www.hotelboulevard.com. You can select from various neighborhood areas (e.g., Eiffel Tower area), give the dates of your visit and preferred price range, and presto—they'll list options with rates. You'll find the hotels listed in this book to be better located and objectively reviewed, though as a last resort these services are handy.

Rue Cler Orientation

Rue Cler, a villagelike pedestrian street, is safe, tidy, and makes me feel like I must have been a poodle in a previous life. How such coziness lodged itself between the high-powered government district and the wealthy Eiffel Tower and Invalides areas, I'll never know. This is a neighborhood of wide, tree-lined boulevards, stately apartment buildings, and lots of Americans. The American Church, American library, American University, and many of my readers call this area home.

Become a local at a rue Cler café for breakfast or join the after-noon crowd for *une bière pression* (a draft beer). On rue Cler, you can eat and browse your way through a street full of tart shops, delis, cheeseries, and colorful outdoor produce stalls. For an after-dinner cruise on the Seine, it's just a short walk to the river and the Bâteaux-Mouches (see "Organized Tours of Paris," above).

Your neighborhood **TI** is at the Eiffel Tower (May–Sept

daily 11:00–18:42, no kidding, tel. 01 45 51 22 15). The Métro
station (Ecole Militaire) and a **post office** are at the end of
rue Cler on avenue de la Motte Piquet, and there's a handy
SNCF office at 78 rue St. Dominique (Mon–Fri 09:00–19:00, Sat
10:00–12:20, 14:00–18:00). The Banque Populaire (across from
Hôtel Leveque) changes money. Rue St. Dominique is the area's
boutique-browsing street. The Epicerie de la Tour **grocery** is
open until midnight (197 rue de Grenelle).

The **American Church and College** is the community center
for Americans living in Paris and should be one of your first stops
if you're planning to stay a while (reception open Mon–Sat 09:00–
22:30, Sun 09:00–19:30, 65 quai d'Orsay, tel. 01 40 62 05 00). Pick
up copies of the *Paris Voice* for a monthly review of Paris entertainment, and *France-U.S.A. Contacts* for information on housing and
employment through the community of 30,000 Americans living
in Paris. The interdenominational service at 11:00 on Sunday, the
coffee hour after church, and the free Sunday concerts (18:00, not
every week, Sept–May only) are a great way to make some friends
and get a taste of émigré life in Paris.

Afternoon *boules* (lawn bowling) on the esplanade des
Invalides is a relaxing spectator sport. Look for the dirt area to
the upper right as you face the Invalides.

You should try at least one of these helpful **bus routes:**
Line #69 runs along rue St. Dominique and serves Les Invalides,
Orsay, Louvre, Marais, and Père-Lachaise cemetery. Line #92
runs along avenue Bosquet and serves the Arc de Triomphe and
Champs-Elysées in one direction and the Montparnasse Tower in
the other. Line #87 runs on avenue de la Bourdonnais and serves
St. Sulpice, Luxembourg Gardens, and the Sevres-Babylone shopping area. Line #28 runs on boulevard La Tour Maubourg and
serves the St. Lazare station.

Sleeping in the Rue Cler Neighborhood
(7th arrondissement, Mo: Ecole Militaire, zip code: 75007)
Rue Cler is the glue that holds this pleasant neighborhood
together. From here you can walk to the Eiffel Tower, Napoleon's
Tomb, the Seine, and the Orsay and Rodin Museums.

Many of my readers stay in this neighborhood. If you want to
disappear into Paris, you'll do it better at the hotels away from the
rue Cler or in the other neighborhoods I list. And if nightlife matters, sleep elsewhere. The first seven hotels listed below are within
Camembert-smelling distance of rue Cler; the others are within a
5- to 10-minute stroll. Warning: The first two hotels are popular
with my readers.

Hôtel Leveque** is ideally located, with a helpful staff
and a singing maid. It's a big place with well-designed rooms
that have all the comforts (S-€53, Db-€84–91, Tb-€114,

breakfast-€7, first breakfast free for readers of this book, CC, air-con planned for 2002, 29 rue Cler, tel. 01 47 05 49 15, fax 01 45 50 49 36, www.hotel-leveque.com, e-mail: info @hotelleveque.com).

Hôtel du Champ de Mars**, with charming, pastel rooms and helpful English-speaking owners Françoise and Stephane and right-hand man Slim, is a cozier rue Cler option. The hotel has a Provence-style, small-town feel from top to bottom. Rooms are small but comfortable and a very good value. Single rooms can work as tiny doubles (Sb-€66, Db-€72–76, Tb-€92, CC, 30 meters off rue Cler at 7 rue de Champ de Mars, tel. 01 45 51 52 30, fax 01 45 51 64 36, www.hotel-du-champ-de-mars.com, e-mail: stg@club-internet.fr).

Hôtel Cadran*** charges too much for its fine location and cozy lobby. Rooms are tight and narrow but air-conditioned (Sb-€148, Db-€165, CC, 10 rue de Champs de Mars, tel. 01 40 62 67 00, fax 01 40 62 67 13, www.cadran.com).

Hôtel Relais Bosquet*** is modern, spacious, and a bit upscale, with snazzy, air-conditioned rooms and big beds (Sb-€123–148, standard Db-€140, spacious Db-€163, extra bed-€31, parking-€14, CC, 19 rue de Champ de Mars, tel. 01 47 05 25 45, fax 01 45 55 08 24, www.relaisbosquet.com).

Hôtel Beaugency***, on a quieter street just off rue Cler, has small but comfortable rooms, a lobby you can stretch out in, and friendly Nadine in charge (Sb-€104, Db-€111, Tb-€127, buffet breakfast, CC, 21 rue Duvivier, tel. 01 47 05 01 63, fax 01 45 51 04 96, www.hotel-beaugency.com).

Hôtel la Motte Piquet**, at the end of rue Cler, is reasonable, spotless, and cozy (Ss-€54, Sb-€60–69, Db-€69–79, CC, most rooms face a busy street, 30 avenue de la Motte Piquet, tel. 01 47 05 09 57, fax 01 47 05 74 36).

Sleeping near rue Cler: The following listings are a 5- to 10-minute walk west of rue Cler and are listed in order of proximity.

Hôtel Prince**, just across avenue Bosquet from the Ecole Militaire Métro stop, has fair-value rooms, many overlooking a busy street (Db-€74–97, CC, 66 avenue Bosquet, tel. 01 47 05 40 90, fax 01 47 53 06 62).

Hôtel le Tourville**** is the most classy and expensive of my Paris listings. This four-star gem is surprisingly intimate and friendly, from its welcoming lobby to its air-conditioned, pastel rooms and vaulted breakfast area (small standard Db-€138, superior Db-€170, Db with private terrace-€215, extra bed-€15.50, CC, 16 avenue de Tourville, Mo: Ecole Militaire, tel. 01 47 05 62 62, fax 01 47 05 43 90, e-mail: hotel@tourville.com).

Hôtel de Turenne**, with comfortable, air-conditioned rooms, is a great value when it's hot, and it has five truly single rooms (Sb-€61, Db-€71–81, Tb-€96, extra bed-€9.50, CC,

Rue Cler Hotels

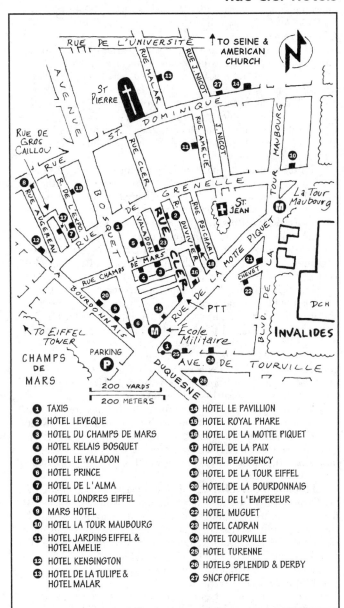

1 TAXIS		**14** HOTEL LE PAVILLION
2 HOTEL LEVEQUE		**15** HOTEL ROYAL PHARE
3 HOTEL DU CHAMPS DE MARS		**16** HOTEL DE LA MOTTE PIQUET
4 HOTEL RELAIS BOSQUET		**17** HOTEL DE LA PAIX
5 HOTEL LE VALADON		**18** HOTEL BEAUGENCY
6 HOTEL PRINCE		**19** HOTEL DE LA TOUR EIFFEL
7 HOTEL DE L'ALMA		**20** HOTEL DE LA BOURDONNAIS
8 HOTEL LONDRES EIFFEL		**21** HOTEL DE L'EMPEREUR
9 MARS HOTEL		**22** HOTEL MUGUET
10 HOTEL LA TOUR MAUBOURG		**23** HOTEL CADRAN
11 HOTEL JARDINS EIFFEL & HOTEL AMELIE		**24** HOTEL TOURVILLE
12 HOTEL KENSINGTON		**25** HOTEL TURENNE
13 HOTEL DE LA TULIPE & HOTEL MALAR		**26** HOTELS SPLENDID & DERBY
		27 SNCF OFFICE

20 avenue de Tourville, tel. 01 47 05 99 92, fax 01 45 56 06 04, e-mail: hotel.turenne.paris7@wanadoo.fr).

Hôtel Londres Eiffel*** is my closest listing to the Eiffel Tower and Champs de Mars park. It offers small but thoughtfully appointed rooms, cozy public spaces, and an Internet station. Helpful Esther and Cedric take good care of their guests (Sb-€90–102, Db-€103–112, Tb-€135, CC, use handy bus #69 or the RER Alma stop, 1 rue Augerau, tel. 01 45 51 63 02, fax 01 47 05 28 96, www.Londres-Eiffel.com).

Mars Hôtel**, with an ambitious, engaging new owner, is a solid midrange value with mostly spacious rooms and a beam-me-up-Jacques, coffin-sized elevator. The front rooms are noisier but have a view of the Eiffel Tower (€70, large Db-€85, extra bed-€18.50, CC, 117 avenue de la Bourdonnais, tel. 01 47 05 42 30, fax 01 47 05 45 91).

Hôtel de la Bourdonnais***, best known for its renowned restaurant, is a perfectly Parisian place. It mixes Old World elegance with professional service, generally spacious rooms, and pleasant public spaces (Sb-€110, Db-€130, Tb-€140, Qb-€150, Qb suite-€200, CC, 111 avenue de la Bourdonnais, tel. 01 47 05 45 42, fax 01 45 55 75 54, www.hotellabourdonnais.fr).

Hôtel Kensington** feels less personal but is a good value with warmly decorated rooms (Sb-€53, Db-€67–82, CC, 79 avenue de la Bourdonnais, tel. 01 47 05 74 00, fax 01 47 05 25 81, www.hotel-kensington.com).

Hôtel de la Paix is bare-bones basic and cheap (S-€29, Ds-€51, Db-€54, Tb-€74, no CC, no elevator, no frills, 19 rue du Gros-Caillou, tel. 01 45 51 86 17, fax 01 45 55 93 28).

Hôtel de la Tulipe** is a unique place two blocks from rue Cler toward the river, with artistically decorated rooms (each one different) above a wood-beamed lounge and a peaceful, leafy courtyard (Db-€105–110, Tb-€140, CC, no elevator, cable TV, 33 rue Malar, tel. 01 45 51 67 21, fax 01 47 53 96 37, www.hoteldelatulipe.com).

Sleeping near Métro stop La Tour Maubourg: The next four listings are within two blocks of the intersection of avenue de la Motte Piquet and Les Invalides.

Hôtel le Pavillon** is a quiet place with unrealized potential, set back from the street. A small courtyard greets clients, its pastel rooms are adequate, but bathrooms need work (Sb-€72, Db-80€, CC, family suites-€105, 54 rue St. Dominique, tel. 01 45 51 42 87, fax 01 45 51 32 79, e-mail: patrickpavillon@aol.com).

Hôtel Les Jardins Eiffel*** is a bit pricey but merits its three stars with professional service, a spacious lobby, outdoor patio, and comfortable, air-conditioned rooms—some with private balconies. Ask for a room *avec petit balcon* (Sb-€92–128, Db-€100–152, extra bed-€21, parking-€17/day,

CC, 8 rue Amelie, tel. 01 47 05 46 21, fax 01 45 55 28 08, e-mail: eiffel@unimedia.fr).

What the roomy **Hôtel de l'Empereur**** lacks in personality, it makes up for in value. Its pleasant rooms offer all the comforts except air-conditioning. Streetside rooms have views but some noise; fifth-floor rooms have small balconies and better views (Sb-€68–72, Db-€73–82, Tb-€103, Qb-€118, CC, 2 rue Chevert, tel. 01 45 55 88 02, fax 01 45 51 88 54, www.hotelempereur.com).

Reserve early for the **Hôtel Muguet****, a peaceful and clean hotel where you get three-star comfort for the price of two. The hotel offers sharp, air-conditioned rooms, a small garden courtyard, and several good family rooms (Sb-€85, Db-€94–102, Tb-€130, CC, 11 rue Chevert, tel. 01 47 05 05 93, fax 01 45 50 25 37, www.hotelmuguet.com).

Lesser values: Given this fine area, these are acceptable last choices. **Hôtel Malar*** (Db-€78–86, CC, 29 rue Malar, tel. 01 45 51 38 46, fax 01 45 55 20 19, www.hotelmalar.com); **Hôtel de la Tour Eiffel**** (Sb-€61, Db-€76, Tb-€79, CC, 17 rue de l'Exposition, tel. 01 47 05 14 75, fax 01 47 53 99 46, Muriel speaks English); **Hôtel Royal Phare**** (Db-€61–74, CC, facing Ecole Militaire Métro stop, 40 avenue de la Motte Piquet, tel. 01 47 05 57 30, fax 01 45 51 64 41); **Hôtel Amelie**** (Db-€87, CC, 5 rue Amelie, tel. 01 45 51 74 75, fax 01 45 56 93 55); **Hôtel de l'Alma***** (Db-€114, CC, 32 rue de l'Exposition, tel. 01 47 05 45 70, fax 01 45 51 84 47, e-mail: almahotel@minitel.net); **Derby Eiffel Hôtel***** (Db-€116–139, CC, air-con, 5 avenue Duquesne, tel. 01 47 05 12 05, fax 01 47 05 43 43, e-mail: info@derbyeiffelhotel.com); **Hôtel Splendid***** (Db-€122–145, CC, most rooms have Eiffel Tower views, 29 avenue Tourville, tel. 01 45 51 24 77, fax 01 44 18 94 60, e-mail: splendid@club-internet.fr); and the basic, overpriced **Hôtel La Serre*** (Db-€84, CC, has good location on rue Cler but generates readers' complaints for its rude staff and bizarre hotel practices—you can't see room in advance or get a refund, 24 rue Cler, across from Hôtel Leveque, Mo: Ecole Militaire, tel. 01 47 05 52 33, fax 01 40 62 95 66).

These are last resorts. The following two hotels are decent and well-located, but are poorly and erratically run by the same rude owner. **Hôtel La Tour Maubourg*****, with spacious Old World rooms, overlooks a lawn within sight of Napoleon's tomb (Sb-€107, Db-€122–137, CC, includes breakfast, immediately at La Tour Maubourg Métro stop, 150 rue de Grenelle, tel. 01 47 05 16 16, fax 01 47 05 16 14). **Hôtel Valadon****, one block west of rue Cler, is small, quiet, and sleekly furnished. Avoid the musty, windowless basement room (Sb-€61, Db-€78–86, CC, 16 rue Valadon, tel. 01 47 53 89 85, fax 01 44 18 90 56).

Marais Orientation

Those interested in a more Soho–Greenwich Village locale should make the Marais their Parisian home. The Marais is a more happening area than rue Cler, with great access to many museums: Picasso, Carnavalet, Jewish History, and Pompidou Center. It's narrow, medieval Paris at its finest, where elegant stone mansions sit side by side with trendy bars, antique shops, and slick boutiques. Only 15 years ago it was a forgotten Parisian backwater, but now the Marais is one of Paris' most popular residential, tourist, and shopping areas.

The nearest **TIs** are in the Louvre (Wed–Mon 10:00–19:00, closed Tue) and Gare de Lyon (daily 08:00–20:00, tel. 08 92 68 31 12, wait for English recording). The **Banque de France** changes money, with good rates and long lines (Mon–Fri 09:00–11:45, 13:30–15:30, closed Sat–Sun, at corner of rue St. Antoine and place de la Bastille). Most banks and other services are on the main drag, rue de Rivoli/St. Antoine. You'll find one **taxi stand** on the north side of rue St. Antoine, where it meets rue Castex, and another on the south side of St. Antoine, in front of the St. Paul church.

The new Bastille opera house, Promenade Plantée Park, place des Vosges (Paris' oldest square), the Jewish Quarter (rue des Rosiers), and nightlife-happening rue de Lappe are all nearby. Be sure to stroll into place des Vosges after dark. The massive budget **department store** is BHV, next to Hôtel de Ville. Marais **post offices** are on rue Castex and on the corner of rues Pavée and Francs Bourgeois.

Helpful **bus routes:** Line #69 on rue St. Antoine takes you to the Louvre, Orsay, Rodin, and Napoleon's Tomb and ends at the Eiffel Tower. Line #86 runs down boulevard Henri IV, crossing Ile St. Louis and serving the Latin Quarter along boulevard St. Germain. Line #96 runs on rues Turenne and Francois Miron and serves the Louvre and boulevard St. Germain (near Luxembourg Gardens). Line #65 serves the train stations Austerlitz, Est, and Nord from place de la Bastille.

Sleeping in the Marais Neighborhood
(4th arrondissement, Mo: St. Paul or Bastille, zip code: 75004)

The Marais runs from the Pompidou Center to the Bastille (a 15-min walk), with most hotels located a few blocks north of the main east-west drag, rue de Rivoli/St. Antoine. It's about 15 minutes on foot from any hotel in this area to Notre-Dame, Ile St. Louis, and the Latin Quarter. Strolling home (day or night) from Notre-Dame along the Ile St. Louis is marvelous.

The St. Paul Métro stop puts you right in the heart of the Marais, while the Hôtel de Ville stop serves its western end, and the Bastille stop serves its eastern limit.

Hôtel Castex** is a clean, well-run, and cheery place—a great value with comfortable rooms, many stairs, and a good location on a relatively quiet street. Reserve by phone and leave your credit-card number (Sb-€47, Db-€55–58, Tb-€74, CC, no elevator, just off place de la Bastille and rue St. Antoine, 5 rue Castex, Mo: Bastille, tel. 01 42 72 31 52, fax 01 42 72 57 91, e-mail: info@castexhotel.com). The owners have another decent-value hotel two Métro stops away in a less-appealing location that often has rooms when others don't: **Hôtel de la République**** (Sb-€53, Db-€61, CC, cable TV, 31 rue Albert Thomas, 75010 Paris, Mo: République, tel. 01 42 39 19 03, fax 01 42 39 22 66, www.republiquehotel.com).

Grand Hôtel Jeanne d'Arc**, a warm, welcoming place with thoughtfully appointed rooms, is ideally located for connoisseurs of the Marais. Rooms on the street can be noisy until the bars close. Sixth-floor rooms have a view, and corner rooms are wonderfully bright in the City of Lights. Reserve this place way ahead (small Db-€70, standard Db-€94, Tb-€109, good Qb-€125, CC, 3 rue Jarente, Mo: St. Paul, tel. 01 48 87 62 11, fax 01 48 87 37 31).

Hôtel Bastille Speria***, a short block off the Bastille, feels family-run while offering business-type service. The 45 plain but cheery rooms have air-conditioning and thin walls. It's English-language friendly, from the *Herald Tribune*s in the lobby to the history of the Bastille posted in the elevator (Sb-€90–98, Db-€100–125, Tb-€143, CC, 1 rue de la Bastille, Mo: Bastille, tel. 01 42 72 04 01, fax 01 42 72 56 38, e-mail: speria@micronet.fr).

Hôtel Lyon-Mulhouse**, with half of its rooms on a busy street just off place de la Bastille, is a good value. Rooms are large and pleasant (Sb-€55–75, Db-€65–85, Tb-€75–95, Qb-€102, CC, 8 boulevard Beaumarchais, tel. 01 47 00 91 50, fax 01 47 00 06 31, e-mail: hotelyonmulhouse@wanadoo.fr).

Hôtel de la Place des Vosges** is well-located on a quiet street just off place des Vosges. The owners plan to renovate all rooms in 2002 (Sb-€84–99, Db-€107–122, prices are estimates, CC, elevator starts one floor up, 12 rue de Biraque, Mo: St. Paul, tel. 01 42 72 60 46, fax 01 42 72 02 64, e-mail: hotel.place.des .vosges@gofornet.com).

Hôtel des Chevaliers***, a little boutique hotel one block northwest of place des Vosges, offers small, pleasant rooms with modern comforts. Rooms off the street are quiet (Db-€114–130, CC, skip overpriced breakfast, 30 rue de Turenne, Mo: St. Paul, tel. 01 42 72 73 47, fax 01 42 72 54 10).

Hôtel Sévigné** is less personal but central, offering sufficient rooms at fair prices with the cheapest breakfast in Paris—€3.50 (Sb-€56, Db-€60–63, Tb-€69, CC, 2 rue Malher, Mo: St. Paul, tel. 01 42 72 76 17, fax 01 42 78 68 26, www.le-sevigne.com).

Marais Hotels

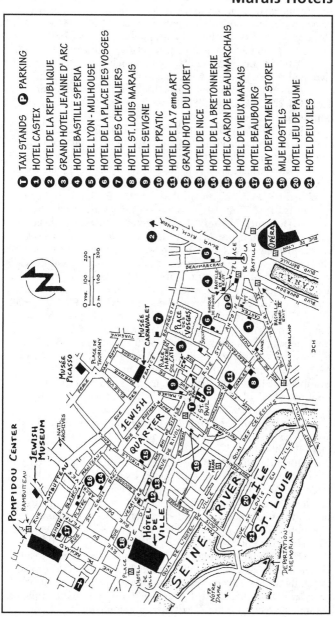

T TAXI STANDS **P** PARKING
1 HOTEL CASTEX
2 HOTEL DE LA REPUBLIQUE
3 GRAND HOTEL JEANNE D' ARC
4 HOTEL BASTILLE SPERIA
5 HOTEL LYON - MULHOUSE
6 HOTEL DE LA PLACE DES VOSGES
7 HOTEL DES CHEVALIERS
8 HOTEL ST. LOUIS MARAIS
9 HOTEL SEVIGNE
10 HOTEL PRATIC
11 HOTEL DE LA 7 eme ART
12 GRAND HOTEL DU LOIRET
13 HOTEL DE NICE
14 HOTEL DE LA BRETONNERIE
15 HOTEL CARON DE BEAUMARCHAIS
16 HOTEL DE VIEUX MARAIS
17 HOTEL BEAUBOURG
18 BHV DEPARTMENT STORE
19 MIJE HOSTELS
20 HOTEL JEU DE PAUME
21 HOTEL DEUX ILES

Hôtel Pratic* has a terrific location on a fun, people-friendly square and charges accordingly. Its stairs are many and its over-priced rooms are modern, but nothing special (Db-€90, CC, no elevator, 9 rue d'Ormesson, Mo: St. Paul, tel. 01 48 87 80 47, fax 01 48 87 40 04, e-mail: practic.hotel@wanadoo.fr).

Hôtel St. Louis Marais**, well-situated between the river and rue St. Antoine, has a fine lobby and cozy if pricey rooms (small Db-€108, standard Db-€125, CC, no elevator, 1 rue Charles V, tel. 01 48 87 87 04, fax 01 48 87 33 26, www .saintlouismarais.com).

Hôtel de 7ème Art**, two blocks south of rue St. Antoine, is a relaxed, Hollywood-nostalgia place, run by young, friendly, hip Marais types, with a full-service café/bar and Charlie Chaplin murals. Most rooms are adequate, but the few large double rooms at €107 are plenty nice (Sb or Db-€82–93, large Db-€107–125, extra bed-€21, CC, 20 rue St. Paul, Mo: St. Paul, tel. 01 44 54 85 00, fax 01 42 77 69 10, e-mail: hotel7art@wanadoo.fr).

MIJE Youth Hostels: The Maison Internationale de la Jeunesse des Etudiants (MIJE) runs three classy old residences clustered a few blocks south of rue St. Antoine. Each offers simple, clean, single-sex, one- to four-bed rooms for families and travelers under the age of 30 (exceptions are made for families). Prices are per person; you can pay more to have your own room or be roomed with as many as three others (Sb-€37, Db-€27, Tb-€24, Qb-€22, no CC, includes breakfast but not towels, which you can get from a machine; required membership card-€2.50 extra/person; rooms locked 12:00–15:00 and at 01:00). **MIJE Fourcy** (cheap dinners, 6 rue de Fourcy, just south of rue Rivoli), **MIJE Fauconnier** (11 rue Fauconnier), and the best, **MIJE Maubisson** (12 rue des Barres), share the same contact information (tel. 01 42 74 23 45, fax 01 40 27 81 64, www.mije.com) and Métro stop (St. Paul). Reservations are accepted.

Sleeping near the Pompidou Center: The remaining hotels are farther west and closer to the Pompidou Center than to place Bastille.

Hôtel de Nice**, on the Marais' busy main drag, is a cozy "Marie Antoinette does tie-dye" place. Its narrow halls are lit-tered with paintings, and rooms are filled with lots of thoughtful touches. Twin rooms, which cost the same as doubles, are larger but on the street side—with effective double-paned windows (23 rooms, Sb-€58, Db-€92, Tb-€110, CC, 42 bis rue de Rivoli, Mo: Hôtel de Ville, tel. 01 42 78 55 29, fax 01 42 78 36 07).

Hôtel de la Bretonnerie***, three blocks north and east of Hôtel de Ville, is a fine Marais splurge. It has elegant decor and tastefully decorated rooms with an antique, open-beam warmth (standard Db-€105, Db with character-€136, the standard Db has enough character for me, family-friendly suites-€175, CC, closed

Aug, between rue du Vielle du Temple and rue des Archives at 22 rue Sainte Croix de la Bretonnerie, Mo: Hôtel de Ville, tel. 01 48 87 77 63, fax 01 42 77 26 78, www.bretonnerie.com).

At the inexpensive, laid-back **Grand Hôtel du Loiret****, you get what you pay for (S-€37, Sb-€47–60, D-€42, Db-€56–73, Tb-€70–82, CC, just north of rue de Rivoli, 8 rue des Garçons Mauvais, Mo: Hôtel de Ville, tel. 01 48 87 77 00, fax 01 48 04 96 56, e-mail: hoteloiret@aol.com).

Hôtel Caron de Beaumarchais***, its lobby cluttered with bits from an elegant 18th-century Marais house, rents rooms that antique collectors would appreciate (Db-€135–150, CC, air-con, 12 rue Vielle du Temple, Mo: Hôtel de Ville, tel. 01 42 72 34 12, fax 01 42 72 34 63, www.carondebeaumarchais.com).

Hôtel de Vieux Marais**, tucked away on a quiet street two blocks east of the Pompidou Center, offers bright and fairly spacious rooms with air-conditioning, simple decor, and we-try-harder owners. Say hello to Leeloo, the hotel hound (Sb-€95–105, Db-€105–120, extra bed-€23, CC, just off rue des Archives at 8 rue du Platre, Mo: Rambuteau/Hôtel de Ville, tel. 01 42 78 47 22, fax 01 42 78 34 32).

Hôtel Beaubourg*** is a good three-star value within spitting distance of the Pompidou Center. The rooms are wood-beam comfy, and public spaces are warm and pleasant (Db-€104–113, some with balconies-€122, includes breakfast, CC, 11 rue Simon Lefranc, Mo: Rambuteau, tel. 01 42 74 34 24, fax 01 42 78 68 11, e-mail: htlbeaubourg@hotellerie.net).

Sleeping near the Marais on Ile St. Louis: The peaceful, residential character of this island and its central location have drawn Americans for decades, allowing hotels to charge top euro for their generally standard though comfortable rooms. There are no budget values here, but the island's coziness and proximity to the Marais, Notre-Dame, and the Latin Quarter compensate for high room rates. These hotels are on the island's main drag, the rue St. Louis en l'Ile, where I list several restaurants (see "Eating," below).

Hôtel Jeu de Paume**** is the most expensive hotel I list in Paris. When you enter its magnificent lobby—with high ceilings and half-timbered walls—you'll understand why. It has fine public spaces and charming rooms, most of which face a central garden (Db-€210–255, Db-suite-€415–445, CC, 54 rue St. Louis en l'Ile, tel. 01 43 26 14 18, fax 01 40 46 02 76, www .JeudePaumehotel.com).

Hôtel Des Deux Iles*** is the best value on the island, with an appealing lobby and well-appointed rooms. The owners charge a small-room price for some larger rooms—ask (Sb-€122, Db-€140, CC, air-con, must cancel 1 week in advance or pay fees, 59 rue St. Louis en l'Ile, tel. 01 43 26 13 35, fax

01 43 29 60 25, www.hotel-ile-saintlouis.com). Its sister hotel,
Hôtel de Lutece***, is next door (#65) with the same rates but
smaller rooms (CC, tel. 01 43 26 13 35, fax 01 43 29 60 25).

Contrescarpe Orientation

This lively, colorful neighborhood is like Montmartre with fewer
tourists. It's just south of the Latin Quarter, encompassing the
area between Luxembourg Gardens and rue Monge.

The nearest **TI** is at the Louvre Museum. The **post office**
(PTT) is between rue Mouffetard and rue Monge at 10 rue de
l'Epée du Bois. Place Monge hosts a colorful **outdoor market**
on Wednesday, Friday, and Sunday until 13:00. The **street
market** at the bottom of rue Mouffetard bustles daily except
Monday (Tue–Sat 08:00–12:00, 15:30–19:00, Sun 08:00–12:00,
5 blocks south of place Contrescarpe). Lively cafés at place
Contrescarpe hop with action from the afternoon into the wee
hours. **Bus #47** runs along rue Monge north to Notre-Dame,
the Pompidou Center, and Gare du Nord.

The flowery Jardin des Plantes park is just east, and the sublime Luxembourg Gardens are just west. Both are ideal for afternoon walks, picnics, naps, and kids. The doorway at 49 rue Monge
leads to a hidden **Roman arena** (Arènes de Lutèce). Today, *boules*
players occupy the stage while couples cuddle on the seats. Admire
the Panthéon from the outside (it's not worth paying to enter), and
peek inside the exquisitely beautiful St. Etienne-du-Mont church.

Sleeping in the Contrescarpe Neighborhood
(5th arrondissement, Mo: place Monge, zip code: 75005)

Hotels here are a 20-minute walk from Notre-Dame, Ile de la
Cité, and Ile St. Louis, and a 5- to 10-minute walk to the Luxembourg Gardens and the grand boulevards St. Germain and St.
Michel. Fewer tourists sleep in Contrescarpe, and I find the hotel
values generally better than in most other neighborhoods. Most
hotels listed are on or very near rue Mouffetard, the spine of this
area, running from the perfectly Parisian place Contrescarpe
south to rue Bazelles. Two thousand years ago, rue Mouffetard
was the principal Roman road south to Italy. Today, this small,
meandering street has a split personality. The lower part thrives in
the daytime as a pedestrian market street. The upper part sleeps
during the day but comes alive after dark, teeming with bars,
restaurants, and nightlife. These hotels are listed in order of proximity to the Seine and Notre-Dame.

Hôtel Central* defines unpretentiousness, with a charming
location; a steep, slippery, castlelike stairway; so-so beds; and simple rooms (all with showers, though toilets are down the hall). It's
a fine budget value (Ss-€27–29, Ds-€37–41, no CC, no elevator,
6 rue Descartes, Mo: Cardinal Lemoine, tel. 01 46 33 57 93).

Contrescarpe Hotels and Restaurants

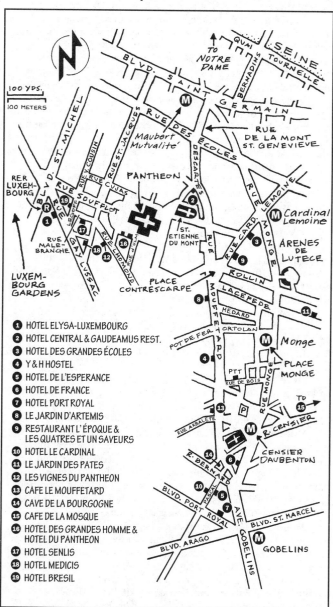

100 YDS.
100 METERS

1. HOTEL ELYSA-LUXEMBOURG
2. HOTEL CENTRAL & GAUDEAMUS REST.
3. HOTEL DES GRANDES ÉCOLES
4. Y & H HOSTEL
5. HOTEL DE L'ESPERANCE
6. HOTEL DE FRANCE
7. HOTEL PORT ROYAL
8. LE JARDIN D'ARTEMIS
9. RESTAURANT L'ÉPOQUE & LES QUATRES ET UN SAVEURS
10. HOTEL LE CARDINAL
11. LE JARDIN DES PATES
12. LES VIGNES DU PANTHEON
13. CAFE LE MOUFFETARD
14. CAVE DE LA BOURGOGNE
15. CAFE DE LA MOSQUE
16. HOTEL DES GRANDES HOMME & HOTEL DU PANTHEON
17. HOTEL SENLIS
18. HOTEL MEDICIS
19. HOTEL BRESIL

Hôtel des Grandes Ecoles*** is simply idyllic. A short alley leads to three buildings that protect a flowering garden courtyard, preserving a sense of tranquility that is rare in a city this size. Rooms are spacious and comfortable with large beds. This romantic place is deservedly popular, so call well in advance (Db-€90–114, extra bed-€15, parking-€20, CC, 75 rue de Cardinal Lemoine, Mo: Cardinal Lemoine, tel. 01 43 26 79 23, fax 01 43 25 28 15, www .hotel-grandes-ecoles.com, mellow Marie speaks some English).

Sleeping between the Panthéon and Luxembourg Gardens: The following five hotels are a five-minute walk from place Contre-scarpe. For these listings, the RER stop Luxembourg (with direct connections to the airports) is closer than the nearest Métro stop, Maubert Mutualité. The first two face the Panthéon's right transept.

Hôtel du Panthéon*** offers a seductively comfy lobby and rooms decorated in "country French." Rooms are well-designed, with air-conditioning and every comfort. Fifth-floor rooms have balconies, but sixth-floor rooms have the best views (Db-€190–220, CC, tel. 01 43 54 32 95, fax 01 43 26 64 65, www.hoteldupantheon.com).

Hôtel des Grandes Hommes*** has spacious, wood-beamed rooms, which are scheduled for renovation in 2002 (Db-€190–230, prices are estimates, CC, 17 place du Panthéon, tel. 01 46 34 19 60, fax 01 43 26 67 32, e-mail: reservation @hoteldesgrandeshommes.com).

Hôtel Senlis** hides quietly two blocks from Luxem-bourg Gardens with modest rooms, all with beamed ceilings and TVs (Sb-€65, Db-€70–85, Tb-€95, Qb-€107, CC, 7 rue Malebranche, tel. 01 43 29 93 10, fax 01 43 29 00 24, e-mail: hoteldesenlis@wanadoo.fr).

Hôtel Brésil** lies one block from Luxembourg Gardens and offers less character, and some smoky rooms, at reasonable rates (Sb-€62, Db-€62–85, CC, 10 rue le Goff, tel. 01 43 54 76 11, fax 01 46 33 45 78, e-mail: hoteldubresil@wanadoo.fr).

Hôtel Medicis is as cheap, stripped-down, and basic as it gets with a soiled linoleum charm, a helpful owner, and a great location (S-€15, D-€30, 214 rue St. Jacques, tel. 01 43 54 14 66, Denis SE).

Hôtel Elysa-Luxembourg*** sits on a busy street at Luxem-bourg Gardens and charges top euro for its plush, air-conditioned rooms (Sb-€107, Db-€134, CC, 6 rue Gay Lussac, tel. 01 43 25 31 74, fax 01 46 34 56 27, www.elysa_luxembourg.fr).

Sleeping at the bottom of rue Mouffetard: Of my recom-mended accommodations in the Contrescarpe neighborhood, these are farthest from the Seine and other tourists and lie in an appealing work-a-day area. They may have rooms when others don't.

Y&H Hostel offers a great location; easygoing, English-speaking management; Internet access; kitchen facilities; and basic but acceptable hostel conditions (beds in 4-bed rooms-€18, beds in double rooms-€21, sheets-€2.50, no CC, rooms closed 11:00–16:00 but reception stays open, 02:00 curfew, reservations require deposit, 80 rue Mouffetard, Mo: Cardinal Lemoine, tel. 01 47 07 47 07, fax 01 47 07 22 24, e-mail: smile@youngandhappy.fr).

Hôtel de l'Esperance** gives you nearly three stars for the price of two. It's quiet, pink, fluffy, and comfortable, with thoughtfully appointed rooms complete with canopy beds, hair dryers, and a flamboyant owner (Sb-€70, Db-€72–86, small Tb-€101, CC, 15 rue Pascal, Mo: Censier-Daubenton, tel. 01 47 07 10 99, fax 01 43 37 56 19).

Hôtel le Cardinal*** is a new, well-designed hotel with pleasing decor, air-conditioning, and modern comforts (Sb-€93, standard Db-€115, large Db-€185, Tb-€205, CC, 20 rue Pascal, tel. 01 47 07 41 92, fax 01 47 07 43 80, e-mail: hotelcardinal@aol.com).

Hôtel de France**, set on a busy street, has fine, modern rooms and hardworking, helpful owners (Jean and Christine). The best and quietest rooms are *sur le cour* (on the courtyard), though streetside rooms are fine (Sb-€62, Db-€74–78, CC, requires 1 night nonrefundable deposit, 108 rue Monge, Mo: Censier-Daubenton, tel. 01 47 07 19 04, fax 01 43 36 62 34, e-mail: hotel.de.fce@wanadoo.fr).

Don't let **Hôtel Port Royal***'s lone star fool you—this place is polished bottom to top and has been well-run by the same family for 66 years. Its clean and comfy rooms come at fair prices. Ask for a room off the street (S-€35–46, Db-€63–73, no CC, climb stairs from rue Pascal to busy boulevard de Port Royal, 8 boulevard de Port Royal, Mo: Gobelins, tel. 01 43 31 70 06, fax 01 43 31 33 67).

Sleeping and Eating near Paris, in Versailles

For a laid-back alternative to Paris within easy reach of the big city by RER train (5/hr, 30 min), Versailles, with easy, safe parking and reasonably priced hotels, can be a good overnight stop (see map on page 213). Park in the château's main lot while looking for a hotel or leave your car there overnight (free from 19:30–08:00). Get a map of Versailles at your hotel or at the TI. Be sure to explore the pleasant town center around place du Marché Notre-Dame (15-min walk, veer left out of the château), where you'll find a variety of reasonable restaurants, cafés, and a few cobbled lanes (market days Sun, Tue, and Fri until 13:00). Rue Satory is another pedestrian-friendly street with restaurants (near recommended Hôtel d'Angleterre, 10-min walk, go right out of the château).

Hôtel Le Cheval Rouge**, built in 1676 as Louis XIV's stables, now houses tourists. It's a block behind place du Marché in a quaint corner of town on a large, quiet courtyard with free, safe parking and sufficiently comfortable rooms (Ds-€49, Db-€58–72, Tb-€86, Qb-€90, CC, 18 rue Andre Chenier, tel. 01 39 50 03 03, fax 01 39 50 61 27).

Ibis Versailles** offers fair value, modern comfort, but no air-conditioning (Db-€71, cheaper weekend rates can't be reserved ahead, CC, across from RER station, 4 avenue du General de Gaulle, tel. 01 39 53 03 30, fax 01 39 50 06 31).

Hôtel du Palais, facing the RER station, has clean, sharp rooms, and the cheapest I list in this area. Ask for a quiet room off the street (Ds-€43, Db-€49, extra person-€11, CC, miles of stairs, 6 place Lyautey, tel. 01 39 50 39 29, fax 01 39 50 80 41).

Hôtel d'Angleterre**, away from the frenzy, is a tranquil old place with comfortable and spacious rooms. Park nearby in the palace lot (Db-€56–72, extra bed-€15, CC, just below palace to the right as you exit, 2 rue de Fontenay, tel. 01 39 51 43 50, fax 01 39 51 45 63).

Hôtel de France***, in an 18th-century townhouse, offers four-star value, with air-conditioned, appropriately royal rooms, a pleasant courtyard, comfy public spaces, a bar, and a restaurant (Db-€125–130, Tb-€168, CC, just off parking lot across from château, 5 rue Colbert, tel. 01 30 83 92 23, fax 01 30 83 92 24, www.hotelfrance-versailles.com).

Eating: You'll find nothing but food establishments lining the old market square (place du Marché). These places are on or near the square and all are good for lunch or dinner. **La Boeuf à la Mode** offers fine, traditional cuisine right on the square (€23 *menu*, 4 rue au Pain, tel. 01 39 50 31 99). **Fenêtres sur Cour** is the romantic's choice; it feels like you're dining in an Impression-ist painting (closed Mon all year and Tue–Wed eves in summer, just below market square in antique village, on place de la Geole, tel. 01 39 51 97 77). **A la Cote Bretonne** is the place to go for crêpes in a cozy setting (a few steps off the square on the traffic-free rue des Deux Ponts, #12).

EATING IN PARIS

Paris is France's wine and cuisine melting pot. While it lacks a style of its own (only French onion soup is truly Parisian), it draws from the best of France. Paris could hold a gourmet's Olympics and import nothing.

Picnic or go to bakeries for quick take-out lunches. Many Parisian department stores have huge supermarkets hiding in the basement, and top-floor cafeterias offering affordable, low-risk, low-stress, what-you-see-is-what-you-get meals.

Stop at a café for a lunch salad or *plat du jour*, but linger longer over dinner. You can eat well, restaurant style, for €15 to €23. Your hotel can usually recommend nearby restaurants in the €15 range. Remember, cafés are happy to serve a *plat du jour* (garnished plate of the day, about €11) or a cheflike salad (about €9) day or night, while restaurants expect you to enjoy a full dinner.

To save piles of euros, review the budget eating tips in this book's introduction and consider dinner picnics (great take-out dishes available at *charcuteries*).

Romantic Picnic Spots: My favorite dinner-picnic places are the pedestrian bridge (pont des Arts) across from the Louvre, with unmatched views and plentiful benches; the Champ de Mars park under the Eiffel Tower; and the western tip of Ile St. Louis, overlooking Ile de la Cité. Bring your own dinner feast and watch the riverboats or the Eiffel Tower light up the city for you.

Restaurants

Restaurants open for dinner around 19:00, and small local favorites get crowded after 21:00. Most of the restaurants listed below accept credit cards.

My recommendations are centered around the same three great neighborhoods I list accommodations for (above); you can come home exhausted after a busy day of sightseeing and have a good selection of restaurants right around the corner. And evening is a fine time to explore any of these delightful neighborhoods, even if you're sleeping elsewhere.

Most restaurants we've listed in these areas have set priced *menus* between €15 and €30. In most cases, the few extra euros you pay for not choosing the least expensive option is money well-spent, as it opens up a variety of better choices. You decide.

If you are traveling outside of Paris, save your splurges for the countryside, where you'll enjoy regional cooking for less money.

Eating in the Rue Cler Neighborhood

The rue Cler neighborhood isn't famous for its restaurants. That's why I enjoy eating here. Several small, family-run places serve great dinner *menus* for €15 and *plats du jour* for €9 to €12. My first two recommendations are easygoing cafés, ideal if what you want is a light dinner (good dinner salads) or more substantial but simple meals.

Café du Marché, with the best seats, coffee, and prices on rue Cler, serves hearty salads and good €9 *plats du jour* for lunch or dinner to a trendy, smoky, mainly French crowd. Arrive before 19:30 or wait at the bar. A chalkboard listing the plates of the day— each a meal—will momentarily be hung in front of you (at the corner of rue Cler and rue Champ de Mars).

Café le Bosquet is a vintage Parisian brasserie. Come here for a bowl of French onion soup, a salad, or a three-course set *menu* (€16 *menu*, many choices, closed Sun, 46 avenue Bosquet, tel. 01 45 51 38 13).

Leo le Lion, a warm, charming souvenir of old Paris, is popular with locals. Expect to spend €23 per person for fine *à la carte* choices (closed Sun, 23 rue Duvivier, tel. 01 45 51 41 77).

Rue Cler Restaurants

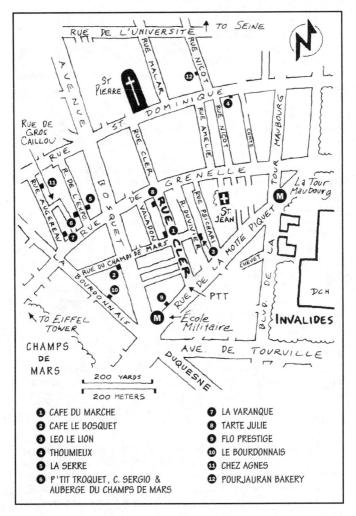

RUE DE L'UNIVERSITÉ   ↑ TO SEINE

ST PIERRE

DOMINIQUE

RUE DE GROS CAILLOU

GRENELLE

RUE CLER

ST. JEAN

La Tour Maubourg

TO EIFFEL TOWER

CHAMPS DE MARS

École Militaire

INVALIDES

AVE. DE TOURVILLE

DUQUESNE

200 YARDS

200 METERS

❶ CAFE DU MARCHE
❷ CAFE LE BOSQUET
❸ LEO LE LION
❹ THOUMIEUX
❺ LA SERRE
❻ P'TIT TROQUET, C. SERGIO & AUBERGE DU CHAMPS DE MARS

❼ LA VARANQUE
❽ TARTE JULIE
❾ FLO PRESTIGE
❿ LE BOURDONNAIS
⓫ CHEZ AGNES
⓬ POURJAURAN BAKERY

Thoumieux, the neighborhood's classy, traditional Parisian brasserie, is deservedly popular. It's big and dressy with formal but good-natured waiters. Skip the *menu* and order *à la carte* (allow €30/person with wine, 79 rue St. Dominique, tel. 01 47 05 49 75).

I like browsing the handful of fine places that line rue de l'Exposition, one block west of avenue Bosquet between rue St. Dominique and rue de Grenelle. Each of these places is a hard-working, mom-and-pop organization with plenty of charm and a distinct ambience. Eat early with tourists or late with locals. **Restaurant La Serre**, at #29, has fun atmosphere but an unpredictable staff (*plats* €8–11, daily from 19:00, often a wait after 21:00, good onion soup and duck specialties, tel. 01 45 55 20 96, Marie-Alice and Philippe speak English). **Le P'tit Troquet**, across the street at #28, is delightfully Parisian, popular with locals, and gracefully run by Dominique—allow €24 per person for dinner (closed Sun–Mon, tel. 01 47 05 80 39). **La Casa di Sergio**, at #20, is where I go in Paris for gourmet Italian cuisine served family style by Sicilian Sergio. Sergio says he's waited his entire life to open a restaurant like this. While not cheap, the food is remarkable. Sit down and let Sergio do the rest (€26–34 *menus*, closed Wed, tel. 01 45 51 37 71). The softly lit tables and red velvet chairs of **Auberge du Champ de Mars**, at #18, draw a romantic crowd (€15 *menu*, expensive wines, closed Sun).

These three places are closer to the Champs de Mars park. Just off rue de Grenelle, the friendly and unpretentious **La Varanque** is a good budget bet, with €9 *plats* and a €12 *menu* (27 rue Augereau, tel. 01 47 05 51 22). **Chez Agnes** is tiny, a good value, and run by engaging Agnes (closed Mon, next to recommended Hôtel Londres Eiffel at 1 rue Augereau, tel. 01 45 51 06 04). For a truly special occasion, the **Le Bourdonnais** has one Michelin star and a warm, intimate feel. Micheline Croat, your hostess, will take good care of you (€64 *menu*, 113 avenue de la Bourdonnais, tel. 01 47 05 47 96).

Picnicking: The rue Cler is a moveable feast that gives "fast food" a good name. The entire street is clogged with connoisseurs of good eating. Only the health-food store goes unnoticed. A festival of food, the street is lined with people whose lives seem to be devoted to their specialty: polished produce, rotisserie chicken, crêpes, or cheese squares.

For a magical picnic dinner at the Eiffel Tower, assemble it in no fewer than five shops on rue Cler and lounge on the best grass in Paris (the police don't mind after dusk), with the dogs, Frisbees, a floodlit tower, and a cool breeze in the Parc du Champ de Mars.

The **crêpe stand** next to Café du Marché does a wonderful top-end dinner crêpe for €4. Asian delis (generically called *Traiteur Asie*) provide tasty low-stress, low-price, take-out treats (2 with tables on rue Cler—1 across from Hôtel Leveque, the other near rue du Champs de Mars). For a variety of savory quiches or a tasty pear-and-chocolate tart, try **Tarte Julie's** (take-out or stools, 28 rue Cler). The elegant **Flo Prestige** *charcuterie* is open until 23:00 and offers mouthwatering meals to go (at the Ecole Militaire Métro stop).

Eating in the Marais Neighborhood

The sidewalks of the Marais are filled with locals and tourists in search of a good meal from, unfortunately, an abundance of average eateries. I've worked hard to find the best in this area where too often you must choose between the quality of the atmosphere or the cuisine. The Ile St. Louis is a short walk away (see below) and offers those staying in the Marais a pleasant alternative for restaurants.

For starters, stroll rue Vieille du Temple (near rue des Rosiers), home to several lively cafés providing traditional fare (some even serve Sunday brunch) and a handful of good restaurants worth the detour. **Au Petit Fer à Cheval,** named for its horseshoe-shaped bar, is an authentic gem with mirrored walls and tiled floors. To avoid crowds, come for lunch, an early dinner, or a nightcap. The restaurant in back serves daily specials to diners seated on old wooden Métro seats (daily until 24:00, 30 rue Vieille du Temple, tel. 01 42 72 47 47,). **Le Colimacon,** at #44, is a romantic little place offering two-course (€14) or three-course (€20) *menus* of traditional cuisine including *magret de canard aux fruits de saison* (duck breast with a sauce of seasonal fruit, closed Tue eves, reservations required, tel. 01 48 87 12 01).

Vegetarians will appreciate the excellent cuisine at popular **Picolo Teatro** (closed Mon, near rue des Rosiers, 6 rue des Ecouffes, tel. 01 42 72 17 79) or **L'As du Falafel,** which serves the best falafels on rue des Rosiers at #34.

You'll find several places that rely more on the quality of their charming location than their cuisine at the tiny square, place du Marché Ste. Catherine. For reliably good cuisine with a Basque emphasis, find **L'Auberge de Jarente** (€18 *menu*, closed Sun–Mon, just off the square at 7 rue Jarente, tel. 01 42 77 49 35).

Dinners under the candlelit arches of place des Vosges are *très* romantic. The mod and pastel **Nectarine** at #16 is a teahouse serving good salads, quiches, and reasonable *plats du jour* both day and night (tel. 01 42 77 23 78). **Ma Bourgogne** is bigger, darker, and more traditional (allow €38/person with wine, open daily, dinner reservations smart, no CC, at northwest corner, tel. 01 42 78 44 64). Just off place des Vosges, **L'Impasse** (or **Chez Robert**) is a cozy neighborhood bistro located on a quiet alley next to a Laundromat. Clean your clothes while you dine from a classic bourgeois *menu* with a variety of €6 first courses, €13.50 second courses, and €6 desserts (closed Sun, 4 impasse Guemenee, tel. 01 42 72 08 45). A few blocks west you'll find **Camille,** a traditional corner brasserie with white-aproned waiters serving €9 salads and very French *plats du jour* for €15 (daily, 24 rue des Francs-Bourgeois at corner of rue Elzevir, tel. 01 42 72 29 50).

The next places sit near the intersection of rues Castex and St. Antoine. For a break from French cooking, find a table at the tiny and *très* tasty **Trattoria Delizie Italiane** (closed

Marais Restaurants

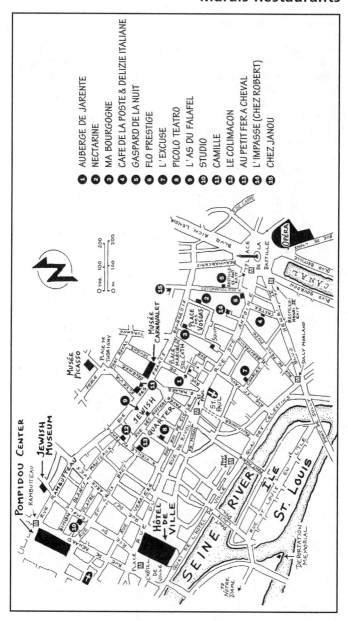

1. AUBERGE DE JARENTE
2. NECTARINE
3. MA BOURGOGNE
4. CAFE DE LA POSTE & DELIZIE ITALIANE
5. GASPARD DE LA NUIT
6. FLO PRESTIGE
7. L'EXCUSE
8. PICOLO TEATRO
9. L'AS DU FALAFEL
10. STUDIO
11. CAMILLE
12. LE COLIMACON
13. AU PETIT FER A CHEVAL
14. L'IMPASSE (CHEZ ROBERT)
15. CHEZ JANOU

Sun–Mon, 6 rue Castex, tel. 01 44 54 00 33). On the other side
of rue St. Antoine, **Gaspard de la Nuit** is cozy and a worthwhile
step up with a good €24 *menu* (a block off rue St. Antoine at 6 rue
des Tournelles, tel. 01 42 77 90 53). If the weather's nice, grab
a table on the terrace at **Chez Janou**, a Provençal bistro, then
make your selection from a tempting *à la carte* menu (CC, at
corner of rue des Tournelles and rue Roger-Verlomme, 2 rue
Roger-Verlomme, tel. 01 42 72 28 41).

  Near Hôtel du 7ème Art, splurge at the romantic and
dressy **L'Excuse** (€30 *menu*, closed Sun, reserve ahead, 14 rue
Charles V, tel. 01 42 77 98 97).

  Closer to the Pompidou Center, the **Studio** is wonderfully
located on a 17th-century courtyard below a dance school.
The tasty salads, €12 *plats du jour*, and Tex-Mex food are good
day or night (41 rue de Temple, tel. 01 42 74 10 38).

  Picnicking: Picnic at the peaceful place des Vosges (park
closes at dusk). Hobos stretch their euros at the supermarket in
the basement of the **Monoprix** department store (near place
des Vosges on rue St. Antoine), and connoisseurs prefer the
gourmet take-out places all along rue St. Antoine, such as **Flo
Prestige** (open until 23:00, on the tiny square where rue Tour-
nelle and rue St. Antoine meet). A few small grocery shops are
open until 23:00 on rue St. Antoine (near intersection with rue
Castex). An **open-air market**, held Sunday morning, is just off
place de la Bastille on boulevard Richard Lenoir.

  For a cheap breakfast, try the tiny *boulangerie/pâtisserie*
where the hotels buy their croissants (coffee machine-€0.50,
baby quiches-€1.50, *pain au chocolat*-€0.75, 1 block off place de
la Bastille, at corner of rue St. Antoine and rue de Lesdiguieres).

Eating in the Contrescarpe Neighborhood

There are a few diamonds in this otherwise rough area for fine
dining. Most come here for the lively and cheap eateries that
line rues Mouffetard and du Pot-de-Fer. Study the many *menus*,
compare crowds, then dive in and have fun (see map on page 235).

  Le Jardin d'Artemis is one of the better values on rue Mouffetard at #34 (€13.50 and €21 *menus*), though **Restaurant l'Epoque**
is the best place I found for fine cuisine at moderate prices (basic
€13.50 *menu*, €19 *menu* is worth the extra euros, a block off place
Contrescarpe at 81 rue Cardinal Lemoine, tel. 01 46 34 15 84).
Across the street, **Les Quatres et Une Saveurs** is a hard-core,
gourmet vegetarian place and worth a detour (closed Mon, 72 rue
Cardinal Lemoine, tel. 01 43 26 88 80). **Le Jardin des Pates** is popular with less strict vegetarians, serving pastas and salads at fair prices
(near Jardins des Plantes, 4 rue Lacepede, tel. 01 43 31 50 71).

  The next two places are near the Panthéon. **Gaudeamus**,
with a low-profile café on one side and a cozy bistro on the other,

has friendly owners and cheap *menus* (daily, just below the Panthéon, 47 rue Montagne Ste. Genevieve, tel. 01 40 46 93 40).
Les Vignes du Panthéon has Old World appeal and is popular
with locals (allow €23 for *à la carte*, closed Sat–Sun, 4 rue des
Fossés, tel. 01 43 54 80 81).

Eating on Ile St. Louis

The Ile St. Louis is popular with Americans for good reason: It's
a romantic and peaceful place to window shop for plenty of promising dinner possibilities. Cruise the island's main street for a
variety of good options, from cozy *crêperies* to romantic restaurants.
After dinner, sample Paris' best sorbet and ice cream at any place
advertising "les glaces Berthillon" (the original Berthillon shop is
at 31 rue St. Louis en l'Ile). Then stroll across to the Ile de la
Cité to see an illuminated Notre Dame.

All listings below line the rue St. Louis en l'Ile and begin at
the end of the island closest Notre Dame. **Café Med**, at #77, serves
inexpensive salads, crêpes, and lighter *menus* in a cheery setting
(open daily). Nearby at #72, **Coin Sud** offers much of the same with
warmer ambience. **La Castafiore**, at #51-53, serves fine Italian in
a black-and-white-tile atmosphere (€28 *menu*). Farther down, **Au
Gourmet de l'Isle**, is a fun, good bet with a €25 *menu* (closed
Mon–Tue). Almost next door, **l'Auberge de la Reine Blanche** is
worth a visit for its consistently good cuisine and pleasant owners
(open daily).

For a crazy, touristy, cellar atmosphere and hearty, fun
food, feast at **La Taverne du Sergeant Recruiter**. The "Sergeant Recruiter" used to get young Parisians drunk and stuffed
here, then sign them into the army. It's all-you-can-eat, including wine and service, for €31 (daily from 19:00, #41, tel. 01 43
54 75 42). There's a near-food-fight clone next door at **Nos
Ancêtres Les Gaulois** ("Our Ancestors the Gauls," daily from
19:00, tel. 01 46 33 66 07).

Transportation Connections—Paris

Paris is Europe's rail hub, with six major train stations, each serving different regions: Gare de l'Est (east-bound trains), Gare du
Nord (northern France and Europe), Gare St. Lazare (northwestern France), Gare d'Austerlitz (southwest France and
Europe), Gare de Lyon (southeastern France and Italy), and
Gare Montparnasse (northwestern France and TGV service to
France's southwest). Any train station can give you schedule
information, make reservations, and sell tickets for any destination. Buying tickets is handier from an SNCF neighborhood
office (e.g., Louvre, Invalides, Orsay, Versailles, airports) or
at your neighborhood travel agency—worth their small fee
(SNCF signs in their window indicate they sell train tickets).

For schedule information, call 08 36 35 35 35 (€0.50/min, English sometimes available).

Gare du Nord: Serves northern France and several international destinations. To **Brussels** (21/day, 1.5 hrs, cheaper by bus, see "Buses," below), **Bruges** (18/day, 2 hrs, change in Brussels, 1 direct), **Amsterdam** (10/day, 4 hrs; cheaper by bus, see "Buses," below), **Copenhagen** (1/day, 16 hrs, 2 night trains), **Koblenz** (6/day, 5 hrs, change in Köln), **London** via Eurostar Chunnel (17/day, 3 hrs, tel. 08 36 35 35 39, www.raileurope.com, www.eurostar.co.uk). **By Banlieue/RER lines to**: **Chantilly-Gouvieux** (hrly, fewer on weekends, 35 min), **Charles de Gaulle airport** (2/hr, 30 min, runs 05:30–23:00, track 4).

Gare de l'Est: Serves eastern France and points east. To **Colmar** (12/day, 5.5 hrs, change in Strasbourg, Dijon, or Mulhouse), **Strasbourg** (14/day, 4.5 hrs, many require changes), **Reims** (12/day, 1.5 hrs), **Verdun** (5/day, 3 hrs, change in Metz or Chalon), **Munich** (5/day, 9 hrs, some require changes, night train), **Vienna** (7/day, 13–18 hrs, most require changes, night train), **Zurich** (10/day, 7 hrs, most require changes, night train), **Prague** (2/day, 14 hrs, night train).

Gare Montparnasse: Serves Lower Normandy and Brittany and offers TGV service to Loire Valley and southwestern France. To **Chartres** (20/day, 1 hr, Banlieue lines), **Pontorson-Mont St. Michel** (5/day, 4.5 hrs, via Rennes, then take bus; or take train to Pontorson via Caen, then bus from Pontorson), **Dinan** (7/day, 4 hrs, change in Rennes and Dol), **Bordeaux** (14/day, 3.5 hrs), **Sarlat** (5/day, 6 hrs, change in Bordeaux, Libourne, or Souillac), **Toulouse** (11/day, 5 hrs, most require change, usually in Bordeaux), **Albi** (7/day, 6–7.5 hrs, change in Toulouse, also night train), **Carcassonne** (8/day, 6.5 hrs, most require changes in Toulouse and Bordeaux, direct trains take 10 hrs), **Tours** (14/day, 1 hr).

Gare du Lyon: Offers TGV and regular service to southeastern France, Italy, and other international destinations. To **Melun** (hrly, 30 min), **Fontainebleau** (nearly hrly, 45 min), **Beaune** (12/day, 2.5 hrs, most require change in Dijon), **Dijon** (15/day, 1.5 hrs), **Chamonix** (9/day, 9 hrs, change in Lyon and St. Gervais, direct night train), **Annecy** (8/day, 4–7 hrs), **Lyon** (16/day, 2.5 hrs), **Avignon** (9/day in 2.5 hrs, 6/day in 4 hrs with change), **Arles** (14/day, 5 hrs, most with change in Marseille, Avignon, or Nîmes), **Nice** (14/day, 5.5–7 hrs, many with change in Marseille), **Venice** (3/day, 3/night, 11–15 hrs, many require changes), **Rome** (2/day, 5/night, 15–18 hrs, many require changes).

Gare St. Lazare: Serves Upper Normandy. To **Giverny** (train to Vernon, 5/day, 45 min; then bus or taxi 10 min to Giverny), **Rouen** (15/day, 75 min), **Honfleur** (6/day, 3 hrs, via Lisieux, then bus), **Bayeux** (9/day, 2.5 hrs, some with change in Caen), **Caen** (12/day, 2 hrs).

Gare d'Austerlitz: Provides non-TGV service to the Loire Valley, southwestern France, and Iberia. To **Amboise** (8/day in 2 hrs, 12/day in 1.5 hrs with change in St. Pierre des Corps), **Cahors** (7/day, 5–7 hrs, most with changes), **Barcelona** (1/day, 9 hrs, change in Montpellier, night trains), **Madrid** (2 night trains only, 13–16 hrs), **Lisbon** (1/day, 24 hrs).

Buses

The main bus station is Gare Routière du Paris-Gallieni (28 avenue du General de Gaulle, in the suburb of Bagnolet, Mo: Gallieni, tel. 01 49 72 51 51). Buses provide cheaper, although less comfortable, transportation to major European cities; you'll pay about $24 to get from Paris to Brussels (compared to $80 second-class by train) and $33 from Paris to Amsterdam, compared to $100 second-class by train (Eurolines tel. 08 36 69 52 52, www.eurolines.com).

Charles de Gaulle Airport

Paris' primary airport has three main terminals: T-1, T-2, and T-9. Air France uses T-2; charters dominate T-9, and U.S. carriers use T-1. Terminals are connected every few minutes by a free *navette* (bus), and the RER (Paris subway) stops at T-1 and T-2 terminals. The TGV train station is at T-2. There is no bag storage at the airport.

Those flying to or from the United States will probably use T-1, and the information that follows is for that terminal. The "Meeting Point" is ground zero for tourist information, with free maps, museum passes, and brochures (daily 07:00–22:00). A Relay store sells Kertel phone cards. A bank (with lousy rates) is near gate 16. An American Express cash machine and an ATM are near gate 32. Car-rental offices are on the arrival level from gates 10 to 22; the SNCF (train) office is at gate 22. For flight information, call 01 48 62 22 80.

Those departing from this terminal will find restaurants, a PTT (post office), a pharmacy, boutiques, and a handy grocery store one floor below the ticketing desks at level 2.

Transportation between Charles de Gaulle Airport and Paris: Three efficient public-transportation routes, taxis, and airport shuttle vans link the airport's T-1 and T-2 terminals with central Paris. At T-1 (where most land), **RER trains** run every 15 minutes to central Paris. From gate 36, take the elevator down to level (*niveau*) 2, walk outside, cross the street, and catch the green bus to *Roissypole*. Transfer to RER trains there (€8, stops at Gare du Nord, Chatelet, St. Michel, and Luxembourg Gardens). When coming to the airport from Paris, T-1 is the first RER stop at Charles de Gaulle, T-2 is the second stop. The **Roissy Bus** runs every 15 minutes between gate 30 and Paris' Opéra Garnier (€8, 40 min, buy ticket inside terminal at gate 30; the Opéra stop is on rue Scribe at the American Express office). The **Air France Bus** leaves every 15 minutes from gate 34 and serves the Arc de Triomphe and Porte Maillot in about 40 minutes for €10, and the Montparnasse Tower in 60 minutes for €11 (from any of these stops you can reach your hotel by taxi). The RER Roissy Rail, Roissy Bus, and Air France bus described above serve the T-2 terminal as efficiently and economically as T-1. For most people, the RER Roissy Rail works best. A **taxi** ride with luggage costs about €38; a taxi stand is at gate 20. The **Disneyland Express bus** departs from gate 32. The **TGV station** is at T-2 (from gate 36, take elevator down to *niveau* 2, walk outside, cross the street, and catch the red bus to T-2).

For a stress-free trip between either of Paris' airports and downtown, consider an **airport shuttle minivan**, ideal for single travelers or families of four or more. Reserve from home, and they'll meet you at the airport (€23 for 1 person, €27 for 2, €41 for 3, €55 for 4, plan on a 30-min wait if you ask them to pick you up at the airport). Choose between **Airport Connection** (tel. 01 44 18 36 02, fax 01 45 55 85 19, www.airport-connection.com) or **Paris Airport Services** (tel. 01 49 62 78 78, fax 01 49 62 78 79, www.magic.fr/pas, e-mail: pas@magic.fr).

Sleeping at or near Charles de Gaulle Airport: Hôtel Ibis**, outside the RER Roissy Rail station for T-1 (the first RER stop coming from Paris), offers standard and predictable accommodations (Db-€85, CC, near *navette* bus stop, free shuttle bus to either terminal takes 2 min, tel. 01 49 19 19 19, fax 01 49 19 19 21, e-mail: h1404@accor-hotels.com), as does **Novotel***** (Db-€133–145, CC, tel. 01 49 19 27 27, fax 01 49 19 27 99). A 15-minute drive from the airport is another Ibis hotel in the village of Roissy with shuttle service.

Drivers wanting to avoid rush-hour traffic may consider sleeping north of Paris in the medieval town of Senlis (15 min north of airport) at **Hostellerie de la Porte Bellon** (Db-€65, CC, in center at 51 rue Bellon, near rue de la République, tel. 03 44 53 03 05, fax 03 44 53 29 94).

Orly Airport

This airport feels small. Orly has two terminals: Sud and Ouest. International flights arrive at Sud, as I assume you will. After exiting Terminal Sud's baggage claim (near gate H), you'll be greeted by signs directing you to city transportation, car rental, and so on. Turn left to enter the main terminal area, and you'll find exchange offices with bad rates, an ATM machine, the ADP (a quasi–tourist office that offers free city maps and basic sightseeing information, open until 23:00), and an SNCF French rail desk (closes at 18:00, sells train tickets and even Eurailpasses, next to the ADP). Downstairs is a sandwich bar, WCs, a bank (same bad rates), a newsstand (buy *télécarte* phone card), and a post office (great rates for cash or American Express traveler's checks). Car-rental offices are located in the parking lot in front of the terminal. For flight info on any airline serving Orly, call 01 49 75 15 15.

Transportation between Paris and Orly Airport: There are three efficient public-transportation routes, taxis, and a couple of airport shuttle services linking Orly Sud and central Paris. The gate locations listed below apply to Orly Sud, but the same transportation services are available from both terminals. The **Air France bus** (outside gate G) runs to Paris' Invalides Métro stop (€8, 4/hr, 30 min) and is best for those staying in or near the rue Cler neighborhood (from Invalides terminal, take the Métro 2 stops to Ecole Militaire to reach recommended hotels). The **Jetbus #285** (outside gate F, €5, 4/hr) is the quickest way to the Paris subway and the best way to the recommended hotels in the Marais and Contrescarpe neighborhoods (take Jetbus to Villejuif Métro stop, buy a *carnet* of 10 Métro tickets, then take the Métro to the Sully Morland stop for the Marais area, or the Censier-Daubenton or place Monge stops for the Contrescarpe area). If coming to the airport, make sure your train serves Villejuif, as the route splits at the end of the line.

The **Orlybus** (outside gate H, €5.50, 4/hr) takes you to the Denfert-Rochereau RER-B line and the Métro, offering subway access to central Paris. The **Orlyval trains** are overpriced (€9) and require a transfer at the Antony stop to reach RER line B (serving Luxembourg, Chatelet, St. Michel, and Gare du Nord stations in central Paris). **Taxis** are to the far right as you leave the terminal, at gate M. Allow €26 for a taxi into central Paris.

Airport shuttle minivans are ideal for single travelers or families of four or more (see "Charles de Gaulle Airport," above, for the companies to contact; from Orly, figure about €18 for 1 person, €12/person for 2, less for larger groups and kids).

Sleeping near Orly Airport: The only reasonable airport hotel is **Hôtel Ibis**** (Db-€61, CC, tel. 01 56 70 50 60, fax 01 56 70 50 70). The **Hôtel Mercure***** provides more comfort for a price (Db-€114, tel. 01 46 87 23 37, fax 01 46 87 71 92). Both have free shuttles to the terminal.

PROVENCE

This magnificent region is shaped like a giant wedge of quiche. From its sunburnt crust fanning out along the Mediterranean coast from Nîmes to Nice, it stretches north along the Rhône Valley to Orange. The Romans were here in force and left many ruins—some of the best anywhere. Seven popes, great artists such as van Gogh, Cézanne, and Picasso, and author Peter Mayle all enjoyed their years in Provence. The region offers a splendid recipe of arid climate (except for occasional brutal winds known as the *mistral*), captivating cities, exciting hill towns, dramatic scenery, and oceans of vineyards.

Explore the ghost town that is ancient Les Baux and France's greatest Roman ruin, Pont du Gard. Spend your starry, starry nights where van Gogh did, in Arles. Uncover its Roman past, then find the linger-longer squares and café corners that inspired Vincent. Youthful but classy Avignon bustles in the shadow of its brooding pope's palace.

Planning Your Time

Make Arles or Avignon your sightseeing base (hotels are a far better value in Arles). Italophiles prefer smaller Arles, while poodles pick urban Avignon. Everything is accessible by public transit. You'll want a full day for sightseeing in Arles (best on Wed or Sat, when the morning market rages), a half day for Avignon, and a day or two for the villages and sights in the countryside.

Getting around Provence

By Car: The yellow Michelin map of this region is essential for drivers. Avignon (population 100,000) is a headache for drivers; Arles (population 35,000) is easier, though it still requires urban

Provence

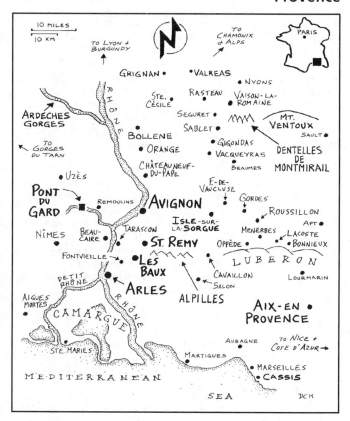

driving skills. Park only in well-watched spaces and leave nothing in your car.

By Bus or Train: Public transit is good between cities and marginal to small towns. Frequent trains link Avignon, Arles, and Nîmes (about 30 min between each), and buses connect smaller towns. Les Baux is accessible by bus from Arles. The Pont du Gard is accessible by bus from Avignon. The TIs in Arles and Avignon have information on bus excursions to regional sights that are hard to reach *sans* car (€18/half day, €30/full day).

Cuisine Scene—Provence

The almost extravagant use of garlic, olive oil, herbs, and tomatoes makes Provence's cuisine France's liveliest. To sample it, order anything *à la Provençale*. Among the area's spicy specialties are *ratatouille* (a thick mixture of vegetables in an herb-flavored tomato sauce), *brandade* (a salt cod, garlic, and cream mousse), *aioli* (a garlicky mayonnaise often served atop fresh vegetables), *tapenade* (a paste of puréed olives, capers, anchovies, herbs, and sometimes tuna), *soupe au pistou* (vegetable soup with basil, garlic, and cheese), and *soupe à l'ail* (garlic soup). Look also for *riz Camarguaise* (rice from the Camargue) and *taureau* (bull meat). Banon (wrapped in chestnut leaves) and Picodon (nutty taste) are the native cheeses. Provence also produces some of France's great wines at relatively reasonable prices. Look for Gigondas, Sablet, Côtes du Rhône, and Côte de Provence. If you like rosé, try the Tavel. This is the place to splurge for a bottle of Châteauneuf-du-Pape.

Provence Market Days

Provençal market days offer France's most colorful and tantalizing outdoor shopping. The best markets are Tuesday in Vaison la Romaine; Wednesday in St. Rémy; Thursday in Nyons; Saturday in Arles, Uzès, and Apt; and, best of all, Sunday in Isle sur la Sorgue. Crowds and parking problems abound at these popular events— arrive by 09:00, or, better, sleep in the town the night before.

Monday:	Cadenet (near Vaison la Romaine)
Tuesday:	Vaison la Romaine, Tarascon, and Gordes
Wednesday:	St. Rémy, Arles, and Violes (near Vaison la Romaine)
Thursday:	Nyons, Beaucaire, Vacqueyras, and Isle sur la Sorgue
Friday:	Remoulins (Pont du Gard), Bonnieux, Châteauneuf-du-Pape, and Lourmarin
Saturday:	Arles, Uzès, Valreas, and Apt (near Luberon hill towns)
Sunday:	Isle sur la Sorgue, Mausanne (near les Baux), Coustelet (local produce only), and Beaucaire

ARLES

By helping Julius Caesar defeat Marseille, Arles earned the imperial nod and was made an important port city. With the first bridge over the Rhône River, Arles was a key stop on the Roman road from Italy to Spain, the Via Domitia. After reigning as a political hotspot of the early Christian church (the seat of an archbishopric for centuries) and thriving as a trading city on and off until the 18th century, Arles all but disappeared from the map. Van Gogh settled here a hundred years ago but left only memories. American bombers destroyed much of Arles in World War II. Today, Arles thrives again with one of France's few communist mayors. This compact city is alive with great Roman ruins, an eclectic assortment of museums, made-for-ice-cream pedestrian zones, and squares that play hide-and-seek with visitors.

Orientation

Arles faces the Mediterranean and turns its back to Paris. Its spaghetti street plan disorients the first-time visitor. Landmarks hide in the medieval tangle of narrow, winding streets. Everything is deceptively close. While Arles sits on the Rhône, it completely ignores the river. The elevated riverside walk provides a direct route to the excellent Ancient History Museum, an easy return to the station, and fertile ground for poorly trained dogs. Hotels have free city maps, but Arles works best if you simply follow street-corner signs pointing you toward the sights and hotels of the town center. Racing cars enjoy Arles' medieval lanes, turning sidewalks into tightropes and pedestrians into leaping targets. The free "Starlette" minibus-shuttle circles the town's major sights every 20 minutes, but does not serve the Ancient History Museum, so it isn't very helpful (just wave at the driver and hop in; Mon–Sat 07:30–19:30, never on Sun). It does serve the train station, the only stop you pay for (€0.80).

Tourist Information: The main TI is on the ring road, esplanade Charles de Gaulle (April–Sept daily 09:00–18:45, Oct–March Mon–Sat 09:00–17:45, Sun 10:30–14:30, tel. 04 90 18 41 20). There's also a TI at the train station (April–Sept Mon–Sat 09:00–13:00, 14:00–18:00, closed Sun, Oct–March 09:00–13:00 only, closed Sun). Both TIs can reserve a hotel room (€0.75 fee). Pick up the good city map and information on the Camargue Wildlife area. Ask about bullfights and bus excursions to regional sights.

Arrival in Arles

By Train and Bus: Both stations are next to each other on the river and a 10-minute walk from the center. Lockers are not available. Pick up a city map at the train station TI and get the bus schedule to Les Baux at the bus station (tel. 04 90 49 38 01). To reach the old town, walk to the river and turn left.

By Car: Follow signs to *centre-ville*, then follow signs toward *gare SNCF* (train station). You'll come to a huge roundabout (place Lamartine) with a Monoprix department store to the right. Park along the city wall or in nearby lots (€1/hr, €2.60/4 hrs; pay attention to "no parking" signs on Wed and Sat until 13:00). Theft is a big problem. From place Lamartine, walk into the city through the two stumpy towers or take bus #1 (€0.80, 2/hr).

Helpful Hints

Supermarket: A big, handy Monoprix supermarket/department store is on place Lamartine (Mon–Sat 08:30–19:25, closed Sun).

Laundromats: One is at 12 rue Portagnel (daily 07:00–21:00). Another, nearby at 6 rue Cavalarie, near place Voltaire (daily 07:00–21:00, later once you're in), has a confusing central-command panel: €3 for wash (push machine number on top row),

€1.50 for 25 minutes of dryer (push dryer number on third row 5 times slowly), €0.30 for flakes (button #11). Dine at the recommended L'Arlatan restaurant (across the street, see "Eating in Arles," below) while you clean.

Public Pools: There are two public pools in Arles (one indoor and one outdoor). Ask at the TI or your hotel.

Taxis: Arles' taxis charge a minimum €9 fee. Nothing in town is worth a taxi ride (figure €33–41 to Les Baux or St. Rémy, tel. 04 90 96 90 03).

Bike Rental: Try the Peugeot store (15 rue du Pont, tel. 04 90 96 03 77). Riding to Les Baux (very steep climb) or into the Camargue work from Arles, providing you're in great shape (forget it in the wind).

Car Rental: Consider ADA (cheapest, 22 avenue Stalingrad, tel. 04 90 52 07 27), Avis (at train station, tel. 04 90 96 82 42), or Europcar (downtown at 2 bis avenue Victor Hugo, tel. 04 90 93 23 24).

Sights—Arles' Museums

The very handy monument pass (*le pass monuments)* covers Arles' many sights and is valid for one week (€10, €7.75 under 18, sold at each sight). Otherwise, it's €3 per sight and museum (€5.50 apiece for the Ancient History Museum and the Arlaten Folk Museum). While any sight is worth a few minutes, many aren't worth the individual admission. Many sights begin closing rooms 30 minutes early.

▲▲▲**Ancient History Museum (Musée de L'Arles Antique)**— Begin your visit of Arles in this superb, air-conditioned museum. Models and original sculpture (with the help of the free English handout) recreate the Roman city of Arles, making work-a-day life and culture easier to imagine. Notice what a radical improvement the Roman buildings were over the simple mud-brick homes of the pre-Roman inhabitants. Models of Arles' arena even illustrate the moveable stadium cover, good for shade and rain. While virtually nothing is left of Arles' chariot racecourse, the model shows that it must have rivaled Rome's Circus Maximus. Jewelry, fine metal and glass artifacts, and well-crafted mosaic floors make it clear that Roman Arles was a city of art and culture. The finale is an impressive row of pagan and early Christian sarcophagi (2nd–5th centuries). In the early days of the Church, Jesus was often portrayed beardless and as the good shepherd—with a lamb over his shoulder.

Built at the site of the chariot racecourse, this museum is a 20-minute walk from Arles along the river. Turn left at the river and follow it to the big modern building just past the new bridge—or take bus #1 (€0.80) from boulevard des Lices and the TI (€5.50, March–Oct daily 09:00–19:00, Nov–Feb 10:00–18:00, tel. 04 90 18 88 88).

Arles

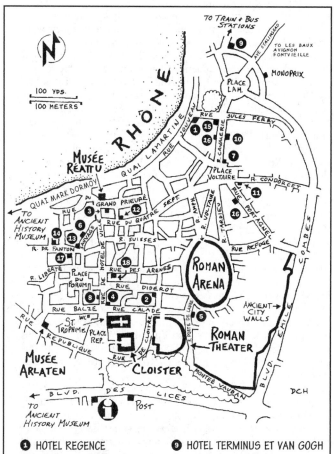

1. HOTEL REGENCE
2. HOTEL DE L'AMPHITHEATRE
3. HOTEL DU MUSEE
4. HOTEL ST. TROPHIME
5. HOTEL CALENDAL
6. HOTEL D'ARLATAN
7. HOTEL VOLTAIRE
8. HOTEL LA GALLIA
9. HOTEL TERMINUS ET VAN GOGH
10. L'ARLATAN RESTAURANT
11. LA GIRAUDIERE RESTAURANT
12. L'OLIVIER RESTAURANT
13. LA VITAMINE RESTAURANT
14. LA PAILLOTTE RESTAURANT
15. HOTEL ACACIAS
16. LAUNDROMATS
17. SOLEILEI'S ICE CREAM
18. LA GUEULE DE COUP REST.

▲▲▲**Roman Arena (Amphithéâtre)**—Nearly 2,000 years ago, gladiators fought wild animals here to the delight of 20,000 screaming fans—cruel. Today matadors fight wild bulls to the delight of local fans—still cruel. While the ancient third row of arches is long gone, three towers survive from medieval times, when the arena was used as a fortress. In the 1800s, it corralled 200 humble homes and functioned as a town within the town. Climb the tower. Walk through the inner corridors of this 132-by-105-meter oval and notice the similarity to modern-day stadium floor plans. And, if you don't mind the gore, a bullfight is an exciting show (€3, May–Sept 09:00–18:30, Oct 09:00–17:30, and Nov–April 10:00–16:30).

Classical Theater (Théâtre Antique)—Precious little survives from this Roman theater, which served as a handy town quarry throughout the Middle Ages. Two lonely Corinthian columns look from the stage out over the audience. The 10,000 mostly modern seats are still used for concerts and festivals. Take a stroll backstage through broken bits of Rome; you can see much of the theater by peeking through the fence (€3, May–Sept 09:00–11:30, 14:00–18:30, Oct and April 09:00–11:30, 14:00–17:30, Nov–March 10:00–11:30, 14:00–16:30).

Musée Réattu—Housed in a beautiful, 15th-century mansion, highlights of this mildly interesting, mostly modern art collection are 57 Picasso drawings (some two-sided and all done in a flurry of creativity—I liked the bullfights best), a room of Henri Rousseau's Camargue watercolors, and an unfinished painting by the neo-classical artist Réattu, none with English explanations (€3, plus €1.50 for special exhibits, April–Sept daily 09:00–12:00, 14:00–18:30, Oct and March until 17:00, Nov–Feb until 16:00, 10 rue de Grand Prieuré, tel. 04 90 96 37 68).

▲**Musée Arlaten**—This cluttered folklore museum, given to Arles by Nobel Prize winner Frederic Mistral (see "Place du Forum," below), overflows with interesting odds and ends of Provence life. It's like a failed 19th-century garage sale: shoes, hats, wigs, old photos, bread cupboards, and a model of a beetle-dragon monster, all crammed too close together to really appreciate. If you're fond of folklore, this museum is for you (€5.50, April–Sept daily 09:00–12:30, 14:00–18:00, Oct–March until 17:00, 29 rue de la République, tel.04 90 96 08 23).

▲▲**St. Trophime Cloisters and Church**—This church, named after a third-century bishop of Arles, sports the finest Romanesque west portal (main doorway) I've seen anywhere. But first enjoy place de la République. Sit on the steps opposite the church. The **Egyptian obelisk** used to be the centerpiece of Arles' Roman Circus. Watch the peasants—pilgrims, locals, and street musicians. There's nothing new about this scene. Like a Roman triumphal arch, the church trumpets the promise of Judgment

Day. The tympanum (the semicircular area above the door) is filled with Christian symbolism. Christ sits in majesty, surrounded by symbols of the four evangelists (Matthew—the winged man, Mark—the winged lion, Luke—the ox, and John—the eagle). The twelve apostles are lined up below Jesus. Move closer. This is it. Some are saved and others aren't. Notice the condemned— a chain gang on the right bunny-hopping over the fires of hell. For them, the tune trumpeted by the three angels on the very top is not a happy one. Ride the exquisite detail back to a simpler age. In an illiterate medieval world, long before the vivid images of our Technicolor time, this message was a neon billboard over the town's square. A chart just inside the church (on the right) helps explain the carvings. On the right side of the nave, a fourth-century early-Christian sarcophagus is used as an altar.

The adjacent **cloisters** are the best in Provence (enter from square, 20 meters to right of church). Enjoy the sculpted capitals of the rounded Romanesque columns (12th century) and the pointed Gothic columns (14th century). The second floor offers only a view of the cloisters from above (same cost and hours as the Roman arena).

More Sights—Arles

▲▲**Place du Forum**—Named for the Roman Forum that stood here, this café-crammed square is always lively and best at night. Only two columns from a second-century temple survive. They are incorporated into the wall of Hôtel Nord Pinus. Van Gogh lounged under these same plane trees—his *Le Café de Nuit* was painted from this square. The bistros on the square, while no place for a fine dinner, put together a good salad, and when you sprinkle in the ambience, that's €8 well spent. The guy on the pedestal is Frederic Mistral; he received the Nobel Prize for literature in 1904. He used his prize money to preserve and display the folk identity of Provence—by founding the Arlaten Folk Museum—at a time when France was rapidly centralizing.

▲▲**Wednesday and Saturday Markets**—On these days until noon, Arles' ring road erupts into an outdoor market of fish, flowers, produce, and you-name-it (boulevard Emile Combes on Wed, boulevard Lices on Sat). Join in, buy flowers, try the olives, sample some wine, and swat a pickpocket. On the first Wednesday of the month, it's a grand flea market.

Fondation Van Gogh—A ▲▲ sight for his fans, this small gallery features works by several well-known contemporary artists who pay homage to Vincent through their thought-provoking interpretations of his art (€4.60, not covered by monument passes, April–mid Oct daily 10:00–19:00, mid-Oct–March Tue–Sun 10:00–12:30, 14:00–17:30, facing Roman arena at 24 bis Rond Point des Arènes).

▲▲**Bullfights (Courses Camarguaise)**—Occupy the same

seats fans have used for nearly 2,000 years and take in one of Arles' most memorable experiences—a bullfight *à la Provençale* in an ancient arena. Three classes of bullfights take place here. The *course protection* is for aspiring matadors; it's a daring dodge-bull game of scraping hair off the angry bull's nose for prize money offered by local businesses (no blood). The *trophée de l'avenir* is the next class, with amateur matadors. The *trophée des as excellence* is the real thing à la Spain: outfits, swords, spikes, and the whole gory shebang (tickets €4.60–9.15; Easter–Oct Sat, Sun, and holidays; skip the "rodeo" spectacle, tel. 04 90 96 03 70 or ask at TI). There are nearby village bullfights in small wooden bullrings nearly every weekend (TI has schedule).

The Camargue—Knocking on Arles' doorstep, this is one of the few truly "wild" areas of France, where pink flamingos, wild bulls, and the famous white horses wander freely amid rice fields, lagoons, and mosquitoes. It's a ▲▲▲ sight for nature-lovers and boring for others. The D-37 that skirts the Etang de Vaccarès lagoon has some of the best views. The **Musée Camarguais** actually does a good job describing (in English) the natural features and traditions of the Camargue and has a 3.5-kilometer (2-mile) nature trail. It's 12 kilometers from Arles on the D-570 toward Ste. Marie de la Mer; at the *Mas du Pont de Rousty* farmhouse, look for signs (€4.60, May–Sept daily 09:15–17:45, Wed–Mon Oct–March 10:15–16:45, closed Tue off-season, tel. 04 90 97 10 82). Buses serve the Camargue (and the museum) from Arles' train station (tel. 04 90 96 36 25).

Sleeping in Arles
(€1.10 = about $1, country code: 33, zip code: 13200)
Sleep Code: **S** = Single, **D** = Double/Twin, **T** = Triple, **Q** = Quad, **b** = bathroom, **s** = shower only, **CC** = Credit Cards accepted, **no CC** = Credit Cards not accepted, **SE** = Speaks English, **NSE** = No English, ***** = French hotel rating system (0–4 stars).

Hotels are a great value here; many are air-conditioned, though few have elevators. All except the last are central. The first three are closer to the train station.

Hôtel Régence** sits on the river with immaculate and comfortable rooms, good beds, safe parking, and easy access to the train station (Db-€30–46, Tb-€40–55, Qb-€56, choose river-view or quiet, air-con courtyard rooms, CC, 5 rue Marius Jouveau, from place Lamartine turn right immediately after passing through towers, tel. 04 90 96 39 85, fax 04 90 96 67 64, www.hotel-regence.com, e-mail: contact@hotel-regence.com).

Hôtel Acacias**, just off place Lamartine and inside the old city walls, is a modern new hotel owned by Hôtel Régence (above). It's a pastel paradise, with rooms that are a smidge too small but have all the comforts, including cable TV, hair dryers, and air-conditioning (Db-€46–65, Tb-€69–74, Qb-€78, buffet breakfast-€5.50, CC, elevator, 1 rue Marius Jouveau, tel. 04 90 96 37 88, fax 04 90 96 32 51, www.hotel-acacias.com, e-mail: contact@hotel-acacias.com).

Hôtel Terminus et van Gogh* has bright, basic rooms in van Gogh colors, facing a busy roundabout at the gate of the old town, a long block from the train station. This building appears in the painting of van Gogh's house; the artist's house was bombed in World War II (Db-€30–37, CC, 5 place Lamartine, tel. & fax 04 90 96 12 32).

Hôtel du Musée** is a quiet, delightful, manor-home hide-away with 20 comfortable air-conditioned rooms, a flowery two-tiered courtyard, and a cool art-gallery lounge. The rooms in the new section are worth the few extra euros and steps. The relaxed Dubreuils speak some English (Sb-€37–46, Db-€46–61, Tb-€60–64, Qb-€75, parking-€7, breakfast-€6, CC, no elevator, 11 rue du Grande Prieuré, follow signs to Musée Réattu, tel. 04 90 93 88 88, fax 04 90 49 98 15, www.hoteldumusee.com.fr, e-mail: contact@hoteldumusee.com.fr).

Hôtel St. Trophime** is another fine old mansion converted to a hotel with a grand entry, charming courtyard, broad halls, large rooms, and (rare in Arles) an elevator, but no air-conditioning (standard Db-€47, larger, off-street Db-€55, Tb-€63, huge Qb-€70, CC, 16 rue de la Calade, near place de la République, tel. 04 90 96 88 38, fax 04 90 96 92 19).

Hôtel de l'Amphithéâtre**, a boutique hotel, is small, friendly, and *très* cozy, with thoughtfully decorated rooms, a pleasant atrium breakfast room, and air-conditioning. Ask about the new family rooms planned for 2002 (Db-€44–64, Tb-€84, CC, parking-€4, 5 rue Diderot, 1 block from arena, tel. 04 90 96 10 30, fax 04 90 93 98 69, www.hotelamphitheatre.fr, SE).

Hôtel Calendal**, located between the Roman arena and classical theater, should be three stars. It's Provençal chic with a large outdoor courtyard, smartly decorated rooms, Internet access, and seductive ambience (Db facing street-€40–55, Db facing garden-€60–65, Db with balcony-€75, Tb-€70, Qb-€80, breakfast-€6.50, CC, air-con, reserve ahead for parking-€10, 5 rue Porte de Laure, just above arena, tel. 04 90 96 11 89, fax 04 90 96 05 84, www.lecalendal.com, SE).

Hôtel d'Arlatan***, built over the site of a Roman basilica, is classy in every sense of the word. It has sumptuous public spaces, a tranquil terrace, designer pool, and antique-filled rooms, most with high wood-beamed ceilings and stone walls. In the lobby of this 15th-century building, a glass floor looks down into Roman ruins (Db-€84–137, Db/Qb suites-€152–229, great €10 buffet breakfast, parking-€11, CC, elevator, air-con, 26 rue du Sauvage, 1 block off place du Forum, tel. 04 90 93 56 66, fax 04 90 49 68 45, www.hotel-arlatan.fr, SE).

Starving artists can afford these two clean but spartan places: friendly **Hôtel Voltaire*** rents 12 small rooms with great balconies overlooking a caffeine-stained square a block below the arena (D-€24, Ds-€27, Db-€30, third or fourth person-€8 each, CC, 1 place Voltaire, tel. 04 90 96 49 18, fax 04 90 96 45 49). **Hôtel La Gallia**, with small but clean rooms, is a steal (Ds-€23, Db-€25, no CC, above lively café, 22 rue de l'Hôtel de Ville, tel. 04 90 96 00 63).

Sleeping near Arles, in Fontvieille

(See also "Sleeping in Les Baux," below.) Many drivers, particularly those with families, prefer staying in the peaceful countryside with good access to the area's sights. Just 10 minutes from Arles and Les Baux, and 20 minutes from Avignon, little Fontvieille slumbers in the shadows of its big-city cousins (though it has its share of restaurants and boutiques). **Le Peiriero*** is a tired mommy or daddy's dream come true with a vast grassy garden, massive pool, Ping-Pong table, badminton, and (believe it or not) three miniature golf holes. This complete retreat also comes with an appealing terrace café, good restaurant, and spacious loft family rooms, capable of sleeping up to five, with full bathrooms on both levels (the higher prices in each category are for rooms over the garden, Db-€69–81, Tb-€76–88, Tb loft-€104, add €7.75 per extra person, breakfast buffet-€7.35, CC, air-con, free parking, 34 avenue de Les Baux, just east of Fontvieille on road to Les Baux, tel. 04 90 54 76 10, fax 04 90 54 62 60, www.hotel-peiriero.com). **Le Domaine de la Forest** is a restored farmhouse with modern apartments for five to six people (kitchen, 2 bedrooms, private terrace). Surrounded by vineyards and rice fields, this rural refuge offers a pool, swings, and a volleyball court. While most spend a full week, shorter stays are possible off-season (nightly-€92, weekly rental required in summer-€534, from Arles take D-17 toward Fontvieille and look for *Gîtes Ruraux* signs, route de L'Aqueduc Romain, just off D-82, 13990 Fontvieille, tel. 04 90 54 70 25, fax 04 90 54 60 50, www.domaine-laforest.com).

Eating in Arles

Great atmosphere and mediocre food at fair prices await on place du Forum; **L'Estaminet** probably does the best dinner. Elsewhere, near Hôtel Régence, **L'Arlatan** is friendly and unpretentious, serving a fine meal and great desserts (€16 *menu*, closed Wed, opposite Laundromat at 7 rue Cavalarie, tel. 04 90 96 24 85). Just up the street on place Voltaire, **La Giraudière** offers good regional cooking (€17.50 *menu*, closed Tue, tel. 04 90 93 27 52). Near Hôtel du Musée, **L'Olivier** is my Arles splurge, offering exquisite Provençale cuisine (€26 *menu*, 1 bis rue Réattu, reserve ahead, tel. 04 90 49 64 88). Locals reserve early for the few tables at **Gueule de Loup** (€23/€38 *menus*, 97 rue des Arenes, tel. 04 90 96 96 69). Vegetarians and carnivores appreciate **La Vitamine**'s good selection of salads and pastas, and the owners appreciate you—show this book and enjoy a free *kir* (closed Sun, just below place du Forum on 16 rue Dr. Fanton, tel. 04 90 93 77 36). Almost next door, **La Paillotte** specializes in traditional Provençale cuisine (€14.50 *menu*, 28 rue Dr. Fanton, tel. 04 90 33 15). For the best ice cream in Arles, find **Soleilei's**; all ingredients are natural, with unusual flavors such as *fadoli*, an olive oil ice cream (across from recommended La Vitamine restaurant at 9 rue Dr. Fanton).

Transportation Connections—Arles

By bus to: Les Baux (4/day, 30 min, none on Sun, less from Nov–March, ideal departure about 08:30 with a return from Les Baux about 11:20 or 12:40), **Camargue/Ste. Marie de la Mer** (8/day Mon–Sat, less on Sun, 1 hr). Buses depart from Arles bus station and from 16 boulevard Clemenceau downtown (tel. 04 90 49 38 01).

By train to: Paris (17/day, 2 direct TGVs in 4 hrs, 15 with change in Avignon in 5 hrs), **Avignon** (14/day, 20 min, check for afternoon gaps), **Carcassonne** (6/day, 3 hrs, 3 with change in Narbonne), **Beaune** (10/day, 4.5 hrs, 9 with change in Nîmes or Avignon and Lyon), **Nice** (11/day, 4 hrs, 10 with change in Marseille), **Barcelona** (2/day, 6 hrs, change in Montpellier), **Italy** (3/day, change in Marseille and Nice; from Arles it's 4.5 hrs to Ventimiglia on the border, 9.5 hrs to the Cinque Terre, 8 hrs to Milan, 11 hrs to Florence, or 13 hrs to Venice or Rome).

AVIGNON

Famous for its nursery rhyme, medieval bridge, and brooding Palace of the Popes, contemporary Avignon bustles and prospers behind its mighty walls. During the 68 years (1309–1377) that Avignon starred as the *Franco Vaticano*, it grew from a quiet village to the thriving city it remains. Today it combines a huge student population with a white-collar, sophisticated city feel. Street mimes play to international crowds enjoying Avignon's sprawling cafés and many boutiques. If you're here in July, be prepared for the rollicking theater festival and reserve your hotel months early. Clean, polished, and popular Avignon is more impressive for its outdoor ambience than its museums and monuments. See the pope's palace, then explore its thriving streets and beautiful vistas from the Parc de Rochers des Doms.

Orientation

The cours Jean Jaurés (which turns into rue de la République) leads from the train station to place de l'Horloge and the Palace of the Popes, splitting Avignon in two. The larger right (eastern) half is where the action is. Climb to the parc de Rochers des Doms for a fine view, enjoy the people scene on place de l'Horloge, meander the back streets (see "Sights—Walking Tour Of Avignon's Back Streets," below), and lose yourself in a quiet square. Avignon's shopping district fills the traffic-free streets where rue de la République meets place de l'Horloge (creamy gelato just off place de l'Horloge, where St. Agricol meets Joseph-Vernet). Walk or drive across Pont Daladier (bridge) for a great view of Avignon and the Rhône River.

Tourist Information: The main TI is between the train station and the old town at 41 cours Jean Juarés (April–Sept Mon–Sat 09:00–18:00, closed Sun; Oct–March Mon–Fri 09:00–18:00, Sat 09:00–13:00, 14:00–17:00, Sun 10:00–12:00, longer hours during July festival, tel. 04 32 74 32 74, www.avignon-tourisme.com). A branch TI is inside the city wall at the entrance to Pont St. Bénezet (April–Oct only, daily 09:00–19:00). Pick up the handy *Guide Pratique* (info on car and bike rental, hotels, and museums) as well as their Avignon discovery guide, which includes several good (but tricky to follow) walking tours. Ask about English walking tours of Avignon (€7.75, Tue and Thu at 10:00, depart from the main TI). They also have regional bus and train schedules and information on bus excursions to popular regional sights (including the Camargue). Many of Avignon's sights are closed on Tuesdays.

Arrival in Avignon

By Train: TGV passengers need to take the free shuttle bus (*navette*, 4/hr, 15 min) from the space-age new TGV station to the main station in central Avignon (car rental is available at the TGV station; nothing within walking distance). All other trains serve the main station (baggage check available). From the main station, walk through the city walls onto the cours Jean Juarés (TI 3 blocks down at #41). The bus station (*gare routière*) and car rentals are 100 meters to the right of the train station, near the Ibis hotel.

By Car: Drivers enter Avignon following *centre-ville* signs. Park close to Pont St. Bénezet, either outside the wall or in the big structure just inside the walls and use that TI. Figure €1.50/hr and €8/day for pay lots. Hotels have advice for smart overnight parking. Leave nothing in your car.

Helpful Hints

Book Ahead for July: During the July festival, rooms are rare—reserve way early or stay in Arles (see "Sleeping in Arles," above).

Laundromat: Handy to most hotels is the Laundromat at 66 place St. Corps, where rue Agricol Perdiguier ends (daily 07:00–20:00).

English Bookstore: Try Shakespeare Bookshop (Tue–Sat 09:30–12:30, 14:00–18:30, closed Mon, 155 rue Carreterie, in Avignon's northeast corner, tel. 04 90 27 38 50).

Sights—Avignon

▲**Palace of the Popes (Palais des Papes)**—In 1309, a French pope was elected (Pope Clement V). At the urging of the French king, His Holiness decided he'd had enough of unholy Italy. So he loaded his carts and moved north to peaceful Avignon for a steady rule under a supportive king. The Catholic Church literally bought Avignon (then a two-bit town), and popes resided here until 1403. From 1378 on, there were twin popes, one in Rome and one in Avignon, causing a schism in the Catholic Church that wasn't fully resolved until 1417.

The pope's palace is two distinct buildings: one old and one older. Along with lots of big, barren rooms, you'll see frescoes, tapestries, and some beautiful floor tiles. The audioguide tour does a decent job of overcoming the lack of furnishings and gives a thorough history lesson while allowing you to tour this largely empty palace at your own pace. Enjoy the view and windswept café at the tower (€7, €8.50 during art exhibits, April–Oct daily 09:00–19:00, July–Aug until 20:00, Nov–March 09:00–17:45, ticket office closes 1 hr earlier, tours in English twice daily March–Oct, call 04 90 27 50 74 to confirm, at north end of town on place du Palais).

Musée du Petit Palais—This palace superbly displays medieval Italian painting and sculpture. Since the Catholic Church was the patron of the arts, all 350 paintings deal with Christian themes. Visiting this museum before going to the Palace of the Popes gives you a sense of art and life during the Avignon papacy (€4.60, Wed–Mon 09:30–13:00, 14:00–17:30, closed Tue, at north end of place du Palais).

▲**Parc de Rochers des Doms and Pont St. Bénezet**—Hike above the Palace of the Popes for a panoramic view over Avignon and the Rhône valley. At the far end, drop down a few steps for a good view of pont St. Bénezet. This is the "Sur le pont d'Avignon" of nursery-rhyme fame, whose construction and location were inspired by a shepherd's religious vision. Imagine a 22-arch, 1,000-meter-long bridge extending across two rivers to the lonely Tower of Philip the Fair, the bridge's former tollgate, on the distant side (equally great view from that tower back over Avignon; see below). The island the bridge spanned is now filled with campgrounds. You can pay €3 to walk along a section of the ramparts and do your own jig on pont St. Bénézet (nice view, otherwise nothing special). The castle on the right, St. André Fortress, was once another island in the Rhône. Cross Daladier Bridge for the best view of the old bridge and Avignon's skyline.

Fondation Angladon-Dubrujeaud—This museum mixes a small but enjoyable collection of art from Post-Impressionists (including Cézanne, van Gogh, Daumier, Degas, and Picasso) with recreated

Avignon

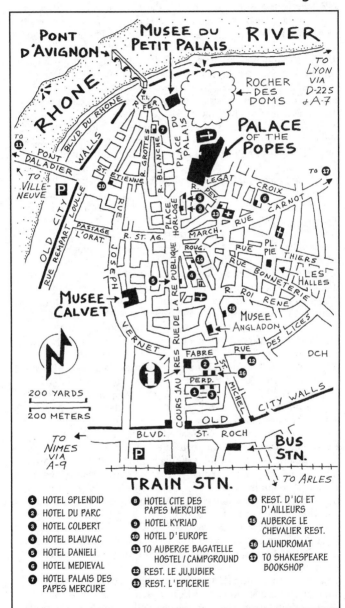

1 HOTEL SPLENDID
2 HOTEL DU PARC
3 HOTEL COLBERT
4 HOTEL BLAUVAC
5 HOTEL DANIELI
6 HOTEL MEDIEVAL
7 HOTEL PALAIS DES
   PAPES MERCURE

8 HOTEL CITE DES
   PAPES MERCURE
9 HOTEL KYRIAD
10 HOTEL D'EUROPE
11 TO AUBERGE BAGATELLE
   HOSTEL / CAMPGROUND
12 REST. LE JUJUBIER
13 REST. L'EPICERIE

14 REST. D'ICI ET
   D'AILLEURS
15 AUBERGE LE
   CHEVALIER REST.
16 LAUNDROMAT
17 TO SHAKESPEARE
   BOOKSHOP

art studios and furnishings from many periods. It's a quiet place with a few superb paintings (€4.60, Tue–Sun 13:00–18:00, closed Mon, 5 rue Laboureur, tel. 04 90 82 29 03).

Musée Calvet—This fine-arts museum impressively displays its good collection without any English explanations (€4.60, Wed–Mon 10:00–12:00, 14:00–18:00, closed Tue, on the quieter west half of town at 65 Joseph Vernet; its antiquities collection is a few blocks away at 27 rue de la République, same hours and ticket).

Discovering Avignon's Back Streets—Use the map in this book and the TI's barely adequate, single-sheet-of-paper city map to help navigate this one-hour walk.

Begin at the Agricol Perdiguier **park** by the TI. This lovely park sits on the site of a medieval monastery/college, reminding us of the critical role that monasteries played in the resurgence of medieval cities. Work your way to the eastern edge of the park, passing the children's play area; exit the small doorway on the right and enter place des Corps Saints.

This triangular square, a one-time cemetery, is typical of many smaller squares in Avignon; the plane trees seem to grow right out of the asphalt, providing essential shade for café clients. Walk north to the rue des Lices and turn right. In the 1200s, a defensive wall lined this street, marking Avignon's city limits (*lices* are the areas running along ramparts where knights would practice jousting).

Stroll east along rue de Lices for about 10 minutes (passing recommended Jujubier restaurant), then turn right on **rue des Tenturiers**, ground zero in Avignon for all that's hip. Earthy cafés, galleries, and a small stream with waterwheels line this tie-dyed street that served as the cloth industry's dying and textile center in the 1800s. Go as far as the second waterwheel, then retrace your steps on rue des Tenturiers, crossing back over rue des Lices onto rue de la Boneterrie.

You'll come face to face with Avignon's recently completed and concrete-ugly market hall, **Les Halles** (produce, meats, fish, closes at 12:30). Wander through the air-conditioned market and onto the broad place Pie.

Pass Avignon's medieval lookout tower as you walk up rue Gal Leclerc (lunches in air-conditioned comfort at **Restaurant Francois**, closed Sun, 6 Gal Leclerc). Turn left on rue Carnot, veer right on the narrow street, rue Petite Saunerie, and continue to the charming place des Chataignes (several inexpensive outdoor cafés). Notice the tower of the pope's palace and work your way counter-clockwise around the church of St. Pierre to the intimate place St. Pierre (recommended restaurant, **L'Epicerie**, see "Eating in Avignon," below). Turn left on rue Corderie to the place Carnot to enter Avignon's thriving network of shopping streets. A right on the pedestrian-only rue des Marchands takes you to place de l'Horloge.

Sights near Avignon, in Villeneuve-lès-Avignon

▲**Tower of Philip the Fair (Tour Phillipe-le-Bel)**—Built
to protect access to the pont St. Bénézet in 1307, this massive
tower offers the best view over Avignon and the Rhône basin.
It's best late in the day (€1.50, April–Sept daily 10:00–12:00,
15:00–19:00, Oct–March Tue–Sun 10:00–12:00, 15:00–17:30,
closed Mon). To reach the tower from Avignon, it's a five-minute
drive (cross pont Daladier bridge, follow signs to Villeneuve-
lès-Avignon), boat ride (Bâteau-Bus departs from Mireio Embar-
cadere near pont Daladier), or a bus ride on #11 (2/hr, catch
bus across from train station inside city wall, in front of post
office, on cours President Kennedy).

Sleeping in Avignon
(€1.10 = about $1, country code: 33, zip code: 84000)
Hotel values in Avignon pale in comparison to Arles. Still, these
are all solid values, listed in the order you would pass them walking north from the train station. The first three are a 10-minute
walk from the station; turn right off cours Jean Jaurés on rue
Agricol Perdiguier.

At **Hôtel Splendid***, the friendly Pre-Lemoines rent
17 cheery rooms with firm beds and small bathrooms for a fair
price (Sb-€26–37, Db-€38–46, breakfast-€4.60, CC, elevator,
17 rue Agricol Perdiguier, tel. 04 90 86 14 46, fax 04 90 85 38 55,
www.avignon-splendid-hotel.com).

Hôtel du Parc*, across the street, is a similar value with
less personality (D-€27–34, Ds-€35–43, Db-€37–46, CC,
ask for room overlooking the park, tel. 04 90 82 71 55, fax
04 90 85 64 86).

Hôtel Colbert** is a fine mid range bet. Parisian refugee
Patrice Medy is your host, and his care for this hotel shows in the
attention to detail (Sb-€38–44, Db-€44–58, Tb-€58–79, CC,
air-con, 7 rue Agricol Perdiguier, tel. 04 90 86 20 20, fax 04 90
85 97 00, e-mail: colberthotel@wanadoo.fr).

Hôtel Blauvac** offers 16 tired rooms (many with an
upstairs loft) and stone walls in a grand old manor home near
the pedestrian zone (Sb-€52–62, Db-€55–73, Tb/Qb-€73–82,
breakfast-€6, CC, 11 rue de La Bancasse, 1 block off rue de
la République, tel. 04 90 86 34 11, fax 04 90 86 27 41, www
.hotel-blauvac.com).

Hôtel Danieli** is a hello-dolly fluff ball of a place, renting
29 good, modern rooms with faded carpets (Sb-€52–63, Db-
€63–72, Tb-€70–78, breakfast-€7, CC, elevator, 17 rue de
la République, tel. 04 90 86 46 82, fax 04 90 27 09 24, www
.avignon-et-provence.com/danieli).

Hôtel Medieval** is a good value in a stone mansion with
unimaginative but comfortable and spacious rooms (Db-€40–56,

Tb-€61, extra bed-€7.65, kitchenettes available but require 3-day minimum stay, breakfast-€6, CC, elevator, 15 rue Petite Saunerie, 5 blocks east of place de l'Horloge, behind Eglise St. Pierre, tel. 04 90 86 11 06, fax 04 90 82 08 64, e-mail: hotel.medieval@wanadoo.fr).

For predictable comfort with air-conditioning, elevators, minibars, cable TVs, and unbeatable locations, try one of two **Hôtel Mercures***** (Db-€100–104, extra bed-€12.25, ask about their family rooms, CC, www.mercure.com). **Palais des Papes Mercure** is just inside the walls, near pont St. Bénézet (87 rooms, no CC, rue Ferruce, tel. 04 90 80 93 93, fax 04 90 80 93 94, e-mail: H0549@accor-hotels.com). **Cité des Papes Mercure** is within spitting distance of the Palace of the Popes (73 rooms, many with views over place de l'Horloge, no CC, 1 rue Jean Vilar, tel. 04 90 80 93 00, fax 04 90 80 93 01, e-mail: H1952@accor-hotels.com),

Hôtel Kyriad** is a basic chain hotel, with 38 uninspired but decent rooms in the thick of things on place de l'Horloge (Sb-€56–82, Db-€73–82, Tb-€82–92, Qb-€92–100, includes good buffet breakfast, CC, elevator, 26 place de l'Horloge, tel. 04 90 82 21 45, fax 04 90 82 90 02, www.kyriad-avignon.com).

At **Hôtel d'Europe******, be a gypsy in the palace at Avignon's most prestigious address—if you get one of the surprisingly reasonable standard rooms (standard Db-€120–150, first class-€210, deluxe Db-€285–385, breakfast-€17.50, CC, garage-€13, elevator, every comfort, 12 place Crillon, near pont Daladier, tel. 04 90 14 76 76, fax 04 90 14 76 71, www.hotel-d-europe.fr).

Auberge Bagatelle's hostel/campground offers dirt cheap beds, a lively atmosphere, busy pool, café, grocery store, Laundromat, great views of Avignon, and campers for neighbors (D-€24, dorm bed-€11, no CC, across pont Daladier on the Island (*Ile de la*) Barthelasse, #10 bus from main post office, tel. 04 90 86 30 39, fax 04 90 27 16 23).

Eating in Avignon

Le Jujubier is a delightful place to experience purely Provençal cuisine (€17 *menu*, closed Sun–Tue, 24 rue des Lices, tel. 04 90 86 64 08). **L'Epicerie**, charmingly located on a tiny square a few blocks east of place de l'Horloge, offers a good selection of *à la carte* items (daily, 10 place St. Pierre, tel. 04 90 82 74 22). **D'Ici et d'Ailleurs** ("from here and elsewhere") is Avignon's budget value for discerning diners, with decor as soothing as the prices (*menu* from €13, closed Sun, 4 rue Galande, tel. 04 90 14 63 65). **Auberge le Chevalier** offers an international flavor at a decent price (€13.60 *menu*, 19 rue des Trois Faucons, tel. 04 90 16 03 96).

Transportation Connections—Avignon

Trains

Remember, there are two train stations in Avignon, the new sub-urban TGV station and the main station in the city center (free shuttle buses connect both stations, 4/hr, 15 min). Some cities are served by slower local trains from the main station and by faster TGV trains from the TGV station; I've listed the most convenient stations for each trip.

By train from Avignon's main station to: Arles (12/day, 20 min), **Orange** (16/day, 20 min), **Nîmes** (14/day, 30 min), **Isle sur la Sorgue** (6/day, 30 min), **Lyon** (10/day, 2 hrs, also from TGV station—see below), **Carcassonne** (8/day, 3 hrs, 7 with change in Narbonne), **Barcelona** (2/day, 6 hrs, change in Montpellier).

By train from Avignon's TGV station to: Nice (10/day, 4 hrs, a few direct, most require transfer in Marseille), **Lyon** (12/day, 1.5 hrs), **Paris'** Gare du Lyon (14 TGVs/day, 2.5 hrs, 3 with change in Lyon), **Paris'** Charles de Gaulle airport (7/day, 3 hrs).

Buses

The bus station (*halte routière*, tel. 04 90 82 07 35) is in the basement of the building to the right as you exit the train station. You can call STD Gard bus company directly at 04 66 29 27 29. Nearly all buses leave from this station. The main exception is the SNCF bus service that runs from the TGV station to Arles (10/day, 30 min). The Avignon TI should have schedules. Service is reduced or nonexistent on Sunday and holidays.

By bus to Pont du Gard (6/day in summer, 4/day off-season, 40 min, see details under "Pont du Gard," below). Consider visiting Pont du Gard, continuing on to Nîmes or Uzès (both merit exploration), and returning to Avignon from there (use the same Pont du Gard bus stop you arrived at to continue on to Nimes and Uzès). Try these plans: Take the 12:00 bus from Avignon, arriving at Pont du Gard at 12:45. Then take either the 14:45 bus from there to Nîmes, where trains run hourly back to Avignon, or a 16:00 bus (Mon–Fri) on to Uzès, arriving at 16:30, with a return bus to Avignon at 18:30. Off-season service can leave you stranded for hours.

More Sights in Provence

A car is a dream come true here. But however you tour this magnificent area, notice the wind-buffeting rows of bamboo and cypress and how buildings are oriented south, with few or no windows facing north.

LES BAUX

Crowning the rugged Alpilles mountains, this rock-top castle and tourist village is a ▲▲▲ sight, worth visiting for the lunar landscape alone. Arrive by 09:00 or after 17:00 to avoid ugly crowds. Sunsets are sacrosanct and nights in Les Baux are pin-drop peaceful; the castle is beautifully illuminated (though closed after dark).

In the tourist-trampled live city, you'll find the **TI** (daily April–Sept 09:00–19:00, Oct–March 09:00–18:00, in Hôtel de Ville, tel. 04 90 54 34 39), too many shops, great viewpoints, and an exhibit of paintings by Yves Brayer, who spent his final years here (€3, 10:00–12:00, 14:00–18:30, in Hôtel des Porcelets).

A 12th-century regional powerhouse, Les Baux was razed in 1632 by a paranoid Louis XIII, who was afraid of these trouble-making upstarts. What remains is the reconstructed "live city" of tourist shops and snack stands and, the reason you came, the "dead city" (*Ville Morte* or *Citadelle des Baux*) ruins carved into, out of, and on top of a 200-meter-high rock. Climb through the "modern village" to the sun-bleached top where la Citadelle awaits (best early in the morning or early-evening light). Find the perfect view from the highest perch and try to imagine 6,000 people living within these stone walls. Survey the small museum as you enter la Citadelle (good exhibits, pick up the English explanations) and don't miss the slide show on Van Gogh, Gaugin, and Cézanne in the little chapel across from the museum (€6 entry to la Citadelle, includes entry to all the town's sights, Easter–Oct 09:00–19:00, until 20:00 July–Aug, Nov–Easter 09:30–17:00).

The best view of Les Baux day or night is one kilometer north on D-27 near **Caves de Sarragnan**, where you can sample wines in a very cool rock quarry that dates from the Middle Ages (daily April–Sept 10:00–12:00, 14:00–19:00, Oct–March closes at 18:00, tel. 04 90 54 33 58). On the way, you'll pass the **Cathédrale d'Images**, a mesmerizing sound-and-slide show that immerses visitors in regional themes by projecting 3,000 images inside a rock quarry (€7, daily 10:00–18:00, just above Les Baux on D-27).

Four daily buses serve Les Baux from the Arles bus station (30 min, see "Transportation Connections—Arles," above).

Sights between Les Baux and Arles

Abbey de Montmajour—You can't miss this brooding structure, just a few minutes from Arles toward Les Baux. A once-thriving abbey and a convenient papal retreat, it dates from 948. The vast, vacant church of St. Pierre is a massive example of Romanesque architecture, though its subtlety is lost on some (€5.50, April–Sept daily 09:00–19:00, Oct–March 10:00–13:00, 14:00–17:00, tel. 04 90 54 64 17).

▲**Roman Aqueduct**—Coming from Arles, take D-17 toward Fontvieille and look for signs on the right to *L'Aqueduc Romain* just before Fontvieille. Follow that road for a few kilometers to the romantically ruined remains of a Roman aqueduct that served Arles (no sign, look for stone walls on either side of the road). A path allows you to explore this fascinating and largely ignored aqueduct.

Sleeping in and near Les Baux
(€1.10 = about $1, country code: 33)
See also "Sleeping near Arles," above.

Hôtel Reine Jeanne** is 50 meters to your right after the main entry to the live city (Db-€46–61, great family suite-€92, CC, most air-con, ask for *chambre avec terasse*, good *menus* from €19, 13520 Les Baux, tel. 04 90 54 32 06, fax 04 90 54 32 33).

Le Mas de L'Esparou *chambre d'hôte*, a few minutes below Les Baux, is welcoming (Jacqueline loves her job, and her lack of English only makes her more animated) and kid-friendly, with spacious rooms, a swimming pool, Ping-Pong, and distant views of Les Baux. Monsieur Roux painted the paintings in your room (Db-€60, extra person-€15.25, no CC, a few kilometers north of Maussane on D-5, look for sign, 13520 Les Baux de Provence, tel. & fax 04 90 54 41 32, NSE).

Le Mazet des Alpilles, a small home with two tidy rooms in the unspoiled village of Paradou, may have space when others don't (Db-€46–52, extra bed-€15.25, no CC, route de Brunelly, 13520 Paradou, tel. 04 90 54 45 89, fax 04 90 54 44 66, e-mail: ricci@netcourrier.com, Annick NSE).

PONT DU GARD
One of Europe's great ▲▲▲ treats, this perfectly preserved Roman aqueduct was built as the critical link of a 56-kilometer (35-mile) canal that, by dropping one foot for every 300, supplied 44 million gallons of water daily to Nîmes, one of western Europe's largest cities. After years of work, the new **Grande Expo** does this sight justice with a phenomenal museum, a 23-minute movie, and a kid's space (called *Ludo*), all designed to improve your appreciation of this remarkable sight.

Start at the *rive gauche* (left bank of the Pont du Gard). You'll be greeted by the Grande Expo's linear new structure, housing the three exhibits. Begin with the informative but silly movie, if the English times are convenient; otherwise, skip it. Spend most of your time in the museum. The multimedia approach will draw you into daily Roman life: You'll learn about the many uses of water in Roman times; see examples of lead pipes, faucets, and siphons; marvel at the many models; walk through a rock quarry; and learn how they moved those huge rocks into place and how those massive arches were made. English video screens and information displays help make things as clear as spring water. The *Ludo* kid's space does the same for kids (English displays), giving them a scratch-and-sniff experience of various aspects of Roman life and the importance of water (€13, €43 for family of 2 adults and up to 4 kids, Easter–Nov daily 09:30–19:00, mid-June–Aug until 21:30, Jan–Easter until 18:00, good cafeteria, tel. 04 66 37 50 99). The high-priced entry fees include all three exhibits and your parking (parking costs €4.60 otherwise).

The actual Pont du Gard **aqueduct** is free and open until midnight (the illumination is beautiful after dark). It's a level, 300-meter walk to the aqueduct from the Grande Expo. Inspect it closely and imagine getting those stones to the top. The entire structure relies on perfect stone placement; there's no mortar holding this together. Signs direct you to "panoramas" above the bridge on either side, but you'll get better views by walking along the riverbank below—either up or downstream—or, more refreshing, by floating flat on your back; bring a swimsuit and sandals for the rocks (always open and free).

Consider **renting a canoe** from Collias to Pont du Gard (€27 per 2-person canoe; they pick you up at Pont du Gard—or elsewhere, if prearranged—and shuttle you to Collias, where you float down the river to nearby town of Remoulins; 2-hr trip, though you can take as long as you like, Collias Canoes, tel. 04 66 22 85 54, SE).

Transportation Connections—Pont du Gard

By car: Pont du Gard is an easy 25-minute drive due west of Avignon (follow signs to Nîmes) and 45 minutes northwest of Arles (via Tarascon). The *rive gauche* parking is off the D-981 that leads from Remoulins to Uzès. (Parking is also available on the *rive droite* side but leaves you farther away from the museum.)

By bus: Buses run to Pont du Gard (*rive gauche*) from Nîmes, Uzès, and Avignon. Combine Uzès (see below) and Pont du Gard for a good day excursion from Avignon (5/day in summer, 3/day off-season, 40 min to Pont du Gard; see "Transportation Connections—Avignon," above). The bus stop at Pont du Gard is in the new parking lot near the Grande Expo on the left bank (rive gauche). The return stop to Avignon is to your left before crossing the traffic circle. Make sure you're waiting for the bus on the correct side of the traffic circle.

Sights near Pont du Gard

Uzès—An intriguing, less-trampled town, Uzès is best seen slowly on foot, with a long coffee break in its beautifully arcaded and mellow main square, the *place aux Herbes* (not so mellow during the colorful Wednesday and bigger Saturday-morning market). The city is the sight; there are no important museums, and most of the center city is traffic-free and tastefully restored. (Uzès is officially in Languedoc, not Provence.)

At the **TI**, pick up the English walking tour brochure (June–Sept Mon–Fri 09:00–18:00, Sat–Sun 10:00–13:00, 14:00–17:00, Oct–March Mon–Fri 09:00–12:00, 13:30–18:00, Sat 10:00–13:00, closed Sun, on the ring road on place Albert 1er tel. 04 66 22 68 88). Skip the dull and overpriced palace of the Duché de Uzès (€9, French-only tour). You can enjoy the unusual Tour Fenestrelle—all that remains of a 12th-century cathedral—from the outside only.

Uzès is a short hop west (by bus) of Pont du Gard and is well-served by bus from Nîmes (9/day) and Avignon (3/day).

THE FRENCH RIVIERA

A hundred years ago, celebrities from London to Moscow flocked here to socialize, gamble, and escape the dreary weather at home. The belle époque is today's tourist craze, as this most sought-after fun-in-the-sun destination now caters to budget travelers as well. Some of the Continent's most stunning scenery and intriguing museums lie along this strip of land—as do millions of heat-seeking tourists.

Nice has world-class museums, a grand beachfront promenade, and a seductive old city. Daytrips are easy: Monte Carlo welcomes all with open cash registers, and Antibes has a romantic port and silky-sandy beaches. Evenings on the Riviera, a.k.a. the Côte d'Azur, were made for the promenade and outdoor dining.

Choose a Home Base

I've listed accommodations for three different places: Nice, Antibes, and Villefranche-sur-Mer. **Nice** is the region's capital and France's fifth-largest city. With excellent public transportation to most regional sights, it's the most practical base for train travelers. Nice also has a full palette of museums and rock-hard beaches, the best selection of hotels in all price ranges, and is ground zero for Rivera nightlife. A car is a headache in Nice. Nearby **Antibes** is smaller, with fewer hotels but fine sandy beaches, good hiking, and the Picasso Museum. It has frequent train service to Nice and Monaco, and is easier for drivers. **Villefranche-sur-Mer** is the romantic's choice, with a serene setting and small-town warmth. It has finely ground pebble beaches, good public transportation (particularly to Nice and Monaco), and easy parking. Its few hotels leap from simple to sublime, letting Nice handle the middle ground.

Planning Your Time

Most should plan a full day for Nice and at least a half day
each for Monaco and Antibes. Monaco is best at night (the
sights are closed but crowds are few, consider eating dinner
here), and Antibes glitters during the day (good beaches and
Picasso Museum).

Getting around the Riviera

Getting around the Côte d'Azur by train or bus is easy (park your
car and leave the driving to others). For some of the Riviera's best
scenery, follow the coast road between Cannes and Fréjus (when
arriving in or leaving the Côte d'Azur), take the short drive along
Moyenne Corniche from Nice to Eze Village. Tune into Riviera-
Radio at FM 106.5 for English radio.

Nice is perfectly located for exploring the region. Monaco,
Eze Village, Villefranche-sur-Mer, and Antibes, are all a 15-
to 60-minute bus or train ride apart from each other.

The TI (and probably your hotel) has information on
minivan excursions from Nice (half day–about €61, full day–
€76-107; Tour Azur is one of many, tel. 04 93 44 88 77,
www.tourazur.com).

Bus service can be cheaper and more frequent than
rail service, depending on the destination. At Nice's efficient bus station (*gare routière*), on boulevard J. Jaures
(see map of Nice on page 279), you'll find a baggage check
(called *messagerie*, available Mon–Sat), clean WCs for €0.40,
and several bus companies offering free return trips to some
destinations (keep your ticket). Get schedules and prices
at the helpful information desk in the bus station. Buy
tickets in the station or on the bus.

Here's an overview of public transport options to key
Riviera destinations from Nice (rt = round-trip, ow = one-way):

Destination	Bus	Train
Monaco	4/hr, 40 min, €3, rt	2/hr, 20 min, €3, ow
Villefranche	4/hr, 15 min, €1.40, rt	2/hr, 10 min, €1.40, ow
Antibes	3/hr, 50 min, €4.25, ow	2/hr, 25 min, €3.35, ow
Cannes	way too long	2/hr, 30 min, €4.90, ow
Eze Village	every 2 hrs, 25 min, €2.30, rt	none

Two bus companies, RCA and Cars Broch, provide service on
the same route between Nice, Villefranche, and Monaco; RCA's
buses run more frequently (tel. 04 93 85 61 81 for info on both).

The French Riviera

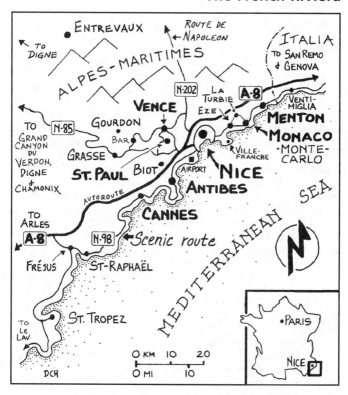

Cuisine Scene—Côte d'Azur

The Côte d'Azur (technically a part of Provence) gives Provence's cuisine a Mediterranean flair. Local specialties are *bouillabaisse* (the spicy seafood stew-soup that seems worth the cost only for those with a seafood fetish), *bourride* (a creamy fish soup thickened with aioli, a garlic sauce), and *salade niçoise* (nee-swaz; a tasty tomato, potato, olive, anchovy, and tuna salad). You'll also find these tasty bread treats: *pissaladière* (bread dough topped with onions, olives, and anchovies), *fougasse* (a spindly, lacelike bread), *socca* (a thin chickpea crepe), and *pan bagnat* (a bread shell stuffed with tomatoes, anchovies, olives, onions, and tuna). Good Italian cuisine is easy to find and generally a good value. White and rosé Bellet and the rich reds and rosés of Bandol are the local wines.

This is the most difficult region in France in which to find reliable restaurant listings. Because most visitors come more for the sun than the cuisine, and because the clientele is predominantly international, most restaurants aim for the middle and are hard to distinguish from each other. Look for views and ambience and lower your expectations.

Art Scene—Côte d'Azur

The list of artists who have painted the Riviera reads like a Who's Who of 20th-Century Art: Renoir, Matisse, Chagall, Braque, Dufy, Leger, and Picasso all lived and worked here. Their simple, semi-abstract, and, above all, colorful works reflect the Riviera. You'll experience the same landscapes they painted in this bright, sun-drenched region punctuated with views of the "azure sea."

But mostly the artists were drawn to the simple lifestyle of fishermen and farmers that has reigned here since time began. These *très* serious artists, as they grew older, retired in the sun and turned their backs on modern art's "isms" and painted with the wide-eyed wonder of children, using bright, primary colors, simple outlines, and simple subjects.

A remarkable concentration of well-organized contemporary art museums (many described below) litter the Riveria, allowing art-lovers to appreciate these artists' work while immersed in the same sun and culture that inspired them. Many of the museums were designed to blend the art with surrounding views, gardens, and fountains, highlighting that modern art is not only stimulating, but sometimes simply beautiful.

NICE

Nice (neece) is the ultimate tourist melting pot. You'll share its international beaches with the chicest of the chic, the cheapest of the cheap, and everyone else in this scramble to be where the mountains meet the water. Nice's spectacular Alps-to-Mediterranean scenery, thriving old city, eternally entertaining seafront promenade, and fine museums make settling into this city easy. Nice may be nice, but it's hot and jammed in July and August. Get a room with air-conditioning (*avec climatization*). Everything you'll want in Nice is walkable or a short bus ride away.

Orientation

Most sights and hotels recommended in this book are located near the avenue Jean Medécin, between the train station and the beach. It's a 20-minute walk from the train station to the beach (or a €9 taxi ride) and a 20-minute walk along the promenade from the fancy Hôtel Negresco to the heart of Old Nice.

Tourist Information: Nice has four helpful TIs: at terminal 1 at the airport, next to the train station, on RN-7 after the airport on the right, and across from the beach at 5 promenade des Anglais (all open daily 08:00–19:00, until 20:00 July–Aug, can book rooms for a small fee, tel. 04 93 87 07 07 or

04 92 14 48 00). Pick up the excellent, free Nice map (which lists all the sights and hours), the extensive *Practical Guide to Nice*, information on regional daytrips (such as maps to Antibes), and the museums booklet.

Consider buying the **museum pass**. The regional *Carte Musées* is a great value for those planning to visit more than one museum in a day or several museums over a few days (€5.50/1 day, €13/3 consecutive days, €24/7 consecutive days, valid at all museums described in this chapter, sold at any TI or participating museum).

Arrival in Nice

By Train: Nice has one main station (*Nice-Ville*, lockers available) where all trains stop and you get off. Avoid the suburban stations. The TI is next door to the left as you exit the train station, car rental is to the right. To reach my recommended hotels, turn left out of the station, then right on avenue Jean Médecin. To get to the beach and the promenade des Anglais from the station, continue on foot for 20 minutes down avenue Jean Médecin or take bus #12 (stop on Jean Médecin). To get to the old city and the bus station (*gare routière*), catch bus #5 from avenue Jean Médecin.

By Car: Avoid arriving at rush hour (Mon–Fri 17:00–19:30). Stop at the roadside TI just past the airport, then park at the lot at the Nice Etoile shopping center on avenue Jean Médecin (ticket booth on 3rd floor, about €13/day, €7.75 from 20:00–8:00). Most Nice street parking is metered, and garages cost from €9 to €14 per day—your hotel can advise you best.

By Plane: Nice's mellow, user-friendly airport is on the Mediterranean, about 25 minutes west of the city center. The TI and international flights use terminal 1; domestic flights use terminal 2 (airport tel. 04 93 21 30 30). At terminal 1 you'll find the TI, banks (so-so rates), and car rental just outside customs. Taxis wait immediately outside the terminal (allow €25–30 to Nice hotels, €45 to Villefranche). Turn left after passing customs to find the bus information office (taxi vouchers to Villefranche sold here for €43). Three bus lines run to Nice: the Nice-Direct express bus to the SNCF train station (stall #6, €3.50, 2/hr until 21:00, 20 min, drops you within a 10-min walk of many of my hotel listings), local bus #23 (also stall #6, €1.40, 4/hr, 40 min, direction: St. Maurice, serves stops between the airport and SNCF station), and the yellow "NICE" bus to the bus station (*gare routière*, stall #1, €3.50, 3/hr, 25 min). To get to Villefranche from the airport, take the yellow "NICE" bus to the bus station (*gare routière*) and transfer to the Villefranche bus (€1.40, 4/hr). Buses also run to Antibes and Monaco from the airport (both hrly, 50 min).

Helpful Hints

Theft Alert: Nice is notorious for pickpockets. Have nothing important on or around your waist, unless it's in a money belt tucked out of sight (no fanny packs, please); don't leave anything visible in your car; be wary of scooters when standing at intersections; don't leave things unattended on the beach while swimming; and stick to main streets in Old Nice after dark.

U.S. Consulate: If you lose your passport, this is the place to go (31 rue Marechal Joffre, tel. 04 93 88 89 55, fax 04 93 87 07 38).

Medical Help: Dr. Veronique Margery speaks English (26 rue Paul Deroulede, tel. 04 93 87 21 25, cellular 06 12 44 97 85).

Taxis: Taxis allow four passengers in Nice and are handy to some museums. They normally only pick up at taxi stands (*tête de station*) or by a telephoned request. You'll pay €1 per bag and supplements for service on Sunday and after 19:00 any day (tel. 04 93 13 78 78).

Rocky Beaches: To make life tolerable on the rocks, swimmers should buy a pair of the cheap plastic beach shoes (flip-flops fall off in the water) sold at many shops.

American Express: AmEx faces the beach at 11 promenade des Anglais (tel. 04 93 16 53 53).

English Bookstore: Try **The Cat's Whiskers** (closed Sun, 26 rue Lamartine, near Hôtel Star).

Laundromats: Self-serve Laundromats abound in Nice; ask your hotelier for suggestions and guard your load.

Internet Access: It's easy in Nice. Ask your hotelier for the nearest Internet café.

Sights—Nice

▲▲**Promenade des Anglais**—Welcome to the Riviera. There's something for everyone along this seafront circus. Watch the Europeans at play, admire the azure Mediterranean, anchor yourself in a blue chair, and prop your feet up on the made-to-order guardrail. Join the evening parade of tans along the promenade. Start at the pink-domed Hôtel Negresco and, like the belle époque (late 19th-century) English aristocrats for whom the promenade was built, stroll to the old city and Castle Hill (20-min walk).

Hôtel Negresco, Nice's finest hotel and a historic monument, offers the city's most costly beds and a free "museum" interior (reasonable attire is necessary to enter). March through the lobby into the exquisite Salon Royal. The tsar's chandelier hangs from an Eiffel-built dome. Read the explanation, check out the room photos, and stroll the circle. On your way out, pop into the Salon Louis XIV (more explanations).

The next block to your left as you exit has a lush park and the Masséna Museum. The TI is beyond that. Cross over to the promenade.

Nice

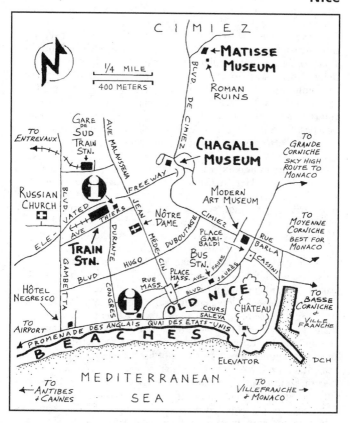

Pull up a chair and admire the scene (beautiful after dark). To your right is the airport, built on a landfill, and, on that tip of land way out there, Cap d'Antibes. Until the late 1800s, Antibes and Nice were in different countries; the Italians gave Nice to the French as thanks for their help during the reunification of Italy in 1860. To the far left lies Villefranche-sur-Mer (beyond that tower at land's end), Monaco, then Italy. Behind you are the pre-Alps (*les Alpes Maritimes*), which gather threatening clouds and leave the Côte d'Azur in sunshine over 300 days per year. Turn around. To the right of Hôtel Negresco sit two other belle époque establishments: the West End and Westminster hotels. These hotels represent Nice's initiation as a tourist mecca 100 years ago, when the combination of leisure time and a stable economy allowed wealthy tourists to find the sun even in winter. Tourism as we know it today took off after World War II (blame planes, trains, and automobiles), allowing even budget travelers to appreciate this once-exclusive resort. Now get down to that beach.

Beaches—Nice is where the jet set relax *à la plage*. After settling into the smooth pebbles, you can play beach volleyball, Ping-Pong, or *boules*; rent paddleboats, jet skis, or windsurfing equipment; explore ways to use your zoom lens as a telescope; or snooze on comfy beach beds with end tables (mattress-€9, mattress and chaise lounge-€11, umbrella-€4.60). Have lunch in your bathing suit (€9 salads and pizzas). Before heading off in search of sandy beaches, try it on the rocks. As you stroll the promenade, look for the *Plage Publique* signs explaining the 15 beach no-nos (translated in English).

▲▲Old City (Vieux Nice)—The thriving old city is characteristic Nice in the buff. Here Italian and French flavors mix to create a spicy Mediterranean dressing. The modern age drove Old Nice into a triangle of spindly streets filling a corner between Castle Hill and the beach. A broad, park-lined boulevard seals it off. The streets, while straight, are anything but predictable. Stealth pigeons fly under tall, pastel, domestic cliffs, while tattoo shops show their work. The Naples-like rue Droite plays host to simple bars, chic art shops, and shaded strolling; stop by Le Four à Bois bakery (at #38) and watch them make *fougasse*. The fresh pasta shops (almost nonexistent elsewhere in France) and many *gelaterias* remind us how close we are to Italy. Cours Saleya, a long broad square, collects people, produce, and flowers as if in a trough between all this and the sea. Restaurant tables tangle with market stalls and browsers. Dinner here is a treat—not for the cuisine, but for the sea of tables and festive feel. The daily flower and produce market becomes a flea market on Monday. Nearby place Rosetti is more intimate and utterly Italian at night (more average restaurants). Duck into the Cathedral St. Reparate for a dose of Italian Baroque. The fish market on place St. Francois isn't worth the detour.

Castle Hill—Climb or, better yet, take the elevator up this saddle horn in the otherwise flat city center only for exercise or the view (elevator is next to Hôtel Suisse where the bay-front road curves to the right, €0.60 one-way, €1 round-trip). The views over Nice, the port (to the east), the Alps foothills, and the Mediterranean make a decent reward, better if you took the elevator, best at sunset (park closes at 20:00 in summer, earlier off-season). You'll find a waterfall, a playground, two cafés (fair prices), and a cemetery, but no castle on Castle Hill. If you walk down, follow signs from just below the upper café to *Vielle Ville* (not *le Port*), and turn right at the cemetery, then look for the walkway down on your left.

▲Russian Cathedral—Even if you've been to Russia, this Russian Orthodox church, which claims to be the finest outside Russia, is interesting. Its one-room interior is filled with icons and candles.

Tsar Nicholas II gave his aristocratic countryfolk—who wintered on the Riviera—this church in 1912. (A few years later, Russian comrades who didn't winter on the Riviera shot him.) Here in the land of olives and anchovies, these proud onion domes seem odd. But, I imagine, so did those old Russians (€1.85, daily 09:00–12:00, 14:30–18:00, services Sat at 18:00, Sun at 10:00, no shorts, 10-min walk behind station at 17 boulevard du Tsarevitch, tel. 04 93 96 88 02).

Nightlife—Nice's bars play host to the Riviera's most happening late-night scene, full of jazz and rock 'n' roll. Most activity focuses on Old Nice, near place Rossetti. If you're out very late, avoid walking alone. Plan on a cover charge or expensive drinks.

Museums—Nice

▲▲**Musée National Marc Chagall**—Even if you're suspicious of modern art, this museum—with the largest collection of Chagall's work anywhere—might appeal to you. After World War II, Chagall returned from the United States to settle in nearby Vence. Between 1954 and 1967, he painted a cycle of 17 large murals designed for and donated to this museum. These paintings, inspired by the books of Genesis, Exodus, and the Song of Songs, make up the "nave," or core, of what Chagall called the "House of Brotherhood."

Each painting is a lighter-than-air collage of images drawing from Chagall's Russian-folk-village youth, his Jewish heritage, Biblical themes, and his feeling that he existed somewhere between heaven and earth. He felt the Bible was a synonym for nature, and color and Biblical themes were key ingredients for understanding God's love for his creation. Chagall's brilliant blues and reds celebrate nature, as do his spiritual and folk themes. Notice the focus on couples. To Chagall, humans loving each other mirrored God's love of creation.

Don't miss the stained-glass windows of the auditorium (enter through the garden), early family photos of the artist, and a room full of Chagall lithographs. The small €3 guidebook begins with an introduction by Chagall (€4.60, €5.80 in summer, July–Sept Wed–Mon 10:00–17:40, Oct–June 10:00–16:40, closed Tue, ask about English tours, tel. 04 93 53 87 20). An idyllic café awaits in the garden.

Getting to Chagall and Matisse Museums: The Chagall Museum is a confusing but manageable 15-minute walk from the top of avenue Jean Médecin and the train station; the Matisse Museum (described below) is a 30-minute uphill walk from the Chagall Museum. Buses #15 and #17 serve Chagall and Matisse from the eastern, Italy side of avenue Jean Medécin (both run 6/hr, €1.30). Consider walking to Chagall and taking the bus to Matisse.

To walk to the Chagall Museum, go to the train-station end of avenue Jean Médecin and turn right onto rue Raimbaldi along the overpasses, then turn left under the overpasses onto avenue Comboul. Once under the overpass, angle to the right up rue Olivetto to the alley with the big wall on your right. A pedestrian path soon emerges, leading up and up to signs for Chagall and Matisse. The bus to Matisse is on avenue Cimiez, two blocks up from Chagall.

▲**Matisse Museum** (▲▲▲ for his fans)—The art is beautifully displayed in this elegant orange mansion and represents the single largest collection of Matisse paintings. While many don't get Matisse, this museum offers a painless introduction to this influential artist whose style was shaped by the southern light and fellow Côte d'Azur artists, Picasso and Renoir. Watch as his style becomes simpler with time. A room on the top floor has models of his famous Chapelle du Rosaire in nearby Vence and illustrates the beauty of his simple design (€4, April–Sept Wed–Mon 10:00–18:00, Oct–March 10:00–17:00, closed Tue, take bus #15 or #17 to Arènes stop, see directions under Chagall Museum listing above, tel. 04 93 81 08 08).

Modern Art Museum (Musée d'Art Moderne et d'Art Contemporain)—This ultramodern museum features an enjoyable collection of art from the 1960s and 1970s, including works by Andy Warhol and Roy Lichtenstein, and frequent special exhibits (€4, Wed–Mon 10:00–18:00, Fri until 22:00, closed Tue, on promenade des Arts near bus station, tel. 04 93 62 61 62).

Other Nice Museums—These museums offer decent rainy-day options (generally open 10:00-12:00, 14:00-18:00). The **Musée des Beaux Arts** (Fine Arts Museum), with 6,000 works from the 17th to 20th centuries, will satisfy your need for a fine-arts fix (€4, 3 avenue des Baumettes, in western end of Nice, tel. 04 92 15 28 28). The **Musée de la Marine** (Naval Museum) is interesting and relevant, given Nice's huge port (€2.30, in Tour Bellanda, halfway up Château Hill, tel. 04 93 80 47 61). The **Musée Masséna** describes Nice's history (€4, facing beach next to Hôtel Negresco at 65 rue de France, tel. 04 93 88 11 34). The **Musée Archeologique** (Archaeological Museum) displays Roman ruins and various objects from the Romans' occupation of this region (€4, near Matisse Museum at 160 avenue des Arenes, tel. 04 93 81 59 57).

Between Nice and Monaco

▲▲▲**The Three Corniches**—Nice and Monaco are linked with three coast-hugging routes, each one higher than the other, all offering sensational views and a different perspective on this billion-dollar slice of real estate. The *Basse Corniche* (the lower cornice, often called *Corniche Inférieure*) strings ports, beaches, and villages together for a ground-floor view. The *Moyenne Corniche* (middle cornice) is far more impressive and slices its way halfway to the top, connecting hill towns such as Eze Village and providing great views over the Mediterranean below. Napoleon's crowning road-construction achievement, the *Grande Corniche* (Great Cornice), caps the cliffs with staggering views from almost 480 meters (1,600 feet) above the sea. For the best of all worlds, take the Moyenne Corniche from Nice to Eze Village, find the Grande Corniche/La Turbie from there, and drop down to Monaco after La Turbie (see "Sights near Villefranche-sur-Mer," below). Buses travel each route; the higher the cornice, the less frequent the buses (get details at Nice's bus station).

Sleeping in Nice
(€1.10 = about $1, country code: 33, zip code: 06000)
Sleep Code: **S** = Single, **D** = Double/Twin, **T** = Triple, **Q** = Quad, **b** = bathroom, **s** = shower only, **CC** = Credit Cards, **no CC** = Credit Cards not accepted, **SE** = Speaks English, **NSE** = No English, * = French hotel rating (0–4 stars). Hotels have elevators unless otherwise noted.

Don't look for charm in Nice. Go for modern and clean with a central location and, in summer, air-conditioning. Reserve early for summer visits. Prices generally drop €5 to €10 from October to April (the rates listed are for May–Sept) and increase during Carnival (Jan 31–Feb 2) and the Monaco Grand Prix (May 23–27). Most hotels near the station are overrun, overpriced, and loud. I sleep halfway between Old Nice (Vieux Nice) and the train station, near avenues Jean Médecin and Victor Hugo. Drivers can park under the Nice Etoile shopping center (on avenue Jean Médecin and boulevard Dubouchage). Hotels are listed in order of proximity to the train station, the latter being closest to Old Nice and the beach.

Hôtel Excelsior***, one block below the station, is a diamond in the rough with 19th-century decor, a lush garden courtyard with fountain, pleasant rooms with real wood furnishings, and an elegant dining room (*menus* from €19). Rooms on the garden are best in the summer; those streetside have balconies and get winter sun (Db-€72–87, Tb-€87–102, CC, 19 avenue Durante, tel. 04 93 88 18 05, fax 04 93 88 38 69, www.excelsiornice.com).

Hôtel Trianon**, with formal owners, is a small, big-city refuge with very fair rates and bright, spotless rooms, half of which overlook a small park (Sb-€44, Db-€53, CC, 15 avenue Auber, tel. 04 93 88 30 69, fax 04 93 88 11 35).

Hôtel du Petit Louvre* is basic, but a solid budget bet, with playful owners (the Vilas), art-festooned walls, and adequate rooms (Ds-€35, Db-€39, Tb-€41–46, CC, payment due on arrival, 10 rue Emma Tiranty, tel. 04 93 80 15 54, fax 04 93 62 45 08, e-mail: petilouvr@aol.com).

Hôtel Clemenceau** is a good value with a homey, family feel and mostly spacious, traditional, and comfortable rooms, some with balconies, all with air-conditioning, but no elevator

Nice Hotels and Restaurants

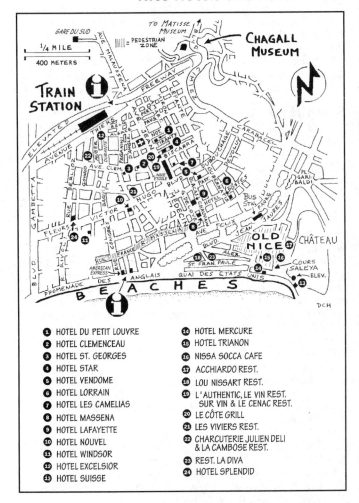

- ❶ HOTEL DU PETIT LOUVRE
- ❷ HOTEL CLEMENCEAU
- ❸ HOTEL ST. GEORGES
- ❹ HOTEL STAR
- ❺ HOTEL VENDOME
- ❻ HOTEL LORRAIN
- ❼ HOTEL LES CAMELIAS
- ❽ HOTEL MASSENA
- ❾ HOTEL LAFAYETTE
- ❿ HOTEL NOUVEL
- ⓫ HOTEL WINDSOR
- ⓬ HOTEL EXCELSIOR
- ⓭ HOTEL SUISSE
- ⓮ HOTEL MERCURE
- ⓯ HOTEL TRIANON
- ⓰ NISSA SOCCA CAFE
- ⓱ ACCHIARDO REST.
- ⓲ LOU NISSART REST.
- ⓳ L'AUTHENTIC, LE VIN REST. SUR VIN & LE CENAC REST.
- ⓴ LE CÔTE GRILL
- ㉑ LES VIVIERS REST.
- ㉒ CHARCUTERIE JULIEN DELI & LA CAMBOSE REST.
- ㉓ REST. LA DIVA
- ㉔ HOTEL SPLENDID

(S-€31, Sb-€38, D-€43, Db-€46, Tb-€61, Qb-€77, kitchenette-€7.75 extra and for long stays only, CC, 3 avenue Clemenceau, 1 block west of avenue Jean Médecin, tel. 04 93 88 61 19, fax 04 93 16 88 96, Marianne SE).

Hôtel St. Georges**, a block away, is bigger and brighter with air-conditioning, a peaceful garden courtyard, reasonably roomy and comfortable rooms, and happy Jacques at the reception (Sb-€55, Db-€64, 3-bed Tb-€80, extra bed-€15, CC, 7 avenue

Clemenceau, tel. 04 93 88 79 21, fax 04 93 16 22 85, e-mail: nicefrance.hotelstgeorges@wanadoo.fr).

Hôtel Star**, a few blocks east of avenue Jean Médecin, is immaculate, air-conditioned, comfortable, and a truly great value. It's run by intense Françoise and mellower Georges (SE) who expect you to respect their high standards (Sb-€33–39, Db-€45–55, Tb-€59–69, breakfast-€4.60, CC, fine beds, beach towels, no elevator, 14 rue Biscarra, reserve by fax or e-mail rather than by phone, tel. 04 93 85 19 03, fax 04 93 13 04 23, e-mail: star-hotel@wanadoo.fr, www.hotel-star.com).

Hôtel les Camelias** reminds me of the Old World places I stayed in as a kid traveling with my parents. A well-located, dark, creaky, and floral place burrowed behind a small parking lot and garden, it has linoleum halls, simple rooms (some lumpy beds), and a loyal clientele who give the TV lounge a retirement-home-after-dinner feeling. Some rooms have balconies—request a *chambre avec balcon* (Ss-€40, Ds-€46, Db-€62, includes breakfast, parking-€4.60, CC, 3 rue Spitaleri, tel. 04 93 62 15 54, fax 04 93 80 42 96, formal Madame Vimont and her son Jean Claude SE). The €11 four-course dinner is simple, hearty, and stressless.

Hôtel Vendome***, a mansion, gives you a whiff of *la belle époque*, with pink pastels, high ceilings, and grand staircases. Rooms are small but adequate; the best have balconies—request a *chambre avec balcon*. The most desirable rooms are on the fifth floor (Sb-€82–89, Db-€98–106, Tb-€110–118, Qb-€128, extra bed-€15.25, CC, air-con, limited off-street parking-€8, cable TV, 26 rue Pastorelli, tel. 04 93 62 00 77, fax 04 93 13 40 78, e-mail: contact@vendome-hotel-nice.com).

Hôtel Lafayette*** looks big and average from the outside, but inside it's a cozy, good value offering 18 sharp, spacious, three-star rooms at two-star rates, all one floor up from the street (Sb-€60–76, Db-€75–96, Tb-€90–111, extra bed-€15.50, CC, no elevator, 32 rue de l'Hôtel des Postes, tel. 04 93 85 17 84, fax 04 93 80 47 56, e-mail: lafayette@nouvel-hotel.com).

Hôtel Masséna****, a few blocks from place Massena in a beautiful old building, is a business hotel offering 100 four-star rooms with all the comforts at reasonable rates (Db-€100–137, larger Db-€168, Tb-€198, Qb-€213, CC, reserve a parking space ahead-€15.50, Internet access in lobby, 58 rue Giofreddo, tel. 04 93 85 49 25, fax 04 93 62 43 27, www.hotel-massena-nice.com, SE).

Hôtel Lorrain** offers kitchenettes in all of its simple but spacious rooms and is conveniently located one block from the bus station and Old Nice (Sb-€38, Db-€46, Tb-€53, Qb-€69, CC, 6 rue Gubernatis, push top buzzer to release door, tel. 04 93 85 42 90, fax 04 93 85 55 54, e-mail: hotellorrain@aol.com).

Hôtel Mercure*** is on the water, behind Cours Saleya, and offers predictable, modern rooms at good rates considering the location (Sb-€84, Db-€94, CC, air-con, some balconies and views, 91 quai des Etats-Unis, tel. 04 93 85 74 19, fax 04 93 13 90 94, e-mail: H0962@accor-hotels.com).

Hôtel Suisse*** offers Nice's best ocean views for the money with many balconied rooms. Rooms are comfortable, with air-conditioning and modern conveniences, and are surprisingly quiet given the busy street below (Db without view-€67, Db with great view-€92–107, extra bed-€20, CC, 15 quai Rauba-Capeu, tel. 04 92 17 39 00, fax 04 93 85 30 70, e-mail: nice@hotels-primotel.com).

Hotels near boulevard Victor Hugo: The next three hotels are on or very near this tree-lined boulevard, several blocks west of avenue Jean Médecin and about five blocks from the beach.

Hôtel Nouvel** is a well-run, spotless place set on a broad sidewalk with modern rooms (Sb-€61–76, Db-€67–84, Tb apartment-€112–136, CC, air-con, 19 bis boulevard Victor Hugo, tel. 04 93 87 15 00, fax 04 93 16 00 67, www.nouvel-hotel.com).

Hôtel Windsor***, a snazzy, airy, garden retreat with many contemporary rooms designed by modern artists, has a swimming pool, free gym, and €9 sauna (Db-€87–120, extra bed-€15, rooms over garden are worth the higher price, CC, 11 rue Dalpozzo, 10 blocks west of Jean Medécin and 5 blocks from sea, tel. 04 93 88 59 35, fax 04 93 88 94 57, e-mail: windsor@webstore.fr, SE).

Hôtel Splendid**** is a worthwhile splurge if you miss your Hilton. The rooftop pool, Jacuzzi, and panoramic breakfast room alone almost justify the cost—throw in luxurious rooms, a free gym, Internet access, and air-conditioning, and you're as good as home (Db-€167–214, suites-€282–300, limited parking-€14, CC, 50 boulevard Victor Hugo, tel. 04 93 16 41 00, fax 04 93 16 42 70, www.splendid-nice.com).

Eating in Nice

Nice's old city overflows with restaurants in all shapes and sizes. The dinner scene on Cours Saleya is as entertaining as the food is average. It's a fun, festive place to compare tans and new outfits. Comparison shopping is half the fun (I go Italian). **La Cambuse** is the lone exception, offering a more refined setting and fine cuisine for a bit more (5 Cours Saleya, tel. 04 93 80 02 40). **Charcuterie Julien** is a good deli that sells an impressive array of local dishes by weight. Buy 200 grams of your choice plopped into a plastic carton to go (*pour emporter*, poor ahn-por-tay) or eat there (Thu–Tue 11:00–19:30, closed Wed, rue de la Poissonnerie, at Castle Hill). **Nissa Socca** café offers good, cheap Italian cuisine in Old Nice in a lively atmosphere (opens at 19:00, closed Sun, arrive early, a block off place Rossetti on rue Ste. Reparate, tel. 04 93 80 18 35). Deeper in the old city, **Acchiardo's** is a budget traveler's best friend, with simple, hearty food at bargain prices and no fluff (closed Sat–Sun, 38 rue Droite, tel. 04 93 85 51 16).

Just below place Masséna, **Lou Nissart** serves regional specialties to appreciative locals in non-air-conditioned rooms (moderate
prices, across place Masséna at 1 rue de l'Opéra, tel. 04 93 85 34 49).
Across the street, **La Diva** is softer, stylish, and popular (€15–22
menus, closed Sun–Mon, 4 rue de l'Opera, tel. 04 93 85 96 15). For
the best, most authentic Niçoise cuisine in this chapter (allow €30
for dinner), reserve a table at the cozy **Les Viviers** (5-min walk
west of avenue Jean Médecin at 22 rue Alphonse Karr, tel. 04 93
16 00 48). For a special occasion, consider the more elegant restaurant next door, run by the same owners.

Several relaxed cafés line the broad sidewalk on rue Biscarra,
just east of avenue Jean Medécin between numbers 16 and 18.
L'Authentic, **Le Vin sur Vin** (with a wine emphasis), and **Le
Cenac** are all reasonable. On the other side of avenue Jean
Medécin, **Le Côte Grill** is bright, cool, and easy, with a salad
bar, air-conditioned rooms, a large selection at reasonable
prices, and a friendly staff (1 avenue Georges Clemenceau,
tel. 04 93 82 45 53).

Transportation Connections—Nice
By train to: Arles (11/day, 3.5 hrs, 10 with change in Marseille), **Paris'** Gare de Lyon (14/day, 5.5–7 hrs, 6 with change
in Marseille), **Venice** (3/day, 3/night, 11–15 hrs, 5 require
changes), **Chamonix** (4/day, 11 hrs, 2–3 changes), **Beaune**
(7/day, 7 hrs, change in Lyon), **Digne/Grenoble** (consider
the scenic little trains that run from Nice to Digne, then on to
Grenoble), **Munich** (2/day, 12 hrs with 2 changes, 1 night train
with a change in Verona), **Interlaken** (1/day, 12 hrs), **Florence**
(4/day, 7 hrs, changes in Pisa and/or Genoa, night train), **Milan**
(4/day, 5–6 hrs, 3 with changes), **Venice** (4/day, 8 hrs, 2 changes
required or a direct night train), **Barcelona** (3/day, 11 hrs, long
change in Montpellier, or a direct night train).

By plane to Paris (hrly, 1 hr, about the same price as a
train ticket).

VILLEFRANCHE-SUR-MER
Come here for upscale, small-town Mediterranean atmosphere.
Villefranche (between Nice and Monte Carlo, with frequent
15-min buses and trains to both) is quieter and more exotic than
Nice. Narrow cobbled streets tumble into the mellow waterfront,
a scenic walkway below the castle leads to the hidden port, and
luxury yachts glisten in the harbor below. Semi-sandy beaches, a
handful of interesting sights, and quick access to Cap Ferrat keep
visitors just busy enough.

The **TI** is in the park François Binon, just below the main
bus stop (July–Aug daily 09:00–19:00, Sept–June Mon–Sat 09:00–
12:00, 14:00–18:30, closed Sun, a 20-min walk or €8 taxi from

train station, tel. 04 93 01 73 68). Pick up the brochure detailing a self-guided walking tour of Villefranche and information on boat rides and the Rothschild Villa Ephrussi's gardens (see "Sights near Villefranche," below).

The dramatic interior of **Chapel of St. Pierre**, decorated by Jean Cocteau, is the town's cultural highlight, but at €1.85 it's not worth it for many (daily 10:00–12:00, 16:00–20:30, below Hôtel Welcome). **Boat rides** (*promenades en mer*) are offered several days a week (June–mid-Sept, €12, 2 hrs, across from Hôtel Welcome). Lively *boules* action takes place each evening just below the huge soccer field. Walk beyond the train station for views back to Villefranche and a quieter beach.

Even if you're sleeping elsewhere, consider an ice cream–licking village stroll. The last bus leaves Nice for Villefranche at about 19:45; the last bus from Villefranche to Nice leaves at about 21:00; and one train runs later (24:00). Beware of taxi drivers who overcharge—the normal weekday, daytime rate to central Nice is about €27; to the airport, €38 to €43.

Sleeping in Villefranche-sur-Mer
(€1.10 = about $1, country code: 33, zip code: 06230)
There's precious little middle ground here. Hotels are linoleum-floor cheap or million-dollar-view expensive. The lone *chambre d'hôte* offers the only normal mid-range comfort.

If your idea of sightseeing is to enjoy the view from your bedroom deck, the dining room, or the pool, stay at **Hôtel La Flore***, where most rooms have unbeatable views (Db-€87–120, Tb-€120–151, Qb loft with huge terrace-€151–198, lower rates are Nov–March, CC, air-con, easy parking, fine restaurant, elevator, just off main road high above harbor, 5 boulevard Princess Grace de Monaco, 2 blocks from TI toward Nice, tel. 04 93 76 30 30, fax 04 93 76 99 99, www.hotel-la-flore.fr, e-mail: Hotel-La-Flore@wanadoo.fr, SE).

Hôtel Welcome* is buried in the heart of the old city, right on the water, with most of the 32 rooms overlooking the harbor. You'll pay top price for all the comforts in a very sharp, professional hotel that seems to do everything right and couldn't be better located (standard Db with view but no balcony-€111, "comfort" Db with view and balcony-€132, superior Db with view and balcony-€168, extra person-€30, CC, air-con, 1 quai Courbet, tel. 04 93 76 27 62, fax 04 93 76 27 66, www.welcome-hotel.com, e-mail: steves@welcomehotel.com, SE). The rooms at both Hôtel La Flore and Hôtel Welcome, while different in cost, are about the same in comfort. La Flore has a pool, Welcome is on the harbor.

The hotelesque **Hôtel Provençal*** needs a face-lift but offers air-conditioning and fine views from well-worn rooms with awful furniture but nifty balconies (Db-€63–92, Tb-€73–85, extra bed-€9, 10 percent off with this book and a two-night stay, CC, skip the cheaper no-view rooms, a block from TI at 4 avenue Maréchal Joffre, tel. 04 93 76 53 53, fax 04 93 76 96 00, e-mail: provencal@riviera.fr).

At **Le Home**, Madame Repellin-Villard rents the town's best budget beds in 10 simple rooms around a garden bursting with color and a welcoming terrace (Db-€37–40, no CC; from main road near TI, walk between cafés Riche and Regence and then climb the steps and turn left, avenue de Grande Bretagne, tel. 04 93 76 79 88).

Hôtel la Darse**, a simple hotel sitting in the shadow of its highbrow brothers, offers a low-key alternative right on the water in Villefranche's old Port. The rooms are quiet and plain with linoleum floors, and those facing the sea have great view balconies (easily worth the extra cost). Room cleanliness has been a problem, but this hotel will have a new owner in 2002 (Db-€40–58, extra person-€9, CC, from TI walk or drive down avenue General de Gaulle to the old Port de la Darse, tel. 04 93 01 72 54, fax 04 93 01 84 37).

Hôtel Vauban*, two blocks down from the TI, is an odd and basic place with homey, red-velvet decor, and a few cheery, simple rooms (Db-€46–53, Db with view-€53–69, no CC, 11 avenue General De Gaulle, tel. 04 93 76 62 18).

Eating in Villefranche-sur-Mer

Pickings are slim in this land of high rollers. The places lining the port are expensive and vary in quality; less expensive places are off the port. If you want to eat well, spring for dinner at **Hôtel la Flore** (see "Sleeping in Villefranche," above). Or, for a cool view and good-enough food at reasonable prices, try **Restaurant Le Marinières** on the beach below the train station (salads and *à la carte*, open daily, tel. 04 93 01 76 06).

Sights near Villefranche-sur-Mer

Cap Ferrat—This is the peninsula you're staring at across the bay from Villefranche. An exclusive, largely residential community, it's off the Nice-Monaco route and receives less traffic than other towns. Drive, bus, or walk here from Villefranche to visit the sublime gardens of the Rothschild Villa Ephrussi, with stunning views east to Villefranche and west toward Monaco; seven lush and varied gardens and several lavishly decorated rooms (€7.75, €2.25 for English tours generally between 11:00 and 14:00, Feb–Oct daily 10:00–18:00, until 19:00 in July–Aug, Nov–Jan Mon–Fri 14:00–18:00, Sat–Sun 10:00–18:00). From Villefranche, it's a scenic 50-minute walk around the bay past the train station or 10 minutes by bus #111. A few kilometers beyond sits the sophisticated port-village of St. Jean Cap Ferrat, offering more yachts, boardwalks, views, and boutiques in a less-frenzied atmosphere.

▲**Eze Village**—Floating high above the sea, Eze Village (don't confuse it with the seafront town of Eze-Bord de la Mer) mixes perfume outlets, upscale boutiques, outrageously priced hotels, steep, cobbled lanes, and magnificent views. About 15 minutes east of Villefranche on the Moyenne Corniche (6 buses/day from Nice, 25 min), this medieval hill town makes a handy stop between Nice and Monaco. You can drop in on the Fragonard or Galli-mard perfume outlets to learn about the interesting fabrication process and shop the fragrant collections (both daily 08:30–18:00, Gallimard breaks for lunch 12:00–14:00). You can also enjoy the charming church (Eglise Paroissial), but skip the Jardins Exotiques (exotic gardens). For a panoramic view and ideal picnic perch (they say on a clear day you can see Corsica), walk up to the hill town from the parking lot, take a left at the top of the first hill, and walk 20 meters down a dirt path.

▲**La Turbie**—Ten minutes east and uphill of Eze Village lies one of this region's most dramatic panoramas. Follow the winding road up from Eze Village to La Grande Corniche and the village of La Turbie; park in the lot near the view. Inspect all viewpoints. The massive Roman monument in front of you (*La Trophée des Alpes*) was erected to commemorate Caesar Augustus' conquering of the Alps, a less than subtle reminder of who was in charge. The view over Monaco is even greater after dark.

ANTIBES

Antibes is busy and massive compared to Villefranche, but far more manageable than Nice. Come here for yachts, sandy beaches, an enjoyable old town, good hiking, and a great Picasso collection. Twenty-five minutes west of Nice by train (skip the 50-min bus), Antibes' glamorous port glistens below its fortifications—boat lovers are welcome to browse. The Fort Carré that dominates the port was the last fortification before Italy in the 1500s. The festive old city is charming in a sandy-sophisticated way and sits atop the ruins of the fourth-century B.C. Greek city of Antipolis. Hotels aren't a very good value here, so I prefer Antibes as a daytrip.

Orientation

The old city lies between the port and boulevards Albert 1er and Robert Soleau. Place Nationale is the hub of activity in the old city. Lively rue Auberon connects the port and the old city. Stroll along the sea between the Picasso Museum and place Albert 1er (where boulevard Albert 1er meets the sea); the best beaches lie just beyond place Albert 1er, and the path is beautiful. Good chil-dren's play areas are on place des Martyrs de la Resistance (near recommended Hôtel Relais du Postillon). Near the port in the old city you'll find **Heidi's English Bookshop** (great selection, daily 10:00–19:00, 24 rue Auberon) and a **Laundromat** (14 rue Thuret).

Tourist Information: The Maison de Tourisme has what you need (July–Aug Mon–Sat 09:00–19:00, Sun 09:00–13:00, Sept–June Mon–Sat 09:00–12:30, 14:00–18:30, closed Sun, located just east of the old city where boulevard Albert 1er and rue de République meet at 11 place de Gaulle, tel. 04 92 90 53 00). Pick up the excellent city map, the interesting walking tour of Old Antibes brochure (in English), ask about tours of the Fort Carré, and get details on the hikes described below. Remember, the Nice TI has Antibes maps; plan ahead.

Arrival in Antibes

By Train: To get to the port (5-min walk), cross the street in front of the station and follow avenue de la Liberation. To reach the TI (15-min walk), exit right from the station on avenue Soleau; follow "Maison du Tourisme" signs to place de Gaulle. A free minibus (*Minibus Gratuit*) circulates around Antibes from the train station and serves place Albert 1er, the old city, and the port (4/hr), or you can call a taxi (tel. 04 93 67 67 67).

By Bus: The bus station is on the edge of the old city on place Guynemer, a block below the TI.

By Car: Follow c*entre ville*, *vieux port* signs and park near the old city walls, as close to the beach as you can (first half hour is free, municipal lots cost about €8/day). Enter the old city through the last arch on the right.

Sights—Antibes

Market Hall (Marché Provençal)—The daily market bustles under a 19th-century canopy and mixes flowers, produce, Provençal products, and beach accessories (in old city behind Picasso Museum on cours Masséna, daily until 13:00, closed Mon off-season). You'll also find antique/flea markets on place Nationale and place Audiberti (next to the port) on Thursdays and Saturdays (7:00–18:00).

▲▲Musée Picasso (Château Grimaldi)—Sitting serenely where the old city meets the sea, this museum offers a remarkable collection of Picasso's work: paintings, sketches, and ceramics. Picasso, who lived and worked here in 1946, said if you want to see work from his Antibes period, you'll have to do it in Antibes. You'll understand why Picasso liked working here. Several photos of the artist make this already intimate museum more so. In his famous *Joie de Vivre* (the museum's highlight), there's a new love in Picasso's life, and he's feelin' groovy (€4.75, June–Sept Tue–Sun 10:00–18:00, closed Mon and Oct–May 12:00–14:00, tel. 04 92 90 54 20).

Musée d'Histoire et d'Archéologie—Featuring Greek, Roman, and Etruscan odds and ends, this is the only place to get a sense

Antibes

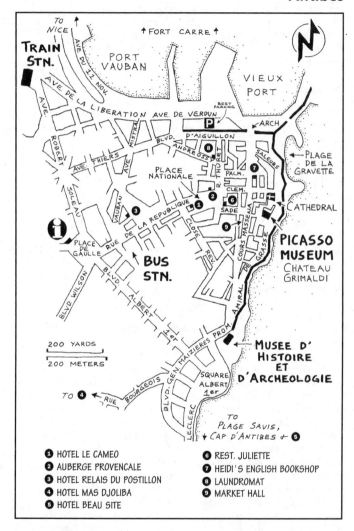

1. HOTEL LE CAMEO
2. AUBERGE PROVENCALE
3. HOTEL RELAIS DU POSTILLON
4. HOTEL MAS DJOLIBA
5. HOTEL BEAU SITE
6. REST. JULIETTE
7. HEIDI'S ENGLISH BOOKSHOP
8. LAUNDROMAT
9. MARKET HALL

of this city's ancient roots. I liked the 2,000-year-old lead anchors (€1.50, no English explanations, Tue–Sun 10:00–12:00, 14:00–18:00, closed Mon, on the water between Picasso Museum and place Albert 1er).

Beaches (Plages)—The best beaches stretch between Antibes' port and Cap d'Antibes, the best (plages Salis and Ponteil) are just south of Place Albert 1er. All are golden and sandy. Plage Salis is busy in summer, but it's manageable, with snack stands every 100 meters and views to the old city. The closest beach to the old city is at the port (plage de la Gravette) and remains relatively calm in any season.

Hikes and Day Trips from Antibes

From place Albert 1er (where boulevard Albert 1er meets the beach), there's a great view of the beach plage Salis and the Cap d'Antibes. That tower on the hill is your destination for the first walk described below. The longer hike along the Cap d'Antibes begins on the next beach, just over that hill (see below).

▲**Chapelle et Phare de la Garoupe**—The chapel and lighthouse, a 20-minute uphill climb from the far end of plage Salis (follow Chemin du Calvaire up to the lighthouse tower), offer magnificent views (best at sunset) over Juan les Pins, Antibes, the pre-Alps, and Nice. Roads allow car access.

Cap d'Antibes Hike (Sentier Touristique de Tirepoll/Sentier Littoral)—At the end of the mattress-ridden plage de la Garoupe (over the hill from the lighthouse) is a well-maintained trail around Cap d'Antibes. The beautiful trail follows the rocky coast for about three kilometers, then heads inland. Take bus #2A from the bus station (2/hr, get return times) or drive to Hôtel Beau Site and walk 10 minutes down to plage de la Garoupe (parking available). The trail begins at the far right end of the beach. Allow two hours for the loop that ends at the recommended Hôtel Beau Site (see "Sleeping in Antibes," below) and use your Antibes map.

Daytrips from Antibes—Antibes is halfway between Nice and Cannes (easy train service to both), and close to the artsy pottery and glass-blowing village of Biot, home of the Fernand Léger Museum (frequent buses, ask at TI). And while Cannes has much in common with its sister city, Beverly Hills, and little of interest for your authors, its beaches and the beachfront promenade are beautiful.

Sleeping in Antibes
(€1.10 = about $1, country code: 33, zip code: 06600)

Central pickings are slim here; most hotel owners seem more interested in their restaurants.

Hôtel Le Cameo** is a rambling, refreshingly unaggressive old place above a bustling bar (what reception there is you'll find in the bar). The public areas are dark, but its nine, very simple linoleum-lined rooms are almost huggable. All open onto the charming place Nationale, which means you don't sleep until the restaurants close (Ss-€35, Sb-€46, Ds-€43, Db-€53, Ts-€53, Tb-€61, CC, 5 place Nationale, tel. 04 93 34 24 17, fax 04 93 34 35 80, NSE).

Auberge Provençale*, on the same square, has seven reasonably nice rooms (those on the square get all the noise, day and night) but nonexistent, couldn't-care-less management and a popular restaurant (Db-€53–76, Tb-€61–84, Qb-€92, CC, reception in restaurant, 61 place Nationale, tel. 04 93 34 13 24, fax 04 93 34 89 88). Their loft room, named "Celine," is huge and faces the rear. It comes with a royal canopy bed and a dramatic open-timbered ceiling and costs no more than the other rooms.

Hôtel Relais du Postillon**, on a thriving square, offers 15 small, tastefully designed rooms, accordion bathrooms, and helpful owners who take more pride in their well-respected restaurant (Db-€42–79, extra bed-€9, breakfast-€6.75, CC, *menus* from €30, 8 rue Championnet, tel. 04 93 34 20 77, fax 04 93 34 61 24, www.relais-postillon.com, SE).

Mas Djoliba*** is a good splurge but best for drivers, as it's a 15-minute walk from the beach and old Antibes, and a 25-minute walk to the station. Reserve early for this tranquil, bird-chirping, flower-filled manor house where no two rooms are the same. Dinner (by the pool) is required from May to September (Db with breakfast and dinner-€67–85 per person, off-season Db-€76–107 for two people—room only; several good family rooms, breakfast-€8.50, CC, 29 avenue de Provence, from boulevard Albert 1er, turn right up avenue Gaston Bourgeois, tel. 04 93 34 02 48, fax 04 93 34 05 81, www.hotel-djoliba.com, e-mail: hotel.djoliba @wanadoo.fr).

Hôtel Beau Site***, my only listing on Cap d'Antibes and a 10-minute drive from the old city, is a good value if you want to get away, but not *too* far away. The friendly owners, nice pool, outdoor terrace, easy parking, and 30 pleasant rooms make it worthwhile (Db-€52–107, CC, 141 boulevard Kennedy, tel. 04 93 61 53 43, fax 04 93 67 78 16, www.hotelbeausite.net). From the hotel, it's a 10-minute walk down to the crowded plage de la Garoupe and a nearby hiking trail.

Eating in Antibes

Gourmets should dine at the recommended hotels **Relais du Postillon** or **Auberge Provençale**, while romantics and those on a budget should buy a picnic dinner and head for the beach. Lively place Nationale is filled with tables and tourists (great ambience), while locals seem to prefer the restaurants along the market hall. Just off place Nationale, **Chez Juliette** offers good budget meals (*menus* from €13, 20 rue Sade).

MONACO

Still impressive despite overdevelopment, high prices, and wall-to-wall daytime tourists, Monaco will disappoint anyone looking for something below the surface. This glittering two-square-kilometer country is a tax haven for its miniscule full-time population (30,000, 83 percent foreigners), who pay no income tax, and is the kind of place you visit once and probably don't need to see again. France surrounds Monaco on all sides but the Mediterranean and provides Monaco's telephones (French phone cards work here), electricity, and water. About the only thing you'll use that's made locally are its stamps.

Orientation

Monaco (the principality) is best understood when separated into its three tourist areas: Monaco-Ville, Monte Carlo, and La Condamine (a fourth area, Fontvieille, is of no interest to tourists). Monaco-Ville, dangling on the rock high above, is the oldest section, housing Prince Rainier's palace and all sights except the casino; Monte Carlo is the area around the casino; and La Condamine (the port) divides the two. A brief bus ride on routes #1 or #2 links all areas (10/hr, €1.40, or €3.50 for 4 tickets). It's a 20-minute uphill walk from the port (and train station) to Prince Rainier's palace, 20 minutes to the casino, and a 40-minute down-and-up walk between the palace and the casino.

Tourist Information: There are several TIs, but you shouldn't need one, as sightseeing is straightforward (a map is helpful). The main TI is near the casino (2 boulevard des Moulins), but the handiest one for most is in the train station; pick up a city map (daily 09:00–19:00, tel. 00-377/92 16 61 66). From June to September, you'll find information kiosks in the Monaco-Ville parking garage and on the port.

Telephone Tip: To call Monaco from France, dial 00, then 377 (Monaco's country code), and the eight-digit number. Within Monaco, simply dial the eight-digit number.

Arrival in Monaco

By Bus from Nice and Villefranche: Keep your receipt for the return ride (RCA buses run twice as often as Cars Broch). There are three stops in Monaco, in order from Nice: in front of a tunnel at the base of Monaco-Ville (place d'Armes), on the port, and below the casino (on avenue d'Ostende). The first stop is the best starting point. To walk up to Monaco-Ville and the palace (10 min straight up), or catch a local bus there (lines #1 or #2), cross the street right in front of the tunnel and walk with the rock on your right—the bus stop and steps up to Monaco-Ville are in 70 meters. The bus stop back to Nice is across the major road from your arrival point at the light. The last bus leaves Monaco for Nice at about 19:00 (the last train leaves about 23:30).

By Train from Nice: A dazzling but confusing new train station provides central access to Monaco. The TI, baggage check, and ticket windows are up the escalator at the end of the tracks. To reach Monaco-Ville, walk along the platform toward Nice following *Sortie la Condamine* then *Access Port* signs. The stop for

Monaco

- 🅣 - ACCESS TO TRAIN STATION

300 YARDS
300 METERS

TO MENTON

F R A N C E

TO MENTON

MOYENNE CORNICHE

🛈

BLVD. MOULINS

LOEWS CASINO

AVE. SPEL.

BLVD. PRINCESSE CHARLOTTE

❺

🅟 PARK

❸

PLACE DU CASINO

CASINO

BLVD. DU JARDIN EXOTIQUE

🅣

AVE. D'OSTENDE

PALAIS DES CONGRES

JARDIN EXOTIQUE

🅣

BLVD. RAINIER III

RUE GRIMALDI

🅣

PORT LOTSA YACHTS!

MONTE-CARLO

TO NICE

BLVD.

TO NICE

🅣

❶ PLACE D'ARMES

BLVD. ALBERT

MONACO-VILLE

❺

RAMPE MAJOR

❷ AVE. DE LA PORTE NEUVE

🅟

MONTE CARLO STORY

BLVD.

❹

PALACE & NAPOLEON COLLECTION

CATHEDRAL

🛈 ❸

COUSTEAU AQUARIUM

FONT-VIEILLE

OLD TOWN

BOTANICAL GARDEN

- ❶ HOTEL DE FRANCE
- ❷ PAN BAGNA SANDWICHES AT RUE BASSE #8
- ❸ LOCAL BUS STOPS
- ❹ BUS STOPS FROM NICE
- ❺ BUS STOPS TO NICE

local buses is in front of the station exit. The port is a few blocks downhill, the casino is uphill along the left side of the port, and Monaco-Ville is uphill to the right of the port. The most direct route to the casino from the station is up the escalator from the platform, left past the TI, and up the elevator. Exit the station and turn left on boulevard Princesse Charlotte.

By Car: You'll be directed to parking structures under Monaco-Ville, under the casino, or above at Jardins Exotique (about €1.50/hr).

Sights—Monaco-Ville

Start with a look at Monaco-Ville from the palace square. Buses #1 or 2 leave you a five-minute walk away; turn right off

the bus and walk past the fountain down rue Marie de Lorraine
to reach the palace (to go directly to the aquarium, walk down
the steps at the bus stop). The walkway up from the port ends
at the **palace square**. Find a seat overlooking the port for a
magnifique view (particularly at night).

This funny little country was born on this rock in 1215
and has managed to stay independent for most of its almost 800
years. A medieval castle sat where the palace is today, its strategic
setting having a lot to do with Monaco's ability to resist attackers.
They still **change guards** the old-fashioned way (11:55 daily,
fun to watch but jammed). As you look back over the port, notice
the faded green roof above to the right—it's the famous casino.
In the mid-1800s, Prince Charles began an aggressive economic
development plan for his tiny, isolated country. He built spas
and a casino to lure a growing aristocratic class with leisure time. It
worked. Today, Monaco has the world's highest per-capita income.

The name Monte Carlo means "Charles' Hill" in Spanish
(the Spanish were traditional protectors of Monaco and have
200 guards present today). The famous Monte Carlo Grand Prix
started in 1929 and still runs right through the streets of the port
and around the casino.

Now walk to the statue of the monk grasping a sword near the
palace. Meet François Grimaldi, a renegade Italian who captured
Monaco dressed as a monk in 1297, and began the dynasty that still
rules the principality. Walk to the opposite side of the square and
more Louis XIV cannon balls. Down below is Monaco's newest
area, Fontvieille, where much of its post–WWII growth has been.
Prince Rainier has continued Monaco's economic growth with land-
fills (like Fontvieille), flashy ports, new beaches, and the new rail
station. Today, thanks to Prince Rainier's efforts, tiny Monaco is
a member of the United Nations.

Hungry? You'll find good *pan bagna* and other sandwiches
at 8 rue Basse, on the street leaving the square to the left. You
can buy stamps (mail from here!) at the PTT located a few blocks
down rue Comte F. Gastaldi.

Palace—Automated and uninspired tours (in English) take you
through part of the prince's lavish palace in 30 merciful minutes
and yet still manage to describe every painting. The rooms are well-
furnished and impressive, but interesting only if you haven't seen
a château lately (€4.60, €6 with Napoleon Collection, June–Sept
daily 09:30–18:30, Oct 10:00–17:00, closed off-season).

Napoleon Collection—Napoleon occupied Monaco after the
French Revolution. This is the prince's private collection of what
Napoleon left behind: military medals, swords, guns, letters, and,
most interesting, his hat. I found this collection more appealing
than the palace (€3, June–Sept daily 09:30–18:30, Oct–May 10:00–
12:30, 14:00–17:00, next to palace entry).

Cathédrale de Monaco—This somber cathedral, built in 1878, is where Princess Grace is buried (near the left transept).

Jardins Botanique—Take in sensational views as you meander back to the bus stop through these immaculately maintained gardens (or pick up a *pan bagna* sandwich in the old city and picnic here).

Musée de l'Océanographique (Cousteau Aquarium)—This monumental building overhangs the Mediterranean. It was inaugurated in 1910 and is the largest of its kind, thanks to the oceanographic zeal of Prince Albert I. It can be jammed and disappoints some, though kids love it (€11, ages 6–18-€5.35, April–Sept daily 09:00–19:00, until 20:00 in July–Aug, March and Oct 09:30–19:00, Nov–Feb 10:00–18:00, CC, at opposite end of Monaco-Ville from palace, down the steps from Monaco-Ville bus stop).

Monte Carlo Story—This informative 35-minute film gives a helpful account (English headphones) of Monaco's history and is a comfortable soft-chair break from all that walking (€6, usually on the hour from 11:00–17:00 March–Oct, until 18:00 July–Aug, 14:00–17:00 only Nov–Feb, frequent extra showings for groups that you can join; from the Monte Carlo side of the Aquarium take the escalator into the parking garage, then take the elevator down and follow the signs, it's just past the café).

Leave Monaco-Ville and ride the shuttle bus (the stop is up the steps across from the aquarium) or stroll down through the pedestrian-pleasant port and up to Monte Carlo.

Sights—Monte Carlo

▲**Casino**—Stand in the park, above the traffic circle in front of the casino (opens at noon). The casino is designed to make the wealthy feel comfortable while losing money. Charles Garnier designed this Casino-Opera House in 1878 in part to thank the prince for his financial help in completing the Paris Opéra, which Garnier also designed. The central doors provide access to slot machines, private gaming rooms, and the Opera House. The private gaming rooms take up much of the left wing of the building. Count the counts and Rolls-Royces in front of Hôtel de Paris (built at the same time). Strut inside past the slots and find the sumptuous atrium. This is the lobby for the Opera House; doors open only during performances. There's a model of the Opera at the end of the room and marble WCs on the right. Anyone (even in shorts, if before 20:00) can get as far as the one-armed bandits (open at 12:00, push the button on the slot machines to claim your winnings), though you'll need decent attire to go any farther, and after 20:00 shorts are off-limits anywhere. Only adults 21 and older are allowed to dive deeper and pay €7.75 for the first rooms, Salons Européens (open at 12:00), or €15.50 for the glamorous private game rooms where you can rub elbows with high rollers (these rooms open at 16:00, some at 21:00, a tie and jacket are not necessary until evening, can be rented at the bag check). The scene is great at night and downright James Bond–like in the €15.50 rooms. The park behind the casino offers a peaceful café and a good view of the casino's rear facade and of Monaco-Ville. Entrance is free to all games in the new, plebeian, American-style Loews Casino, adjacent to the old casino. The return bus stop to Nice is at the top of the park above the casino on rue des Moulins. To return to the train station from the casino, walk up the parkway in front of the casino, turn left on boulevard des Moulins, right on impasse de la Fontaine, climb the steps, and turn left on boulevard Princesse Charlotte (the entrance is next to Parking de la gare).

Near Monte Carlo: Menton

Grand, beautiful, and overlooked Menton is a peaceful and relaxing spa/beach town with a fine beachfront promenade and a sandy-cobbled old town (TI tel. 04 93 57 57 00). It's just a few minutes by train (8/day) from Monte Carlo or 40 minutes from Nice.

Sleeping in Monaco
(€1.10 = about $1, country code: 377)

Since Monaco is by far best after dark, consider sleeping here. The perfectly pleasant **Hôtel de France**** is reasonable (Sb-€63, Db-€81, Tb-€100, includes breakfast, CC, 6 rue de la Turbie, near west exit from train station, tel. 00-377/93 30 24 64, fax 00-377/92 16 13 34, e-mail: hotel-france@monte-carlo.mc). You'll find a few affordable restaurants on rue de la Turbie and up in Monaco-Ville.

BAVARIA
AND TIROL

Two hours south of Munich, between Germany's Bavaria and Austria's Tirol, is a timeless land of fairy-tale castles, painted buildings shared by cows and farmers, and locals who still yodel when they're happy.

In Germany's Bavaria, tour "Mad" King Ludwig's ornate Neuschwanstein Castle, Europe's most spectacular. Stop by the Wieskirche, a textbook example of Bavarian rococo bursting with curly curlicues, and browse through Oberammergau, Germany's wood-carving capital and home of the famous Passion Play.

In Austria's Tirol, hike to the Ehrenberg ruined castle, scream down a nearby ski slope on an oversized skateboard, then catch your breath for an evening of yodeling and slap dancing.

In this chapter I'll cover Bavaria first, then Tirol. Austria's Tirol is easier and cheaper than touristy Bavaria. My favorite home base for exploring Bavaria's castles is actually in Austria, in the town of Reutte. Füssen, in Germany, is a handier home base for train travelers.

Planning Your Time

While locals come here for a week or two, the typical speedy American traveler will find two days' worth of sightseeing. With a car and more time you could enjoy three or four days, but the basic visit ranges anywhere from a long day trip from Munich to a three-night, two-day visit. If the weather's good and you're not going to Switzerland, be sure to ride a lift to an alpine peak.

A good schedule for a one-day circular drive from Reutte is: 07:00-Breakfast, 07:30-Depart hotel, 8:00-Arrive at Neuschwanstein to get admission times for two castles, tour both Hohenschwangau and Neuschwanstein, 13:00-Drive to the Wieskirche (20-min stop)

Highlights of Bavaria and Tirol

and on to Linderhof, 14:30-Tour Linderhof, 16:30-Drive along
scenic Plansee back into Austria, 17:30-Back at hotel, 19:00-Dinner
at hotel and perhaps a folk evening (or the Ludwig II Musical).
In peak season you might arrive later at Linderhof to avoid the
crowds. The next morning you could stroll through Reutte, hike
to the Ehrenberg ruins, and ride the luge on your way to Innsbruck,
Munich, Venice, Switzerland, or wherever.

Train travelers can base in Füssen and bus or bike the five-
kilometer distance to Neuschwanstein. Reutte is connected by bus
with Füssen (except on Sun). If you base in Reutte, you can bike
to the Ehrenberg ruins (just outside Reutte) and to Neuschwanstein
Castle/Tegelberg luge (90 min), or hike through the woods to
Neuschwanstein from the recommended Gutshof zum Schluxen
hotel (60 min).

Getting around Bavaria and Tirol

By Car: This region is ideal by car. All the sights are within an easy 100-kilometer (60-mile) loop from Reutte or Füssen.

By Train and Bus: It can be frustrating by public transportation. Local bus service in the region is spotty for sightseeing. If you're rushed and without wheels, Reutte, Wieskirche, Linderhof, and the luge rides are probably not worth the trouble (but the Tegelberg luge near Neuschwanstein is within walking distance of the castle).

Füssen (with a 2-hr train ride to/from Munich every hr, some with a transfer in Buchloe) is five kilometers from Neuschwanstein Castle with easy bus and bike connections (see "Getting to the Castles from Füssen or Reutte," below). Reutte is a 30-minute bus ride from Füssen (Mon–Fri 5/day, Sat 3/day, none Sun; taxis from Reutte are €21 one-way).

To visit Oberammergau, catch one of the buses going from Füssen to Garmisch (6–10/day, less off-season, 1.75 hr, some with transfer in Echelsbacherbrücke, confirm with driver that bus will stop in Oberammergau, 4–6 buses/day return from Oberammergau to Füssen). From Munich, Oberammergau is easier to visit directly by train (hrly, 1.75 hrs, change in Murnau) than going to Füssen to catch the bus.

Füssen to Linderhof is a hassle but doable without a car in the summer. The first bus to Oberammergau (direction: Garmisch) has hourly bus connections to Linderhof from June to mid-October (mid-Oct–May only 2 buses/day). Bus trips to Garmisch and Linderhof are cheaper if you buy a *Tagesticket*, a round-trip special fare—even if you're only going one way.

Confirm all bus schedules in Füssen by checking the big board at the bus stop across from the train station, getting a bus timetable (€0.25) at the TI or train station, or calling 08362/939-0505.

By Rental Car: You can rent a car in Füssen for €51 to €77 per day (see below; or in Reutte, if you're a guest at the Hotel Maximilian).

By Tour: If you're interested only in Bavarian castles, consider an all-day organized bus tour of the Bavarian biggies as a side trip from Munich.

By Bike: This is great biking country. Shops in or near train stations rent bikes for €8 to €11 per day. The ride from Reutte to Neuschwanstein and the Tegelberg luge (90 min) is great for those with the time and energy.

By Thumb: Hitchhiking, always risky, is a slow-but-possible way to connect the public transportation gaps.

FÜSSEN

Füssen has been a strategic stop since ancient times. Its main street sits on the Via Claudia Augusta, which crossed the Alps (over Brenner Pass) in Roman times. The town was the southern terminus of a medieval trade route now known among modern tourists as the "Romantic Road." Dramatically situated under a renovated castle on the lively Lech River, Füssen just celebrated its 700th birthday.

Unfortunately, in the summer Füssen is entirely overrun by tourists. Traffic can be exasperating, but by bike or on foot it's not bad. Off-season the town is a jester's delight.

Apart from Füssen's cobbled and arcaded town center, there's little real sightseeing here. The striking-from-a-distance castle houses a boring picture gallery. The mediocre city museum in the monastery below the castle exhibits lifestyles of 200 years ago and the story of the monastery, and offers displays on the development of the violin, for which Füssen was famous (€3, April–Oct Tue–Sun 11:00–16:00, closed Mon, shorter hrs off-season, ask for English explanation sheet, tel. 08362/903-145). Halfway between Füssen and the border (as you drive, or a woodsy walk from the town) is the Lechfall, a thunderous waterfall with a handy potty stop.

Orientation (area code: 08362)

Füssen's train station is a few blocks from the TI, the town center (a cobbled shopping mall), and all my hotel listings (see "Sleeping," below). The modern, sometimes surly TI has a room-finding service (June–mid-Sept Mon–Fri 8:30–18:30, Sat 9:00–12:30, Sun 10:00–12:00, less off-season, 3 blocks down Bahnhofstrasse from station, tel. 08362/93850, fax 08362/938-520, www.fuessen.de). After-hours the little self-service info pavilion (7:00–0:30) near the front of the TI features an automated room-finding service.

Arrival in Füssen: Exit left as you leave the train station (lockers available) and walk a few straight blocks to the center of town and the TI. To go to Neuschwanstein or Reutte, catch a bus from in front of the station.

Bike Rental: Rent from friendly Christian at Preisschranke next to the station (€8/day, June–Aug Mon–Sat 9:00–20:00, Sept–May Mon–Sat 9:00–19:00, closed Sun, tel. 08362/921-544) or, for a bigger selection and a less convenient location, check out Rad Zacherl (€7/day, mountain bikes-€10/day, passport number for deposit, May–Sept Mon–Fri 9:00–18:00, Sat 9:00–13:00, closed Sun, less off-season, 2 km out of town at Kempterstrasse 119, tel. 08362/3292, www.rad-zacherl.de).

Car Rental: Peter Schlichtling (Kemptenerstrasse 26, tel. 08362/922-122, www.schlichtling.de) is cheaper and more central than Hertz (Füssenerstrasse 112, tel. 08362/986-580).

Laundry: You can drop off your laundry at Pfronter Reinigung Wäscherei (Mon–Fri 9:00–12:00, 14:00–18:00, closed Wed afternoon and Sat–Sun, in the parking lot of the huge Hotel

Hirsch, 2 blocks past TI on the way out of town, Sebastianstrasse 3, tel. 08362/4529).

Sights—Neuschwanstein Castle Area, Bavaria

The most popular tourist destination in Bavaria is the "King's Castles" (*Königschlosser*). With fairy-tale turrets in a fairy-tale alpine setting built by a fairy-tale king, it's understandably popular. The well-organized visitor can have a great four-hour visit. Others will just stand in line and perhaps not even see the castle. The key: arrive early. You can see both castles, consider fun options nearby (mountain lift, luge course, Füssen town), and get out by early afternoon.

Ludwig II (a.k.a. "Mad" King Ludwig), a tragic figure, ruled Bavaria for 23 years until his death in 1886 at the age of 41. Politically, his reality was to "rule" either as a pawn of Prussia or a pawn of Austria. Rather than deal with politics in Bavaria's capital, Munich, Ludwig frittered away most of his time at his family's hunting palace, Hohenschwangau. He spent most of his adult life constructing his fanciful Neuschwanstein Castle—much like a kid builds a tree house—on a neighboring hill upon the scant ruins of a medieval castle. Although Ludwig spent 17 years building Neuschwanstein, he lived in it only 172 days. Ludwig was a true Romantic living in a Romantic age. His best friends were artists, poets, and composers such as Richard Wagner. His palaces are wallpapered with misty medieval themes—especially those from Wagnerian operas. Eventually he was declared mentally unfit to rule Bavaria and taken away from Neuschwanstein. Two days after this eviction, Ludwig was found dead in a lake. To this day people debate whether the king was murdered or committed suicide.

▲▲▲**Neuschwanstein Castle**—Imagine King Ludwig as a boy, climbing the hills above his dad's castle, Hohenschwangau (details below), dreaming up the ultimate fairy-tale castle. He had the power to make his dream concrete and stucco. Neuschwanstein was designed by a painter first...then an architect. It looks medieval, but it's only about as old as the Eiffel Tower. It feels like something you'd see at a home show for 19th-century royalty. Built from 1869 to 1886, it's a textbook example of the Romanticism that was popular in 19th-century Europe. Construction stopped with Ludwig's death (only a third of the interior was finished) and within six weeks tourists were paying to go through it. Guides herd groups of 60 through the castle giving an interesting if rushed 30-minute tour. You'll go up and down more than 300 steps through lavish Wagnerian dream rooms, a royal state-of-the-19th-century-art kitchen, the king's gilded-lily bedroom, and his extravagant throne room. You'll see 15 rooms with their original furnishings and fanciful wall paintings. After the tour you'll see a room lined with fascinating drawings (described in

Neuschwanstein

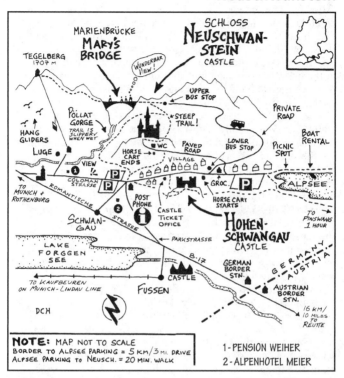

MARIENBRÜCKE
MARY'S BRIDGE

SCHLOSS
NEUSCHWAN-STEIN
CASTLE

TEGELBERG
1707 M

WUNDERBAR VIEW!

UPPER BUS STOP

PRIVATE ROAD

PÖLLAT GORGE
TRAIL IS SLIPPERY WHEN WET

HANG GLIDERS

LUGE

STEEP TRAIL!

BOAT RENTAL

WC

PAVED ROAD

LOWER BUS STOP

PICNIC SPOT

HORSE CART ENDS

VILLAGE

VIEW

ALPSEE

COLOMAN STRASSE

TO MUNICH + ROTHENBURG

ROMANTISCHE STRASSE

POST PHONE

CASTLE TICKET OFFICE

GROC.

HORSE CART STARTS

TO PINSWANG 1 HOUR

SCHWAN-GAU

HOHEN-SCHWANGAU CASTLE

← PARKSTRASSE

LAKE FORGGEN SEE

B-17

GERMAN BORDER STN.

GERMANY AUSTRIA

AUSTRIAN BORDER STN.

TO KAUFBEUREN ON MUNICH-LINDAU LINE

FÜSSEN

CASTLE

16 KM / 10 MILES TO REUTTE

DCH

NOTE: MAP NOT TO SCALE
BORDER TO ALPSEE PARKING = 5 KM/3 MI. DRIVE
ALPSEE PARKING TO NEUSCH. = 20 MIN. WALK

1 - PENSION WEIHER
2 - ALPENHOTEL MEIER

English) of the castle plans, construction, and drawings from 1883 of Falkenstein—a fanciful over-the-top but never-built castle that makes Neuschwanstein look stubby. Falkenstein occupied Ludwig's fantasies the year he died. After the tour, a 20-minute slide show (alternating German and English) plays continuously. If English is on, pop in. If not, it's not worth waiting for.

▲▲**Hohenschwangau Castle**—Standing quietly below Neuschwanstein, the big yellow Hohenschwangau Castle was Ludwig's boyhood home. Originally built in the 12th century, it was ruined by Napoleon. Ludwig's father Maximilian rebuilt it, and you'll see it as it looked in 1836. It's more lived-in and historic, and excellent 30-minute tours actually give a better glimpse of Ludwig's life than the more visited and famous Neuschwanstein castle tour.

Getting Tickets for the Castles: Every tour bus in Bavaria converges on Neuschwanstein, and tourists flush in each morning from Munich. A handy reservation system (see below) sorts out the chaos for smart travelers. Tickets come with admission times. (Miss this time and you don't get in.) To tour both castles you must do Hohenschwangau first (logical since this gives a better introduction to Ludwig's short life). You'll get two castle tour times: Hohenschwangau and then, two hours later, Neuschwanstein.

If you arrive late without a reservation you'll spend two hours in the ticket line and may find all tours for the day booked. A ticket center for both Neuschwanstein and Hohenschwangau castles is located at street level between the two castles, a few blocks from the TI toward the Alpsee (April–Sept daily 07:30–18:00, Oct–March daily 8:30–16:00). First tours start around 9:00. Arrive by 8:00 and you'll likely be touring by 9:00. Warning: During the summer, tickets for English tours can run out by 16:00.

It's best to reserve ahead in peak season (July–Sept). You can make reservations a minimum of 48 hours in advance by contacting the ticket office by phone (tel. 08362/930-8322 or 08362/930-8324), fax (08362/930-8320), or e-mail (info @ticket-center-hohenschwangau.de; www.ticket-center -hohenschwangau.de). Tickets reserved in advance cost €1.50 extra, and ticket holders must be at the ticket office at least one hour before the appointed entry time (allowing time to make your way up to the castle).

Cost and Hours: Each castle costs €7, a *Königsticket* for both castles costs €13.50, and children under 18 are free (April–Sept daily 9:00–18:00, Thu until 20:00, Oct–March daily 10:00–16:00).

Getting to the Castles: From the ticket booth, Hohenschwangau is an easy five-minute climb. Neuschwanstein is a steep 30-minute hike. To minimize hiking to Neuschwanstein, you can take a shuttle bus (from in front of Hotel Lisl, just above ticket office and to the left) or horse carriage (from in front of Hotel Müller, just above ticket office and to the right), but neither gets you to the castle doorstep. The frequent shuttle buses drop you off at Mary's Bridge, leaving you a steep 10-minute downhill walk to the castle—be sure to see the view from Mary's Bridge before hiking down to castle (€1.80 up; €3 round-trip not worth it since you have to hike up to bus stop for return trip). Horse carriages (€4 up, €2 down) are slower than walking and stop below Neuschwanstein, leaving you a five-minute uphill hike. Note: If it's less than an hour until your Neuschwanstein tour time, you'll need to hike—at a brisk pace it's still at least 20 minutes.

Mary's Bridge: Before or after the tour, climb up to Mary's Bridge to marvel at Ludwig's castle, just as Ludwig did. This bridge was quite an engineering accomplishment 100 years ago. From the bridge, the frisky can hike even higher to the "Beware—Danger of Death" signs and an even more glorious castle view.

For the most interesting descent (15 min longer and extremely slippery when wet), follow signs to the Pöllat Gorge.

Castle Village: The "village" at the foot of Europe's "Disney" castle feeds off the droves of hungry, shop-happy tourists. The Bräustüberl serves the cheapest grub (often with live folk music). The Alpsee lake is ideal for a picnic; the souvenir shop (open daily) nearest the Bräustüberl restaurant has the makings for a skimpy lunch. Picnic at the lakeside park or in one of the old-fashioned rowboats (rented by the hour in summer). Between the ticket office and TI, you'll find plenty of bratwurst stands. The bus stop, telephones, ATM, and helpful TI cluster around the main intersection (TI open April–June daily 9:00–17:00, July–Sept daily 9:00–18:00, Oct–March daily 9:00–16:00, tel. 08362/819-840).

Getting to the Castles from Füssen or Reutte: There's plenty of parking (all lots-€4). Get there early, and you'll park conveniently at lot D near the TI (lot E next to the lake is more scenic but farther away). Those without cars can catch the bus from Füssen (€1.40 one-way, €3 round-trip, hrly, 10 min, 5 km, catch bus at train station), take a taxi (€10 one-way), or ride a rental bike. From Reutte, take the bus to Füssen (Mon–Fri 5/day, Sat 3/day, none Sun, 30 min), then hop a city bus to the castle.

For a romantic twist, hike or mountain bike from the trailhead at the recommended hotel Gutshof zum Schluxen in Pinswang (see "Sleeping near Reutte," below). When the dirt road forks at the top of the hill, go right (downhill), cross the Austria-Germany border (marked by a sign and deserted hut), and follow the narrow paved road to the castles. It's a 60- to 90-minute hike or a great circular bike trip (allow 90 min from Reutte or 30 min from Gutshof zum Schluxen; cyclists can return to Schluxen from the castles on a different 30-min bike route via Füssen).

▲**Tegelberg Gondola**—Just north of Neuschwanstein is a fun play zone around the mighty Tegelberg gondola. Hang gliders circle like vultures. Their pilots jump from the top of the Tegelberg Gondola. For €14 you can ride the lift to the 1,690-meter (5,500-foot) summit and back down (May–Oct daily 9:00–17:00, Dec–April daily 9:00–16:30, closed Nov, last lift goes up 10 min before closing time, in bad weather call first to confirm, tel. 08362/98360). On a clear day you get great views of the Alps and Bavaria and the vicarious thrill of watching hang gliders and parasailors leap into airborne ecstasy. Weather permitting, scores of German thrill seekers line up and leap from the launch ramp at the top of the lift. With one leaving every two or three minutes, it's great spectating. Thrill seekers with exceptional social skills may talk themselves into a tandem ride with a parasailor. From the top of Tegelberg, it's a steep 2.5-hour hike down to Ludwig's castle. At the base of the gondola, you'll find a playground, cheery eatery, and a very good luge ride.

▲**Tegelberg Luge**—Next to the lift is a luge course. A luge is like a bobsled on wheels (for more details, see "Sights—Tirol, Near Reutte," below). This track, made of stainless steel, is often open when drizzly weather shuts down the concrete luges. It's not as scenic as Bichlbach and Biberwier (see below), but it's handy (€2.30/ride, July–Sept daily 9:00–18:00, otherwise same hours as gondola, in winter sometimes opens later due to wet track, in bad weather call first to confirm, tel. 08362/98360). A funky cable system pulls lugers (in their sleds) to the top without a ski lift.

▲**Ludwig II Musical**—A spectacular opera/musical based on the romantic life and troubled times of Ludwig plays in a grand lakeside theater. While called a musical, "Ludwig II, Longing for Paradise" felt like opera to me—with an orchestra in the pit, creative stage sets, fine singing, wonderful acoustics, and an easy-to-follow story line about Ludwig abandoning the normal, guy-thing rush of political power to pal around with his muses (3 vampy women dressed in purple). It's Bismarck the realistic politician on one side versus Wagner the romantic composer on the other as "art triumphs" (and Ludwig disappears into the lake).

The music is wonderful and the show's a hit with Germans. It's clearly top classical quality, but the superscripts in English are tough to read and tickets are pricey. The state-of-the-art theater is romantically set on a lake (Forgensee) with a view of floodlit Neuschwanstein in the distance (€44–118 per seat, nightly at 19:30, plus a matinee Sat–Sun at 14:30, English subtitles, 3 hrs including intermission, plenty of chances to eat a good light meal, parking-€3—have coins, about 1.5 km north of Füssen—follow signs for "musical," book well in advance, for tickets call 01805/583-944, www.ludwigmusical.com).

More Sights—Bavaria

These are listed in driving order from Füssen:

▲▲**Wies Church (Wieskirche)**—Germany's greatest rococo-style church, Wieskirche ("the church in the meadow") is newly restored and looking as brilliant as the day it floated down from heaven. Overripe with decoration but bright and bursting with beauty, this church is a divine droplet, a curly curlicue, the final flowering of the Baroque movement. The ceiling depicts the Last Judgment—but the most positive one around. Jesus, rather than sitting on the throne to judge, rides high on a rainbow, giving any sinner the feeling that there is still time to repent and plenty of mercy on hand.

This is a pilgrimage church. In the early 1700s, a carving of Christ too graphic to be accepted by that generation's church was the focus of worship in a peasant's private chapel. Miraculously, it wept. And pilgrims came from all around.

Bavaria's top rococo architects, the Zimmermann brothers, were then commissioned to build the Wieskirche, which features the amazing carved sculpture above its altar and still attracts countless pilgrims (donation requested, daily in summer 8:00–19:00, winter 8:00–17:00, tel. 00862/932-930). Take a commune-with-nature-and-smell-the-farm detour back through the meadow to the car park.

Wieskirche is 30 minutes north of Neuschwanstein. The northbound Romantic Road bus tour stops here for 15 minutes. You can take a bus from Füssen to the Wieskirche, but you'll spend more time waiting for the bus back than you will seeing the church. By car, head north from Füssen, turn right at Stein-gaden, and follow the signs.

If you can't visit Wieskirche, visit one of the other churches that came out of the same heavenly spray can: Oberammergau's church, Munich's Asam Church, Würzburg's Residenz Chapel, the splendid Ettal Monastery (free and near Oberammergau), and, on a lesser scale, Füssen's cathedral.

If you're driving from Wieskirche to Oberammergau, you'll cross the Echelsbacher Bridge, which arches 70 meters over the Pöllat Gorge. Thoughtful drivers let their passengers walk across (for the views) and meet them at the other side. Any kayakers? Notice the painting of the traditional village wood-carver (who used to walk from town to town with his art on his back) on the first big house on the Oberammergau side, a shop called Almdorf Ammertal. It has a huge selection of overpriced carvings and commission-hungry tour guides.

▲**Oberammergau**—The Shirley Temple of Bavarian villages and exploited to the hilt by the tourist trade, Oberammergau wears way too much makeup. If you're passing through anyway, it's worth a wander among the half-timbered houses painted with Bible scenes and famous fairy-tale characters. Browse through wood-carvers' shops—small art galleries filled with very expensive whittled works. Pilat's house on Ludwig Thomastrasse is a living workshop full of wood-carvers and painters in action (daily 13:00–18:00, closed Nov, Jan, March–April). Or see folk art at the town's Heimatmuseum (TI tel. 08822/92310, closed weekends off-season, www.oberammergau.de).

Visit the church, a poor cousin of the one at Wies. This church looks richer than it is. Put your hand on the "marble" columns. If they warm up, they're painted fakes. Wander through the graveyard. Ponder the deaths that two wars dealt Germany. Behind the church are the photos of three Schneller brothers, all killed within two years in World War II.

Passion Play: Still making good on a deal the townspeople made with God when they were spared devastation by the Black Plague several centuries ago, once each decade Oberammergau presents the Passion Play. For 100 summer days in a row, the town performs an all-day dramatic story of Christ's crucifixion (in 2000, 5,000 people attended per day). Until the next performance in 2010, you'll have to settle for reading the Book, seeing Nicodemus tool around town in his VW, or browsing through the theater's exhibition hall (€2, daily 10:00–12:00, 13:00–16:00, tel. 08822/32278). Consider a guided tour of the Passion Play theater (call TI for details).

Sleeping: Gasthaus zum Stern is friendly, serves good food (restaurant closed Wed Nov–May), and is a good value for this touristy town (Sb-€26, Db-€51, no CC, Dorfstrasse 33, 82487 Oberammergau, tel. 08822/867, fax 08822/7027). **Hotel Bayerische Lowe** is central with a good restaurant and comfortable rooms (Db-€56, no CC, Dedlerstrasse 2, tel. 08822/1365). **Pension Rudhart** comes with a lot of rules (no laundry in sinks, no flushing after 23:00) but has an idyllic location next to a stream, a 15-minute walk from the center (Db-€56, no CC, 5 min from swimming pool, Ludwig-Lang Strasse 41, 8103 Oberammergau, tel. 08822/4487). Oberammergau's modern **youth hostel** is on the river a short walk from the center (€12 beds, no CC, open year-round, tel. 08822/4114, fax 08822/1695).

Connections: From Oberammergau, four to six buses run daily to Füssen, fewer in winter (1.75 hrs). Drivers entering the town from the north should cross the bridge, take the second left, follow "Polizei" signs, and park by the huge gray Passionsspielhaus. Leaving town, head out past the church and turn toward Ettal on Road 23. You're 30 kilometers (20 miles) from Reutte via the scenic Plansee.

▲▲**Linderhof Castle**—This homiest of "Mad" King Ludwig's castles is small and comfortably exquisite—good enough for a minor god. Set in the woods 15 minutes from Oberammergau by car or bus (hrly bus, June–mid-Oct, only 2/day off-season) and surrounded by fountains and sculpted, Italian-style gardens, it's the only palace I've toured that actually had me feeling envious. Don't miss the grotto—15-minute tours are included with the palace ticket (€6, April–Sept daily 9:00–18:00, Thu until 20:00, Oct–March daily 10:00–16:00, parking-€2, fountains often erupt on the hour, English tours when 15 gather—easy in summer but sparse off-season, tel. 08822/92030). Plan for lots of walking and a two-hour stop to fully enjoy this royal park. Pay at the entry and get an admission time. Visit outlying sights in the garden to pass any wait time.

▲▲**Zugspitze**—The tallest point in Germany is a border crossing. Lifts from Austria and Germany go to the 3,075-meter (10,000-foot) summit of the Zugspitze. Straddle the border between two great nations while enjoying an incredible view. Restaurants, shops, and telescopes await you at the summit.

On the German side, the 75-minute trip from Garmisch costs €42 round-trip; family discounts are available (buy a combo ticket for cogwheel train to Eibsee and cable-car ride to summit, drivers can park for free at cable-car station at Eibsee, tel. 08821/7970). Allow plenty of time for afternoon descents: if bad weather hits in the late afternoon, cable cars can be delayed at the summit, causing tourists to miss their train from Eibsee back to Garmisch. Hikers enjoy the easy 10-kilometer walk around the lovely Eibsee (German side, 5 min downhill from cable car "Seilbahn").

On the Austrian side, from the less crowded Talstation Obermoos above the village of Erwald, the tram zips you to the top in 10 minutes (€31 round-trip, cash only, late May–Oct daily 8:40–16:40, tel. in Austria 05673/2309).

The German ascent is easier for those without a car, but buses do connect the Erwald train station and the Austrian lift almost every hour.

Sleeping in Füssen
(€1.10 = about $1, country code: 49, area code: 08362, zip code: 87629)
Sleep Code: **S** = Single, **D** = Double/Twin, **T** = Triple, **Q** = Quad, **b** = bathroom, **s** = shower only, **CC** = Credit Cards accepted, **no CC** = Credit Cards not accepted, **SE** = Speaks English, **NSE** = No English.

Unless otherwise noted, breakfast is included, hall showers are free, and English is spoken. Prices listed are for one-night stays. Large price ranges usually indicate high versus low season. Some places give a discount for longer stays. Always ask. Competition is fierce, and off-season prices are soft.

While I prefer sleeping in Reutte (see below), convenient Füssen is just five kilometers from Ludwig's castles and offers a cobbled, riverside retreat. But it also happens to be very touristy (notice *das* sushi bar). It has just about as many rooms as tourists, though, and the TI has a free room-finding service. All places I've listed (except the hostel) are within a few blocks of the train station and the town center. They are used to travelers getting in after the Romantic Road bus arrives (20:15) and will hold rooms with a telephone promise. Parking is easy at the station.

Hotel Kurcafé is deluxe, with spacious rooms and all of the amenities. Its bakery can ruin your budget—and your diet—any time of year (Sb-€52–83, Db-€78–101, Tb-€93–124, Qb-€108–139, €10 more for weekends and holidays, CC, some nonsmoking rooms, lots of stairs and no elevator, on tiny traffic circle a block in front of station at Bahnhofstrasse 4, tel. 08362/6369, fax 08362/39424, www.kurcafe.com). The attached restaurant has good and reasonable daily specials.

Altstadthotel zum Hechten offers all the modern comforts

Füssen

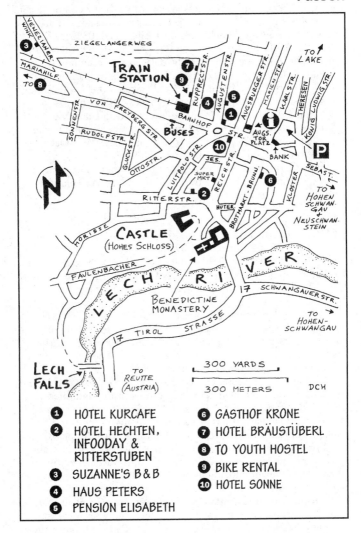

ZIEGELANGERWEG

TRAIN STATION

TO LAKE

MARIAHILF.

TO

VON FREYBERG STR

BAHNHOF

BUSES

RUDOLFSTR.

RITTERSTR.

SUPER MKT

CASTLE
(Hohes Schloss)

FAULENBACHER

LECH RIVER

BENEDICTINE
MONASTERY

SCHWANGAUER STR.

TIROL STRASSE

TO HOHEN-SCHWANGAU

LECH FALLS

TO REUTTE (AUSTRIA)

300 YARDS

300 METERS

DCH

❶ HOTEL KURCAFE
❷ HOTEL HECHTEN, INFOODAY & RITTERSTUBEN
❸ SUZANNE'S B & B
❹ HAUS PETERS
❺ PENSION ELISABETH
❻ GASTHOF KRONE
❼ HOTEL BRÄUSTÜBERL
❽ TO YOUTH HOSTEL
❾ BIKE RENTAL
❿ HOTEL SONNE

in a friendly, traditional shell right under Füssen Castle in the old-town pedestrian zone (S-€33, Sb-€41–46, D-€56, Db-€72–82, Tb-€100, Qb-€114, no CC, free parking with this book in 2002, cheaper off-season and for multinight stays, fun mini-bowling alley in basement, nearby church bells ring every 15 min at night; from TI, walk down pedestrian street, take second right

to Ritterstrasse 6, tel. 08362/91600, fax 08362/916-099, www
.hotel-hechten.com, Frau Margaret has taken fine care of
travelers for 40 years). The hotel runs two fine restaurants (see
"Eating," below).

Suzanne's B&B is a tidy, delightful place run by a plain-
spoken, no-nonsense American woman who strikes some travelers
as brusque and others as warm. Suzanne offers local travel advice,
backyard-fresh eggs, local cheese, a children's yard, affordable laundry, bright and spacious rooms, and feel-good balconies. Families
should ask about her "attic special," four beds in a loft with a private
bathroom and very low ceilings (Db-€75, Tb-€105, Qb-€125, attic
special: €68 for 2, €95 for 3, €113 for 4; another room holds up to
6—ask for details, no CC, nonsmoking, exit station right and backtrack 2 blocks along tracks, cross tracks at Venetianerwinkel to #3,
tel. 08362/38485, fax 08362/921-396, www.suzannes.org, e-mail:
svorbrugg@t-online.de).

The funky, old, ornately furnished **Pension Garni Elisabeth**
exudes an Addams-family friendliness. Floors creak, dust balls
wander, and the piano is never played (S-€28, D-€56–61, Db-
€61–92, T-€84–92, Tb-€92–100, hall showers-€3, no CC,
Augustenstrasse 10, 2 blocks from station toward town, take
second left, tel. 08362/6275).

Hotel Sonne is a splurge in the heart of the town with 32
quaint yet plush rooms with all the extras (Sb-€54–82, Db-
€77–100, Tb-€92–123, CC, free parking, kitty-corner from
TI at Reichenstrasse 37, tel. 08362/9080, fax 08362/908-100,
www.hotel-sonne.de).

Gasthof Krone, a rare bit of pre-glitz Füssen in the pedestrian zone, has dumpy halls and stairs and standard, comfy rooms
at good prices (S-€30, D-€54, extra bed-€27, prices drop €3
for 2-night stays, CC, reception in restaurant, from TI head
down pedestrian street, take first left to Schrannengasse 17, tel.
08362/7824, fax 08362/37505, www.krone-fuessen.de).

Hotel Bräustüberl has decent rooms at fair rates attached
to a gruff and musty old beer hall–type place (Sb-€42, Db-€62,
no CC, Rupprechtstrasse 5, a block from station, tel. 08362/7843,
fax 08362/923-951).

Haus Peters, across the street from Pension Garni Elisabeth
(listed above), is comfy, smoke free, and friendly, but tends to be
closed often in summer (Ds/Db-€46, Tb-€61, no CC, Augustenstrasse 5 1/2, tel. 08362/7171).

Füssen Youth Hostel, a fine, German-run youth hostel,
welcomes travelers under 27 (€14-dorm beds in 2- to 6-bed
rooms, D-€34, €3 more for nonmembers, includes breakfast
and sheets, no CC, dinner-€5, laundry-€3/load, nonsmoking,
from station backtrack 10 min along the tracks, Mariahilferstrasse
5, tel. 08362/7754, fax 08362/2770).

Sleeping in Hohenschwangau, near Neuschwanstein Castle
(country code: 49, area code: 08362, zip code: 87645)
Inexpensive farmhouse *Zimmer* (B&Bs) abound in the Bavarian countryside around Neuschwanstein and are a decent value. Look for signs that say "Zimmer Frei" ("room free," or vacancy). The going rate is about €50 to €65 for a double including breakfast.

Pension Weiher has lots of balconies and floodlit Neuschwanstein views (S-€19–41, D-€41–44, Db-€46–51, no CC, Hofwiesenweg 11, tel. & fax 08362/81161). **Pension Schwansee** has clean, basic rooms (Ds-€50–55, Db-€61–66, Tb-€92–97, CC, free use of bikes, 2.5 km from the castle, on the road to Füssen at Parkstrasse 9, 87645 Alterschrofen, tel. 08362/8353, fax 08362/787-320).

For more of a hotel, try **Alpenhotel Meier**. It's located in a rural setting within walking distance of the castle, just beyond the lower parking lot (Sb-€41–46, Db-€66–77, 2-night discounts, no CC, all rooms have porches or balconies, larger rooms available, sauna, easy parking, just before the tennis courts at Schwangauerstrasse 37, tel. 08362/81152, fax 08362/987-028, www.alpenhotel-allgaeu.de, e-mail: alpenhotelmeier @firemail.de).

Eating in Füssen
For hearty, traditional Bavarian fare, consider **Zum Hechten**, which specializes in pike (*Hecht*), pulled from the Lech River (Thu–Tue 11:30–14:30, 17:30–21:00, closed Wed, under Füssen Castle in Altstadthotel zum Hechten Hotel, Ritterstrasse 6). The hotel also runs **Infooday** next door, a clever and modern self-service eatery that sells its hot meals and salad bar by weight and offers English newspapers (filling salad-€3, meals-€5, Mon–Fri 10:30–18:30, Sat 10:30–14:30, closed Sun, Ritterstrasse 6).

Next door, **Ritterstuben** offers reasonable and delicious fish and salads (Tue–Sun 11:30–14:30, 17:30–23:00, closed Mon, Ritterstrasse 4, tel. 08362/7759). A couple of blocks away, **Pizza Blitz** is a dive that offers good take-out or eat-at-the-counter pizzas and hearty salads for about €5 apiece (Mon–Sat 11:00–23:00, Sun 12:00–23:00, Luitpoldstrasse 14, tel. 08362/38354). Picnickers can shop at **Woolworth's** plentiful supermarket (Mon–Fri 8:45–19:00, Sat 8:30–16:00, closed Sun, Reichenstrassse 11, tel. 08362/91840). Satisfy your gelato needs at **Eis Café Hohes Schloss** (Riechenstrasse 14, across from Woolworth's).

Transportation Connections—Füssen
To: Neuschwanstein (hrly buses, 10 min, €1.35 one-way, €2.70 round-trip; taxis cost €10 one-way), **Reutte** (Mon–Fri 5 buses/day, Sat 3/day, none Sun, 30 min; taxis cost €21

one-way), **Munich** (hrly trains, 2 hrs, some change in Buchloe). Train info: tel. 01805-996-633.

Romantic Road Buses: The northbound Romantic Road bus departs Füssen at 8:00; the southbound bus arrives at Füssen at 20:15 (bus stops at train station). Railpasses get you a 60 percent discount on the Romantic Road bus (and, best of all, the ride doesn't use up a day of a flexipass)—this is a great value. For more information, see the Rothenburg chapter.

REUTTE, AUSTRIA
(€1.10 = about $1)
Reutte (ROY-teh, rolled "r"), a relaxed town of 5,500, is located 20 minutes across the border from Füssen. It's far from the international tourist crowd but popular with Germans and Austrians for its climate. Doctors recommend its "grade 1" air. Reutte's one claim to fame with Americans: As Nazi Germany was falling in 1945, Hitler's top rocket scientist Werner von Braun joined the Americans (rather than the Russians) here in Reutte. You could say the American space program began in Reutte.

Reutte isn't featured in any other American guidebook. Its charms are subtle, though its generous sidewalks are filled with smart boutiques and lazy coffeehouses. It never was rich or important. Its castle is ruined, its buildings have painted-on "carvings," its churches are full, its men yodel for each other on birthdays, and lately its energy is spent soaking its Austrian and German guests in *Gemütlichkeit*. Most guests stay for a week, so the town's attractions are more time-consuming than thrilling. If the weather's good, hike to the mysterious Ehrenberg ruins, ride the luge, or rent a bike. For a slap-dancing bang, enjoy a Tirolean folk evening. For accommodations, see "Sleeping," below.

Orientation (area code: 05672)
Tourist Information: Reutte's TI is a block in front of the train station (Mon–Fri 8:00–12:00, 14:00–17:00, Sat 8:30–12:00, closed Sun, tel. 05672/62336 or, from Germany, 00-43-5672/62336). Go over your sightseeing plans, ask about a folk evening, pick up city and biking maps, and ask about discounts with the hotel guest cards.

Bike Rental: In the center, the Heinz Glätzle shop rents good bikes (city and mountain bikes–€15, kids' bikes–€7.50, inside toy store at Obermarkt 61, tel. 05672/62752). Several recommended hotels loan or rent bikes to guests. Most of the sights described in this chapter make good biking destinations. Ask about the bike path (*Radwanderweg*) along the Lech River.

Laundry: Don't ask the TI about a Laundromat. Unless you can infiltrate the local campground, Hotel Maximilian, or Gutshof zum Schluxen (see "Sleeping," below), the town has none.

Reutte

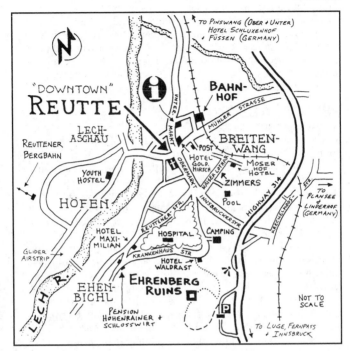

Sights—Reutte

▲▲**Ehrenberg Ruins**—The brooding ruins of Ehrenberg Castle are 1.5 kilometers outside of Reutte on the road to Lermoos and Innsbruck. This is a pleasant walk or a short bike ride from Reutte; bikers can use the trail—*Radwanderweg*—along the Lech River (the TI has a good map).

Ehrenberg, a 13th-century rock pile, provides a great contrast to King Ludwig's "modern" castles and a super opportunity to let your imagination off its leash.

At the parking lot at the base of the ruin-topped hill, you'll find the café/guest house Gasthof Klaus (closed Wed), which offers a German-language flier about the castle and has a wall painting of the intact castle.

The parking lot lies on the ancient Roman road, Via Claudia, and the medieval salt road. The **fortification** at the parking lot was a castle built over the road to control traffic and levy tolls on all that passed this strategic valley. (This will open as a museum of European castle ruins in about 2004.)

Hike up 20 minutes from the parking lot for a great view

from your own private ruins. Facing the hill from the parking lot, find the gravelly road at the Klaus sign. Follow the road to the saddle between the two hills. From the saddle, notice how the castle stands high on the horizon. This is Ehrenberg (which means "mountain of honor"), built in 1290. Thirteenth-century castles were designed to stand boastfully tall. With the advent of gunpowder, castles dug in. Notice the **ramparts** around you. They are 18th century. Approaching Ehrenberg castle, look for the small door to the left. It's the night entrance (tight and awkward, therefore safer in a surprise invasion).

Hiking up the hill you go through two doors. Castles allowed step-by-step retreat, giving defenders time to regroup and fight back against invading forces.

Before making the final and steepest ascent, follow the path around to the right to a big, grassy courtyard with commanding views and a fat, newly restored **turret**. This stored gunpowder and held a big cannon that enjoyed a clear view of the valley below. In medieval times, all the trees approaching the castle were cleared to keep an unobstructed view.

Look out over the valley. The pointy spire marks **Breitenwang**, which was a stop on the ancient Via Claudia. In A.D. 46, there was a Roman camp there. In 1489, after the Reutte bridge crossed the Lech River, Reutte (marked by the onion-domed church) was made a market town and eclipsed Breitenwang in importance. Any gliders circling? They launch from just over the river in Hofen (see "Flying and Gliding," below).

For centuries, this castle was the seat of government—ruling an area called the "judgement of Ehrenberg" (roughly the same as today's "district of Reutte"). When the emperor came by, he stayed here. In 1604, the ruler moved downtown into more comfortable quarters and the castle was no longer a palace.

Climb the steep hill to the top of the castle. Take the high ground. There was no water supply here, just kegs of wine, beer, and a cistern to collect rain.

Ehrenberg repelled 16,000 Swedish soldiers in the defense of Catholicism in 1632. Ehrenberg saw three or four other battles, but its end was not glorious. In the 1780s, a local businessman bought the castle in order to sell off its parts. Later, when vagabonds moved in, the roof was removed to make squatting miserable. With the roof gone, deterioration quickened, leaving this evocative shell and a whiff of history.

Folk Museum—Reutte's Heimatmuseum, offering a quick look at the local folk culture and the story of the castle, is more cute than impressive. Ask to borrow the packet of information in English (€2, Tue–Sun 10:00–12:00, 14:00–17:00, closed Mon and Nov–April, in the bright green building on Untermarkt, around corner from Hotel Goldener Hirsch).

▲▲**Tirolean Folk Evening**—Ask the TI or your hotel if there's a Tirolean folk evening scheduled. About once a week in summer (July–Sept) Reutte or a nearby town puts on an evening of yodeling, slap dancing, and Tirolean frolic usually worth the €6 to €9 and short drive. Off-season, you'll have to do your own yodeling. There are also weekly folk concerts in the park (summer only, ask at TI).

Swimming—Plunge into Reutte's Olympic-size swimming pool to cool off after your castle hikes (€5.25, June–Aug daily 10:00–21:00, Sept–May Tue–Sun 14:00–21:00, closed Mon; playground on site, 5 min on foot from Reutte center, head out Obermarkt and turn left on Kaiser Lothar Strasse).

Reuttener Bergbahn—This mountain lift swoops you high above the tree line to a starting point for several hikes and an alpine flower park with special paths leading you past countless local varieties (good bike ride with an uphill at the end).

Flying and Gliding—For a major thrill on a sunny day, drop by the tiny airport in Hofen across the river, and fly. A small single-prop plane can buzz the Zugspitze and Ludwig's castles and give you a bird's-eye peek at Reutte's Ehrenberg ruins (2 people for 30 min–€110, 1 hr–€220, tel. 05672/62827, phone rarely answered, and then not in English, so your best bet is to show up at Hofen airport on good-weather afternoons). Or, for something more angelic, how about *Segelfliegen*? For €37 you get 30 minutes in a glider for two (you and the pilot). Just watching the towrope launch the graceful glider like a giant, slow-motion rubber-band gun is thrilling (late May–Oct 11:00–19:00, in good weather only, tel. 05672/71550).

Sights—Tirol, Near Reutte

▲▲**The Luge** (*Sommerrodelbahn*)—Near Lermoos, on the road from Reutte to Innsbruck, you'll find two exciting luge courses, or *Sommerrodelbahn*. To try one of Europe's great $5 thrills, take the lift up, grab a sledlike go-cart, and luge down. The concrete course banks on the corners, and even a novice can go very, very fast. Most are cautious on their first run, speed demons on their second (and bruised and bloody on their third). A woman once showed me her journal illustrated with her husband's dried five-inch-long luge scab. He disobeyed the only essential rule of luging: Keep both hands on your stick. To avoid getting into a bumper-to-bumper traffic jam, let the person in front of you get way ahead before you start. No one emerges from the course without a windblown hairdo and a smile-creased face. Both places charge the same price (€6 per run, 5- and 10-trip discount cards) and shut down at the least hint of rain (call ahead to make sure they're open; you're more likely to get luge info in English if you call the TIs, see below). If you're without a car, these are not worth the trouble (consider the luge near Neuschwanstein instead, see "Tegelberg Luge," above).

The short and steep luge: Bichlbach, the first course (100-meter drop over 800-meter course), is six kilometers beyond Reutte's castle ruins. Look for a chair lift on the right and exit on the tiny road at the Almkopfbahn Rosthof sign (open from mid-May Sat–Sun 10:00–17:00 only, June–Oct daily 10:00–17:00, sometimes opens earlier in spring depending on weather, call first, tel. 05674/5350, or contact the local TI at 05674/5354).

The longest luge: The Biberwier Sommerrodelbahn is a better luge and, at 1,300 meters, the longest in Austria (15 min farther from Reutte than Bichlbach, just past Lermoos in Biberwier—the first exit after a long tunnel). The only drawbacks are its short season and hours (open mid-May–June Sat–Sun 9:00–16:30 only, July–Sept daily 9:00–16:30, call first, tel. 05673/2111 or 05673/2323, TI tel. 05673/2922).

▲**Fallerschein**—Easy for drivers and a special treat for those who may have been Kit Carson in a previous life, this extremely remote log-cabin village is a 1,230-meter-high (4,000 feet), flower-speckled world of serene slopes and cowbells. Thunderstorms roll down the valley like it's God's bowling alley, but the pint-size church on the high ground, blissfully simple in a land of Baroque, seems to promise that this huddle of houses will survive, and the river and breeze will just keep flowing. The couples sitting on benches are mostly Austrian vacationers who've rented cabins here. Many of them, appreciating the remoteness of Fallerschein, are having affairs. Fallerschein, at the end of the two-kilometer Berwang Road, is near Namlos and about 45 minutes southwest of Reutte.

Sleeping in and near Reutte
(€1.10 = about $1, country code: 43, area code: 05672, zip code: 6600)
Reutte is a mellow Füssen with fewer crowds and easygoing locals with a contagious love of life. Come here for a good dose of Austrian ambience and lower prices. Those with a car should home-base here; those without should consider it. (To call Reutte from Germany, dial 00-43-5672, then the local number.) You'll drive across the border without stopping. Reutte is popular with Austrians and Germans who come here year after year for one- or two-week vacations. The hotels are big, elegant, and full of comfy, carved furnishings and creative ways to spend so much time in one spot. They take great pride in their restaurants, and the owners send their children away to hotel management schools. All include a generally great breakfast but few accept credit cards.

Hotels and Guest Houses
Moserhof Hotel is a plush Tirolean splurge with polished service and facilities, including an elegant dining room (Sb-€49–53, Db-€82–89, extra person-€32–35, discounts for 2 or more nights, no

CC, all rooms have balconies, parking garage, elevator, from downtown Reutte walk to post office roundabout then to Planseestrasse 44, in village of Breitenwang, tel. 05672/62020, fax 05672/620-2040, www.hotel-moserhof.at).

Hotel Goldener Hirsch, located in the center of Reutte just two blocks from the station, is a grand old hotel renovated with a mod Tirolean Jugendstil flair. It includes mini-bars, cable TV, and one lonely set of antlers (Sb-€44–48, Db-€67–70, Tb-€102–106, Qb-€124–131, 2-night discounts, CC, a few family rooms, elevator, quality food in their restaurant, 6600 Reutte-Tirol, tel. 05672/62508, fax 05672/625-087, www .goldener-hirsch.at, Monika, Helmut, and daughter Vanessa).

In Ehenbichl: The next four listings are a few kilometers upriver from Reutte in the village of Ehenbichl; all are along an enjoyable hike to Ehrenberg ruins.

Hotel Maximilian is a fine splurge. It includes free bicycles, Ping-Pong, a children's playroom, and the friendly service of the Koch family. Daughter Gabi speaks flawless English and is clearly in charge. The Kochs host many special events, and their hotel has lots of wonderful extras such as a sauna, a masseuse, and a beauty salon (Sb-€35–38, Db-€70–78, family deals, CC, laundry service available even to nonguests, Internet access, good restaurant, A-6600 Ehenbichl-Reutte, tel. 05672/62585, fax 05672/625-8554, www.maxihotel.com, e-mail: maxhotel@netway.at). From central Reutte, go south on Obermarkt and turn right on Reuttener-strasse. They rent cars to guests only (1 VW Golf, 1 VW van, must book in advance).

Pension Hohenrainer is a quiet, good value with some castle-view balconies (Sb-€23–29, Db-€41–53, no CC). The same family runs the simpler **Gasthof Schlosswirt** across the green field (S-€19, D-€32–35, no CC, traditional Tirolean-style restaurant). Both are up the road behind Hotel Maximilian (turn right and continue 100 meters to Unterreid 3, A-6600 Ehenbichl, both cheaper after 3 nights, tel. 05672/62544, fax 05672/62052, www.hohenrainer.at).

Gasthof-Pension Waldrast, separating a forest and a meadow, is run by the farming Huter family and their huge, friendly dog, Bari. The place feels hauntingly quiet and has no restaurant, but it does include 10 very nice rooms with sitting areas and castle-view balconies (Sb-€30, Db-€51–55, Tb-€66, Qb-€88, no CC, includes small breakfast, nonsmoking, 1.5 km from Reutte just off main drag toward Innsbruck, past camp-ground and under castle ruins, on Ehrenbergstrasse, 6600 Reutte-Ehenbichl, tel. & fax 05672/62443, www.waldrast.com, e-mail: waldrast@aon.at).

In Pinswang: Closer to Füssen but still in Austria, **Gutshof zum Schluxen**, run by helpful Hermann, gets the "remote-old-hotel-in-an-idyllic-setting" award. This family-friendly working farm offers modern rustic elegance draped in goose down and pastels, and a chance to pet a rabbit and feed the deer. Its picturesque meadow setting will turn you into a dandelion picker, and its proximity to Neuschwanstein will turn you into a hiker. King Ludwig II himself is said to have slept here (Sb-€41, Db-€82, extra person-€22, 3-night discounts, CC, free pickup from Reutte and Füssen, good restaurant, fun bar, self-service laundry, mountain bike rental, between Reutte and Füssen in village of Pinswang, A-6600 Pinswang-Reutte, tel. 05677/8903, fax 05677/890-323, www.schluxen.com, e-mail: welcome@schluxen.com).

Private Homes in Breitenwang, near Reutte

The Reutte TI has a list of more than 50 private homes (*Zimmer*) that rent out generally good rooms with facilities down the hall, pleasant communal living rooms, and breakfast. Most charge €15 per person per night and speak little if any English. Reservations are nearly impossible for one- or two-night stays. But short stops are welcome if you just drop in and fill in available gaps. Most *Zimmer* charge €1.25 to €1.50 extra for heat in winter (worth it). The TI can always find you a room when you arrive.

Right next door to Reutte is the older and quieter village of Breitenwang. It has all the best *Zimmer*, the recommended Moserhof Hotel (above), and a bakery (a 20-min walk from Reutte train station—at post office roundabout, follow Planseestrasse past onion dome to pointy straight dome; unmarked Kaiser Lothar Strasse is first right past this church). The following three *Zimmer* are comfortable, quiet, have few stairs, and are within two blocks of the Breitenwang church steeple: **Helene Haissl** (the best of the bunch, D-€28, 2-night discounts, no CC, children's room available, beautiful garden, separate entrance for rooms, free bikes, laundry service, across from big Alpenhotel Ernberg at Planseestrasse 63, tel. 05672/67913); **Inge Hosp** (S-€15, D-€30, no CC, an old-fashioned place, includes antlers over breakfast table, Kaiser Lothar Strasse 36, tel. 05672/62401); and **Walter and Emilie Hosp**, Inge's more formal in-laws, who have a modern house across the street (D-€32, extra person-€12, cheaper after 3 nights, no CC, Kaiser Lothar Strasse 29, tel. 05672/65377).

Hostel

The homey hostel **Jugendgästehaus Graben** has two to six beds per room and includes breakfast and sheets. The Reyman family keeps the place traditional, clean, and friendly and serves a great €6.60 dinner for guests only. This is a super value. If you've never hosteled and are curious (and have a car or don't mind a bus ride), try it. They accept nonmembers of any age (dorm bed-€17,

Db-€43, no CC, laundry service, Internet access, no curfew, smoke-free rooms, bus connection to Neuschwanstein; about 3 km from Reutte, from downtown Reutte, cross bridge and follow main road left along river, or take the bus—1 bus/hr until 18:00, ask for Graben stop; Graben 1, A-6600 Reutte-Höfen, tel. 05672/626-440, fax 05672/626-444, www.tirol.com/jgh -hoefen, e-mail: jgh-hoefen@tirol.com).

Eating in Reutte

Hotels in this region take great pleasure in earning the loyalty of their guests by serving local cuisine at reasonable prices. Rather than go to a cheap restaurant, eat at your hotel. For cheap food, **Metzgerei Storf,** across from the Heimatmuseum, is good (Mon–Fri 07:30–12:30, 14:00–18:00, Sat 07:30–12:00, above deli, Untermarkt Street). The modern **Alina** in Breitenwang is a fine Italian establishment with decent prices (Tue–Sun 10:00–24:00, closed Mon, near recommended *Zimmer*, follow Planseestrasse past Moserhof Hotel on the way out of town, then turn left at Bachweg to #17, tel. 05672/65008).

Transportation Connections—Reutte

Reutte's train station, always in danger of closing, should be open at least through June 2002.

By train to: Innsbruck (7/day, 2.5 hrs, transfer in Garmisch and sometimes also in Mittenwald), **Munich** (hrly, 2.5–3 hrs, transfer in Garmisch, Pfronten-Steinach, or Kempten).

By bus to: Füssen (Mon–Fri 5 buses/day, Sat 3/day, none Sun, 30 min; taxis cost €21 one-way).

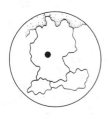

ROTHENBURG AND THE ROMANTIC ROAD

From Munich or Füssen to Frankfurt, the Romantic Road takes you through Bavaria's medieval heartland, a route strewn with picturesque villages, farmhouses, onion-domed churches, Baroque palaces, and walled cities.

Dive into the Middle Ages via Rothenburg (ROE-ten-burg), Germany's best-preserved walled town. Countless travelers have searched for the elusive "untouristy Rothenburg." There are many contenders (such as Michelstadt, Miltenberg, Bamberg, Bad Windsheim, and Dinkelsbühl), but none holds a candle to the king of medieval German cuteness. Even with crowds, over-priced souvenirs, Japanese-speaking night watchmen, and, yes, even with *Schneebälle*, Rothenburg is best. Save time and mileage and be satisfied with the winner.

Planning Your Time

The best one-day look at the heartland of Germany is the Romantic Road bus tour. Eurail travelers, who get a 60 percent discount, pay only €29 for the ride (daily, Frankfurt to Füssen or Rothenburg to Munich, and vice versa). Drivers can follow the route laid out in the tourist brochures (available at any TI along the route). The only stop worth more than a few minutes is Rothenburg. Twenty-four hours is ideal for this town. Two nights and a day are a bit much, unless you're actually relaxing on this trip.

Rothenburg in a day is easy, with four essential experiences: the Medieval Crime and Punishment Museum, the Riemen-schneider wood carving in St. Jakob's Church, the city walking tour, and a walk along the wall. With more time there are several mediocre but entertaining museums, walking and biking in the nearby countryside, and lots of cafés and shops. Make a point

Rothenburg

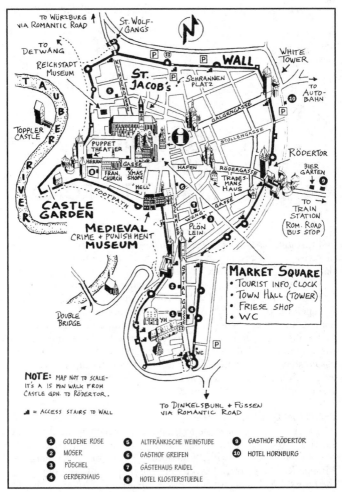

❶	GOLDENE ROSE	❺	ALTFRÄNKISCHE WEINSTUBE	❾	GASTHOF RÖDERTOR	
❷	MOSER	❻	GASTHOF GREIFEN	❿	HOTEL HORNBURG	
❸	PÖSCHEL	❼	GÄSTEHAUS RAIDEL			
❹	GERBERHAUS	❽	HOTEL KLOSTERSTUEBLE			

to spend at least one night. The town is yours after dark when the groups vacate and the town's floodlit cobbles wring some romance out of any travel partner.

ROTHENBURG

In the Middle Ages, when Frankfurt and Munich were just wide spots on the road, Rothenburg was Germany's second-largest free imperial city, with a whopping population of 6,000. Today it's her best-preserved medieval walled town, enjoying tremendous tourist popularity without losing its charm. Get medievaled in Rothenburg.

During Rothenburg's heyday, from 1150 to 1400, it was the crossing point of two major trade routes: Tashkent-Paris and Hamburg-Venice. Today the great trade is tourism; two-thirds of the townspeople are employed to serve you. Too often Rothenburg brings out the shopper in visitors before they've had a chance to appreciate the historic city. True, this is a great place to do your German shopping, but first see the town. While 2.5 million people visit each year, a mere 500,000 spend the night. Rothenburg is most enjoyable early and late, when the tour groups are gone.

Orientation (area code: 09861)
To orient yourself in Rothenburg, think of the town map as a human head. Its nose—the castle garden—sticks out to the left, and the neck is the skinny lower part, with the hostel and my favorite hotels in the Adam's apple. The town is a joy on foot. No sight or hotel is more than a 15-minute walk from the train station or each other.

Most of the buildings you'll see were built by 1400. The city was born around its long-gone castle—built in 1142, destroyed in 1356—which was located on the present-day site of the castle garden. You can see the shadow of the first town wall, which defines the oldest part of Rothenburg, in its contemporary street plan. A few gates from this wall still survive. The richest and biggest houses were in this central part. The commoners built higgledy-piggledy (read: picturesquely) farther from the center near the present walls.

Tourist Information
The TI is on Market Square (April–Oct Mon–Fri 09:00–12:00, 13:00–18:00, Sat 10:00–15:00, closed Sun, shorter hours off-season, after-hours board lists rooms still available, tel. 09861/ 40492, www.rothenburg.de). Pick up a free map, a virtual walking guide to the town. The free "Hotels and Pensions of Rothenburg" map has the greatest detail and names all of the streets. Confirm sightseeing plans and ask about the daily 14:00 walking tour (May–Oct) and evening entertainment. The TI also posts a weekly list of events. The best town map is available free at the Friese shop, two doors from the TI in the direction of Rothenburg's "nose."

Arrival in Rothenburg: Exit left from the train station and turn right on the first busy street (Ansbacher Strasse). It'll take you to Rothenburg's Market Square within 10 minutes. Day trippers can leave luggage in station lockers (€2, on platform) or at the Friese shop on Market Square. The travel agency in the station is the place to arrange train and *couchette*/sleeper reservations (Mon–Fri 09:00–18:00, Sat 09:00–13:00, €1.50 for print-outs of 2 or more itineraries). The nearest WCs are at the snack bar next door to the station. The taxis waiting at the station can take you to any hotel for €5. Drivers will find many parking lots outside the town walls that range from no cost to €3.60 per day. Park outside of town and walk five minutes to the center. Only those with a hotel reservation can park within the walls after hours (but not during festivals).

Festivals: Rothenburgers dress up in medieval costumes and beer gardens spill out into the street to celebrate Mayor Nusch's Meistertrunk victory (May 17–20 in 2002, see story below under "Sights—Meistertrunk Show") and 700 years of history in the Imperial City Festival (Sept 6–8 in 2002, first weekend in Sept, with fireworks).

Tours of Rothenburg

The TI on Market Square offers one-hour guided walking tours in English (€3, May–Oct daily at 14:00 from Market Square). A bit less informative but wonderfully entertaining, the **Night Watchman's Tour** takes tourists on his one-hour rounds each evening at 20:00 (€3, April–Dec, in English, meet at Market Square). This is the best evening activity in town. Or you can hire a **private guide**. For €50, a local historian who's an intriguing character as well brings the ramparts alive. Hundreds of years of history are packed between Rothenburg's cobbles. Anita Weinzierl (tel. 09868/7993) and Manfred Baumann (tel. 09861/4146) are good guides. **Horse-and-buggy rides** last 30 minutes and cost €5.10 per person for a minimum of three people (start at Schrannenplatz or Market Square).

Sights—Rothenburg's Town Hall Square

▲▲**Town Hall Tower**—The best view of Rothenburg and the surrounding countryside and a close-up look at the interior of an old tiled roof are yours for €1 and a rigorous but interesting climb (214 steps, 62 meters/200 feet, daily April–Oct 09:30–12:30, 13:30–17:00, off-season weekends 12:00–15:00 only). The entrance is on Market Square. Women, beware: Some men find the view best from the bottom of the ladder just before the top.

Meistertrunk Show—Be on Market Square at 11:00, 12:00, 13:00, 14:00, 15:00, 20:00, 21:00, or 22:00 for the ritual gathering of the tourists to see the less-than-breathtaking reenactment of the Meistertrunk story. In 1631, the Catholic army took the Protestant town and was about to do its rape, pillage, and plunder thing when, as the story goes, the mayor said, "Hey, if I can drink this entire three-liter tankard of wine in one gulp, will you leave us alone?" The invading commander, sensing he was dealing with an unbalanced person, said, "Sure." Mayor

Nusch drank the whole thing, the town was saved, and the mayor slept for three days. Hint: For the best show, don't watch the clock; watch the open-mouthed tourists gasp as the old windows flip open. At the late shows, the square flickers with flash attachments. While you wait for the show, give yourself the spin tour below.

Market Square Spin Tour—Stand at the bottom of Market Square (3 meters/10 feet below the last wooden post) and spin 360 degrees clockwise starting with the city hall tower. Now, do it slower following these notes: 1) The city's tallest **tower**, at 62 meters (200 feet), stands atop the old city hall, a white, Gothic, 13th-century building. Notice the tourists enjoying the view from the black top of the tower. 2) When the town had more money and Gothic went out of style, a new **town hall** was built in front of the old one. This is in Renaissance style from 1570. (Access to the old town hall tower is through the middle of the new town hall arcade.) 3) At the top of the square stands the proud **Councilors' Tavern** (clock tower, from 1466). In its day, the city council drank here. Today it's the TI and the focus of all the attention when the little doors on either side of the clock flip open and the wooden figures (from 1910) reenact the Meistertrunk. 4) Across the street, the green building is the oldest **pharmacy** in town—Löwen Apotheke, from 1374—peek inside. 5) On the bottom end of the square, the cream building is a fine **print shop** (see "Shopping," below, free brandy). 6) Adjoining that is the **Baumeister's House**, a good restaurant with a fine courtyard (see "Eating," below), with its famous Renaissance facade featuring statues of the seven virtues and the seven vices—the former supporting the latter. 7) The green house below that is the former house of Mayor Toppler, today the fine old **Greifen Hotel**; next to it is a famous Scottish restaurant (with arches). 8) Continue circling to the big 17th-century **St. George's fountain**. The long metal gutters slid, routing the water into the villagers' buckets. Rothenburg's many fountains had practical functions beyond providing drinking water. The water was used for fighting fires, and the fountains were stocked with fish during times of siege. Two fine buildings behind the fountain show the old-time lofts with warehouse doors and pulleys on top for hoisting. All over town, lofts were filled with grain and corn. A year's supply was required by the city so they could survive any siege. The building on the left is a free art gallery showing off the work of Rothenburg's top artists. The other is another old-time pharmacy. 9) The broad street running under the town hall tower is **Herrngasse**. The town originated with its castle (1142). Herrngasse leads from the castle (now gone) to Market Square where you stand now.

▲**Historical Town Hall Vaults**—Under the town hall tower is a city history museum that gives a waxy but good look at medieval

Rothenburg. With the best English descriptions in town, it offers a look at "the fateful year 1631," a replica of the famous Meistertrunk tankard, and a dungeon complete with three dank cells and some torture lore (€1.80, May–Oct daily 09:00–18:00, less off-season).

Sights—Rothenburg

▲▲**Walk the Wall**—Just over 1.5 kilometers around, providing great views and a good orientation, this walk can be done by those under six feet tall and without a camera in less than an hour, and requires no special sense of balance. Photographers go through lots of film, especially before breakfast or at sunset, when the lighting is best and the crowds are fewest. The best fortifications are in the Spitaltor (south end). Walk from there counterclockwise to the "forehead." Climb the Rödertor en route. The names you see along the way are people who donated money to rebuild the wall after World War II.

▲**Rödertor**—The wall tower nearest the train station is the only one you can climb. It's worth the hike up (135 steps) for the view and a fascinating rundown on the bombing of Rothenburg in the last weeks of World War II when the northeast corner of the city was destroyed (€1.30, April–Oct daily 09:00–16:00, closed Nov–March, photos of WWII damage with English translations).

▲▲**St. Jakob's Church**—Built in the 14th century, it's been Lutheran since 1544. Take a close look at the Twelve Apostles altar in front (from 1546, left permanently in its open festival-day position). Six saints are below Christ. St. James (Jakob in German) is the one with the staff. He's the saint of pilgrims, and this was on the medieval pilgrimage route to Santiago de Compostela in Spain. Study the painted panels. Around the back (upper left) is a great painting of Rothenburg's Market Square in the 15th century looking like it does today. Before leaving the front of the church, notice the old medallions above the carved choir stalls featuring the coats of arms of Rothenburg's leading families and portraits of early Reformation preachers.

Next, climb the stairs in the back. Behind the pipe organ stands the artistic highlight of Rothenburg and perhaps the most wonderful wood carving in all Germany: the glorious 500-year-old, 10-meter-high *Altar of the Holy Blood*. Tilman Riemenschneider, the Michelangelo of German wood-carvers, carved this from 1499 to 1504 to hold a precious rock crystal capsule set in a cross containing a drop of the holy blood (1270). Below, in the scene of the Last Supper, Jesus gives Judas a piece of bread, marking him as the traitor while John lays his head on Christ's lap. On the left: Jesus entering Jerusalem. On the right: Jesus praying in the Garden of Gethsemane (€1.30, Mon–Sat 09:00–17:30, Sun 10:45–17:30, off-season 10:00–12:00, 14:00–16:00, free helpful English info sheet, no flash photos).

▲▲**Medieval Crime and Punishment Museum**—It's the best of its kind, full of fascinating old legal bits and *Kriminal* pieces, instruments of punishment and torture, even a special cage complete with a metal gag—for nags. Exhibits are well described in English (€3, €5.10 combo includes Imperial City Museum, daily 09:30–17:15, shorter hrs off-season, fun cards and posters).

Museum of the Imperial City (Reichsstadt Museum)—This less sensational museum, housed in the former Dominican Convent, gives a more scholarly look at old Rothenburg. Highlights include *The Rothenburg Passion*, a 12-panel series of paintings from 1492 showing scenes leading up to Christ's crucifixion, an exhibit of Jewish culture through the ages in Rothenburg, and a 14th-century convent kitchen (€2.60, April–Oct daily 09:30–17:30, Nov–March 13:00–16:00, last entry 30 min before closing, English info sheet and descriptions, no photos, tel. 09861/939-043). Next door, the convent garden (free) is a peaceful place to work on your tan.

▲**Toy Museum**—Two floors of historic *Kinder* cuteness is a hit with many (€3, €6.20 per family, daily 09:30–18:00, just off Market Square, downhill from the fountain, Hofbronneng 13).

▲▲**Herrngasse and the Castle Garden**—Any town's *Herrngasse*, where the richest patricians and merchants (the *Herren*) lived, is your chance to see its finest old mansions. Wander from Market Square down Herrngasse (past Rothenburg's old official measurement rods on the city hall wall) and drop into the lavish front rooms of a ritzy hotel or two. Pop into the Franciscan Church (free, Mon–Sat 10:00–12:00, 14:00–16:00, Sun 14:00–16:00, built in 1285—the oldest in town, with a Riemenschneider altarpiece), continue on down past the old-fashioned puppet theater, through the old gate (notice the tiny after-curfew door in the big door and the frightening mask mouth from which hot Nutella was poured onto attackers), through the garden and to the end of what used to be the castle (great picnic spots and Tauber Riviera views at sunset). This is the popular kissing spot for romantic Rothenburg teenagers.

▲**Walk in the Countryside**—Just below the *Burggarten* (castle garden) in the Tauber Valley is the cute, skinny, 600-year-old castle/summer home of Mayor Toppler (€1.50, Fri–Sun 13:00–16:00, closed Mon–Thu, 1.5 km from town center). On the top floor, notice the photo of bombed-out Rothenburg in 1945. Then walk on past the covered bridge and huge trout to the peaceful village of Detwang. Detwang (from 968, the second-oldest village in Franconia) is actually older than Rothenburg and also has a Riemenschneider altarpiece in its church. For a scenic return, loop back to Rothenburg through the valley along the river, past a café with outdoor tables, great desserts, and a town view to match.

Swimming—Rothenburg has a fine modern recreation center with an indoor/outdoor pool and sauna. It's just a few minutes' walk down the Dinkelsbühl Road (Fri–Wed 09:00–20:00, Thu 10:00–20:00, pool: €3 adults, €1.50 kids ages 5–17, swimsuit and towel rental–€1.50 each, Nordlingerstrasse 20, tel. 09861/4565). **Sightseeing Lowlights**—St. Wolfgang's Church is a fortified Gothic church built into the medieval wall at Klingentor. Its dungeonlike passages and shepherd's dance exhibit are pretty lame (€1.30, April–Oct daily 10:00–13:00, 14:00–17:00, closed Nov–March). The cute-looking Bäuerliches Museum (farming museum) next door is even worse. The Rothenburger Handwerkerhaus (tradesman's house, 700 years old) shows the typical living situation of a Rothenburger in the town's heyday (€2, April–Dec daily 09:00–18:00, closed Jan–March, Alter Stadtgraben 26, near Markus Tower).

Sights—Near Rothenburg

Franconian Bike Ride—For a fun, breezy look at the countryside around Rothenburg, rent a bike from Rad & Tat (€10.25/day, Mon–Fri 09:00–18:00, Sat 09:00–14:00, closed Sun, Bensenstrasse 17, outside of town behind the "neck," near corner of Bensenstrasse and Erlbacherstrasse, no deposit except passport number, bike maps–€3-12.80, tel. 09861/87984). Return the bike the next morning before 10:00. For a pleasant half-day pedal, bike south down to Detwang via Topplerschlosschen. Go north along the level bike path to Tauberscheckenbach, then huff and puff uphill about 20 minutes to Adelshofen and south back to Rothenburg.
Franconian Open-Air Museum—A 20-minute drive from Rothenburg in the undiscovered "Rothenburgy" town of Bad Windsheim is a small, open-air folk museum that, compared with others in Europe, isn't much. But it's trying very hard and gives you the best look around at traditional rural Franconia (€4.10, daily 09:00–18:00, closed Nov–Feb and Mon off-season, tel. 09841/66800).

Shopping

Be careful…Rothenburg is one of Germany's best shopping towns. Do it here and be done with it. Lovely prints, carvings, wine glasses, Christmas-tree ornaments, and beer steins are popular. Warning: Shipping is so expensive that it's probably not worth it for purchases under $200.

The Käthe Wohlfahrt Christmas trinkets phenomenon is spreading across the half-timbered reaches of Europe. In Rothenburg tourists flock to two **Käthe Wohlfahrt Christmas Villages** (on either side of Herrngasse, just off Market Square). This Christmas wonderland is filled with enough twinkling lights to require a special electric hookup, instant Christmas mood music (best appreciated on a hot day in July), and American and Japanese tourists hungrily filling little woven shopping baskets with €5–8 goodies to hang on their trees. (OK, I admit it, my Christmas tree sports a few KW ornaments.) Note: Prices have tour-guide kickbacks built into them (Mon–Fri 09:00–18:00, Sat 09:00–16:00, Sun 10:00–18:00, 1 store usually closed Jan–Feb, tel. 09861/4090, www .wohlfahrt.de). The new **Christmas Museum** upstairs (€2.60) is overkill, geared for shoppers who want to see 5,000 more Christmas items and learn about various Christmas traditions—before being dumped back in the store, primed to buy, compelled now by historical imperative. The Käthe Wohlfahrt **discount store** sells damaged and discontinued items. It's unnamed, across from the entrance of St. Jakob's Church, at Kirchgasse 5 (may move in 2002; ask at main shops about new location).

The **Friese shop** offers a charming contrast (just off Market Square, west of TI, on corner across from public WC). Cuckoo with friendliness, it gives shoppers with this book tremendous service: a 10 percent discount, 16 percent tax deducted if you have it mailed, and a free map. Anneliese, who runs the place with her sons Frankie and Berni and grandson Rene, charges only her cost for shipping, changes money at the best rates in town with no extra charge, and lets tired travelers leave their bags in her back room for free. For fewer crowds and better service, visit after 14:00 (Mon–Sat 08:00–17:00, Sun 09:30–17:00, tel. & fax 09861/7166).

The Ernst Geissendörfer **print shop** sells fine prints, etchings, and paintings. If you show this book, they'll offer 10 percent off marked prices for all purchases in cash (or credit-card purchases of at least €51) and a free shot of German brandy whether you buy anything or not (Mon–Sat 10:00–18:00, Sun 10:00–17:00, late Dec–April closed Sun, enter through bear shop in cream building on corner where Market Square hits Schmiedgasse, go up 1 floor, tel. 09861/2005).

For characteristic wine glasses, oinkology gear, and local wine from the town's oldest winemakers, drop by the **Weinladen am Plönlein** (Mon–Fri 08:30–18:00, see Ringhotel Glocke under "Evening Fun," below, for info on wine tasting, Plönlein 27).

Shoppers who mail their goodies home can get handy €1.50 boxes at the **post office** in the shopping center across from the train station (Mon–Fri 09:00–17:30, Sat 09:00–12:00).

Those who prefer to eat their souvenirs shop the *Bäckereien* (bakeries). Their succulent pastries, pies, and cakes are pleasantly distracting. Skip the bad-tasting Rothenburger *Schneebälle*.

Sleeping in Rothenburg
**(€1.10 = about $1, country code: 49,
area code: 09861, zip code: 91541)**
Sleep Code: **S** = Single, **D** = Double/Twin, **T** = Triple, **Q** = Quad, **b** = bathroom, **s** = shower only, **CC** = Credit Cards accepted, **no CC** = Credit Cards not accepted, **SE** = Speaks English, **NSE** = No

English. Unless otherwise indicated, room prices include break-fast. Rothenburg is crowded with visitors. But when the sun sets, most retreat to the predictable plumbing of their big-city high-rise hotels. Except for the rare Saturday night and festivals (see "Orientation," above), room finding is easy throughout the year. Unless otherwise noted, enough English is spoken.

Many hotels and guest houses will pick up tired, heavy pack-ers at the station. You may be greeted at the station by *Zimmer* skimmers who have rooms to rent. If you have reservations, resist and honor your reservation. But if you haven't booked ahead, try talking yourself into one of these more desperate bed-and-break-fast rooms for a youth-hostel price. Be warned: These people are notorious for taking you to distant hotels and then charging you for the ride back if you decline a room.

A handy **Laundromat** is near the station off Ansbacher Strasse (€5.10/load, includes detergent, English instructions, Johannitergasse 8, tel. 09861/2775).

Hotels

I like **Hotel Goldene Rose**, where scurrying Karin serves breakfast and stately Henni keeps everything in good order. The hotel has one shower on each floor of rooms, but the rooms are clean, and you're surrounded by cobbles, flowers, and red-tiled roofs. The hotel also has a spacious family apartment and a separate annex (S-€20.50, D-€35, Ds-€46, Db-€49, some triples, apartment: for 4-€107, for 5-€128; CC; streetside rooms can be noisy, closed Jan–Feb, kid friendly, ground-floor rooms in annex, Spitalgasse 28, tel. 09861/4638, fax 09861/86417, Henni SE). The Favetta family also serves good, reasonably priced meals (restaurant closed Wed). Remember to keep your key to get in after they close (at the side gate in the alley). The hotel is a 15-minute walk from the station or a seven-minute walk downhill from Market Square.

Gasthof Greifen, once the home of Mayor Toppler, is a big, traditional, 600-year-old place with large rooms and all the comforts. It's run by a fine family staff and creaks just the way you want it to (small Sb-€38, Sb-€48, one big D-€40, Db-€59–77, Tb-€97, Qb-€117, 10 percent off for 3-night stay, CC, self- or full-service laundry, free and easy parking, half a block downhill from Market Square at Obere Schmiedgasse 5, tel. 09861/2281, fax 09861/86374, e-mail: info@gasthof-greifen.rothenburg.de, Brigitte and Klingler family).

Hotel Gerberhaus, a classy new hotel in a 500-year-old building, is warmly run by Inge and Kurt, who mix modern comforts into bright and airy rooms while maintaining a sense of half-timbered elegance. Enjoy the great buffet breakfasts and pleasant garden in back (Sb-€44–56, Db-€56–79 depending on size, Tb-€90, Qb-€100, CC or pay cash for 5 percent off and a free *Schneebälle*, €2.60 less for 2 or more nights, all with TV and telephones, parking-€5/day, self-service laundry-€3.60, nonsmoking rooms, Spitalgasse 25, tel. 09861/94900, fax 09861/86555, www.gerberhaus.rothenburg.de, e-mail: gerberhaus@t-online.de). The downstairs café serves good soup and salad.

Hotel Klosterstueble, deep in the old town near the castle garden, is even classier. Jutta greets her guests while husband Rudolf does the cooking (Sb-€50, Db-€85–90, Tb-€110, family rooms-€110–155, luxurious apartment with kitchen and balcony-€105–200, €3 extra on weekends, family deals, CC, Heringsbronnengasse 5, tel. 09861/6774, fax 09861/6474, www.klosterstueble.de).

Bohemians enjoy the **Hotel Altfränkische Weinstube am Klosterhof**. Mario and lovely Hanne run this dark and smoky pub in a 600-year-old building. Upstairs they rent six cozy rooms with upscale Monty Python atmosphere, TVs, modern showers, open-beam ceilings, and "Himmel" beds—canopied four-poster "heaven" beds (Sb-€40, Db-€46–56, Tb-€61, CC, most rooms have tubs with hand-held showers, kid friendly, walk under St. Jakob's Church, take second left off Klingengasse at Klosterhof 7, tel. 09861/6404, fax 09861/6410). Their pub is a candlelit classic, serving hot food until 22:30 and closing at 01:00. Drop by on Wednesday evening (19:30–24:00) for the English Conversation Club.

Gasthof Marktplatz, right on Market Square, has nine tidy rooms with 70s-era wallpaper and a warm family atmosphere (S-€21, D-€38, Ds-€43, Db-€47, T-€50, Ts-€57, Tb-€63, no CC, Grüner Markt 10, tel. & fax 09861/6722, www.gasthof-marktplatz.de, Herr Rosner SE).

Gästehaus Raidel, a creaky 500-year-old house packed with antiques, offers 14 large rooms with cramped facilities down the hall. Run by grim people who make me want to sing the *Addams Family* theme song, it works in a pinch (S-€20, Sb-€35, D-€38, Db-€48, Tb-€71, no CC, Wenggasse 3, tel. 09861/3115, fax 09861/935-255, www.romanticroad.com/raidel, e-mail: gaestehaus-raidel@t-online.de, Herr Raidel speaks a little English).

Sleeping Outside the Wall

Gasthof Rödertor offers 15 decent rooms in a quiet setting one block outside the Rödertor tower. The guest house has a pleasant breakfast room with a farmhouse flair, a popular beer garden, and a restaurant dedicated to the potato (see "Evening Fun and Beer Drinking," below). Guest rooms in an annex inside the wall are slightly cheaper (Db-€61–82, Tb-€102, Qb-€123, kid's bed-€10.25, CC, most rooms with TV and phone, Ansbacher Strasse 7, tel. 09861/2022, fax 09861/86324, e-mail: hotel@roedertor.com).

Hotel Hornburg, a splurge with all the comforts, has groomed grounds and 10 spacious, tastefully decorated rooms a two-minute walk outside the wall (Sb-€49–67, Db-€69–95,

Tb-€90–110, CC, ground-floor rooms, nonsmoking rooms, cordless phones, cable TV, parking-€1/day, bikes for guests-€10.25/day, 10-min walk from station, exit station and go straight on Ludwig-Siebert Strasse, turn left on Mann Strasse and take first left to Hornburgweg 28, tel. 09861/8480, fax 09861/5570, www.hotelhornburg.rothenburg.de, e-mail: hotelhornburg @t-online.de, friendly Gabriele).

In the modern world, a block from the train station, **Pension Then** has six tidy pastel rooms and is worth a look (D-€40, Ds/Db-€44, no CC, basement rooms are dark but decent, Johannitergasse 8A, tel. 09861/5177, fax 09861/86014, Frau Then NSE).

Top Private Rooms Within the Wall

For the best real, with-a-local-family, comfortable, and homey experience, stay with **Herr und Frau Moser** (D-€36, T-€51, no CC, no single rooms, 2 rooms share 1 shower, no sign, look for Spitalgasse 12, 91541 Rothenburg o.d.t., tel. 09861/5971). This charming retired couple speak little English but try very hard. Speak slowly, in clear, simple English. Reserve by phone and please reconfirm by phone one day ahead of arrival.

Pension Pöschel is friendly with seven bearskin-cozy rooms on the second floor of a concrete but pleasant building. A great garden sits out back (S-€20, D-€35, T-€45, small kids free, no CC, Wenggasse 22, tel. 09861/3430, e-mail: pension.poeschel @t-online.de, Bettina).

Gästehaus Viktoria is a cheery little place right next to the town wall. Lovely gardens surround the house and its three rooms stuffed with furniture, ribbons, and silk flowers (Db-€38–49, no CC, breakfast served around the corner at Hotel Altfränkische, hand-held showers, Klingenschütt 4, tel. 09861/87682, Hanne).

Frau Liebler rents two large ground-floor rooms with kitchenettes and hardwood floors (Db-€41, no CC, breakfast in room, off Market Square behind Christmas shop, Pfaffleinsgasschen 10, tel. 09861/709215, fax 09861/709216, some English).

More Accommodations

These are decent places, just lesser values compared to the places mentioned above. **Pension Kreuzerhof** has seven big, modern, ground-floor, motel-style rooms on a quiet street (Sb-€29–32, Db-€47, Tb-€67.50, Qb-€75, no CC, nonsmoking rooms, parking, Millergasse 6, tel. 09861/3424, fax 09861/936-730, e-mail: kreuzerhof.rothenburg@t-online.de, NSE).

Pension Elke, run by the spry Erich Endress, offers eight airy, comfy rooms above his grocery store (S-€23, Sb-€33, D-€36–46, Db-€56, extra bed-€15, no CC, reception in grocery store until 19:00, otherwise go around corner onto Alter Stadt-graben to first door on left and ring bell at top of stairs, near

Markus Tower at Rodergasse 6, tel. 09861/2331, fax 09861/935-355). **Cafe Uhl** offers 10 fine rooms over a bakery. A top-floor twin room has a nice valley view if you don't mind the stairs (Sb-€30–44, Db-€50–61, third person-€18, fourth person-€13, CC, reception in café, nonsmoking rooms, parking-€3/day, closed Jan, Plönlein 8, tel. 09861/4895, fax 09861/92820, www.hotel-uhl.de, e-mail: info@hotel-uhl.de, Robert the baker SE).

   Gästehaus Flemming has seven plain yet comfortable rooms behind St. Jakob's Church (Db-€50, Tb-€72, no CC, Klingengasse 21, tel. & fax 09861/92380, Regina speaks a little English). The **Zum Schmoelzer** restaurant at Rosengasse 21 rents 14 nice but drab-colored rooms located around the corner (Sb-€28, Db-€46, no CC, parking, Stollengasse 29, tel. 09861/3371, fax 09861/7204, www.hofmann.rothenburg.de, e-mail: pension-hofmann-schmoelzer@t-online.de, SE).

Hostel
Here in Bavaria, hosteling is limited to those under 27, except for families traveling with children under 18. The fine **Rossmühle Youth Hostel** has 184 beds in two buildings. The droopy-eyed building (the old town horse mill, used when the town was under siege and the river-powered mill was inaccessible) houses groups and the office. The adjacent hostel is mostly for families and individuals (dorm beds-€14, Db-€34, no CC, includes breakfast and sheets, dinner-€5.10, self-serve laundry-€4, Internet access, Muhlacker 1, tel. 09861/94160, fax 09861/941-620, www.djh.de, e-mail: jhrothenburg@djh-bayern.de, SE). This popular place takes reservations (even more than a year in advance) and will hold rooms until 18:00 (or later if you call ahead on your arrival date).

Sleeping in Nearby Detwang and Bettwar
The town of Detwang, a 15-minute walk below Rothenburg, is loaded with quiet *Zimmer*. The clean, quiet, and comfortable old **Gasthof zum Schwarzes Lamm** in Detwang (Sb-€44, D-€46, Db-€56–72, Tb-€77, Qb-€87, CC, tel. 09861/6727, fax 09861/86899, e-mail: hotelschwarzeslamm@t-online.de, SE) has 30 rooms and serves good food, as does the popular and very local-style **Eulenstube** next door. **Gästehaus Alte Schreinerei** offers good food and 18 quiet, comfy, reasonable rooms a little farther down the road in Bettwar (Db-€39, less for 3 or more nights, no CC, 91628 Bettwar, tel. 09861/1541, fax 09861/86710, e-mail: alte.schreinerei@t-online.de, Christine SE).

Eating in Rothenburg
Most places serve meals only from 11:30 to 13:30 and 18:00 to 20:00. At **Goldene Rose** (see "Sleeping," above), Reno cooks up traditional German fare at good prices (Tue 11:30–14:00,

Thu–Mon 11:30–14:00, 17:30–20:30, closed Wed, in sunny weather the leafy garden terrace is open in the back, Spitalgasse 28).

Perhaps the most elegant place in town is the courtyard of **Baumeister Haus**, tucked deep behind a streetside pastry counter and antlered dining room. Squeeze past the commotion in front to grab a table in this classy, glass-domed space (€6–14, daily 08:00–23:00, behind statue-festooned facade a few doors below Market Square, Obere Schmiedgasse 3, tel. 09861/94700).

For cellar dining under medieval murals and pointy pikes consider **Burgerkeller** (€7–10, daily 12:00–14:00, 18:00–21:00, Herrngasse 24, tel. 09861/2126). Next to St. Jakob's, the pricier **Reichs-Küchenmeister** has a pleasant tree-shaded terrace and tidy plaid dining room (€8–16, daily 11:00–21:30, CC, nonsmoking room, nouveau German menu, some veggie choices, Kirchplatz 8, tel. 09861/2046).

Small meals, good cakes, and coffee are served in the beautifully restored **Allstadt-Café Alter Keller**, its walls festooned with old pots and jugs. Herr Hufnagel, a baker and pastry chef, whips up giant meringue cookies and other treats (Wed–Mon 11:00–20:00, until 18:00 on Sun, closed Tue, Alter Keller 8, tel. 09861/2268).

Galgengasse (Gallows Lane) has two cheap and popular standbys. **Pizzeria Roma** is the locals' favorite for €6.50 pizza, but service can be slow (daily 11:30–24:00, also has schnitzel fare, Galgengasse 19, tel. 09861/4540). Next door, **Landsknechtstuben** serves salads for €7 and dinners from €6 to €10 (Wed–Mon 11:00–15:00, 18:00–22:00, closed Tue, Galgengasse 21, tel. 09861/3323).

For a break from schnitzel, **Lotus China** serves good Chinese food daily and is home to a jolly buddha (€8 dinners, daily 11:30–14:30, 17:30–23:00, 2 blocks behind TI near church, Eckele 2, tel. 09861/86886).

Two **supermarkets** are near the wall at Rödertor. The one outside the wall is cheaper (Mon–Fri 08:00–20:00, Sat 08:00–16:00, on left as you exit wall); the one inside is nicer (Mon–Fri 08:00–19:00, Sat 08:00–16:00). Both are closed Sunday.

Evening Fun and Beer Drinking

For beer-garden fun on a balmy summer evening (dinner or beer), you have two fine choices. The locals' top pick in Rothenburg is **Gasthof Rödertor**, just outside the wall at the Rödertor (May–Sept daily 17:00–24:00, wood gate, near discos, see below).

The Gasthof Rödertor's *Kartoffeln Stube* inside is dedicated to the potato, complete with German-style "potato bar" (€6–10, daily 11:30–14:00, 17:30–23:00, tel. 09861/2022). In the valley along the river and worth the 20-minute hike is the **Unter den Linden** beer garden (daily 10:00–24:00, better for beer than food, tel. 09861/5909).

Trinkstube zur Hölle (Hell) is dark and foreboding. But they serve good ribs from 18:00 and offer thick wine-drinking atmosphere until late (Jan–March closed on Wed, a block past Criminal Museum on Burggasse, with devil hanging out front, tel. 09861/4229). Wine lovers enjoy **Ringhotel Glocke**'s *weinstube*, run by Rothenburg's oldest winemakers, the Thürauf family. For €4, you can sample five of their Franconian wines (Mon–Sat 10:30–23:00, Sun 10:30–14:00, Plönlein 1, tel. 09861/958-990). The mellow, red-velvet-classy **Löchle** pours wine until 01:00 (Tue–Sun from 18:00, closed Mon, next door to recommended Reichs-Küchenmeister restaurant, see above).

Two popular **discos** are near the Gasthof Rödertor's beer garden, a few doors farther out by the Sparkasse bank (Black Out at Ansbacher 15, in alley next to bank, open Wed, Fri–Sat 22:00–03:00; the other is Club 23, around corner from bank on Adam Hörber Strasse, open Thu–Sat from 22:00).

For a rare chance to mix it up with locals who aren't selling anything, bring your favorite slang and tongue twisters to the **English Conversation Club** at Mario's Altfränkische Weinstube (Wed 19:30–24:00, Anneliese from Friese shop is a regular). This dark and smoky pub is an atmospheric hangout any night but Tuesday (Jan–May), when it's closed (€5–11 entrées, Klosterhof 7, off Klingengasse, behind St. Jakob's Church, tel. 09861/6404).

Transportation Connections—Rothenburg

By bus: The Romantic Road bus tour takes you in and out of Rothenburg each afternoon (April–Oct) heading to Munich, Frankfurt, or Füssen. See the Romantic Road bus schedule on page 339 (or check www.euraide.de/ricksteves).

By train: A tiny train line connects Rothenburg to the outside world via **Steinach** (almost hrly, 15 min). If you plan to arrive in Rothenburg by train, note that the last train to Rothenburg departs nightly from Steinach at 20:30 (if you arrive in Steinach after 20:30, call one of the **taxi** services to get you to Rothenburg for about €20; ideally order the taxi an hour or more in advance: tel. 09861/2000, tel. 09861/7227, and tel. 09861/95100). For those leaving Rothenburg by train, the first train to Steinach departs at 06:00, the last train to Steinach at 20:00.

Steinach by train to: Rothenburg (almost hrly, 15 min, last train at 20:30), **Würzburg** (hrly, 1 hr), **Munich** (hrly, 3 hrs, 2 changes), **Frankfurt** (hrly, 2.5 hrs, change in Würzburg). The train often leaves from track 5. Train connections in Steinach are usually within a few minutes. Train info: tel. 01805-996-633.

ROMANTIC ROAD

The Romantic Road (*Romantische Strasse*) winds you past the most beautiful towns and scenery of Germany's medieval heartland. Once Germany's medieval trade route, now it's the best way to connect the dots between Füssen, Munich, and Frankfurt.

Wander through quaint hills and rolling villages, and stop wherever the cows look friendly or a town fountain beckons. My favorite sections are from Füssen to Landsberg and Rothenburg to Weikersheim. (If you're driving with limited time, you can connect Rothenburg and Munich by autobahn, but don't miss these two best sections.) Caution: The similarly promoted "Castle Road," which runs between Rothenburg and Mannheim, sounds intriguing but is nowhere near as interesting.

Throughout Bavaria you'll see colorfully ornamented may-poles decorating town squares. Many are painted in Bavaria's colors, blue and white. The decorations that line each side of the pole symbolize the crafts or businesses of that community. Each May Day they are festively replaced. Traditionally, rival communi-ties try to steal each other's maypole. Locals will guard their new pole night and day as May Day approaches. Stolen poles are ran-somed only with lots of beer for the clever thieves.

Getting around the Romantic Road

By Bus: The Deutsche Touring bus company runs buses daily between Frankfurt and Füssen in each direction (April–Oct). A second route goes daily between Munich and Rothenburg (you can transfer at Rothenburg to the other route). Buses leave promptly from train stations in towns served by a train. The €71, 11-hour ride is offered at a 60 percent discount (only €29, less if going part-way; add €1.50 per bag) to travelers who have a German railpass, Eurailpass, Europass, or a Eurail Selectpass—if Germany is one of the selected countries. Buses stop in Rothenburg (about 2 hrs) and Dinkelsbühl (about 1 hr) and briefly at a few other attractions. The driver usually hands out maps and brochures, and a taped recording narrates highlights of the journey in English. There is no quicker or easier way to travel across Germany and get such a hearty dose of its countryside. Bus reservations are free, easy, and smart—without one you can lose your seat to someone who has one (especially on summer weekends; call Munich's EurAide office at 089/593-889 at least 1 day in advance to reserve). You can start, stop, and switch over where you like, but you'll be guaranteed a seat only if you reserve each segment.

By Car: Follow the brown *Romantische Strasse* signs.

Sights along the Romantic Road

These sights are listed from south to north.

Füssen—This town, the southern terminus of the Romantic Road, is five kilometers (3 miles) from the startlingly beautiful Neuschwan-stein Castle, worthy of a stop on any sightseeing agenda. (See the Bavaria and Tirol chapter for description and accommodations.)

Romantic Road Bus Schedule (Daily, April–October)

Frankfurt	8:00	—
Würzburg	10:00	—
Arrive Rothenburg	12:45	—
Depart Rothenburg	14:30	14:30
Arrive Dinkelsbühl	15:25	15:25
Depart Dinkelsbühl	15:30	16:15
Munich	—	19:50
Füssen	20:15	—
Füssen	8:00	—
Arrive Wieskirche	8:42	—
Depart Wieskirche	8:55	—
Munich	—	9:00
Arrive Dinkelsbühl	12:45	12:45
Depart Dinkelsbühl	14:00	14:00
Arrive Rothenburg	14:30	14:50
Depart Rothenburg	16:15	—
Depart Würzburg	18:45	—
Frankfurt	20:30	

Note: These times are based on the 2001 schedule. Check www.euraide.de/ricksteves for any changes.

▲▲**Wieskirche**—This is Germany's most glorious Baroque-rococo church. Heavenly! This lovingly restored church is in a sweet meadow. Northbound Romantic Road buses stop here for 15 minutes. (See the Bavaria and Tirol chapter.)

Rottenbuch—This is a nondescript village with an impressive church in a lovely setting.

▲**Dinkelsbühl**—Rothenburg's little sister is cute enough to merit a short stop. A moat, towers, gates, and a beautifully preserved medieval wall surround this town and its interesting local museum. The Kinderzeche children's festival turns Dinkelsbühl wonderfully on end each July (July 12–21 in 2002). The helpful TI on the main street sells maps with a short walking tour (€0.25) and can help find rooms for €1.50

The Romantic Road

(Mon–Fri 09:00–18:00, Sat 10:00–13:00, 14:00–16:00, Sun
10:00–13:00, shorter hours off-season, tel. 09851/90240,
www.dinkelsbuehl.de). On Neustädtlein (outside town wall),
you'll find doubles with breakfast and TVs at friendly **Pension
Fritz Küffner** (Sb-€24, Db-€44, no CC, tel. 09851/1247,
e-mail: fritz.kueffner@t-online.de, Frau Küffner SE) and **Zur
Linde** (Sb-€25, Db-€36–41, no CC, tel. 09851/3465, Frau
Mögel NSE).

▲▲▲**Rothenburg**—See opening of this chapter for information
on Germany's best medieval town.

▲**Herrgottskapelle**—This peaceful church, graced with Tilman
Riemenschneider's greatest carved altarpiece (Easter–Oct daily
09:15–17:30, less off-season, tel. 07933/508), is 1.5 kilometers
south of Creglingen (TI tel. 07933/631) and across the street
from the Fingerhut thimble museum (€1.30, April–Oct daily
09:00–18:00, less off-season, tel. 07933/370). The southbound

Romantic Road bus stops here for 15 minutes, long enough to see one or the other.

Weikersheim—This untouristy town has a palace with fine Baroque gardens (luxurious picnic spot), a folk museum, and a picturesque town square.

▲▲**Würzburg**—This historic city, though freshly rebuilt since World War II, is worth a stop for its impressive Prince Bishop's Residenz, the bubbly Baroque chapel (*Hofkirche*) next door, and the palace's sculpted gardens. The helpful TI is on the Marktplatz (Mon–Fri 10:00–18:00, Sat 10:00–14:00, summer Sun 10:00–14:00, tel. 0931/372-398, www.wuerzburg.de). The Residenz is a Franconian Versailles, with grand rooms, 3-D art, and a tennis-court-sized fresco by Tiepolo (€4.10, April–Oct daily 9:00–18:00, summer Thu until 20:00, Nov–March daily 10:00–16:00, last entry 30 min before closing, no photos, tel. 0931/355-170). English tours are offered daily at 11:00 and 15:00 (May–Oct, confirm at TI or call ahead). Or consider the TI's walking tour at 11:00, which includes a tour of the Residenz along with a walk through the "old" city (€8, daily May–Nov, 2 hrs, all in English, includes admission to Residenz, meet at TI). The elaborate *Hofkirche* chapel is next door (as you exit the palace, go left) and the entrance to the picnic-worthy garden is just beyond. Easy parking is available. Don't confuse the Residenz (a 15-min walk from the train station) with the fortress on the hilltop.

RHINE AND
MOSEL VALLEYS

These valleys are storybook Germany, a fairy-tale world of Rhine legends and robber-baron castles. Cruise the most castle-studded stretch of the romantic Rhine as you listen for the song of the treacherous Loreley. For hands-on castle thrills, climb through the Rhineland's greatest castle, Rheinfels, above the town of St. Goar. Then, for a sleepy and laid-back alternative, mosey through the neighboring Mosel Valley.

Spend your nights in a castle-crowned village. On the Rhine, choose between St. Goar and Bacharach. On the Mosel, choose Zell.

Planning Your Time

The Rhineland does not take much time to see. The blitziest tour is an hour at the Köln cathedral (see below) and an hour looking at the castles from your train window. For a better look, however, cruise in, tour a castle or two, sleep in a genuine medieval town, and take the train out. If you have limited time, cruise less and be sure to get into a castle.

Ideally, spend two nights here, sleep in Bacharach, cruise the best hour of the river (from Bacharach to St. Goar), and tour the Rheinfels Castle. Those with more time can ride the riverside bike path. With two days and a car, visit the Rhine and the Mosel. With two days by train, see the Rhine. With three days, actually relax on the Rhine, and with four days include a sleepy night in the Mosel River Valley.

If your train travels take you through Köln, pop out to see Germany's greatest Gothic cathedral (located next to station and TI), then continue on your way (Köln has nearly hourly train connections to nearby Rhine villages).

Rhine and Mosel Valleys

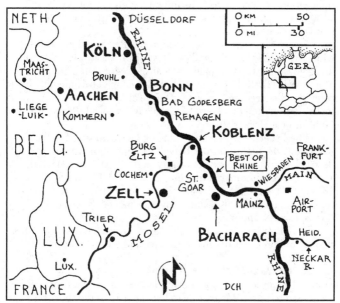

THE RHINE

Ever since Roman times, when this was the Empire's northern boundary, the Rhine has been one of the world's busiest shipping rivers. You'll see a steady flow of barges with 1,000- to 2,000-ton loads. Tourist-packed buses, hot train tracks, and highways line both banks.

Many of the castles were "robber-baron" castles, put there by petty rulers (there were 300 independent little countries in medieval Germany) to levy tolls on passing river traffic. A robber baron would put his castle on, or even in, the river. Then, often with the help of chains and a tower on the opposite bank, he'd stop each ship and get his toll. There were 10 customs stops in the 100-kilometer (60-mile) stretch between Mainz and Koblenz alone (no wonder merchants were early proponents of the creation of larger nation-states).

Some castles were built to control and protect settlements, and others were the residences of kings. As times changed, so did the lifestyles of the rich and feudal. Many castles were abandoned for more comfortable mansions in the towns.

Most Rhine castles date from the 11th, 12th, and 13th centuries. When the pope successfully asserted his power over the

German emperor in 1076, local princes ran wild over the rule of their emperor. The castles saw military action in the 1300s and 1400s, as emperors began reasserting their control over Germany's many silly kingdoms.

The castles were also involved in the Reformation wars, in which Europe's Catholic and "protesting" dynasties fought it out using a fragmented Germany as their battleground. The Thirty Years' War (1618–1648) devastated Germany. The outcome: Each ruler got the freedom to decide if his people would be Catholic or Protestant, and one-third of Germany was dead. Production of Gummi Bears ceased entirely.

The French—who feared a strong Germany and felt the Rhine was the logical border between them and Germany—destroyed most of the castles prophylactically (Louis XIV in the 1680s, the revolutionary army in the 1790s, and Napoleon in 1806). They were often rebuilt in neo-Gothic style in the Romantic Age—the late 1800s—and today are enjoyed as restaurants, hotels, hostels, and museums.

For more information on the Rhine, visit www.loreleytal.com (heavy on hotels but has maps, photos, and a little history).

Getting around the Rhine

While the Rhine flows north from Switzerland to Holland, the scenic stretch from Mainz to Koblenz hoards all the touristic charm. Studded with the crenelated cream of Germany's castles, it bustles with boats, trains, and highway traffic. Have fun exploring with a mix of big steamers, tiny ferries, bikes, and trains.

By Boat: While many travelers do the whole trip by boat, the most scenic hour is from St. Goar to Bacharach. Sit on the top deck with your handy Rhine map-guide (or the kilometer-keyed tour in this chapter) and enjoy the parade of castles, towns, boats, and vineyards.

There are several boat companies, but most travelers sail on the bigger, more expensive, and romantic Köln-Düsseldorf (K-D) line (free with a consecutive-day Eurailpass or with dated Eurail Flexipass, Europass, Eurail Selectpass, or German railpass—but it uses up a day of any flexipass; otherwise about €8.25 for the first hour, then progressively cheaper per hr; the recommended Bacharach-St. Goar trip costs €8.25 one-way, €10 round-trip; tel. 06741/1634 in St. Goar, tel. 06743/1322 in Bacharach, www .k-d.com). Boats run daily in both directions from April through October, with no boats off-season. Complete, up-to-date schedules are posted in any station, Rhineland hotel, TI, bank, current Thomas Cook Timetable, or at www.euraide.de/ricksteves. Purchase tickets at the dock up to five minutes before departure. The boat is rarely full. (Confirm times at your hotel the night before.)

The smaller Bingen-Rüdesheimer line is 25 percent cheaper

than K-D (railpasses not valid, buy tickets on boat, tel. 06721/ 14140), with three two-hour round-trip St. Goar-to-Bacharach trips daily in summer (about €6.50 one-way, €9 round-trip; departing St. Goar at 11:00, 14:10, and 16:10, departing Bacharach at 10:10, 12:00, and 15:00).

Drivers have these options: (1) skip the boat; (2) take a round-trip cruise from St. Goar or Bacharach; (3) draw pretzels and let the loser drive, prepare the picnic, and meet the boat; (4) rent a bike, bring it on the boat for free, and bike back; or (5) take the boat one-way and return by train.

By Train: Hourly milk-run trains down the Rhine hit every town: St. Goar–Bacharach, 12 min; Bacharach–Mainz, 60 min; Mainz–Frankfurt, 45 min. Some train schedules list St. Goar but not Bacharach as a stop, but any schedule listing St. Goar also stops at Bacharach. Tiny stations are unmanned—buy tickets at the platform machines or on the train. Prices are cheap (e.g., €2.60 between St. Goar and Bacharach).

By Bike: In Bacharach try Hotel Hillen (€5/half day, €8/day, cheaper for guests, 20 bikes) or Hotel Gelberhof (€13/day for 10-speeds or trekking bikes, €2.60 for child's seat, tel. 06743/910-100, ring bell when closed).

You can bike on either side of the Rhine, but, if you want a designated bike path, stay on the west side. The path runs between Koblenz and Bingen, about 60 kilometers (35 miles). The pleasant stretch between Bacharach and Bingen hugs the riverside (leaving Bacharach, after you pass campground, head down to path bordering river). The path is also good from St. Goar to Bacharach, but it's closer to the highway.

Consider renting a bike in Bacharach and taking it on the boat to Bingen and biking back, visiting Rheinstein Castle (you're on your own to wander the well-furnished castle) and Reichenstein Castle (admittance with groups), and maybe even taking a ferry across the river to Kaub (where a tiny boat shuttles sightseers to the better-from-a-distance castle on the island).

By Ferry: While there are no bridges between Koblenz and Mainz, there are car-and-passenger ferries about every five kilometers, running constantly and cheaply (adult round-trip-€1, car and driver round-trip-€4.60). Ferries near St. Goar and Bacharach run daily in the summer from about 06:00 to 20:00 and connect: Bingen–Rüdesheim, Lorch–Niederheimbach, Engelsburg–Kaub, and St. Goar–St.Goarshausen. Ask at the TI for more details.

Sights—The Romantic Rhine

These sights are listed from north to south, Koblenz to Bingen.
▲▲▲**Der Romantische Rhein Blitz Zug Fahrt**—One of Europe's great train thrills is zipping along the Rhine in this fast train tour. Here's a quick and easy, from-the-train-window tour

Best of the Rhine

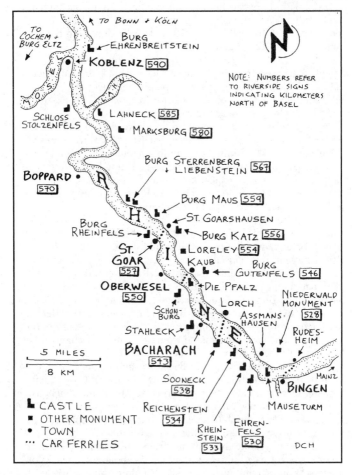

NOTE: NUMBERS REFER
TO RIVERSIDE SIGNS
INDICATING KILOMETERS
NORTH OF BASEL

L CASTLE
■ OTHER MONUMENT
● TOWN
··· CAR FERRIES

(also works for car, bike, or best by boat, you can cut in anywhere) that skips the syrupy myths that fill normal Rhine guides. For more information than necessary, buy the handy *Rhine Guide from Mainz to Cologne* (€3.60 book with foldout map, at most shops or TIs).

Sit on the left (river) side of the train or boat going south from Koblenz. While nearly all the castles listed are viewed from this side, clear a path to the right window for the times I yell, "Crossover!"

You'll notice large black-and-white kilometer markers along the riverbank. I erected these years ago to make this tour easier to follow. They tell the distance from the Rhinefalls where the Rhine

Rhine Cruise Schedule

Koblenz	Boppard	St. Goar	Bacharach
—	09:00	10:15	11:25
09:00	11:00	12:20	13:35
11:00	13:00	14:15	15:25
14:00	16:00	17:15	18:25
11:05*	11:30*	11:50*	12:10*
13:00	11:50	10:55	10:15
14:20	12:50	11:55	11:15
—	13:50	12:55	12:15
18:00	16:50	15:55	15:15
20:00	18:50	17:55	17:15

*Hydrofoil, Koblenz–Bacharach, €46 round-trip, railpass holders receive discount but must pay supplement.

Note: These times are based on the 2001 schedule. Check www.euraide.de/ricksteves for any changes. Boats run May through September and part of April and October; no boats run November through March.

leaves Switzerland and becomes navigable. Now the river-barge pilots have accepted these as navigational aids as well. We're tackling just 58 kilometers (36 miles) of the 1,320-kilometer-long (820-mile) Rhine. Your Blitz Rhine Tour starts at Koblenz and heads upstream to Bingen. If you're going the other direction, it still works. Just hold the book upside down.

Km 590: Koblenz—This Rhine blitz starts with Romantic Rhine thrills—at Koblenz. Koblenz is not a nice city (it was really hit hard in World War II), but its place as the historic *Deutsche Ecke* (German corner)—the tip of land where the Mosel joins the Rhine—gives it a certain historic charm. Koblenz, Latin for "confluence," has Roman origins. Walk through the park, noticing the reconstructed memorial to the Kaiser. Across the river, the yellow Ehrenbreitstein Castle now houses a hostel. It's a 30-minute hike from the station to the Koblenz boat dock.

Km 585: Burg Lahneck—Above the modern autobahn bridge over the Lahn River, this castle (*Burg*) was built in 1240 to defend local silver mines, ruined by the French in 1688 and rebuilt in the 1850s in neo-Gothic style. Burg Lahneck faces the yellow Schloss Stolzenfels (out of view above the train, a 10-min climb from tiny car park, open for touring, closed Mon).

Km 580: Marksburg—This castle (black and white with the three modern chimneys behind it, just after town of Spay) is the best looking of all the Rhine castles and the only surviving medieval castle on the Rhine. Because of its commanding position, it was never attacked. It's now open as a museum with a medieval interior second only to the Mosel's Burg Eltz (€4.50, daily 10:00–17:00, call ahead to see if a rare English tour is scheduled, tel. 02627/206, www.marksburg.de).

Km 570: Boppard—Once a Roman town, Boppard has some impressive remains of fourth-century walls. Notice the Roman towers and the substantial chunk of Roman wall near the train station, just above the main square. Below the square is a fascinating church. Notice the carved Romanesque crazies at the doorway. Inside, to the right of the entrance, you'll see Christian symbols from Roman times. Also notice the painted arches and vaults. Originally most Romanesque churches were painted this way. Down by the river, look for the high water (*Hochwasser*) marks on the arches from various flood years. (You'll find these flood marks throughout the Rhine and Mosel Valleys.)

Km 567: Burg Sterrenberg and Burg Liebenstein—These are the "Hostile Brothers" castles across from Bad Salzig. Take the wall between the castles (actually designed to improve the defenses of both castles), add two greedy and jealous brothers and a fair maiden, and create your own legend. The castles are restaurants today.

Km 559: Burg Maus—The Maus ("Mouse") got its name because the next castle was owned by the Katzenelnbogen family. ("Katz" means "cat.") In the 1300s, it was considered a state-of-the-art fortification . . . until Napoleon had it blown up in 1806 with state-of-the-art explosives. It was rebuilt true to its original plans around 1900.

Km 557: St. Goar and Rheinfels Castle—Cross to the other side of the train. The pleasant town of St. Goar was named for a sixth-century hometown monk. It originated in Celtic times (really old) as a place where sailors would stop, catch their breath, send home a postcard, and give thanks after surviving the seductive and treacherous Loreley crossing. St. Goar is worth a stop to explore its mighty Rheinfels Castle. (For information on a guided castle tour and accommodations, see below.)

Km 556: Burg Katz—From the town of St. Goar, you'll see Burg Katz (Katzenelnbogen) across the river. Together, Burg Katz (built in 1371) and Rheinfels Castle had a clear view up and down the river and effectively controlled traffic. There was absolutely no duty-free shopping on the medieval Rhine. Katz got Napoleoned in 1806 and rebuilt around 1900. Today it's an expensive tourist hotel.

About Km 555: You'll see the statue of the Loreley, the beautiful but deadly nymph (see next listing for legend), at the

River Trade and Barge Watching

The river is great for barge watching. Since ancient times this has been a highway for trade. Today the world's biggest port (Rotterdam) waits at the mouth of the river. Barge workers are almost a subculture. Many own their own ships. The captain (and family) live in the stern. Workers live in the bow. The family car often decorates the bow like a shiny hood ornament. In the Rhine town of Kaub there's even a boarding school for the children of the Rhine merchant marine. The flag of the boat's home country flies in the stern (German, Swiss, Dutch—horizontal red, white, and blue; or French—vertical red, white, and blue). Logically, imports go upstream (Japanese cars, coal, and oil) and exports go downstream (German cars, chemicals, and pharmaceuticals). A clever captain manages to ship goods in each direction.

At this point tugs can push a floating train of up to five barges at once. Upstream it gets steeper and they can push only one at a time. Before modern shipping, horses dragged boats upstream (the faint remains of the towpaths survive at points along the river). From 1873 to 1900 they actually laid a chain from Bonn to Bingen, and boats with cogwheels and steam engines hoisted themselves slowly upstream. Today 265 million tons are shipped each year along the 850 navigable kilometers (528 miles) from Basel on the Swiss border to Rotterdam on the Atlantic.

While riverside navigational aids are ignored by camera-toting tourists, they are of vital interest to captains who don't wish to meet the Loreley. Boats pass on the right unless they clearly signal otherwise with a large blue sign. Since downstream ships can't stop or maneuver as freely, upstream boats are expected to do the tricky do-si-do work. Cameras monitor traffic all along and relay warnings of oncoming ships via large triangular signals posted before narrow and troublesome bends in the river. There may be two or three triangles per signpost, depending upon how many "sectors," or segments, of the river are covered. The lowest triangle indicates the nearest stretch of river. Each triangle tells if there's a ship in that sector. When the bottom side of a triangle is lit, that sector is empty. When the left side is lit, an oncoming ship is in that sector.

end of a long spit—built to give barges protection from vicious icebergs that occasionally rage down the river in the winter. The actual Loreley, a cliff, is just ahead.

Km 554: The Loreley—Steep a big slate rock in centuries of legend and it becomes a tourist attraction, the ultimate Rhine-stone. The Loreley (two flags on top, name painted near shore-line), rising 135 meters (450 feet) over the narrowest and deepest point of the Rhine, has long been important. It was a holy site in pre-Roman days. The fine echoes here—thought to be ghostly voices—fertilized the legendary soil.

Because of the reefs just upstream (at kilometer 552), many ships never made it to St. Goar. Sailors (after days on the river) blamed their misfortune on a *wunderbares Fräulein* whose long blonde hair almost covered her body. Heinrich Heine's *Song of Loreley* (the Cliffs Notes version is on local postcards) tells the story of a count who sent his men to kill or capture this siren after she distracted his horny son, causing him to drown. When the soldiers cornered the nymph in her cave, she called her father (Father Rhine) for help. Huge waves, the likes of which you'll never see today, rose from the river and carried Loreley to safety. And she has never been seen since.

But alas, when the moon shines brightly and the tour buses are parked, a soft, playful Rhine whine can still be heard from the Loreley. As you pass, listen carefully ("Sailors…sailors…over my bounding mane").

Km 552: Killer reefs, marked by red-and-green buoys, are called the "Seven Maidens."

Km 550: Oberwesel—Cross to the other side of the train. Oberwesel was a Celtic town in 400 B.C., then a Roman military station. It now boasts some of the best Roman wall and tower remains on the Rhine and the commanding Schönburg Castle. Notice how many of the train tunnels have entrances designed like medieval turrets—they were actually built in the Romantic 19th century. OK, back to the riverside.

Km 546: Burg Gutenfels and Pfalz Castle: The Classic Rhine View—Burg Gutenfels (see white painted "Hotel" sign) and the shipshape Pfalz Castle (built in the river in the 1300s) worked very effectively to tax medieval river traffic. The town of Kaub grew rich as Pfalz raised its chains when boats came and lowered them only when the merchants had paid their duty. Those who didn't pay spent time touring its prison, on a raft at the bottom of its well. In 1504, a pope called for the destruction of Pfalz, but a six-week siege failed. Notice the overhanging outhouse (tiny white room with faded medieval stains between two wooden ones). Pfalz is tourable but bare and dull (€1.50 ferry from Kaub, €2 entry, Tue–Sun 09:00–13:00, 14:00–17:00, closed Mon, tel. 06774/570).

In Kaub, a green statue honors the German General Blücher.

He was Napoleon's nemesis. In 1813, as Napoleon fought his way back to Paris after his disastrous Russian campaign, he stopped at Mainz—hoping to fend off the Germans and Russians pursuing him by controlling that strategic bridge. Blücher tricked Napoleon. By building the first major pontoon bridge of its kind here at the Pfalz Castle, he crossed the Rhine and outflanked the French. Two years later Blücher and Wellington teamed up to defeat Napoleon once and for all at Waterloo.

Km 544: The "Raft Busters"—Immediately before Bacharach, at the top of the island, buoys mark a gang of rocks notorious for busting up rafts. The Black Forest is upstream. It was poor, and wood was its best export. Black Foresters would ride log booms down the Rhine to the Ruhr (where their timber fortified coal-mine shafts) or to Holland (where logs were sold to shipbuilders). If they could navigate the sweeping bend just before Bacharach and then survive these "raft busters," they'd come home reckless and romantic, the German folkloric equivalent of American cowboys after payday.

Km 543: Bacharach and Burg Stahleck—Cross to the other side of the train. Bacharach is a great stop (see details and accommodations below). Some of the Rhine's best wine is from this town, whose name means "altar to Bacchus." Local vintners brag that the medieval Pope Pius II ordered it by the cartload. Perched above the town, the 13th-century Burg Stahleck is now a hostel.

Km 540: Lorch—This pathetic stub of a castle is barely visible from the road. Notice the small car ferry (3/hr, 10 min), one of several between Mainz and Koblenz, where there are no bridges.

Km 538: Castle Sooneck—Cross back to the other side of the train. Built in the 11th century, this castle was twice destroyed by people sick and tired of robber barons.

Km 534: Burg Reichenstein, and **Km 533: Burg Rheinstein**—Stay on the other side of the train to see two of the first castles to be rebuilt in the Romantic era. Both are privately owned, tourable, and connected by a pleasant trail.

Km 530: Ehrenfels Castle—Opposite Bingerbrück and the Bingen station, you'll see the ghostly Ehrenfels Castle (clobbered by the Swedes in 1636 and by the French in 1689). Since it had no view of the river traffic to the north, the owner built the cute little *Mäuseturm* (Mouse Tower) on an island (the yellow tower you'll see near the train station today). Rebuilt in the 1800s in neo-Gothic style, today it's used as a Rhine navigation signal station.

Km 528: Niederwald Monument—Across from the Bingen station on a hilltop is the 36-meter-high (120-foot) Niederwald monument, a memorial built with 32 tons of bronze in 1877 to commemorate "the reestablishment of the German Empire." A lift takes tourists to this statue from the famous and extremely touristy wine town of Rüdesheim.

Our tour is over. From Bingen you can continue your journey (or return to Koblenz) by train or boat.

BACHARACH

Once prosperous from the wine and wood trade, Bacharach is now just a pleasant half-timbered village working hard to keep its tourists happy.

The **TI** is on the main street in the Posthof courtyard next to the church (Mon–Fri 09:00–17:00, Sat 10:00–16:00, closed Sun, shorter hrs off-season, Internet access–€6/hr, Oberstrasse 45, from station turn right and walk down main street with castle high on your left and walk about 5 blocks, tel. 06743/919-303). The TI stores bags for daytrippers, provides ferry schedules, and sells the handy *Rhine Guide from Mainz to Cologne* (€3.60).

The **Jost** beer-stein stores carry most everything a shopper could want. One shop is across from the church in the main square, the other—which offers more deals—is a block away on Rosenstrasse 16 in a building that also houses the **post office** (post office closed 12:30–14:00; Jost store hours: Mon–Fri 08:30–18:00, Sat 08:30–17:00, Sun 10:00–17:00, Rosenstrasse shop closed Sun, ships overseas, 10 percent discount with this book, CC, tel. 06743/1224, www.phil-jost-germany.com, e-mail: phil.jost@t-online.de). The Josts can offer sightseeing advice, send faxes, and reserve German hotels for travelers (reasonable charge for phone and fax fees).

Woodburn House, which engraves woody signs and knick-knacks, lets travelers store bags while they look for a room and gives readers with this book a 10 percent discount on purchases (across from Altes Haus, Oberstrasse 60, Frances Geuss SE).

Get acquainted with Bacharach by taking a **walking tour**. Charming Herr Rolf Jung, retired headmaster of the Bacharach school, is a superb English-speaking guide (€26, 90 min, call him to reserve a tour, tel. 06743/1519). The TI also has a list of other English-speaking guides, or take the self-guided walk, described below. For accommodations, see "Sleeping on the Rhine," below.

Sights—Bacharach

▲▲**Introductory Bacharach Walk**—Start at the Köln-Düsseldorf ferry dock (next to a fine picnic park). View the town from the parking lot—a modern landfill. The Rhine used to lap against Bacharach's town wall, just over the present-day highway. Every few years the river floods, covering the highway with several meters of water. The **castle** on the hill is a youth hostel. Two of its original 16 towers are visible from here (up to five if you look real hard). The huge roadside wine keg declares this town was built on the wine trade.

Reefs up the river forced boats to unload upriver and reload here. Consequently, Bacharach became the biggest wine trader

Bacharach

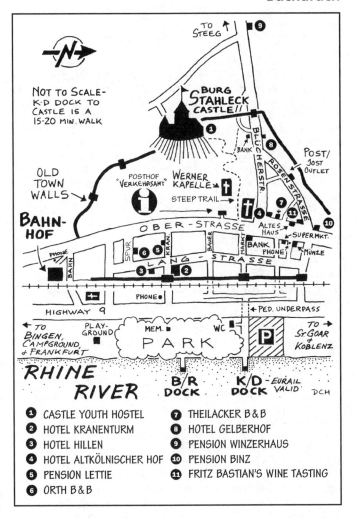

NOT TO SCALE-
K·D DOCK TO
CASTLE IS A
15-20 MIN. WALK

TO STEEG

BURG STAHLECK CASTLE

OLD TOWN WALLS

BAHN-HOF

POSTHOF "Verkehrsamt"

WERNER KAPELLE

STEEP TRAIL

BANK

BLÜCHERSTR.

POST/ JOST OUTLET

ROSEN-STRASSE

O B E R - S T R A S S E

ALTES HAUS

SUPERMKT.

SPUR

KRAN

BAUER

MARKT

L A N G - S T R A S S E

BANK PHONE

MÜNZE

PHONE

BAHN

PHONE

HIGHWAY 9

PED. UNDERPASS

TO BINGEN, CAMPGROUND, + FRANKFURT

PLAY-GROUND

MEM.

WC

P A R K

P

TO St.GOAR + KOBLENZ

RHINE RIVER

B/R DOCK

K/D DOCK – EURAIL VALID

DCH

❶ CASTLE YOUTH HOSTEL
❷ HOTEL KRANENTURM
❸ HOTEL HILLEN
❹ HOTEL ALTKÖLNISCHER HOF
❺ PENSION LETTIE
❻ ORTH B & B
❼ THEILACKER B & B
❽ HOTEL GELBERHOF
❾ PENSION WINZERHAUS
❿ PENSION BINZ
⓫ FRITZ BASTIAN'S WINE TASTING

on the Rhine. A riverfront crane hoisted huge kegs of prestigious "Bacharach" wine (which in practice was from anywhere in the region). The tour buses next to the dock and the flags of the biggest spenders along the highway remind you today's economy is basically tourism.

At the big town map and (dirty) public WC, take the underpass, ascend on the right, make a U-turn, then walk under the train tracks through the medieval gate (one out of an original six 14th-century gates) and to the two-tone Protestant **church**, which marks the town center.

From this intersection, Bacharach's main street (Oberstrasse) goes right to the half-timbered, red-and-white Altes Haus (from 1368, the oldest house in town) and left way down to the train station. To the left (or south) of the church, the golden horn hangs over the old **Posthof** (and TI). The post horn symbolizes the postal service throughout Europe. In olden days, when the postman blew this, traffic stopped and the mail sped through. Step into the courtyard. Notice the fascist eagle (from 1936, on the left as you enter) and the fine view of a chapel and church. This post station dates from 1724, when stagecoaches ran from Köln to Frankfurt.

Two hundred years ago this was the only road along the Rhine. Napoleon widened it to fit his cannon wagons. The steps alongside the church lead to the castle. Return to the church.

Inside the church you'll find grotesque and brightly painted capitals and a mix of round Romanesque and pointed Gothic arches. In the upper left corner, some medieval frescoes survive where an older Romanesque arch was cut by a pointed Gothic one.

Continue down Oberstrasse past the Altes Haus to the **old mint** (*Münze*), marked by a crude coin in its sign. Across from the mint, the wine garden of Fritz Bastian is the liveliest place in town after dark. Above you in the vineyards stands a ghostly black-and-gray tower—your destination.

Take the next left (Rosenstrasse) and wander 30 meters (98 feet) up to the **well**. Notice the sundial and the wall painting of 1632 Bacharach with its walls intact. Climb the tiny-stepped lane behind the well up into the vineyard and to the tower. The slate steps lead to a small path that deposits you at a viewpoint atop the stubby remains of the old town wall, just above the tower's base (if signs indicate that the path is closed, get as close to the tower base as possible).

A grand medieval town spreads before you. When Frankfurt had 15,000 residents, medieval Bacharach had 6,000. For 300 years (1300–1600) Bacharach was big, rich, and politically powerful.

From this perch you can see the chapel ruins and six of the nine surviving **city towers**. Visually trace the wall to the castle, home of one of seven electors who voted for the Holy Roman Emperor in 1275. To protect their own power, these elector princes did their best to choose the weakest guy on the ballot. The elector from Bacharach helped select a two-bit prince named Rudolf von Hapsburg (from a two-bit castle in Switzerland). The underestimated Rudolf brutally silenced the robber barons along the Rhine and established the mightiest dynasty in European history. His family line, the Hapsburgs, ruled the Austro-Hungarian Empire until 1918.

Plagues, fires, and the Thirty Years' War (1618–1648) finally did Bacharach in. The town has slumbered for several centuries, with a population of about a thousand.

In the mid-19th century, artists and writers such as Victor Hugo were charmed by the Rhineland's romantic mix of past glory, present poverty, and rich legend. They put this part of the Rhine on the old "grand tour" map as the "Romantic Rhine." Victor Hugo pondered the ruined 15th-century chapel, which you can see under the castle. In his 1842 travel book, *Rhein Reise* (*Rhine Travels*), he wrote, "No doors, no roof or windows, a magnificent skeleton puts its silhouette against the sky. Above it, the ivy-covered castle ruins provide a fitting crown. This is Bacharach, land of fairy tales, covered with legends and sagas." If you're enjoying the Romantic Rhine, thank Victor Hugo and company.

To get back into town, take the path that leads along the wall up the valley to the next tower, then down onto the street. Follow the road under the gate and back into the center.

ST. GOAR

St. Goar is a classic Rhine town—its hulk of a castle overlooking a half-timbered shopping street and leafy riverside park busy with sightseeing ships and contented strollers. From the boat dock, the main drag—a pedestrian mall—cuts through town before winding up to the castle. Rheinfels Castle, once the mightiest on the Rhine, is the single best Rhineland ruin to explore.

The St. Goar **TI**, which books rooms and offers a €0.50 left-luggage service, is on the pedestrian street, three blocks from the K-D boat dock (May–Oct Mon–Fri 08:00–12:30, 14:00–17:00, Sat 10:00–12:00, closed Sun and earlier in winter, sells *Rhine Guide from Mainz to Cologne*; if you're coming from train station, take a quick right, go around church, walk toward river and turn left on Heer Strasse, TI is 100 meters down on the right; tel. 06741/383).

St. Goar's waterfront park is hungry for a picnic. The small EDEKA **supermarket** on the main street is great for picnic fixings (Mon–Fri 08:00–18:30, Sat 08:00–16:00, limited hrs on Sun in summer).

The friendly and helpful Montag family in the shop under Hotel Montag has Rhine guidebooks (Koblenz-Mainz, €4), fine steins, and copies of this year's *Rick Steves' Germany, Austria & Switzerland* guidebook. They offer 10 percent off any of their souvenirs for travelers with this book (€5 minimum purchase) and offer Internet access (€8/hr).

For a good two-hour **hike** from St. Goar to the Loreley viewpoint, catch the ferry across to St. Goarshausen (€1.30 round-trip, 4/hr), hike up past the Katz castle (now a pricey hotel for tourists), and traverse along the hillside, always bearing right toward the river. You'll pass through a residential area, hike

St. Goar

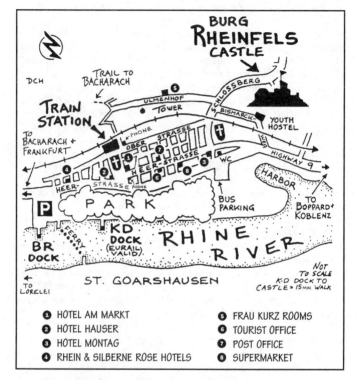

1 HOTEL AM MARKT
2 HOTEL HAUSER
3 HOTEL MONTAG
4 RHEIN & SILBERNE ROSE HOTELS
5 FRAU KURZ ROOMS
6 TOURIST OFFICE
7 POST OFFICE
8 SUPERMARKET

down a 50-meter (165-feet) path through trees, then cross a wheat field until you reach an amphitheater adjacent to the Loreley overview (restaurant available). From here it's a steep 15-minute hike down to the river where a riverfront trail takes you back to the St. Goarshausen–to–St. Goar ferry.

Sights—St. Goar's Rheinfels Castle

▲▲▲**Self-Guided Tour**—Sitting like a dead pit bull above St. Goar, this mightiest of Rhine castles rumbles with ghosts from its hard-fought past. Burg Rheinfels (built in 1245) withstood a siege of 28,000 French troops in 1692. But in 1797 the French Revolutionary army destroyed it.

Rheinfels was huge. In fact, it was the biggest castle on the Rhine and was used as a quarry. Today this hollow but interesting shell offers your single best hands-on ruined-castle experience on the river (€3, daily 09:00–18:00, last entry at 17:00, only Sat–Sun in winter, gather 15 English-speaking tourists and get an English tour, tel. 06741/7753). The castle map is mediocre; the English booklet is better, with history and illustrations (€1.80).

If planning to explore the underground passages, bring a flashlight, buy a tiny one (€2.60 at entry), or do it by candlelight (museum sells candles with matches, €0.50). To get to the castle from St. Goar's boat dock or train station, take a steep 15-minute hike, a €5 taxi ride (€6 for a minibus, tel. 06741/7011), or the goofy tourist train (€2.60, 3/hr, daily 10:00–17:00, runs from square between station and dock, also stops at Hotel Montag, complete with lusty music). A handy WC is in the castle court-yard under the stairs to the restaurant entry. If it's damp, be careful of slippery stones.

Rather than wander aimlessly, visit the castle by following this tour: From the ticket gate, walk straight and uphill. Pass *Grosser Keller* on the left (where we'll end this tour), walk through an internal gate past the *zu den gedeckten Wehrgängen* sign on the right (where we'll pass later) to the museum (daily 09:00–12:00, 13:00–17:30) in the only finished room of the castle.

1. Museum and castle model: The two-meter-tall (7-foot) carved stone (*Keltische Säule von Pfalzfeld*) immediately inside the door—a tombstone from a nearby Celtic grave—is from 600 years before Christ. There were people here long before the Romans... and this castle. The chair next to the door is an old library chair. Fold it up and it becomes stairs for getting to the highest shelves.

The castle history exhibit in the center of the room is well described in English. The massive fortification was the only Rhineland castle to withstand Louis XIV's assault during the 17th century. At the far end of the room is a model reconstruction of the castle showing how much bigger it was before French revolutionary troops destroyed it in the 18th century. Study this. Find where you are (hint: look for the tall tower). This was the living quarters of the original castle, which was only the smallest ring of buildings around the tiny central courtyard (13th century, marked by red well). The ramparts were added in the 14th century. By 1650, the fortress was largely complete. Ever since its destruction by the French in 1797, it's had no military value. While no WWII bombs were wasted on this ruin, it served St. Goar as a quarry for generations. The basement of the museum shows the castle phar-macy and an exhibit on Rhine region odds and ends, including tools and an 1830 loom.

Exit the museum and walk 30 meters (100 feet) directly out, slightly uphill into the castle courtyard.

2. Medieval castle courtyard: Five hundred years ago the entire castle circled this courtyard. The place was self-sufficient and ready for a siege with a bakery, pharmacy, herb garden, ani-mals, brewery, well (top of yard), and livestock. During peacetime, 300 to 600 people lived here; during a siege there would be as

St. Goar's Rheinfels Castle

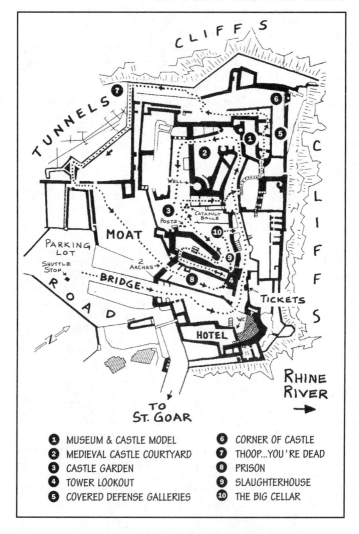

1 MUSEUM & CASTLE MODEL	**6** CORNER OF CASTLE
2 MEDIEVAL CASTLE COURTYARD	**7** THOOP...YOU'RE DEAD
3 CASTLE GARDEN	**8** PRISON
4 TOWER LOOKOUT	**9** SLAUGHTERHOUSE
5 COVERED DEFENSE GALLERIES	**10** THE BIG CELLAR

many as 4,500. The walls were plastered and painted white. Bits of the original 13th-century plaster survive.

Continue through the courtyard, out *Erste Schildmauer*, turn left into the next courtyard, and walk to the two old, black, upright posts. Find the pyramid of stone catapult balls.

3. Castle garden: Catapult balls like these were too expensive not to recycle. If ever used, they'd be retrieved after the battle. Across from the balls is a well—essential for any castle during the age of sieging. The old posts are for the ceremonial baptizing of new members of the local trading league. While this guild goes back centuries, today it's a social club that fills this court with a huge wine party the third weekend of each September.

If weary, skip to 5; otherwise, climb the cobbled path up to the castle's best viewpoint up where the German flag waves.

4. Highest castle tower lookout: Enjoy a great view of the river, castle, and the forest that was once all part of this castle. Remember, the fortress once covered five times the land it does today. Originally this castle was no bigger than the two you see over the river. Notice how the other castles don't poke above the top of the Rhine canyon. That would make them easy for invading armies to see.

Return to the catapult balls, walk down the road, go through the tunnel, veer left through the arch marked *zu den gedeckten Wehrgängen*, go down two flights of stairs, and turn left into the dark covered passageway. We now begin a rectangular walk taking us completely around the perimeter of the castle.

5. Covered defense galleries: Soldiers—the castle's "minutemen"—had a short commute: defensive positions on the outside, home in the holes below on the left. Even though these living quarters were padded with straw, life was unpleasant. A peasant was lucky to live beyond age 28.

Continue straight through the gallery and to the corner of the castle, where you'll see a white painted arrow at eye level.

6. Corner of castle: Look up. A three-story, half-timbered building originally rose beyond the highest stone fortification. The two stone tongues near the top just around the corner supported the toilet. (Insert your own joke here.) Turn around. The crossbow slits below the white arrow were once steeper. The bigger hole on the riverside was for hot pitch, etc.

Follow that white arrow along the outside to the next corner. Midway you'll pass stairs leading down *zu den Minengängen* (sign on upper left). Adventurers with flashlights can detour here. You may come out around the next corner. Otherwise, stay with me, walking level to the corner. At the corner, turn left.

7. Thoop . . . you're dead. Look ahead at the smartly placed crossbow arrow slit. While you're lying there, notice the stone work. The little round holes were for scaffolds used as they built up. They indicate this stonework is original. Notice also the fine stonework on the chutes. More boiling oil . . . now you're toast too. Continue along. At the railing, look up the valley and uphill where the fort existed. Below, just outside the wall, is land where attackers would gather.

To the left you'll find a metal gate and stairs. Walk down into small, dark tunnels that were once filled with explosives and ran under the land just outside the walls. Keep your bearings by following the faded white marks on the ceiling. To protect their castle, the Rheinfellers cleverly built tunnels topped by thin slate roofs and packed with explosives. By detonating the explosives when under attack, they could kill hundreds of approaching invaders without damaging the castle. In 1626, a handful of underground Protestant Germans blew 300 Catholic Spaniards to—they figured—hell.

Continue along the perimeter, jog left, go down five steps and into an open field, and walk toward the wooden bridge. You may detour here into the passageway marked *13 Hals Graben*. The old wooden bridge is actually modern. Angle left through two arches and through the rough entry to *Verlies* on the left.

8. Prison: This is one of six dungeons. You walked through a door prisoners only dreamed of 400 years ago. They came and went through the little square hole in the ceiling. The holes in the walls supported timbers that politely gave as many as 15 residents something to sit on to keep them out of the filthy slop that gathered on the floor. Twice a day they were given bread and water. Some prisoners actually survived five years in here. The town could torture and execute; the castle had permission only to imprison criminals in these dungeons.

Continue through the next arch, under the white arrow, and turn left and walk 36 meters (120 feet) to the *Schlachthaus.*

9. Slaughterhouse: A castle was prepared to survive a six-month siege. With 4,000 people, that's a lot of provisions. The cattle that lived within the walls were slaughtered here. Notice the drainage gutters for water and blood. "Running water" came through from above... one bucket at a time.

Back outside, climb the modern stairs to the left. A skinny passage leads you into...

10. The big cellar: This *Grosser Keller* was a big pantry. When the castle was smaller, this was the original moat—you can see the rough lower parts of the wall. The original floor was 1.5 meters (5 feet) deeper. When the castle expanded, the moat became the cellar. Above the entry, holes mark spots where timbers made a storage loft, perhaps filled with grain. Kegs of wine lined the walls. Part of a soldier's pay was three liters of wine a day. In the back, an arch leads to the wine cellar where finer wine was kept. The castle consumed 200,000 liters of wine a year. The count owned the surrounding farmland. Farmers got to keep 20 percent of their production. Later, in more liberal feudal times, the nobility let them keep 40 percent. Today the German government leaves the workers with 60 percent... and provides a few more services.

Climb out, turn right, and leave. For coffee on a great view terrace, visit the Rheinfels Castle Hotel, opposite the entrance (WC at base of steps).

Sleeping on the Rhine
(€1.10 = about $1)

Sleep Code: **S** = Single, **D** = Double/Twin, **T** = Triple, **Q** = Quad, **b** = bathroom, **s** = shower only, **CC** = Credit Cards accepted, **no CC** = Credit Cards not accepted, **SE** = Speaks English, **NSE** = No English. All hotels speak some English. Breakfast is included unless otherwise noted.

The Rhine is an easy place for cheap sleeps. *Zimmer* and *Gasthäuser* with €20 beds abound (and *Zimmer* normally discount their prices for longer stays). A few exceptional Rhine-area hostels offer €14 beds (for travelers of any age). Each town's TI is eager to set you up, and finding a room should be easy any time of year (except for winefest weekends in September and October). Bacharach and St. Goar, the best towns for an overnight stop, are about 16 kilometers (10 miles) apart, connected by milk-run trains, riverboats, and a riverside bike path. Bacharach is more interesting, but St. Goar has the famous castle (see "St. Goar," above). Parking in Bacharach is simple along the highway next to the tracks (3-hr daytime limit is generally not enforced) or in the boat parking lot. Parking in St. Goar is tighter; ask at your hotel.

Sleeping in Bacharach
(country code: 49, area code: 06743, zip code: 55422)

See map on page 353 for location. A few guest houses (and restaurants) in Bacharach post signs reading "Recommended by Rick Steves." This is not always true. If they're not listed in the current edition of this book, I don't recommend them.

Hotels

Hotel Kranenturm gives you castle ambience without the climb. It offers a good combination of comfort and hotel privacy with *Zimmer* coziness, a central location, and a medieval atmosphere. Every room is different. Run by hardworking Kurt Engel, his intense but friendly wife, Fatima, and attentive Schumi the waiter, this hotel is actually part of the medieval fortification. Its former *Kran* (crane) towers are now round rooms—great for medievalists. When the riverbank was higher, cranes on this tower loaded barrels of wine onto Rhine boats. Hotel Kranenturm is five meters (16 feet) from the train tracks, but a combination of medieval sturdiness, triple-paned windows, and included earplugs makes the riverside rooms sleepable (Sb-€41–43, Db-€54–60, Tb-€74–80, Qb-€92–95, the lower price is for off-season or stays of at least 2 nights in high season, family deals, CC but prefer cash, Rhine views come with ripping train noise, back rooms—some with castle views—are quieter, all rooms with cable TV, kid friendly, Langstrasse 30, tel. 06743/1308, fax 06743/1021, e-mail: hotel-kranenturm@t-online.de). Kurt, a good cook,

serves €6 to €14 dinners; try his ice-cream special for dessert.
Trade travel stories on the terrace with new friends over dinner,
letting screaming trains punctuate your conversation. Drivers park
along the highway at the Kranenturm tower. Eurailers walk down
Oberstrasse, then turn right on Kranenstrasse.

Hotel Hillen, a block south of the Hotel Kranenturm, has
less charm and similar train noise, with friendly owners, great
food, and lots of rental bikes. To minimize train noise, ask for
ruhige Seite, the quiet side (S-€26, Sb-€33, D-€41, Ds-€46,
Db-€51–€56, Tb-€74, 10 percent less for 3 nights, CC, closed
Nov–March, Langstrasse 18, tel. 06743/1287, fax 06743/1037,
e-mail: hotel-hillen@web.de, Iris speaks some English).

Hotel Altkölnischer Hof, a grand old building near the
church, rents 20 rooms with modern furnishings and bathrooms,
some with balconies over an Old World restaurant. Public rooms
are old-time elegant (Sb-€49–54, Db-€61–72, Db with terrace-
€82–87, with balcony-€77–97, less expensive for 3 nights, CC,
TV in rooms, elevator, closed Nov–April, tel. 06743/1339 or
06743/2186, fax 06743/2793, www.hotel-bacharach-rhein.de,
e-mail: tscherba@sparkasse.net, SE).

Hotel Gelberhof, a few doors up from the Jost store, has
spiffy public spaces but unimaginative rooms (S-€31, Sb-€44–49,
small Db-€64, Db-€69–79, Tb-€95–100, 3-night discounts, CC,
nonsmoking rooms, popular with groups, elevator, bike rental,
Blücherstrasse 26, tel. 06743/910-100, fax 06743/910-1050,
www.hotel-gelber-hof.com).

Pensions and Private Rooms

At **Pension Lettie**, effervescent and eager-to-please Lettie offers
four bright rooms. Some readers view Lettie as a highlight of their
trip (because she treats them like friends), others mention that the
rooms could be cleaner. Lettie speaks good English (worked for
the U.S. Army before we withdrew), does laundry (€10.50 per
load), and has a handy list of train schedules (Sb-€34, Db-€45,
Tb-€61 with cash, discount for 2-night stays, no CC, family deals,
strictly nonsmoking, no train noise, a few doors inland from Hotel
Kranenturm, Kranenstrasse 6, tel. & fax 06743/2115, e-mail:
pension.lettie@t-online.de).

Pension Winzerhaus, a 10-room place run by friendly Herr
and Frau Petrescu, is 200 meters (655 feet) up the valley from
the town gate, so the location is less charming, but it has no train
noise and easy parking. Rooms are simple, clean, and modern
(Sb-€30, Db-€45, Tb-€50, Qb-€60, 10 percent off with this
book excluding weekends and 1-night stays, no CC, free bikes
for guests, nonsmoking rooms, Blücherstrasse 60, tel. 06743/1294,
fax 06743/937-779, e-mail: winzerhaus@compuserve.de, SE).

Just off the main street, the cozy home of **Herr und Frau**

Theilacker is a German-feeling *Zimmer* offering four comfortable rooms, vine-covered trellises, and a pleasant stay. It's likely to have a room when others don't (S-€15, D-€31, no CC, in the town center behind Altkölnischer Hof, take short lane between Altkölnischer Hof and Altes Haus straight ahead to Oberstrasse 57, no outside sign, tel. 06743/1248, NSE).

Pension Binz offers four large, bright rooms and a plain apartment in a serene location (Sb-€33, Db-€51, third person-€18, apartment-€61–77, CC, fine breakfast, Koblenzer Strasse 1, tel. 06743/1604, cheery Carla speaks a little English).

Delightful **Ursula Orth** rents five stale-smelling but decent rooms around the corner from Pension Lettie (Sb-€18, D-€31, Db-€31–33, Tb-€38, no CC, nonsmoking, Rooms 4 and 5 on ground floor—easy access, from station walk down Oberstrasse, turn right on Spurgasse, her *Zimmer* is on the right, look for *Orth* sign, ring any of 3 door buzzers, Spurgasse 3, tel. 06743/1557, minimal English spoken).

Bacharach's hostel, **Jugendherberge Stahleck**, is a 12th-century castle on the hilltop—500 steps above Bacharach—with a royal Rhine view. Open to travelers of any age, this is a newly redone gem with eight beds and a private modern shower and WC in most rooms. A steep 15-minute climb on the trail from the town church, the hostel is warmly run by Evelyn and Bernhard Falke (FALL-kay), who serve hearty, €5 buffet, all-you-can-eat dinners. The hostel pub serves cheap local wine until midnight (€14.20 dorm beds with breakfast and sheets, €4 extra without a card or in a double, couples can share doubles, groups pay €20 per bed with breakfast and dinner, no CC, no smoking in rooms, easy parking, 22:00 curfew, washing machine, beds normally available but call and leave your name, they'll hold a bed until 18:00, tel. 06743/1266, fax 06743/2684, e-mail: jh-bacharach@djh-info.de, SE).

Eating in Bacharach

You can easily find inexpensive (€10–15), atmospheric restaurants offering indoor and outdoor dining. Two restaurants offering good values and great ambience are **Altes Haus**, the oldest building in town (€8–15, Thu–Tue 12:00–15:30, 18:00–21:30, closed Wed and Dec–Easter, dead center by the church), and the classier, candlelit **Kurpfälzische Münze** (€6–19, daily 10:00–23:00, in the old mint, a half block down from Altes Haus; claims to be even older). **Weingut zum Gruner Baum** offers delicious appetizers (also next to Altes Haus with good ambience indoors and out). **Hotel Kranenturm** is another good value with hearty meals and good main course salads (restaurant closed Jan–Feb, see hotel listing above).

Wine Tasting: Drop in on entertaining Fritz Bastian's **Weingut zum Grüner Baum** wine bar (just past Altes Haus, eves only, closed Thu, tel. 06743/1208). As the president of the local vintner's club, Fritz's mission is to give travelers an understanding of the subtle differences among the Rhine wines. Groups of two to six people pay €14 for a "carousel" of 15 glasses of 14 different white wines, one lonely red, and a basket of bread. Your mission: Team up with others with this book to rendezvous here after dinner. Spin the lazy Susan, share a common cup, and discuss the taste. Fritz insists, "After each wine, you must talk to each other."

Sleeping in St. Goar
(country code: 49, area code: 06741, zip code: 56329)
Hotel am Markt, well run by Herr and Frau Velich, is rustic with all the modern comforts. It features a hint of antler with a pastel flair and bright rooms and a good restaurant. It's a good value and a stone's throw from the boat dock and train station (S-€35, Sb-€43, Db-€59, Tb-€82, Qb-€88, cheaper off-season, closed Dec–Feb, CC, Am Markt 1, tel. 06741/1689, fax 06741/1721, e-mail: hotel.am.markt@gmx.de).

Hotel Hauser, facing the boat dock, is another good deal, warmly run by another Frau Velich. Its 12 rooms sit over a fine restaurant (S-€21.50, D-€45, Db-€50, great Db with Rhine-view balconies-€56, show this book to get these prices, Db cheaper in off-season, CC but prefer cash, small bathrooms, Heer Strasse 77, telephone reservations easy, tel. 06741/333, fax 06741/1464, SE).

Hotel Montag is on the castle end of town just across the street from the world's largest free-hanging cuckoo clock. Manfred and Maria Montag and their son Mike speak New Yorkish. Even though the hotel gets a lot of bus tours, it's friendly, laid-back, and comfortable (Sb-€41, Db-€77, Tb-€87, price can drop if things are slow, CC, Internet access-€8/hr, Heer Strasse 128, tel. 06741/1629, fax 06741/2086, e-mail: hotelmontag@1019freenet.de). Check out their adjacent crafts shop (heavy on beer steins).

A few doors down from Hotel Hauser, **Hotel Silberne Rose** is musty with older decor. Some rooms have Rhine views (Sb-€31–36, Db-€51–61, Tb-€64–72, cheaper price for longer stays, CC, 14 rooms, across from K-D dock, Heer Strasse 63, tel. 06741/7040, fax 06741/2865, earnest Herr Jankovic NSE).

Nearby, the strangely vacant **Rhein Hotel** has modern, unimaginative rooms (Sb-€36–41, Db-€46–66, no CC, Heer Strasse 71, tel. & fax 06741/2835, e-mail: blecic@t-online.de).

St. Goar's best *Zimmer* deal is the home of **Frau Kurz**, which comes with a breakfast terrace, garden, fine view, homemade marmalade, and most of the comforts of a hotel (S-€20, D-€32–35, Db-€36, showers-€2.60, 1-night stays cost extra, no CC, free and easy parking, confirm prices, honor your reservation or call to cancel, Ulmenhof 11, tel. & fax 06741/459, little English spoken). It's a steep five-minute hike from the train station (exit left from station, take immediate left at the yellow phone booth, pass under tracks to paved path, go up stairs, follow zigzag path, and climb a few more stairs to Ulmenhof, *Zimmer* is just past tower).

The Germanly run **St. Goar Hostel**, the big beige building under the castle (on road to castle veer right just after railroad bridge), has 2 to 12 beds per room, a 22:00 curfew, and hearty €6 dinners (€12 beds with breakfast, no CC, open all day, check-in preferred 17:00–18:00 and 19:00–20:00, Bismarckweg 17, tel. 06741/388, e-mail: jl-st-goar@djh-info.de, SE).

Rheinfels Castle Hotel is the town splurge. Actually part of the castle but an entirely new building, this luxury 57-room place is good for those with money and a car (Db-€128–148 depending on river views and balconies, cheaper for 3 or more nights, CC, elevator, free parking, indoor pool and sauna, dress-up restaurant, Schlossberg 47, tel. 06741/8020, fax 06741/802-802, www .schlosshotel-rheinfels.de, e-mail: rheinfels.st.goar@t-online.de).

Eating in St. Goar
Hotel Am Markt and **Hotel Hauser** offer excellent meals at fair prices (€5–18). For your Rhine splurge, walk, taxi, or drive up to **Rheinfels Castle Hotel** for its incredible view and elegant setting, and consider a sunset drink on the view terrace (€8–10 dinners, daily 18:30–21:15, reserve a table by the window, see hotel listing above).

Transportation Connections—Rhine
Milk-run trains stop at all Rhine towns each hour starting as early as around 06:00. Koblenz, Boppard, St. Goar, Bacharach, Bingen, and Mainz are each about 15 minutes apart. From Koblenz to Mainz takes 75 minutes. To get a faster big train, go to Mainz (for points east and south) or Koblenz (for points north, west, and along Mosel). Train info: tel. 01805-996-633.

From Mainz to: Bacharach/St. Goar (hrly, 1 hr), **Cochem** (hrly, 2.5 hrs, change in Koblenz), **Köln** (3/hr, 90 min, change in Koblenz), **Baden-Baden** (hrly, 1.5 hrs), **Munich** (hrly, 4 hrs), **Frankfurt** (3/hr, 45 min), **Frankfurt Airport** (4/hr, 25 min).

From Koblenz to: Köln (4/hr, 1 hr), **Berlin** (2/hr, 5.5 hrs, up to 2 changes), **Frankfurt** (3/hr, 1.5 hrs, 1 change), **Cochem** (2/hr, 50 min), **Trier** (2/hr, 2 hrs), **Brussels** (12/day, 4 hrs, change in Köln), **Amsterdam** (12/day, 4.5 hrs, up to 5 changes).

From Frankfurt to: Bacharach (hrly, 1.5 hrs, change in Mainz; first train to Bacharach departs at 06:00, last train at 20:45), **Koblenz** (hrly, 90 min, changes in Mannheim or Wiesbaden), **Rothenburg** (hrly, 3 hrs, transfers in Würzburg and Steinach), **Würzburg** (hrly, 2 hrs), **Munich** (hrly, 4 hrs, 1 change), **Amsterdam** (8/day, 5 hrs, up to 3 changes), **Paris** (9/day, 6.5 hrs, up to 3 changes).

From Bacharach to Frankfurt Airport (hrly, 1.5 hrs, change in Mainz, first train to Frankfurt airport departs 05:40, last train 21:30).

MOSEL VALLEY

The misty Mosel is what some visitors hoped the Rhine would be—peaceful, sleepy, romantic villages slipped between the steep vineyards and the river; fine wine; a sprinkling of castles; and lots of friendly *Zimmer*. Boat, train, and car traffic here is a trickle compared to the roaring Rhine.

While the swan-speckled Mosel moseys 500 kilometers (300 miles) from France's Vosges Mountains to Koblenz, where it dumps into the Rhine, the most scenic piece of the valley lies between the towns of Bernkastel-Kues and Cochem. I'd savor only this section. Zell makes a pleasant home base.

Throughout the region on summer weekends and during the fall harvest time, wine festivals with oompah bands, dancing, and colorful costumes are powered by good food and wine.

Getting around the Mosel Valley

By Train and Bus: The train zips you to Cochem, Bullay, or Trier in a snap. Bullay has bus connections with Zell (nearly hrly, 10 min) and with Beilstein (4/day). Cochem has more frequent bus connections with Beilstein (hrly, 20 min, last bus departs Beilstein about 18:50). A one-way taxi from Cochem to Beilstein costs about €15. Pick up bus schedules at train stations or TIs.

By Boat: A few daily departures on the Undine-Kolb Line allow you to cruise the most scenic stretch between Cochem, Beilstein, and Zell: between Cochem and Zell (2/day, May–Oct, but none on Fri and Mon May–June, 3 hrs, €13 one-way, €19 round-trip), between Cochem and Beilstein (5/day, 60 min, €8 one-way, €10 round-trip), and between Zell and Beilstein (1/day May–Oct, 2 hrs, €10 one-way, €14 round-trip, tel. 02671/7387).

The K-D (Köln-Düsseldorf) line sails once a day in each direction but only between Cochem and Koblenz (May–late Oct, Koblenz to Cochem 09:45–14:30, or Cochem to Koblenz 15:40–20:10, free with consecutive-day Eurailpass or a dated Eurail flexipass, Europass, Eurail Selectpass, or German railpass, uses up a day of a flexipass, tel. 02671/980-023). In early- to mid-June, the locks close for 10 days of annual maintenance, and no boats run between Cochem, Koblenz, Beilstein, and Zell.

By Car: The easygoing Mosel Wine Route turns anyone into a relaxed Sunday driver. Pick up a local map at a TI or service station. Koblenz and Trier are linked by two-lane roads that run along both riverbanks. Between Koblenz and Karden (south of Burg Eltz), road 416 runs along the west side of the river, and road 49 along the east bank. At Karden, road 49 jumps the river and runs on the west bank to Cochem. Just south of Zell, road 49 crosses the river again and becomes—and stays—road 53 all the way to Trier. Koblenz, Cochem, and Trier have car-rental agencies.

Mosel Valley

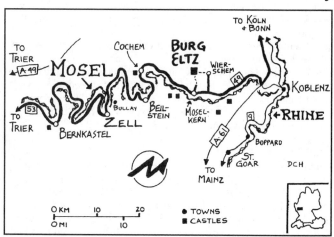

By Bike: You can rent bikes in most Mosel towns (see village listings below). A fine bike path follows the river from Koblenz to Zell.

By Ferry: About a dozen car-and-passenger ferries (*fähre*) cross the Mosel between Koblenz and Trier. These are marked "AF" for "auto" and "PF" for "pedestrian" on the *Moselle Wine Road* brochure (this *Mosellauf* brochure is sold for €2.60 at local TIs and tourist shops).

Cochem

With a majestic castle and picturesque medieval streets, Cochem is the very touristic hub of this part of the river.

Tourist Information: The information-packed TI is by the bridge at the main bus stop. Most of the pamphlets are kept behind the desk, so ask. They keep a thorough 24-hour room listing in the window. Their free map includes a walking tour, and a separate brochure tells the town's history. Ask about public transportation to Burg Eltz (see below) and pick up info on area hikes and the well-done *Moselle Wine Road* (*Mosellauf*) brochure (€2.60). The TI also has information on special events and wine tastings held by local vintners. The *Tips and Information from A to Z* brochure lists everything from car rental agencies to saunas and babysitters (May–Oct Mon–Sat 09:00–17:00, also Sun 10:00–12:00 in July–Nov, off-season closed weekends and at lunch, tel. 02671/60040, www.cochem.de). For accommodations, see "Sleeping," below.

Arrival in Cochem: Make a hard right out of the station (lockers available, €2/day, no WC) and walk about 10 minutes to the town center and TI (just past the bus lanes). Drivers can park near the bridge (TI right there). To get to the main square (*Markt*), continue under the bridge, then angle right and follow Bernstrasse.

Helpful Hints: The Edeka **supermarket** is on Ravene-strasse, a five-minute walk from the TI toward the train station. For **Internet access**, try COCbit-Kommunikation (€2.60/30 min, €5/hr, Mon–Fri 10:00–18:00, Sat 10:00–13:00, closed Sun, on street facing river, across from boat ticket booths, Moselprome-nade 7, tel. 02671/211). Cochem's biggest **wine festival** is held the last weekend in August.

Sights—Cochem

Cochem Castle—This pointy castle is the work of overly imagi-native 19th-century restorers (€3.60, daily mid-March–Oct 09:00–17:00, Nov–Dec only Sat–Sun 11:00–15:00, closed Jan–mid-March, 20-min walk from Cochem, follow one of the fre-quent German-language tours while reading English explanation sheets or gather 12 English speakers and call a day ahead to sched-ule an English tour, tel. 02671/255, www.reichsburg-cochem.de). A little yellow train shuttles castle-seekers between the bridge near the TI and the road below the castle (€2 one-way, 2/hr, last shuttle about 16:45, walk last 10 min uphill to castle).

River Activities—Stroll along the pleasant paths that line the river and **hike** up to the Aussichtspunkt (the cross on the hill) for a great view. You can rent **bikes** from the K-D boat kiosk at the dock (summers only, €3.60/4 hrs, €7/day) or year-round from Kreutz near the station on Ravenstrasse 42 (€3.60/4 hrs, €7/day, includes helmet, CC, no deposit required, just your passport number, tel. 02671/91131). Consider taking a bike on the boat and riding back. For **cruises**, see "Getting around the Mosel Valley," above.

Transportation Connections—Cochem

By train to: Koblenz (hrly, 60 min), **Bullay** (hrly, 10 min), and **Trier** (hrly, 60 min). Train info: tel. 01805-996-633. Bus info: tel. 02671/8976.

Sights—Mosel Valley

▲▲▲**Burg Eltz**—My favorite castle in all of Europe lurks in a mysterious forest. It's been left intact for 700 years and is furnished throughout as it was 500 years ago. Thanks to smart diplomacy and clever marriages, Burg Eltz was never destroyed. (It survived one five-year siege.) It's been in the Eltz family for 820 years. The countess arranges for new flowers in each room weekly. The only way to see the castle is with a 45-minute tour (included in admission ticket). German tours (with helpful English fact sheets, €0.50) go constantly. Call ahead to see if an English-language tour is scheduled, or organize your own by corralling 20 English speakers in the inner courtyard—they'll thank you for it. Then push the red button on the white porch and politely beg for an English guide. This is well worth a short wait (€5, April–Nov daily 09:30–17:30, tel. 02672/950-500, www.burg-eltz .de). To get to Burg Eltz from Cochem, you can taxi (€36 one-way for up to 4 people, tel. 02671/980-098), drive, or train-and-hike.

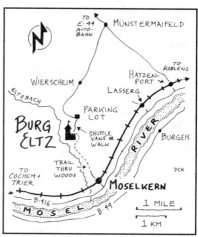

Burg Eltz Area

Arrival by Train: Get off at the Moselkern station midway between Cochem and Koblenz (no lockers at station, but, if you ask politely, clerk will store luggage in office). When leaving the station, exit right and follow "Burg Eltz" signs for about 20 minutes through town (signs are sparse but have faith and stay on the main road). Then take the marked trail (slippery when wet, slightly steep near end). It's a pleasant 75-minute hike between the station and castle through a pine forest where sparrows carry crossbows, and maidens, disguised as falling leaves, whisper "watch out."

Arrival by Car: Drivers often get lost on the way to Burg Eltz. Use your map and do this: Leave the river at Hatzenport following the white "Burg Eltz" signs through the towns of Münstermaifeld and Wierschem. The castle parking lot (€1/day, 09:00–18:00) is two kilometers (1.25 miles) past Wierscheim. From the lot, hike 10 minutes downhill to the castle or wait for the red castle shuttle bus (€1 one-way). There are three "Burg Eltz" parking lots; only this lot (2 km south of Wierscheim) is close enough for an easy walk. Another option is to park at the Moselkern station (free) and follow the "park and walk" signs (see "Arrival by Train," above).

▲**Beilstein**—Farther upstream is the quaintest of all Mosel towns (see "Sleeping," below). Beilstein is Cinderella land. Explore the narrow lanes, ancient wine cellar, resident (and very territorial) swans, and ruined castle. The small €1 ferry goes constantly back and forth across the river. A shop rents bikes for the pleasant riverside ride (toward Zell is best). The TI is in Café Klapperburg (summer Tue–Sun 09:00–18:00, closed Mon and Nov–March, tel. 02673/900-191).

▲**Zell**—This is the best Mosel town for an overnight stop (see "Sleeping," below). It's peaceful, with a fine riverside promenade, a pedestrian bridge over the water, plenty of *Zimmer*, and a long pedestrian zone filled with colorful shops, restaurants, *Weinstuben* (wine bars), and a fun oompah folk band on weekend evenings on the main square.

The **TI** is on the pedestrian street, four blocks downriver from the pedestrian bridge (Mon–Fri 08:00–12:30, 13:30–17:00, Sat 10:00–13:00, off-season closed Sat, tel. 06542/4031, www.zell -mosel.de). The fine little Wein und Heimatmuseum features Mosel history (same building as TI, Wed and Sat 15:00–17:00). Walk up to the medieval wall's gatehouse and through the cemetery to the old munitions tower for a village view. You can rent **bikes** from Frau Klaus (€6/day, Hauptstrasse 5, tel. 06542/2589). For **Internet access**, try the relaxing Berliner Kaffe-Kannchen (€1.50/15 min, Thu–Tue 07:00–18:30, closed Wed, across pedestrian bridge opposite bus stop at Baldninen Strasse 107, tel. 06542/5450).

Locals know Zell for its Schwarze Katz (Black Cat) wine. Franz Josef Weis (who was once a POW in England) and his son Peter give an entertaining and free tour of their 40,000-bottle-per-year **wine cellar**. The clever 20-minute tour starts at 17:00 (call ahead to reserve, tel. 06542/41398, SE); buy a bottle or two to keep this fine tour going. A green-and-yellow flag marks their *Weinkeller* south of town, past the bridge, at Notenau 30. They also rent two fine apartments (see "Sleeping in Zell," below).

Ernst—Drivers will find this tiny town filled with many pleasant *Zimmer* and inviting *Weinstuben* (5 km south of Cochem on road 49).

Sleeping on the Mosel
(€1.10 = about $1)

Sleeping in Cochem
(country code: 49, area code: 02671, zip code: 56812)
All rooms come with breakfast. Kapro Reinigung, just off the main square, will do your **laundry** (Mon–Fri 08:00–18:00, Sat 09:00–12:30, closed Sun, Oberbach Strasse).

Weingut Rademacher offers a good value and beautiful rooms, wedged between vineyards and train tracks, with a pleasant garden and a big common kitchen. Charming hostess Andrea and her husband (both SE) give tours of their wine cellar when time permits (earlier is better); houseguests enter for free. If there is no tour, visitors are welcome to taste the wine (Sb-€25.50, Db on train side-€41, Db on vineyard side-€47, less for 3 or more nights, CC, all 6 rooms are nonsmoking, family deals, ground-floor rooms, from station take a quick right on Ravenestrasse, turn right on Pinner-strasse, pass under train tracks, curve right for another 50 meters, Pinnerstrasse 10, tel. 02671/4164, fax 02671/91341).

Just above a local *Weinstube*, the light-hearted and ever-so-funky **Gasthaus Ravene** offers six rooms varying in size and comfort (several are spacious and airy). The stairway needs new carpeting, but the rooms are fine (Sb-€36, Db-€46–61, Tb-€77, CC, family deals, Ravenestrasse 43, tel. 02671/980-177, fax 02671/91119, www.gasthaus-ravene.de, friendly Silvia Boegel NSE). Silvia closes the *Weinstube* Monday–Friday until 15:00 and on Sunday until 18:00. If you want to check in early, call one day before or when you arrive at the train station so she can let you in (no doorbell at *Gasthaus*).

The rustic **Hotel Lohspeicher**, just off the main square on a tiny-stepped street, is for those who want a real hotel—with much higher prices—in the thick of things (Sb-€49, Db-€77–87, CC, includes breakfast in a fine stone-and-timber room, restaurant, elevator, parking-€4/day, closed Feb, Obergasse 1, tel. 02671/3976, fax 02671/1772, Ingo SE).

Haus Andreas has 10 squeaky-clean, modern rooms at fair prices (Sb-€21, Db-€36–41, Tb-€54, Sb is less for 2 or more nights, no CC, Schlosstrasse 9, tel. 02671/1370 or 02671/5155, fax 02671/1370, Frau Pellny speaks a little English). From the main square, take Herrenstrasse; after a block, angle right up the steep hill on Schlosstrasse.

For a top-dollar view of Cochem, cross the bridge and find the balconied rooms at **Hotel Am Hafen** (Db-€60–110, Tb-€90–110, skip cheaper no-view rooms, CC, nonsmoking rooms, air-con, Uferstrasse 3, cross bridge to reach hotel, tel. 02671/97720, fax 02671/977-227, e-mail: hotel-am-hafen@t-online.de, SE).

Sleeping in Zell
(country code: 49, area code: 06542, zip code: 56856)
If the Mosel charms you into spending the night, do it in Zell. By car, this is a natural. It's also easy by boat (2/day from Cochem) or train (go to Bullay—hrly from Cochem or Trier—from Bullay the bus takes you to little Zell, €1.50, 2/hr, 10 min; bus stop is across street from Bullay train station, check yellow MB schedule for times, last bus at about 19:00). The central Zell stop is called Lindenplatz.

Zell's hotels are a disappointment, but its private homes are great. The owners speak almost no English and discount their rates if you stay more than one night. They can't take reservations long in advance for one-night stays; just call a day ahead. My favorites are on the south end of town, a five-minute walk from the town hall square (TI) and the bus stop. Breakfast is included unless otherwise noted. These places are listed in the order you would find them from the pedestrian bridge.

Friendly **Natalie Huhn** (no sign), your German grandmother, has the cheapest beds in town in her simple but comfortable house

(D-€33, cheaper for 2-night stays, no CC, 3 rooms, closed
Nov–April, 2 blocks to left of church at Jakobstrasse 32, tel.
06542/41048).
   Weinhaus zum Fröhlichen Weinberg offers cheap, basic
rooms (D-€36, €31 for 2 or more nights, no CC, family *Zimmer*,
Mittelstrasse 6, tel. 06542/4308, fax 06542/5781) above a *Weinstube* disco (noisy on Friday and Saturday nights).
   Homey **Gästehaus am Römerbad** is a few blocks from
the church and a decent value (Sb-€21, Db-€41, no CC, 6
rooms, Am Römerbad 5, tel. 06542/41602, Elizabeth Münster).
   Zell's best *Zimmer* values lie at the end of the pedestrian
street about five blocks from the pedestrian bridge:
   Gasthaus Gertrud Thiesen is classy, with a TV-living-
breakfast room and a river view. The Thiesen house has big,
bright rooms and is on the town's first corner overlooking the
Mosel from a great terrace (D-€41, €36 for 2 or more nights,
no CC, closed Nov–Feb, Balduinstrasse 1, tel. 06542/4453, SE).
Notice the high-water flood marks on the wall across the street.
   Gästezimmer Rosa Mesenich is another little place facing
the river (Db-€36–41, no CC, Brandenburg 48, tel. 06542/4297,
NSE). The vine-strewn doorway of **Gastehaus Eberhard** leads
to gregarious owners, cushy rooms, and potential wine tastings
(Db-€38, no CC, near Gästezimmer Rosa Mesenich, Brandenburg 42, tel. 06542/41216, NSE).
   If you're looking for room service, a sauna, a pool, and an
elevator, sleep at **Hotel Grüner Kranz** (Sb-€45–60, Db-€86–
130, CC, 32 rooms, nonsmoking rooms, tel. 06542/98610, fax
06542/986-180).
   Weinhaus Mayer, a classy—if stressed-out—old pension next
door, is perfectly central with Mosel-view rooms (Db-€66–72, no
CC, Balduinstrasse 15, tel. 06542/4530, fax 06542/61160, NSE).
They have newly renovated rooms with top comforts, many with
river-view balconies (ask for *Neues Gastehaus*, view Db-€82–92, big
Tb-€123, no CC, tel. 06542/61169, fax same as above). Both guest
houses are closed December through March.
   The freshly remodeled **Hotel Ratskeller** (above a classy
pizzeria) has 14 rooms on the pedestrian street that are less cozy
but sharp with tile flooring and fair rates (Sb-€44, Db-€61,
Db €10 more on summer weekends, CC, Balduinstrasse 36,
tel. 06542/98620, fax 06542/986-244).
   Franz Josef Weis and son Peter of the **Schwarze Katz** winery rent two luxurious apartments with kitchens and free use of
a funky old grape-pressing room (Db-€55, less for 2 or more
nights, extra person-€6, breakfast-€6, CC, look for green-and-
yellow flag marking their *Weinkeller* south of town, past bridge,
at Notenau 30, tel. 06542/41398, fax 06542/961-178, e-mail:
f.j.weis@t-online.de, SE).

Sleeping in Beilstein
(country code: 49, area code: 02673, zip code: 56814)

Cozier and farther north, Beilstein (BILE-shtine) is very small and quiet (no train; hrly buses to nearby Cochem, fewer buses on weekends, 15 min; taxi from Cochem-€15). Breakfast is included.

Hotel Haus Lipmann is your chance to live in a medieval mansion with hot showers and TVs. A prizewinner for atmosphere, it's been in the Lipmann family for 200 years. The creaky wooden staircase and the elegant dining hall, with long wooden tables surrounded by antlers, chandeliers, and feudal weapons, will get you in the mood for your castle sightseeing, but the riverside terrace may mace your momentum (Sb-€75, Db-€85, no CC, 5 rooms, closed Nov–April, tel. 02673/1573, fax 02673/1521, e-mail: hotel.haus.lipmann@t-online.de, SE).

Gasthaus Winzerschenke an der Klostertreppe is comfortable and a great value, right in the tiny heart of town (Db-€38, bigger Db-€49, no CC, discount for 2-night stays, 5 rooms, closed Nov–Easter, tel. & fax 02673/1354, Frau Sausen NSE, her son Christian SE).

The half-timbered, riverfront **Altes Zollhaus Gästezimmer** has packed all the comforts into eight tight, bright, and modern rooms (Db-€56, deluxe Db-€77, no CC, closed Nov–March, tel. 02673/1574, fax 02673/1287, e-mail: lipmann@t-online.de).

Hotel Gute Quelle offers more half-timbers, 13 comfortable rooms, and a good restaurant (Db-€41–61, CC, closed Dec–March, Marketplatz 34, tel. 02673/1437, fax 02673/1399, e-mail: info@hotel-gute-quelle.de, helpful Susan SE).

BERLIN

No tour of Germany is complete without a look at its historic and reunited capital, a construction zone called Berlin. Stand over ripped-up tracks and under a canopy of cranes and watch the rebirth of a European capital. Enjoy the thrill of walking over what was the Wall and through Brandenburg Gate.

Berlin has had a tumultuous recent history. After the city was devastated in World War II, it was divided by the Allied powers: with the American, British, and French sectors being West Berlin, and the Russian sector, East Berlin. The division was set in stone when the East built the Berlin Wall in 1961. The Berlin Wall lasted 28 years. In 1990, less than a year after the Wall fell, Germany was formally reunited. When the dust settled, Berliners from both sides of the once-divided city faced the monumental challenge of reunification.

The last decade has taken Berlin through a frenzy of rebuilding. And, while there's still plenty of work to be done, a new Berlin is emerging. Berliners joke they don't need to go anywhere because the city's always changing. Spin a postcard rack to see what's new. A five-year-old guidebook on Berlin covers a different city.

Unification has had its negative side, and locals are fond of saying "the Wall survives in the minds of some people." Some "Ossies" (impolite slang for Easterners) miss their security. Some "Wessies" miss their easy ride (military deferrals, subsidized rent, and tax breaks). To free spirits, walled-in West Berlin was a citadel of freedom within the East.

The city government has been eager to charge forward with little nostalgia for anything that was "Eastern." Big corporations and the national government have moved in, and the dreary swath of land that was the Wall has been transformed. City planners are boldly taking Berlin's reunification and the return of the national government as a good opportunity to make Berlin a great capital once again.

During the grind of World War II, Hitler enjoyed rolling out the lofty plans for a post-war Berlin as capital of a Europe united under his rule. As Europe unites, dominated by a muscular Germany with its shiny new capital in the works, Hitler's dream of a grand post-war Berlin seems about to come true....

Planning Your Time

Because of the city's location, try to enter and/or leave by either night train or plane. Berlin is worth a busy two days, and I'd spend them this way:

Day 1: 10:00-Take a guided walking tour (offered by Original Berlin Walks, see "Tours of Berlin," below). After lunch, take my Do-It-Yourself Orientation Tour (described below), stopping midway to scale the new dome of the Reichstag building, then finishing with a walk through eastern Berlin. Stop at the Deutscher Dom (German Cathedral) to devour the "Questions on Germany History" exhibit. Finish your day among Greek treasures at the Pergamon Museum.

Day 2: Spend the morning lost in the painted art of the Gemäldegalerie, hike or taxi via Potsdamer Platz to the Topography of Terror exhibit and along the surviving Zimmerstrasse stretch of Wall to the Museum of the Wall at Checkpoint Charlie.

If you are maximizing your sightseeing, you could squeeze a hop-off hop-on bus tour into Day 1 and start Day 2 with a visit to the Egyptian and Picasso museums at Charlottenburg. Remember that the Museum of the Wall is open late and most museums are closed on Monday.

Orientation (area code: 030)

Berlin is huge, with nearly 4 million people. But the tourist's Berlin can be broken into four digestible chunks:

1. The area around Bahnhof Zoo and the grand Kurfürstendamm Boulevard, nicknamed Ku'damm (transportation, tours, information, hotel, shopping hub).

2. Former downtown East Berlin (Brandenburg Gate, Unter den Linden Boulevard, Pergamon Museum, and the area around Oranienburger Strasse).

3. The new center: Kulturforum museums, Potsdamer Platz, and Wall-related sights.

4. Charlottenburg Palace and museums, on the outskirts of the city.

Tourist Information

Berlin's TIs are run by a for-profit agency working for the city's big hotels, which colors the information they provide. The main TI

Berlin Sightseeing Modules

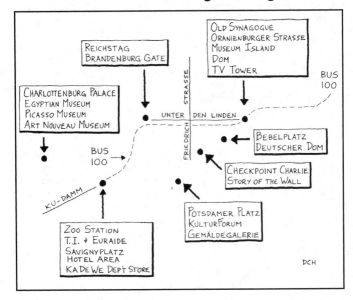

is five minutes from the Bahnhof Zoo train station, in the Europa Center (with Mercedes symbol on top, enter outside to left, on Budapester Strasse, Mon–Sat 08:30–20:30, Sun 10:00–18:00, tel. 030/264-7480, www.btm.de). A smaller TI is in the Brandenburg Gate (daily 09:30–18:00). The TIs sell city maps (€0.50—get it), the *Berlin Programm* (a €1.50 German-language monthly listing upcoming events and museum hours, www.berlin.de), the Museumspass (€4, 3-day pass to several museums, including many of the biggies, see "Helpful Hints," below), and the German-English quarterly *Berlin* magazine (€2, with timely features on Berlin and a partial calendar of events). The TIs also offer a €3 room-finding service (but only to hotels that give them kickbacks—many don't). Most hotels have free city maps.

EurAide's information office, in the Bahnhof Zoo, provides a great service. They have answers to all your questions about Berlin or train travel around Europe. Staffed by Americans, communication is simple, and they have a knack for predicting your needs and then publishing free fliers to answer them (June–Sept daily 08:00–18:00, Oct–May daily 8:00–16:30, always with a 12:00–13:00 lunch break, at the back of station near lockers, great opportunity to get all future *couchette* reservations nailed down ahead of time, Prague Excursion passes available, www.euraide.de). EurAide also sells one-day bus/metro passes (€6) and city maps (making a trip to the TI probably unnecessary). To get the most out of EurAide, organize your questions and needs before your visit. Euraide sells an excellent €5 *Berlin for Young People* book listing plenty of creative, inexpensive, and fun ways to spend your days and nights here.

Arrival in Berlin

By Train at Bahnhof Zoo: Berlin's central station is called Bahnhof Zoologischer Garten (because it's near Berlin's famous zoo)..."Zoo" for short. Coming from Western Europe, you'll probably land at Zoo (rhymes with "toe"). It's small, well organized, and handy.

Upon arrival by train, orient yourself like this: Inside the station, follow signs to Hardenbergplatz. Step into this busy square filled with city buses, taxis, the transit office, and derelicts. "The Original Berlin Walks" start from the curb immediately outside the station at the top of the taxi stand (see "Tours of Berlin," below). Between you and the McDonald's across the street is the stop for bus #100 (departing to the right for the Do-It-Yourself Orientation Tour, described below). Turn right and tiptoe through the riffraff to the eight-lane highway, Hardenbergstrasse. Walk to the median strip and stand with your back to the tracks. Ahead you'll see the black, bombed-out hulk of the Kaiser Wilhelm Memorial Church and the Europa Center (Mercedes symbol spinning on roof), which houses the main TI. Just ahead on the left amid the traffic is the BVG transport information kiosk. (Buy a €6 day pass covering the subway and buses, and pick up a free subway map.) If you're facing the church, my recommended hotels are behind you to your right.

If you arrive at Berlin's other train stations (trains from most of Eastern Europe arrive at Ostbahnhof), no problem: Ride another train (fastest option) or the S-Bahn or U-Bahn (runs every few min) to Bahnhof Zoo and pretend you arrived here.

By Plane: See "Transportation Connections," below.

Getting around Berlin

Berlin's sights spread far and wide. Right from the start, commit yourself to the fine public transit system. The *On the Move* booklet (from BVG and EurAide) explains it all.

By Subway and Bus: The U-Bahn, S-Bahn, and all buses are consolidated into one "BVG" system that uses the same tickets. Here are your options:

• Basic ticket (*Einzel Fahrschein*) for two hours of travel on buses or subways (€2.25; *Erwachsener* means adult—anyone 14 or older).

• A day pass (*Tages Karte*) covering zones A and B—the city proper—€6, good until 03:00 the morning after. To get out to Potsdam, you need a ticket covering zone C (€6.50).

• A cheap short-ride ticket (*Kurzstrecke Erwachsener*) for a single short ride of six bus stops or three subway stations, with one transfer (€1.30).

• Berlin/Potsdam WelcomeCard gives you three days of transportation and three days of minor sightseeing discounts (€16, valid for an adult and up to 3 kids—generally only worthwhile for traveling families).

Buy your tickets or cards from machines at U- or S-Bahn stations or at the BVG pavilion in front of Bahnhof Zoo. To use the machine, first select the type of ticket you want, then load in the coins or paper. Punch your ticket in a red or yellow clock machine to validate it (or risk a €31 fine). The double-decker buses are a joy (can buy ticket on bus), and the subway is a snap. The S-Bahn (but not U-Bahn) is free with a validated Eurailpass (but it uses up a day of a flexipass).

By Taxi: Taxis are easy to flag down, and taxi stands are common. A typical ride within town costs €5 to €8. A local law designed to help people get safely and affordably home from their subway station late at night is handy for tourists any time of day: A short ride of no more than two kilometers (1.25 miles) is a flat €3. (Ask for "*Kurzstrecke, drei euro, bitte.*") Cabbies aren't crazy about the law, so insist on the price and be sure to keep it short.

By Bike: In western Berlin you can rent bikes at the Bahnhof Zoo left-luggage counter (€10/day); in the east, go to Fahhradstation at Hackesche Höfe (€13/day, Mon–Fri 08:00–20:00, Sat 10:00–16:00, closed Sun, Rosenthaler Strasse 40, tel. 030/2045-4500). Be careful: in Berlin, motorists don't brake for bikers. Fortunately some roads have special bike lanes.

Helpful Hints

Monday Activities: Most museums are closed on Monday. Save Monday for Berlin Wall sights, the Reichstag building, the Do-It-Yourself Orientation Tour (see below), walking/bus tours, churches, the zoo, or shopping along Kurfurstendamm (Ku'damm) Boulevard or at the Kaufhaus des Westens (KaDeWe) department store. (When Monday is a holiday—as it is several times a year—museums are open then and closed Tuesday.)

Museums: All **state museums**, including the Pergamon Museum and Gemäldegalerie (plus others as noted in "Sights," below) are free on the first Sunday of each month. These museums are all also covered by a single **Museumspass** (€4/1 day, €8.25/3 consecutive days, not valid for special exhibitions, purchase at TI or participating museum). This means that if you buy a ticket for one of the participating museums, it automatically gets you into all of the others on the same day.

Addresses: Many Berlin streets are numbered with odd and even numbers on the same side of the street, often with no connection to the other side (i.e., Ku'damm #212 can be across the street from #14). To save steps, check the white street signs on curb corners; many list the street numbers covered on that side of the block.

Travel Agency: Reisebüro im Europa Center specializes in **last-minute tickets** (e.g., fly to London tomorrow for €102, next to TI in Europa Center, tel. 030/2655-1050, www .lastminuteflugboerse.de).

Tours of Berlin

▲▲▲**City Walking Tours**—"The Original Berlin Walks" offers a variety of worthwhile tours led by enthusiastic guides who are native English speakers. The company, run by Englishman Nick Gay, offers a three-hour "Discover Berlin" introductory walk daily year-round at 10:00 and also at 14:30 from April through October for €9 (€8 if you're under 26). Just show up at the taxi rank in front of Zoo Station. Their high-quality, high-energy guides also offer tours of "Infamous Third Reich Sites" every morning except Mondays and Fridays in high season at 10:00, "Jewish Life in Berlin" Mondays and Fridays at 10:00, and Potsdam (see "Sights—Near Berlin," below). Many of the Third Reich and Jewish history sites are difficult to pin down without these excellent walks. New for 2002 is a six-hour trip to the Sachsenhausen Concentration Camp, intended "to challenge preconceptions," according to Nick. This tour runs most mornings from April through October (€15, requires transit day ticket with zone C or buy from guide, call office for tour specifics). Confirm tour schedules at EurAide or by phone with Nick or his wife and partner Serena (private tours also available, tel. 030/301-9194, www.berlinwalks.com, e-mail: berlinwalks@berlin.de).

▲**City Bus Tours**—For bus tours you have two choices:

1) Full-blown, three-hour bus tours. Contact Severin & Kühn (€22, daily 10:00 and 14:00 in summer, live guides in 2 languages, from Ku'damm 216, tel. 030/880-4190) or take BVG buses from Ku'damm 225 (tel. 030/885-9880).

2) Hop-on hop-off circle tours. Several companies do the "City-Circle Sightseeing" tour. The tour offers unlimited hop-on hop-off privileges for its 12-stop route with a good English narration (€18, 2–4/hr, April–Oct, 2-hr loop, taped guides, frequent buses). The TI has the brochures. Just hop on where you like and pay the driver. On a sunny day when the double-decker buses go topless, these are a photographer's delight, cruising slowly by just about every top sight in town.

Do-It-Yourself Orientation Tour

Here's an easy ▲▲▲ introduction to Berlin. Half the tour is by bus, the other half is on foot. Berlin's bus #100 (direction Mollstrasse and Prenzlauer Allee) is a sightseer's dream, stopping at Bahnhof Zoo, Europa Center/Hotel Palace, Siegessäule, Reichstag, Brandenburg Gate, Unter den Linden, Pergamon Museum, and ending at Alexanderplatz. If you have the €18 and two hours for a hop-on hop-off bus tour (described above), take that instead. But this short €2.25 tour is a fine city introduction. Buses leave from Hardenbergplatz in front of the Zoo Station (and nearly next door to the Europa Center TI, in front of Hotel Palace). Buses come every 10 minutes, and single tickets are good for two hours—so take advantage of hop on and off privileges. Climb aboard, stamp your ticket (giving it a time), and grab a seat on top. You could ride the bus all the way, but I'd get out at the Reichstag and walk to Alexanderplatz.

Part 1: By Bus #100 from Bahnhof Zoo to the Reichstag

(This is about a 10-min ride. Note: The next stop lights up on the reader board inside the bus.)

☛ On your left and then straight ahead, before descending into the tunnel, you'll see: the bombed-out hulk of the Kaiser Wilhelm Memorial Church, with its post-war sister church (described below) and the Europa Center. This is the west end shopping district with the big department stores nearby and a bustling people zone. Emerging from the tunnel on your immediate right you'll see the Berlin tourist information office.

☛ At the stop in front of Hotel Palace: on the left, the elephant gates mark the entrance to the Berlin Zoo and its aquarium (described below).

☛ Driving down Kurfürstenstrasse, you'll pass several Asian restaurants—a reminder that, for most, the best food in Berlin is not German. Turning left, with the huge Tiergarten park in the distance ahead, you'll cross a canal and see the famous Bauhaus on the right (an off-white, blocky building). Built in the 1920s, this revolutionary building ushered in a new age of modern architecture that emphasized function over beauty, giving rise to the blocky steel-and-glass skyscrapers in big cities around the world. On the left is Berlin's new embassy row. The big turquoise wall marks the communal home of all five Nordic embassies.

☛ The bus enters a 167-acre park called the Tiergarten, packed with cycle paths, joggers, and nude sunbathers. The Victory Column (Siegessäule, with the gilded angel, described below) towers above this vast city park that was once a royal hunting grounds, now nicknamed the "green lungs of Berlin."

☛ On the left, a block after leaving the Siegessäule: The 18th-century late-rococo Bellevue Palace is the German "White House." Formerly a Nazi VIP guest house, it's now the residence of the federal president (whose "power" is mostly ceremonial). If the flag's out, he's in.

Berlin

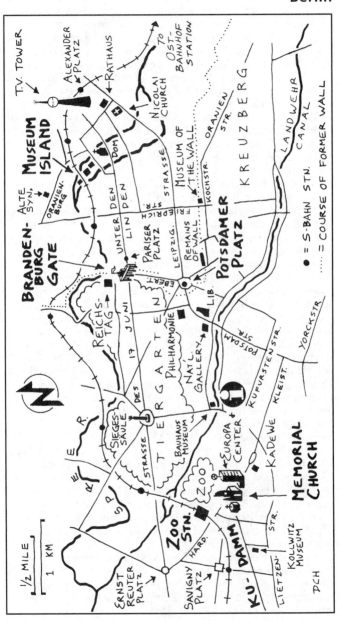

☛ Driving along the Spree River: This park area was a residential district before World War II. Now, on the left-hand side, it's filled with the buildings of the new national government. The huge brick "brown snake" complex was built to house government workers—but it didn't sell—so now its apartments are available to anyone. A Henry Moore sculpture floats in front of the slope-roofed House of World Cultures (on left side, sculpture nick-named "the pregnant oyster"). The modern tower (next on left) is a carillon with 68 bells (1987).

☛ While you could continue on bus #100, it's better on foot from here. Leap out at the Platz der Republik. Through the trees on the left you'll see Germany's new and sprawling chancellory. Started during the more imperial rule of Helmut Kohl, today it's considered overly grand.

☛ Just down the street stands the Reichstag. As you approach the old building with the new dome, look for the row of slate slabs imbedded in the ground near the curb closest to the bus stop (looks like a fancy slate bicycle rack). This is a memorial for politi-cians who were sent to concentration camps because their politics didn't agree with Chancellor Hitler's. Each slab is marked with a name and the party that politician belonged to—mostly KPD (Communists) and SPD (Socialists). Now visit the Reichstag (open late, no lines in evening) and continue the walk below.

▲▲▲**Reichstag Building**—The Parliament building—the heart of German democracy—has a short but complicated and emotional history. When it was inaugurated in the 1890s, the last emperor, Kaiser Wilhelm, disdainfully called it the "house for chatting." It was from here that the German Republic was proclaimed in 1918. In 1933 this symbol of democracy nearly burned down. It's believed Hitler planned the fire, using it as a handy excuse to frame the Communists and grab power. As World War II drew to a close, Stalin ordered his troops to take the Reichstag from the Nazis by May 1 (the worker's holiday). More than 1,500 Nazis made their last stand here—extending World War II by two days. On April 30, 1945, it fell to the Allies. It was not used from 1933 to 1999. For its 101st birthday, in 1995, the Bulgarian artist Christo wrapped it in silvery-gold cloth. It was then wrapped again in scaffolding, rebuilt by British architect Sir Norman Foster, and turned into the new parliamentary home of the Bundestag (Germany's lower house). To many Germans, the proud resurrection of the Reichstag—which no longer has a hint of Hitler—symbolizes the end of a terrible chapter in German history.

The **glass cupola** rises 48 meters (155 feet) above the ground, and a double staircase winds 230 meters (755 feet) to the top for a grand view. Inside the dome, a cone of 360 mirrors reflects natural light into the legislative chamber below. Lit from inside at night, this gives Berlin a memorable nightlight.

Hours: Visit the Reichstag (free, daily 08:00–24:00, last entry 22:00, most crowded 10:00–16:00, wait in line to go up—good street musicians, some hour-long English tours, tel. 030/2273-2152).

Self-guided tour: As you approach the building, look above the door, surrounded by stone patches from WWII bomb damage, to see the motto and promise: *Dem Deutschen Volke* (to the German people). The open and airy lobby towers 30 meters high (100 feet) with 20-meter-tall colors of the German flag. Glass doors show the **central legislative chamber**. The message: there will be no secrets in government. Look inside. The seats are "Reichstag blue," a lilac blue color designed by the architect to brighten the otherwise gray interior. The German eagle (a.k.a. the "fat hen") spreads his wings behind the podium. Notice the doors marked "yes," "no," or "abstain" ... the Bundestag's traditional "sheep jump" way of counting votes (for critical and close votes, all 669 members leave and vote by walking through the door of their choice).

Ride the elevator to the base of the glass **dome**. Take time to study the photos and read the circle of captions—an excellent exhibition telling the Reichstag story. Then study the surrounding architecture: a broken collage of old on new, like Germany's history. Notice the dome's giant and unobtrusive sunscreen that moves as necessary with the sun. Peer down through the skylight to look over the shoulders of the elected representatives at work. For Germans, the best view is down—keeping a close eye on their government.

Start at the ramp nearest the elevator and wind up to the top of the **double staircase**. Take a 360-degree survey of the city as you hike: First, the big park is the **Tiergarten**, the "green lung" of Berlin. Beyond that is the **Teufelsberg**—Devil's Hill (built of rubble from the bombed city in the late 1940s and famous during the Cold War as a powerful ear of the West—notice the telecommunications tower on top). Given the violent and tragic history of Berlin, a city blown apart by bombs and covered over by bulldozers, locals say, "You have to be suspicious when you see the nice green park." Find the **Seigessäule**, the Victory Column (moved by Hitler in the 1930s from in front of the Reichstag to its present position in the Tiergarten). Next, scenes of the new Berlin spiral into your view—**Potsdamer Platz** marked with the conical glass tower that houses Sony's European headquarters. The yellow building to the right is the Berlin Philharmonic Concert Hall. Continue circling left, and find the green chariot atop the **Brandenburg Gate**. A monument to the Gypsy Holocaust will be built between the Reichstag and Brandenburg Gate. (Gypsies, as disdained by the Nazis as the Jews, lost the same percentage of their population to Hitler.) Another Holocaust memorial will be built just south of Brandenburg Gate. Next, you'll see **former East Berlin** and the city's next huge construction zone, with a forest

of 100-meter-tall (300 feet) skyscrapers in the works. Notice the
TV tower (with the Pope's Revenge—explained below), the Berlin
Cathedral's massive dome, the red tower of the city hall, the
golden dome of the New Synagogue, and the Reichstag's **roof
garden restaurant** (Dachgarten, €15–26 meals with a view,
09:00–16:00, tel. 030/2262-9933). Follow the train tracks in the
distance to the left toward a huge construction zone marking the
future central Berlin train station. Complete your spin tour with
the blocky **Chancellory**, nicknamed by locals "the washing
machine." It may look like a pharaoh's tomb, but it's the office of
Germany's most powerful person, the Chancellor and his team.

Part 2: Walking Tour from Brandenburg Gate up Unter den Linden to Alexanderplatz

Allow a comfortable hour for this walk through eastern Berlin,
including time for dawdling but not museum stops.

▲▲**Brandenburg Gate**—The historic Brandenburg Gate (1791,
the last survivor of 14 gates in Berlin's old city wall—which led to
the city of Brandenburg), crowned by a majestic four-horse chariot
with the Goddess of Peace at the reins, was the symbol of Berlin
and then the symbol of divided Berlin. Napoleon took the statue
to the Louvre in Paris in 1806. When the Prussians got it back,
she was renamed the Goddess of Victory. The gate sat, part of a
sad circle dance called The Wall, for more than 25 years. (TI
within gate, open daily 09:30–18:00.)

Now postcards all over town show the ecstatic day—November 9, 1989—when the world enjoyed the sight of happy Berliners
jamming the gate like flowers on a parade float. Pause a minute
and think about struggles for freedom—past and present. (There's
actually a "quiet room" built into the gate for this purpose.)

▲**Pariser Platz**—From Brandenburg Gate, face Pariser Platz
(toward the east). Unter den Linden leads to the TV tower in the
distance (the end of this walk). The space used to be filled with
important government buildings—all bombed to smithereens.
Today, Pariser Platz is unrecognizable from the deserted no-
man's land it became under the Communist regime. Sparkling
new banks, embassies (the French embassy rebuilt where it was
before World War II), and a swanky hotel have filled in the void.

Crossing through the Gate, look to your right to a stretch of
empty land—formerly the "death strip." The U.S. Embassy once
stood here. Plans to rebuild it here are stalled because the Americans want to set it back (for safety purposes), but the Germans
want to keep the location the same. The new Holocaust memorial
(a 3-year construction project, beginning in late 2001) will stand
behind that: over 2,500 gravestone-like pillars.

Brandenburg Gate, the center of old Berlin, sits on a
major boulevard, running east-west through Berlin. The

Unter den Linden

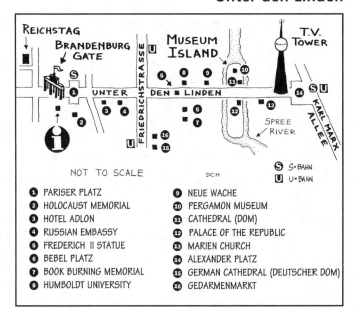

REICHSTAG
BRANDENBURG GATE
MUSEUM ISLAND
T.V. TOWER
FRIEDRICHSTRASSE
UNTER DEN ■ LINDEN
SPREE RIVER
KARL MARX ALLEE

NOT TO SCALE

DCH

S S-BAHN
U U-BAHN

❶ PARISER PLATZ
❷ HOLOCAUST MEMORIAL
❸ HOTEL ADLON
❹ RUSSIAN EMBASSY
❺ FREDERICH II STATUE
❻ BEBEL PLATZ
❼ BOOK BURNING MEMORIAL
❽ HUMBOLDT UNIVERSITY
❾ NEUE WACHE
❿ PERGAMON MUSEUM
⓫ CATHEDRAL (DOM)
⓬ PALACE OF THE REPUBLIC
⓭ MARIEN CHURCH
⓮ ALEXANDER PLATZ
⓯ GERMAN CATHEDRAL (DEUTSCHER DOM)
⓰ GEDARMENMARKT

western segment, called Strasse des 17 Juni, stretches for six kilometers (4 miles) from the Siegessäule (past the flea market—see below) to the Olympic Stadium. For our walk, we'll follow this city axis in the opposite direction, east, up what is known as Unter den Linden, into the core of old imperial Berlin and past what was once the palace of the Hohenzollern family who ruled Prussia and then Germany. The palace—the reason for just about all you'll see—is a phantom sight…long gone.

▲▲**Unter den Linden**—This is the heart of former East Berlin. In Berlin's good old days, Unter den Linden was one of Europe's grand boulevards. In the 15th century, this carriageway led from the palace to the hunting grounds (today's big park). In the 17th century, Hohenzollern princes and princesses moved in and built their palaces here so they could be near the Prussian emperor.

Named centuries ago for its thousand linden trees, this was the most elegant street of Prussian Berlin before Hitler's time and the main drag of East Berlin after his reign. Hitler replaced the venerable trees—many 250 years old—with Nazi flags. Popular discontent actually drove him to replant linden trees. Today Unter den Linden is no longer a depressing Cold War cul-de-sac, and its pre-Hitler strolling café ambience is returning.

As you walk toward the giant TV tower, the first big building you see on your right is the **Hotel Adlon**. It hosted such notables as Charlie Chaplin, Albert Einstein, and Greta Garbo. (This was where Garbo said, "I want to be alone," during the filming of *Grand Hotel*.) Destroyed in World War II, the grand Adlon was rebuilt in 1996. See how far you can get inside.

The Unter den Linden S-Bahn station ahead of you is one of Berlin's former "**ghost subway stations**." During the Cold War, most underground train tunnels were simply blocked at the border. But a few Western lines looped through the East. To make a little hard Western cash, the Eastern government rented the use of these tracks to the West, but the stations (which happened to be in East Berlin) were strictly off-limits. For 28 years, the stations were unused as Western trains slowly passed through seeing only eerie DDR guards and lots of cobwebs. Literally within days of the fall of the Wall, these stations were reopened, and today they are a time warp with the dreary old green tiles and the original traditional signs. Walk along the track and exit following signs to *Russische Botschaft* . . . the Russian embassy.

The **Russian embassy** was the first big post-war building project in East Berlin. It's built in the powerful, simplified, neo-classical style Stalin liked. While not as important now as it was a few years ago, it's immense as ever. It flies the Russian white, red, and blue. Find the hammer-and-sickle motif decorating the window frames. Continuing past the Aeroflot Airline offices, you come to the back of the **Komische Oper** (comic opera; program and view of ornate interior posted in window). While the exterior is ugly, the fine old theater interior, amazingly missed by WWII bombs, survives. The shop here is an amusing mix of antiques, local guidebooks, knickknacks, and East Berlin–nostalgia souvenirs.

The West lost no time in consuming the East; consequently, some are feeling a wave of nostalgia—**Ost-algia**—for the old days of East Berlin. But one symbol of that era has been given a reprieve. At Friedrichstrasse, look at the DDR–style pedestrian lights, and you'll realize someone had a sense of humor back then. The perky red and green men—*Ampelmännchen*—were under threat of replacement by the far less jaunty Western signs. Fortunately, the DDR signals will be kept after all.

At **Friedrichstrasse**, look right. Before the war, the Unter den Linden/Friedrichstrasse intersection was the heart of Berlin. In the '20s, Berlin was famous for its anything-goes love of life. This was the cabaret drag, a springboard to stardom for young and vampy entertainers like Marlene Dietrich. (Born in 1901, Dietrich starred in the first German "talkie" and headed from there straight to Hollywood.) Today, this boulevard, lined with super department stores (such as Galeries Lafayette, with its cool marble and glass waste-of-space interior; belly up to its amazing ground floor viewpoint) and big-time hotels (such as the Hilton and Four Seasons), hopes to replace Ku'damm as the grand commerce and café boulevard of Berlin. American Express is across from Galeries Lafayette (handy for any train ticket needs, Mon–Sat 09:00–19:00, tel. 030/201-7400).

You'll notice big colorful water pipes throughout Berlin. As long as the city remains a big construction zone, it will be laced with these drainage pipes—key to any building project. Berlin's high water table means any new basement comes with lots of pumping out.

Continue down Unter den Linden a few more blocks, past the large equestrian statue of **Frederick II** ("the Great"), and turn right into the square (Bebelplatz). Stand on the glass window in the center. (Construction of an underground parking lot might prevent you from reaching the glass plate, depending on the timing of your visit.)

Frederick the Great—who ruled from 1740 to 1786—established Prussia as a military power. This square was the center of the "new Rome" Frederick envisioned. Much of Frederick's palace actually survived World War II but was torn down by the Communists since it symbolized the imperialist past.

Bebelplatz is bounded by great buildings. The German State Opera was bombed in 1941, rebuilt to bolster morale and to celebrate its centennial in 1943, and bombed again in 1945. The former state library is where Lenin studied much of his exile away (climb to the second floor of the library to see a stained glass window depicting his life's work with almost biblical reverence). And the round Catholic St. Hedwig's Church was built to placate the subjects of Catholic lands Frederick added to his empire. (Step inside to see the cheesy DDR government renovation.)

Humboldt University (across Unter den Linden) was one of Europe's greatest. Marx and Lenin (not the brothers or the sisters) studied here along with Grimm (both brothers) and 22 Nobel Prize winners. Einstein—who was Jewish—taught here until taking a spot at Princeton in 1932 (smart guy).

Look down through the glass you're standing on: The room of empty bookshelves is a memorial to the notorious Nazi **book burning**. It was on this square in 1933 that staff and students from the university threw 20,000 newly forbidden books (like Einstein's) into a huge bonfire on the orders of the Nazi propaganda minister Joseph Goebbels. Continue down Unter den Linden. The next square on your right holds the Opernpalais' restaurants (see "Eating," below).

On the university side of Unter den Linden, the Greek templelike building is the **Neue Wache** (the emperor's New Guardhouse, from 1816). When the Wall fell, this memorial to the victims of fascism was transformed into a new national memorial. Look inside where a replica of the Käthe Kollwitz statue, *Mother* *with Her Dead Son*, is surrounded by thought-provoking silence. This marks the tombs of Germany's unknown soldier and the unknown concentration camp victim. The inscription in front reads, "To the victims of war and tyranny." Read the entire statement in English (on wall, right of entry).

After the Neue Wache, detour down Hinter dem Giesshaus to see the new I.M. Pei–designed spiraling glass staircase of the new **German History Museum** (scheduled to open in 2003). Until then, the current (and worthwhile) German History Museum is across the street (Tue–Sun 10:00–18:00, closed Mon).

Just before the bridge, wander left along the canal through a tiny but colorful flea market (weekends only). Canal tour boats leave from here.

Cross the bridge to **Museum Island**, home of Germany's first museums and today famous for its Pergamon Museum (described below). The museum complex starts with an imposing red neoclassical facade on the left (a musty museum of antiquities; Pergamon is behind it). For 300 years the square (Lustgarten) has flip-flopped between military parade ground and people-friendly park—depending upon the political tenor of the time. In 1999 it was made into a park again (read the history posted in the corner opposite the church).

The towering church is the 100-year-old **Berlin Cathedral**, or *Dom* (€4, €5 including access to the dome, Mon–Sat 09:00– 20:00, Sun 11:30–18:00, organ concerts offered most Wed, Thu, and Fri at 15:00, free with regular admission). Inside, the great reformers (Luther, Calvin, and company) stand around the brilliantly restored dome like stern saints guarding their theology. Frederick I rests in an ornate tomb (right transept, near entry to dome). The crypt downstairs is not worth a look.

Across the street is the decrepit **Palace of the Republic** (with the copper-tinted windows). A symbol of the Communist days, it was East Berlin's parliament building and futuristic entertainment complex. Although it officially has a date with the wrecking ball, many Easterners want it saved, and its future is still uncertain.

Before crossing the next bridge (and leaving Museum Island), look right. The pointy twin spires of the 13th-century Nikolai Church mark the center of medieval Berlin. This *Nikolai-Viertel* (district) was restored by the DDR and was trendy in the last years of socialism. Today it's dull and, with limited time, not worth a visit. As you cross the bridge, look left in the distance to see the gilded **New Synagogue**, rebuilt after WWII bombing (described below).

Walk toward **Marien Church** (from 1270, interesting but very faded old *Dance of Death* mural inside door) at the base of the TV tower. The big, red-brick building past the trees on the right is the city hall, built after the revolution of 1848 and arguably the first democratic building in the city.

The **Fernsehturm (TV Tower)**, at 364 meters tall (1,200 feet), offers a fine view from 182 meters (€6, March–Oct daily 09:00–01:00, Nov–Feb daily 10:00–24:00, tel. 030/242-3333). Consider a kitschy trip to the top for the view and lunch in its revolving restaurant. Built (with Swedish know-how) in 1969, the tower was meant to show the power of the atheistic state at a time when DDR leaders were having the crosses removed from church domes and spires. But when the sun shined on their tower, the greatest spire in East Berlin, a huge cross reflected on the mirrored ball. Cynics called it "The Pope's Revenge."

Farther east, pass under the train tracks into **Alexanderplatz**. This—especially the Kaufhof—was the commercial pride and joy of East Berlin. Today it's still a landmark, with a major U-Bahn and S-Bahn station.

For a ride through work-a-day eastern Berlin, with its Lego-hell apartments (dreary even with their new face-lifts), hop back on bus #100 from here. It loops five minutes to the end of the line and then, after a couple minutes' break, heads on back. (This bus retraces your route, finishing at Bahnhof Zoo.) Consider extending this foray into eastern Berlin to Karl Marx Allee (described below).

Sights—Western Berlin

Western travelers still think of Berlin's "West End" as the heart of the city. While it's no longer that, the West End still has the best infrastructure to support your visit and works well as a home base. Here are a few sights within an easy walk of your hotel and the Zoo station.

▲**Kurfürstendamm**—In the 1850s, when Berlin became a wealthy and important capital, her new rich chose Kurfürstendamm as their street. Bismarck made it Berlin's Champs-Élysées. In the 1920s, it became a chic and fashionable drag of cafés and boutiques. During the Third Reich, as home to an international community of diplomats and journalists, it enjoyed more freedom than the rest of Berlin. Throughout the Cold War, economic subsidies from the West made sure that capitalism thrived on Ku'damm, as western Berlin's main drag is popularly called. And today, while much of the old charm has been hamburgerized, Ku'damm is still a fine place to feel the pulse of the city and enjoy the elegant shops (around Fasanenstrasse), department stores, and people watching. Ku'damm, starting at Kaiser Wilhelm Memorial Church, does its commercial cancan for three kilometers (2 miles).

▲**Kaiser Wilhelm Memorial Church (Gedächtniskirche)**— The church was originally a memorial to the first emperor of Germany, who died in 1888. Its bombed-out ruins have been left standing as a memorial to the destruction of Berlin in World War II. Under a fine mosaic ceiling, a small exhibit features interesting photos about the bombing (free, Mon–Sat 10:00–16:00, closed

Western Berlin

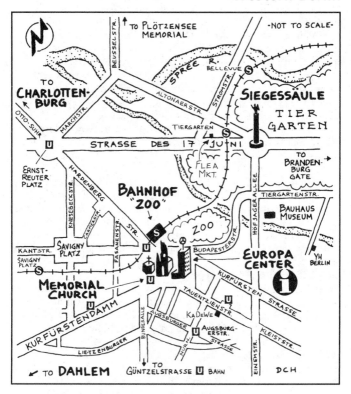

Sun). Next to it, a new church (1961) offers a world of 11,000
little blue windows (free, daily 09:00–19:00). The blue glass was
given to the church by the French as a reconciliation gift. The
lively square between this and the Europa Center (a shiny high-
rise shopping center built as a showcase of Western capitalism
during the Cold War) usually attracts street musicians.

▲**Käthe Kollwitz Museum**—This local artist (1867–1945),
who experienced much of Berlin's stormiest century, conveys
some powerful and mostly sad feelings about motherhood, war,
and suffering through the black-and-white faces of her art (€4,
Wed–Mon 11:00–18:00, closed Tue, a block off Ku'damm at
Fasanenstrasse 24, tel. 030/882-5210).

▲**Kaufhaus des Westens (KaDeWe)**—The "department store
of the West," with a staff of 2,100 to help you sort through its
vast selection of 380,000 items, claims to be the biggest department
store on the Continent. You can get everything from a haircut and

train ticket to souvenirs (third floor). A cyber bar is on the fourth floor. The theater and concert box office on the sixth floor charges an 18 percent booking fee, but they know all your options. The sixth floor is also a world of gourmet taste treats. This biggest selection of deli and exotic food in Germany offers plenty of classy opportunities to sit down and eat. Ride the glass elevator to the seventh floor's glass-domed Winter Garden self-service cafeteria— fun but pricey (Mon–Fri 09:30–20:00, Sat 09:00–16:00, closed Sun, tel. 030/21210, U-Bahn: Wittenbergplatz). The Wittenbergplatz U-Bahn station (in front of KaDeWe) is a unique opportunity to see an old-time station in Berlin. Enjoy its interior.

Berlin Zoo—More than 1,400 different kinds of animals call Berlin's famous zoo home—or so the zookeepers like to think. Germans enjoy seeing the pandas at play (straight in from the entry). I enjoy seeing the Germans at play (€8 for zoo or world-class aquarium, €12 for both, children half price, daily 09:00–18:30, in winter until 17:30, aquarium closes at 18:00, feeding times—*Fütterungszeiten*— posted on map just inside entry, enter near Europa Center in front of Hotel Palace, Budapester Strasse 32, tel. 030/254-010).

Erotic Art Museum—This offers three floors of graphic (mostly 18th-century) Oriental art, a tiny theater showing erotic silent movies from the early 1900s, and a special exhibit on the queen of German pornography, the late Beate Uhse. This amazing woman, a former test pilot for the Third Reich and ground-breaking pur-veyor of condoms and sex ed in the 1950s, was the female Hugh Hefner of Germany and CEO of a huge chain of porn shops. If you're traveling far and are sightseeing selectively, the sex museums in Amsterdam or Copenhagen are much better. This one, while well described in English, is little more than prints and posters (€5, daily 09:00–24:00, hard-to-beat gift shop, at corner of Kant-strasse and Joachimstalerstrasse, a block from Bahnhof Zoo, tel. 030/886-0666). If you just want to see sex, you'll see much more for half the price in a private video booth next door.

Sights—Central Berlin
Hitler and The Third Reich—While many come to Berlin to see Hitler sights, these are essentially invisible. The German Resis-tance Museum (described below) is in German only and difficult for the tourist to appreciate. The Topography of Terror (SS and Gestapo headquarters) is a fascinating exhibit but—again—only in German, and all that remains of the building is its foundation. (Both museums have helpful audioguides in English.) "Hitler's Bunker" is completely gone (near the balloon site at Potsdamer Platz). Your best bet for "Hitler sights" is to take the "Infamous Third Reich Sites" walking tour offered by Berlin Walks (see "City Walking Tours," above). EurAide has a good flier listing and explaining sights related to the Third Reich.

Tiergarten/Siegessäule—Berlin's "Central Park" stretches three
kilometers (2 miles) from Bahnhof Zoo to Brandenburg Gate.
Its centerpiece, the Siegessäule (Victory Column), was built to
commemorate the Prussian defeat of France in 1870. The pointy-
helmeted Germans rubbed it in, decorating the tower with French
cannons and paying for it all with francs received as war reparations.
The three lower rings commemorate Bismarck's victories. I imagine
the statues of Moltke and other German military greats—which
lurk in the trees nearby—goose-stepping around the floodlit angel
at night. Originally standing at the Reichstag, the immense tower
was actually moved to this position by Hitler in 1938 to complement his anticipated victory parades. At the first level, notice how
WWII bullets chipped the fine marble columns. Climbing its 285
steps earns you a breathtaking Berlin-wide view and a close-up look
at the gilded angel made famous in the U2 video (€1, April–Sept
Mon–Thu 09:30–18:30, Fri–Sun 09:30–19:00, Oct–March daily
09:30–17:30, bus #100). From the tower, the grand Strasse des 17
Juni (named for a workers' uprising against the DDR government
in the 1950s) leads east to the Brandenburg Gate.

Flea Market—A colorful flea market with great antiques, over
200 stalls, collector-savvy merchants, and fun German fast-food
stands thrives weekends beyond Siegessäule on Strasse des 17
Juni (S-Bahn: Tiergarten).

**German Resistance Memorial (Gedenkstätte Deutscher
Widerstand)**—This memorial and museum tells the story of the
German resistance to Hitler. The Benderblock was a military
headquarters where an ill-fated attempt to assassinate Hitler was
plotted. Stauffenberg and his co-conspirators were shot in the
courtyard. While explanations are in German only, the spirit that
haunts the place is multilingual (free, Mon–Fri 09:00–18:00, Thu
until 20:00, Sat–Sun 10:00–18:00, €3 printed English translation,
free English audioguide, just south of Tiergarten at Stauffen-
bergstrasse 13, bus #129, tel. 030/2699-5000).

▲Potsdamer Platz—The Times Square of Berlin and possibly
the busiest square in Europe before World War II, it was cut in
two by the Wall and left a deserted no-man's-land for 40 years.
This immense commercial/residential/entertainment center (with
the European corporate headquarters of Sony and others), sitting
on a futuristic transportation hub, was a vision begun in 1991
when it was announced that Berlin would resume its position as
capital of Germany. Sony, Daimler-Chrysler, and other huge
corporations have turned it once again into a center of Berlin.

While most of the complex just feels big (the arcade is like
any huge modern American mall), the Sony Center Platz, under
a towering tent roof, is remarkable. At night, multicolored flood-
lights play on the underside of the tent. Office workers and
tourists eat here by the fountain, enjoying the parade of people.

The modern Bavarian Lindenbrau beer hall—the Sony boss wanted a *Bräuhall*—serves good traditional food (big salads, meter-long taster boards of 8 different beers, tel. 030/2575-1280). The adjacent Josty Bar is built around a surviving bit of a venerable hotel that was a meeting place for Berlin's rich and famous before the bombs. You can browse the futuristic Sony Style Store, visit the Film-haus (a museum with an exhibit on Marlene Dietrich), and do some surfing at the Web Free TV shop. Across Leipziger Strasse, the public is welcome to ride an elevator to a sky-scraping rooftop terrace.

Sights—Kulturforum, in Central Berlin

Just off Potsdamer Platz, with several top museums and Berlin's concert hall, is the city's cultural heart (admission to all sights covered by €4 day card, free on first Sun of month). Of its sprawling museums, only the Gemäldegalerie is a must. The telephone number for all Kulturforum museums is 030/2660. To reach the Kulturforum, take the S- or U-Bahn to Potsdamer Platz, then walk along Potsdamer Platz and Potsdamer Strasse. From the Zoo station, you can also take bus #200 to Philharmonie.

▲▲▲**Gemäldegalerie**—Germany's top collection of 13th-through 18th-century European paintings (over 1,400 canvases) is beautifully displayed in a building that is a work of art in itself. Follow the excellent and free audioguide. The North Wing starts with German paintings of the 13th to 16th centuries—including eight by Dürer. Then come the Dutch and Flemish—Jan van Eyck, Brueghel, Rubens, Van Dyck, Hals, and Vermeer. The wing finishes with German, English, and French 18th-century art—Gainsborough and Watteau. An octagonal hall at the end features a fine stash of Rembrandts. The South Wing is saved for the Italians—Giotto, Botticelli, Titian, Raphael, and Caravaggio (€4, covered by Museumspass, Tue–Sun 10:00–18:00, Thu until 22:00, closed Mon, clever little loaner stools, great salad bar in cafeteria upstairs, Matthäikirchplatz 4).

New National Gallery (Neue Nationalgalerie)—This features 20th-century art (€4, covered by Museumspass, Tue–Fri 10:00–18:00, Thu until 22:00, Sat–Sun 11:00–18:00, closed Mon, tel. 030/266-2662).

Museum of Arts and Crafts (Kunstgewerbemuseum)—This shows off a thousand years of applied arts—porcelain, fine Jugendstil furniture, art deco, and reliquaries. There are no crowds and no English descriptions (€2, covered by Museumspass, Tue–Fri 10:00–18:00, Sat–Sun 11:00–18:00, closed Mon). The huge National Library is across the courtyard (free, English periodicals).

▲**Music Instruments Museum**—This impressive hall is filled with 600 exhibits from the 16th century to modern times. Wander among old keyboard instruments and funny-looking tubas. There's no English, aside from a €0.10 info sheet, but it's fascinating if you're into pianos (€2, Tue–Fri 09:00–17:00, Sat–Sun 10:00–17:00, closed Mon, the low-profile white building east of the big, yellow Philharmonic Concert Hall, tel. 030/254-810). Poke into the lobby of Berlin's Philharmonic Concert Hall and see if there are tickets available for your stay (ticket office open Mon–Fri 15:00–18:00, Sat–Sun 11:00–14:00, must purchase tickets in person, box office tel. 030/2548-8132).

Sights—Eastern Berlin

▲▲**Pergamon Museum**—Of the museums on Museumsinsel (Museum Island), just off Unter den Linden, only the Pergamon Museum is essential. Its highlight is the fantastic Pergamon Altar. From a second-century B.C. Greek temple, it shows the Greeks under Zeus and Athena beating the giants in a dramatic pig pile of mythological mayhem. Check out the action spilling onto the stairs. The Babylonian Ishtar Gate (glazed blue tiles from sixth century B.C.) and many ancient Greek and Mesopotamian treasures are also impressive (€4, covered by Museumspass, Tue–Sun 10:00–18:00, Thu until 22:00, closed Mon, free on first Sun of month, café, behind Museum Island's red stone museum of antiquities, tel. 030/2090-5555 or 030/2090-5577). The excellent audioguide (free with admission) covers the museum's highlights.

Old National Gallery—Also on the museum island, this gallery (scheduled to open in this new location in 2002) shows 19th-century German Romantic art: man against nature, Greek ruins dwarfed in enchanted forests, medieval churches, and powerful mountains (€4, covered by Museumspass, Tue–Sun 10:00–18:00, Thu until 22:00, closed Mon, free on first Sun of month).

▲▲**The Berlin Wall**—The 160-kilometer (100-mile) "Anti-Fascist Protective Rampart," as it was called by the East German government, was erected almost overnight in 1961 to stop the outward flow of people (3 million leaked out between 1949 and 1961). The Wall, which was four meters high (13 feet), had a five-meter tank ditch, a no-man's-land that was 9 to 50 meters wide (30 to 160 feet), and 300 sentry towers. In its 28 years there were 1,693 cases when border guards fired, 3,221 arrests, and 5,043 documented successful escapes (565 of these were East German guards). The carnival atmosphere of those first years after the Wall fell is gone, but hawkers still sell "authentic" pieces of the Wall, DDR (East German) flags, and military paraphernalia to gawking tourists. Pick up the free brochure *Berlin: The Wall*, available at EurAide or the TI, which traces the history of the Wall and helps you find the remaining chunks and other Wall-related sights in Berlin.

▲▲▲**Haus am Checkpoint Charlie Museum**—While the famous border checkpoint between the American and Soviet

Eastern Berlin

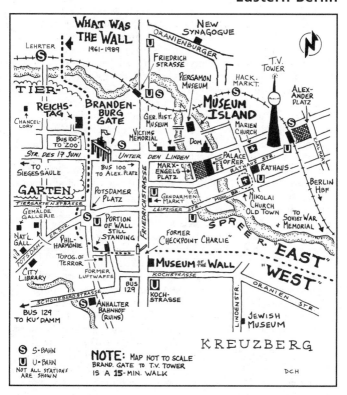

WHAT WAS THE WALL 1961-1989

LEHRTER Ⓢ

TIER-

REICHS-TAG

CHANCELLORY

BUS 100 TO ZOO

STR. DES 17 JUNI

TO .. SIEGESSÄULE

GARTEN

TIERGARTENSTRASSE

GEMÄLDE GALLERIE

NAT'L. GALL.

PHIL-HARMONIE

CITY LIBRARY

TOPOG. OF TERROR

FORMER LUFTWAFFE

SCHÖNEBERGSTRASSE

BUS 129 TO KU'DAMM

ANHALTER BAHNHOF (RUINS)

BRANDEN-BURG GATE

BUS 100 TO ALEX. PLATZ

POTSDAMER PLATZ

PORTION OF WALL STILL STANDING

UNTER DEN LINDEN

GER. HIST. MUSEUM

VICTIMS MEMORIAL

MARX-ENGELS PLATZ

DOM

LEIPZIGER STR.

GENDARMEN-MARKT

FORMER CHECKPOINT CHARLIE"

Ⓤ MUSEUM OF THE WALL

KOCHSTRASSE

KOCH-STRASSE

NEW SYNAGOGUE

ORANIENBURGER

FRIEDRICH STRASSE

PERGAMON MUSEUM

HACK. MARKT.

MUSEUM ISLAND

MARIEN CHURCH

PALACE OF REP.

RATHAUS STR.

RATHAUS

MÜHL. BR.

NIKOLAI CHURCH Old Town

SPREE R.

TO SOVIET WAR MEMORIAL

"EAST" "WEST"

LINDENSTR.

ORANIEN STR.

JEWISH MUSEUM

KREUZBERG

T.V. TOWER

ALEX-ANDER PLATZ

BERLIN HBF

TO SOVIET WAR MEMORIAL

N

Ⓢ S-BAHN
Ⓤ U-BAHN
NOT ALL STATIONS ARE SHOWN

NOTE: MAP NOT TO SCALE
BRAND. GATE TO T.V. TOWER
IS A **15**-MIN. WALK

DCH

sectors is long gone, its memory is preserved by one of Europe's most interesting museums: The House at Checkpoint Charlie. During the Cold War, it stood defiantly—spitting distance from the border guards—showing off all the clever escapes over, under, and through the Wall.

Today, while the drama is over and hunks of the Wall stand like victory scalps at its door, the museum still tells a gripping history of the Wall, recounts the many ingenious escape attempts (early years with a cruder wall saw more escapes), and includes plenty of video and film coverage of those heady days when people-power tore down the Wall (€6, assemble 10 tourists and you all get in for €3 each, daily 09:00–22:00, U-Bahn: Kochstrasse, Friedrichstrasse 44, tel. 030/253-7250). If you're pressed for time, this is a good after-dinner sight.

Americans—the Cold War victors—have the biggest appetite for Wall-related sights. Where the gate once stood, notice the thought-provoking post with larger-than-life posters of a young American soldier facing east and a young Russian soldier facing west. Around you are reconstructions of the old checkpoint (named not after any guy, but "number three," as in alpha, bravo, charlie). Charlie was the most famous because this was the only place through which foreigners could pass. A few meters away (on Zimmerstrasse) a glass panel describes the former checkpoint. From there, a double row of cobbles in Zimmerstrasse marks where the Wall once stood (these innocuous cobbles run throughout the city, tracing the former Wall's path). Follow it a long block to Wilhelmstrasse and a surviving stretch of Wall.

When it fell, the Wall was literally carried away by the euphoria. What survived has been nearly devoured by a decade of persistent "wall peckers." The park behind the Zimmerstrasse/Wilhelmstrasse bit of wall marks the site of the command center of Hitler's Gestapo and SS (explained by English plaques throughout). It's been left undeveloped as a memorial to the tyranny once headquartered here. In the park is . . .

The Topography of Terror—Because of the horrible things planned here, rubble of the Gestapo and SS buildings will always be left as rubble. The SS, Hitler's personal body guards, grew to become a state-within-a-state with its talons in every corner of German society. Along an excavated foundation of the building, an exhibit tells the story of National Socialism and its victims in Berlin (free, info booth open May–Sept daily 10:00–20:00, Oct–April daily 10:00–18:00, free English audioguide with your passport as a deposit, written English translations-€1, tel. 030/2548-6703).

Across the street (beyond the Wall) is the German Finance Ministry. Formerly the Nazi headquarters of the air force, this is the only major Hitler-era government building that survived the war's bombs. Walk down Wilhelmstrasse to see an entry gate that looks today much like it did when Germany occupied nearly all of Europe. At the far end of the building (farther down Wilhelmstrasse) is a wonderful example of Communist art. The mural (from the 1950s) is classic "Social Realism"—showing the entire society . . . industrial laborers, farm workers, women, and children all happily singing the same patriotic song.

East Side Gallery—The biggest remaining stretch of the Wall is now "the world's longest outdoor art gallery." It stretches for over a kilometer (a half mile) and is covered with murals painted by artists from around the world. The murals are routinely whitewashed so new ones can be painted. This length of the Wall makes a poignant walk. For a quick look, just go to Ostbahnhof station and look around (the freshest and most colorful art is at this end). The gallery only survives until a land ownership dispute can be solved when it will likely be developed like the rest of the city. (Given the recent history, imagine the complexity of finding rightful owners of all this suddenly very valuable land.) If you walk the entire length, there's a small Wall souvenir shop at the end where you'll find a bridge crossing the river to a subway station at Schlesisches Tor (in Kreuzberg).

Kreuzberg—This district—once butted against the dreary Wall and inhabited largely by poor Turkish guest laborers and their families—is still run-down, with graffiti-riddled buildings and plenty of student and Turkish street life. It offers a gritty look at melting-pot Berlin in a city where original Berliners are as rare as old buildings. Berlin is the fourth-largest Turkish city in the world, and Kreuzberg is its "downtown." But to call it a "little Istanbul" insults the big one. You'll see *döner kebab* stands, spray paint–decorated shops, and mothers wearing scarves. For a dose of Kreuzberg without getting your fingers dirty, joyride on bus #129. For a colorful stroll, take U-Bahn to Kottbusser Tor and wander—ideally on Tuesday and Friday from 12:00 to 18:00, when the Turkish Market sprawls along the bank of the Maybachufer Canal.

▲▲**Gendarmenmarkt**—This delightful and historic square is bounded by twin churches and the concert hall (designed by Schinkel, the man who put the neoclassical stamp on Berlin) for the Berlin symphony. The name of the square—part French and part German—reminds us that in the 17th century a fifth of all Berliners were French émigrés, Protestant Huguenots fleeing Catholic France. Back then, tolerant Berlin was a magnet for the persecuted. The émigrés vitalized the city with new ideas and know-how.

The German Cathedral (described below) has the most important German history exhibit in town. The Franzosischer Dom (French Cathedral) houses a humble museum to the Huguenots (€1.50, Tue–Sun 12:00–17:00, closed Mon) and a chance to climb 254 steps to the top for a grand city view (€1.50, daily 09:00–19:00).

Two classy lunch spots (Lang and Spitz) and the world's biggest **chocolate store** (Rassbender & Rausch) are clustered behind the concert hall, on Charlottenstrasse (see "Eating in Eastern Berlin," below).

▲▲**German Cathedral**—The Deutscher Dom houses the great and thought-provoking "Questions on German History" exhibit, a wonderful coverage of the story of German nationalism from medieval times to unification. It's impressive how openly and honestly Germany is dealing with its fascist past. There are no English descriptions, but you can follow a fine and free hour-long audioguide (to start, follow the blue arrows upstairs until you see *Ebene 2*) or buy the excellent €5 book (free, June–Aug Tue–Sun 10:00–19:00, closed Mon, Sept–May Tue–Sun 10:00–18:00, closed Mon, on Gendarmenmarkt just off Friedrichstrasse, tel. 030/2273-0431).

▲▲**New Synagogue**—A shiny gilded dome marks the New Synagogue, now a museum and cultural center on Oranienburger Strasse. Only the dome and facade have been restored, and a window overlooks a vacant field marking what used to be the synagogue. The largest and finest synagogue in Berlin before World War II, it was desecrated by Nazis on "Crystal Night" in 1938, bombed in 1943, and partially rebuilt in 1990. Inside, past tight security, there's a small but moving exhibit on the Berlin Jewish community through the centuries with some good English descriptions (ground floor and first floor). The *Vergesst es nie* message on its facade means "Never forget." It was put up by East Berlin Jews in 1966. East Berlin had only a few hundred Jews, but, now that the city is united, the Jewish community numbers about 10,000 (€3, Sun–Thu 10:00–18:00, Fri 10:00–14:00, closed Sat, U-Bahn: Oranienburger Tor, tel. 030/8802-8316).

Oren, a popular near-kosher café, is next to the synagogue (see "Eating," below). If you're heading for the Pergamon Museum next, take a shortcut by turning left after leaving the synagogue, then right on Monbijoustrasse. Cross the canal and turn left to the museum.

A block from the synagogue, walk 50 meters (160 feet) down Grosse Hamburger Strasse to a little park. This street was known for 200 years as the "street of tolerance" for its many religions. Hitler turned it into the street of death (*Todes Strasse*), bulldozing 12,000 graves of the city's oldest Jewish cemetery and turning a Jewish old-folks home into a deportation center. Note the two memorials—one erected by the former East Berlin government and one built later by the city's unified government. Somewhere nearby a plainclothes police officer keeps watch on this park.

▲**Oranienburger Strasse**—Berlin is developing so fast it's impossible to predict what will be "in" next year. The area around Oranienburger Strasse is definitely trendy (but is being challenged by hip Friedrichshain farther east).

While the area immediately around the Synagogue is dull, 100 meters (300 feet) away things get colorful. The streets behind Grosse Hamburger Strasse flicker with atmospheric cafés, *Kneipen* (pubs), and art galleries.

At night "techno-prostitutes" line Oranienburger Strasse. Prostitution is legal here, but there's a big debate about taxation. Since they don't get unemployment insurance, why should they pay taxes?

A block in front of the Hackescher Markt S-Bahn station is Hackesche Höfe—with eight courtyards bunny-hopping through a wonderfully restored 1907 Jugendstil building. It's full of trendy restaurants, theaters, and cinema (playing movies in their original languages). This is a fine example of how to make huge city blocks livable—Berlin's apartments are organized around courtyard after courtyard off the main roads.

Jewish Museum Berlin—This new Jewish Museum is housed in a striking zinc-walled building with no doors—you can only reach the museum through a tunnel leading from the 18th-century Baroque building next door. Designed by the American architect Daniel Libeskind, the building's zigzag shape is pierced by voids symbolic of the irreplaceable cultural loss caused by the Holocaust. The focus of this museum is artifacts from Berlin's Jewish community, not the Holocaust. The Holocaust section of the museum—a dark, eerily empty tower—is set apart from the rest of the building and can be reached only through another tunnel. The museum is in a nondescript neighborhood a 10-minute walk from the Checkpoint Charlie museum. For a similar but more central sight, see the wonderful exhibits at the New Synagogue (described above) instead of trekking out here (€5, Sun–Fri 10:00–20:00, closed Sat, Lindenstrasse 9, tel. 030/2599-3300).

Karl Marx Allee—The buildings along Karl Marx Allee in eastern Berlin (just beyond Alexanderplatz) were completely leveled by the Soviets in 1945. When Stalin decided this main drag should be a showcase street, he had it rebuilt with lavish Soviet aid and named it Stalin Allee. Today this street, done in the bold Stalin Gothic style so common in Moscow back in the 1950s, has been restored (and named after Karl Marx), providing a rare look at Berlin's Communist days. Cruise down Karl Marx Allee by taxi or ride the U-Bahn to Strausberger Platz and walk to Schillingstrasse. There are some fine Social Realism reliefs on the buildings, and the lampposts incorporate the wings of a phoenix (rising from the ashes) in their design.

Natural History Museum (Museum für Naturkunde)—This place is worth a visit just to see the largest dinosaur skeleton ever assembled. While you're there, meet "Bobby" the stuffed ape (€3, Tue–Sun 09:30–17:00, closed Mon, U-6: Zinnowitzer Strasse, Invalidenstrasse 43, tel. 030/2093-8591).

Sights—Around Charlottenburg Palace

The Charlottenburg District—with a cluster of fine museums across the street from a grand palace—makes a good side trip from downtown. Ride U-2 to Sophie-Charlotte Platz and walk 10 minutes up the tree-lined boulevard (following signs to *Schloss*), or—much faster—catch bus #145 (direction: Spandau) direct from Bahnhof Zoo. For a Charlottenburg lunch, the Luisen Bräu is a comfortable brew-pub restaurant with a copper and woody atmosphere, good local "microbeers" (*dunkles*—dark, *helles*—light), and traditional German grub (€5–8 meals, daily 09:00–01:00, fun for groups, across from palace at Luisenplatz 1, tel. 030/341-9388).

▲**Charlottenburg Palace (Schloss)**—If you've seen the great palaces of Europe, this Baroque Hohenzollern palace comes in at about number 10 (behind Potsdam, too). It's even more disappointing since the main rooms can be toured only with a German guide (€8 includes 45-min tour, €2 to see just upper

Charlottenburg Palace Area

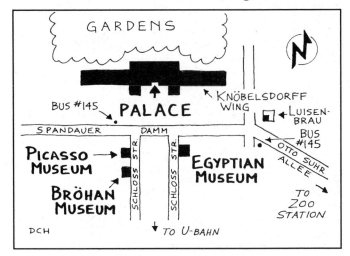

floors without tour, €7 to see palace grounds excluding tour areas, last tour 1 hour before closing, Tue–Fri 10:00–17:00, Sat–Sun 11:00–17:00, closed Mon, tel. 030/3209-1275).

The **Knöbelsdorff Wing** features a few royal apartments. Go upstairs and take a substantial hike through restored-since-the-war, gold-crusted, white rooms filled with Frederick the Great's not-so-great collection of Baroque paintings (€5 depending on special exhibitions, free English audioguide, Tue–Fri 10:00–18:00, Sat–Sun 11:00–18:00, last entry 30 min before closing, when facing the palace walk toward the right wing, tel. 030/3209-1202).

▲▲**Egyptian Museum**—Across the street from the palace, the Egyptian Museum offers one of the great thrills in art appreciation—gazing into the still-young and beautiful face of 3,000-year-old Queen Nefertiti, the wife of King Akhenaton (€4, covered by Museumspass, Tue–Sun 10:00–18:00, closed Mon, free on first Sun of month, free English audioguide, Schlossstrasse 70, tel. 030/3435-7311).

This bust of Queen Nefertiti, from 1340 B.C., is perhaps the most famous piece of Egyptian art in Europe. Discovered in 1912, she was the Marilyn Monroe of the early 20th century, with all the right beauty marks: long neck, symmetrical face, and just the right makeup. The bust never left its studio but served as a master model for all other portraits of the queen. (That's probably why the left eye was never inlaid.) Buried over 3,000 years, she was found by a German team who, by agreement with the Egyptian government, got to take home any workshop models they found.

Although this bust is not representative of Egyptian art, it's become a symbol for Egyptian art by popular acclaim. Don't overlook the rest of the impressive museum, wonderfully lit and displayed but with little English aside from the audioguide.

▲▲**Berggruen Collection: Picasso and His Time**—This tidy little museum is a pleasant surprise. Climb three floors through a fun and substantial collection of Picasso. Along the way you'll see plenty of notable work by Matisse, van Gogh, and Cézanne, and enjoy a great chance to meet Paul Klee (4€, covered by Museumspass, Tue–Fri 10:00–18:00, Sat–Sun 11:00–18:00, closed Mon, free the first Sun of month, Schlossstrasse 1, tel. 030/3269-5815).

▲**Bröhan Museum**—Wander through a dozen beautifully furnished Art Nouveau (*Jugendstil*) and art deco living rooms, a curvy organic world of lamps, glass, silver, and posters. While you're there, go to the second floor to see a fine collection of Impressionist paintings by Karl Hagemeister (€4, Tue–Sun 10:00–18:00, closed Mon, free the first Sun of month, Schlossstrasse 1A, tel. 030/3269-0600).

Sights—Near Berlin

▲**Sanssouci Palace, New Palace, and Park, Potsdam**—With a lush park strewn with the extravagant whimsies of Frederick the Great, the sleepy town of Potsdam has long been Berlin's holiday retreat. Frederick's super-rococo Sanssouci Palace is one of Germany's most dazzling. His equally extravagant New Palace (Neues Palais), built to disprove rumors that Prussia was running out of money after the costly Seven Years' War, is on the other side of the park (it's a 30-minute walk between palaces).

Your best bet for seeing Sanssouci Palace is to take the Potsdam TI's walking tour (see below). Otherwise, to make sense of all the ticket and tour options for the two palaces, stop by the palaces' TI (TI is across the street from windmill near Sanssouci entrance, helpful English-speaking staff, tel. 0331/969-4202).

Sanssouci Palace: Even though *Sanssouci* means "without a care," it can be a challenge for an English speaker to have an enjoyable visit. The palaces of Vienna, Munich, and even Würzburg offer equal sightseeing thrills with far fewer headaches. While the grounds are impressive, the interior of Sanssouci Palace can be visited only by a one-hour tour in German (with a borrowed English text), and these tours get booked up quickly. The only English option is the Potsdam TI's tour (see below).

If you take a German tour of Sanssouci, you must be at the palace in person to get your ticket and the appointment time for your tour. In the summer, if you arrive by 09:00, you'll get right in. If you arrive after 10:00, plan on a wait. If you arrive after 12:00, you may not get in at all (€8, April–Oct Tue–Sun 09:00–17:00, closed Mon, shorter hours off-season, tel. 0331/969-4190).

Greater Berlin

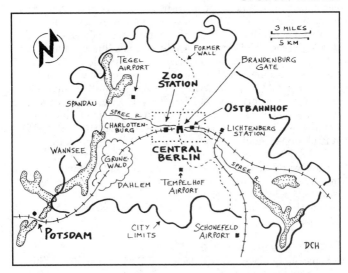

New Palace: Use the free audioguide to tour Frederick's New Palace (€5, plus €1 for optional live tour in German, mid-May–Oct Tue–Sun 09:00–17:00, closed Mon, shorter hours off-season). If you also want to see the king's apartments, you must take a required 45-minute tour in German (€6, offered daily at 11:00 and 14:00). Off-season (Nov–March) you can visit the New Palace only on a German tour (€5); it can take up to an hour for enough people to gather.

Walking Tours: The Potsdam TI's handy walking tour includes Sanssouci Palace, offering the only way to get into the palace with an English-speaking guide (€20 covers walking tour, palace, and park, 11:00 daily except Mon, 3.5 hrs, departs from Film Museum across from TI, reserve by phone, in summer reserve at least 2 days in advance, tel. 0331/275-5850, Potsdam TI hours: April–Oct Mon–Fri 09:00–19:00, Sat–Sun 10:00–16:00, less off-season, 5-min walk from Potsdam S-Bahn station, walk straight out of station and take first right onto An Der Orangerie, Friedrich-Ebert Strasse 5, tel. 0331/275-5850).

A "Discover Potsdam" walking tour (which doesn't include Sanssouci Palace) is offered by "The Original Berlin Walks" and led by a native English-speaking guide. The tour leaves from Berlin at 09:00 on Tuesday, Thursday, and Saturday (€14, or €11 if under age 26, meet at taxi stand at Zoo Station, public transportation not included but can buy ticket from guide, no booking necessary, tel. 030/301-9194). The guide takes you to Cecilienhof Palace (site of post-war Potsdam conference attended by Churchill, Stalin, and Truman), through pleasant green landscapes to the historic heart of Potsdam for lunch, and to Sanssouci Park.

What to Avoid: Potsdam's much-promoted Wannsee boat rides are torturously dull.

Getting to Potsdam: Potsdam is easy to reach from Berlin (30 min direct on S-Bahn #7 from Bahnhof Zoo to Potsdam station; Potsdam not included in a day ticket unless you buy zone C). If you're taking the Potsdam TI's tour, walk to the TI from the Potsdam S-Bahn stop (see "Walking Tours," above, for directions). If not taking the TI tour, catch bus #695 from the Potsdam station to the palaces (3/hr, 20 min). Use the same bus to shuttle between the sights in the park. For a more scenic approach, take tram #96 or #X98 from the station to Luisenplatz, then walk 15 minutes through the park and enjoy a classic view of Sansoucci.

Other Day Trips—EurAide has researched and printed a *Get Me Outta Here* flier describing good day trips to small towns and another on the nearby Sachsenhausen Concentration Camp (which many think is as interesting as Dachau; Sachsenhausen day trip also offered by Original Berlin Walks, see "City Walking Tours," above).

Nightlife in Berlin

For the young and determined sophisticate, *Zitty* and *Tip* are the top guides to alternative culture (in German, sold at kiosks). The TI's *Berlin Programm* lists a nonstop parade of concerts, plays, exhibits, and cultural events (www.berlin.de).

Tourists stroll the Ku'damm after dark. Oranienburger Strasse's trendy scene (described above) is already being eclipsed by the action at Friedrichshain and Kollwitzplatz farther east.

Visit KaDeWe's ticket office for your music and theater options (sixth floor, 18 percent fee but access to all tickets). Ask about "competitive improvisation" and variety shows.

For jazz (blues and boogie, too) near recommended Savigny-platz hotels, consider **A Trane Jazz Club** (Bleibtreustrasse 1, tel. 030/313-2550) and **Quasimodo Live** (Kantstrasse 12a, under Delphi Cinema, tel. 030/312-8086). For quality blues and New Orleans–style jazz, stop by **Ewige Lampe** (from 21:00, Niebuhr-strasse 11a).

For modern-day cabaret a short walk from the recommended hotels, consider **Bar Jeder Vernunft**. This variety show under a classic old tent perched atop a modern parking lot is a hit with German speakers but probably not worthwhile for non-German speakers. Tickets are generally around €15, and shows change regularly (shows start at 20:30, closed Sun, Schaperstrasse 24, tel. 030/883-1582).

To spend an evening enjoying Europe's largest revue theater, consider **Revue Berlin** at the Friedrichstadt Palast. The show basically depicts the history of Berlin, and is choreographed in a funny and musical way that's popular with the Lawrence Welk–type German crowd. It's even entertaining for your entire English-speaking family (€13-51, Tue–Sat 20:00, Sat–Sun at 16:00 also, U-Bahn: Oranienburger Tor, tel. 030/284-8830, www.friedrichstadtpalast.de).

Sleeping in Berlin
(€1.10 = about $1, country code: 49, area code: 030)
Sleep Code: **S** = Single, **D** = Double/Twin, **T** = Triple, **Q** = Quad, **b** = bathroom, **s** = shower only, **CC** = Credit Cards accepted, **no CC** = Credit Cards not accepted, **SE** = Speaks English, **NSE** = No English. Unless otherwise noted, a buffet breakfast is included.

I've concentrated my hotel recommendations around Savignyplatz. While the Bahnhof Zoo and Ku'damm are no longer the center of Berlin, the trains, TI, and walking tours are all still handy to Zoo. And the streets around the tree-lined Savignyplatz (a 7-min walk behind the station) have a neighborhood charm. While towering new hotels are being built in the new center, simple, small, and friendly good-value places abound only here. My listings are generally located a couple of flights up in big, run-down buildings. Inside they are clean, quiet, and spacious enough so that their well-worn character is actually charming. Rooms in back are on quiet courtyards.

The city is packed, and hotel prices go on holidays, including Green Week in mid-January, Easter weekend, first weekend in May, Ascension weekend in May, the Love Parade (a huge techno-Woodstock, second weekend in July), Germany's national holiday (Oct 2–4), Christmas, and New Year's.

During slow times, the best values are actually business-class rooms on the push list booked through the TI. But as the world learns what a great place Berlin is to visit, a rising tide of tourists will cause these deals to fade away.

Sleeping near Zoo Station at Savignyplatz
(zip code: 10623, unless otherwise noted)
These hotels and pensions are a 5- to 15-minute walk from Bahnhof Zoo (or take S-Bahn to Savignyplatz). Hotels on Kantstrasse have street noise. Ask for a quieter room in back. The area has an artsy charm going back to the cabaret days in the 1920s, when it was the center of Berlin's gay scene. Wasch Salon is a handy **Laundromat** (daily 06:00–22:00, €4–8 wash and dry, Leibnizstrasse 72, near intersection with Kantstrasse).

Business-Class Splurges near Zoo
Hotel Astoria is a friendly, three-star, business-class hotel with 32 comfortably furnished rooms and affordable summer and

weekend rates (high season Db-€153; prices drop to Sb-€107, Db-€124 during low season of July–Aug, Nov–Feb, or any 2 weekend nights or if slow; rooms with showers are cheaper than rooms with baths, CC, elevator, around corner from Bahnhof Zoo at Fasanenstrasse 2, tel. 030/312-4067, fax 030/312-5027, www.hotelastoria.de, e-mail: astoriahotel@t-online.de).

Heckers Hotel is an ultramodern, four-star business hotel with all the sterile Euro-comforts (Sb-€133, Db-€159, breakfast-€15, summer and weekends breakfast included, CC, some smoke-free rooms, between Savignyplatz and Ku'damm at Grolmanstrasse 35, tel. 030/88900, fax 030/889-0260, www .heckers-hotel.com).

Hotel Askanischerhof is the oldest *Zimmer* in Berlin. Posh as can be, you get porters, valet parking, and 16 sprawling antique-furnished rooms. Photos on the walls brag of famous movie-star guests. Frau Glinicke offers Old World service and classic Berlin atmosphere (Sb-€100–107, Db-€128–143, CC, some smoke-free rooms, elevator, Ku'damm 53, tel. 030/881-8033, fax 030/881-7206, www.askanischer-hof.de, e-mail: aska_hof_berlin@brnet.net).

Inexpensive Pensions near Savignyplatz
These hotels are clean but well worn, unless otherwise stated.

Pension Peters, run by a German-Swedish couple, is sunny and central with a cheery breakfast room. Decorated sleek Scandinavian, with every room renovated, it's a winner (S-€31–41, Ss-€46–51, D-€51–56, Ds-€61–66, Db-€66–77, extra bed-€8, kids under 12 free, family room, CC, Internet access, 10 meters off Savignyplatz at Kantstrasse 146, tel. 030/3150-3944, fax 030/ 312-3519, e-mail: penspeters@aol.com, Annika and Christoph SE). They also rent apartments (ideal for small groups and longer stays) and bikes (€5/day).

Hotel Crystal Garni is professional with small, well-worn but comfortable rooms and a *vollkorn* breakfast room (S-€36, Sb-€41, D-€46, Ds-€56, Db-€66–77, CC, elevator, a block past Savignyplatz at Kantstrasse 144, tel. 030/312-9047, fax 030/312-6465, run by John and Dorothy Schwarzrock and Herr Glasgow Flasher).

Pension Alexis is a classic old-European four-room pension in a stately 19th-century apartment run by Frau and Herr Schwarzer. The shower and toilet facilities are older and cramped, but this, more than any other Berlin listing, has you feeling at home with a faraway aunt (S-€39–41, D-€56–61, T-€84, Q-€114, no CC, big rooms, hand-held showers, Carmerstrasse 15, tel. 030/312-5144, enough English spoken).

Hotel Carmer 16, with 40 bright, airy rooms, feels like a big professional hotel with all the comfy extras (S-€56, Sb-€72–92, D-€72–82, Db-€92–114, CC, elevator, Carmerstrasse 16,

Berlin's Savignyplatz Neighborhood

❶ PENSION PETERS	❽ HOTEL ASTORIA	⓮ HOTEL BOGOTA
❷ HOTEL CRYSTAL GARNI	❾ PENSION SAVOY & IMPERATOR	⓯ HOTEL PENSION FUNK
❸ PENSION ALEXIS	❿ HOTEL ATLANTA	⓰ DICKE WIRTIN
❹ HOTEL CARMER 16	⓫ HECKERS HOTEL	⓱ ZILLEMARKT REST
❺ JUGENDGASTEHAUS AM ZOO	⓬ HOTEL ASKANISCHERHOF	⓲ SCHELL REST
❻ HOTEL PENSION EDEN AM ZOO	⓭ HOTELS AUSTRIANA, RÜGEN,	⓳ KÄTHE KOLLEWITZ
❼ PENSION SILVA	CURTIS, HOTEL-PENSION BELLA,	MUSEUM
	WEYERS CAFE RESTAURANT	⓴ TO LAUNDROMAT

tel. 030/3110-0500, fax 030/3110-0510, e-mail: carmer16 @t-online.de).

Pension Silva is a basic place just off Savignyplatz with 15 spacious well-furnished rooms (S-€28, Sb-€46, Db-€51, Tb-€77, €5 less without breakfast, no CC, Knesebeckstrasse 29, tel. 030/881-2129, fax 030/885-0435).

Pension Savoy rents 16 rooms with all the amenities. You'll love the cheery old pastel breakfast room (Ss-€61, Sb-€72, Db-€100–107, CC, Meinekestrasse 4, 10719 Berlin, elevator, tel. 030/881-3700, fax 030/882-3746, www.hotel-pension-savoy.de, e-mail: info@hotel-pension-savoy.de).

Hotel-Pension Imperator fills a sprawling floor of a grand building with 11 big quiet and Old-World-elegant rooms (S-€41, Sb-€61, D-€77, Ds-€87, Db-€97, breakfast is classy but an extra

€6–10, no CC, elevator, Meinekestrasse 5, tel. 030/8814181, fax 030/8851919).

Hotel Atlanta is in an older building half a block south of Ku'damm. It's next to Gucci, on an elegant shopping street, with big leather couches (Ss-€56–72, Sb-€66–90, Db-€82–100, extra person-€5, some smoke-free rooms, CC, Fasanenstrasse 74, 10719 Berlin, tel. 030/881-8049, fax 030/ 881-9872, www.hotelatlanta.de, e-mail: hatlanta68266759@aol.com).

Hotel Bogota has 125 big and comfortable rooms in a sprawling, drab old building. The service is brisk and hotelesque. Pieces of the owner's modern art collection lurk around every corner. Take a peek at the bizarre collage in the atrium—with mannequins suspended from the ceiling (S-€44, Ss-€51, Sb-€66, D-€66, Ds-€74, Db-€97, T-€84, Tb-€114, children under 15 free, elevator, CC, smoke-free rooms, bus #109 from Bahnhof Zoo to Schlüterstrasse 45, tel. 030/881-5001, fax 030/883-5887, www.hotelbogota.de, e-mail: hotel.bogota@t-online.de).

Hotel-Pension Funk, the former home of a 1920s silent-movie star, is delightfully quirky. It offers 14 elegant, richly furnished old rooms (S-€36–46, Ss-€56, Sb-€66, D-€66, Ds-€77, Db-€87, extra person-€23, CC but prefer cash, Fasanenstrasse 69, a long block south of Ku'damm, tel. 030/882-7193, fax 030/883-3329).

Hotel Pension Eden am Zoo is another nondescript place with well-worn rooms in a big, old, well-located building (25 rooms, S-€36, Ss-€41, Sb-€51, D-€51, Ds-€61, Db-€77, no CC, Uhlandstrasse 184, tel. 030/881-5900, fax 030/881-5732, www.rheingold-hotel.de).

Jugendgastehaus am Zoo is a bare-bones, cash-only youth hostel that takes no reservations and hardly has a reception desk. It's far less comfortable and only marginally cheaper than simple hotels (85 beds, €18-dorm beds, S-€24, D-€44, includes sheets, breakfast not included, no CC, Hardenbergstrasse 9a, tel. 030/ 312-9410, fax 030/312-5430).

Sleeping South of Ku'damm
(zip code: 10707)

Several small hotels are nearby in a charming, café-studded neighborhood 300 meters south of Ku'damm near the intersection of Sächsische Strasse and Pariser Strasse (bus #109 from Bahnhof Zoo, direction: Airport Tegel). They are less convenient from the station than the Savignyplatz listings above.

Hotel Austriana, with 25 modern and bright rooms, is warmly and energetically run by Thomas (S-€39, Ss-€44–49, Sb-€51–66, Ds-€61–72, Db-€77–92, cheaper off-season, CC, elevator, Pariser Strasse 39, tel. 030/885-7000, fax 030/8857-0088, www.austriana.de, e-mail: austriana@t-online.de). Two other pensions are in the same building: the ornate and eastern-feeling

Hotel Rügen (S-€28, Ss-€39, D-€51, Ds-€61–66, Db-€77–82, CC, Pariser Strasse 39, tel. 030/884-3940, fax 030/884-39-437, www.insel-ruegen.hotel.de, e-mail: ir-hotel@t-online.de), and the hip, piney, and basic **Pension Curtis** (S-€36–39, Ds-€56–69, Ts-€84–87, Qs-€102, no CC, cheaper for slow-time drop-ins, Pariser Strasse 39, tel. 030/883-4931, fax 030/885-0438).

Hotel-Pension Bella, a clean, simple, masculine-feeling place with high ceilings and a cheery, attentive management, rents nine big, comfortable rooms (S-€41, Ss/Sb-€51–66, D-€56–61, Ds-€71–82, Db-€72–82, Ts-€87, Qs-€102, CC, bus #249 from Zoo, Ludwigkirchstrasse 10a, tel. 030/881-6704, fax 030/8867-9074, www.pension-bella.de, e-mail: pension.bella@t-online.de).

More Berlin Hotels

Near Augsburgerstrasse U-Bahn stop: Consider **Hotel-Pension Nürnberger Eck** (S-€46, Sb-€61, D-€72, Db-€87–92, no CC, Nürnberger Strasse 24a, tel. 030/235-1780, fax 030/2351-7899) or, just upstairs, **Pension Fischer** (D-€36, Ds-€41–46, Db-€62–67, no CC, breakfast-€5, Nürnberger Strasse 24a, tel. 030/218-6808, fax 030/213-4225), or **Hotel Arco** (Sb-€64–74, Db-€51–92, no CC, Geisbergerstrasse 30, tel. 030/235-1480, fax 030/2147-5178, www.arco-hotel.de).

Near Güntzelstrasse U-Bahn stop: Pension Güntzel (Ds-€56, Db-€66–77, single rooms €15 less, no CC, Guntzelstrasse 62, tel. 030/857-9020, fax 030/853-1108, www.pension-gruenzel.de), **Pension Finck** (Ss-80, Ds-€56, no CC, Güntzelstrasse 54, tel. 030/861-2940, fax 030/861-8158), or the **Hotel Pension München** (D-€41, Db-€59–66, breakfast-€5, also Güntzelstrasse 62, tel. 030/857-9120, fax 030/8579-1222).

In eastern Berlin: The **Hotel Unter den Linden** is ideal for those nostalgic for the days of Soviet rule, although nowadays at least, the management tries to be efficient and helpful. Formerly one of the best hotels in the DDR, this huge blocky hotel, right on Unter den Linden in the heart of what was East Berlin, is reasonably comfortable and reasonably priced. Built in 1966 with prisonlike corridors, its 331 rooms are modern, plain, and comfy (Sb-€61–123, standard Db-€92–128, superior Db-€103–154, only a tiny difference between standard and superior, some nonsmoking rooms, CC, at intersection of Friedrichstrasse, Unter den Linden 14, 10117 Berlin, tel. 030/238-110, fax 030/2381-1100, e-mail: reservation@hotel-unter-den-linden.de).

Berlin Hostels

Berlin has plenty of great hostels in eastern Berlin. Four good bets are: **Studentenhotel Meininger 10** (D-€45, €21-per-bed quads, includes sheets and breakfast, no curfew, elevator, free parking, near city hall on JFK Platz, Meiningerstrasse 10, U-Bahn:

Rathaus Schoneberg, tel. 030/7871-7414, fax 030/7871-7412, www.studentenhotel.de, e-mail: info@studentenhotel.de), **Mitte's Backpacker Hostel** (€12–15 dorm beds, D-€21, T-€19, Q-€18, sheets-€2, no CC, breakfast-€4, funky "theme" rooms, no curfew, Internet access, bike rental-€5, English newspapers, U-Bahn: Zinnowitzerstrasse, Chauseestrasse 102, tel. 030/262-5140, fax 030/2839-0935, www.backpacker.de, e-mail: info@backpacker.de), **Circus** (dorm bed-€13, S-€25, D-€20, T-€17, Q-€15, apartments-€50–92, no CC, breakfast-€2, sheets-€2, no curfew, Internet access, laundry machines, U-Bahn: Alexanderplatz, Rosa-Luxemburg Strasse 39, tel. 030/2839-1433, fax 030/2839-1484, e-mail: circus@mind.de), or **Clubhouse** (dorm bed-€14, bed in 5- to 7-bed room-€16, S-€31, D-€23, T-€20, no CC, breakfast-€4, sheets-€2, on second floor, nightclub below, Internet access, in hip Oranienburger Strasse area, S- or U-Bahn: Friedrichstrasse, Kalkscheunenstrasse 4, tel. 030/2809-7979, fax 030/2809-7977, www.clubhouse-berlin.de, e-mail: mailto@clubhouse-berlin.de).

Eating in Berlin

Don't be too determined to eat "Berlin style." The city is known only for its mildly spicy sausage. Still, there is a world of restaurants in this ever-changing city to choose from. Your best approach may be to choose a neighborhood rather than a particular restaurant.

For quick and easy meals, colorful pubs—called *Kneipen*—offer light meals and the fizzy local beer, Berliner Weiss. Ask for it *mit Schuss* for a shot of fruity syrup in your suds. If the kraut is getting wurst, try one of the many Turkish, Italian, or Balkan restaurants. Eat cheap at *Imbiss* snack stands, bakeries (sandwiches), and falafel/kebab places. Bahnhof Zoo has several bright and modern fruit-and-sandwich bars and a grocery (daily 06:00–24:00).

Eating in Western Berlin

Near Bahnhof Zoo

Self-service Cafeterias: The top floor of the famous department store, **KaDeWe**, holds the Winter Garden Buffet view cafeteria, and its sixth-floor deli/food department is a picnicker's nirvana. Its arterials are clogged with more than 1,000 kinds of sausage and 1,500 types of cheese (Mon–Fri 09:30–20:00, Sat 09:00–16:00, closed Sun, U-Bahn: Ku'damm). The **Wertheim** department store, a half block from the Memorial Church, has cheap food counters in the basement and a city view from its fine self-service cafeteria, Le Buffet, located up six banks of escalators (Mon–Fri 09:30–20:00, Sat 09:00–16:00, closed Sun, U-Bahn: Ku'damm). The **Marche**, popping up in big cities all over Germany, is another inexpensive self-service cafeteria within a half block of the Kaiser Wilhelm church (daily 08:00–24:00,

CC, plenty of salads, fruit, made-to-order omelets, Ku'damm 14, tel. 030/882-7578).

At the Zoo station: Terrasan am Zoo is a good restaurant right in the station (upstairs, next to track 1), offering peaceful decency amidst a whirlwind of travel activity.

Near Savignyplatz
Several good places are on or within 100 meters (300 feet) of Savignyplatz. Take a walk and survey these: **Dicke Wirtin** is a smoky old pub with good *Kneipe* atmosphere, famously cheap *Gulaschsuppe*, and salads (Mon–Thu 12:00–03:00, Fri–Sun 12:00–04:00, just off Savignyplatz at Carmerstrasse 9, tel. 030/312-4952). **Die Zwölf Apostel** restaurant is trendy for leafy candlelit ambience and Italian food. A dressy local crowd packs the place for €10 pizzas and €15 meals. Late-night partygoers appreciate Apostel's great breakfast (daily, 24 hrs, immediately across from Savigny S-Bahn entrance, Bleibtreustrasse 49, tel. 030/312-1433). **Ristorante San Marino**, on the square, is another good Italian place, serving cheaper pasta and pizza (daily 10:00–01:00, Savignyplatz 12, tel. 030/313-6086). **Zillemarkt Restaurant** feels like an old-time Berlin beer garden. It serves traditional Berlin specialties in the garden or in the rustic candlelit interior (€10 meals, daily 09:00–01:00, no English menu—that's good, near the S-Bahn tracks at Bleibtreustrasse 48a, tel. 030/881-7040).

Schell Restaurant is a dressy place (named for a gas station that once stood there) serving high Italian cuisine to a completely German crowd that seems "in the know" (€21 dinner plates, daily, a block off Savignyplatz at Knesebackstrasse 22, reservations smart, tel. 030/312-8310). **Café Hegel** is a mellow little Russian piano bar with light meals right on Savignyplatz. Late at night there may be some balalaika music (open nightly from 20:00 on, Savignyplatz 2, tel. 030/312-1948).

Weyers Cafe Restaurant, serving quality international and German cuisine, is a great value and worth a short walk. It's sharp, with white tablecloths, but not stuffy (€10 dinner plates, CC, daily 08:00–24:00, seating indoors or outside on the leafy square, Pariser Strasse 16, reservations smart after 20:00, tel. 030/881-9378).

Ullrich Supermarkt is the neighborhood grocery store (Mon–Fri 09:00–20:00, Sat 09:00–16:00, closed Sun, Kantstrasse 7, under the tracks near Bahnhof Zoo). There's plenty of fast food near Bahnhof Zoo and on Ku'damm.

Eating in Eastern Berlin
Along Unter den Linden near Pergamon Museum
The Opernpalais, preening with fancy pre-war elegance, hosts a number of pricey restaurants. Its **Operncafé** has the best desserts

(longest dessert bar in Europe, daily 08:00–24:00, across from university and war memorial at Unter den Linden 5, tel. 030/202-683). Sit down and enjoy perhaps the classiest coffee stop in Berlin. The shady beer and tea garden in front has a cheap self-service *Imbiss* (wurst, meatball sandwiches, and so on) and a *creperie* (from 10:00, depending on weather). More students and fewer tourists eat in the student facilities at Humboldt University across the street (go through courtyard, enter building through main door, follow signs to cafeteria on right or mensa on left, both closed weekends).

Oren Restaurant and Café is a trendy, stylish, near-kosher/vegetarian place next to the New Synagogue. The food is pricey but good, and the ambience is happening (Sun–Thu 12:00–24:00, Fri–Sat 10:00–02:00, north of Museum Island about 5 blocks away at Oranienburger Strasse 28, tel. 030/282-8228).

Near Checkpoint Charlie
Lekkerbek is a busy little bakery and cafeteria selling inexpensive and tasty salads, soups, pastas, and sandwiches (Mon–Sat, closed Sun, a block from Checkpoint Charlie museum at Kochstrasse subway stop on Friedrichstrasse). For a classier sit-down meal, try **Café Adler** across the street from the museum.

Near Gendarmenmarkt
For information on this pleasant square, look up Gendarmenmarket in "Sights—Eastern Berlin," above.

Elegant lunch spots are tucked away behind the concert hall. **Restaurant Lang** (at Charlottenstrasse 59) and the **Spitz Restaurant** next door are both deservedly popular with local businesspeople. **Fassbender & Rausch**, on the corner near the Lang and Spitz restaurants, is Europe's biggest **chocolate store**. After 150 years of chocolate making, this family-owned business proudly displays its sweet delights—200 different kinds—on a 15-meter-long (50-foot) buffet. Truffles are sold for about €0.50 each. The shop's evangelical Herr Ostwald (a.k.a. Benny) would love you to try his bestseller: tiramisu (Mon–Fri 10:00–20:00, Sat 10:00–16:00, closed Sun, corner of Mohrenstrasse at Charlottenstrasse 60, tel. 030/2045-8440).

Transportation Connections—Berlin
Berlin has three train stations. Bahnhof Zoo was the West Berlin train station and still serves Western Europe: Frankfurt, Munich, Hamburg, Paris, and Amsterdam. The Ostbahnhof (former East Berlin's main station) still faces east, serving Prague, Warsaw, Vienna, and Dresden. The Lichtenberg Bahnhof (eastern Berlin's top U- and S-Bahn hub) also handles a few eastbound trains. Expect exceptions. All stations are conveniently connected by subway and even faster by train. Train info: tel. 01805-996-633.

By train to: Frankfurt (14/day, 5 hrs), **Munich** (14/day,
7 hrs, 10 hrs overnight), **Köln** (hrly, 6.5 hrs), **Amsterdam** (4/day,
7 hrs), **Budapest** (2/day, 13 hrs), **Copenhagen** (4/day, 8 hrs,
change in Hamburg), **London** (4/day, 15 hrs), **Paris** (6/day, 13
hrs, change in Köln, 1 direct night train), **Zurich** (12/day, 10 hrs,
1 direct night train), **Prague** (4/day, 5 hrs, no overnight trains),
Warsaw (4/day, 8 hrs), **Vienna** (2/day, 12 hrs via Czech Republic;
for second-class ticket, Eurailers pay an extra €23 if under age 26
or €31 if age 26 or above; otherwise, take the Berlin-Vienna via
Passau train—nightly at 20:00).

Eurailpasses don't cover the Czech Republic. The **Prague
Excursion pass** picks up where Eurail leaves off, getting you from
any border into Prague and then back out to Eurail country again
within seven days (first class-€46, second class-€36, youth second
class-€26, buy at EurAide in Berlin at the Bahnhof Zoo and get
reservations—€3—at the same time).

There are **night trains** from Berlin to Amsterdam, Munich,
Köln, Brussels, Paris, Vienna, Budapest, Stuttgart, Basel, and
Zurich, but there are no night trains from Berlin to anywhere
in Italy or Spain. A *Liegeplatz*, or berth (€15–21), is a great deal;
inquire at EurAide at Bahnhof Zoo for details. Beds cost the same
whether you have a first- or second-class ticket or railpass. Trains
are often full, so get your bed reserved a few days in advance from
any travel agency or major train station in Europe. Note: Since
the Paris–Berlin night train goes through Belgium, railpass
holders cannot use a Europass or Eurail Selectpass to cover
this ride unless they've added or selected Belgium.

Berlin's Three Airports

Allow €20 for a taxi ride to or from any of Berlin's airports.
Tegel Airport handles most flights from the United States and
Western Europe (6 km from center, catch the faster bus #X9 to
Bahnhof Zoo or bus #109 to Ku'damm and Bahnhof Zoo for €2).
Flights from the east usually arrive at **Schönefeld Airport** (20 km
from center, short walk to S-Bahn, catch S-9 to Zoo Station).
Templehof Airport's future is uncertain (in Berlin, bus #119
to Ku'damm or U-Bahn 6 or 7). The central telephone number
for all three airports is 01805-000-186. For British Air, call 01805-
266-522, Delta at 01803-337-880, SAS at 01803-234-023, or
Lufthansa at 01803-803-803.

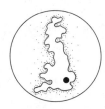

LONDON

London is more than 600 square miles of urban jungle. With 9 million struggling people—many of whom speak English—it's a world in itself and a barrage on all the senses. On my first visit I felt very, very small. London is much more than its museums and famous landmarks. It's a living, breathing, thriving organism.

London has changed dramatically in recent years, and many visitors are surprised to find how "un-English" it is. Whites are now a minority in major parts of the city that once symbolized white imperialism. Arabs have nearly bought out the area north of Hyde Park. Chinese take-outs outnumber fish-and-chips shops. Many hotels are run by people with foreign accents (who hire English chambermaids), while outlying suburbs are home to huge communities of Indians and Pakistanis. London is learning—sometimes fitfully—to live as a microcosm of its formerly vast empire. Many see the English Channel Tunnel as another foreign threat to the Britishness of Britain.

With just a few days here, you'll get no more than a quick splash in this teeming human tidal pool. But, with a quick orientation, you'll get a good look at its top sights, history, and cultural entertainment, as well as its ever-changing human face.

Have fun in London. Blow through the city on the open deck of a double-decker orientation tour bus, and take a pinch-me-I'm-in-Britain walk through downtown. Ogle the crown jewels at the Tower of London, hear the chimes of Big Ben, and see the Houses of Parliament in action. Hobnob with the tombstones in Westminster Abbey, duck WWII bombs in Churchill's underground Cabinet War Rooms, and brave the earthshaking

Imperial War Museum. Overfeed the pigeons at Trafalgar Square. Visit with Leonardo, Botticelli, and Rembrandt in the National Gallery. Whisper across the dome of St. Paul's Cathedral and rummage through our civilization's attic at the British Museum. Cruise down the Thames River. At the National Portrait Gallery, watch the parade of British greats who created history—from kings and queens to the artists in between. You'll enjoy some of Europe's best people-watching at Covent Garden and snap to at Buckingham Palace's Changing of the Guard. Just sit in Victoria Station, at a major tube station, at Piccadilly Circus, or in Trafalgar Square, and observe. Spend one evening at a theater and the others catching your breath.

Planning Your Time

The sights of London alone could easily fill a trip to Britain. It's a great one-week getaway. On a short tour of Britain I'd give it three busy days. If you're flying in, consider starting your trip in Bath and make London your British finale. Especially if you hope to enjoy a play or concert, a night or two of jet lag is bad news.

Here's a suggested schedule:

Day 1: 09:00–Tower of London (Beefeater tour, crown jewels), 12:00–Munch a sandwich on the Thames while cruising from the Tower to Westminster Bridge, 13:00–Follow the self-guided Westminster Walk (see below) with a quick visit to the Cabinet War Rooms, 15:30–Trafalgar Square and National Gallery, 17:30–Visit the Britain Visitors Centre near Piccadilly, planning ahead for your trip, 18:30–Dinner in Soho. Take in a play or 19:30 concert at St. Martin-in-the-Fields.

Day 2: 09:00–Take the Round London bus tour (consider hopping off near the end for the 11:30 Changing of the Guard at Buckingham Palace), 12:30–Covent Gardens for lunch and people watching, 14:00–Tour the British Museum. Have a pub dinner before a play, concert, or evening walking tour.

Days 3 and 4: Choose among these remaining London highlights: Tour Westminster Abbey (tour, evensong), British Library, Imperial War Museum, the two Tates (Tate Modern on the south bank for modern art, Tate Britain on the north bank for British art), St. Paul's Cathedral (tour, dome climb, evensong), Museum of London, or London Eye Ferris Wheel (reserve in advance); cruise to Kew or Greenwich; do some serious shopping at one of London's elegant department stores or open-air markets; or consider another historic walking tour.

After considering nearly all of London's tourist sights, I have pruned them down to just the most important (or fun) for a first visit of up to seven days. You won't be able to see all of these, so don't try. You'll keep coming back to London. After 25 visits myself, I still enjoy a healthy list of excuses to return.

Orientation (area code: 020)

To grasp London comfortably, see it as the old town without the modern, congested sprawl. Most of the visitor's London lies between the Tower of London and Hyde Park—about a three-mile walk. Mentally—maybe even physically—scissor down your map to include only the area between the Tower, King's Cross Station, Paddington Station, the Victoria and Albert Museum, and Victoria Station. With this focus and a good orientation, you'll find London manageable and even fun.

Tourist Information

The **Britain Visitors Centre** is the best information service in town (Mon–Fri 09:00–18:30, Sat–Sun 10:00–16:00, phone not answered after 17:00 Mon–Fri and not at all Sat–Sun, booking service, just off Piccadilly Circus at 1 Lower Regent Street, tel. 020/8846-9000, www.visitbritain.com). It's great for London information; buy your city map here (Bensons £2 Mapguide is best, also sold at newsstands). If you're traveling beyond London, take advantage of its well-equipped London/England desk, Wales desk (tel. 020/7808-3838), Ireland desk (tel. 020/7808-3841), and Scotland desk. At the center's extensive bookshop, gather whatever guidebooks, hostel directories, maps, and information you'll need. For trips through Britain, consider the *Michelin Green Guide to Britain* (£9.25; Green Guide just for London also available), the Britain road atlas (£10), and Ordnance Survey maps for areas you'll be exploring by car. The tourist office has a travel agency upstairs plus computers displaying only their Web site: www.visitbritain.com.

Nearby you'll find the **Scottish Tourist Centre** (mid-June–mid-Sept Mon–Fri 09:00–18:00, Sat 10:00–17:00, off-season Mon–Fri 09:30–17:30, Sat 12:00–16:00, Cockspur Street, tel. 0131/472-2035, www.visitscotland.com) and the slick **French National Tourist Office** (Mon–Fri 10:00–18:00, Sat until 17:00, closed Sun, 178 Piccadilly Street).

Unfortunately, **London's Tourist Information Centres** are now owned by the big hotels' exchange bureaus and are simply businesses selling advertising space to companies with fliers to distribute. They are reasonably helpful but biased. Locations include Heathrow Airport's tube station, which serves Terminals 1, 2, and 3 (daily 08:00–18:00, most convenient and least crowded); Victoria Station (daily 08:00–20:00, crowded and commercial); and Waterloo International Terminal Arrivals Hall (daily 08:30–22:30, serving trains from Paris; if you arrive by train when the TI is mobbed, skip it, buy city map at newsstand upstairs in station lobby, then return downstairs to catch the tube or a taxi to your hotel).

Bring your itinerary and a checklist of questions to any of the TIs and pick up these publications: *London Planner* (a great

It's Party Time Again

It's been two years since the big millennium bash, so it's about time for another party.

In 2002 Britain hosts a Golden Jubilee Celebration to commemorate the 50-year reign of Queen Elizabeth. You can expect festivities throughout the U.K. as the queen makes her rounds from May through July. The biggest party is in London from June 1 through 4, with concerts at Buckingham Palace (classical on June 1, pop on June 3—when the queen rocks), bell-ringing across the U.K. (June 2), fireworks (June 3), and a Procession to St. Paul's plus a Carnival Pageant (June 4). In honor of the queen's reign, a new covered Jubilee Bridge will cross the Thames come June, to the delight of pedestrians frustrated by the wobbly Millennium Bridge. This new bridge (attached to the Cannon Railway Bridge between Southwark and London Bridges) does what the Millennium Bridge was supposed to do—it provides a pedestrian-friendly way to connect North and South Bank sights. As part of the Jubilee celebration, a London String of Pearls festival (www.stringofpearls.org.uk) showcases sights all along the Thames, with exhibitions, tours, and performances throughout the summer. Britain knows how to throw a royal party. For your invitation, see www.goldenjubilee.gov.uk.

free monthly that lists all the sights, events, and hours), walking-tour schedule fliers, a theater guide, Central London bus guide, and the Thames River Services brochure.

TIs sell BT phone cards, long-distance bus tickets and passes, British Heritage Passes, and tickets to plays (20 percent booking fee). And they book rooms (avoid their £5 booking fee by calling hotels directy).

The **London Pass** gives free entrance to most of the city's sights, but—especially with many museums lowering or eliminating their entrance fees in 2002 and with the cluttery decisions a pass adds to your trip (should I go here, there, or everywhere . . . ?)—it's worthwhile only for torrid sightseers (£18/1 day, £27/2 days, £32/3 days, £43/6 days). London does have many mildly interesting sights worth a quick look but perhaps not their steep £6 admission fee. With the pass, you can just go crazy.

TIs also sell **"Fast Track" tickets** to some of London's attractions (at no extra cost), allowing you to skip the queue at the sights. They're worthwhile for places notorious for long ticket lines such as the Tower of London, London Eye Ferris wheel, and Madame Tussaud's Wax Museum.

Helpful Hints

U.S. Embassy: 24 Grosvenor Square (for passport concerns, open Mon–Fri 08:30–11:30 plus Mon, Wed, Fri 14:00–16:00, tube: Bond Street, tel. 020/7499-9000).

Theft Alert: The Artful Dodger is alive and well in London. Be on guard, particularly when using public transportation and in places crowded with tourists. Tourists, considered naive and rich, are targeted. Over 7,500 handbags are stolen annually at Covent Garden alone. Thieves paw you so you don't feel the pickpocketing.

Changing Money: ATMs are the way to go. For changing traveler's checks, standard transaction fees at banks are £2 to £4. American Express offices offer a fair rate and change any brand of traveler's checks for no fee. Handy AmEx offices are at Heathrow's Terminal 4 tube station (daily 07:00–19:00) and near Piccadilly (June–Sept Mon–Fri 08:30–19:00, Sat 09:00–18:30, Sun 10:00–17:00; Oct–May Mon–Sat 09:00–17:30, Sun 10:00–17:00; 30 Haymarket, tel. 020/7484-9600). Marks & Spencer Department stores offer good rates with no fees.

Avoid changing money at exchange bureaus. Their latest scam: They advertise very good rates with a same-as-the-banks fee of 2 percent. But the fine print explains that the fee of 2 percent is for buying pounds. The fee for *selling* pounds is 9.5 percent. Ouch!

What's Up: For the best listing of what's happening (plays, movies, restaurants, concerts, exhibitions, protests, walking tours, shopping, and children's activities) and a look at the trendy London scene, pick up a current copy of *Time Out* (£2, www .timeout.co.uk) or *What's On* at any newsstand. The TI's free monthly *London Planner* lists sights, plays, and events at least as well. For a chatty, *People Magazine*–type Web site on London's entertainment, theater, restaurants, and news, visit www .thisislondon.com. For plays, try www.officiallondontheatre.co.uk.

Sights: There's talk of making most sights free of charge in 2002. Currently the British Museum, British Library, National Gallery, National Portrait Gallery, Tate Britain (British art), and Tate Modern (modern art), along with many other top London museums, are free—though special exhibitions cost extra.

Telephoning first to check hours and confirm plans, especially off-season when hours can shrink, is always smart.

Internet Access: The astonishing easyEverything offers up to 500 computers per store, 24 hours daily. Depending on demand, a mere £2 ticket buys anywhere from 80 minutes to six hours of computer time. The ticket is valid for four weeks and multiple visits at any of their five branches: Victoria Station (across from front of station, near taxis and buses, long lines), Trafalgar Square, Tottenham Court Road, Oxford Street, and Kensington High Street (www.easyEverything.com).

Travel Bookstores: Stanfords Travel Bookstore is good

and stocks current editions of my books at Covent Garden (12 Long Acre, tel. 020/7836-1321) and 156 Regent Street (tel. 020/7434-4744). There are two impressive Waterstones Bookstores: the biggest in Europe on Piccadilly and one on the corner of Trafalgar Square (next to Coffee Republic café, tel. 020/7839-4411).

Travel Agency: The student travel agency, USIT, across from Victoria Station, has great deals on flights for people of all ages (Mon–Fri 09:00–18:00, Sat 10:00–17:00, Sun 11:00–15:00, Buckingham Palace Road, tel. 020/7823-5363, www.usitcampus .co.uk). Also, take a look in the Sunday *Times* travel section for cheap flights.

Beatles: Fans of the still-Fabulous Four can take one of the Beatles walks (5/week, offered by Original London Walks, under "Tours of London," below), visit the Beatles Shop (231 Baker Street, next to Sherlock Holmes Museum, tube: Baker Street), or go to Abbey Road and walk the famous crosswalk (at intersection with Grove End, tube: St. John's Wood).

Luggage Lockers: Victoria Station has a huge room full of lockers (3 sizes: £4, £5, and £8/24 hrs, daily 07:00–22:15, up ramp behind platform 8). The airports also have places to check bags. If leaving London and returning later, it may be possible to leave a box or bag at your hotel for free—assuming you'll be staying there again.

Arrival in London
By Train: London has eight train stations, all connected by the tube (subway) and all with exchange offices and luggage storage. From any station, ride the tube or taxi to your hotel.

By Bus: The bus station is one block southwest of Victoria Station, which has a TI and tube entrance.

By Plane: For detailed information on getting from London's airports to downtown London, see "Transportation Connections" at the end of this chapter.

Getting Around London
London's taxis, buses, and subway system make a private car unnecessary. To travel smart in a city this size, you must get comfortable with public transportation. For tube and bus information 24 hours a day, call 020/7222-1234 (www.transportforlondon.gov.uk).

By Taxi: London is the best taxi town in Europe. Big, black, carefully-regulated cabs are everywhere. I never met a crabby cabbie in London. They love to talk and know every nook and cranny in town. I ride in one a day just to get my London questions answered. Rides start at £1.50 and cost about £1.50 per tube stop. Connecting downtown sights is quick and easy and will cost you about £4 (e.g., St. Paul's to the Tower of London). For a short ride, three people in a cab travel at tube prices. Groups of four or five should taxi everywhere (though families save money, if not

London

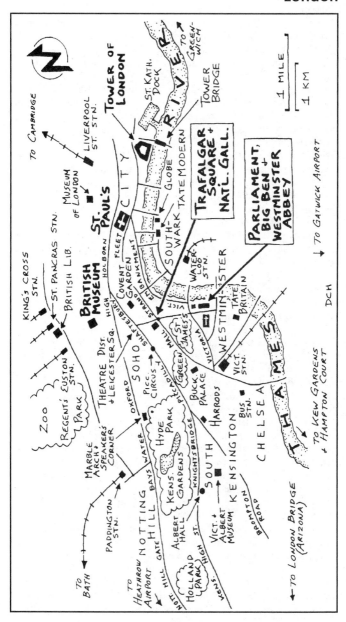

time, with the "One Day Family Travel Card" sold at tube stops). If a cab's top light is on, just wave it down. (Drivers flash lights when they see you.) They have a tiny turning radius, so you can wave at cabs going in either direction. If waving doesn't work, ask someone where you can find a taxi stand. While telephoning a cab gets one in minutes, it's generally not necessary and adds to the cost. London is such a great wave-'em-down taxi town that most cabs don't even have a radio phone. Don't worry about meter cheating. British cab meters come with a sealed computer chip and clock that ensures you'll get the regular tariff #1 most of the time, tariff #2 during "unsociable hours" (18:00–06:00 and Sat–Sun), and tariff #3 only on holidays. All extra charges are explained in writing on the cab wall. The only way a cabbie can cheat you is by taking a needlessly long route. There are alternative cab companies driving normal-looking, non-metered cars that charge fixed rates based on postal codes of your start and end points. These are generally honest and can actually be cheaper when snarled traffic drives up the cost of a metered cab.

By Bus: London's extensive bus system is easy to follow. Just pick up a free "Central London Bus Guide" map from a TI or tube station. Signs at stops list routes clearly. There are two kinds of buses. Those without a conductor (pay the driver as you enter) and those with a conductor (just hop on, take a seat, relax, and sooner or later the conductor will come by and collect £1). Any ride in downtown London costs £1. (The best views are upstairs.) If you have a Travel Card (see below), get in the habit of hopping buses for quick little straight shots, even just to get to a metro stop. During bump-and-grind rush hours (8:00–10:00 and 16:00–19:00), you'll go faster by tube. Consider two special bus deals: all day for £2 and a ticket six-pack for £4.

By Tube: London's subway is one of this planet's great people movers and the fastest—and cheapest—long-distance transport in town (runs daily about 05:00–24:00). Any ride in the Central Zone (on or within the Circle Line, including virtually all my recommended sights and hotels) costs £1.50. You can avoid ticket-window lines in tube stations by buying tickets from coin-op machines; practice on the punchboard to see how the system works (hit "adult single" and your destination). Again, nearly every ride will be £1.50. (These tickets are valid only on the day of purchase.) Beware: Overshooting your zone nets you a £10 fine.

Most city maps include a tube map with color-coded lines and names (free at any station window). Each line has a name (such as Circle, Northern, or Bakerloo) and two directions (indicated by end stop). In stations you'll have a choice of two platforms per line. Navigate by signs leading to the platforms (usually labeled north, south, east, or west) that clearly list the stops served by each line, or ask a local or a blue-vested staff person for help.

All city maps have north on top. If you know which general direction you're heading, tube navigation suddenly becomes easier. Some tracks are shared by several lines, and electronic signboards announce which train is next and the minutes remaining until various arrivals. Each train has its final destination or line name above its windshield. Depending on the particular line, trains run roughly every 3 to 10 minutes. Bring something to do to make your wait productive. The system is fraught with construction delays and breakdowns (pay attention to signs and announcements explaining necessary detours, etc). The Circle Line is notorious for problems. And always...mind the gap.

You can't leave the system without feeding your ticket to the turnstile. Save time by choosing the best street exit (look at the maps on the walls or ask any station personnel). "Subway" means pedestrian underpass in "English."

London Tube and Bus Passes: Consider using these passes, valid on both the tube and buses (all passes are available for more zones and are purchased as easily as a normal ticket at any station):

One-Day passes: If you figure you'll take three rides in a day, a day pass is a good deal. The "One Day Travel Card," covering Zones 1 and 2, gives you unlimited travel for a day, starting after 09:30 and anytime on weekends, for £4. The all-zone version of this card costs £4.90 (and includes Heathrow Airport). The "One Day LT Card," covering Zones 1 and 2 with no time restriction, costs £5.10. Families save with the "One Day Family Travel Card" (price varies depending on number in family).

Weekend pass: The "Weekend Travel Card," which covers Saturday, Sunday, and Zones 1 and 2 for £6, costs 25 percent less than two one-day cards.

Seven-day pass: The "7-Day Travel Card" costs £19, covers Zones 1 and 2, and requires a passport-type photo (cut one out of any snapshot and bring it from home). If you have no photo, the TI at Heathrow Airport sells a similar "Visitor's Card" for about the same price without requiring a photo.

Ten rides: If you want to travel a little each day or if you're part of a group, an £11.50 "carnet" is a great deal: You get 10 separate tickets for tube travel in Zone 1 (£1.15 per ride rather than £1.50). Wait for the machine to lay all 10 tickets. Groups of 10 or more can travel all day on the tube for £3 each (not on buses).

Tours of London

▲▲▲**Hop-on Hop-off Double-Decker Bus Tours**—Two competitive companies ("Original" and "Big Bus") offer essentially the same tours with buses that have live (English-only) guides as well as some marked buses with a tape-recorded, dial-a-language narration. This two-hour, once-over-lightly bus tour drives by all the famous sights, providing a stressless way to get your bearings and at least see the biggies. You can sit back and enjoy the entire two-hour orientation tour (a good idea if you like the guide and the weather) or "hop-on and hop-off" at any of the nearly 30 stops and catch a later bus. Buses run about every 10 to 15 minutes in summer, every 20 minutes in winter. It's an inexpensive form of transport as well as an informative tour. Grab one of the maps from a TI and study it. Buses run daily (from about 09:00 until early evening in summer, until late afternoon in winter) and stop at Victoria Street (1 block north of Victoria Station), Marble Arch, Piccadilly Circus, Trafalgar Square, and elsewhere.

Each company offers a core two-hour overview tour, two other routes, and a narrated Thames boat tour covered by the same ticket (buy ticket from driver, credit cards are accepted at major stops such as Victoria Station, ticket good for 24 hrs, bring a sweater and extra film). Note: If you start at Victoria at 09:00, you'll finish near Buckingham Palace in time to see the Changing of the Guard (at 11:30); ask your driver for the best place to hop off. Sunday morning—when the traffic is light and many museums are closed—is a fine time for a tour. The last full loop leaves Victoria at 18:00. Both companies have entertaining and boring guides. The narration is important. If you don't like your guide, jump off and find another. If you like your guide, settle in for the entire loop.

Original London Sightseeing Bus Tour: Live guided buses have a Union Jack flag and a yellow triangle on the front of the bus. If the front has many flags or a green triangle, it's a tape-recorded multilingual tour—avoid it, unless you have kids who'd enjoy the entertaining recorded kids' tour (£14, £2.50 discount with this book—limit 2 discounts per book, they'll rip off the corner of this page—raise bloody hell if they don't honor this discount, ticket good for 24 hrs, tel. 020/8877-1722). Your ticket includes a 50-minute-long circular boat tour from the London Eye (2/hr until 22:00, tape-recorded narration).

Big Bus Hop-on Hop-off London Tours: These are also good. For £15 you get the same basic tour plus coupons for four different one-hour London walks and the scenic and usually entertainingly guided Thames boat ride (normally £5) between Westminster Pier and the Tower of London. The pass and extras are valid for 24 hours. Buses with live guides are marked in front with a picture of a blue bus; buses with tape-recorded spiels display a picture of a yellow bus and headphones. While the price is steeper, Big Bus guides seem more dynamic than the Original guides (office a block from Victoria Station at 48 Buckingham Palace Road, daily 08:30–17:30, tel. 020/7233-9533, www.bigbus.co.uk).

At Night: The London by Night Sightseeing Tour runs basically the same circuit as the other companies after hours. While the narration is pretty lame (the driver does little more than call out the names of famous places as you roll by), the views at twilight are grand (£9, pay driver or buy tickets at Victoria Station TI, April–Oct, 2-hr tour with live guide, can hop on and off, departs at 20:00, 21:00, and 22:00 from Victoria Station, Taxi Road, at front of station near end of Wilton Road, tel. 020/8646-1747).

▲▲**Walking Tours**—Many times a day top-notch local guides lead (often big) groups through specific slices of London's past. Schedule fliers litter the desks of TIs, hotels, and pubs. *Time Out* lists many but not all scheduled walks. Simply show up at the announced location, pay £5, and enjoy two chatty hours of Dickens, the Plague, Shakespeare, Legal London, the Beatles, Jack the Ripper, or whatever is on the agenda. Original London Walks, the dominant company, lists their extensive daily schedule in a beefy, plain black-and-white *The Original London Walks* brochure. They also run Explorer daytrips, a good option for those with limited time and transportation (different trip daily: Stonehenge/Salisbury, Oxford/Cotswolds, York, Bath, and so on; walks offered year-round—even Christmas, get schedule at hotel or TI, private tours for £80, tel. 020/7624-3978, www.walks.com).

Standard rates for London's registered guides are £85 for four hours, £136 for eight hours (tel. 020/7403-2962, www.touristguides.org.uk). Robina Brown leads tours with small groups in her Toyota Previa (£185/3 hrs, £270–400/day, tel. 020/7228-2238, e-mail: robina.brown@which.net). Brit Lonsdale, an energetic mother of twins, is another registered London guide (tel. 020/7386-9907). Chris Salaman is a clearinghouse for guides who do specialty tours (just dream up a topic: industrial, famous London women, you name it) and tours of London's characteristic boroughs for a low rate (£40/group for a private 2-hr tour, tel. 020/8672-1270).

▲▲**Cruise the Thames**—Boat tours with entertaining commentaries sail regularly from **Westminster Pier** (at the base of Westminster Bridge under Big Ben). You can cruise to the **Tower of London** (£5—included with Big Bus London tour, £6 round-trip, daily 09:00–21:00, until 15:45 Nov–March, 2/hr, 30 min, tel. 020/7930-9033); **Greenwich** (£6.30, £7.60 round-trip, 10:00–17:00, 2/hr, 1 hr, likely narrated only downstream, tel. 020/7930-4097); and **Kew Gardens** (£7, £11 round-trip, 5/day, generally departing 10:00–14:00, 90 min, 30 min narrated, some boats continue on to **Hampton Court** for extra £3, tel. 020/7930-2062). For pleasure and efficiency, consider combining a one-way cruise with a tube ride back. Fifty minute round-trip cruises leave regularly from the London Eye (included with Original London Bus tickets—see above).

Frog Tours—A bright-yellow amphibious vehicle takes you streetside past some famous sights (Big Ben, Buckingham Palace, Piccadilly Circus), then splashes into the Thames for a 30-minute cruise (£15, daily 10:00–18:00, 80 min, live commentary, these

book up in advance, departs from County Hall near London
Eye Ferris Wheel, tube: Waterloo or Westminster, tel. 020/
7928-3132, www.frogtours.com).

Sights—From Westminster Abbey to Trafalgar Square

▲▲**Westminster Walk**—Just about every visitor to London
strolls the historic Whitehall boulevard from Big Ben to Trafalgar
Square. Beneath London's modern traffic and big-city bustle lies
2,000 fascinating years of history. This three-quarter-mile, self-
guided orientation walk (see map on page 425) gives you a whirlwind tour and connects the sights listed in this section.

Start halfway across **Westminster Bridge** (#1 on map) for
that "Wow, I'm really in London!" feeling. Get a close-up view
of the **Houses of Parliament** and **Big Ben** (floodlit at night).
Downstream you'll see the **London Eye Ferris wheel**. Down
the stairs are boats to the Tower of London and Greenwich.

En route to Parliament Square, you'll pass a statue of **Boadicea**
(#2), the Celtic queen defeated by Roman invaders in A.D. 60.

To thrill your loved ones (or bug the envious), call home
from a pay phone near Big Ben at about three minutes before the
hour. You'll find a phone on Great George Street, across from
Parliament Square. As Big Ben chimes, stick the receiver outside
the booth and prove you're in London: Ding dong ding dong...
dong ding ding dong.

Wave hello to Churchill in Parliament Square (#3). To his
right is **Westminster Abbey** with its two stubby, elegant towers.

Walk north up Parliament Street (which turns into White-
hall) toward Trafalgar Square. You'll see the thought-provoking
Cenotaph (#5) in the middle of the street, reminding passersby of
Britain's many war dead. To visit the Cabinet War Rooms (see
"Sights," below) take a left before the Cenotaph, on King Charles
Street (#4).

Continuing on Whitehall, stop at the barricaded and guarded
little **10 Downing Street** to see the British "White House" (#6),
home of the prime minister. Break the bobby's boredom and ask
him a question.

Nearing Trafalgar Square, look for the **Horse Guards**
behind the gated fence (11:00 inspection Mon–Sat, 10:00 on Sun;
dismounting ceremony daily at 16:00) and the 17th-century
Banqueting House across the street (#7; see "Sights," below).

The column topped by Lord Nelson marks **Trafalgar Square**
(#8). The stately domed building on the far side of the square is
the **National Gallery** (free), which has a classy café (upstairs in
the Sainsbury wing). To the right of the National Gallery is
St. Martin-in-the-Fields Church and its Café in the Crypt.

To get to Piccadilly from Trafalgar Square, walk up

Westminster Walk

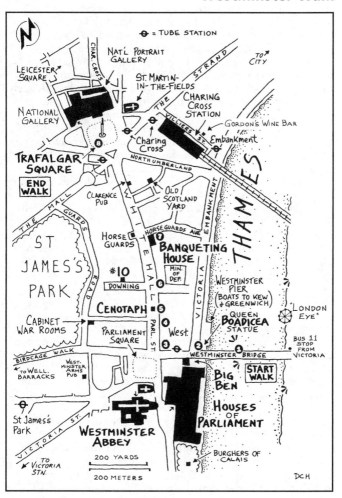

⊕ = TUBE STATION

N

NAT'L PORTRAIT
GALLERY

LEICESTER
SQUARE

ST. MARTIN-
IN-THE-FIELDS

CHARING
CROSS
STATION

NATIONAL
GALLERY

CHARING CROSS RD

STRAND

THE STRAND

TO
CITY

GORDON'S WINE BAR

VILLIERS ST.

Embankment

Charing
Cross

TRAFALGAR
SQUARE

NORTHUMBERLAND

END
WALK

CLARENCE
PUB

OLD
SCOTLAND
YARD

THE MALL

GUARDS RD.

THAMES

ST
JAMES'S
PARK

HORSE
GUARDS

HORSE GUARDS AVE

BANQUETING
HOUSE

#10
DOWNING

THE MALL

MIN.
OF
DEF.

WESTMINSTER
PIER
(BOATS TO KEW
& GREENWICH)

CENOTAPH

PARL. ST.

VICTORIA

LONDON
EYE

CABINET
WAR ROOMS

PARLIAMENT
SQUARE

West.

QUEEN
BOADICEA
STATUE

BUS 11
STOP
FROM
VICTORIA

BIRDCAGE WALK

WEST-
MINSTER
ARMS
PUB

WESTMINSTER BRIDGE

TO WELL.
BARRACKS

START
WALK

St James's
Park

VICTORIA ST.

WESTMINSTER
ABBEY

BIG
BEN

HOUSES
OF
PARLIAMENT

TO
VICTORIA
STN.

200 YARDS

BURGHERS OF
CALAIS

200 METERS

DCH

Cockspur Street to Haymarket, then take a short left on Coventry
Street to colorful **Piccadilly Circus**.

Near Piccadilly you'll find the **Britain Visitors Centre**
and piles of theaters. **Leicester Square** (with its half-price ticket
booth for plays) thrives just a few blocks away. Walk through
seedy **Soho** (north of Shaftesbury Avenue) for its fun pubs
(see "Eating," below, for "Food is Fun" Dinner Crawl). From
Piccadilly or Oxford Circus, you can taxi, bus, or tube home.

▲▲▲**Westminster Abbey**—As the greatest church in the English-speaking world, Westminster Abbey has been the place where England's kings and queens have been crowned and buried since 1066. A thousand years of English history—3,000 tombs, the remains of 29 kings and queens, and hundreds of memorials—lie within its walls and under its stone slabs. Like a stony refugee camp huddled outside St. Peter's gates, this place has a story to tell and the best way to enjoy it is with a **tour** (audioguide-£2, live-£3; many prefer the audioguide because it's self-paced, both tours include entry to cloister museums). Experience an **evensong** service—awesome in a nearly-empty church (weekdays except Wed at 17:00, Sat–Sun at 15:00). The free **organ recital** on Sunday is another highlight (17:45, 40 min). Organ concerts here are great and inexpensive; look for signs with schedule details.

Enter on the Big Ben side (often with a sizable line, visit early to avoid crowds) and then follow a one-way route through this English hall of fame around the church and cloisters (with the 3 small museums), back through the nave, and out (£6 for abbey entry, Mon–Fri 09:15-16:45, Wed also 18:00–19:45, Sat 09:30–14:45, last admission 1 hr before closing, photography prohibited, closed on Sun except for worship, coffee in cloister, tube: Westminster or St. James' Park, call for tour schedule, tel. 020/7222-7110). Since the church is often closed to the public for special services, it's wise to call first.

Three tiny **museums** ring the cloister (£1 covers all, on top of your abbey ticket; or free with either the audioguide or live tour): the Chapter House (where the monks held their daily meetings, notable for its fine architecture and well-described but faded medieval art), the Pyx Chamber (containing an exhibit on the king's treasury), and the Abbey Museum (which tells of the abbey's history, royal coronations, and burials). Look into the impressively realistic eyes of Henry VII's funeral effigy (one of a fascinating series of wax-and-wood statues that, for three centuries, graced royal coffins during funeral processions).

For a free peek inside and a quiet sit in the nave, you can tell a guard at the west end (where the tourists exit) that you'd like to pay your respects to Britain's Unknown Soldier.

▲▲**Houses of Parliament (Palace of Westminster)**—This neo-Gothic icon of London, the royal residence from 1042 to 1547, is now the meeting place of the legislative branch of government. Tourists are welcome to view debates in either the bickering House of Commons or the genteel House of Lords (when in session—indicated by a flag flying atop the Victoria Tower). While the actual action is generally extremely dull, it is a thrill to be inside and see the British government inaction (House of Commons: Mon–Wed 14:30–22:30, Thu 11:30–19:30, Fri 09:30–15:00, generally less action and no lines after 18:00, use

St. Stephen's entrance, tube: Westminster, tel. 020/7219-4272 for schedule, www.parliament.uk). The House of Lords has more pageantry, shorter lines, and less-interesting debates (Mon–Wed 14:30 until they finish, Thu from 15:00 on, sometimes Fri from 11:00 on, tel. 020/7219-3107 for schedule). If confronted with a too-long House of Commons line, see the House of Lords first. Once you've seen the Lords (hide your HOL flier), you can often slip directly to the House of Commons and join the gang waiting in the lobby. If there's only one line outside, it's for the House of Commons. Go to the gate and tell the guard you want the Lords. You may pop right in.

After passing security, slip to the left and study the big dark **Westminster Hall**, which survived the 1834 fire. The hall is from the 11th century, and its famous self-supporting hammer-beam roof was added in 1397. The Houses of Parliament are located in what was once the Palace of Westminster, long the palace of England's medieval kings, until it was largely destroyed by fire in 1834. The palace was rebuilt in Victorian Gothic style (a move away from neoclassicism back to England's Christian and medieval heritage, true to the Romantic Age). It was completed in 1860.

Houses of Parliament tours are given in August and September (£3.50, Mon, Fri, Sat 09:15–16:30, Tue–Thu 13:15–16:30, 75 min). Meet your Blue Badge guide (at the Sovereign's Entrance—far south end) for a behind-the-scenes peek at the royal chambers and both the House of Commons and House of Lords. Tickets are sold at the Westminster Hall ticket booth (Mon–Sat 08:45-13:00, closed Sun, or tel. 020/7344-9966).

The **Jewel Tower** is (along with Westminster Hall) all that survives of the old Palace of Westminster. It contains a fine little exhibit on Parliament: first floor—history; second floor—Parliament today, with a 25-minute video and lonely picnic-friendly benches (£1.60, daily April–Sept 10:00–18:00, Oct 10:00–17:00, Nov–March 10:00–16:00, across street from St. Stephens Gate, tel. 020/7222-2219).

Big Ben, the clock tower (315 feet high), is named for its 13-ton bell, Ben. The light above the clock is lit when the House of Commons is sitting. The face of the clock is huge—you can actually see the minute hand moving. For a hip HOP view, walk halfway over Westminster Bridge.

▲▲**Cabinet War Rooms**—This is a fascinating walk through the underground headquarters of the British government's fight against the Nazis in the darkest days of the Battle for Britain. The 21-room nerve center of the British war effort was used from 1939 to 1945. Churchill's room, the map room, and other rooms are just as they were in 1945. For all the blood, sweat, toil, and tears details, pick up an audioguide at the entry and follow the included and excellent 45-minute tour; be patient—it's worth it (£5, daily

April–Oct 09:30–18:00, Nov–March 10:00–18:00, last entry 45 min before closing, on King Charles Street 200 yards off Whitehall, follow the signs, tube: Westminster, tel. 020/7930-6961). For a nearby pub lunch, try Westminster Arms (food served downstairs, on Storey's Gate, a couple blocks south of War Rooms).

Horse Guards—The Horse Guards are inspected daily at 11:00 (10:00 on Sun), and there's a colorful dismounting ceremony daily at 16:00. The rest of the day they just stand there—terrible for camcorders (on Whitehall, between Trafalgar Square and #10 Downing Street, tube: Westminster). While Buckingham Palace pageantry is canceled when it rains, the horse guards change regardless of the weather.

▲**Banqueting House**—England's first Renaissance building was designed by Inigo Jones around 1620. It's one of the few London landmarks spared by the 1666 fire and the only surviving part of the original Palace of Whitehall. Don't miss its Rubens ceiling, which, at Charles I's request, drove home the doctrine of the legitimacy of the divine right of kings. In 1649—divine right ignored—Charles I was beheaded on the balcony of this building by a Cromwellian parliament. Admission includes a restful 20-minute audiovisual history, which shows the place in banqueting action; a 30-minute tape-recorded tour—interesting only to history buffs; and a look at an exquisite banqueting hall (£3.90, Mon–Sat 10:00–17:00, closed Sun, last entry at 16:30, subject to closure for government functions, aristocratic WC, immediately across Whitehall from the Horse Guards, tube: Westminster, tel. 020/7930-4179). Just up the street is Trafalgar Square.

Sights—Trafalgar Square

▲▲**Trafalgar Square**—London's central square is a thrilling place to just hang out. Lord Nelson stands atop his 185-foot-tall fluted granite column, gazing out to Trafalgar (off Spain's southern coast), where he lost his life but defeated the French fleet. Part of this 1842 memorial is made from the melted-down cannons of his victims at Trafalgar. He's surrounded by giant lions, hordes of people, and—until recently—even more pigeons. London's new mayor, nicknamed "Red Ken" for his passion for an activist government, decided that London's "flying rats" were a public nuisance and evicted the venerable seed salesmen. This high-profile square is the climax of most marches and demonstrations (tube: Charing Cross).

▲▲▲**National Gallery**—Displaying Britain's top collection of European paintings from 1250 to 1900 (works by Leonardo, Botticelli, Velázquez, Rembrandt, Turner, van Gogh, and the Impressionists), this is one of Europe's great galleries. While the collection is huge, following the 30-stop route suggested on the map on the next page will give you my best quick visit.

National Gallery Highlights

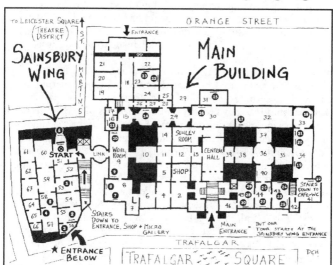

Medieval and Early Renaissance
1. Wilton Diptych
2. UCCELLO—Battle of San Romano
3. VAN EYCK—Arnolfini Marriage
4. CRIVELLI—Annunciation with St. Emidius
5. BOTTICELLI—Venus and Mars

High Renaissance
6. LEONARDO DA VINCI— Virgin and Child (painting and cartoon)
7. MICHELANGELO—Entombment
8. RAPHAEL—Pope Julius II

Venetian Renaissance
9. TITIAN—Bacchus and Ariadne
10. TINTORETTO —Origin of the Milky Way

Northern Protestant Art
11. VERMEER—Young Woman
12. REMBRANDT—Belshazzar's Feast
13. REMBRANDT—Self-Portrait

Baroque and Rococo
14. RUBENS—The Judgment of Paris
15. VAN DYCK—Charles I on Horseback
16. VELÁZQUEZ—The Rokeby Venus
17. CARAVAGGIO—Supper at Emmaus
18. BOUCHER—Pan and Syrinx

British
19. CONSTABLE—The Hay Wain
20. TURNER—The Fighting Téméraire
21. TURNER—Rain, Steam, Speed
22. DELAROCHE—The Execution of Lady Jane Grey

Impressionism and Beyond
23. MONET—Gare St. Lazare
24. MONET—The Water Lily Pond
25. MANET—The Waitress (La Servante de Bocks)
26. RENOIR—Boating on the Seine
27. SEURAT—Bathers at Asnières
28. DEGAS—Miss La La at the Cirque Fernando
29. VAN GOGH—Sunflowers
30. CÉZANNE—Bathers

The audioguide tours are the best I've used in Europe (entirely voluntary £4 donation requested). Don't miss the "Micro Gallery," a computer room even your dad could have fun in (closes 30 min earlier than museum); you can study any artist, style, or topic in the museum and even print out a tailor-made tour map (free, daily 10:00–18:00, likely Thu–Sat until 21:00 in 2002, free 1-hr overview tours daily at 11:30 and 14:30 plus Wed at 18:30, photography prohibited, on Trafalgar Square, tube: Charing Cross or Leicester Square, tel. 020/7747-2885).

▲▲**National Portrait Gallery**—Put off by halls of 19th-century characters who meant nothing to me, I used to call this "as interesting as someone else's yearbook." But a selective walk through this 500-year-long Who's Who of British history is quick and free and puts faces on the story of England. A bonus is the chance to admire some great art by painters such as Holbein, Van Dyck, Hogarth, Reynolds, and Gainsborough. The collection is well described, not huge, and in historical sequence, from the 16th century on the second floor to today's royal family on the ground floor.

Some **highlights**: Henry VIII and wives; several fascinating portraits of the "Virgin Queen" Elizabeth I, Sir Francis Drake, and Sir Walter Raleigh; the only real-life portrait of Shakespeare; Oliver Cromwell and Charles I with his head on; self-portraits and other portraits by Gainsborough and Reynolds; the Romantics (Blake, Byron, Wordsworth, and company); Queen Victoria and her era; and the present royal family, including the late Princess Diana.

The excellent audioguide tours (£3 donation requested) describe each room (or era in British history) and more than 300 paintings. You'll learn more about British history than art and actually hear interviews with 20th-century subjects as you stare at their faces (free, daily 10:00–18:00, Thu–Fri until 21:00, entry 100 yards off Trafalgar Square, around corner from National Gallery, opposite Church of St. Martin-in-the-Fields, tel. 020/7306-0055, www.npg.org.uk). The elegant Portrait Restaurant on the top floor comes with views and high prices (cheaper Potrait café in basement).

▲**St. Martin-in-the-Fields**—This church, built in the 1720s, with a Gothic spire placed upon a Greek-type temple, is an oasis of peace on the wild and noisy Trafalgar Square. St. Martin cared for the poor. "In the fields" was where the first church stood on this spot (in the 13th century), between Westminster and the city. Stepping inside, you still feel a compassion for the needs of the people in this community. A free flier provides a brief yet worthwhile self-guided tour. The church is famous for its concerts. Consider a free lunchtime concert (Mon, Tue, and Fri at 13:05) or an evening concert (£6–16, Thu–Sat at 19:30, CC, box office tel. 020/7839-8362, church tel. 020/7766-1100). Downstairs you'll find a ticket office for concerts, a good shop, a brass-rubbing center, and a fine support-the-church cafeteria (see "Eating," below).

London's Top Squares

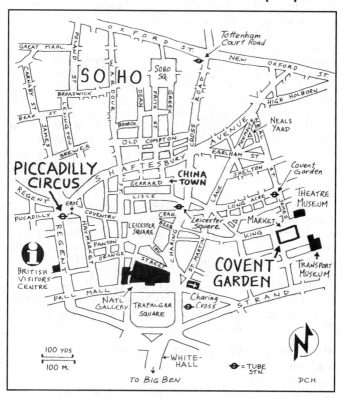

More Top Squares: Piccadilly, Soho, and Covent Garden

▲▲**Piccadilly Circus**—London's most touristy square got its name from the fancy ruffled shirts—*picadils*—made in the neighborhood long ago. Today the square is surrounded by fascinating streets and is swimming with youth on the rampage. The **Rock Circus** offers a gimmicky history of rock music with Madame Tussaud wax stars. While overpriced, it's an entertaining hour for wealthy rock 'n' roll romantics (£8.25, daily 10:00–17:30, plenty of photo ops, tube: Piccadilly Circus, tel. 020/7734-7203). For overstimulation, drop by the extremely trashy **Pepsi Trocadero Center**'s "theme park of the future" for its Segaworld virtual-reality games, nine-screen cinema, and thundering IMAX theater (admission to Trocadero is free; individual attractions cost £2–8; find a discount ticket at brochure racks at TI or hotels before paying full price for IMAX; between Coventry and Shaftesbury, just off Piccadilly). Chinatown, to the east, has swollen since Hong Kong lost its independence. Nearby Shaftesbury Avenue and Leicester Square teem with fun seekers, theaters, Chinese restaurants, and street singers.

Soho—North of Piccadilly, seedy Soho is becoming trendy and is well worth a gawk. Soho is London's red-light district, where "friendly models" wait in tiny rooms up dreary stairways and voluptuous con artists sell strip shows. While venturing up a stairway to check out a model is interesting, anyone who goes into any one of the shows will be ripped off. Every time. Even a £5 show in a "licensed bar" comes with a £100 cover or minimum (as it's printed on the drink menu) and a "security man." You may accidentally buy a £200 bottle of bubbly. And suddenly, the door has no handle. By the way, telephone sex is hard to avoid these days in London. Phone booths are littered with racy fliers of busty ladies "new in town." Some travelers gather six or eight phone booths' worth of fliers and take them home for kinky wallpaper.

▲▲**Covent Garden**—This boutique-ish shopping district is a people watcher's delight with cigarette eaters, Punch-and-Judy acts, food that's good for you (but not your wallet), trendy crafts, sweet whiffs of marijuana, two-tone hair (neither natural), and faces that could set off a metal detector (tube: Covent Garden). For better Covent Garden lunch deals, walk a block or two away from the eye of this touristic hurricane (check out the places a block or two north of the tube station along Endell and Neal Streets).

Museums near Covent Garden

▲▲**Somerset House**—Just opened to the public, this grand 18th-century civic palace provides Londoners with a marvelous new public space and riverside terrace (between the Strand and the Thames). The palace, which once housed the national registry that records Britain's births, marriages, and deaths ("where they hatched 'em, latched 'em, and dispatched 'em"), now houses three collections of fine art. Step into the courtyard to enjoy the fountain. Go ahead...walk through it; the 55 jets get playful twice an hour. Surrounding you are three small and sumptuous sights: the Courtauld Gallery (paintings), Gilbert Collection (fine arts), and Hermitage Rooms (finest art of czarist Russia). All have the same hours (Mon–Sat 10:00–18:00, Sun 12:00–18:00, easy bus #6, #9, #11, #13, #15, or #23 from Trafalgar Square, tube: Temple or Covent Garden, tel. 020/7848-2526, www.somerset-house.org.uk). The Web site lists a busy schedule of tours, kids' events, and concerts. The riverside terrace is picnic-friendly (deli inside lobby).

While the **Courtauld Gallery** is far less impressive than the National Gallery, its wonderful collection of paintings is a joy. The gallery is part of the Courtauld Institute of Art, and the thoughtful

Central London

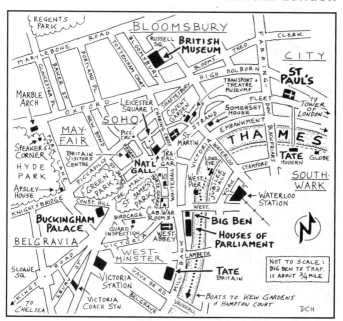

REGENTS PARK — BLOOMSBURY — RUSSELL — BRITISH MUSEUM — CLERK — CITY — MARYLEBONE — ROAD — BLOOMSBURY — THEO — P A R — ST PAUL'S — GLOUCESTER ST. — BAKER ST. — PORTLAND PL. — TOTTENHAM COURT — HIGH — HOLBORN — MARBLE ARCH — O X F O R D — NEW BOND ST. — LEICESTER SQUARE — SHAFTESBURY — COVENT GARDEN — STRAND — SOMERSET HOUSE — FLEET — TRANSPORT & THEATRE MUSEUMS — TO TOWER OF LONDON — MAY-FAIR — SOHO — PICC. CIRC. — ST. MARTIN — CHARING CROSS — EMBANKMENT — THAMES — BLACKFRIARS — SPEAKER'S CORNER — BRITAIN VISITORS CENTRE — PICCADILLY — NAT'L GALL. — TRAF. SQ. — VICTORIA — LOND. EYE — STAMFORD — TATE MODERN — GLOBE — HYDE PARK — GREEN PARK — #10 — WHITEHALL — WEST. PIER — JUBILEE — YORK — SOUTH-WARK — APSLEY HOUSE — THE MALL — ST. JAMES PARK — WEST. — WATERLOO STATION — KNIGHTSBRIDGE — CONST. HILL — BIRDCAGE — CAB. WAR ROOMS — BIG BEN — BUCKINGHAM PALACE — GUARD INSPECTION — WEST. ABBEY — HOUSES OF PARLIAMENT — BELGRAVIA — VICTORIA — WEST-MINSTER — LAMBETH — SLOANE SQ. — ROAD — ST. — VICTORIA STATION — VAUX BR RD — MILL — TATE BRITAIN — NOT TO SCALE: BIG BEN TO TRAF. IS ABOUT ¾ MILE — TO CHELSEA — KINGS — VICTORIA COACH STN. — BELGRAVE — VAUXHALL — BOATS TO KEW GARDENS & HAMPTON COURT — DCH

descriptions of each piece of art remind visitors that the gallery is still used for teaching. You'll see medieval European paintings, works by Rubens, Impressionists (Manet, Monet, Degas, Seurat), Post-Impressionists (such as Cézanne), and more (£4, free Mon 10:00–14:00).

The **Hermitage Rooms** offer a taste of Romanov imperial splendor. Since tourists are staying away from Russia because of its struggles, someone had the bright idea to send the best Russian art to London to raise some hard cash. These five rooms host a different collection each six months with a standard intro to the czar's winter palace in St. Petersburg (£6, includes great live video of the square, tel. 020/7420-9410). The excellent audio-guide costs £3 . . . consider it charity for Russia.

The **Gilbert Collection** displays 800 pieces of the finest in European decorative arts, from gold, diamond-studded snuff boxes to intricate Italian mosaics. Maybe you've seen Raphael paintings and Botticelli frescoes, but this lush collection is refreshingly different (£4, includes free audioguide with a highlights tour and a kid-friendly family tour, free Mon 10:00–14:00).

▲**London Transport Museum**—This wonderful museum is a delight for kids. Whether you're cursing or marveling at the buses and tube, the growth of Europe's biggest city has been made possible by its public transit system. Watch the growth of the tube, then sit in the simulator to "drive" a train (£6, kids under 16 free, Sat–Thu 10:00–18:00, Fri 11:00–18:00, 30 yards southeast of Covent Garden's marketplace, tel. 020/7379-6344).

Theatre Museum—This earnest museum, probably worthwhile only for theater buffs, traces the development of British theater from Shakespeare to today (£4.50, kids under 16 free, Tue–Sun 10:00–18:00, closed Mon, call about guided tours, makeup demos, and costume workshops, a block east of Covent Garden's marketplace down Russell Street, tel. 020/7943-4700).

Sights—North London

▲▲▲**British Museum, Great Court, and Reading Room**— Simply put, this is the greatest chronicle of civilization … anywhere. A visit here is like taking a long hike through Encyclopedia Britannica National Park. Enjoy the museum's recent facelift: Entering on Great Russell Street, you'll step into the Great Court, the new glass-domed hub of a two-acre cultural complex, containing restaurants, shops, and lecture halls plus the just-reopened Round Reading Room.

The most popular sections of the museum fill the ground floor: Egyptian, Mesopotamian, and ancient Greek—with the famous Elgin Marbles from the Pantheon. Huge winged lions (which guarded Assyrian palaces 800 years before Christ) guard these great ancient galleries. For a brief tour, connect these ancient dots:

Start with the **Egyptian**. Wander from the Rosetta Stone past the many statues. At the end of the hall, climb the stairs to mummy land.

Back at the winged lions, wander through the dark, violent, and mysterious **Assyrian** rooms. The Nimrud Gallery is lined with royal propaganda reliefs and wounded lions.

The most modern of the ancient art fills the **Greek** section. Find room 11 behind the winged lions and start your walk through Greek art history with the simple and primitive Cycladic fertility figures. Later, painted vases show a culture really into partying. The finale is the Elgin Marbles. The much-wrangled-over bits of the Athenian Parthenon (from 450 B.C.) are even more impressive than they look. To best appreciate these ancient carvings, take the free audioguide tour (available in this gallery).

Be sure to venture upstairs to see artifacts from Roman Britain (room 50) that surpass anything you'll see at Hadrian's Wall or elsewhere in Britain. Nearby, the Dark Age Britain exhibits (especially the Sutton Hoo Ship Burial artifacts from a 7th-century royal burial on the east coast of England—room 41) offer a worthwhile peek at that bleak era. Room 90 contains a rare Michelangelo cartoon.

The British Museum is revving up for its 250th birthday in 2003. The immense yet empty King's Library (once the home of the treasures of the British Library—now housed elsewhere) lines the east side of the Great Court. The plan: restore it to its Regency splendor (1827), restock the shelves with the leather-bound volumes from the House of Commons Library, and fill the hall with a special exhibit featuring museums of the Enlightenment.

The newly opened **Queen Elizabeth II Great Court** is Europe's largest covered square—bigger than a football field. This people-friendly court—delightfully out of the London rain— was for 150 years one of London's great lost spaces...closed off and gathering dust. While the vast British Museum wraps around the court, its centerpiece is the stately **Reading Room**—famous as the place Karl Marx hung out while formulating his ideas on communism and writing *Das Kapital*. The Reading Room—one of the fine cast-iron buildings of the 19th century—is free to wander, but there's little to see that you can't see from the doorway.

The British Museum and the Reading Room are both free (£2 donation requested, daily 10:00–17:30, Thu–Fri until 20:30, least crowded weekday late afternoons, Great Russell Street, tube: Tottenham Court Road, tel. 020/7323-8000 or 020/7388-2227, www.thebritishmuseum.ac.uk). The museum offers three kinds of **tours** of its immense collection: Highlights (£7, 90 min), Focus (£5, 1 hr), and Eye Openers (free, nearly hrly, 50 min). For tour times, call ahead or check schedule and brochures at entry.

▲▲▲**British Library**—The British Empire built its greatest monuments out of paper. And it's in literature that England made her lasting contribution to civilization and the arts. Opened in 1998, Britain's national archives has more than 12 million books, 180 miles of shelving, and the deepest basement in London. But everything that matters for your visit is in one delightful room labeled "The Treasures." This room is filled with literary and historical documents that changed the course of history. You'll trace the evolution of European maps over 800 years. Follow the course of the Bible—from the earliest known gospels (written on scraps of papyrus) to the first complete Bible to the original King James version and the Gutenberg Bible. You'll see Leonardo's doodles, the Magna Carta, Shakespeare's First Folio, the original *Alice in Wonderland* in Lewis Carroll's handwriting, and manuscripts by Beethoven, Mozart, Lennon, and McCartney. Finish in the fascinating *Turning the Pages* exhibit, which lets you actually browse through virtual manuscripts of a few of these treasures on a computer (free, Mon–Fri 09:30–18:00, Tue until 20:00, Sat until 17:00, Sun 11:00–17:00; 1-hr tours for £5 usually offered Mon, Wed, and Fri–Sun at 15:00, also Tue 18:30, Sat 10:30, and Sun 11:30, tel. 020/7412-7332 to confirm schedule and reserve, tube: King's Cross, turn right out of station and walk a block to

96 Euston Road, library tel. 020/7412-7000, www.bl.uk). The ground-floor café is next to a vast and fun pull-out stamp collection, and the cafeteria upstairs serves good hot meals.

▲**Madame Tussaud's Waxworks**—This is expensive but dang good. The original Madame Tussaud did wax casts of heads lopped off during the French Revolution (e.g., Marie Antoinette). She took her show on the road and ended up in London. And now it's much easier to be featured. The gallery is one big Who's Who photo-op—a huge hit with the kind of travelers who skip the British Museum. Don't miss the "make a model" exhibit (showing Jerry Hall getting waxed) or the gallery of has-been heads that no longer merit a body (such as Sammy Davis Jr. and Nikita Khruschev). After looking a hundred famous people in their glassy eyes and surviving a silly hall of horror, you'll board a Disney-type ride and cruise through a kid-pleasing "Spirit of London" time trip (£11.50, children-£8, under 5 free, Jan–Sept daily 09:00–17:30, Oct–Dec Mon–Fri 10:00–17:30, Sat–Sun 09:30–17:30, last entry 30 min before closing, Marylebone Road, tube: Baker Street; combined ticket for Tussaud's and Planetarium is £14 for adults, £9.50 for kids). The waxworks are popular. Avoid a wait by either booking ahead to get a ticket with an entry time (tel. 0870-400-3000, online at www.madame-tussaud.com, or any London TI) or arriving late in the day—90 minutes is plenty of time for the exhibit.

Sir John Soane's Museum—Architects and fans of eclectic knick-knacks love this quirky place (free, Tue–Sat 10:00–17:00, closed Sun–Mon, 5 blocks east of British Museum, tube: Holborn, 13 Lincoln's Inn Fields, tel. 020/7405-2107).

Sights—Buckingham Palace

▲**Buckingham Palace**—This lavish home has been Britain's royal residence since 1837. When the queen's at home, the royal standard flies; otherwise the Union Jack flaps in the wind (£11 for state apartments and throne room, open early Aug–Sept only, daily 09:30–16:30, only 8,000 visitors a day—come early to get an appointed visit time or call 020/7321-2233 and reserve a ticket with CC, tube: Victoria).

The Royal Mews—Actually the queen's working stables, visitors can wander among stalls, talk to the horse-keeper, and see the well-groomed horses. Marvel at the gilded coaches paraded during royal festivals, see fancy horse gear—all well-described—and learn how skeptical the attendants were when the royals first parked a car in the stables (£5, Aug–Sept daily 10:30–16:30, Oct–July Mon–Thu 12:00–16:00, on Buckingham Palace Road, tel. 020/7839-1377).

▲▲**Changing of the Guard at Buckingham Palace**—The guards change with much fanfare at 11:30 daily April through August and generally every even-numbered day September through March (no band when wet; worth a 50p phone call any day to confirm that they'll change, tel. 090-505-452). Join the mob behind the palace (the front faces a huge and extremely private park). You'll need to be early or tall to see much of the actual changing of the guard, but for the pageantry in the street you can pop by at 11:30. Stake out the high ground on the circular Victoria Monument for the best general views. The marching troops and bands are colorful and even stirring, but the actual changing of the guard is a nonevent. It is interesting, however, to see nearly every tourist in London gathered in one place at the same time. Hop into a big black taxi and say, "Buck House, please." The show lasts about 30 minutes: Three troops parade by, the guard changes with much shouting, the band plays a happy little concert, and then they march out. On a balmy day, it's a fun happening.

For all the color with none of the crowds, see the **Inspection of the Guard Ceremony** at 11:00 in front of the **Wellington Barracks**, 500 yards east of the palace on Birdcage Walk. Afterward, stroll through nearby St. James' Park (tube: Victoria, St. James' Park, or Green Park).

Sights—West London

▲**Hyde Park and Speakers' Corner**—London's "Central Park"—originally Henry VIII's hunting grounds—has more than 600 acres of lush greenery, a huge man-made lake, the royal Kensington Palace (not worth touring), and the ornate neo-Gothic Albert Memorial across from the Royal Albert Hall. Early afternoons on Sunday, Speakers' Corner offers soapbox oratory at its best (tube: Marble Arch). "The grass roots of democracy" is actually a holdover from when the gallows stood here, and the criminal was allowed to say just about anything he wanted to before he swung. I dare you to raise your voice and gather a crowd—it's easy to do.

▲**Apsley House (Wellington Museum)**—Having beaten Napoleon at Waterloo, the Duke of Wellington was the most famous man in Europe. He was given London's ultimate address, #1 London. His newly refurbished mansion offers one of London's best palace experiences. An 11-foot-tall marble statue (by Canova) of Napoleon clad only in a fig leaf greets you. Downstairs is a small gallery of Wellington memorabilia (including a pair of Wellington boots). The lavish upstairs shows off the duke's fine collection of paintings, including works by Velázquez and Steen (£4.50, Tue–Sun 11:00–17:00, closed Mon, well-described by included audioguide, 20 yards from Hyde Park Corner tube station, tel. 020/7499-5676). Hyde Park's pleasant and picnic-wonderful rose garden is nearby.

▲▲**Victoria and Albert Museum**—The world's top collection of decorative arts is a gangly (150 rooms over 12 miles of corridors) but surprisingly interesting assortment of artistic stuff from the West as well as Asian and Islamic cultures. The V & A, which

West London

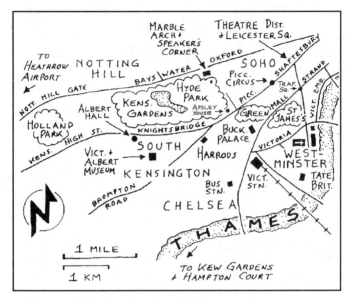

grew out of the Great Exhibition of 1851—that ultimate festival celebrating the Industrial Revolution and the greatness of Britain—was
originally for manufactured art. But after much support from Queen
Victoria and Prince Albert, it was renamed after the royal couple,
and its present building was opened in 1909. The idealistic Victorian notion that anyone can be continually improved by education
and example remains the driving force behind this museum.

While just wandering works well here, consider catching one
of the free 60-minute orientation tours (daily, at :30 past each hr
from 10:30–15:30) or buying the fine £5 *Hundred Highlights* guidebook or the handy 80p *What to See at the V & A* brochure (outlines
5 speedy self-guided tours). Experts give free tours on various topics daily at 13:00. Or walk through these ground-floor **highlights**:
Medieval Treasury (room 43, well-described treasury of Middle
Age European art), the finest collection of Indian decorative art
outside India (room 41), the Dress Gallery (room 40, 400 years
of English fashion corseted into 40 display cases), the Raphael
Gallery (room 48a, 7 huge watercolor cartoons painted as designs
for tapestries to hang in the Sistine Chapel, among the greatest art
treasures in Britain and the best works of the High Renaissance),
reliefs by the Renaissance sculptor Donatello (room 16), a close-up
look at medieval stained glass (room 28, much more upstairs), the
fascinating Cast Courts (rooms 46a and 46b, filled with plaster

copies of the greatest art of our civilization—such as Trajan's *Column* and Michelangelo's *David*—made for the benefit of 19th-century art students who couldn't afford a railpass), and the hall of "great" fakes and forgeries (room 46). Upstairs you can walk through the newly-renovated British Galleries for centuries of British furniture, clothing, glass, jewelry, and sculpture (free, possible fee for special exhibits, daily 10:00–17:45, open Wed and last Fri of month until 22:00 except mid-Dec–mid-Jan; tube: South Kensington, a long tunnel leads directly from tube station to museum, tel. 020/7942-2000, www.vam.ac.uk).

▲**Natural History Museum**—Across the street from the Victoria and Albert Museum, this mammoth museum is housed in a giant and wonderful Victorian neo-Romanesque building. Built in the 1870s specifically to house the huge collection (50 million specimens), it presents itself in two halves: the Life Galleries (creepy-crawlies, human biology, the origin of species, "our place in evolution," and awesome dinosaurs) and the Earth Galleries (meteors, volcanoes, earthquakes, and so on). Exhibits are wonderfully explained with lots of creative interactive displays. Free 45-minute tours occur daily about every hour from 11:00–16:00 (free, possible fee for special exhibits, Mon–Sat 10:00–17:50, Sun 11:00–17:50, a long tunnel leads directly from South Kensington tube station to museum, tel. 020/7942-5000, www.nhm.ac.uk). Pop in if only for the wild collection of dinosaurs and the roaring *T. Rex.*

Sights—East London: "The City"

▲▲**The City of London**—When Londoners say "The City," they mean the one-square-mile business, banking, and journalism center that 2,000 years ago was Roman Londinium. The outline of the Roman city walls can still be seen in the arc of roads from Blackfriars Bridge to Tower Bridge. Within the City are 24 churches designed by Christopher Wren, mostly just ornamentation around St. Paul's Cathedral. Today, while home to only 5,000 residents, the City thrives with more than 500,000 office workers coming and going daily. It's a fascinating district to wander, but since almost nobody actually lives there, it's dull on Saturday and Sunday.

▲**Old Bailey**—To see the British legal system in action—lawyers in little blond wigs speaking legalese with a British accent—spend a few minutes in the visitors' gallery at "Old Bailey" (free, Mon–Fri 10:00–13:00 and 14:00–14:30 most weeks, no kids under 14, no bags or cameras, purses OK, you can check your bag at the SPAR grocery across the street for £1, tube: St. Paul's, 2 blocks northwest of St. Paul's on Old Bailey Street, follow signs to public entrance, tel. 020/7248-3277).

▲▲▲**St. Paul's Cathedral**—Wren's most famous church is the great St. Paul's, its elaborate interior capped by a 365-foot dome. The crypt (included with admission) is a world of historic bones

East London: "The City"

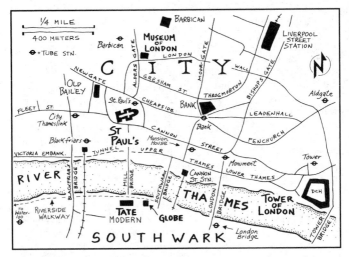

and memorials, including Admiral Nelson's tomb and interesting cathedral models. The great West Door is opened only for great occasions, such as the wedding of Prince Charles and the late Princess Diana in 1981. Stand in the back of the church and imagine how Diana felt before making the hike to the altar with the world watching. Sit under the second-largest dome in the world and eavesdrop on guided tours.

Since World War II, St. Paul's has been Britain's symbol of resistance. Despite 57 nights of bombing, the Nazis failed to destroy the cathedral, thanks to the St. Paul's volunteer fire watch who stayed on the dome. Climb the dome for a great city view and some fun in the whispering gallery—where the precisely designed barrel of the dome lets sweet nothings circle audibly around to the opposite side (£5 entry; Mon–Sat 08:30–16:30, last entry 16:00, closed Sun except for worship; allow 1 hr to climb up and down dome—closed Sun; no photography allowed within church; £2.50 for guided 90-min "super tours" of cathedral and crypt offered at 11:00, 11:30, 13:30, and 14:00; £3.50 for an audioguide tour anytime; Sun services at 08:00, 10:15, 11:30, 15:15, and 18:00; inexpensive and cheery café in crypt; tube: St. Paul's; tel. 020/7236-4128). The **evensong** services are free, but nonpaying visitors are not allowed to linger afterward (Mon–Sat at 17:00, Sun at 15:15, 40 min).

▲**Museum of London**—London, a 2,000-year-old city, is so littered with Roman ruins that when a London builder finds Roman antiquities he doesn't stop work. He simply documents the finds, moves the artifacts to a museum, and builds on. If you're asking,

"Why did the Romans build their cities underground?" a trip to the creative and entertaining London Museum is a must. Stroll through London history from pre-Roman times through the Blitz up to today. This regular stop for the local school kids gives the best overview of London history in town (£5, free after 16:30, Mon–Sat 10:00–18:00, Sun 12:00–18:00, tube: Barbican or St. Paul's, tel. 020/7600-3699).

Geffrye Decorative Arts Museum—Walk through English front rooms from 1600 to 1990 (free, Tue–Sat 10:00–17:00, Sun 12:00–17:00, closed Mon, tube: Liverpool Street, then bus #149 or #242 north, tel. 020/7739-9893).

▲▲▲Tower of London—The Tower has served as a castle in wartime, a king's residence in peace, and, most notoriously, as the prison and execution site of rebels. This historic fortress is host to more than 3 million visitors a year. Enjoy the free and entertaining 50-minute Beefeater tour (leaves regularly from inside the gate, last one is usually at 15:30). The crown jewels, dating from the Restoration, are the best on Earth—and come with hour-long lines for most of the day. To avoid the crowds, arrive at 09:00 and go straight for the jewels, doing the Beefeater tour and White Tower later—or do the jewels after 16:30 (£11.50, 1-day combo ticket with Hampton Court Palace-£19, March–Oct Mon–Sat 09:00–18:00, Sun 10:00–18:00, Nov–Feb Tue–Sat 09:00–17:00, Sun–Mon 10:00–17:00, last entry 1 hr before closing, the long but fast-moving ticket line is worst on Sun, no photography allowed of jewels or in chapels, tube: Tower Hill, tel. 020/7709-0765, recorded info: tel. 020/7680-9004). You can avoid the long lines by picking up your ticket at any London TI or the Tower Hill tube station ticket office.

Ceremony of the Keys: Every night at 21:30, with pageantry-filled ceremony, the Tower of London is locked up (as it has been for the last 700 years). To attend this free 30-minute event, you need to request an invitation at least two to three months before your visit. Write to: Ceremony of the Keys, H.M. Tower of London, London EC3N 4AB. Include your name; the addresses, names, and ages of all people attending (up to 7 people, nontransferable, no kids under 8 allowed); requested date; alternative dates; and an international reply coupon (buy at U.S. post office).

Sights next to the Tower—The best remaining bit of London's **Roman Wall** is just north of the tower (at Tower Hill tube station). Freshly painted and restored, **Tower Bridge Experience**—the neo-Gothic maritime gateway to London—has an 1894-to-1994 history exhibit (£6.25, daily 10:00–18:30, last entry at 17:15, good view, poor value, tel. 020/7403-3761). The chic **St. Katherine Yacht Harbor**, just east of the Tower Bridge, has mod shops and the classic old Dickens Inn, fun for a drink or pub lunch. Across the bridge is the South Bank, with the upscale Butlers Wharf area, museums, and promenade.

Sights—South London, on the South Bank

The South Bank is a thriving arts and cultural center tied together by a riverside path. This trendy, pub-crawling walk—called the Jubilee Promenade—stretches from the Tower of London bridge past Westminster Bridge, where it offers grand views of the Houses of Parliament. (The promenade hugs the river except just east of London Bridge, where it cuts inland for a couple of blocks.)

▲▲▲**London Eye Ferris Wheel**—Built by British Air, the wheel towers above London opposite Big Ben. At 450 feet, this is the world's highest observational wheel, giving you a chance to fly British Air without leaving London. Built like a giant bicycle wheel, it's a pan-European undertaking: British steel and Dutch engineering, with Czech, German, French, and Italian mechanical parts. It's also very "green," running extremely efficiently and virtually silently. Twenty-five people ride in each of its 32 air-conditioned capsules for the 30-minute rotation (each capsule has a bench, but most people stand). From the top of the wheel—the highest public viewpoint in the city—Big Ben looks small. You only go around once; save a shot on top for the glass capsule of people next to yours.

A big hit with Londoners and tourists alike, the ride gets booked up fast, especially on weekends. To save time and guarantee a spot, book a time slot a day ahead—at a London TI, in person at the office near the base of the wheel, at the Big Bus Information Centre (daily 08:30–17:30, 48 Buckingham Palace Road, a block from Victoria Station), possibly through your hotel (ask), or online at www.ba-londoneye.com. You can also book by phone, but allow at least five days before your ticket is available (pick up ticket at wheel office, 50p charge, automated booking tel. 0870-500-0600). Whether you book ahead or just stand in line, you'll be assigned—or you can request—a half-hour time slot. You must arrive at the wheel during this time (earlier is better) to ensure getting on. Advance booking, which costs nothing extra, allows you to skip the queue to buy tickets. No one escapes the second queue, the ticket-holders' line to get on the wheel (line starts forming 10 min before your 30-min time slot begins; listen for announcement).

Freewheeling types who don't care for lines or prebooking can usually avoid the line by riding at night. It's open until 22:00 in peak season (last boarding 21:30). If you're lucky, you can waltz right on (£9, daily 09:30–22:00, mid-Sept–March 10:00–20:00, at County Hall, shop with binoculars for rent, tube: Waterloo or Westminster, www.ba-londoneye.com).

The Dalí Universe—Cleverly located next to the hugely popular London Eye Ferris wheel, this exhibit features 500 works of mind-bending art by Salvador Dalí. While pricey, it's entertaining if you like surrealism and want to learn about Dalí (£7, daily 10:00–17:30, generally summer eves until 20:00, tel. 020/7620-2720).

▲▲Imperial War Museum—This impressive museum covers the wars of the last century, from heavy weaponry to love notes and Varga Girls, from Monty's Africa campaign tank to Schwartzkopf's Desert Storm uniform. You can trace the development of the machine gun; watch footage of the first tank battles; see one of over a thousand V2 rockets (each with over a ton of explosives) Hitler rained on Britain in 1944; hold your breath through the gruesome WWI trench experience; and buy WWII-era toys in the fun museum shop. The "Secret War" section gives a fascinating peek into the intrigues of espionage in World War I and World War II. The new Holocaust Exhibit is one of the best on the subject anywhere. Rather than glorify war, the museum does its best to shine a light on the powerful human side of one of mankind's most persistent traits (£6.50, free for kids under 16 and over 60, free for anyone after 16:30, daily 10:00–18:00, 90 min is enough time for most visitors, tube: Lambeth North or bus #12 from Westminster, tel. 020/7416-5000). The museum is housed in what was the Royal Bethlam Hospital. Also known as "the Bedlam asylum," the place was so wild it gave the world a new word for chaos: "bedlam." Back in Victorian times, locals—without trash-talk shows and cable TV—came here for their entertainment. The asylum actually opened the place to the paying public on weekends to view the "bedlam."

Bramah Tea and Coffee Museum—Aficionados of tea or coffee will find this small museum fascinating. It tells the story of each drink almost passionately. The owner, Mr. Bramah, comes from a big tea family and wants the world to know how the advent of commercial television, with breaks not long enough to brew a proper pot of tea, required a faster hot drink. In came the horrible English instant coffee. Tea countered with finely chopped leaves in tea bags, and it's gone downhill ever since (£4, daily 10:00–18:00, in the Butlers Wharf complex just across the bridge from the tower, behind Design Museum, tel. 020/7378-0222). Its café, which serves more kinds of coffees and teas than cakes, is open to the public (same hrs as museum).

▲▲Shakespeare's Globe—The original Globe Theater has been rebuilt—half-timbered and thatched—exactly as it was in Shakespeare's time. (This is the first thatch in London since they were outlawed after the great fire of 1666.) The Globe originally accommodated 2,000 seated and another 1,000 standing. (Today, leaving space for reasonable aisles, the theater holds 900 seated and 600 groundlings.) Its promoters brag that the theater forges "the three A's": actors, audience, and architecture, with each contributing to the play. Open as a museum and working theater, it hosts authentic old-time performances of Shakespeare's plays. The theater can be toured when there are no plays. The Globe's exhibition on Shakespeare is the world's largest, with interactive displays and film presentations, a sound lab, a script factory, and costumes (£7.50, mid-May–Sept daily 09:00–12:00, Oct–mid-May 10:00–17:00, includes guided 30-min tour offered on the half hr, on South Bank directly across the Thames over Southwark Bridge from St. Paul's, tube: Mansion House or London Bridge, tel. 020/7902-1500, www.shakespeares-globe.org, for details on seeing a play see "Entertainment," below).

▲▲**Tate Modern**—Dedicated in the spring of 2000, this striking new museum across the river from St. Paul's opened the new century with art from the old one (remember the 20th century?). Its powerhouse collection of Monet, Matisse, Dalí, Picasso, Warhol, and much more is displayed in a converted power house (museum free, fee for special exhibitions, daily 10:00–18:00, Fri–Sat until 22:00—a good time to visit, various audioguide tours-£1, free guided tours, call for schedule, view café on top floor, walk the Millennium Bridge—if it's open—from St. Paul's, or get off at the Southwark tube stop for a 7-min walk, tel. 020/7887-8008, www.tate.org.uk).

A river-bus service connects Tate Modern with Tate Britain (either free or minimal charge, runs May–Sept—maybe longer; ask for schedule at information desk at either Tate).

▲**Millennium Bridge**—This new pedestrian bridge was supposed to link St. Paul's Cathedral and Tate Modern across the Thames. Nicknamed "a blade of light" for its sleek minimalist design—370 yards long, 4 yards wide, stainless steel with teak planks—it includes clever aerodynamic handrails to deflect wind over the heads of pedestrians. But since it wiggles with people on it, it was closed days after it opened. The $25 million bridge will cost $7 million to stabilize, and skeptics doubt it will reopen in 2002. Try instead the new Jubilee Bridge (one bridge east), due to open in June.

▲▲**The Old Operating Theatre Museum and Herb Garret**—Climb a tight and creaky wooden spiral staircase to a church attic where you'll find: a garret used to dry medicinal herbs, a fascinating exhibit on Victorian surgery, cases of well-described 19th-century medical paraphernalia, and a special look at "anesthesia, the defeat of pain." Then you stumble upon Britain's oldest operating theater, where limbs were sawed off way back in 1821 (£3.50, daily 10:30–17:00, tube: London Bridge, 9a St. Thomas Street, tel. 020/8806-4325).

▲▲**Vinopolis: City of Wine**—While it seems illogical to have a huge wine museum in London, Vinopolis makes a good case. It's built over a Roman wine store and fills the massive vaults of an old wine warehouse. Visitors follow an excellent audioguide through a light yet earnest history of wine. Sipping your various wines, ports, and champagnes—immersed in your headset as you stroll—you learn about wine from its Georgian origins to Chile to a Vespa ride through Chianti country in Tuscany. Allow yourself some time, as the tour takes 90 minutes (the sipping can slow things down wonderfully, £11.50 with 5 tastes, £14 for 10, don't worry... for £2.50 you can buy 5 more tastes inside, daily 11:00–18:00, last entry 16:00, tube: London Bridge, between the Glove and Southwark Cathedral at 1 Bank End, tel. 0870-241-4040).

More South Bank Sights, in Southwark

These sights are mediocre but worth knowing about. The area stretching from Tate Modern to London Bridge, known as Southwark (suth-uck), was for centuries the place Londoners would go to escape the rules and decency of the city and let their medieval hair down. Bear-baiting, brothels, rollicking pubs and theater—you name it, your dreams could be fulfilled just across the Thames. Through the 20th century a run-down warehouse district, in the last decade it's been gentrified with classy restaurants, office parks, pedestrian promenades, major new sights (such as the Tate Modern and the Globe Theatre), and this colorful collection of lesser sights. The area is easy on foot and a scenic—though circuitous—way to connect St. Paul's and the Tower of London.

Southwark Cathedral—While made a cathedral only in 1905, this has been the neighborhood church since the 13th century and comes with some interesting history (Mon–Sat 10:00–18:00, Sun 11:00–17:00, evensong services weekdays at 17:30, tel. 020/7367-6711). The adjacent church-run **Long View of London Exhibition** tells the story of Southwark (£3, same hrs as church).

The Clink Prison—Proudly the "original clink," this was where law-abiding citizens threw Southwark troublemakers until 1780. Today it's a low-tech torture museum filling grotty old rooms with papier-mâché gore. Unfortunately, there's little to seriously deal with the fascinating problem of law and order in Southwark, where 18th-century Londoners went for a good time (overpriced at £4, daily 10:00–18:00, 1 Clink Street, tel. 020/7378-1558).

Rose Theatre—Here, in the basement of an 11-story office building, you can see the scant remains of the 16th-century theater that once stood here. The Rose Theatre was built in 1587, 12 years before the original Globe, and excavated in 1989. In this barren site, you view a 25-minute video on the history of theater in the days of Shakespeare (£4, daily 11:00–17:00).

Golden Hinde—This is a full-size replica of the 16th-century warship in which Sir Francis Drake circumcised the globe from 1577 to 1580. Commanding this boat, Drake earned the reputation as history's most successful pirate. The original is long gone but this boat has logged over 100,000 miles, including its own voyage around the world. While fun to see, the interior is not worth touring (£2.50, daily 09:30–17:30).

HMS *Belfast*—"The last big gun–armored warship of World War II" clogs the Thames just upstream from the Tower Bridge.

The South Bank

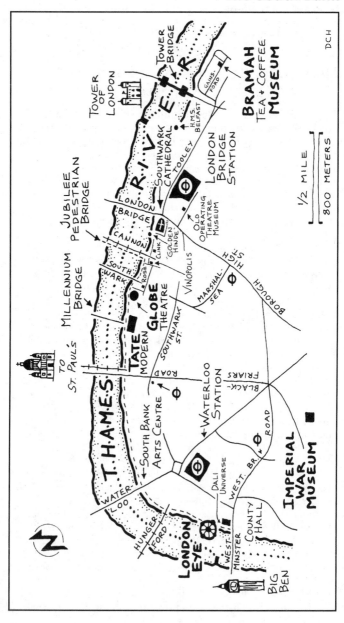

DCH

This huge vessel—now manned with wax sailors—thrills kids who always dreamed of sitting in a turret shooting off their imaginary guns. If you're into WWII warships, this is the ultimate... otherwise it's just lots of exercise with a nice view of the Tower Bridge (£5.40, daily 10:00–18:00).

Sights—South London, on the North Bank

▲▲**Tate Britain**—One of Europe's great art houses, Tate Britain specializes in British painting: 16th century through the 20th, including Pre-Raphaelites. Commune with the mystical Blake and romantic Turner (free, daily 10:00–17:50, fine £3 audioguide, free tours: 11:30—Turner, 14:30 and 15:30—British Highlights, call to confirm schedule, no photography allowed, tube: Pimlico, then 7-min walk, or arrive directly at museum by taking bus #88 from Oxford Circus or #77A from National Gallery, tel. 020/7887-8000, recorded info tel. 020/7887-8008, www.tate.org.uk). A river-bus service connects Tate Britain with Tate Modern (either free or minimal charge, runs May–Sept—maybe longer; ask for schedule at information desk at either Tate).

Sights—Greater London

▲**Kew Gardens**—For a fine riverside park and a palatial greenhouse jungle to swing through, take the tube or the boat to every botanist's favorite escape, Kew Gardens. While to most visitors the Royal Botanic Gardens of Kew is simply a delightful opportunity to wander among 33,000 different types of plants, it's also notable because it's run by a hardworking organization committed to understanding and preserving the botanical diversity of our planet. The Kew tube station drops you in a little business community a two-block walk from Victoria Gate (the main garden entry). Pick up a map brochure and check at the gate for a monthly listing of best blooms.

Garden lovers could spend days exploring Kew's 300 acres. For a quick visit, spend a fragrant hour wandering through three buildings: the Palm House, a humid Victorian world of iron, glass, and tropical plants built in 1844; a Waterlily House that Monet would swim for; and the Princess of Wales Conservatory, a modern greenhouse with many different climate zones growing countless cacti, bug-munching carnivorous plants, and more (£6.50, £4.50 at 16:45, Mon–Fri 09:30–18:30, Sat–Sun 09:30–19:30, until 16:30 or sunset off-season, galleries and conservatories close at 17:30, consider £2.50 narrated floral joyride on little train departing from 11:00–15:30 from Victoria Gate, tube: Kew Gardens, tel. 020/8332-5000). For a sun–dappled lunch, walk 10 minutes from the Palm House to the Orangery (£6 hot meals, daily 10:00–17:30).

▲**Hampton Court Palace**—Fifteen miles up the Thames from downtown (£15 taxi ride from Kew Gardens) is the 500-year-old palace of Henry VIII. Actually, it was the palace of his minister,

Greater London

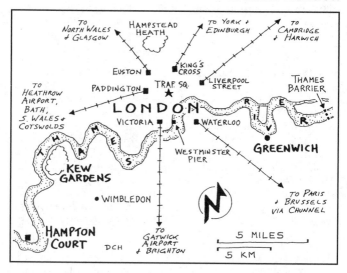

Cardinal Wolsey. When Wolsey, a clever man, realized Henry
VIII was experiencing a little palace envy, he gave it to his king.
The Tudor palace was also home to Elizabeth I and Charles I.
Parts were updated by Christopher Wren for William and Mary.
The palace stands stately overlooking the Thames and includes
some impressive Tudor rooms, including a Great Hall, with its
magnificent hammer-beam ceiling. The industrial-strength Tudor
kitchen was capable of keeping 600 schmoozing courtesans
thoroughly—if not well—fed. The sculpted garden features a
rare Tudor tennis court and a popular maze.

The palace, fully restored after a 1986 fire, tries hard to please,
but it doesn't quite sparkle. From the information center in the main
courtyard, visitors book times for tours with tired costumed guides
or pick up audioguides for self-guided tours of various wings of the
palace (all free). The Tudor Kitchens, Henry VIII's Apartments, and
the King's Apartments are most interesting. The Georgian Rooms
are pretty dull. The maze in the nearby garden is a curiosity some
find fun (maze free with palace ticket, otherwise £2.50). The train
(2/hr, 30 min) from London's Waterloo station drops you just across
the river from the palace (£10.80, 1-day combo ticket with Tower of
London-£19, Mon 10:15–18:00, Tue–Sun 09:30–18:00, Nov–March
until 16:30, tel. 020/8781-9500).

Royal Air Force Museum—A hit with aviation enthusiasts, this
huge aerodrome and airfield contain planes from World War II
through the Battle of Britain up to the Gulf War. You can climb

inside some of the planes, try your luck in a cockpit, and fly with the Red Arrows in a flight simulator (£7.50, daily 10:00–18:00, café, shop, parking, tube: Colindale—on the Northern Line, Grahame Park Way, tel. 020/8205-2266, www.rafmuseum.org.uk).

Disappointments of London

The venerable BBC broadcasts from Broadcasting House. Of all its productions, its "BBC Experience" tour for visitors is among the worst. On the South Bank, the London Dungeon, a much-visited but amateurish attraction, is just a highly advertised, overpriced haunted house—certainly not worth the £10 admission, much less your valuable London time. It comes with long and rude lines. Wait for Halloween and see one in your hometown to support a better cause. The Design Museum (next to the Bramah Tea and Coffee Museum) and "Winston Churchill's Britain at War Experience" (next to London Dungeon) waste your time. The Kensington Palace State Apartments are lifeless and not worth a visit.

Shopping in London

Harrods—Filled with wonderful displays, Harrods is London's most famous and touristy department store. Big yet classy, Harrods has everything from elephants to toothbrushes. The food halls are sights to savor. If anything, ride the ornate Egyptian escalator (Mon–Sat 10:00–19:00, closed Sun, on Brompton Road, tube: Knightsbridge, tel. 020/7730-1234). Many readers report that Harrods is now overpriced (its £1 toilets are the most expensive in Europe), snooty, and teeming with American and Japanese tourists. Still, it's the palace of department stores. The nearby Beauchamp Place is lined with classy and fascinating shops.

Harvey Nichols—Princess Diana's favorite, this remains the department store *du jour* (Mon, Tue, Sat 10:00–19:00, Wed–Fri until 20:00, Sun 12:00–18:00, near Harrods, tube: Knightsbridge, 109 Knightsbridge, www.harveynichols.com). Its fifth floor is a veritable food fest with a gourmet grocery store, a fancy (smoky) restaurant, a Yo! Sushi bar, and a lively café. Consider a take-away tray of sushi to eat on a bench in the Hyde Park rose garden two blocks away. On Friday nights, the café hosts a popular "Film on Five" event: a three-course dinner followed by recently-released films shown on big-screen televisions (£35, 20:00–24:00, for reservations tel. 020/7201-8562).

Toys—The biggest toy store in Britain is **Hamleys**, with seven floors buzzing with 28,000 toys managed by a staff of 200. At the "Bear Factory," kids can get a made-to-order teddy bear by picking out a "bear skin" and watch while it's stuffed and sewn (Mon–Sat 10:00–20:00, Sun 12:00–18:00, tube: Oxford Circus, 188 Regent Street, tel. 020/7494-2000).

Street Markets—Antique buffs, people watchers, and folks who brake for garage sales love London's street markets. There's good early-morning market activity somewhere any day of the week. The best are **Portobello Road** (roughly Mon–Sat 09:00–17:00, go on Sat for antiques until 17:30—plus the regular junk, clothes, and produce; tube: Notting Hill Gate, tel. 020/7229-8354) and **Camden Market** (daily 10:00–18:00, trendy arts and crafts, tube: Camden Town, tel. 020/7284-2084). The TI has a complete, up-to-date list. If you like to haggle, there are no holds barred in London's street markets. Warning: Markets attract two kinds of people—tourists and pickpockets.

Famous Auctions—London's famous auctioneers welcome the curious public for viewing and bidding. For schedules, call **Sotheby's** (Mon–Fri 09:00–16:30, 34-35 New Bond Street, tube: Oxford Circus, tel. 020/7293-5000, www.sothebys.com) or **Christie's** (Mon–Fri 09:00–16:30, Tue 09:00–20:00, 8 King Street, tube: Green Park, tel. 020/7839-9060, www.christies.com).

Entertainment and Theater in London

London bubbles with top-notch entertainment seven days a week. Everything's listed in the weekly entertainment magazines, available at newsstands. Choose from classical, jazz, rock, and far-out music, Gilbert and Sullivan, dance, comedy, Baha'i meetings, poetry readings, spectator sports, film, and theater.

London's **theater** rivals Broadway's in quality and beats it in price. Choose from the Royal Shakespeare Company, top musicals, comedy, thrillers, sex farces, and more. Performances are nightly except Sunday, usually with one matinee a week. Matinees, held on Wednesday, Thursday, or Saturday, are cheaper and rarely sell out. Tickets range from about £8 to £35.

Most theaters, marked on tourist maps, are in the Piccadilly/ Trafalgar area. Box offices, hotels, and TIs offer a handy "Theater Guide." To book a seat, simply call the theater box office directly, ask about seats and dates available, and buy a ticket with your credit card. You can call from the United States as easily as from England (photocopy your hometown library's London newspaper theater section or check out www.officiallondontheatre.co.uk). Pick up your ticket 15 minutes before the show. You can also book through www.ticketmaster.co.uk (fee).

Ticket agencies are scalpers with an address. Booking through an agency (at most TIs or scattered throughout London) is quick and easy, but prices are inflated by a standard 25 percent fee. If buying from an agency, look at the ticket carefully (your price should be no more than 30 percent over the printed face value; the 17.5 percent VAT tax is already included in the face value) and understand where you're sitting according to the floor plan (if your view is restricted it will state this on ticket). Agencies are worthwhile only if a show you've got to see is sold out at the box office. They scarf up hot tickets, planning to make a killing after the show is sold out. U.S. booking agencies get their tickets from another agency, adding even more to your expense by involving yet another middleman. Many tickets sold on the streets are forgeries. With cheap international phone calls and credit cards, there's no reason not to book direct.

Theater lingo: stalls (ground floor), dress circle (1st balcony), upper circle (2nd balcony), balcony (sky-high 3rd balcony).

Cheap theater tricks: Most theaters offer returned-ticket, standing-room, matinee, and senior or student stand-by deals. These "concessions" are indicated with a "conc" or "s" in the listings. Picking up a late return can get you a great seat at a cheap-seat price. If a show is "sold out," there's usually a way to get a seat. Call the theater box office and ask how. I buy the second-cheapest tickets directly from the theater box office.

The famous "half-price booth" in Leicester (LES-ter) Square sells discounted tickets for good seats to shows on the push list the day of the show only (Mon–Sat 12:00–18:30, matinee tickets Tue–Sun from noon, cash only). The real half-price booth is a freestanding kiosk at the edge of the garden in Leicester Square. Several dishonest outfits advertise "official half-price tickets" at agencies closer to the tube station. Avoid these.

Many theaters are so small that there's hardly a bad seat. After the lights go down, "scooting up" is less than a capital offense. Shakespeare did it.

Royal Shakespeare Company—If you'll ever enjoy Shakespeare, it'll be in Britain. The RSC performs at London's Barbican Centre from December through May (office open daily 09:00–20:00, box office tel. 020/7638-8891, recorded information tel. 020/7628-9760) and in Stratford year-round (tel. 01789/403-403). To get a schedule, you can call (numbers listed above), write (Royal Shakespeare Theatre, Stratford-upon-Avon, CV37 6BB Warwickshire), or visit www.rsc.org.uk.

Tickets range in price from £10 to £30 (discounts for young and old). Book direct by telephone and credit card and pick up your ticket at the door (Barbican Centre, Silk Street, tube: Barbican).

Shakespeare at Shakespeare's Globe—To see Shakespeare in a replica of the theater for which he wrote his plays, attend a play at the Globe. This thatch-roofed, open-air round theater does the plays much as Shakespeare intended (with no amplification). The play's the thing from mid-May through September (usually Tue–Sat 14:00 and 19:30, Sun at either 13:00 and 18:30 or 16:00 only, no plays Mon). You'll pay £5 to stand and £10 to £26 to sit (usually on a backless bench; only a few rows and the pricier Gentlemen's Rooms have seats with backs). The £5 "groundling" tickets—while the only ones open to rain—are most fun. Scurry in early to stake out a spot on the stage's edge leaning rail—where the most interaction with the actors occurs. You're a crude peasant. You lean your elbows on the stage, munch a picnic dinner, or walk around. I've never enjoyed Shakespeare as much as here, performed as it was meant to be in the "wooden O." Plays can be long. Many groundlings leave before the end. If you like, hang out an hour before the finish and beg or buy a ticket from someone leaving early (groundlings are allowed to come and go).

The theater is on the South Bank directly across the Thames over Southwark Bridge from St. Paul's (tube: Mansion House, or walk across the Millennium Bridge—if it's open— from St. Paul's, tel. 020/7902-1500, box office tel. 020/7401-9919, www.shakespeares-globe.org). The Globe is inconvenient for public transport, but the courtesy phone in the lobby gets a minicab in minutes. (These have set fees—e.g., £8 to South Kensington—but generally cost less than a metered cab and provide fine and honest service.)

Music—For easy, cheap, or free concerts in historic churches, check the TI's listings for lunch concerts (especially Wren's St. Bride's Church; St. James at Piccadilly—free lunch concerts on Mon, Wed, and Fri at 13:00, info tel. 020/7381-0441; and St. Martin-in-the-Fields—free lunch concerts on Mon, Tue, and Fri at 13:05, church tel. 020/7766-1100). St. Martin-in-the-Fields also hosts fine evening concerts by candlelight (£6–16, Thu–Sat at 19:30, CC, box office tel. 020/7839-8362). For a fun classical event (mid-June–early Sept), attend a "Prom Concert." This is an annual music festival with nightly concerts in the Royal Albert Hall at give-a-peasant-some-culture prices (£3 standing-room spots sold at the door, £5 restricted view seats, most £21.50, CC, tube: South Kensington, tel. 020/7589-8212, www.royalalberthall.com).

Cruises—Of the Thames River evening cruises that offer four-course meals and dancing, London Showboat offers the best value (£48, April–Oct Wed–Sun, departs 19:00 from Westminster Pier, Thu–Sat evening cruises through the winter, 3.5 hrs, tel. 020/7237-5134, www.citycruises.com). For more on cruising, get the Thames River Services brochure from a London TI.

Daytrips from London

You could fill a book with the many easy and exciting daytrips from London (Earl Steinbicker did: *Daytrips London: Fifty-One Day Adventures by Rail or Car, in and around London and Southern England*). **Original London Walks** offers a variety of Explorer daytrips using the train for about £10 plus transportation costs (destinations include Bath, Stonehenge, Windsor Castle, Hampton Court Palace, and more; see their walking-tour brochure, tel. 020/7624-3978, www.walks.com).

Several **bus-tour companies** take London-based travelers out and back every day. If you're going to Bath and want to stay

London Daytrips

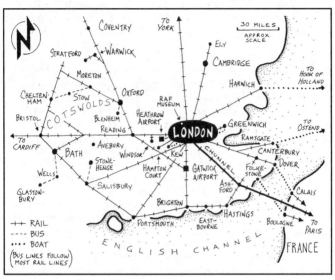

COVENTRY
TO YORK
ELY
CAMBRIDGE
STRATFORD — WARWICK
MORETON
HARWICH
TO HOOK OF HOLLAND
CHELTENHAM — STOW
OXFORD
RAF MUSEUM
COTSWOLDS
BLENHEIM
HEATHROW AIRPORT
BRISTOL
READING
LONDON
GREENWICH
TO OSTEND
TO CARDIFF
AVEBURY
WINDSOR
KEW
RAMSGATE
CHUNNEL
CANTERBURY
BATH
STONEHENGE
HAMPTON COURT
GATWICK AIRPORT
FOLKESTONE
DOVER
WELLS
SALISBURY
ASHFORD
CALAIS
GLASTONBURY
BRIGHTON
HASTINGS
PORTSMOUTH
EASTBOURNE
BOULOGNE
TO PARIS

30 MILES
APPROX. SCALE

++ RAIL
---- BUS
•••• BOAT
(BUS LINES FOLLOW MOST RAIL LINES)

E N G L I S H   C H A N N E L   FRANCE

overnight, consider taking a day tour to Bath and skipping the trip back to London. Depending on the type and availability of tour, you'll pay about £48, which also includes a visit to Stonehenge (compare to a £31 one-way 2nd-class train ticket from London to Bath). Evan Evans' tour leaves from the Victoria Coach station daily every morning at 09:00 (you can stow your bag under the bus), stops in Stonehenge (45 min), and then stops in Bath for lunch and a city tour before returning to London (£48, offered year-round, fully-guided, admissions included). You can book the tour at the Victoria Coach station; the Evan Evans' office (258 Vauxhall Bridge Road, near Victoria Coach station, tel. 020/7950-1777, www.evanevans.co.uk); or the Green Line Travel Office (4a Fountain Square, across from Victoria Coach station, tel. 020/7950-1777). Golden Tours offers a similar daily and fully-guided tour of Stonehenge and Bath for comparable prices (departs from Fountain Square, across from Victoria Coach station, tel. 020/7233-6668, www.goldentours.co.uk).

The British rail system uses London as a hub and normally offers round-trip fares (after 09:30) that cost virtually the same as one-way fares. For daytrips, "day return" tickets are best (and cheapest). You can save a little money if you purchase Super Advance tickets before 18:00 on the day before your trip. But given the high cost of big-city living and the charm of small-town England, rather than side tripping, I'd see London and get out.

Sleeping in London
(£1 = about $1.50, country code: 44, area code: 020)
Sleep Code: **S** = Single, **D** = Double/Twin, **T** = Triple, **Q** = Quad, **b** = bathroom, **s** = shower only, **CC** = Credit Cards accepted, **no CC** = Credit Cards not accepted. Unless otherwise noted, prices include a generous breakfast and all taxes.

London is expensive. For £50 ($75) you'll get a double with breakfast in a safe, cramped, and dreary place with minimal service. For £60 ($90) you'll get a basic, clean, reasonably cheery double in a usually cramped, cracked-plaster building or a soulless but comfortable room without breakfast in a huge Motel 6–type place. My London splurges, at £100 to £150 ($150–230), are spacious, thoughtfully-appointed places you'd be happy to entertain or make love in. Hearty English or generous buffet breakfasts are included unless otherwise noted, and TVs are standard in rooms.

Reserve your London room with a phone call or e-mail as soon as you can commit to a date. To call a London hotel from the United States or Canada, dial 011-44-20 (London's area code without the initial zero), then the local eight-digit number. A few places will hold a room with no deposit if you promise to arrive by midday. Most take your credit-card number as security. Many inexpensive places don't take credit cards and require a cash deposit (generally a personal check if 6 weeks in advance, otherwise a bank draft in pounds). The pricier ones have expensive cancellation policies (such as no refund if you cancel with less than 2 weeks' notice). Some fancy £120 rooms rent for a third off if you arrive late on a slow day and ask for a deal.

Sleeping in Victoria Station Neighborhood, Belgravia
The streets behind Victoria Station teem with budget B&Bs. It's a safe, surprisingly tidy, and decent area without a hint of the trashy touristy glitz of the streets in front of the station. Here in Belgravia, your neighbors include Andrew Lloyd Webber and Margaret Thatcher (her policeman stands outside 73 Chester Square). Decent eateries abound (see "Eating," below). Cheaper rooms are relatively dumpy. Don't expect £90 cheeriness in a £50 room. Off-season it's possible to save money by arriving late without a reservation and looking around. Fierce competition softens prices, especially for multinight stays. Particularly on hot summer nights, request a quiet back room. All are within a five-minute walk of the Victoria tube, bus, and train stations. There's a £15-per-day (with a hotel voucher) garage, a nearby **launderette** (daily 08:00–20:30, self-service or full-service, past Warwick Square at 3 Westmoreland Terrace, tel. 020/7821-8692), and an easygoing little dance club (Club D'Jan, £5 includes drink, Wed–Sat, 63 Wilton Road).

Winchester Hotel is family run and perhaps the best value,

London, Victoria Station Neighborhood

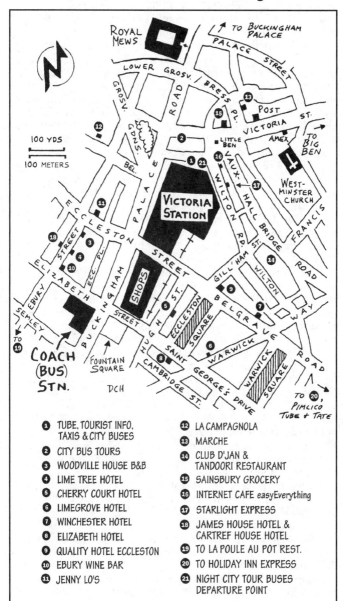

❶ TUBE, TOURIST INFO, TAXIS & CITY BUSES

❷ CITY BUS TOURS

❸ WOODVILLE HOUSE B&B

❹ LIME TREE HOTEL

❺ CHERRY COURT HOTEL

❻ LIMEGROVE HOTEL

❼ WINCHESTER HOTEL

❽ ELIZABETH HOTEL

❾ QUALITY HOTEL ECCLESTON

❿ EBURY WINE BAR

⓫ JENNY LO'S

⓬ LA CAMPAGNOLA

⓭ MARCHE

⓮ CLUB D'JAN & TANDOORI RESTAURANT

⓯ SAINSBURY GROCERY

⓰ INTERNET CAFE easyEverything

⓱ STARLIGHT EXPRESS

⓲ JAMES HOUSE HOTEL & CARTREF HOUSE HOTEL

⓳ TO LA POULE AU POT REST.

⓴ TO HOLIDAY INN EXPRESS

㉑ NIGHT CITY TOUR BUSES DEPARTURE POINT

with 18 fine rooms, no claustrophobia, and a wise and caring management (Db-£85, Tb-£110, Qb-£140, no CC, no groups, no infants, 17 Belgrave Road, London SW1V 1RB, tel. 020/7828-2972, fax 020/7828-5191, run by Jimmy).

In **Woodville House** the quarters are dollhouse tight, showers are down the hall, and several of its 12 rooms are on the noisy street (doubles on quiet backside, twins and singles on street). Still, this well-run, well-worn place is a good value, with lots of travel tips and friendly chat—especially about the local rich and famous—from Rachel Joplin (S-£42, D-£62, bunky family deals-£80–110 for 3–5 people, CC, 107 Ebury Street, SW1W 9QU, tel. 020/7730-1048, fax 020/7730-2574, www.woodvillehouse .co.uk, e-mail: woodville.house@cwcom.net).

Lime Tree Hotel, enthusiastically run by David and Marilyn Davies, comes with spacious and thoughtfully-decorated rooms and a fun-loving breakfast room. While priced a bit steep, the place has character (Sb-£75, Db-£105–115, Tb-£145, family room-£160, CC but possible discount with cash, David deals in slow times and is creative at helping travelers in a bind, 135 Ebury Street, SW1W 9RA, tel. 020/7730-8191, fax 020/7730-7865, www.limetreehotel.co.uk).

James House and **Cartref House** are two nearly-identical, well-run, smoke-free, 10-room places on either side of Ebury Street (S-£50, Sb-£60, D-£68, Db-£82, T-£90, Tb-£105, family bunkbed quad-£130, CC, 5 percent discount with cash, all rooms with fans; James House at 108 Ebury Street, tel. 020/7730-2511; Cartref House at 129 Ebury Street, tel. 020/7730-6176, fax for both: 020/7730-7338, www.jamesandcartref.co.uk, e-mail: jandchouse@cs.com).

Elizabeth Hotel is a stately old place overlooking Eccleston Square with fine public spaces and 37 spacious and decent rooms (D-£68, small Db-£83, big Db-£95, Tb-£108, Qb-£120, Quint with b-£125, CC, 37 Eccleston Square, tel. 020/7828-6812, fax 020/7828-6814, www.elizabeth-hotel.com, e-mail: info@elizabeth-hotel.com). Be careful not to confuse this hotel with the Elizabeth House. This one is big and comfy, the other small and dumpy.

Elizabeth House feels institutional and bland—as you might expect from a former YMCA—and it's run-down and none too clean. But the price is right (S-£30, D-£40, Db-£50, T-£60, Q-£70, plus extra £10/room for D or Db in July–Aug, CC, 118 Warwick Way, SW1 4JB, tel. 020/7630-0741, fax 020/7630-0740, e-mail: elizabethhouse@ehlondon.fsnet.co.uk).

Quality Hotel Eccleston is big, modern, well-located, and a fine value for no-nonsense comfort (Db-£125, on slow days drop-ins can ask for "saver prices"—33 percent off on first night, breakfast extra, CC, nonsmoking floor, elevator, 82 Eccleston Square, SW1V 1PS, tel. 020/7834-8042, fax 020/7630-8942, e-mail: admin@gb614.u-net.com).

Georgian House Hotel has 50 rooms and a cheaper annex that works well for backpackers (tiny D on 4th floor-£42, Db-£66, annex Db-£56, Tb-£82, Qb-£90, CC, Internet access, 35 St. George's Drive, SW1V 4DG, tel. 020/7834-1438, fax 020/7976-6085, www.georgianhousehotel.co.uk, e-mail: georgian@wildnet.co.uk).

Enrico Hotel, with 26 simple rooms, is basic, well-worn, and affordable (S-£45, D-£55, Ds-£60, CC, nonsmoking, 77 Warwick Way, SW1V 1QP, tel. 020/7834-9538, fax 020/7233-9995, www.enricohotel.fsnet.co.uk).

Cherry Court Hotel, run by the friendly and industrious Patel family, offers tight, basic rooms for good value in a central location (Sb-£42, Db-£48, Tb-£70, Qb-£90, Quint/b-£100, prices promised with this book through 2002, CC, using CC adds 5 percent extra, fruit-basket breakfast in room, nonsmoking, Internet access, 23 Hugh Street, SW1V 1QJ, tel. 020/7828-2840, fax 020/7828-0393, www.cherrycourthotel.co.uk, e-mail: info@cherrycourthotel.co.uk).

Holiday Inn Express fills an old building with 52 fresh, modern, and efficient rooms (Db-£97, Tb-£107, CC, up to 2 kids free, some discounts on Web site, nonsmoking floor, elevator, tube: Pimlico, 106 Belgrave Road, Victoria, tel. 020/7630-8888 or 0800-897-121, fax 020/7828-0441, www.hiexpress.com, e-mail: expressvictoria@hotmail.com).

Big, Cheap, Modern Hotels

These places—popular with budget tour groups—are well-run and offer elevators and all the modern comforts in a no-frills practical package. The doubles for £60 to £75 are a great value for London.

London County Hall Travel Inn, literally down the hall from a $400-a-night Marriott Hotel, fills one end of London's massive former City Hall. This place is wonderfully located near the base of the London Eye Ferris wheel and across the Thames from Big Ben. Its 300 slick and no-frills rooms come with all the necessary comforts (Db-£75 for 2 adults and up to 2 kids under age 15, couples can request a bigger family room—same price, CC, breakfast extra, book in advance, no-show rooms are released at 16:00, elevator, some smoke-free and easy-access rooms, 500 yards from Westminster tube stop and Waterloo Station where the Chunnel train leaves for Paris, Belvedere Road, SE1 7PB, you can call 0870-242-8000 or 020/7902-1600 but you'll be put on hold, you can fax at 020/7902-1619 but you might not get a response, it's easiest to book online at www.travelinn.co.uk).

Other London Travel Inns charging about £65 per room include **London Euston** (a big, blue Lego-type building on a handy but noisy street packed with Benny Hill families on vacation, 141 Euston Road, NW1 2AU, tube: Euston,

tel. 020/7554-3400), **Tower Bridge** (tube: London Bridge,
tel. 020/7940-3700), and **London Putney Bridge** (farther out,
tube: Putney Bridge, tel. 020/7471-8300). For any of these,
call 0870-242-8000, fax 0870-241-9000, or best, book online
at www.travelinn.co.uk.

Hotel Ibis London Euston, which feels classier than
a Travel Inn, is located on a quiet street a block behind
Euston Station (380 rooms, Db-£70, CC, no family rooms,
breakfast extra, nonsmoking floor, 3 Cardington Street,
NW1 2LW, tel. 020/7388-7777, fax 020/7388-0001, e-mail:
h0921@accor-hotels.com).

Jurys Inn rents 200 mod, compact, and comfy rooms near
King's Cross Station (Db/Tb-£89, 2 adults and 2 kids—under age
12—can share 1 room, breakfast extra, CC, nonsmoking floors,
60 Pentonville Road, Islington, N1 9LA, tube: Angel, tel.
020/7282-5500, fax 020/7282-5511, www.jurys.com).

Premier Lodge opens in the spring of 2002 near Shakespeare's
Globe Theatre on the South Bank (55 rooms, Db for up to 2
adults and 2 kids-£70, Bankside, 34 Park Street, London SE1,
tel. 0870-700-1456, www.premierlodge.com).

"South Kensington," She Said, Loosening His Cummerbund

To live on a quiet street so classy it doesn't allow hotel signs,
surrounded by trendy shops and colorful restaurants, call "South
Ken" your London home. Shoppers like being a short walk from
Harrods and the designer shops of King's Road and Chelsea.
When I splurge, I splurge here. Sumner Place is just off Old
Brompton Road, 200 yards from the handy South Kensington
tube station (on Circle Line, 2 stops from Victoria Station, direct
Heathrow connection). There's a taxi rank in the median strip at
the end of Harrington Road. The handy "Wash & Dry" **Laun-
dromat** is on the corner of Queensberry Place and Harrington
Road (daily 08:00–21:00, bring 20p and £1 coins).

Aster House Hotel—run by friendly and accommodating
Simon and Leona Tan—has a sumptuous lobby, lounge, and
breakfast room. Its newly renovated rooms are comfy and quiet,
with TVs, phones, air-conditioning, and refrigerators. Enjoy
breakfast or just lounging in the whisper-elegant Orangery, a
Victorian greenhouse (Sb-£75–99, Db-£135, bigger Db-£150,
deluxe 4-poster Db-£180, CC, entirely nonsmoking, 3 Sumner
Place, SW7 3EE, tel. 020/7581-5888, fax 020/7584-4925,
www.asterhouse.com).

Five Sumner Place Hotel was recently voted "the best small
hotel in London." The rooms in this 150-year-old building are
tastefully decorated and the breakfast room is a Victorian-style
conservatory/greenhouse (13 rooms, Sb-£100, Db-£153, third

London, South Kensington Neighborhood

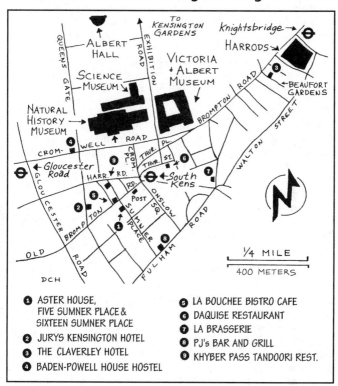

QUEEN'S GATE

TO KENSINGTON GARDENS

Knightsbridge →

HARRODS →

ALBERT HALL

EXHIBITION ROAD

VICTORIA & ALBERT MUSEUM

SCIENCE MUSEUM

BROMPTON ROAD

← BEAUFORT GARDENS

NATURAL HISTORY MUSEUM

WALTON STREET

CROM- WELL ROAD

THUR. PL.

THUR. PL.

CROM. RD.

THUR. ST.

← Gloucester Road

HARR. RD.

← South Kens

GLOUCESTER ROAD

BROMPTON ROAD

SUMNER PLACE

Post SQ.

ONSLOW

FULHAM ROAD

OLD ROAD

DCH

N

¼ MILE

400 METERS

❶ ASTER HOUSE, FIVE SUMNER PLACE & SIXTEEN SUMNER PLACE

❷ JURYS KENSINGTON HOTEL

❸ THE CLAVERLEY HOTEL

❹ BADEN-POWELL HOUSE HOSTEL

❺ LA BOUCHEE BISTRO CAFE

❻ DAQUISE RESTAURANT

❼ LA BRASSERIE

❽ PJ's BAR AND GRILL

❾ KHYBER PASS TANDOORI REST.

bed-£22, CC; TV, phones, and fridge in rooms by request; non-smoking rooms, elevator, 5 Sumner Place, South Kensington, SW7 3EE, tel. 020/7584-7586, fax 020/7823-9962, www.sumnerplace .com, e-mail: reservations@sumnerplace.com, Tom).

Sixteen Sumner Place, a lesser value for classier travelers, has over-the-top formality and class packed into its 37 un-numbered but pretentiously-named rooms, plush lounges, and quiet garden (Db-£170 with shower, £200 with bath, CC, breakfast in your room, elevator, 16 Sumner Place, SW7 3EG, tel. 020/7589-5232, fax 020/7584-8615, U.S. tel. 800/592-5387, e-mail: reservations@numbersixteenhotel.co.uk).

Jurys Kensington Hotel is big and stately with a greedy pricing scheme (Sb/Db/Tb-£100–220 depending upon "availability," ask for a deal, breakfast extra, CC, piano lounge, nonsmoking floor, elevator, Queen's Gate, South Kensington, SW7 5LR, tel. 020/7589-6300, fax 020/7581-1492).

The Claverley, two blocks from Harrods, is on a quiet street similar to Sumner Place. The 30 fancy dark-wood and marble rooms come with all the comforts (S-£70, Sb-£85–120, Db-£120–150, sofa bed Tb-£190–215, prices may be flexible Dec–March, CC, plush lounge, nonsmoking rooms, elevator, may renovate in 2002, 13-14 Beaufort Gardens, SW3 1PS, tube: Knightsbridge, tel. 020/7589-8541, fax 020/7584-3410, U.S. tel. 800/747-0398, www.claverleyhotel.co.uk).

Baden-Powell House Hostel is a huge, modern, institutional place built to inexpensively house Boy and Girl Scouts and their families in central London. Those with a relative in a scouting organization get about a 30 percent discount. It's a big, bright, smoke-free place that feels safe and is well-run (180 single beds, Sb-£65, Scout rate Sb-£44, Db-£88, Scout rate Db-£66, Tb-£114, Scout rate Tb-£90, extra bed-£12, dorm beds-£27, Scout rate dorm beds-£22, CC, air-con, cheap meals served, rooms are spacious with yacht-type bathrooms, receive discount with a letter from your Boy or Girl Scout troop saying you're "family," across from Natural History Museum on corner of Cromwell Road and Queen's Gate at 65 Queen's Gate, tube: South Kensington, tel. 020/7584-7031, fax 020/7590-6902, www.scoutbase.org.uk, e-mail: bph.hostel@scout.org.uk).

Sleeping in Notting Hill Gate Neighborhood

Residential Notting Hill Gate has quick bus and tube access to downtown, is on the A2 Airbus line from Heathrow, and, for London, is very "homely." It has a self-serve launderette, an artsy theater, a late-hours supermarket, and lots of fun budget eateries (see "Eating," below).

Westland Hotel is comfortable, convenient, and hotelesque, with a fine lounge and spacious 1970s-style rooms (Sb-£88, Db-£105, cavernous deluxe Db-£121, sprawling Tb-£122, gargantuan Qb-£149, 10 percent discount with this book through 2002, CC, elevator, free garage with 7 spaces, between Notting Hill Gate and Queensway tube stations, 154 Bayswater Road, W2 4HP, tel. 020/7229-9191, fax 020/7727-1054, www.westlandhotel.co.uk, e-mail: reservations@westlandhotel.co.uk).

Vicarage Private Hotel, understandably popular, is family-run and elegantly British in a quiet, classy neighborhood. It has 18 rooms furnished with taste and quality, a TV lounge, and facilities on each floor. Mandy, Richard, and Tere maintain a homey and caring atmosphere (S-£46, D-£76, Db-£100, T-£93, Q-£100, no CC, 6-min walk from the Notting Hill Gate and High Street Kensington tube stations, near Kensington Palace at 10 Vicarage Gate, Kensington, W8 4AG, tel. 020/7229-4030, fax 020/7792-5989, www.londonvicaragehotel.com, e-mail: reception@londonvicaragehotel.com).

London, Notting Hill Gate Neighborhood

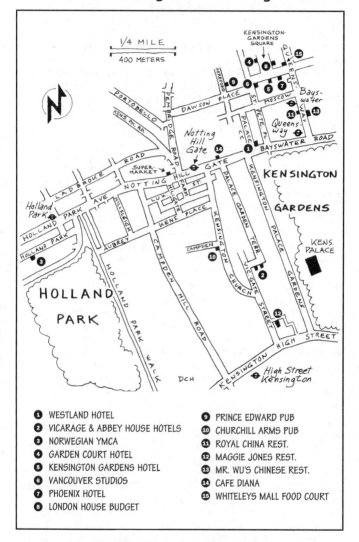

1. WESTLAND HOTEL
2. VICARAGE & ABBEY HOUSE HOTELS
3. NORWEGIAN YMCA
4. GARDEN COURT HOTEL
5. KENSINGTON GARDENS HOTEL
6. VANCOUVER STUDIOS
7. PHOENIX HOTEL
8. LONDON HOUSE BUDGET
9. PRINCE EDWARD PUB
10. CHURCHILL ARMS PUB
11. ROYAL CHINA REST.
12. MAGGIE JONES REST.
13. MR. WU'S CHINESE REST.
14. CAFE DIANA
15. WHITELEYS MALL FOOD COURT

Abbey House Hotel, next door, is similar but has no lounge and is not as cozy (16 rooms, S-£45, D-£74, T-£90, Q-£100, Quint-£110, no CC, 11 Vicarage Gate, Kensington, W8 4AG, tel. 020/7727-2594, fax 020/7727-1873, www.abbeyhousekensington .com, Rodrigo).

Norwegian YWCA (Norsk K.F.U.K.) is for women under 30 only (and men with Norwegian passports). Located on a quiet, stately street, it offers nonsmoking rooms, a study, TV room, piano lounge, and an open-face Norwegian ambience. They have mostly quads, so those willing to share with strangers are most likely to get a place (July–Aug: Ss-£29, shared double-£27.50/bed, shared triple-£23/bed, shared quad-£20/bed, with breakfast; Sept–June: same prices include dinner; CC, 52 Holland Park, W11 3RS, tel. & fax 020/7727-9897, www.kfuk.dial.pipex.com). With each visit I wonder which is easier to get—a sex change or a Norwegian passport?

Sleeping on Kensington Gardens

Several big old hotels line the quiet Victorian Kensington Gardens, a block off the bustling Queensway shopping street near the Bayswater tube station. Popular with young international travelers, Queensway is a multicultural festival of commerce and eateries (such as Mr. Wu's Chinese Buffet and the Whiteleys Mall Food Court—see "Eating," below). These hotels come with the least traffic noise of all my downtown recommendations. **Brookford Wash & Dry**, at Queensway and Bishop's Bridge Road (daily 07:00–19:30, service from 09:00–17:30, computerized pay point takes all coins), is one of several Laundromats in the area.

Garden Court rents 34 comfortable rooms and is one of London's best values. It's friendly and has a garden (S-£40, Sb-£59, D-£59, Db-£89, T-£73, Tb-£99, Q-£83, Qb-£120, 10 percent discount with this book, CC, 30 Kensington Gardens Square, W2 4BG, tel. 020/7229-2553, fax 020/7727-2749, www.gardencourthotel .co.uk, e-mail: info@gardencourthotel.co.uk, Edward Connolly).

Kensington Gardens Hotel laces 16 decent rooms together in a tall, skinny place with lots of stairs (Ss-£55, Sb-£62, Db-£85, Tb-£105, CC, 9 Kensington Gardens Square, W2 4BH, tel. 020/7221-7790, fax 020/7792-8612, www .kensingtongardenshotel.co.uk).

Vancouver Studios offers 45 modern rooms with all the amenities, and gives you a fully-equipped kitchenette (utensils, stove, microwave, and fridge) rather than breakfast (small Sb-£56, big Sb-£77, small Db-£97, big Db-£112, Tb-£130, extra bed-£10, CC, homey lounge and private garden, 30 Prince's Square, W2 4NJ, tel. 020/7243-1270, fax 020/7221-8678, www.vienna-group .co.uk, e-mail: vancouverstudios@vienna-group.co.uk).

Phoenix Hotel, a Best Western modernization of a 125-room hotel, offers American business-class comforts; spacious and plush public spaces; and big, fresh, modern-feeling rooms (Sb-£94, Db-£120, Tb-£165, CC, elevator, 1-8 Kensington Gardens Square, W2 4BH, tel. 020/7229-2494, fax 020/7727-1419, U.S. tel. 800/528-1234, www.phoenixhotel.co.uk).

London House Budget Hotel is a threadbare, nose-ringed slumber-mill renting 240 beds in 93 stark rooms (S-£40, Sb-£50, twin-£54, Db-£68, dorm bed-£17, includes continental breakfast, CC, lots of school groups, 81 Kensington Gardens Square, W2 4DJ, tel. 020/7243-1810, fax 020/7243-1723, e-mail: londonhousehotel@aol.com).

Sleeping in Other Neighborhoods

Paddington Station: **The Royal Norfolk Hotel** is a 60-room place on a busy corner just one short block from the Paddington Station terminus of the Heathrow Express train (Db-£100, superior Db-£111, Tb-£130, 25 percent discount for 3-night stay, CC, elevator, 25 London Street, tel. 020/7723-3386, fax 020/7724-8442, www.royalnorfolk.co.uk, e-mail: 106165.1413 @compuserve.com).

Euston Station: The **Methodist International Centre**, a modern, youthful Christian residence, fills its lower floors with international students and its top floor with travelers. Rooms are modern and simple yet comfortable, with fine bathrooms, phones, and desks. The atmosphere is friendly, safe, clean, and controlled, with a spacious lounge and game room (Sb-£48, Db-£69, 2-course buffet dinner-£8, CC, nonsmoking rooms, elevator, on a quiet street a block southwest of Euston Square, 81-103 Euston Street, not Euston Road, W1 2EZ, tube: Euston Station, tel. 020/7380-0001, fax 020/7387-5300, e-mail: sales@micentre.com). In June, July, and August, when the students are gone, they rent simple £38 singles.

Cottage Hotel is tucked away a block off the west exit of Euston Station. Established in 1950, it's a bit tired, cramped, and smoky. But it's cheap and quiet (40 rooms, D-£50, Db-£60, T-£65, Tb-£75, Qb-£85, CC, 10 percent discount for 2-night cash-only stays, 67 Euston Street, tel. 020/7387-6785, fax 020/7383-0859, managed by Ali).

Downtown near Baker Street: For a less-hotelesque alternative in the center, consider renting one of the 18 stark, hardwood, comfortable rooms in **22 York Street B&B** (Db-£100, Tb-£141, CC, strictly smoke-free, inviting lounge, social breakfast, from Baker Street tube station walk 2 blocks down Baker Street and take a right, 22 York Street, tel. 020/7224-3990, fax 020/7224-1990, www.myrtle-cottage.co.uk/callis.htm, energetically run by Liz and Michael).

Near Buckingham Palace: **Vandon House Hotel**, formerly run by the Salvation Army, is now run by the Central University of Iowa. While filled by students most of the year, they rent their 33 rooms to travelers from late May through August at great prices. The rooms, while institutional, are comfy, and the location is excellent (S-£40, D-£62, Db-£79, Tb-£115, Qb-£145, prices promised with this book through 2002, CC, only single beds, nonsmoking, elevator, on a tiny road 2 blocks west of St. James Park tube station, near east end of Petty France Street at 1 Vandon Street, tel. 020/7799-6780, fax 020/7799-1464, www.vandonhouse.com, e-mail: info@vandonhouse.com).

Near St. Paul's: The **City of London Youth Hostel** is clean, modern, friendly, and well-run. You'll pay about £25 for a bed in their three- to eight-bed rooms, £28 for a single (hostel membership required, 200 beds, CC, cheap meals, tube: St. Paul's, 36 Carter Lane, EC4V 5AD, tel. 020/7236-4965, fax 020/7236-7681, e-mail: city@yha.org.uk).

Sleeping near Gatwick and Heathrow Airports

Near Gatwick Airport: The **Gatwick Travelodge** is a budget hotel two miles from the airport (Db-£50, CC, breakfast extra, free shuttle from south terminal, Church Road, Lowfield Heath, Crawley, tel. 0870-905-6343, www.travelodge.co.uk). The **London Gatwick Airport Travel Inn** also rents cheap rooms (Db-£50, CC, located at airport, tel. 01293/568-158, www .travelinn.co.uk).

Barn Cottage, a converted 17th-century barn, sits in the peaceful countryside with a tennis court, small swimming pool, and a good pub within walking distance. It has two wood-beamed rooms, antique furniture, and a large garden that makes you forget Gatwick is 10 minutes away (S-£35–40, D-£55, no CC, can drive you to airport or train station for £6, Leigh, Reigate, Surrey, RH2 8RF, tel. 01306/611-347, warmly run by Pat and Mike Comer).

The **Wayside Manor Farm** is another rural alternative to a bland airport hotel. This four-bedroom countryside place is a 10-minute drive from the airport (Db-£60, Norwood Hill, near Charlwood, tel. 01293/862-692, www.waysidefm.freeserve.co.uk).

Near Heathrow Airport: It's so easy to get to Heathrow from central London, I see no reason to sleep there. But for budget beds near the airport, consider **Heathrow Ibis** (Db-£60, Db-£40 on Fri–Sun nights, breakfast extra, CC, £2.50 shuttle bus to/from terminals except T-4, 112 Bath Road, tel. 020/8759-4888, fax 020/ 8564-7894, www.ibishotel.com, e-mail: h0794@accor-hotels.com). **Heathrow Airport Travelodge** is another option (300 rooms, Db-£70, Db-£50 Fri–Sun, 2 kids sleep free, CC, free shuttle to/from all terminals, Bath Road, off A4, behind Le Meridien Excelsior Hotel, half-mile from airport, tel. 0870-905-6343, www.travelodge.co.uk).

Eating in London

If you want to dine (as opposed to eat), check out the extensive listings in the weekly entertainment guides sold at London newsstands (or catch a train for Paris). The thought of a £30 meal in Britain generally ruins my appetite, so my London dining is limited mostly to easygoing, fun, but inexpensive alternatives. I've listed places by neighborhood—handy to your sightseeing or hotel.

Your £7 budget choices are pub grub, a café, fish and chips, pizza, ethnic, or picnic. Pub grub is the most atmospheric budget option. Many of London's 7,000 pubs serve fresh, tasty buffets under ancient timbers, with hearty lunches and dinners priced from £6 to £8. (While pubs are going strong, the new phenomenon is coffee shops: Starbucks and its competitors have sprouted up all over town, providing cushy and social watering holes with comfy chairs, easy WCs, £2 lattes, and a nice break between sights.)

Ethnic restaurants from all over the world add spice to England's lackluster cuisine scene. Eating Indian or Chinese is "going local" in London. It's also going cheap (cheaper if you take it out). Most large museums (and many churches) have inexpensive, cheery cafeterias. Sandwich shops (try "tikka chicken"—curry flavored) are a hit with local workers eating on the run. Of course, picnicking is the fastest and cheapest way to go. Good grocery stores and sandwich shops, fine park benches, and polite pigeons abound in Britain's most expensive city.

Eating near Trafalgar Square

For a tasty meal on a monk's budget sitting on somebody's tomb in an ancient crypt, descend into the **St. Martin-in-the-Fields Café in the Crypt** (£5–7 cafeteria plates, cheaper sandwich bar, Mon–Sat 10:00–20:00, Sun 12:00–20:30, profits go to the church; underneath St. Martin-in-the-Fields on Trafalgar Square, tel. 020/7839-4342).

Chandos Bar's Opera Room floats amazingly apart from the tacky crush of tourism around Trafalgar Square. Look for the pub opposite the National Portrait Gallery (corner of William Street and St. Martin's Lane) and climb the stairs to the Opera Room. They serve £6 pub lunches and dinners (kitchen open daily 11:00–19:00, tel. 020/7836-1401). This is a fine Trafalgar rendezvous point—smoky, but wonderfully local.

Gordon's Wine Bar is ripe with atmosphere. A simple steep staircase leads into a 14th-century cellar filled with dusty old wine bottles, faded British memorabilia, local nine-to-fivers, and candlelight (hot meals only for lunch, fine plate of cheeses or various cold cuts with salad buffet all day until 21:00—1 plate of each feeds 2 for £7). While it's crowded, you can normally corral two chairs and grab the corner of a table (Mon–Sat 12:00–22:00, closed Sun, arrive before 18:00 to get a seat, 2 blocks from Trafalgar Square, bottom of Villiars Street at #47, near Embankment tube station, tel. 020/7930-1408).

Down Whitehall (toward Big Ben), a block south of Trafalgar

Square, you'll find the touristy but atmospheric **Clarence Pub** (lunch only, decent grub) and several cheaper cafeterias and pizza joints.

For a classy lunch in the National Gallery, treat your palate to the moderately-priced light Mediterranean cuisine at **Crivelli's Garden** (daily 10:00–17:00, 1st floor of Sainsbury Wing).

Simpson's on the Strand serves a stuffy, aristocratic, old-time carvery dinner—where the chef slices your favorite red meat from a fancy trolley at your table—in their elegant, smoky old dining room (£20, Mon–Sat 12:15–14:30, 17:30–22:45, no tennis shoes or T-shirts, at #100 the Strand, tel. 020/7836-9112).

Eating near Piccadilly

Hungry and broke in the theater district? Head for Panton Street (off Haymarket, 2 blocks southeast of Piccadilly Circus) for cheap Thai, Chinese, and two famous London eateries. **Stockpot** is a mushy-peas kind of place, famous and rightly popular for its edible, cheap meals (daily 07:00–22:00, 38 Panton Street). The **West End Kitchen** (across the street at #5, same hrs and menu) is a direct competitor that's just as good.

The palatial **Criterion Brasserie** serves a special £15 two-course "Anglo-French" *menu* (or £18 for 3 courses) under gilded tiles and chandeliers in a dreamy Byzantine-church setting from 1880. It's right on Piccadilly Circus but a world away from the punk junk. The house wine is great and so is the food (specials available Mon–Sat 12:00–14:30 and 17:30–18:30, dinner served until 23:00, CC, closed Sun lunch, tel. 020/7930-0488). Anyone can drop in for coffee or a drink.

The "Food Is Fun" Dinner Crawl:
From Covent Garden to Soho

London has a trendy generation X scene that most Beefeater seekers miss entirely. For a multicultural movable feast and a chance to sample some of London's most popular eateries, consider sampling these. Start around 18:00 to avoid lines, get in on early specials, and find waiters willing to let you split a meal. Prices, while reasonable by London standards, add up. Servings are large enough to share. All are open nightly.

Suggested nibbler's dinner crawl for two: Arrive before 18:00 at **Belgo** and split the early-bird dinner special: a kilo of mussels, fries, and dark Belgian beer. At **Yo! Sushi**, have beer or sake and a few dishes. Slurp your last course at **Wagamama**. Then, for dessert, people watch at Leicester Square, where the serf's always up.

Belgo Centraal is a space-station world overrun with Trappist monks serving hearty Belgian specialties. The classy restaurant section requires reservations, but just grabbing a bench in the boisterous beer hall (no reservations possible) is more fun.

From Covent Garden to Soho, "Food is Fun"

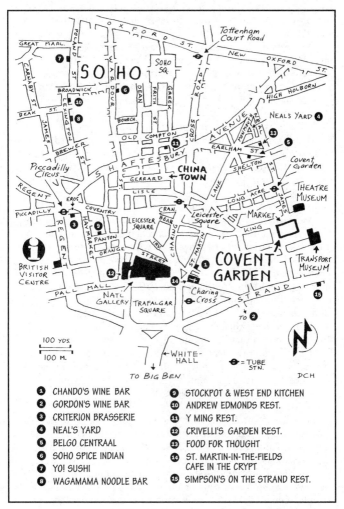

1	CHANDO'S WINE BAR	**9**	STOCKPOT & WEST END KITCHEN
2	GORDON'S WINE BAR	**10**	ANDREW EDMONDS REST.
3	CRITERION BRASSERIE	**11**	Y MING REST.
4	NEAL'S YARD	**12**	CRIVELLI'S GARDEN REST.
5	BELGO CENTRAAL	**13**	FOOD FOR THOUGHT
6	SOHO SPICE INDIAN	**14**	ST. MARTIN-IN-THE-FIELDS
7	YO! SUSHI		CAFE IN THE CRYPT
8	WAGAMAMA NOODLE BAR	**15**	SIMPSON'S ON THE STRAND REST.

The same menu and specials work on both sides. Belgians claim they eat as well as the French and as heartily as the Germans. Specialties include mussels, great fries, and a stunning array of dark, blond, and fruity Belgian beers. Belgo actually makes things Belgian trendy—a formidable feat (£14 meals; open daily till very late; Mon–Fri 17:00–18:30 "beat the clock" meal specials cost only the time…£5-6.30, and you get mussels, fries, and beer; no meal splitting after 18:30 and they are not licensed to serve anyone just a beer; daily £5 lunch special 12:00–17:00; 1 block north of Covent Garden tube station at intersection of Neal and Shelton Streets, 50 Earlham Street, tel. 020/7813-2233).

Yo! Sushi is a futuristic Japanese-food-extravaganza experience. With thumping rock, Japanese cable TV, a 60-meter-long conveyor-belt, the world's longest sushi bar, a robotic drink trolley, and automated sushi machines, just sipping a sake on a bar stool here is a trip. For £1 you get *miso* soup, unlimited tea (on request), or water (from spigot at bar, with or without gas). Grab dishes as they rattle by (priced by color of dish; check the chart) and a drink off the trash-talking robot. Weekdays from 15:00–19:00 they serve a "rainbow special"—five different colored plates for £10 (daily 12:00–24:00, 2 blocks south of Oxford Street, where Lexington Street becomes Poland Street, 52 Poland Street, tel. 020/7287-0443). For more-serious drinking on tatami mats, go downstairs into "Yo Below."

Wagamama Noodle Bar is a noisy, pan-Asian organic slurp-athon. As you enter, check out the kitchen and listen to the roar of the basement, where benches rock with happy eaters. Everybody sucks. Stand against the wall to feel the energy of all this "positive eating" (daily 12:00–23:00, crowded after 20:00, non-smoking, 10A Lexington Street, tel. 020/7292-0990). If you like this place, there are now branches all over town (including a handy one near the British Museum on Streatham Street).

Soho Spice Indian is where modern Britain meets Indian tradition—fine Indian cuisine in a trendy jewel-tone ambience. The £15 "Tandoori selections" meal is the best "variety" dish and big enough for two (daily 11:30–24:00, nonsmoking section available Sun–Tue, CC, 5 blocks north of Piccadilly Circus at 124 Wardour Street, tel. 020/7434-0808).

Y Ming Chinese Restaurant, across Shaftesbury Avenue from the ornate gates, clatter, and dim sum of Chinatown, has clean European décor, serious but helpful service, and authentic Northern Chinese cooking (good £10 meal deal offered 12:00–18:00, Mon–Sat 12:00–23:30, closed Sun, 35 Greek Street, tel. 020/7734-2721).

Andrew Edmunds Restaurant is a tiny candlelit place where you'll want to hide your camera and guidebook and act as local as possible. The modern-European cooking is worth the splurge (3 courses for £25, daily 12:30–15:00, 18:00–22:45, 46 Lexington Street in Soho, reservations are generally necessary, tel. 020/7437-5708).

For cheap, hip, and healthy near Covent Garden, the area around Neal's Yard is busy with fun, hippie-type cafés. One of the best is **Food for Thought** (good £5 vegetarian meals, Mon–Sat 12:00–20:30, Sun 12:00–17:00, nonsmoking, 2 blocks north of tube: Covent Garden, 31 Neal Street, tel. 020/7836-0239). Neal's Yard itself is a food circus of trendy, healthy eateries.

Eating near Recommended
Victoria Station Accommodations

Here are places a couple of blocks southwest of Victoria
Station where I've enjoyed eating (see map on page 455).

Jenny Lo's Tea House is a simple, for-the-joy-of-
good-food kind of place serving up eclectic Chinese-style
meals to locals in the know (£5–7, Mon–Fri 11:30–15:00,
18:00–22:00, Sat 12:00–15:00, 18:00–22:00, closed Sun,
no CC, 14 Eccleston Street, tel. 020/7259-0399 or
020/7823-6331).

The small but classy **La Campagnola** is Belgravia's
favorite budget Italian restaurant (£12–15, Mon–Sat 12:00–
15:00, 18:00–23:30, closed Sun, CC, 10 Lower Belgrave Street,
tel. 020/7730-2057).

The **Ebury Wine Bar**, filled with young professionals,
provides a classy atmosphere and pricey but delicious meals
(£15–18, daily 12:00–15:00, 18:00–22:30, CC, 139 Ebury
Street, at intersection with Elizabeth Street, near bus station,
tel. 020/7730-5447). Several cheap places are around the
corner on Elizabeth Street (#23 for take-out or eat-in super-
absorbent fish and chips).

The **Duke of Wellington** pub is a good, if smoky, neigh-
borhoody place for dinner (£6 meals, Mon–Sat 11:00–23:00,
Sun 12:00–22:30, 63 Eaton Terrace, at intersection with
Chester Row, tel. 020/7730-1782).

La Poule au Pot, ideal for a romantic splurge, offers
a classy candlelit ambience with well-dressed patrons and
expensive but fine Mediterranean and Provencal-style French
food (£20–25 dinners, daily 12:30–14:30, 19:00–23:00, Sun
until 22:00, leafy patio dining, reservations smart, end of
Ebury, at intersection with Pimlico, 231 Ebury Street, tel.
020/7730-7763).

Jomuna Tandoori serves quality Indian cuisine (daily
12:00–15:00, 18:00–23:30, 74 Wilton Road, near Eccleston
Hotel, tel. 020/7828-7509).

The **Marche** is an easy but pricey cafeteria a couple
of blocks north of Victoria Station at Bressenden Place
(Mon–Sat 07:30–23:00, Sun 11:00–21:00, CC, tel. 020/
7630-1733). If you miss America, there's a mall-type
food circus at Victoria Place, upstairs in Victoria Station.
Café Rouge offers the best food there (£8–11 dinners,
daily 09:30–22:30).

Groceries: The late-hours **Whistle Stop** at the station
has decent sandwiches, fresh fruit, snacks, and beverages
(daily, 24 hrs). A larger grocery, **Sainsbury Local**, is on
Victoria Street in front of the station, just past the buses
(Mon–Fri 07:00–22:00, Sat 07:00–21:00, Sun 10:00–16:00).

Eating near Recommended Notting Hill Gate B&Bs and Bayswater Hotels

Queensway is lined with lively and inexpensive eateries. See map on page 461.

The exuberantly rustic and very English **Maggie Jones** serves my favorite £20 London dinner. You'll get solid English cuisine, including huge plates of crunchy vegetables—by candlelight (daily 12:30–14:30, 18:30–23:00, much-less-expensive lunch menu, CC, 6 Old Court Place, just east of Kensington Church Street, near High Street Kensington tube stop, reservations recommended—request upstairs for noisy but less-cramped section, tel. 020/7937-6462). If you eat well once in London, eat here (and do it soon, before it burns down).

The **Churchill Arms** pub is a local hangout, with good beer and old-English ambience in front and hearty £6 Thai plates in an enclosed patio in the back. You can bring the Thai food into the smoky but wonderfully atmospheric pub section. Arrive by 18:00 to avoid a line (Mon–Sat 12:00–14:30, 18:00–21:30, Sun 12:00–14:30, 119 Kensington Church Street, tel. 020/7792-1246).

Prince Edward Pub serves good traditional pub grub with great pub ambience (£8 meals, daily 12:00–15:00, 18:00–22:00, CC, indoor/outdoor seating, 2 blocks north of Bayswater Road at the corner of Dawson Place and Hereford Road, 73 Prince's Square, tel. 020/7727-2221).

Cafe Diana is a healthy little eatery serving sandwiches and Middle Eastern food. It's decorated with photos of Princess Diana because she used to drop by for pita sandwiches (daily 08:00–22:30, 5 Wellington Terrace, on Bayswater Road, opposite Kensington Palace Garden Gates—where Diana once lived, tel. 020/7792-9606).

The **Royal China Restaurant** is filled with London's Chinese who consider this one of the city's best eateries. It's black, white, chrome, and candles with brisk waiters and fine food (£7–9 dishes, dim sum, daily 12:00–17:00, CC, 13 Queensway, tel. 020/7221-2535).

Mr. Wu's Chinese Restaurant serves a 10-course buffet in a bright and cheery little place. Just grab a plate and help yourself (£4.50, daily 12:00–23:00, check quality of buffet—right inside entrance—before committing, pickings can get slim, across from Bayswater tube station, 54 Queensway, tel. 020/7243-1017).

Whiteleys Mall Food Court offers a fun selection of ethnic and fast-food eateries in a delightful mall (good salads at Café Rouge, 2nd floor, corner of Porchester Gardens and Queensway).

Supermarket: Europa is a half block from the Notting Hill Gate tube stop (Mon–Fri 08:00–23:00, Sun 12:00–18:00, 112 Notting Hill Gate, near intersection with Pembridge Road).

Eating near Recommended Accommodations in South Kensington

Popular eateries line Old Brompton Road and Thurloe Street (tube: South Kensington). See map on page 459.

La Bouchee Bistro Café is a classy hole-in-the-wall touch of France serving early-bird three-course meals for £11 before 19:00 and *plats du jour* for £8 all *jour* (daily 12:00–23:00, CC, 56 Old Brompton Road, tel. 020/7589-1929).

Daquise, an authentic-feeling Polish place, is ideal if you're in the mood for kielbasa and kraut. It's fast, cheap, family-run, and a part of the neighborhood (£10 meals, daily until 23:00, CC, nonsmoking, 20 Thurloe Street, tel. 020/7589-6117).

The **Khyber Pass Tandoori Restaurant** is a nondescript but handy place serving great Punjabi-style Indian cuisine. Locals in-the-know eat here (£10 dinners, daily 12:00–14:30, 18:00–23:30, CC, 21 Bute Street, tel. 020/7589-7311).

La Brasserie fills a big "nicotine yellow" room with ceiling fans, a Parisian ambience, and good traditional French cooking at reasonable prices (2-course £16 "regional *menu*," £13 bottle of house wine, CC, nightly until 23:30, 272 Brompton Road, tel. 020/7581-3089).

PJ's Bar and Grill is lively with the yuppie Chelsea crowd for a good reason. Traditional "New York Brasserie"–style yet trendy, it's dressy tables surround a centerpiece bar. It serves pricey, cosmopolitan cuisine from a menu that changes with the seasons (£20 meals, CC, nightly until 24:00, 52 Fulham Road, at intersection with Sydney Street, tel. 020/7581-0025).

Eating Elsewhere in London

Near St. Paul's, in the City: The **Counting House**, formerly an elegant old bank, offers great £7 meals, nice homemade meat pies, fish, and fresh vegetables (Mon–Fri 12:00–20:00, closed Sat–Sun, gets really busy with the buttoned-down 9-to-5 crowd after 12:15, near Mansion House in the City, 50 Cornhill, tel. 020/7283-7123).

Near the British Library: Drummond Street (running just east of Euston Station) is famous in London for very cheap and good Indian and vegetarian food. Consider **Chutneys** and **Ravi Shankar** for a good *thali*.

Transportation Connections—London

Flying into London's Heathrow Airport

Heathrow Airport is the world's fourth busiest. Think about it: 60 million passengers a year on 425,000 flights from 200 destinations riding 90 airlines...some kind of global Maypole dance. While many complain about it, I like it. It's user-friendly. Read signs, ask questions. For Heathrow's airport, flight, and transfers **information**, call the switchboard at 0870-000-0123. It has four **terminals**: T-1 (mostly domestic flights with some European), T-2 (mostly European flights), T-3 (mostly flights from the United States), and T-4 (British Air transatlantic flights and BA flights to Paris, Amsterdam, and Athens). Taxis know which terminal you'll need.

Each terminal has an airport information desk, car-rental agencies, exchange bureaus and ATMs, a pharmacy, a VAT refund desk (VAT info tel. 020/8910-3682; you must present the VAT claim form from the retailer here to get your 15 percent tax rebate on items purchased in Britain), and a £3.50/day baggage-check desk (open 05:30–23:00). There are **post offices** in T-2 and T-4. Each terminal has cheap eateries (such as the cheery Food Village self-service cafeteria in T-3). The American Express desk, in the tube station at Terminal 4 (daily 07:00–19:00), has rates similar to the exchange bureaus upstairs, but they don't charge a commission (typically 1.5 percent) for cashing any type of traveler's check.

Heathrow's small **TI** gives you all the help that London's Victoria Station does, but with none of the crowds (daily 08:30–18:00, 5-min walk from Terminal 3 in the tube station, follow signs to "underground"; bypass the queue for transit info to reach the window for London questions). If you're riding the Airbus into London, have your partner stay with the bags at the terminal. At the TI, get a free map and brochures, and if you're taking the tube into London, buy a Travel Card day pass to cover the ride (see below). Heathrow's "Internet Exchange" provides **Internet access** 24 hours a day (Terminal 3).

Transportation to London from Heathrow Airport
By Tube (Subway): For £3.50, the tube takes you 14 miles to downtown London in 50 minutes (6/hr, depending on your destination, may require a change). Even better, buy a £4.90 Travel Card that covers your trip into London and all your tube travel for the day (starting at 09:30). Buy it at the ticket window at the tube. You can hop on the tube at any terminal.

By Airport Bus: The Airbus, running between the airport and London's King's Cross Station, serves the Notting Hill Gate and Bayswater neighborhoods (£7, £10-round-trip, 2/hr, 1 hr, 06:30–21:15, departs from each terminal, buy ticket from driver). The tube works fine, but with baggage I prefer the Airbus (assuming it serves my hotel neighborhood) because there are no connections underground and there's a lovely view from the top of the double-decker bus. Ask the driver to remind you when to get off. For people heading to the airport, exact pick-up times are clearly posted at each bus stop.

If you're staying in London's Victoria Station neighborhood, consider the National Express bus that runs between Heathrow's central bus station and the Victoria Coach Station, which is one block from Victoria Station (£6, kids go free, 2/hr, 40 min, 05:40–21:45 from Heathrow, 07:45-24:00 from Victoria, tel. 08705-808-080).

By Taxi: Taxis from the airport cost about £40. For four people traveling together this can be a deal. Hotels can often line up a cab back to the airport for £30. For the cheapest taxi to the airport don't order one from your hotel. Simply flag down a few and ask them for their best "off-meter" rate (I managed a ride for £25).

By Heathrow Express Train: This slick train service zips you between Heathrow Airport and London's Paddington Station. At Paddington Station you're in the thick of the tube system, with easy access to any of my recommended neighborhoods—Notting Hill Gate is just two stops away (£12, but ask about discount promos at Heathrow ticket desk, children under 16 ride free if you buy tickets before boarding, £2 surcharge for tickets purchased on train, CC, covered by Britrail pass; 4/hr, daily 05:10–23:30, 15 min to downtown from Terminals 1, 2, 3; 20 min from T-4; works as a free transfer between terminals, tel. 0845-600-1515, www.heathrowexpress.co.uk); a "Go Further" ticket (£13.50) includes one tube ride from Paddington to get you to your hotel (valid only on same day and in Zone 1, saves time). For one person, combining the Heathrow Express with either a tube or taxi ride (between your hotel and Paddington) is as fast as and half the cost of taking a cab directly to (or from) the airport.

If you're flying out of Heathrow, check in at London's Paddington station. Take advantage of the calm, easy airline check-in at Paddington. If you're using any of the 26 represented airlines (including British Airways, British Midland, American, Lufthansa, SAS, Swiss Air, United Airlines, Air Canada, and Canadian Airlines), you can get a boarding pass and check your luggage (daily 05:00–21:00, last check-in 1 hour before departure with a carry-on, 2 hrs with bags to check). You'll avoid the crowded chaos of check-in at Heathrow and, even better, you'll have a little more time to sightsee before heading out to the airport. (On the morning of my most recent departure, I checked my luggage at Paddington—6 hrs before my flight—then went on the London Eye Ferris wheel, which I'd booked the day before.) You can also check bags here and then ride the cheaper tube out to Heathrow.

Buses from Heathrow to Destinations beyond London

The **National Express Central Bus Station** offers direct bus connections to **Gatwick Airport** (2/hr, 75 min). There are two services: Speedlink for £17 and Jetlink for £12 (from central bus station, a 5-min walk to terminals 1, 2, or 3). Several direct buses run daily to **Bath** (11/day, 2.5 hrs, £12.50, direct, tel. 08705-757-747). Britrail passholders may prefer the 2.5-hour Heathrow-Bath bus/train connection via Reading (free with pass, otherwise £29.20, payable at desk in terminal, CC); catch the twice-hourly RailAir Link shuttle bus to Reading (RED-ding), then hop on the hourly express train to Bath. Most Heathrow buses depart from the common area serving terminals 1, 2, and 3, although some depart from T-4 (bus tel. 08705-747-777).

Flying into London's Gatwick Airport
More and more flights, especially charters, land at Gatwick Airport, halfway between London and the southern coast (airport recorded info tel. 0870-000-2468). Trains—clearly the best way into London from here—shuttle conveniently between Gatwick and London's Victoria Station (£10.20, £19.50 round-trip, 4/hr during day, 1–2/hr at night, 40 min, runs 24 hrs daily, can purchase tickets on train at no extra charge, tel. 08705-301-530, www.gatwickexpress.co.uk). To get to Bath from Gatwick, catch the Flight Link bus to Heathrow and the bus to Bath from there.

London's Other Airports
If you're flying into or out of **Stansted** (airport tel. 0870-0000-303), you can take the Airbus between the airport and downtown London's Victoria Coach Station (£8, 2/hr, 90 min, runs 04:00–24:00, picks up and stops throughout London, tel. 08705-747-777) or take the Stansted Airport Rail Link (departs London's Liverpool Station, 40 min, 2–4/hr, 05:00–23:00).

For **Luton** (airport tel. 01582/405-100, www.london-luton .com), try Green Line's bus #757, which runs between the airport and London's Victoria Station at Buckingham Palace Road—stop 6 (£7.50, 2/hr, 1–1.25 hrs depending on time of day, runs 04:30–24:00, tel. 0870-608-7261, www.greenline.co.uk).

Discounted Flights from London
BMI British Midland has been around the longest, but Virgin Express and Ryanair generally offer cheaper flights.

BMI British Midland, the local discount airline, can be cheaper than the train. You can fly inexpensively to Edinburgh (as little as £75 round-trip if you stay over Sat); to Dublin, Ireland (as little as £103 round-trip over Sat); to Paris (as little as £75 round-trip over Sat); and elsewhere. For the latest, call British tel. 0870-607-0555 or U.S. tel. 800/788-0555 (www.flybmi.com). The further you book in advance (up to about 9–12 months or as few as 3 weeks), the cheaper the fares. You can book right up until the flight departs, but the cheap seats will have sold out long before, leaving the expensive seats for latecomers.

Virgin Express is a British-owned company with good rates (book by phone and pick up ticket at airport 1 hour before your flight, tel. 020/7744-0004, www.virgin-express.com). Virgin Express flies from London Heathrow and Brussels. From its hub in Brussels you can connect cheaply to Barcelona, Madrid, Nice, Malaga, Copenhagen, Rome, or Milan (round-trip from Brussels to Rome for as little as £105). Their prices stay the same whether or not you book in advance.

Ryanair is a creative Irish airline that prides itself on offering the lowest fares. They fly from London (mostly Stansted airport) to obscure airports in Dublin, Glasgow, Frankfurt, Stockholm, Oslo, Venice, Turin, and elsewhere. Sample fares: London-Dublin—£78 round-trip, London-Frankfurt—£67 round-trip (Irish tel. 01/609-7881, British tel. 0870-333-1231, www.ryanair.com). Because they offer promotional deals any time of year, it's not essential that you book long in advance to get the best deals.

Trains and Buses

London has a different train station for each region. Waterloo handles the Eurostar to Paris. King's Cross covers northeast England and Scotland (tel. 08457-225-225). Paddington covers west and southwest England (Bath) and South Wales (tel. 08457-000-125). For the others, call 08457-484-950.

National Express' excellent bus service is considerably cheaper than taking the train. (For a busy signal, call 08705-808-080, or visit www.nationalexpress.co.uk or the bus station a block southwest of Victoria Station.)

To Bath: Trains leave London's Paddington Station every hour (at a quarter after) for the 75-minute ride to Bath (costs roughly £31 if you leave after 09:30). As an alternative, consider taking a guided bus tour from London to Stonehenge and Bath and abandoning the tour in Bath. Evan Evans' tour comes fully guided, with admissions, for £48 (for details, see "Daytrips from London," on page 452). Golden Tours also runs a fully-guided Stonehenge-Bath tour for a similar price (departs from Fountain Square, across from Victoria Coach Station, tel. 020/7233-6668, www.goldentours.co.uk).

To points north: Trains run hourly from London's King's Cross Station, stopping in York (2 hrs), Durham (3 hrs), and Edinburgh (5 hrs).

To Dublin, Ireland: The boat/rail journey takes between 10 and 11 hours and goes all day or all night (£24–35, 7/day, tel. 08705-143-219, www.eurolines.co.uk). Consider a cheap 70-minute Ryanair flight instead (see above).

Crossing the English Channel

By Eurostar Train: The fastest and most convenient way to get from Big Ben to the Eiffel Tower is by rail. In London, advertisements claim "more businessmen travel from London to Paris on the Eurostar than on all airlines combined." Eurostar is the speedy passenger train that zips you (and up to 800 others in 18 sleek cars) from downtown London to downtown Paris (15/day, 3 hrs) or Brussels (9/day, 3 hrs) faster and more easily than flying. The train goes 80 miles per hour in England and 190 miles per hour on the Continent. (When the English segment gets up to speed the journey time will shrink to 2 hrs.) The actual tunnel crossing is a 20-minute, black, silent, 100-mile-per-hour nonevent. Your ears won't even pop. You can go direct to Disneyland Paris (1/day, more frequent with transfer at Lille) or change at Lille to catch a TGV to Paris' Charles de Gaulle Airport.

Channel fares (essentially the same to Paris or Brussels) are reasonable but complicated. For the latest, call 800/EUROSTAR in the United States. These are prices from 2001: The "Leisure Ticket" is cheap ($139 second class, $219 first class, 50 percent refundable up to 3 days before departure). "Full Fare" first class costs $279 and includes a meal (a dinner departure nets you more grub than breakfast); second class (or "standard") costs $199 (fully refundable even after departure date). Discounts are available to travelers holding railpasses that include France, Belgium, or Britain ($155 for first class, $75 for second); seniors over 60 ($189 for first class); youths under 26 ($79 in second class); and children under 12 (about half the fare of your ticket).

Cheaper seats can sell out. Book from home if you're ready to commit to a date and time. Compare fares sold by U.S. rail agents (www.raileurope.com) and British agents (www.eurostar .co.uk). If you're ready to commit to a date, time, and U.S. prices, you can book by calling 800/EUROSTAR, visiting www .raileurope.com, or having your travel agent do it all for you (prices do not include FedEx ticket delivery). For the British fares, book by calling 08705-186-186 or visiting www.eurostar .co.uk (pick up ticket at station).

Buying a Eurostar ticket in London is easy. Here are some sample London-Paris standard—that's second-class—fares from 2001 (London-Brussels fares are about the same). Avoid the "standard flexi" fare: one-way for £165, round-trip for £300. Those with a railpass pay £50 one-way, any day. Without a railpass, a same-day round-trip on a Saturday or Sunday costs £70. The various second-class round-trip Leisure Tickets (for stays over a Sat) are affordable: Leisure Flexi—£160 (partially refundable if not used), Leisure—£120 (not refundable), Leisure Apex 7—£95 (not refundable, purchase at least 7 days in advance), Leisure Apex 14—£70 (not refundable, purchase at least 14 days in advance, stay 2 nights or over a Sat). Many cheaper fares sell out in advance. One-way tickets for departures after 14:00 Friday or anytime Saturday or Sunday cost £105. Youth tickets (for those under 26) are £45 one-way to either Paris or Brussels (£75 round-trip, exchangeable but not refundable). First-class and business-class fares are much higher. Remember, round-trip tickets over a Saturday are much cheaper than the basic one-way fare...you know the trick.

In Europe you can get your Eurostar ticket at any major train station (in any country) or at any travel agency that handles train tickets (expect a booking fee). In Britain you can book and pay for tickets over the phone with a credit card by calling 08705-186-186 and pick up your tickets at London's Waterloo station an hour before the Eurostar departure. Note: Britain's time zone is one hour earlier than the Continent's. Times listed on tickets are local times.

By Bus and Boat or Train and Boat: The old-fashioned way of crossing the channel is cheaper than crossing via Eurostar. It's also twice as romantic, complicated, and time-consuming. You'll get better prices arranging your trip in London than you would in the United States. Taking the bus is cheapest, and round-trips are a bargain.

By **bus** to Paris, Brussels, or Amsterdam from Victoria Coach Station (via boat or chunnel): £32 one-way, £52 round-trip; 7 hrs to Paris—7/day; 7 hrs to Brussels—10/day; 11.25 hrs to Amsterdam—6/day; day or overnight, on Eurolines (tel. 08705-143-219, www.eurolines.co.uk).

The **Hoverspeed ferry** runs between Dover, England, and Calais, France (tel. 08705-240-241, www.hoverspeed.com). Hoverspeed sells rail and ferry packages for trips between London and Paris: £39 one-way; £49 round-trip with five-day return; and £58 round-trip over more than five days. You can buy this package deal in person at Waterloo or Charing Cross stations. If you book by phone (number listed above), you must book at least two weeks in advance and the ticket will be mailed to you (no ticket pick-up at station for bookings by phone).

By **P&O Stena Line ferry** from Dover to Calais: £26 one-way; £48 round-trip with five-day return; £52 round-trip over more than five days (tel. 0870-600-0613, www.posl.com). Prices are for the ferry only; you need to book your own train tickets.

By Plane: Typical fares are £110 regular, less for student standby. Call in London for the latest fares. Consider BMI British Midland (see "Discounted Flights," above) for its cheap round-trip fares to Paris.

BATH

Any tour of Britain that skips Bath stinks. Two hundred years ago this city of 80,000 was the trendsetting Hollywood of Britain. If ever a city enjoyed looking in the mirror, Bath's the one. It has more "government-listed" or protected historic buildings per capita than any other town in England. The entire city, built of the creamy warm-tone limestone called "Bath stone," beams in its cover-girl complexion. An architectural chorus line, it's a triumph of the Georgian style. Proud locals remind visitors that the town is routinely banned from the "Britain in Bloom" contest to give other towns a chance to win. Bath's narcissism is justified. Even with its mobs of tourists (2 million a year), it's a joy to visit.

Long before the Romans arrived in the first century, Bath was known for its hot springs. What became the Roman spa town of Aquae Sulis has always been fueled by the healing allure of its 116-degree mineral hot springs. The town's importance carried through Saxon times, when it had a huge church on the site of the present-day Abbey and was considered the religious capital of Britain. Its influence peaked in 973, when England's first king, Edgar, was crowned in the Abbey. Bath prospered as a wool town.

Bath then declined until the mid-1600s, when it was just a huddle of huts around the Abbey and some hot springs, with 3,000 residents oblivious to the Roman ruins 18 feet below their dirt floors. Then, in 1687, Queen Mary, fighting infertility, bathed here. Within 10 months she gave birth to a son...and a new age of popularity for Bath.

The town boomed as a spa resort. Ninety percent of the buildings you'll see today are from the 18th century. Local architect John Wood was inspired by the Italian architect Palladio to build a "new Rome." The town bloomed in the neoclassical style, and streets were lined not with scrawny sidewalks but with wide "parades," upon which the women in their stylishly wide dresses could spread their fashionable tails.

Beau Nash (1673–1762) was Bath's "master of ceremonies." He organized both the daily regimen of the aristocratic visitors and the city, lighting and improving street security, banning swords, and opening the Pump Room. Under his fashionable baton, Bath became a city of balls, gaming, and concerts and the place to see and be seen in England. This most civilized place became even more so with the great neoclassical building spree that followed.

Planning Your Time

Bath needs two nights even on a quick trip. There's plenty to do, and it's a joy to do it.

Here's how I'd spend a day in Bath: 09:00–Tour the Roman Baths, 10:30–Catch the free city walking tour, 12:30–Picnic on the open deck of a Guide Friday tour bus, 14:30–Free time in the shopping center of old Bath, 15:30–Tour the Costume Museum. Evening: After a pub or classy dinner, consider a Bizarre Bath walking tour.

Orientation (area code: 01225)

Bath's town square, three blocks in front of the bus and train station, is a bouquet of tourist landmarks, including the Abbey, Roman and medieval baths, and the royal Pump Room.

Tourist Information: The TI is in the Abbey churchyard (Mon–Sat 09:30–18:00, Sun 10:00–16:00; Oct–April Mon–Sat until 17:00, tel. 01225/477-101, www.visitbath.co.uk). Pick up the 50p Bath miniguide, which includes a 50p map and the free, info-packed *This Month in Bath*. Browse through scads of fliers, books, and maps (including the Cotswolds). Skip their room-finding service (£5) and book direct. The TI sells a **Bath Pass**, giving you free entry to all the sights in town, but you have to work pretty hard to make it pay (£19/1 day, £29/2 days, £39/3 days). An American Express office is tucked into the TI (decent rates, no commission on any checks, open same hrs as TI).

Arrival in Bath: The Bath train station is a pleasure (small-town charm, an international tickets desk, and a Guide Friday office masquerading as a TI). The bus station is immediately in front of the train station. To get to the TI, walk two blocks up Manvers Street from either station and turn left at the triangular "square," following the small TI arrow on a signpost. My recommended B&Bs are all within a 10- or 15-minute walk or a £3.50 taxi ride from the station.

Driving within Bath is a nightmare of one-way streets. Nearly everyone gets lost. Ask for advice from your hotelier and minimize driving in town. Even consider hiring and following a taxi to your place.

Helpful Hints

Festivals: The International Music Festival bursts into song from May 17 to June 2 in 2002 (classical, folk, jazz, contemporary, tel. 01225/462-231), overlapped by the eclectic Fringe Festival from late May to mid-June (theater, walks, talks, bus trips, tel. 01225/480-079, www.bathfringe.co.uk). Bath's box office sells tickets for most every event and can tell you exactly what's on tonight (2 Church Street, tel. 01225/463-362, www.bathfestivals.org.uk).

Internet Access: The Click Café has two branches, one across from the train station on Manvers Street and the other on 19 Broad Street, near the YMCA (£2.50/30 min, daily 10:00–22:00, tel. 01225/337-711). Other places offering Internet access are the Itchy Feet Café & Travel Store (4 Bartlett Street, near Costume Museum) and the Bath Backpackers Hostel (13 Pierrepont Street; coming from train station, you pass hostel on your way to the TI).

Farmers' Market: This is held on the first and third Saturday of the month at Green Park Station (9:00–15:00).

Car Rental: Avis (behind the station and over the river at Unit 4B Riverside Business Park, Lower Bristol Road, tel. 01225/446-680), Enterprise (Lower Bristol Road, tel. 01225/443-311), and Hertz (just outside the train station, tel. 01225/442-911) are all trying harder. Most offices are a 10-minute walk from most recommended accommodations. Consider hotel delivery (usually £5, free with Enterprise). Most offices close Saturday afternoon and all day Sunday, complicating weekend pickups. Ideally, pick up your car only on the way out and into the countryside. Take the train or bus from London to Bath and rent a car as you leave Bath rather than in London.

Tours of Bath

▲▲**City Bus Tours**—The Guide Friday green-and-cream opentop tour bus makes a 70-minute figure-eight circuit of Bath's main sights with an exhaustingly informative running commentary. For one £8.50 ticket (buy from driver), tourists can stop and go at will for a whole day. The buses cover the city center and the surrounding hills (17 signposted pick-up points, 3/hr spring and fall—runs 09:30–17:00, 4/hr in summer—9:30–18:00, 1/hr in winter—9:30–15:30, tel. 01225/464-446). This is great in sunny weather and a feast for photographers. You can munch a sandwich, work on a tan, and sightsee at the same time. Several competing hop-on hop-off tour-bus companies offer basically the same tour, but in 45 minutes and without the swing through the countryside, for a couple pounds less. Generally, the Guide Friday guides are better. (These tour buses are technically "public service vehicles"—a loophole they use to be able to run the same routes as transit buses. Consequently, tour buses are required to take

passengers across town for the normal £1 fare. Nervy tourists have
the right to hop on and just ask for a "single fare" and pay £1.)
▲▲▲**Walking Tours**—These free two-hour tours, offered by
"The Mayor's Corps of Honorary Guides"—volunteers who want
to share their love of Bath with its many visitors—are a chatty,
historical, gossip-filled joy, essential for your understanding of
this town's amazing Georgian social scene. How else will you
learn that the old "chair ho" call for your sedan chair evolved into
today's "cheerio" greeting? Tours leave from in front of the Pump
Room (year-round daily at 10:30 plus Sun–Fri at 14:00; evening
walks offered May–Sept at 19:00 on Tue, Fri, and Sat). For Ghost
Walks and Bizarre Bath Comedy Walks, see "Nightlife," below.
For a private walking tour, call the local guide's bureau (£45/2 hrs,
tel. 01225/337-111).

Sights—Bath
▲▲▲**Roman and Medieval Baths**—In ancient Roman times,
high society enjoyed the mineral springs at Bath. From Londinium, Romans traveled so often to Aquae Sulis, as the city was
called, to "take a bath" that finally it became known simply as
Bath. Today a fine museum surrounds the ancient bath and is,
with its well-documented displays, a one-way system leading you
past Roman artifacts, mosaics, a temple pediment, and the actual
mouth of the spring, piled high with Roman pennies. Enjoy some
quality time looking into the eyes of Minerva, goddess of the hot
springs. The included self-guided tour audioguide makes the visit
easy and plenty informative. For those with a big appetite for
Roman history, in-depth 40-minute tours leave from the end of
the museum at the edge of the actual bath (included, on the hour,
a poolside clock is set for the next departure time). You can revisit
the museum after the tour (£7.50, £9.50 combo ticket includes
Costume Museum at a good savings, family combo-£25, combo
tickets good for 1 week; April–Sept daily 09:00–18:00, in July–
Aug until 22:15—last entry at 21:00, Oct–March until 17:00,
tel. 01225/477-000).
Bath Spa—In October of 2002, Bath's natural thermal springs
will once again be used for bathing and treatments in a complex
combining restored old buildings and a new, state-of-the-art
leisure spa (£17/2 hrs, £23/half day, £35/day).
▲**Pump Room**—For centuries, Bath was forgotten as a spa. Then,
in 1687, the previously barren Queen Mary bathed here, became
pregnant, and bore a male heir to the throne. Word of its wonder
waters spread and once again Bath was back on the aristocratic map.
High society soon turned the place into one big pleasure palace.
The Pump Room, an elegant Georgian hall just above the Roman
baths, offers the visitor's best chance to raise a pinky in this Chip-
pendale elegance. Drop by to sip coffee or tea or enjoy a light meal

Bath

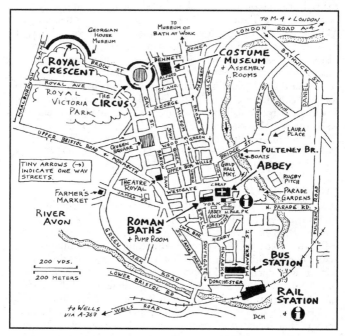

(09:30–12:00 Morning Coffee, 12:00–14:30 lunch—£12 2-course menu, 14:30–17:30 traditional High Tea—£8, 17:30–20:30 dinner, £7 tea/coffee and pastry available anytime except during lunch, string trio or live pianist 10:00–17:00, tel. 01225/444-477). Above the newspaper table and sedan chairs a statue of Beau Nash himself sniffles down at you. Now's your chance to have a famous (but for-gettable) "Bath bun" and split (and spit) a 50p drink of the awfully curative water. Convenient public WCs are in the entry hallway that connects the Pump Room with the Baths.

▲**Abbey**—Bath town wasn't much in the Middle Ages. But an important church has stood on this spot since Anglo-Saxon times. In 973, Edgar, the first king of England, was crowned here. Dominating the town center, the present church—the last great medieval church of England—is 500 years old and a fine example of Late Perpendicular Gothic, with breezy fan vaulting and enough stained glass to earn it the nickname "Lantern of the West" (worth the £2 donation, Mon–Sat 09:00–18:00, Sun 13:00–14:30, 15:30–17:30, closes at 16:30 in winter, handy flier narrates a self-guided 19-stop tour). The schedule for concerts, services, and **evensong** (Sun at 15:30 year-round, plus most Sat in Aug at 17:00) is posted on the door. Take a moment to really appreciate the Abbey's architecture from the Abbey Green square.

The Abbey's **Heritage Vaults**, a small but interesting exhibit, tells the story of Christianity in Bath since Roman times (£2, Mon–Sat 10:00–16:00, closed Sun, entrance just outside church, south side).

▲**Pulteney Bridge, Parade Gardens, and Cruises**—Bath is inclined to compare its shop-lined Pulteney Bridge to Florence's Ponte Vecchio. That's pushing it. To best enjoy a sunny day, pay £1 to enter the Parade Gardens below the bridge (daily 10:00–19:00, until 20:00 June– Aug, free after 20:00, includes deck chairs, ask about the concerts held some Sun at 15:00 in summer).

Across the bridge at Pulteney Weir, tour boats run cruises from under the bridge (£4.50, up to 7/day if the weather's good, 50 min to Bathampton and back, WCs on board). Just take whatever boat is running. Avon Cruisers stop in Bathampton if you'd like to walk back; Pulteney Cruisers come with a sundeck ideal for picnics.

▲▲**Royal Crescent and the Circus**—If Bath is an architectural cancan, these are the kickers. These first elegant Georgian "condos" by John Wood (the Elder and the Younger) are well explained in the city walking tours. "Georgian" is British for "neoclassical," or dating from the 1770s. As you cruise the Crescent, pretend you're rich. Pretend you're poor. Notice the "ha ha fence," a drop in the front yard offering a barrier, invisible from the windows, to sheep and peasants. The round Circus is a colosseum turned inside out. Its Doric, Ionic, and Corinthian capital decorations pay homage to its Greco-Roman origin.

▲▲**Georgian House at #1 Royal Crescent**—This museum (on the corner of Brock Street and the Royal Crescent) offers your best look into a period house. It's worth the £4 admission to get behind one of those classy exteriors. The volunteers in each room are determined to fill you in on all the fascinating details of Georgian life . . . like how high-class women shaved their eyebrows and pasted on carefully trimmed strips of furry mouse skin in their place (Tue–Sun 10:30–17:00, closed Mon, closes at 16:00 in Nov, closed Dec–mid-Feb, "no stiletto heels, please," tel. 01225/428-126).

▲▲▲**Costume Museum**—One of Europe's great museums, displaying 400 years of fashion—one frilly decade at a time— is housed within Bath's Assembly Rooms. Follow the included, excellent audioguide tour. On display through October 2002 are 14 dresses worn by Queen Elizabeth II—a special exhibit marking the queen's 50-year reign (£4.20, a £9.50 combo ticket covers Roman Baths, family combo-£25, daily 10:00–17:00, tel. 01225/477-789). The Assembly Rooms, which you'll see en route to the museum, are big, elegant, empty rooms where card games, concerts, tea, and dances were held in the 18th century before the advent of fancy hotels with grand public spaces made them obsolete.

▲▲▲**Museum of Bath at Work**—This is the official title for
Mr. Bowler's Business, a 1900s engineer's shop, brass foundry,
and fizzy-drink factory with a Dickensian office. It's just a pile of
meaningless old gadgets until a volunteer guide lovingly resurrects
Mr. Bowler's creative genius. Fascinating hour-long tours go regularly; just join the one in session upon arrival (£3.50, April–Oct
daily 10:00–17:00, weekends only in winter, 2 blocks up Russell
Street from Assembly Rooms, call to be sure a volunteer is available to give a tour, café upstairs, tel. 01225/318-348).

Jane Austen Centre—This new exhibition focuses on Jane
Austen's five years in Bath (around 1800) and the influence
Bath had on her writing. While the exhibit is thoughtfully done
and is a hit with "Jane-ites," there is little of historic substance
here. You'll walk through a Georgian townhouse that she didn't
live in and see mostly enlarged reproductions of things associated
with her writing. After a live intro explaining how this romantic
but down-to-earth girl dealt with the silly, shallow, and arrogant
aristocrat's world where "the doing of nothings all day prevents
one from doing anything," you see a 13-minute video and wander
through the rest of the exhibit (£4, Mon–Sat 10:00–17:30, Sun
10:30–17:30, 40 Gay Street between Queen's Square and the
Circus, tel. 01225/443-000, www.janeausten.co.uk).

The Building of Bath Museum—This offers a fascinating look
behind the scenes at how the Georgian city was actually built. It's
just one large room of exhibits, but those interested in construction find it worth the £4 (Tue–Sun 10:30–17:00, closed Mon, near
the Circus on a street called "the Paragon," tel. 01225/333-895).

▲**Impossible Microworld**—This dark two-room museum glows
with a couple dozen illuminated glass bubbles that contain magnifying glasses, helping you focus on the smallest sculptures you've ever
seen. These tiny creations by two artists are almost invisible. Ussa's
work borders on hokey (flea riding a bicycle), but Wigan's work is
remarkable. Wigan actually carves his minute work out of sugar
grains, match heads, or bits of boxwood (look for the Statue of Liberty in the eye of a needle and Samson splitting a human hair). As
a dyslexic kid, labeled "nothing" by a racist teacher, he was determined to make something out of nothing (£4, daily 10:00–18:00,
Kingsmead Square, near Theatre Royal, tel. 01225/333-003).

Views—For the best views of Bath, try Alexander Park (south of
city, 10-min walk from train station), Camden Crescent (10–15
min walk north), or Becksford Tower (steep 20-min walk north
up Lansdown Road, www.bath-preservation-trust.org.uk).

▲**American Museum**—I know, you need this in Bath like you
need a Big Mac. But this museum offers a fascinating look at
colonial and early-American lifestyles. Each of 18 completely
furnished rooms (from the 1600s to the 1800s) is hosted by an eager
guide waiting to fill you in on the candles, maps, bedpans, and

various religious sects that make domestic Yankee history surprisingly interesting. One room is a quilter's nirvana (£5.50, Tue–Sun 14:00–17:00, closed Mon and early Nov–late March, at Claverton Manor, tel. 01225/460-503). The museum is outside of town and a headache to reach if you don't have a car (15-min walk from the nearest Guide Friday stop or a 10-min walk from bus #18).

Activities in Bath

Walking, Biking, and Swimming—The Bath Skyline Walk is a six-mile wander around the hills surrounding Bath (70p leaflet at TI). For more options, get *Country Walks around Bath*, by Tim Mowls (£4.50 at TI).

Consider the idyllic **walk** up the canal path to Bathampton: from downtown, walk over Pulteney Bridge, through Sydney Gardens, turn left on canal, and in 30 minutes you'll hit Bathampton, with its much-loved Old George Pub. Sailors enjoy the river cruise up to Bathampton; hikers like walking back (see "Pulteney Bridge and Cruises," above). From Bathampton it's two hours farther along the canal to the fine old town of Bradford-on-Avon, from which you can train back to Bath. You can **bike** this route (rent bikes at Avon Valley Cyclery behind train station, £9/4 hrs, £14/8 hrs, £18/24 hrs, no helmets, tel. 01225/442-442). Plenty of other scenic paths are described in the TI's literature.

The Bath Sports and Leisure Centre has a **swimming pool**—great for laps—and lots of slides and gadgets for kids (£2.70, towels rentable, daily 08:00–22:00, just across North Parade Bridge, call for open swim times, tel. 01225/462-565).

The Bath Boating Station, in an old Victorian boathouse, rents **boats** and punts (£4.50/first hr per person, then £1.50/hr, April–Sept 10:00–18:00, Forester Road, a mile northeast of center, tel. 01225/466-407).

Shopping—There's great browsing between the Abbey and the Assembly Rooms (Costume Museum). Shops close at 17:30, later on Thursday. Explore the antique shops lining Bartlett Street just below the Assembly Rooms. You'll find the most stalls open on Wednesday. Pick up the local paper (usually out on Friday) and shop with the dealers at estate sales and auctions listed in "What's On."

Nightlife in Bath

This Month in Bath (free, available at TI) lists events.
Plays—The Theatre Royal, newly restored and one of England's loveliest, offers a busy schedule of London West End–type plays, including many "pre-London" dress-rehearsal runs (£11–25, cheaper matinees as low as £5, tel. 01225/448-844). Forty standby tickets per evening show go on sale starting at 12:00 on the day of the performance (either pay cash at box office or call and book

with CC, 2 tickets maximum). Or you can buy a £10 last-minute seat 30 minutes before "curtain up."

Evening Walks—Take your choice: comedy, ghost, or history. For an immensely entertaining walking comedy act "with absolutely no history or culture," follow J. J. or Noel Britten on their creative and entertaining **Bizarre Bath** walk. This 90-minute "tour," which plays off local passersby as well as tour members, is a belly laugh a minute (£5, April–Sept nightly at 20:00, smaller groups Mon–Thu, heavy on magic, careful to insult all minorities and sensitivities, just racy enough but still good family fun; leave from Huntsman pub near the Abbey, confirm at TI or call 01225/335-124, www.bizarrebath .co.uk). **Ghost Walks** are another way to pass the after-dark hours (£4, 20:00, 2 hrs, unreliably Mon–Sat April–Oct; in winter Fri only; leave from Garrick's Head pub near Theatre Royal, tel. 01225/463-618). The TI offers **free evening walks** in summer (May–Sept at 19:00 on Tue, Fri, and Sat, 2 hrs, leave from Pump Room, confirm at TI); for more information, see "Tours of Bath," above.

Sleeping in Bath
(£1 = about $1.50, country code: 44, area code: 01225)
Sleep Code: **S** = Single, **D** = Double/Twin, **T** = Triple, **Q** = Quad, **b** = bathroom, **s** = shower only, **CC** = Credit Cards accepted, **no CC** = Credit Cards not accepted.

Bath is a busy tourist town. To get a good B&B, make a telephone reservation in advance. Competition is stiff, and it's worth asking any of these places for a weekday, three-nights-in-a-row, or off-season deal. Friday and Saturday nights are tightest, especially if you're staying only one night, since B&Bs favor those staying longer. If staying only Saturday night, you're very bad news. At B&Bs (and cheaper hotels), expect lots of stairs and no lifts.

Launderettes: The Spruce Goose Launderette is around the corner from Brock's Guest House on the pedestrian lane called Margaret's Buildings (£4-self-service, £7-full-service on same day if dropped off at 08:00, Sun–Fri 08:00–20:00, Sat 08:00–19:00, tel. 01225/483-309). Anywhere in town, "Speedy Wash" can pick up your laundry for same-day service (£6.50/bag, most hotels work with them, tel. 01225/427-616). East of Pulteney Bridge, the humble Lovely Wash is on Daniel Street (daily 09:00–21:00, self-service only).

Sleeping in B&Bs near the Royal Crescent
These listings are all a 15-minute uphill walk or an easy £3.50 taxi ride from the train station. Or take the Guide Friday bus tour from the station and get off at the stop nearest your B&B (for Brock's: Assembly Rooms; for Marlborough listings: Royal Avenue; confirm with driver), check in, then finish the tour later in the day. All of these B&Bs are non-smoking.

Brock's Guest House will put bubbles in your Bath experience. Marion and Geoffrey Dodd have redone their Georgian townhouse (built by John Wood in 1765) in a way that would make the famous architect proud. It's located between the prestigious Royal Crescent and the elegant Circus (Db-£64–72, 1 deluxe Db-£72–77, Tb-£85–87, Qb-£99–105, CC, reserve with CC number far in advance, little library on top floor, 32 Brock Street, BA1 2LN, tel. 01225/338-374, fax 01225/334-245, www.brocksguesthouse.co.uk, e-mail: marion@brocksguesthouse.co.uk).

On Marlborough Lane: The **Woodville House** is run by Anne and Tom Toalster. This grandmotherly little house has three tidy, charming rooms, one shared shower/WC, an extra WC, and a TV lounge. Breakfast is served at a big, family-style table (D-£40, minimum 2 nights, no CC, some parking, below the Royal Crescent at 4 Marlborough Lane, BA1 2NQ, tel. & fax 01225/319-335, e-mail: toalster@compuserve.com).

Elgin Villa, also thoughtfully run and a fine value, has five comfy, well-maintained rooms (Ss-£32, Sb-£45, Ds-£45, Db-£65, Tb-£85, no CC, more expensive for 1 night, discounted for 3 nights, continental breakfast served in room, parking, 6 Marlborough Lane, BA1 2NQ Bath, tel. & fax 01225/424-557, www.elginvilla.co.uk, Alwyn and Carol Landman).

Athelney Guest House, which also serves a continental breakfast in your room, has three spacious rooms with two shared bathrooms (D-£40–42, T-£60–63, no CC, parking, 5 Marlborough Lane, BA1 2NQ, tel. & fax 01225/312-031, e-mail: colin-davies @supanet.com, Sue and Colin Davies).

Marlborough House Hotel is both Victorian and vegetarian, with seven comfortable rooms—well furnished with antiques— and optional £15 organic-veggie dinners (Sb-£45–75, Db-£65–85, Tb-£75–95, price depending on season, CC, varied breakfast menu, room service, 1 Marlborough Lane, BA1 2NQ, tel. 01225/318-175, fax 01225/466-127, www.marlborough-house.net, Americans Laura and Charles).

Prior House B&B, with four well-kept rooms, is run by helpful Lynn and Keith Shearn (D-£40, Db-£45, CC, 3 Marlborough Lane, tel. 01225/313-587, fax 01225/443-543, e-mail: priorhouse@greatplaces.co.uk).

Parkside Guest House rents four Edwardian rooms but lacks B&B warmth (Db-£65, small breakfast, no CC, 11 Marlborough Lane, BA1 2NQ, tel. & fax 01225/429-444, e-mail: parkside@lynall.freeserve.co.uk, Erica and Inge Lynall).

Sleeping in B&Bs East of the River

These listings are about a 10-minute walk from the city center.

Near North Parade Road: The **Holly Villa Guest House**, with a cheery garden, six bright rooms, and a cozy TV lounge, is enthusiastically and thoughtfully run by Jill and Keith McGarrigle (Ds-£45, Db-£50, Tb-£75, no CC, strictly nonsmoking, easy parking, 8-min walk from station and city center, 14 Pulteney Gardens, BA2 4HG, tel. 01225/310-331, e-mail: hollyvilla.bb@ukgateway .net). From the city center, walk over North Parade Bridge, take the first right, and then take the second left.

Near Pulteney Road: **Muriel Guy's B&B** is another good value, mixing Georgian elegance with homey warmth and artistic taste (5 rooms, S-£25, Db-£50, Tb-£60, no CC, nonsmoking, go over bridge on North Parade Road, left on Pulteney Road, cross to church, Raby Place is first row of houses on hill, 14 Raby Place, BA2 4EH, tel. 01225/465-120, fax 01225/465-283, e-mail: no way).

The Ayrlington, next door to a lawn-bowling green, has attractive rooms that hint of a more genteel time. Though this well-maintained hotel fronts a busy street, it feels tranquil inside, with double-paned windows. Rooms in the back have pleasant views of sports greens and Bath beyond. For the best value, request a standard double with a view of Bath (standard Db-£90–110, superior Db-£100–125, deluxe Db with Jacuzzi-£110–145, high prices on Fri, Sat, and Sun, no Sat night only, CC, access to garden in back, easy parking, 24/25 Pulteney Road, BA2 4EZ, tel. 01225/425-495, fax 01225/469-029, www.ayrlington.com, Simon and Mee-Ling).

In Sydney Gardens: The **Sydney Gardens Hotel** is a classy Casablanca-type place with six tastefully decorated rooms, an elegant breakfast room, garden views, and an entrance to Sydney Gardens park (Db-£75, Tb-£100, CC, request garden view, easy parking, located on busy road between park and canal, Sydney Road, BA2 6NT, tel. 01225/464-818, fax 01225/484-347, www.sydneygardens.co.uk, Geraldine and Peter Beaven).

Sleeping East of Pulteney Bridge

These are just a few minutes' walk from the city center.

Driving in from the M4 on the A4 London Road be sure to turn left at the lights, just before the town center, onto the A36 Warminster road. (Miss this and you're toast.) Crossing the Cleveland Bridge onto Bathwick Street, take the second right onto Henrietta Road and you're nearly there.

Kennard Hotel is comfortable, with 14 charming Georgian rooms and a dazzling breakfast room. Richard Ambler runs this place warmly, giving careful attention to guests (S-£48, Db-£88–98 depending upon size, CC, no kids under 12, nonsmoking, just over Pulteney Bridge, turn left at Henrietta, 11 Henrietta Street, BA2 6LL, tel. 01225/310-472, fax 01225/460-054, www.kennard.co.uk, e-mail: reception@kennard.co.uk).

Laura Place Hotel is another elegant Georgian place (8 rooms, 2 on the ground floor, rooftop D-£62, Db-£70–92 from

Bath Hotels

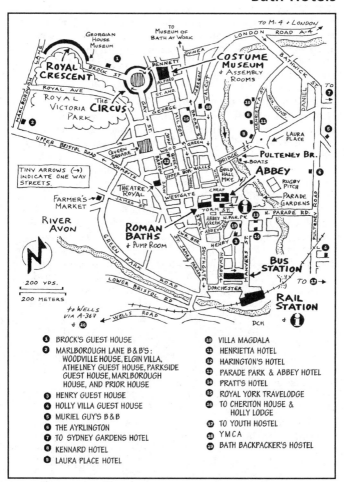

1 BROCK'S GUEST HOUSE

2 MARLBOROUGH LANE B & B'S:
WOODVILLE HOUSE, ELGIN VILLA,
ATHELNEY GUEST HOUSE, PARKSIDE
GUEST HOUSE, MARLBOROUGH
HOUSE, AND PRIOR HOUSE

3 HENRY GUEST HOUSE

4 HOLLY VILLA GUEST HOUSE

5 MURIEL GUY'S B & B

6 THE AYRLINGTON

7 TO SYDNEY GARDENS HOTEL

8 KENNARD HOTEL

9 LAURA PLACE HOTEL

10 VILLA MAGDALA

11 HENRIETTA HOTEL

12 HARINGTON'S HOTEL

13 PARADE PARK & ABBEY HOTEL

14 PRATT'S HOTEL

15 ROYAL YORK TRAVELODGE

16 TO CHERITON HOUSE &
HOLLY LODGE

17 TO YOUTH HOSTEL

18 YMCA

19 BATH BACKPACKER'S HOSTEL

small and high up to huge and palatial, CC, 2-night minimum
stay, must show this book to get 10 percent discount with cash,
family suite, nonsmoking, easy parking, just over Pulteney Bridge,
3 Laura Place, Great Pulteney Street, BA2 4BH, tel. 01225/
463-815, fax 01225/310-222, Patricia Bull).

Villa Magdala, with 18 rooms in a freestanding Victorian
townhouse opposite a park, is formal and hotelesque (Db-£85–
105, depending on size, type of bed, and plumbing; no CC,
nonsmoking, in quiet residential area, inviting lounge, parking,

Henrietta Road, Bath BA2 6LX, tel. 01225/466-329, fax 01225-483-207, www.villamagdala.co.uk).

Henrietta Hotel, with simple basic rooms and lots of stairs, gives you a budget-hotel option in this elegant neighborhood (10 rooms, Db-£45-75, discounts for cash and 2-night stay Sun–Thu, CC, 32 Henrietta Street, tel. 01225/447-779, fax 01225/444-150, Mary).

Sleeping in the City Center

Harington's of Bath Hotel, with 13 newly renovated rooms on a quiet street in the town center, is run by Susan and Desmond Pow (Db-£88–108, Tb-£100–130, prices decrease midweek and increase Fri–Sat, 10 percent discount with this book Sun–Thu, CC, nonsmoking, lots of stairs, attached restaurant/bar serves simple meals and pastries all day, extremely central at 10 Queen Street, BA1 1HE, tel. 01225/461-728, fax 01225/444-804, www.haringtonshotel.co.uk).

Parade Park Hotel, in a Georgian building, has a central location, helpful owners, and comfortable rooms decorated in a modern style (35 rooms, S-£35, D-£50, Db-£60–80, Tb-£90, Qb-£120, CC, nonsmoking, beaucoup stairs, 10 North Parade, BA2 4AL, tel. 01225/463-384, fax 01225/442-322, www.paradepark .co.uk, e-mail: info@paradepark.co.uk, Nita and David Derrick).

Pratt's Hotel is as proper and old English as you'll find in Bath. Its creaks and frays are aristocratic. Its public places make you want to sip a brandy, and its 46 rooms are bright, spacious, and come with all the comforts (Sb-£75, Db-£110, advanced reservations get high rack rates, drop ins often enjoy 25 percent discount, dogs-£4.95 but children free, CC, attached restaurant/bar, elevator, 2 blocks immediately in front of the station on South Parade, BA2 4AB, tel. 01225/460-441, fax 01225/448-807, e-mail: hotel@prattshotel.demon.co.uk).

The **Royal York Travelodge** offers American-style, characterless, comfortable rooms—worrying B&Bs and hotels alike with its reasonable prices (Db-£60, £70 on Fri–Sun, breakfast extra, CC, 1 York Bldg, George Street, BA1 3EB, tel. 01225/ 448-999, www.travelodge.co.uk).

Best Western–style **Abbey Hotel** has 60 decent rooms, some on the ground floor, a super location, and a rare elevator (standard Db-£120, deluxe Db-£130, CC, attached restaurant, nonsmoking rooms available, North Parade, BA1 1LF, tel. 01225/461-603, fax 01225/447-758, e-mail: ahres@compasshotels.co.uk).

Henry Guest House is a plain, simple, old, vertical, eight-room, family-run place two blocks in front of the train station on a quiet side street. Nothing matches—not the curtains, wallpaper, carpeting, throw rugs, or bedspreads—but it is the cheapest hotel in the center (S-£22.50, D-£45, T-£55, TVs in rooms, lots of narrow stairs,

3 showers and WCs for all, 6 Henry Street, BA1 1JT, tel. 01225/424-052, e-mail: cox@thehenrybath.freeserve.co.uk, Rosemary).

Sleeping in B&Bs South of the Train Station

Up a hill a 15-minute walk south of the train station are a string of classy B&Bs in a car-friendly residential neighborhood. Here are two good ones: **Cheriton House**, with 11 well-furnished rooms (Sb-£42–60, Db-£64–85, 10 percent discount for 2 nights or more by showing this book, CC, nonsmoking, garden, 9 Upper Oldfield Park, BA2 3JX, tel. 01225/429-862, e-mail: cheriton@which.net, Iris and John Chiles); and **Holly Lodge**, with six frilly, Victorian-style rooms and a gazebo in the garden (Sb-£48–55, Db-£79–97, CC, nonsmoking, phones in rooms, tel. 01225/339-187, fax 01225/481-138, e-mail: stay@hollylodge.co.uk, Mr. George Hall).

Sleeping in Dorms

The **YMCA**, wonderfully central on a leafy square down a tiny alley off Broad Street, has 200 beds in industrial-strength rooms and scuff-proof halls (S-£16, D-£28, T-£42, Q-£56, beds in big dorms-£11, includes meager continental breakfast, CC, families offered a day nursery for kids under 5, cheap dinners, no lockers, dorms closed from 10:00–16:00, Broad Street Place, BA1 5LH, tel. 01225/460-471, fax 01225/462-065, e-mail: info@ymcabath.u-net.com).

White Hart Hostel is a simple, new place offering adults and families good cheap beds in two- to six-bed dorms (£12.50/bed, D-£30, no CC, family rooms, kitchen, smoke free, no breakfast, 5-min walk behind train station at Widcombe—where Widcombe Hill hits Claverton Street, tel. 01225/313-985, e-mail: sue @whitehartinn.freeserve.co.uk, run by Mike and Sue).

Bath Backpackers Hostel bills itself as a totally fun-packed, mad place to stay. This Aussie-run dive/hostel rents bunk beds in 6- to 10-bed rooms (£12/bed, 2 D-£30, lockers, Internet access for nonguests as well, bar, kitchen, a couple of blocks toward city center from train station, 13 Pierrepont Street, tel. 01225/446-787, e-mail: stayinbath @backpackers-uk.demon.co.uk).

The **youth hostel** is in a grand old building on Bathwick Hill outside of town (£11/bed in 2- to 10-bed rooms, D-£31, Db-£36, non-members pay £2 extra, breakfast not included, bus #18 from station, tel. 01225/465-674).

Eating in Bath

While not a great pub-grub town, Bath is bursting with quaint and stylish eateries. There's something for every appetite and budget—just stroll around the center of town. A picnic dinner of deli food or take-out fish 'n' chips in the Royal Crescent Park is ideal for aristocratic hobos.

Eating between the Abbey and the Station

Three fine and popular places share North Parade Passage, a block south of the Abbey: **Tilley's Bistro** serves healthy French, English, and vegetarian meals with candlelit ambience. Their fun menu lets you build your meal choosing from an interesting array of £6 starters (Mon–Sat 12:00–14:30, 18:30–23:00, closed Sun, CC, reservations smart, nonsmoking, North Parade Passage, tel. 01225/484-200). **Sally Lunn's House** is a cutesy, quasi-historic place for expensive doily meals, tea, pink pillows, and lots of lace (£7–10, nightly, CC, smoke-free, 4 North Parade Passage, tel. 01225/461-634). It's fine for tea and buns, and customers get a free peek at the basement Kitchen Museum (otherwise 30p). Next door, **Demuth's Vegetarian Restaurant** serves good £15 meals (daily 10:00–22:00, CC, vegan options available, reservations wise, tel. 01225/446-059).

Crystal Palace Pub, with typical pub grub under rustic timbers or in the sunny courtyard, is a handy standby (£6 meals, Mon–Fri 11:00–20:30, Sat 11:00–16:30, Sun 12:00–16:00, children welcome on patio but not indoors, 11 Abbey Green, tel. 01225/482-666).

Evans is decent for fish 'n' chips (Mon–Fri 11:30–15:30, Sat 11:30–19:00, closed Sun, on Abbeygate, near Marks & Spencer). Also greasy is **Seafoods** (daily 12:00–23:00, 27 Kingsmeads Street, just off Kingsmead Square). For more cheap meals, try **Spike's Fish and Chips** (open very late) and the neighboring café just behind the bus station.

Eating between the Abbey and the Circus

George Street is lined with cheery eateries: Thai, Italian, wine bars, and so on. **Martini Restaurant** is purely Italian with class and jovial waiters (£11 entrées, £7 pizzas, daily 12:00–14:30, 18:00–22:30, CC, reservations smart, smoke-free section, 9 George Street, tel. 01225/460-818, Nunzio, Franco, and Luigi).

Bengal Brasserie, a Bangaladeshi place specializing in Tandoori and curries, is unpretentious with good food at good prices (lunch from 12:00, dinner from 18:00, 32 Milsom Street, tel. 01225/447-906).

Jamuna makes a mean curry (Mon–Sun 12:00–14:30, 18:00–24:00, Abbey views, 9-10 High Street, tel. 01225/464-631).

The **Old Green Tree Pub** on Green Street is a rare pub with good grub, locally brewed real ales, and a nonsmoking room (lunch only, served 12:00–14:30, no children, live jazz Sun–Mon 20:30 until closing, tel. 01225/448-259).

Browns, a popular, modern chain, offers affordable—though not great—English food throughout the day (£6 lunch special, Mon–Sat 11:00–23:30, Sun 12:00–23:30, CC, kid-friendly, half block east of the Abbey, Orange Grove, tel. 01225/461-199).

The Moon and Sixpence, prized by locals, offers "modern

Bath Restaurants

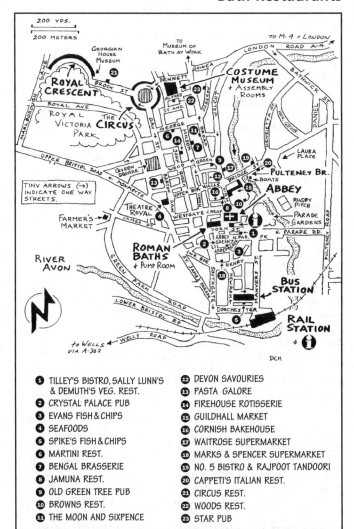

1. TILLEY'S BISTRO, SALLY LUNN'S & DEMUTH'S VEG. REST.
2. CRYSTAL PALACE PUB
3. EVANS FISH & CHIPS
4. SEAFOODS
5. SPIKE'S FISH & CHIPS
6. MARTINI REST.
7. BENGAL BRASSERIE
8. JAMUNA REST.
9. OLD GREEN TREE PUB
10. BROWNS REST.
11. THE MOON AND SIXPENCE
12. DEVON SAVOURIES
13. PASTA GALORE
14. FIREHOUSE ROTISSERIE
15. GUILDHALL MARKET
16. CORNISH BAKEHOUSE
17. WAITROSE SUPERMARKET
18. MARKS & SPENCER SUPERMARKET
19. NO. 5 BISTRO & RAJPOOT TANDOORI
20. CAPPETI'S ITALIAN REST.
21. CIRCUS REST.
22. WOODS REST.
23. STAR PUB

English fusion" cuisine, giving British cooking a needed international flair and flavor (£7 2-course lunch, £21 3-course dinner menu, daily 12:00–14:30, 17:30–22:30, CC, indoor/outdoor seating, 6a Broad Street, tel. 01225/460-962).

Devon Savouries serves greasy-but-delicious take-out

pasties, sausage rolls, and vegetable pies (Mon–Sat 09:00–17:30, hours vary on Sun, on Burton Street, the main walkway between New Bond Street and Upper Borough Walls).

Pasta Galore serves decent (sometimes so-so) Italian food and homemade pasta outside on a patio or inside. The ground floor beats the basement (daily 12:00–14:30, 18:00–22:30, CC, 31 Barton Street, tel. 01225/463-861).

If you're missing California, try the popular **Firehouse Rotisserie** (Mon–Sat 12:00–14:30, 18:00–23:00, closed Sun, make reservations, near Queen Square on John Street, tel. 01225/482-070).

Guildhall Market, across from Pulteney Bridge, is fun for browsing and picnic shopping, with an inexpensive Market Café if you'd like to sip tea surrounded by stacks of used books, bananas on the push list, and honest-to-goodness old-time locals (Mon–Sat 09:00–17:00, closed Sun, a block north of the Abbey, main entrance on High Street).

The **Cornish Bakehouse**, near the Guildhall Market, has good take-away pasties (11a The Corridor, off High Street, tel. 01225/426-635).

Supermarkets: **Waitrose**, at the Podium shopping center, is great for groceries (Mon–Fri 08:30–20:00, Sat 08:30–19:00, Sun 11:00–17:00, salad bar, just west of Pulteney Bridge and across from post office on High Street). **Marks & Spencer**, near the train station, has a good grocery at the back of its department store (Mon–Sat 09:00–17:30, Sun 11:00–17:00, Stall Street).

Eating East of Pulteney Bridge

For a stylish, intimate setting and "new English" cuisine worth the splurge, dine at **No. 5 Bistro** (£12–15 main courses with vegetables, Mon–Sat 18:30–22:00, closed Sun, Mon–Tue are "bring your own bottle of wine" nights—no corkage fee, smart to reserve, CC, just over Pulteney Bridge at 5 Argyle Street, tel. 01225/444-499). **Rajpoot Tandoori**, next door to No. 5, serves good Indian food. You'll hike down deep into a cellar where the classy Indian atmosphere and award-winning cooking makes paying the extra pounds OK (4 Argyle Street, tel. 01225/466-833). **Cappeti's Italian Restaurant** is a checkered-tablecloth place in another deep cellar serving good Italian (Tue–Sat 12:00–14:00, 18:30–22:30, closed Sun–Mon, CC, 12 Argyle Street, tel. 01225/442-299).

Eating near the Circus and Brock's Guest House

Circus Restaurant is intimate and a good value, with Mozartian ambience and candlelit prices: £17 for a three-course dinner special including great vegetables and a selection of fine desserts (daily 12:00–14:00, 18:30–22:00, reservations smart, CC, 34 Brock Street, tel. 01225/318-918, run by Felix Rosenow).

Woods Restaurant serves modern English cuisine to

well-dressed locals in a sprawling candlelit brasserie (£8-lunches, £13–25 3-course dinners, daily 12:00–15:00, 18:00–22:30, closed Sun eve, CC, 9-13 Alfred Street, near Assembly Rooms, tel. 01225/314-812).

For real ale (but no food), try the **Star Pub** (top of Paragon Street).

Transportation Connections—Bath

Bath's train station is called Bath Spa. The National Express bus office (Mon–Sat 08:00–17:30, closed Sun) is one block in front of the train station.

To London from Bath Spa: By train to Paddington Station (2/hr, 75 min, £31 one-way after 09:30), or cheaper by National Express bus to Victoria Station (nearly 1/hr, up to 3 hrs, £12.50 one-way, £20 round-trip). To get from London to Bath, consider an all-day Stonehenge-and-Bath organized bus tour from London (for details see "Daytrips from London" on page 452). Train info: tel. 08457-484-950.

To London's airports: By National Express bus to **Heathrow** Airport and continuing on to London (10/day, 2.5 hrs, £11.50, tel. 08705-808-080) and to **Gatwick** (2/hr, 4.5 hrs, £19.50). Trains are faster but more expensive (1/hr, 2.5 hrs, £29.20). For information on getting to Bath, see "Transportation Connections" in the London chapter.

To the Cotswolds: By train to **Moreton-in-Marsh** (1/hr, 2 hrs, transfer in Oxford). By National Express bus to **Cheltenham** (1 direct bus/day, 2.5 hrs, more buses with transfer), **Stratford** (1/day, 4 hrs, transfer in Bristol or Birmingham), and **Oxford** (1 direct/day, 2 hrs, more buses with transfer). Bus info: tel. 08705/808-080.

By train to: Oxford (1/hr, 1 hr), **Heathrow** (1/hr, transfer at Reading to bus), **Gatwick** (1/hr, 3 hrs), **Birmingham** (1/hr, 2.5 hrs, transfer in Bristol), and **points north** (from Birmingham, a major transportation hub, trains depart for Blackpool, York, Durham, Scotland, and North Wales; use a train/bus combination to reach Ironbridge Gorge and the Lake District).

YORK

Historical York is loaded with world-class sights. Marvel at the York Minster, England's finest Gothic church. Ramble through the Shambles, York's wonderfully preserved medieval quarter. Enjoy a walking tour led by an old Yorker. Hop a train at Europe's greatest Railway Museum, travel to the 1800s in York Castle Museum, and head back a thousand years to Viking York at the Jorvik exhibit.

York has a rich history. In A.D. 71 it was Eboracum, a Roman provincial capital. Constantine was actually proclaimed emperor here in A.D. 306. In the fifth century, as Rome was toppling, a Roman emperor sent a letter telling England it was on its own, and York became Eoforwic, the capital of the Anglo-Saxon kingdom of Northumbria. A church was built here in 627, and the town became an early Christian center of learning. The Vikings later took the town, and from about 860 to 950 it was a Danish trading center called Jorvik. The invading and conquering Normans destroyed then rebuilt the city, giving it a castle and the walls you see today. Medieval York, with 9,000 inhabitants, grew rich on the wool trade and became England's second city. Henry VIII spared the city's fine minster in order to use York as his Anglican church's northern capital. The Archbishop of York is second only to the Archbishop of Canterbury in the Anglican Church. In the Industrial Age, York was the railway hub of North England. When it was built, York's train station was the world's largest. Today, York's leading industry is tourism. Its leading drug? Starbucks and Costa are doing their best to turn high tea into high coffee.

Planning Your Time

York rivals Edinburgh as the best sightseeing city in Britain after London. On even a short trip through Britain, it deserves two nights and a day. For the best 36 hours, follow this plan: Catch the 19:00 city walking tour on the evening of your arrival. The next morning, be at the Castle Museum at 09:30 when it opens—it's worth a good two hours. Then browse and sightsee through the day. Train buffs love the National Railway Museum, and scholars give the Yorkshire Museum three stars. Tour the minster at 16:00 before catching the 17:00 evensong service (at 16:00 Sat–Sun). Finish your day with an early evening stroll along the wall and perhaps through the abbey gardens. This schedule assumes you're there in the summer (evening orientation walk) and that there's an evensong on. Confirm your plans with the TI.

Orientation (area code: 01904)

The sightseer's York is small. Virtually everything is within a few minutes' walk: the sights, train station, TI, and B&Bs. The longest walk a visitor might take (from a B&B across the old town to the Castle Museum) is 15 minutes.

Bootham Bar, a gate in the medieval town wall, is the hub of your York visit. At Bootham Bar (and on Exhibition Square facing it) you'll find the TI, the starting points for most walking tours and bus tours, handy access to the medieval town wall, and Bootham Street, which leads to the recommended B&Bs. (In York, a "bar" is a gate and a "gate" is a street. Go ahead, blame the Vikings.) When finding your way, navigate by sighting the tower of the minster or the strategically-placed green signposts pointing out all places of interest to tourists.

Tourist Information: The TI at Bootham Bar sells an 80p *York Map and Guide*. Ask for the free monthly *What's On* guide and the monthly *Gig Guide* for live music (April–Oct Mon–Sat 09:00–18:00, Sun 10:00–16:00, sometimes longer in summer, always shorter in winter but no one really knows, pay WCs next door, tel. 01904/621-756). The TI books rooms for a £4 fee and sells theater tickets. The train-station TI is smaller but provides all the same information and services (April–Sept Mon–Sat 09:00–18:00, Sun 09:30–16:00, shorter hrs off-season).

Arrival in York: The train station, which stores luggage for daytrippers (£1.50, Mon–Sat 08:00–20:30, Sun 09:00–20:30, platform 1), is a five-minute walk from town; turn left down Station Road and follow the crowd toward the Gothic towers of the minster. After the bridge, a block before the Minster, signs to the TI send you left on St. Leonard's Place. Recommended B&Bs are a five-minute walk from there. (For a shortcut to B&B area from station, walk 1 block toward the minster, cut through parks to riverside, cross railway bridge/pedestrian walkway, cross parking lot for B&Bs on St. Mary's Street, or duck through pedestrian walkway under tracks to B&Bs on Sycamore and Queen Anne's Road.) **Taxis** zip new arrivals to their B&B for £3.

York

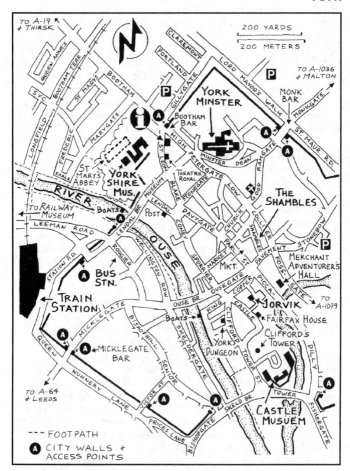

Helpful Hints

Study Ahead: York has a great Web site: www.york.gov.uk.

Internet Access: Get online at Internet Exchange (Mon–Sat 08:00–21:00, Sun 10:00–18:00, 13 Stonegate), Gateway (Mon–Wed 10:00–20:00, Thu–Sat 10:00–23:00, Sun 12:00–22:00, 26 Swinegate, tel. 01904/646-446) or Comms.port (near Betty's at Coney Street 2a, first floor, tel. 01904/658-270).

Festivals: The Viking Festival in late February is a lot of fun, with lur-blowing, warrior drills, and re-created battles. The Early Music Festival zings its strings in mid-July. The York Festival of

Food and Drink takes a 10-day bite out of the last half of September. Book a room well in advance during festival times and weekends any time of year.

Bike Rental: Trotters, just outside Monk Bar, has free cycling maps. The riverside path is fun (£8/day, helmets-£2, Mon–Sat 09:00–17:30, Sun 10:00–16:00, tel. 01904/622-868). Europcar at the train station also rents bikes (£9/day, helmets-£1, platform 1, tel. 01904/656-161).

Car Rental: If you're nearing the end of your trip, consider dropping your car upon arrival in York. The money saved by turning it in early nearly pays for the train ticket that whisks you effortlessly to Edinburgh or London. Here are some car-rental agencies in York: Avis (Mon–Sat, closed Sun, 3 Layerthorpe, tel. 01904/610-460), Hertz (April–Sept daily 09:00–13:00, at train station, tel. 01904/612-586), Kenning Car & Van Rental (Mon–Fri, closed Sun, inconveniently 3 miles out of town at Clifton Moor Industrial Estate, tel. 01904/659-328), Budget (daily 09:00–11:00, 1 mile past recommended B&Bs at Clifton 82, tel. 01904/644-919), and Europcar (daily 09:00–13:00, train station platform 1, tel. 1904/656-161). Beware, car-rental agencies close Saturday afternoon and some close all day Sunday—when dropping off is OK but picking up is impossible.

Tours of York

▲▲▲**Walking Tours**—Charming local volunteer guides give energetic, entertaining, and free two-hour walks through York (daily 10:15 all year, plus 14:15 April–Oct, plus 19:00 June–Aug, from Exhibition Square across from TI). There are many other commercial York walking tours. YorkWalk Tours, for example, has reliable guides and many themes from which to choose, such as Roman York, City Walls, or Snickleways—small alleys (£5, tel. 01904/622-303, TI has schedule). The ghost tours, all offered after nightfall, are more fun than informative. Haunted Walk relies a bit more on storytelling and history rather than masks and surprises (£3, April–Nov nightly at 20:00, 90 min, just show up, depart from Exhibition Square, across street from TI, end in the Shambles, tel. 01904/411-578).

▲**Guide Friday Hop-on Hop-off Bus Tours**—York's Guide Friday offers tour guides who can talk enthusiastically to three sleeping tourists in a gale on a topless double-decker bus for an hour without stopping. Buses make the 60-minute circuit, covering secondary York sights that the city walking tours skip—the work-a-day perimeter of town (£6.50, pay driver cash, can also buy from TI with CC, fliers at TI give £1 off on tickets, departures every 15 min from 09:15 until around 17:00, tel. 01904/640-896). While you can hop on and off all day, the York route is of no value from a transportation-to-the-sights point of view. I'd catch it at the Bootham Bar TI and ride it for an orientation all the way around or get off at the Railway Museum, skipping the last five minutes. Guide Friday's competitors give you a little less for a little less.

Boat Cruise—Even though York turns its back on its river, the York Boat does a lazy 60-minute lap along the River Ouse (£5, Feb–Nov daily from 10:30 on, narrated cruise, leaves from Lendal Bridge and King's Staith landing), and also offers themed evening cruises: ghost, dinner, floodlit, and so on (boat rentals possible, tel. 01904/628-324, www.yorkboat.co.uk).

Sights—York Minster

▲▲▲**Minster**—The pride of York, this largest Gothic church north of the Alps (540 feet long, 200 feet tall) brilliantly shows that the High Middle Ages were far from dark. The word "minster" means a place from which people go out to minister or spread the word of God.

Your first impression might be the spaciousness and brightness of the nave (built 1280–1350). The nave—from the middle period of Gothic, called "Decorated Gothic"—is one of the widest Gothic naves in Europe. Notice the Great West Window (1338) above the entry. The heart in the tracery is called "the heart of Yorkshire."

Look down the nave. The mysterious gold-and-red dragon's head (in the middle of the nave, sticking out of the side) was probably used as a crane to lift a font cover.

The north and south transepts are the oldest parts of today's church (1220–1270). The oldest complete window in the minster is the entire wall of glass in the north transept (1260). Known as the Five Sister's Window, these 50-foot-high panels were made of modern-looking grisaille (gray-silver) glass.

The fanciful choir and the east end (high altar) is from the last stage of Gothic, Perpendicular (1360–1470). The Great East Window (1405), the largest medieval glass window in existence, shows the beginning and the end of the world, with scenes from Genesis and the book of Revelation. A chart (on the right, with a tiny, more helpful chart within) highlights the core Old Testament scenes in this hard-to-read masterpiece. Enjoy the art close up on the chart and then step back and find the real thing.

There are three more extra visits to consider. The **Chapter House**, an elaborately decorated 13th-century Gothic dome—the largest in England without a central supporting pillar—features playful details carved in the stonework (pointed out in the flier that comes with the £1 admission, enter from north transept). You can scale the 275-step **tower** for £3 and enjoy a great view (south transept). The **Undercroft**, also in the south transept, consists of the crypt, treasury, and foundations (£3). The crypt is an actual bit of the Romanesque church, featuring 12th-century Romanesque art, excavated in modern times. The foundations give you a chance to climb down—archaeologically and physically—through the centuries to see the roots of the much smaller, but still huge, Norman church (Romanesque, 1100) that stood on this spot and, below that, the Roman excavations. Constantine was proclaimed Roman emperor here in A.D. 306. Peek also at the modern concrete save-the-church foundations.

Hours and Tours: The cathedral opens daily at 07:00. The closing time flexes with the season (roughly 20:30 July–Aug, 19:30 May–June and Sept, 18:00 Oct–April, £2 to use your camera, tel. 01904/557-222). The Chapter House, tower, and Undercroft have shorter hours (usually 09:30–18:30, Oct–April 10:00–16:30). The minster is open for sightseeing from 12:30 on Sundays.

While a donation of £2.50 to visit the church is reasonably requested, I skip that and pay for admission to all the little overpriced extra spots inside—eventually giving more than the £2.50.

When you enter go directly to the welcome desk, pick up the worthwhile "Welcome to the York Minster" flier, and ask when the next free guided tour departs (tours go frequently, even with just 1 or 2 people; you can join one in progress). The helpful blue-armbanded minster guides are happy to answer your questions.

Evensong and Church Bells: To experience the cathedral in musical and spiritual action, attend an evensong (Tue–Sat 17:00, Sat–Sun 16:00, 45 min). When the choir is off on school break (mid-July–Aug), visiting choirs usually fill in. Arrive 10 minutes early and wait just outside the choir in the center of the church from where you'll be ushered in and can sit in one of the big wooden stalls. If you're a fan of church bells, Sunday morning (around 10:00) and the Tuesday-evening practice (19:30–21:30) are heavenly.

Sights—York

▲**City Walls**—The historic walls of York provide a fine two-mile walk. Walk from Bootham Bar (gate) to Monk Bar for outstanding cathedral views. They're free and open from dawn until dusk (barring attacks).

▲**The Shambles**—This is the most colorful old York street in the half-timbered, traffic-free core of town. Ye olde downtown York, while very touristy, is a window-shopping, busker-filled, people-watcher's delight. Don't miss the more frumpy Newgate Market or the old-time Hamilton's candy store just opposite the bottom end of the Shambles. For a cheap lunch, consider the cute, tiny **St. Crux Parish Hall**. This medieval church is now used by a medley of charities selling tea, homemade cakes, and light meals. They each book the church for a day, often a year in advance. Chat up the volunteers (Mon–Sat 10:00–16:00, closed Sun, at bottom end of the Shambles, at intersection with Pavement).

▲▲▲**Castle Museum**—Truly one of Europe's top museums, this is a Victorian home show, the closest thing to a time-tunnel experience England has to offer. It includes the 19th-century Kirkgate (a collection of old shops well stocked exactly as they were 150 years ago); a "From Cradle to Grave" exhibit; and a fine costume collection. The one-way plan allows you to see everything: a working water mill (April–Oct), prison cells, World War II fashions, and old toys. Bring 10p coins to jolt a mechanical Al Jolson into song. The museum's £2.50 guidebook isn't necessary but makes a fine souvenir (£6, April–Oct daily 09:30–17:00, Nov–March until 16:30, gift shop, parking, cafeteria midway through museum, CC, tel. 01904/653-611).

Clifford's Tower (across from Castle Museum, not worth the £2, daily 10:00–18:00, until 16:00 Oct–March) is all that's left of York's castle (13th century, site of a 1190 massacre of local Jews—read about this at base of hill). If you do climb inside, there are fine city views from the top of the ramparts.

▲**Jorvik**—Sail the "Pirates of the Caribbean" north and back 800 years and you get Jorvik—more a ride than a museum. Innovative 10 years ago, the commercial success of Jorvik (yor-vik) inspired copycat ride/museums all over England. You'll ride a little Disney-type train car for 13 minutes through the re-created Viking street of Coppergate. It's the year 975, and you're in the village of Jorvik. Next, your little train takes you through the actual excavation site that inspired this. Finally you'll browse through a small gallery of Viking shoes, combs, locks, and other intimate glimpses of that redheaded culture (£7, daily from 09:00 with last entry at 17:30, Nov–March closing varies from 15:30–16:30, tel. 01904/643-211, www.vikingjorvik.com).

Midday lines can be an hour long. Avoid the line by going very early or very late in the day or by pre-booking (call 01904/543-403, you're given a time slot, £1 booking fee, CC). Some love this "ride"; others call it a gimmicky rip-off. If you're looking for a grown-up museum, the Viking exhibit at the Yorkshire Museum is far better. If you're thinking Disneyland with a splash of history, Jorvik's fun. To me, Jorvik is a commercial venture designed for kids with nearly as much square footage devoted to its shop as to the museum.

▲▲**National Railway Museum**—If you like model railways, this is train-car heaven. The thunderous museum shows 150 fascinating years of British railroad history. Fanning out from a grand roundhouse is an array of historic cars and engines, including Queen Victoria's lavish royal car and the very first "stagecoaches on rails." There's much more, including exhibits on dining cars, post cars, sleeping cars, train posters, and videos. At the "Works" section you can see live train switchboards. And don't miss the English Channel Tunnel video (showing the first handshake at

breakthrough). Red-shirted "explainers" are everywhere, eager
to talk trains. This biggest and best railroad museum anywhere
is interesting even to people who think "Pullman" means "don't
push" (£7.50, under 17 and over 60 free, daily 10:00–18:00, CC,
tel. 01904/621-261). Cute little "street trains" shuttle you between
the minster and the Railway Museum (£1.50 each way, leaves
Railway Museum every 30 min from 12:00–17:30 at the top and
bottom of the hour; leaves minster—from Duncombe Place—
every 30 min 15 and 45 min after the hour).

▲▲Yorkshire Museum—Located in a lush and lazy park next to
the stately ruins of St. Mary's Abbey, Yorkshire Museum is the city's
forgotten, serious "archaeology of York" museum. While the hordes
line up at Jorvik, the best Viking artifacts are here—with no crowds
and a better historical context. A stroll around this museum takes
you through Roman (wonderfully described battle-bashed skull in
first case), Saxon (great Anglo-Saxon helmet from A.D. 750), Viking,
Norman, and Gothic York. Its prize piece is the delicately etched
15th-century pendant called the Middleham Jewel—for which the
museum raised $4 million to buy. The 20-minute video about the
creation of the abbey is worth a look (£4, various exhibitions can
increase price, daily 10:00–17:00, tel. 01904/551-800).

Theatre Royal—A full variety of dramas, comedies, and works by
Shakespeare is put on to entertain the locals (£10–15, 19:30 or 20:00
almost nightly, tickets easy to get, closes for 6-week period starting
in June, CC, on St. Leonard's Place next to TI and a 5-min walk
from recommended B&Bs, recorded info tel. 01904/610-041,
booking tel. 01904/623-568, www.theatre-royal-york.co.uk).

Honorable Mention

York has a number of other sights and activities (described in TI
material) that, while interesting, pale in comparison to the biggies.
Fairfax House is perfectly Georgian inside, with docents happy to
talk with you (£4, Sat–Thu 11:00–17:00 except Sun 13:30–17:00,
Fri by tour only at 11:00 and 14:00, a tour helps bring this well-
furnished building to life, on Castlegate, near Jorvik, tel.
01904/655-543). The **Hall of the Merchant Adventurers** claims
to be the finest medieval guildhall in Europe (from 1361). It's basically a vast half-timbered building with marvelous exposed beams
and 15 minutes worth of interesting displays about life and commerce back in the days when York was England's second city (£2,
Mon–Sat 09:00–17:30, Sun 12:00–16:00, early Nov–mid-March
until 15:30, below the Shambles off Piccadilly). The **Richard III
"Museum"** is interesting only for Richard III enthusiasts (£1.50,
daily 09:00–17:00, Nov–Feb until 16:00, Monk Bar). **The York
Dungeon** is gimmicky but, if you insist on papier-mâché gore, is
better than the London Dungeon (£6.50, daily 10:30–18:00, less
off-season, 12 Clifford Street).

Visitors are welcome at the **lawn bowling green** on Sycamore Place (near recommended B&Bs, tell them which B&B
you're staying at); you can buy a pint of beer and watch the action
(best in evenings). Another green is in front of the Coach House
Hotel Pub on Marygate.

York—with its medieval lanes lined with classy as well as tacky
little shops—is a hit with shoppers. I find the **antique malls** interesting. Three places within a few blocks of each other are filled
with stalls and cases owned by antique dealers from the countryside.
The malls sell the dealers' bygones on commission. Serious shoppers do better heading for the countryside, but York's shops are
a fun browse: Stonegate Antiques Centre (daily 09:00–18:00,
41 Stonegate, tel. 01904/613-888), the antique mall at 2 Lendal
(Mon–Sat 10:00–17:00, closed Sun), and the Red House Antiques
Centre (daily 09:30–17:30, as late as 20:00 in the summer, a block
from the Minster at Duncombe Place, tel. 01904/637-000).

Sights—Near York

Eden Camp—Once an internment camp for German and Italian
POWs during World War II, this is now a theme museum on
Britain's war experience. Various barracks detail the rise of Hitler
and the fury of the Blitz (with the sound of bombs, the acrid smell
of burning, and quotes such as "Hitler will send no warning—so
always carry your gas mask.") This award-winning museum energetically conveys the spirit of a country Hitler couldn't conquer.
Don't miss hut #10, which details the actual purpose of the
camp—as a prison for captured Nazis during World War II. Consider the relative delight of being in the care of the gentlemanly
English rather than in a Nazi camp. It's no wonder the Germans
settled right in (£4, daily 10:00–17:00, closed late-Dec–mid-Jan,
mess-kitchen cafeteria, Malton, 18 miles northeast of York, tel.
01653/697-777, www.edencamp.co.uk). To get to the camp from
York, catch the Coastliner bus at the York Railway Station (leaves
from front of station, on station side of road). Buses are marked
with the destination "Whitby" or "Pickering" and are numbered
#840, #842, or #X40, depending on the time of day (£4 round-trip,
Mon–Sat 11/day, fewer on Sun, 50 min). From York, drivers take
A169 toward Scarborough, then follow signs to the camp.

Sleeping in York
(£1 = about $1.50, country code: 44, area code: 01904)
Sleep Code: **S** = Single, **D** = Double/Twin, **T** = Triple, **Q** = Quad,
b = bathroom, **s** = shower only, **CC** = Credit Cards accepted, **No
CC** = Credit Cards not accepted.

I've listed peak-season, book-direct prices. Don't use the TI.
Outside of July and August some prices go soft. B&Bs will sometimes turn away one-night bookings, particularly for peak-season

Saturdays. (York is worth 2 nights.) Remember to book ahead during festival times (late Feb, mid-July, latter half of Sept) and weekends year-round.

Sleeping in B&Bs near Bootham

These recommendations are in the handiest B&B neighborhood, a quiet residential area just outside the old-town wall's Bootham gate, along the road called Bootham. All are within a five-minute walk of the minster and TI and a 10-minute walk or taxi ride (£3) from the station. If driving, head for the cathedral and follow the medieval wall to the gate called Bootham Bar. Bootham "street" leads away from Bootham Bar.

These B&Bs are all small, nonsmoking, and family run. They come with plenty of steep stairs but no traffic noise. For a good selection, call well in advance. B&Bs will generally hold a room with a phone call and work hard to help their guests sightsee and eat smartly. Most have permits for street parking. And most don't take credit cards.

Laundry: Regency Dry Cleaning does small loads for £8 (Mon–Fri 08:30–18:00, Sat 09:00–17:00, closed Sun, drop off by 9:30 for same-day service, 75 Bootham, at intersection with Queen Anne's, tel. 01904/613-311). The next-nearest place is a long 15-minute walk away (Washeteria Launderette, 124 Haxby Road, tel. 01904/623-379).

Airden House, the most central of my Bootham-area listings, has eight spacious rooms, a grandfather clock–cozy TV lounge, and brightness and warmth throughout. Susan and Keith Burrows, a great source of local travel tips, keep their place tastefully simple, clean, comfortable, and friendly (D–£40–42, Db–£50–52, no CC, 1 St. Mary's, York YO30 7DD, tel. 01904/ 638-915, www.airdenhouse.co.uk, e-mail: info@airdenhouse.co.uk).

The Sycamore, run by Margaret and David Tyce, is a fine value, with seven homey rooms strewn with silk flowers and personal touches. It's at the end of a dead end opposite a fun-to-watch bowling green (S–£20–24, D–£32–34, Db–£42–44, T–L48–50, no CC, 19 Sycamore Place off Bootham Terrace, YO30 7DW, tel. & fax 01904/624-712, e-mail: thesycamore@talk21.com).

Abbeyfields Guest House has nine cozy, bright rooms and a quiet lounge. This doily-free place, which lacks the usual clutter, has been designed with care (S–£23, Sb–£33, Db–£52, no CC, 19 Boothham Terrace, YO30 7DH, tel. & fax 01904/636-471, www.abbeyfields.co.uk, Richard and Gwen Martin).

23 St. Mary's is extravagantly decorated. Mrs. Hudson has done everything super-correctly and offers nine comfortable rooms, a classy lounge, and all the doily touches (Sb–£34–36, Db–£64–75 depending on season and size, no CC, 23 St. Mary's, YO30 7DD, tel. 01904/622-738, fax 01904/621-168).

York's Hotels and Restaurants

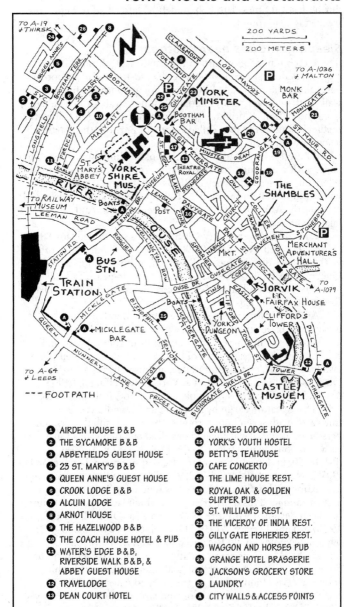

1. AIRDEN HOUSE B & B
2. THE SYCAMORE B & B
3. ABBEYFIELDS GUEST HOUSE
4. 23 ST. MARY'S B & B
5. QUEEN ANNE'S GUEST HOUSE
6. CROOK LODGE B & B
7. ALCUIN LODGE
8. ARNOT HOUSE
9. THE HAZELWOOD B & B
10. THE COACH HOUSE HOTEL & PUB
11. WATER'S EDGE B & B, RIVERSIDE WALK B & B, & ABBEY GUEST HOUSE
12. TRAVELODGE
13. DEAN COURT HOTEL
14. GALTRES LODGE HOTEL
15. YORK'S YOUTH HOSTEL
16. BETTY'S TEAHOUSE
17. CAFE CONCERTO
18. THE LIME HOUSE REST.
19. ROYAL OAK & GOLDEN SLIPPER PUB
20. ST. WILLIAM'S REST.
21. THE VICEROY OF INDIA REST.
22. GILLY GATE FISHERIES REST.
23. WAGGON AND HORSES PUB
24. GRANGE HOTEL BRASSERIE
25. JACKSON'S GROCERY STORE
26. LAUNDRY

Ⓐ CITY WALLS & ACCESS POINTS

Queen Anne's Guest House has seven clean, cheery rooms (May–Sept D-£34, Db-£36, Oct–April D-£30, Db-£32, prices good through 2002 with this book, CC, 1 family room, lounge, 24 Queen Anne's Road, Y030 7AA, tel. 01904/629-389, fax 01904/619-529, e-mail: info@queenannes.fsnet.co.uk, Judy and David).

Crook Lodge B&B, with seven charming, tight rooms, is a bit more elegant than the rest (Db-£50–56, no CC, parking, quiet, 26 St. Mary's, Y030 7DD, tel. & fax 01904/655-614, www.crooklodge.co.uk, e-mail: crooklodge@hotmail.com, Susan and John Arnott).

Alcuin Lodge is a good value, with seven flowery rooms and solid-wood furnishings (Db-£42–50, 1 small top-floor D-£35, no kids, CC, 15 Sycamore Place, Y030 7DW, tel. 01904/632-222, fax 01904/626-630, e-mail: Alcuinlodg@aol.com, Susan Taylor and her husband, General Patton).

Arnot House, run by a hard-working daughter-and-mother team, is homey, cluttered, and lushly decorated with early-1900s memorabilia. The four well-furnished rooms have little libraries (Db-£54–58, CC, minimum 2-night stay, 17 Grosvenor Terrace, Y030 7AG, tel. & fax 01904/641-966, www.arnothouseyork.co.uk, e-mail: kim.robbins@virgin.net, Kim and Ann Robbins).

The Hazelwood, my most hotelesque listing in this neighborhood, is plush, though it lacks the intimacy of a B&B. This spacious house has 14 beautifully decorated rooms with modern furnishings and lots of thoughtful touches (Db-£75–85–95 depending on room size, CC, 2 ground-floor rooms, classy breakfast, quiet for being so central, laundry service-£5; a fridge, ice, and great travel library in the pleasant basement lounge; 24 Portland Street, Gillygate, YO31 7EH, tel. 01904/626-548, fax 01904/628-032, e-mail: hazwdyork@aol.com.

The Coach House Hotel is a labyrinthine, funky old place—a little musty, but well-located facing a bowling green and the abbey walls. It offers 12 comfortable old-time rooms and a crackerjack lounge (Sb-£32, D-£60, Db-£64, CC, free parking, 20 Marygate, Bootham, tel. 01904/652-780, fax 01904/679-943, e-mail: coach_house@btclick.com).

Sleeping in B&Bs along the Riverside

Three fine smoke-free places front the River Ouse midway between the train station and the minster. Each faces a pedestrian path and comes with a delightful front garden and absolutely no traffic noise. Front rooms overlook the river; back rooms watch a sprawling car park.

Water's Edge B&B, a pastel place with five comfy rooms a teddy bear would like, is well-run by Julie Mett (Db-£50, 4-poster river-view Db-£55–60, CC, 5 Earlsborough Terrace, Marygate,

Y030 7BQ, tel. 01904/644-625, fax 01904/731-516, www
.watersedgeyork.co.uk, e-mail: julie@watersedgeyork.co.uk).

Riverside Walk B&B has 14 small shipshape rooms, steep
stairs, and narrow hallways (Db-£52–55, CC for 2.5 percent extra,
free parking, 8 Earlsborough Terrace, Marygate, Y030 7BQ,
tel. 01904/620-769, fax 01904/646-249, www.riversidewalkbb
.demon.co.uk, Mr. Summers).

Abbey Guest House is similar with seven rooms (S-£25,
Sb-£30, D-£45, Db-£55, Tb-£65, Qb-£70, CC adds a small fee,
free parking, Internet access, 14 Earlsborough Terrace, Marygate,
Y030 7BQ, tel. 01904/627-782, fax 01904/671-743, e-mail:
abbey@rsummers.cix.co.uk, Hilary Summers).

Sleeping in Hotels in the Center

Travelodge offers 90 identical, affordable rooms near the Castle
Museum (Db-£60, Oct–June Db discounted to £50, kids' bed free,
CC, some smoke-free rooms, 90 Piccadilly, central reservations
tel. 0870-085-0950, www.travelodge.co.uk).

Dean Court Hotel, facing the minster, is a big, stately Best
Western–style place that has classy lounges and 40 comfortable
rooms (small Db-£105, standard Db-£130, superior Db-£145,
spacious deluxe Db-£160, CC, some nonsmoking rooms, tearoom,
restaurant, elevator to most rooms, Duncombe Place, YO1 7EF, tel.
01904/625-082, fax 01904/620-305, www.deancourt-york.co.uk).

Galtres Lodge Hotel, a block from the minster, offers comfy
rooms above a restaurant in the old-town center (S-£28, Sb-£40,
Db-£70, 1 refurbished Db-£75 and worth it, CC, nonsmoking,
54 Low Petergate, Y01 7HZ, tel. 01904/622-478, fax 01904/
627-804, www.yorkshireholidays.com).

York's Youth Hotel is well run, with a kitchen, launderette,
bar, game room, and 120 beds (S-£16, bunk bed D-£30, £14 beds
in 4- to 6-bed dorms, £9 beds in larger dorms, CC, less for multinight stays, same-sex or coed possible, no breakfast, 10-min
walk from station at 11 Bishophill Senior Road, YO1 1EF, tel.
01904/625-904, fax 01904/612-494, e-mail: info@yorkyouthhotel
.demon.co.uk).

Eating in York

Traditional Tea

York is famous for its elegant teahouses. Drop into one around
16:00 for tea and cakes. Ladies love **Betty's Teahouse** where you
pay £5 for a cream tea (tea and scones) or £9 for a full traditional
English afternoon tea (tea, elegant sandwich, scones, and sweets).
Your table is so full of doily niceties that the food is served on a
little three-tray tower. While Betty's food is nothing special, the
ambience and people watching are hard to beat (daily 09:00–21:00,

piano music nightly 18:00–21:00, CC, mostly nonsmoking, St. Helen's Square; fine view of street scene from a window seat on the main floor, downstairs near WC is a mirror signed by WWII bomber pilots—read the story). If there's a line, it moves quickly. I'd wait for a seat by the windows on ground level rather than sit in the much bigger basement.

Eating near the Minster

Of these listings, the first faces the minster, the last two are behind the minster, and the rest are on Goodramgate near the minster.

Café Concerto, a French-style bistro with a fun menu, has an understandably loyal following. Their food is the best I've had in York (great £8 lunches, £15 dinners, daily 10:00–22:00, serves meals all day, CC, smoke-free, smart to reserve for dinner, facing the minster, Petergate 21, tel. 01904/610-478).

The **Lime House Restaurant** is a small, modern, candlelit place enthusiastically run by chef Adam Fisher. His menu features European dishes revolving with the seasons and always includes a good vegetarian plate. Adam offers a free glass of house wine to anyone with this book (£10 plates, 10 percent off on orders before 19:00, Tue–Sat 12:00–14:00, 18:00–22:00, closed Sun–Mon, lunch specials, CC, 55 Goodramgate, tel. 01904/632-734).

For **Italian**, three popular places compete along Goodramgate.

There's a pub serving grub on every block. Eat where you see lots of food. The **Royal Oak** offers £5 pub grub throughout the day, a small nonsmoking room, and hand-pulled ale (daily 11:00–20:00, heavy meat dishes, fat fries, but don't look in their kitchen, CC, Goodramgate, a block from Monk Bar, a block east of the minster, tel. 01904/653-856). The **Golden Slipper**, next door, is also a classic for basic pub grub and darts.

St. Williams Restaurant, just behind the great east window of the minster in a wonderful half-timbered, 15th-century building (read the history), serves quick and tasty lunches and elegant candlelit dinners (2 courses-£14, 3 courses-£17, daily 10:00–17:00 plus Tue–Sat 18:00–22:00, traditional and Mediterranean, CC, College Street, tel. 01904/634-830).

The Viceroy of India—just outside Monk Bar and therefore outside the tourist zone—serves great Indian food at good prices to mostly locals. If you've yet to eat Indian on your trip, do it here (£8 plates, nightly 18:00–24:00, friendly staff, CC, continue straight through Monk Bar—pass the big old "nightly bile beans keep you healthy, bright-eyed, and slim" sign on your left—to 26 Monkgate, tel. 01904/622-370).

Eating near Bootham Bar and Your B&B

Gillygate Fisheries is a wonderfully traditional little fish-and-chips joint where tattooed people eat in and housebound mothers take out

(Mel serves £4–5 meals, "eat your mushy peas," Mon 17:00–23:30, Tue–Fri 11:30–14:00, 17:00–23:30, Sat 11:30–23:30, closed Sun, smoke-free seating, 2 blocks from the TI at 59 Gillygate).

The **Waggon and Horses** pub has local color and serves cheap "pub food with attitude" in a cozy smoke-free room or with the smoking beer drinkers (Mon–Sat 11:30–21:00, Sun 12:00–15:00, fresh vegetables, across from Wackers at Gillygate 48, tel. 01904/654-103).

The well-worn **Coach House** serves good-quality food with fresh vegetables but can be smoky (£8–11, nightly 18:30–21:30, CC, 20 Marygate, tel. 01904/652-780).

The **Grange Hotel's Brasserie**, a couple of blocks from the B&Bs, is classier than a pub and serves a smattering of traditional European dishes. Go downstairs—avoid the pricey ground-floor restaurant (£9 meals, Mon–Sat 12:00–14:00, 18:00–22:00, Sun 19:00–22:00, CC, 1 Clifton, tel. 01904/644-744).

Jacksons **grocery store** is open every day from 07:00–23:00 (near B&Bs, outside Bootham Bar, on Bootham). For an atmospheric **picnic spot,** try the Museum Gardens (near Bootham Bar) at the evocative 12th-century ruins of St. Mary's Abbey.

Transportation Connections—York
By train to: Durham (4/hr, 45 min), **Edinburgh** (2/hr, 2.5 hrs), **London** (2/hr, 2 hrs), **Bath** (1/hr, 5 hrs, change in Bristol), **Cambridge** (nearly hrly, 2 hrs, change in Peterborough), **Birmingham** (2/hr, 2.5 hrs), **Keswick** (with transfers to Penrith then bus, 4.5 hrs). **Train info:** tel. 08457-484-950.

Connections with London's Airports: **Heathrow** (1/hr, allow 2.5–3 hrs, take Heathrow Express train to London's Paddington station, tube to King's Cross, train to York—2/hr, 2 hrs), **Gatwick** (from Gatwick catch low-profile Thameslink train to King's Cross-Thameslink station in London; from there, walk 100 yards to King's Cross station, train to York—2/hr, 2 hrs).

The **York Bus Information Centre** is at 20 Hudson Street, near the train station (Mon–Fri 08:30–17:00, tel. 01904/551-400, phone answered Mon–Sat 08:00–20:00, Sun 08:00–14:00).

EDINBURGH

Edinburgh, the colorful city of Robert Louis Stevenson, Sir Walter Scott, and Robert Burns, is Scotland's showpiece and one of Europe's most entertaining cities. Historical, monumental, fun, and well organized, it's a tourist's delight.

Promenade down the Royal Mile through Old Town. Historic buildings pack the Royal Mile between the castle (on the top) and Holyrood Palace (on the bottom). Medieval skyscrapers stand shoulder to shoulder, hiding peaceful courtyards connected to High Street by narrow lanes or even tunnels. This colorful jumble is the tourist's Edinburgh.

Edinburgh (ED'n-burah) was once the most crowded city in Europe—famed for its skyscrapers and filth. The rich and poor lived atop one another. In the Age of Enlightenment, a magnificent Georgian city, today's New Town, was laid out to the north giving the town's upper class a respectable place to promenade. Georgian Edinburgh, like the city of Bath, shines with broad boulevards, straight streets, square squares, circular circuses, and elegant mansions decked out in colonnades, pediments, and sphinxes in the proud, neoclassical style of 200 years ago.

While the Georgian city celebrated the union of Scotland and England (with streets and squares named after English kings and emblems), "devolution" is the latest craze. In a 1998 election, the Scots voted for more autonomy and to bring their parliament home. Though Edinburgh has been the historic capital of Scotland for centuries, parliament had not met in Scotland since 1707. In 2000—while London still calls the strategic shots—Edinburgh resumed its position as home to the Scottish Parliament. A strikingly modern new parliament building, opening in 2003, will be one more jewel in Edinburgh's crown.

Planning Your Time

While the major sights can be seen in a day, I'd linger longer and give Edinburgh two days and three nights.

Day 1: Tour the castle. Then consider catching one of the city bus tours (from a block below the castle at Tolbooth church) for a 60-minute loop, returning to the castle. Explore the Royal Mile, going downhill—lunching, museum-going, shopping, taking a walking tour (one leaves at 14:00 from Mercat Cross). If you tour Holyrood Palace, do it near the end of the day and the bottom of the Mile. In the evening, take in live music at a pub, a literary pub crawl, or a haunted walk.

Day 2: Tour the Museum of Scotland. After lunch, stroll through the Princes Street Gardens and the Scottish National Gallery. Then tour the good ship *Britannia*.

Orientation (area code: 0131)

The center of Edinburgh holds the Princes Street Gardens park and Waverley Bridge, where you'll find the TI, Princes Mall, train station, bus info office (starting point for most city bus tours), National Gallery, and a covered dance-and-music pavilion. Weather blows in and out—bring your sweater.

Tourist Information: The crowded TI is as central as can be atop the Princes Mall and train station (May–June and Sept Mon–Sat 09:00–19:00, Sun 10:00–19:00; July–Aug daily until 20:00; Nov–March daily until 17:00; ATM outside entrance, tel. 0131/473-3800). Unfortunately, all their information—even which car-rental companies "exist" and their assessment of museums— is skewed by tourism payola. Buy a map (£1 if in stock, or the excellent £3.50 Collins Illustrated Edinburgh map, which comes with opinionated commentary and locates virtually every major shop and sight), and ask for the free monthly entertainment *Gig Guide* if you're interested in late-night music. The *Essential Guide to Edinburgh* (£1), while not essential, lists additional sights and services. Book your room direct without the TI's help (B&Bs charge more for rooms booked through the TI, and you pay the TI a £3 finder's fee). Browse the racks (tucked away in hallway at back of TI) for brochures on the various Scottish folk shows, walking tours, and regional bus tours. Connect@edinburgh, a small Internet café, is beyond the brochure racks (see "Hints," below). The best monthly entertainment listing, *The List*, is sold for £1.95 at newsstands.

Haggis Backpackers Ltd. has budget travel information and sells cheap one- to six-day tours around Scotland (Mon–Sat 09:00–18:00, summer Sun 14:00–18:00, 60 High Street, at Blackfriars Street, tel. 0131/557-9393, www.radicaltravel.com).

Arrival in Edinburgh: Arriving by train at Waverley Station puts you in the city center and below the TI (go up the many stairs until you surface at street level, TI to your left) and the

Edinburgh

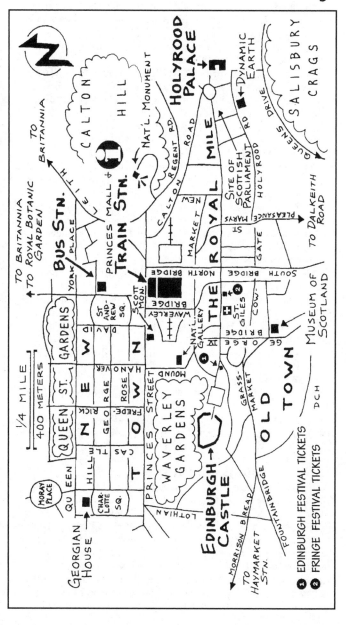

city bus to my recommended B&Bs (see "Sleeping," below, for directions to B&B neighborhood by bus). Both Scottish Citylink and National Express buses use the bus station two blocks north of the train station on St. Andrew Square in New Town.

Edinburgh's slingshot-of-an-**airport** is 10 miles northwest of the center and well-connected by taxi (£14, 30 min) and by shuttle buses with Waverley Bridge (LRT "Airline" bus #100, £3.30 or £4.20 with all-day "Airsaver" city-bus pass, 6/hr, 30 min, roughly 05:00–23:00). Flight info: tel. 0131/333-1000, BMI British Midland tel. 0870-607-0555, British Air tel. 0845-773-3377, Aer Lingus tel. 0845-973-7747.

Helpful Hints

Sunday Activities: Many sights close on Sunday, but there's still a lot to do: Royal Mile walking tour, Edinburgh Castle, St. Giles Cathedral, Holyrood Palace, Royal Botanic Gardens, climb Arthur's Seat, and city bus tour. An open-air market including antiques is held every Sunday from 10:00 to 16:00 at New Street Car Park near the train station. The Georgian House and National Gallery are open Sunday afternoon.

Internet Access: It's a cinch to get plugged in. Try Connect@edinburgh at the TI (£1/20 min, Mon–Sat 09:00–18:00, Sun 10:00–18:00, as you enter TI head back to the left down a corridor) or International Telecom Centre on the Royal Mile (£1/15 min, daily 09:00–23:00, also has cheap phones with rare sit-down booths, 52 High Street, half block east of Tron Kirk and South Bridge).

Late-Night Pharmacy: Try Boots at 48 Shandwick Place (tel. 0131/225-6757).

Car Rental: Consider Avis (5 West Park Place, tel. 0131/337-6363, airport tel. 0131/344-3900); Europcar (24 East London Street, tel. 0131/557-3456, airport tel. 0131/333-2573); Hertz (Pickardy Place, tel. 0131/556-8311, airport tel. 0131/333-1019); or Budget (394 Ferry Road, tel. 0131/551-3322, airport tel. 0131/333-1926).

Getting around Edinburgh

Nearly all Edinburgh sights are within walking distance of each other. City **buses** are handy and inexpensive (about 80p/ride, buy tickets on bus, LRT transit office at Old Town end of Waverley Bridge has schedules and route maps, tel. 0131/555-6363). Tell the driver where you're going, have change handy (most buses require exact change; you lose any excess), take your ticket as you board, push the stop button as you near your stop (so your stop isn't skipped), and exit from the middle door. Two companies handle the city routes: LRT (or Lothian) does most of it and First does the rest (e.g., to get from the city center to the recommended

B&Bs on Dalkeith Road, you can catch LRT buses #14, #21, and #33 or First buses #C3 and #86). Day passes sold by each company are valid only on their buses (£2.20, or £1.50 after 09:30 weekdays and all day weekends, buy from driver). Buses run from about 06:00 to 23:00. **Taxis** are reasonable (easy to flag down, average ride between downtown and B&B district-£4).

Bus Tours of Edinburgh

▲**Hop-on Hop-off City Bus Tours**—Three companies offer 60-minute bus tours that circle the town center stopping at the biggies—Waverley Bridge, the castle, Royal Mile, Georgian New Town, and Princes Street—with an informative narration and pickups about every 10 to 15 minutes. You can hop on and off with one ticket all day, but not 24 hours. Hop on at any stop or go to Waverley Bridge to comparison shop between your bus-tour options.

Guide Friday has a live guide (£8.50, £10 combo ticket includes round-trip transportation to Britannia—which normally costs £3.50, ticket gives 10 percent discount off castle admission, tel. 0131/556-2244). LRT's "Edinburgh Classic Tour," which runs a little more frequently, uses headphones with a recorded narration (£7.50, tel. 0131/555-6363). Mac Tours' "Edinburgh by Vintage Bus" has a live guide, fewer buses, and a shorter route (£7.50, 3/hr, 50 min, ticket bought after 17:00 also valid the next day).

On sunny days they go topless (the buses), but they also suffer from traffic noise and congestion. Buses run year-round. First and last buses leave Waverley Bridge around 09:00 and continue until 19:00 mid-June through early September (last buses leave earlier off-season).

Sights—Edinburgh

▲▲▲**Edinburgh Castle**—The fortified birthplace of the city 1,300 years ago, this imposing symbol of Edinburgh sits proudly on a rock high above the city. While the castle has been both a fort and a royal residence since the 11th century, most of the buildings today are from its more recent use as a military garrison. It's a fascinating and multifaceted sight deserving several hours (£7.50, daily 09:30–18:00, Oct–March 09:30–17:00, CC, cafeteria, tel. 0131/225-9846; consider avoiding the long uphill walk from the nearest city bus stop by taking a cab to the castle gate).

Entry Gate: Start with the wonderfully droll 30-minute guided introduction tour (free with admission, departs 2–4 times/hr from entry, see clock for next departure; few tours run off-season). The audioguide is excellent, with four hours of quick digital dial descriptions (free with admission, pick up at entry gate before meeting the live guide). The clean WC at the entry annually wins "British Loo of the Year" awards (marvel at the plaques near men's room), but they use a one-way mirror showing the sink area in the women's room (women: pop your head into office near men's room to complain or make sure mirror is curtained).

In the castle there are five essential stops: Crown Jewels, Royal Palace, Scottish National War Memorial, St. Margaret's Chapel with city view, and the excellent National War Museum of Scotland. The first four are at the highest and most secure point—on or near the castle square, where your introductory guided tour ends. The War Museum is 50 yards below by the cafeteria and big shop.

1. Crown Jewels: The line of tourists leads from the square directly to the jewels. Skip this line and enter the building around to the left (next to WC) where you'll get to the jewels via a wonderful *Honors of Scotland* exhibition about the crown jewels and how they survived the harrowing centuries.

Scotland's **Crown Jewels** are older than England's. While Cromwell destroyed England's, the Scots hid theirs successfully. Longtime symbols of Scottish nationalism, they were made in Edinburgh—of Scottish gold, diamonds, and gems—in 1540 for a 1543 coronation. They were last used to crown Charles II in 1651. While the Act of Union, which dissolved Scotland's parliament into England's to create the United Kingdom in 1707, was forced upon the Scots, part of the deal was that they could keep their jewels locked up in Edinburgh. They remained hidden for over 100 years. In 1818 Walter Scott and a royal commission rediscovered the jewels intact.

The **Stone of Scone** sits plain and strong next to the jewels. This big gray chunk of rock is the coronation stone of Scotland's ancient kings (9th century). Swiped by the English, it sat under the coronation chair at Westminster Abbey from 1296 until 1996. With major fanfare, Scotland's treasured Stone of Scone returned to Edinburgh on Saint Andrew's Day, November 30, 1996. Talk to the guard for more details.

2. The Royal Palace (facing castle square under the flag pole) has two historic yet unimpressive rooms (through door reading 1566) and the Great Hall (separate entrance from the same castle square). Remember, Scottish royalty only lived here when safety or protocol required. They preferred the **Holyrood Palace** at the bottom of the Royal Mile. Enter the **Mary Queen of Scots room**, where in 1566 the queen gave birth to James VI of Scotland, who later became King James I of England. The **Presence Chamber** leads into **Laich Hall** (Lower Hall), the dining room of the royal family.

The **Great Hall** was the castle's ceremonial meeting place in the 16th and 17th centuries. In modern times it was a barracks and a hospital. While most of what you see is Victorian, two medieval elements survive: the fine hammer-beam roof and the big iron-barred peephole (above fireplace on right). This allowed the king to spy on his partying subjects.

3. The Scottish National War Memorial commemorates the 149,000 Scottish soldiers lost in World War I, the 58,000 lost in World War II, and the 750 lost in British battles since. Each bay is dedicated to a particular Scottish regiment. The main shrine, featuring a green Italian-marble memorial containing the original WWI rolls of honor, actually sits upon an exposed chunk of the castle rock. Above you, the archangel Michael is busy slaying the dragon. The bronze frieze accurately shows the attire of various wings of Scotland's military. The stained glass starts with Cain and Abel on the left and finishes with a celebration of peace on the right. If the importance of this place is hard to understand, consider that one out of every three adult Scottish men died in World War I.

4. St. Margaret's Chapel, the oldest building in Edinburgh, is dedicated to Queen Margaret, who died here in 1093 and was sainted in 1250. Built in 1130 in the Romanesque style of the Norman invaders, it is wonderfully simple, with classic Norman zigzags decorating the round arch that separates the tiny nave from the sacristy. Used as a powder magazine for 400 years, very little survives. You'll see an 11th-century gospel book of St. Margaret's and small windows featuring St. Margaret, St. Columba (who brought Christianity to Scotland via Iona), and William Wallace (the brave defender of Scotland). The place is popular for weddings and, since it seats only 20, particularly popular with brides' fathers.

Mons Meg—a huge and once-upon-a-time frightening 15th-century siege cannon that fired 330-pound stones nearly two miles—stands in front of the church.

Belly up to the bannister (outside the chapel below the cannon) to enjoy the great view. Below you are the guns—which fire the one o'clock salute—and a sweet little line of doggie tombstones, the soldiers' pet cemetery. Beyond stretches the Georgian New Town (read the informative plaque).

5. The National War Museum of Scotland thoughtfully covers four centuries of Scottish military history. Instead of the usual musty, dusty displays of endless armor, this museum has an interesting mix of short films, uniforms, weapons, medals, mementos, and eloquent excerpts from soldiers' letters. A pleasant surprise just when you thought your castle visit was about over, this rivals any military museum you'll see in Europe.

When leaving the castle, turn around and look back at the gate. There stand King Robert the Bruce (on the left, 1274–1329) and Sir William Wallace (Braveheart—on the right, 1270–1305). Wallace (newly famous, thanks to Mel Gibson) fought long and hard against English domination before being executed in

London—his body cut to pieces and paraded through the far corners of jolly olde England. Bruce beat the English at Bannockburn in 1314. Bruce and Wallace still defend the spirit of Scotland. The Latin inscription above the gate between them reads (basically) "What you do to us...we will do to you."

Sights—Along the Royal Mile

These are listed in walking order, from top to bottom. (Bus #35 runs along the Mile, handy for going up after you've hit bottom.)

▲▲▲**Royal Mile**—This is one of Europe's most interesting historic walks. Start at the top and amble down to the palace. The Royal Mile, which consists of a series of four different streets—Castlehill, Lawnmarket, High Street, and Canongate (each with its own set of street numbers)—is actually 200 yards longer than a mile. And every inch is packed with shops, cafés, and lanes leading to tiny squares. As you walk, remember that originally, there were two settlements here, divided by a wall: Edinburgh lined the ridge from the castle at the top. The lower end, Cannongate, was outside the wall until 1856. By poking down the many side alleys, you'll find a few rough edges of a town well on its way to becoming a touristic mall. See it now. In a few years tourists will be slaloming through the postcard racks on bagpipe skateboards.

Royal Mile Terminology: A "close" is a tiny alley between two buildings (originally with a door that closed it at night). A close usually leads to a "court" or courtyard. A "land" is a tenement block of apartments. A "pend" is an arched gateway. A "wynd" is a narrow winding lane. And "gate" is from an old Scandinavian word for street.

Royal Mile Walking Tours: Mercat Tours offers two-hour guided walks of the Mile—more entertaining than historic (£6, April–Sept daily at 11:00 and 14:00, Oct–March daily 11:15 only, from Mercat Cross on the Royal Mile, tel. 0131/557-6464). The guides, who enjoy making a short story long, ignore the big sights, taking you behind the scenes with piles of barely historic gossip, bully-pulpit Scottish pride, and fun but forgettable trivia. They also offer a variety of other tours. In August only, the Voluntary Guides Association leads free tours of Edinburgh; call for a schedule (tel. 0131/664-7180).

Castle Esplanade—At the top of the Royal Mile, the big parking lot leading up to the castle was created as a military parade ground in 1816. It's often cluttered with bleachers under construction for the Military Tattoo—a spectacular massing of the bands that fills the square nightly for most of August (see "Edinburgh Festival," below). At the bottom, on the left (where the square hits the road), a plaque above the tiny witch's fountain memorializes 300 women who were accused of witchcraft and burned here. Scotland burned more witches per capita than any other country—17,000 between

Royal Mile

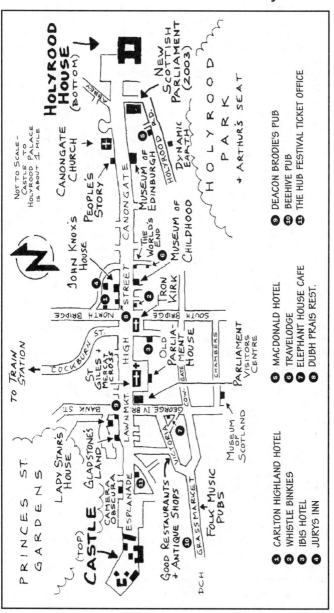

NOT TO SCALE –
CASTLE TO
HOLYROOD PALACE
IS ABOUT 1 MILE

HOLYROOD HOUSE (BOTTOM)

NEW SCOTTISH PARLIAMENT (2003)

CANONGATE CHURCH

PEOPLE'S STORY

MUSEUM OF EDINBURGH

DYNAMIC EARTH

HOLYROOD PARK + ARTHUR'S SEAT

JOHN KNOX'S HOUSE

THE WORLD'S END

MUSEUM OF CHILDHOOD

TRON KIRK

CANONGATE

NORTH BRIDGE

SOUTH BRIDGE

COCKBURN ST.

ST. ANDREW SQ.

HIGH STREET

OLD PARLIAMENT HOUSE

ST. GILES + MERCAT CROSS

PARLIAMENT VISITORS CENTRE

CHAMBERS

GEORGE IV BR.

COWGATE

VICTORIA

MUSEUM OF SCOTLAND

TO TRAIN STATION

PRINCES ST. GARDENS

LADY STAIR'S HOUSE

GLADSTONE'S LAND

CAMERA OBSCURA

ESPLANADE

BANK ST.

LAWN MKT.

GOOD RESTAURANTS + ANTIQUE SHOPS

FOLK MUSIC PUBS

GRASSMARKET

CASTLE (TOP)

DCH

① CARLTON HIGHLAND HOTEL
② WHISTLE BINKIES
③ IBIS HOTEL
④ JURYS INN

⑤ MACDONALD HOTEL
⑥ TRAVELODGE
⑦ ELEPHANT HOUSE CAFE
⑧ DUBH PRAIS REST.

⑨ DEACON BRODIE'S PUB
⑩ BEEHIVE PUB
⑪ THE HUB FESTIVAL TICKET OFFICE

1479 and 1722. But in a humanitarian gesture, rather than burning them alive as was the custom in the rest of Europe, Scottish "witches" were strangled to death before they were burned. The plaque shows two witches: one good and one bad. (For 90 minutes of this kind of Royal Mile trivia, take the guided tour described above.)

Camera Obscura—A big deal when built in 1853, this observatory topped with a mirror reflected images onto a disc before the wide eyes of people who had never seen a photograph or captured image. Today you can climb 100 steps for an entertaining 15-minute demonstration (3/hr). At the top enjoy the best view anywhere of the Royal Mile. Then work your way down through three floors of illusions, holograms, and early photos. This is a big hit with kids (£4.75, daily 09:30–19:30, less off-season, tel. 0131/2263709).

Scotch Whiskey Heritage Centre—This touristy ambush is designed only to distill £6.50 out of your pocket. You get a video history, a short talk, and a little whiskey-keg train-car ride before downing a free sample and finding yourself in the shop 45 minutes later. Those in a hurry are offered the unadvertised quickie— a sample and a whiskey-keg ride for £4.25. People do seem to enjoy it, but that might have something to do with the sample (tel. 0131/220-0441).

The Hub/Tolbooth Church—This neo-Gothic church (1844), with the tallest spire in the city, is now The Hub, Edinburgh's Festival Ticket and Information Centre. From here, Johnston Terrace leads down to Grassmarket Street's lively pub scene (see "Nightlife in Edinburgh," below).

▲▲Gladstone's Land—Take a good look at this typical 16th- to 17th-century merchant's house, complete with a lived-in furnished interior and guides in each room who love to talk (£3.50, Mon–Sat 10:00–17:00, Sun 14:00–17:00, last entry at 16:30). For a good Royal Mile photo, lean out the upper-floor window (or simply climb the curved stairway outside the museum to the left of the entrance). Notice the snoozing pig outside the front door. Just like every house has a vacuum cleaner today, in the 14th century a snorting rubbish collector was a standard feature of any well-equipped house.

▲Writers' Museum at Lady Stair's House—This interesting house, built in 1622, is filled with well-described manuscripts and knickknacks of Scotland's three greatest literary figures: Robert Burns, Sir Walter Scott, and Robert Louis Stevenson. It's worth a few minutes for anyone and is fascinating for fans (free, Mon–Sat 10:00–17:00, closed Sun). Wander around the courtyard here. Edinburgh was a wonder in the 17th and 18th centuries. Tourists came here to see its skyscrapers, which towered 10 stories and higher. No city in Europe was so densely populated as "Auld Reekie."

Deacon Brodie's Tavern—This is a decent place for a light meal (see "Eating," below). Read the story of its notorious name-sake on the wall facing Bank Street. Then check out both sides of the hanging signpost.

Visitors Centre of the Scottish Parliament—Scotland's Parliament goes back to 1293, was dissolved by England in 1707, and returned in 1999. This new center, kitty-corner to Deacon Brodie's on George IV Bridge, proudly introduces the new Scottish Parliament. Exhibits explain how the parliament works, and models show the building where it will work (currently an expensive hole in the ground near Holyrood Palace, due to open in 2003). At the Visitors Centre (free, Mon–Fri 10:00–17:00, closed Sat–Sun), you can sign up to witness the new Scottish Parliament debating and creating Scottish history in their tempo-rary quarters, a few steps off the Royal Mile, tucked away in Mylnes Court, across from The Hub (debates Wed 14:30–17:30, Thu 09:30–12:30, 14:30–17:30, tel. 0131/348-5411).

Heart of Midlothian—Near the street in front of the cathedral, find the outline of a heart in the brickwork. This marks the spot of a gallows and a prison now long gone. Traditionally, locals stand on the rim of the heart and spit into it. Hitting the middle brings good luck. Go ahead...do as the locals do.

▲▲St. Giles Cathedral—Wander through Scotland's most impor-tant church. Stepping inside, find John Knox's statue. Look into his eyes for 10 seconds from 10 inches away. Knox, the great reformer and founder of austere Scottish Presbyterianism, first preached here in 1559. His insistence that every person should be able to read the word of God gave Scotland an educational system 300 years ahead of the rest of Europe. For this reason it was Scottish minds that led the way in math, science, medicine, engineering, and so on. Voltaire called Scotland "the intellectual capital of Europe."

Knox preached Calvinism. Consider that the Dutch and the Scots were about the only nations to embrace this creed of hard work, thrift, and strict ethics. This helps explain why the English and the Scottish are so different (and why the Dutch and the Scots—both famous for their thriftiness and industriousness—are so much alike).

Speaking of intellects, look up at the modern window filling the West Wall celebrating Scotland's favorite poet, Robert Burns. It was made in 1985 by an Icelandic artist (Leifur Breidfjord).

The oldest parts of the cathedral—the four massive central pillars—date from 1120. After the English burnt the cathedral in 1385, it was rebuilt bigger and better than ever, and in 1495 its famous crown spire was completed. During the Reformation—when Knox preached here (1559–1572)—the place was simplified and whitewashed. Before this, with the emphasis on holy services provided by priests, there were lots of little niches. With the new focus on sermons rather than rituals, the floorplan was opened up and the grand pulpit took center stage. The organ (1992, Austrian-built) is one of the best in Europe and comes with a glass panel in the back for peeking into the mechanism.

The neo-Gothic **Chapel of the Knights of the Thistle** (in the far right corner, from 1911), with its intricate wood carving, was built in two years entirely with Scottish material and labor. Find the angel tooting the bagpipes (from inside chapel, above the door to the right). The Scottish crown steeple from 1495 is a proud part of Edinburgh's skyline (Mon–Sat 09:00–17:00, open later and on Sun in summer; ask about concerts—some are free, usually Thu at 13:00; café and WC downstairs; see "Eating," below).

John Knox is buried out back—austerely, under the parking lot, at spot 44. The statue among the cars shows King Charles II riding to a toga party back in 1685.

Parliament House—Stop in to see the grand hall with its fine 1639 hammer-beam ceiling and stained glass. This hall housed the Scottish Parliament until the Act of Union in 1707 (explained in history exhibition under the big stained-glass depiction of the initiation of the first Scottish High Court in 1532). It now holds the law courts and is busy with wigged and robed lawyers hard at work in the old library (peek through the door) or pacing the hall deep in discussion. The friendly doorman is helpful (free, public welcome Mon–Fri 09:00–16:30, best action midmornings Tue–Fri, open-to-the-public trials 10:00–16:00—doorman has day's docket, entry behind St. Giles Cathedral near parking spot 21).

Mercat Cross—This chunky pedestal, on the downhill side of St. Giles, holds a slender column topped with a white unicorn. Royal proclamations have been read from here since the 14th century. The tradition survives. In 1952, three days (traditionally the time it took for a horse to speed here from London) after the actual event, a town cryer heralded the news that England had a new queen. Today Mercat Cross is the meeting point of various walking tours—both historic and ghostly. Pop into the police information center, a few doors downhill, for a little local law-and-order history (free, May–Aug daily 10:00–22:00, less off-season).

Tron Kirk—This fine old building, used as a sales base for a local walking-tour company, sits over an old excavation site and houses a free Old Town history display.

Cockburn Street—Across from Tron Kirk, this street was cut through High Street's dense wall of medieval skyscrapers in the 1860s to give easy access to the new Georgian town and the train station. Notice how the sliced buildings were thoughtfully capped with facades in a faux 16th-century Scottish Baronial style. In medieval times, only tiny lanes (like the Fleshmarket Lane just uphill from Cockburn Street) interrupted the long line of Royal Mile buildings. Continue downhill to the old half-timbered building jutting out (John Knox House). Across the street is the...

Scottish Words

aye	yes	**inch, innis**	island
ben	mountain	**inver**	river, mouth
bonnie	beautiful	**kyle**	strait
carn	heap of stones	**loch**	lake
creag	rock, cliff	**neeps**	turnips
tattie	potato	**cello tape**	scotch tape

haggis   rich assortment of oats and sheep organs stuffed into a chunk of sheep intestine, liberally seasoned, boiled, and eaten mostly by tourists. Usually served with "neeps and tatties." Tastier than it sounds.

▲**Museum of Childhood**—This five-story playground of historical toys and games—called the noisiest museum in the world because of its delighted tiny visitors—is rich in nostalgia and history (free, Mon–Sat 10:00–17:00, closed Sun). Just downhill is a fragrant fudge shop offering free samples.

▲**John Knox House**—Fascinating for Reformation buffs, this fine 16th-century house offers a well-explained look at the life of the great reformer (£2.25, Mon–Sat 10:00–17:00, closed Sun, 43 High Street). While Knox never actually lived here, it was called "his house" to save it from the wrecking ball in 1850.

The World's End—For centuries, a wall halfway down the Royal Mile marked the end of Edinburgh and the beginning of Cannongate, a community associated with the Holyrood Abbey. Today, where the mile hits St. Mary's and Jeffrey Streets, High Street becomes Cannongate. Just below John Knox House (at #43) notice the hanging sign showing the old gate. At the intersection, find the brass bricks tracing the gate (demolished in 1764). Look down St. Mary's Street to see a surviving bit of that old wall. Then, entering Cannongate, you leave what was Edinburgh...

▲**People's Story**—This interesting exhibition traces the lot of the working class through the 18th, 19th, and 20th centuries (free, Mon–Sat 10:00–17:00, closed Sun). Curiously, while this museum is dedicated to the proletariat, immediately around the back is the tomb of Adam Smith—the author of *Wealth of Nations* and the father of modern capitalism (1723–1790).

▲**Museum of Edinburgh**—Another old house full of old stuff, this one is worth a look for its early Edinburgh history and handy ground-floor WC. Don't miss the original copy of the National Covenant (written in 1638 on an animal skin), sketches of pre-Georgian Edinburgh (which show a lake, later filled in to become

Princes Street Gardens when New Town was built), and early golf balls (free, Mon–Sat 10:00–17:00, closed Sun).

White Horse Close—Step into this 17th-century courtyard (bottom of Canongate, on the left, a block before Holyrood Palace). It was from here that the Edinburgh stagecoach left for London. Eight days later, the horse-drawn carriage pulled into its destination: Scotland Yard. Across the street is the extravagant new Scottish Parliament building (described below).

▲**Holyrood Palace**—A palace since the 14th century, this marks the end of the Royal Mile. The queen spends a week in Scotland each summer, during which this is her official residence and office. The abbey—part of a 12th-century Augustinian monastery—stood here first. It was named for a piece of the cross brought here as a relic by queen-then-saint Margaret. Scotland's royalty preferred living here to the blustery castle on the rock, and, gradually, the palace grew. The building is rich in history and decor. But without information or a guided tour ("there's none of either," snickered the guy who sells the boring £3.70 museum guidebooks), you're just another peasant in the dark. Docents in each room are happy to give you the answer if you know the question. After wandering through the elegantly furnished rooms and a few dark older rooms filled with glass cases of historic bits and Scottish pieces that must be fascinating, you're free to wander through the ruined abbey and the queen's gardens (£6.50, daily 09:30–18:00, Nov–April until 16:30, while no tours are offered during peak season guided tours are mandatory off-season—2/hr, last admission 45 min before closing, CC; closed last 2 weeks in May, 10 days in early July, when the queen's home, and whenever a prince drops in, tel. 0131/556-7371).

▲**New Scottish Parliament Building**—Slated to open in 2003, the parliament building is being constructed at the base of the Royal Mile next to Holyrood Palace. England forced the union in 1707 and only in 1999 did Scotland win back its parliament and autonomy (at least for domestic concerns). The Visitor Centre (free, daily 10:00–16:00, between Holyrood Palace and big white Dynamic Earth tent) makes a valiant effort to sell this extravagant and therefore controversial building to the Scotch public (don't miss the 10-min video in a room filled with interior/exterior photos of Europe's other great parliament buildings). As a conversation starter, ask a local what he/she thinks about the building's architect, expense, design, and so on.

Dynamic Earth—This immense exhibit, filling several underground floors under a vast Gortex tent appropriately pitched at the base of the Salisbury Crags, tells the story of our planet. It's designed for younger kids and does the same thing an American science exhibit would do—but with a charming Scottish accent. Standing in a time tunnel, you watch time rewind from Churchill to dinosaurs to that first big poof. After several short films on stars, tectonic plates, and ice caps, you're free to wander past salty pools, a re-created rain forest, and various TV screens, ending your visit with a 12-minute video finale (£8, family deals, April–Oct daily 10:00–18:00, Nov–March Wed–Sun 10:00–17:00, last ticket sold 70 min before closing, on Holyrood Road, between the palace and mountain, tel. 0131/550-7800).

▲▲▲**Museum of Scotland**—This huge new museum has amassed more historic artifacts than everything I've seen in Scotland combined. It's all wonderfully displayed with fine descriptions offering a best-anywhere hike through the history of Scotland: prehistoric, Roman, Viking, the "birth of Scotland," all the way to life in the 20th century. Audioguides (£2, worthwhile if planning to spend a couple of hours) offer a pleasant (if slow) description of various rooms and exhibits and even provide mood music for your wanderings (free, Mon–Sat 10:00–17:00, Tue until 20:00, Sun 12:00–17:00, free 1-hr orientation tours daily at 14:00, 2 long blocks south of Royal Mile from St. Giles Church, Chambers Street, off George IV Bridge, tel. 0131/247-4422, www.nms.ac.uk).

The **Royal Museum**, next door, fills a fine iron-and-glass Industrial-Age building (built to house the museum in 1851) with all the natural sciences as it "presents the world to Scotland." It's great for school kids, but of no special interest to foreign visitors (free, same hrs as Museum of Scotland). The famous statue of Greyfriars Bobby (Edinburgh's favorite dog—a terrier immortalized by Disney—who stood by his master's grave for 14 years) is across the street. Every business nearby is named for the pooch that put the fidelity into Fido.

More Bonnie Wee Sights

▲**Georgian New Town**—Cross Waverley Bridge and walk through Georgian Edinburgh. According to the 1776 plan, it was three streets (Princes, George, and Queen) flanked by two squares (St. Andrew and Charlotte), woven together by alleys (Thistle and Rose). George Street—20 feet wider than the others (so a 4-horse carriage could make a U-turn)—was the main drag. And, while Princes Street has gone down market, George Street still maintains its old elegance. The entire elegantly-planned New Town—laid out when George was king—celebrated the hard-to-sell notion that Scotland was an integral part of the United Kingdom. The streets and squares are named after the British royalty (Hanover was the royal family surname). Even Thistle and Rose Streets are emblems of the two happily paired nations. Rose Street, mostly pedestrian-only, is famous for its rowdy pubs. Where it hits St. Andrew's Square, Rose Street is flanked by the venerable Jenners department store and a Sainsbury supermarket. Sprinkled with popular restaurants and bars, stately New Town is turning trendy.

▲▲**Georgian House**—This refurbished Georgian house, set on

Edinburgh's finest Georgian square, is a trip back to 1796. A volunteer guide in each of the five rooms is trained in the force-feeding of stories and trivia. Start your visit with two interesting videos (£5, Mon–Sat 10:00–17:00, Sun 14:00–17:00, videos total 30 min and cover architecture and Georgian lifestyles, shown in the basement, 7 Charlotte Square, tel. 0131/225-2160). A walk down George Street after your visit here can be fun for the imagination.

▲▲**National Gallery**—This elegant neoclassical building has a delightfully small but impressive collection of European master-pieces, from Raphael, Titian, and Rubens to Gainsborough, Monet, and van Gogh. And it offers the best look you'll get at Scottish paintings. The gallery's free, but investing £2 in the fine audioguide makes the museum's highlights yours as well (Mon–Sat 10:00–17:00, Sun 12:00–17:00, tel. 0131/624-6200). After your visit, if the sun's out, enjoy a wander through Princes Street Gardens.

Princes Street Gardens—This grassy park, a former lake bed, separates Edinburgh's New and Old Towns and offers a wonderful escape from the city. Once the private domain of the local wealthy, it was opened to the public in about 1870, not as a democratic ges-ture, but because it was thought that allowing the public into the park would increase sales for the Princes Street department stores. There are plenty of free concerts and country dances in the summer and the oldest floral clock in the world. Join the local office workers for a picnic lunch break.

▲**Walter Scott Monument**—Built in 1840, this elaborate, neo-Gothic monument honors the great author, one of Edinburgh's many illustrious sons. Scott, who died in 1832, is considered the father of the romantic historical novel. The 200-foot monument shelters a marble statue of Scott and his dog Maida, surrounded by busts of 16 great Scottish poets and 64 characters from his books. Scott was a great dog lover. Of the 30 dogs he had in his lifetime, his favorite was a deerhound named Maida. Climb 287 steps for a fine view of the city (£2.50, March–Oct Mon–Sat 09:00–18:00, Nov–Feb until 16:00, closed Sun).

Royal Botanic Garden—Britain's second-oldest botanical garden, established in 1670 for medicinal herbs, is now one of Europe's best (free, March and Sept 09:30–18:00, April–Aug 09:30–19:00, Nov–Jan 09:30–16:00, Feb and Oct 09:30–17:00, 90-min "rain forest to desert" tours April–Sept daily at 11:00 and 14:00 for £2, 1 mile north of center at Inverleith Row, tel. 0131/552-7171).

Sights—Near Edinburgh

▲*Britannia*—This much-revered vessel, which carted around Britain's royal family for over 40 years and 900 voyages, is retired, permanently moored at Edinburgh's Port of Leith. It's open to the public and worth the 15-minute bus or taxi ride from the center. After watching a video about the ship, wander through the museum filled with fascinating royal-family-afloat history. Then, armed with your included audioguide, hike the stairs to the ship's top deck and begin working your way down. You'll tour the bridge, dining room, and living quarters, following in the historic footsteps of such notables as Churchill, Gandhi, and Reagan. It's easy to see how the royals must have loved the privacy this floating retreat offered (£8, April–Oct daily 09:30–18:00, Oct–March daily 10:00–17:00, last ticket sold 1.5 hrs before closing; to get to ship from Edinburgh, catch city bus X50 at Waverley Bridge—£3 round-trip, or take the Guide Friday bus—£3.50 round-trip—covered by Guide Friday's £10 combo city-tour ticket; cheap café on site, tel. 0131/555-5566, www.royalyachtbritannia.co.uk).

Edinburgh Crystal—Blowing, molding, cutting, polishing, and engraving, the Edinburgh Crystal Company glassworks tour smashes anything you'll see in Venice (£3, daily 10:00–16:30, kids under 8 not admitted). There is a shop full of "bargain" second-quality pieces, a video show, and a cafeteria. A free minibus shuttle departs from Waverley Bridge at the top of the hour (summer daily 10:00–15:00), or you can drive 10 miles south of town on A701 to Penicuik. You can schedule a more expensive VIP tour (£5) where you actually blow and cut glass (tel. 01968/675-128).

Activities in Edinburgh

▲▲**Arthur's Seat Hike**—A 45-minute hike up the 822-foot volcanic mountain (surrounded by a fine park overlooking Edinburgh), starting from the Holyrood Palace, rewards you with a commanding view. You can drive up most of the way from behind (follow the one-way street from the palace, park by the little lake) or run up like they did in *Chariots of Fire*. From the parking lot (immediately south of Holyrood Palace), you'll see two trails going up. For an easier grade, take the wide path to the left and skip the steeper path that begins with steps and skirts the base of the cliffs. You can also hike up to the Seat from the Dalkeith B&B neighborhood. Take the road (Holyrood Park Road) that borders the Commonwealth pool, turn right (on Queen's Drive), and continue to a small car park. From here, it's a 20-minute hike.

Brush Skiing—If you'd rather be skiing, the Midlothian Ski Centre in Hillend has a hill on the edge of town with a chair-lift, two slopes, a jump slope, and rentable skis, boots, and poles. While you're actually skiing over what seems like a million toothbrushes, it feels like snow skiing on a slushy day. Beware: Local doctors are used to treating an ailment called "Hillend Thumb"—thumbs dislocated when people fall here and get tangled in the brush (£6.60/first hr, then £2.70/hr, includes gear, Mon–Fri 09:30–21:00, Sat–Sun 09:30–17:00, closed last 2 weeks of June, probably closed if it snows, LRT bus #4 from Princes Street—garden side, tel. 0131/445-4433).

▲**Royal Commonwealth Games Swimming Pool**—This immense pool is open to the public, with a well-equipped fitness center (£5.80, includes swim), sauna (£6.50 extra, BYO suit), and a cafeteria overlooking the pool (£3 for pool admission only, Mon–Fri 06:00–21:30, Sat–Sun 10:00–16:30, closed 09:00–10:00 every Wed, no towels or suit rentals, tel. 0131/667-7211).

More Hikes—You can hike along the river (called Water of Leith) through Edinburgh. Locals favor the stretch between Roseburn and Dean Village, but the 1.5-mile walk from Dean Village to the Royal Botanic Garden is also good. This and other hikes are described in the TI's *Walks in and around Edinburgh* (ask for the free 1-page flyer, not their £2 guide to walks).

Shopping—For shopping consider: Princes Street (the elegant old Jenners department store is nearby on Rose Street, at St. Andrew's Square), Victoria Street (antiques galore), Nicolson Street (south of the Royal Mile for a line of interesting second-hand stores), and the Royal Mile (touristy but competitively-priced, shops usually open 09:00–17:30, later on Thu, some closed Sun).

Bus Tours to Countryside—Many companies offer daytrips to regional sights (such as Loch Ness). Comparison-shop at the TI's brochure rack. Haggis Backpackers (see "Orientation," above) runs very cheap daytrips (£21, choose between distillery visit and northern Highlands or Loch Lomond and southern Highlands) and overnight trips for young backpackers (but welcoming travelers of all ages) wanting a quick look at the bonnie countryside. Three-daytrips (£80, overnights in hostels on Isle of Skye and Loch Ness) and six-daytrips (£140, overnights in hostels in Oban, Isle of Skye, and Loch Ness) include a tour guide and transport on a 22-seat bus, but hostels cost extra.

Edinburgh Festival

One of Europe's great cultural events, Edinburgh's annual festival turns the city into a carnival of culture. There are enough music, dance, art, drama, and multicultural events to make even the most jaded traveler drool with excitement. Every day is jammed with formal and spontaneous fun. A number of festivals—official, fringe, book, film, and jazz and blues—rage simultaneously for about three weeks each August, with the Military Tattoo starting a week earlier (the best overall Web site is www.edinburghfestivals.co.uk). Many city sights run on extended hours, and those that normally close on Sunday (Writers' Museum, Museum of Edinburgh, People's Story, and Museum of Childhood) open in the afternoon. It's a glorious time to be in Edinburgh.

The official festival (August 11–31 in 2002) is the original, more formal, and likely to get booked up first. Major events sell out well in advance. The ticket office is at The Hub, located in a former church (with café, ATM, and WC) near the top of the

Royal Mile (tickets-£4-55, CC, booking from mid-April on, office open Mon–Sat 10:00–17:00 or longer, in Aug until 20:00 plus Sun 10:00–17:00, tel. 0131/473-2000, fax 0131/473-2003). Or book online at www.eif.co.uk.

The less-formal **Fringe Festival** features "on the edge" comedy and theater (CC, Aug 4–26 in 2002, ticket/info office just below St. Giles Cathedral on the Royal Mile, 180 High Street, tel. 0131/226-0001, bookings tel. 0131/226-0000, can book online from mid-June on, www.edfringe.com). Tickets are usually available at the door, but popular shows can sell out.

Other festivals in August: jazz and blues (tel. 0131/467-5200, www.jazzmusic.co.uk), film (tel. 0131/229-2550, www.edfilmfest .org.uk), and book (tel. 0131/228-5444, www.edbookfest.co.uk).

The **Military Tattoo** is a massing of the bands, drums, and bagpipes with groups from all over what was the British Empire. Displaying military finesse with a stirring lone-piper finale, this grand spectacle fills the castle esplanade nightly except Sunday, normally from a week before the festival starts until a week before it finishes (Aug 2–24 in 2002). Shows occur Monday through Friday at 21:00 and on Saturdays at 19:30 and 22:30 (£10–28, CC, booking starts in Dec, Fri–Sat shows sell out first; office open Mon–Fri 10:00–16:30, during Tattoo open until showtime and Sat 10:00–19:30 and Sun 12:00–17:00; 33 Market Street, behind—and south of—Waverley train station, tel. 0131/225-1188, www.edintattoo.co.uk). If nothing else, it is a really big show.

If you do manage to hit Edinburgh during the festival, book a room far in advance and extend your stay by a day or two. While Fringe tickets and most Tattoo tickets are available the day of the show, you may want to book a couple of official events in advance. Do it directly by telephone, leaving your credit-card number. Pick up your ticket at the office the day of the show. Several publications—including the festival's official schedule, the *Edinburgh Festivals Guide Daily*, *The List*, the *Fringe Program*, and the *Daily Diary*—list and evaluate festival events.

Nightlife in Edinburgh

▲**Ghost Walks**—These walks are an entertaining and cheap night out (offered nightly, usually 19:00 and 21:00, easy socializing for solo travelers). The theatrical and creatively staged **Witchery Tours**, the most established of the ghost tours, offer two different walks: "Ghosts and Gore" and "Murder and Mystery" (£7, 90 min, reservations required, leave from the top of the Royal Mile near Castle esplanade, tel. 0131/225-6745).

▲▲**Literary Pub Tour**—This two-hour walk is interesting even if you think Walter Scott was an arctic explorer. You'll follow the witty dialogue of two actors as they debate whether the great literature of Scotland was the creative re-creation of fun-loving louts fueled by a love of whiskey or high art. You'll wander from the Grassmarket, over Old Town to New Town, with stops in three pubs as your guides share their takes on Scotland's literary greats. The tour meets at the Beehive Pub on Grassmarket (£7, nightly in summer at 19:30, with earlier and later tours according to demand, most nights off-season; call 0131/226-6665 to confirm).

▲**Scottish Folk Evenings**—These £35 to £40 dinner shows, generally for tour groups and Japanese travelers intent on photographing old cultural clichés, are held in huge halls of expensive hotels. (Prices are bloated to include 20 percent commissions.) Your "traditional" meal is followed by a full slate of swirling kilts, blaring bagpipes, and Scottish folk dancing with an "old-time music hall"–type emcee. You can often see the show without dinner for about half the price. The TI has fliers on all the latest venues. **Carlton Highland Hotel** offers its Scottish folk evening with or without dinner, nearly nightly (£15 for show only at 20:45–22:30, £39.50 includes super-traditional dinner at 19:30, CC, at High Street and North Bridge, tel. 0131/556-7277).

▲▲**Folk Music in Pubs**—Edinburgh used to be a good place for folk music, but in the last few years, pub-owners—out of economic necessity—are catering to twenty-somethings more interested in beer drinking than traditional music. Pubs that were regular venues for folk music have gone popular. Especially on weekends, you're unlikely to find much live folk music. The monthly *Gig Guide* (free at TI and various pubs, www.gigguide.co.uk) lists most of the live-music action. **Whistle Binkies** still offers nightly ad-lib traditional music, which can start as early as 19:30 or as late as 22:30 and goes until the wee hours (just off the Royal Mile on South Bridge, another entrance on Niddry Street, tel. 0131/557-5114).

Grassmarket Street (below the castle) is sloppy with live music and rowdy people spilling out of the pubs and into what was once upon a time a busy market square. It's fun to just wander through Grassmarket late at night. **Finnigan's Wake** has live music—often Irish rock—nightly (starts at 22:00, a block off Grassmarket at 9 Victoria Street, tel. 0131/226-3816). The **Fiddlers Arms**, **Biddy Mulligan**, and **White Hart Inn**, among others, all feature live music. By the noise and crowds you'll know where to go and where not to. Have a beer and follow your ear.

Theater—Even outside of festival time, Edinburgh is a fine place for lively and affordable theater. Pick up *The List* for a complete rundown of what's on (£1.95 at newsstands).

Sleeping in Edinburgh
(£1 = about $1.50, country code: 44, area code: 0131)
Sleep Code: **S** = Single, **D** = Double/Twin, **T** = Triple, **Q** = Quad, **b** = bathroom, **s** = shower only, **CC** = Credit Cards accepted, **no CC** = Credit Cards not accepted.

The advent of big, cheap hotels has made life tough for B&Bs. Still, book ahead, especially in August when the annual festival fills Edinburgh. Conventions, school holidays, and weekends can make finding a room tough at almost any time of year. For the best prices, book directly rather than through the TI, which charges a higher room fee and levies a £3 booking fee. "Standard" rooms, with toilets and showers a tissue-toss away, save you £10 a night.

Room prices in this section are usually listed as a range, from low season (winter) to high season (July–Sept). I have not listed the higher "festival prices"—which are limited to August. Prices get soft off-season, for longer visits, and sometimes for midweek stays outside of summer.

Sleeping off Dalkeith Road

These recommendations are south of town near the Royal Commonwealth Pool, just off Dalkeith Road. This comfortable and safe neighborhood is a 20-minute walk or 10-minute bus ride from the Royal Mile. All listings are nonsmoking, on quiet streets, a two-minute walk from a bus stop, and well-served by city buses. B&Bs are unlikely to accept bookings for one-night stays in August.

Near the B&Bs you'll find plenty of eateries (see "Eating," below), easy free parking, and **Laundromats**—one at 208 Dalkeith Road (Mon–Sat 08:30–17:00, closed Sun, £4-self-service, £5.50-full-service, drop off by 11:00 for same-day service, June–Sept they'll deliver your clean clothes to your B&B for free, tel. 0131/667-0825) and another at 13 South Clerk Street (Mon–Fri 08:00–20:00, Sat 09:00–17:00, Sun 10:00–16:00, opposite Queens Hall).

To reach the hotel neighborhood from the train station, TI, or Scott Monument, cross Princes Street and wait at the **bus stop** under the small C&A sign on the department store (80p; LRT buses #14, #21, and #33, or First buses #86 and #C3; tell driver your destination is "Dalkeith Road;" red bus: exact change or pay more; green bus: makes change; ride 10 min to first or second stop—depending on B&B—after the pool, push the button, exit middle door). These buses also stop at the corner of North Bridge and High Street on the Royal Mile. Buses run from 06:00 to 23:00, and after 09:00 on Sunday morning. **Taxi** fare between the station or Royal Mile and the B&Bs is about £4.

B&Bs off Dalkeith Road

Dunedin Guest House (dun-EE-din)—bright, plush, and elegantly Scottish, with seven huge rooms—is a fine value (S-£20–35, Db-£40–70, no CC, family rooms for up to 5, 8 Priestfield Road, EH16 5HH, tel. 0131/668-1949, fax 0131/668-3636, www.dunedinguesthouse.co.uk, e-mail: dunedin-guesthouse @edinburgh-EH16.freeserve.co.uk, Marsella Bowen).

Turret Guest House is teddy-on-the-beddy cozy, with a great

Edinburgh, Our Neighborhood

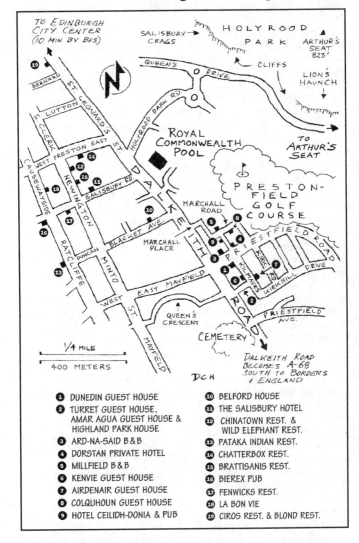

1 DUNEDIN GUEST HOUSE	**10** BELFORD HOUSE
2 TURRET GUEST HOUSE, AMAR AGUA GUEST HOUSE & HIGHLAND PARK HOUSE	**11** THE SALISBURY HOTEL
	12 CHINATOWN REST. & WILD ELEPHANT REST.
3 ARD-NA-SAID B & B	**13** PATAKA INDIAN REST.
4 DORSTAN PRIVATE HOTEL	**14** CHATTERBOX REST.
5 MILLFIELD B & B	**15** BRATTISANIS REST.
6 KENVIE GUEST HOUSE	**16** BIEREX PUB
7 AIRDENAIR GUEST HOUSE	**17** FENWICKS REST.
8 COLQUHOUN GUEST HOUSE	**18** LA BON VIE
9 HOTEL CEILIDH-DONIA & PUB	**19** CIROS REST. & BLOND REST.

bay-windowed family room and a vast breakfast menu that includes haggis and vegetarian options (7 rooms, S-£20–23, Sb-£23–28, D-£42–48, Db-£44–58, £2/person discount with this book and cash, no CC, 8 Kilmaurs Terrace, EH16 5DR, tel. 0131/667-6704, fax 0131/668-1368, www.turret.clara.net, Mrs. Jackie Cameron).

Amar Agua Guest House, next door to Turret, is an inviting Victorian home away from home (7 rooms, S-£18–27, Db-£36–58, £2/person discount with this book, no CC, 10 Kilmaurs Terrace, EH16 5DR, tel. 0131/667-6775, fax 0131/6677687, www.amaragua.co.uk, run by energetic young couple Dawn-Ann and Tony Costa).

Ard-Na-Said B&B is an elegant 1875 Victorian house with a comfy lounge and five classy rooms (1 S-£22–28, Db-£44–56, family deals, no CC, 5 Priestfield Road, EH16 5HH, tel. 0131/6 67-8754, fax 0131/271-0960, www.ardnasaid.freeserve.co.uk, enthusiastically run by Jim and Olive Lyons).

Dorstan Private Hotel is more formal, professional, and hotelesque, with all the comforts. Several of its 14 thoughtfully-decorated rooms are on the ground floor (2 Ds-£60, Db-£66, family rooms, CC, no clothes washing except for "smalls," 7 Priest-field Road, EH16 5HJ, tel. 0131/667-6721, fax 0131/668-4644, e-mail: reservations@dorstan-hotel.demon.co.uk, Mairae Campbell).

Millfield B&B, run graciously by Liz Broomfield, is thought-fully furnished with antique class, a rare sit-and-chat ambience, and a comfy TV lounge. Since the showers are down the hall, you'll get spacious rooms and great prices (S-£21–23, D-£38–40, T-£48–52, no CC, reconfirm reservation by phone, 12 Marchhall Road, EH16 5HR, tel. & fax 0131/667-4428). Decipher the break-fast prayer by Robert Burns. Then try the "Taste of Scotland" breakfast option. See how many stone (14 pounds) you weigh in the elegant throne room.

Kenvie Guest House, well run by Dorothy Vidler, comes with six pleasant rooms and lots of personal touches (1 small twin-£40, D-£42, Db-£50, family deals, 3 percent more with CC, 16 Kilmaurs Road, EH16 5DA, tel. 0131/668-1964, fax 0131/668-1926, www.kenvie.co.uk, e-mail: dorothy@kenvie.co.uk).

Airdenair Guest House, offering views and homemade scones (made by the owner's mom), has five attractive rooms with a lofty above-it-all feeling (Sb-£25–35, Db-£40–50, CC, 29 Kilmaurs Road, EH16 5DB, tel. 0131/668-2336, http://airdenair.edinburghnet.co.uk/, Jill McLennan).

Highland Park House has bright, basic rooms (S-£20–25, D-£40–44, Db-£44–52 with this book, family deals, no CC, 16 Kilmaurs Terrace, EH16 5DR, tel. & fax 0131/667-9204, e-mail: highlandparkhouse@hotmail.com, Margaret and Brian Love).

Colquhoun Guest House, in an elegant building, has seven fine rooms, several on the ground floor (S-£22–25, D-£40, Db-£50, family room, no CC, 5 Marchhall Road, EH16 5HR, tel. 0131-667-8481, run by amazing Grace McAinsh).

Hotel Ceilidh-Donia is a work in progress with 14 basic rooms and a fun pub (Db-£45–60, CC, 14 Marchhall Crescent, tel. 0131/667-2743, run by Max, a creative man with a big vision).

Belford House is a tidy, homey place offering seven good rooms and a warm welcome (D-£40–44, Db-£50–54, family deals, CC, 5 percent off with cash, 13 Blacket Avenue, tel. 0131/667-2422, fax 0131/667-7508, e-mail: mailbox@belfordguesthouse .com, Isa and Tom Borthwick).

The Salisbury, more like a hotel than its neighbors, fills a classy old Georgian building with 12 rooms, a large lounge, tired carpeting, and even a dumbwaiter in the breakfast room (D-£44–52, Db-£50–56, 5 percent off with cash and this book, CC, free parking, 45 Salisbury Road, EH16 5AA, tel. & fax 0131/667-1264, http://members.edinburgh.org/salisbury/, Brenda Wright).

Big, Modern Hotels

Four of these listings are cheap as hotels go and offer more comfort than character. One's a splurge. In each case I'd skip the institutional breakfast and eat out.

Sleeping cheap near the Royal Mile: **Travelodge**, the cheapest hotel in the center, has 193 no-nonsense, central rooms all decorated in dark blue. All rooms are the same and suitable for two adults with two kids or three adults. While sleepable, it has a cheap feel with a quickly-revolving staff (Sb, Db, Tb all £50 except £70 Fri–Sun in Aug, breakfast-£8, CC, 33 St. Mary's Street, a block off the Royal Mile, tel. 08700-850-950, www.travelodge.co.uk).

Ibis Hotel, mid–Royal Mile behind Tron Church, is well-run and perfectly located. It has 98 soulless but clean and comfy rooms drenched in pre-fab American charm (Sb-£54–70, Db-£60–70, top price July–Aug, discounted in off-season, lousy continental breakfast-£4, CC, nonsmoking rooms, elevator, 6 Hunter Square, EH1 1QW, tel. 0131/240-7000, fax 0131/240-7007, e-mail: H2039@accor-hotels.com).

Jurys Inn, another cookie-cutter place with 186 dependably comfortable rooms, is well-located a short walk from the station and capably run (Sb, Db, Tb all £90 Fri–Sat, £70 Sun–Thu, much cheaper in off-season, CC, breakfast-£8, 2 kids sleep free, nonsmoking rooms, some views, pub/restaurant, on quiet street just off Royal Mile, 43 Jeffrey Street, EH1 1DG, tel. 0131/200-3300, fax 0131/200-0400, www.jurys.com).

Splurge near the Royal Mile: **MacDonald Hotel**, my only fancy listing, is an opulent five-star splurge across the street from the new parliament. With its classy marble-and-wood decor, fitness center, and pool, it's hard to leave. On a gray winter day in Edinburgh, this could be worth it. Prices vary wildly (50 rooms, Db-£170, breakfast-£13, CC, near bottom of Mile, across from Dynamic Earth, Holyrood Road, EH8 6AE, tel. 0131/550-4500, fax 0131/550-4545, www.macdonaldhotels.co.uk). Beg for free breakfast before reserving and you'll likely get it.

Away from the center: **Travel Inn**, the biggest hotel in Edinburgh, has even less character—with a clientele to match—but a great price and a mediocre location about a mile west of the Mile. Each of its 280 rooms is modern and comfortable, with a sofa that folds out for two kids if necessary (Db-£52 for 2 adults and up to 2 kids under 15, breakfast is extra, CC, elevators, nonsmoking rooms, weekends booked long in advance, near Haymarket station west of the castle at 1 Morrison Link, EH3 8DN, tel. 0131/228-9819, fax 0131/228-9836, www.travelinn.co.uk).

Hostels
Although Edinburgh's hostels are well-run and open to all—providing Internet access, laundry facilities, and £12 bunk beds in 8- to 16-bed single-sex dorms (about a £9–12 savings over B&Bs)—they are scruffy and don't include breakfast.

Castle Rock Hostel is hip and easygoing, offering cheap beds, plenty of friends, and a great central location just below the castle and above the pubs with all the folk music (15 Johnston Terrace, tel. 0131/225-9666). Their sister hostels are nearly across the street from each other: **High Street Hostel** (laundry-£2.50, kitchen, 8 Blackfriars Street, just off High Street/Royal Mile, tel. 0131/557-3984) and **Royal Mile Backpackers** (105 High Street, tel. 0131/557-6120).

For more regulations and less color, try the IYH hostels: **Bruntsfield Hostel** (6–12 beds/room, near golf course, 7 Bruntsfield Crescent, buses #11, #15, #16, and #17 from Princes Street, tel. 0131/447-2994) and **Edinburgh Hostel** (4–10 beds/room, 5-min walk from Haymarket station, 18 Eglinton Crescent, tel. 0131/337-1120).

Eating in Edinburgh
Eating along the Royal Mile
Historic pubs and doily cafés with reasonable, unremarkable meals abound. Here are some handy, affordable places for a good bite to eat (listed in downhill order). **Deacon Brodie's Pub** serves soup, sandwiches, and snacks on the ground floor and good £8 meals upstairs in the restaurant. As in all Edinburgh pubs, kids are allowed only in the restaurant section (daily 12:00–22:00, CC, tel. 0131/225-6531). Or munch prayerfully in the **Lower Aisle** restaurant under St. Giles Cathedral (Mon–Fri 08:30–16:30, Sun 10:00–14:00, closed Sat except in Aug). The **Filling Station**, a big noisy bar decorated with car parts, has an American-type menu, serves good burgers, and rocks at night (daily 12:00–22:30, 235 High Street, near North Bridge, tel. 0131/226-2488). **Bann UK**, a vegetarian café, serves healthy cuisine that goes way beyond tofu and granola (daily 11:00–23:00, CC, just off South Bridge behind Tron Church

at 5 Hunter Square, tel. 0131/226-1112). **Dubh Prais Scottish Restaurant**—the only serious restaurant on this list—is a dressy little place filling a cellar 10 steps and a world away from the High Street bustle. The owner/chef promises to serve Scottish fayre at its very best. The only thing not Scottish here is the wine list and some of the guests (£10 lunches Tue–Fri 12:00–14:00, £25 dinners Tue–Sat 18:30–22:30, closed Sun–Mon, CC, reservations smart at night, opposite Crowne Plaza at 123b High Street, tel. 0131/557-5732). **Food Plantation** has good, inexpensive, fresh sandwiches to eat in or take out (Mon–Fri 10:00–15:30, closed Sat–Sun, 274 Canongate). **The Tea Room** serves light lunches, scones, and fine tea in yellow elegance (Mon–Sat 10:30–16:45, Sun 11:00–16:45, next to Museum of Edinburgh at 158 Canongate). **Clarinda's Tea Room**, near the bottom of the Royal Mile, is a charming and tasty place to relax after touring the Mile or palace (daily 09:00–16:45, 69 Cannongate, tel. 0131/557-1888).

For a break from the touristic grind just off the top end of the Royal Mile, consider the **Elephant House**, where locals browse newspapers in the stay-awhile back room, listen to classic rock, and sip coffee or munch a light meal (Mon–Fri 08:00–23:00, Sat–Sun 09:00–23:00, 2 blocks south of Royal Mile near Museum of Scotland at 21 George IV Bridge, tel. 0131/220-5355).

Grassmarket Street, below the castle, is lined with lots of eateries and noisy pubs. This is the place for live music and absorbent food.

Eating in the New Town
Princes Mall Food Court, below the TI and above the station, is a circus of sticky fast-food joints littered with paper plates and shoppers (Mon–Sat 08:30–18:00, Thu until 19:00, Sun 11:00–17:00). If you'd prefer pubs, browse the nearby Rose Street.

The Dome Restaurant serves decent meals around a classy bar under the elegant 19th-century skylight dome of what was a fancy bank. With soft jazz and dressy, white-tablecloth ambience, it feels a world apart (£10 lunches until 17:00, £16 dinners until 24:00, daily 12:00–24:00, modern cuisine, borderline smoky, open for a drink anytime under the dome or in the adjacent art deco bar, 14 George Street, tel. 0131/624-8624). Notice the façade of this former bank building—the various ways to make money fill the pediment with all the nobility of classical gods.

The **Undercroft**, in the basement of St. Andrew's church, is the cheapest place in town for lunch (£1 sandwich or soup and roll, Mon–Fri 12:00–14:00, closed Sat–Sun, on George Street, just off St. Andrew's Square).

Café Royal is a movie producer's dream pub—the perfect *fin de siècle* setting for a coffee, beer, or light meal (parts of *Chariots of Fire* were filmed in here). Drop in, if only to admire the 1880

Edinburgh's New Town

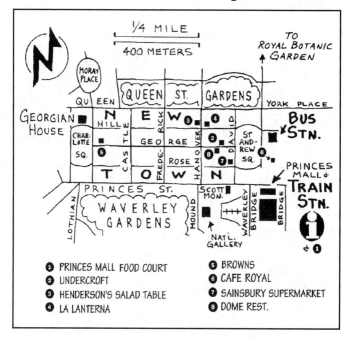

¼ MILE
400 METERS

TO ROYAL BOTANIC GARDEN

MORAY PLACE

QUEEN ST. GARDENS
QUEEN
YORK PLACE

GEORGIAN HOUSE

NEW
HILL ST.
CASTLE ST.
FREDERICK ST.
GEORGE
ROSE
HANOVER ST.

TOWN

ST. ANDREW SQ.

BUS STN.

PRINCES MALL & TRAIN STN.

PRINCES ST.

LOTHIAN RD.

WAVERLEY GARDENS

SCOTT MON.

MOUND

NAT'L. GALLERY

WAVERLEY BRIDGE

BRIDGE

❶ PRINCES MALL FOOD COURT
❷ UNDERCROFT
❸ HENDERSON'S SALAD TABLE
❹ LA LANTERNA
❺ BROWNS
❻ CAFE ROYAL
❼ SAINSBURY SUPERMARKET
❽ DOME REST.

tiles featuring famous inventors (2 blocks from Princes Mall on West Register Street).

A generation of New Town vegetarians have munched hearty cuisine and salads at **Henderson's Salad Table and Wine Bar** (£5–6, Mon–Sat 08:00–22:45, closed Sun, CC, nonsmoking section, strictly vegetarian, pleasant live jazz nightly in Wine Bar, between Queen and George Streets at 94 Hanover Street, tel. 0131/225-2131). Henderson's has two different seating areas, but both use the same self-serve cafeteria line. They also run Henderson's Bistro upstairs with table service.

Local office workers pile into the friendly and family-run **La Lanterna** for good Italian food (Mon–Sat 12:00–14:00, 17:15–22:00, closed Sun, CC, dinner reservations wise, 2 blocks off Princes Street, 83 Hanover Street, tel. 0131/226-3090).

Supermarket: The glorious **Sainsbury** supermarket, with a tasty assortment of take-away food and specialty coffee, is just one block from the Walter Scott Monument and the lovely picnic-perfect Princes Street Gardens (Mon–Sat 07:00–22:00, Sun 10:00–19:00, CC, on corner of Rose Street, on St. Andrew's Square, across the street from Jenners, the classy department store).

Eating in Dalkeith Road Area, near Your B&B

All these places are within a 10-minute walk of the recommended B&Bs. Most are on or near the intersection of Newington and East Preston Streets. For location, see map on page 532.

Ethnic Restaurants: **Chinatown**—an oasis of Asian calm— is a delightful Chinese restaurant with sharp service and loyal local clientele (£7–10, Tue–Fri 12:00–14:00, 17:30–23:30, Sat–Sun 17:30–23:00, closed Mon, CC, reservations smart on weekend nights, take-away food is 25 percent off, Newington Road, tel. 0131/662-0555).

Pataka Indian and Bengali Restaurant, a 10-table "Indian bistro" with attentive service and great food, is understandably popular with locals. Portions are big, but not overly spicy, and prices are small. This tight little restaurant can be a bit smoky (£7 dishes, nightly 17:30–23:30, CC, also offers take-away, 190 Causewayside, tel. 0131/668-1167).

Wild Elephant, a few doors down from recommended Chinatown restaurant, is a plain, cheap place serving decent Thai food to locals who dress like grunge is the new craze (£4–7, Wed–Mon 16:30–22:00, closed Tue, they don't serve wine but you can BYO wine for £1 corkage fee, CC, also does take-away, 21 Newington Road, tel. 0131/662-8822).

Scottish/French Restaurants: Several classy little eight-table places feature "Auld Alliance" cuisine—Scottish cooking with a French flair (seasoned with a joint, historic disdain for England). They offer small menus with three or four items per course for two- or three-course meals (about £10 for a 2-course lunch, £20 for a 3-course dinner). These popular places take credit cards, and reservations are smart on weekends evenings. Many offer less-expensive meals outside of weekends.

Fenwicks is cozy and reliable, with tasty food and no French fries (daily 12:00–14:00, dinner 18:00–late, open all day Sun, CC, 15 Salisbury Place, tel. 0131/667-4265).

Ciros Restaurant is a hard-working, well-established family affair (£10 2-course lunches, £24 3-course dinners, £15 dinner Tue–Thu; open Tue–Sat 12:00–14:00, 18:30–21:45, closed Sun–Mon; 93 St. Leonards Street, tel. 0131/668-4207, run by Christine, Jean, and Stuart Stevenson).

La Bon Vie Restaurant is perhaps the liveliest with the most enticing menu (Mon–Sat 18:00–22:00, closed Sun, 49 Causewayside, tel. 0131/667-1110).

Blond Restaurant, with a more eclectic and European menu, is less expensive and bigger than the others with no set-price dinners (about £12 for 2 courses, Tue–Sun 12:00–14:00, 18:00–22:00, closed Mon, 75 St. Leonard's Street, tel. 0131/668-2917).

Pubs: **Hotel Ceilidh-Donia's pub** serves good grub with live folk music most nights and offers free Internet access to diners (£6–7, Mon–Fri eves plus Sun lunch 12:00–14:30, CC, within a block of most recommended B&Bs at 14 Marchhall Crescent, tel. 0131/667-2743, Max).

Bierex, a modern and youthful pub, is the neighborhood favorite for edible grub and a social atmosphere (132 Causewayside, tel. 0131/667-2335).

Cheaper Choices: **Chatterbox**, a grandmotherly little place, is fine for a light meal with tea (£4 meals, Thu–Mon, open only until 18:00, closed Wed, around corner from Chinatown on East Preston Street).

Brattisanis is your basic fish-and-chips joint serving lousy milkshakes and great haggis. Add a cheap touch of class by bringing in a beer or half bottle of wine from next door (daily 11:30–23:00, 87 Newington Road).

On Dalkeith Road, the huge Commonwealth Pool's noisy **cafeteria** is for hungry swimmers and budget travelers alike (Mon–Fri 10:00–20:00, Sat–Sun 10:00–17:00, pass the entry without paying).

Supermarket: The nearest supermarket, **Tesco**, is located between the Royal Mile and the Dalkeith B&B neighborhood (Mon–Sat 08:00–21:00, Sun 09:00–19:00, 5 long blocks south of the Royal Mile, on Nicolson, just south of intersection with West Richmond Street).

Transportation Connections—Edinburgh

By train to: Inverness (7/day, 4 hrs), **Oban** (3/day, change in Glasgow, 4.5 hrs), **York** (1/hr, 2.5 hrs), **London** (1/hr, 5 hrs), **Durham** (1/hr, 2 hrs, less frequent in winter), **Newcastle** (1/hr, 1.5 hrs), **Keswick**, the Lake District (south past Carlisle to Penrith, then catch bus to Keswick, 1/hr except Sun 6/day, 40 min), **Birmingham** (6/day, 4.5 hrs), **Crewe** (6/day, 3.5 hrs), **Bristol**, near Bath (1/hr, 6–7 hrs). Train info: tel. 08457-484-950.

By bus to: Oban (1/day, 09:15 departure, 4 hrs, not on Sun), **Fort William** (1/day, 4 hrs), **Inverness** (1/hr, 4 hrs), **Blackpool** (requires change in Glasgow, 5 hrs), **York** (1/day at 09:45, 5 hrs). For bus info, call Scottish Citylink (tel. 08705-505-050, www.citylink.co.uk) or National Express (tel. 08705-808-080). You can get info and tickets at the bus desk inside the Princes Mall TI.

DUBLIN

With reminders of its stirring history and rich culture on every corner, Ireland's capital and largest city is a sightseer's delight. Dublin's fair city will have you humming "Alive, alive-O."

Founded as a Viking trading settlement in the ninth century, Dublin grew to be a center of wealth and commerce second only to London in the British Empire. Dublin, the seat of English rule in Ireland for 700 years, was the heart of a "civilized" Anglo-Irish area (eastern Ireland) known as "the Pale." Anything "beyond the Pale" was considered uncultured and almost barbaric...purely Irish.

The Golden Age of English Dublin was the 18th century. Britain was on a roll, and Dublin was right there with it. Largely rebuilt during this Georgian era, Dublin—even with its tattered edges—became an elegant and cultured capital.

Then nationalism and human rights got in the way. The ideas of the French Revolution inspired Irish intellectuals to buck British rule and, after the revolt of 1798, life in Dublin was never quite the same. But the 18th century left a lasting imprint on the city. Georgian (that's British for neoclassical) squares and boulevards gave the city an air of grandness. The National Museum, National Gallery, and many government buildings are in the Georgian section of town. Few buildings (notably Christchurch Cathedral and St. Patrick's Cathedral) survive from before this Georgian period.

In the 19th century, with the closing of the Irish Parliament, the famine, and the beginnings of the struggle for independence, Dublin was treated—and felt—more like a colony than a partner. The tension culminated in the Rising of 1916, independence, and the tragic civil war. With many of its elegant streets left in ruins, Dublin emerged as the capital of the only former colony in Europe.

While bullet-pocked buildings and dramatic statues keep memories of Ireland's recent struggle for independence alive, it's boom time now, and the city is looking to a bright future. Locals are enjoying the "Celtic Tiger" economy—the best in Europe— while visitors enjoy a big-town cultural scene wrapped in a small-town smile.

Planning Your Time

Dublin deserves three nights and two days. Consider this aggressive sightseeing plan:

Day 1: 10:15–Trinity College guided walk, 11:00–*Book of Kells* and Old Library, 12:00–Browse Grafton Street, lunch there or picnic on Merrion Square, 13:30–Visit Number Twenty-Nine Georgian House, 15:00–National Museum, 17:00–Return to hotel, rest, have dinner—eat well for less during "early-bird specials," 19:30–Evening walk (musical or literary), 22:00–Irish music in Temple Bar area.

Day 2: 10:00–Dublin Castle tour, 11:00–Historic town walk, 13:00–Lunch, 14:00–O'Connell Street walk, 16:00–Kilmainham Jail, 18:00–Guinness Brewery tour finishing with view of city, Evening–Catch a play, concert, or Comhaltas traditional music in Dun Laoghaire.

Orientation (area code: 01)

Greater Dublin sprawls with over a million people—nearly a third of the country's population. But the center of touristic interest is a tight triangle between O'Connell Bridge, St. Stephen's Green, and Christchurch Cathedral. Within this triangle you'll find Trinity College (*Book of Kells*), Grafton Street (top pedestrian shopping zone), Temple Bar (trendy nightlife center), Dublin Castle, and the hub of most city tours and buses.

The River Liffey cuts the town in two. Focus on the southern half (where nearly all your sightseeing will take place). Dublin's main drag, O'Connell Street (near Abbey Theater and the outdoor produce market) runs north of the river to the central O'Connell Bridge then continues as the main city axis— mostly as Grafton Street—to St. Stephen's Green. The only major sights outside your easy-to-walk triangle are the Kilmainham Jail and the Guinness Brewery (both west of the center).

Tourist Information

Dublin's main tourist information office (TI) is a big shop with little to offer other than promotional fliers and long lines (Mon– Sat 09:00–17:30, Sun July–Aug only 10:30–15:00, located in a former church on Suffolk Street, 1 block off Grafton Street, tel. 01/605-7700, www.visitdublin.com). It has an American Express office, car-rental agency, bus-info desk, café, and traditional

Dublin

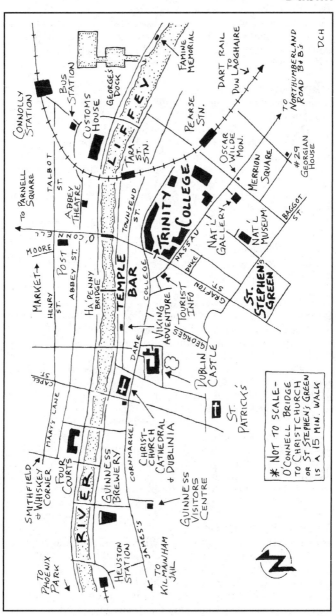

DCH

* NOT TO SCALE —
O'CONNELL BRIDGE
TO CHRISTCHURCH
OR ST STEPHEN'S GREEN
IS A 15 MIN. WALK

knickknacks. But perhaps its greatest value is the chance to peruse the rack opposite the info counter and pick up brochures for destinations throughout Ireland. There's also a TI at the airport (daily 08:00–22:00) as well as the Dun Laoghaire ferry terminal.

While you can buy the TI's lousy map for €0.50, its free newspaper (*The Guide to Dublin*) has the same one on its staple page. The handy *Dublin's Top Visitor Attractions* booklet has a small map and the latest on all of the town's sights—many more than I list here (€3.25, sold at TI bookshop without any wait). For a schedule of happenings in town, check the minimal calendar of events inside *The Guide to Dublin* newspaper (free at TI), or better, buy the informative *In Dublin* at any newsstand (published fortnightly, €2.50).

The excellent *Collins Illustrated Dublin Map* (€7.75 at TIs and newsstands) is the ultimate city map, listing just about everything of interest, along with helpful opinions.

Arrival in Dublin

By Train: Dublin has two stations. Heuston Station, on the west end of town, serves west and southwest Ireland. Connolly Station, which serves the north, northwest, and Rosslare, is closer to the center (a 10-min walk from O'Connell Bridge). Each station has a luggage-check facility and ATMs. Bus #90 runs along the river, connecting both train stations, the bus station, and the city center (€0.85, 6/hr).

By Bus: Bus Eireann, Ireland's national bus company, uses the Busaras Central Bus Station next to Connolly Station (10-min walk or short ride on bus #90 to the city center).

By Ferry: Irish Ferries dock at the mouth of the River Liffey (near the town center), while the Stena Line docks at Dun Laoghaire (easy DART train connections into Dublin, at least 3/hr, 20 min).

By Plane: The airport has ATMs, change bureaus, car-rental agencies, baggage check, a café, and a supermarket at the parking lot. Taxis from the airport into Dublin cost about €16.50, to Dun Laoghaire about €32.

Airport Buses: Consider buying a bus pass that covers the Airlink bus into town (see "Getting Around Dublin," below), but read this first to see if Airlink is best for you. To get to the recommended accommodations in the **city center**, take Airlink bus #748 (not #747) and ask the driver which stop is closest to your hotel (€4.50, €2.50 with Aer Lingus boarding pass, pay driver, 4/hr, 40 min, connects airport with Heuston train station and Busaras bus station, near Connolly train station). For the **St. Stephen's Green** neighborhood, the Aircoach is your best bet (€5, 4/hr, runs 05:30–22:30; pay driver and confirm best stop for your hotel). If you're staying in **Dun Laoghaire**, take Airlink bus #746 direct to Dun Laoghaire.

City Bus: To get to Dublin cheaply, take the city bus from
the airport; buses marked #16, #41A, #41B, and #41C go to
Marlborough Street, a five-minute walk from O'Connell Bridge
(€1.50, exact change required, 3/hr, 40 min).

Helpful Hints

Tourist Victim Support Service: This thoughtful service can
be helpful if you run into any problems (tel. 01/478-5295, 24-hr
help-line tel. 800-661-771).

U.S. Embassy: It's on 42 Elgin Road in the Ballsbridge
neighborhood (Mon–Fri 08:30–12:00 for passport concerns, tel.
01/668-7122 or 01/668-8777, www.usembassy.ie).

Internet Access: There are Internet cafés on nearly every
street. The one at the top of Dame Street (facing Kinlay House)
is fast and open 24 hours a day.

Car Rental: Consider Avis (tel. 01/605-7502, www.avis.com)
or Hertz (tel. 01/660-2255, www.hertz.com).

Festivals: St. Patrick's Day is a five-day extravaganza in
Dublin (www.stpatricksday.ie). June 16 is Bloomsday, dedicated
to the Irish author James Joyce and featuring the Messenger Bike
Rally. On rugby weekends (about 4 per year), hotels raise their
prices and are packed. Book ahead during festival times and for
any weekend.

Getting around Dublin

You'll do most of Dublin on foot. Big green buses are cheap
and cover the city thoroughly. Most lines start at the four quays
(pronounced "keys," piers) nearest O'Connell Bridge. If you're
away from the center, nearly any bus takes you back downtown.
Tell the driver where you're going, and he'll ask for €0.85, €1,
or €1.35, depending on the number of stops. Bring exact change
or lose any excess. To get to Heuston station from the city
center, catch bus #90 on the south side of the river; to get to
Connolly station and the bus station, catch #90 on the north
side of the river.

Passes: The bus office at 59 Upper O'Connell Street has
free "route network" maps and sells city-bus passes. The three-
day Rambler costs €8 (covers Airlink airport bus but not DART
trains) and the four-day adult Explorer pass costs €13 (includes
DART but not Airlink). Passes are also sold at each TI (bus info
tel. 01/873-4222).

DART: Speedy commuter trains connect Dublin with Dun
Laoghaire (ferry terminal and recommended B&Bs, at least 3/hr,
20 min, €1.50).

Taxi: Taxis are honest, plentiful, friendly, and good sources
of information (under €5 for most downtown rides, €26 per hour
for a guided joyride available from most any cab).

Tours of Dublin

While the physical treasures of Dublin are mediocre by European standards, the city has a fine story to tell and people with a natural knack for telling it. It's a good town for walking tours and the competition is fierce. Pamphlets touting creative walks are posted all over town. There are medieval walks, literary walks, 1916 Easter Rising walks, Georgian Dublin walks, and more. The evening walks are great ways to meet other travelers.

▲▲**Historical Walking Tour**—This is your best introductory walk. A group of hardworking history graduates—many of whom claim to have done more than just kiss the Blarney Stone—enliven Dublin's basic historic strip (Trinity College, Old Parliament House, Dublin Castle, and Christchurch Cathedral) with the story of their city, from its Viking origin to the present. As you listen to your guide's story, you stand in front of buildings that aren't much to see but are lots to talk about. Guides speak at length about the roots of Ireland's struggle with Britain (daily May–Sept at 11:00 and 15:00, Oct–April only Fri, Sat, and Sun at 12:00). From May to September, the same group offers more focused tours at noon (1916 Easter Rising walks on Mon, Wed, and Fri; and juicy, slice-of-old-life Dublin walks on Tue and Thu). All walks last two hours and cost €8 (but get the student discount with this book, depart from front gate of Trinity College, private walks also available, tel. 01/878-0227, www.historicalinsights.ie).

Another group offers **1916 Rebellion Walks** (€9 but get student price with this book, 2 hrs, daily mid-April–Sept Mon–Sat at 11:30, Sun at 13:00, depart from International Bar at 23 Wicklow Street, tel. 01/6762493, www.1916rising.com).

▲**Dublin Literary Pub Crawl**—Two actors take 30 or so tourists on a walk, stopping at four pubs. Half the time is spent enjoying their entertaining banter, which introduces the novice to the high *craic* (conversation) of Joyce, O'Casey, and Yeats. The two-hour tour is punctuated with 20-minute pub breaks (free time). While the beer lubricates the social fun, it dilutes the content of the evening (€9, April–Oct daily at 19:30, plus Sun at noon; Nov–March Thu–Sun only; meet upstairs in Duke Pub, off Grafton on Duke Street, tel. 01/670-5602, www.dublinpubcrawl.com).

▲▲**Traditional Irish-Music Pub Crawl**—This is similar to the Literary Pub Crawl but features music. You meet upstairs at 19:30 at Gogarty's Pub (Temple Bar area, corner of Fleet and Anglesea) and spend 40 minutes each in the upstairs rooms of three pubs listening to two musicians talk about, play, and sing traditional Irish music. While having only two musicians makes the music a bit thin (Irish music aficionados will tell you you're better off just finding a good session), the evening, while touristy, is not gimmicky. It's an education in traditional Irish music. The musicians demonstrate a few instruments and really enjoy introducing rookies to their art (€9, boss Vinnie offers a €1.30 discount with this book, beer extra, April–Oct nightly; Nov and Feb–March Fri–Sat only, allow 2.5 hrs, expect up to 50 tourists, tel. 01/478-0193).

▲**Hop-on Hop-off Bus Tours**—Two companies (Guide Friday and Dublin City Tours) offer hop-on hop-off bus tours of Dublin, doing virtually identical 90-minute circuits, allowing you to hop on and off at your choice of about 12 stops. Buses are mostly topless—with running live commentaries. They go to Guinness Brewery but not to Kilmainham Jail. Buy your ticket on board. Each company's map, free with ticket, details various discounts you'll get on Dublin's sights. Your ticket's valid the entire day—not 24 hours (April–Oct 4/hr from 09:30–17:30, until 18:30 in summer, fewer buses Nov–March with shorter hours: 09:30–15:30). **Dublin City Tour** runs the green-and-cream buses (€10.25, driver narrates, tel. 01/873-4222). **Guide Friday** (€11.50, black-and-gold buses, tel. 01/676-5377) costs a bit more but includes Phoenix Park and comes with a guide and a driver, rather than a driver who guides.

▲**Viking Splash Tours**—If you'd like to ride in a WWII amphibious vehicle—driven by a Viking-costumed guide who is as liable to spout history as he is to growl—this is for you. The tour starts with a group roar from the Viking within us all. At first the guide talks as if he were a Viking ("When we came here in 841 . . . "), but quickly the patriot emerges as he tags Irish history to the sights you pass. Near the end of the 75-minute tour (punctuated by occasional group roars at passersby), you don a life jacket for a slow spin up and down a boring canal. Kids who expect a Viking splash may feel they've been trapped in a classroom, but historians will enjoy the talk more than the gimmick (€12.75, mid-March–Nov Tue–Sun 10:00–17:00, sometimes later in summer, closed Mon, about hrly, depart from Bull Alley, beside St. Patrick's Cathedral; on gray days boat is covered but still breezy—dress warmly, tel. 01/855-3000, www.vikingsplashtours.com).

Sights—Dublin's Trinity College

▲**Trinity College**—Founded in 1592 by Queen Elizabeth I to establish a Protestant way of thinking about God, Trinity has long been Ireland's most prestigious college. Originally the student body was limited to rich Protestant males. Women were admitted in 1903, and Catholics, while allowed entrance by the school much earlier, were given formal permission to study at Trinity in the 1970s. Today half of Trinity's 12,500 students are women, and 70 percent are culturally Catholic (although only about 20 percent of Irish youth are churchgoing).

▲▲**Trinity College Tour**—Inside the gate of Trinity, students organize and lead 30-minute tours of their campus. You'll get a rundown on the mostly Georgian architecture; a peek at student

Dublin Center

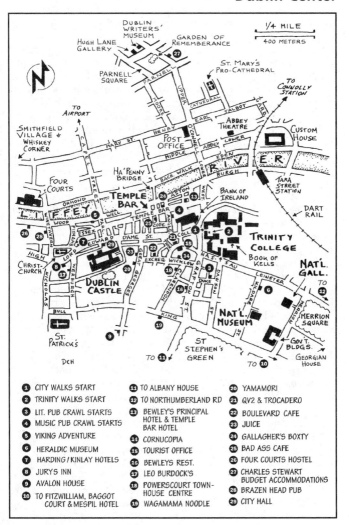

DUBLIN WRITERS' MUSEUM
HUGH LANE GALLERY
GARDEN OF REMEMBERANCE
PARNELL SQUARE
PARNELL
ST. MARY'S PRO-CATHEDRAL
TO CONNOLLY STATION
TO AIRPORT
SMITHFIELD VILLAGE & WHISKEY CORNER
HENRY
MARY ST.
POST OFFICE
MIDDLE
ABBEY THEATRE
ABBEY LOWER
CUSTOM HOUSE
RIVER
EARL
TALBOT
CATHEDRAL
UPPER
HA'PENNY BRIDGE
BACK WALK
EDEN
BURGH
FOUR COURTS
ORMOND
WOOD
ESSEX
LIFFEY
WELL
TEMPLE BAR
TEMPLE BAR
COPE
BANK OF IRELAND
TARA STREET STATION
DART RAIL
HIGH
LORD
EDWARD
DAME ST.
EXCHEQ
WICKLOW
COLL.
TRINITY COLLEGE
BOOK OF KELLS
NAT'L. GALL.
CHRIST-CHURCH
NICHOLAS
DUBLIN CASTLE
GREAT GEORGES
DUKE
NASSAU
LEINSTER
KILDARE
TO
BULL
ST. PATRICK'S
DCH
KING
NAT'L. MUSEUM
MERRION SQUARE
GOV'T. BLDGS.
GEORGIAN HOUSE
ST STEPHEN'S GREEN
TO

1/4 MILE
400 METERS

N

TO FITZWILLIAM, BAGGOT COURT & MESPIL HOTEL

❶ CITY WALKS START
❷ TRINITY WALKS START
❸ LIT. PUB CRAWL STARTS
❹ MUSIC PUB CRAWL STARTS
❺ VIKING ADVENTURE
❻ HERALDIC MUSEUM
❼ HARDING / KINLAY HOTELS
❽ JURYS INN
❾ AVALON HOUSE
❿ TO FITZWILLIAM, BAGGOT COURT & MESPIL HOTEL

⓫ TO ALBANY HOUSE
⓬ TO NORTHUMBERLAND RD
⓭ BEWLEY'S PRINCIPAL HOTEL & TEMPLE BAR HOTEL
⓮ CORNUCOPIA
⓯ TOURIST OFFICE
⓰ BEWLEYS REST.
⓱ LEO BURDOCK'S
⓲ POWERSCOURT TOWN-HOUSE CENTRE
⓳ WAGAMAMA NOODLE

⓴ YAMAMORI
㉑ QV2 & TROCADERO
㉒ BOULEVARD CAFE
㉓ JUICE
㉔ GALLAGHER'S BOXTY
㉕ BAD ASS CAFE
㉖ FOUR COURTS HOSTEL
㉗ CHARLES STEWART BUDGET ACCOMMODATIONS
㉘ BRAZEN HEAD PUB
㉙ CITY HALL

life, both in the early days and today; and enjoy the company of a witty Irish college kid who talks about the school (late May–Sept daily 10:15–15:30; Oct and late April–early May usually weekends only, weather permitting; look for small blue kiosk inside gate, the €7.75 tour fee includes the €5.75 fee to see the *Book of Kells*, where the tour leaves you).

▲▲▲*Book of Kells* **in the Trinity Old Library**—The only Trinity campus interior welcoming tourists—just follow the signs—is the Old Library with its precious *Book of Kells*. The first-class *Turning Darkness into Light* exhibit puts the 680-page illuminated manuscript in its historical and cultural context and prepares you for the original book and other precious manuscripts in the treasury. The exhibit is a one-way affair leading to the actual treasury, which shows only four books under glass in one display case. Make a point to spend at least half an hour in the exhibit (before reaching the actual *Book of Kells*). The video clips showing the exacting care that went into the "monkuscripts" and the ancient art of bookbinding are especially interesting.

Written on vellum (baby calfskin) in the eighth or early ninth century—probably by Irish monks in Iona, Scotland—this enthusiastically decorated copy of the four Gospels was taken to the Irish monastery at Kells in A.D. 806 after a series of Viking raids. Arguably the finest piece of art from what is generally called the Dark Ages, the *Book of Kells* shows that monastic life in this far fringe of Europe was far from dark. It has been bound into four separate volumes. At any given time, two of the four gospels are on display. The crowd around the one glass case with the treasures can be off-putting, but hold your own and get up close. You'll see four richly decorated, 1,200-year-old pages—two text and two decorated cover pages. The library treasury also displays two other books—likely the *Book of Armagh* (A.D. 807) and the *Book of Durrow* (A.D. 680)—neither of which can be checked out.

Next, a stairway leads to the 60-meter-long main chamber of the Old Library (from 1732), stacked to its towering ceiling with 200,000 of the library's oldest books. Here you'll find one of a dozen surviving original copies of the Proclamation of the Irish Republic. Patrick Pearse read these words outside the General Post Office on April 24, 1916, to start the Easter Rising that led to Irish independence. Read the entire thing…imagining it was yours. Notice the inclusive opening phrase and the seven signatories (each was executed). Another national icon is nearby—the oldest surviving Irish harp, from the 15th century (€5.75, at Trinity College Library, year-round Mon–Sat 09:30–17:00, Sun 09:30–16:30, Oct–May Sun 12:00–16:30, tel. 01/608-2308). A long line often snakes out of the building. It's the line to purchase a ticket—not to actually get in. If you take the Trinity College tour or if you buy the combo-ticket at the Dublin Experience, you've already bought your *Book of Kells* ticket and can scoot right past the line and into the exhibit.

▲**Dublin Experience**—This 40-minute fancy slideshow giving a historic introduction to Dublin is one more tourist movie with the sound turned up. It's good—offering a fine sweeping introduction to the story of Ireland—but pricey and riding on the coattails of the *Book of Kells*. Considering that the combo-ticket gets you this for half-price and gets you past any Kells line, it's not a bad value (€4.25, or half-price with a €8.25 combo Kells/Dublin Experience ticket, June–Sept daily, showings on the hr 10:00–17:00, in modern arts building across from Trinity Old Library).

Sights—Dublin, South of the River Liffey

▲▲**Dublin Castle**—Built on the spot of the first Viking fortress, this castle was the seat of British rule in Ireland for 700 years. Located where the Poddle and Liffey Rivers came together, making a black pool ("dubh linn" in Irish), Dublin Castle was the official residence of the Viceroy, who implemented the will of the British royalty. It was the stirring setting where, in 1922, the Brits handed power over to Michael Collins and the Irish. Today it's used for fancy state and charity functions. The 45-minute tours offer a room-by-room walk through the lavish state apartments of this most English of Irish palaces (€4.25, 4/hr, Mon–Fri 10:00–17:00, Sat–Sun 14:00–17:00, tel. 01/677-7129). The tour finishes with a look at the foundations of the Norman tower and the best remaining chunk of the 13th-century town wall.

Dublin City Hall—The first neoclassical building in this very neoclassical city stands proudly overlooking Dame Street, in front of the gate to Dublin Castle. Built in 1779 as the Royal Exchange, it introduced the neoclassical style (then very popular on the continent) to Ireland. Step inside (it's free) to feel the prosperity and confidence of Dublin in her 18th-century glory days. In 1852 it became the city hall. Under the grand rotunda, a cycle of heroic paintings tell the city's history. Pay your respects to the 18-foot-tall statue of Daniel O'Connell (the great orator and "liberator" who won Catholic emancipation in 1829 from those vile Protestants over in London). The greeter sits like the Maytag repairman at the information desk, eager to give you more information. Downstairs is a simple "Story of the Capital" exhibition (storyboards and video clips of Dublin's history (€4, Mon–Sat 10:00–17:00, Sun 14:00–17:00).

▲**Dublin's Viking Adventure**—For kids, this really is an adventure. You start in a box of seats that transforms into a Viking ship. Your chieftain—who hasn't washed since he left Norway—joins you, and suddenly you're in a storm: Waves splash, smoke rolls, and you land in a kind of Viking summer camp. You then spend 30 minutes being shuttled from one friendly original Dubliner to the next (a trader, a sassy maiden, a monk building a church, and so on). After a guide takes you through a reconstructed excavation sight, you'll see a replica of a Viking ship, watch a film on shipbuilding, and tour a small museum. It feels hokey, but the cast is certainly hardworking. You leave feeling as though you've visited if not a Viking town, at least the set for a B-grade Viking movie.

It's on Essex Street, a block off the riverside Essex Quay in Temple Bar—where the Vikings established their first Dublin settlement in 841 A.D. (€7, Tue–Sat 10:00–17:30, last tour at 16:30, allow 60 min total, closed Sun–Mon, tel. 01/679-6040).

Dublinia—This tries valiantly, but fails, to be a "bridge to Dublin's medieval past." The amateurish look at the medieval town starts with a walk through dim rooms of tableaus, followed by several rooms of medieval exhibits, a scale model of old Dublin, and an interesting room devoted to medieval fairs. Then, after piles of stairs, you get a tower-top, skyline view of Dublin's churches and breweries (€5, €6.50 includes Christchurch Cathedral, saving you €1.30; April–Sept daily 10:00–17:00, Oct–March daily 11:00–16:00, brass rubbing, coffee shop, across from Christchurch Cathedral, tel. 01/679-4611).

Christchurch Cathedral—The first church here, built of wood in about 1040 by King Sitric, dates back to Viking times. The present structure dates from a mix of periods: Norman and Gothic, but mostly Victorian neo-Gothic (1870s restoration work). The unusually large crypt under the cathedral—actually the oldest building in Dublin—contains stocks, statues, and the cathedral's silver (€2.50 donation to church, €2.50 extra for crypt silver exhibition, free brochure with self-guided tour, daily 10:00–17:00). Because of Dublin's British past, neither of its top two churches is Catholic. Christchurch Cathedral and the nearby St. Patrick's Cathedral are both Church of Ireland. In Catholic Ireland they feel hollow and are more famous than visit-worthy.

Evensong: At Christchurch, a 45-minute evensong service is sung regularly (less regularly during the summer) several times a week (18:00 Wed–schoolgirl choir, 18:00 Thu–adult choir, 17:00 Sat–adult choir, 15:30 Sun–adult choir). The 13th-century St. Patrick's Cathedral, where Jonathan Swift (author of *Gulliver's Travels*) was dean in the 18th century, also offers evensong (Sun 15:15, Mon–Fri 17:30, but not Wed July–Aug).

▲▲▲**National Museum**—Showing off the treasures of Ireland from the Stone Age to modern times, this museum is a national treasure and wonderfully digestible under one dome. Ireland's Bronze Age gold fills the center. Up four steps, the prehistoric Ireland exhibit rings the gold. In a corner (behind a 2,000-year-old body), you'll find the treasury with the most famous pieces (brooches, chalices, and other examples of Celtic metalwork) and an 18-minute video (played on request), giving an overview of Irish art through the 13th century. The collection's superstar is the gold, enamel, and amber eighth-century Tara Brooch. Jumping way ahead (and to the opposite side of the hall), a special corridor features "The Road to Independence," with guns, letters, and death masks recalling the fitful birth of the "Terrible Beauty" (1900–1921, with a focus on the 1916 Easter Rising). The best

Viking artifacts in town are upstairs with the medieval collection. If you'll be visiting Cong (in Connemara, near Galway), seek out the original Cross of Cong (free entry, Tue–Sat 10:00–17:00, Sun 14:00–17:00, closed Mon, good café, Kildare Street 2, between Trinity College and St. Stephen's Green). Greatest-hits tours are given several times a day (€1.30, 40 min, tel. 01/677-7444 in morning for schedule). For background information, read "Irish Art" in the appendix.

▲**National Gallery**—Along with a hall featuring the work of top Irish painters, this has Ireland's best collection of European masters. It's impressive—unless you've been to London or Paris (free, Mon–Sat 09:30–17:30, Thu until 20:30, Sun 13:00–17:00, guided tours on weekends, Merrion Square West, tel. 01/661-5133, www.nationalgallery.ie).

▲▲**Grafton Street**—Once filled with noisy traffic, today Grafton Street is Dublin's liveliest pedestrian shopping mall. A five-minute stroll past street musicians takes you from Trinity College up to St. Stephen's Green (and makes you wonder why American merchants are so terrified of a car-free street). Walking by a buxom statue of "sweet" Molly Malone (known by locals as "the tart with the cart"), you'll soon pass two venerable department stores: the Irish Brown Thomas and the English Marks & Spencer. An alley leads to the Powerscourt Townhouse Shopping Centre, which tastefully fills a converted Georgian mansion. The huge, glass-covered St. Stephen's Green Shopping Centre and the peaceful and green Green itself mark the top of Grafton Street.

▲**St. Stephen's Green**—This city park, originally a medieval commons, was enclosed in 1664 and gradually surrounded with fine Georgian buildings. Today it provides 22 acres of grassy refuge for Dubliners. On a sunny afternoon, it's a wonderful world apart from the big city.

▲▲**Number Twenty-Nine Georgian House**—The carefully restored house at Number 29 Lower Fitzwilliam Street gives an intimate glimpse of middle-class Georgian life—which seems pretty high-class. Start with an interesting 12-minute video (you're welcome to bring in a cup of coffee from the café) before joining your guide, who takes you on a fascinating 35-minute walk through this 1790 Dublin home (€3.25, Tue–Sat 10:00–17:00, Sun 14:00–17:00, closed Mon and last half of Dec, tel. 01/702-6165).

▲**Merrion Square**—Laid out in 1762, the square is ringed by elegant Georgian houses decorated with fine doors—a Dublin trademark—with elegant knobs and knockers. The park, once the exclusive domain of the residents, is now a delightful public escape. More inviting than St. Stephens Green, it's ideal for a picnic. If you want to know what "snogging" is, walk through the park on a sunny day. Oscar Wilde, lounging wittily on the corner nearest the town center and surrounded by his clever quotes, provides a fun photo op.

▲**Temple Bar**—This was a Georgian center of craftsmen and merchants. As it fell on hard times in the 19th century, the lower rents attracted students and artists, giving the neighborhood a bohemian flair. With recent government tax incentives and lots of development money, the Temple Bar district has become a thriving cultural (and beer-drinking) hotspot. Today this much-promoted center of trendy shops, cafés, theaters, galleries, pubs with live music, and restaurants feels like the heart of Dublin. Dublin's "Left Bank"—actually on the right bank—fills the cobbled streets between Dame Street and the river. ("Bar" means a walkway along the river.) The central **Meeting House Square** (just off Essex Street) hosts free street theater, a lively organic-produce market (Sat 09:30–15:00), and a book market (Sat 11:00–18:00). The square is surrounded by interesting cultural centers. For a listing of events and galleries, visit the **Temple Bar Information Centre** (Eustace Street, tel. 01/671-5717, www.temple-bar.ie). Rather than follow particular pub or restaurant recommendations (mine are below under "Eating"), venture down a few side lanes off the main drag to see what looks good. The pedestrian-only **Ha' Penny Bridge**, named for the halfpence toll people used to pay to cross it, leads from Temple Bar over the River Liffey to the opposite bank and more sights.

Sights—Dublin, North of the River Liffey

▲▲**O'Connell Bridge**—This bridge spans the River Liffey, which has historically divided the wealthy, cultivated south side from the poorer, cruder north side. While there's plenty of culture north of the river, even today "the north" is considered rougher and less safe. (Currently, the big investment seems to be directed to this area which, in time, is expected to be another fresh and lively prosperity zone.)

From the bridge look upriver (west) as far upstream as you can see. The big concrete building houses the city planning commission. Maddening to locals, this eyesore is in charge of making sure new buildings in the city are built in good taste. It marks (and covers) the place where the Vikings established Dublin in the ninth century. Across the river stands the Four Courts, today's Supreme Court building, bombed and burned in 1922 during the tragic civil war that followed Irish independence. The closest bridge upstream—the elegant, iron Ha' Penny Bridge—leads left into the Temple Bar nightlife district. Just beyond that old-fashioned 19th-century bridge is Dublin's pedestrian Millennium Bridge, inaugurated in 2000. (Note that buses leave from O'Connell Bridge—specifically Aston Quay—for Guinness and the Kilmainham Jail.) Turn 180 degrees and look downstream to see the tall union headquarters—for now the tallest building in the Republic—and lots of cranes. Booming Dublin is developing downstream.

The Irish (forever clever tax fiddlers) have subsidized and revitalized this formerly dreary quarter with great success. A short walk downstream along the north bank leads to a powerful series of modern statues memorializing the great famine of 1845–49.

▲▲**O'Connell Street Stroll**—Dublin's grandest street leads from O'Connell Bridge through the heart of north Dublin. Since the 1740s, it has been a 45-yard-wide promenade. Ever since the first O'Connell Bridge connected it to the Trinity side of town in 1794, it's been Dublin's main drag. (But it was only named O'Connell after independence was won in 1922.) The street, while lined with fast-food and souvenir shops, echoes with history. Take the following stroll:

Statues line O'Connell Street, celebrating great figures in Ireland's fight for independence. At the base of the street stands Daniel O'Connell (1775–1847), known as "the Liberator," who founded the Catholic Association and was a strong voice for Irish Catholic rights in the British parliament.

Looking a block east down Abbey Street you can see the famous Abbey Theatre—rebuilt after a fire and now a nondescript modern building. It's still the much-loved home of the Irish National Theatre.

The statue of James Larkin honors the founder of the Irish Workers' Union. The one monument that didn't wave an Irish flag—a tall column crowned by a statue of the British hero of Trafalgar, Admiral Nelson—was blown up in 1966... the IRA's contribution to the local celebration of the 50th anniversary of the Easter Rising. This vacant spot will be marked by the 120-yard-tall steel spike called the O'Connell Street Monument (planned for 2002).

The **General Post Office** is not just any P.O. It was from here that Patrick Pearse read the Proclamation of Irish Independence in 1916 and kicked off the Easter Rising. The GPO building itself—a kind of Irish Alamo—was the rebel headquarters and scene of a five-day bloody siege that followed the proclamation. Its facade remains pockmarked with bullet holes. Step inside and trace the battle by studying the well-described cycle of 10 paintings that circle the main hall (open for business and sightseers Mon–Sat 08:00–20:00, Sun 10:00–18:00).

The **Moore Street Market** is nearby. After the GPO, detour left two blocks down people-filled Henry Street and then wander to the right into the busy Moore Street Market (Mon–Sat 08:00–18:00). Many of its merchants have manned the same stall for 30 years. Start a conversation. It's a great work-a-day scene. You'll see lots of mums with strollers—a reminder that Ireland is Europe's youngest country, with about 40 percent of the population under the age of 25. An immense glass canopy is planned to cover the street market.

Back on O'Connell Street, cross to the meridian and continue your walk. Find what locals call the "Floozie in the Jacuzzi." This statue of Anna Livia, the mythological being who represents the spirit of the city, was built as part of Dublin's 1,000th birthday celebration in 1988.

St. Mary's Pro-Cathedral, a block east of O'Connell down Cathedral Street, is Dublin's leading Catholic church. But, curiously, it's not a cathedral, since the pope declared Christchurch one in the 12th century—and later, St. Patrick's. (Stubbornly, the Vatican has chosen to ignore the fact that Christchurch and St. Patrick's haven't been Catholic for centuries.) Completed in 1821, it's done in the style of a Greek temple.

Continuing up O'Connell Street, you'll find a statue of **Father Matthew**—a leader of the temperance movement of the 1830s who, historians claim, was responsible for enough Irish peasants staying sober to enable Daniel O'Connell to organize them into a political force. (Perhaps understanding this dynamic, the USSR was careful to keep the price of vodka affordable.) The fancy Gresham Hotel is a good place for an elegant tea or beer.

Charles Stewart Parnell stands boldly at the top of O'Connell Street. The names of the four ancient provinces of Ireland and all 32 Irish counties (north *and* south, since this was erected before Independence) ring the statue, honoring the member of Parliament who nearly won Home Rule for Ireland in the late 1800s. (A sex scandal cost him the support of the Church, which let the air out of any chance for a free Ireland.)

Continue straight up Parnell Square East. The Gate Theater (on the left) was where Orson Welles and James Mason got their acting starts.

The Garden of Remembrance (top of the square, on left) honors the victims of the 1916 Rising. The park was dedicated by Eamon de Valera in 1966 on the 50th anniversary of the uprising that ultimately led to Irish independence. The bottom of the cross-shaped pool is a mosaic of Celtic weapons, symbolic of how the early Irish would proclaim peace by throwing their weapons into the river. The Irish flag flies above the park: green for Catholics, orange for Protestants, and white for the hope that they can live together in peace. Across the street...

The **Dublin Writers' Museum** fills a splendidly-restored Georgian mansion. No country so small has produced such a wealth of literature. As interesting to fans of Irish literature as it is boring to those who aren't, this three-room museum features the lives and works of Dublin's great writers (€4, Mon–Sat 10:00–17:00, Sun 11:00–17:00, June–Aug Mon–Fri until 18:00, helpful audioguide available, 18 Parnell Square North, tel. 01/872-2077). With hometown wits such as Swift, Yeats, Joyce, and Shaw, there is a checklist of residences and memorials to see. Those into James Joyce may want to hike 350 meters east to see the James Joyce Center at 35 North Great George Street (more Joyce memorabilia is in Dun Laoghaire's James Joyce Museum).

Hugh Lane Gallery (next door to the Dublin Writers' Museum) is a fine little gallery in a grand neoclassical building with a bite-size selection of Pre-Raphaelite, French Impressionist, and 19th- and 20th-century Irish paintings (same hrs at Writers' Museum). Sir Hugh went down on the *Lusitania* in 1915; due to an unclear will, his collection is shared by this gallery and the National Gallery in London.

(Your walk is over. Here on the north end of town, you'll never be closer to the Gaelic Athletic Association Museum—described below. Otherwise, hop on your skateboard and return to the river.)

Sights—Dublin's Smithfield Village

Until recently a run-down industrial area, huge investments hope to make Smithfield Village the next Temple Bar. It's worth a look for "Cobblestores" (a redeveloped Duck Lane lined with fancy crafts and gift shops), the Old Jameson whiskey tour, and a chimney observatory with big Dublin views. The sights are clustered close together, two blocks north of the river behind the Four Courts—the Supreme Court building.

The Old Jameson Distillery—Whiskey fans enjoy visiting the old distillery. You get a 10-minute video, 20-minute tour, and a free shot in the pub. Unfortunately, the "distillery" feels fake and put together for tourism. The Old Bushmills tour in Midleton near Cork (in the huge, original factory) is a better experience (tel. 021/461-3594). If you do take the Jameson tour, volunteer energetically when offered the chance to take the "whiskey taste test" at the end (€6.50, daily 09:30–18:00, last tour at 17:30, Sow Street, tel. 01/807-2355).

The Chimney—Built in 1895 for the distillery, the chimney is now an observatory. Ride the elevator 175 feet up for a Dublin panorama not quite as exciting as the view from the Guinness Brewery's Gravity Bar (overpriced at €6.50, daily 10:00–17:30, tel. 01/817-3800).

Sights—Outer Dublin

The jail and the Guinness Brewery are the main sights outside of the old center. Combine them in one visit.

▲▲▲**Kilmainham Gaol (Jail)**—Opened in 1796 as the Dublin County Jail and a debtors' prison and considered a model in its day, it was used frequently as a political prison by the British. Many of those who fought for Irish independence were held or executed here, including leaders of the rebellions of 1798, 1803, 1848, 1867, and 1916. National heroes Robert Emmett and

Charles Stewart Parnell (1846–1891)

Parnell, who led the Irish movement for Home Rule, did time in Kilmainham Jail. A Cambridge-educated Protestant and member of Parliament, he had a vision of a modern and free Irish Republic filled mostly with Catholics but not set up as a religious state. Momentum seemed to be on his side. With the British Prime Minister of the time, Gladstone, in favor of a similar form of Home Rule, it looked as if all of Ireland was ripe for independence. Then a sex scandal broke around Parnell and his mistress. The press, egged on by the powerful Catholic bishops (who didn't want a free but secular Irish state), battered and battered away at the scandal until finally Parnell was driven from office. Sadly, after that, Ireland became mired in the troubles of the 20th century: an awkward independence (1921) featuring a divided island, a bloody civil war, and sectarian violence ever since. It's said Parnell died of a broken heart. Before he did, this great Irish statesman requested to be buried outside of Ireland.

Charles Stewart Parnell each did time here. The last prisoner to be held here was Eamon de Valera (later president of Ireland). He was released on July 16, 1924, the day Kilmainham was finally shut down. The buildings, virtually in ruins, were restored in the 1960s. Today it's a shrine to the Nathan Hales of Ireland.

Start your visit with a guided tour (1 hr, 2/hr, includes 25 min in prison chapel for a rebellion-packed video, spend waiting time in museum). It's touching to tour the cells and places of execution while hearing tales of terrible colonialism and heroic patriotism alongside Irish schoolkids who know these names well. The museum is an excellent exhibit on Victorian prison life and Ireland's fight for independence. Don't miss the museum's dimly lit "Last Words 1916" hall upstairs, displaying the stirring last letters patriots sent to loved ones hours before facing the firing squad (€4.50, April–Sept daily 09:30–18:00, last admission 1 hr before closing; Oct–March Sun–Fri 09:30–17:00, likely closed Sat; €4.50 taxi, bus #51b, #78a, or #79 from Aston Quay or Guinness, tel. 01/453-5984). I'd taxi to the jail and catch the bus from there to Guinness (leaving the prison, take three lefts, crossing no streets, to the bus stop and hop #51b or #78a).

▲Guinness Brewery—A visit to the Guinness Brewery is, for many, a pilgrimage. Arthur Guinness began brewing the famous stout here in 1759. By 1868 it was the biggest brewery in the world. Today the sprawling brewery fills several city blocks. Around the world, Guinness brews more than 10 million pints a day. The home of Ireland's national beer welcomes visitors (for a price) with a sprawling new museum. It fills the old fermentation plant, used from 1902 through 1988, vacated, and then opened in 2000 as a huge shrine-like place that most tourists just have to visit. Stepping into the middle of the ground floor, look up. A tall beer glass–shaped glass atrium—14 million pints big—leads past four floors of exhibitions and cafés to the skylight. Atop the building, the "Gravity Bar" provides visitors with a commanding 360-degree view of Dublin—with vistas all the way to the sea—and a free beer. The actual exhibit makes brewing more grandiose than it is and treats Arthur like the god of human happiness. Highlights are the cooperage (with old film clips showing the master wood-keg makers plying their now-extinct trade), a display of the brewery's clever ads, and the Gravity Bar, which really is spectacular (€11.50—including a €4 pint, daily 09:30–19:00, enter on Market Street, bus #78A from Aston Quay near O'Connell Bridge, or bus #123 from Dame Street and O'Connell Street, tel. 01/408-4800). Hop-on hop-off bus tours stop here.

▲**Gaelic Athletic Association Museum**—The GAA was founded in 1884 as an expression of an Irish cultural awakening. While created to foster the development of Gaelic sports—specifically Irish football and hurling (and to ban English sports such as cricket and rugby)—it played an important part in the fight for independence. This museum, at the newly-expanded 97,000-seat Croke Park Stadium, offers a high-tech, interactive introduction to Ireland's favorite games. Relive the greatest moments in hurling and Irish-football history. Then get involved. Pick up a stick and try hurling, kick a football, and test your speed and balance. A 15-minute film clarifies the connection between sports and Irish politics (€3.75, May–Sept daily 09:30–17:00; Oct–April Tue–Sat 10:00–17:00, Sun 12:00–17:00, closed Mon; on game Sundays the museum is open 12:00–17:00 to new stand ticket-holders only; under the new stand at Croke Park, from O'Connell Street walk 20 min or catch bus #3, #11, #11a, #16, #16a, or #123; tel. 01/855-8176).

Hurling or Irish Football at Croke Park—Actually seeing a match here, surrounded by incredibly spirited Irish fans, is a fun experience. Hurling is like airborne hockey with no injury time-outs, and Irish football is a rugged form of soccer. Matches are held on most Sunday afternoons outside of winter. Tickets—which cost €12.75 to €25.50—are available at the stadium except during championships.

Greyhound Racing—For an interesting lowbrow look at another local pastime, consider going to the dog races and doing a little gambling (€6.50, generally Wed, Thu, and Sat at 20:00, Shelbourne Park, tel. 01/668-3502). Greyhounds race on the other days at Harold's Cross Racetrack (Mon, Tue, and Fri at 20:00, tel. 01/497-1081).

Shopping

Shops are open roughly Monday to Saturday from 09:00 to 18:00, and until 20:00 on Thursday. They have shorter hours on Sunday (if they're open at all). The best shopping area is Grafton, with its neighboring streets and arcades (such as the fun Great George's Arcade between Great George's and Drury Streets), and nearby shopping centers (Powerscourt and St. Stephen's Green). For antiques, try Francis Street. For a street market, consider Mother Redcaps (all day Fri–Sun, bric-a-brac, antiques, crafts, Back Lane, Christchurch). For produce, noise, and color, visit Moore Street (Mon–Sat, near General Post Office). For raw fish, get a whiff of Michan Street (Tue–Sat 07:00–15:00, behind Four Courts building). Saturdays at Temple Bar's Meeting House Square, it's food in the morning (from 09:00) and books in the afternoon (until 18:00). Temple Bar is worth a browse any day for its art, jewelry, new-age paraphernalia, books, music, and gift shops.

Entertainment and Theater in Dublin

Ireland has produced some of the finest writers in both English and Irish, and Dublin houses some of Europe's finest theaters. While Handel's *Messiah* was first performed in Dublin (1742), these days Dublin is famous for its rock bands (U2, Thin Lizzie, and Sinead O'Connor all got started here).

You have much from which to choose. **Abbey Theatre** is Ireland's national theater, founded by W. B. Yeats in 1904 to preserve Irish culture during British rule (Lower Street, tel. 01/878-7222). **Gate Theatre** does foreign plays as well as Irish classics (Cavendish Row, tel. 01/874-4045). **Point Theatre**, once a railway terminus, is now the country's top live-music venue (North Wall quay, tel. 01/836-3633). At the **National Concert Hall**, the National Symphony Orchestra performs most Friday evenings (Earlsfort Terrace, off St. Stephen's Green, tickets €10.50–18, tel. 01/475-1666, www.nch.ie). Street theater takes the stage in Temple Bar on summer evenings.

Pub Action: Folk music fills the pubs, and street entertainers are everywhere. For the latest on live theater, music, cultural happenings, restaurant reviews, pubs, and current museum hours, pick up a copy of the twice-monthly *In Dublin* (€2.50, any newsstand).

The Temple Bar area thrives with music—traditional, jazz, and pop. It really is *the* comfortable and fun place for tourists and locals (who come here to watch the tourists). **Gogarty's Pub** (corner of Fleet and Anglesea) has top-notch sessions upstairs nightly from 21:00. Use this as a kick-off for your Temple Bar evening fun.

A ten-minute hike up the river west of Temple Bar takes you to a twosome with a local and less-touristy ambience. **The Brazen Head**, famous as Dublin's oldest pub, is a hit for an early dinner and late live music, with smoky, atmospheric rooms and a courtyard made to order for balmy evenings (on Bridge Street, tel. 01/677-9549). **O'Shea's Merchant Pub**, just across the street, is encrusted in memories and filled with locals taking a break from the grind. They have live traditional music nightly (the front half is a restaurant, the magic is in the back half).

Irish Music in nearby Dun Laoghaire

For an evening of pure Irish music, song, and dance, check out the **Comhaltas Ceoltoiri Eireann**, an association working to preserve this traditional slice of Irish culture. It got started when Elvis and company threatened to steal the musical heart of the new generation. Judging by the pop status of traditional Irish music these days, Comhaltas accomplished its mission. Their "Fonntrai" evening is a stage show mixing traditional music, song, and dance (€7.75, July–Aug Mon–Thu at 21:00, followed by informal music session at 22:30). Fridays all year long they have a *ceilidh* (kay-lee) where everyone does set dances (€6.50 includes friendly pointers, 21:30–00:30). Wednesdays, Fridays, and Saturdays at 21:30 there are informal sessions by the fireside. All musicians are welcome. Performances are held in the Cuturlann na Eireann, near the Seapoint DART stop or a 20-minute walk from Dun Laoghaire, at 32 Belgrave Square, Monkstown (tel. 01/280-0295, www .comhaltas.com). Their bar is free and often filled with music.

Sleeping in Dublin
(€1.10 = about $1, country code: 353, area code: 01)

Sleep Code: **S** = Single, **D** = Double/Twin, **T** = Triple, **Q** = Quad, **b** = bathroom, **s** = shower only, **CC** = Credit Cards accepted, **no CC** = Credit Cards not accepted. Breakfast is included unless otherwise noted. To locate hotels, see map on page 547.

Dublin is popular and rooms can be tight. Book ahead for weekends anytime of year, particularly in summer and during rugby weekends. Prices are often discounted on weeknights (Mon–Thu) and from November through February.

Big and practical places (both cheap and moderate) are most central at Christchurch on the edge of Temple Bar. For classy, older Dublin accommodations, you'll pay more and stay a bit farther out (east of St. Stephen's Green). For a small-town escape with the best budget values, take the convenient DART train (at least 3/hr, 20 min) from nearby Dun Laoghaire (see page 564).

Laundry in Dublin: Capricorn Launderette, a block southwest of Jury's Inn Christchurch on Patrick Street, is full-service only. Allow four hours and about €8 (Mon–Fri 07:30–20:00, Sat 09:00–18:00, Sun 10:00–16:00, tel. 01/473-1779). The All-American Launderette offers self- and full-service options (Mon–Sat 08:30–19:00, Sun 10:00–18:00, 40 South George's Street, tel. 01/677-2779).

Sleeping near Christchurch

These places face Christchurch Cathedral, a great locale a five-minute walk from the best evening scene at Temple Bar and 10 minutes from the sightseeing center (Trinity College and Grafton Street). Full Irish breakfasts, which cost €9 at the hotels, are half the price at the many small cafés nearby (consider the Applewood café at 1b Werburgh Street, next to Burdoch's Fish & Chips). For cheap hostels (with some double rooms) in this neighborhood, see "Hostels in the Center," below.

Harding Hotel is a hardwood, 21st-century, Viking-style place with 53 institutional-yet-hotelesque rooms. The rooms are simpler than Jurys (below), but they're also more intimate (Sb-€60, Db/Tb-€92, tell them Rick sent you and get 10 percent off, breakfast-€5–7.50, CC, Internet access, Copper Alley across street from Christchurch, tel. 01/679-6500, fax 01/679-6504, www.hardinghotel.ie).

Jurys Christchurch Inn (like its sisters across town, in Galway, and in Belfast) is central and offers business-class comfort in all of its identical rooms. This no-nonsense, modern, American-style hotel chain has a winning keep-it-simple-and-affordable formula. If ye olde is getting old (and you don't mind big tour groups), there's no better value in town. All 182 rooms cost the same: €95 for one, two, or three adults or two adults and two kids (breakfast extra). Each room has a modern bathroom, direct-dial telephone, and TV. Two floors are strictly nonsmoking. Request a room far from the noisy elevator (book long in advance for weekends, CC, parking €10.25/day, Christchurch Place, Dublin 8, tel. 01/454-0000, fax 01/454-0012, U.S. tel. 800/843-3311, www.jurys.com, e-mail: christchurch_inn@jurysdoyle.com). Another Jurys is near the Connelly train station (see below).

Sleeping between Trinity College and Temple Bar

Bewley's Principal Hotel rents 70 decent rooms. For its size, it has an intimate feel, with character (Sb-€109, Db-€137, often mid-week deals, breakfast extra, CC, nonsmoking rooms, request a quiet room off the street, 19-20 Fleet Street, tel. 01/670-8122, fax 01/670-8103, www.bewleysprincipalhotel.com).

Temple Bar Hotel is a 130-room business-class place, very centrally located midway between Trinity College and the Temple Bar action (Sb-€133, Db-€178, Tb-€241, often discounted, CC, smoke-free rooms, Fleet Street, Temple Bar, Dublin 2, tel. 01/677-3333, fax 01/677-3088, e-mail: templeb@iol.ie).

Sleeping near St. Stephen's Green

Albany House's 33 rooms come with classic furniture, high ceilings, Georgian elegance, and some street noise. Request the huge "superior" rooms, which are the same price (Sb-€89, Db-€127, €114 in slow times, Tb-€140, Una promises 10 percent off with this book in 2002, includes breakfast, CC, back rooms are quieter, smoke-free, just 1 block south of St. Stephen's Green at 84 Harcourt Street, Dublin 2, tel. 01/475-1092, fax 01/475-1093, e-mail: albany@indigo.ie).

The Fitzwilliam has an inviting lounge and rents 13 decent rooms (Sb-€70, Db-€121, CC, 10 percent discount with this book, children under 16 sleep free, 41 Upper Fitzwilliam Street, Dublin 2, tel. 01/662-5155, fax 01/676-7488, Declan Carney).

Baggot Court Accommodations rents 11 similar rooms a block farther away and without a lounge (Sb-€83, Db-€140, Tb-€210, CC, entirely nonsmoking, free parking, 92 Lower Baggot Street, Dublin 2, tel. 01/661-2819, fax 01/661-0253, e-mail: baggot@indigo.ie).

Sleeping Away from the Center, East of St. Stephen's Green

Mespil Hotel is a huge, modern, business-class hotel renting 260 identical three-star rooms (each with a double and single bed, phone, TV, voicemail, and modem hookup) at a good price with all the comforts. This is a cut above the Jurys Inns for a little more money (Sb, Db, or Tb-€121, breakfast extra, CC, elevator, nonsmoking floor, apartments for weeklong stays, 10-min walk southeast of St. Stephen's Green or bus #10, Mespil Road, Dublin 4, tel. 01/667-1222, fax 01/667-1244, www.leehotels.ie, e-mail: mespil@leehotels.ie).

On Northumberland Road: The next two listings are on Northumberland Road, southeast of the city center. Trinity College is a 15-minute walk away, or catch bus #5, #6, #7, #8, or #45, which lumber down Northumberland Road into downtown Dublin every 10 minutes.

Northumberland Lodge has eight elegant rooms in a quiet mansion (Sb-€57–70, Db-€83–114, highest on weekends and in summer, CC, video library in lounge, 68 Northumberland Road, Ballsbridge, Dublin 4, car park, tel. 01/660-5270, fax 01/668-8679, e-mail: info@northumberlandlodge.com).

Glenveagh Town House rents 13 rooms—Victorian upstairs, modern downstairs (Sb-€63–70, Db-€95–102, less in slow times, includes breakfast, CC, car park, 31 Northumberland Road, tel. 01/668-4612, fax 01/668-4559, e-mail: glenveagh@eircom.net).

Sleeping near Connolly Train Station

Jurys Inn Custom House, on Custom House Quay, offers the same value as the Jurys at Christchurch. Bigger (with 234

rooms) and not quite as well-located (in a boring neighborhood, a 10-min riverside hike from O'Connell Bridge), this
Jurys is more likely to have rooms available (Db-€88, CC,
tel. 01/607-5000, fax 01/829-0400, U.S. tel. 800/843-3311,
e-mail: info@jurys.com).

Charles Stewart Budget Accommodations is a big, basic
place offering lots of forgettable rooms, many long and narrow
with head-to-toe twins, in a great location for a good price
(D-€32, Sb-€63, D-€76, Db-€89, Tb-€121, Qb-€140, CC,
includes cooked breakfast, just beyond top of O'Connell Street
at 5 Parnell Square, Dublin 1, tel. 01/878-0350, fax 01/878-1387,
e-mail: cstuart@iol.ie).

Hostels in the Center

Near Christchurch: **Kinlay House**, around the corner from Jurys
Christchurch Inn, is the backpackers' equivalent—definitely the
place to go for cheap beds in a central location and an all-
ages-welcome atmosphere. This huge, red-brick, 19th-century
Victorian building has 149 metal, prison-style beds in spartan,
smoke-free rooms. There are singles, doubles, and four-to-six-
bed coed dorms (good for families), as well as a few giant dorms.
It fills up most days. Call well in advance, especially for singles,
doubles, and summer weekends (S-€33, D-€52, Db-€57, dorm
beds-€15.25–23.50, cheaper off-season, includes continental
breakfast, CC, kitchen access, launderette-€6.50, Internet access-
€6.50/hr, left luggage, travel desk, TV lounge, small lockers,
lots of stairs, Christchurch, 2-12 Lord Edward Street, Dublin 2,
tel. 01/679-6644, fax 01/679-7437, www.kinlayhouse.ie, e-mail:
kinlay.dublin@usitworld.com).

Four Courts Hostel is a new 230-bed hostel beautifully
located immediately across the river from the Four Courts, a
five-minute walk from Christchurch and Temple Bar. It's bare
and institutional (as hostels are), but expansive and well-run with
a focus on security and efficiency (dorm beds from €15.25–20.25,
bunk D-€56, bunk Db-€65, includes small breakfast, girls'
floor and boys' floor, elevator, no smoking, Internet access,
game room, laundry service, some parking, lockers, 15 Merchant's
Quay, Dublin 8, tel. 01/672-5839, fax 01/672-5862, www.
fourcourtshostel.com, e-mail: info@fourcourtshostel.com,
bus #90 from train or bus station).

Near Grafton Street: **Avalon House** rents 300 backpacker beds much like the places listed above (S-€29, Sb-€33,
D/twin-€51, Db/twin-€56, dorm beds-€13–23, includes continental breakfast, CC, elevator, Ireland bus tickets, Internet
access, launderette across street, a few minutes off Grafton
Street at 55 Aungier Street, tel. 01/475-0001, fax 01/475-0303,
www.avalon-house.ie).

Sleeping and Eating in nearby Dun Laoghaire
(€1.10 = about $1, country code: 353, area code: 01, mail: County Dublin)

Dun Laoghaire (dun leary) is seven miles south of Dublin. This beach resort, with the ferry terminal for Wales and easy connections to downtown Dublin, is a great small-town base for the big city.

While buses run between Dublin and Dun Laoghaire, the **DART commuter train** is much faster (6/hr in peak times, at least 3/hr otherwise, 20 min, runs Mon–Sat about 06:30–23:15, Sun from 09:00, €1.50 one-way, €2.75 round-trip, Eurail valid but uses day of flexipass; for a longer stay consider the €13 4-day Explorer ticket covering DART and Dublin buses). If you're coming from Dublin, catch a DART train marked "Bray" and get off at the Sandy Cove or Dun Laoghaire stop, depending on which B&B you choose; if you're leaving Dun Laoghaire, catch a train marked "Howth" to get to Dublin—get off at the central Tara Street station.

The Dun Laoghaire harbor was strategic enough to merit a line of Martello Towers (built to defend against an expected Napoleonic invasion). By the mid-19th century, the huge break-waters—reaching like two muscular arms into the Irish Sea—were completed, protecting a huge harbor. Ships sailed regularly from here to Wales (60 miles away), and the first train line in Ireland connected the terminal with Dublin. While still a busy transportation hub, today the nearly mile-long breakwaters are also popular with strollers, bikers, birders, and fishermen. Hike out to the lighthouse at the end of the interesting East Pier.

The **Dun Laoghaire TI** is in the ferry terminal (Mon–Sat 10:00–18:00 year-round, closed Sun). Comhaltas Ceoltoiri Eireann, an association that preserves Irish folk music, offers lively shows in Dun Laoghaire (see "Irish Music in nearby Dun Laoghaire," above). Taxi fare from Dun Laoghaire to central Dublin is about €13, to the airport about €32. With easy free parking and DART access into Dublin, this area is ideal for those with cars (which cost €19 a day to park in Dublin). A **Laundromat** is located in Sandycove "Village" (self- and full-serve, 2 Glasthule, across from church). The Net House Café, down-town on George's Street, provides a fast **Internet** connection 24 hours a day.

Near Sandycove DART station: These listings are within several blocks of the Sandycove DART station and a seven-minute walk to the Dun Laoghaire DART station/ferry landing.

Mrs. Kane's **Seaview B&B** is a modern house with three big, cheery rooms and a welcoming guests' lounge with a computer for guests to jump online. While a few blocks farther out than the

Dun Laoghaire

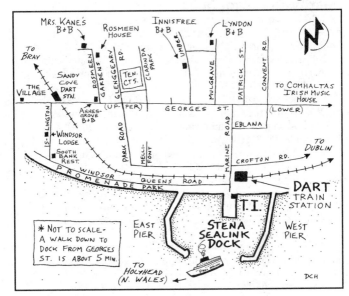

others, it's worth the walk for its bright and friendly feeling (Db-€61 through 2002 with this book, no CC, strictly smoke-free, just above Rosmeen Gardens at 2 Granite Hall, tel. & fax 01/280-9105, e-mail: seaviewbedandbreakfast@hotmail.com).

Windsor Lodge rents four fresh, cheery rooms on a quiet street a block off the harbor and a block from the DART station (Db-€56–63, family deals, no CC, nonsmoking, 3 Islington Avenue, Sandycove, Dun Laoghaire, tel. & fax 01/284-6952, e-mail: winlodge@eircom.net, Mary O'Farrell).

Annesgrove B&B has four tidy rooms decorated in beige and brown (D-€56, Db-€63, includes breakfast, no CC, parking, close to park and beach, 28 Rosmeen Gardens, tel. 01/280-9801, Anne D'Alton). **Rosmeen House** is a similar grandfather-clock kind of place renting four smoke-free rooms (S-€32, Db-€63, no CC, 13 Rosmeen Gardens, tel. 01/280-7613, Joan Murphy).

Near Dun Laoghaire DART Station: **Lynden B&B**, with a classy 150-year-old interior hiding behind a somber front, rents four big rooms (D-€48, Db-€56, 10 percent discount with this book, no CC, past Mulgrave Street to 2 Mulgrave Terrace, tel. 01/280-6404).

Innisfree B&B has a fine lounge and six big, bright, and comfy rooms (D-€44, Db-€50, 10 percent discount with this book, CC, from George Street hike up the plain but quiet

Northumberland Avenue to #31, tel. 01/280-5598, fax 01/280-3093, e-mail: djsmith@club1.ie, Brendan and Mary Smith).

On the same street, you'll find two places renting four big, well-worn rooms each: **Mrs. Howard's B&B** (S-€32, D-€46, no CC, TV lounge, 36 Northumberland Avenue, tel. 01/280-3262) and **Mrs. O'Sullivan's Duncree B&B** (D-€48, Db-€53, no CC, family room, no smoking, 16 Northumberland Ave, tel. 01/280-6118).

Eating in Dun Laoghaire: If staying in Dun Laoghaire, I'd definitely eat here and not in Dublin. Glasthule (called simply "The Village" locally, just down the street from the Sandycove DART station) has a stunning array of fun, little, hardworking restaurants.

Bistro Vino is the rage lately, with cozy, candlelit, Mediterranean ambience and great food (€10–20 meals, seafood, pasta, CC, arrive early or have a reservation, nightly early-bird special 17:00–19:00, 56 Glasthule Road, tel. 01/280-6097).

Duzy's Café fills a classy but garishly painted, mod-feeling old room above the Eagle House Pub with happy eaters and French-Irish cuisine. The menu is a joy and their €16.50 early-bird special—three courses with coffee on weeknights until 19:00—is a super value (€19 plates, nightly from 18:00, CC, 18 Glasthule Road, tel. 01/230-0210, run by John Dunne and Stephane Couzy).

The big **Eagle House** pub serves hearty €8 pub meals (until 21:00 except Sun) in a wonderful but smoky atmosphere. This is a great local joint for a late drink. The nearby **Daniel's Restaurant and Wine Bar** is less atmospheric but also good (€19 meals, closed Mon, 34 Glasthule Road, tel. 01/284-1027).

South Bank Restaurant, a jolly place filled with happy piano music, faces the water and serves fish and European cuisine (€19 main courses, nightly except Mon in winter, 1 Martello Terrace, directly down from Sandycove DART station, reservations smart, tel. 01/280-8788).

Walters Public House and Restaurant is a bright, modern place above a similar pub, offering good food to a dressy crowd (nightly 17:30–23:00, €13–19 meals, 68 Upper George's Street, tel. 01/230-1086).

George's Street, three blocks inland and Dun Laoghaire's main drag, has plenty of eateries and pubs, many with live music. A good bet for families is the kid-friendly **Bits and Pizza** (off George's Street on Patrick Street).

Eating in Dublin

As Dublin does its boom-time jig, fine and creative eateries are popping up all over town. While you can get decent pub grub for €9 on just about any corner, consider saving pub grub for the countryside. And there's no pressing reason to eat Irish in cosmopolitan Dublin. Dublin's good restaurants are packed from 20:00 on, especially on weekends. Eating early (18:00–19:00) saves time and money (as many better places offer an early-bird special).

Eating Quick and Easy around Grafton Street

Cornucopia is a small, earth-mama-with-class, proudly vegetarian, self-serve place two blocks off Grafton. It's friendly and youthful, with hearty €7.75 lunches and €9 dinner specials (Mon–Sat 08:30–20:00, closed Sun, 19 Wicklow Street, tel. 01/677-7583).

Graham O'Sullivan Restaurant and Coffee Shop is a cheap, cheery cafeteria serving soup and sandwiches with a salad bar in unpretentious ambience (Mon–Fri 08:00–18:30, Sat 09:00–17:00, closed Sun, smoke-free upstairs, 12 Duke Street). Two pubs on the same street—**The Duke** and **Davy Burns**—serve pub lunches. The **Cathach Rare Books** shop (10 Duke Street) displays a rare edition of *Ulysses* among other treasures in its window.

Bewley's Restaurant is an old-time local favorite offering light meals from €5.75 and full meals from €9. Sit on the ground floor among Harry Clarke windows and Art Deco lamps or upstairs in the bright atrium decorated by local art students (self-service 07:30–23:00, CC, 78 Grafton Street, tel. 01/635-5470).

Wagamama Noodle Bar, like its popular sisters in London, is a pan-Asian slurp-athon with great and healthy noodle and rice dishes (€8–12) served by walkie-talkie-toting waiters at long communal tables (daily 12:00–23:00, CC, nonsmoking, no reservations, often a line, South King Street, underneath St. Stephen's Green Shopping Centre, tel. 01/478-2152).

South Great Georges Street is lined with hardworking little eateries. **Juice** keeps vegetarians happy (daily 11:00–23:00, 73 South Great Georges Street, tel. 01/475-7856).

Yamamori is a plain, bright, and mod Japanese place serving seas of sushi and noodles (€9 lunches daily 12:30–17:30, dinners €10.25–15.25, 17:30–23:00, CC, 71 South Great Georges Street, tel. 01/475-5001).

Marks & Spencer department store (on Grafton Street) has a fancy grocery store in the basement with fine take-away sandwiches and salads (Mon–Fri 09:00–19:00, Thu until 21:00, Sat 09:00–19:00, Sun 12:00–18:00). Locals prefer **Dunne's** department store for its lower prices (same hrs, grocery in basement, in St. Stephen's Green Shopping Centre).

Eating Fast and Cheap near Christchurch

Many of Dublin's **late-night grocery stores** (such as the Spar off the top of Dame Street on Parliament Street) sell cheap salads, microwaved meat pies, and made-to-order sandwiches.

A €5 picnic dinner back at the hotel might be a good option after a busy day of sightseeing.

Leo Burdocks Fish & Chips is popular with locals (takeout only, daily 12:00–24:00, 2 Werburgh Street, off Christchurch Square).

Dining at Classy Restaurants and Cafés

These three restaurants are located within a block of each other, just south of Temple Bar and Dame Street, near the main TI.

QV2 Restaurant serves "international with an Irish twist"—great cooking at reasonable prices with a happy-colors-and-candle-light atmosphere (€32 meals, Mon–Sat 12:00–15:00, 18:00–23:00, closed Sun, nonsmoking section, CC, 14 St. Andrew Street, tel. 01/677-3363, run by John Count McCormack—grandson of the famous tenor). They offer a quick €11.50 lunch special and the same lunch menu for early birds ordering before 19:30.

Trocadero, across the street, serves beefy European cuisine to locals interested in a slow, romantic meal. The dressy red-velvet interior is draped with photos of local actors. Come early or make a reservation. This place is a favorite with Dublin's theatergoers (€26 meals, Mon–Sat 18:00–24:00, closed Sun, nonsmoking section, CC, 3 St. Andrew Street, tel. 01/677-5545). The three-course early-bird special at €18 is a fine value (18:00–19:15, leave by 20:30).

Boulevard Café is a mod, local, likeable, trendy place serving Mediterranean cuisine, heavy on the Italian. They serve salads, pasta, and sandwiches for around €6.50, three-course lunch specials for €10.25 (Mon–Sat 12:00–16:00), and dinner plates for €13–15.50 (daily 18:00–24:00, CC, 27 Exchequer Street, smart to reserve for dinner, tel. 01/679-2131).

Eating at Temple Bar

Gallagher's Boxty House is touristy and traditional, a good, basic value with creaky floorboards and old Dublin ambience. Its specialty is boxties—the generally bland-tasting Irish potato pancake filled and rolled with various meats, veggies, and sauces. The "Gaelic Boxty" is liveliest (€13–15, also serves stews and corned beef, daily 12:00–23:30, nonsmoking section, CC, 20 Temple Bar, tel. 01/677-2762). Popular Gallagher's takes same-day reservations only; to reserve for dinner, stop by between 12:00 and 15:00.

Bad Ass Café is a grunge diner serving cowboy/Mex/veggie/pizzas to old and new hippies. No need to dress up (€6.50 lunch and €16.50 3-course dinner deals, kids' specials, daily 11:30–24:00, CC, Crown Alley, just off Meeting House Square, tel. 01/671-2596).

Luigi Malone's, with its fun atmosphere and varied menu of pizza, ribs, pasta, sandwiches, and fajitas, is just the place to take your high-school date (€10-20, daily 12:00–23:00, corner of Cecila and Fownes Streets).

The Shack, while a bit pricey and touristy, has a reputation for quality and serves traditional Irish, chicken, seafood, and steak dishes (€15–26 entrées, CC, daily 12:00–23:00, across from Dublin Castle on Dame Street, tel. 01/670-9785). Their second location is in the center of Temple Bar (24 East Essex Street, tel. 01/679-0043).

Transportation Connections—Dublin

By bus to: Belfast (7/day, 3 hrs), **Trim** (4/day, 1 hr), **Ennis** (11/day, 4.5 hrs), **Galway** (13/day, 3.5 hrs), **Limerick** (13/day, 3.5 hrs), **Tralee** (6/day, 6 hrs), **Dingle** (4/day, 8 hrs, €21.50, transfer at Tralee). Bus info: tel. 01/836-6111.

By train from Heuston Station to: Tralee (6/day, 4 hrs, talking timetable tel. 805-4266), **Ennis** (2/day, 4 hrs), **Galway** (5/day, 3 hrs, talking timetable tel. 01/805-4222).

By train from Connolly Station to: Rosslare (3/day, 3 hrs), **Portrush** (6/day, 5 hrs, €30 one-way, €41 round-trip, transfer in Belfast or Portadown), **Belfast** (8/day, 2 hrs, talking timetable tel. 01/836-3333). The **Dublin-Belfast train** connects the two Irish capitals in two hours at 90 miles per hour on one continuous, welded rail (€27 one-way, €41 round-trip; round-trip the same day only €27 except Fri and Sun; from the border to Belfast one-way €14, €19 round-trip). Train info: tel. 01/836-6222. North Ireland train info: tel. 048/9089-9400.

Dublin Airport: The airport is well-connected to the city center 11 kilometers away (airport info: tel. 01/814-1111; also see "Arrival in Dublin," above). Ryanair is an Irish cut-rate airline with cheap fares to London (€76 round-trip) and other European destinations (Irish tel. 01/609-7800, www.ryanair.com). British Air offers pricier flights to London's Gatwick Airport (7/day, from €139 round-trip, Irish tel. 01/814-5201 or toll-free tel. 1-800-626-747 in Ireland, U.S. tel. 800/247-9297, www.britishairways.com), as do Aer Lingus (tel. 01/886-8888, www.aerlingus.ie) and BMI British Midland (Irish tel. 01/283-8833, U.S. tel. 800/788-0555, www.flybmi.com).

Transportation Connections— Ireland and Britain

Dublin and London: The journey by boat plus train or bus takes 7 to 10 hours, all day or all night (bus: 4/day, €31–44, British tel. 08705-143-219, www.eurolines.co.uk; train: 4/day, €51-87, Dublin train info: tel. 01/836-6222).

If you're going directly to London, flying is your best bet. Check Ryanair first (Irish tel. 01/609-7878, www.ryanair.com). BMI British Midland offers reasonable flights, such as Dublin–

Heathrow (8/day, 90 min, about €217 one-way, as little as €170 round-trip); to get the lowest fares, book months in advance and go round-trip (you can forget to return), leaving and returning on a weekday (Mon–Thu), and staying over a Saturday. For reservations and information, call Irish tel. 01/407-3036. The U.S. office of BMI British Midland sells Discover Europe air passes (these must be purchased before you leave)—flights out of Dublin that are less than 500 miles cost $218 plus tax; flights over 500 miles cost $268 plus tax (discounts sometimes offered to American and Canadian youths and seniors, U.S. tel. 800/788-0555). For more info, visit www.flybmi.com.

Dublin and Holyhead: Irish Ferries sails between Dublin and Holyhead in North Wales (dock is a mile east of O'Connell Bridge, 5/day: 2 slow, 3 fast; slow boats: 3.25 hrs, €25.50 one-way walk-on fare; fast boats: 1.75 hrs, €32; Dublin tel. 01/661-0511, Holyhead tel. 08705-329-129, www.irishferries.ie).

Dublin and Liverpool: NorseMerchant Ferries sails most mornings (Tue–Sat) and every evening year-round from Dublin Harbor (8 hrs, €32–44 one-way by day, €26–39 one-way overnight, cabins extra, car transport possible, Dublin tel. 01/819-2999, British tel. 0870-800-4321, www.norsemerchant.com).

Dun Laoghaire and Holyhead: Stena Line sails between Dun Laoghaire (near Dublin) and Holyhead in North Wales (4/day, 2 hrs on *HSS Catamaran*, €46 one-way walk-on fare, reserve by phone—they book up long in advance on summer weekends, Dun Laoghaire tel. 01/204-7777, recorded info tel. 01/204-7799, can book online at www.stenaline.ie).

Ferry Connections—Ireland and France

Irish Ferries connect Ireland (Rosslare) with France (Cherbourg and Roscoff) every other day (less Jan–March). While Cherbourg has the quickest connection to Paris, your overall time between Ireland and Paris is about the same (18 hrs) regardless of which port is used on the day you sail. One-way fares vary from €51 to €102. Eurailers go for half the price. In both directions, departures are generally between 16:00 and 18:00 and arrive late the next morning. While passengers can nearly always get on, reservations are wise in summer and easy by phone. If you anticipate a crowded departure, you can reserve a seat for €8. Doubles (or singles) start at €43. The easiest way to get a bed (except during summer) is from the information desk upon boarding. The cafeteria serves bad food at reasonable prices. Upon arrival in France, buses and taxis connect you to your Paris-bound train (Irish Ferries: Dublin tel. 01/313-131 or 01/661-0511, recorded info tel. 01/661-0715, Paris tel. 01 44 94 20 40, www.irishferries.com, e-mail: info@irishferries.com, European Ferry Guide: www.youra .com/ferry/intlferries.html).

DINGLE PENINSULA

Dingle Peninsula, the westernmost tip of Ireland, offers just the right mix of far-and-away beauty, ancient archaeological wonders, and desolate walks or bike rides—all within convenient reach of its main town. Dingle Town is just large enough to have all the necessary tourist services and a steady nocturnal beat of Irish folk music.

While the big tour buses clog the neighboring Ring of Kerry before heading east to slobber all over the Blarney Stone, Dingle—while crowded in the summer—still feels like the fish and the farm really matter. Forty fishing boats sail from Dingle, tractor tracks dirty the main drag, and a faint whiff of peat fills its nighttime streets.

For 20 years, my Irish dreams have been set here on this sparse but lush peninsula where locals are fond of saying, "The next parish is Boston." There's a feeling of closeness to the land on Dingle. When I asked a local if he was born here, he thought for a second and said, "No, it was about six miles down the road." When I told him where I was from, a faraway smile filled his eyes, he looked out to sea and sighed, "Ah, the shores of Americy." I asked his friend if he'd lived here all his life. He said, "Not yet."

Dingle feels so traditionally Irish because it's a Gaeltacht, a region where the government subsidizes the survival of the Irish language and culture. While English is always there, the signs, menus, and songs come in Gaelic. Children carry hurling sticks to class, and even the local preschool brags, "ALL Gaelic."

Of the peninsula's 10,000 residents, 1,300 live in Dingle Town. Its few streets, lined with ramshackle but gaily-painted shops and pubs, run up from a rain-stung harbor always busy with fishing boats and yachts. Traditionally, the buildings were drab gray or whitewashed. Thirty years ago Ireland's "tidy town" competition prompted everyone to paint their buildings in playful pastels.

It's a peaceful town. The courthouse (1832) is open one hour a month. The judge does his best to wrap up business within a half hour. During the day you'll see teenagers—already working on ruddy beer-glow cheeks—roll kegs up the streets and into the pubs in preparation for another night of music and *craic* (fun conversation).

Dingle History

The wet sod of Dingle is soaked with medieval history. In the darkest depths of the Dark Ages, peace-loving, bookwormish monks fled the chaos of the Continent and its barbarian raids. They sailed to the drizzly fringe of the known world—places like Dingle. These monks kept literacy alive in Europe. Charlemagne, who ruled much of Europe in the year 800, imported Irish monks to be his scribes.

It was from this peninsula that the semi-mythical explorer monk, St. Brendan, is said to have set sail in the sixth century in search of a legendary western paradise. Some think he beat Columbus to North America by nearly a thousand years.

Dingle (*An Daingean* in Gaelic) was a busy seaport in the late Middle Ages. Along with Tralee, it was the only walled town in Kerry—castles stood at the low and high ends of Main Street, protecting the Normans from the angry and dispossessed Irish outside. Dingle was a gateway to northern Spain—a three-day sail due south. Many 14th- and 15th-century pilgrims left from Dingle for the revered Spanish church, Santiago de Compostela, thought to house the bones of St. James.

In Dingle's medieval heyday, locals traded cowhides for wine. When Dingle's position as a trading center ended, the town faded in importance. In the 19th century it was a linen-weaving center. Until 1970 fishing dominated. The only visitors were scholars and students of old Irish ways. In 1970 the movie *Ryan's Daughter* introduced the world to Dingle. The trickle of Dingle fans has grown to a flood as word of its musical, historical, gastronomical, and scenic charms—not to mention its friendly dolphin—has spread.

The Voyage of St. Brendan

It has long been part of Irish lore that St. Brendan the Navigator (A.D. 484–577) and 12 followers sailed from the southwest of Ireland to "The Land of Promise" (what is now North America) in a currach—a wood-framed boat covered with oxen hide and tar. According to a 10th-century monk who poetically wrote of the journey, Brendan and his crew encountered a paradise of birds, were attacked by a whale, and suffered the smoke of a smelly island in the north before finally reaching their Land of Promise.

Dingle Peninsula

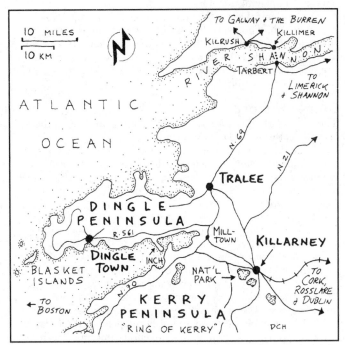

The legend and its precisely-described locations still fascinate modern readers. A British scholar of navigation, Tim Severin, re-created the entire journey from 1976 to 1977. He and his crew set out from Brendan Creek in County Kerry in a currach. The prevailing winds blew them to the Hebrides, the Faeroe Islands, Iceland, and finally to Newfoundland. While this didn't prove that St. Brendan successfully sailed to North America, it did prove that he could have.

Brendan fans have been emboldened by an intriguing arch-aeological find in Connecticut. Called the "Gungywamp," the site includes a double circle of stones and a beehive-like chamber built in the same manner as the stone igloos seen on the Dingle Peninsula. The Gungywamp beehive chamber has been carbon-dated to approximately A.D. 600. Outside the chamber, a stone slab is inscribed with a cross that resembles the unique style of the Irish cross.

According to his 10th-century biographer, "St. Brendan sailed from the Land of Promise home to Ireland. And from that time on, Brendan acted as if he did not belong to this world at all. His mind and his joy were in the delight of heaven."

Planning Your Time

For the shortest visit, give Dingle two nights and a day. It takes six to eight hours to get there from Dublin, Galway, or the boat dock in Rosslare. I like two nights because you feel more like a local on your second evening in the pubs. You'll need the better part of a day to explore the 30-mile loop around the peninsula by bike, car, or tour bus (see "Circular Tour" on page 584). To do any serious walking or relaxing, you'll need two or three days. It's not uncommon to find Americans slowing way, way down in Dingle town.

Orientation (area code: 066)

Dingle—extremely comfortable on foot—hangs on a medieval grid of streets between the harborfront (where the bus from Tralee stops) and Main Street (3 blocks inland). Nothing in town is more than a five-minute walk away. Street numbers are used only when more than one place is run by a family of the same name. Most locals know most locals, and people on the street are fine sources of information. Remember, locals love their soda bread, and tourism provides the butter. You'll find a warm and sincere welcome.

Tourist Information: The TI is a privately owned, for-profit business—little more than a glorified shop with a green staff that's disinclined to really know the town (June-Sept Mon–Sat 09:00–18:00, Sun 10:00–17:00; shorter hours in spring and fall and closed Sun–Mon, closed Dec–Feb; on Strand Street by the water, tel. 066/915-1188). For more knowledgeable help, drop by the Mountain Man shop (on Strand Street, see "Dingle Activities," below) or talk to your B&B host.

Helpful Hints

Before You Go: The local Web site (www.dingle-peninsula.ie) lists festivals and events. Celticwave.com is a good bet for music and arts listings. Look up old issues of *National Geographic* (April '76 and Sept '94).

Crowds: Crowds trample Dingle's charm throughout July and August. The absolute craziest are the Dingle Races (2nd weekend in Aug), Dingle Regatta (3rd weekend in Aug), and the Blessing of the Boats (end of Aug, beginning of Sept). The first Mondays in May, June, and August are bank holidays giving Ireland's workers three-day weekends—and ample time to fill up Dingle. Dingle's metabolism (prices, schedules, activities) rises and falls with the tourist crowds—October through April is sleepy.

Banking: Two banks in town, both on Main Street, offer the same rates (Mon 10:00–17:00, Tue–Fri 10:00–16:00, closed Sat–Sun) and have cash machines. The TI happily changes cash and traveler's checks at mediocre rates. Expect to use cash (rather than credit cards) to pay for most peninsula activities.

Supermarket: The Super Valu supermarket/department

store, at the base of town, has everything and is ideal for assembling a peninsula picnic (Mon–Sat 08:00–21:00, Sun 08:00–19:00, until 22:00 in summer). Smaller groceries are scattered throughout the town. Try Centra on Main Street (Mon–Sat 08:00–21:00, Sun 08:00–18:00).

Post Office: It's on Main Street near Benners Hotel (Mon–Fri 09:00–17:30, Sat 09:00–13:00, closed Sun).

Internet Access: Dingle Internet Café is on Main Street (€2.50/20 min, cheaper before noon, Mon–Sat 09:00–22:00, Sun 10:00–20:00, shorter hours Oct–April, tel. 066/915-2478).

Bike Rental: Bike-rental shops abound. The best is Paddy's Bike Hire (€9/day or 24 hrs, €11.50 for better bikes, daily 09:00–19:00, includes helmets, on Dykegate next to Grapevine Hostel, tel. 066/915-2311). Foxy John's (Main Street), Mountain Man (no helmets), and the Ballintaggert Hostel also rent bikes. If you're biking the peninsula, get a bike with skinny street tires, not slow and fat mountain-bike tires. Plan on leaving a credit card, driver's license, or passport as security.

Dingle Activities: The Mountain Man, a hiking shop run by a local guide, Mike Shea, is a clearinghouse for information, local tours, and excursions (July–Sept daily 09:00–21:00, Oct–June 09:00–18:00, just off harbor at Strand Street, tel. 066/915-2400, e-mail: irasc@eircom.net). Stop by for ideas on biking, hiking, horse riding, climbing, peninsula tours (which they offer), and trips to the Blaskets. They are the Dingle Town contact for the Dunquin-Blasket Islands boats and shuttle-bus rides to the harbor (see "Blasket Islands," below).

Travel Agency: Maurice O'Connor at Galvin's Travel Agency can book train, long-distance bus, and plane tickets, and boat rides to France (Mon–Fri 09:30–18:00, Sat 09:30–17:00, closed Sun, John Street, tel. 066/915-1409).

Farmers Market: Every Saturday (10:00–14:00), local farmers fill the St. James churchyard (on Main Street) with their fresh produce and homemade marmalade.

Sights—Dingle Town

▲▲**The Harry Clark Windows of Diseart**—Just behind Dingle's St. Mary Church stands the St. Joseph's Convent and Diseart (dee-zhart). The sisters of this order, who came to Dingle in 1829 to educate local girls, were heroic in their work during the famine. Their neo-Gothic chapel, built in 1884, was graced in 1922 with 12 windows—the work of Ireland's top stained-glass man, Harry Clark. Long enjoyed only by the sisters, these special windows—showing six scenes from the life of Christ—are now open to the public. The convent has become a center for sharing Christian Celtic culture and spirituality (free, Mon–Sat 10:00–17:00, closed Sun). Enjoy a meditative 15 minutes following the free taped

Dingle Town

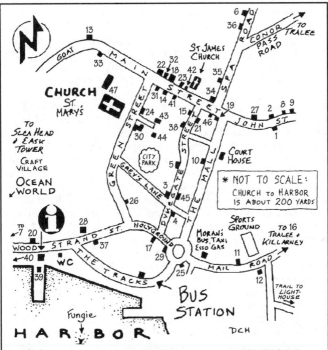

St James Church

To Tralee

Conor Pass Road

Church St. Mary's

To Slea Head & Eask Tower

Craft Village

Ocean World

City Park

Court House

* NOT TO SCALE: Church to Harbor is about 200 yards

Green St.

Grey's Lane

Holyground

To 7

Wood

Strand St.

The Tracks

WC

Moran's Bus, Taxi Esso Gas

Sports Ground

To 16 Tralee & Killarney

Mail Road

Trail to Lighthouse

Bus Station

Fungie

HARBOR

DCH

John St.

SLEEPING:

1. O'NEILL'S B & B
2. SRAID EOIN B & B AND GALVIN'S TRAVEL AGENCY
3. CORNER HOUSE B & B
4. O COILEAN B & B, KIRRARY B & B AND SCIUIRD TOURS
5. CONNOR'S B & B
6. ARD NA GREINE HOUSE B & B
7. OCEAN VIEW B & B, COASTLINE B & B AND HEATONS GUESTHOUSE
8. KELLIHERS BALLYEGAN HOUSE
9. GREENMOUNT HOUSE
10. CAPTAIN'S HOUSE B & B
11. ALPINE GUEST HOUSE
12. BAMBURY'S GUESTHOUSE
13. BARR NA SRAIDE INN

14. BENNERS HOTEL
15. GRAPEVINE HOSTEL
16. BALLINTAGGART HOSTEL

EATING & DRINKING:

17. SUPERMARKET
18. ADAM'S BAR AND REST.
19. THE OLD SMOKEHOUSE
20. MAIRE DE BARRA'S REST. AND PAUDIE BROSNAN'S PUB
21. AN CAFÉ LITEARTA
22. GLOBAL VILLAGE REST.
23. THE MYSTIC CELT REST.
24. EL TORO REST.
25. CHART HOUSE REST.
26. BEGINISH REST.
27. DOYLE'S SEAFOOD BAR AND HALF DOOR REST
28. O'FLAHERTY'S PUB
29. MURPHY'S PUB
30. DICK MACK PUB

31. FOXY JOHN'S PUB
32. O CURRAIN'S PUB
33. MAC CARTHY'S PUB
34. THE SMALL BRIDGE BAR
35. AN CONAIR PUB
36. HILLGROVE HOTEL BAR

SERVICES:

37. MOUNTAIN MAN
38. BIKE RENTAL
39. CRUISEBOAT OFFICES
40. DINGLE SAILING CLUB
41. POST
42. BANK
43. LAUNDRY
44. CRAFT GALLERIES
45. CINEMA
46. DINGLE INTERNET CAFÉ
47. HARRY CLARK WINDOWS IN CHAPEL

audioguide that explains the chapel one window at a time. The scenes (clockwise from the back entrance): the visit of the Magi, the Baptism of Jesus, "Let the little children come to me," the Sermon on the Mount, the Agony in the Garden, and Jesus appearing to Mary Magdalene. Each face is lively and animated in the imaginative, devout, medieval, and fun-loving art of the man locals talk about as if he's the kid next door . . . Harry Clark. While the "Mother Superior" sat in the covered stall in the rear, the sisters—filling the carved stalls—would chant responsively from side to side.

▲**Oceanworld**—The only place charging admission in Dingle is worth considering. This aquarium offers a little peninsula history, 300 different species of local fish in thoughtfully described tanks, and the easiest way to see Fungie the dolphin . . . on video. Walk through the tunnel while fish swim overhead. The only creatures not local—other than you—are the sharks. The aquarium's mission is to teach, and you're welcome to ask questions. The petting pool is fun. Splashing attracts the rays—they're unplugged (€7.10, families-€19, July–Aug daily 10:00–20:30, until 18:00 Sept–June, cafeteria, just past the harbor on the west edge of town, tel. 066/915-2111).

▲**Fungie**—In 1983 a dolphin moved into Dingle Harbor and became a local celebrity. Fungie (foon-gee) is now the darling of the town's tourist trade and one reason you'll find so many tour buses parked along the harbor. With a close look at Fungie as bait, tour boats are thriving. The hardy little boats motor 7 to 40 passengers out to the mouth of the harbor, where they troll around looking for Fungie. You're virtually assured of seeing the dolphin, but you don't pay unless you do (€9, kids-€3.80, 1-hr trips depart 10:00–19:00 depending upon demand, book behind TI at Dolphin Trips office, tel. 066/915-2626). To actually swim with Fungie, rent wetsuits and catch the early-morning trip from 08:00 to 10:00 (€32 includes wetsuits—unless you've brought your own).

▲**Short Harbor Walk from Dingle**—For an easy stroll along the harbor out of town (and a chance to see Fungie, 90 min round-trip), head east from the roundabout past the Esso station. Just after Bambury's B&B, take a right, following signs to Skelligs Hotel. At the beach, climb the steps over the wall and follow the seashore path to the mouth of Dingle Harbor (marked by a tower—some 19th-century fat cat's folly). Ten minutes beyond that is a lighthouse. This is Fungie's neighborhood. If you see tourist boats out, you're likely to see the dolphin. The trail continues to a dramatic cliff.

The Harbor: The harbor was built on land reclaimed (with imported Dutch expertise) in 1992. The string of old stone shops facing the harbor was the loading station for the narrow-gauge railway that hauled the fish from Dingle to Tralee (1891–1953). Make a point to walk out to the end of the breakwater—newly paved and lit at night. The Eask Tower on the distant hill is a marker built in 1847 during the famine as a make-work project. In pre-radar days, it helped ships locate Dingle's hidden harbor. The fancy mansion across the harbor is Lord Ventry's 17th-century manorhouse (see "Circular Tour," below).

Sailing—The Dingle Marina Center offers diving, sailing, traditional currach rowing, and a salty little restaurant. Sailors can join the club for a day to sail (€19, July–Aug, tel. 066/915-1984). Currachs—stacked behind the building—are Ireland's traditional lightweight fishing boats, easy to haul and easy to make. Cover a wooden frame with canvas (originally cowhide) and paint with tar—presto. The currachs, owned by the Dingle Rowing Club, go out many summer evenings (tel. 087-699-2925).

Dingle Pitch & Putt—For 18 scenic holes and a driving range, hike 10 minutes past Oceanworld (€3.80 with gear, driving range €3.80 for 100 balls, daily 10:00–20:00, over bridge take first left and follow signs, Milltown, tel. 066/915-1819).

Horseback Riding—Dingle Horse Riding takes out beginners (€25.50/hr with instruction) and experienced riders for half-day (€76) and longer excursions. Bob along beaches or mountains on an English-style ride. Book at Greenlane Gallery (Green Street, tel. 066/915-2018, www.dinglehorseriding.com).

Shopping in Dingle—Dingle is filled with shops showing off local craftsmanship. The **West Kerry Craft Guild**—a co-op selling the work of 15 local artists—is a delight even if you're just browsing. The prices here are very good since you're buying directly from "low-overhead craftspeople" (18 Main Street). The **Niamh Utsch Jewelry** shop next door is much respected for its unique work. **Lisbeth Mulcahy Weaver**, filled with traditional but stylish woven wear, is also the Dingle sales outlet of the well-known potter from out on Slea Head (Green Street, tel. 066/915-1688).

Nightlife in Dingle Town

▲▲▲**Folk Music in Dingle Pubs**—Even if you're not into pubs, take a nap and then give these a whirl. Dingle is renowned among traditional musicians as a place to get work ("€40 a day, tax-free, plus drink"). The town has piles of pubs. There's music every night and rarely a cover charge. The scene is a decent mix of locals, Americans, and Germans. Music normally starts around 21:30, and the last call for drinks is "half eleven" (23:30), sometimes later on weekends. For a seat near the music, arrive early. If the place is chockablock, power in and find breathing room in the back. By midnight the door is usually closed and the chairs are stacked. For more information on Irish traditional music, check the fine local-music Web site, www.celticwave.com.

While two pubs, the Small Bridge Bar (An Droighead Beag) and O'Flaherty's, are the most famous for their good beer and folk music, make a point to wander the town and follow your ear.

Smaller pubs may feel a bit foreboding to a tourist, but people—locals as well as travelers—are out for the *craic*. Irish culture is so accessible in the pubs; they're highly interactive museums waiting to be explored. But if you sit at a table, you'll be left alone. Stand or sit at the bar and you'll be engulfed in conversation with new friends. Have a glass in an empty no-name pub and chat up the publican. Pubs are smoky and hot (leave your coat home). The more offbeat pubs are more likely to erupt into leprechaun karaoke.

Pub crawl: The best pub crawl is along Strand Street to O'Flaherty's. Murphy's is lively, offering rock as well as ballads and traditional music. O'Flaherty's, with a high ceiling and less smoke, dripping in old-time photos and town memorabilia, is touristy but lots of fun, with nightly music in the summer.

Then head up Green Street. Dick Mack, across from the church, is nicknamed "the last pew." This is a tiny leather shop by day, expanding into a pub at night, with several rooms, a fine snug (private booth, originally designed to allow women to drink discreetly), reliably good beer, and a smoky and strangely fascinating ambience. Notice the Hollywood-type stars on the sidewalk recalling famous visitors. Established in 1899, the grandson of the original Dick Mack now runs the place. A painting in the window shows Dick Mack II with the local gang.

Green Street climbs to Main Street where two more Dick Mack–type places are filled with smoke and locals deep in conversation (but no music): Foxy John's (a hardware shop by day) and O Currain's (across the street, a small clothing shop by day).

A bit higher up Main Street is McCarthy's Pub, a smoke-stained relic. It's less touristy and has some fine traditional music sessions and occasional plays on its little stage. Wander downhill to the Small Bridge Bar at the bottom. With live music nightly, it's popular for good reason. While the tourists gather around the music, poke around the back, which leads to a nook actually closest to the musicians. Finally, head up Spa Road a few doors to An Conair—a.k.a. John Benny's, a clean, modern pub that offers good music and is often less crowded than the others. Farther up Spa Road, the big hotel has late-night dancing (see below).

Off-season: From October through April, the bands play on, though at fewer pubs: Small Bridge Bar (live music nightly), An Conair (Mon, Wed, Thu), McCarthy's (Fri, Sat), and Murphy's (Sat).

Music shops: Danlann Gallery sells musical instruments and woodcrafts (Mon–Fri 10:00–18:00, later in summer, "flexible" on weekends, CC, owner makes violins, Dykegate Street). Siopa an Phiobaire, exclusively a music shop, sells traditional wind instruments, drums, and CDs (Mon–Sat 09:30–18:00, closed Sun, CC, Craft Centre, on edge of town a few minutes' walk

past Oceanworld, tel. 066/915-1778). Dingle Bodhrans sells
homemade traditional goatskin drums and gives lessons
(1-hr lesson-€25.50–51, rates are on "sliding scale," Mon–Sat
10:30–18:00, closed Sun, Green Street, enter red iron gate of
small alley opposite church, tel. 087-245-7689, Andrea).
Folk Concerts—Top local musicians offer a quality evening of
live acoustic, classic Irish music in the fine little St. James Church
on Main Street (€9, Mon and Thu at 19:30, June–Aug only, see
sign on church gate or drop by Murphy's Ice Cream for details).
Dancing—Some pubs host "set dancing" with live music (An
Conair Bar on Mon at 21:30, Small Bridge Bar on Thu). Hillgrove
Hotel, up Spa Road a few hundred yards, is a modern hotel with
traditional dances every Thursday at 23:00 and pop dancing other
nights in summer. Locals say the Hillgrove "is a good time if
you're pissed."
Theater—Dingle's great little theater is The Phoenix on Dykegate. Its film club (50–60 locals) meets here Tuesdays year-round
at 20:30 for coffee and cookies, followed by a film at 21:00 (€5.10
for film, anyone is welcome). The leader runs it almost like a
religion, with a sermon on the film before he rolls it. The regular
film schedule for the week is posted on the door.

Sleeping in Dingle Town
**(€1.10 = about $1, country code: 353,
area code: 066, mail: Dingle, County Kerry)**
Sleep Code: **S** = Single, **D** = Double/Twin, **T** = Triple, **Q** = Quad,
b = bathroom, **s** = shower only, **CC** = Credit Cards accepted, **no
CC** = Credit Cards not accepted. Prices vary with the season,
with winter cheap and August tops.

The **launderette** is full-service only—drop off a load and
pick it up dry and folded three hours later (tiny load-€5.75,
regular load-€7.75, Mon–Fri 09:00–17:30, closed Sat–Sun; Oct–
April open only Mon, Wed, Fri 09:00–17:00, on Green Street
down alley opposite church, tel. 066/915-1837).

Good B&Bs
O'Neill's B&B is a homey, friendly place with six decent rooms
on a quiet street at the top of town (Db-€51 with this book
through 2002, family deals, no CC, strictly nonsmoking, parking,
John Street, tel. 066/915-1639, Mary O'Neill).

Sraid Eoin B&B, with four spacious, modern, pastel rooms
and giant bathrooms, is warmly run by Kathleen and Maurice
O'Connor (Db-€56, family deals, 10 percent discount with this
book and cash, CC, smoke free, John Street, tel. 066/915-1409, fax
066/915-2156, e-mail: sraideoinhouse@hotmail.com). Maurice runs
Galvin's Travel Agency on the ground floor (same phone number).

Corner House B&B is my longtime Dingle home. It's a

simple, traditional place with five large, uncluttered rooms run with a twinkle and a grandmotherly smile by Kathleen Farrell (S-€25.50, D-€46, T-€65, plenty of plumbing but it's down the hall, no CC, reserve with a phone call and reconfirm a day or 2 ahead, central as can be on Dykegate Street, tel. 066/915-1516). Mrs. Farrell, one of the original three B&B hostesses in a town now filled with them, is a great storyteller.

The following two B&Bs, which take up a quiet corner in the town center, are run by the same Collins—*Coileain* in Gaelic—family that does archaeological tours of the peninsula (below). Both offer pleasant rooms (O Coileain's are a bit bigger), bike rental (€7.75), identical prices (Db-€51–56), and a homey friendliness. **O Coileain B&B** is run by a young family—Rachel, Michael, and their two cute little girls (tel. 066/915-1937, e-mail: archeo@eircom.net). **Kirrary B&B**, just over the fence, is grandma's place with a homely charm (tel. & fax 066/915-1606, e-mail: colinskirrary@eircom.net, Eileen Collins).

The nearby **Connor's B&B**, with 15 basic rooms, is a lesser value (Db-€51–57, CC, quiet and central on Dykegate Street, tel. 066/915-1598, fax 066/915-2376, Mrs. Connor).

Ard Na Greine House B&B is a charming, windblown, modern house on the edge of town. Mrs. Mary Houlihan rents four well-equipped, comfortable rooms (with fridges) to non-smokers only (Sb-€44, Db-€48–58, Tb-€72, CC, parking, on the edge of town, an 8-min walk up Spa Road, 3 doors beyond Hillgrove Hotel, tel. 066/915-1113).

Ocean View B&B rents three tidy rooms (2 with views) in a humble little waterfront row house overlooking the bay (S-€21.50, D-€39, CC, welcome treat on arrival, 5-min walk from center, 100 yards past Oceanworld at 133 The Wood, tel. 066/915-1659, e-mail: thewood@gofree.indigo.ie, Mrs. Brosnan).

Kellihers Ballyegan House is a big, plain building with six fresh, comfortable rooms on the edge of town and great harbor views (Db-€46–53, Tb-€76, family deals, 10 percent off through 2002 with this book, no CC, nonsmoking, parking, TVs in rooms, Upper John Street, tel. 066/915-1702, Hannah and James Kelliher).

Fancier B&Bs and Guest Houses
Greenmount House sits among chilly palm trees in the country-side at the top of town. A five-minute hike up from the town center, this guest house commands a fine view of the bay and mountains. John and Mary Curran run one of Ireland's best B&Bs, with five superb rooms (Db-€57–83—top price through the summer) and seven sprawling suites (Db-€76–114) in a modern building with lavish public areas and breakfast in a solarium (CC, reserve in advance, no singles during high season, no children under 8, most rooms at ground level, parking, top of

John Street, tel. 066/915-1414, fax 066/915-1974, e-mail: mary@greenmounthouse.com).

Captain's House B&B is a shipshape place fit for an admiral in the town center, with eight classy rooms, peat-fire lounges, a stay-awhile garden, and a magnificent breakfast. Mary, whose mother ran a guest house before Dingle was discovered, loves her work and is very good at it (Sb-€44, Db-€76, great suite-€114, super breakfast in conservatory, CC, The Mall, tel. 066/915-1531, fax 066/915-1079, e-mail: captigh@eircom.net, Jim and Mary Milhench).

Alpine Guest House looks like a monopoly hotel, but that means comfortable and efficient. Its 13 spacious, bright, and fresh rooms come with wonderful sheep-and-harbor views, a cozy lounge, great breakfast, and friendly owners (Db-€51–76, Tb-€76–102, prices vary with room size and season, 10 percent discount with this book, CC, parking, Mail Road, tel. 066/915-1250, fax 066/915-1966, www.alpineguesthouse.com, e-mail: alpinedingle@eircom.net, Paul). If you're driving into town from Tralee, you'll see this a block uphill from the Dingle roundabout and Esso station.

Bambury's Guesthouse, big and modern with views of grazing sheep and the harbor, rents 12 airy, comfy rooms (Db-€51–76, prices depend on size and season, family deals, CC; coming in from Tralee it's on your left on Mail Road, 2 blocks before Esso station; tel. 066/915-1244, fax 066/915-1786, e-mail: bamburysguesthouse@eircom.net).

Barr Na Sraide Inn, central and hotelesque, has 22 comfortable rooms (Db-€63-89, family deals, CC, self-service laundry, bar, parking, past McCarthy's pub, Upper Main Street, tel. 066/915-1331, fax 066/915-1446, e-mail: barrnasraide@eircom.net).

Benners Hotel was the only place in town a hundred years ago. It stands bewildered by the modern world on Main Street, with sprawling public spaces and 52 abundant, overpriced rooms—only its nonsmoking rooms smell fresh (Db-€178 July–Aug, €140 May–June, €127 Sept–May, kids under 7-€19 extra, CC, tel. 066/915-1638, fax 066/915-1412, e-mail: benners@eircom.net).

The next two places, virtually next door, are located on the water just west of town at the end of Dingle Bay—a five-minute walk past Oceanworld on The Wood.

Coastline Guesthouse is a modern, sterile place with seven bright, spacious rooms (Sb-€51, Db-€51–76, Tb-€99, deals for 3-night stays, CC, nonsmoking, parking, The Wood, tel. 066/915-2494, fax 066/915-2493, www.coastlinedingle.com, e-mail: coastlinedingle@eircom.net, Vivienne O'Shea).

Heatons Guesthouse, big, peaceful, and American in its comforts, rents 16 thoughtfully-appointed rooms with all the amenities (Db-€99, suite Db-€152, CC, creative breakfasts,

parking, The Wood, tel. 066/915-2288, fax 066/915-2324,
e-mail: heatons@iol.ie, Cameron and Nuala Heaton).

Hostels in Dingle Town

Grapevine Hostel is a clean and friendly establishment, quietly
yet very centrally located, with a cozy fireplace lounge and a fine
members' kitchen. Each three- to eight-bed dorm has its own
bathroom. Dorms are coed, but there's a girls' room established
(32 beds, €11.50–12.75 each, laundry-€5.10, open all day,
Dykegate Lane, tel. 066/915-1434, e-mail: grapevine@dingleweb
.com, run by Siobhan—pron: sheh-vahn).

Ballintaggart Hostel, a backpacker's complex, is housed
in a stylish old manorhouse used by Protestants during the famine
as a soup kitchen (for those hungry enough to renounce their
Catholicism). It comes complete with laundry service (€5.70), a
classy study, a family room with a fireplace, and a resident ghost
(130 beds, €11.50 in 10-bed dorms, €14 beds in Qb, Db-€39,
no breakfast but there's a kitchen, bike rental, a mile east of town
on Tralee Road, tel. 066/915-1454, fax 066/915-2207, e-mail:
info@dingleaccommodation.com). Ask the Tralee bus to drop
you here before arriving in Dingle. The hostel's shuttle bus
does a nightly pub run in summer.

Eating in Dingle Town

For a rustic little village, Dingle is swimming in good food.

Budget tips: The **supermarket** stays open late—if you're
considering a grand view picnic out on the end of the new pier
walk. Fancy restaurants serve early-bird specials from 18:00 to
19:00. Many "cheap and cheery" places close at 18:00, and pubs
do good €8 dinners all over town. Most pubs stop serving food
around 21:00 (to make room for their beer drinkers).

Adam's Bar and Restaurant is a tight, smoky place popular
with locals for traditional food at great prices. Try their stew, corned
beef and cabbage, or lemon chicken sandwiches (€6.40 lunches,
Mon–Sat 12:00–17:30 only, closed Sun, Upper Main Street).

The Old Smokehouse, your best moderate-value eating
in town with fresh Dingle Bay fish and good vegetables, serves
happy locals in a rustic woody setting (€15.25 plates, Tue–Sun
18:00–22:00, closed Mon, CC, tel. 066/915-1061).

Maire De Barra's is a smoky pub serving the best €9
fresh-fish dinners in town, and traditional Irish fare as well (daily
12:30–21:30, music after 21:30, The Pier). **Paudie Brosnan's**
pub, a few doors down, is also popular (and smoky).

An Cafe Litearta, a popular eatery hidden behind an inviting
bookstore, serves tasty soup and sandwiches to a good-natured crowd
of Gaelic-speaking smokers (daily 10:00–17:30, Dykegate Street).

The **Global Village Restaurant** is where Martin Bealin

serves his favorite dishes, gleaned from his many travels around the world. It's an eclectic, healthy, meat-eaters' place that's popular with the locals for its interesting cuisine (€9 lunches, €16.50 dinners, good salads and great Thai curry, Mon 18:00–22:00, Wed–Sun 12:00–15:30, 18:00–22:00, closed Tue, CC, top of Main Street, tel. 066/915-2325).

The Mystic Celt is run by husband-and-wife chefs with a passion for preserving ancient Irish recipes. Portions are huge, excellent, and lovingly prepared (€19 dinners, daily 18:00–21:30, closed Wed off-season and Nov–Feb, veggie options, CC, Main Street, tel. 066/915-2117, Paul and Sylvia Smith).

El Toro offers a candlelit splash of the Mediterranean, with good seafood, salads, and pizzas (€10.25–19 meals, daily 18:00–22:00, Oct–April closed Tue–Wed, Green Street, tel. 066/915-1820).

Dingle's Four Fancy Restaurants

Chart House Restaurant serves contemporary cuisine with a menu dictated by what's fresh and seasonal. Settle back into the sharp, clean, lantern-lit harborside ambience (€25.50 dinners, CC, Wed–Mon 18:30–22:00, closed Tue, at roundabout at base of town, tel. 066/915-2255).

Beginish Restaurant, serving modern European fare with a fish forte in an elegant Georgian setting, is probably your best dressy splurge meal in town (€23 plates, €28 daily 3-course meal, dinner only, Tue–Sun 18:00–22:00, closed Mon, CC, you'll be glad you reserved ahead, Green Street, tel. 066/915-1321).

Two of Dingle's long-established top-notch restaurants— **Doyle's Seafood Bar** (more famous, tel. 066/915-1174) and **The Half Door** (heartier portions, tel. 066/915-1600)—are neighbors on John Street. While they are in all the guidebooks (and therefore filled with tourists), they serve good food. Both take credit cards, have the same hours (Mon–Sat 18:00–22:00, closed Sun), offer an early-bird special (3-course meal-€27, 18:00–19:00), and take reservations (wise).

Transportation Connections—Dingle Town

The nearest train station is in Tralee.

By bus from Dingle to: Galway (4/day, 6.5 hrs), **Dublin** (3/day, 8 hrs), **Rosslare** (2/day, 9 hrs), **Tralee** (4/day, 75 min, €8), fewer departures on Sundays. Most bus trips out of Dingle require at least one or two (easy) transfers. Dingle has no bus station and only one bus stop, on the waterfront behind Super Valu supermarket (bus info tel. 01/830-2222 or Tralee station at 066/712-3566).

Drivers choose two roads into town, the easy southern route or the much more dramatic, scenic, and treacherous Conor Pass. It's 30 miles from Tralee either way.

Dingle Peninsula: Circular Tour by Bike or Car

A three-star sight, the Dingle Peninsula loop trip is about 30 miles long. It's easy by car, or it's a demanding three hours by bike—if you don't stop (do in clockwise direction).

While you can take the basic guided tour of the peninsula (offered by several companies; see "Dingle Peninsula Tours," below), it's not necessary with the route described in this section. A fancy map is also unnecessary with my instructions. I've keyed in mileage to help locate points of interest. If you're driving, as you leave Dingle, reset your odometer at Oceanworld. Even if you get off track or are biking, derive distances between points from my mileage key.

To get the most out of your circle trip, read through this entire section before departing. Then go step by step (staying on R559 and following "The Slea Head Drive" signs). Note: Roads are very congested in August.

The Dingle Peninsula is 10 miles wide and runs 40 miles from Tralee to Slea Head. The top of its mountainous spine is Mount Brandon—at 3,130 feet, the second-tallest mountain in Ireland. While only tiny villages lie west of Dingle Town, the peninsula is home to 500,000 sheep.

Leave Dingle Town west along the waterfront (0.0 miles at Oceanworld). There's an eight-foot tide here. The seaweed was used to make formerly-worthless land arable. (Seaweed was a natural source of potash—organic farming before that was trendy.) Across the water, the fancy Milltown House B&B (with flags) was Robert Mitchum's home for a year during the filming of *Ryan's Daughter*. Look back out the harbor to see the narrow mouth of this blind harbor (where Fungie frolics) and the "Ring of Kerry" beyond that. Dingle Bay is so hidden, ships needed the tower (1847) on the hill to find its mouth.

0.4 miles: At the roundabout, turn left over the bridge. The hardware-store building on the right was a corn-grinding mill in the 18th century.

0.8 miles: The Milestone B&B is named for the pillar stone (*Gallaun* in Gaelic) in its front yard. This may have been a prehistoric grave, or boundary, marker between two tribes. The stone extends below the earth as far as it sticks up. The peninsula, literally an open-air museum, is dotted with more than 2,000 such monuments dating from the Neolithic Age (4,000 B.C.) through early Christian times. Another pillar stone stands in the field across the street in the direction of the yellow manorhouse of Lord Ventry (in the distance).

Lord Ventry, whose family came to Dingle as post-Cromwell War landlords in 1666, built this mansion about 1750. Today it houses an all-Gaelic boarding school for 140 high school–age girls.

Dingle Peninsula Tour

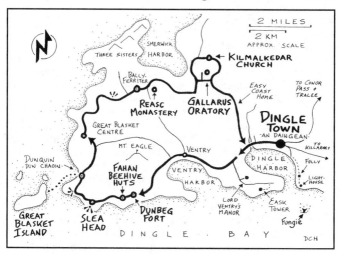

As you drive past the Ventry estate, you'll pass palms, magnolias, fuchsias, and exotic flora introduced to Dingle by Lord Ventry. Because of the mild climate (cradled by the gulf stream), fuchsias—imported from Chile and spreading like weeds—line the roads all over the peninsula and redden the countryside from June to September. The mild climate—it never snows—is fine for subtropical plants. And over 100 inches a rain a year gives this area its "40 shades of green."

Ten yards past the Tobair Michael B&B (on left) a tiny white wall with a blue marker marks the St. Michael's Well. A Christianized Celtic holy well, it's still the site of a Mass on St. Martin's day. St. Martin was the Christian antidote to pagan holy places. Generally, when you see something dedicated to him, it sits upon something pre-Christian people worshiped.

3 miles: Stay off the "soft margin" as you enjoy views of Ventry Bay, its four-mile-long beach (to your right as you face the water), and distant views of Skellig Michael, which you'll see all along this part of the route. Skellig Michael—jutting up like France's Mont St. Michel—contains the rocky remains of an eighth-century monastic settlement. Hermit monks lived here in obscure beehive huts—their main contact with the outside world being trading ships stopping between Spain and Scandinavia. Next to it is a smaller island, Little Skellig—a breeding ground for gannets (seagull-like birds with 6-foot wingspans). In 1865 Western Union laid the first transatlantic cable from here to Newfoundland. It was in use until 1965. Mount Eagle (1,660 feet),

rising across the bay, marks the end of Ireland. In the village of
Ventry, Gaelic is the first language. The large hall at the end of
the village is used by big-city students who come here on field
trips to be immersed in the Gaelic language.

4.7 miles: The rushes on either side of the road are the
kind used to make the local thatched roofs. Thatching, which nearly
died out because of the fire danger, is more popular now that anti-
flame treatments are available. Black and white magpies fly.

5.3 miles: The Irish football star Paidi O Se (Paddy O'Shea)
is a household name in Ireland. He now trains the Kerry team
and runs the pub on the left. (Easy beach access from here.)

5.6 miles: The blue house hiding in the trees 100 yards off the
road on the left (view through the white gate) was kept cozy by Tom
Cruise and Nicole Kidman during the filming of *Far and Away*.

6.6 miles: "Taisteal go Mall" means "go slowly"; there's a
peach-colored, two-room schoolhouse on the right (20 students,
2 teachers). On the left is the small Celtic and Prehistoric Museum,
a strange private collection of prehistoric artifacts with no real
connection to Dingle (overpriced at €3.80, daily 09:00–18:00).

6.9 miles: The circular mound on the right is a late–Stone
Age ring fort. In 500 B.C. it was a petty Celtic chieftain's headquarters, a stone-and-earth stockade filled with little stone houses.
These survived untouched through the centuries because of super-
stitious beliefs that they were "fairy forts." While this is unexcavated,
recent digging has shown that people have lived on this peninsula
since 4000 B.C.

7.3 miles: Look ahead up Mount Eagle at the patchwork
fields created by the stone fences.

7.7 miles: Dunbeg Fort, a series of defensive ramparts
and ditches around a central clochan, while ready to fall into
the sea, is open to tourists. Though there are no carvings
to be seen, the small (*beg*) fort (*dun*) is dramatic (€1.30, daily
09:30–20:00, descriptive handout). Forts like this are the
most important relics left from Ireland's Iron Age (500 B.C.
to A.D. 500). Since erosion will someday take this fort, it has
been excavated. Alongside the road, the new stone-roofed
house was built to blend in with the landscape and the region's
ancient rock-slab architecture (A.D. 2000, tea inside, traditional
currach boat in parking lot).

8.2 miles: A group of beehive huts, or *clochans*, is a short
walk uphill (€1.30, daily 09:30–19:00, WC). These mysterious
stone igloos, which cluster together within a circular wall, are a
better sight than the similar group of beehive huts a mile down
the road. Look over the water for more Skellig views.

Farther on, you'll ford a stream. There has never been a bridge
here; this bit of road—nicknamed the "upside down bridge"—
was designed as a ford.

9.2 miles: Pull off to the left at this second group of beehive huts. Look downhill at the scant remains of the scant home that was burned as the movie equivalent of Lord Ventry tried to evict the tenants in *Far and Away*. Even without Hollywood, this is a bleak and godforsaken land. Look above at the patches of land slowly made into farmland by the inhabitants of this westernmost piece of Europe. Rocks were cleared and piled into fences. Sand and seaweed were laid on the clay, and in time it was good for grass. The created land, generally not tillable, was used only for grazing. Much has fallen out of use now. Look behind at the Ring of Kerry in the distance and ahead at the Blasket Islands.

9.9 miles: At Slea Head, marked by a crucifix, a pullout, and great views of the Blasket Islands (described below), you turn the corner on this tour. On stormy days, the waves are "racing in like white horses."

10.4 miles: Pull into the little parking lot (signed "Dunchaoin") to view the Blaskets and Dunmore Head (the westernmost point in Europe) and to review the roadside map (which traces your route) posted in the parking lot. The scattered village of Dunquin has many ruined rock homes abandoned during the famine. They were built with small windows to minimize taxation. Some are fixed up, as this is a popular place these days for summer homes. You can see more good examples of land reclamation, patch by patch, climbing up the hillside. Mount Eagle was the first bit of land Charles Lindberg saw after crossing the Atlantic on his way to Paris in 1927. Villagers here were as excited as he was—they had never seen anything so big in the air. Ahead, down a road on the left, a plaque celebrates the 30th anniversary of the filming of *Ryan's Daughter*.

11.9 miles: The Blasket Islanders had no church or cemetery on the island. This was their cemetery. The famous Blasket storyteller Peig Sayers (1873–1958) is buried in the center. At the next intersection, drive down the little lane that leads left (100 yards) to a small stone marker remembering the 1588 shipwreck of the *Santa Maria de la Rosa* of the Spanish Armada. Below that is the often-tempestuous Dunquin Harbor, from which the Blasket ferry departs. Island farmers—who on a calm day could row across in 20 minutes—would dock here and hike 12 miles into Dingle to sell their produce. When transporting sheep, farmers would lash their pointy little hoofs together and place the sheep carefully upside down in the currach—so they wouldn't puncture their frail little craft's canvas skin.

12 miles: Back on the main road, follow signs to the Great Blasket Centre.

13.5 miles: Leave the Slea Head Road left for the Great Blasket Centre (described below).

13.7 miles: Back at the turnoff, head left (sign to Louis Mulcahy Pottery).

14.5 miles: Passing land that was never reclaimed, think of the work it took to pick out the stones, pile them into fences, and bring up sand and seaweed to nourish the clay and make soil for growing potatoes. Look over the water to the island aptly named the "Sleeping Giant"—hand resting happily on his beer belly.

15.1 miles: The view is spectacular. Ahead, on the right, study the top fields, untouched since the planting of 1845, when the potatoes didn't grow, but rotted in the ground. The faint vertical ridges of the potato beds can still be seen—a reminder of the famine (easier to see a bit later). Before the famine, 50,000 people lived on this peninsula. After the famine starved the population down, there was never again a need to farm so high up. Today only 10,000 live on the peninsula. Coast downhill. The distant hills are crowned by lookout forts built back when Britain expected Napoleon to invade.

18.3 miles: Ballyferriter (*Baile an Fheirtearaigh*), established by a Norman family in the 12th century, is the largest town on this side of Dingle. The pubs serve grub, and the old schoolhouse is a museum (€2, Easter-Sept daily 10:00–16:30, closed off-season). The early-Christian cross next to the schoolhouse looks real. Tap it…it's fiberglass—a prop from *Ryan's Daughter*.

19.1 miles: At the T-junction, signs direct you to Dingle (*An Daingean*, 11 km) either way. Go left, via Gallarus (and still following Slea Head Way). Take a right over the bridge, still following signs to Gallarus.

19.5 miles: Just beyond the bridge and a few yards before the sign to Mainistir Riaise (Reasc Monastic enclosure), detour right up the lane. After 0.2 miles (the unsigned turnout on your right), you'l find the scant remains of the walled Reasc Monastery (dating from the 6th–12th centuries). The inner wall divided the community into work and religious sections. In 1975 only the pillar stone was visible as the entire site was buried. The layer of black felt marks where the original rocks stop and the excavators' reconstruction begins. The pillar stone is Celtic (c. 500 B.C.). When the Christians arrived in the fifth century, they didn't throw out the Celtic society. Instead, they carved a Maltese-type cross over the Celtic scrollwork. The square building was an oratory (church—you'll see an intact oratory at the next stop). The round buildings would have been clochans—those stone igloo-type dwellings. The monasteries had cottage industries. Just outside the wall (opposite the oratory, past the duplex clochan, at the bottom end), find a stone hole with a passage facing the southwest wind. This was a kiln—fanned by the wind, used for cooking, drying grain, and making pottery. Locals would bring their grain to be dried and ground, and the monks would keep a "tithe." With the arrival of the Normans in the 12th century, these small religious communities were replaced by relatively big-time state and church governments.

20 miles: Return to the main road, continue to the right.

21.1 miles: At the big hotel (Smerwick Harbor), turn left following the sign to Gallarus Oratory.

21.8 miles: At the big building (with camping sign), go right up a lane marked with a sign for the oratory. Another sign directs you to a small tourist center—with a shop, WC, and video theater. For €2 you get a 17-minute video overview of Dingle Peninsula's historic sights. (Bikers and hikers can avoid the entry fee by ignoring the visitors center sign and continuing up the lane 200 yards to a free entrance.)

The Gallarus Oratory, built about 1,300 years ago, is one of Ireland's best-preserved early-Christian churches. Shaped like an upturned boat, its finely fitted drystone walls are still waterproof. Notice the holes for some covering at the door and the fine alternating stonework on the corners.

From the Oratory the little lane leads directly up and over the hill home to Dingle. To complete this tour, however, you should return to the main road and continue (following sign to An Mhuirioch).

22.9 miles: Turn right at the fork and immediately take a right (at the blue "shop" sign) at the next fork. Pass a 19th-century church.

24.2 miles: The ruined Kilmalkedar church was the Norman center of worship for this end of the peninsula. It was built when England replaced the old monastic settlements in an attempt to centralize their rule. The 12th-century Irish Romanesque church is surrounded by a densely populated graveyard (which has risen noticeably above the surrounding fields over the centuries). In front of the church you'll find the oldest medieval tombs, a stately early-Christian cross (substantially buried by the rising graveyard and therefore oddly proportioned), and a much older "ogham" stone. This stone, which had already stood here 900 years when the church was built, is notched with the mysterious Morris code–type script the Celts used from the third to seventh centuries. It marked a grave, indicating this was a pre-Christian holy spot. The hole was drilled through here centuries ago as a place where people would come to seal a deal—standing on the graves of their ancestors and in front of the house of God, they'd "swear to God" by touching fingers through this stone. You can still use this to renew your marriage vows (free). The church fell into ruin during the Reformation. As Catholic worship went underground until the early 19th century, Kilmalkedar was never rebuilt.

24.6 miles: Continue uphill, overlooking the water. You'll pass another "fairy fort" (Ciher Dorgan) dating back to 1000 B.C. (free, go through the rusty "kissing gate").

25.5 miles: At the crest of the hill, enjoy a three-mile coast back into Dingle Town (in the direction of the Eask Tower).

28.3 miles: Tog Bog E means "take it easy." At the T-junction, turn left. Then turn right at the roundabout.

29 miles: You're back into Dingle Town. Well done.

Dingle Peninsula Tours

▲▲**Sciuird Archaeology Tours**—Sciuird (screw-id) tours are offered by a father-son team with Dingle history—and a knack for sharing it—in its blood. Tim Collins (a retired Dingle police officer) and his son Michael give serious 2.5-hour minibus tours (€12.75, departing at 10:30 and 14:00, depending upon demand). Drop by the Kirrary B&B (Dykegate and Grey's Lane) or call 066/915-1606 to put your name on the list. Call early. Tours fill quickly in summer. Off-season (Oct–April) you may have to call back to see if the necessary four people signed up to make a bus go. While skipping the folk legends and the famous sights (such as Slea Head), your guide will drive down tiny farm roads (the Gaelic word for road means "cow path"), over hedges, and up ridges to hidden Celtic forts, mysterious stone tombs, and forgotten castles with sweeping seaside views. The running commentary gives an intimate peek into the history of Dingle. Sit as close to the driver as possible to get all the information. They do two completely different tours: west (Gallarus Oratory) and east (Minard Castle and a wedge tomb). I enjoyed both. Dress for the weather. In a literal gale with horizontal winds, Tim kept saying, "You'll survive it."

Moran's Tour does a quickie minibus tour around the peninsula. You'll get a meager narration and a short stop at the Gallarus Oratory (€10.25 to Slea Head, normally May–Sept at 10:00 and 14:00 from Dingle TI, 2.5 hrs; Moran's is at Esso station at roundabout, tel. 066/915-1155 or cellular 087-275-3333). There are always enough seats. But if no one shows up, consider a private Moran taxi trip around the peninsula (€32 for 3 people, cabby narrates 2.5-hour ride). The **Mountain Man** also offers three-hour minibus tours of the peninsula (€10.25 for 3 hours, 3 tours daily June-Aug with demand, tel. 066/915-2400).

Blasket Islands

This rugged group of six islands off the tip of Dingle Peninsula seems particularly close to the soul of Ireland. The population of Great Blasket Island, home to as many as 160 people, dwindled until the government moved the last handful of residents to the mainland in 1953. Life here was hard. Each family had a cow, a few sheep, and a plot of potatoes. They cut their peat from the high ridge and harvested fish from the sea. There was no priest, pub, or doctor. These people formed the most traditional Irish community of the 20th century—the symbol of antique Gaelic culture.

Their special closeness to their island—combined with their knack for vivid storytelling—is inspirational. From this primitive but proud fishing/farming community came three writers of international repute whose Gaelic work—basically tales of life on Great Blasket—is translated into many languages. You'll find *Peig* (by Peig Sayers*)*, *Twenty Years a-Growing* (Maurice O'Sullivan), and *The Islander* (Thomas O'Crohan) in shops everywhere.

In the summer there's a café and hostel (cellular 086-852-2321) on the island, but it's little more than a ghost town overrun with rabbits on a peaceful, grassy, three-mile-long poem. The Blasket ferry runs hourly, and in summer every half hour, depending on weather and demand (€18 round-trip, May–Sept, sometimes into Oct). There may be a bus from Dingle Town to Dunquin—leaving in the morning and picking up in the late afternoon—coordinated with the ferry schedule (€11.50 round-trip offered by Mountain Man, tel. 066/915-2400; or a €12.75 taxi service by Moran, tel. 066/915-1155; Dunquin ferry tel. 066/915-6422). Dunquin has a fine hostel (tel. 066/915-6121). There is a fast boat service from Dingle to the Blaskets on the *Peig Sayers* in the summer (€32 round-trip, 30-min ride with free time to explore the island, or an overnight trip, call Mary at 066/915-1344).

▲▲**Great Blasket Centre**—This state-of-the-art Blasket and Gaelic heritage center gives visitors the best look possible at the language, literature, and way of life of the Blasket Islanders. See the fine 20-minute video (shows on the half hr), hear the sounds, read the poems, browse through old photos, and then gaze out the big windows at those rugged islands and imagine. Even if you never got past limericks, the poetry of these people—so pure and close to each other and nature—will have you dipping your pen into the cry of the birds (€3.20, Easter-Oct daily 10:00–18:00, until 19:00 July–Aug, cafeteria, on the mainland facing the islands, well-signposted, tel. 066/915-6444). Visit this center before visiting the islands.

▲▲**Blasket Islands Adventure Cruise**—Three-hour cruises take visitors among the islands and provide a wild Atlantic dose of birds, fish, and natural scenery (€25.50, May–Sept 2/day: late morning and afternoon, weather permitting; bring barf bag, pack for rain and cold, coffee and snacks included, booking required, departs from Dunquin Pier, reach Dunquin from Dingle via shuttle bus—€8 round-trip—with Moran or Mountain Man; cruise tel. 066/915-6533 or 066/915-6422, cellular 087-228-0460, www.blaskettours.com).

Eco-Cruises—Dingle Marine Eco Tours offers two-hour birds-and-rocks boat tour of the peninsula for €19. The guided tour sails either east toward Minard Castle or west toward the Blaskets.

ROME
(ROMA)

Rome is magnificent and brutal at the same time. Your ears will ring, if you're careless you'll be run down or pickpocketed, you'll be frustrated by the kind of chaos that only an Italian can understand. You may even come to believe Mussolini was a necessary evil. But Rome is required, and still aglow after the improvements made for Jubilee 2000, it's more exciting and easier than ever.

If your hotel provides a comfortable refuge, if you pace yourself and accept and even partake in the siesta plan, if you're well organized for sightseeing, and if you protect yourself and your valuables with extra caution and discretion, you'll do fine. You'll see the sights and leave satisfied.

Rome at its peak meant civilization itself. Everything was either civilized (part of the Roman Empire, Latin- or Greek-speaking) or barbarian. Today Rome is Italy's political capital, the capital of Catholicism, and a splendid... "junk pile" is not quite the right term... of Western civilization. As you peel through its fascinating and jumbled layers, you'll find its buildings, cats, laundry, traffic, and 2.6 million people endlessly entertaining. And then, of course, there are its magnificent sights.

Tour St. Peter's, the greatest church on earth, and scale Michelangelo's 100-meter-tall dome, the world's largest. Learn something about eternity by touring the huge Vatican Museum. You'll find the story of creation—bright as the day it was painted—in the newly restored Sistine Chapel. Do the "Caesar Shuffle" through ancient Rome's Forum and Colosseum. Savor Europe's most sumptuous building—the Borghese Gallery—and take an early evening "Dolce Vita Stroll" down the Via del Corso with Rome's beautiful people. Enjoy an after-dark walk from Trastevere to the Spanish Steps, lacing together Rome's Baroque and bubbly night spots.

Rome Area

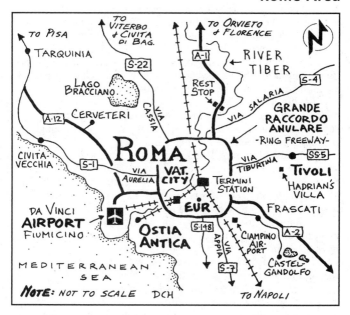

TO PISA
TARQUINIA
TO VITERBO & CIVITA DI BAG.
TO ORVIETO & FLORENCE
RIVER TIBER
S-22
A-1
S-4
REST STOP
LAGO BRACCIANO
VIA CASSIA
VIA SALARIA
GRANDE RACCORDO ANULARE
-RING FREEWAY-
A-12
CERVETERI
CIVITA-VECCHIA
S-1
RoMA
VIA AURELIA
VAT. CITY
TERMINI STATION
VIA TIBURTINA
SS5
TIVOLI
HADRIAN'S VILLA
DA VINCI AIRPORT
FIUMICINO
EUR
OSTIA ANTICA
S-148
VIA APPIA
CIAMPINO AIRPORT
A-2
FRASCATI
MEDITERRANEAN SEA
S-7
CASTEL-GANDOLFO
NOTE: NOT TO SCALE   DCH
TO NAPOLI

Planning Your Time

For most travelers, Rome is best done quickly. It's a great city, but it's exhausting. Time is normally short, and Italy is more charming elsewhere. To "do" Rome in a day, consider it as a side trip from Orvieto or Florence and maybe before the night train to Venice. Crazy as that sounds, if all you have is a day, it's a great one.

Rome in a day: Vatican (2 hours in the museum and Sistine Chapel and 1 hour in St. Peter's), taxi over the river to the Pantheon (picnic on its steps), then hike over Capitol Hill, through the Forum, and to the Colosseum. Have dinner on Campo de' Fiori and dessert on Piazza Navona.

Rome in two days: Do the "Caesar Shuffle" from the Colosseum and Forum over Capitol Hill to the Pantheon. After a siesta, join the locals strolling from Piazza del Popolo to the Spanish Steps (see my recommended "Dolce Vita Stroll," below). Have dinner near your hotel.

On the second day, see the Vatican City (St. Peter's, climb the dome, tour the Vatican Museum). Spend the evening walking from Trastevere to Campo de' Fiori—an atmospheric place for dinner—to the Trevi Fountain (see "Night Walk Across Rome," below). With a third day, add the Borghese Gallery (reservations required) and the National Museum of Rome.

Orientation

Sprawling Rome actually feels manageable once you get to know it. It's the old core—within the triangle formed by the train station, Colosseum, and Vatican. Get a handle on Rome by considering it in these layers:

The ancient city had a million people. Tear it down to size by walking through just the core. The best of the classical sights stand in a line from the Colosseum to the Pantheon.

Medieval Rome was little more than a hobo camp of 50,000—thieves, mean dogs, and the pope, whose legitimacy required a Roman address. The medieval city, a colorful tangle of lanes, lies between the Pantheon and the river.

Window-shoppers' Rome twinkles with nightlife and ritzy shopping near Rome's main drag—Via del Corso—in the triangle formed by Piazza del Popolo, Piazza Venezia, and the Spanish Steps.

Vatican City is a compact world of its own with two great, huge sights: St. Peter's Basilica and the Vatican Museum.

Trastevere, the seedy, colorful, wrong-side-of-the-river neighborhood/village, is Rome at its crustiest—and perhaps most "Roman."

Baroque Rome is an overleaf that embellishes great squares throughout the town with fountains and church facades.

Since no one is allowed to build taller than St. Peter's dome, the city has no modern skyline. And the Tiber River is ignored. It's not navigable, and after the last floods (1870) the banks were built up very high and Rome turned its back on its naughty, unnavigable river.

Tourist Information

While Rome has three main tourist information offices, the dozen or so TI kiosks scattered around the town at major tourist centers are handy and just as helpful. If all you need is a map, forget the TI and pick up one at your hotel.

You'll find TIs at the airport (daily 08:15–19:00, tel. 06-6595-6074) and the train station (daily 08:00–21:00, off-season 09:00–20:00, near track 3, accessible from platforms or lobby, marked "Informazioni Turistiche/Tourist Info," crowded, combined with travel agency, tel. 06-4890-6300).

The central TI office, near Piazza della Repubblica's huge fountain, covers the city and the region. It's a five-minute walk out the front of the train station (Mon–Sat 08:15–19:00, air-con, next to car dealership, Via Parigi 5, seats, table, free Internet access for tourist info: www.romaturismo.com, tel. 06-488-991). It's, less crowded, and more helpful than the station TI.

At any TI, ask for a city map, a listing of sights and hours (in the free *Tesori di Roma* booklet), and *L'Evento*, the free bimonthly periodical entertainment guide for evening events and fun.

Rome

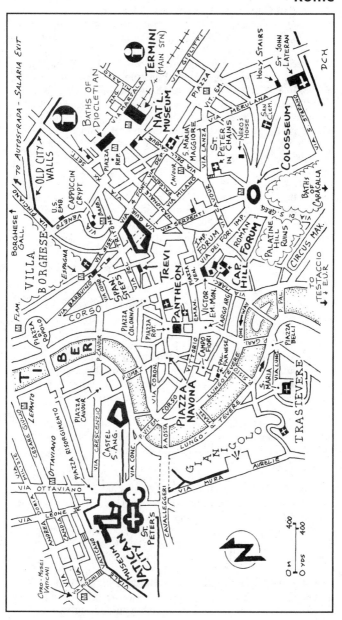

All hotels list an inflated rate to cover the hefty commission any TI room-finding service charges. Save money by booking direct.

Smaller TIs (daily 09:00–18:00) include kiosks near the Forum (on Piazza del Tempio della Pace), at Via del Corso (on Largo Goldoni), in Trastevere (on Piazza Sonnino), on Via Nazionale (at Palazzo delle Esposizioni), at Castel Sant' Angelo, Santa Maria Maggiore, and at San Giovanni in Laterano. For more information, call 06-3600-4399 (daily 09:00–19:00, www.comune.roma.it).

Roma c'è is a cheap little weekly entertainment guide with a helpful English section (at the back) on musical events and the pope's schedule for the week (new edition every Thu, sold at newsstands for €1, www.romace.it, Web site in Italian). Fancy hotels carry a free English monthly, *Un Ospite a Roma* (A Guest in Rome).

Arrival in Rome

By Train: Rome's main train station, Termini, is a minefield of tourist services: a TI (daily 08:00–21:00, off-season 09:00–20:00, near track 3), train info office (daily 07:00–21:45), ATMs, late-hours banks, public showers (downstairs), luggage lockers (near track 24), 24-hour thievery, a pharmacy (daily 07:30–22:00, in the modern mall downstairs), the main city-bus hub (in front of train station), a subway stop, a grocery (oddly named "Drug Store," daily 07:00–24:00, downstairs), and the handy, cheery Chef Express Self-Service Ristorante (daily 11:00–22:30, easy WC at entrance, near east end of station; although there are several Chef Express bars scattered throughout station, the most comfortable is this sit-down Ristorante). The closest Internet point is downstairs near Dunkin Donuts (Thenetgate, daily 06:00–23:30, cheapest to buy a €5.50 60-minute card, can return or use at branches at Trevi Fountain or Vatican). The station has some sleazy sharks with official-looking cards. In general, avoid anybody selling anything at the station if you can.

Most of my hotel listings are easily accessible by foot (those near the train station) or by Metro (those in the Colosseum and Vatican neighborhoods). The train station has its own Metro stop (Termini).

By Bus: Long-distance buses (e.g., from Siena and Assisi) arrive at Rome's small **Tiburtina** station, which is on Metro line B, with easy connections to the main train station (a straight shot 4 stops away) and the entire Metro system.

By Plane: If you arrive at the airport, catch a train (hrly, 30 min, €9) to Rome's train station or take (or share) a taxi to your hotel. For details, see "Transportation Connections," below.

Dealing with (and Avoiding) Problems

Theft Alert: With sweet-talking con artists meeting you at the station, well-dressed pickpockets on buses, and thieving gangs of children at the ancient sites, Rome is a gauntlet of rip-offs. There's no great physical risk, but green tourists will be ripped off. Thieves strike when you're distracted. Don't trust kind strangers. Keep nothing important in your pockets. Assume you're being stalked. (Then relax and have fun.) Be most on guard while boarding and leaving buses and subways. Thieves crowd the door, then stop and turn while others crowd and push from behind. The sneakiest thieves are well-dressed businessmen (generally with something in their hands); lately many are posing as tourists with Tevas, fanny packs, and cameras. Scams abound: Don't give your wallet to self-proclaimed "police" who stop you on the street, warn you about counterfeit (or drug) money, and ask to see your wallet.

If you know what to look out for, the gangs of children picking the pockets and handbags of naive tourists are no threat but an interesting, albeit sad, spectacle. Gangs of city-stained children (sometimes as young as 8–10 years old), too young to prosecute but old enough to rip you off, troll through the tourist crowds around the Colosseum, Forum, Piazza Repubblica, and train and Metro stations. Watch them target tourists who are overloaded with bags or distracted with a video camera. The kids look like beggars and hold up newspapers or cardboard signs to confuse their victims. They scram like stray cats if you're onto them. A fast-fingered mother with a baby is often nearby. The terrace above the bus stop near the Colosseum Metro stop is a fine place to watch the action and maybe even pick up a few moves of your own.

Reporting Losses: To report lost or stolen passports and documents or to file an insurance claim, you must file a police report (with Polizia at track 1 or with Carabinieri at track 20, also at Piazza Venezia). To replace a passport, file the police report, then go to your embassy (see below). To report lost traveler's checks, call your bank (Visa tel. 800-874-155, Thomas Cook/MasterCard tel. 800-872-050, American Express tel. 800-872-000; these toll-free 800 numbers are Italian, not American), then file a police report. To report stolen or lost credit cards, call the company (Visa tel. 800-877-232, MasterCard tel. 800-870-866, American Express tel. 800-874-333), then file a police report.

Embassies: United States (Mon–Fri 08:30–13:00, 14:00–17:30, Via Veneto 119, tel. 06-46741) and Canada (Via Zara 30, tel. 06-445-981).

Emergency Numbers: Police tel. 113. Ambulance tel. 118.

Hit and Run: Walk with extreme caution. Scooters don't need to stop at red lights, and even cars exercise what drivers call the "logical option" of not stopping if they see no oncoming traffic. As Vespa scooters become electric, they'll get quieter (hooray) but more dangerous for pedestrians. Follow locals like a shadow when you cross a street (or spend a good part of your visit stranded on curbs).

Staying/Getting Healthy: The siesta is a key to survival in summertime Rome. Lie down and contemplate the extraordinary power of gravity in the eternal city. I drink lots of cold, refreshing water from Rome's many drinking fountains (the Forum has three). There's a pharmacy (marked by a green cross) in every neighborhood, including a handy one in the train station (daily 07:30–22:00, located downstairs, at west end) and a 24-hour pharmacy on Piazza dei Cinquecento 51 (next to train station on Via Cavour, tel. 06-488-0019). Embassies can recommend English-speaking doctors. Consider MEDline, a 24-hour home medical service (tel. 06-808-0995, doctors speak English). Anyone is entitled to free emergency treatment at public hospitals. The hospital closest to the train station is Policlinico Umberto 1 (entrance for emergency treatment on Via Lancisi, translators available, Metro: Policlinico). The American Hospital is a private hospital on the edge of town accustomed to helping Yankees (tel. 06-225-571).

Helpful Hints
Web Sites on Rome: www.romaturismo.com (music, exhibitions, events, kid stuff, in English), www.wantedinrome.com (job openings and real estate, but also festivals and exhibitions, in English), and www.vatican.va (the pope's Web site, in English).

  Bookstore: The American Bookstore sells fiction and all the major guidebooks (Via Torino 136, Metro: Repubblica, tel. 06-474-6877).

  Train Tickets and Reservations: Get train tickets and rail-pass-related reservations and supplements at travel agencies rather than dealing with the congested train station. The cost is either the same or there's a minimal charge. Your hotel can direct you to the nearest travel agency. Quo Vadis, near the Pantheon, is handy (Via dei Cestari 21, tel. 06-413-1831).

Getting around Rome
Sightsee on foot, by city bus, or by taxi. I've grouped your sightseeing into walkable neighborhoods.

  Public transportation is efficient, cheap, and part of your Roman experience. It starts running around 05:30 and stops around 23:30, sometimes earlier. After midnight there are a few very crowded night buses, and taxis become more expensive and hard to get. Don't try to hail one—go to a taxi stand.

  Buses and subways use the same ticket. You can buy tickets at newsstands, tobacco shops, or at major Metro stations or bus stops, but not on board (€0.80, good for 75 minutes—one Metro ride and unlimited buses); all-day bus/Metro passes cost €3.25 (for more info, visit www.atac.roma.it).

  Buses (especially the touristic #64) and the subway are havens for thieves and pickpockets. Assume any commotion is a thief-created distraction.

Metropolitana: Rome's Subway

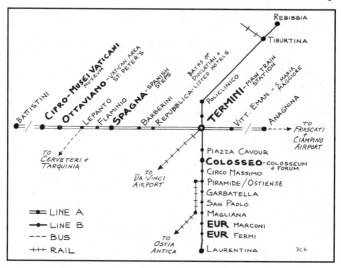

By Metro: The Roman subway system (Metropolitana) is simple, with two clean, cheap, fast lines. While much of Rome is not served by its skimpy subway, these stops are helpful: Termini (train station, National Museum of Rome at Palazzo Massimo, recommended hotels), Repubblica (Baths of Diocletian/Octagonal Hall, main TI, recommended hotels), Barberini (Cappuccin Crypt, Trevi Fountain), Spagna (Spanish Steps, Villa Borghese, classy shopping area), Flaminio (Piazza del Popolo, start of recommended Dolce Vita Stroll down Via del Corso), Ottaviano (St. Peter's and Vatican City), Cipro-Musei Vaticani (Vatican Museum, recommended hotels), Colosseo (Colosseum, Roman Forum, recommended hotels), and E.U.R. (Mussolini's futuristic suburb).

By Bus: Bus routes are clearly listed at the stops. Punch your ticket in the orange stamping machine as you board (even if you've already stamped it for the Metro)—or you are cheating. Riding without a stamped ticket on the bus, while relatively safe, is stressful. Inspectors fine even innocent-looking tourists €52. If you hop a bus without a ticket, locals who use tickets rather than a monthly pass can sell you a ticket from their wallet bundle. Ideally buy a bunch of tickets from a tobacco shop so you can hop a bus without first having to search for a tobacco shop that's open.

Here are a few buses worth knowing about:

#64: Termini (train station), Piazza della Repubblica (sights), Via Nazionale (recommended hotels), Piazza Venezia (near Forum), Largo Argentina (near Pantheon), St. Peter's Basilica.

Ride it for a city overview and to watch pickpockets in action (can get horribly crowded).

#8: This tram connects Largo Argentina with Trastevere (get off at Piazza Mastai).

Electrico **#116:** Through the medieval core of Rome from Campo de' Fiori to Piazza Barberini via the Pantheon.

Electrico **#117:** San Giovanni in Laterano, Colosseo, Via dei Serpenti, Trevi Fountain, Piazza di Spagna, Piazza del Popolo.

"J" buses are bigger, come with a hostess, and provide more convenient access to some places farther out, such as St. Peters (Cavalleggeri stop) and the catacombs. Purchase tickets (€1) on the bus (info: tel. 800-076-287).

By Taxi: Taxis start at about €2.75 (surcharges of €1 on Sun, €2.75 for night hours of 22:00–7:00, €1 surcharge for luggage, €7.25 extra for airport, tip about 10 percent by rounding up to the nearest euro). Sample fares: Train station to Vatican-€9; train station to Colosseum-€6; Colosseum to Trastevere-€7. Three or four companions with more money than time should taxi almost everywhere. It's tough to wave down a taxi in Rome. Find the nearest taxi stand. (Ask a local or in a shop *"Dov'è* [DOH-vay] *una fermata dei tassi?"* Some are listed on my maps.) Unmarked, unmetered taxis at train stations and the airport are usually a rip-off. Taxis listing their telephone number on the door have fair meters—use them. To save time and energy, have your hotel call a taxi; the meter starts when the call is received. (To call a cab on your own, dial 06-3570, 06-4994, or 06-88177.)

Tours of Rome

Scala Reale—Tom Rankin (an American architect in love with Rome and his Roman wife) runs Scala Reale, a company committed to sorting out the rich layers of Rome for small groups with a long attention span. Their excellent walking tours vary in length from two to four hours and start at €16 per person. Try to book in advance since their groups are limited to six and fill up fast. Their fascinating "Rome Orientation" walks lace together lesser-known sights from antiquity to the present, helping you get a sense of how Rome works (tel. 06-474-5673, U.S. tel. 888/467-1986, www.scalareale.org, e-mail: info@scalereale.org).

Through Eternity—This company offers four walking tours, all led by native English speakers with relevant university degrees and an emphasis on storytelling: St. Peter's and Vatican Museum (€31, museum entry not included, 5.5 hrs, daily except Sun); Colosseum and Roman Forum (€18, 2.5 hrs, daily); Rome at Twilight (€18, nightly); and a Wine Sampling Tour (€26, nightly, includes a glass at 4 or 5 wine bars). Call to get the schedule and to book in advance (max of 25 people, tel. 06-700-9336, cellular 347-336-5298, private tours possible, www.througheternity.com).

Walks of Rome—Students working for "Walks of Rome" give tours in fluent American or British English. They offer group tours (that individuals can join) and private tours (at a higher cost). Sample group tours include: Rome Through the Centuries (€34, 3 hrs, Mon, Wed, Fri at 10:00), Vatican City Walk (€52, includes admission to Vatican Museum, 4.5 hrs, Tue, Thu, Sat at 10:00), and the Colosseum (€19, includes admission, 1.5 hrs, offered daily). See their Web site for the latest (www .walksofeurope.com) and book in advance by e-mail (info @walksofeurope.com) or phone (tel. 06-484-853, cellular 347-795-5175). You'll need to give your hotel name and phone number. Your guide will call to let you know the meeting place. Their pub crawl tours meet at 20:00 at the Colosseum Metro stop (year-round) and finish at a disco six pubs later around midnight (€16, no need to reserve). I've never seen 50 young, drunk people having so much fun.

Hop-on Hop-off Bus Tour—The ATAC city bus tour offers your best budget orientation tour of Rome. In 1.75 hours you'll have 80 sights pointed out to you (by a live guide in English and maybe one other language) and have a chance to get out at nine different stops and catch a later bus. While the guide's spiel is limited to simple identification of the sights, this tour provides an efficient and economical orientation to Rome. The stops are: Piazza Barberini, Via Veneto, Villa Borghese, Piazza Cavour, St. Peter's Square, Corso Vittorio Emanuele (for Piazza Navona), Piazza Venezia, Colosseum, and Via Nazionale (€7.75, bus #110 departs every 30 minutes—at top and bottom of hour—from front of train station, near platform C, buy tickets at info kiosk there—marked "i bus," runs March–Sept 09:00–20:00, Oct–Feb 10:00–18:00, tel. 06-4695-2252).

Archeobus—This handy new hop-on-and-hop-off bus runs hourly from Piazza Venezia way out the Appian Way (buy €7.75 ticket on the bus, good from 09:00–17:00, 16-seat bus with hostess, pick up the guided tour flier in English, tel. 06-4695-4695). They have cheap bike rental at the appropriate Appian Way stop as well.

Sights—From the Colosseum Area to Capitol Hill

Beware of gangs of young thieves, particularly between the Colosseum and the Forum; they're harmless if you know their tricks (see Theft Alert in "Helpful Hints," above).

▲**St. Peter-in-Chains Church (San Pietro in Vincoli)**—Built in the fifth century to house the chains that held St. Peter, this church is most famous for its Michelangelo statue. Check out the much-venerated chains under the high altar, then focus on Moses (free, but pop in a coin to light the statue, Mon–Sat 07:00–12:30, 15:30–19:00, Sun 07:30–12:30, a short walk uphill from the Colosseum, modest dress required).

Museum Tips for Rome

Plan ahead. The marvelous Borghese Gallery and Nero's Golden House both require reservations. For the Borghese Gallery, it's safest to make reservations well in advance of your trip (for specifics, see page 614). You can wait until you're in Rome to reserve a time at Nero's Golden House, though it's easy to book farther ahead (see listing on this page).

Some museums may stay open later in summer (usually on Sat). Get a current listing of museum hours from one of Rome's TIs: ask for the booklet *Tesori di Roma* (Treasures of Rome).

A **special combo ticket**—covering the National Museum of Rome, Colosseum, Palatine Hill, Baths of Caracalla, and a couple of other museums—costs €16 (allows you to see 7 sights for price of 3, purchase at participating sites, valid for 5 days). When you buy this, you can upgrade to a "Coupon Servizi" pass for an extra €5, giving you tours or audioguides at each site (they usually cost €3.60 each). The big plus of this ticket is that you avoid the long lines at the Colosseum (if you purchase it at a participating site other than the Colosseum).

Pope Julius II commissioned Michelangelo to build a massive tomb, with 48 huge statues, crowned by a grand statue of this egomaniac pope. The pope had planned to have his tomb placed in the center of St. Peter's Basilica. When Julius died, the work had barely been started, and no one had the money or necessary commitment to Julius to finish the project. Michelangelo finished one statue—Moses—and left a few unfinished statues: Leah and Rachel flanking Moses in this church, the "prisoners" now in Florence's Accademia, and the "slaves" now in Paris' Louvre.

This powerful statue of Moses—mature Michelangelo—is worth studying. He worked on it in fits and starts for 30 years. Moses has received the Ten Commandments. As he holds the stone tablets, his eyes show a man determined to stop his tribe from worshiping the golden calf and idols...a man determined to win salvation for the people of Israel. Why the horns? Centuries ago, the Hebrew word for "rays" was mistranslated as "horns."

▲**Nero's Golden House (Domus Aurea)**—The barren remains of Emperor Nero's "Golden House" was reopened to the public in 1999. The original entrance to the house was all the way over at the Arch of Titus in the Forum. This massive house once sprawled across the valley (where the Colosseum now stands)

The Forum Area

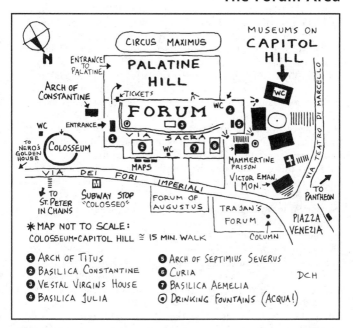

- ❶ ARCH OF TITUS
- ❷ BASILICA CONSTANTINE
- ❸ VESTAL VIRGINS HOUSE
- ❹ BASILICA JULIA
- ❺ ARCH OF SEPTIMIUS SEVERUS
- ❻ CURIA
- ❼ BASILICA AEMELIA
- ◎ DRINKING FOUNTAINS (ACQUA!)

DCH

and up the hill—the part you tour today. Larger even than Bill Gates' place, it was a pain to vacuum. A colossal, 33-meter-tall bronze statue of Nero towered over everything. The house incorporated an artificial lake (where the Colosseum was later built) and a forest stocked with game. It was decorated with the best multicolored marble and the finest frescoes. No expense was too great for Nero—his mistress soaked daily in the milk of 500 wild asses kept for her bathing pleasure.

Nero (ruled A.D. 54–68) was Rome's most notorious emperor. He killed his own mother, kicked his pregnant wife to death, crucified St. Peter, and—most galling to his subjects—was a bad actor. When Rome burned in A.D. 64, Nero was accused of torching it to clear land for an even bigger house. The Romans rebelled and Nero stabbed himself in the neck, crying, "What an artist dies in me!"

While only hints of the splendid, colorful frescoes survive, the towering vaults and the basic immensity of the place are impressive. As you wander through rooms that are now underground, look up at the holes in the ceiling. Imagine how much of old Rome still hides underground...and why the subway is limited to two lines.

Visits are allowed only with an escort (30 people every 15 minutes) and a reservation (€6.20, Wed–Mon 09:00–19:45, last entry at 18:45, closed Tue, tour lasts 45 min, escort speaks Italian only, audioguides-€1.60 but listen to the intro before entering or you'll be forever behind, 200 meters northeast of Colosseum, through a park gate, up a hill and on the left). To reserve a place, call 06-3996-7700. If you just show up (particularly on a late afternoon on a weekday), you could luck out and get on a tour; if tours aren't booked up, the remaining seats are sold to drop-ins.

▲▲▲**Colosseum**—This 2,000-year-old building is *the* great example of Roman engineering. Using concrete, brick, and their trademark round arches, Romans constructed much larger buildings than the Greeks. But in deference to the higher Greek culture, notice how they finished their no-nonsense megastructure by pasting all three orders of Greek columns (Doric, Ionic, and Corinthian) as exterior decorations. The Flavian Amphitheater's popular name, "Colosseum," comes from the colossal statue of Nero that once stood in front of it.

Romans were into "big." By putting two theaters together, they created a circular amphitheater. They could fill and empty its 50,000 numbered seats as quickly and efficiently as we do our superstadiums. Teams of sailors hoisted canvas awnings over the stadium to give fans shade. This was where ancient Romans, whose taste for violence was the equal of modern America's, enjoyed their Dirty Harry and *Terminator*. Gladiators, criminals, and wild animals fought to the death in every conceivable scenario. The floor of the Colosseum is missing, exposing underground passages. Animals in cages were kept here and then lifted up in elevators; they'd pop out from behind blinds into the arena. The gladiator didn't know where, when, or by what he'd be attacked.

Cost, Hours, Tours: €7, covered by €16 combo-ticket, daily 09:00–19:00, off-season 09:00–15:00 (Metro: Colosseo, tel. 06-3974-9907). To avoid the long lines here, buy your ticket elsewhere. Individual tickets for the Colosseum are sold at the entrances to Palatine Hill: just inside the Forum entry, and on Via di San Gregorio (facing Forum entry, with your back to the Colosseum, go left on street to reach other Palatine entrance). If you buy a €16 combo-ticket (sold at Palatine Hill entrances, National Museum of Rome, Baths of Caracalla, and more), you can walk right into the Colosseum. For details, see "Museum Tips for Rome," page 602. Public WCs are behind the Colosseum (face ticket entrance and go right—WC under stairway). The modern-day gladiators outside the Colosseum expect payment if you snap a photo of them; negotiate—they have swords.

▲**Arch of Constantine**—The well-preserved arch, which stands between the Colosseum and the Forum, commemorates a military coup and, more importantly, the acceptance of Christianity in the Roman Empire. In A.D. 312, the ambitious Emperor Constantine (who had a vision he could win under the sign of the cross) defeated his rival Maxentius. Constantine became sole emperor and promptly legalized Christianity.

▲▲▲**Roman Forum (Foro Romano)**—This is ancient Rome's birthplace and civic center, and the common ground between Rome's famous seven hills (free admission to Forum, €6.20 for Palatine Hill, both keep the same hours: daily 09:00–19:15 or an hour before dark, off-season 09:00–15:00, Metro: Colosseo, tel. 06-3974-9907).

To help resurrect this confusing pile of rubble, study the before-and-after pictures in the cheap city guidebooks sold on the streets. (Check out the small red *Rome, Past and Present* books with plastic overlays to un-ruin the ruins; they're priced at €11—pay no more than €8.) With the help of the map in this section, follow this basic walk. Enter the Forum near the Arch of Constantine:

1. Start by the small **Arch of Titus** (drinking fountain opposite) overlooking the remains of what was the political, social, and commercial center of the Roman Empire. The Via Sacra—the main street of ancient Rome—cuts through the Forum from here to Capitol Hill and the Arch of Septimius Severus on the opposite side. On the left, a ticket booth welcomes you to the Palatine Hill (described below)—once filled with the palaces of Roman emperors. Study the Arch of Titus—carved with propaganda celebrating the A.D. 70 defeat of the Jews, which began the Diaspora that ended with the creation of Israel in 1947. Notice the gaggle of soldiers carrying the menorah.

2. Ahead of you on the right are the massive ruins of the **Basilica of Constantine.** Follow the path leading there from the Via Sacra. Only the giant barrel vaults remain, looming crumbly and weed-eaten. As you stand in the shadow of the Basilica of Constantine, reconstruct it in your mind. The huge barrel vaults were just side niches. Extend the broken nub of an arch out over the vacant lot and finish your imaginary Roman basilica with rich marble and fountains. People it with plenty of toga-clad Romans. Yeow.

3. Next hike past the semicircular Temple of Vesta to the **House of the Vestal Virgins.** Here, the VVs kept the eternal flame lit. A set of ponds and a marble chorus line of Vestal Virgins mark the courtyard of the house.

4. The grand **Basilica Julia,** a first-century law court, fills the corner opposite the Curia. Notice how the Romans passed their time; ancient backgammon-type game boards are cut into the pavement.

5. The **Arch of Septimius Severus,** from about A.D. 200, celebrates that emperor's military victories. In front of it a stone called Lapis Niger covers the legendary tomb of Romulus. To the left of the arch, the stone bulkhead is the Rostra, or speaker's platform. It's named for the ship's prows that used to decorate it as big shots hollered, "Friends, Romans, countrymen . . . . "

6. The plain, intact brick building near the Arch of Septimius Severus was the **Curia,** where the Roman senate sat. (Peek inside.) Roman buildings were basically brick and concrete, usually with a marble veneer, which in this case is long lost.

7. The **Basilica Aemilia** (2nd century B.C.) shows the floor plan of an ancient palace. This pre-Christian "basilica" design was later adopted by medieval churches. From here a ramp leads up and out (past a WC and a fun headless statue to pose with).

▲**Palatine Hill**—The hill above the Forum contains scanty remains of the Imperial palaces and the Roman Quadrata (Iron Age huts and the legendary house of Romulus—under corrugated tin roof in far corner). We get our word *palace* from this hill, where the emperors chose to live. The Palatine was once so filled with palaces that later emperors had to build out. (Looking up at it from the Forum you see the substructure that supported these long-gone palaces.) The Palatine museum has sculptures and fresco fragments but is nothing special. From the pleasant garden, you'll get an overview of the Forum. On the far side, look down into an emperor's private stadium and then beyond at the dusty Circus Maximus, once a chariot course. Imagine the cheers, jeers, and furious betting. But considering how ruined the ruins are, the heat, the hill to climb, the €6.20 entry fee, and the relative difficulty in understanding what you're looking at, the Palatine Hill is a disappointment (covered by €16 combo-ticket, same hours as Forum, above; the entrance and ticket office—which also sells Colosseum tickets, enabling smart sightseers to avoid that long line—is near the Arch of Titus at the south end of the Forum).

▲**Mammertine Prison**—The 2,500-year-old, cisternlike prison, that once held Saints Peter and Paul, is worth a look (donation requested, daily 09:00–12:30, 14:30–18:30, at the foot of Capitol Hill, near Forum's Arch of Septimius Severus). When you step into the room, you'll hit a modern floor. Ignore that and look up at the hole in the ceiling, from which prisoners were lowered. Then take the stairs down to the level of the actual prison floor. As you descend, you'll walk past a supposedly miraculous image of Peter's face, created when a guard pushed him into the wall. Downstairs you'll see the column to which Peter was chained. It's said that a miraculous fountain sprang up in this room so Peter could baptize other prisoners. The upside-down cross commemorates Peter's upside-down crucifixion.

Imagine humans, amid fat rats and rotting corpses, awaiting slow deaths. On the walls near the entry are lists of notable prisoners (Christian and non-Christian) and the ways they were executed: *strangolati, decapitato, morto di fame* (died of hunger) . . . .

Sights—Capitol Hill Area

There are several ways to get to the top of Capitol Hill. If you're coming from the north (Piazza Venezia), take the grand stairs located to the right of the big, white Victor Emmanuel Monument (described below). Coming from the Forum, take either the steep staircase or the winding road, which converge at a great Forum overlook and a refreshing water fountain. Block the spout with your fingers; water spurts up for drinking. Romans, who call this *il nasone* (the nose), joke that a cheap Roman boy takes his date out for a drink at *il nasone*.

▲▲**Capitol Hill (Campidoglio)**—This hill was the religious and political center of ancient Rome. It's still the home of the city's government. Michelangelo's Renaissance square is bounded by two fine museums and the mayoral palace. Its centerpiece is a copy of the famous equestrian statue of Marcus Aurelius (the original is behind glass in the museum a few steps away).

Michelangelo intended that people approach the square from the grand stairway off Piazza Venezia. From the top of the stairway, you see the new Renaissance face of Rome with its back to the Forum, facing the new city. Notice how Michelangelo gave the buildings the "giant order"—huge pilasters make the existing two-story buildings feel one-storied and more harmonious with the new square. Notice also how the statues atop these buildings welcome you and then draw you in. The terraces just downhill (past either side of the mayor's palace) offer fine views of the Forum.

▲▲**Capitol Hill Museum**—This museum encompasses two buildings (Palazzo dei Conservatori and Palazzo Nuovo), connected by an underground passage that leads to the vacant Tabularium and a panoramic overlook of the Forum (€8, free on last Sun of month, Tue–Fri and Sun 09:00–19:00, Sat 09:30–23:00, closed Mon, last entry 60 min before closing, tel. 06-3996-7800).

For an orientation to the museum's two buildings, face the equestrian statue on Capitol Hill Square (with your back to the grand stairway). The Palazzo Nuovo is on your left and the Palazzo dei Conservatori is on your right (closer to the river). Ahead is the mayor's palace (Palazzo Senatorio); below it and out of sight is the Tabularium and underground passage.

You can buy your ticket at either building (but if you want to rent a €3.75 audioguide, go to Palazzo dei Conservatori).

The **Palazzo dei Conservatori** is one of the world's oldest museums, at 500 years old. Outside the entrance, notice the marriage announcements and, very likely, wedding-party photo ops. Inside the courtyard, have a look at giant chunks of a statue of Emperor Constantine; when intact, this imposing statue held court in the Basilica of Constantine in the Forum. The museum is worthwhile, with lavish rooms and several great statues. Tops is the original (500 B.C.) Etruscan *Capitoline Wolf* (the little statues

of Romulus and Remus were added in the Renaissance). Don't
miss the *Boy Extracting a Thorn* or the enchanting *Commodus
as Hercules*. The second-floor painting gallery—except for two
Caravaggios—is forgettable. The café upstairs has a splendid
patio with city views (lovely at sunset).

Connect the two museums with the underground passage
that leads to the **Tabularium**. Built in the first century A.D., this
once held the archives of ancient Rome. The word *Tabularium*
comes from tablet, on which the Romans wrote their laws. You
won't see any tablets, but you will see a superb head-on view of
the Forum from the windows.

The **Palazzo Nuovo** houses mostly portrait busts of forgotten
emperors. But it has three must-see statues: the *Dying Gaul*, the
Capitoline Venus (both on the first floor up), and the original
gilded bronze equestrian statue of Marcus Aurelius (behind glass
in museum courtyard). This greatest surviving equestrian statue
of antiquity was the original centerpiece of the square. While
most such pagan statues were destroyed by Dark Age Christians,
Marcus was mistaken as Constantine (the first Christian emperor)
and therefore spared.

From Capitol Hill to Piazza Venezia—Leaving Capitol Hill,
descend the stairs leading to Piazza Venezia. At the bottom of the
stairs, look left several blocks down the street to see a condominium
actually built around surviving ancient pillars and arches of Teatro
Marcello—perhaps the oldest inhabited building in Europe.

Still at the bottom of the stairs, look up the long stairway
to your right (which pilgrims climb on their knees) for a good
example of the earliest style of Christian church. While pilgrims
find it worth the climb, sightseers can skip it. As you walk toward
Piazza Venezia, look down into the ditch on your right and see
how modern Rome is built on the forgotten frescoes and mangled
mosaics of ancient Rome.

Piazza Venezia—This vast square is the focal point of modern
Rome. The Via del Corso, which starts here, is the city's axis,
surrounded by Rome's classiest shopping district. In the 1930s,
Mussolini whipped up Italy's nationalistic fervor here from a
balcony above the square (to your right with back to Victor
Emmanuel Monument). Fascist masses filled the square screaming, "Four more years!" or something like that. Fifteen years
later, they hung him from a meat hook in Milan.

Victor Emmanuel Monument—This oversized monument to
an Italian king was part of Italy's rush to overcome the new country's strong regionalism and to create a national identity after
unification in 1870. It's now open to the public, offering a new
view of the Eternal City (free, just climb the big stairs, long hours).

Romans think of the monument not as an altar of the father-
land but as "the wedding cake," "the typewriter," or "the dentures."

It wouldn't be so bad if it weren't sitting on a priceless acre of ancient Rome and if they had chosen better marble (this is too in-your-face white and picks up the pollution horribly). Soldiers guard Italy's *Tomb of the Unknown Soldier* as the eternal flame flickers. At this level, stand with your back to the flame and see how Via del Corso bisects Rome.

▲**Trajan's Column, Market, and Forum**—This offers the grandest column and best example of "continuous narration" from antiquity. Over 2,500 figures scroll around the 40-meter-high column telling of Trajan's victorious Dacian campaign (circa A.D. 103, in present-day Romania), from the assembling of the army at the bottom to the victory sacrifice at the top. The ashes of Trajan and his wife were held in the mausoleum at the base while the sun once glinted off a polished bronze statue of Trajan at the top. Today St. Peter is on top. Study the propaganda that winds up the column like a scroll, trumpeting Trajan's wonderful military exploits. You can view this close-up for free (always open and viewable, just off Piazza Venezia, across the street from the Victor Emmanuel Monument). Viewing balconies once stood on either side, but it seems likely Trajan fans only came away with a feeling that the greatness of their emperor and empire was beyond comprehension (for a rolled-out version of the Column's story, visit the Museum of Roman Civilization at E.U.R., below). This column marked **Trajan's Forum**, built to handle the shopping needs of a wealthy city of over a million. Commercial, political, religious, and social activities all mixed in the Forum.

For a fee, you can go inside **Trajan's Market** (boring) and part of Trajan's Forum; the entrance is uphill from the column on Via IV Novembre. The market was once filled with shops selling goods from all over the Roman Empire (€6.20, summer Tue–Sun 09:00–18:30, winter 09:00–16:30, closed Mon, entrance is uphill from the column on Via IV Novembre, tel. 06-3600-4399).

Pantheon Area

▲▲▲**Pantheon**—For the greatest look at the splendor of Rome, antiquity's best-preserved interior is a must (free, Mon–Sat 08:30–19:30, Sun 09:00–13:00, 14:00–18:00, tel. 06-6830-0230). Because it became a church dedicated to the martyrs just after the fall of Rome, the barbarians left it alone, and the locals didn't use it as a quarry. The portico is called Rome's umbrella—a fun local gathering in a rainstorm. Walk past its one-piece granite columns (biggest in Italy, shipped from Egypt) and through the original bronze doors. Sit inside under the glorious skylight and enjoy classical architecture at its best.

The dome, 47 meters (142 feet) high and wide, was Europe's biggest until the Renaissance. Michelangelo's dome at St. Peter's, while much higher, is one meter smaller. The brilliance of its

Heart of Rome

construction astounded architects through the ages. During the
Renaissance, Brunelleschi was given permission to cut into the
dome (see the little square hole above and to the right of the
entrance) to analyze the material. The concrete dome gets thinner
and lighter with height—the highest part is volcanic pumice.

This wonderfully harmonious architecture greatly inspired
Raphael and other artists of the Renaissance. Raphael, along
with Italy's first two kings, chose to be buried here.

As you walk around the outside of the Pantheon, notice the
"rise of Rome"—about five meters (15 feet) since it was built.
▲▲**Churches near the Pantheon**—The **Church of San
Luigi dei Francesi** has a magnificent chapel painted by Caravaggio (free, Fri–Wed 07:30–12:30, 15:30–19:00, Thu 07:30–
12:30, sightseers should avoid Mass at 07:30 and 19:00, modest
dress recommended).

The only Gothic church you'll see in Rome is **Santa
Maria sopra Minerva**. On a little square behind the Pantheon
to the east, past the Bernini statue of an elephant carrying an
Egyptian obelisk, this Dominican church was built *sopra* (over)

a pre-Christian temple of Minerva. Before stepping in, notice the high-water marks on the wall (right of door). Inside you'll see that the lower parts of the frescoes were lost to floods. (After the last great flood, in 1870, Rome built the present embankments, finally breaking the spirit of the Tiber River.)

Rome was at its low ebb, almost a ghost town, through much of the Gothic period. Little was built during this time (and much of what was built was redone Baroque). This church is a refreshing exception.

St. Catherine's body lies under the altar (her head is in Siena). In the 1300s, she convinced the pope to return from France to Rome, thus saving Italy from untold chaos.

Left of the altar stands a little-known Michelangelo statue, *Christ Bearing the Cross*. Michelangelo gave Jesus an athlete's or warrior's body (a striking contrast to the more docile Christ of medieval art) but left the face to one of his pupils. Fra Angelico's simple tomb is farther to the left, on the way to the back door. Before leaving, head over to the right (south transept), pop in a coin for light, and enjoy a fine Filippo Lippi fresco showing scenes from the life of St. Thomas Aquinas.

Exit the church via its rear door (behind the Michelangelo statue), walk down Fra Angelico lane (spy any artisans at work), turn left, and walk to the next square. On your right, you'll find the **Chiesa di St. Ignazio** church, a riot of Baroque illusions. Study the fresco over the door and the ceiling in the back of the nave. Then stand on the yellow disk on the floor between the two stars. Look at the central (black) dome. Keeping your eyes on the dome, walk under and past it. Church building project runs out of money? Hire a painter to paint a fake, flat dome. (Both churches open early, take a siesta—Santa Maria sopra Minerva closes at 12:00, St. Ignazio at 12:30—reopen around 15:30, and close at 19:00. Modest dress is recommended.)

A few blocks away, back across Corso Vittorio Emmanuele, is the rich and Baroque **Gesu Church** (daily 06:00–12:30, 16:00–19:15), headquarters of the Jesuits in Rome. The Jesuits powered the Church's Counter-Reformation. With Protestants teaching that all roads to heaven did not pass through Rome, the Baroque churches of the late 1500s were painted with spiritual road maps that said they did.

Walk out the Gesu Church and two blocks down Corso V. Emmanuele to the **Sacred Area** (Largo Argentina), an excavated square facing the boulevard, about four blocks south of the Pantheon. Stroll around this square and look into the excavated pit at some of the oldest ruins in Rome. Julius Caesar was assassinated near here. Today, it's a refuge for cats—some 250 of them are cared for by volunteers. You'll see them (and their refuge) at the far (west) side of the square.

▲**Trevi Fountain**—This bubbly Baroque fountain of Neptune with his entourage is a minor sight to art scholars but a major nighttime gathering spot for teens on the make and tourists tossing coins (for more information, see "Self-Guided Walks in Rome," page 627).

East Rome: Near the Train Station

These sights are within a 10-minute walk of the train station. By Metro, use the Termini stop for the National Museum and the Piazza Repubblica stop for the rest.

▲▲▲**National Museum of Rome in Palazzo Massimo**—This museum houses the greatest collection of ancient Roman art anywhere, including busts of emperors and a Roman copy of the *Greek Discus Thrower*. The ground floor is a historic yearbook of marble statues from the second century B.C. to the second century A.D., with rare Greek originals.

The first floor is peopled by statues from the first through fourth centuries A.D. The second floor (which requires an appointment, request when you buy ticket) contains frescoes and mosaics that once decorated the walls and floors of Roman villas. Finally, descend into the basement to see fine gold jewelry, dice, an abacus, and vault doors leading into the best coin collection in Europe, with fancy magnifying glasses maneuvering you through cases of coins from ancient Rome to modern times.

Cost and Hours: €6.20, covered by €16 combo-ticket, Tue–Sun 09:00–19:45, closed Mon, open some summer Saturdays until 23:00, last entry 45 min before closing, audioguide-€3.60 (Metro: Termini, tel. 06-481-5576). The museum is about 100 meters from the Termini train station. As you leave the station, it's the sandstone-brick building on your left. Enter at the far end, at Largo di Villa Peretti.

Baths of Diocletian—Around A.D. 300, Emperor Diocletian built the largest baths in Rome. This sprawling meeting place, with baths and schmoozing spaces to accommodate 3,000 bathers at a time, was a big deal in ancient Rome. While much of it is still closed, three sections are open: the Octagonal Hall, the Church of St. Mary of the Angels and Martyrs (both face Piazza della Repubblica), and the Museum of the Bath (across from the train station).

▲▲**Octagonal Hall**—The Aula Ottagona or Rotunda of Diocletian was a private gymnasium in the Baths of Diocletian. Built around A.D. 300, these functioned until 537, when the barbarians cut Rome's aqueducts. The floor would have been seven meters lower (look down the window in the center of the room). The graceful iron grid supported the canopy of a 1928 planetarium. Today, the hall's a gallery, showing off fine bronze and marble statues—the kind that would have decorated the baths of imperial Rome. Most are Roman copies of Greek originals...gods, athletes, portrait busts. Two merit a close look:

the *Defeated Boxer* (first century B.C, Greek and textbook Hellenistic) and the *Roman Aristocrat*. The aristocrat's face is older than the body. This bronze statue is typical of the day: take a body modeled on Alexander the Great and pop on a portrait bust (free, Tue–Sat 09:00–14:00, Sun 09:00–13:00, closed Mon, faces Piazza Repubblica).

▲**Church of St. Mary of the Angels and Martyrs (Santa Maria degli Angeli e dei Martiri)**—From Piazza della Repubblica, step through the Roman wall into what was the great central hall of the baths and is now a church (since the 16th century) designed by Michelangelo. When the church entrance was moved to Piazza Repubblica, the church was reoriented 90 degrees, turning the nave into long transepts and the transepts into a short nave. The 12 red granite columns still stand in their ancient positions. The classical floor was five meters (15 feet) lower. Project the walls down and imagine the soaring shape of the Roman vaults.

Museum of the Bath (Museo Nazionale Romano Terme di Diocleziano)—This museum, located on the grounds of the ancient Baths of Diocletian, has a misleading name. Rather than featuring the baths, it displays ancient Roman inscriptions on tons of tombs, steles, and tablets. Although well displayed and described in English, the museum is difficult to appreciate quickly, and most travelers will find more history presented on a grander scale in the National Museum of Rome a block away (€4.20, Tue–Sun 09:00–19:45, closed Mon, Viale E. De Nicola 79, entrance faces Termini station, tel. 06-488-0530).

▲**Santa Maria della Vittoria**—This church houses Bernini's statue of a swooning *St. Teresa in Ecstasy* (free, daily 07:00–12:00, 16:00–19:00, on Largo Susanna, about 5 blocks northwest of train station, Metro: Repubblica). Once inside the church, you'll find St. Teresa to the left of the altar.

Teresa has just been stabbed with God's arrow of fire. Now the angel pulls it out and watches her reaction. Teresa swoons, her eyes roll up, her hand goes limp, she parts her lips...and moans. The smiling, Cupidlike angel understands just how she feels. Teresa, a 16th-century Spanish nun, later talked of the "sweetness" of "this intense pain," describing her oneness with God in ecstatic, even erotic, terms.

Bernini, the master of multimedia, pulls out all the stops to make this mystical vision real. Actual sunlight pours through the alabaster windows; bronze sunbeams shine on a marble angel holding a golden arrow. Teresa leans back on a cloud and her robe ripples from within, charged with her spiritual arousal. Bernini has created a little stage setting of heaven. And watching from the "theater boxes" on either side are members of the family that commissioned the work.

North Rome: Villa Borghese and nearby Via Veneto

▲**Villa Borghese**—Rome's scruffy "Central Park" is great for people watching (plenty of modern-day Romeos and Juliets). Take a row on the lake or visit its fine museums.

▲▲▲**Borghese Gallery**—This private museum, filling a cardinal's mansion in the park, offers one of Europe's most sumptuous art experiences. Because of the gallery's slick mandatory reservation system, you'll enjoy its collection of world-class Baroque sculpture—including Bernini's *David* and his excited statue of Apollo chasing Daphne, as well as paintings by Caravaggio, Raphael, Titian, and Rubens—with manageable crowds.

The essence of the collection is the connection of the Renaissance with the classical world. Notice the second-century Roman reliefs with Michelangelo-designed panels above either end of the portico as you enter. The villa was built in the early 17th century by the great art collector Cardinal Borghese, who wanted to prove that the glories of ancient Rome were matched by the Renaissance.

In the main entry hall, opposite the door, notice the thrilling relief of the horse falling (first century A.D., Greek). Pietro Bernini, father of the famous Bernini, completed the scene by adding the rider.

Each room seems to feature a Baroque masterpiece. The best of all is in Room 3: Bernini's Apollo chasing Daphne. It's the perfect Baroque subject—capturing a thrilling, action-filled moment. In the mythological story, Apollo races after Daphne. Just as he's about to reach her, she turns into a tree. As her toes turn to roots and branches spring from her fingers, Apollo is in for one rude surprise. Walk slowly around. It's more air than stone.

Cost and Hours: €7.25, Tue–Sun 09:00–19:00, June–Sept may be open until 23:00 on Sat, closed Mon. No photos are allowed.

Reservations: Reservations are mandatory and easy to get in English over the Internet (www.ticketeria.it) or by phone: call 06-32810 (if you get an Italian recording, press 2 for English; office hours: Mon–Fri 09:00–18:00, Sat 09:00–13:00). Reserve a *minimum* of several days in advance for a weekday visit, at least a week ahead for weekends.

Every two hours, 360 people are allowed to enter the museum. Entry times are 09:00, 11:00, 13:00, 15:00, and 17:00 (plus 19:00 and 21:00 if open late on Sat June–Sept). When you reserve, request a day and time (which you'll be given if available), and you'll get a claim number. While you'll be advised to come 30 minutes before your appointed time, you can arrive a few minutes beforehand, but don't be late, as no-show tickets are sold to stand-bys.

Visits are strictly limited to two hours. Concentrate on the first floor but leave yourself 30 minutes for the paintings of the Pinacoteca upstairs; highlights are marked by the audioguide icons. The fine bookshop and cafeteria are best visited outside your two-hour entry window.

If you don't have a reservation, just show up (or call first and ask if there are openings; a late afternoon on a weekday is usually your best bet). Reservations are tightest at 11:00 and on weekends. No-shows are released a few minutes after the top of the hour. Generally, out of 360 reservations, a few will fail to show (but more than a few may be waiting to grab them).

Tours: Guided English tours are offered at 09:10 and 11:10 for €4.20; reserve with entry reservation (or consider the excellent audioguide tour for €4.20).

Location: The museum is in the Villa Borghese park. A taxi (tell the cabbie your destination: gah-leh-REE-ah bor-GAY-zay) can get you within 100 meters of the museum. Otherwise, Metro to Spagna and take a 15-minute walk through the park.

Etruscan Museum (Villa Giulia Museo Nazionale Etrusco)— The Etruscan civilization thrived in this part of Italy around 600 B.C., when Rome was an Etruscan town. The Etruscan civilization is fascinating, but the Villa Giulia Museum is extremely low-tech and in a state of disarray. I don't like it, and Etruscan fans will prefer the Vatican Museum's Etruscan section. Still, the Villa Giulia does have the famous "husband and wife sarcophagus" (a dead couple seeming to enjoy an everlasting banquet from atop their tomb; 6th century B.C from Cerveteri), the *Apollo from Veio* statue (of textbook fame), and an impressive room filled with gold sheets of Etruscan printing and temple statuary from the Sanctuary of Pyrgi (€4.20, Tue–Sun 09:00–19:00, plus June–Sept Sat 21:00–23:45, closed Mon, closes earlier off-season, Piazzale di Villa Giulia 9, tel. 06-320-1951).

▲**Cappuccin Crypt**—If you want bones, this is it. The crypt is below the church of Santa Maria della Immaculata Concezione on Via Veneto, just up from Piazza Barberini. The bones of more than 4,000 monks who died between 1528 and 1870 are in the basement, all artistically arranged for the delight—or disgust—of the always-wide-eyed visitor. The soil in the crypt was brought from Jerusalem 400 years ago, and the monastic message on the wall explains that this is more than just a macabre exercise. Pick up a few of Rome's most interesting postcards (donation, Fri–Wed 09:00–12:00, 15:00–18:00, closed Thu, Metro: Barberini). A painting of St. Francis by Caravaggio is upstairs. Just up the street, you'll find the American embassy, Federal Express, and fancy Via Veneto cafés filled with the poor and envious looking for the rich and famous.

Ara Pacis (Altar of Peace)—This will reopen in 2005 once restoration is complete. In 9 B.C, after victories in Gaul and Spain, Emperor Augustus celebrated the beginning of the Pax Romana by building this altar of peace. Peace is almost worshiped here. The north and south walls show a procession with realistic portraits of the imperial family in Greek Hellenistic style. It's a fine combination of Roman grandeur and Greek elegance. Even when the altar is not open, it can sometimes be seen through the windows (a long block west of Via del Corso on Via di Ara Pacis, on east bank of river near Ponte Cavour, nearest Metro: Spagna).

West Rome: Vatican City Area

Vatican City is a tiny independent country (just over 100 acres) that contains two huge sights: the Vatican Museum (with Michelangelo's Sistine Chapel) and St. Peter's Basilica (with Michelangelo's exquisite *Pietà*). A helpful **TI** is just to the left of St. Peter's Basilica (Mon–Sat 08:30–18:30, closed Sun, tel. 06-6988-1662, Vatican switchboard tel. 06-6982, www.vatican.va). The entrances to St. Peter's and to the Vatican Museum are a 15-minute walk apart (follow the outside of the Vatican wall, which links the two sights). The nearest Metro stops still involve a 10-minute walk to either sight: for St. Peter's, the closest stop is Ottaviano; for the Vatican Museum, it's Cipro-Musei-Vaticani.

Post Office: The Vatican post, with an office in the Vatican Museum and one on St. Peter's Square, is more reliable than the Italian mail service (comfortable writing rooms, Mon–Sat 08:30–18:30). The stamps are a collectible bonus (Vatican stamps are good throughout Rome; Italian stamps are not good at the Vatican).

Tours: The Vatican TI conducts free 90-minute tours of St. Peter's (depart from TI at 15:00 on Mon, Wed, and Fri, confirm schedule at TI, tel. 06-6988-1662). Tours of the Vatican Gardens offer the only way to see the gardens; book tours at least one day in advance by calling 06-6988-4466 (€9, Mon–Sat 10:00–12:00, tours start at Vatican Museum tour desk and finish on St. Peter's Square). To tour the necropolis of St. Peter's and the saint's tomb, call the Excavations Office at 06-6988-5318 (€8, 2 hrs, office open Mon–Fri 09:00–17:00, tel. 06-6988-5318).

Seeing the Pope: Your best chances for a sighting are on Sundays and Wednesdays. Because he's a travelin' man, the following schedule can vary. The pope gives a blessing at noon on Sunday from his apartment on St. Peter's Square (except Aug–Sept when he speaks at his summer residence at Castel Gandolfo, 40 km from Rome; train leaves Rome's Termini station at 08:35, returns after his talk). On Wednesday at 10:00, the pope blesses the crowds at St. Peter's from a balcony or canopied platform on the square (except in winter, when he speaks at 11:00 in 7,000-seat Aula Paola VI Auditorium, next to St. Peter's Basilica). To find out the pope's schedule or to book a free spot for the Wednesday blessing (either for a seat on the square or in the auditorium), call 06-6988-3017. Smaller ceremonies celebrated by the pope require reservations. The weekly entertainment guide *Roma c'è* always has

Vatican City Overview

① HOTEL ALIMANDI
② HOTEL SPRING HOUSE
③ HOTEL GERBER
④ HOSTARIA BASTIONI REST.
⑤ LA RUSTICHELLA REST.
⑥ ENTRANCE TO VATICAN MUSEUM
⑦ TOURIST INFO, POST & WC
⑧ HOTEL SANT' ANNA
⑨ HOTEL BRAMANTE

a "Seeing the Pope" section. If you don't want to see the pope, minimize crowd problems by avoiding these times.

▲▲▲**St. Peter's Basilica**—There is no doubt: This is the richest and most impressive church on earth. To call it vast is like calling God smart. Marks on the floor show where the next-largest churches would fit if they were put inside. The ornamental cherubs would dwarf a large man. Birds roost inside, and thousands of people wander about, heads craned heaven-ward, hardly noticing each other. Don't miss Michelangelo's

Pietà (behind bullet-proof glass) to the right of the entrance. Bernini's altar work and seven-story-tall bronze canopy (*baldacchino*) are brilliant.

For a quick self-guided walk through the basilica, follow these points (see map on next page):

1. The atrium is larger than most churches. Notice the historic doors (the Holy Door, on the right, won't be opened until the next Jubilee Year, in 2025—see point 13 below).

2. The purple circular porphyry stone marks the site of Charlemagne's coronation in A.D. 800 (in the first St. Peter's church that stood on this site). From here get a sense of the immensity of the church, which can accommodate 95,000 worshippers standing on its six acres.

3. Michelangelo planned a Greek-cross floor plan rather than the Latin-cross standard in medieval churches. A Greek cross, symbolizing the perfection of God and by association the goodness of man, was important to the humanist Michelangelo. But accommodating large crowds was important to the Church in the fancy Baroque age, which followed Michelangelo, so the original nave length was doubled. Stand halfway up the nave and imagine the stubbier design Michelangelo had in mind.

4. View the magnificent dome from the statue of St. Andrew. See the vision of heaven above the windows: Jesus, Mary, a ring of saints, rings of angels, and, on the very top, God the Father.

5. The main altar sits directly over St. Peter's tomb and under Bernini's 21-meter-tall (70 feet) bronze canopy.

6. The stairs lead down to the crypt to the foundation, chapels, and tombs of popes. (Do this last since it leads you out of the church.)

7. The statue of St. Peter, with an irresistibly kissable toe, is one of the few pieces of art that predate this church. It adorned the first St. Peter's church.

8. St. Peter's throne and Bernini's star-burst dove window is the site of a daily Mass (Mon–Sat at 17:00, Sun at 17:45).

9. St. Peter was crucified here when this location was simply "the Vatican Hill." The obelisk now standing in the center of St. Peter's square marked the center of a Roman racecourse long before a church stood here.

10. For most, the treasury (in the sacristy) is not worth the admission.

11. The church is filled with mosaics, not paintings. Notice the mosaic version of Raphael's *Transfiguration*.

12. Blessed Sacrament Chapel.

13. Michelangelo sculpted his *Pietà* when he was 24 years old. A pietà is a work showing Mary with the dead body of Christ taken down from the cross. Michelangelo's mastery of the body is obvious in this powerfully beautiful masterpiece. Jesus is believably

St. Peter's Basilica

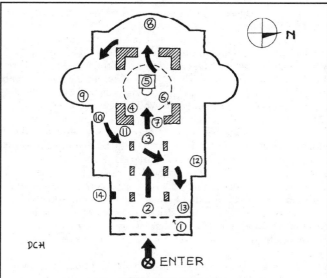

ST. PETER'S SQUARE

DCH

1. Holy Door
2. Site of Charlemagne's coronation, 800 AD
3. Extent of the original "Greek Cross" church plan
4. St. Andrew statue (view the dome from here)
5. Main altar directly over Peter's tomb. BERNINI's 70-foot bronze canopy covers the altar
6. Stairs down to the crypt: the foundation of old St. Peter's, chapels and tombs of popes (the entrance moves around)
7. Statue of St. Peter with irresistibly kissable toe
8. BERNINI - Dove window and "St. Peter's Throne"
9. Site of Peter's crucifixion
10. Museum entrance
11. RAPHAEL - "Transfiguration" mosaic
12. Blessed Sacrament Chapel
13. MICHELANGELO - Pieta
14. Elevator to roof and dome-climb (this entrance moves around - sometimes it is even outside)

dead, and Mary, the eternally youthful "handmaiden" of the Lord, still accepts God's will...even if it means giving up her son.

The Holy Door (just to the right of the *Pietà*) was bricked shut at the end of the Jubilee Year 2000 and won't be opened until 2025. Every 25 years the Church celebrates an especially festive year derived from the Old Testament idea of the Jubilee

Year (originally every 50 years), which encourages new beginnings and the forgiveness of sins and debts. In the Jubilee Year 2000, the pope tirelessly—and with significant success—promoted debt relief for the world's poorest countries.

14. An elevator leads to the roof and the stairway up the dome (€4.20, allow an hour to go up and down). The dome, Michelangelo's last work, is (you guessed it) the biggest anywhere. Taller than a football field is long, it's well worth the sweaty climb for a great view of Rome, the Vatican grounds, and the inside of the basilica—particularly heavenly while there is singing. Look around—Rome has no modern skyline. No building is allowed to exceed the height of St. Peter's. The elevator takes you to the rooftop of the nave. From there, a few steps take you to a balcony at the base of the dome looking down into the church interior. After that the one-way, 300-step climb (for some people claustrophobic) to the cupola begins. The rooftop level (below the dome) has a gift shop, WC, drinking fountain, and a commanding view.

Dress Code: The church strictly enforces its dress code: no shorts or bare shoulders (men and women); no miniskirts. You might be required to check any bags at a free cloakroom near the entry.

Hours of Church: May–Sept daily 07:00–19:00, Oct–April daily until 18:00 (ticket booth to treasury closes 1 hour earlier). All are welcome to join in the hour-long Mass at the front altar (Mon–Sat at 17:00, Sun at 17:45). The church is particularly moving at 07:00, while tourism is still sleeping. Volunteers who want you to understand and appreciate St. Peter's give free 90-minute tours (3/week, see "Tours," above); these are generally excellent but non-Christians can find them preachy. Seeing the *Pietà* is neat; understanding it is divine.

Cost and Hours of Dome: The view from the dome is worth the climb (€4.20 elevator plus 300-step climb, May–Sept daily 08:00–18:00, Oct–April daily 08:30–17:00).

▲▲▲**Vatican Museum**—The six kilometers of displays in this immense museum—from ancient statues to Christian frescoes to modern paintings—are topped by the Raphael Rooms and Michelangelo's glorious Sistine Chapel. (If you have binoculars, bring them.)

Even without the Sistine, this is one of Europe's top three or four houses of art. It can be exhausting, so plan your visit carefully, focusing on a few themes. Allow two hours for a quick visit, three or four for time to enjoy it. The museum has a nearly impossible-not-to-follow, one-way system (although, for the rushed visitor, the museum does clearly mark out 4 color-coded visits of different lengths—A is shortest, D longest). Tip: The Sistine Chapel has an exit (optional) that leads directly to St. Peter's Basilica, saving you the 10-minute walk back to the Vatican Museum exit; if you want to squirt out at the Sistine, see the Pinacoteca painting gallery first (described below) and don't get an audioguide (which needs to be returned at the entry/exit).

Start, as civilization did, in Egypt and Mesopotamia. Next, the Pio Clementino collection features **Greek and Roman statues**. Decorating its courtyard are some of the best Greek and Roman statues in captivity, including the *Laocoön* group (1st century B.C., Hellenistic) and the *Apollo Belvedere* (a 2nd-century Roman copy of a Greek original). The centerpiece of the next hall is the *Belvedere Torso* (just a 2,000-year-old torso, but one that had a great impact on the art of Michelangelo). Finishing off the classical statuary are two fine fourth-century porphyry sarcophagi; these royal purple tombs hold the remains of Constantine's mother and daughter. Crafted in Egypt at a time when a declining Rome was unable to do such fine work, the details are fun to study.

After long halls of tapestries, old maps, broken penises, and fig leaves, you'll come to what most people are looking for: the Raphael Rooms (or *stanza*), and Michelangelo's Sistine Chapel.

These outstanding works are frescoes. A fresco (meaning "fresh" in Italian) is technically not a painting. The color is mixed into wet plaster, and, when the plaster dries, the painting is actually part of the wall. This is a durable but difficult medium, requiring speed and accuracy as the work is built slowly, one patch at a time.

After fancy rooms illustrating the "Immaculate Conception of Mary" (a hard-to-sell, 19th-century Vatican doctrine) and the triumph of Constantine (with divine guidance, which led to his con-version to Christianity), you enter the first room completely done by **Raphael** and find the newly restored *School of Athens*. This is remarkable for its blatant pre-Christian classical orientation wall-papering the apartments of Pope Julius II. Raphael honors the great pre-Christian thinkers—Aristotle, Plato, and company—who are portrayed as the leading artists of Raphael's day. The bearded figure of Plato is Leonardo da Vinci. Diogenes, history's first hippie, sprawls alone in bright blue on the stairs, while Michelangelo broods in the foreground—supposedly added late. Apparently Raphael snuck a peek at the Sistine Chapel and decided that his arch competitor was so good he had to put their personal differences aside and in-clude him in this tribute to the artists of his generation. Today's St. Peter's was under construction as Raphael was working. In the *School of Athens*, he gives us a sneak preview of the unfinished church.

Next (unless you detour through the refreshingly modern Catholic art section) is the brilliantly restored **Sistine Chapel**. The Sistine Chapel, the pope's personal chapel, is where, upon the death of the ruling pope, a new pope is elected. The College of Cardinals meets here and votes four times a day until a two-thirds-plus-one majority is reached and a new pope is elected.

The Sistine is famous for Michelangelo's pictorial culmination of the Renaissance, showing the story of Creation, with a powerful God weaving in and out of each scene through that busy first week. This is an optimistic and positive expression of the High Renaissance and a stirring example of the artistic and theological maturity of the 33-year-old Michelangelo, who spent four years on this work.

Later, after the Reformation wars had begun and after the Catholic army of Spain had sacked the Vatican, the reeling Church began to fight back. As part of its Counter-Reformation, a much older Michelangelo was commissioned to paint the *Last Judgment* (behind the altar). Brilliantly restored, the message is as clear as the day Michelangelo finished it: Christ is returning, some will go to hell and some to heaven, and some will be saved by the power of the rosary.

In the recent and controversial restoration project, no paint was added. Centuries of dust, soot (from candles used for lighting and Mass), and glue (added to make the art shine) were removed, revealing the bright original colors of Michelangelo. Photos are allowed (without a flash) elsewhere in the museum, but as part of the deal with the company who did the restoration, no photos are allowed in the Sistine Chapel.

For a shortcut, a small door at the rear of the Sistine Chapel allows groups and individuals (without an audioguide) to escape directly to St. Peter's Basilica. If you exit here, you're done with the museum. The Pinacoteca is the only important part left. Consider doing it at the start. Otherwise it's a 10-minute, heel-to-toe slalom through tourists from the Sistine Chapel to the entry/exit.

After this long march, you'll find the **Pinacoteca** (the Vatican's small but fine collection of paintings, with Raphael's *Transfiguration*, Leonardo's unfinished *St. Jerome*, and Caravaggio's *Deposition*), a cafeteria (long lines, mediocre food), and the underrated early-Christian art section, before you exit via the souvenir shop.

Cost and Hours: €9.30, March–Oct Mon–Fri 08:45–16:45, Sat 08:45–13:45, Nov–Feb Mon–Sat 08:45–13:45, closed Sun except last Sun of the month when it's free and crowded. The last entry is 75 minutes before closing time. The Sistine Chapel shuts down 30 minutes early. The museum is closed on many holidays (mainly religious ones), including—for 2002: Jan 1 and 6, Feb 11, March 19, Easter and Easter Monday, May 1, 9, and 30, June 29, Aug 14 and 15, Nov 1, Dec 8, 25, and 26. Modest dress (no short shorts or bare shoulders for men or women) is appropriate and often required. Museum tel. 06-6988-4947.

▲**Castel Sant' Angelo**—Built as a tomb for the emperor; used through the Middle Ages as a castle, prison, and place of last refuge for popes under attack; and today, a museum, this giant pile of ancient bricks is packed with history.

Ancient Rome allowed no tombs—not even the emperor's—within its walls. So Hadrian grabbed the most commanding position just outside the walls and across the river and built a towering tomb (circa A.D. 139) well within view of the city. His mausoleum was a huge cylinder (64 meters wide, 21 meters high) topped by a cypress grove and crowned by a huge statue of Hadrian himself riding a chariot. For nearly a hundred years, Roman emperors (from Hadrian to Caracalla in A.D. 217) were buried here.

In the year 590, the Archangel Michael appeared above the mausoleum to Pope Gregory the Great. Sheathing his sword, the angel signaled the end of a plague. The fortress that was Hadrian's mausoleum eventually became a fortified palace, renamed for the "holy angel."

Since Rome was repeatedly plundered by invaders, Castel Sant' Angelo was a handy place of last refuge for threatened popes. The elevated corridor connecting Castel Sant' Angelo with the Vatican was built in 1277. In anticipation of long sieges, rooms were decorated with papal splendor (you'll see paintings by Crivelli, Signorelli, and Mantegna). In the 16th century, during a sack of Rome by troops of Charles V of Spain, the pope lived inside the castle for months with his entourage of hundreds (an unimaginable ordeal considering the food service at the top-floor bar).

After you walk around the entire base of the castle, take the small staircase down to the original Roman floor. In the atrium, study the model of the castle in Roman times and imagine the niche in the wall filled with a towering "welcome to my tomb" statue of Hadrian. From here a ramp leads to the right, spiraling 125 meters. While some of the fine brickwork and bits of mosaic survive, the marble veneer is long gone (notice the holes in the wall which held it in place). At the end of the ramp, stairs climb to the room where the ashes of the emperors were kept. These stairs continue to the top, where you'll find the papal apartments. Don't miss the Sala del Tesoro (treasury), where the wealth of the Vatican was locked up in a huge chest. Do miss the 58 rooms of the military museum. The views from the top are great—pick out landmarks as you stroll around—and a restful coffee with a view of St. Peter's is worth the price.

Cost, Hours, Tours: €5, Tue–Sun 09:00–19:00, plus June–Sept Sat 21:00–23:45, closed Mon. You can take an English-language tour with an audioguide (€3.60) or live guide (€4.20, Tue–Fri at 15:00, Sat at 12:15 and 16:30, confirm times, tel. 06-3996-7600, Metro: Lepanto or bus #64, near Vatican City).

Ponte Sant' Angelo—The bridge leading to Castel Sant' Angelo was built by Hadrian for quick and regal access from downtown to his tomb. The three middle arches are actually Roman originals and a fine example of the empire's engineering expertise. The angels were designed by Bernini and finished by his students.

South Rome

Baths of Caracalla (Terme di Caracalla)—Today it's just a shell—a huge shell—with all of its sculptures and most of its mosaics moved to museums. Inaugurated by Emperor Caracalla in A.D. 216, this massive complex could accommodate 1,600 visitors at a time. Today you'll see a huge two-story, roofless brick building surrounded by a garden, bordered by ruined walls. The two large rooms at either end of the building were used for exercise. In between the exercise rooms was a pool flanked by two small mosaic-floored dressing rooms. Niches in the walls once held statues. In its day, this was a remarkable place to hang out. For ancient Romans, the baths were a social experience.

The Baths of Caracalla functioned until Goths severed the aqueducts in the sixth century. In modern times, operas were performed here from 1938 to 1993. For the same reason concerts no longer take place in the Forum—to keep the ruins from becoming more ruined—the performances were discontinued (€4.20, covered by €16 combo-ticket, Mon 09:00–14:00, Tue–Sun 09:00–19:15, ask if audioguides are available, fine €8 guidebook—can read in shaded garden while sitting on a chunk of column, Metro: Circus Maximus, and a 5-minute walk south along Via delle Terme di Caracalla, tel. 06-574-5748). Several of the Baths' statues are now in Rome's Octagonal Hall; the immense *Toro Farnese* (a marble sculpture of a bull surrounded by people) snorts in Naples' Archaeological Museum.

E.U.R.—In the late 1930s, Italy's dictator Benito Mussolini planned an international exhibition to show off the wonders of his fascist society. But these wonders brought us World War II, and Il Duce's celebration never happened. The unfinished mega-project was completed in the 1950s and now houses government offices and big, obscure museums.

If Hitler and Mussolini won the war, our world might look like E.U.R. (pronounced "ay-oor"). Hike down E.U.R.'s wide, pedestrian-mean boulevards. Patriotic murals, aren't-you-proud-to-be-an-extreme-right-winger pillars, and stern squares decorate the soulless, planned grid and stark office blocks. Boulevards named for Astronomy, Electronics, Social Security, and Beethoven are more exhausting than inspirational. Today E.U.R. is worth a trip for its Museum of Roman Civilization (described below).

The Metro skirts E.U.R. with three stops (10 min from the Colosseum): Use E.U.R. Magliana for the "Square Colosseum" and E.U.R. Fermi for the Museum of Roman Civilization (both described below). Consider walking 30 minutes from the palace to the museum through the center of E.U.R.

From the Magliana subway stop, stairs lead uphill to the **Palace of the Civilization of Labor (Palazzo del Civilta del Lavoro)**, the essence of fascist architecture. With its giant, no-questions-asked, patriotic statues and its black-and-white simplicity, this is E.U.R.'s tallest building and landmark. It's understandably nicknamed the "Square Colosseum." Around the corner, Café Palombini is still decorated in a 1930s style and is now quite trendy with young Romans (daily 07:00–24:00, good gelato, pastries, and snacks, Piazzale Adenauer 12, tel. 06-591-1700).

The **Museum of Roman Civilization (Museo della Civilta Romana)** fills 59 rooms with plaster casts and models illustrating the greatness of classical Rome. Each room has a theme, from military tricks to musical instruments. One long hall is filled with casts of the reliefs of Trajan's Column. The museum's highlight is the 1:250 scale model of Constantine's Rome—circa A.D. 300 (€4.20, Tue–Sat 09:00–18:45, Sun 09:00–13:00, closed Mon, Piazza G. Agnelli, from Metro: E.U.R. Fermi, walk 10 min up Via dell Arte, you'll see its colonnade on the right, tel. 06-592-6041).

Ancient Appian Way (Via Appia Antica)

Since the fourth century B.C., this has been Rome's gateway to the East. The first section was perfectly straight. It was the largest, widest, fastest road ever, the wonder of its day, called the "Queen of Roads." Eventually this most important of Roman roads stretched 700 kilometers to the port of Brindisi—where boats sailed for Greece and Egypt.

Tourist's Appian Way: The road starts about three kilometers south of the Colosseum at the massive San Sebastian Gate. The Museum of the Walls, located at the gate, offers an interesting look at Roman defense and a chance to scramble along a stretch of the ramparts (€2.60, Tue–Sun 09:00–19:00, closed Mon, tel. 06-7047-5284). A kilometer down the road are the two most historic and popular catacombs, those of San Callisto and San Sebastian (described below). Beyond that, the road becomes pristine and traffic-free, popular for biking and evocative hiking.

To reach the Appian Way, you can hop on the new Archeobus (see "Tours of Rome," above) or take the Metro to the Colli Albani stop, then catch bus #660 to Via Appia Antica—its last stop and the start of an interesting stretch of the ancient road (the café next to the stop sometimes rents bikes). The segment between the third and 11th milestones is most interesting.

▲▲**Catacombs**—The catacombs are burial places for (mostly) Christians who died in ancient Roman times. By law, no one was allowed to be buried within the walls of Rome. While pagan Romans were into cremation, Christians preferred to be buried. But land was expensive and most Christians were poor. A few wealthy landowning Christians allowed their land to be used as burial places.

The 40 or so known catacombs circle Rome about five kilometers from its center. From the first through the fifth centuries,

Christians dug an estimated 600 kilometers of tomb-lined tunnels with networks of galleries as many as five layers deep.

In the 800s, when barbarian invaders started ransacking the tombs, Christians moved the relics of saints and martyrs to the safety of churches in the city center. For a thousand years, the catacombs were forgotten. Around 1850, they were excavated and became part of the romantic Grand Tour of Europe.

The underground tunnels, while empty of bones, are rich in early Christian symbolism. The dove symbolized the soul. You'll see it quenching its thirst (worshiping), with an olive branch (at rest), or happily perched (in paradise). Peacocks, known for their "incorruptible flesh," symbolized immortality. The shepherd with a lamb on his shoulders was the "good shepherd," the first portrayal of Christ as a kindly leader of his flock. The fish was used because the first letters of these words—"Jesus Christ, Son of God, Savior"— spelled "fish" in Greek. And the anchor is a cross in disguise. A second-century bishop had written on his tomb: "All who understand these things, pray for me." You'll see pictures of people praying with their hands raised up—the custom at the time.

Catacomb tours are essentially the same. Which one you visit is not important. The **Catacombs of San Callisto**, the official cemetery for the Christians of Rome and burial place of third-century popes, is the most historic. Sixteen bishops (early popes) were buried here. Buy your €4.20 ticket and wait for your language to be called. They move lots of people quickly. If one group seems ridiculously large (over 50 people), wait for the next English tour (Thu–Tue 08:30–12:00, 14:30–17:30, closed Wed and Feb, closes at 17:00 in winter, Via Appia Antica 110, tel. 06-5130-1580).

The **Catacombs of San Sebastian** are 300 meters farther down the road (€4.20, Mon–Sat 08:30–12:00, 14:30–17:30, closed Sun and Nov, closes at 17:00 in winter, Via Appia Antica 136, tel. 06-5130-1580). Dig this: The catacombs have a Web site— www.catacombe.roma.it.

Sights—Near Rome

▲▲**Ostia Antica**—Rome's ancient seaport, less than an hour from downtown Rome, is the next best thing to Pompeii. Ostia had 80,000 people at the time of Christ, later became a ghost town, and is now excavated. Start at the 2,000-year-old theater, buy a map, explore the town, and finish with its fine little museum (note that museum closes at 14:00). To get there, take the Metro's B Line to the Piramide stop (consider popping out to see an ancient Roman pyramid tomb); from the Piramide stop, catch the Lido train to Ostia Antica (2/hr), then follow the signs to (or ask for) "*scavi* Ostia Antica" (€4.20, Tue–Sun 08:30–18:00 in summer, 09:00–16:00 in winter, closed Mon, museum closes for lunch, tel. 06-5635-8099). Just beyond is Rome's filthy beach (*lido*).

Self-Guided Walks in Rome

▲▲▲**Night Walk Across Rome: Trastevere to the Spanish Steps**—Rome can be grueling. But a fine way to enjoy this historian's rite of passage is an evening walk lacing together Rome's floodlit night spots. Enjoying fine urban spaces, observing real-life theater vignettes, sitting so close to a Bernini fountain that traffic noises evaporate, watching water flicker its mirror on the marble, jostling with local teenagers to see all the gelato flavors, enjoying lovers straddling more than the bench, jaywalking past flak-proof vested *polizia*, marveling at the ramshackle elegance that softens this brutal city for those who were born here and can imagine living nowhere else—these are the flavors of Rome best tasted after dark. This walk is about three kilometers (2 miles) long; for a shortcut, start at Campo de' Fiori.

Taxi or ride the bus (from Vatican area, take #23; from Via Nazionale hotels, take #64, #70, #115, or #640 to Largo Argentina and then transfer to #8) to Trastevere, the colorful neighborhood across (*tras*) the Tiber (*tevere*) River. Consider dinner here (see "Eating," below).

Trastevere offers the best look at medieval-village Rome. The action all marches to the chime of the church bells. Go to Trastevere and wander. Wonder. Be a poet on Rome's Left Bank. This proud neighborhood was long an independent working-class area. Now becoming trendy, high rents are driving out the source of so much color. Still, it's a great people scene, especially at night. Start your exploratory stroll at Piazza di Santa Maria in Trastevere. While today's fountain is 17th century, there's been a fountain here since Roman times.

Santa Maria in Trastevere, one of Rome's oldest churches, was made a basilica in the fourth century, when Christianity was legalized (free, daily 07:30–13:00, 15:00–19:00). It was the first church dedicated to the Virgin Mary. The portico (covered area just outside the door) is decorated with fascinating ancient fragments filled with early Christian symbolism. Most of what you see today dates from around the 12th century, but the granite columns come from an ancient Roman temple, and the ancient basilica floor plan (and ambience) survives. The 12th-century mosaics behind the altar are striking and notable for their portrayal of Mary—the first showing her at the throne with Jesus in heaven. Look below the scenes from the life of Mary to see ahead-of-their-time paintings (by Cavallini, from 1300) that predate the Renaissance by 100 years.

Before leaving Trastevere, wander the back streets. Then, from the church square (Piazza di Santa Maria), take Via del Moro to the river and cross on Ponte Sisto, a pedestrian bridge with a good view of St. Peter's dome. Continue straight ahead for one block. Take the first left, which leads down Via di Capo di Ferro

Trastevere

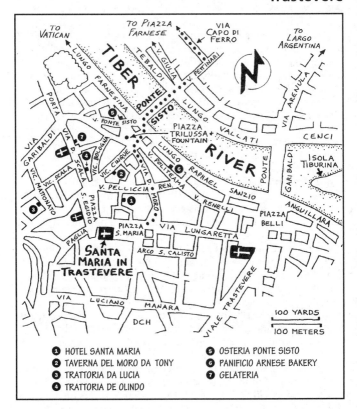

1 HOTEL SANTA MARIA
2 TAVERNA DEL MORO DA TONY
3 TRATTORIA DA LUCIA
4 TRATTORIA DE OLINDO
5 OSTERIA PONTE SISTO
6 PANIFICIO ARNESE BAKERY
7 GELATERIA

through the scary and narrow darkness to Piazza Farnese, with its imposing Palazzo Farnese. Michelangelo contributed to the facade of this palace, now the French embassy. The fountains on the square feature huge one-piece granite hot tubs from the ancient Roman Baths of Caracalla.

One block from there (opposite the palace) is **Campo de' Fiori** (Field of Flowers), which is my favorite outdoor dining room after dark (see "Eating," below). The statue of Giordano Bruno, a heretic who was burned in 1600 for believing the world was round and not the center of the universe, marks the center of this great and colorful square. Bruno overlooks a busy produce market in the morning and strollers after dark. This neighborhood is still known for its free spirit. When the statue of Bruno was erected in 1889, local riots overcame Vatican protests against honoring a heretic. Bruno faces his executioner, the Vatican

From Campo de' Fiori to the Spanish Steps

Chancellory (the big white building in the corner a bit to his right), while his pedestal reads: "And the flames rose up." The square is lined and surrounded by fun eateries. Bruno also faces La Carbonara restaurant, the only real restaurant on the square. The Forno, next door, is a popular place for hot and tasty take-out *pizza bianco* (plain but spicy pizza bread).

If Bruno did a hop, step, and jump forward and turned right and marched 200 meters, he'd cross the busy Corso Vittorio Emanuele and find **Piazza Navona**. Rome's most interesting night scene features street music, artists, fire eaters, local Casanovas, ice cream, outdoor cafés (splurge-worthy if you've got time to sit and enjoy the human river of Italy), and fountains by Bernini, the father of Baroque art. The Tartufo "death by chocolate" ice cream (€3, €6.50 at a table) made the Tre Scalini café (left of obelisk) world-famous among connoisseurs of ice cream and chocolate alike. This oblong piazza is molded around the long-gone Stadium of Domitian, an ancient chariot racetrack.

Leave Piazza Navona directly across from Tre Scalini café, go (east) past rose peddlers and palm readers, jog left around the guarded building, and follow the brown sign to the **Pantheon** straight down Via del Salvatore (cheap pizza place on left just before the Pantheon, easy WC at McDonald's). Sit for a while and ponder under the Pantheon's floodlit, moonlit portico.

With your back to the Pantheon, head right, passing Bar Pantheon on your right. The Tazza d'Oro Casa del Caffè, one of Rome's top coffee shops, dates back to the days when this area was licensed to roast coffee beans. Look back at the fine view of the Pantheon from here.

With the coffee shop on your right, walk down Via degli Orfani to Piazza Capranica, with the big plain Florentine Renaissance–style Palazzo Capranica. Big shots, like the Capranica family, built stubby towers on their palaces—not for any military use...just to show off. Leave the piazza to the right of the palace, between the palace and the church. Via in Aquiro leads to a sixth-century B.C. Egyptian **obelisk** (taken as a trophy by Augustus after his victory in Egypt over Mark Antony and Cleopatra). Walk into the guarded square past the obelisk and face the huge parliament building. A short detour to the left (past Albergo National) brings you to some of Rome's most famous gelato. **Gelateria Caffè Pasticceria Giolitti** is cheap to go or elegant, pricey, and worthwhile for a sit among classy locals (open daily until very late, your choice: cone or *bicchierini*—cup, Via Uffici del Vicario 40). Gelato fans will want to visit the nearby **Gelateria della Palma**, also two blocks away, with better gelato (Via della Maddalena 20). Or head directly from the parliament into the next, even grander, square.

Piazza Colonna features a huge second-century column honoring Marcus Aurelius, the philosopher-emperor. The big, important-looking palace is the prime minister's residence. Cross Via del Corso, Rome's noisy main drag, and jog right (around the Y-shaped shopping gallery from 1928) and head down Via dei Sabini to the roar of the water, light, and people of the Trevi Fountain.

The **Trevi Fountain** is an example of how Rome took full advantage of the abundance of water brought into the city by its great aqueducts. This watery Baroque avalanche was built in 1762 by Nicola Salvi, hired by a pope celebrating his reopening of the ancient aqueduct that powers it. Salvi used the palace behind the fountain as a theatrical backdrop for Neptune's "entrance" into the square. Neptune surfs through his watery kingdom while Triton blows his conch shell.

Romantics toss two coins over their shoulder thinking it will give them a wish and assure their return to Rome. That

may sound silly, but every year I go through this touristic ritual...
and it actually seems to work.

Take some time to people watch (whisper a few breathy *bello*s
or *bella*s) before leaving. Facing the fountain, go past it on the
right down Via delle Stamperia to Via del Triton. Cross the busy
street and continue to the Spanish Steps (ask, "*Dov'è Piazza di
Spagna?*"; doh-vay pee-aht-zah dee spahn-yah) a few blocks and
thousands of dollars of shopping opportunities away.

The **Piazza di Spagna** (rhymes with "lasagna"), with the
very popular Spanish Steps, got its name 300 years ago, when this
was the site of the Spanish embassy. It's been the hangout of many
Romantics over the years (Keats, Wagner, Openshaw, Goethe,
and others). The Boat Fountain at the foot of the steps, which was
done by Bernini's father, Pietro Bernini, is powered by an aqueduct. The piazza is a thriving night scene. Facing the steps, walk
to your right about a block to tour one of the world's biggest and
most lavish McDonald's. About a block on the other side of the
steps is the Spagna Metro stop, which (usually until 23:30) will
zip you home.

▲**The Dolce Vita Stroll down Via del Corso**—This is the city's
chic and hip "cruise" from Piazza del Popolo (Metro: Flaminio)
down a wonderfully traffic-free section of Via del Corso and up
Via Condotti to the Spanish Steps each evening around 18:00
(Sat and Sun are best). Strollers, shoppers, and flirts on the prowl
fill this neighborhood of Rome's most fashionable stores (open
after siesta 16:30–19:30). Throughout Italy, early evening is
time to stroll.

Start on **Piazza Popolo**. Historians: This area was once
just inside medieval Rome's main entry. The delightfully car-free
square is marked by an obelisk that was brought to Rome by
Augustus after he conquered Egypt. (It once stood in the Circus
Maximus.) The Baroque Church of **Santa Maria del Popolo**—
with Raphael's Chigi Chapel (pron. kee-gee, third chapel on left)
and two Caravaggio paintings (side paintings in chapel left of
altar)—is next to the gate in the old wall, on the far side of Piazza
del Popolo, to the right as you face the gate (church open Mon–
Sat 07:00–12:00, 16:00–19:00, Sun 08:00–13:30, 16:30–19:30).

From Piazza del Popolo, shop your way down **Via del Corso**.
To rest your feet, join the locals sitting on the steps of various
churches along the street.

At Via Pontefici, historians turn right and walk a block to
see the massive, rotting, round brick **Mausoleum of Augustus**,
topped with overgrown cypress trees. Beyond it, next to the river,
is Augustus' Ara Pacis, or Altar of Peace (which should reopen
in 2005).

From the mausoleum, return to Via del Corso and the 21st
century, continuing straight until **Via Condotti**. Shoppers, take

a left on Via Conditti to join the parade to the **Spanish Steps**. The streets that parallel Via Condotti to the south (Borgogno and Frattini) are just as popular. You can catch a taxi home at the taxi stand a block south of the Spanish Steps (at Piazza Mignonelli, near American Express and McDonald's).

Historians: Ignore Via Condotti. Continue a kilometer down Via del Corso—straight since Roman times—to the Victor Emmanuel Monument. Climb Michelangelo's stairway to his glorious (especially when floodlit) square atop Capitol Hill. From the balconies at either side of the mayor's palace, catch the lovely views of the Forum as the horizon reddens and cats prowl the unclaimed rubble of ancient Rome.

Sleeping in Rome
(€1.10 = about $1, country code: 39)

Sleep Code: **S** = Single, **D** = Double/Twin, **T** = Triple, **Q** = Quad, **b** = bathroom, **s** = shower only, **CC** = Credit Cards accepted, **no CC** = Credit Cards not accepted, **SE** = Speaks English, **NSE** = No English. Breakfast is included in all but the cheapest places.

The absolute cheapest beds (dorms or some cramped doubles) in Rome are €18 in small, backpacker-filled hostels. A nicer hotel (around €130 with a bathroom and air-con) provides an oasis and refuge, making it easier to enjoy this intense and grinding city. If you're going door to door, prices are soft—so bargain. Built into a hotel's official price list is a kickback for a room-finding service or agency; if you're coming direct, they pay no kickback and may lower the price for you. Many hotels have high-season (mid-March–June, Sept–Oct) and low-season prices. If traveling outside of peak times, ask about a discount. Room rates are lowest in sweltering August. Easter, September, and Christmas are most crowded and expensive. On Easter, April 25, and May 1, the entire city gets booked up.

English works in all but the cheapest places. Traffic in Rome roars. My challenge: To find friendly places on quiet streets. With the recent arrival of double-paned windows and air-conditioning, night noise is not the problem it was. Even so, light sleepers should always ask for a *tranquillo* room. Many prices here are promised only to people who show this book and reserve directly, without using a room-finding service. And many places prefer hard cash.

Bed-and-breakfasts are booming in Rome, offering comfy doubles in the old center for around €80. The Beehive hostel is a good contact for booking B&Bs in Rome (www.cross-pollinate .com, see "Sleeping in Hostels and Dorms," below).

Your hotel can point you to the nearest **Laundromat** (usually open daily 08:00–22:00, about €6 to wash and dry a 15-pound load). The Bolle Blu chain comes with Internet access (€4.25/hr, near train station at Via Milazzo 20, Via Palestro 59, and Via Principe Amedeo 116, tel. 06-446-5804).

Most hotels are eager to connect you with a shuttle service to the airport. It's reasonable and easy for leaving, but upon arrival I think it's easiest to simply catch a cab or the shuttle train.

Almost no hotels have parking but nearly all have a line on spots in a nearby garage (about €21/day).

Sleeping on Via Firenze (zip code: 00184)

I generally stay on Via Firenze because it's safe, handy, central, and relatively quiet. It's a 10-minute walk from the central train station and airport shuttle, and two blocks beyond Piazza della Repubblica and the TI. The Defense Ministry is nearby, and you've got heavily armed guards watching over you all night. Virtually all the orange buses that rumble down Via Nazionale (#64, #70, #115, #640) take you to Piazza Venezia (Forum) and Largo Argentina (Pantheon). From Largo Argentina, electric trolley #8 goes to Trastevere (first stop after crossing the river) and #64 (jammed with people and thieves) continues to St. Peter's. Farmacia Piram (Via Nazionale 228, tel. 06-488-4437) is the neighborhood 24-hour pharmacy.

Hotel Oceania is a peaceful slice of air-conditioned heaven. This 16-room manor house–type hotel is spacious and quiet, with newly renovated and spotless rooms, run by a pleasant father-and-son team (Sb-€105, Db-€135, Tb-€165, Qb-€192, these prices through 2002 with this book only, additional 25 percent off in Aug and winter, phones, CC, Via Firenze 38, 3rd floor, tel. 06-482-4696, fax 06-488-5586, www.hoteloceania.it, e-mail: hoceania@tin.it, son Stefano SE, dad Armando serves world-famous coffee).

Hotel Aberdeen, while more formal and hotelesque, offers the same great value, with mini-bars, phones, and showers in its 36 modern, air-conditioned, and smoke-free rooms. It's warmly run by Annamaria, with support from her cousins Sabrina and Cinzia, and trusty Massimo riding shotgun after dark (Sb-€92, Db-€129, Tb-€154, Qb-€180, prices through 2002 with this book only, €30 less per room in Aug and winter, CC, free Internet access, nearby parking—€21/day, Via Firenze 48, tel. 06-482-3920, fax 06-482-1092, check for deals on Web, www.travel.it/roma/aberdeen, e-mail: hotel.aberdeen@travel.it, SE).

Residence Adler, with its wide halls, breakfast on a garden patio, and eight quiet, elegant, and air-conditioned rooms in a great locale, is another good deal. It's run the old-fashioned way by a charming family (Db-€103, Tb-€145, Qb-€176, prices through 2002 with this book only, CC, additional 5 percent off for cash, elevator, Via Modena 5, 2nd floor, tel. 06-484-466, fax 06-488-0940, gracious Sr. Brando Massini NSE but tries).

Residenza Cellini is a gorgeous new place with six rooms. It offers "ortho/anti-allergy beds" and four-star comforts and service on a small scale (Db-€155, larger Db-€181, €26 discount

Rome's Train Station Neighborhood

1. HOTEL OCEANIA & NARDIZZI
2. HOTEL ABERDEEN
3. RESIDENCE ADLER & RESIDENZA CELLINI
4. HOTEL REX
5. HOTEL BRITANNIA
6. HOTEL SONYA
7. HOTEL PENSIONE ITALIA
8. HOTEL CORTINA & CAFFETTERIA NAZIONALE
9. YWCA CASA STUDENTESSE
10. SUORE SANTA ELISABETTA
11. HOTEL MONTREAL
12. HOTEL FENICIA & MAGIC
13. ALBERGO SILEO
14. HOTEL DUCA D'ALBA
15. HOTEL GRIFO
16. SUORE DI SANT ANNA
17. SNACK BAR GASTRONOMIA
18. PASTICCERIA DAGNINO
19. HOSTARIA ROMANA
20. RISTORANTE GIOVANNI
21. PHARMACY
22. RIST. CINESE INT'L.
23. BEEHIVE HOSTEL & MONTE D.O.C. VINERIA
24. CASA OLMATA HOSTEL
25. PENSIONE PELLIGRINI
26. CLARIN HOTEL
27. TO HOTEL CASA KOLBE
28. HOTEL LANCELOT
29. HOTEL PABA
30. GULLIVER'S HOUSE ROME
31. REST. NERONE

in off-season—Nov–March plus Aug, these prices with this book and payment in cash through 2002, elevator, air-con, Via Modena 5, tel. 06-4782-5204, fax 06-4788-1806, www.residenzacellini.it, e-mail: residenzacellini@tin.it, SE).

Hotel Nardizzi Americana, with 18 simple, pleasant, air-conditioned rooms and a delightful rooftop terrace, is loosely run (Sb-€83, Db-€109, Tb-€129, Qb-€140, prices through 2002 with this book only, discounts for off-season and long stays, CC, additional 10 percent off with cash, elevator, Via Firenze 38, 4th floor, tel. 06-488-0368, fax 06-488-0035, SE).

Hotel Seiler is a quiet, serviceable place with 33 decent rooms (Sb-€83, Db-€119, Tb-€145, Qb-€165, these discounted prices good only with this book, CC, fans, elevator, Via Firenze 48, tel. 06-485-550, fax 06-488-0688, e-mail: acropoli@rdn.it, Silvio and Alessia SE).

Hotel Texas Seven Hills, a stark, institutional throwback to the 1960s, rents 18 dreary rooms (D-€83, Db-€93, often soft prices, CC, single-paned windows, Via Firenze 47, first elevator on the right to 3rd floor, tel. 06-481-4082, fax 06-481-4079, e-mail: reserva@texas7hills.com, NSE). Note: This place may go three stars in 2002.

Sleeping between Via Nazionale and Basilica Santa Maria Maggiore
(zip code: 00184 unless otherwise noted)

Hotel Pensione Italia, in a busy, interesting, and handy locale, is placed safely on a quiet street next to the Ministry of the Interior. Thoughtfully run by Andrea, Lena, and Alberico, it has 31 comfortable, airy, clean, and bright rooms (Sb-€67, Db-€93, Tb-€124, Qb-€145, air-con for €8 extra, prices through 2002 with this book and cash only, all rooms 20 percent off in mid-July–Aug and winter, elevator, Via Venezia 18, just off Via Nazionale, tel. 06-482-8355, fax 06-474-5550, www.hotelitaliaroma.com, e-mail: hitalia@pronet.it, SE). Most rooms have a fan. Their fine singles are all on the quiet courtyard, and the eight annex rooms across the street are a cut above the rest.

Clarin Hotel, a plain and worn slumbermill with 21 rooms, is quiet, safe, and run with a smile (Db-€88, Tb-€109, Qb-€129, prices good with this book and cash, 3 percent extra with CC, Via Palermo 36, tel. 06-4782-5170, fax 06-4788-1393, e-mail: clarinhotel@hotmail.com, Renaldo, Franco, and Marco SE).

Hotel Sonya is a small, family-run, but impersonal place with 20 comfortable, well-equipped rooms, a great location, and decent prices (Db-€119, Tb-€134, Qb-€155, Quint/b-€170, CC, air-con, elevator, facing the Opera at Via Viminale 58, tel. 06-481-9911, fax 06-488-5678, e-mail: hotelsonyaroma @katamail.com, Francesca SE).

Hotel Cortina rents 14 modern, air-conditioned rooms on a busy street. Ask for a quieter room on the courtyard or side street (Db-€129 in 2002 with this book, CC, Via Nazionale 18, tel. 06-481-9794, fax 06-481-9220, www.travel.it /roma/hotelcortina, e-mail: hotelcortina@pronet.it, John Carlo and Angelo SE).

Hotel Montreal, run with care, is a bright, solid, business-class place on a big street a block southeast of Santa Maria Maggiore (Db-usually €103 but €88 July–Aug and €78 in winter, CC, 21 of its 27 rooms have air-con; elevator, good security, 1 block from Metro: Vittorio, 3 blocks west of train station, Via Carlo Alberto 4, 00185 Roma, tel. 06-445-7797, fax 06-446-5522, www.hotelmontrealroma.com).

Splurges: **Hotel Britannia** stands like a marble fruitcake, offering all the comforts in tight quarters. Lushly renovated with over-the-top classical motifs, its 32 air-conditioned rooms are small but comfortable with bright, modern bathrooms (Db-€233 in May–June and Sept–Oct, Db-€152 in Aug, Db-€207 the rest of the year, extra bed-€52, CC, free parking, Via Napoli 64, tel. 06-488-3153, fax 06-488-2343, www.hotelbritannia.it, e-mail: info@hotelbritannia.it).

Hotel Rex is a business-class, Art Deco fortress—a quiet, plain, and stately four-star place with 50 rooms and all the comforts (Sb-€201, Db-€253, Tb-€294, CC, elevator, air-con, Via Torino 149, tel. 06-482-4828, fax 06-488-2743, e-mail: hotel.rex@alfanet.it, SE).

YWCA and Convents: **YWCA Casa Per Studentesse** accepts men and women. It's an institutional place, filled with white-uniformed maids, more-colorful Third World travelers, and 75 single beds (€26 per person in 3- and 4-bed rooms, S-€36, Sb-€46, D-€62, Db-€73, includes breakfast except on Sun, no CC, elevator, Via C. Albo 4, tel. 06-488-0460, fax 06-487-1028). The YWCA faces a great little street market.

Suore di Santa Elisabetta is a heavenly Polish-run convent. While often booked long in advance and a challenge in communication, it's an incredible value (S-€27, Sb-€34, D-€48, Db-€63, Tb-€80, Qb-€98, CC, elevator, fine view roof terrace, a block southwest of Basilica Santa Maria Maggiore at Via dell' Omata 9, tel. 06-488-8271, fax 06-488-4066).

Pensione Per Pelligrini is another nun-run place with 39 big, simple rooms and lots of twin beds. There's a language barrier, but the price is right (S-€34, Sb-€41, D-€67, Db-€78, Tb-€89, breakfast-€4.25, closed Aug, no CC, peaceful garden, elevator, just off Piazza Vittorio Emmanuel II, Istituto Buon Salvatore, Via Leopardi 17, from station take bus #714, #649, or #360 or Metro: Vittorio Emmanuel, tel. 06-446-7147 or 06-446-7225, fax 06-446-1382, Sister Anna Maria SE).

Sleeping Cheap, Northeast of the Train Station (zip code: 00185)

The cheapest hotels in town are northeast of the station. Some travelers feel this area is weird and spooky after dark, but these hotels feel plenty safe. With your back to the train tracks, turn right and walk two blocks out of the station. The first two hotels are located in the same building.

Hotel Fenicia rents 11 comfortable, well-equipped rooms at a fine price. The bigger rooms upstairs are quieter, but there's no elevator (Sb-€47, Db-€73, Tb-€98, bigger and fancier Db-€83, prices through 2002 with this book only, air-con-€10.50/day, breakfast-€5.25, says she takes CC but doesn't, Via Milazzo 20, tel. & fax 06-490-342, www.fenicia.web-page.net, e-mail: fenicia@tiscalinet.it, Georgio and Anna SE).

Hotel Magic, a clean, marbled, family-run place with 10 rooms, is high enough off the road to escape the traffic noise (Sb-€52, Db-€73, Tb-€103, Qb-€114, air-con-€10.50/day, breakfast-€3.75, prices through 2002 with this book only, cheaper in Aug and winter, CC, thin walls, midnight curfew, Via Milazzo 20, 3rd floor, tel. & fax 06-495-9880, little English spoken).

Albergo Sileo is a shiny-chandeliered, 10-room place with an elegant touch that has a contract to house train conductors who work the night shift. Most of the simple, pleasant rooms are rented from 19:00 to 09:00 only. If you can handle this, it's a great value. During the day, they store your luggage, and, though you won't have access to a room, you're welcome to hang out in their lobby or bar (D-€39, Db-€47, Tb-€62, Db for 24 hours-€62—a steal, elevator, Via Magenta 39, tel. & fax 06-445-0246, friendly Alessandro and Maria Savioli NSE).

Sleeping near the Colosseum (zip code: 00184)

These places are buried in a very Roman world of exhaust-stained medieval ambience. Take the subway one stop from the train station to Metro: Cavour. The handy *electrico* bus line #117 (San Giovanni in Laterano, Colosseo, Via dei Serpenti, Trevi Fountain, Piazza di Spagna, and Piazza del Popolo) connects you with the sights.

Hotel Paba is a little six-room place, chocolate-box tidy and lovingly cared for by Alberta and Pasquale Castelli. While overlooking busy Via Cavour just two blocks from the Colosseum, it's quiet enough (Db-€124, extra bed-€21, show this book for 5 percent discount, breakfast served in room, CC, air-con, elevator, Via Cavour 266, tel. 06-4782-4902, fax 06-4788-1225, www.hotelpaba.com, e-mail: info@hotelpaba.com).

Hotel Duca d'Alba, a tight and modern pastel-marble-hardwood place, is more professional than homey (Sb-€134, Db-€201, much cheaper July–Aug and winter, extra bed-€21, CC, air-con, safes, phones, TV, elevator, Via Leonina 14, tel. 06-484-471, fax 06-488-4840, check Web site for deals, www.hotelducadalba.com, SE).

Hotel Grifo has a homey, tangled floor plan with 20 modern rooms and a roof terrace. The double-paned windows almost keep out the Vespa noise (Db-€119, €109 July–Aug, CC, elevator, air-con, some rooms have terraces, 2 blocks off Via Cavour at Via del Boschetto 144, tel. 06-487-1395, fax 06-474-2323, e-mail: alez@dds.nl, SE).

Suore di Sant Anna was built for Ukrainian pilgrims. The sisters are sweet. It's difficult (little English plus 23:00 curfew), but once you're in, you've got a comfortable home in a classic Roman-village locale (Sb-€41, Db-€67, Tb-€101, consider dinner for €15, no CC, off the corner of Via dei Serpenti and Via Baccina at Piazza Madonna dei Monti 3, tel. 06-485-778, fax 06-487-1064, e-mail: santasofia@tiscalinet.it).

Behind the Colosseum: **Hotel Lancelot**, a favorite among United Nations workers, is a big 60-room place with a shady courtyard, rooftop terrace, bar, and restaurant. It's quiet, safe, well-run by Faris and Lubna Khan, and popular with returning guests (Sb-€88–103, Db-€139, Tb-€163, Qb-€178, add €11 for balcony, CC, air-con, no elevator, parking-€11/day, behind Colosseum near San Clemente Church at Via Capo D'Africa 47, tel. 06-7045-0615, fax 06-7045-0640, www.venere.com/roma /lancelot/lancelot.html, e-mail: lancelot@italyhotel.com).

Near the Palatine: The **Hotel Casa Kolbe**, located in a former monastery, rents out 63 monkish, spartan rooms with no fans or air-conditioning. With vast public spaces and a peaceful garden, it's popular with groups. But the location is great: on the river side of the Palatine ruins, on a quiet side street about a block from a little-used entrance to the Forum (Sb-€62, Db-€78, Tb-€98, Qb-€109, breakfast-€5.25, CC, elevator, garden, courtyard, not handy to public transit so taxi from the station, Via S. Teodoro 44, tel. 06-679-4974 or 06-679-8866, fax 06-6994-1550, Maurizio and Antonio SE).

Sleeping near Campo de' Fiori (zip code: 00186)

You pay a premium to stay in the old center, but each of these places is romantically set deep in the tangled back streets near the idyllic Campo de' Fiori and are, for many, worth the extra money.

Casa di Santa Brigida overlooks the elegant Piazza Farnese. With soft-spoken sisters gliding down polished hallways, and pearly gates instead of doors, this lavish 23-room convent makes exhaust-stained Roman tourists feel like they've died and gone to heaven. If you're unsure of your destiny (and don't need a double bed), this is worth the splurge (Sb-€78, Db-€134, 3 percent extra with CC, great €16 dinners, roof garden, plush library, air-con, physical address: Monserrato 54,

mailing address: Piazza Farnese 96, 00186 Roma, tel. 06-6889-2596, fax 06-6889-1573, www.brigidine.org/case/italy/welcome
.html, e-mail: brigida@mclink.it, many of the sisters are from
India and speak English). If you get no response to your fax or
e-mail within three days, consider that a "no." Groups are very
welcome here.

Hotel Smeraldo, while well-run, clean, and air-conditioned,
is noisy at night, and its 50 rooms can be somewhat smoky (Sb-
€73, D-€73, Db-€103, Tb-€124, CC, Civolo dei Chiodaroli 9,
midway between Campo de' Fiori and Largo Argentina, tel.
06-687-5929, fax 06-6880-5495, www.hotelsmeraldoroma.com,
e-mail: albergosmeraldoroma@tin.it).

Hotel Arenula, the only hotel in Rome's old Jewish quarter
or ghetto, is a fine place in the thick of old Rome with 50 comfy
rooms (Sb-€88, Db-€114, Tb-€134; €26 less in July, Aug, and
winter; air-con- €10.50/day, CC, just off Via Arenula at Via Santa
Maria de' Calderari 47, tel. 06-687-9454, fax 06-689-6188, www
.hotelarenula.com, e-mail: hotel.arenula@flashnet.it).

Sleeping near the Pantheon (zip code: 00186)
These four places are buried in the pedestrian-friendly heart of
ancient Rome, each within a four-minute walk of the Pantheon.
You'll pay more here—but save time and money by being exactly
where you want to be for your early and late wandering.

Hotel Due Torri hides out on a tiny, quiet street. It feels
professional yet homey, with an accommodating staff, generous
public spaces, and 26 comfortable-if-small rooms—four with
balconies (Sb-€98, Db-€165, family apartment-€222 for 3 and
€248 for 4, CC, air-con, Vicolo del Leonetto 23, a block off
Via della Scrofa, tel. 06-6880-6956, fax 06-686-5442, www
.hotelduetorriroma.com, e-mail: hotelduetorri@interfree.it).

Piazza Navona: **Hotel Navona**, while pretty ramshackle, is
a fine value, offering 35 basic rooms in an ancient building (with
a perfect locale) a block off Piazza Navona. Top-floor rooms
come with more character (wood beams) and more stairs (D-€98,
Db-€109, air-con-€16/day, family rooms, no CC, Via dei Sediari
8, tel. 06-686-4203, fax 06-6880-3802, www.hotelnavona.com,
e-mail: info@hotelnavona.com, run by a friendly Australian named
Corry, his Italian wife Patricia, and her dad Pino).

Residenza Zanardelli is a sumptuous little place with six
classy and quiet rooms. Also owned by Corry, it's two blocks
north of Piazza Navona (Db-€134, air-con-€10.50/day, no CC,
on busy street but double-paned windows minimize noise, Via G.
Zanardelli 7, tiny name next to doorbell, tel. 06-6821-1392 or
06-6880-9760, fax 06-6880-3802).

Hotel Nazionale, a four-star landmark, is a 16th-century
palace sharing a well-policed square with the national Parliament.

Hotels and Restaurants in the Heart of Rome

1. CASA DI SANTA BRIGIDA
2. HOTEL SMERALDO
3. TO HOTEL ARENULA
4. HOTEL DUE TORRI
5. HOTEL NAVONA
6. RESIDENZA ZANARDELLI
7. HOTEL NAZIONALE
8. TAVERNA REST., VINERIA REST. & LA CARBONARA REST.
9. OSTARIA DA GIOVANNI AR GALLETTO
10. OSTERIA ENOTECA AL BRIC
11. FILETTI DE BACCALA & TRATTORIA DER PALLARO
12. RIST. GROTTE DEL TEATRO DI POMPEO
13. CUL DE SAC BAR & L'INSALATA RICCA REST.
14. BREK REST.
15. IL DELFINO REST.
16. OSTERIA DA MARIO REST.
17. REST. MYOSOTIS DI MARSILI
18. ENOTECA SPIRITI
19. TO RIST. ALLA RAMPA
20. RIST. LA TAVERNA DEGLI AMICI
21. RIST. PIZZERIA SACRO & PROFANO
22. GIOLITTI GELATERIA
23. GELATERIA DELLA PALMA

Its 90 rooms are served by lush public spaces, fancy bars, and a uniformed staff. It's a big hotel with a revolving front door, but it's a worthy splurge if you want security, comfort, and the heart of old Rome at your doorstep (Sb-€186, Db-€289, extra person-€62, suite-€439, less in Aug and winter, CC, air-con, elevator, free loaner motorbikes, Piazza Montecitorio 131, tel. 06-695-001, fax 06-678-6677, www.nazionaleroma.it, e-mail: hotel@nazionaleroma .it, SE). See their Web site for weekend and summer discounts of about 25 percent.

Sleeping in Trastevere (zip code: 00153)

Hotel Santa Maria sits like a lazy hacienda in the midst of Trastevere. Surrounded by a medieval skyline, you'll feel as if you're on some romantic stage set. Its 18 small but well-equipped rooms—former cells in a cloister—are all ground floor, circling a gravelly courtyard of orange trees and stay-awhile patio furniture. Because this is the only hotel in Trastevere, you'll pay about 25 percent more—but for poets, it's a deal (Db-€155, Tb-€191, Qb-€217, for this special price it's cash only, prices good with this book through 2002, 3-night min, CC, air-con, a block north of Piazza Maria Trastevere at Vicolo del Piede 2, tel. 06-589-4626, fax 06-589-4815, www.htlsantamaria.com, e-mail: hotelsantamaria @libero.it, Stefano SE).

Sleeping "Three Stars" near the Vatican Museum (zip code: 00192)

To locate hotels, see map on page 617.

Hotel Alimandi is a good value, run by the friendly and entrepreneurial Alimandi brothers: Paolo, Enrico, and Luigi, and the next generation: Marta and Germano. Their 35 rooms are air-conditioned, modern, and marbled in white (Sb-€85, Db-€145, Tb-€168, 5 percent discount with this book and cash, CC, elevator, a grand buffet breakfast is served in their great roof garden, self-service washing machines, Internet access, pool table, grand piano lounge, free parking, down the stairs directly in front of the Vatican Museum, Via Tunisi 8, near Metro: Cipro-Musei Vaticani, reserve by phone, no reply to fax means they are full, tel. 06-3972-6300, toll-free in Italy tel. 800-122-121, fax 06-3972-3943, www.alimandi .org, e-mail: alimandi@tin.it, SE). They offer free airport pickup and drop-off, though you must reserve when you book your room and wait for a scheduled shuttle (every 2 hours, see their Web site). Maria Alimandi rents out three rooms in her apartment a 20-minute bus ride from the Vatican (Db-€78, see www.alimandi.org).

Hotel Spring House, with a hotelesque feel, offers 51 attractive rooms—some with balconies or terraces (Db-€129, Tb-€155, mention this book, 15 percent discount July–Aug and winter plus additional 5 percent discount for cash payment, weekend deals,

CC, Internet access, air-con, elevator, free loaner bikes, Metro: Cipro-Musei Vaticani, Via Mocenigo 7, 2 blocks from Vatican Museum, tel. 06-3972-0948, fax 06-3972-1047, www.hotelspringhouse.com, Stefano Gabbani SE).

Hotel Gerber is sleek, modern, and air-conditioned, with 27 businesslike rooms set in a quiet residential area (S-€62, Sb-€98, Db-€129, Tb-€150, Qb-€170, 10 percent discount with this book, CC, air-con, Via degli Scipioni 241, a block from Metro: Lepanto, at intersection with Ezio, tel. 06-321-6485, fax 06-321-7048, www.hotelgerber.it, Peter and Simonetta SE).

Hotel Sant' Anna is pricier than the rest, located on a charming-for-Rome pedestrian street that fills up with restaurant tables at dinnertime. Its 20 rooms are overly decorated with classical themes, but the furnishings are comfy (Sb-€145, Db-€181, Db-€145 in July–Aug and winter, CC, air-con, elevator, courtyard, Borgo Pio 133, near intersection with Mascherino, a couple blocks from entrance to St. Peter's, tel. 06-6880-1602, fax 06-6830-8717, www.travel.it/roma/santanna, SE).

Hotel Bramante sits like a grand medieval lodge in the shadow of the fortified escape wall that runs from the Vatican to Castel San Angelo. The public spaces and the 16 rooms are generously sized, with rough wood beams and high ceilings (Sb-€129, Db-€181, Tb-€217, Qb-€253, 8 percent discount with this book, CC, air-con, no elevator, Vicolo delle Palline 24, tel. 06-6880-6426, fax 06-687-9881, www.hotelbramante.com, e-mail: bramante@excalhq.it, Loredana SE).

Sleeping in Hostels and Dorms *(zip code: 00184)*

For easy communication with young, friendly entrepreneurs, cheap dorm beds, and the very cheapest doubles in town—within a 10-minute hike of the train station—consider the following places:

Casa Olmata is a laid-back backpackers' place midway between the Termini train station and Colosseum (dorm beds €16–18, S-€34, bunk bed D-€36, one queen-size D-€55, no CC, lots of stairs, laundry service, free Internet access, video rentals, games, rooftop terrace with views, communal kitchen, dinners twice weekly, a block southwest of Basilica Santa Maria Maggiore, Via dell' Omata 36, 3rd floor, tel. 06-483-019, fax 06-474-2854, www.casaolmata.com, e-mail: casaolmata30@hotmail.com, Mirella and Marco).

The Beehive is especially good for older vagabonds. This tidy little place has two six-bed dorms (€16 beds) and a guests' kitchen on the main floor. Upstairs are five hotel-type rooms that are a great value (Sb-€39, D-€52, T-€78, Q-€103). It's thoughtfully run by a friendly young American couple, Steve and Linda (CC, dorms closed 13:00–16:00, 2 blocks south of Basilica Santa Maria Maggiore at Via Giovanni Lanza 99, tel. 06-474-0719, www.the-beehive.com). They also run a B&B booking service (fine private rooms in the old center, offering comparable quality for €65–95—about half the cost of a hotel, www .cross-pollinate.com).

Gulliver's House Rome is a fun little hostel in a very safe and handy locale, run by Simon and Sara. Its 24 beds in cramped quarters work fine for backpackers (€18 per bunk bed in 8-bed dorm, D–€57, no CC, closed 12:00–16:00, Via Palermo 36, tel. 06-481-7680, www.gullivershouse.com, e-mail: info@gullivershouse.com).

Eating in Rome

Romans spend their evenings eating rather than drinking, and the preferred activity is simply to enjoy a fine, slow meal, buried deep in the old city. Rome's a fun and cheap place to eat, with countless little eateries serving memorable $20 meals.

Although I've listed a number of restaurants, I recommend that you just head for a scenic area and explore. Piazza Navona, the Pantheon area, Campo de' Fiori, and Trastevere are neighborhoods packed with characteristic eateries. Sitting with tourists on a famous square enjoying the scene works fine or, for places more out of the way, consider my recommendations.

For Rome's best gelato, see "Eating near the Pantheon," below.

Eating in Trastevere

Colorful Trastevere is also now pretty touristy. Still, Romans join the tourists to eat on the rustic side of the Tiber River. Start at the central square (Piazza Santa Maria in Trastevere). Then choose: eat with tourists enjoying the ambience of the famous square, or wander the back streets in search of a mom-and-pop place with barely a menu. Consider these places before making a choice (all are in the tangle of lanes between Ponte Sisto and the Piazza Santa Maria in Trastevere—see map on page 628):

At **Taverna del Moro da Tony**, Tony scrambles—with a great antipasti table—to keep his happy eaters (mostly tourists) well-fed and returning. Until we start telling him to "hold the mayo," his bruschetta will come buried in it (Tue–Sun 12:00–24:00, closed Mon, off Via del Moro at Vicolo del Cinque 36, tel. 06-580-9165).

For good home cooking Roman-style, consider these two fun little places (within a block of each other): **Trattoria da Lucia** (closed Mon, indoor or outdoor seating, Vicolo del Mattonato 2, tel. 06-580-3601) and the homey **Trattoria de Olindo** (closed Sun, Vicolo della Scala 8, tel. 06-581-8835).

Osteria Ponte Sisto, a rough-and-tumble little place, specializes in traditional Roman cuisine. Since it's just outside of the tourist zone, it offers the best value and caters mostly to Romans. It's also easiest to find: As you approach Trastevere, crossing Ponte Sisto (pedestrian bridge), continue across the little square (Piazza Trilussa), and it's on the right (open daily, Via Ponte Sisto 80, tel. 06-588-3411).

Panificio Arnese could be the most respected traditional bakery in town (daily 09:00–21:00, Via del Politeama 27). Pop in and eat something fresh out of the oven. And the fine little *gelateria* (across from the church on Piazza della Scala) dishes up oh-wow pistachio.

Eating on and near Campo de' Fiori

While touristy, Campo de' Fiori offers a classic, romantic square setting. And since it is so close to the collective heart of Rome, it remains popular with locals. For greater atmosphere than food value, circle the square, considering each place. Bars and pizzerias seem overwhelm the square. The **Taverna** and **Vineria** at numbers 16 and 15 offer good perches from which to people-watch and nurse a glass of wine. The only real restaurant is **La Carbonara**. While not the birthplace of pasta carbonara, it does serve good food (closed Tue, Piazza Campo de Fiori 23, tel. 06-686-4783). Meals on small nearby streets are a better value but lack that Campo de' Fiori magic.

Nearby, on the more elegant and peaceful Piazza Farnese, **Ostaria Da Giovanni Ar Galletto** has a dressier, local crowd, great outdoor seating, and moderate prices. Giovanni and his son Angelo serve fine food; but unfortunately single diners have been turned away (closed Sun, tucked in corner of Piazza Farnese at #102, tel. 06-686-1714). Of all my listings, Giovanni offers perhaps the best *al fresco* dining experience.

Osteria Enoteca al Bric is a mod Italian/French bistro-type place run by a man who loves to cook and serve good wine. Wine case lids decorate the wall like happy memories. With candlelit elegance and no tourists, it's perfect for the wine snob in the mood for pasta and fine cheese. Choose your bottle (or half bottle) from the huge selection lining the walls as you enter (open from 19:30, closed Mon, CC, 100 meters off Campo dei' Fiori at Via del Pellegrino 51, tel. 06-687-9533).

Filetti de Baccala is a tradition for many Romans. Basically a fish bar with paper tablecloths and cheap prices, it features grease-stained, hurried waiters who serve old-time favorites— fried cod fillets, a strange, bitter *puntarelle* salad, and delightful anchovies with butter—to nostalgic locals (Mon–Sat 17:30–23:00, closed Sun, a block east of Campo de' Fiori tumbling onto a tiny and atmospheric square, Largo dei Librari 88, tel. 06-686-4018).

Trattoria der Pallaro has no menu but plenty of return eaters. Paola Fazi—with a towel wrapped around her head— turban-style—and her family serve up a five-course festival of typically Roman food for €17.50, including wine, coffee, and a wonderful mandarin liqueur. Their slogan: "Here, you'll eat what we want to feed you." Make like Oliver Twist asking for more soup and get seconds on the mandarin liqueur (Tue–Sun 12:00–15:30, 19:30–24:00, closed Mon, indoor/outdoor seating on quiet square, a block south of Corso Vittorio Emmanuele, down Largo del Chiavari to Largo del Pallaro 15, tel. 06-6880-1488).

Ristorante Grotte del Teatro di Pompeo, sitting atop an ancient theater, serves good food at fair prices with a smile (closed Mon, Via del Biscione 73, tel. 06-6880-3686). This is great if you want to dine on a characteristic street busy with people strolling.

Between Campo de Fiori and Piazza Navona: For interesting bar munchies, try **Cul de Sac** on Piazza Pasquino (often crowded, daily 12:00–18:00, 19:00–24:00, a block southwest of Piazza Navona). **L'Insalata Ricca**, next door, is a popular chain that specializes in hearty and healthy salads (daily 12:00–15:45, 18:45–22:00, Piazza Pasquino 72, tel. 06-6830-7881). Another branch is nearby with more spacious outdoor seating (just off Corso Vittorio Emmanuele on Largo del Chiavari).

Eating near the Pantheon

You'll find a mix of cafeterias, groceries, restaurants, wine bars, and gelato shops.

Cafeterias: **Brek**, on Largo Argentina just south of the Pantheon, is an appealing, self-service restaurant with modern efficient atmosphere and really cheap prices (daily 12:00–15:30, 18:30–23:00, skip the sandwiches and pizza slices downstairs and go to the cafeteria upstairs, northwest corner of square, Largo Argentina 1, tel. 06-6821-0353).

Il Delfino, also on Largo Argentina, is a tired but handy self-service cafeteria that serves throughout the day (daily 07:00–21:00, not cheap but fast). Across the side street, **Frullati di Frutta** sells refreshing fruity frappés.

Grocery: The *alimentari* on the Pantheon square will make you a sandwich for a temple-porch picnic. Sit at the base of a column in the shade and munch lunch.

Restaurants: **Osteria da Mario**, a great little mom-and-pop joint with a no-stress menu, serves delicious traditional favorites. You'll feel right at home with locals who know a good value. The pop (Mario), who passed away—you'll see his photo on the wall—would be happy with the way his wife and kids are carrying on (Mon–Sat 13:00–15:00, 19:30–23:00, closed Sun, 2 blocks in front of Pantheon and to the left at Piazza delle Coppelle 51, tel. 06-6880-6349).

Ristorante Myosotis di Marsili, a dressy place with black-tie waiters and a coat check, is popular with local politicians and diners classy enough to look into the fish locker and make a knowledgeable choice. It has a traditional yet imaginative menu with a good wine list (Mon–Sat 12:30–15:30, 19:30–23:30, closed Sun, reservations smart, near Osteria da Mario 2 blocks in front of Pantheon at Vicolo Della Vaccarella 3, tel. 06-686-5554).

Wine Bar: **Enoteca Spiriti**, a wine bar two blocks from the Pantheon, is run by Raffaele, son Matteo, and daughter Daria. They serve great wine ("*corposo*" means full-bodied) by the glass and light meals with integrity. Raffaele and I have designed a treat for travelers with this book: "A Taste of Italy for Two" includes two glasses of fine Amarone wine (or the equivalent in value), fresh bread, and a plate decorated with a tasty variety of Italian cheeses and meats for a total of €16. Choose: Cool jazz interior or classic Roman sidewalk exterior (open at 12:30, very busy with local office workers at 13:30, dinner from 19:30, facing Pantheon walk around to the right and take 2 rights to Via S. Eustachio 5).

Gelato: Two of Rome's top ice-cream joints are a minute's walk in front of the Pantheon. The venerable **Giolitti's** (just off Piazza Colonna and Piazza Monte Citorio on Via Uffici del Vicario) is good with cheap take-away prices and elegant Old World seating. But **Gelateria della Palma** is the new king of gelato— fresher, tastier, and with more options, including sugar-free and frozen yogurt varieties (100 flavors, 2 blocks in front of Pantheon at Via della Maddalena 20, tel. 06-6880-6752).

Eating near the Spanish Steps

Ristorante Alla Rampa is a classic old restaurant tucked away just around the corner from the touristy crush of the Spanish Steps. You'll get quality Roman cooking here with great indoor/outdoor ambience for a moderate price. They take no reservations, so arrive by 19:30 or be prepared to wait (closed Sun, 100 meters east of Spanish Steps at Piazza Mignanelli 18, tel. 06-678-2621).

Eating near Piazza Venezia

Ristorante La Taverna degli Amici is a dressy yet friendly candlelit place draped in ivy and tucked away on a sleepy square two blocks toward the Pantheon from the Victor Emmanuel Monument. This is a great and peaceful spot for a break before or after your Capital Hill sightseeing. The waiters are friendly, and the clientele is local and upscale (reserve for dinner to avoid the basement, Tue–Sun 12:30–15:00, 19:30–24:00, closed Mon, Piazza Margana 36, tel. 06-6920-0493).

Eating near the Trevi Fountain

Ristorante Pizzeria Sacro e Profano is a bright and trendy place energetically filling an old church with spicy south Italian (Calabrian) cuisine and great pizzas. Run by friendly and helpful Pasquale and friends, this is just far enough away from the

Trevi mobs (a block off Via del Tritone at Via dei Maroniti 29, tel. 06-6791-836).

Eating between the Colosseum and St. Peter-in-Chains Church

You find good views but poor value in the restaurants directly behind the Colosseum. To get your money's worth, eat a block away from the Colosseum. There are two handy eateries at the top of Terme Di Tito a block uphill from the Colosseum, near St. Peter-in-Chains Church (of Michelangelo's *Moses* fame).

For a real restaurant meal, try **Ostaria da Nerone**. The Santis family serves traditional Roman cuisine in a homey indoor or outdoor setting (Mon–Sat 12:00–15:00, 19:00–23:00, closed Sun, Via delle Terme di Titi 96, tel. 06-481-7952). Next door at **Caffè dello Studente**, Pina and Mauro serve typical "bar gastronomia" fare (pizza, toasted sandwiches, various drinks). Stand up at the crowded bar, take away, or enjoy the outdoor tables (Mon–Sat 07:30–21:30, closed Sun, tel. 06-488-3240).

Eating near Via Firenze and Via Nazionale Hotels

Snack Bar Gastronomia is a great local hole-in-the-wall for lunch or dinner (daily 07:00–24:00, fresh meat or veggie sandwiches, fresh squeezed juices, and Greek-style yogurt—yummy with fruit—ask the price first, Via Firenze 34). There's a classic old-fashioned *alimentari* (grocery) across the street (7:00–19:30).

Pasticceria Dagnino—popular for its top-quality Sicilian specialties, especially pastries and ice cream—is frequented by people who work at my recommended hotels (daily 07:00–22:00, in Galleria Esedra off Via Torino, tel. 06-481-8660). Their *arancino*—a rice, cheese, and ham ball—is a greasy Sicilian favorite, and their cannoli is sweet. Direct the construction of your meal at the bar, pay for your trayful at the cashier, and climb upstairs, where you'll find the dancing Sicilian girls (free).

Hostaria Romana is a great place for traditional Roman cuisine. For an air-conditioned, classy, local favorite run by a jolly group of men who enjoy their work, eat here (closed Sun, midway between Trevi Fountain and Piazza Barberini, Via del Boccaccio 1, at intersection with Via Rasella, no reservations needed before 20:00, tel. 06-474-5284). Go ahead and visit the antipasto bar in person to assemble your plate. They're happy to serve an *antipasti misto della casa* and pasta dinner. Take a hard look at their *Specialita Romane* list.

Ristorante da Giovanni is a serviceable, hardworking place, feeding locals and tired travelers now for 50 years (tired €12 menu, Mon–Sat 12:00–15:00, 19:00–22:30, closed Sun, CC, just off Via XX Settembre at Via Antonio Salandra 1, tel. 06-485-950).

Cafeteria Nazionale, with woody elegance, offers light

lunches—including salads—at reasonable prices (Mon–Sat 07:00–20:00, closed Sun, CC, Via Nazionale 26-27, at intersection with Via Agostino de Pretis, tel. 06-4899-1716). Their lunch buffet is a delight (€7.50, 12:30–15:00).

Ristorante Cinese Internazionale is your best neighborhood bet for Chinese (daily 12:00–15:00, 18:00–23:00, inexpensive, no pasta, just off Via Nazionale behind Hotel Luxor at Via Agostino de Pretis 98, tel. 06-474-4064).

Restaurant Target is a soulless, modern, but handy place serving decent pizza and pasta near recommended hotels (open daily, indoor and outdoor seating, don't expect great service, Via Torino 33, tel. 06-474-0066).

The **McDonald's** restaurants on Piazza della Repubblica (free piazza seating outside), Piazza Barberini, and Via Firenze offer air-conditioned interiors and salad bars.

Flann O'Brien Irish Pub is an entertaining place for a quick light meal (of pasta or something *other* than pasta, served early or late when other places are closed), fine Irish beer, live sporting events on TV, and perhaps the most Italian crowd of all (daily 07:30–01:00, Via Nazionale 17, at intersection with Via Napoli, tel. 06-488-0418).

Eating near Santa Maria Maggiore

For a classy taste of Tuscany in a woody wine bar filled with local office workers, drop by **Monti D.O.C. Vineria** Wine Bar for lunch (chalkboard shows the daily specials, daily 10:00–24:00, 2 blocks from basilica next to recommended Beehive hostel at Via Giovanni Lanza 93, tel. 06-487-2696).

Eating near the Vatican Museum and St. Peter's

Avoid the restaurant pushers handing out fliers near the Vatican: bad food, expensive menu tricks. Try any of these instead:

Antonio's Hostaria dei Bastioni is tasty and friendly. It's conveniently located midway on your hike from St. Peters' to the Vatican Museum, with noisy streetside seating and a quiet interior (Mon–Sat 12:00–15:00, 19:00–23:30, closed Sun, €5.25–6.25 pastas, €7.75 *secondi*, no cover charge, at corner of Vatican wall, Via Leone IV 29, tel. 06-3972-3034). Antonio is your gracious host.

La Rustichella serves a sprawling antipasti buffet (€7.75 for a meal-sized plate). Arrive when they open at 19:30 to avoid a line and have the pristine buffet to yourself (Tue–Sun 12:30–15:00, 19:30–23:00, closed Mon, near Metro: Cipro-Musei Vaticani stop, opposite church at end of Via Candia, Via Angelo Emo 1, tel. 06-3972-0649). Consider the fun and fruity **Gelateria Millennium** next door.

Viale Giulio Cesare is lined with cheap **Pizza Rustica** shops and fun eateries, such as **Cipriani Self-Service Rosticcería** (closed Mon, pleasant outdoor seating, near Ottaviano subway stop, Viale Guilio Cesare 195). Restaurants such as **Tre Pupazzi** lining the pedestrian-only Borgo Pio, a block from Piazza San Pietro, are worth a look.

Turn your nose loose in the wonderful **Via Andrea Doria** open-air market three blocks north of the Vatican Museum (Mon–Sat roughly 07:00–13:30, until 16:30 on Tue and Fri except summer, between Via Tunisi and Via Andrea Doria). If the market is closed, try the nearby **IN's supermarket** (Mon–Sat 08:30–13:30, 16:00–20:00 but closed Thu eve, a half block straight out from Via Tunisi entrance of open-air market, Via Francesco 18).

Transportation Connections—Rome

Termini is the central station (see "Arrival in Rome," on page 596; Metro: Termini). Tiburtina is the bus station (4 Metro stops away from train station; Metro: Tiburtina).

By train from Rome to: Venice (6/day, 5–8 hrs), **Florence** (12/day, 2 hrs, most stop at Orvieto en route), **Pisa** (8/day, 3–4 hrs), **Genova** (7/day, 6 hrs, overnight possible), **Milan** (12/day, 5 hrs, overnight possible), **Naples** (6/day, 2 hrs), **Brindisi** (2/day, 9 hrs), **Amsterdam** (2/day, 20 hrs), **Bern** (5/day, 10 hrs), **Frankfurt** (4/day, 14 hrs), **Munich** (5/day, 12 hrs), **Nice** (2/day, 10 hrs), **Paris** (5/day, 16 hrs), **Vienna** (3/day, 13–15 hrs). All-Italy train info: tel. 848-888-088.

By bus to: Assisi (3/day, 3 hrs), **Siena** (7/day, 3 hrs).

Rome's Airports

Rome's two airports—Fiumicino (a.k.a. Leonardo da Vinci) and the small Ciampino—share the same Web site (www.adr.it).

Fiumicino Airport: Rome's major airport has a TI (Mon–Sat 08:00–19:00, closed Sun, tel. 06-6595-4471), ATMs, banks, luggage storage, shops, and bars.

A slick, direct train connects the airport and Rome's central Termini train station in 30 minutes. Trains run twice hourly in both directions from roughly 07:30 to 22:00. From the airport, trains depart at :07 and :37 past the hour (from airport's arrival gate, follow signs to "Stazione/Railway Station"; buy ticket from a machine or the Biglietteria office; €9, CC). From the Termini train station, trains depart at :21 and :51 past the hour usually from track 25; look for signs that say "Fiumicino" and confirm with an official or a local on the platform that the train is indeed going to the airport (€9, buy ticket from any *tabacchi* shop in station or at Alitalia desk near entrance to track 25; to reach track 25, walk along track 24 midway through the station, then follow signs that take you inside—to Alitalia desk—and down the escalator). Read your ticket: if it requires validation, stamp it in a yellow machine near the platform before boarding.

Your hotel can arrange a taxi to the airport at any hour for about €40. To get from the airport into town cheaply by taxi, try teaming up with any tourist also just arriving (most are heading for hotels near yours in the center). Splitting a taxi and hopping out once downtown at a taxi stand to take another to your hotel will save you about €15. Avoid unmarked, unmetered taxis.

For airport information, call 06-65951. To inquire about flights, call 06-6595-3640 (Alitalia: tel. 06-65643, British Air: toll-free tel. 848-812-266, Delta: toll-free tel. 800-864-114, KLM/Northwest: tel. 06-6501-1441, Lufthansa: tel. 06-6568-4004, SAS: tel. 06-6501-0771, Swiss Air: tel. 06-847-0555, United: tel. 0266-7481).

Ciampino Airport: Rome's smaller airport (tel. 06-794-941) handles budget and charter flights. To get to downtown Rome from the airport, take the LILA/Cotral bus (2/hrly) to the Anagnina Metro stop, where you can connect by Metro to the stop nearest your hotel.

Driving in Rome

Greater Rome is circled by the Grande Raccordo Anulare. This ring road has spokes that lead you into the center. Entering from the north, leave the autostrada at the Settebagni exit. Following the ancient Via Salaria (and the black-and-white "Centro" signs), work your way doggedly into the Roman thick of things. This will take you along the Villa Borghese park and dump you right on Via Veneto (where there's an Avis office). Avoid rush hour and drive defensively: Roman cars stay in their lanes like rocks in an avalanche. Parking in Rome is dangerous. Park near a police station or get advice at your hotel. The Villa Borghese underground garage is handy (€18/day, Metro: Spagna).

Consider this: Your car is a worthless headache in Rome. Avoid a pile of stress and save money by parking at the huge, easy, and relatively safe lot behind the Orvieto station (follow "P" signs from autostrada) and catch the train to Rome (14/day, 75 min).

FLORENCE
(FIRENZE)

Florence, the home of the Renaissance and birthplace of our modern world, is a "supermarket sweep," and the groceries are the best Renaissance art in Europe.

Get your bearings with a Renaissance walk. Florentine art goes beyond paintings and statues—there's food, fashion, and handicrafts. You can lick Italy's best gelato while enjoying some of Europe's best people watching.

Planning Your Time

If you're in Europe for three weeks, Florence deserves a well-organized day. For a day in Florence, see Michelangelo's *David*, tour the Uffizi Gallery (best Italian paintings anywhere), tour the underrated Bargello (best statues), and do the Renaissance ramble (explained below). Art lovers will want to chisel another day out of their itinerary for the many other Florentine cultural treasures. Shoppers and ice-cream lovers may need to do the same. Plan your sightseeing carefully. Some sights close Mondays and afternoons. While many spend several hours a day in lines, thoughtful travelers avoid this by making reservations or going late in the day. Places open at night are virtually empty.

Orientation

The Florence we're interested in lies mostly on the north bank of the Arno River. Everything is within a 20-minute walk of the train station, cathedral, or Ponte Vecchio (Old Bridge). The less impressive but more characteristic Oltrarno (south bank) area is just over the bridge. The huge red-tiled dome of the cathedral (the Duomo) and its tall bell tower (Giotto's Tower) mark the center of historic Florence.

Florence Overview

Tourist Information

There are three TIs in Florence: at the station, near Santa Croce, and on Via Cavour (www.firenze.turismo.toscana.it).

The TI across the square from the train station is most crowded—expect long lines (Mon–Sat 08:30–19:00, Sun 08:30–13:00; off-season Mon–Sat 08:30–17:30, Sun 08:30–13:00; with your back to tracks, it's across square in wall near corner of church; Piazza Stazione, tel. 055-212-245). Note: In the station, avoid the Hotel Reservations "Tourist Information" window (marked Informazioni Turistiche Alberghiere) near the McDonald's; it's not a real TI but a hotel reservation business.

The TI near Santa Croce Church is pleasant, helpful, and uncrowded (Mon–Sat 09:00–19:00, Sun 09:00–14:00, shorter hours off-season, Borgo Santa Croce 29 red, tel. 055-234-0444).

Another winner is the TI three blocks north of the Duomo (Mon–Sat 08:15–19:15, Sun 08:30–13:30, closed winter Sun, Via Cavour 1 red, tel. 055-290-832 or 055-290-833; international bookstore across street, see "Helpful Hints," below).

At any TI pick up a map, a current museum-hours listing (extremely important since no guidebook—including this one—has ever been able to predict next year's hours), and any information on entertainment. The free monthly *Florence Concierge Information* magazine lists museums plus lots that I don't: concerts and events, markets, sporting events, church services, shopping ideas, bus and train connections, and an entire similar section on Siena. Get yours at the TI or from any expensive hotel (pick one up, as if you're staying there).

Greater Florence

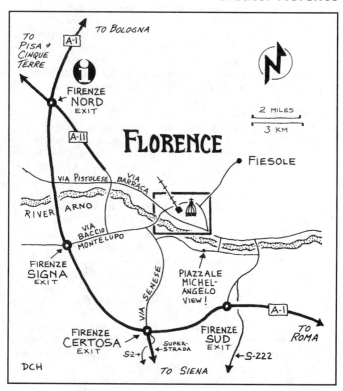

To Bologna

TO PISA & CINQUE TERRE

A-1

FIRENZE NORD EXIT

A-11

N

2 MILES
3 KM

FLORENCE

● FIESOLE

VIA PISTOLESE · VIA BARRACA

RIVER ARNO

VIA BACCIO MONTELUPO

FIRENZE SIGNA EXIT

VIA SENESE

PIAZZALE MICHEL-ANGELO VIEW!

A-1

FIRENZE CERTOSA EXIT

SUPER-STRADA

S2→

FIRENZE SUD EXIT

TO ROMA

←S-222

DCH

TO SIENA

Arrival in Florence

By Train: The station soaks up time and generates dazed and sweaty crowds. Try to get your tourist information and train tickets elsewhere. (You can get onward tickets and information at American Express—see "Helpful Hints," below.) With your back to the tracks, to your left are most of my recommended hotels; a 24-hour pharmacy (Farmacia Comunale, near McDonald's); city buses; and the entrance to the underground mall/passage that goes across the square to the church Santa Maria Novella (but because the tunnel, especially the surface point near the church, is frequented by pickpockets, stay above ground).

By Car: From the *autostrada* (north or south), take the Certosa exit (follow signs to *Centro*; at Porta Romana go to the left of the arch and down Via Francesco Petrarca). After driving and trying to park in Florence, you'll understand why Leonardo never invented the car. Cars flatten the charm of Florence. Don't

drive in Florence and don't risk parking illegally (fines up to
€150). The city has plenty of lots. For a short stay, park underground at the train station (€2/hr). The Fortezza da Basso is
clearly marked in the center (€18.50/24 hrs). The least expensive
lots are: Parcheggio Parterre (Firenze Parcheggi, €10.50/24 hrs,
perhaps cheaper with hotel reservation) and Parcheggio Oltrarno
(near Porta Romana—pass through gate and on left, €10.50 per
day). For parking information, call 055-500-1994.

Helpful Hints

Hours of Sights Can Change Suddenly: Because of labor
demands, hours of sights change without warning. Pick up the
latest listing of museum hours at a TI, or you'll miss out on something you came to see. Don't delay; you never know when a place
will unexpectedly close for a holiday, strike, or restoration.

Make Reservations to Avoid Lines: Florence has a great
reservation system for its top five sights—Uffizi, Accademia,
Bargello, Medici Chapel, and the Pitti Palace. You can show up
and wait in line or, make a quick and easy telephone booking.

Two sights come with long lines: the Accademia (*David*)
and the Uffizi (two-hour lines on busy days). These lines are
easily avoided by making a reservation. Frankly, it's stupid not to.

While you can generally make a reservation a day in advance
(upon arrival in Florence), you'll have a wider selection of entry
times by calling a few days ahead. You dial 055-294-883 (Mon–Fri
08:30–18:30, Sat 08:30–12:00), an English-speaking operator walks
you through the process, and two minutes later you say *grazie* with
appointments (15-minute entry window) and six-digit confirmation
numbers for each of the top museums and galleries.

If you don't book ahead, remember that many sights (a breeze
at the minor, less crowded sights) can reserve and sell tickets to
other museums—often for admissions the same day—allowing
you to skip right past the dreary mob scene.

More Tips on Sightseeing: Some museums close at 14:00
and stop selling tickets 30 minutes before that. The biggies (Uffizi
and Accademia) close on Monday. The *Concierge Information* magazine thoughtfully lists which sights are open afternoons, Sundays,
and Mondays (best attractions open Mon: Museo dell' Opera del
Duomo, Giotto's Tower, Brancacci Chapel, Michelangelo's Casa
Buonarroti, Dante's House, Science Museum, Palazzo Vecchio, and
churches). Churches usually close from 12:30 to 15:00 or 16:00.

I like the €2.60 "new map" of Florence that lists the sights
(sold at newsstands). Local guidebooks are cheap and give you a
map and a decent commentary on the sights.

Theft Alert: Florence has particularly hardworking thief
gangs. They specialize in tourists and hang out where you do:
near the train station, the station's underpass (especially where

the tunnel surfaces), and major sights. Also, be on guard at two squares frequented by drug pushers (Santa Maria Novella and Santo Spirito). American tourists—especially older ones—are considered easy targets.

Medical Help: For a doctor who speaks English, call 055-475-411 (reasonable hotel calls, cheaper if you go to the clinic at Via L. Magnifico 59). The TI has a list of English-speaking doctors. A 24-hour pharmacy is at the train station.

Addresses: Street addresses list businesses in red and residences in black or blue (color-coded on the actual street number and indicated by a letter following the number in printed addresses: n = black, r = red). *Pensioni* are usually black but can be either. The red and black numbers each appear in roughly consecutive order on streets but bear no apparent connection with each other. I'm lazy and don't concern myself with the distinction (if one number's wrong, I look for the other) and find my way around fine.

American Express: AmEx offers all the normal services but is most helpful as an easy place to get your train tickets, reservations, supplements (all the same price as at station), or even just information on train schedules. It's three short blocks north of Palazzo Vecchio on Via Dante Alighieri 22 red (Mon–Fri 09:00–17:30, Sat money exchange only 09:00–12:30, CC, tel. 055-50981).

Long-Distance Telephoning: Small newsstand kiosks sell PIN phone cards giving you cheap international phone calls (6 minutes/$1).

Books: Feltrinelli International, a fine bookstore that sells fiction and guidebooks in English, is a few blocks north of the Duomo and across the street from the TI on Via Cavour (Mon–Sat 09:00–19:30, Via Cavour 20 red). Paperback Exchange also sells fiction and guidebooks (daily 09:00–19:30, shorter hours in Aug, at corner of Via Fiesolana and Via dei Pilastri, 6 blocks east of Duomo, tel. 055-247-8154).

Getting around Florence

I organize my sightseeing geographically and do it all on foot. A €0.75 ticket gives you one hour on the buses, €1.30 gives you three hours, and €3.10 gets you 24 hours (tickets not sold on bus—except after 21:00; buy in *tabacchi* shops or newsstands, validate on bus).

The minimum cost for a taxi ride is €4, or, after 22:00, €5 (rides in the center of town should be charged as tariff #1). A taxi ride from the train station to Ponte Vecchio costs about €8. Taxi fares and supplements are clearly explained in each cab.

Tours of Florence

Walking Tours of Florence—This company offers a variety of tours (up to 4 a day Mon–Sat) featuring downtown Florence,

Uffizi highlights, or the countryside, presented by informative, entertaining, native English-speaking guides (€24 for 3-hr Original Florence walk, office open Mon–Sat 08:30–18:00, closed for lunch off-season, Piazza Santo Stefano 2 black, a short block north of Ponte Vecchio; go east on tiny Vicolo San Stefano, in Piazza Santo Stefano at #2; booking necessary for Uffizi tour, private tours also available, tel. 055-264-5033 or cellular 0329-613-2730, www .florencewalkingtour.com). The "Original Florence" walk hits the main sights but gets off-beat to weave a picture of Florentine life in medieval and Renaissance times. You can expect lots of talking, which is great if you like history. Tours start at their office (year-round, regardless of weather, maximum of 22, extra guides available if more show up). For a private tour, consider Rosanne Magers (tel. 055-264-5033, e-mail: walkingtours@artviva.com).

Scholarly Tours—Simone Gaddini runs Firenze Antica with a group of art historians. They offer top-notch private and "semi-private" tours of Florence and Tuscany, good for thoughtful and well-heeled travelers (semi-private tours start at $45 per person, max 8 per group; private tours start at $180 for half-day tour; reserve in advance, tel. 055-225-535, www.firenzeantica.org, e-mail: info@firenzeantica.org).

A Florentine Renaissance Walk

Even during the Dark Ages people knew they were in a "middle time." It was especially obvious to the people of Italy—sitting on the rubble of Rome—that there was a brighter age before them. The long-awaited rebirth, or Renaissance, began in Florence for good reason. Wealthy because of its cloth industry, trade, and banking; powered by a fierce city-state pride (locals would pee into the Arno with gusto, knowing rival city-state Pisa was downstream); and fertile with more than its share of artistic genius (imagine guys like Michelangelo and Leonardo attending the same high school)—Florence was a natural home for this cultural explosion.

Take a walk through the core of Renaissance Florence by starting at the Accademia (home of Michelangelo's *David*) and cutting through the heart of the city to Ponte Vecchio on the Arno River. (A 10-page, self-guided tour of this walk is outlined in my museum guidebook, *Rick Steves' Mona Winks;* otherwise, you'll find brief descriptions below.)

At the Accademia you'll look into the eyes of Renaissance man—humanism at its confident peak. Then walk to the cathedral (Duomo) to see the dome that kicked off the architectural Renaissance. Step inside the baptistery to view a ceiling covered with preachy, flat, 2-D, medieval mosaic art. Then, to learn what happened when art met math, check out the realistic 3-D reliefs on the doors. The painter, Giotto, designed the bell tower—

Florence

an early example of a Renaissance genius excelling in many areas. Continue toward the river on Florence's great pedestrian mall, Via de' Calzaiuoli (or "Via Calz")—part of the original grid plan given the city by the ancient Romans. Down a few blocks, compare medieval and Renaissance statues on the exterior of the Orsanmichele Church. Via Calz connects the cathedral with the central square (Piazza della Signoria), the city palace (Palazzo Vecchio), and the Uffizi Gallery, which contains the greatest collection of Italian Renaissance paintings in captivity. Finally, walk through the Uffizi courtyard—a statuary think tank of Renaissance greats—to the Arno River and Ponte Vecchio.

Sights—On Florence's Renaissance Walk

▲▲▲**Accademia (Galleria dell' Accademia)**—This museum houses Michelangelo's *David* and powerful (unfinished) *Prisoners*. Eavesdrop as tour guides explain these masterpieces. More than any other work of art, when you look into the eyes of *David*, you're looking into the eyes of Renaissance man. This was a radical break with the past. Hello humanism. Man was now a confident individual, no longer a plaything of the supernatural. And life was now more than just a preparation for what happened after you died.

The Renaissance was the merging of art, science, and humanism. In a humanist vein, *David* is looking at the crude giant of medieval darkness and thinking, "I can take this guy." (David was an apt mascot for a town surrounded by big bully city-states.) Back on a religious track, notice *David*'s large and overdeveloped right hand. This is symbolic of the hand of God that powered David to slay the giant…and enabled Florence to rise above its crude neighboring city-states.

Beyond the magic marble are two floors of interesting pre-Renaissance and Renaissance paintings, including a couple of lighter-than-air Botticellis.

Cost, Hours, Location: €7.75. Open Tue–Sun, 08:15–18:50, maybe summer Sat until 22:00, closed Mon (Via Ricasoli 60, tel. 055-238-8609).

Nearby: Piazza Santissima Annunziata, behind the Accademia, features lovely Renaissance harmony. Brunelleschi's Hospital of the Innocents (Spedale degli Innocenti, not worth going inside), with terra-cotta medallions by Luca della Robbia, was built in the 1420s and is considered the first Renaissance building. The 15th-century Santissima Annunziata church facing the same square is worth a peek.

▲▲**Duomo**—Florence's Gothic Santa Maria del Fiori cathedral has the third-longest nave in Christendom (free, Mon–Wed and Fri–Sat 10:00–17:00, Thu 10:00–15:30, Sun 13:30–17:00, first Sat of month 10:00–15:30). The church's noisy neo-Gothic facade from the 1870s is covered with pink, green, and white Tuscan marble. Since nearly all of its great art is stored in the Museo dell' Opera del Duomo (behind the church), the best thing about the interior is the shade. The inside of the dome is decorated by one of the largest paintings of the Renaissance, a huge (and newly restored) *Last Judgment* by Vasari and Zuccari.

Think of the confidence of the age: the Duomo was built with a hole awaiting a dome in its roof. This was before the technology to span it with a dome was available. No matter. They knew that someone soon could handle the challenge…and the local architect Brunelleschi did. The cathedral's claim to artistic fame is Brunelleschi's magnificent dome—the first Renaissance dome and the model for domes to follow.

▲**Climbing the Cathedral's Dome**—For a grand view into the cathedral from the base of the dome, a peek at some of the tools used in the dome's construction, a chance to see Brunelleschi's "dome-within-a-dome" construction, a glorious Florence view from the top, and the equivalent of 463 plunges on a Stairmaster, climb the dome (€5.20, Mon–Fri 08:30–19:00, Sat 08:30–17:40, closed Sun, first Sat of month 08:30–15:20, enter from outside church on south or river side, expect a long, dreadfully slow-moving line if you don't arrive by 08:30, tel. 055-230-2885). When planning St. Peter's in Rome, Michelangelo rhymed (not in English), "I can build its sister—bigger, but not more beautiful, than the dome of Florence."

▲**Giotto's Tower**—Climbing Giotto's 82-meter-tall tower (or Campanile) beats climbing the neighboring Duomo's dome because it's 50 fewer steps, faster, not so crowded, and offers the same view plus the dome (€5.20, daily 08:30–19:30).

▲▲**Museo dell' Opera del Duomo**—The underrated cathedral museum, behind the church at #9, is great if you like sculpture. It has masterpieces by Donatello (a gruesome wood carving of Mary Magdalene clothed in her matted hair, and the *cantoria*, a delightful choir loft bursting with happy children) and by Luca della Robbia (another choir loft, lined with the dreamy faces of musicians praising the Lord). Look for a late Michelangelo *Pietà* (Nicodemus, on top, is a self-portrait), Brunelleschi's models for his dome, and the original restored panels of Ghiberti's doors to the baptistery. This is one of the few museums in Florence open on Monday (€5.20, Mon–Sat 09:00–19:30, Sun 09:00–13:40, tel. 055-230-2885). If you find all this church art intriguing, look through the open doorway of the Duomo art studio, which has been making and restoring church art since the days of Brunelleschi (a block toward the river from the Duomo at 23a Via dello Studio).

▲**Baptistery**—Michelangelo said its bronze doors were fit to be the gates of Paradise. Check out the gleaming copies of Ghiberti's bronze doors facing the Duomo. Making a breakthrough in perspective, Ghiberti used mathematical laws to create the illusion of receding distance on a basically flat surface. The earlier, famous competition doors are around to the right (north); Ghiberti, who beat Brunelleschi, got the job of designing these doors.

A local document from 860 A.D. already refers to Florence's oldest building as "ancient." Inside, sit and savor the medieval mosaic ceiling where it's Judgment Day and Jesus is giving the ultimate thumbs up and thumbs down. Compare that to the "new, improved" art of the Renaissance (€2.60 interior open Mon–Sat 12:00–19:00, Sun 08:30–14:00, bronze doors are on the outside so always "open"; original panels are in the Museo dell' Opera del Duomo).

▲**Orsanmichele**—This 9th-century loggia (a covered courtyard) was a market used for selling grain (stored upstairs). Later, it was closed in to make a church. Notice the grain spouts on the pillars inside. The glorious tabernacle by Orcagna takes you back (1359).

Study the sculpture in the niches outside. You can see man stepping out of the literal and figurative shadow of the church in the great Renaissance sculptor Donatello's *St. George.* Look into George's face; he's a sensitive new-age guy (SNAG). The predella at the base of this statue shows St. George slaying the dragon to protect the wispy melodramatic maiden. This was ground-breaking Renaissance emotion and perspective (free, daily 09:00–12:00, 16:00–18:00, closed first and last Mon of month, on Via Calz-aiuoli; can be closed due to staffing problems, try going through the back door). The iron bars spanning the vaults were the Italian Gothic answer to the French Gothic external buttresses. Across the street is Museo Orsanmichele...

▲**Museo Orsanmichele**—For some peaceful time alone with the original statues that filled the niches of Orsanmichele, climb to the top of the church (entry behind church, across street). Be there at 09:00, 10:00, and 11:00 daily when the door is open and art lovers in the know climb four flights of stairs to this little known museum, containing statues by Ghiberti, Donatello, and others (info in Italian, but picture guides on wall help you match art with artists). Upstairs is a tower room with city views (free). A block away, you'll find...

▲**Mercato Nuovo**—This market loggia is how Orsanmichele looked before it became a church. Originally a silk and straw market, Mercato Nuovo still functions as a rustic market today (at intersection of Via Calimala and Via Porta Rossa). Prices are soft. Notice the circled X in the center, marking the spot where those who fell into bankruptcy hit after being hoisted up to the top and dropped as punishment. You'll also find Porcellino (a wild boar nicknamed "little pig"), which people rub and give coins to in order to insure their return to Florence. Nearby is a wagon selling tripe (cow innards) sandwiches.

▲**Piazza della Repubblica**—This large square sits on the site of Florence's original Roman Forum. The lone column is the only remaining bit of Roman Florence except for the grid street plan. Look at the map to see the ghost of Rome: a rectangular fort lined up with the compass oblivious to the river with this square marking the intersection of the two main roads (Via Corso and Via Roma). The piazza you see today is really a nation-alistic statement from just after the unification of Italy. Florence, the capital of the country (1865-1870) until Rome was liberated, lacked a square worthy of this grand new country. So the neigh-borhood here was razed to open up a grand modern forum surrounded by grand circa 1890 buildings.

Medieval writers described Florence as so densely built up that when it rained, pedestrians didn't get wet. Torches were used to light the lanes in midday. The city was prickly with noble family towers (like San Gimignano) and had Romeo and Juliet-type family feuds. But with the rise of the Medici (c. 1300), no noble family was allowed to have an architectural ego trip taller then their tower and nearly all were taken down.

▲**Palazzo Vecchio**—This fortified palace, once the home of the Medici family, is a Florentine landmark. But if you're visiting only one palace interior in town, the Pitti Palace is better. The Palazzo Vecchio interior is wallpapered with mediocre magnificence, worthwhile only if you're a real Florentine art and history fan. The museum's most famous statues are Michelangelo's *Genius of Victory*, Donatello's static *Judith and Holerfernes*, and Verrocchio's *Winged Cherub* (a copy tops the fountain in the free courtyard at entrance, original inside).

Scattered throughout the museum are a dozen computer terminals with information in English on the Medici family, Palazzo Vecchio, and the building's architecture and art, including an animation of the relocation of Michelangelo's *David* (€5.70, Sun 09:00–14:00, Mon–Wed and Fri–Sat 09:00–19:00, Thu 09:00–14:00, in summer open until 23:00 on Mon and Fri, WC in second courtyard, tel. 055-276-8465).

Even if you don't go to the museum, do step into the free courtyard (behind the fake *David*) just to feel the essence of the Medici. Until 1873 Michelangelo's *David* stood at the entrance, where the copy is today. While the huge statues in the square are important only as the whipping boys of art critics and rest stops for pigeons, the nearby Loggia dei Lanzi has several important statues. Look for Cellini's bronze statue of Perseus (with the head of Medusa). The plaque on the pavement in front of the fountain marks the spot where the monk Savonarola was burned in MCCCCXCVIII (for more on the monk, see "Museum of San Marco" listing, below).

▲▲▲**Bargello (Museo Nazionale)**—This underrated sculpture museum is behind Palazzo Vecchio in a former prison that looks like a mini-Palazzo Vecchio. It has Donatello's painfully beautiful *David* (the very influential first male nude to be sculpted in a thousand years), works by Michelangelo, and rooms of Medici treasures cruelly explained in Italian only—mention that English descriptions would be wonderful (€4, daily 08:15–13:50 but closed first, third, and fifth Sun and second and fourth Mon of each month, Via del Proconsolo 4, tel. 055-238-8606).

▲▲▲**Uffizi Gallery**—The greatest collection of Italian paintings anywhere is a must, with plenty of works by Giotto, Leonardo, Raphael, Caravaggio, Rubens, Titian, and Michelangelo and a roomful of Botticellis, including his *Birth of Venus*. Because only

780 visitors are allowed inside the building at any one time, during the day there's generally a very long wait. The good news: no Louvre-style mob scenes. The museum is nowhere near as big as it is great: Few tourists spend more than two hours inside. The paintings are displayed on one comfortable floor in chronological order from the 13th through 17th centuries.

Essential stops are (in this order): Gothic altarpieces (narrative, pre-Realism, no real concern for believable depth) including Giotto's altarpiece, which progressed beyond "totem-pole angels"; Uccello's *Battle of San Romano*, an early study in perspective (with a few obvious flubs); Fra Filippo Lippi's cuddly Madonnas; the Botticelli room, filled with masterpieces, including a pantheon of classical fleshiness and the small *La Calumnia*, showing the glasnost of Renaissance free-thinking being clubbed back into the darker age of Savonarola; two minor works by Leonardo; the octagonal classical sculpture room with an early painting of Bob Hope and a copy of Praxiteles' *Venus de Medici*—considered the epitome of beauty in Elizabethan Europe; a view through the window of Ponte Vecchio—dreamy at sunset; Michelangelo's only surviving easel painting, the round *Holy Family;* Raphael's noble *Madonna of the Goldfinch;* Titian's voluptuous *Venus of Urbino;* and Duomo views from the café terrace at the end (WC near café).

Cost, Hours, Reservations: €9.30, Tue–Sun 08:15 to 18:50, maybe summer Sat until 22:00, closed Mon (last entry 45 min before closing; take elevator or climb 4 long flights of stairs).

Avoid the two-hour peak season midday wait by making a telephone reservation. It's easy, slick, and costs only €1.60 (tel. 055-294-883) explained in "Helpful Hints," above). At the Uffizi, walk briskly past the 200-meter-long line—pondering the IQ of this gang—to the special entrance for those with reservations (labeled in English "Entrance for Reservations Only"), give your number, pay (cash only), and scoot right in. You can reserve in advance for other museums—including the Bargello, Accademia (*David*), Medici Chapel, and Pitti Palace, though the only other one I'd consider reserving would be the Accademia.

If you haven't called ahead, you may be able to book directly at the Uffizi. Ask the clerk (who stands at the entrance for people with reservations) if you can make a reservation in person. He may direct you to the ticket office where you can secure a reservation for later in the day or the next day (depends on luck and availability). Also, Walking Tours of Florence does a guided tour of the museum Tuesday through Saturday (€31 includes admission and reservation, departs from their office at 15:30, 2 hrs, 18 people; see "Tours of Florence," above).

Enjoy the Uffizi square, full of artists and souvenir stalls. The surrounding statues honor the earthshaking: artists, philosophers (Machiavelli), scientists (Galileo), writers (Dante), explorers

(Amerigo Vespucci), and the great patron of so much Renaissance thinking, Lorenzo (the Magnificent) de Medici.

▲**Ponte Vecchio**—Florence's most famous bridge is lined with shops that have traditionally sold gold and silver. A statue of Cellini, the master goldsmith of the Renaissance, stands in the center, ignored by the flood of tacky tourism. Notice the "prince's passageway" above. In less secure times, the city leaders had a fortified passageway connecting the Palace Vecchio and Uffizi with the mighty Pitti Palace, to which they could flee in times of attack. This passageway, called the Vasari Corridor, is open to the persistent by request only (€6.20, Tue–Sat at 09:30, closed Mon, tel. 055-265-4321).

More Sights—Central Florence

▲▲**Santa Croce Church**—This 14th-century Franciscan church, decorated by centuries of precious art, holds the tombs of great Florentines (free, Mon–Sat 09:30–17:30, Sun 15:00–17:30, in winter Mon–Sat 09:30–12:30, 15:00–17:30, Sun 15:00–17:30, modest dress code enforced, tel. 055-244-619). The loud 19th-century Victorian Gothic facade faces a huge square ringed with tempting touristy shops and littered with tired tourists. Escape into the church.

Working counterclockwise from the entrance you'll find the tomb of Michelangelo (with the allegorical figures of painting, architecture, and sculpture), a memorial to Dante (no body . . . he was banished by his hometown), the tomb of Machiavelli (the originator of hardball politics), a relief by Donatello of the Annunciation, and the tomb of the composer Rossini. To the right of the altar, step into the sacristy where you'll find a bit of St. Francis' cowl and old sheets of music with the medieval and mobile C clef (two little blocks on either side of the line determined to be middle C). In the bookshop, notice the photos high on the wall of the devastating flood of 1966. Beyond that is a touristy—but mildly interesting—"leather school." The chapels lining the front of the church are richly frescoed. The Bardi Chapel (far left of altar) is a masterpiece by Giotto featuring scenes from the life of St. Francis. On your way out you'll pass the tomb of Galileo (allowed in by the church long after his death). The neighboring Pazzi Chapel (by Brunelleschi) is considered one of the finest pieces of Florentine Renaissance architecture.

▲▲**Museum of San Marco**—One block north of the Accademia on Piazza San Marco, this museum houses the greatest collection anywhere of medieval frescoes and paintings by the early Renaissance master Fra Angelico. You'll see why he thought of painting as a form of prayer and couldn't paint a crucifix without shedding tears. Each of the monks' cells has a Fra Angelico fresco. Don't miss the cell of Savonarola, the charismatic monk who rode in from the Christian right, threw out the Medici, turned Florence into a theocracy, sponsored "bonfires of the vanities" (burning books, paintings, and so on), and was finally burned himself when Florence decided to change channels (€4, daily 08:15–13:50, Sat and Sun until 19:00, but closed the first, third, and fifth Sun and the second and fourth Mon of each month, tel. 055-238-8608). They can sell tickets (often with immediate reservation) to Uffizi and Accademia.

▲**Medici Chapel (Cappella dei Medici)**—This chapel, containing two Medici tombs, is drenched in lavish High Renaissance architecture and sculpture by Michelangelo (€5.70, daily 08:15–17:00 but closed the second and fourth Sun and the first, third, and fifth Mon of each month, tel. 055-238-8602). Behind San Lorenzo on Piazza Madonna is a lively market scene that I find just as interesting. Take a stroll through the huge double-decker central market one block north.

Science Museum (Museo di Storia della Scienza)—This is a fascinating collection of Renaissance and later clocks, telescopes, maps, and ingenious gadgets. One of the most talked-about bottles in Florence is the one here containing Galileo's finger. Loaner English guidebooklets are available. It's friendly, comfortably cool, never crowded, and just downstream from the Uffizi (€6.20, Mon and Wed–Fri 09:30–17:00, Tue and Sat 09:30–13:00, closed Sun, Piazza dei Giudici 1, tel. 055-239-8876).

▲**Michelangelo's Home, Casa Buonarroti**—Fans enjoy Michelangelo's house, which has some of his early, much-less-monumental statues and sketches (€6.20, Wed–Mon 09:30–14:00, closed Tue, English descriptions, Via Ghibellina 70).

Casa di Dante—Dante's house consists of five rooms in an old building with little of substance to show but lots of photos relating to the life and work of Dante. Although it's well described in English, it's interesting only to literary buffs (€2.60, Mon and Wed–Sat 10:00–18:00, Sun 10:00–14:00, closed Tue, across the street and around the corner from Bargello, at Via S. Margherita 1).

Church of Santa Maria Novella—This 13th-century Dominican church is rich in art. Along with crucifixes by Giotto and Brunelleschi, there's the early Renaissance mastery of perspective: *The Holy Trinity* by Masaccio; it's opposite the entrance (€2.60, Mon–Thu and Sat 09:30–17:00, Fri and Sun 13:00–17:00).

A palatial **perfumery** is around the corner 100 meters down Via della Scala at #16 (free but shopping encouraged, Mon–Sat 09:30–19:30, closed Sun). Thick with the lingering aroma of centuries of spritzes, it started as the herb garden of the Santa Maria Novella monks. Well-known even today for its top-quality products, it is extremely Florentine. Pick up the history sheet at the desk and wander deep into the shop. From the back room you can peek at the S. M. Novella cloister, with its dreamy frescoes, and imagine a time before Vespas and tourists.

Museum of Precious Stones (Museo dell' Opificio delle Pietre Dure)—This unusual gem of a museum features mosaics of inlaid marble and semiprecious stones. You'll see remnants of the Medici workshop from 1588, including 500 different semiprecious stones, the tools used to cut and inlay them, and room after room of the sumptuous finished product. The fine loaner booklet describes it all in English (€2, Mon–Sat 08:15–14:00, Thu until 19:00, closed Sun, Via degli Alfani 78, around corner from Accademia). This ticket booth can also sell tickets with reservations (perhaps today) to the Uffizi and Accademia.

Sights—Florence, South of the Arno River

▲▲**Pitti Palace**—From the Uffizi follow the elevated passageway (closed to non-Medicis) across the Ponte Vecchio bridge to the gargantuan Pitti Palace, which has five separate museums.

The **Palatine Gallery/Royal Apartments** features palatial room after chandeliered room, its walls sagging with paintings by the great masters. Its Raphael collection is the biggest anywhere (first floor, €7.25, Tue–Sun 08:15–18:50, perhaps summer Sat until 22:00, closed Mon).

The **Modern Art Gallery** features Romanticism, neoclassicism, and Impressionism by 19th- and 20th-century Tuscan painters (second floor, €4, daily 08:15–13:50 but closed second and fourth Sun and first, third, and fifth Mon).

The **Grand Ducal Treasures**, or Museo degli Argenti, is the Medici treasure chest entertaining fans of applied arts with jeweled crucifixes, exotic porcelain, gilded ostrich eggs, and so on (ground floor, €7.75, nearly the same hours as Modern Art Gallery).

Behind the palace, the huge landscaped **Boboli Gardens** offer a shady refuge from the city heat (€2, daily 09:00–18:30, until 19:30 June–Aug, until 16:30 in winter, but closed first and last Mon of month).

▲**Brancacci Chapel**—For the best look at the early Renaissance master Masaccio, see his restored frescoes here (€3, Mon and Wed–Sat 10:00–17:00, Sun 13:00–17:00, closed Tue, cross Ponte Vecchio and turn right a few blocks to Piazza del Carmine). Since only a few tourists are let in at a time, seeing the chapel often involves a wait. The neighborhoods around here are considered the last surviving bits of old Florence.

▲**Piazzale Michelangelo**—Across the river overlooking the city (look for the huge statue of *David*), this square is worth the 30-minute hike, drive, or bus ride (either #12 or #13 from the train station) for the view of Florence and the stunning dome of the Duomo. After dark it's packed with local schoolkids, feeding their dates slices of watermelon. Just beyond it is the stark and beautiful, crowd-free Romanesque San Miniato Church.

Oltrarno Walk—If you never leave the touristy center you don't really see Florence. There's more to the city than tourism. Ninety percent of its people live and work—mostly in small shops—where tourists rarely venture. This self-guided tour follows a perfectly straight line (you can't get lost). Cross the Ponte Vecchio and walk west on the road toward Pisa—it changes names, from Borgo San Jacopo and Via di Santo Spirito to Borgo Frediano—until you reach the city wall at Porta San Frediano. Along this route you can check out several of my favorite restaurants (described below). As you walk, consider these points:

After one block, at the fancy **Hotel Lungarno**, belly up to the Arno River viewpoint for a great look at Ponte Vecchio. Recall the story of Kesserling, the Nazi commander-in-chief of Italy who happened to be an art lover. As the Nazis retreated in 1944, he was commanded to blow up all the bridges. Rather than destroy the venerable Ponte Vecchio, he disabled it by blowing up the surrounding neighborhood. Turn around and cross the street to see the ivy-covered nub of a medieval tower—ruined August 6, 1944.

Along this walk you'll see plenty of artisans at work and inviting little **shops**. You're welcome to drop in but remember, it's rude not to say "*Buon giorno*" and "*Ciao*." "Can I take a look?" is "*Posso guardare?*" (pron. poh-soh gwahr-dah-ray).

The streets are busy with *motorini* (Vespas and other motor bikes). While these are allowed in the city, non-resident cars are not (unless they are electric). Notice that parked cars have a *residente* permit on their dash. You'll see a police officer (likely a woman) later on the walk, keeping traffic out.

Look for little architectural details. Tiny shrines protect the corners of many blocks. Once upon a time, the iron spikes on the walls impaled huge candles, which provided a little light. Electricity changed all that, but notice there are no electric wires visible. They're under the streets.

This street is lined with apartment flats punctuated by the occasional palazzo. The skyline and architecture is typical of the 13th to 16th centuries. Huge **palazzos** (recognized by their immense doors, lush courtyards, and grand stonework) were for big-shot merchants. Many have small wooden doors designed to look like stones (e.g., 3b on Borgo San Frediano). While originally for one family, these buildings are now subdivided, evidenced by the huge banks of doorbells at the door.

The **Church of Santa Maria del Carmine**, with its famous Brancacci Chapel and Masaccio frescoes, is a short detour off Borgo San Frediano (described above).

A couple of blocks before Porta San Frediano (and its tower), look left up Piazza dei Nerli. The bold yellow schoolhouse was built during Mussolini's rule—grandly proclaiming the resurrection of the Italian empire.

Porta San Frediano, from about 1300, is part of Florence's medieval wall, which stretches grandly from here to the river. The tower was originally twice as high, built when gravity ruled warfare. During the Renaissance, when gunpowder dominated warfare, the tower—now just an easy target—was topped. In medieval times, a kilometer-wide strip outside the wall was cleared to deny attackers any cover. Notice the original doors—immense and studded with fat iron nails to withstand battering rams. Got a horse? Lash it to a ring.

Tour over. You passed several fun eateries, and the colorful Trattoria Sabatino is just outside the wall (all described in "Eating," below). *Ciao.*

Experiences—Florence

▲▲**Gelato**—Gelato is an edible art form. Italy's best ice cream is in Florence—one souvenir that can't break and won't clutter your luggage. But beware of scams at touristy joints on busy streets that turn a simple request of a cone into a €10 "tourist special."

The **Gelateria Carrozze** is very good (daily 11:00–24:00, closes at 21:00 in winter, on riverfront 30 meters from Ponte Vecchio toward the Uffizi, Via del Pesce 3). **Gelateria dei Neri** is another local favorite worth finding (2 blocks east of Palazzo Vecchio at Via Dei Neri 20 red, daily in summer 12:00–23:00, closed Wed in winter).

Vivoli's is the most famous (Tue–Sun 08:00–01:00, closed Mon, the last 3 weeks in Aug, and winter; opposite the Church of Santa Croce, go down Via Torta a block, turn right on Via Stinche; before ordering, try a free sample of their *riso* flavor—rice). The **Cinema Astro**, across the street from Vivoli's, plays English/American movies in their original language (closed Mon).

If you want an excuse to check out the little village-like neighborhood across the river from Santa Croce, enjoy a gelato at the tiny **no-name gelateria** at Via San Miniato 5 red (just before Porta San Miniato).

Shopping

Florence is a great shopping town. Busy street scenes and markets abound, especially near San Lorenzo, near Santa Croce, on Ponte Vecchio, and at Mercato Nuovo (a covered market square 3 blocks north of Ponte Vecchio, listed above in "Sights"). Leather (often better quality for less than the U.S. price), gold, silver, art prints, and tacky plaster "mini-*Davids*" are most popular. Shops usually have promotional stalls in the market squares. Prices are soft in markets. Many spend entire days shopping.

For ritzy Italian fashions, browse along Via de Tornabuoni, Via della Vigna Nuova, and Via Strozzi. Typical chain department stores are Coin (Mon–Sat 09:30–20:00, Sun 11:00–20:00, on Via Calzaiuoli, near Orsanmichele church) and Standa

(Mon–Sat 09:00–19:55, closed Sun, at intersection of Via Panzani and Via del Giglio, near train station).

For shopping ideas, ads, and a list of markets, see the *Florence Concierge Information* magazine described under "Tourist Information," above (free from TI and many hotels).

Side Trips to Fiesole and Siena

For a candid peek at **Fiesole**—a Florentine suburb—ride bus #7 (3/hr, departs from Piazza Adua at the northeast side of the station and also from Piazza San Marco) for about 25 minutes through neighborhood gardens, vineyards, orchards, and large villas to the last stop—Fiesole. This town is a popular excursion from Florence because of its small eateries and its good views of Florence. Catch the sunset from the terrace just below the La Reggia restaurant; from the Fiesole bus stop, face the bell tower and take the very steep Via San Francisco on your left. You'll find the view terrace near the top of the hill.

Connoisseurs of peace and small towns who aren't into art or shopping (and who won't be seeing Siena otherwise) should consider riding the bus to **Siena** (75 min by bus). This can be a daytrip or an evening trip. Siena is magic after dark. Confirm when the last bus returns. For more information, see the Siena chapter.

Sleeping in Florence
(€1.10 = about $1, country code: 39)

Sleep Code: **S** = Single, **D** = Double/Twin, **T** = Triple, **Q** = Quad, **b** = bathroom, **s** = shower only, **CC** = Credit Cards accepted, **no CC** = Credit Cards not accepted, **SE** = Speaks English, **NSE** = No English. Unless otherwise noted, breakfast is included (but usually optional). English is generally spoken.

The accommodations scene varies wildly with the season. Spring and fall are very tight and expensive, while mid-July through August is wide open and discounted. November through February is also generally empty. With good information and a phone call ahead, you can find a stark, clean, and comfortable double with breakfast for about €65, with a private shower for €90 (less at the smaller places, such as the *soggiornos*). You get elegance for €125. Many places listed are old and rickety; I can't imagine Florence any other way. Rooms with air-conditioning cost around €100—worth the extra money in the summer. Virtually all of the places are central, within minutes of the great sights. Few hotels escape Vespa noise at night.

Call direct to the hotel. Do not use the TI, which costs your host and jacks up the price. In slow times, budget travelers call around and find soft prices. Ask if you'll get a discount for paying in cash, for staying for three or more nights (or both), or for using this book. And ask if you can skip breakfast (these overpriced breakfasts are legally optional, though some hotels pretend otherwise).

Call ahead. I repeat, call ahead. Places will hold a room until early afternoon. If they say they're full, mention you're using this book.

Laundromats: The Wash & Dry Lavarapido chain offers long hours and efficient self-service Laundromats at several locations (daily 08:00–22:00, tel. 055-580-480). Close to recommended hotels: Via dei Servi 105 red (near *David*), Via del Sole 29 red and Via della Scala 52 red (between station and river), and Via dei Serragli 87 red (across the river in Oltrarno neighborhood). East of the station another handy modern launderette is just off Via Cavour at Via Guelfa 22 red (daily 08:00–22:00, 12 pounds washed and dried for €6.20).

Sleeping between the Station and Duomo
(zip code: 50123)
Hotel Accademia is an elegant two-star hotel with marble stairs, parquet floors, attractive public areas, 22 pleasant rooms, and a floor plan that defies logic (Sb-€83, Db-€124, Tb-€155, these discounted prices are promised through 2002 only with this book, CC, air con, TV, tiny courtyard, Via Faenza 7, tel. 055-293-451, fax 055-219-771, www.accademiahotel.net, e-mail: info@accademiahotel.net).

Hotel Bellettini rents 33 bright, cool, well-cared-for rooms with inviting lounges and a touch of class. Its five rooms in an annex two blocks away are of higher quality with all the comforts, but you need to come to the main hotel for breakfast (Sb-€83, Db-€108, Tb-€145, Qb-€181, CC, 5 percent discount with this book only if you claim it upon arrival, air con, free Internet access, Via de' Conti 7, tel. 055-213-561, fax 055-283-551, www.firenze.net/hotelbellettini, e-mail: hotel.bellettini@dada.it, frisky Gina SE).

Residenza Dei Pucci, a block north of the Duomo, has 12 tastefully decorated rooms—in soothing earth tones—with aristocratic furniture and tweed carpeting. It's fresh and bright (Sb-€130, Db-€145, Tb-€165, suite with grand Duomo view-€207 for 2 people, €233 for 4, claim a 10 percent discount through 2002 with this book, breakfast served in room, CC, Via dei Pucci 9, tel. 055-281-886, fax 055-264-314, http ://residenzapucci.interfree.it/, SE).

Palazzo Castiglioni offers 16 grand rooms with all the conveniences in a peaceful 19th-century palazzo package. Most rooms are spacious, several have frescoes, and all make a fine splurge (Db-€170, Db suite-€232, air-con, elevator, Via del Giglio 8, tel. 055-214-886, fax 055-274-0521, e-mail: torre .guelfa@flashnet.it, Laura SE).

Hotels in Florence

200 YARDS
200 METERS

❶ HOTEL ACCADEMIA
❷ HOTEL MORANDI ALLA CROCETTA
❸ CASA RABATTI
❹ SOGGIORNO PEZZATI
❺ HOTEL ENZA
❻ SOGGIORNO MAGLIANI
❼ HOTEL LOGGIATO DEI SERVITI
❽ DUE FONTANE HOTEL
❾ OBLATE SISTERS OF THE ASSUMPTION
❿ RESIDENZA DEI PUCCI
⓫ PALAZZO CASTIGLIONI & HOTEL ALDOBRANDINI
⓬ HOTEL BELLETTINI
⓭ HOTEL BASILEA
⓮ PENSIONE CENTRALE
⓯ HOTEL SOLE
⓰ SOGGIORNO BATTISTERO
⓱ HOTEL PENDINI
⓲ PENSIONE MAXIM
⓳ ALBERGO FIRENZE
⓴ HOTEL ELITE
㉑ TORRE GUELFA, HOTEL APOSTOLI & ALESSANDRA HOTELS
㉒ PENSIONE BRETAGNA
㉓ FLORENCE WALKING TOURS

Pensione Centrale, a happy and traditional-feeling place with 18 spacious rooms, is indeed central. Run by aristocratic Marie Therese Blot, spunky Margherita, and Franco, you'll feel right at home (D-€93, Db-€109, CC, quiet, some air-con rooms, often filled with American students, elevator, Via de' Conti 3, tel. 055-215-761, fax 055-215-216, e-mail: info@pensionecentrale.it). They sometimes send people to a nearby, noisier pension; confirm that your reservation is for this place.

Hotel Aldobrandini, a good budget choice, has 15 decent, clean, affordable rooms, with the San Lorenzo market at its doorstep and the entrance to the Medici Chapel a few steps away (Ss-€42, Sb-€52, D-€67, Db-€83, CC, lots of night noise, fans, Piazza Madonna Degli Aldobrandini 8, tel. 055-211-866, fax 055-267-6281, Ignazio and Anna SE).

Sleeping near the Central Market
(zip code: 50129)

Hotel Basilea offers predictable three-star, air-conditioned comfort in its 38 modern rooms (Db-€109–150 depending on season, CC, elevator, terrace, free e-mail service, Via Guelfa 41, at intersection with Nazionale—a busy street, ask for rooms in the back, tel. 055-214-587, fax 055-268-350, www.florenceitaly .net, e-mail: basilea@dada.it).

Casa Rabatti is the ultimate if you always wanted to be a part of a Florentine family. Its four simple, clean rooms are run with motherly warmth by Marcella and her husband Celestino, who speak minimal English (D-€47, Db-€54, €20 per bed in shared quad or quint, prices good with this book, no breakfast, fans, no sign other than on doorbell, 5 blocks from station, Via San Zanobi 48 black, tel. 055-212-393, e-mail: casarabatti@inwind.it).

Soggiorno Pezzati Daniela is another little place with six homey rooms (Sb-€44, Db-€60, Tb-€83, cheaper off-season, no breakfast, all rooms have a fridge, air con extra; marked only by small sign near door, Via San Zanobi 22, tel. 055-291-660, fax 055-287-145, e-mail: 055291660@iol.it, Daniela SE). If you get an Italian recording when you call, hang on—your call is being transferred to a cell phone.

Hotel Enza rents 16 quirky rooms for a decent price (S-€42, Sb-€52, D-€57, Ds-€65, Db-€75, T-€78, Tb-€93, family loft, CC, Via San Zanobi 45 black, tel. 055-490-990, fax 055-473-672, www.hotelenza.it, e-mail: info@hotelenza.it, Katia and Tatyana SE).

Central and humble, with seven rooms, **Soggiorno Magliani** feels and smells like a great-grandmother's place (S-€33, D-€43, cash only but secure reservation with CC, double-paned windows, near Via Guelfa at Via Reparata 1, tel. 055-287-378, e-mail: hotel-magliani@libero.it, run by a friendly family duo, Vincenza and English-speaking daughter Cristina).

Sleeping East of the Duomo

The first two listings are near the Accademia, on Piazza Annunziata (zip code: 50122).

Hotel Loggiato dei Serviti, at the most prestigious address in Florence on the most Renaissance square in town, gives you Renaissance romance with hair dryers. Stone stairways lead you under open-beam ceilings through this 16th-century monastery's elegant public rooms. The 29 cells, with air-conditioning, TVs, mini-bars, and telephones, wouldn't be recognized by their original inhabitants. The hotel staff is both professional and friendly (Sb-€140, Db-€202, family suites from €258, book a month ahead during peak season, discounts in Aug and winter, CC, elevator, Piazza S.S. Annunziata 3, tel. 055-289-592, fax 055-289-595, www.loggiatodeiservitihotel.it, Simonetta, Francesca, and Andrea SE).

Le Due Fontane Hotel faces the same great square but fills its old building with a smoky, 1970s, business-class ambience. Its 57 air-conditioned rooms are big and comfortable (Sb-€103, Db-€140, Tb-€196, these discounted prices are promised through 2002 but only if you claim them upon reserving, CC, elevator, Piazza S.S. Annunziata 14, tel. 055-210-185, fax 055-294-461, e-mail: leduefontane@dada.it, SE).

At **Hotel Morandi alla Crocetta**, a former convent, you're enveloped in a 16th-century cocoon. Located on a quiet street, with period furnishings, parquet floors, and wood-beamed ceilings, it draws you in (Sb-€93, Db-€150, CC, Via Laura 50, a block off Piazza S.S. Annunziata, tel. 055-234-4747, fax 055-248-0954, www.hotelmorandi.it, e-mail: welcome@hotelmorandi.it).

The **Oblate Sisters of the Assumption** run a 20-room hotel in a Renaissance building with a dreamy garden and a quiet, institutional feel (S-€34, D-€62, Db-€67, elevator, Borgo Pinti 15, 50121 Firenze, tel. 055-248-0582, fax 055-234-6291, NSE).

Sleeping on or near Piazza Repubblica
(zip code: 50123)

These are the most central of my accommodations recommendations, though given Florence's walkable core, nearly every hotel can be considered central.

Hotel Pendini, a very well-run three-star hotel with 42 old-time rooms (8 with views of the square), is popular and central, overlooking Piazza Repubblica (Sb-€83–109, Db-€109–150 depending on season, CC, elevator, fine lounge and breakfast room, air con, Via Strozzi 2, reserve ASAP, tel. 055-211-170, fax 055-281-807, www.florenceitaly.net, e-mail: pendini@dada.it).

Pensione Maxim, right on Via Calz, is a big, institutional-feeling place as close to the sights as possible. Its halls are narrow, but the 29 rooms are comfortable and well-maintained (Sb-€83, Db-€93, Tb-€124, Qb-€155, add €5 per person per day for air con June–Sept, CC but pay first night in cash, Internet access, elevator, no curfew, Via dei Calzaiuoli 11, tel. 055-217-474, fax 055-283-729, www.firenzealbergo.it/home/hotelmaxim, e-mail: hotmaxim@tin.it, Paolo and Nicola Maioli).

Soggiorno Battistero, next door to the Baptistery, has seven simple, airy rooms, most with urban noise but also great views, overlooking the Baptistery and square. You're in the heart of Florence (S-€52, Db-€93, Tb-€124, breakfast served in room, Internet access, CC, Piazza San Giovanni 1, third floor, tel. 055-295-143, fax 055-268-189, www.soggiornobattistero.it, e-mail: battistero@dada.it, lovingly run by Italian Luca and American wife Kelly).

Albergo Firenze, a big efficient place, offers good, basic, and spacious rooms in a wonderfully central, reasonably quiet locale two blocks behind the Duomo (Sb-€62, Db-€83, cash only, must prepay first night with a bank draft or traveler's check, elevator, off Via del Corso at Piazza Donati 4, tel. 055-214-203, fax 055-212-370, SE).

Sleeping South of the Train Station near Piazza Santa Maria Novella (zip code: 50123)

From the station (with your back to the tracks), cross the wide square to reach the church and continue to the Piazza Santa Maria Novella in front of the church (or you can take the underground Galleria S.M. Novella tunnel from the station—with your back to the tracks, it's outside on the left—but beware of thieves in the tunnel, where the tunnel surfaces, and at night). Piazza Santa Maria Novella is a pleasant square by day that becomes a little sleazy after dark.

Hotel Pensione Elite, run warmly by Maurizio and Nadia, is a fine basic value, with eight comfortable rooms and a charm rare in this price range (Ss-€52, Sb-€72, Ds-€67, Db-€83, breakfast-€5, fans, at south end of square with back to church, go right to Via della Scala 12, second floor, tel. & fax 055-215-395, SE).

Hotel Sole, a clean, cozy, family-run place with eight bright, modern rooms, is just off Santa Maria Novella toward the river (Sb-€47, Db-€75, Tb-€103, no breakfast; air con, elevator, Via del Sole 8, third floor, tel. & fax 055-239-6094, friendly Anna NSE).

Sleeping near Arno River and Ponte Vecchio (zip code: 50123)

Pensione Bretagna is an Old World-ramshackle place run by helpful Antonio and Maura. Imagine eating breakfast under

a painted, chandeliered ceiling overlooking the Arno River
(S-€47, Sb-€57, small Db-€93, big Db-€96, Tb-€120,
Qb-€133, family deals, prices special with this book through
2002, CC, air con, just past Ponte San Trinita, Lungarno Corsini
6, tel. 055-289-618, fax 055-289-619, www.bretagna.it, e-mail:
hotel@bretagna.it). They also run Soggiorno Althea, a cheaper
place with nicer rooms, near Piazza San Spirito in the Oltrarno
neighborhood (6 rooms, Db-€67, no breakfast, no reception
desk, call Bretagna to book).

Hotel Torre Guelfa is topped with a fun medieval tower
with a panoramic rooftop terrace and has a huge living room. Its
16 rooms vary wildly in size (small Db-€129, standard Db-€170,
Db suite-€232). Number 15, with a private terrace—€200—
is worth reserving several months in advance (elevator, air con, a
couple blocks northwest of Ponte Vecchio, Borgo S.S. Apostoli 8, tel.
055-239-6338, fax 055-239-8577, www.hoteltorreguelfa.com, e-mail:
torre.guelfa@flashnet.it, Giancarlo, Carlo, and Sandro all SE).

Residenza Apostoli, in the same building, is bright, spacious,
and modern, with parquet floors and 12 air-conditioned rooms
(Db-€134, Tb-€155, breakfast in room, CC, 10 percent discount with this book in 2002, elevator, Borgo Santi Apostoli 8,
tel. 055-284-837, fax 055-268-790, e-mail: residenza.apostoli
@infinito.it, run by Mirella and Cinzia).

Hotel Pensione Alessandra is an old 16th-century, peaceful
place with 25 big rooms (S-€72, Sb-€109, D-€109, Db-€140,
T-€140, Tb-€181, Q-€155, Qb-€202, CC but 5 percent discount with cash, air con, Internet access, Borgo S.S. Apostoli 17,
tel. 055-283-438, fax 055-210-619, www.hotelalessandra.com).

Sleeping in Oltrarno, South of the River
(zip code: 50125)
Across the river in the Oltrarno area, between the Pitti Palace
and Ponte Vecchio, you'll still find small traditional crafts shops,
neighborly piazzas, and family eateries. The following places are
a few minutes' walk from Ponte Vecchio.

Hotel La Scaletta, an elegant, dark, cool place with 13
rooms, a labyrinthine floor plan, lots of Old World lounges, and
a romantic and panoramic roof terrace, is run by Barbara, her
son Manfredo, and daughters Bianca and Diana (S-€52, Sb-€93,
D-€98, Db-€113–124, Tb-€129–145, Qb-€145–155, higher
price is for quieter rooms in back, €5–10 discount if you pay
cash, CC, air con in 8 rooms and fans in others, elevator, bar
with fine wine at good prices, Via Guicciardini 13b, 150 meters
south of Ponte Vecchio, tel. 055-283-028, fax 055-289-562,
www.lascaletta.com, e-mail: info@lascaletta.it). Secure your
reservation with a personal check or traveler's check. Manfredo
loves to cook. If he's cooking dinner, eat here. He serves a

Florence's Oltrarno Neighborhood

1 HOTEL LA SCALETTA	**9** RISTORANTE BIBO
2 TO HOTEL SILLA	**10** BORGO ANTICO REST., OSTERIA
3 PENSIONE SORELLE BANDINI	SANTO SPIRITO, & RICCHI CAFE
4 HOTEL LUNGARNO	**11** TRATTORIA CASALINGA
5 SOGGIORNO PEZZATI ALESSANDRA	**12** CAMMILLO TRATTORIA
6 ISTITUTO GOULD	**13** OSTERIA DEL CINGHIALE BIANCO
7 OSTELLO SANTA MONACA	**14** TRATTORIA ANGIOLINO
8 TRATTORIA BORDINO	**15** TO TRATTORIA SABATINO

€10 "Taste of Tuscany" deal (plate of quality Tuscan meats and cheeses with bread and 2 glasses of robust Chianti)—ideal for a light lunch on the terrace.

Hotel Silla, a classic three-star hotel with 36 cheery, spacious, pastel, and modern rooms, is a fine value. It faces the river and overlooks a park opposite the Santa Croce Church (Db-€160, Tb-€196, mention this book for a discount, CC, elevator, air con, Via dei Renai 5, 50125 Florence, tel. 055-234-2888, fax 055-234-1437, www.hotelsilla.it, e-mail: hotelsilla@tin.it, Laura SE).

Pensione Sorelle Bandini is a ramshackle, 500-year-old palace on a perfectly Florentine square, with cavernous rooms, museum-warehouse interiors, a musty youthfulness, cats, a balcony lounge-loggia with a view, and an ambience that, for romantic bohemians, can be a highlight of Florence. Mimmo or Sr. Romeo will hold a room until 16:00 with a phone call (D-€96, Db-€116, T-€133, Tb-€159, includes breakfast—which during low times is optional, saving €9 per person—elevator, Piazza Santo Spirito 9, tel. 055-215-308, fax 055-282-761).

Hotel Lungarno is the place to stay if money is no object. This deluxe, four-star hotel with 70 rooms strains anything stressful or rough out of Italy and gives you only service with a salute, physical elegance everywhere you look, and fine views over the Arno and Ponte Vecchio (Sb-€222, Db-€346, Db facing the river-€424, fancier suites, great riverside public spaces, 100 meters from Ponte Vecchio at Borgo San Jacopo 14, tel. 055-27261, fax 055-268-437, www.lungarnohotels.com, e-mail: bookings@lungarnohotels.com).

Soggiorno Pezzati Alessandra is a warm and friendly place renting five great rooms in the Oltrarno neighborhood (Sb-€44, Db-€60, Tb-€83, Qb-€104, cheaper off-season, no breakfast, all rooms have a fridge, air con extra, Via Borgo San Frediano 6, tel. 055-290-424, fax 055-218-464, e-mail: alex170169@libero.it, Alessandra). If you get an Italian recording when you call, hang on—your call is being transferred to a cellular phone.

Istituto Gould is a Protestant Church-run place with 33 clean but drab rooms with twin beds and modern facilities (S-€30, Sb-€35, D-€41, Db-€48, Tb-€62, €20 per person in quads, no breakfast, quieter rooms in back, Via dei Serragli 49, tel. 055-212-576, fax 055-280-274, e-mail: gould.reception@dada.it). You must arrive when the office is open (Mon–Fri 09:00–13:00, 15:00–19:00, Sat 09:00–13:00, no check-in Sun).

Ostello Santa Monaca, a cheap hostel, is a few blocks south of Ponte Alla Carraia, one of the bridges over the Arno (€15.50 beds, 4- to 20-bed rooms, breakfast extra, 01:00 curfew, Via Santa Monaca 6, tel. 055-268-338, fax 055-280-185).

Sleeping Away from the Center

Hotel Ungherese is good for drivers. It's northeast of the city center (near Stadio, en route to Fiesole), with easy, free street parking and quick bus access (#11 and #17) into central Florence (Sb-€60, Db-€114, extra bed-€30, these discounted prices available with this book, pay cash for additional 7 percent discount, rooms are 20 percent less off-season, includes breakfast, CC, most rooms air-con, Via G. B. Amici 8, tel. & fax 055-573-474, www.hotelungherese.it, e-mail: hotel.ungherese@dada.it). It has great singles and a backyard garden terrace (ask for a room on the garden). They can recommend good eateries nearby.

Villa Camerata, classy for an IYHF hostel, is on the outskirts of Florence (€14.50 per bed with breakfast, 4- to 12-bed rooms, must have IYHF card, ride bus #17 to Salviatino stop, Via Righi 2, tel. 055-601-451).

Eating in Florence

To save money and time for sights, you can keep lunches fast and simple, eating in one of the countless self-service places and pizzerias or just picnicking (try juice, yogurt, cheese, and a roll for €5). For good sit-down meals, consider the following. Remember, restaurants like to serve what's fresh. If you're into flavor, go for the seasonal best bets—featured in the *Piatti del Giorno* (special of the day) sections of the menus.

Eating in Oltrarno, South of the River

For a change of scene, eat across the river in Oltrarno. Here are a few good places just over Ponte Vecchio.

At Piazza San Felicita: A block south of Ponte Vecchio is the unpretentious and happy Piazza San Felicita, with two good restaurants. The cozy and candlelit **Trattoria Bordino**, just up the street and actually built into the old town wall (c. 1170), serves tasty and beautifully-presented Florentine cuisine "with international influence" (moderate prices, Mon–Sat 12:00–14:30, 19:30–22:30, closed Sun, Via Stracciatella 9 red, tel. 055-213-048). Right on the square, the more touristy **Ristorante Bibo** serves *"cucina tipica Fiorentina"* with a pink-tablecloth-and-black-bowties dressiness and leafy candlelit outdoor seating (good €15 3-course meal, CC, reserve for out-door seating, Wed–Mon 12:00–15:00, 19:00–23:00, closed Tue, Piazza San Felicita 6 red, tel. 055-239-8554).

At Piazza Santo Spirito: This classic Florentine square (lately a hangout for drug pushers, therefore a bit seedy-feeling and plagued by Vespa bag-snatchings) has two popular little restaurants offering good local cuisine every night of the week, indoor and on-the-square seating (reserve for on-the-square), moderate prices, and impersonal service: **Borgo Antico** (Piazza Santo Spirito 6 red, tel. 055-210-437) and **Osteria Santo Spirito** (pricier, more peaceful outdoor seating, Piazza Santo Spirito 16 red, tel. 055-238-2383).

The **Ricchi Caffè**, next to Borgo Antico, has fine *gelato* and shaded outdoor tables. Notice the plainness of the facade of the Brunelleschi church facing the square. Then step inside the café, grab a coffee, and pick your favorite of the many ways it might be finished.

Trattoria Casalinga is an inexpensive standby. Famous for its home-cooking, it's now filled with tourists rather than locals. But it sends them away full, happy, and with euros left for *gelato* (Mon–Sat 12:00–14:30, 19:00–21:45, closed Sun and all of Aug, CC, just off Piazza Santo Spirito, near the church at Via dei Michelozzi 9 red, after 20:00 reserve or wait, tel. 055-218-624).

Florence's Restaurants

1. OSTERIA BELLEDONNE
2. RIST. LA SPADA
3. TRATTORIA MARIONE
4. TRATTORIA SOSTANZA-TROIA
5. TRATTORIA IL CONTADINO
6. TRATTORIA DA GIORGIO
7. LA GROTTA DI LEO
8. MERCATO CENTRALE MARKET
9. TRATTORIA LA BURRASCA & OSTERIA LA CONGREGA
10. SELF-SERVICE REST. LEONARDO
11. RIST. IL CAVALLINO
12. OSTERIA VINI E VECCHI SAPORI
13. CANTINETTA DEI VERRAZZANO & RIST. PAOLI
14. I FRATELLINI WINE & SANDWICH SHOP
15. TRATTORIA ICCHE C'E C'E
16. PICNIC SPOT IF IT'S NOT TOO HOT

On Via di Santo Spirito/Borgo San Jacopo: Several good and colorful restaurants line this multi-named street a block off the river in Oltrarno. I'd survey the scene (perhaps following the self-guided Oltrarno walk described above) before making a choice.

At **Cammillo Trattoria**, while Cammillo is slurping spaghetti in heaven, his granddaughter Chiara carries on his tradition, mixing traditional Tuscan with "creative" modern cuisine. With a charcoal grill and a team of white-aproned waiters cranking out wonderful food in a fun, dressy-but-down-to-earth ambience, this place is a hit (full dinners about €36 plus wine, Thu–Tue 12:00–14:30, 19:30–22:30, closed Wed, CC, Borgo San Jacopo 57 red, reservations smart, tel. 055-212-427).

Other inviting places along this street include: **Osteria del Cinghiale Bianco** is popular but cramped (around €30 for dinner plus wine, Borgo San Jacopo 43 red, air con, closed Tue–Wed, reservations wise, tel. 055-215-706). The more relaxed **Trattoria Angiolino** serves good old-fashioned local cuisine (about €20 for dinner plus wine, closed Mon, Via di Santo Spirito 36 red, tel. 055-239-8976). **Trattoria Sabatino** is spacious and disturbingly cheap, with family character, red-checkered tablecloths, a simple menu, and the fewest tourists of all. A wonderful place to watch locals munch, it's just outside the Porta San Frediano (medieval gate), a ten-minute walk from Ponte Vecchio (12:00–14:30, 19:20–22:00, Mon–Fri only—because it caters to locals rather than tourists, Via Pisana 2 red, tel. 055-225-955). If you eat here, read my guided walk before hiking out to the gate.

Eating North of the River

Eating near Santa Maria Novella and the Train Station

Osteria Belledonne is a crowded and cheery bohemian hole-in-the-wall serving great food at good prices. I loved the meal but had to correct the bill—read it carefully. They don't take too many reservations. Arrive early or wait (Mon–Fri 12:00–14:30, 19:00–22:30, closed Sat–Sun, Via delle Belledonne 16 red, tel. 055-238-2609).

Ristorante La Spada, nearby, is another local favorite serving typical Tuscan cuisine with less atmosphere and more menu (€11 lunch special, about €20 for dinner plus wine, daily 12:00–14:30, 19:00–22:30, air con, near Via della Spada at Via del Moro 66 red, evening reservations smart, tel. 055-218-757).

Trattoria Marione serves good home-cooked-style meals to a local crowd in a happy food-loving ambience (closed Sun, dinners run about €15 plus wine, pretty smoky, Via della Spada 27 red, tel. 055-214-756).

Trattoria Sostanza-Troia is a characteristic and

well-established place with shared tables and a loyal local following. Whirling ceiling fans and walls strewn with old photos create a time-warp ambience. They offer two seatings, requiring reservations: one at 19:30 and one at 21:00 (dinners for about €15 plus wine, lunch 12:00–14:00, great for steaks, closed Sat, Via del Porcellana 25 red, tel. 055-212-691).

Two smoky chowhouses for local workers offer a €9, hearty, family-style, fixed-price menu with a bustling working-class/budget-Yankee-traveler atmosphere (Mon–Sat 12:00–14:30, 18:15–21:30, closed Sun, 2 blocks south of train station): **Trattoria il Contadino** (Via Palazzuolo 69 red, tel. 055-238-2673) and **Trattoria da Giorgio** (across the street at Via Palazzuolo 100 red). Arrive early or wait. The touristy **La Grotta di Leo** (a block away) has a cheap, straightforward menu and edible food and pizza (daily 11:00–01:00, Via della Scala 41 red, tel. 055-219-265). Because these places are a block from the station, they are handy but the street scene is grotty.

Eating near the Central and San Lorenzo Markets

For mountains of picnic produce or just a cheap sandwich and piles of people watching, visit the huge Central Market—**Mercato Centrale** (Mon–Sat 07:00–14:00, closed Sun, a block north of the San Lorenzo street market).

Trattoria la Burrasca is a funky family-run place ideal for Tuscan home cooking. It's small—10 tables—and inexpensive—pasta for €4—but Anna and Antonio Genzano have cooked and served here with passion since 1982. If Andy Capp was Italian, he'd eat here for special nights out. Everything but the desserts is homemade. And if you want good wine cheap, order it here (Fri–Wed 12:00–15:00, 19:00–22:00, closed Thu, Via Panicale 6b, at north corner of Central Market, tel. 055-215-827, NSE).

Osteria La Congrega brags it's a Tuscan wine bar designed to help you lose track of time. In a fresh and romantic two-level setting, creative chef/owner Mahyar has designed a fun, easy menu featuring modern Tuscan cuisine with top-notch local meat and produce. He offers fine vegetarian dishes but only one main meat course per evening. With just 10 uncrowded tables, reservations are required for dinner (moderate with €13 dinner plates, CC, daily 12:00–15:00, 19:00–23:00, Via Panicale 43 red, tel. 055-2645027).

Eating near the Accademia and Museum of San Marco

Gran Caffè San Marco, conveniently located on Piazza San Marco, offers reasonably-priced pizzas, sandwiches, and desserts (no cover charge, self-service and restaurant, Piazza San Marco 11 red, across square from entrance to Museum of San Marco, tel. 055-215-833).

Eating near the Cathedral (Duomo)

Self-service Restaurant Leonardo is fast, cheap, air-conditioned and very handy, just a block from the Duomo behind the Baptistery (€3 pastas, €4 main courses, Sun–Fri 11:45–14:45, 18:45–21:45, closed Sat, upstairs at Via Pecori 5, tel. 055-284-446). Luciano ("like Pavarotti") runs the place with enthusiasm.

Eating near Palazzo Vecchio

Piazza Signoria, the square facing the old city hall, is ringed by beautifully-situated yet touristic eateries. Any will do for a reasonably-priced pizza. Perhaps the best value is **Ristorante il Cavallino** (€10 fixed-price lunch menu, €15.50 fixed-price dinner menu, great outdoor seating in shadow of palace, tel. 055-215-818).

Osteria Vini e Vecchi Sapori is a colorful hole-in-the-wall serving traditional food, including plates of mixed sandwiches (€0.75 each—you choose), half a block north of Palazzo Vecchio (Tue–Sun 10:00–23:00, closed Mon, Via dei Magazzini 3 red, facing the bronze equestrian statue in Piazza della Signoria, go behind its tail into the corner and to your left, Emore NSE).

Cantinetta dei Verrazzano is a long-established bakery/café/wine bar, serving delightful sandwich plates in an elegant old-time setting and hot focaccia sandwiches to go. The *Specialita Verrazzano* is a fine plate of four little *crostini* (like mini *bruschetta*) featuring different local breads, cheeses, and meats (€7). The *Tagliere di Focacce*, a sampler plate of mini focaccia sandwiches, is also fun. Either of these dishes with a glass of Chianti makes a fine, light meal. Paolo describes things to make eating educational. As office workers pop in for a quick bite, it's traditional to share tables at lunchtime (Mon–Sat 12:30–21:00, closed Sun, just off Via Calzaiuoli on a side street across from Orsanmichele church at Via dei Tavolini 18, tel. 055-268-590).

At **I Fratellini,** a colorful hole-in-a-wall place, the "little brothers" have served peasants rustic sandwiches and cheap glasses of Chianti wine since 1875. Join the local crowd, then sit on a nearby curb or windowsill to munch, placing your glass on the wall rack before you leave (€4 for sandwich and wine, 20 meters in front of Orsanmichele church on Via dei Cimatori).

Ristorante Paoli serves great local cuisine to piles of happy eaters under a richly frescoed Gothic vault. Because of its fame and central location it's filled mostly with tourists, but for a dressy, traditional splurge meal, this is my choice (Wed–Mon 12:00–14:00, 07:00–22:00, closed Tue, smart to reserve for dinner, €19 tourist menu, à la carte is pricier, CC, midway between the old square and the cathedral at Via de Tavolini 12 red, tel. 055-216-215). Salads are flamboyantly cut and mixed from a trolley right at your table.

Trattoria Icche C'è C'è (dialect for "whatever is, is"; pron. ee-kay chay chay) is a small family-style place where fun-loving Gino serves good traditional meals (moderate, not too touristy, closed Mon, midway between the Bargello and river at Via Magalotti 11 red, tel. 055-216-589).

Transportation Connections—Florence

By train to: Assisi (3/day, 2 hrs, more frequent with transfers, direction: Foligno), **Orvieto** (6/day, 2 hrs), **Pisa** (2/hr, 1 hr), **La Spezia** (for the Cinque Terre, 2/day direct, 2 hrs, or change in Pisa), **Venice** (7/day, 3 hrs), **Milan** (12/day, 3–5 hrs), **Rome** (hrly, 2.5 hrs), **Naples** (2/day, 4 hrs), **Brindisi** (3/day, 11 hrs with change in Bologna), **Frankfurt** (3/day, 12 hrs), **Paris** (1/day, 12 hrs overnight), **Vienna** (4/day, 9–10 hrs). Train info: tel. 848-888-088.

Buses: The SITA bus station, a block west of the Florence train station, is user-friendly (but remember, bus service drops dramatically on Sunday). Schedules are posted everywhere with TV monitors indicating imminent departures. You'll find buses to: **San Gimignano** (hrly, 1.75 hrs), **Siena** (hrly, 75-min *corse rapide* fast buses, faster than the train, avoid the 2-hr *diretta* slow buses), and the **airport** (hrly, 15 min). Bus info: tel. 055-214-721 from 09:30 to 12:30; some schedules are in the *Florence Concierge Information* magazine.

Taxi to Siena: For around €100 you can arrange a ride directly from your Florence hotel to your Siena hotel. For a small group or people with more money than time, this can be a good value.

VENICE
(VENEZIA)

Soak all day in this puddle of elegant decay. Venice is Europe's best-preserved big city. This car-free urban wonderland of a hundred islands—laced together by 400 bridges and 2,000 alleys—survives on the artificial respirator of tourism.

Born in a lagoon 1,500 years ago as a refuge from barbarians, Venice is overloaded with tourists and is slowly sinking (unrelated facts). In the Middle Ages, the Venetians, becoming Europe's clever middlemen for east-west trade, created a great trading empire. By smuggling in the bones of St. Mark (San Marco, A.D. 828), Venice gained religious importance as well. With the discovery of America and new trading routes to the Orient, Venetian power ebbed. But as Venice fell, her appetite for decadence grew. Through the 17th and 18th centuries, Venice partied on the wealth accumulated through earlier centuries as a trading power.

Today Venice is home to about 65,000 people in its old city, down from a peak population of nearly 200,000. While there are about 500,000 in greater Venice (counting the mainland, not counting tourists), the old town has a small-town feel. Locals seem to know everyone. To see small-town Venice away from the touristic flak, escape the Rialto-San Marco tourist zone and savor the town early and late without the hordes of vacationers daytripping in from cruise ships and nearby beach resorts. A 10-minute walk from the madness puts you in an idyllic Venice few tourists see.

Planning Your Time

Venice is worth at least a day on even the speediest tour. Hyper-efficient train travelers take the night train in and/or out. Sleep in the old center to experience Venice at its best: early and late. For a one-day visit, cruise the Grand Canal, do the major sights

Venice

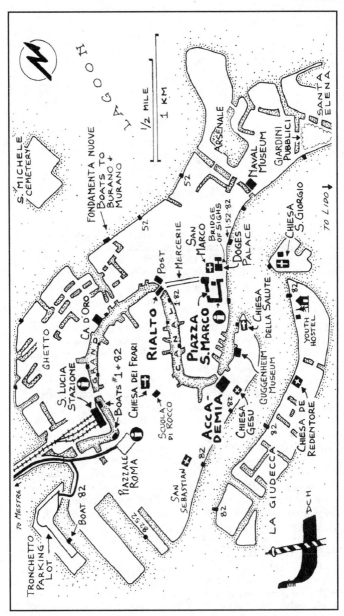

on St. Mark's Square (the square itself, Doge's Palace, and St. Mark's Basilica), see the Church of the Frari (Chiesa dei Frari) for art, and wander the back streets on a pub crawl (see "Eating," below). Venice's greatest sight is the city itself. Make time to simply wander. While doable in a day, Venice is worth two. It's a medieval cookie jar, and nobody's looking.

Orientation

The island city of Venice is shaped like a fish. Its major thorough-fares are canals. The Grand Canal winds through the middle of the fish, starting at the mouth where all the people and food enter, passing under the Rialto Bridge, and ending at St. Mark's Square (San Marco). Park your 21st-century perspective at the mouth and let Venice swallow you whole.

Venice is a carless kaleidoscope of people, bridges, and odor-less canals. The city has no real streets, and addresses are hope-lessly confusing. Each district has about 6,000 address numbers. Luckily it's easy to find your way, since many street corners have a sign pointing you to the nearest major landmark, such as San Marco, Accademia, Rialto, and Ferrovia (the train station). To find your way, navigate by landmarks, not streets. Obedient visit-ors stick to the main thoroughfares as directed by these signs and miss the charm of backstreet Venice.

Tourist Information

There are TIs at the train station (daily 08:00–20:00, crowded and surly), at St. Mark's Square (Mon–Sat 09:45–15:15, with your back to St. Mark's, it's in far corner of square to your left), and near St. Mark's Square *vaporetto* stop (a *vaporetto* is a motorized bus-boat) on the lagoon (daily 09:00–18:00, sells *vaporetto* tickets, rents audioguides for self-guided walking tours). Smaller offices are at Tronchetto, Piazzale Roma, and the airport. For a quick question, save time by phoning (tel. 041-529-8711 or 041-522-5150, www.turismovenezia .it). At any TI, pick up a free city map and the free *Leo* bimonthly magazine, which comes with an insert, *Leo Bussola*, that lists museum hours, exhibitions, and musical events (in Italian and English). Confirm your sightseeing plans. Ask for the fine brochures outlining three offbeat Venice walks. The free periodical entertainment guide *Un Ospite de Venezia* (a monthly listing of events, nightlife, museum hours, train and *vaporetto* schedules, emergency telephone numbers, and so on) is available at the TI or fancy hotel reception desks.

Maps: The €3.10 Venice map on sale at postcard racks has much more detail than the TI's free map, but the new "Illustrated Venice Map" by Magnetic North is by far the best ever (€6.20, listing nearly every shop, hotel, and restaurant). Also consider the little guidebook (sold alongside the postcards), which comes with a city map and explanations of the major sights.

Arrival in Venice

A three-kilometer-long causeway (with highway and train lines) connects Venice to the mainland. Mestre, Venice's sprawling mainland industrial base, has fewer crowds, cheaper hotels, plenty of parking lots, but no charm. Don't stop here, unless you're parking your car in a lot. Trains regularly connect Mestre with Venice's Santa Lucia station (6/hr, 5 min). Don't leave your train at Venezia-Mestre—the next stop is Venezia Santa Lucia (end of the line for Venice).

By Train: Venice's Santa Lucia train station plops you right into the old town on the Grand Canal, an easy *vaporetto* ride or fascinating 40-minute walk from St. Mark's Square. Upon arrival, skip the station's crowded TI (the two TIs at St. Mark's Square are better); it's not worth a long wait for a miminal map (buy a good one from a newsstand with no wait). Confirm your departure plan (stop by train info desk or just study the *partenze*—departure—posters on walls). Consider storing unnecessary heavy bags, although lines for baggage check may be very long (baggage check at platform 14, €2.60/12 hrs, €5.20/24 hrs, daily 03:45–00:30; or lockers at platform 1—€1.60–2.60, often either in use or broken). Then walk straight out of the station to the canal. The dock for *vaporetti* #1 and #82 is on your left (for downtown Venice, most recommended hotels, and Grand Canal Tour); the dock for #51 and #52 is on your right (for some recommended hotels). Buy a €3.10 ticket (or €9.25 all-day pass) at the ticket window and hop on a boat for downtown (direction: Rialto or San Marco).

By Car: The freeway ends at Venice. Follow the green lights directing you to a parking lot with space, probably Tronchetto (across the causeway and on the right), which has a huge, multi-storied garage (€15.50/day, half price with discount coupon from your hotel, tel. 041-520-7555). From there you'll find travel agencies masquerading as TIs and *vaporetto* docks for the boat connection (#82) to the town center. Don't let taxi boatmen con you out of the cheap €3.10 *vaporetto* ride. Parking in Mestre is easy and cheap (open-air lots €4.10/day, €5.20/day garage across from Mestre train station).

By Plane: Romantics can jet to St. Mark's Square by Alilaguna speedboat (€9.75, hrly, 70 min, 06:15–24:00 from airport, 04:50–22:50 from St. Mark's Square, generally departing at :50 after each hour). A water taxi zips you directly to your hotel in 30 minutes for €80. Or, buses connect the airport and Piazzale Roma *vaporetto* stop: either the handy blue ATVO shuttle bus (€2.60, 2/hr, 20 min, 05:30–20:40 to airport, 08:30–24:00 from airport, www.atvo.it) or the cheaper orange ACTV bus #5 (€0.75, 1–3/hr, 20–40 min, 04:40–01:00). Airport info: tel. 041-260-611, flight info: tel. 041-260-9260.

Helpful Hints

Venice is expensive for locals as well as tourists. The demand is huge and running a business is costly. Things just cost more here. Perhaps the best way to enjoy Venice is to just succumb to its charms and blow a lot of money. Accept the fact that Venice was a tourist town 400 years ago. It was, is, and always will be crowded. While 80 percent of Venice is actually an untouristy place, 80 percent of the tourists never notice. Hit the back streets.

Get Lost: Venice is the ideal town to explore on foot. Walk and walk to the far reaches of the town. Don't worry about getting lost. Get as lost as possible. Keep reminding yourself, "I'm on an island, and I can't get off." When it comes time to find your way, just follow the directional arrows on building corners or simply ask a local, *"Dov'è San Marco?"* ("Where is St. Mark's?"). People in the tourist business (that's most Venetians) speak some English. If they don't, listen politely, watching where their hands point, say *"Grazie,"* and head off in that direction. If you're lost, pop into a hotel and ask for their business card—it comes with a map and a prominent "you are here."

Rip-Offs, Theft, and Help: While pickpockets work the crowded main streets, docks, and *vaporetti* (wear your money-belt and carry your daybag in front), the dark, late-night streets of Venice are safe. A service called Venezia No Problem tries to help tourists who've been mistreated by any Venetian business (toll-free tel. 800-355-920, for complaints only, not for information).

Water: Venetians pride themselves on having pure, safe, and tasty tap water piped in from the foothills of the Alps; you can actually see the mountains from Venice bell towers on crisp, clear winter days.

Money: ATMs are plentiful and the easiest way to go. Bank rates vary. I like the Banca di Sicilia, a block toward St. Mark's Square from Campo San Bartolomeo. The American Express change desk is just off St. Mark's Square (see "Travel Agencies," below). Nonbank exchange bureaus such as Exacto will cost you $10 more than a bank for a $200 exchange. A 24-hour cash machine near the Rialto *vaporetto* stop exchanges U.S. dollars and other currencies at fair rates.

Travel Agencies: If you need to get train tickets, pay supplements, or make reservations, avoid the time-consuming trip to the crowded station by using a downtown travel agency. Kele & Teo Viaggi e Turismo is good and handy (cash only, Mon–Fri 08:30–18:00, Sat 09:00–12:00, at Ponte dei Bareteri on the Mercerie midway between Rialto and St. Mark's Square, tel. 041-520-8722).

While American Express provides other travel services, it no longer sells train tickets and is of no help with reservations (Mon–Fri 09:00–17:30; change desk: Mon–Sat 08:30–20:00; about

2 blocks off St. Mark's Square at 1471, en route to the Accademia, tel. 041-520-0844).

Post Office: A large post office is off the far end of St. Mark's Square (on the side of square opposite the St. Mark's church, Mon–Sat 08:10–18:00, shorter hours off-season), and a branch is near the Rialto (on St. Mark's side, Mon–Fri 08:10–13:30, Sat 08:10–12:30).

Church Services: The San Zulian Church (the only church in Venice which you can actually walk around) offers a Mass in English at 09:30 on Sunday (May–Sept, 2 blocks toward Rialto off St. Mark's Square). Gregorians would enjoy the sung Gregorian Mass at 11:00 on Sunday at San Giorgio Maggiore church (on island of San Giorgio Maggiore, visible from Doge's Palace, catch *vaporetto* #82 from San Zaccaria dock). Confirm times of Mass at TI.

The "Rolling Venice" Youth Discount Pass: This worthwhile €2.60 pass gives those under 30 discounts on sights and transportation plus information on cheap eating and sleeping. In summer, they have may have a kiosk in front of the train station (July–Sept daily 08:00–20:00). Their main office, near St. Mark's Square, is open year-round (Mon–Fri 09:00–14:00, from American Express head toward St. Mark's Square, first left, first left again through "Contarina" tunnel, follow white sign to Commune di Venezia and see the sign, Corte Contarina 1529, third floor, tel. 041-274-7651).

Pigeon Poop: If bombed by a pigeon, resist the initial response to wipe it off immediately—it'll just smear into your hair. Wait until it dries and flake it off cleanly.

Laundry: There are two full-service laundrys, both closed on weekends. **Lavanderia Gabriella** is near St. Mark's Square (Mon–Fri 08:00–19:00, 985 Rio Terra Colonne, from San Zulian Church go over Ponta dei Ferali, take first right down Calle dei Armeni, tel. 041-522-1758). **Lavanderia S.S. Apostoli** is near the Rialto on the St. Mark's side (Mon–Fri 08:30–12:00, 15:30–19:00, closed Sat-Sun, just off Campo S.S. Apostoli on Salizada del Pistor, tel. 041-522-6650). At either place you can get nine pounds of laundry washed and dried for €16—confirm price carefully. Drop it off in the morning; pick it up that afternoon. (Call to be sure they're open.) Don't expect to get your clothes back ironed, folded, or even entirely dry.

Across the canal from the train station, you'll find the modern and much cheaper **Bea Vita** self-serve *lavanderia* (daily 08:00–22:00, from station go over bridge, take first right, first left, first right).

Etiquette: Walk on the right and don't loiter on bridges. Picnicking is technically forbidden (keep a low profile). Dress modestly. Men should keep their shirts on. When visiting St. Mark's or other major churches, men, women, and even children should cover their knees and shoulders (or risk being turned away).

Haircuts: I've been getting my hair cut at Coiffeur Benito for 15 years. Benito has been keeping local men and women trim for 25 years. He's an artist—actually a "hair sculptor"— and a cut here is a fun diversion from the tourist grind (€18, Tue–Sat 08:30–13:30, 15:30–19:30, behind San Zulian Church near St. Mark's Square, Calle S. Zulian Gia del Strazzanol 592A, tel. 041-528-6221).

Getting around Venice

By Vaporetto: The public transit system is a fleet of motorized bus-boats called *vaporetti*. They work like city buses except that they never get a flat, the stops are docks, and if you get off between stops, you may drown. For most, only two lines matter: #1 is the slow boat, taking 45 minutes to make every stop along the entire length of the Grand Canal, and #82 is the fast boat that zips down the Grand Canal in 25 minutes, stopping mainly at Tronchetto (car park), Piazzale Roma (bus station), Ferrovia (train station), Rialto Bridge, San Tomá (Church of the Frari), the Accademia Bridge, and San Marco. Buy a €3.10 ticket ideally before boarding (at the booth at the dock) or from a conductor on board. Families of three or more pay €2.60 per person. A round-trip (*andata e ritorno*) costs €5.20 (good for 2 trips within a day on any line).

A 24-hour pass (€9.25, cheaper for families) pays for itself in three trips. Also consider the 72-hour (€18) and one-week (€31) passes. It's fun to be able to hop on and off spontaneously. Technically, luggage costs the same as dogs—€3.10—but I've never been charged. Riding free? There's a one-in-ten chance a conductor will fine you €20.

Only three bridges cross the Grand Canal, but *traghetti* (little €0.50 ferry gondolas, marked on better maps) shuttle locals and in-the-know tourists across the Grand Canal at several handy locations (see Downtown Venice map). Take advantage of these time savers. They can also save money. For instance, while most tourists take the €3.10 *vaporetto* to connect St. Mark's with Salute Church, a €0.50 *traghetto* also does the job.

By Taxi: Venetian taxis, like speedboat limos, hang out at most busy points along the Grand Canal. Prices—which average €30–40 (about €75 to the airport)—are a bit soft. Negotiate and settle before stepping in. With lots of luggage or small groups they can be a worthwhile and time-saving convenience—and extremely scenic to boot.

Walking Tours of Venice

Audioguide Tours—The TI rents audioguides for self-guided walking tours of Venice (2 hours-€5, 24 hrs-€10, just punch the number of what you'd like described—exteriors only, available at TI at lagoon near St. Mark's Square).

American Express Tours—AmEx runs several basic guided

Downtown Venice

- ① HOTEL RIVA
- ② LOCANDA PIAVE
- ③ LOCANDA CASA QUERINI
- ④ HOTEL CAMPIELLO
- ⑤ ALBERGO PAGANELLI
- ⑥ ALBERGO DONI
- ⑦ HOTEL FONTANA
- ⑧ ALBERGO CORONA
- ⑨ HOTEL ASTORIA
- ⑩ LOCANDA GAMBERO
- ⑪ HOTEL BEL SITO
- ⑫ ALLOGGI ALLA SCALA
- ⑬ LOCANDA STURION & HOTEL LOCANDA OVIDIUS
- ⑭ ALBERGO GUERRATO
- ⑮ HOTEL CANADA
- ⑯ HOTEL GIORGIONE
- ⑰ LOCANDA LA CORTE
- ⑱ FORESTERIA DELLA CHIESA VALDESE

tours daily (€16–28, 2–3 hrs, depart from AmEx office, about 2 blocks off St. Mark's Square in direction of Accademia, past TI in arcade, tel. 041-520-0844).

Classic Venice Bars Tour—Debonair local guide Alessandro Schezzini is a connoisseur of Venetian *bacaros*—classic old bars serving traditional *cicchetti* (local munchies). He offers evening tours that involve stopping, eating, and drinking at three of these. The fee (about €26 per person) includes wine, *cicchetti*, and a great insight into this local tradition (4–8 per group, depart at 18:00, tel. & fax 041-534-5367, cellular 33-5530-9024, e-mail: venische@tiscalinet.it).

Venicescapes—Michael Broderick's private theme tours of Venice are demanding intellectually and beyond the attention span of most mortal tourists, but for the curious with stamina, he's enthralling. Michael's challenge: to help visitors gain a more solid understanding of Venice. For a description of all six of his itineraries, see www.venicescapes.org (book well in advance, 6-hour tour: $275 for 2, $25 per person after that, plus admissions and transportation, tel. 041-520-6361, e-mail: info@venicescapes.org).

Local Guides—Alessandro Schezzini gets into offbeat Venice (€90, 2.5 hrs, listed above in "Classic Venice Bars Tour"). Elisabetta Morelli is a good, licensed, local guide (€130, 2 hrs, tel. 041-526-7816, cellular 328-753-5220, e-mail: bettamorelli@inwind.it).

Grand Canal Tour of Venice

For a ▲▲▲ joyride, introduce yourself to Venice by boat. Cruise the entire Canale Grande from Tronchetto (car park) or Ferrovia (train station) all the way to San Marco. You can ride boat #1 (slow and ideal, 45 min) or #82 (too fast, 25 min, be certain you're on a "San Marco via Rialto" boat because some boats don't go farther than Rialto).

If you can't snag a front seat, lurk nearby and take one when it becomes available or find an outside seat in the stern. This ride has the best light and fewest crowds early or late. Twilight is magic. After dark, chandeliers light up the building interiors. While Venice is a barrage on the senses that hardly needs a narration, these notes give the cruise a little meaning and help orient you to this great city. Some city maps (on sale at postcard racks) have a handy Grand Canal map on the back.

Venice, built in a lagoon, sits on pilings driven nearly five meters (15 feet) into the clay (alder wood worked best). About 40 kilometers (25 miles) of **canals** drain the city, dumping like streams into the Grand Canal. Technically, there are three canals: Grand, Giudecca, and Cannaregio. The other 45 "canals" are referred to as *rio* (rivers), but the only natural river is this main street of Venice, about five meters deep. Because of its faster current, sediment never settled here.

Venice is a city of **palaces**. The most lavish were built
fronting the Grand Canal. This cruise is the only way to really
appreciate the front doors of this unique and historic chorus line
of mansions dating from the days when Venice was the world's
richest city. Strict laws prohibit any changes in these buildings,
so while landowners gnash their teeth, we can enjoy Europe's
best-preserved medieval city—slowly rotting. Many of the grand
buildings are now vacant. Others harbor chandeliered elegance
above mossy, empty ground floors. Ages ago the city was nicknamed "Venice the Red" for the uniform red brick dust-colored
stucco of its buildings. Today you'll see a bit of the original red
along with the modern colors.

Start at **Tronchetto** (the bus and car park) or the **train station**. The station, one of the few modern buildings in town, was
built in 1954. It's been the gateway into Venice since 1860, when
the first station was built. "F.S." stands for "Ferrovie dello Stato,"
the Italian state railway system. The bridge at the station is the
first of only three that cross the Canale Grande.

The **ghetto** is shortly after the train station, on the left.
Look down Cannaregio Canal (opposite the Riva di Biasio stop).
The twin pink six-story buildings, known as the "skyscrapers,"
are a reminder of how densely populated the world's original
ghetto was. Set aside as the local Jewish quarter in 1516, the area
became extremely crowded. This urban island (behind the San
Marcuola stop) developed into one of the most closely knit business and cultural quarters of all Jewish communities in Italy
(Jewish Museum described in "Sights," below).

As you cruise, notice the traffic signs. Venice's main thoroughfare is busy with traffic. You'll see all kinds of **boats**: taxis, police
boats, garbage boats, ambulances, and even brown-and-white UPS
boats. Venice's sleek, black, graceful **gondolas** are a symbol of the
city. While used gondolas cost around $10,000, new ones run up to
$30,000 apiece. Today, with over 400 gondoliers joyriding around
the churning *vaporetti*, there's a lot of congestion on the Grand
Canal. Watch your *vaporetto* driver curse the gondoliers.

Opposite the San Stae stop look for the faded frescoes.
Imagine the grand facades of the Grand Canal in its day.

At the Ca d'Oro stop notice the lacy Gothic palace. Named
the **"House of Gold"**—the frilly edge of the roof was once
gilded—it's considered the most elegant Venetian Gothic palace
on the canal. Unfortunately there's little to see inside (€3.10,
Mon 08:15–14:00, Tue–Sun 08:15–19:15, free peek through hole
in door of courtyard). "Ca" refers to "house." Because only the
house of the doge (Venetian ruler) could be called a palace, all
other palaces are technically "Ca."

On the right, the outdoor **fish and produce market** bustles
with people in the morning but is quiet the rest of the day. (This

is a great scene to wander through—even though new European hygiene standards required a less-colorful remodeling job last year.) Find the *traghetto* gondola ferrying shoppers—standing like Washington crossing the Delaware—back and forth.

Ahead, above the post office, the golden angel of the Campanile (bell tower) faces the wind and marks St. Mark's Square, where this tour will end. The huge **post office**, with *servizio postale* boats moored at its blue posts, is on the left just before the Rialto Bridge.

A major landmark of Venice, the **Rialto Bridge** is lined with shops and tourists. The third bridge on this spot, it was built in 1592. Earlier Rialto Bridges could open to let in big ships. After 1592, much of the Grand Canal was closed to shipping and became a canal of palaces. With a span of 42 meters and foundations stretching 200 meters on either side, the Rialto was an impressive engineering feat in its day. Locals call the summit of this bridge the "icebox of Venice" for its cool breeze. Tourists call it a great place to kiss. *Rialto* means "high river bank." The restaurants with views of the bridge feature high prices and low quality.

Rialto, a separate town in the early days of Venice, has always been the commercial district, while San Marco was the religious and governmental center. Today a street called the Mercerie connects the two, providing travelers with human traffic jams and a mesmerizing gauntlet of shopping temptations.

Beyond the Rialto on the left, notice the long stretch of important **merchants' palaces**, each with proud and different facades. Since ships couldn't navigate beyond the Rialto Bridge (to reach the section of the Grand Canal you just came from), the biggest palaces—with the major shipping needs—lie ahead. Many feature the Roman palace design of twin towers flanking a huge set of central windows. These were showrooms designed to let in maximum sunlight.

Take a deep whiff of Venice. What's all this nonsense about stinky canals? All I smell is my shirt. By the way, how's your captain? Smooth dockings? To get to know him, stand up in the bow and block his view.

The rising water level takes its toll. Many canal-level floors are abandoned. Notice how many buildings have a foundation of waterproof white stone (*pietra d'Istria*) upon which the bricks sit high and dry. The posts—historically painted gaily with the equivalent of family coats of arms—don't rot under water. But the wood at the water line does rot. Notice how the rich marble facades are just a veneer covering no-nonsense brick buildings. Look up at the characteristic funnel-shaped chimneys. These forced embers through a loop-the-loop channel until dead—required in the days when stone palaces were surrounded by humble wooden buildings and a live spark could make a merchant's workforce homeless.

After the San Silvestro stop you'll see (on the right) the

palace of a 13th-century **"captain general of the sea."** The Venetian equivalent of five-star admirals were honored with twin obelisks decorating their palaces.

After the San Tomá stop look down the side canal (on the right) before the bridge to see the traffic light, the **fire station**, and the fireboats ready to go.

These days, when buildings are being renovated, huge murals with images of the building mask the ugly scaffolding. Corporations hide the scaffolding out of goodwill (and to get their name on the mural).

The wooden Accademia Bridge crosses the Grand Canal and leads to the **Accademia Gallery** (neoclassical facade just after the British consulate on the right), filled with the best Venetian paintings. The bridge was put up in 1932 as a temporary one. Locals liked it, so it stayed.

Cruising under the bridge, you'll get a classic view of the **Salute Church** ahead (daily 09:00–12:00, 15:00–18:00). This Church of Saint Mary of Good Health was built to coax God into delivering them from the devastating plague of 1630 (which eventually killed about a third of the city's population). It's claimed that more than a million trees were piled together to build a foundation reaching below the mud to the solid clay.

Much of the surrounding countryside was deforested by Venice. Trees were exported and consumed locally to fuel the furnaces of Venice's booming glass industry, build Europe's biggest merchant marine, and to prop up this city in the mud.

The low white building on the right (between the bridge and the church) is the **Peggy Guggenheim Collection**. She willed the city a fine collection of modern art.

Next to this notice the early Renaissance building (flat-feeling facade just decorated with Renaissance motifs). The Salviati building (with the fine mosaic) is a glass factory.

Just before the Salute stop (on the right), the house with the big view windows and the red and wild Andy Warhol painting on the living-room wall (often behind white drapes) was lived in by Mick Jagger. In the 1970s this was famous as Venice's rock-and-roll-star party house.

The building on the right with the golden ball is the **Dogana da Mar**, a 16th-century customs house (not open to the public today). Its two bronze Atlases hold a statue of Fortune riding the ball. While there are few hotels on this side, all the buildings on the left are fancy Grand Canal hotels.

As you prepare to deboat at San Marco, look from left to right out over the lagoon. A wide harborfront walk leads past the town's most elegant hotels to the green area in the distance. This is the public garden, the only park in Venice. Farther out is the

lido, Venice's beach. It's tempting, with its sand and casinos, but its car traffic breaks into the medieval charm of Venice.

The dreamy church that seems to float is the architect Palladio's **San Giorgio Maggiore**. It's just a *vaporetto* ride away (#82 from San Zaccaria dock); if you visit the church, find the Tintoretto paintings (such as the *Last Supper*) and take the elevator up the tower for a terrific view (€2.10 for tower; €5.20 for tower, church, and museum; daily 09:30–12:30, 14:30–18:30, Gregorian Mass at 11:00 on Sun, tel. 041-522-7827). Across the lagoon (to your right) is a residential island called Giudecca.

Get out at the San Marco stop. Directly ahead is Harry's Bar. Hemingway drank here when it was a characteristic no-name *osteria* and the gondoliers' hangout. Today, of course, it's the overpriced hangout of well-dressed Americans who don't mind paying triple for their Bellinis (peach juice with Prosecco wine) to make the scene. St. Mark's Square is just around the corner.

For more *vaporetto* fun, ride a boat around the city and out into the lagoon and back (ask for the *circulare*; pron. cheer-koo-LAH-ray). Plenty of boats leave from San Marco for the beach (*lido*), and speedboats offer tours of nearby islands: Burano is a quiet, picturesque fishing and lace town, Murano specializes in glassblowing, and Torcello has the oldest churches and mosaics but is otherwise dull and desolate. Boat #12 takes you to these remote points slower and cheaper.

Sights—Venice, on St. Mark's Square

▲▲▲**St. Mark's Square (Piazza San Marco)**—Surrounded by splashy and historic buildings, Piazza San Marco is filled with music, lovers, pigeons, and tourists by day and is your private rendezvous with the Middle Ages late at night. Europe's greatest dance floor is the romantic place to be. St. Mark's Square is about the first place in Venice to flood (you might see stacked wooden benches; when the square floods, these are put end to end to make elevated sidewalks).

Venice's best TIs (and WCs) are here; one TI is on the square, the other on the lagoon. To find the TI on the square, stand with your back to the church, and go to the far corner on your left; the office is tucked away in the arcade (daily 09:00–17:00, near this TI is a €0.50 WC open daily 08:00–21:00—it's a few steps beyond St. Mark's Square en route to American Express office and Accademia; see "Albergo Diorno" sign marked on pavement). The other TI is on the lagoon (daily 10:00–18:00, walk out to the water by Doge's Palace, go right; nearby WCs open daily 09:00–19:00).

With your back to the church, survey one of Europe's great urban spaces and the only square in Venice to merit the title "Piazza." Nearly two football fields long, it's surrounded by the offices of the republic. On the right are the "old offices"

(16th-century Renaissance). On the left are the "new offices" (17th-century Baroque). Napoleon, after enclosing the square with the more simple and austere neoclassical wing across the far end, called this "the most beautiful drawing room in Europe."

The clock tower, a Renaissance tower built in 1496, marks the entry to the Mercerie, the main shopping drag, which connects St. Mark's Square with the Rialto. From the piazza you can see the bronze men (Moors) swing their huge clappers at the top of each hour. In the 17th century one of them knocked an unsuspecting worker off the top and to his death—probably the first-ever killing by a robot. Notice the world's first "digital" clock on the tower facing the square (with dramatic flips every 5 minutes).

For a slow and pricey evening thrill, invest €6.20 (plus €4 if the orchestra plays) in a beer or coffee at one of the elegant cafés with the dueling orchestras. (Caffè Florian is described below in "Nightlife in Venice.") If you're going to sit awhile and savor the scene, it's worth the splurge. If all you have is €1, buy a bag of pigeon seed and become popular in a flurry. To get everything airborne, toss your sweater in the air.

▲▲St. Mark's Basilica—Since about A.D. 830 this basilica has housed the saint's bones. The mosaic above the door at the far left of the church shows two guys carrying Mark's coffin into the church. Mark looks pretty grumpy after the long voyage from Egypt.

The church, built in eastern style to underline Venice's connection with Byzantium (thus protecting it from the ambition of Charlemagne and his Holy Roman Empire), is decorated by booty from returning sea captains—a kind of architectural Venetian trophy chest.

To enter the church, modest dress is required even of kids (no shorts or bare shoulders). In peak season, there can be long lines of people waiting to get into the church. People who ignore the dress code hold up the line while they plead fruitlessly with—or put on extra clothes under the watchful eyes of—the dress code police.

The church has 4,000 square meters of Byzantine mosaics, the best and oldest of which are in the atrium (turn right as you enter and stop under the last dome—this may be roped off, but dome is still partially visible). Facing the church, gape up (it's OK, no pigeons), and read clockwise the story of Adam and Eve that rings the bottom of the dome. Now, facing the piazza, look dome-ward for the story of Noah, the ark, and the flood (two by two, the wicked being drowned, Noah sending out the dove, a happy rainbow, and a sacrifice of thanks).

Step inside the church (stairs on right lead to bronze horses) and notice the marble floor richly decorated in mosaics. As in many Venetian buildings, because the best foundation pilings were made around the perimeter, the interior floor rolls. As you shuffle under the central dome, look up for the Ascension (free, Mon–Sat 09:30–17:00, Sun 14:00–17:00, no photos, tel. 041-522-5205). See the schedule board in the atrium, listing free English guided tours (schedules vary but April–Oct there can be up to 4 a day). The church is particularly beautiful when lit (unpredictable schedule, maybe middays 11:00–12:00, Sat–Sun 14:00–17:00 plus 18:45 Mass on Sat). During peak times the line can be very long. Free reservations are available at www.alata.it (just print out your time and present it when you enter to the left of the general entry).

In the **Galleria and Museum** upstairs, you can see an up-close mosaic exhibition, a fine view of the church interior, a view of the square from the horse balcony, and (inside, in their own room) the newly-restored original bronze horses. These well-traveled horses, made during the days of Alexander the Great (4th century B.C.), were taken to Rome by Nero, to Constantinople/Istanbul by Constantine, to Venice by crusaders, to Paris by Napoleon, back "home" to Venice when Napoleon fell, and finally indoors and out of the acidic air (€1.60, daily 09:45–16:00, summer until 17:00, enter from atrium either before or after you tour church).

San Marco's **treasury** (with included and informative audioguide free for the asking) and **altarpiece** (€2.10 each, daily 09:45–17:10, 16:10 in winter) give you the best chance outside of Istanbul or Ravenna to see the glories of Byzantium. Venetian crusaders looted the Christian city of Constantinople and brought home piles of lavish loot (until the advent of TV evangelism, perhaps the lowest point in Christian history). Much of this plunder is stored in the treasury (*tesoro*) of San Marco. As you view these treasures, remember most were made in A.D. 500, while Western Europe was still rutting in the mud. Beneath the high altar lies the body of St. Mark ("Marxus") and the Pala d'Oro, a golden altarpiece made with 80 Byzantine enamels (A.D. 1000–1300). Each shows a religious scene set in gold and precious stones. Both of these sights are interesting and historic, but neither is as much fun as two bags of pigeon seed.

▲▲▲**Doge's Palace (Palazzo Ducale)**—The seat of the Venetian government and home of its ruling duke, or doge, this was the most powerful half-acre in Europe for 400 years (April–Oct daily 09:00–19:00, Nov–March daily 09:00–17:00, last entry 90 min before closing, €5 audioguide, tel. 041-522-4951). The €9.25 combo-ticket includes admission to a number of lesser museums: Museo Correr (see below), Palazzo Mocenigo (textiles and costumes, closed Mon), Museo del Vetro di Murano (glass museum on Murano, closed Wed), and Museo del Merletto di Burano (lace museum on Burano, closed Tue). The ticket is valid for three months. If the line is very long here, consider buying the combo-ticket at the Correr Museum across the square. With that, you can go directly through the Doge's turnstile.

The fine "Secret Itineraries Tour," which follows the Doge's footsteps through rooms not included in the general admission price, must be booked in advance (€12.50, at 10:00 and 11:30 in English, 1.25 hrs, call 041-522-4951). As they take only 25 people per tour, call two or three days in advance to confirm times and reserve a spot. The cost includes admission only to the Doge's Palace (and allows you to bypass the long line) and while the tour skips the main halls inside, the tour finishes inside the palace and you're welcome to visit those on your own.

The Doge's palace was built to show off the power and wealth of the republic and remind all visitors that Venice was number one. In typical Venetian Gothic style, the bottom has pointy arches, and the top has an Eastern or Islamic flavor. Its columns sat on pedestals, but in the thousand years since they were erected, the palace has settled into the mud, and the bases have vanished.

Enjoy the newly-restored facades from the courtyard. Notice a grand staircase (with nearly naked Moses and Paul Newman at the top). Even the most powerful visitors climbed this to meet the doge. This was the beginning of an architectural power trip. The doge, the elected-for-life duke or leader of this "dictatorship of the aristocracy," lived with his family on the first floor near the halls of power. From his lavish quarters you'll follow the one-way tour through the public rooms of the top floor, finishing with the Bridge of Sighs and the prison. The place is wallpapered with masterpieces by Veronese and Tintoretto. Don't worry much about the great art. Enjoy the building.

In room 12, the **Senate Room**, the 200 senators met, debated, and passed laws. From the center of the ceiling, Tintoretto's *Triumph of Venice* shows the city in all her glory. Lady Venice, in heaven with the Greek gods, stands high above the lesser nations who swirl respectfully at her feet with gifts.

The **Armory**—a dazzling display originally assembled to intimidate potential adversaries—shows remnants of the military might the empire employed to keep the east-west trade lines open (and the local economy booming). Squint out the window at the far end for a fine view of Palladio's San Giorgio Maggiore Church and the *lido* (cars, casinos, crowded beaches) in the distance.

The giant **Hall of the Grand Council** (55 meters/180 feet long, capacity 2,000) is where the entire nobility met to elect the senate and doge. Ringing the room are portraits of 76 doges (in chronological order). One, a doge who opposed the will of the Grand Council, is blacked out. Behind the doge's throne, you can't miss Tintoretto's monsterpiece, *Paradise*. At 520 square meters (1,700 square feet), this is the world's largest oil painting.

Christ and Mary are surrounded by a heavenly host of 500 saints. Its message to electors who met here: make wise decisions and you'll ultimately join that holy crowd.

Walking over the Bridge of Sighs, you'll enter the prisons. In the privacy of his own home, a doge could sentence, torture, and jail his opponents secretly. As you walk back over the bridge, squeeze your arm through the marble lattice window and wave to the gang of tourists gawking at you.

▲▲**Museo Civico Correr**—The city history museum is now included (whether you like it or not) with the admission to the Doge's Palace. In the Napoleon Wing you'll see fine neoclassical works by Canova. Then peruse armor, banners, and paintings re-creating festive days of the Venetian Republic. The top floor lays out a good overview of Venetian art. And just before the cafeteria is a room filled with traditional games. There are English descriptions and great Piazza San Marco views through-out (€9.25 combo-ticket with Doge's Palace and other museums, enter in arcade directly opposite church, daily April–Oct 09:00–19:00, Nov–March 09:00–17:00, last entry 60 min before closing, tel. 041-522-4951).

▲**Campanile di San Marco**—The towering bell tower was once half as tall—a lighthouse marking the entry of the Grand Canal and part of the original fortress/palace which guarded its entry. Ride the elevator 92 meters (300 feet) to the top of the bell tower for the best view in Venice. This tower crumbled into a pile of bricks in 1902, a thousand years after it was built. For an ear-shattering experience, be on top when the bells ring (€5.20, daily 09:00–21:00 in summer, until 19:00 otherwise). The golden angel at its top always faces into the wind. Beat the crowds and enjoy crisp air at 09:00.

More Sights—Venice

▲▲**Galleria dell' Accademia**—Venice's top art museum, packed with highlights of the Venetian Renaissance, features paintings by Bellini, Veronese, Tiepolo, Giorgione, Testosterone, and Canaletto. It's just over the wooden Accademia Bridge. Expect long lines in the late morning because they allow only 300 visitors in at a time; visit early or late to miss crowds (€6.20, Mon 08:15–14:00, Tue–Sun 08:15–19:15, audioguide-€3.60 or €5.20 with 2 earphones, English info sheets in some rooms, guidebook-€7.75, no photos, tel. 041-522-2247). Hour-long guided tours run daily at 10:00, 11:00, and 12:00 for €5.20 (you can skip to the front of the line if buying a tour).

There's a decent pizzeria at the bridge (Pizzeria Accademia Foscarini; see "Eating," below), a public WC under it, and usually a classic shell game being played on top of it (study the system as partners in the crowd win big money).

▲**Peggy Guggenheim Collection**—This popular collection of far-out art offers one of Europe's best reviews of the art styles of the 20th century. Stroll through Cubism (Picasso, Braque), surrealism (Dalí, Ernst), futurism (Boccione, Carra), American abstract expressionism (Pollock), and a sprinkling of Klee, Calder, and Chagall (€6.20, Wed–Mon 10:00–18:00, Sat until 22:00 April–Oct, closed Tue, audioguide-€5.20, guidebook-€5.20, free baggage check, pricey café, photos allowed only in garden and terrace—a fine and relaxing perch overlooking Grand Canal, near Accademia, tel. 041-240-5411). The place is run (cheaply) by American interns working on art history degrees.

▲▲**Chiesa dei Frari**—My favorite art experience in Venice is seeing art in the setting for which it was designed—at the Chiesa dei Frari. The Franciscan "church of the friars" and the art that decorates it is warmed by the spirit of St. Francis. It features the work of three great Renaissance masters: Donatello, Bellini, and Titian—each showing worshippers the glory of God in human terms.

In Donatello's wood carving of St. John the Baptist (just to the right of the high altar), the prophet of the desert—dressed in animal skins and almost anorexic from his diet of bugs 'n honey—announces the coming of the Messiah. Donatello was a Florentine working at the dawn of the Renaissance.

Bellini's *Madonna and the Saints* painting (in the chapel farther to the right) came later, done by a Venetian in a more Venetian style—soft focus without Donatello's harsh realism. While Renaissance humanism demanded Madonnas and saints that were accessible and human, Bellini places them in a physical setting so beautiful it creates its own mood of serene holiness. The genius of Bellini, perhaps the greatest Venetian painter, is obvious in the pristine clarity, believable depth, and reassuring calm of this three-paneled altarpiece. Notice the rich colors of Mary's clothing and how good it is to see a painting *in situ*.

Finally, glowing red and gold like a stained glass window over the high altar, Titian's *Assumption* sets the tone of exuberant beauty found in the otherwise sparse church. Titian the Venetian—a student of Bellini—painted steadily for 60 years…you'll see a lot of his art. As stunned apostles look up past the swirl of arms and legs, the complex composition of this painting draws you right to the radiant face of the once-dying, now-triumphant Mary as she joins God in heaven.

Be comfortable discreetly freeloading off of passing tours. For many, these three pieces of art make a visit to the Accademia Gallery unnecessary (or they may whet your appetite for more). Before leaving, check out the neoclassical, pyramid-shaped tomb of Canova and (opposite that) the grandiose tomb of Titian. Compare the carved marble Assumption behind his tombstone portrait with the painted original above the high altar (€2.10, Mon–Sat 09:00–18:00, Sun 13:00–18:00, modest dress recommended, tel. 041-522-2637).

▲**Scuola di San Rocco**—Next to the Frari Church, another

lavish building bursts with art, including some 50 Tintorettos. The best paintings are upstairs, especially the *Crucifixion* in the smaller room. View the neck-breaking splendor with one of the mirrors (*specchio*) available at the entrance (€5.20, daily 09:00–17:00, or see a concert here and enjoy the art as an evening bonus—see "Nightlife in Venice," below). For *molto* Tiepolo (14 stations of the cross), drop by the nearby Church of San Polo.

▲**Ca' Rezzonico and the Museum of the Venetian 18th Century**—This grand Grand Canal *palazzo* offers the best look in town at the life of Venice's rich and famous in the 1700s. Wandering among furnishings from that most decadent century, you'll see the art of Guardi, Canaletto, Longhi, and Tiepolo (€6.70, Wed–Mon 10:00–18:00, closed Tue, easy *vaporetto* access via Ca' Rezzonico stop, tel. 041-520-4036).

Dalmatian School (Scuola Dalmata dei San Giorgio)—This school (which means "meeting place") is a reminder that Venice was Europe's most cosmopolitan place in its heyday. It was here that the Dalmatian community (people from the present-day region of Croatia) worshipped in their own way, held neighborhood meetings, and worked to preserve their culture. The chapel on the ground floor happens to have the most exquisite Renaissance interior in Venice, with a cycle painted by Carpaccio ringing the room (€2.60, Tue–Sat 09:30–12:30, 15:30–18:30, Sun 09:30–12:30, closed Mon between St. Mark's and Arsenale, on Calle dei Furlani, 3 blocks southeast of Campo San Lorenzo).

Jewish Ghetto—The word "ghetto" is Venetian for foundry, and was inherited by Venice's Jewish community when it was confined to the site of Venice's former copper foundries in 1516. Notice how an island—dominated by the Campo del Ghetto Nuovo square and connected with the rest of Venice by only three bridges—would be easy to isolate. While little survives from that time or the Jewish community, in its day the square was densely populated—lined with proto-skyscrapers seven to nine stories high. This original ghetto becomes most interesting after touring the Jewish Museum. Entry is by guided tour only, leaving hourly (€2.60, June–Sept Sun–Fri 10:00–19:00, Oct–May Sun–Fri 10:00–17:30, closed Sat; guided tours hourly; look for Campo di Ghetto Nuovo on map; tel. 041-715-359).

Santa Elena—For a pleasant peek into a completely untouristy residential side of Venice, catch the boat from St. Mark's Square to the neighborhood of Santa Elena (at the fish's tail). This 100-year-old suburb lives as if there were no tourism. You'll find a kid-friendly park, a few lazy restaurants, and beautiful sunsets over San Marco.

Gondola Rides

A rip-off for some, this is a traditional must for romantics. Gondoliers charge about €62 for a 50-minute ride during the day; from

20:00 on, figure on €77 to €103 (for *musica*—singer and accordionist, it's an additional €88 during day, €98 after 20:00). You can
divide the cost—and the romance—among up to six people. Glide
through nighttime Venice with your head on someone else's shoulder. Follow the moon as it sails past otherwise unseen buildings.
Silhouettes gaze down from bridges while window glitter spills
onto the black water. You're anonymous in the city of masks as the
rhythmic thrust of your striped-shirted gondolier turns old crows
into songbirds. This is extremely relaxing (and I think worth the
extra cost to experience at night). Since you might get a narration
plus conversation with your gondolier, talk with several and choose
one you like who speaks English well. Women beware…while
gondoliers can be extremely charming, local women say anyone
who falls for one of these guys "has hams over her eyes."

For a glimpse at the most picturesque gondola workshop in
Venice, visit the Accademia neighborhood. Walk down the Accademia side of the canal called Rio San Trovaso. As you approach
Giudecca Canal you'll see the beached gondolas on your right
across the canal.

For cheap gondola thrills, stick to the €0.50 one-minute
ferry ride on a Grand Canal *traghetto* or hang out on a bridge
along the gondola route and wave at (or drop leftover pigeon
seed on) romantics.

Festivals

Venice's most famous festival is **Carnevale** (Feb. 2–12 in 2002).
Carnevale, which means "farewell to meat," originated centuries ago
as a wild two-month-long party leading up to the austerity of Lent.
In Carnevale's heyday—the 1600s and 1700s—you could do pretty
much anything with anybody from any social class if you were wearing a mask. These days it's a tamer 10-day celebration, culminating
in a huge dance lit with fireworks on St. Mark's Square. Sporting
masks and costumes, Venetians from kids to businessmen join in the
fun. Drawing the biggest crowds of the year, Carnevale has nearly
been a victim of its success, driving away many Venetians (who skip
out on the craziness to go ski in the Dolomites).

Other typically Venetian festival days filling the city's hotels
with visitors and its canals with decked-out boats are: **Feast of
the Ascension Day** (May 12, 2002), **Feast and Regatta of the
Redeemer** (parade and fireworks, July 20 and 21, 2002), and
the **Historical Regatta** (old-time boats and pageantry, Sept 1 in
2002). Each November 21 is the **Feast of Our Lady of Good
Health.** On this local "Thanksgiving," a bridge is built over the
Grand Canal so the city can pile into the Salute Church and
remember how this city survived the gruesome plague of 1630.
On this day, Venetians eat smoked lamb from Dalmatia (which
was the cargo of the first ship let in when the plague lifted).

Every other year the city hosts the **Venice Biennale International Art Exhibition** (next scheduled for 2003), a world-class contemporary art exhibition spread over the sprawling Castello Gardens and the Arsenale. Artists representing 65 nations from around the world offer the latest in contemporary art forms: video, computer art, performance art, and digital photography, along with painting and sculpture (€13, open daily generally March–Nov 10:00–18:00, Sat until 22:00; for details, see www.labiennale.org).

Venice is always busy with special musical and artistic events. The free monthly **Un Ospite de Venezia** lists all the latest in English (free at TI or from fancy hotels).

Shopping

Shoppers like Carnevale masks, lace (a specialty of Burano, see below, but sold in Venice as well), empty books with handmade covers, and paintings—especially of Venice. If you're buying a substantial amount from nearly any shop, bargain. It's accepted and almost expected. Offer less and offer to pay cash; merchants are very conscious of the bite taken by credit-card companies.

Popular **Venetian glass** is available in many forms: vases, tea sets, decanters, glasses, jewelry, lamps, sculptures (such as solid-glass aquariums), and on and on. Shops will ship it home for you; snap a photo of it before it's packed up. For simple, easily-packable souvenirs, consider glass-bead necklaces (sold cheap at vendors' stalls, expensive at shops).

If you're serious about glass, visit the small shops on Murano Island. Murano's glass-blowing demonstrations are fun; you'll usually see a vase and a "leetle 'orse" made from molten glass.

In Venice, glass-blowing demos are given by various companies around St. Mark's Square for tour groups. **Galleria San Marco**, a tour-group staple, offers great demos just off Piazza San Marco every few minutes. They have agreed to let individual travelers flashing this book sneak in with tour groups to see the show (and sales pitch). And, if you buy anything, show this book and they'll take 20 percent off the price listed. (The gallery faces the square behind the orchestra nearest the church at #153, go through it, cross the alley, get in good with the guard, and climb the stairs with the next group, daily 09:30–12:00, 14:00–17:00, manager Adriano Veronese, tel. 041-271-8650).

Salizada San Samuele is a nontouristy street with several artsy shops. Livio de Marchi's wood sculpture shop is delightful even when it's closed. Check out the window displays for his latest creations: socks, folded shirts, teddy bears, "paper" sacks, all carved from wood (Mon–Fri 09:30–12:30, 13:30–18:30, nearest major landmark is Accademia Bridge—on St. Mark's side, Salizada San Samuele 3157, *vaporetto* stop: San Samuele, or if approaching by foot, follow signs to Palazzo Grassi, tel. 041-528-5694, www.liviodemarchi.com).

Venice Lagoon

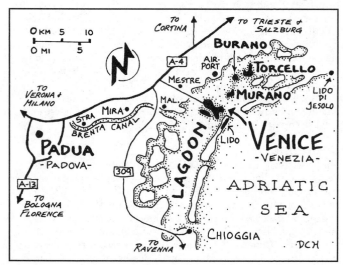

Sights—Venice Lagoon

Several interesting islands hide out in the Venice Lagoon.

Burano, famous for its lace, is a sleepy island with a sleepy community—village Venice without the glitz. Lace fans enjoy Scuola di Merletti (€4.10, Wed–Mon 10:00–17:00, closed Tue, tel. 041-730-034). While the main drag leading from the *vaporetto* stop into town is lined with shops and packed with tourists, simply wander to the far side of the island and the mood shifts. Explore to the right of the leaning tower for a peaceful yet intensely pastel small-town lagoon world.

Torcello, another lagoon island, is dead except for its church, which claims to be the oldest in Venice (€5.20 for church, tower, and museum, Tue–Sun 10:30–17:30, closed Mon, tel. 041-730-761). It's impressive for its mosaics but not worth a look on a short visit unless you really have your heart set on Ravenna, but can't make it there.

The island of **Murano**, famous for its glass factories, has the Museo Vetrario, which displays the very best of 700 years of Venetian glassmaking (€4.10, Thu–Tue 10:00–17:00, closed Wed, tel. 041-739-586). You'll be tempted by salesmen offering free speedboat shuttles from Piazza San Marco to the island. If you're interested in glass, it's handy. You must watch the show, but then you're free to buy or escape and see the rest of the island.

The islands are reached easily, cheaply, and slowly by *vaporetto* (depart from San Zaccaria dock nearest the Bridge of

Sighs/Doge's Palace, line #12 connects all 3 islands, can also take #41 to Murano, then #12 to the other islands). Four-hour speedboat tours of these three lagoon destinations leave twice a day from the dock near the Doge's Palace (usually at 09:30 and 14:30; 1/day winter at 14:30, €16, tel. 041-523-8835); the tours are indeed speedy, stopping for roughly 35 minutes at each island.

Nightlife in Venice

Venice is quiet at night, as tour groups are back in the cheaper hotels of Mestre on the mainland, and the masses of daytrippers return to their beach resorts. **Gondolas** can cost nearly double but are doubly romantic and relaxing under the moon. *Vaporettos* are nearly empty, and it's a great time to cruise the Grand Canal on slow boat #1.

Take your pick of traditional Vivaldi **concerts** in churches throughout town. Vivaldi is as trendy here as Strauss in Vienna and Mozart in Salzburg. In fact, you'll find frilly young Vivaldis all over town hawking concert tickets. The TI has a list of this week's Baroque concerts (tickets from €18, shows start at 21:00 and generally last 90 min). If you see a concert at Scuola di San Rocco, you can enjoy the art (which you're likely to pay €5.20 for during the day) for free during the intermission. The general rule of thumb: musicians in wigs and tights offer better spectacle, musicians in black-and-white suits are better performers. Consider the venue carefully.

On St. Mark's Square, the dueling **café orchestras** entertain. Every night, enthusiastic musicians play the same songs, creating the same irresistible magic. Hang out for free behind the tables (which allows you to easily move on to the next orchestra when the musicians take a break) or spring for a seat and enjoy a fun and gorgeously set concert. If you sit awhile it can be €10.20 well spent (€6.20 drink plus a one-time €4 fee for entertainment).

Caffè Florian, on St. Mark's Square, is the most famous Venetian café and one of the first places in Europe to serve coffee. It's been the place for a discreet rendezvous in Venice since 1720. Today it's most famous for its outdoor seating and orchestra, but do walk through its 18th-century richly-decorated rooms where Casanova, Lord Byron, Charles Dickens, and Woody Allen have all paid too much for a drink (reasonable prices at bar in back, tel. 041-520-5641).

You're not a tourist, you're a living part of a soft Venetian night...an alley cat with money. Streetlamp halos, live music, flood-lit history, and a ceiling of stars make St. Mark's magic at midnight. In the misty light, the moon has a golden hue. Shine with the old lanterns on the gondola piers where the sloppy Grand Canal splashes at the Doge's Palace...reminiscing. Comfort the small statues of the four frightened tetrarchs (ancient Byzantine emperors) where the Doge's Palace hits the basilica. Cuddle history.

Sleeping in Venice
(€1.10 = about $1, country code: 39)
Sleep Code: **S** = Single, **D** = Double/Twin, **T** = Triple, **Q** = Quad,
b = bathroom, **s** = shower only, **CC** = Credit Cards accepted, **no
CC** = Credit Cards not accepted, **SE** = Speaks English, **NSE** =
No English. Breakfast is included unless otherwise noted. Air-
conditioning, when available, is usually only turned on in summer.
See map on page 690 for hotel locations. Virtually all of these
hotels are central.

Reserve a room as soon as you know when you'll be in town.
Book direct—not through any tourist agency. Most places take a
credit card number for a deposit. If everything's full, don't despair.
Call a day or two in advance and fill in a cancellation. If you arrive
on an overnight train, your room may not be ready. Drop your
bag at the hotel and dive right into Venice.

I've listed prices for peak season: April, May, June, September,
and October. Prices can get soft in July, August, and winter. Hotels
sometimes give discounts if you stay at least three nights and/or pay
cash. If on a budget, ask for a cheaper room or a discount. Always
ask. I've listed rooms in two neighborhoods: in the Rialto-San
Marco action and in a quiet Dorsoduro area behind the Accademia
Gallery. If a hotel has a Web site, check it. Hotel Web sites are
particularly valuable for Venice, because they often come with a
map that at least gives you the illusion you can easily find the place.

Sleeping between St. Mark's Square and Campo Santa Maria di Formosa
(zip code: 30122)

Hotel Riva, with gleaming marble hallways and bright modern
rooms, is romantically situated on a canal along the gondola
serenade route. You could actually dunk your breakfast rolls in
the canal (but don't). Sandro may hold a corner (*angolo*) room if
you ask. Confirm prices and reconfirm reservations, as readers
have had trouble with both (Sb-€77, 2 D with adjacent showers-
€93, Db-€108, Tb-€155, Qb-€232, Ponte dell' Angelo, #5310
Castello, 30122 Venezia, tel. 041-522-7034, fax 041-528-5551,
Dante works the night shift). Face St. Mark's cathedral, walk
behind it on the left along Calle de la Canonica, take the first
left (at blue "Pauly & C" mosaic in street), continue straight,
go over the bridge, and angle right to the hotel.

Locanda Piave, with 19 fine rooms above a bright and classy
lobby, is fresh, modern, and comfortable (Db-€139, Tb-€181, family suites-€200 for 3, €212 to €232 for 4 or 5 people, prices good
through 2002 with this book, CC but 10 percent discount with cash,
air con; *vaporetto* #51 or #82 to San Zaccaria, to the left of Hotel
Danieli is Calle de le Rasse, take it, turn left at end, turn right nearly
immediately at square—S.S. Filippo e Giacomo—on Calle Rimpeto

La Sacrestie, go over bridge, take second left, hotel is 2 short blocks ahead on Ruga Giuffa #4838/40, Castello, 30122 Venezia, tel. 041-528-5174, fax 041-523-8512, www.elmoro.com/alpiave, e-mail: hotel.alpiave@iol.it, Mirella, Paolo, and Ilaria SE, faithful Molly NSE). They have a couple of apartments for €181 to €227 (for 3–5 people, cash only, includes kitchenette, cheaper in Aug).

Locanda Casa Querini is a plush little six-room place on a quiet square tucked away behind St. Marks (Db-€165, CC, 5 percent discount with this book, air-con, exactly halfway between San Zaccaria *vaporetto* stop and Campo Santa Maria Formosa at Castello Campo San Giovanni Novo 4388, tel. 041-241-1294, fax 041-241-4231, e-mail: casaquerini@italyhotel.com, Sylvia SE).

Sleeping on or near the Waterfront, East of St. Mark's Square

These places, about one canal down from the Bridge of Sighs, on or just off the Riva degli Schiavoni waterfront promenade, rub drainpipes with Venice's most palatial five-star hotels. The first three—while pricey because of the location—are professional and comfortable. Ride *vaporetto* to San Zaccaria (#51 from train station, #82 from Tronchetto car park).

Hotel Campiello, a lacy and bright little 16-room, air-conditioned place, was once part of a 19th-century convent. It's ideally located 50 meters off the waterfront (Sb-€114, Db-€119–170, CC, 8 percent discount with cash, 30 percent discount mid-Nov–Feb excluding Christmas and Carnevale; behind Hotel Savoia, up Calle del Vin off the waterfront street—Riva degli Schiavoni, San Zaccaria #4647, tel. 041-520-5764, fax 041-520-5798, www.hcampiello.it, e-mail: campiello@hcampiello.it, family-run for 4 generations, sisters Monica and Nicoletta).

Albergo Paganelli is right on the waterfront—on Riva degli Schiavoni—and has a few incredible view rooms (S-€88, Sb-€119, Db-€140–€181, Db with view-€192, request *"con vista"* for view, CC, air con, prices often soft, at San Zaccaria *vaporetto* stop, Riva degli Schiavoni #4182, Castello, 30122 Venezia, tel. 041-522-4324, fax 041-523-9267, www.hotelpaganelli.com, e-mail: hotelpag@tin.it). With spacious rooms, carved and gilded headboards, chandeliers, and hair dryers, this hotelesque place is a good value. Seven of their 22 rooms are in a less interesting but equally comfortable *dependencia* a block off the canal.

Albergo Doni is a dark, hardwood, clean, and quiet place with 12 dim-but-classy rooms run by a likable smart aleck named Gina (D-€77, Db-€103, T-€103, Tb-€139, ceiling fans, air con for €10 extra per night, secure telephone reservations with CC but must pay in cash, Riva degli Schiavoni, San Zaccaria N. #4656 Calle del Vin, tel. & fax 041-522-4267, e-mail: albergodoni@libero.it, Niccolo and Gina SE). Leave Riva Degli Schiavoni on Calle del Vin and go 100 meters with a left jog.

Hotel Fontana is a cozy, two-star, family-run place with 14 rooms and lots of stairs on a touristy square two bridges behind St. Mark's Square (Sb-€52–103, Db-€77–155, family rooms, fans, 10 percent discount with cash, CC; *vaporetto* #51 to San Zaccaria, find Calle de le Rasse—to left of Hotel Danieli— take it, turn right at end, continue to first square, Campo San Provolo, Castello 4701, tel. 041-522-0579, fax 041-523-1040, www.hotelfontana.it, e-mail: htlcasa@gpnet.it).

Albergo Corona is a dingy, confusing, Old World place with eight basic rooms (D-€57, lots of stairs and no breakfast; *vaporetto* #1 to San Zaccaria dock, take Calle de le Rasse— to left of Hotel Danieli, turn left at end, take right at square— Campo S.S. Filippo e Giacomo—on Calle Rimpeto La Sacrestie, take first right, then next left on Calle Corona to #4464, tel. 041-522-9174).

Sleeping North of St. Mark's Square

Hotel Astoria has 24, simple rooms tucked away a few blocks off St. Mark's Square (D-€103, Db-€124, €10 discount July–Aug if you pay cash, closed mid-Nov–mid-March, CC, 2 blocks from San Zulian Church at Calle Fiubera #951; from Rialto *vaporetto* #1 dock go straight inland on Calle le Bembo, which becomes Calle dei Fabbri, turn left on Calle Fiubera, tel. 041-522-5381, fax 041-528-8981, e-mail: info@hotelastoriavenezia.it, Alberto SE).

Locanda Gambero, with 27 rooms, is comfortable and very central in the San Marco area (Db-€129, Tb-€170, CC; from Rialto *vaporetto* #1 dock go straight inland on Calle le Bembo, which becomes Calle dei Fabbri; or from St. Mark's Square go through Sotoportego dei Dai then down Calle dei Fabbri to #4687, at intersection with Calle del Gambero, tel. 041-522-4384, fax 041-520-0431, e-mail: hotgamb@tin.it). Gambero runs the pleasant Art Deco–style La Bistrot on the corner, which serves old-time Venetian cuisine.

Sleeping West/Northwest of St. Mark's Square

Hotel Bel Sito, friendly for a three-star hotel, has Old World character and a picturesque location—facing a church on a small square between St. Mark's Square and the Accademia. With solid wood furniture, its rooms feel elegant (Sb-€123, Db-€186, CC, air con, elevator, some rooms with canal or church views, *vaporetto* #1 to Santa Maria del Giglio stop, take narrow alley to square, hotel at far end to your right, San Marco 2517, Santa Maria del Giglio, west of St. Mark's Square, tel. 041-522-3365, fax 041-520-4083, e-mail: belsito@iol.it).

Alloggi Alla Scala, a seven-room place run by Senora Andreina della Fiorentina, is homey, central, and tucked away on a quiet square that features a famous spiral stairway called Scala Contarini del Bovolo (small Db-€73, big Db-€83, extra bed-€26, breakfast-€7.75, 5 percent discount for payment in cash, sometimes overbooks and sends overflow to her sister's lesser accomodations, Campo Manin #4306, San Marco, northwest of St. Mark's Square, tel. 041-521-0629, fax 041-522-6451, daughter SE). From Campo Manin follow signs to (on statue's left) "Scala Contarini del Bovolo" (€2.10, daily 10:00–17:30, views from top).

Sleeping near the Rialto Bridge
(zip code: 30125)
The first three hotels are on the west side of the Rialto Bridge (away from St. Mark's Square) and the last three are on the east side of the bridge (on St. Mark's side). *Vaporetto* #82 quickly connects the Rialto with both the train station and the Tronchetto car park.

On West Side of Rialto Bridge: **Locanda Sturion**, with air-conditioning and all the modern comforts, is pricey because it over-looks the Grand Canal (Db-€129–191, Tb-€181–232, family deals, canal-view rooms cost about €16 extra, CC, piles of stairs, 100 meters from Rialto Bridge opposite *vaporetto* dock, San Polo, Rialto, Calle Sturion #679, 30125 Venezia, tel. 041-523-6243, fax 041-522-8378, www.locandasturion.com, e-mail: info@locandasturion.com, SE). They require a personal check or traveler's check for a deposit.

Hotel Locanda Ovidius, with an elegant Grand Canal view terrace, wood-beamed-ceilinged breakfast room, and nine bright, comfortable rooms, is also on the Grand Canal (Sb-€77–155, Db-€103–201, Db with view-€155–232, CC, air con, Calle del Sturion #677a, tel. 041-523-7970, fax 041-520-4101, www.hotelovidius.com, e-mail: info@hotelovidius.com).

Albergo Guerrato, overlooking a handy and colorful pro-duce market one minute from the Rialto action, is run by friendly, creative, and hardworking Roberto and Piero. Giorgio takes the night shift. Their 800-year-old building is Old World simple, airy, and wonderfully characteristic (D-€77, Db-€103, big top floor Db-€124, T-€98, Tb-€129, Q-€103, Qb-€150, including a €2.10 city map, prices promised through 2002 with this book, cash only; walk over the Rialto away from St. Mark's Square, go straight about 3 blocks, turn right on Calle drio la Scimia—not Scimia, the block before—and you'll see the hotel sign, Calle drio la Scimia #240a, 30125 San Polo, tel. & fax 041-522-7131 or 528-5927, e-mail: hguerrat@tin.it, SE). My tour groups book this place for 50 nights each year. Sorry. If you fax without calling first, no reply within three days means they are booked up. (It's best to call first.) They rent family apartments in the old center (great for groups of 4 to 8) for around $50 per person.

On East Side of Rialto Bridge: **Locanda Novo Venezia,** a
charming six-room place run by industrious Claudio and Ivan, is on
a great square—Campo dei S.S. Apostoli, just north of the Rialto
Bridge (Db-€124 with this book, family deals for up to 6 in a room,
CC, air con, Cannaregio #4529, tel. 041-241-1496, fax 041-241-
5989, www.locandanovo.com, e-mail: info@locandanova.com).

Hotel Canada has 25 small, pleasant rooms (S-€83, Sb-€119,
D-€124, Db-€150, Tb-€181, Qb-€227, CC, air con-€7.75 extra
per night, rooms on canal come with view, noise, and aroma, rooms
facing church are quiet and fresh, Castello San Lio #5659, 30122
Venezia, tel. 041-522-9912, fax 041-523-5852, SE). This hotel is
ideally located on a small, lively square, just off Campo San Lio
between the Rialto and St. Mark's Square.

Hotel Giorgione, a four-star hotel in a 15th-century palace
on a quiet lane, is super-professional, with plush public spaces,
pool tables, Internet access, a garden terrace, and 70 spacious
over-the-top rooms with all the comforts. They have perfect
price discrimination down to a science (Sb-€88–145, Db-€129–
€248, pricier superior rooms and suites available, extra bed-€52,
20 percent off July–Aug, check Web for discounts, CC, elevator,
air con, Piazza S.S. Apostoli #4587, tel. 041-522-5810, fax
041-523-9092, www.hotelgiorgione.com).

Sleeping near S.S. Giovanni e Paoli
Locanda la Corte, a three-star hotel, has 16 attractive, high-
ceilinged, wood-beamed rooms—done in pastels—bordering a small,
quiet courtyard (Sb-€93, standard Db-€165, superior Db-€181,
suites available, CC, air con; *vaporetto* #52 from train station to Fon-
damente Nove, exit boat to your left, follow waterfront, turn right
after second bridge to get to S.S. Giovanni e Paolo square; facing
Rosa Salva bar, take street to left—Calle Bressana, hotel is a short
block away at bridge; Castello 6317, tel. 041-241-1300, fax 041-241-
5982, www.locanda.lacorte.it, e-mail: info@locanda.lacorte.it).

Sleeping near the Accademia
When you step over the Accademia Bridge, the commotion of
touristy Venice is replaced by a sleepy village laced with canals.
This quiet area, next to the best painting gallery in town, is a
10-minute walk from St. Mark's Square and the Rialto. The fast
vaporetto #82 connects the Accademia Bridge with both the train
station (in about 15 min) and St. Mark's Square (5 min). The
hotels are located near the south end of the Accademia Bridge,
except for the last listing (Fondazione Levi), which is at the north
end of the bridge (St. Mark's side).

Pensione Accademia fills the 17th-century Villa Maravege.
While its 27 comfortable and air-conditioned rooms are nothing
extraordinary, you'll feel aristocratic gliding through its grand public

Accademia Area Hotels and Restaurants

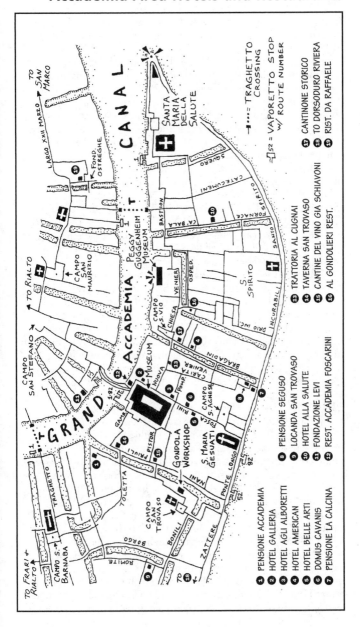

- **1** PENSIONE ACCADEMIA
- **2** HOTEL GALLERIA
- **3** HOTEL AGLI ALBORETTI
- **4** HOTEL AMERICAN
- **5** HOTEL BELLE ARTI
- **6** DOMUS CAVANIS
- **7** PENSIONE LA CALCINA
- **8** PENSIONE SEGUSO
- **9** LOCANDA SAN TROVASO
- **10** HOTEL ALLA SALUTE
- **11** FONDAZIONE LEVI
- **12** REST. ACCADEMIA FOSCARINI
- **13** TRATTORIA AL CUGNAI
- **14** TAVERNA SAN TROVASO
- **15** CANTINE DEL VINO GIA SCHIAVONI
- **16** AL GONDOLIERI REST.

---- = TRAGHETTO CROSSING
☐52 = VAPORETTO STOP w/ ROUTE NUMBER

- **17** CANTINONE STORICO
- **18** TO DORSODURO RIVIERA
- **19** RIST. DA RAFFAELE

spaces and lounging in its breezy garden (Sb-€83–119, standard Db-€129–181, superior Db-€155–227, one big family-of-5 room with grand canal view, family deals, CC; facing Accademia Gallery, take first right, cross first bridge, go right, Dorsoduro #1058, 30123 Venezia, tel. 041-523-7846, fax 041-523-9152, www .pensioneaccademia.it, e-mail: info@pensioneaccademia.it).

Hotel Galleria has 10 compact and velvety rooms, most with views of the Grand Canal (S-€62, D-€88–93, Db-€103, 2 big canal-view Db-€129, includes breakfast in room, CC, fans, some rooms narrow, near Accademia Gallery and next to recommended Foscarini restaurant, Dorsoduro #878a, 30123 Venezia, tel. 041-523-2489, tel. & fax 041-520-4172, www.galleria.it, e-mail: galleria@tin.it, SE).

Hotel Agli Alboretti is a cozy, family-run, 25-room place in a quiet neighborhood a block behind the Accademia Gallery. With red carpeting and wood-beamed ceilings, it feels elegant (Sb-€96, 2 small Db-€116, Db-€145, Tb-€170, Qb-€196, CC, air con; 100 meters from the Accademia *vaporetto* stop on Rio Terra a Foscarini at #884 Accademia; facing Accademia Gallery, go left, then forced right, tel. 041-523-0058, fax 041-521-0158, www.aglialboretti.com, e-mail: alborett@gpnet.it, SE).

Hotel American is a small, cushy, three-star hotel on a lazy canal next to the delightful Campo San Vio (a tiny overlooked square facing the Grand Canal). At this Old World hotel with 18 rooms, you'll get better rates Sundays through Thursdays (Sb-€103–155, Db-€155–207, Db with view-€155–232, extra bed-€26–52, CC, air con, 30 meters off Campo San Vio and 200 meters from Accademia Gallery; facing Accademia Gallery, go left, forced right, take second left—following yellow sign to Guggenheim Museum, cross bridge, take immediate right, #628 Accademia, 30123 Venezia, tel. 041-520-4733, fax 041-520-4048, check www.hotelamerican.com for deals, e-mail: reception@hotelamerican.com, Marco SE).

Hotel Belle Arti is a good bet if you want to be in the old center without the commotion and intensity of Venice. With a grand entry and all the American hotel comforts, it's a big 67-room, modern, three-star place sitting on a former schoolyard (Sb-€114–134, Db-€145–196, Tb-€186–238, the cheaper rates apply to July–Aug and winter, CC, plush public areas, air con, elevator, 100 meters behind Accademia Gallery; facing Gallery, take left, then forced right, Via Dorsoduro #912, tel. 041-522-6230, fax 041-528-0043, www.hotelbellearti.com, info@hotelbellearti.com).

Domus Cavanis, across the street from—and owned by— Belle Arti, is a big, practical, plain place with a garden renting 27 quiet and simple rooms (Db-€103, extra beds €21, includes breakfast at Hotel Belle Arti, elevator, TV, phones, Dorsoduro #896, tel. 041-528-7374, fax 041-522-8505, e-mail: info@hotelbellearti.com).

Pensione La Calcina, the home of English writer John Ruskin in 1876, comes with all the three-star comforts in a professional yet intimate package. Its 29 rooms are squeaky-clean, with good wood furniture, hardwood floors, and a peaceful canalside setting facing Giudecca (S-€65–77, Sb-€88, Sb with view-€103, Db-€124–139, Db with view-€155–176, prices vary with room size and season, CC, air con, rooftop terrace, killer sundeck on canal and canalside buffet breakfast terrace, Dorsoduro #780, at south end of Rio di San Vio, tel. 041-520-6466, fax 041-522-7045, e-mail: la.calcina@libero.it). They also rent apartments nearby (max 2 people, from €130–€233, air con and amenities). From the Tronchetto car park or station, catch *vaporetto* #51 to Zattere (at *vaporetto* stop, exit right, and walk along canal to hotel).

Next door, **Pensione Seguso** is almost an Addams-Family-on-vacation time warp. Sra. Seguso runs her place as her parents did, with the beds, freestanding closets, lamps, and drapes all feeling like your great-grandmother's. The upside is the commanding canal-side setting. The downside is that dinner is required during high season (Db with dinner-€207 for 2 maximum price, slow season Db-€124 without dinner, CC, elevator, tel. 041-522-2340, fax 041-528-6096, e-mail: what's that?).

Locanda San Trovaso is sparkling new, with seven classy, spacious rooms—three with canal views—and a peaceful location on a small canal (Sb-€77–88, Db-€103–124, CC, small roof terrace, Dorsoduro #1351, take *vaporetto* #82 from Tronchetto or #51 from Piazzale Roma or train station, get off at Zattere, exit left, cross bridge, turn right at tiny Calle Trevisan, cross bridge, cross adjacent bridge, take immediate right, then first left, tel. 041-277-1146, fax 041-277-7190, www.locandasantrovaso.com, e-mail: s.trovaso@tin.it, Mark and his son Alessandro SE).

The basic **Hotel Alla Salute** is buried deep in Dorsoduro, ideal for those wanting a quiet Venice with three-star comforts (Db-€134, CC, facing the canal Rio delle Fornace near the Salute church, tel. 041-523-5404, fax 041-522-2271, e-mail: hotel.salute.dacici@iol.com).

Fondazione Levi, a guest house run by a foundation that promotes research on Venetian music, offers 21 quiet, institutional yet comfortable rooms (Sb-€62, Db-€103, Tb-€119, Qb-€134, only twin beds, elevator; 80 meters from base of Accademia Bridge on St. Mark's side; from Accademia *vaporetto* stop, cross Accademia Bridge, take immediate left—crossing the bridge Ponte Giustinian and going down Calle Giustinian directly to the Fondazione, buzz the "Foresteria" door to the right, San Vidal #2893, 30124 Venezia, tel. 041-786-711, fax 041-786-766, www.foresterialevi@libero.it, SE).

Sleeping near the Train Station

Hotel Marin is three minutes from the train station but completely out of the touristic bustle. Just renovated, cozy, and cheery, it seems like a 19-bedroom home the moment you cross the threshold. This is one of the best values in town (S-€57, D-€70, Db-€85, T-€93, Tb-€112, Q-€111, Qb-€122, prices good with this book and if you pay cash, pricier with CC, San Croce #670b, tel. 041-718-022, fax 041-721-485, www.hotelmarin.it). It's family run by helpful, friendly, English-speaking Bruno, Nadia, and son Samuel (they have city maps). It's immediately across the canal from the train station, behind the green dome (over bridge, right, first left, first right, first right). There's an Internet café and handy Laundromat nearby.

Dormitory Accommodations
Foresteria della Chiesa Valdese, warmly run by the local Methodist church, offers cheap dorm beds and doubles, halfway between St. Mark's Square and the Rialto Bridge. This run-down but charming old place has elegant paintings on the ceilings (dorm bed-€18, D-€52, Db-€67, some family apartments-€103 for 5, must check in and out when office is open: 09:00–13:00, 18:00–20:00, from Campo Santa Maria di Formosa, walk past Bar all' Orologio to end of Calle Lunga and cross the bridge, Castello #5170, tel. & fax 041-528-6797, fax 041-241-6328, e-mail: veneziaforesteria@chiesavaldese.org).

Venice's **youth hostel** on Giudecca Island is crowded, cheap, and newly remodeled (€16 beds with sheets and breakfast in 10- to 16-bed rooms, membership required, office open daily 07:00–9:30, 13:30–23:00, catch *vaporetto* #82 from station to Zittele, tel. 041-523-8211). Their budget cafeteria welcomes nonhostelers (nightly 17:00–23:30).

Eating in Venice
While touristy restaurants are the scourge of Venice, and most restauranteurs believe you can't survive in Venice without catering to tourists, there are plenty of places which are still popular with locals and respect the tourists who happen in. First trick: Walk away from triple-language menus. Second trick: Order daily specials.

For a fun change from restaurant fare, consider a pub crawl. You can stop at various, atmospheric pubs to make a meal out of appetizers, called *cicchetti* (pron. cheh-KET-tee). For details, see "The Stand-Up Progressive Venetian Pub-Crawl Dinner," below.

To supplement Venice's skimpy hotel breakfasts, drop by any bar and ask for toast (which gets you a grilled ham-and-cheese sandwich).

Eating between Campo Santi Apostoli and Campo S.S. Giovanni e Paolo
Antiche Cantine Ardenghi de Lucia e Michael is a leap of local faith and an excellent splurge. Effervescent Michael and his wife, Lucia, cook proudly Venetian for a handful of people each night

by reservation only. You must call first. You pay €41 per person and trust them to wine, dine, and serenade you with Venetian class. The evening can be quiet or raucous depending on who and how many are eating. While the menu is heavy on crustaceans, Michael promises to serve plenty of veggies and fruit as well. Find #6369. There's no sign, the door's locked, and the place looks closed. But knock, say the password (La Repubblica Serenissima), and you'll be let in. From Campo S.S. Giovanni e Paolo, pass the churchlike hospital (notice the illusions painted on its facade), go over the bridge to the left, and take the first right on Calle della Testa to #6369 (Tue–Sat 20:00–24:00, closed Sun–Mon, tel. 041-523-7691, cellular 389-523-7691).

The following two colorful *osterias* are good for *cicchetti* (munchies), wine tasting, or a simple, rustic, sit-down meal, surrounded by a boisterous local ambience:

Osteria da Alberto has decent *cicchetti* (18:00–19:30) and great sit-down meals after 19:30 (closed Sun, CC, midway between Campo Santi Apostoli and Campo S.S. Giovanni e Paolo, next to Ponte de la Panada on Calle Larga Giacinto Gallina, tel. 041-523-8153)

Osteria Al Promessi Sposi does *cicchetti* with gusto and offers a little garden for sit-down meals. This place is proudly Venetian (great cod and polenta) and has a fun ambience (Thu–Tue 09:00–23:00, closed Wed, a block off Campo S.S. Apostoli and a block inland from Strada Nova at Calle dell' Oca, tel. 041-522-8609). You'll find more pubs in the side streets opposite Campo St. Sofia across Strada Nova.

Eating in Dorsoduro, near the Accademia

See map on page 711 for location.

Restaurant/Pizzeria Accademia Foscarini, next to the Accademia Bridge and Galleria, offers decent €5 to €7 pizzas in a great canalside setting (Wed–Mon 07:00–23:00, closed Tue).

Trattoria Al Cugnai is an unpretentious place run by three gruff sisters serving good food at a good price (Tue–Sun 12:00–15:00, 19:00–22:30, closed Mon, midway between Accademia Gallery and the forgotten and peaceful Campo San Vio, tel. 041-528-9238). Enjoy a quiet sit on Campo San Vio (benches with Grand Canal view) for dessert.

Taverna San Trovaso is an understandably popular restaurant/pizzeria. Arrive early or wait (Tue–Sun 12:00–14:50, 19:00–21:50, closed Mon, CC, air con, 100 meters from Accademia Gallery on San Trovaso canal; facing Accademia take a right, then a forced left at canal). On the same canal, **Enoteca Cantine del Vino Gia Schiavi**—much loved for its *cicchetti*—is a good place for a glass of wine and appetizers (tel. 041-523-0034). You're welcome to enjoy your wine and finger-food while sitting on the bridge.

Al Gondolieri is considered one of the best restaurants for meat—not fish—in Venice. Its sauces are heavy and prices are high, but carnivores love it (closed Tue, behind Guggenheim Gallery on west end of Rio delle Torreselle, reservations smart, tel. 041-5286396).

Cantinone Storico, also in this neighborhood, is described below under "Romantic Canalside Settings."

Eating near St. Mark's Square
Osteria Da Carla, two blocks west of St. Mark's Square, is a fun and very local hole-in-the-wall where the food is good and the price is right. They have hearty tuna salads and a daily pasta special along with traditional antipasti, polenta, and decent wine by the glass. While you can eat outside, you don't want table #3 (Mon–Sat 07:00–23:00, closed Sun; from American Express head toward St. Mark's Square, first left down Frezzeria, first left again through "Contarina" tunnel, at Sotoportego e Corte Contarina, tel. 041-523-7855, Carlo SE).

The Stand-Up Progressive Venetian Pub-Crawl Dinner
A tradition unique to Venice in Italy is a *giro di ombre* (pub crawl)—ideal in a city with no cars. My favorite Venetian dinner is a pub crawl. I've listed plenty of pubs in walking order for a quick or extended crawl below. If you've crawled enough, most of these bars make a fine one-stop, sit-down dinner. *Ombre* means shade, from the old days when a portable wine bar scooted with the shadow of the Campanile across St. Mark's Square.

Venice's residential back streets hide plenty of characteristic bars with countless trays of interesting toothpick-munchie food (*cicchetti*). This is a great way to mingle and have fun with the Venetians. Real *cicchetti* pubs are getting rare in these fast-food days, but locals appreciate the ones that survive.

Try fried mozzarella cheese, gorgonzola, calamari, artichoke hearts, and anything ugly on a toothpick. Meat and fish (*pesce:* PAY-shay) munchies can be expensive; veggies (*verdure*) are cheap, around €3.10 for a meal-sized plate. In many places there's a set price per munchie (e.g., €1). Ask for a *piatto misto* (mixed plate). Or try a plate of assorted appetizers for €5 (or more, depending on how hungry you are); ask for *"Un classico piatto di cicchetti misti da €5"* (pron. oon KLAH-see-koh pee-AH-toh dee cheh-KET-tee MEE-stee dah CHEEN-kway ay-OO-roh). Bread sticks (*grissini*) are free for the asking.

Drink the house wines. A small glass of house red or white wine (*ombre rosso* or *ombre bianco*) or a small beer (*birrino*) costs about €1. A liter of house wine costs around €3.60. *Vin bon,* Venetian for fine wine, may run you from €1.60 to €2.60 per little glass. Remember, *corposo* means full-bodied. A good last drink is *fragolino,* the local

Venice Restaurants

❶ CANTINA DO MORI	⓫ CIP CIAP PIZZA
❷ OSTERIA SORA AL PONTE	⓬ OSTERIA AL MASCARON
❸ CANTINA DO SPADE	⓭ ENOTECA MASCARETA
❹ OSTERIA ALLA BOTTE	⓮ GELATERIA
❺ ROSTICCERIA SAN BARTOLOMEO	⓯ LA BOUTIQUE GELATERIA
❻ PASTICCERIA PONTE DELLE PASTE	⓰ ANTICHE CANTINE ARDENGHI
❼ OSTERIA AL PORTEGO	⓱ OSTERIA DA ALBERTO
❽ DEVIL'S FOREST PUB & BORA BORA PIZZERIA	⓲ OSTERIA AL PROMESSI SPOSI
❾ OSTERIA AL DIAVOLO E L'AQUASANTA	⓳ REST. AL VAGON
❿ BAR ALL'OROLOGIO	⓴ BENITO'S HAIR SALON

sweet wine—*bianco* or *rosso*. It often comes with a little cookie (*biscotti*) for dipping. Bars don't stay open very late, and the *cicchetti* selection is best early, so start your evening by 18:00. Most bars are closed on Sunday. You can stand around the bar or grab a table in the back—usually for the same price.

Cicchetteria *West of the Rialto Bridge*
Cantina Do Mori is famous with locals (since 1462) and savvy travelers (since 1982) as a classy place for fine wine and *francobollo* (a spicy selection of 20 tiny sandwiches called "stamps"). Choose from the featured wines in the barrel on the bar. Order carefully, or they'll rip you off. From Rialto Bridge walk 200 meters down

Ruga degli Orefici away from St. Mark's Square—then ask
(Mon–Sat 17:00–20:30, closed Sun, stand up only, arrive early
before *cicchetti* are gone, San Polo 429, tel. 041-522-5401).

A few steps from the Rialto fish market you'll find Campo
delle Becarie and two little places serving traditional munchies.
On this square, as you face the restaurant Vini da Pinto, **Ostaria
Sora al Ponte** is to your right, just over the bridge (each item
€1.30, assemble by pointing, Tue–Sun until 24:00, closed Mon),
and **Cantina do Spade** is in the alley directly behind Vini da
Pinto (head around building to your left, take a right through
archway; closed Sun).

Eating near the Rialto Bridge and
Campo San Bartolomeo (East of the Rialto Bridge)
Osteria "Alla Botte" Cicchetteria is an atmospheric place
packed with a young, local, bohemian jazz clientele. It's good for
a *cicchetti* snack with wine at the bar (see the posted, enticing selection of wines by the glass) or for a light meal in the small, smoke-
free room in the back (2 short blocks off Campo San Bartolomeo
in the corner behind the statue—down Calle de la Bissa, notice
the "day after" photo showing a debris-covered Venice after the
notorious 1989 Pink Floyd open-air concert, closed Mon and
Wed, tel. 041-520-9775).

If the statue on the Campo San Bartolomeo walked backward
20 meters, turned left, and went under a passageway, he'd hit
Rosticceria San Bartolomeo. This cheap—if confusing—self-
service restaurant has a likably surly staff (good €4.70 pasta, great
fried mozzarella *al* prosciutto for €1.20, delightful fruit salad, and
€1 glasses of wine, prices listed on wall behind counter, no cover or
service charge, daily 09:30–21:30, tel. 041-522-3569). Take out or
grab a table.

From Rosticceria San Bartolomeo, continue over a bridge to
Campo San Lio (a good landmark). Here, turn left, passing Hotel
Canada and following Calle Carminati straight about 50 meters
over another bridge. On the right is the pastry shop (*pasticceria*) and
straight ahead is Osteria Al Portego (at #6015), both listed below:

Pasticceria Ponte delle Paste is a feminine and pastel salon
de tè, popular for its pastries and apéritifs. Italians love a 15-minute
break, sipping a "spriz" apéritif with friends after a long day's
work before heading home. Ask spritely Monica for a "spriz al
bitter" (white wine, amaro, and soda water, €1.30, or choose from
the menu on the wall) and munch some of the free goodies on the
bar (Wed–Mon after 18:00, closed Tue, Ponte delle Paste).

Osteria Al Portego is a friendly, local-style bar serving great
cicchetti and good meals (Mon–Fri 09:00–22:00, closed Sat–Sun, tel.
041-522-9038). The *cicchetti* here can make a great meal, or consider
sitting down for an actual meal. They have a fine little menu.

The **Devil's Forest Pub**, an air-conditioned bit of England tucked away a block from the crowds, is—strangely—more Venetian these days than the *tipico* places. Locals come here for good English and Irish beer on tap, big salads (€6.70, lunch only), hot bar snacks, and an easy-going ambience (no cover or service charge, fine prices, backgammon and chess boards available-€2.10, meals daily 12:00–15:30, bar snacks all the time, closed Sun in Aug, a block off Campo San Bartolomeo on Calle dei Stagneri, tel. 041-520-0623). Across the street, **Bora Bora Pizzeria** serves pizza and salads from an entertaining menu (daily 12:00–15:00, 19:00–22:30, closed Wed in winter, CC, tel. 041-523-6583).

Osteria al Diavolo e L'Aquasanta, three blocks west of the Rialto, serves good pasta and makes a handy lunch stop for sightseers (Wed–Mon 12:00–15:00, 19:00–22:00, closed Tue, hiding on a quiet street just off Rua Vecchia S. Giovanni, on Calle della Madonna, tel. 041-277-0307).

Eating on or near Campo Santa Maria di Formosa

Campo Santa Maria di Formosa is just plain atmospheric (as most squares with a Socialist Party office seem to be). For a balmy outdoor sit, you could split a pizza with wine on the square. **Bar all' Orologio** has a good setting and friendly service but mediocre "freezer" pizza (happy to split a pizza for pub crawlers, Mon–Sat 06:00–23:00, closed Sun). For a picnic pizza snack on the square, cross the bridge behind the canalside *gelateria* and grab a slice to go from **Cip Ciap Pizza** (Wed–Mon 09:00–21:00, closed Tue; facing *gelateria*, take bridge to the right; Calle del Mondo Novo). Pub crawlers get a salad course at the fruit-and-vegetable stand next to the water fountain (open until about 19:30, closed Sun).

From Campo Santa Maria di Formosa, follow the yellow sign to "S.S. Giov e Paolo" down Calle Longa Santa Maria di Formosa and head down the street to **Osteria al Mascaron,** a delightful little restaurant seemingly made to order for pirates gone good (#5225, Gigi's bar, Mon–Sat 12:00–15:00, 19:00–23:00, closed Sun, reservations smart, tel. 041-522-5995). Their *antipasto della casa* (a €13 plate of mixed appetizers) is fun, and the Pasta Scogliera (€26, rock fish spaghetti for 2) makes a grand meal.

Enoteca Mascareta, a wine bar with much less focus on food, is 30 meters farther down the same street (#5183, Mon–Sat 18:00–01:00, closed Sun, tel. 041-523-0744).

The *gelateria* on the canal at Campo Santa Maria di Formosa is handy (for more, see "Gelato," below).

Eating on Campo S. Angelo

Ristorante Aqua Pazza (literally "crazy water") provides good pizza in a wonderful setting on a square midway between the Rialto, Accademia, and St. Mark's. The owner is from Naples and he delights locals with Amalfi/Naples cuisine. That means perhaps the best—and most expensive—pizza in Venice (Tue–Sun 12:00–15:00, 19:00–23:30, closed Mon, Campo S. Angelo, tel. 041-277-0688).

Eating in Cannaregio

For great local cuisine far beyond the crowds in a rustic Venetian setting, hike to **Osteria Al Bacco** (closed Mon, Fondamenta Cappuccine, Cannaregio #3054, halfway between train station and northernmost tip of Venice, reservations recommended, tel. 041-717-493).

Eating with a Romantic Canalside Setting

Of course, if you want a canal view, it comes with lower quality or a higher price. But the memory is sometimes most important.

Restaurant Al Vagon is popular with tourists because nearly everyone gets a seat right on the canal. The food and prices are acceptable and the ambience glows (moderate prices, a 3-minute walk north of Rialto just before Campo S.S. Appostoli, overlooking canal called Rio dei Santi Apostoli, tel. 041-523-7558).

Ristorante da Raffaele is *the* place for classy food on a quiet canal. It's filled with top-end tourists and locals who want to pay well for the best seafood. The place was a haunt of the avant-garde a few generations ago. Today it's on a main gondolier thoroughfare—in fact, many guests arrive or depart by gondola. Make a reservation if you want a canalside table (you do). While their multilingual menu is designed for the tourists, locals stick with their daily specials (expensive, exactly halfway between Piazza San Marco and the Accademia Bridge at Ponte delle Ostreghe, CC, tel. 041-523-2317). Before leaving, wander around inside to see the owner's fabulous old weapons collection.

Ristorante Cantinone Storico sits on a peaceful canal in Dorsoduro between the Accademia Bridge and the Peggy Guggenheim Collection. It's dressy, specializes in fish, has six or eight tables on the canal, and is worth the splurge (on the canal Rio de S. Vio, reservations wise, tel. 041-523-9577).

Dorsoduro Riviera, the long promenade along the south side of the Dorsoduro (a 5-min walk south of Accademia Bridge), is lined with canal-side restaurants away from the crush of touristic Venice. Places immediately south of the Accademia Bridge (near the Zattere *vaporetto* stop) are decent but more touristic. At the west end (near the S. Basilio *vaporetto* stop), **Trattoria B. Basilio** and **Pizzeria Riviera** (a local fave for pizza), both come with local crowds and wet views.

For a Grand Canal view from the Rialto Bridge, consider **Al Buso**, at the northeast end of the Rialto Bridge. Of the several restaurants that hug the canal near the Rialto, this is recommended by locals as offering the best value (daily 09:00–24:00, Ponte di Rialto #5338, tel. 041-528-9078).

Cheap Meals

A key to cheap eating in Venice is bar snacks, especially stand-up mini-meals in out-of-the-way bars. Order by pointing. *Panini* (sandwiches) are sold fast and cheap at bars everywhere. Basic reliable ham-and-cheese sandwiches (white bread, crusts trimmed) come toasted—simply ask for "toast." Pizzerias are cheap and easy—try for a sidewalk table at a scenic location. For budget eating, I like small *cicchetti* bars (see "Pub-Crawl Dinner," above); for speed, value, and ambience, you can get a filling plate of local appetizers at nearly any of the bars.

The **produce market** that sprawls for a few blocks just past the Rialto Bridge (best 08:00–13:00, closed Sun) is a great place to assemble a picnic. The adjacent fish market is wonderfully slimy. Side lanes in this area are speckled with fine little hole-in-the-wall munchie bars, bakeries, and cheese shops.

The **Mensa DLF**, the public transportation workers' cafeteria, is cheap and open to the public (daily 11:00–14:30, 18:00–22:00). Leaving the train station, turn right on the Grand Canal, walk about 150 meters along the canal, up eight steps, and through the unmarked door.

Gelato

La Boutique del Gelato is one of the best *gelaterias* in Venice (daily 10:00–20:30, closed Dec–Jan, 2 blocks off Campo Santa Maria di Formosa on corner of Salizada San Lio and Calle Paradiso, next to Hotel Bruno, #5727—just look for the crowd).

For late-night gelato at Rialto, try **Michielangelo**, next to the McDonald's on Campo San Bartolomeo, on the St. Mark's side of the Rialto Bridge (daily 10:00–23:30, closed Wed in winter). At St. Mark's Square, the **Al Todaro** *gelateria* opposite the Doge's Palace is open late (daily 08:00–24:00, closed Mon in winter).

Transportation Connections—Venice

By train to: Verona (hrly, 90 min), **Florence** (6/day, 3 hrs), **Dolomites** (8/day to Bolzano, 4 hrs with 1 transfer; catch bus from Bolzano into mountains), **Milan** (hrly, 3–4 hrs), **Rome** (6/day, 5 hrs, slower overnight), **Naples** (change in Rome, plus 2–3 hrs), **Brindisi** (3/day, 11 hrs), **Cinque Terre** (2 La Spezia trains go directly to Monterosso al Mare daily, 6 hrs, at 09:58 and 14:58), **Bern** (4/day, change in Milan, 8 hrs), **Munich** (5/day, 8 hrs), **Paris** (3/day, 11 hrs), **Vienna** (4/day, 9 hrs). Train and *couchette* reservations (about €18) are easily made at a downtown travel agency. Venice train info: 848-888-088.

SIENA

Break out of the Venice-Florence-Rome syndrome and savor Italy's hill towns. Experience the texture of Tuscany, the slumber of Umbria, and the lazy towns of Lazio.

For starters, here's one of my favorites. Tuscany's Siena seems to be every Italy connoisseur's pet town. In my office, whenever Siena is mentioned, someone moans, "Siena? I luuuv Siena!"

Seven hundred years ago, Siena was a major military power in a class with its rivals Florence, Venice, and Genoa. With a population of 60,000, Siena was even bigger than Paris. In 1348 a disastrous plague weakened Siena. Then, in the 1550s, her bitter enemy, Florence, really "salted" her, forever making Siena a nonthreatening backwater. Siena's loss became our sight-seeing gain, as its political and economic irrelevance pickled it purely Gothic. Today Siena's population is still 60,000, compared to Florence's 420,000.

Siena's thriving historic center, with red-brick lanes cascading every which way, offers Italy's best Gothic city experience. Most people do Siena, just 50 kilometers south of Florence, as a day trip, but it's best experienced at twilight. While Florence has the blockbuster museums, Siena has an easy-to-enjoy soul: Courtyards sport flower-decked wells, alleys dead-end at rooftop views, and the sky is a rich blue dome. Right off the bat, Siena becomes an old friend.

For those who dream of a Fiat-free Italy, pedestrians rule in the old center of Siena. Sit at a café on the red-bricked main square that slopes peacefully down to the City Hall. Take time to savor the first European city to eliminate automobile traffic from its main square (1966) and then, just to be silly, wonder what would happen if they did it in your city.

Hill Towns

Planning Your Time

On a quick trip, consider spending three nights in Siena (with a whole-day side trip into Florence and a day to relax and enjoy Siena). Whatever you do, enjoy a sleepy medieval evening in Siena to watch the sky turn an unforgettable blue from the main square. After an evening in Siena, its major sights can be seen in half a day.

If you're basing in Florence and have time to daytrip to only one nearby town—Pisa, San Gimignano, and Siena—choose Siena.

Orientation

Siena lounges atop a hill, stretching its three legs out from Il Campo. This main square, the historic meeting point of Siena's neighborhoods, is pedestrians only. And most of those pedestrians are students from the local university. Everything I mention is within a 15-minute walk of the square. Navigate by landmarks,

Hill Towns: Public Transportation

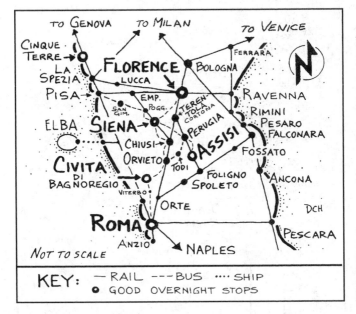

KEY: — RAIL --- BUS •••• SHIP
      ● GOOD OVERNIGHT STOPS

following the excellent system of street-corner signs. The typical visitor sticks to the San Domenico-Il Campo axis.

Siena is one big sight. Its essential individual sights come in two little clusters: the square (city hall, museum, tower) and the cathedral (baptistery, cathedral museum with its surprise viewpoint). Check these sights off and you're free to wander.

Tourist Information: Pick up a free town map from the main TI at #56 on Il Campo; look for the yellow "Change" sign— bad rates, good information (mid-March–mid-Nov Mon–Sat 08:30–19:30, mid-Nov–mid-March Mon–Sat 08:30–14:00, 15:00– 19:00, tel. 0577-280-551, www.siena.turismo.toscana.it). The little TI at San Domenico is for hotel promotion only and sells a Siena map for €0.60.

Museum Passes: Siena offers a variety of passes. If you're staying for two days or more, consider getting the €16 combo ticket (called Siena Itinerari d'Arte) that covers eight sights, includ- ing Museo Civico, Santa Maria della Scala, Museo dell' Opera, Baptistery, Piccolomini Library (in the cathedral), and more (valid for 7 days, sold at participating sites). This pass covers a wider range of sights than the other passes that cost and cover less (e.g., just religious sights or just city museums). In general, if you see two- thirds of the sights covered by a pass, you'll save money.

Helpful Hints

Local Guide: Roberto Bechi, a hardworking Sienese guide, specializes in off-the-beaten-path tours of Siena and the surrounding countryside. Married to an American (Patti) and having run restaurants in Siena and the U.S., Roberto communicates well with Americans. His passions are Sienese culture, Tuscan history, and local cuisine. Book well in advance for full-day tours (ranging in cost from $60–90 per person). Half days ($30–50 per person) cannot be pre-booked during high season but may be available at the last minute (tel. & fax 0577-704-789, www.toursbyroberto.com, e-mail: tourrob@tin.it; for U.S. contact, fax Greg Evans at 540/434-4532).

Internet Access: In this university town, there are lots of places to get plugged in. **Internet Point** is just off Piazza Matteotti, on Via Paradiso (across street from McDonald's), and **Internet Train** is near Il Campo, at Via di Città 121 (tel. 0577-226-366).

Markets: On Wednesday morning, the weekly market—consisting mainly of clothes—sprawls near Piazza Gramsci along Viale Cesare Maccabi and the adjacent Viale XXV Aprile. The produce market is held a block from Il Campo, behind the city hall (Mon–Sat mornings).

Arrival in Siena

By Train: The small train station has a bar, bus office, luggage storage (€2), and lockers (€2.25–2.75, at far end of station, to your left with back to tracks). If you're daytripping, note that luggage can be stored only until 18:30 (that goes for lockers, too).

The station is located on the outskirts of town. To get to the city center, take a taxi or a city bus. The **taxi stand** is to your far right as you exit the station; allow about €8 to your hotel (for taxis at station, call 0577-44504, for taxis at Piazza Matteotti in the center, call 0577-49222). For the **city bus**, buy a €0.75 ticket from the Bus Ticket Office in the station lobby (daily 06:15–19:30, ask for city map—it's free and just a bus route map, but helps get you started). You can also buy a bus ticket from the blue machine in the lobby (touch screen for English and select "urban" for type of ticket). Then cross the parking lot and the street to reach the sheltered bus stop. Catch any orange city bus to get into town (punch ticket in machine on bus to validate it). You'll end up at one of three stops—Piazza Gramsci/Lizza, Piazza Sale, or Stufa Secca—all within several blocks of each other (buses run about every 7 min, fewer on Sun; if you get off at Stufa Secca's tiny square, you're soon faced with two uphill roads—take the one to the right for one block to reach the main drag, Banchi di Sopra.

To get to Siena's train station from the center of Siena, catch the city bus at Piazza del Sale or Stufa Secca; note that bus stops are rarely marked with a "bus stop" sign but instead with a posted schedule and sometimes with yellow lines painted on the pavement, showing a bus-sized rectangle and the word "bus." Confirm with the driver that the bus is going to the *stazione* (stat-zee-OH-nay). Remember to purchase your ticket in advance from a *tabacchi* shop.

By Bus: Some buses arrive in Siena at the train station (see "Arrival By Train," above), others at Piazza Gramsci (a few blocks from city center), and some stop at both. The main bus companies are Sena and Tran. You can store baggage underneath Piazza Gramsci in Sotopassaggio la Lizza (€2.75, daily 07:00–19:30, no overnight).

By Car: Drivers coming from the autostrada take the Porta San Marco exit and follow the "Centro" then "Stadio" signs (stadium, soccer ball). The soccer-ball signs take you to the stadium lot (Parcheggio Stadio, €1.50/hr, €12.50/day) at the huge, bare-brick San Domenico Church. The Fortezza lot nearby charges the same. Or park in the lot underneath the railway station. You can drive into the pedestrian zone (a pretty ballsy thing to do) only to drop bags at your hotel. You can park free in the lot below the Albergo Lea, in white-striped spots behind Hotel Villa Liberty, and behind the Fortezza. (The signs showing a street cleaner and a day of the week indicate which day the street is cleaned; there's a €105 tow-fee incentive to learn the days of the week in Italian.)

Sights—Siena's Main Square

▲▲▲**Il Campo**—Siena's great central piazza is urban harmony at its best. Like a people-friendly stage set, its gently tilted floor fans out from the tower and city hall backdrop. It's the perfect invitation to loiter. Think of it as a trip to the beach without sand or water. Il Campo was located at the historic junction of Siena's various competing districts, or *contrada*, on the old marketplace. The brick surface is divided into nine sections, representing the council of nine merchants and city bigwigs who ruled medieval Siena. At the square's high point, look for the Fountain of Joy, the two naked guys about to be tossed in, and the pigeons politely waiting their turn to gingerly tightrope down slippery spouts to slurp a drink (you can see parts of the original fountain, of which this is a copy, in an interesting exhibit at Siena's Santa Maria della Scala museum, listed below). At the square's low point is the city hall and tower. The chapel located at the base of the tower was built in 1348 as thanks to God for ending the Black Plague (after it killed more than a third of the population). The market area behind the city hall, a wide-open expanse since the Middle Ages, originated as a farming area within the city walls to feed the city in times of siege. Now the morning produce market is held here Monday through Saturday. (The closest public WCs to Il Campo are each about a block away: at Via Beccheria—a few steps off Via de Città—and on Casato di Sotto; €0.60.)

To say Siena and Florence have always been competitive is an understatement. In medieval times, a statue of Venus stood on

Siena

1 PICCOLO HOTEL ETRURIA
2 ALBERGO TRE DONZELLE
3 ALBERGO LA PERLA
4 TO HOTEL DUOMO
5 HOTEL CANNON D' ORO
6 LOCANDA GARIBALDI
7 ALBERGO BERNINI
8 ALMA DOMUS

9 HOTEL CHIUSARELLI
10 TO ALBERGO LEA & HOTEL LIBERTY
11 JOLLY HOTEL SIENA
12 PIZZERIA SPADAFORTE
13 RISTORANTE GALLO NERO
14 OSTERIA IL TAMBURINO
15 OSTERIA DA DIVO

16 IL VERROCHIO
17 CIAO CAFETERIA
18 PALIO MOVIE
19 TO PENSIONE PAL. RAVIZZA
20 HOTEL SANTA CATARINA & PALAZZO VALLI
21 SOTTOPASSAGGIO LA LIZZA
22 LAUNDROMATS

Il Campo (where the Fountain of Joy is today). After the plague hit Siena, the monks blamed this pagan statue. The people cut it to pieces and buried it along the walls of Florence.

▲**Museo Civico**—The Palazzo Publico (City Hall), at the base of the tower, has a fine and manageable museum housing a good sample of Sienese art. In the following order you'll see the Sala Risorgimento, with dramatic scenes of Victor Emmanuel's unification of Italy (surrounded by statues that don't seem to care); the chapel, with impressive inlaid wood chairs in the choir; and the Sala del Mappamondo, with Simone Martini's *Maesta* (Enthroned Virgin) facing the faded *Guidoriccio da Fogliano* (a mercenary providing a more concrete form of protection). Next is the Sala della Pace—where the city's fat cats met. Looking down on the oligarchy during their meetings were two interesting frescoes showing the effects of good and bad government. Notice the whistle-while-you-work happiness of the utopian community ruled by the utopian government (in the better-preserved fresco) and the fate of a community ruled by politicians with more typical values (in a terrible state of repair). The message: Without justice there can be no prosperity. The rural view out the window is essentially the view from the top of the big stairs—enjoy it from here (€6.25, combo-ticket with tower-€9.50, daily March–Oct 10:00–19:00, July–Sept 10:00–23:00, Nov–Jan 10:00–16:00, last entry 45 min before closing, audioguide-€3.75 for 1 person, €5.25 for 2, tel. 0577-292-111).

▲**City Tower (Torre del Mangia)**—Siena gathers around its city hall, not its church. It was a proud symbol; its "declaration of independence" is the tallest secular medieval tower in Italy. The 100-meter-tall Torre del Mangia was named after a hedonistic watchman who consumed his earnings like a glutton consumes food (his chewed-up statue is in the courtyard, to the left as you enter). Its 300 steps get pretty skinny at the top, but the reward is one of Italy's best views (€5.25, combo-ticket with Museo Civico-€9.50, daily 10:00–19:00, mid-July–mid-Sept until 23:00, closed in rain, sometimes long lines, limit of 30 towerists at a time, avoid midday crowd).

▲**Pinacoteca (National Picture Gallery)**—Siena was a power in Gothic art. But the average tourist, wrapped up in a love affair with the Renaissance, hardly notices. This museum takes you on a walk through Siena's art, chronologically from the 12th through the 15th centuries. For the casual sightseer, the Sienese art in the city hall and cathedral museums is adequate. But art fans enjoy this opportunity to trace the evolution of Siena's delicate and elegant art (€4.25, Sun–Mon 08:30–13:15, Tue–Sat 08:15–19:15, plus possibly 20:30–23:30 on Sat in summer, tel. 0577-281-161). From Il Campo, walk out Via di Città to Piazza di Postierla and go left on San Pietro.

Sights—Siena's Cathedral Area

▲▲▲**Duomo**—Siena's cathedral is as Baroque as Gothic gets. The striped facade is piled with statues and ornamentation, and the interior is decorated from top to bottom. The heads of 172 popes peer down from the ceiling, over the fine inlaid art on the floor. This is one busy interior.

To orient yourself in this *panforte* of Italian churches, stand under the dome and think of the church floor as a big clock. You're the middle, and the altar is high noon: you'll find the *Slaughter of the Innocents* roped off on the floor at 10:00, Pisano's pulpit between two pillars at 11:00, Bernini's chapel at 3:00, two Michelangelo statues (next to doorway leading to a shop, snacks, and WC) at 07:00, the library at 08:00, and a Donatello statue at 09:00. Take some time with the floor mosaics in the front. Nicola Pisano's wonderful pulpit is crowded with delicate Gothic storytelling from 1268. To understand why Bernini is considered the greatest Baroque sculptor, step into his sumptuous *Cappella della Madonna del Voto*. This last work in the cathedral, from 1659, is enough to make a Lutheran light a candle. Move up to the altar and look back at the two Bernini statues: Mary Magdalene in a state of spiritual ecstasy, and St. Jerome playing the crucifix like a violinist lost in beautiful music.

The Piccolomini altar is most interesting for its two Michelangelo statues (the lower big ones). Paul, on the left, may be a self-portrait. Peter, on the right, resembles Michelangelo's more famous statue of Moses. Originally contracted to do 15 statues, Michelangelo left the project early (1504) to do his great *David* in Florence.

The Piccolomini Library—worth the €1.50 entry—is brilliantly frescoed with scenes glorifying the works of a pope from 500 years ago. It contains intricately decorated, illuminated music scores and a statue (a Roman copy of a Greek original) of the Three Graces (library open Sun 14:30–19:30, Tue–Sat same as church hours, below). Donatello's bronze statue of St. John the Baptist, in his famous rags, is in a chapel to the right of the library.

Hours: The church is open mid-March–Oct daily 09:00–19:30 but Sun 10:15–13:30 is reserved for worship only, Nov–mid-March Mon–Sat 10:00–13:00, 14:30–17:00, Sun 14:30–17:30 (modest dress required). In September, when much of the elaborate mosaic floor is uncovered, you'll pay a fee to enter the church (€2.75 for Pavimento Cattedrale).

Audioguides: There's a daunting number of audioguides. An audioguide for just the church costs €2.75; to add the library it's €3.75; and to add the Cathedral Museum (Museo dell' Opera de Panorama), pay €5.25. For the church and museum only, it's €4.25. Two headphones are available at a price break.

▲▲**Santa Maria della Scala**—This renovated old hospital-turned-museum (opposite the Duomo entrance) was used as a hospital as recently as the 1980s. Now it displays a lavishly frescoed hall, a worthwhile exhibit on Quercia's *Fountain of Joy* (downstairs), and a so-so archaeological museum (subterranean, in labyrinthine tunnels). The entire museum is a maze, with various exhibitions and paintings plugged in to fill the gaps.

The frescoes in the **Pellegrinaio Hall** show medieval Siena's innovative health care and social welfare system in action (c. 1442, wonderfully described in English). The hospital was functioning as early as the 11th century, nursing the sick and caring for abandoned children (see frescoes). The good work paid off, as bequests and donations poured in, creating the wealth that's evident in the chapels elsewhere on this floor. The Old Sacristy was built to house precious relics, including a Holy Nail thought to be from Jesus' cross.

Downstairs, the engaging exhibit on Jacopo della Quercia's early 15th-century *Fountain of Joy* doesn't need much English description—fortunately—because there isn't much. In the 19th century, the *Fountain of Joy* in Il Campo was deteriorating. It was dismantled and plaster casts were made of the originals. Then replicas were made, restoring the pieces as if brand-new. The *Fountain of Joy* that stands in Il Campo today is a replica. In this exhibit, you'll see the plaster casts of the original, eroded panels paired with their restored twins. Statues originally stood on the edges of the fountain (see the statues and drawings). In general, the pieces at the beginning and end of the exhibit are original. If there's a piece in a dim room near the exit of the exhibit, it's likely an original chunk awaiting cleaning.

The **Archaeological Museum**, way downstairs, consists mainly of pottery fragments in cases lining tunnels after tunnels. It's like being lost in a wine cellar without the wine. Unless there's an exhibition, it's not worth the trip.

Cost and Hours: €5.25, daily 10:00–18:00, Fri–Sat in summer until 23:00, off-season 11:00–16:30. The chapel just inside the door to your left is free (English description inside chapel entrance).

▲**Baptistery**—Siena is so hilly that there wasn't enough flat ground on which to build a big church. What to do? Build a big church and prop up the overhanging edge with the baptistery. This dark and quietly tucked-away cave of art is worth a look (and €2) for its cool tranquility and the bronze panels and angels—by Ghiberti, Donatello, and others—adorning the pedestal of the baptismal font (daily mid-March–Sept 09:00–19:30, Oct 09:00–18:00, Nov–mid-March 10:00–13:00, 14:30–17:00).

▲▲**Cathedral Museum (Museo dell' Opera e Panorama)**—Siena's most enjoyable museum, on the Campo side of the church (look for the yellow signs), was built to house the cathedral's art. The ground floor is filled with the cathedral's original Gothic sculpture by Giovanni Pisano (who spent 10 years in the late 1200s carving and orchestrating the decoration of the cathedral) and a fine Donatello *Madonna and Child.* Upstairs to the left awaits a private audience with Duccio's *Maesta* (Enthroned Virgin). Pull up a chair and study one of the great pieces of medieval art. The flip side of the *Maesta* (displayed on the opposite wall), with 26 panels—the medieval equivalent of pages—shows scenes from the Passion of Christ. Climb onto the "Panorama dal Facciatone." From the first landing, take the skinnier second spiral for Siena's surprise view. Look back over the Duomo and consider this: When rival republic Florence began its grand cathedral, proud Siena decided to build the biggest church in all Christendom. The existing cathedral would be used as a transept. You're atop what would have been the entry. The wall below you, connecting the Duomo with the museum of the cathedral, was as far as Siena got before a plague killed the city's ability to finish the project. Were it completed, you'd be looking straight down the nave—white stones mark where columns would have stood (€5.25, worthwhile €2.75, 40-minute audioguide, daily mid-March–Sept 09:00–19:30, Oct 09:00–18:00, Nov–mid-March 09:00–13:30, tel. 0577-283-048).

Sights—Siena's San Domenico Area

Church of San Domenico—This huge brick church is worth a quick look. The bland interior fits the austere philosophy of the Dominicans. Walk up the steps in the rear for a look at various paintings from the life of Saint Catherine, patron saint of Siena. Halfway up the church on the right you'll see a metal bust of Saint Catherine and her finger in a case. And in the adjacent chapel (to the left) you'll see her actual head (free, daily May–Oct 07:00–13:00, 15:00–19:00, Nov–April 09:00–13:00, 15:00–18:00; WC for €0.60 at far end of parking lot—facing church entrance, it's to your right).

Sanctuary of Saint Catherine—Step into Catherine's cool and peaceful home. Siena remembers its favorite hometown girl, a simple, unschooled, but almost mystically devout girl who, in the mid-1300s, helped convince the pope to return from France to Rome. Pilgrims have come here since 1464. Since then, architects and artists have greatly embellished what was probably a humble home (her family worked as wool dyers). Enter through the court-yard and walk to the far end. The chapel on your right was built over the spot where Saint Catherine received the stigmata while praying. The chapel on your left used to be the kitchen. Go down the stairs to the left of the chapel/kitchen to reach the saint's room. The saint's bare cell is behind see-through doors. Much of the art throughout the sanctuary depicts scenes from the saint's life (free, daily 09:00–12:30, 14:30–18:00, winter 09:00–12:30, 15:30–18:00, Via Tiratoio). It's a few downhill blocks toward the center from San Domenico (follow signs to the Santuario di Santa Caterina).

Nightlife—Join the evening *passeggiata* (peak strolling time is
19:00) along Via Banchi di Sopra with gelato in hand. **Nannini's**
at Piazza Salimbeni has fine gelato (daily 11:00–24:00).

The **Enoteca Italiana** is a good wine bar in a cellar in the
Fortezza/Fortress (Mon 12:00–20:00, Tue–Sat 12:00–24:00,
closed Sun, sample glasses in 3 different price ranges: €1.50,
€2.75, €5.25, bottles and snacks available, CC, cross bridge
and enter fortress, go left down ramp, tel. 0577-288-497).

Shopping—Shops line Via Banchi di Sopra, the *passeggiata* route.
For a department store, try Upim on Piazza Matteotti (Mon–Sat
09:30–19:50, closed Sun). The large, colorful scarves/flags, each
depicting the symbol of one of Siena's 17 different neighborhoods
(such as the wolf, the turtle, and snail, etc.), are easy-to-pack
souvenirs, fun for decorating your home (€7.25 apiece for large
size, sold at souvenir stands).

Siena's Palio

In the Palio, the feisty spirit of Siena's 17 *contrada* (neighborhoods)
lives on. These neighborhoods celebrate, worship, and compete
together. Each even has its own historical museum. *Contrada* pride is
evident any time of year in the colorful neighborhood banners and
parades. (If you hear distant drumming, run to it for some medieval
action.) But *contrada* pride is most visible twice a year—on July 2 and
August 16—when they have their world-famous Palio di Siena. Ten
of the 17 neighborhoods compete (chosen by lot), hurling themselves with medieval abandon into several days of trial races and
traditional revelry. On the big day, jockeys and horses go into their
contrada's church to be blessed ("Go and win," says the priest). It's
considered a sign of luck if a horse makes droppings in the church.

On the evening of the big day, Il Campo is stuffed to the brim
with locals and tourists, as the horses charge wildly around the
square in this literally no-holds-barred race. A horse can win even
if its rider has fallen off. Of course, the winning neighborhood is
the scene of grand celebrations afterward. The grand prize: simply
proving your *contrada* is numero uno. All over town, sketches and
posters depict the Palio. This is not some folkloristic event. It's a
real medieval moment. If you're packed onto the square with 15,000
people who each really want to win, you won't see much, but you'll
feel it. While the actual Palio packs the city, you could side trip in
from Florence to see horse-race trials each of the three days before
the big day (usually at 09:00 and around 19:30).

▲**Palio al Cinema**—This 20-minute film, *Siena, the Palio, and its
History*, helps recreate the craziness of the Palio. See it at the
Cinema Moderno in Piazza Tolomei, two blocks from Il Campo
(€5.25, with this book pay €4.25, or €7.75 for 2; Mon–Sat 09:30–
17:30, English showings generally hourly at :30 past the hour,
schedule posted on door, closed Sun, air-con, tel. 0577-289-201).

Call or drop by to confirm when the next English showing is scheduled—there are usually seven a day. At the ticket desk, you can buy the same show on video (discounted from €13 to €10.50 with this book, video must be labeled "NTSC American System" or it'll be a doorstop at your home).

Sleeping in Siena
(€1.10 = about $1, country code: 39, zip code: 53100)
Sleep Code: **S** = Single, **D** = Double/Twin, **T** = Triple, **Q** = Quad, **b** = bathroom, **s** = shower only, **CC** = Credit Cards accepted, **no CC** = Credit Cards not accepted, **SE** = Speaks English, **NSE** = No English. Breakfast is generally not included. Have breakfast on Il Campo or in a nearby bar.

Finding a room is tough during Easter or the Palio in early July and mid-August. Call ahead any time of year, as Siena's few budget places are listed in all the budget guidebooks. While daytripping tour groups turn the town into a Gothic amusement park in midsummer, Siena is basically yours in the evenings and off-season. Nearly all listed hotels lie between Il Campo and the Church of San Domenico (see page 727). About a third of the listings don't take credit cards, no matter how earnestly you ask. Cash machines are plentiful on the main streets.

Siena has two modern, self-service **Laundromats**: Lavarapido Wash and Dry (daily 08:00–22:00, Via di Pantaneto 38, near Logge del Papa) and Onda Blu (daily 08:00–22:00, Via del Casato di Sotto 17, 50 meters from Il Campo).

Sleeping near Il Campo
Each of these first listings is forgettable but inexpensive, and just a horse wreck away from one of Italy's most wonderful civic spaces.

Piccolo Hotel Etruria, a good bet for a hotel with 19 decent rooms but not much soul, is just off the square (S-€39, Sb-€44, Db-€73, Tb-€91, Qb-€114, breakfast-€4.75, CC, with your back to the tower, leave Il Campo to the right at 2:00, Via Donzelle 1-3, tel. 0577-288-088, fax 0577-288-461, e-mail: hetruria@tin.it, Fattorini family).

Albergo Tre Donzelle has 27 plain, institutional rooms next door to Piccolo Hotel Etruria that makes sense only if you think of Il Campo as your terrace (S-€34, D-€47, Db-€60, CC, Via Donzelle 5, tel. 0577-280-358, fax 0577-223-933, Signora Iannini SE).

Hotel Cannon d'Oro, a few blocks up Via Banchi di Sopra, is spacious and group friendly (30 rooms, Sb-€62, Db-€76.50, Tb-€101, Qb-€119, these discounted prices promised through 2002 with this book, family deals, breakfast-€5, CC, Via Montanini 28, tel. 0577-44321, fax 0577-280-868, e-mail: cannondoro@libero.it, Maurizio and Debora SE).

Locanda Garibaldi is a modest, very Sienese restaurant/

albergo. Gentle Marcello wears two hats, as he runs a fine, busy restaurant downstairs and seven pleasant rooms up a funky, artsy staircase (Db-€67, Tb-€78, family deals, no CC, takes reservations only a few days in advance, half a block downhill off the square at Via Giovanni Dupre 18, tel. 0577-284-204, NSE).

Albergo La Perla is a funky, jumbled, 13-room place. Its narrow maze of hallways, stark rooms, old bedspreads, miniscule bathrooms, and laissez-faire environment works for backpackers (Sb-€41, Db-€57, Tb-€78, no CC, a block off the square on Piazza Independenza at Via della Terme 25, tel. 0577-47144). Attilio and his American wife, Deborah, take reservations only a day or two ahead. Ideally, call the morning you'll arrive.

Splurges: **Hotel Duomo** is a classy place with 23 spacious rooms (Sb-€103, Db-€129, Tb-€170, Qb-€186, includes breakfast, CC, air-con, picnic-friendly roof terrace, free parking, follow Via di Città, which becomes Via Stalloreggi, to Via Stalloreggi 38, 10-min walk to Il Campo, tel. 0577-289-088, fax 0577-43043, www.hotelduomo.it, e-mail: hduomo@comune.siena.it, Stefania SE). If you arrive by train, take a taxi (€8); if you drive, go to Porta San Marco and follow the signs to the hotel, drop off your bags, and then park in nearby "Il Campo" lot.

Pensione Palazzo Ravizza has an aristocratic feel and a peaceful garden. Elegant and friendly, it's a 10-minute walk from Il Campo (Db-€196–212, suites available, includes breakfast and dinner, cheaper mid-Nov–Feb, CC, elevator, back rooms face open country, good restaurant, parking, Via Pian dei Mantellini 34, tel. 0577-280-462, fax 0577-221-597, www.palazzoravizza.it).

Sleeping near San Domenico Church

These hotels are listed in order of closeness to Il Campo—a maximum 10-minute walk. The first two enjoy views of the old town and cathedral (which sits floodlit before me as I type) and are the best values in town.

Albergo Bernini makes you part of a Sienese family in a modest, clean home with nine fine rooms. Friendly Nadia and Mauro welcome you to their spectacular view terrace for breakfast and picnic lunches and dinners (the resident bird on the terrace is named Romeo). Outside of breakfast and checkout time, Mauro, an accomplished accordionist, might play a song for you if you ask (Sb-€67, D-€62, Db-€78, breakfast-€6.25, less in winter, no CC, midnight curfew, on the main San Domenico-Il Campo drag at Via Sapienza 15, tel. & fax 0577-289-047, www.albergobernini.com, e-mail: hbernin@tin.it, their son, Alessandro, SE).

Alma Domus is ideal—unless nuns make you nervous, you need a double bed, or you plan on staying out past the 23:30 curfew (no mercy given). This quasi-hotel (not a convent) is run with firm but angelic smiles by sisters who offer clean and quiet rooms for a steal and save the best views for foreigners. Bright lamps, quaint balconies, fine views, grand public rooms, top security, and a friendly atmosphere make this a great value. The check-out time is strictly 10:00, but they will store your luggage in their secure courtyard (Db-€57, Tb-€70, Qb-€88, breakfast-€5.75—not always available, no CC, ask for view room—*con vista*, elevator, from San Domenico walk downhill with the church on your right toward the view, turn left down Via Camporegio, make a U-turn at the little chapel down the brick steps to Via Camporegio 37, tel. 0577-44177 and 0577-44487, fax 0577-47601, NSE).

Hotel Chiusarelli, a proper hotel in a beautiful building with a handy location, comes with lots of traffic noise at night—ask for a quieter room in the back (50 rooms, S-€55, Sb-€70, Db-€101, Tb-€134, includes big buffet breakfast, CC, suites available, air-con, pleasant garden terrace, across from San Domenico at Viale Curtatone 15, tel. 0577-280-562, fax 0577-271-177, www.essentia.org/chiusarelli, e-mail: chiusare@tin.it, SE).

Jolly Hotel Siena, for people who want a four-star hotel, has 126 rooms that are modern but not plush. Across the street from Piazza Gramsci, it's convenient if you're arriving by bus and if you've got lots of luggage—and money (Sb-€124–160, Db-€170–233, includes breakfast, CC, nonsmoking floor, Piazza La Lizza, tel. 0577-288-448, fax 0577-41272, e-mail: siena@jollyhotels.it).

Hotel Villa Liberty has 18 big, bright, comfortable rooms (S-€78, Db-€124, includes breakfast, CC, only 1 room with twin beds, elevator, bar, air-con, TVs, courtyard, etc., facing fortress at Viale V. Veneto 11, tel. 0577-44966, fax 0577-44770, www.villaliberty.it, SE).

Albergo Lea is a sleepable place in a residential neighborhood a few blocks away from the center (past San Domenico) with 11 rooms and easy parking (S-€52, Db-€85, Tb-€105, cheaper in winter, includes breakfast, CC, rooftop terrace, Viale XXIV Maggio 10, tel. & fax 0577-283-207, SE).

Sleeping Farther from the Center

The first three listings are near Porta Romana.

Hotel Santa Caterina is a three-star, 18th-century place best for drivers who need air-conditioning. Professionally run with real attention to quality, it has 22 comfortable rooms with a delightful garden (Sb-€98, small Db-€98, Db-€133, Tb-€179, mention this book to get these prices, includes breakfast, CC; garden side is quieter but street side—with multipaned windows—isn't bad, fridge in room, parking-€12/day—request when you reserve, 100 meters outside Porta Romana at Via E.S. Piccolomini 7, tel. 0577-221-105, fax 0577-271-087, www.sienanet.it/hsc,

e-mail: hsc@sienanet.it, SE). A city bus runs frequently (Mon–Sat
4/hr, Sun 2/hr) to the town center. A taxi to/from the station
runs around €8.

Palazzo di Valli, with 11 spacious rooms and a garden, is 800
meters beyond Porta Romana (the Roman gate) and feels like it's
in the country. Catch the city bus into town (Db-€140, Tb-€170,
includes breakfast, CC, parking, Via E.S. Piccolomini, bus to
center Mon–Sat 4/hr, Sun 2/hr; tel. 0577-226-102, fax 0577-
222-255, Camarda family). From the autostrada, exit at Siena
Sud in the direction of Porta Romana.

Casa Laura has five clean, well-maintained rooms, some
with brick-and-beam ceilings (Db-€83 with breakfast, €73
without; cheaper off-season CC, Via Roma 3, 10-min walk
from Il Campo, tel. 0577-226-061, fax 0577-225-240, e-mail:
labenci@tin.it).

Frances' Lodge is a small farmhouse B&B 1.5 kilometers
out of Siena. English-speaking Franca and Franco rent four
modern rooms in a rustic yet elegant old place with a swimming
pool, peaceful garden, eight acres of olive trees and vineyards,
and great Siena views (Db-€135–165, easy parking, near shuttle
bus into town, Strada di Valdipugna 2, tel. & fax 0577-281-061,
www.franceslodge.it).

Hostel: Siena's **Guidoriccio Youth Hostel** has 120 cheap
beds, but, given the hassle of the bus ride and the charm of downtown Siena at night, I'd skip it (office open 15:00–01:00, €13 beds
in doubles, triples, and dorms with sheets and breakfast, CC,
bus #10 from train station or bus #15 from Piazza Gramsci, Via
Fiorentina 89 in Stellino neighborhood, tel. 0577-52212, SE).

Eating in Siena

Sienese restaurants are reasonable by Florentine and Venetian
standards. Even with higher prices, lousy service, and lower-
quality food, consider eating on Il Campo—a classic European
experience. **Pizzeria Spadaforte**, at the edge of Il Campo, has a
decent setting, mediocre pizza, and tables steeper than its prices
(daily 12:00–16:00, 19:30–22:30, CC, to far right of city tower
as you face it, tel. 0577-281-123).

For authentic Sienese dining at a fair price, eat at **Locanda
Garibaldi**, down Via Giovanni Dupre at #18, within a block of
Il Campo (€14.50 *menu*, Sun–Fri opens at 12:00 for lunch and
19:00 for dinner, arrive early to get a table, closed Sat). Marcello
does a nice, little *piatto misto dolce* for €2.75, featuring several
local desserts with sweet wine.

Ristorante Gallo Nero is a friendly "grotto" for authentic
Tuscan cuisine. This "black rooster" serves a mean *ribollita*
(hearty Tuscan bean soup) and offers a €21 "medieval menu,"
as well as several Tuscan *menus*, starting at €14.50 (daily

12:00–15:30, 19:00–24:00, CC, 3 blocks down Via del Porrione from Il Campo at #65, tel. 0577-284-356).

Il Verrochio, a block away—tucked between a church and loggia, serves a decent €11.50 *menu* in a cozy, wood-beamed setting (daily 12:00–14:30, 19:00–22:00, closed Wed in winter, CC, Logge del Papa 1, tel. 0577-284-062).

Antica Osteria Da Divo is the place for a fine €40 meal. The kitchen is creative, the food is fresh and top notch, and the ambience is candlelit. You'll get a basket of exotic fresh breads. The "black pearls"—with a truffle sauce—are sumptuous. The lamb goes baaa in your mouth. And the chef is understandably proud of his desserts (daily 12:00–14:30, 19:00–22:00, CC, Via Franciosa 29, facing baptistery door, take the far right and walk one long curving block, reserve for summer eves, tel. 0577-284-381).

Osteria la Chiacchera, while touristy, is an atmospheric, tasty, and affordable hole-in-the-brick-wall (daily 12:00–15:30, 19:00–24:00, CC, 2 rooms, below Pension Bernini at Costa di San Antonio 4, reservations wise, skip the *trippa*—tripe, tel. 0577-280-631).

Osteria Nonna Gina wins praise from locals for its good quality and prices (Tue–Sun 12:30–14:30, 19:30–20:30, closed Mon, CC, Piano dei Mantellini 2, 10-min walk from Il Campo, near Hotel Duomo, tel. 0577-287-247).

Trattoria La Tellina has patient waiters and great food, including homemade tiramisu. Arrive early to get a seat (Via dell Terme 52, between St. Catherine's House and Piazza Tolomei—where Palio film is shown, tel. 0577-283-133).

Le Campane, two blocks off Il Campo, is classy and a little pricey (daily 12:15–14:30, 19:15–22:00, closed Mon in winter, CC, indoor/outdoor seating, a few steps off Via di Città at Via delle Campane 6, tel. 0577-284-035).

Osteria il Tamburino is friendly, small, and intimate and serves up tasty meals (Mon–Sat 12:00–14:30, 19:00–20:30, closed Sun, CC, follow Via di Città off Il Campo, becomes Stalloreggi, Via Stalloreggi 11, tel. 0577-280-306).

Snack with a view from a small balcony overlooking Il Campo. Survey these three places from Il Campo to see which has a free table. On Via di Città, you'll find **Gelateria Artigiana**, which has perhaps Siena's best ice cream, and **Barbero d'Oro**, which serves cappuccino and *panforte* (€1.75/100 grams; balcony with 2 tables, closed Sun). **Bar Paninoteca** is on Vicolo di S. Paolo, on the stairs leading down to Il Campo (sandwiches, has a row of chairs on balcony, closed Mon).

At the bottom of Il Campo, a **Ciao** cafeteria offers easy self-service meals, no ambience, and no views. The crowded **Spizzico**, a pizza counter in the front half of Ciao, serves huge, inexpensive quarter pizzas; on sunny days, people take the pizza, trays and all, out on Il Campo for a picnic (daily 12:00–15:00, 19:00–21:00, nonsmoking section— *non fumatori*—in back, CC only in cafeteria, to left of city tower as you face it).

Cheap Meals and Picnics: Budget eaters look for *pizza al taglio* shops, scattered throughout Siena, selling pizza by the slice. Picnickers enjoy the market held mornings (except Sun) behind Il Campo, on Piazza del Mercato. Of the grocery shops scattered throughout town, the biggest is called simply **Alimentari**; it's one block off Piazza Matteotti, toward Il Campo. Their pesto is the besto (Mon–Sat 08:00–19:30, Via Pianigiani).

Sienese Sweets: All over town, Prodotti Tipici shops sell Sienese specialties. Siena's claim to caloric fame is its *panforte*, a rich, chewy concoction of nuts, honey, and candied fruits that impresses even fruitcake haters (although locals prefer a white macaroon-and-almond cookie called *ricciarelli*).

Transportation Connections—Siena

By bus to: Florence (2/hr, 1.25–2 hrs, by Tran bus), **Rome** (7/day, 3 hrs, by Sena bus, arrives at Rome's Tiburtina station), **Assisi** (2/day, 2 hrs, by Sena bus; the morning bus goes direct to Assisi, the afternoon bus might terminate at Santa Maria Angeli, from here catch a local bus to Assisi, 2/hr, 20 min), **San Gimignano** (6/day, 1.25 hrs, by Tran bus, more frequent with transfer in Poggibonsi). Schedules get sparse on Sunday.

Buses depart Siena from Piazza Gramsci, the train station, or both; confirm when you purchase your ticket. You can get tickets for Tran buses or Sena buses at the train station (Tran bus office: Mon–Sat 05:50–19:30; for Sena, buy tickets at *tabacchi* shop unless they've opened a separate office in the station), or easier and more central, under Piazza Gramsci at Sottopassaggio La Lizza (Tran bus office: daily 05:50–19:30, tel. 0577-204-246, toll-free 800-373-760; Sena bus office: Mon–Sat 07:45–19:45, Sun 15:30–19:30, tel. 0577-283-203).

Sottopassaggio La Lizza, under Piazza Gramsci, has a cash machine (neither bus office accepts credit cards), luggage storage (€2.75/day, €1.50/half day, daily 07:00–19:30, no overnight storage), posted bus schedules, TV monitors (listing imminent departures), an elevator, and expensive WCs (€0.55). If you decide to depart Siena after the bus offices close, you can buy the ticket directly from the driver.

On schedules, the fastest buses are marked *corse rapide*. Note that if a schedule lists your departure point as Via Tozzi or La Lizza, you catch the bus at Piazza Gramsci (Via Tozzi is the street that runs alongside Piazza Gramsci and La Lizza is the name of the bus station).

By train to: Florence (9/day, 1.75 hrs, last one at 21:00).

ASSISI

Assisi is famous for its hometown boy, St. Francis, who made very good.

Around the year 1200, a simple friar from Assisi challenged the decadence of church government and society in general with a powerful message of non-materialism, simplicity, and a "slow down and smell God's roses" lifestyle. Like Jesus, Francis taught by example. A huge monastic order grew out of his teachings, which were gradually embraced (some would say co-opted) by the church. Clare, St. Francis' partner in poverty, founded the Order of the Poor Clares. Catholicism's purest example of simplicity is now glorified in beautiful churches. In 1939, Italy made Francis and Clare its patron saints.

Francis' message of love and sensitivity to the environment has a broad and timeless appeal. But any pilgrimage site will be commercialized, and the legacy of St. Francis is Assisi's basic industry. In summer, this Umbrian town bursts with flash-in-the-pan Francis fans and Franciscan knickknacks. Those able to see past the tacky friar mementos can actually have a "travel on purpose" experience.

Planning Your Time

Assisi is worth a day and a night. The town has half a day of sightseeing and another half a day of wonder. The essential sight is the Basilica of St. Francis. For a good visit, take the Assisi Welcome Walk (below), ending at the basilica. Schedule time to linger on the main square. Hikers enjoy sunset at the castle.

Most visitors are daytrippers. While the town's a zoo by day, it's a delight at night. Assisi after dark is closer to a place Francis could call home.

Orientation

Crowned by a ruined castle at the top, Assisi spills downhill to its famous Basilica of St. Francis. The town is beautifully preserved and rich in history. The 1997 earthquake did more damage to the tourist industry than to the local buildings. Fortunately tourists are returning—whether art-lovers or pilgrims or both—drawn by Assisi's powerful sights.

Tourist Information: The TI is in the center of town on Piazza del Comune (Mon–Sat 08:00–14:00, 15:30–18:30, Sun 09:00–13:00, tel. 075-812-534; visit www.umbria2000.it for info on Umbria).

Also on (or just off) Piazza Commune, you'll find the Roman temple of Minerva, a Romanesque tower, banks, a finely frescoed pharmacy, and an underground Roman Forum. A combo ticket (*biglietto cumulativo*) for €5.25 covers three sights—Rocca Maggiore, Pinacoteca (paintings), and Roman Forum; you'd need to see all three sights to save money (sold at participating sites). Your hotel may give you an Assisi Card, which offers discounts at some restaurants and on parking. Market day is Saturday on the Piazza Matteotti.

Arrival in Assisi

By Train and Bus: Buses connect Assisi's train station with the old town of Assisi on the hilltop (€0.60, 2/hr, about 15–20 min), stopping at Piazza Unita d'Italia (near Basilica of St. Francis), then Largo Properzio (near Basilica of St. Clare), and finally Piazza Matteotti (top of old town). Going to the old town, buses usually leave from the station at :16 and :46 past the hour. Going to the station from the old town, buses usually run from Piazza Matteotti at :10 and :40 past the hour, and from Piazza Unita d'Italia at :17 and :47 past the hour. At Piazza Unita d'Italia, there are two bus stops (*fermata bus*): one sign reads *per f.s. S.M. Angeli* (take this bus to get to the train station), and the other reads *per P. Matteotti* (this bus goes to the top of the old town).

By Taxi: Taxis from the station to the old town run about €10. There are legitimate extra charges for luggage and night service, but beware: Many taxis rip off tourists by using tariff #2; the meter should be set on tariff #1 (€2.50 drop). You can check bags at the train station (€2.50, daily 07:00–19:30) but not in the old town. When departing the old town of Assisi, you'll find taxi stands at Piazza Unita d'Italia and the Basilica of St. Clare (or have your hotel call for you, tel. 075-812-600).

By Car: Drivers just coming in for the day should follow the signs to Piazza Matteotti's wonderful underground parking garage at the top of the town (which comes with bits of ancient Rome in the walls, €1.20/hr, or €11.50/day with Assisi Card—offered by many hotels; open 07:00–21:00, until 23:00 in summer).

Helpful Hints

Travel Agency: You can get bus and train tickets at Agenzia Viaggi Stoppini, between Piazza del Comune and the Basilica of St. Clare (Mon–Fri 09:00–12:30, 15:30–19:00, Sat 09:00–12:30, closed Sun, Corso Mazzini 31, tel. 075-812-597). Note that they don't sell tickets to Siena; you buy these on the bus (see "Transportation Connections," below).

Internet Access: Internet World has several computers and a nonsmoking room (Thu–Tue 11:00–13:00, 14:00–22:00, Wed 16:00–22:00, Via San Gabriele 25, a long block off Piazza Comune, tel. 075-812-327).

Guide: Anne Robichaud, an American who has lived here since 1975, gives pricey though informative tours of the town and the countryside. Make it clear what you want (half-day/from $60 per person, full day/from $90, tel. 075-802-334, fax 075-813-698, www.annesitaly.com). Thanks to Anne for her help with the following self-guided walk.

Assisi Welcome Walk

There's much more to Assisi than St. Francis and what all the blitz tour groups see.

This walk, rated ▲▲, covers the town from Piazza Matteotti at the top, down to the Basilica of St. Francis at the bottom. To get to Piazza Matteotti, ride the bus from the train station (or from Piazza Unita d'Italia) to the last stop, or drive there (underground parking with Roman ruins).

The Roman Arena: Start 50 meters beyond Piazza Matteotti (at intersection at far end of parking lot, away from the city center—see map). A lane, named Via Anfiteatro Romano, leads to a cozy circular neighborhood built around a Roman arena. Assisi was an important Roman town. Circle the arena counterclockwise (the chain stretched across the road is to keep cars out, not you). Imagine how colorful the town laundry must have been in the last generation when the women of Assisi gathered here to do their wash. Adjacent to the laundry is a small rectangular pool filled with water; above it are the coats of arms of the town's leading families. A few steps farther, hike up the stairs to the top of the hill for an aerial view of the oval arena. The Roman stones have long been absorbed into the medieval architecture. It was Roman tradition to locate the arena outside of town . . . which this was. Continue on. The lane leads down to a city gate.

Umbrian View: Leave Assisi at the Porta Perlici for a commanding view. Umbria, called the "green heart of Italy," is the country's geographical center and only landlocked state. Enjoy the greens: silver green on the valley floor (olives), emerald green 10 meters below you (grape vines), and deep green on the hillsides (evergreen oak trees). Also notice Rocca Maggiore (big castle),

Assisi

① HOTEL ASCESI
② HOTEL BELVEDERE
③ CAMERE ANNALISA
④ HOTEL IDEALE
⑤ ALBERGO DUOMO
⑥ HOTEL FORTEZZA
⑦ SRA. GAMBACORTA'S STORE
⑧ LA PALLOTTA ROOMS
⑨ LA PALLOTTA REST.
⑩ HOTEL SOLE & PRIORI
⑪ HOTEL UMBRA

*NOT TO SCALE...
PIAZZA COMUNE TO:
• BASILICA = 10 MIN. WALK DOWNHILL
• ROCCA MAGGIORE = 10 MIN. WALK UPHILL
• ROCCA MINORE = 15 MIN. WALK UPHILL

ROCCA MINORE
5 KM TO HERMITAGE
PORTA PERLICI
START WALK
PORTA CAPP.
ROCCA MAGGIORE
ROCCA
PIAZZA MATTEOTI
EREMO CARC.
TEMPLE OF MINERVA
COLLE
S. RUFINO
PORTA NUOVA AND LARGO PROP.
PORTA S. GIACOMO
ALESSI
VIA S. CROCE
S. PABLO
PIAZZA COMUNE
ARETINO
METASTASIO
SEM.
AGNESE
BASILICA S. CHIARA
BASILICA OF ST FRANCIS
VIA S. FRANCESCO
FONTEBELLA
CRISTOFANI
S. APOLL.
WALLS
VIA BORGO S.P.
CITY
PIAZZA UNITA D' ITALIA
TO PERUGIA & FLORENCE
3 KILOMETERS TO TRAIN STATION & S.M. ANGELI
DCH

a fortress providing townsfolk a refuge in times of attack, and, behind you, atop the hill, Rocca Minore (little castle). Now walk back to Piazza Matteotti. Go to the opposite end of this piazza, to the corner with the blobby stone tower. As you walk down the lane next to this tower, you'll see the big dome of the Church of San Rufino. Walk to the courtyard of the church; the big bell tower is on your left.

Church of San Rufino: While Francis is Italy's patron saint, Assisi's is Rufino—the town's first bishop (he was martyred and buried here in the third century). The church is 12th-century Romanesque with a neoclassical interior. Enter the church (daily 07:00–12:00, 14:00–19:00). To your right (in the back corner of the church) is the baptismal font where Francis and Clare were baptized. Traditionally, the children of Assisi are still baptized here.

The striking glass panels in the church floor reveal ancient foundations dating from Roman times, discovered only recently. You're walking on history. After the 1997 earthquake, the church was checked from ceiling to floor by structural inspectors. When they looked under the paving stones, they discovered bodies (it used to be a common practice to bury people in church, until

Napoleon decreed otherwise) and underneath the graves, Roman foundations and some animal bones (suggesting the possibility of animal sacrifice). There might have been a Roman temple here. It's plausible, because churches were often built on the sites of ruined Roman temples. Standing at the back of the church (facing the altar), look left at the Roman cistern (enclosed with a black iron fence). This was once the town's water source when under attack.

Underneath the church, alongside the Roman ruins, are the foundations of an earlier Church of San Rufino, now the crypt. When it's open in summer, you can go below to see the saint's sarcophagus.

Medieval Architecture: When you leave the church, take a sharp left (on Via Dono Doni—say it fast three times), following the sign to Santa Chiara. Take the first right, down the stairway. At the bottom, notice the pink limestone pavement. The medieval town survives. The arches built over doorways indicate that the buildings date from the 12th through the 14th century. The vaults that turn lanes into tunnels are reminders of medieval urban expansion (mostly 15th century). While the population grew, people wanted to live protected within the walls, so Assisi became more dense. Medieval Assisi had five times the population density of today's Assisi. Notice the floating gardens. Assisi has a flowering balcony competition each June. When you arrive at a street, turn left, going slightly uphill for a block, then jog right, following the "S. Chiara" sign down to the Basilica of St. Clare.

When you reach the basilica, turn left and walk to the arch sprouting out of the back of the church. Across the street from the arch is a remarkable manger scene, created by Silvano Gion-bolina. Jesus and mom are in the foreground of a village that is going about its business, as an angel with gently fluttering wings perches on the manger. People chat and stroll, the sheep graze in motion, and a worker scoops water from a well. On the manger is written, *Io sono la via, la verita, e la vita*, translated "I am the way, the truth, and the light." No one in the town seems to be listening except his mom.

Basilica of St. Clare (Santa Chiara): For a description, see "More Sights—Assisi," below.)

Another Umbrian View: Belly up to the viewpoint in front of the basilica. On the left is the convent of St. Clare; below you, the olive grove of the Poor Clares since the 13th century; and, in the distance, a grand Umbrian view. Assisi overlooks the richest and biggest valley in otherwise hilly and mountainous Umbria. The municipality of Assisi has 29,000, but only 1,000 live in the old town. The lower town grew up with the coming of the railway in the 19th century. In the haze, the blue-domed church is St. Mary of the Angels (Santa Maria degli Angeli, see description below), the cradle of the Franciscan order, marking the place

St. Francis lived and worked. This church, a popular pilgrimage sight today, is the first Los Angeles. Think about California. The Franciscans named L.A. (after this church), San Francisco, and even Santa Clara.

Arches and Artisans: From Via Santa Chiara, you can see two arches over the street. The arch at the back of the church dates from 1265. (Beyond it—out of view, the Porta Nuova, from 1316, marks the final expansion of Assisi.) Toward the city center (on Via Santa Chiara, the high road), an arch indicates the site of the Roman wall.

Forty meters before this arch, pop into the souvenir shop at #1b. The plaque over the door explains that the old printing press (a national monument now, just inside the door) was used to make fake documents for Jews escaping the Nazis in 1943 and 1944. The shop is run by a couple of artisans: the man makes frames out of medieval Assisi timbers; the woman makes the traditional Assisi, or Franciscan, cross-stitch.

Just past the gate and on your left is the La Pasteria natural products shop at Corso Mazzini 18b (across from entrance of Hotel Sole). Cooks love to peruse Umbrian wines, herbs, pâtés, and truffles, and sample an aromatic "fruit infusion." Ahead at Corso Mazzini 14d, the small shop (Poiesis) sells olive-wood carvings. Drop in. It's said that St. Francis made the first nativity scene to help teach the Christmas message. That's why you'll see so many of these in Assisi. Even today, nearby villages are enthusiastic about their "living" manger scenes. The Lisa Assisi shop (at Corso Mazzini 25b, across the street and to your right) has a delightful bargain basement with surviving bits of a 2000-year-old mortarless Roman wall. Ahead of you, the columns of the Temple of Minerva mark the Piazza del Comune (described below). Sit at the fountain on the square for a few minutes of people-watching—don't you love Italy? Within 200 meters of this square, on either side, were the medieval walls. Imagine a commotion of 5,000 people confined within these walls. No wonder St. Francis needed an escape for some peace and quiet. I'll meet you over at the temple on the square.

Roman Temple/Christian Church: Assisi has always been a spiritual center. The Romans went to great lengths to make this Temple of Minerva a centerpiece of their city. Notice the columns cutting into the stairway. It was a tight fit here on the hilltop. The stairs probably went down triple the distance you see today. The church of Santa Maria sopra (over) Minerva was added in the ninth century. The bell tower is 13th century. Pop inside the temple/church (Mon–Sat 07:15–19:00, from 08:30 on Sun, closes at 17:00 in winter). Today's interior is 17th-century Baroque. Flanking the altar are the original Roman temple floor stones. You can even see the drains for the bloody sacrifices that took place here. Behind the statues of Peter and Paul, the original Roman embankment peeks through.

A few doors back toward the fountain, step into the 16th-century vaults from the old fish market. Notice the Italian flair for design. Even a smelly fish market was finely decorated. The art style is "grotesque"—literally a painting in a grotto. This was painted in the early 1500s, a few years after Columbus brought turkeys back from the New World. The turkeys painted here may just be that bird's European debut. (Public WCs are a few steps off Piazza del Comune; near the fountain, go through Via dell' Arco dei Priori, then down the street on the left.)

Church of San Stefano: From the main square, hike past the temple up the high road, Via San Paolo. After 200 meters, a sign directs you down a lane to San Stefano, which used to be outside the town walls in the days of St. Francis. Legend is that its bells miraculously rang on October 3, 1226, the day St. Francis died. Surrounded by cypress, fig, and walnut trees, it's a delightful bit of offbeat Assisi. Step inside. This is the typical rural Italian Romanesque church—no architect, just built by simple stone masons who put together the most basic design. The lane zigzags down to Via San Francesco. Turn right and walk under the arch toward the Basilica of St. Francis.

Via San Francesco: This was the main drag leading from the town to the basilica holding the body of St. Francis. Francis was a big deal even in his own day. He died in 1226 and was made a saint in 1228—the same year the basilica's foundations were laid—and his body was moved in by 1230. Assisi was a big-time pilgrimage center, and this street was a booming place. Notice the fine medieval balcony just below the arch. A few meters farther down (on the left), cool yourself at the fountain. The hospice next door was built in 1237 to house pilgrims. Notice the three surviving faces of its fresco: Jesus, Francis, and Clare.

Basilica of St. Francis

A ▲▲▲ sight, the Basilica de San Francesco is one of the artistic and religious highlights of Europe. In 1226, St. Francis was buried (with the outcasts he had stood by) outside of his town on the "Hill of the Damned." Now called the "Hill of Paradise," it's frescoed from top to bottom by the leading artists of the day: Cimabue, Giotto, Simone Martini, and Pietro Lorenzetti. A 13th-century historian wrote, "No more exquisite monument to the Lord has been built."

From a distance you see the huge arcades "supporting" the basilica. These were 15th-century quarters for the monks. The arcades lining the square leading to the church housed medieval pilgrims.

There are three parts to the church: the upper basilica, the lower basilica, and the saint's tomb (below the lower basilica). In the 1997 earthquake, the lower basilica (with nine-foot-thick walls) was undamaged. The upper basilica (with three-foot-thick walls and bigger windows) was damaged. After restoration was completed, the entire church was reopened to visitors in late '99 (free, daily 06:30–19:00, relic chapel in lower basilica closes at 18:30, tel. 075-819-0084, e-mail: assisisanfrancesco@krenet.it; a WC is a half block away—from basilica's courtyard, look up the road at the squat brick building; walk alongside the right of it to find the WC). Note that modest dress is required in the basilica—no sleeveless tops or shorts for men or women.

The Basilica of St. Francis, a theological work of genius, can be difficult for the 21st-century tourist/pilgrim to appreciate. Since the basilica is the reason most visit Assisi, and the message of St. Francis has even the least devout blessing the town Vespas, I've designed a *Mona Winks*–type tour with the stress on the place's theology rather than art history. It's adapted from the excellent *The Basilica of Saint Francis—A Spiritual Pilgrimage*, by Goulet, McInally, and Wood (€2 in bookshop).

Start at the lower entrance in the courtyard. The information center (Mon–Sat 09:00–12:00, 14:00–17:00, Sun 14:00–17:00, tel. 075-819-0084) is opposite the entry to the lower basilica. At the doorway of the lower basilica, look up and see St. Francis (in a small gold triangle), who greets you with a Latin inscription (arching over the doorway). Sounding a bit like John Wayne, he says the equivalent of "Slow down and be joyful, pilgrim. You've reached the Hill of Paradise, and this church will knock your spiritual socks off." Start with the tomb (turn left into the nave, midway down the nave to your right follow signs and go downstairs to the tomb). Grab a pew (for more light to read by, sit in back).

The message: Francis' message caused a stir. He traded a life of power and riches for one of obedience, poverty, and chastity. The Franciscan existence (Brother Sun, Sister Moon, and so on) is a space where God, man, and the natural world frolic harmoniously. Franciscan friars, known as the "Jugglers of God," were a joyful part of the community. In an Italy torn by fighting between towns and families, Francis promoted peace and the restoration of order. (He set an example by reconstructing a crumbled chapel.) While the Church was waging bloody Crusades, Francis pushed ecumenism and understanding. Even today the leaders of the world's great religions meet here for summits.

This rich building seems to contradict the teachings of the poor monk it honors, but it was built as an act of religious and civic pride to remember the hometown saint. It was also designed, and still functions, as a pilgrimage center and a splendid classroom.

The tomb: In medieval times, pilgrims came to Assisi because St. Francis was buried here. Holy relics were the "ruby slippers" of medieval Europe. They gave you power—got your prayers answered and helped you win wars—and ultimately helped you get back to your eternal Kansas. Assisi made no bones about promoting the saint's relics but hid his tomb for obvious reasons of security. Not until 1818 was the tomb opened to the public. The saint's remains are above the altar in the stone box with the iron ties. His four closest friends are buried in the corners of the room. Opposite the altar, up four steps in between the entrance and exit, notice the small gold box behind the metal grill; this contains the remains of Francis' rich Roman patron, Jacopa dei Settesoli. Climb back to the lower nave.

The lower basilica is appropriately Franciscan, subdued and Romanesque. The nave was frescoed with parallel scenes from the lives of Christ and Francis—connected by a ceiling of stars. Unfortunately, after the church was built and decorated, the popularity of the Franciscans meant side chapels needed to be built. Huge arches were cut out of some scenes, but others survive. In the fresco directly above the entry to the tomb, Christ is being taken down from the cross (just the bottom half of his body can be seen, to the left), and it looks like the story is over. Defeat. But in the opposite fresco (above the tomb's exit), we see Francis preaching to the birds, reminding the faithful that the message of the Gospel survives.

These stories directed the attention of the medieval pilgrim to the altar, where, through the sacraments, he met God. The church was thought of as a community of believers sailing toward God. The prayers coming out of the nave (*navis*, or ship) fill the triangular sections of the ceiling—called *vele*, or sails—with spiritual wind. With a priest for a navigator and the altar for a helm, faith propels the ship.

Stand behind the altar (toes to the bottom step) and look up. The three scenes in front of you are, to the right, "Obedience" (Francis wearing a yoke); to the left, "Chastity" (in a tower of purity held up by two angels); and straight ahead, "Poverty." Here Jesus blesses the marriage as Francis slips a ring on Lady Poverty. In the foreground two "self-sufficient" merchants (the new rich of a thriving North Italy) are throwing sticks and stones at the bride. But Poverty, in her patched wedding dress, is fertile and strong, and even those brambles blossom into a rosebush crown.

Putting your heels to the altar and bending back like a drum major, look up at Francis, who traded a life of earthly simplicity for glory in heaven. Now, turn to the right and march...

In the corner, steps lead down into the relic chapel. Circle the room clockwise. You'll see the silver chalice and plate Francis used for the bread and wine of the Eucharist (in small dark windowed case set into wall, marked *Calice con Patena*). Francis believed that his personal possessions should be simple, but the items used for worship should be made of the finest materials. In the corner display case is a small section of the hair cloth worn by Francis as penitence. In the next corner is the tunic and slippers Francis wore during his last days. Next find a prayer (in a fancy silver stand) that St. Francis wrote for Brother Leo, signed with his tau cross. Next is a papal document (1223) legitimizing the Franciscan order and assuring his followers that they were not risking a (deadly) heresy charge. Finally, see the tunic lovingly patched and stitched by followers of the five-foot, four-inch-tall St. Francis.

Return up the stairs to the lower basilica. You're in the transept. This church brought together the greatest Sienese (Martini and Lorenzetti) and Florentine (Cimabue and Giotto) artists of the day. Look around at the painted scenes. In 1300 this was radical art—believable homespun scenes, landscapes, trees, real people. Study the crucifix (by Giotto) with the eight sparrowlike angels. For the first time, holy people are expressing emotion: One angel turns her head sadly at the sight of Jesus, and another scratches her hands down her cheeks, drawing blood. Mary, previously in control, has fainted in despair. The Franciscans, with their goal of bringing God to the people, found a natural partner in Europe's first modern painter, Giotto.

To see the Renaissance leap, look at the painting to the right. This is by Cimabue—it's Gothic, without the 3-D architecture, natural backdrop, and slice-of-life reality of the Giotto work. Cimabue's St. Francis is considered by some to be the earliest existing portrait of the saint. To the left, at eye level, enjoy the Martini saints and their exquisite halos.

Francis' friend, "Sister Death," was really not all that terrible. In fact, Francis would like to introduce you to her now (above and to the right of the door leading into the relic chapel). Go ahead, block the light and meet her. I'll wait for you upstairs, in the courtyard, next to the fine bookstore. By the way, monks in robes are not my idea of easy-to-approach people, but the Franciscans are still God's jugglers (and most of them speak English).

From the courtyard, climb the stairs to the **upper basilica**. Built later than the lower, the upper basilica is brighter, Gothic (the first Gothic church in Italy, 1228), and nearly wallpapered by Giotto. This gallery of frescoes by Giotto and his assistants shows 28 scenes from the life of St. Francis.

Look for these scenes:

• **A common man spreads his cape before Francis** (immediately to right of altar, as you're facing altar) out of honor and recognition to a man who will do great things. Symbolized by the rose window, God looks over the 20-year-old Francis, a dandy imprisoned in his selfishness. A medieval pilgrim fluent in symbolism would understand this because the Temple of Minerva (which

you saw today on Assisi's Piazza del Comune) was a prison at
that time. The rose window, which never existed, is symbolic
of God's eye.

• **Francis offers his cape to a needy stranger** (next panel).
Prior to this act of kindness, Francis had been captured in battle,
held as a prisoner of war, and then released.

• **Francis is visited by the Lord in a dream** (next panel)
and told to leave the army and go home.

• **Francis relinquishes his possessions** (two panels down),
giving his dad his clothes, his credit cards, and even his time-share
condo on Capri. Naked Francis is covered by the bishop, symbolizing his transition from a man of the world to a man of the church.

• **The pope has a vision** (next panel) of a simple man
propping up his teetering church. This led to the papal acceptance of the Franciscan reforms.

• **Christ appears to Francis** being carried by a seraph—
a six-winged angel (other side of church, fourth panel from the
door). For the strength of his faith, Francis is given the marks
of his master, the "battle scars of love"...the stigmata: Throughout his life Francis was interested in chivalry; now he's joined
the spiritual knighthood.

• **Francis preaches to the birds** (to the right of the exit).
Francis was more than a nature lover. The birds, of different
species, represent the diverse flock of humanity and nature, all
created and loved by God and worthy of each other's love.

Before you leave, look at the ceiling above the altar and
front entrance to see large tan patches; these careful repairs were
made after the basilica was damaged in the 1997 earthquake.
It's a blessing that so many of the frescoes remain.

Near the outside of the upper basilica is the Latin *pax* (peace)
and the Franciscan *tau* cross in the grass. Tav, the last letter in
the Hebrew alphabet, is symbolic of faithfulness to the end.
Francis signed his name with this simple character. Tav and pax.
(For more pax, take the high lane back to town, up to the castle,
or into the countryside.)

More Sights—Assisi
▲**Basilica of Saint Clare (Basilica di Santa Chiara)**—Dedicated
to the founder of the order of the Poor Clares, this Umbrian Gothic
church is simple, in keeping with the Poor Clares' dedication to a
life of contemplation. The church was built in 1265, and the huge
buttresses were added in the next century. The interior's fine frescoes were whitewashed in Baroque times. The Chapel of the
Crucifix of San Damiano, on the right (actually an earlier church
incorporated into this one), has the crucifix that supposedly spoke
to St. Francis, leading to his conversion in 1206. Stairs lead from
the nave down to the tomb of Saint Clare. Her tomb is at the far

end. The walls depict scenes from Clare's life and death (1193–1253); the saint's robes are in a large case between the stairs. The attached cloistered community of the Poor Clares has flourished for 700 years (church open 09:00–12:00, 14:00–19:00).

Unless you've already seen it on the "Assisi Welcome Walk" (above), make sure you dip into the wondrous mechanical, water-powered manger scene of Silvano Gionbolina (Via Sermei 2b, opposite arch at back end of church).

Roman Forum (Foro Romano)—For a look at Assisi's Roman roots, tour the Roman Forum, which is actually under the Piazza del Comune. The floor plan is sparse, the odd bits and pieces obscure, but it's well explained in English (a 10-page booklet is loaned to you when you enter), and you can actually walk on an ancient Roman road. For an orientation, look at the poster for sale at the entry to get an idea of the original setting of Forum and Temple (€2, or included in €5.25 combo-ticket, daily 10:00–13:00, 15:00–19:00, closes at 17:00 in winter; from Piazza Comune, go one-half block down Via San Francesco, it's on your right).

Pinacoteca—This small museum attractively displays its 13th- to 17th-century art (mainly frescoes), with general information in English in nearly every room. There's a Giotto Madonna (damaged) and a rare secular fresco (to right of Giotto), but it's mainly a peaceful walk through a pastel world, best for art lovers (€2.75, included in €5.25 combo-ticket, daily 10:00–13:00, 15:00–18:00, Via San Francesco 10, on main drag between Piazza del Comune and Basilica of St. Francis, tel. 075-812-033).

▲Rocca Maggiore—The "big castle" offers a good look at a 14th-century fortification and a fine view of Assisi and the Umbrian countryside (€2.75, included in €5.25 combo-ticket, daily 10:00–sunset, opens at 09:00 July–Aug). If you're counting euros, the view is just as good from outside the castle, and the interior is pretty bare. For a picnic with the same birdsong and views that inspired St. Francis, leave all the tourists and hike to the Rocca Minore (small castle) above Piazza Matteotti.

Santa Maria degli Angeli

This flat, modern part of Assisi has one major sight: The basilica that marks the spot where Francis lived, worked, and died.

▲▲St. Mary of the Angels (Basilica di Santa Maria degli Angeli)—This huge basilica, towering above the buildings below Assisi, was built around the tiny but historic Porziuncola Chapel (now directly under the dome). When the pope gave Francis his blessing, he was given his *porziuncola*, or "small portion"— a little land with a fixer-upper chapel—from which Francis and his followers established their order. As you enter, notice the sketch on the door showing the original little chapel with the monks' huts around it and Assisi before it had its huge basilica.

Francis lived here after he founded the Franciscan Order in 1208, and this was where he consecrated St. Clare as the Bride of Christ. A chapel called Cappella del Transito marks the place where Francis died (behind and to the right of the Porziuncola Chapel). Follow signs to the Roseta (Rose Garden). Francis, fighting off a temptation that he never named, threw himself onto roses. As the story goes, the thorns immediately dropped off the roses. Ever since, thornless roses have grown here. Look through the window at the rose garden (to the right of the statue of Francis petting a sheep). The Rose Chapel (Cappella delle Rose) is built over the place where Francis lived. The bookshop has some books in English and the free *museo* has a few monastic cells interesting to pilgrims (museum open Mon–Sat 09:30–12:00, 15:30–18:30, Sun 15:30–18:30).

Hours: The basilica is open May–Oct 07:00–18:30, Nov–April 07:00–12:00, 14:00–sunset. There's a little TI with unpredictable hours (to your right as you face the church, tel. 075-80511). A WC is 40 meters to the right of the TI, behind the hedge.

Transportation Connections: To get to Basilica di Santa Maria degli Angeli from Assisi's train station, it's quicker to walk (exit station left, take first left—at McDonald's, 5-minute walk) than to take the orange city bus' circuitous route (though with lots of luggage, you might prefer the bus). When you're leaving the basilica, you can catch the bus directly to the station and on to the old town of Assisi (as you leave church, stop is to your right, next to basilica). The orange city buses run twice hourly (buses to the old town depart the basilica at :10 and :40 after the hour; tickets cost €0.60 if you buy at *tabacchi* or newsstand, €1.10 if you buy from driver; 15–20 minute ride up to old town).

It's efficient to visit this basilica either on your way to the old town of Assisi or when you leave. You can easily walk to the basilica from the station (baggage check available, €2.75, access through shop). If you're heading to Siena next, visit the basilica right before you leave, because that's where you'll catch the bus to Siena (as you leave basilica, stop is to your right, across the street, buy ticket on bus); see "Transportation Connections—Assisi," below.

Sleeping in Assisi
(€1.10 = about $1, country code: 39, zip code: 06081)
Sleep Code: **S** = Single, **D** = Double/Twin, **T** = Triple, **Q** = Quad, **b** = bathroom, **s** = shower only, **CC** = Credit Cards accepted, **no CC** = Credit Cards not accepted, **SE** = Speaks English, **NSE** = No English.

The town accommodates large numbers of pilgrims on religious holidays. Finding a room any other time should be easy. See map on page 742 for hotel locations.

Splurges

Hotel Umbra, the best splurge in the center, feels like a quiet villa in the middle of town (25 rooms, Sb-€67, Db-€88–103 depending upon season and size of room, Tb-€109, includes breakfast, CC, air-con, peaceful garden and view terrace, most rooms have views, good restaurant, 100 meters below Piazza di Comune at Via degli Archi 6, tel. 075-812-240, fax 075-813-653, www.charmerelax.com/en73.html, family Laudenzi).

Hotel Dei Priori is a three-star, palace-type place in the old center with big, quiet rooms that have all the comforts (Db-€103–116, superior Db-€140–150, includes breakfast, CC, elevator, air-con, Corso Mazzini 15, tel. 075-812-237, fax 075-816-804, www.assisihotel.net, e-mail: hpriori@edisons.it).

Hotels

Hotel Belvedere, which offers 16 comfortable rooms and good views, is run by friendly Enrico and his American wife, Mary (Db-€73, breakfast-€5.25, elevator, 2 blocks past Basilica of St. Clare at Via Borgo Aretino 13, tel. 075-812-460, fax 075-816-812, e-mail: assisihotelbelvedere@hotmail.com, SE). Their attached restaurant is good.

Hotel Ideale is on the top edge of town overlooking the valley, and has 12 bright, modern rooms, view balconies, peaceful garden, free parking, and a warm welcome (Sb-€47, Db-€78, includes big-for-Italy breakfast, CC, most rooms with views, Piazza Matteotti 1, tel. 075-813-570, fax 075-813-020, e-mail: hotelideale@libero.it, sisters Lara and Ilaria SE).

Hotel Sole is well-located, with 35 spacious, comfortable rooms in a 15th-century building (Sb-€41, Db-€62, Tb-€81, breakfast-€6.25, CC, half its rooms are in a newer annex across the street, some rooms have views and balconies, elevator in annex, Corso Mazzini 35, 100 meters before Basilica of St. Clare, tel. 075-812-373, fax 075-813-706, e-mail: sole@tecnonet.it, NSE).

Hotel Ascesi has an inviting little lobby, nine pleasant rooms, and a tiny terrace, located within a block of the Basilica of St. Francis (Sb-€34, Db-€52, breakfast-€3.75, CC, air-con, Via Frate Elia 5, walk up from Piazza Unita d'Italia, take a left at Piazzetta Ruggero Bonghi, see sign on right, tel. & fax 075-812-420, e-mail: hotelideale@libero.it). Both of these hotels—at the top and bottom of town—are close to bus stops (and parking lots), handy if you're packing lots of luggage.

Hotel La Fortezza is a simple, modern, and quiet place with seven rooms (Db-€49, Tb-€67, Qb-€78, CC, a short block above Piazza del Comune at Vicolo della Fortezza 19b, tel. 075-812-993, fax 075-819-8035, www.lafortezzahotel.com, SE).

Albergo Il Duomo is tidy and *tranquillo* with nine rooms on a stair-step lane one block up from San Rufino (S-€26, Sb-€28,

D-€35, Db-€41, breakfast-€4.25, CC, Vicolo S. Lorenzo 2; from Church of San Rufino follow sign, then turn left on stair-stepped alley; tel. 075-812-742, fax 075-812-762, e-mail: ilduomo@retein.it, Carlo SE).

Other Accommodations

Camere Annalisa Martini is a cheery home swimming in vines and roses in the town's medieval core. Annalisa speaks English and enthusiastically accommodates her guests with a picnic garden, a washing machine (small load-€2.75), a refrigerator, and six homey rooms (S-€20, Sb-€23, D-€31, Db-€36, Tb-€47, Qb-€57, 3 rooms share 2 bathrooms, no breakfast, no CC, 1 block from Piazza del Comune, go downhill toward basilica, turn left on Via S. Gregorio to #6, tel. & fax 075-813-536).

La Pallotta, a recommended restaurant (see "Eating," below), offers seven clean, bright rooms (note that rooms and restaurant are in different locations). Rooms #12 and #18 have views (Db-€47, CC, view terrace, Via San Rufino 4, go up short flight of stairs outside building to reach entrance, a block off Piazza del Comune, tel. & fax 075-812-307, www.pallottaassisi.it).

Signora Gambacorta rents several decent rooms and has a roof terrace on a quiet lane (Via Sermei 9) just above St. Chiara. There is no sign or reception desk, so you'll need to check in at her shop a half block east of Piazza del Comune at San Gabriele 17—look for the sign "Bottega di Gambacorta" (S-€20, Db-€40, Tb-€60, 2-night stays preferred, no breakfast; store is open Mon–Wed and Fri–Sat 08:00–13:00, 16:30–19:30, Thu 08:00–13:00, closed Sun— if you can't arrive when store is open, call when you arrive, tel. 075-812-454, fax 075-813-186, www.ilbongustaio.com/inglese /eerooms.htm, e-mail: geo@umbrars.com, NSE). She also has two apartments for stays of at least four nights (3 rooms-€90/day, 5 rooms-€140/day, kitchen, no breakfast).

Hostel: Francis probably would have bunked with the peasants in Assisi's **Ostello della Pace** (€13 beds in 4- to 8-bed rooms, Qb-€15 apiece, includes breakfast, dinner-€7.75, no CC, laundry, get off at Assisi's Piazza Unita d'Italia stop on the station–town bus, then a 10-min walk to Via di Valecchie 177, tel. & fax 075-816-767, SE).

Eating in Assisi

For a fine Assisian perch and good regional cooking, relax on a terrace overlooking Piazza del Comune at **Taverna dei Consoli** (€13 4-course *menu*, also à la carte, Thu–Tue 12:00–14:30, 19:00– 21:30, closed Wed, CC, tel. 075-812-516, friendly owner Moreno SE and recommends the *bruschetta*, *stringozzi*—noodles, *agnello*— lamb, and *cinghiale*—boar).

La Pallotta, a local favorite run by a friendly, hardworking family, offers excellent regional specialties, such as *piccione* (pigeon), *coniglio* (rabbit), and more typical food (€13.50 *menu*, Wed–Mon 12:00–14:30, 19:15–22:00, closed Tue, CC, also rents rooms—see listing above, a few steps off Piazza del Comune, through gate across from temple/church, Vicolo della Volta Pinta, tel. 075-812-649).

Osteria Piazzetta Dell Erba is a fun, little, family-run place a block above Piazza del Comune, serving good, basic Umbrian specialties next to the Gambacorta grocery (Tue–Sun 12:00–14:00, 19:00–21:45, closed Mon, CC, Via San Gabriele, tel. 075-815-352).

Pizzeria/Tavola Calda Dal Carro is popular, affordable, and friendly (good pizzas and €11.50 *menu*, closed Wed, Vicolo di Nepis 2, leave Piazza del Comune on Via San Gabriele, then take first right—down a stepped lane, tel. 075-815-249).

Ristorante San Francesco is the place to splurge for dinner (Thu–Tue 12:00–14:30, 19:30–22:00, closed Wed, CC, facing Basilica of St. Francis at Via San Francesco 52, tel. 075-812-329).

Transportation Connections—Assisi
To train to: Rome (5/day, 1.75–2.5 hrs), **Florence** (5/day, 2–2.75 hrs, more with transfers at Terontola and Cortona), **Orvieto** (7/day, 2 hrs, transfer in Terontola), **Siena** (6/day, 3.25 hrs, transfers in Chiusi and Terontola; bus is more efficient). Train station: 075-804-0272, train info: tel. 848-888-088.

By bus to: Siena (1/day, 2 hrs, €8.25, departs Basilica di Santa Maria degli Angeli near Assisi train station—as you face basilica, stop is to your left across the street), **Rome** (3/day, 3 hrs, departs Assisi's Piazza Unita d'Italia, arrives at Rome's Tiburtina station). Unless you like getting up really early, don't take the bus to **Florence** (1/day, departs Assisi's Piazza Unita d'Italia at 06:45, 2.75 hrs); the train is better.

ORVIETO
AND CIVITA

Orvieto, one of the most famous hill towns, is an ideal springboard for a trip (by car or bus) to the tiny hill town of Civita di Bagnoregio. Stranded alone on its pinnacle in a vast canyon, Civita's lovable. If you have more time and a car, you'll find sun-soaked regions of Tuscany, Umbria, and Le Marche spiked with hill towns.

Planning Your Time

These two towns are worth a day and an overnight—ideally an afternoon, night, and morning. Most people start with Orvieto, which is an easy train stop on the Florence-Rome line, then continue to Civita by bus.

Orvieto has a good half day of sightseeing. Spend the night in Orvieto if you want a variety of restaurants, or in Civita if you want peace. Civita is also worth a half day; a chunk of that time is spent hiking to and from the town from Bagnoregio (connected by bus with Orvieto, daily except Sun).

ORVIETO

Umbria's grand hill town, while no secret, is worth a quick look. Just off the freeway, with three popular claims to fame (cathedral, Classico wine, and ceramics), it's loaded with tourists by day and quiet by night. Drinking a shot of wine in a ceramic cup as you gaze up at the cathedral lets you experience Orvieto all at once.

The town sits majestically on a big chunk of tufa rock. Streets are lined with exhaust-stained buildings made from the volcanic stuff.

Piazza Cahen is a key transportation hub at the entry to the hilltop town. As you exit the funicular, the town center is straight ahead.

Tourist Information: The TI is at Piazza Duomo 24 on

Orvieto and Civita Area

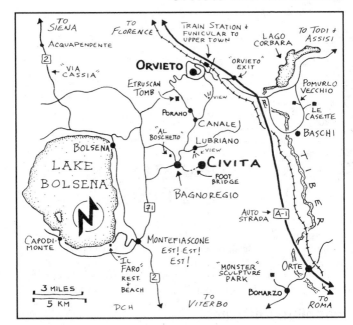

the cathedral square (Mon–Fri 08:15–14:00, 16:00–19:00, Sat 10:00–13:00, 16:00–19:00, Sun 10:00–12:00, 16:00–18:00, tel. 0763-341-772). Pick up the free city map and ask about train and bus schedules. The TI sells a €1.50 admission ticket for the Chapel of St. Brizio (within the cathedral). For a longer visit, consider buying the €10.50 "Carta Unica" which covers entry to the chapel, Archaeological Museum (Museo Claudio Faina e Museo Civico), Underground Orvieto Tours, and Torre del Moro (tower), plus your public transportation (bus and funicular) for one day (or 5 hrs of parking at *parcheggio* Campo della Fiera).

Market Days: Drop by Piazza del Popolo with your cloth shopping bag on Tuesday and Saturday mornings.

Arrival in Orvieto

By Train: If you're daytripping, you can check your bag at the station (€2.75, access from platform, knock if door closed).

A handy funicular/bus shuttle will take you quickly from the train station and car park to the top of the town. Buy your ticket at the entrance to the *funiculare*; look for the *biglietteria* sign (4–6/hr, €0.85, ticket includes the minibus from Piazza Cahen to Piazza Duomo—where you'll find everything that matters; or pay €0.65

for funicular only—best choice if you're staying at Hotel Corso; funicular runs Mon–Sat 07:20–20:30, Sun 08:00–20:30).

As you exit the funicular at the top, to your left is a ruined fortress with a garden, WC, and a commanding view, and to your right—St. Patrick's Well (described below), Etruscan ruins, and another sweeping view. Just in front of you is an orange bus waiting to shuttle you to the town center. It'll drop you off at the TI (last stop, in front of cathedral).

If you forgot to check at the station for the train schedule to your next destination (and now the station is far, far below), Orvieto is ready for you. You can peruse the loose-leaf timetable at the TI or the train schedule posted at the top of the *funiculare*.

By Car: Drivers park at the base of the hill at the huge, free lot behind the Orvieto train station (follow the "P" and "funiculare" signs) or at the pay lot to the right of Orvieto's cathedral (€0.75, for first hour, €0.60/hr thereafter).

Sights—Orvieto's Piazza Duomo
▲▲**Duomo**—The cathedral has Italy's most striking facade (from 1330), thanks to architect Lorenzo Maitani and many others. Grab a gelato (to the left of the church) and study this fascinating, gleaming mass of mosaics and sculpture.

At the base of the cathedral, the broad marble pillars carved with Biblical scenes tell the story of the world from left to right. The pillar on the far left shows the Creation (see the snake and Eve), next is the Tree of Jesse, next the New Testament (look for Mary in a manger, etc.), and on the far right—the Last Judgment (with hell, of course, at the bottom). Each pillar is topped by a bronze symbol of one of the evangelists: angel (Matthew), lion (Mark), eagle (John), and bull (Luke). The bronze doors are modern, by Emilio Greco. (A museum devoted to Greco's work is to the right of the church; it's labeled simply "Museo.") In the mosaic below the rose window, Mary is transported to heaven. In the uppermost mosaic, Mary is crowned.

Why such an impressive church in a little tufa town? Because of a blood-stained cloth. In the 1260s, a Bohemian priest—who doubted that the bread used in communion was really the body of Christ—came to Rome on a pilgrimage. On his return journey, he worshiped in Bolsena, near Orvieto. During Mass, the bread bled, staining a linen cloth. The cloth was brought to the pope, who was visiting Orvieto at the time. Such a miraculous relic required a magnificent church. You can see the actual cloth from the Miracle of Bolsena displayed in the chapel to the left of the altar.

Hours: The cathedral is open daily April–Sept 07:30–12:45, 14:30–19:15, closing at 18:15 March and Oct, and at 17:15 Nov–Feb. Admission is free, but there is a charge for the Chapel of St. Brizio.

Orvieto

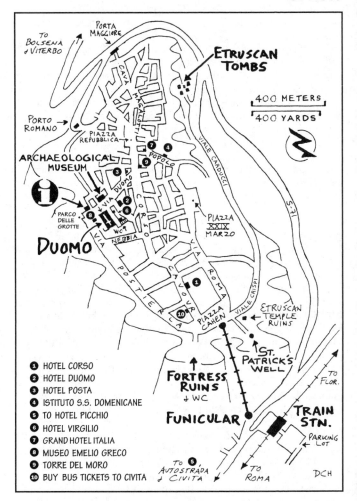

Cost and Hours of Chapel: Buy the €1.50 ticket at the TI or the shop across the square; it's included in Carta Unica. The chapel is usually free 07:30–10:00—drop by to check; Mon–Sat 10:00–12:45, 14:30–19:15, Sun 14:30–17:45, it closes an hour earlier in winter; only 25 people are allowed in the chapel at a time.

Chapel of St. Brizio: This chapel, to the right of the altar, features Luca Signorelli's brilliantly lit frescoes of the Apocalypse

(1449–1451). Step into the chapel and you're surrounded by vivid scenes, including the *Preaching of the Antichrist* (to your left as you enter—the figure standing on far left is a self-portrait of Signorelli, next to Fra Angelico, who worked on the ceiling); the *Calling of the Elect to Heaven* (left of altar—hear that celestial band); the *Damned in Hell* (right of altar—the scariest mosh pit ever); and the *Resurrection of the Bodies* (to your right as you enter; people dreamily climb out of the earth as skeletons chatter in the corner, wondering where to snare some skin). On the same wall is a gripping Pietà. Fra Angelico started the ceiling and Signorelli finished it, turning the entire room into Orvieto's artistic must-see sight.

After leaving the cathedral, if you want a break at a viewpoint park, exit left and pass the small parking lot. The nearest WCs are in the opposite direction (exit cathedral to the right), down the stairs from the left transept.

Archaeological Museum (Museo Claudio Faina e Museo Civico)—Across from the entrance to the cathedral is a fine Etruscan art museum (two upper floors) combined with a miniscule city history museum on the ground floor, featuring a sarcophagus and temple bits. The Faina art—consisting largely of Etruscan vases, plates, and coins, with some jewelry and bronze dishes—was collected by Mauro Faina and his nephew starting in the late 19th century. They bought some of the art and dug up the rest in haphazardly conducted excavations. Many of the vases came from the Etruscan necropolis (Crocifisso del Tufo) just outside Orvieto. The English placards in most rooms offer some information, especially on the Faina family (€4.25, included in Carta Unica, April–Sept Tue–Sun 09:30–18:00, Oct–March 10:00–17:00, closed Mon, audioguide, WC after ticket desk and on top floor, tel. 0763-341-216). Look out the windows at the Duomo's glittering facade.

▲Museo Emilo Greco—This museum displays the work of Emilio Greco (1913–1995), the Sicilian artist who designed the doors of Orvieto's cathedral. His sketches and bronze statues show his absorption with gently twisting and turning nudes. In the back left corner of the museum, look for the sketchy outlines of women—simply beautiful. The artful installation in a palazzo, with walkways and even a spiral staircase up to the ceiling, allow you to view his work from different directions (€2.75, €4.25 includes St. Patrick's Well, April–Sept daily 10:30–13:00, 14:00–18:30, closes 1 hour earlier Oct–March, no English but not essential, next to Duomo, marked *Museo*, tel. 0763-344-605).

Underground Orvieto Tours (Parco delle Grotte)—Guides weave a good archaeological history into an hour-long look at about 100 meters of caves (€5.25, included in Carta Unica, tours daily at 11:00, 12:15—English, 16:00, and 17:15—English, tel. 0763-344-891 or the TI). Orvieto is honeycombed with Etruscan and medieval caves. You'll see only the remains of an old olive press, two impressive 40-meter-deep Etruscan well shafts, and the remains of a primitive cement quarry, but, if you want underground Orvieto, this is the place to get it.

More Sights—Orvieto

Torre del Moro—For yet another viewpoint, this distinctive square tower comes with 250 steps and an elevator. The elevator goes only partway, leaving you with a mere 173 steps to scurry up (€2.75, included in Carta Unica, April–Oct daily 10:00–19:00, July–Aug until 20:00, Nov–Dec 10:30–13:00, 14:30–17:00, terrace on top, at intersection of Corso Cavour and Via Duomo).

St. Patrick's Well (Posso de S. Patrizio)—Engineers are impressed by this deep well (53 meters deep and 13 meters wide), designed in the 16th century with a double-helix design. The two spiral stairways allow an efficient one-way traffic flow, intriguing now, but critical then. Imagine donkeys and people, balancing jugs of water, trying to go up and down the same stairway. At the bottom is a bridge that people could walk on to scoop up water.

The well was built because a pope got nervous. After Rome was sacked in 1527 by renegade troops of the Holy Roman Empire, the pope fled to Orvieto. He feared that even this little town (with no water source on top) would be besieged. He commissioned a well, which was started in 1527 and finished 10 years later. It was a huge project. Even today, when a local is faced with a difficult task, people say, "It's like digging St. Patrick's Well." The unusual name came from the well's supposed resemblance to the Irish saint's cave. It's not worth climbing up and down a total of 495 steps; a quick look is painless but pricey (€3.25, €4.25 includes Museo Emilio Greco; bring a sweater if you descend to the chilly depths; the well is to your right as you exit *funiculare*).

View Walks—For short pleasant walks, climb the medieval wall (at western end of town, between Piazza S. Gionvenale and Via Garibaldi) or stroll the promenade park on the northern edge of town, along Viale Carducci, which becomes Gonfaloniera).

Sights Near Orvieto

Wine Tasting—Orvieto Classico wine is justly famous. For a short tour of a local winery with Etruscan cellars, visit Tenuta Le Velette, where English-speaking Corrado and Cecilia Bottai will welcome you—if you've called ahead to set up an appointment (€8 for tour and tasting, Mon–Fri 08:30–12:00, 14:00–17:00, Sat 08:30–12:00, closed Sun, tel. 0763-29144, fax 076-329-114). From their sign (5 min past Orvieto at top of switchbacks just before Canale, on Bagnoregio road), cruise down a long tree-lined drive, then park at the striped gate (must call ahead; no drop-ins).

Sleeping in Orvieto
(€1.10 = about $1, country code: 39, zip code: 05018)

All of these are in the old town (see page 758) except the last one, in a more modern neighborhood near the station.

Hotel Corso is small, clean, and friendly, with 18 comfy, modern rooms, some with balconies and views (Sb-€57, Db-€78, 10 percent discount with this book, buffet breakfast-€6.50, CC, elevator, air-con at no extra charge, garage on the main street up from funicular toward Duomo at Via Cavour 339, tel. & fax 0763-342-020, www.argoweb.it/hotel _corso, e-mail: hotelcorso@libero.it).

Hotel Virgilio is a decent hotel with bright and modern— if overpriced—rooms shoehorned into an old building, ideally located on the main square facing the cathedral (Sb-€62, Db-€85, breakfast-€7.75, send personal or traveler's check for first night's deposit, CC, elevator, noisy church bells every 15 min, Piazza Duomo 5, tel. 0763-341-882, fax 0763-343-797, SE). They also have a cheaper *dependencia*—a double and quad in a one-star hotel a few doors away (Db-€57, Qb-€103, e-mail: hotel.virgilio@orvienet.it).

Hotel Duomo, centrally located, is super-duper modern, with splashy art and 17 sleek rooms named after artists who worked on the Duomo (Db-€93, Db suite-€114, includes break-fast, CC, elevator, air-con, double-paned windows keep out noise, a block from Duomo, behind *gelateria* at Via di Maurizio 7, tel. 0763-341-887, fax 0763-394-973).

Hotel Posta is a five-minute walk from the cathedral into the medieval core. It's a big, old, formerly elegant but well-cared-for-in-its-decline building with a breezy garden, a grand old lobby, and 20 spacious, clean, plain rooms with vintage rickety furniture and good mattresses (S-€31, Sb-€36, D-€39, Db-€49–54, break-fast-€5.25, no CC, some air-con, Via Luca Signorelli 18, tel. & fax 0763-341-909).

The sisters of the **Istituto SS Domenicane** rent 15 spot-less twin rooms in their heavenly convent with a peaceful terrace (Sb-€36, Db-€52, 2-night min, breakfast-€5.25, no CC, elevator, parking, just off Piazza del Populo at Via del Populo 1, tel. & fax 0763-342-910, www.argoweb.it/istituto _sansalvatore/istituto.uk.html).

Hotel Picchio is a concrete-and-marble place, more comfortable but with less character than others in the area. It's in the lower, plain part of town, 300 meters from the train station (Sb-€34, Db-€46, Tb-€57, ask for the Rick Steves discount; some rooms with air-con, fridge, and phone; Via G. Salvatori 17, 05019 Orvieto Scalo, tel. & fax 0763-301-144, family-run by Marco and Picchio). A trail leads from here up to the old town.

Eating in Orvieto

Near the Duomo, consider **Pergola**—its affordable menu is popular with locals (Thu–Tue 12:30–14:30, 17:30–19:45, closed Wed,
Via dei Magoni 9). **La Palomba** is also a good bet (Thu–Tue
12:30–14:15, 19:30–22:00, closed Wed, Via Cipriano Manenta,
just off Piazza della Republica). For a bit of a splurge, try **Antico
Bucchero** for its classy candlelit ambience and fine food (Thu–
Tue 12:30–15:00, 19:00–24:00, closed Wed, CC, indoor/outdoor
seating, Via de Cartori, a half block south of Corso Cavour,
between Torre del Moro and Piazza della Repubblica). **Osteria
San Patrizio**, near the funicular, is good (closed Sun eve and
Mon, Corso Cavour 312, tel. 0763-341-245).

For dessert, try the *gelateria* **Pasqualetti** (daily 12:30–01:00,
until 20:00 Nov–March, Piazza Duomo 14, next to left transept
of church; another branch is at Corso Cavour 56).

Transportation Connections—Orvieto

By train to: Rome (14/day, 75 min, consider leaving your car
at the large car park behind the Orvieto station), **Florence**
(8/day, 2.25 hrs), **Siena** (8/day, 2–3 hrs, change in Chiusi; all
Florence-bound trains stop in Chiusi). The train station's Buffet
della Stazione is surprisingly good for a quick focaccia sandwich
or pizza picnic for the train ride.

By bus to Bagnoregio (near Civita): It's a 70-minute, €1.50
bus ride. Departures in 2001 from Orvieto's Piazza Cahen on the
blue Cotral bus, daily except Sunday: 05:30, 06:50, 09:50, 10:10,
13:00, 14:25, 17:20. During the school year (roughly Sept–June),
buses also run at 06:35, 13:35, and 16:40. Buy your ticket at the
tabacchi stop on Corso Cavour (also confirm the schedule) a block
up from *funiculare*. To find the bus stop, face the *funiculare*; the
stop is at the far left end of Piazza Cahen where the blue buses are
parked (no schedule posted; confirm departure and return times
with driver; schedule *is* posted at bus stop in Bagnoregio). Each
bus stops at Orvieto's train station five minutes later.

CIVITA DI BAGNOREGIO

Perched on a pinnacle in a grand canyon, the traffic-free village
of Civita is Italy's ultimate hill town. Curl your toes around its
Etruscan roots.

Civita is terminally ill. Only 15 residents remain as, bit by
bit, it's being purchased by rich big-city Italians who come here to
escape. Apart from its permanent (and aging) residents and those
who have weekend homes here, there is a group of Americans—
introduced to the town through a small University of Washington
architecture program—who have bought into the rare magic of
Civita. When the program is in session, 15 students live with
residents and study Italian culture and architecture.

Civita is connected to the world and the town of Bagno-regio by a long pedestrian bridge—and a new Web site (www .civitadibagnoregio.it). While Bagnoregio lacks the pinnacle-town romance of Civita, it is a pure and lively bit of small-town Italy. It's actually a healthy, vibrant community (unlike Civita, the suburb it calls "the dead city"). Get a haircut, sip a coffee on the square, walk down to the old laundry (ask, *"Dov'è la lavanderia vecchia?"*). A Grand Spesa supermarket is 300 meters from the bus stop (Mon–Sat 08:30–13:00, 17:00-20:00, closed Sun; take main drag from town gate—away from Civita, angle right at pyramid monument). A lively market fills the bus parking lot each Monday.

From Bagnoregio, yellow signs direct you along its long, skinny spine to its older neighbor, Civita. Enjoy the view as you walk up the bridge to Civita. Be prepared for the little old ladies of Civita, who can be aggressive at getting money out of visitors—tourists are their only source of support. Off-season Civita, Bag-noregio, and Al Boschetto (see "Sleeping," below) are all deadly quiet—and cold. I'd side-trip in quickly from Orvieto or skip the area altogether.

Arrival in Bagnoregio, near Civita

If you're arriving by bus from Orvieto, you'll get off at the bus stop in Bagnoregio. Look at the posted bus schedule and write down the return times to Orvieto. (Drivers, see "Transportation Connections," below.)

Baggage Check: While there's no official baggage-check service in Bagnoregio, I've arranged with Laurenti Mauro, who runs the Bar/Enoteca/Caffè Gianfu, to let you leave your bags there (€1/bag, Fri–Wed 07:00–24:00 with a 13:00–13:30 lunch break, closed Thu; to get to café from Orvieto bus stop where you got off, continue in same direction the Orvieto bus headed and round the corner).

From Bagnoregio to Civita

From Bagnoregio, you can walk or take the little shuttle bus to the base of the bridge to Civita. From here, you have to walk the rest of the way. It's a 10-minute hike up a pedestrian bridge that gets steeper near the end. There's no bus—only you and your profound regret that you didn't get in better shape before your trip.

You can take the small shuttle **bus** from Bagnoregio to the base of the bridge (€1, 10-min ride, first bus at 07:39, last at 18:20, 1–2/hr except during 13:00–15:30 siesta, catch bus at stop across from gas station). If you'll want to return to Bagnoregio by bus, check the schedule posted near the bridge (at edge of car park, where bus let you off) before you head up to Civita.

To **walk** from Bagnoregio to the base of Civita's bridge (about 20 min, fairly level), take the road going uphill (overlooking the big parking lot), then take the first right and an immediate left onto the main drag, Via Roma. Follow this straight out to the *belvedere* for a superb viewpoint. From the viewpoint, backtrack a few steps, and take the stairs down to the road leading to the bridge.

Civita Orientation Walk

Civita was once connected to Bagnoregio. The saddle between the separate towns eroded away. Photographs around town show the old donkey path, the original bridge. It was bombed in World War II and replaced in 1965 with the new **bridge** you're climbing today. The town's hearty old folks hang on the bridge's hand railing when fierce winter weather rolls through.

Entering the town, you'll pass through a cut in the rock (made by Etruscans 2,500 years ago) and under a 12th-century Romanesque **arch**. This was the main Etruscan road leading to the Tiber Valley and Rome.

Inside the town gate, on your left is the old **laundry** (in front of the WC). On your right a fancy wooden door and windows (above the door) lead to thin air. This was the facade of a Renaissance palace—one of five that once graced Civita. It fell into the valley riding a chunk of the ever-eroding rock pinnacle. Today the door leads to a remaining chunk of the palace—complete with Civita's first hot tub—owned by the "Marchesa," a countess who married into Italy's biggest industrialist family.

Peek into the museum next door if it's open (Wed and Sat–Sun 10:00–13:00, marked *Benvenuti a Civita*) and check out the **viewpoint** a few steps away. Nearby is the long-gone home of Civita's one famous son, Saint Bonaventure, known as the "second founder of the Franciscans."

Now wander to the **town square** in front of the church, where you'll find Civita's only public phone, bar, and restaurant—and a wild donkey race on the first Sunday of June and the second Sunday of September. The church marks the spot where an Etruscan temple, and then a Roman temple, once stood. The pillars that stand like giants' bar stools are ancient—Roman or Etruscan.

Go into the **church**. You'll see frescoes and statues from "the school of Giotto" and "the school of Donatello," a portrait of the patron saint of your teeth (notice the scary-looking pincers), and an altar dedicated to Marlon Brando (or St. Ildebrando).

The basic grid street plan of the ancient town survives. Just around the corner from the church, on the main street, is Rossana and Antonio's cool and friendly **wine cellar** (their sign reads: *bruschette con prodotti locali*). Pull up a stump and let them or their

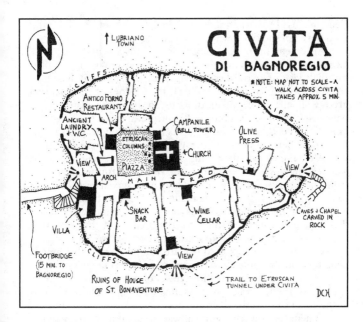

children, Arianna and Antonella, serve you *panini* (sandwiches), *bruschetta* (garlic toast with optional tomato topping), wine, and a local cake called *ciambella*. Climb down into the cellar and note the traditional wine-making gear and the provisions for rolling huge kegs up the stairs. Tap on the kegs in the cool bottom level to see which are full.

The rock below Civita is honeycombed with ancient cellars (for keeping wine at the same temperature all year) and cisterns (for collecting rainwater, since there was no well in town). Many of these date from Etruscan times.

Explore farther down the street but, remember, nothing is abandoned. Everything is still privately owned. After passing an ancient Roman tombstone on your left, you'll come to Vittoria's **Antico Mulino**, an atmospheric collection of old olive presses. The huge press in the entry is about 1,500 years old and was in use as recently as the 1960s (donation requested, give about €1). Her sons Sandro and Felice, running the local equivalent of a lemonade stand, toast delicious *bruschetta* on weekends and holidays (roughly 11:00–19:00). Choose your topping (chopped tomato is super) and get a glass of wine for a fun, affordable snack.

Farther down the way and to your left, Maria (for a donation of about €1) will show you through her **garden** with a grand view (Maria's Giardino) and share historical misinformation (she says Civita and Lubriano were once connected). Maria's husband,

Peppone, used to carry goods on a donkey back and forth on the path between the old town and Bagnoregio.

At the end of town, the main drag winds downhill past small **Etruscan caves** to your right. The first two were used as stables until last year. The third cave is an unusual chapel, cut deep into the rock, with a barred door—this is the **Chapel of the Incarcerated** (Cappella del Carcere). In Etruscan times, the chapel may have originally been a tomb, and in medieval times it was used as a jail. When Civita's few residents have a religious procession, they come here, in honor of the Madonna of the Incarcerated.

After the chapel, the paving-stone path peters out into a dirt trail leading down and around to the right to a **tunnel**. Dating from the Etruscan era, the tunnel may have served as a shortcut to the river below. It was widened in the 1930s so farmers could get between their scattered fields more easily, and now the residents use it as a shortcut in fall to collect chestnuts from the trees that cover the hillside. Backtrack to the town square.

Evenings on the town square are a bite of Italy. The same people sit on the same church steps under the same moon, night after night, year after year. I love my cool, late evenings in Civita. If you visit in the cool of the morning, have cappuccino and rolls at the small café on the town square.

Whenever you visit, stop halfway up the donkey path and listen to the sounds of rural Italy. Reach out and touch one of the monopoly houses. If you know how to turn the volume up on the crickets, do so.

Sleeping in Civita and Bagnoregio
(€1.10 = about $1, country code: 39, zip code: 01022)
When you leave the tourist crush, life as a traveler in Italy becomes easy, and prices tumble. Finding a room is easy in small-town Italy.

Franco Sala, who runs Civita's only restaurant, **Antico Forno**, rents three comfortable rooms overlooking Civita's main square. Call a minimum of one day in advance. English-speaking Franco might meet you at the base of the bridge to beam up your luggage (Db-€67, D-€57, €13 more for optional half-pension, CC, Piazza Del Duomo Vecchio, 01022 Civita di Bagnoregio, tel. 0761-760-016, cellular 34-7611-5426, e-mail: fsala@pelagus.it).

For information about a fully furnished and equipped two-bedroom **Civita apartment** with a terrace and cliffside garden that's rentable May through October ($800/week, one-week minimum Sat to Sat, personal checks OK), call Carol Watts in Kansas (tel. 785/539-0815, evenings or weekends, http://homepage.mac.com/cmwatts/civita.html).

Hotel Fidanza, in Bagnoregio near the bus stop, is tired but decent and the only hotel in town. Of its 25 rooms, #206 and #207 have views of Civita (Sb-€52, Db-€62, breakfast-€5.50, no CC, attached restaurant, Via Fidanza 25, Bagnoregio/Viterbo, tel. & fax 0761-793-444).

Just outside Bagnoregio is **Al Boschetto.** The Catarcia family speaks no English, so have an English-speaking Italian call for you (Sb-€34, D-€44, Db-€49, breakfast-€3, CC, Strada Monterado, Bagnoregio/Viterbo, tel. 0761-792-369). Most of the 25 rooms, while very basic, have private showers. The Catarcia family (Angelino, his wife Perina, sons Gianfranco and Domenico, daughter-in-law Giuseppina, and the grandchildren) offers a candid look at rural Italian life. Meals are uneven in quality, and the men are often tipsy (which can pose a problem for women). If the men invite you down deep into the gooey, fragrant bowels of the cantina, be warned: The theme song is *"Trinka Trinka Trinka,"* and there are no rules unless the female participants set them. The Orvieto bus drops you at the town gate (no bus on Sun). The hotel is a 15-minute walk out of town past the old arch (follow *Viterbo* signs); turn left at the pyramid monument and right at the first fork (follow *Montefiascone* sign). Civita is a pleasant 45-minute walk (back through Bagnoregio) from Al Boschetto.

Eating in and near Civita

In Civita, try **Trattoria Antico Forno**, which serves up pasta at affordable prices (daily for lunch at 12:00 and sporadically for dinner at 19:00, on the main square, also rents rooms—see above, tel. 0761-760-016). From October through March, Franco shifts his restaurant from outdoors (on the square) inside to an atmospheric dining room in his Antico Forno B&B, a few steps away and also on the square. At **Da Peppone**, the small café/bar on the square, you can get a simple sandwich and treats (daily 09:30–12:30, 14:30–19:00, closed in winter Mon or Tue).

Hostaria del Ponte offers light, creative cuisine at the car park at the base of the bridge to Civita (Tue–Sat 12:30–16:00, 19:30–24:00, Sun 12:30–16:00, closed Mon, great view terrace, tel. 0761-793-565).

In Bagnoregio, check out **Ristorante Nello il Fumatore** (Sat–Thu 12:00–15:00, 19:00–22:00, closed Fri, on Piazza Fidanza). At **Al Boschetto,** you'll get country cooking such as bunny (just outside Bagnoregio; see "Sleeping," above).

Transportation Connections—Bagnoregio

To Orvieto: Public buses (7/day, 70 min) connect Bagnoregio to the rest of the world via Orvieto. Departures in 2001 from Bagnoregio, daily except Sunday: 06:20, 09:10, 12:40, 13:55, 15:45, 17:40, 18:20. During the school year (roughly Sept–June), there are additional departures at 07:20 and 07:50 (for info on Orvieto, see "Connections—Orvieto," above).

Driving from Orvieto to Bagnoregio: Orvieto overlooks
the autostrada (and has its own exit). The shortest way to Civita
from the freeway exit is to turn left (below Orvieto) and follow
the signs to Lubriano and Bagnoregio.

The more winding and scenic route takes 20 minutes longer:
From the freeway, pass under hill-capping Orvieto (on your right,
signs to Lago di Bolsena, on Viale I Maggio); take the first left
(direction: Bagnoregio), winding up past great Orvieto views
through Canale, and through farms and fields of giant shredded
wheat to Bagnoregio.

Either way, just before Bagnoregio, follow the signs left to
Lubriano and pull into the first little square by the church on
your right for a breathtaking view of Civita. Then return to the
Bagnoregio road. Drive through Bagnoregio (following yellow
"Civita" signs) and park at the base of the steep pedestrian bridge
leading up to the traffic-free, 2,500-year-old, canyon-swamped
pinnacle town of Civita di Bagnoregio.

THE CINQUE TERRE

The Cinque Terre (CHINK-wuh TAY-ruh), a remote chunk of the Italian Riviera, is the traffic-free, lowbrow, under appreciated alternative to the French Riviera. There's not a museum in sight. Just sun, sea, sand (well, pebbles), wine, and pure unadulterated Italy. Enjoy the villages, swimming, hiking, and evening romance of one of God's great gifts to tourism. For a home base, choose among five villages, each of which fills a ravine with a lazy hive of human activity—calloused locals, sunburned travelers, and no Vespas. While the place is now well discovered (www.cinqueterre .it), I've never seen happier, more relaxed tourists. Vernazza is my favorite home base.

The area was first described in medieval times as "the five castles." Tiny communities grew up in the protective shadows of the castles ready to run inside at the first hint of a Turkish "Saracen" pirate raid. Many locals were kidnapped and ransomed or sold into slavery somewhere far to the east. As the threat of pirates faded, the villages grew, with economies based on fish and grapes. Until the advent of tourism in this generation, the towns were remote. Even today, traditions survive, and each of the five villages comes with a distinct dialect and proud heritage. The region has just become a national park, and its natural and cultural wonders will be carefully preserved.

Now that the Cinque Terre is a national park, you need to pay a park entrance fee. You have two options: buying a Hiking Pass or a Cinque Terre Card. The Hiking Pass costs €2.60 (kids under 4 free; comes with map) and is valid for one day. The pricier Cinque Terre Card covers the park entrance fee and your transportation on the local trains (from Levanto to La Spezia, including all Cinque Terre towns) plus the shuttle buses that run twice per hour within

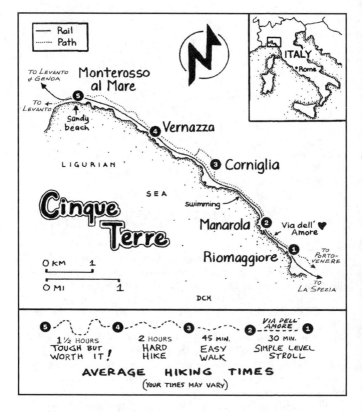

each Cinque Terre town (€5.20/1 day, €10.50/3 days, €15.50/ week, kids 4-12 pay half price, under 4 free; includes map, brochure, and train schedule). Cards and passes are sold at participating train stations, some trailheads, and some hotels. Validate your Cinque Terre Card at a train station (punch into machine). The cards and passes are valid until midnight of the day they expire.

Over the next decade, Italy has quiet plans for the Cinque Terre. For the sake of tranquility, a new train line will be built inland for the noisy fast trains, leaving the Cinque Terre tracks for just the pokey milk-run trains.

Sadly, a few ugly, noisy Americans are giving tourism a bad name here. Even hip young locals are put off by loud, drunken tourists. They say (and I agree) that the Cinque Terre is a special place. It deserves a special dignity. Party in Viareggio or Porto-fino but be mellow in the Cinque Terre. Talk softly. Help keep it clean. In spite of the tourist crowds, it's still a real community and we are guests.

Planning Your Time

The ideal minimum stay is two nights and a completely uninterrupted day. The Cinque Terre is served by the milk-run train from Genoa and La Spezia. Speed demons arrive in the morning, check their bags in La Spezia, take the five-hour hike through all five towns, laze away the afternoon on the beach or rock of their choice, and zoom away on the overnight train to somewhere back in the real world. But be warned: The Cinque Terre has a strange way of messing up your momentum.

The towns are each just a few minutes apart by hourly train or boat. There's no checklist of sights or experiences; just a hike, the towns themselves, and your fondest vacation desires. Study this chapter in advance and piece together your best day, mixing hiking, swimming, trains, and a boat ride. For the best light and coolest temperatures, start your hike early.

Market days are Tuesday in Vernazza, Wednesday in Levanto, Thursday in Monterosso, and Friday in La Spezia (08:00–13:00).

Getting around the Cinque Terre

By Train: At La Spezia, the gateway to the Cinque Terre, you'll transfer to the milk-run Cinque Terre train. There might be a TI at the station. If not, skip the 20-minute hike to La Spezia's main TI at Via Mazzini near the waterfront (daily in summer 09:00–13:00, 15:00–18:00; winter Mon–Sat 09:00–13:00, 14:00–17:00, Sun 09:00–13:00; tel. 0187-718-997).

At the station, buy your €1.20 ticket or Cinque Terre Card (see page 769) and take the half-hour train ride into the Cinque Terre town of your choice. Once in the Cinque Terre, you'll get around the villages cheaper by train but more scenically by boat.

Cinque Terre Train Schedule: Since the train is the Cinque Terre lifeline, many shops and restaurants post the current schedule. Try to get a photocopied schedule—it'll come in handy (included with Cinque Terre Card).

Trains leave La Spezia for the Cinque Terre villages (last year's schedule) at 07:17, 08:10, 10:00, 11:23, 12:40, 13:20, 14:16, 15:00, 16:27, 17:19, 18:16, 19:16, 21:09, and 23:05.

Trains leave Monterosso al Mare for La Spezia (departing Vernazza about 10 minutes later, last year's schedule) at 06:30, 07:04, 08:07, 09:04, 10:16, 11:00, 12:13, 13:05, 13:41, 14:08, 15:12, 16:15, 17:23, 18:24, 19:14, 20:07, 22:13, and 23:31.

Do not rely on these train times. Check the current posted schedule and then count on half the trains being 15 minutes or so late (unless you're late, in which case they are right on time).

To orient yourself, remember that directions are "*per* [to] Genoa" or "*per* La Spezia," and any train that stops at any of the villages other than Monterosso will stop at all five. (Note that many trains leaving La Spezia skip them all or stop only in Monterosso.)

The five towns are just minutes apart by train. Know your stop. After leaving the town before your destination, go to the door to slip out before mobs pack in. Since the stations are small and the trains are long, you might get off the train deep in a tunnel, and you might need to flip open the handle of the door yourself.

The train stations should be staffed at all five Cinque Terre towns. Stations sell train tickets, the one-day Hiking Passes (€2.60), and Cinque Terre Cards, which cover the park entry fee and local buses and trains (€5.20/1 day, €10.50/3 days, and €15.50/week).

The Cinque Terre Card, which includes the national park entry fee, is convenient, but if you're on a tight budget, you can save a bit of money by paying separately for a one-day Hiking Pass (€2.60) and your train travel.

It's cheap to buy individual train tickets to travel between the towns. Since a one-town hop costs the same as a five-town hop (€0.90) and every ticket is good for six hours with stopovers, save money and explore the region in one direction on one ticket. Stamp the ticket at the station machine before you board.

If you have a Eurailpass, don't spend one of your valuable flexi-days on the cheap Cinque Terre.

By Boat: From Easter to late October (through Nov if weather is good), a daily boat service connects Monterosso, Vernazza, Manarola, Riomaggiore, and Portovenere. This provides a scenic way to get from town to town and survey what you just hiked. It's also the only efficient way to visit the nearby resort of Portovenere (the alternative is a tedious train/bus connection via La Spezia). In peaceful weather, the boats are more reliable than the trains. Boats go about hourly, from 10:00 until 18:00 (about €3 per single hop or €11.50 for an all-day pass to the Cinque Terre towns, buy tickets at little stands at each town's harbor, tel. 0187-777-727). A more frequent boat service connects Monterosso and Vernazza (tel. 0187-817-452). Schedules are posted at docks, harbor bars, and hotels.

By Foot: A scenic trail runs along the coast, connecting each of the five Cinque Terre towns (see "Hiking," below). Sometime severe rains can wash out trails, especially in winter. Ask around if the trails are open.

Tour of the Cinque Terre

For a guided tour, consider spending a day with a hard-working and likable American student, Sean Risotti, who liked the Cinque Terre so much he moved in (€40, almost daily April–Oct, departing Monterosso at 10:00 or Vernazza at 10:45, book at cinqueterretrek @hotmail.com or at the Fishnet Internet Lounge in Monterosso). The day—which is a great way to meet other travelers—includes a hike from Vernazza to Manarola, lots of information, special glimpses of the area, and a dinner that evening.

Events on the Cinque Terre

May 11   Monterosso: Lemon Festival
June 2   Monterosso: Corpus Domini (procession on carpet of flowers)
June 24   Riomaggiore and Monterosso: Festival in honor of St. John the Baptist
June 29   Corniglia: Festival of St. Peter and St. Paul
July 20   Vernazza: Festival for patron saint, St. Margaret
Aug 10   Manarola: Festival for patron saint, St. Lawrence
Aug 15   All towns: Ascension of Mary
Sept 8   Monterosso: Maria Nascente, or "Rising Mary" (fair with handicrafts)
End of Sept   Monterosso: Walnut Festival (games with walnuts)

VERNAZZA

With the closest thing to a natural harbor—overseen by a ruined castle and an old church—and only the occasional noisy slurping up of the train by the mountain to remind you of the modern world, Vernazza is my Cinque Terre home.

The action is at the harbor, where you'll find a kids' beach, plenty of sunning rocks, outdoor restaurants, a bar hanging on the edge of the castle (great for evening drinks), and a tailgate-party street market every Tuesday morning. In the summer, the beach becomes a soccer field where teams fielded by local bars and restaurants provide late-night entertainment. In the dark, locals fish off the promontory, using glowing bobs that shine in the waves.

The town's 500 residents, proud of their Vernazzan heritage, brag that "Vernazza is locally owned. Portofino has sold out." Fearing the change it would bring, keep-Vernazza-small proponents stopped the construction of a major road into the town and region. Families are tight and go back centuries; several generations stay together. Leisure time is devoted to the *passeggiata*—strolling lazily together up and down the main street. Sit on a bench and study the passersby. Then explore the characteristic alleys called *carugi*. In October the cantinas are draped with drying grapes. In the winter the population shrinks, as many people move to more comfortable big-city apartments.

A steep five-minute hike in either direction from Vernazza gives you a classic village photo op (for the best light, head toward Corniglia in the morning, toward Monterosso in the evening). Franco's Bar, with a panoramic terrace, is at the tower on the trail toward Corniglia.

Vernazza

NARROW ROAD!
(TO AUTOSTRADA)

P BANK · POST · BAR
SORRISO'S ANNEX

TO
CEMETERY

· TEL.

PENSION
SORRISO

LA TORRE REST.

TRAIL TO
CORNIGLIA

TUNNEL

TRAIN
STN.

TUNNEL

TO/PER
MONTEROSSO
& GENOVA

TO / PER
LA SPEZIA
& PISA

BLUE MARLIN
BAR & LAUNDRY

BAKERY

"MAIN STRADA"
(A.K.A. VIA ROMA)

TRAIL TO
MONTEROSSO

PIZZA

FARMACIA

ALBERGO
BARBARA

GROC.

TRAT.
PIVA

BARS, RESTAURANTS,
GROC. STORES & TEL

SUNNING
& SWIMMING

CHURCH

PIAZZA
MARCONI

GELATI

KIDS BEACH

TRAT.
GIANNI

FRANZI
ROOMS

HARBOR

CASTLE

TO
MONTEROSSO

BREAKWATER

SHOWERS

BAR/
REST.

CASTELLO
RESTAURANT
(GREAT VIEW!)

LIGURIAN

SUNNING
& SWIMMING

STATI
UNITI

SEA

DOCK

★ **NOTE:** MAP NOT TO
SCALE – TRAIN STN. TO BREAK-
WATER IS A 5 MINUTE WALK.
(BUT DON'T RUSH IT!)

⊞ = STEPPED
ALLEYS

DCH

Vernazza has ATMs and two banks (center and top of town). A shuttle bus runs twice an hour up and down the main street (free with Cinque Terre Card, otherwise €1). The slick new Internet Point, run by Alberto and Isabella, is in the village center (fast connections, daily 09:30–23:30, tel. 0187-812-949). The Blue Marlin bar (run by Franco and Massimo, open daily in Aug, otherwise closed Thu) also offers Internet access plus a self-service laundry (€4.70 wash, €4.70 dry, super easy machines with automatic detergent and English instructions, buy tokens at Blue Marlin bar any day except Thu, laundry open daily 08:00–22:00—earlier if the bar is open and every day in Aug, Via Roma 49, 30 meters below train station).

You can buy train tickets, Hiking Passes, and Cinque Terre

Cards and store luggage (€0.50/hr) at the Vernazza train station (open daily in summer 08:00–19:30, in winter 08:00–18:00, tel. 0187-812-533, a little English spoken). Accommodations are listed near the end of this chapter.

Sights—Vernazza

▲▲**Vernazza Top-Down Orientation Walk**—Walk uphill until you hit the parking lot—with a bank, a post office, and a barrier that keeps all but service vehicles out. The tidy new square is called Fontana Vecchia, after a long-gone fountain. Older locals remember the river filled with townswomen doing their washing. Begin your saunter downhill to the harbor.

Just before the "Pension Sorriso" sign you'll see the ambulance barn (big brown wood doors) on your right. A group of volunteers is always on call for a dash to the hospital, 30 minutes away in La Spezia. Opposite that is a big empty lot next to Pension Sorriso. Like many landowners, Sr. Sorriso had plans to expand, but the government said no. The old character of these towns is carefully protected.

Across from Pension Sorriso is the honorary clubhouse for the ANPI (members of the local WWII resistance). Only five ANPI old-timers survive. Cynics consider them less than heroes. After 1943 Hitler called up Italian boys over 15. Rather than die on the front for Hitler, they escaped to the hills. Only to remain free did they become "resistance fighters."

A few steps farther you'll see a monument (marble plaque in wall to your left) to those killed in World War II. Not a family was spared. Study this: Soldiers *morti in combattimento* fought for Mussolini, some were deported to *Germania*, and "partisans" were killed later fighting against Mussolini.

The tiny monorail *trenino* (as you're facing plaque, look up on the wall on your right) is parked quietly here except in September and October, when it's busy helping locals bring down the grapes. The path to Corniglia leaves from here (it runs above plaque, starting at your left). Behind you is a tiny square playground, decorated with three millstones, which no longer grind local olives into oil. From here, Vernazza's tiny river goes underground.

In the tunnel under the railway tracks, you'll see a door marked *Croce Verde Vernazza* (Green Cross). Posted on the other side of the tunnel is the "P.A. Croce Verde Vernazza" (in a small green display case), the list of volunteers ready for ambulance duty each day of the month.

The train tracks are above you. The second set of tracks (nearer the harbor) was recently renovated to lessen the disruptive noise; locals say it made no difference.

Follow the road downhill. Until the 1950s, Vernazza's river ran open through the center of town from here to the *gelateria*.

Wandering through this main business center you'll pass many locals doing their *vasca* (laps) past the entrepreneurial Blue Marlin bar (about the only nightspot in town) and the tiny Chapel of Santa Marta (the small stone building with iron grillwork over the window, across from Il Baretto), where Mass is celebrated only on special Sundays. Next you'll see a grocery, *gelateria*, bakery, pharmacy, another grocery, and another *gelateria*.

On the left, in front of the second *gelateria*, an arch leads to what was a beach where the river used to flow out of town. Continue on down to the harbor square and breakwater. Vernazza, with the only natural harbor of the Cinque Terre, was established as the sole place boats could pick up the fine local wine. (The town is named for a kind of wine.) Peek into the tiny street behind the Vulnetia restaurant with the commotion of arches. Vernazza's most characteristic side streets, called *carugi*, lead up from here. The trail (above the church toward Monterosso) leads to the classic view of Vernazza (best photos just before sunset).

▲▲▲**The Burned-Out Sightseer's Visual Tour of Vernazza**— Sit at the end of the harbor breakwater (perhaps with a glass of local white wine or something more interesting from Bar Capitano— borrow the glass, they don't mind), face the town, and see . . .

The harbor: In a moderate storm you'd be soaked, as waves routinely crash over the *molo* (breakwater, built in 1972). The train line (to your left), constructed 130 years ago to tie a newly united Italy together, linked Turin and Genoa with Rome. A second line (hidden in a tunnel at this point) was built in the 1960s. The yellow building alongside the tracks was Vernazza's first train station. You can see the four bricked-up alcoves where people once waited for trains. Vernazza's fishing fleet is down to three small fishing boats (with the net spools); the town's restaurants buy up everything they catch. Vernazzans are more likely to own a boat than a car. In the '70s tiny Vernazza had one of the top water polo teams in Italy, and the harbor was their "pool." Later, when a real pool was required, Vernazza dropped out of the league.

The castle: On the far right, the castle, which is now a grassy park with great views, still guards the town (€1, daily 10:00–18:30, from harbor, take stairs by Trattoria Gianni and follow signs to Castello restaurant, tower is a few steps beyond, see the photo and painting gallery rooms). It's called *Belforte*, or "loud screams," for the warnings it made back in pirating days. The highest umbrellas mark the recommended Castello restaurant (see "Eating," below). The square, squat tower on the water is great for a glass of wine (follow the rope to the Belforte Bar, open Wed–Mon 08:00–24:00, closed Tue; inside the submarine-strength door, a photo of a major storm shows the entire tower under a wave).

The town: Vernazza has two halves. *Sciuiu*, on the left (literally "flowery"), is the sunny side, and *luvegu*, on the right (literally "dank"), is the shady side. The houses below the castle were connected by an interior arcade—ideal for fleeing attacks. The pastel colors are regulated by a commissioner of good taste in the community government. The square before you is locally famous for some of the region's finest restaurants. The big red central house, the 12th-century site where Genoan warships were built, used to be a kind of guardhouse.

Above the town: The small round tower above the guardhouse, another part of the city fortifications, reminds us of Vernazza's importance in the Middle Ages, when it was an important ally of Genoa (whose arch enemies were the other maritime republics of Pisa, Amalfi, and Venice). Franco's Bar, just behind the tower, welcomes hikers finishing, starting, or simply contemplating the Corniglia-Vernazza hike with great town views. Vineyards fill the mountainside beyond the town. Notice the many terraces. Someone calculated that the vineyard terraces of the Cinque Terre have the same amount of stonework as the Great Wall of China. Wine production is down nowadays, as the younger residents choose less physical work. But locals still work their plots and proudly serve their family wine. A single steel train line winds up the gully behind the tower. This is for the vintner's *trenino*, the tiny service train.

The church, school, and city hall: Vernazza's Ligurian Gothic church, built with black stones quarried from Punta Mesco (the distant point behind you), dates from 1318. The gray-and-red house above and to the left of the spire is the local elementary school (which about 25 children attend). High school is in the "big city," La Spezia. The red building to the right of (and below) the schoolhouse is the former monastery and present city hall. Vernazza and Corniglia function as one community. Through most of the 1990s, the local government was communist. In 1999 they elected a coalition of many parties working to rise above ideologies and simply make Vernazza a better place. Finally, on the top of the hill, with the best view of all, is the town cemetery, where most locals plan to end up.

Cinque Terre Hiking and Swimming

▲▲▲**Hiking**—All five towns are connected by good trails. Experience the area's best by hiking from one end to the other. The entire 11-kilometer (7-mile) hike can be done in about four hours, but allow five for dawdling. While you can detour to dramatic hilltop sanctuaries (one trail leads from Vernazza's cemetery uphill), I'd keep it simple by following the easy red-and-white-marked low trails between the villages. Good hiking maps (about €5, sold everywhere, not necessary for this described walk) cover the expanded version of this hike, from Portovenere through all five Cinque Terre towns to Levanto, and more serious hikes in the high country. Get local advice to make sure trails are open, particularly in spring.

Since I still get the names of the Cinque Terre towns mixed up, I think of the towns by number: Riomaggiore (town #1), Manarola (#2), Corniglia (#3), Vernazza (#4), and resorty Monterosso (#5).

Riomaggiore-Manarola (20 min): Facing the front of the train station in Riomaggiore (town #1), go up the stairs to the right, following signs for the Via dell' Amore. The film-gobbling promenade—wide enough for baby strollers—leads down the coast to Manarola. While there's no beach here, stairs lead down to sunbathing rocks.

Manarola-Corniglia (45 min): The walk from Manarola (#2) to Corniglia (#3) is a little longer and a little more rugged than that from #1 to #2.

Ask locally about the more difficult six-mile inland hike to Volastra. This tiny village, perched between Manarola and Corniglia, hosts the Five-Terre wine co-op; stop by the Cantina Sociale. If you take this high road between Manarola and Corniglia, allow two hours; in return, you'll get sweeping views and a closer look at the vineyards.

Corniglia-Vernazza (90 min): The hike from Corniglia (#3) to Vernazza (#4)—the wildest and greenest of the coast— is most rewarding. From the Corniglia station and beach, zigzag up to the town (taking the steeper corkscrew stairs, the longer road, or the shuttlebus). Ten minutes past Corniglia toward Vernazza you'll see the well-hung Guvano beach far below (see below). The trail leads past a bar and picnic tables, through lots of fragrant and flowery vegetation, and scenically into Vernazza.

Vernazza-Monterosso (90 min): The trail from Vernazza (#4) to Monterosso (#5) is a scenic up-and-down-a-lot trek. Trails are rough (and some readers report "very dangerous") but easy to follow. Camping at the picnic tables midway is frowned upon. The views just out of Vernazza are spectacular.

▲**Swimming**—Wear your walking shoes and pack your swim gear. Several of the beaches have showers (no shampoo, please) that may work better than your hotel's. Underwater sightseeing is full of fish—goggles are sold in local shops. Sea urchins can be a problem if you walk on the rocks; consider using fins or aquasocks.

Here's a beach review:

Riomaggiore: The beach is rocky but clean and peaceful. It's a two-minute walk from the harbor: face the harbor, then take the path to your left. At the La Conchiglia bar, go down the stairs to the right of the bar. Follow the path to the beach.

Manarola: Manarola has no sand but the best deepwater swimming of all. The first "beach," with a shower, ladder, and wonderful rocks (with daredevil high divers), is my favorite.

The second has tougher access and no shower but feels more remote and pristine (follow paved path around point).

Corniglia: This hilltop town has a rocky man-made beach below its station. It's clean and uncrowded, and the beach bar has showers, drinks, and snacks.

The nude Guvano (GOO-vah-noh) beach (between Corniglia and Vernazza) made headlines in Italy in the 1970s as clothed locals in a makeshift armada of dinghies and fishing boats retook their town beach. But big-city nudists still work on all-around tans in this remote setting. From the Corniglia train station, follow the road north, go over the tracks, then zigzag below the tracks, following signs to the tunnel in the cliff (walk past the *proprieta privata* sign). When you buzz the intercom, the hydraulic *Get Smart*-type door is opened from the other end. After a 15-minute hike through a cool, moist, and dimly lit unused old train tunnel, you'll emerge at the Guvano beach—and be charged €5 (€4 with this guidebook). The beach has drinking water, but no WC. A steep (free) trail leads from the beach up to the Corniglia-Vernazza trail. The crowd is Italian counterculture: pierced nipples, tattooed punks, hippie drummers in dreads, and nude exhibitionist men. The ratio of men to women is about three to two. About half the people on the pebbly beach keep their swimsuits on.

Vernazza: The village has a children's sandy cove, sunning rocks, and showers by the breakwater. There's a ladder on the breakwater for deepwater access. The tiny *acque pendente* (waterfall) cove which locals call their *laguna blu*, between Vernazza and Monterosso, is accessible only by small hired boat.

Monterosso: The town's beaches, immediately in front of the train station, are easily the Cinque Terre's best and most crowded. It's a sandy resort with everything rentable...lounge chairs, umbrellas, paddleboats, and usually even beach access. Beaches are free only where you see no umbrellas.

Cinque Terre Towns

(Note: Readers of this book fill Vernazza. For this reason you might prefer to stay in one of these towns with fewer Americans. See "Sleeping," below, for accommodations for each town.)

▲▲**Riomaggiore (town #1)**—The most substantial nonresort town of the group, Riomaggiore is a disappointment from the train station. But walk through the tunnel next to the train tracks (or ride the elevator through the hillside to the top of town) and you land in a fascinating tangle of pastel homes leaning on each other as if someone stole their crutches. There's homemade gelato at the Bar Central on main street, and, if Ivo is there, you'll feel right at home. When Ivo closes, the gang goes down to the harborside with a guitar.

Riomaggiore's **TI** is inside the train station (Mon–Fri 10:30–12:00, 14:30–17:30, Sat–Sun 10:30–12:00, 15:00–17:30, tel.

Riomaggiore and Manarola

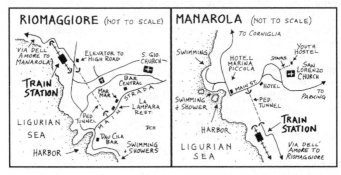

0187-920-633). The bus shuttles locals and tourists up and down Riomaggiore's steep main street (free with Cinque Terre Card, 2/hr, just flag it down); a larger blue bus helps out in the morning.

Here's an easy loop trip through Riomaggiore that maximizes views and minimizes walking uphill (this is easiest if you arrive by train; if you arrive by boat, take the tunnel alongside the tracks to the station and start from there). From the train station, take the elevator up to the top of town (€1, included with Cinque Terre Card, entrance at railway tunnel). At the top, go right, following the walkway—with spectacular sea views—around the cliff. Ignore the steps marked *Marina Seacost* (harbor). Instead, continue on the path; it's a five-minute, fairly level walk to the church. Continue past the church and then take a right down the stairs to Via Columbo, Riomaggiore's main street. Stroll down Via Columbo. Just past the WC you'll see flower boxes on the street, sometimes blocking it; these slide back electrically to let the little bus get past. On your way down the hill, you'll pass colorful, small shops, including a bakery and a couple of groceries. When Via Columbo dead-ends, on your left you'll find the stairs down to the harbor, boat dock, and a 200-meter trail to the beach (*spiaggia*). To your right is the tunnel, running alongside the tracks, that takes you directly to the station. Either take a train or hop a boat (from the harbor) to your next destination.

For hikes from Riomaggiore, consider the cliff-hanging trail that leads from the beach to a hilltop botanical garden (free entrance with Cinque Terre Card) and old WWII bunkers. Another climbs scenically to the Madonna di Montenero sanctuary high above the town. Riomaggiore also has a diving center (scuba, snorkeling, boats, Via San Giacomo, tel. 0187-920-011).

▲**Manarola (town #2)**—Like town #1, #2 is attached to its station by a 200-meter-long tunnel. Manarola is tiny and picturesque, a tumble of buildings bunny-hopping down its ravine

Corniglia and Monterosso

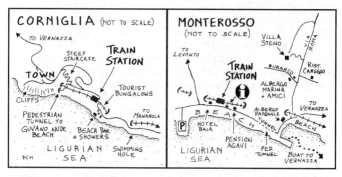

to the fun-loving harbor. Notice how the I-beam crane launches the boats. Facing the harbor, look at the hillside to your right, dotted with a bar in the middle. It's Punta Bonfiglio, an entertaining park/game area/bar with the best view playground on the coast. The gate farther up the hillside is the entrance to the cemetery. From here you can get poster-perfect views of Manarola (2-minute walk from the harbor on path to Corniglia).

Within Manarola, the small bus shuttles people between main street and the parking lot (free with Cinque Terre Card, 2/hr, just flag it down). In the middle of town, across from the railway tunnel, you'll see Bar Aristide, which sometimes shows outdoor movies on weekends in August by hanging a screen over part of the tunnel entrance (closed Mon, Via Discovolo 138, tel. 0187-920-000). At the top of the town you'll find great views, the church, and a cluster of accommodations, including a super hostel (see "Sleeping," below).

The simple, wooden, religious scenes that you'll likely see on the hillside are the work of local resident Mario Andreoli. Before his father died, Mario promised him he'd replace the old cross on the family's vineyard. Mario's been adding figures ever since. After recovering from a rare illness, he redoubled his efforts. The scenes, which do change (a sheep here, an apostle there), are sometimes left up year-round. On religious holidays, everything's lit up: the Nativity, the Last Supper, the Crucifixion, the Resurrection, and more.

▲▲**Corniglia (town #3)**—From the station a footpath zigzags up nearly 400 stairs to the only town of the five not on the water. Take the bus (free with Cinque Terre Card, 2/hr). Originally settled by a Roman farmer who named it for his mother, Cornelia (which is how Corniglia is pronounced), its ancient residents produced a wine so famous that vases found at Pompeii touted its virtues. Today its wine is still its lifeblood. Follow the pungent smell of ripe grapes into an alley cellar and get a local to let you dip a straw into her keg. Remote and less visited, Corniglia has fewer tourists, cooler temperatures, a windy belvedere (on its promontory), a few restaurants, and plenty of private rooms for rent. Continue past the train station (toward Manarola) to find Corniglia's beach. The nude Guvano beach is in the opposite direction (toward Vernazza).

▲▲▲**Vernazza (town #4)**—See beginning of chapter.

▲▲**Monterosso al Mare (town #5)**—This is a resort with cars, hotels, rentable beach umbrellas, and crowds. The town is split into the old and new, connected by a tunnel. The train station is in the new town, along with the TI (daily Mon–Sat 09:30–12:30, 15:30–17:30, closed Sun and Nov–Easter, exit station and go left a few doors, tel. 0187-817-506), several recommended accommodations, and a statue—*Il Gigante*. This 14-meter-tall statue, which once held a trident, looks as if it were hewn from the rocky cliff, but it's made of reinforced concrete, and dates from the beginning of the 20th century.

Monterosso's old town contains Old World charm, small crooked streets, and plenty of Internet access. Kate's Fishnet Internet Lounge is a welcoming, well run, and good center for local information (daily until 24:00, Via Roma 17, can book rooms, tel. 0187-817-373, www.fishnet.it). Or try The Net (Via Vittorio Emanuele 55, also books rooms, guides, tel. 0187-817-288, www.cinqueterrenet.com). From the old town harbor, boats run nearly hourly to Vernazza and points beyond. From the breakwater (and the new town), look for all the towns of the Cinque Terre.

The shuttle buses that run along the waterfront connect the old and newtowns with outlying areas (free with Cinque Terre Card, otherwise €1, 2/hr).

You can easily stroll the short tunnel between the new and old towns, but hikers prefer the trail. It's like a mini-Cinque Terre trail, combining scenery and greenery. Heading from the train station to the old town, take the path to the right of the tunnel entrance. The path leads to views of a German WWII bunker below on the rocks (worth seeing, but not worth climbing down to).

Continuing on the path gets you into the old town. Or, at the point where you see the bunker, take the path up to the top of the hill (where you'll see a statue of St. Francis), and up farther still through the woods to reach a gate (marked *Convento e Chiesa Cappuccini*) leading to a church with a Van Dyck painting of the Crucifixion (accommodations next to church, see "Sleeping," below). You're a world away from the resort town below.

A trail to the right of the church leads up to the cemetery; appreciate its flowers, photos, and your beating heart. Backtrack to the St. Francis statue, and take the trail down into the old town. (Reversing this, if you're going from the old town to the new, take

the trail to the right of the tunnel entrance; go right on Zii di Frati
to see the church, or continue straight to get to the new town).
Allow a total of 30 minutes if you include the church and cemetery.

Cinque Terre Cuisine 101

A few menu tips: *Accuighe* (pron. ah-CHOO-gay) are anchovies,
a local specialty—always served the day they're caught. If you've
always hated anchovies (the harsh, cured-in-salt American kind),
try them fresh here. *Tegame alla Vernazza* is the most typical main
course in Vernazza: anchovies, potatoes, tomatoes, white wine, oil,
and herbs. *Pansotti* is ravioli with ricotta and spinach, often served
with a hazelnut sauce... delightful and filling. While antipasto is
cheese and salami in Tuscany, here you'll get *antipasti di mare*,
a big plate of mixed fruits of the sea and a fine way to start a meal.
For many, splitting this and a pasta dish is plenty. Try the fun
local dessert: "grandmother's cake" with a glass of *sciacchetrà* for
dunking (see "Wine," below).

▲▲**Pesto**—This is the birthplace of pesto. Basil, which loves the
temperate Ligurian climate, is mixed with cheese (half *Parmigiano*
cow cheese and half pecorino sheep cheese), garlic, olive oil, and
pine nuts, and then poured over pasta. Try it on spaghetti, *trenette*,
or *trofie* (made of flour with a bit of potato, designed specifically
for pesto). Many also like pesto lasagna. If you become addicted,
small jars of pesto are sold in the local grocery stores.

▲▲**Wine**—The *vino delle Cinque Terre*, respected throughout
Italy, flows cheap and easy throughout the region. It is white—
great with the local seafood. D.O.C. is the mark of top quality.
Red wine is better elsewhere. For a sweet dessert wine, the local
sciacchetrà wine is worth the splurge (€2.60 per glass, often served
with a cookie). While 10 kilos of grapes yield seven liters of local
wine, *sciacchetrà* is made from near-raisins, and 10 kilos of grapes
make only 1.5 liters of *sciacchetrà*. The word means "push and
pull"... push in lots of grapes, pull out the best wine. If your
room is up a lot of steps, be warned: *sciacchetrà* is 18 percent
alcohol, while regular wine is only 11 percent. In the cool, calm
evening, sit on the Vernazza breakwater with a glass of wine
and watch the phosphorescence in the waves.

Sleeping and Eating on the Cinque Terre
(€1.10 = about $1, country code: 39)
Sleep Code: **S** = Single, **D** = Double/Twin, **T** = Triple, **Q** = Quad,
b = bathroom, **s** = shower only, **CC** = Credit Cards accepted,
no CC = Credit Cards not accepted, **SE** = Speaks English,
NSE = No English. Breakfast is included only in real hotels.

If you're trying to avoid my readers, stay away from Vernazza.
Monterosso is a good choice for the younger crowd (more nightlife) and rich, sun-worshiping softies (who prefer firm reservations

for hotels with private bathrooms). Wine lovers and mountain goats like Corniglia. Sophisticated Italians and Germans choose Manarola. Travelers who show up without reservations enjoy Riomaggiore for its easy room-booking services.

While the Cinque Terre is too rugged for the mobs that ravage the Spanish and French coasts, it's popular with Italians, Germans, and Americans in the know. Hotels charge the most and are packed on Easter, in August, and on summer Fridays and Saturdays. August weekends are worst. But €60 doubles abound throughout the year. Outside of August weekends, you can land a comfortable €60 double in a private home on any day by just arriving in town (ideally by noon) and asking around at bars and restaurants or simply approaching locals on the street. This seems scary, but it's true.

For the best value, visit three private rooms and snare the best. Going direct cuts out a middleman and softens prices. Plan on paying cash. Private rooms are generally bigger and more comfortable than those offered by the pensions.

If you want the security of a reservation, make it long in advance for a hotel (small places generally don't take reservations made weeks ahead). If you don't get a reply to your faxed request for a room, assume the place is fully booked.

Sleeping in Vernazza
(zip code: 19018)

Vernazza, the essence of the Cinque Terre, is my favorite. There are three pensions and piles of private rooms for rent. Anywhere you stay here will require some climbing. Night noises can be a problem if you're near the station. Address letters to 19018 Vernazza, Cinque Terre, La Spezia. Better yet, call, fax, or e-mail. A new parking lot and a hard-working shuttle service makes driving to Vernazza a reasonable option for drivers with nerves of steel. The little shuttle bus runs twice an hour (generally with helpful English-speaking Beppi behind the wheel).

Usually when a price range is listed, the lower price is charged during winter (roughly Nov–March) and the higher price the rest of the year.

Pensions

Albergo Barbara, on the harbor square, is run by kindly Giuseppe and his Swiss wife, Patricia. Their nine, clean, modern rooms share three public showers and WCs (S-€36–47 depending on season, D without view-€43, D with small view-€45, D with big view-€55, bunky family Q-€67, 2-night stay preferred, loads of stairs, fans, closed Dec–Jan, Piazza Marconi 30, call to reserve instead of fax, tel. & fax 0187-812-398, cellular 338-7933261, SE). The two big doubles on the main floor come with grand harbor views and are the best value (top-floor doubles have small windows and small views). The office is on the top floor of the big, red, vacant-looking building facing the harbor.

Trattoria Gianni rents 23 small rooms just under the castle. The funky ones are artfully decorated à la shipwreck and are up lots of tight, winding, spiral stairs, and most have tiny balconies and grand views. The new, comfy rooms lack views but have modern bathrooms and a super scenic, cliff-hanger private garden. Marisa (who doles out smiles like a rich gambler on a losing streak) requires a two-night minimum and check-in before 16:00 (S-€34, D-€47, sinks and bathrooms down the hall; Db-€65, Tb-€78, CC but 10 percent discount for cash, Piazza Marconi 5, closed Jan–Feb, tel. & fax 0187-812-228, tel. 0187-821-003). Pick up your keys at Trattoria Gianni's restaurant/reception on the harbor square and hike up dozens of stairs to #41 (funky, *con vista mare*) or #47 (new, *nuovo*) at the top. As a matter of principle, no English is spoken here. (Note: My tour company books this place 50 nights of the season.) Telephone three days in advance and leave your first name and time of arrival.

Pension Sorriso offers 20 good rooms without views or an exuberant welcome. Prices include breakfast and an obligatory dinner (D-€103, Db-€113, 50 meters up from station, reception in bar, closed Nov–Feb, tel. 0187-812-224, fax 0187-821-198, some English spoken). While train sounds rumble through the front rooms of the main building, the annex up the street is quieter.

Private Rooms (Affitta Camere)

These are the best values in Vernazza. The town is honey-combed year-round with pleasant, rentable private rooms and apartments with kitchens (cheap for families). They are usually reluctant to reserve rooms far in advance. It's easiest to call a day or two ahead or simply show up in the morning and look around. The rooms cost about €45 to €60 for a double, depending on the view and plumbing. Some have killer views, and cost the same as a small dark place on a back lane over the train tracks. Little or no English is spoken at these places. Any main-street business has a line on rooms for rent.

Franca Maria rents two sharp, comfortable rooms overlooking the harbor square (Db-€47–72, Qb-€83–103 depending on season, the 2 side-by-side doubles can turn into a quad, Piazza Marconi 30, tel. 0187-812-002, fax 0187-812-956, son's e-mail: metalgearsolid@inwind.it). It's just a few steps up from the harbor—a rarity in vertical Vernazza.

Martina Callo rents three fine, lofty rooms overlooking square, up piles of steps near the church tower (Db-€47–57, Qb-€93–103; room #1-Qb with harbor view, room #2-Qb is huge family room with no view, room #3-Db with grand view terrace;

heating in winter; ring bell at Piazza Marconi 26, tel. & fax 0187-812-365, e-mail: roomartina@supereva.it).

Affitta Camere da Anna-Maria offers three pleasant rooms up spiral staircases (D-€60, Db-€65 with view or terrace—the terrace room is best, Via Carattino 64, turn left at pharmacy, climb Via Carattino to #64, tel. 0187-821-082).

Tonino Basso rents four super rooms—clean and modern—near the post office, in the only building in Vernazza that has an elevator. Rooms come with a private bath but no views (Sb-€47, Db-€62, Tb-€78, CC, tel. 0187-821-264, fax 0187-821-260, e-mail: toninobasso@libero.it, cellular 335-269-436; when you arrive, call cellular number from train station—phones at bottom of stairs—and Tonino will meet you; or the Gambero Rosso restaurant at harbor can find him—but then you'll have to backtrack to get to his rooms).

Mike and Franca Castiglione, who speak New Yorkish, rent a small, basic room that has a private ramshackle garden with a sea view (€57, Via Carratino 16, turn left at pharmacy, climb Via Carattino to #16, tel. 0187-812-374).

Giuseppina's Villa, a cozy apartment with a low-ceilinged loft, has one window, no view, and a kitchen. The woman at the grocery store nearest the harbor (with *Salumi e Formaggi* on the awning) can check if it's available (Db-€42, Qb-€83, Via S. Giovanni Battista 7, only a short climb from harbor, tel. 0187-812-026). She also has a double room up the street (Db-€47, no view, but has a garden).

Nicolina rents four decent rooms: a large one with a view, two overlooking Vernazza's main drag, and one without any view. Inquire at Pizzeria Vulnetia on the harbor square or reserve in advance by phone (Db-€62, Qb with terrace and view-€127, Piazza Marconi 29, tel. & fax 0187-821-193, Frederica).

Armanda rents a one-room apartment without a view near the Castello (€62, Piazza Marconi 15, tel. 0187-812-218, cellular 347-306-4760).

Giuliano Basso rents three fine rooms that share a view balcony (Db-€62, CC, open year-round, above train station, direction: Corniglia, take a right before Sorriso's, then take left fork, 5-min walk to harbor, cellular 333-341-4792, www.cdh.it/giuliano).

Eating in Vernazza

If you enjoy Italian cuisine, Vernazza's restaurants are worth the splurge. All take pride in their cooking and have similar prices. Wander around at about 20:00 and compare the ambience.

The **Castello**, run by gracious and English-speaking Monica, her husband Massimo, kind Mario, and the rest of her family, serves great food with great views, just under the castle (Thu–Tue 12:00–15:00 for lunch, 15:00–19:00 for drinks and snacks,

19:00–22:00 for dinner, closed Wed and Nov–April, tel. 0187-812-296).

Four fine places fill the harborfront with happy eaters: **Gambero Rosso**, considered Vernazza's best restaurant, feels classy and costs only a few euros more than the others (Tue–Sun 12:00–15:00, 19:00–22:00, closed Mon and Nov–March, CC, Piazza Marconi 7, tel. 0187-812-265). **Trattoria del Capitano** might serve the best food for the money (Thu–Tue 12:00–15:00, 19:00–22:30, closed Wed except in Aug, closed Dec–Jan, CC, Paolo speaks English, tel. 0187-812-201). **Trattoria Gianni** is also good, especially for seafood (daily 12:30–15:00, 18:30–22:00 in July–Aug, otherwise closed Wed). **Pizzeria Vulnetia** serves the best harborside pizza (Tue–Sun 12:00–16:00, 18:30–23:00, closed Mon, Piazza Marconi 29).

Trattoria da Sandro, on the main drag, mixes Genovese and Ligurian cuisine with friendly service and can be a peaceful alternative to the harborside scene (Wed–Mon 12:00–15:00, 19:00–22:00, closed Tue, CC, just below train station, Via Roma 60, tel. 0187-812-223, Gabriella SE). The more offbeat and intimate **Trattoria da Piva** may come with late-night guitar strumming (Tue–Sun 12:00–15:30, 19:00–01:00, closed Mon, Via Carattino 6, around corner from pharmacy).

For basic grub, a grand view, and perfect peace, hike to Franco's **Ristorante "La Torre"** for a dinner at sunset (Wed–Mon 20:00–21:30, closed Tue, on trail toward Corniglia, tel. 0187-821-082).

The main street is creatively determining tourists' needs and filling them. The **Blue Marlin** bar offers a good selection of sandwiches, salads, and *bruschetta*. Try the **Forno** bakery for good focaccia and veggie tarts, and the several bars for sandwiches and pizza by the slice. Grocery stores make inexpensive sandwiches to order (Mon–Sat 07:30–13:00, 17:00–19:30, Sun 07:30–13:00). The town's two *gelaterias* are good. **La Cantina del Molo**, the new wine shop, will uncork the bottle you buy and supply cups to go (daily 11:00–20:00, until 22:00 in summer, owner makes 5 of the wines, tasting possible). Most harborside bars will let you take your glass on a breakwater stroll.

Breakfast: Locals take breakfast about as seriously as flossing. A cappuccino and a pastry or a piece of focaccia does it. The two harborfront bars offer the most ambience (you can walk out with the cup, grab a view picnic bench, and return the cup when you're done). The bakery opens early, offering freshly-made focaccia. The Blue Marlin serves a special €6.20 breakfast: ham and cheese focaccia, an assortment of fresh local pastries, juice, and cappuccino (Fri–Wed 06:45–24:00, closed Thu; open daily in Aug; just below station, tel. 0187-821-149, www.bluemarlin5terre.com).

Sleeping in Riomaggiore
(zip code: 19017)

Riomaggiore has organized its private room scene better than its neighbors. Several agencies within a few meters of each other on the main drag (with regular office hours, English-speaking staff, and e-mail addresses) manage a corral of local rooms for rent. Expect lots of stairs. The town's shuttle bus service makes getting in and out of town from the parking lot easier.

Room-Finding Services

Edi's Rooms rents five fine rooms and 12 apartments—half have views (Db-€52–78, Qb-€83–124 depending on view, season, and number of people, CC, office open 08:00–20:00 in summer, otherwise 09:00–13:00, 15:00–19:00, Via Colombo 111, tel. & fax 0187-920-325, tel. 0187-760-842, e-mail: edi-vesigna@iol.it).

Mar Mar Rooms, run by Mario Franceschetti, has pleasant rooms and a mini-hostel (€21 dorm beds, Db-€47–62, bunky family deals, can request kitchen and balcony, CC, Internet access and small self-service laundry in office, 30 meters above train tracks on the main drag next to Lampara restaurant, Via Malborghetto 8, tel. & fax 0187-920-932, e-mail: marmar@5terre.com). Mar Mar also rents kayaks (double kayaks €8/hr, cheaper by the half day).

Luciano and Roberto Fazioli have five apartments, nine rooms, and a basic 11-bed mini-hostel (€15.50–21 for dorm bed, D-€31–41, Db-€47–62, apartments-€21–52 per person, prices increase with view and in summer, Via Colombo 94, tel. 0187-920-904 or 0187-920-822, e-mail: robertofazioli@libero.it).

At **Bar Central**, friendly Ivo and Alberto can help you find a room (daily 07:00–01:00, closed Mon in winter only, Via Colombo 144, tel. 0187-920-208, e-mail: barcentr@tin.it). Ivo lived in San Francisco, fills his bar with only the best San Franciscan rock, and speaks great English. His Bar Central, a good stop for breakfast, cheeseburgers, Internet access, and live music (sometimes in summer), is a shaded place to relax with other travelers. It's got the only lively late-night action in town. And there's prize-winning gelato next door.

Accommodations

In the center: **Michielini Anna** rents four clean, attractive apartments with kitchens and no views (€26 per person mid-April–Sept, otherwise €21 per person, CC to reserve but please pay cash, cheaper for longer stays, 2 nights preferred June–Sept, across from Bar Central at Colombo 143, door opens hard, tel. 0187-920-950 for friendly Daniela who speaks good English, tel. & fax 0187-920-411 for *solo-Italiano*-speaking mother, e-mail: anna.michielini@tin.it, another e-mail: michielinis@yahoo.it).

At the top of town: **Albergo Caribana** has six new rooms, with views and shared terraces. At the edge of town, it's a five-minute walk to the center. The easy parking makes this especially appealing to drivers (Db-€62–83, depending on season, includes breakfast, Via Sanctuario 114, tel. 0187-920-773, tel. & fax 0187-920-932, e-mail: marmar@5terre.com)

For a real hotel, consider **Villa Argentina**. It's on the top ridge of town, with 15 crisply clean modern rooms, fine balconies (for 9 rooms), and sea views. While this is a good choice for drivers, the little bus which shuttles people (and their luggage) between the top and bottom of town makes this hotel a possibility for train travelers (Db-€114, includes breakfast, no CC, Via de Gasperi 37, go through tunnel from station, wait for bus or walk 15 min uphill, then take a left at the parking booth, tel. 0187-920-213, fax 0187-920-213, e-mail: villaargentina@libero.it).

Eating in Riomaggiore

Ristorante La Lampara serves a *frutti di mare* pizza, *trenete al pesto*, and the aromatic *spaghetti al cartoccio*—spaghetti with mixed seafood cooked in foil (€13 tourist menu, Wed–Mon 12:00–15:30, 18:00–24:00, closed Tue, CC, on Via Colombo just above tracks, tel. 0187-920-120). Groceries and delis (such as Da Simone) on Via Colombo sell food to go including pizza slices (picnic at the harbor). While the late-night fun is at Ivo's Bar Central, take a walk down to the harborside **Dau Cila** bar (closed Tue) for jazz, nets, and mellow *limoncino*—a drink of lemon juice, sugar, and pure alcohol (a.k.a. *limoncello* elsewhere in Italy).

Sleeping in Manarola
(zip code: 19010)

Manarola has plenty of private rooms. Ask in bars and restaurants. Otherwise you'll find a modern three-star place halfway up the main drag, a cluster of great values around the church at the peaceful top of town a five-minute hike above the train tracks, and a salty place on the harbor. The town's handy shuttle bus service makes getting to and from your car easier.

Up the hill, the utterly normal **Albergo ca' d'Andrean** is quiet, comfortable, modern, and very hotelesque, with 10 big, sunny rooms and a cool garden oasis complete with lemon trees (Sb-€52, Db-€67, breakfast-€5, closed Nov, Via A. Discovolo 101, tel. 0187-920-040, fax 0187-920-452, www.cadandrean.it, e-mail: cadandrean@libero.it, Simone SE).

Affitta Camere de Baranin rents eight airy, refreshing rooms (Db-€55, Db with view and breakfast-€85, Internet access, CC to reserve but please pay cash, climb stairway against wall beyond church square—with your back to the church, stairway is at 07:00, follow sign to Trattoria dal Billy, Via Rollandi 29, tel. & fax 0187-920-595, www.baranin.com, Sara and Silvia SE).

La Torretta has four compact apartments with kitchens, five doubles, and one quad, all attractively designed by the young English-speaking architect/manager Gabriele Baldini (student Db-€26–36, Db-€52–72, Db apartment-€57–77, Qb-€83–124, prices vary with season, reserve with CC, views, big garden, with your back to church, it's at 10:00—look left across the square toward the sea, Piazza della Chiesa, Vico Volto 14, tel. & fax 0187-920-327, check Web for deals involving their Tuscan mountain villa, www.cinqueterre.net/torretta/, e-mail: torretta@cdh.it).

Casa Capellini rents four fine rooms; one has a view balcony, another a 360-degree terrace (D-€42, €36 for 2 or more nights; Db-€47, €42 for 2 or more nights; the *alta camera* on the top, with a kitchen, private terrace, and knockout view-€57, €52 for 2 or more nights; 2 doors down the hill from the church, with your back to the church, it's at 2:00, Via Ettore Cozzani 12, tel. 0187-920-823 or 0187-736-765, e-mail: casa.capellini@tin.it, NSE).

Ostello 5-Terre, Manarola's modern and well-run hostel, stands like a Monopoly hotel behind the church square. It's smart to reserve at least two weeks in advance in high season (one week in off-season). You book with your credit card number; if you cancel with less than three days' notice, you'll be charged (May–Sept: beds-€15.50, Qb-€62, off-season: beds-€13, Qb-€52, closed early Jan–mid-Feb, CC, 48 beds in 4- to 6-bed rooms, not co-ed except for families, office closed 13:00–17:00, rooms closed 10:00–17:00, curfew–01:00, off-season: office and rooms closed until 16:00 and curfew's at 24:00, open to anyone of any age, laundry, safes, phone cards, Internet access, book exchange, elevator, breakfast and dinner, great roof terrace with showers and sunsets, Via B. Riccobaldi 21, tel. 0187-920-215, fax 0187-920-218, www.cinqueterre.net/ostello/, e-mail: ostello@cdh.it). They rent bikes, kayaks, and snorkeling gear.

Marina Piccola has 10 bright, modern rooms on the water, so they figure a warm welcome is unnecessary (Db-€72 for 1-day stays, otherwise half-pension required at €67 per person, CC, Via Discovolo 192, tel. 0187-920-103, fax 0187-920-966, www.marinapiccola.com).

Sleeping in Corniglia
(zip code: 19010)

Perched high above the sea on a hilltop, Corniglia has plenty of private rooms (generally Db-€52). To get to the town from the station, catch the shuttle bus or take a 15-minute uphill hike. If you hike, choose between a long road or lots of stairs. At the top of the stairs, turn left to reach the town (if you've taken the road, just stay on the road). The main drag is Via Fieschi, stretching to the tip of the promontory and its viewpoint park.

For this first listing, take the road (rather than the stairs) up from the station. **Domenico Spora** has eight apartments scattered throughout town, all with views and private bath (Db-€65, Qb-€110, Via Villa 19, tel. 0187-812-293, NSE). Her place is about three-fourths of the way up the hill from the station.

For the following listings, if you've taken the stairs up from the station, turn left at the top of the stairs. These are listed in the order you'll encounter them as you walk up Via Fieschi. At the main square, you'll see **La Lanterna** bar, which rents 10 sleepable rooms in town, some with a view (Db-€52, also has 6 new rooms in Comeneco a 30-min walk away—better for drivers, tel. 0187-812-291).

Continue up Via Fieschi. Detour left—up the stairs—on Via Solferino (then go right, left, and left) to find #34 for **Pelligrini** (3 comfortable rooms including 1 with balcony, terrace for all, tel. 0187-812-184 or 0187-821-176). Return to Via Fieschi.

Next on the main drag is **Villa Sandra**, which has five good rooms (D-€47—2 have terraces, Db-€52) and an apartment (Db-€57; Via Fieschi 212, tel. & fax 0187-812-384).

Next...**Louisa Cristiana** rents a great apartment with three doubles and a big comfy living room/kitchen with a view terrace on the tiny soccer court at the top of the town (Db-€52, grand apartment for 2 people-€103, for 4 people-€114, for 6 people-€130, cheaper in winter, Via Fieschi 215, call English-speaking daughter Cristiana at 0187-812-236—she works at Bar Matteo on Via Fieschi, below main square; also tel. & fax 0187-812-345; daughter rents small apartment for €57). Finally, near the town promontory, you'll see the door for **Signora Silvana** (Via Fieschi 220, tel. 0187-513-830) and next door, **La Rocca** (Via Fieschi 222, tel. 0187-812-178); both offer rooms at this scenic cliff-hanging edge of town.

Villa Cecio is more of a hotel (Db-€60, views, on the main road 200 meters toward Vernazza, tel. 0187-812-043).

Sleeping in Monterosso
(zip code: 19016)

Monterosso al Mare, the most beach-resorty of the five Cinque Terre towns, offers maximum comfort and ease. There are plenty of hotels and rentable beach umbrellas, shops, and cars. The TI (Pro Loco) can give you a list of €30-per-person doubles (pricier for a single) in private homes (Mon–Sat 10:00–12:00, 15:30–17:30, Sun 10:00–12:00; exiting station, TI is to your left; tel. 0187-817-506).

Monterosso is 30 minutes off the freeway (exit: Carrodano). Parking is easy in the huge beachfront guarded lot (€6.20/day). A self-serve **laundry** is in the old town (daily 09:00–12:30, 15:00–20:00, Via Mazzini 4, just off Via Roma).

Recommended hotels are listed for the old town and the
new town (connected by a tunnel), with a convent-run place in
between. My favorite is the Hotel Villa Steno in the old town.
To get to the old town from the station, exit left, walk along the
waterfront, and go through the tunnel.

Sleeping in the Old Town: These are listed in the order
you'll encounter them, whether you're emerging from the tunnel
or getting off the boat.

Albergo Pasquale is next to the tunnel entrance, train
tracks, and boat dock. Run by the same family who own Hotel
Villa Steno (see listing below), this is a decent place with more
comfort than character. It's just a few steps from the beach. The
air-conditioning (used with closed windows) minimizes the train
noise (Sb-€80, Db-€120, Tb-€140, Qb-€160, includes breakfast,
CC, €10 discount per room per night if you pay cash and show
this book, readers get a free glass of the local sweet wine—
sciacchetrà—at check-in, Via Fegina 4, tel. 0187-817-550 or
0187-817-477, fax 0187-817-056, e-mail: pasquale@pasini.com,
Felicita and Marco SE).

The next two places, next door to each other on a quiet
street, both require half-pension during peak season: the fancy
Albergo degli Amici (36 modern rooms, Db-€77–90, breakfast
extra, Db with half-pension-€129—required July-Aug, CC, no
views from rooms, peaceful above-it-all view garden with "sun
beds"—lawn chairs with movable sun shades, Via Buranco 36,
tel. 0187-817-544, fax 0187-817-424, www.cinqueterre.it/hotel
_amici/) and the less fancy **Albergo Marina** (23 decent rooms,
Db with required half-pension April–Aug-€103–124, CC,
elevator, air con, garden with lemon trees, next door at Via
Buranco 40, tel. & fax 0187-817-242 or 0187-817-613, www
.cinqueterre.it/hotel_marina/). To get to the Amici and Marina
from the old town harbor, go to the left of the arcaded building
with the bell tower and turn left after a block; for the next listing
go to the right of the arcaded building up Via Roma.

Ristorante al Carugio rents 10, no-view rooms in an
apartment flat at the no-character top end of town (Db-€70,
CC, office at Via S. Pietro 15—just off Via Roma, rooms at
Via Roma 100, tel. & fax 0187-817-453).

Hotel La Colonnina, a comfy, modern place on a sleepy
side street, takes reservations in advance only for three-night stays.
For a shorter stay, just call a day or two ahead to see if they have
space (Db-€88, no breakfast, elevator, garden, rooftop terrace,
Via Zuecca 6, tel. 0187-817-439). By the tracks, look for the playground and the square with a statue of Garibaldi; Via Zuecca is
directly behind him (the hotel is one block up, to the right).

Farther on is the best place in town: the lovingly managed
Hotel Villa Steno, featuring great view balconies, private

gardens off some rooms, TVs, telephones, air-conditioning, and the friendly help of English-speaking Matteo. Of his 16 rooms, 12 have view balconies (Sb-€80, Db-€120, Tb-€140, Qb-€160, includes hearty buffet breakfast, CC, €10 discount per room per night if you pay cash and show this book, Internet access, self-service laundry—guests only, 10-min hike from the station to the top of the old town at Via Roma 109, tel. 0187-817-028 or 0187-818-336, fax 0187-817-354, www.pasini.com, e-mail: steno @pasini.com). Readers get a free glass of the local sweet wine, *sciacchetrà*, when they check in—ask. The Steno has a tiny parking lot (free, but call to reserve a spot).

Sleeping Between the Old and New Towns: The religious **Convento dei Cappuccini** rents 14 spartan rooms, named after monks, on the hill above the tunnel that connects the old and new parts of town. Their terrace, overlooking the garden and a long stretch of coastline, has a tremendous panoramic view. On foot it's a steep hike, or you can take a taxi (€8) to the cemetery 200 meters away—go around or walk through cemetery to reach the convent (S-€34, Sb-€39, D-€72, Db-€78, all twins, includes breakfast, dinner extra and optional, attached church and cloister, reserve ahead, must send a deposit of 30 percent—personal check okay, 19016 Monterosso, tel. 0187-817-531, e-mail: monterosso .convento@libero.it, truly NSE). If you're hiking from the station, exit left, go through the tunnel, then take a hairpin left. Zigzag up the side of the hill until you reach the gate, the church (Chiesa Cappuccin), and *convento* (15-min walk from station).

Sleeping in the New Town: Turn left out of the station to **Pension Agavi,** which has eight bright, airy rooms (Sb-€47, Db-€83, refrigerators, Fegina 30, tel. 0187-817-171, fax 0187-818-264, cellular 336-258-467, spunky Hillary SE).

Turn right leaving the station for the rest of the listings.

The central, waterfront **Hotel Baia** has appealing, high-ceilinged rooms, but the staff is rude (Db-€129, includes breakfast, CC, slow elevator, balconies, request view—same price, Via Fegina 88, tel. 0187-817-512, fax 0187-818-322).

Consider the newly remodeled **Hotel Punta Mesco** (Db-€100, no views, exit right from station, take first right, Via Molinelli 35, tel. 0187-817-495, www.cinqueterre.it/belvedere).

Villa Mario, good for backpackers, has five basic rooms with a view terrace and a squawky bird learning to talk (Db-€62–72, exit right from station, take second right, walk 5 min uphill, Via Padre Semeria 28, tel. & fax 0187-818-030).

Villa Adriana, run by brusque Austrian nuns, has 55 decent, clean rooms divided between a 19th-century villa and an adjacent, modern annex. With a strict 23:00 curfew, a lofty setting (up off the street with a tropical garden as its front yard), and a religious, institutional atmosphere, it's peaceful (Sb-€65, Db-€120, includes breakfast; half-pension required June–Aug: Sb-€69, Db-€130; CC, double and twins available, some views, attached chapel, parking, exit right from station, walk along waterfront, turn right at Via IV Novembre, 300 meters off beach, Via IV Novembre 23, reception at back of building, tel. 0187-818-109, fax 0187-818-128, SE).

Eating in Monterosso

Ristorante Belvedere is a good bet for good value in the old town (Wed–Mon 12:00–14:30, 19:00–22:00, closed Tue, CC, right on the harbor, across from Albergo Pasquale, tel. 0187-817-033). Lots of shops and bakeries sell pizza and focaccia for an easy picnic at the beach. **Il Frantoia** makes tasty pizza to go (Wed–Fri 09:00–14:00, 16:00–20:00, closed Thu, Via Gioberti 1, just off Via Roma in old town).

Transportation Connections—Cinque Terre

The five towns of the Cinque Terre are on a milk-run train line described earlier in this chapter. Hourly trains connect each town with the others, La Spezia, and Genoa. While a few of the milk-run trains go to more distant points (Milan or Pisa), it's faster to change in La Spezia or Monterosso to a bigger train. Train info: Monterosso tel. 0187-817-458 or 848-888-088.

From La Spezia by train to: Rome (10/day, 4 hrs), **Pisa** (hrly, 1 hr, direction: Livorno, Rome, Salerno, Naples, etc.), **Florence** (hrly, 2.5 hrs, change at Pisa), **Milan** (hrly, 3 hrs, 3 direct; or 4 hrs with change in Genoa), **Venice** (2 direct 6-hr trains/day).

From Monterosso by train to: Venice (2/day, 6 hrs), **Milan** (3/day, 3 hrs), **Genova** (9/day, 1.25 hrs), **Pisa** (3/day, 1.5 hrs), **Sestri Levante** (hrly, 15 min, most trains to Genova stop here), **La Spezia** (nearly hrly, 20 min), **Levanto** (nearly hrly, 6 min).

Parking Tips for Drivers

It is possible to snake your car down the treacherous little road into the Cinque Terre and park in the new parking lot above Vernazza, then take the shuttle bus into town. Monterosso has a big, guarded beachfront parking lot that fills only on August weekends (€6.20/day). Riomaggiore and Manarola both offer parking and a shuttle bus to get you into town.

You can park your car near the train stations in La Spezia or Levanto (the first town past Monterosso). Confirm that parking is OK and leave nothing inside to steal. In La Spezia, a nearby garage can store your car for about €13 per day.

AMSTERDAM

Amsterdam is a progressive way of life housed in Europe's most 17th-century city. Physically, it's a city built upon millions of pilings. But, more than that, it's a city built on good living, cozy cafés, great art, street-corner jazz, stately history, and a spirit of live and let live. It has 800,000 people and as many bikes. It also has more canals than Venice and as many tourists. While Amsterdam may box your Puritan ears, this great, historic city is an experiment in freedom.

Planning Your Time
While I'd sleep in nearby Haarlem (see next chapter), Amsterdam is worth a full day of sightseeing on even the busiest itinerary. While the city has a couple of must-see museums, its best sight is its own breezy ambience. The city's a joy on foot. It's a breezier and faster joy by bike. And the sights are conveniently laced together by circular tram #20. Here are the essential stops for a day in Amsterdam:

Start the day with an orientation tour on tram #20 (described below). Break this morning overview with a stop at the city's two great art museums: the Van Gogh and Rijksmuseum (cafeteria lunch). Because of a special exhibit at the Van Gogh, those visiting before June 2, 2002, will need a reservation with an entry time to get into this museum (explained below).

After the museums, if you have limited time, you can pick up tram #20 where you got off and complete the circle back to the station.

With more time, walk from the museums to Spui via Leidsestraat. Spend midafternoon taking a relaxing hour-long canal cruise from the dock at Spui. Near Spui, consider seeing the peaceful

Begijnhof, Amsterdam
Historical Museum, and
flower market.

   Visiting the Anne
Frank House after 18:00
(it's open until 21:00) will
save you an hour in line.

   On a balmy evening,
Amsterdam has a Greek-
island ambience. Wander
the Jordaan for the idyllic
side of town and wander
down Leidsestraat to
Leidseplein for the roaring
café and people scene.
Wander the Red-Light
District while you're at it.

   With extra time:
With two days in Holland,
I'd side-trip by bike, bus,
or train to an open-air folk

Amsterdam

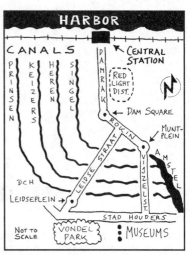

museum and visit Edam or Haarlem. With a third day, I'd
do the other great Amsterdam museums. With four days,
I'd do the "historic triangle" of Enkhuizen, Hoorn, and
Medemblik, or visit The Hague (for details, see "Sights—
Near Haarlem and Amsterdam," in the next chapter).

Orientation (area code: 020)

Amsterdam's central train station is your starting point (TI,
bike rental, and trams—including #20—fanning out to all points).
Damrak is the main street axis, connecting the station with Dam
Square (people watching and hangout center) and its Royal Palace.
From this spine, the city spreads out like a fan, with 90 islands,
hundreds of bridges, and a series of concentric canals (named
"Prince's," "Gentleman's," and "King's") laid out in the 17th
century, Holland's Golden Age. Amsterdam's major sights are
within walking distance of Dam Square.

Tourist Information

Avoid Amsterdam's inefficient VVV offices if you can ("VVV"
is Dutch for tourist information office; TI inside train station open
Mon–Sat 08:00–20:00, Sun 09:00–17:00). Most people wait 30 minutes just to pick up information brochures and get a room. At the
VVV in front of the station (daily 09:00–17:00), avoid this line by
studying the display of publications for sale and going straight to the
sales desk (where everyone ends up anyway, since any information of
substance will cost you). Consider buying a city map (€2), *Day by*

Day entertainment calendar (€1.25), and any of the €1 walking-tour brochures (*Discovery Tour through the Center, The Former Jewish Quarter, Walks through Jordaan*). The Amsterdam Pass, offering free or discounted admissions to some sights and boat rides, isn't worth the clutter or cost (€29, doesn't include Anne Frank House). Nor does it make sense to stand in line at the VVV to buy prepaid same-cost admissions to various Amsterdam sights.

The TI on Leidsestraat is less crowded (daily 09:00–17:00). But for €0.50 a minute, you can save yourself a trip by calling the tourist information toll line at 0900-400-4040 (Mon–Fri 09:00–17:00). If you're staying in nearby Haarlem, use the helpful, friendly, and rarely crowded Haarlem TI (see next chapter) to answer most of your Amsterdam questions and provide you with the brochures.

At Amsterdam's Central Station, **GWK Change** has two hotel reservations windows that sell phone cards and cheaper city maps (€1.60) and answer basic tourist questions with shorter lines. They also change money, including coins, for a hefty €2.25 fee (one office is at track 4/5, the other is in the west tunnel at the right end of the station as you leave the platform, tel. 020/627-2731).

Don't use the TI (or GWK) to book a room; you'll pay €2.25 and your host loses the 13 percent deposit. The phone system is easy, everyone speaks English, and the listings in this book are a better value than the potluck booking you'd be charged for at the TI.

Helpful Hints

Theft Alert: Tourists are considered green and rich, and the city has more than its share of hungry thieves—especially on trams. Wear your money belt.

Street Smarts: A *plein* is a square, *gracht* means canal, and most canals are lined by streets with the same name.

Shop Hours: Many shops close all day Sunday and Monday morning.

Telephones: Calling the United States from a phone booth is now very cheap—you'll get about five minutes for a dollar. Handy telephone cards (€4.50, €11.50, or €23) are sold at TIs, the GVB public-transit office (in front of station), tobacco shops, post offices, and train stations.

Happy Birthday: On the Queen's Birthday on April 30, Amsterdam turns into a gigantic garage sale/street market.

Internet Access: It's easy at cafés all over town. The Internet Café is a couple blocks from the station and is open until the wee hours (20 min free with each drink you buy, Sun–Thu 09:00–24:00, Fri–Sat 09:00–03:00, must buy at least 1 beverage, Martelaarsgracht 11, tel. 020/627-1052). A monstrous Internet café, easyEverything, has several hundred computers and cheap access (daily 24 hrs, at Damrak 33, across the bridge and then a block in front of the station, and another branch at Reguliersbreestraat 22, next to Rembrandtplein). "Coffee shops" (which sell marijuana) also offer Internet access, letting you surf the Net with a special bravado.

Arrival in Amsterdam

By Train: Amsterdam swings, and the hinge that connects it to the world is its perfectly central Central Station. Walk out the door, and you're in the heart of the city. You'll nearly trip over trams ready to take you anywhere your feet won't. Straight ahead is Damrak Street, leading to Dam Square. With your back to the entrance of the station, the TI and GVB public-transit offices and circular tram #20A are just ahead and to your left. And on your right is a vast, multistoried "bike garage."

By Plane: From Schiphol Airport, take the train to Amsterdam (6/hr, 20 min, €3). If you're staying in Haarlem, take a direct express bus to Haarlem (#236 or #362, 2/hr, 30 min, €3.25).

Getting around Amsterdam

The helpful GVB transit-information office is next to the TI. Its free multilingual *Public Transport Amsterdam Tourist Guide* includes a transit map and explains ticket options and tram connections to all the sights.

By Bus, Tram, and Métro: Individual tickets cost €1.50 and give you an hour on the buses, trams, and Métro system (on trams and buses pay as you board; buy Métro tickets from machines). **Strip cards** are cheaper than individual tickets. Any downtown bus or tram ride costs two strips (good for 1 hr of transfers). A card with 15 strips costs €5.75 at the GVB public-transit office, train stations, post offices, airport, or tobacco shops throughout the country; shorter strip tickets (2, 3, and 8 strips) are also sold on some buses and trams. Strip cards are good on buses all over the Netherlands (e.g., 6 strips for Haarlem to the airport), and you can share them with your partner. A €5 **Day Card** gives you unlimited transportation on the buses and Métro for a day in Amsterdam; you'll almost break even if you take three trips (valid until 06:00 the following morning; buy as you board or at the GVB public-transit office, which also sells a better-value 2-day version for €8; sometimes costs €0.50 more if you buy it on board). If you get lost in Amsterdam, 10 of the city's 17 trams take you back to the central train station.

By Foot: The longest walk a tourist would take is 45 minutes from the station to the Rijksmuseum. Watch out for silent but potentially painful bikes, trams, and crotch-high curb posts.

By Bike: One-speed bikes, with "brrringing" bells and two locks (use them both; bike thieves are bold and brazen here), rent for €5.75 per day at the central train station (daily 08:00–22:00, €91 deposit or your credit-card imprint and passport required;

as you exit the station go left, then down the ramp; at east end of station; tel. 020/624-8391). In the summer, arrive early or make a telephone reservation (they hold bikes until 11:00). If the station has rented all its bikes, walk 10 minutes to Rent-a-Bike Damstraat near Dam Square (€7/day, daily 09:00–18:00, deposit of €22.75 plus I.D., or a credit-card imprint, just down alley that begins at Damstraat 20, tel. 020/625-5029).

By Boat: While the city is great on foot or bike, there is a "Museum Boat" with an all-day ticket that shuttles tourists from sight to sight. Tickets cost €12.50 (with discounts to sights worth about €2.25). The sales booths in front of the central train station (and the boats) offer handy free brochures with museum times and admission prices. The narrated ride takes 90 minutes if you don't get off (every 30 min in summer, every 45 min off-season, 6 stops, live quadrilingual guide, departures 10:00–17:00, discounted after 13:00 to €10.25, tel. 020/530-1090). A similar "Canal Bus" is nearby. If you're looking for a floating nonstop tour, the real canal tour boats (without the stops) give more information, cover more ground, and cost less (see "Tours of Amsterdam," below).

By Taxi: Amsterdam's taxis are expensive (€2.75 drop and €1.40 for each kilometer). Given the fine tram system, taxis are only a good value for airport connections (Schiphol Airport to Amsterdam costs €27.25).

By Car: Forget it—frustrating one-ways, terrible parking.

Circle Tram #20 Orientation Tour

If this is still running in 2002 (light use is threatening its existence), Amsterdam's Circle Tram #20 offers a great one-hour, self-guided tour for €1.50. Catch this designed-for-tourists circle route at the train station. Board #20A (not #20B) from tram lane (or *spoor*) #2 on the left as you leave the station. The free tourist guidebooklet—there's a stack on the desk in the transit office 50 meters away—comes with a route map and lists each stop. Tram #20 runs daily every 10 minutes from 09:00 to 18:00 only.

0. Train Station: Leaving the station, you pass both the canal bus and museum boat docks (left). The *Rondvaart* sign (right) means round-trip. Boats like these all over town offer similar one-hour city tours. Gliding up the tacky commercial cancan called the Damrak (which was once the Amstel River), you're following the same route taken by boats loaded with spices and goodies from the East Indies in the city's early trading days. The buildings across the water are Amsterdam's oldest. Behind them are the Red-Light District and the old sailor's quarter. The huge redbrick Beurs building (left) is the Dutch stock exchange.

1. Dam Square: This is the city center, where the original dam was built across the Amstel River, giving the town its name. To your right is the Royal Palace (1655); next to it is the New

Amsterdam

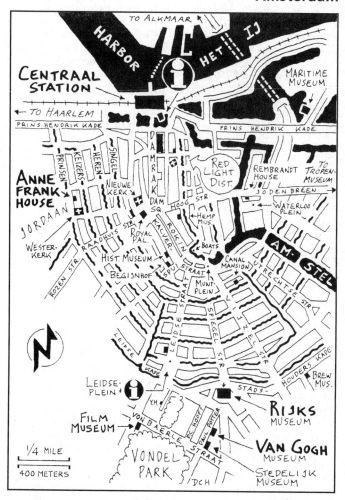

Church, the coronation church of Dutch royalty. To your left is the World War I Memorial, now becoming a generic peace memorial; behind that is a strip of head shops. Straight ahead is one of many diamond-polishing centers. Beyond Dam Square, you continue down Rokin. Parallel and a block to the right is the bustling Kalverstraat pedestrian shopping mall.

2. Spui Square: This marked the end of the city in the 14th century. Spui (rhymes with cow) is near the Begijnhof and the University of Amsterdam's archaeology museum, which has a fine Egyptian collection.

3. Muntplein: This lively area is marked by the Mint Tower from 1620 (on the right). Behind that, a charming flower market lines the Singel Canal (see the row of greenhouses, thriving Mon–Sat 09:00–17:00). Turning left you enter a noisy neon nightlife center.

4. Rembrandtplein: Look for Rembrandt's statue in the leafy park (right). This is the center of gay Amsterdam; you'll pass lots of discos and a Planet Hollywood. A bridge will take you over the Amstel River. The modern brown-and-white building (left) is City Hall. Adjacent is the round Opera House. Notice the charming counterbalance bridges (right).

5. Waterlooplein: This is famous for its flea market (daily except Sun, on left). The Jewish Quarter (right) features the impressive Jewish History Museum (renovated brick synagogues with blue-and-white banner). Crossing the bridge (funny paintings revealed when opened), you enter green Amsterdam (gardens and hothouses of University of Amsterdam all around, zoo nearby).

6. Plantage Kerklaan: Immediately to the right of this tram stop, the white facade of the old Dutch Theater (Hollandsche Schouwburg) survives. Used by Nazis as a holding zone for Jews being deported, today it's a memorial. The Dutch Resistance Museum and the zoo are half a block to the left. Passing through many University of Amsterdam buildings, notice the "XXX" symbol of the city (the three Xs stand for the adversities that Amsterdammers have overcome throughout their history: fire, plague, and floods). Crossing the Amstel River again, see the City Hall and the Opera House again in the distance (right), the palatial Amstel Hotel (behind on the left), and, farther off, Holland's tallest skyscraper—the Philips Electronics corporate headquarters.

7. Frederiksplein: Notice the houseboats; they're a common sight in Amsterdam. Also in Frederiksplein, you'll see the huge Albert Cuyp Market. Perhaps the town's most interesting market, it shows off Amsterdam's ethnic mix daily except Sunday. Now, passing through a nondescript area, notice how the city works: Shops at street level—with homes above—keep neighborhoods vital, people friendly, and safe. Bike lanes even have their own little traffic lights. New buildings still lean out and come with planks and pulleys for hoisting furniture past too-narrow stairways. Many of these are brick and built in the Art Deco "Amsterdam School" from the 1920s—a time when architects considered entire blocks as integrated works of art. Notice street signs with the district listed. You're in the *oud-zuid* (old south) quarter. Mail slots have green and orange decals saying yes or no to junk mail. And now public phone booths stand next to curbside computers for Internet access (locals use prepaid "chip cards"—the first step toward the cash-free society of the future—to access things such as these).

8. Museumplein: A huge park (right) leads to the grand, redbrick Rijksmuseum (built in 1885 by the same guy who designed Central Station). The new addition to the Van Gogh Museum juts into the park in the foreground. The Concertgebouw (on the left) is Amsterdam's main concert hall. A huge underground parking lot keeps things uncluttered.

9. Van Baerlestraat: Rounding the corner, you stop at the Stedelijk Modern Art Museum (right) and the Van Gogh Museum (see crowd on right). An ice rink (right) faces the Coster Diamond House (left).

10. Hobbemastraat: This is the stop for the Rijksmuseum (right). A fancy gate marks the entrance to the sprawling, in-love-with-life Vondelpark (left). Pass a casino (right) as you cross a canal and enter the noisy, people-filled Leidseplein area.

11. Leidseplein: Your tram just skirts Amsterdam's liveliest café, people watching, and entertainment district. Be sure to loiter in Leidseplein later on. The huge modern parking lot (Texaco station, left) marks the line between the protected old town (right) and the anything-goes new one (left). Turning right you cut through the proud, fashionable, and trendy Jordaan district. Ahead stands the much-loved tallest church spire in town, marking the Westerkerk (West Church). Anne Frank hid out just down the street. As you continue ahead, the canal system is evident as you cross the Prinsen (prince's), Keizers (king's), Herren (gentlemen's, actually medieval business fat cats), and Singel Canals and head toward the back side of the Royal Palace we saw at Dam Square. Hop out here or glide back to your starting point at the Central Station.

Sights—Amsterdam's Museum Neighborhood

▲▲▲**Rijksmuseum**—Built to house the nation's greatest art, the Rijksmuseum packs several thousand paintings into 200 rooms. To survive, focus on the Dutch masters: Rembrandt, Hals, Vermeer, and Steen. For a list of the top 20 paintings, pick up the cheap €.50 leaflet *A Tour of the Golden Age* and plan your attack (or follow the self-guided tour, one of 25, in my *Mona Winks* guidebook, written with Gene Openshaw). Audioguide tours are available, allowing you to dial up descriptions of over 200 paintings (€4).

Follow the museum's chronological layout to see painting evolve from narrative religious art, to religious art, to the Golden Age, when secular art dominated. With no local church or royalty to commission big canvases in the post-1648 Protestant Dutch republic, artists had to find different patrons. They specialized in portraits of the wealthy city class (Hals), pretty still lifes (Claesz), and nonpreachy slice-of-life art (Steen). The museum has four quietly wonderful Vermeers. And, of course, a thoughtful brown soup of Rembrandt, including *The Night Watch*. Works by Rembrandt show his excellence as a portraitist for hire (*De Staalmeesters*) and offer some powerful psychological studies, such as *St. Peter's Denial*—with a betrayed Jesus in the murky background (€8, daily 10:00–17:00, great bookshop, decent cafeteria, tram #2, #5, or #20 from station, Stadhouderskade 42, tel. 020/674-7000).

▲▲▲**Van Gogh Museum**—Near the Rijksmuseum, this outstanding and user-friendly museum houses the 200 paintings owned by Vincent's younger brother Theo. It's a stroll through a beautifully displayed garden of van Gogh's work and life. While the main floor dominates, don't miss the top two floors (€7.25, daily 10:00–18:00, Paulus Potterstraat 7, www.vangoghmuseum.nl, tel. 020/570-5200). The museum also focuses on the late-19th-century art that influenced van Gogh (much of which happened to be in his brother Theo's collection). The new exhibition hall (usually included with admission) features temporary art exhibits from 1840 to 1920. The €4 audioguide includes insightful commentaries about van Gogh's paintings, along with related quotations from Vincent himself. *Note that until June 2, 2002, this museum is only open by appointment as the special van Gogh and Gauguin Exhibition takes it over (see details below).*

▲▲▲**Van Gogh and Gauguin Exhibition (Feb 9–June 2, 2002)**—The Van Gogh Museum hosts a major exhibition examining the personal and artistic development of van Gogh and Gauguin. With 120 works from 65 lenders from around the world assembled in the museum's exhibition wing, art lovers are able to explore the intense and almost legendary relationship of these two artists like never before. The climax of the exhibition is the work they produced during their short but turbulent collaboration at the Yellow House in Arles, France, in late 1888. Together they evolved ambitious plans to reinvigorate modern art through what van Gogh called a "Studio of the South." Ultimately, the alliance couldn't survive their philosophical differences. Van Gogh wanted to paint what he saw and show the actual process of painting. Gauguin wanted the painter's technique to remain unnoticed while portraying things beyond what the eye could see. This philosophical debate got physical, culminating in the famous argument in which van Gogh threatened his friend with a razor and then cut off a piece of his own ear. Anticipating huge crowds, the museum is selling tickets with admission time blocks. Visitors can only enter with a reservation and within the time block assigned. Once inside, they can stay as long as they like. Since only a few tickets are available at the museum, assure your entry by getting tickets in advance at www.vangoghgauguin.com or in Amsterdam at Uit Buro (Leidseplein 26), VVV Ticketpoints, or Tracks Multitronics (at Schiphol Airport). For more information, see the above Web site. During this special exhibition, the museum costs more (€13, includes audio-guide) and is open longer (Tue–Wed and Fri–Sun 09:00–21:00, Mon and Thu 09:00–18:00). If crowds are huge, a reservation several days in advance will be necessary. If crowds are moderate, you can drop by the ticket window and get a time that same day. Do this early in the day and plan to visit the Rijksmuseum if you need to kill a couple of hours.

Stedelijk Modern Art Museum—Next to the Van Gogh Museum, this place is fun, far-out, and refreshing. It has mostly post-1945 art but also a sometimes-outstanding collection of Monet, van Gogh, Cézanne, Picasso, and Chagall, and a lot of special exhibitions (€4.50, daily 11:00–17:00, tel. 020/573-2737).

Sights—Near Dam Square

▲▲**Anne Frank House**—A pilgrimage for many, this house offers a fascinating look at the hideaway of young Anne during the Nazi occupation of the Netherlands during World War II. Pick up the English pamphlet at the door. Recently expanded, the exhibit now offers more thorough coverage of the Frank family, the diary, the stories of others who hid, and the Holocaust. Why do thousands endure hour-long daytime lines when they can walk right in by arriving after 18:00? Last entrance is 20:30. Visit after dinner (€6.50, April–Aug daily 09:00–21:00, Sept–March daily 09:00–19:00, Prinsengracht 263, near Westerkerk church, tel. 020/556-7100, www.annefrank.nl). For an interesting glimpse of Holland under the Nazis, rent the powerful movie *Soldier of Orange* before you leave home.

Westerkerk—Near the Anne Frank House, this landmark church has a barren interior, Rembrandt somewhere under the pews, and Amsterdam's tallest steeple. It's worth climbing for the view (€1.40, ascend only with a guide, departures on the hour, April–Sept Mon–Sat 10:00–17:00, last trip at 16:00, closed Sun and in winter, tel. 020/612-6856).

Royal Palace (Koninklijk Paleis)—The palace, right on Dam Square, was built as a lavish city hall for Amsterdam, when the country was a proud new Dutch Republic and Amsterdam was awash in profit from trade. When constructed (around 1660), this building was one of Europe's finest. Today it's the official (but not actual) residence of the Queen and has a sumptuous interior (€4.50, €2.25 audioguide, June–Aug daily 11:00–17:00, Sept daily 12:30–17:00, closed off-season, tel. 020/624-8698).

▲**Begijnhof**—Stepping into this tiny, idyllic courtyard in the city center, you escape into the charm of old Amsterdam. Notice house #34, a 500-year-old wooden structure (rare since repeated fires taught city fathers a trick called brick). Peek into the "hidden" Catholic church, dating from the time when post-Reformation Dutch Catholics couldn't worship in public. It's opposite the

English Reformed church, where the Pilgrims worshiped while waiting for their voyage to the New World (marked by a plaque near the door). Be considerate of the people who live around the courtyard (free, daily 10:00–17:00, on Begijnensteeg Lane, just off Kalverstraat between #130 and #132, pick up flier at office near entrance, open weekdays 10:00–16:00).

Amsterdam Historical Museum—Offering the town's best look into the age of the Dutch masters, this creative and hardworking museum features Rembrandt's paintings, fine English descriptions, and a carillon loft. The loft comes with push-button recordings of the town bell tower's greatest hits and a self-serve carillon "keyboard" to ring a few bells yourself (€6.50, Mon–Fri 10:00–17:00, Sat–Sun 11:00–17:00, good-value restaurant, next to Begijnhof, Kalverstraat 92, tel. 020/523-1822). Its free pedestrian corridor—lined with old-time group portraits—is a powerful teaser.

Sights—East Amsterdam

To reach these sights from the train station, take tram #9, #14, or #20. The first six sights listed make an interesting walk.

▲**Rembrandt's House**—Rembrandt's reconstructed house is filled with exactly what his bankruptcy inventory of 1656 said he owned. You'll find no paintings but 65 of his etchings and a workshop with demonstrations (€7, Mon–Sat 10:00–17:00, Sun 13:00–17:00, 10-min English video explains reconstruction of home, Jodenbreestraat 4, tel. 020/520-0400).

Holland Experience—Bragging "Experience Holland in 30 minutes," this show takes you traveling with three clowns through an idealized montage of Dutch clichés. There are no words but lots of images and special effects as you rock with the boat and get spritzed with perfume while viewing the tulips (€8, 2 enter for price of 1 with this book, or show this book and get €1.25 off the €11.50 combo Rembrandt's House/Experience ticket, daily 10:00–18:00, Jodenbreestraat 8, near Rembrandt's House and Waterlooplein street market, Métro: Waterlooplein, tel. 020/ 422-2233. www.holland-experience.nl). The men's urinal is a trip to the beach. Plan for it.

Waterlooplein Flea Market—For over a hundred years, the Jewish Quarter flea market has raged daily except Sunday behind the Rembrandt House.

▲**Jewish History Museum**—Four historic synagogues have been joined by steel and glass to make one modern complex telling the story of the Jews in Amsterdam through the centuries (€4.50, daily 11:00–17:00, good kosher café, Jonas Daniel Meijerplein 2, tel. 020/626-9945).

▲**Dutch Theatre (Hollandsche Schouwburg)**—This is a moving memorial. Once a great theater in the Jewish neighborhood, this was used as an assembly hall for local Jews destined for Nazi

Central Amsterdam

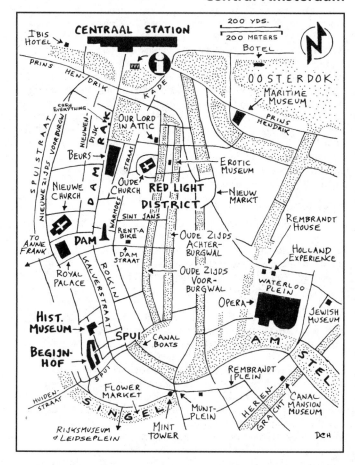

concentration camps. On the wall, 6,700 family names pay tribute to the 104,000 Jews deported and killed by the Nazis. Upstairs is a small history exhibit on Jews here during World War II. Otherwise, there's little to actually see but plenty to think about (free, daily 11:00–16:00, Plantage Middenlaan 24, tel. 020/626-9945).

▲▲**Dutch Resistance Museum (Verzetsmuseum)**—This is an impressive look at how the Dutch resisted their Nazi occupiers from 1940 to 1945. You'll see propaganda movie clips, study forged ID cards under a magnifying glass, and read of ingenious, clever, and courageous efforts to hide local Jews from the Germans. And at the end of the war, Nazi helmets were turned into bedpans (€4.50, Tue–Fri 10:00–17:00, Sat–Mon 12:00–17:00, closed April 30, well described in English, café, tram #9 or #20A from station, Plantage Kerklaan 61, tel. 020/620-2535). Amsterdam's famous zoo is just across the street.

▲**Tropenmuseum (Tropical Museum)**—As close to the Third World as you'll get without lots of vaccinations, this imaginative museum offers wonderful re-creations of tropical-life scenes and explanations of Third World problems (€7, daily 10:00–17:00, tram #9 to Linnaeusstraat 2, tel. 020/568-8215).

Netherlands Maritime (Scheepvaart) Museum—This huge collection of model ships, maps, and sea-battle paintings fills the 300-year-old Dutch Navy Arsenal. Given the Dutch seafaring heritage, I expected a more interesting museum. Sailors may disagree, but—even with its recreation of an 18th-century Dutch East India Company ship manned with characters in old costumes—I found the place pretty lifeless (€6.75, daily 10:00–17:00, closed Mon off-season, English explanations, don't waste your time with 30-min movie, bus #22 or #32 to Kattenburgerplein 1, tel. 020/523-2222).

Sights—Red-Light District

▲**Our Lord in the Attic (Amstelkring)**—Near the station, in the Red-Light District, you'll find a fascinating hidden Catholic church (1661) filling the attic of a hollowed-out row of 17th-century merchants' houses (€4.50, Mon–Sat 10:00–17:00, Sun 13:00–17:00, Oudezijds Voorburgwal 40, tel. 020/624-6604).

▲**Red-Light District**—Europe's most touristed ladies of the night shiver and shimmy as they have since 1700 in 450 display-case windows between the Oudezijds Achterburgwal and Oudezijds Voorburgwal, surrounding the Oude Kerk (Old Church). Druggies make the streets uncomfortable late at night, but it's a fascinating walk at any other time after noon.

The neighborhood, one of Amsterdam's oldest, has had prostitutes since 1200. Back then they were run by the sheriff and his men. Prostitution is entirely legal here and woman are generally entrepreneurs, renting a space and running their own business. Women typically rent their space for eight-hour shifts for about €60 a day. Popular prostitutes make €300 a day (S&F, €34–45), fill out tax returns, and many belong to a loose union called the Red Thread. Rather than pimps, prostitutes are protected by the law. Each one has a buzzer. If she needs help, she rings this to call the police.

The **Prostitution Information Center** welcomes visitors. They have a map showing exactly where prostitution is legal and print a small and frank booklet answering most common questions tourists have about Amsterdam's Red-Light District (free, Tue, Wed, Fri, and Sat 11:30–19:30, facing Old Church at Enge Kerksteeg 3, www.pic-amsterdam.com).

Amsterdam has two **sex museums**, one in the Red-Light

District and one a block in front of the train station on Damrak. While visiting one can be called sightseeing, visiting both is hard to explain. Here's a comparison:

The Red-Light District sex museum is less offensive, with five sparsely decorated rooms relying heavily on badly dressed dummies acting out the roles that women of the neighborhood play. It also has videos, phone-sex phones, and a lot of uninspired paintings, old photos, and sculpture (€2.25, daily 11:00–24:00, along the canal at Oudezijds Achterburgwal 54).

The Damrak sex museum goes deeper and has more rooms. It tells the story of pornography from Roman times through 1960. Every sexual deviation is uncovered in its various displays, and the nude and pornographic art is a cut above that of the other sex museum. Also interesting are the early French pornographic photos and memorabilia from Europe, India, and Asia. You'll find a Marilyn Monroe tribute and some S&M displays, too (€2.25, daily 10:00–23:30, Damrak 18, a block in front of station).

More Sights—Amsterdam

▲**Herengracht Canal Mansion (Willet Holthuysen Museum)**—This 1687 patrician house offers a fine look at the old rich of Amsterdam, with a good 15-minute English introductory film and a 17th-century garden in back (€4.50, Mon–Fri 10:00–17:00, Sat–Sun 11:00–17:00, tram #1, #2, #4, #5, or #9 to Herengracht 605, tel. 020/523-1870).

Vondelpark—This huge and lively city park is popular with the Dutch—families with little kids, romantic couples, hippies sharing blankets and beers, oldsters strolling, and free summer concerts. On a sunny afternoon, it's a hedonistic scene that seems to say "parents...relax" (tel. 020/523-7790).

Amsterdam Film Museum—This museum, next to Vondelpark, has a massive archive and a theater that shows a variety of films, from small foreign productions to 70-mm classics (€5.75, at least 3 showings/night, often English subtitles, Vondelstraat 69, tel. 020/523-7790, www.filmmuseum.nl).

Heineken Brewery—The popular brewery welcomes visitors (€5 for self-guided tour, price includes 3 drinks, must be over age 18, in full slosh Tue–Sun 10:00–18:00, closed Mon, tram #16, #24, or #25, Stadhouderskade 78, near Rijksmuseum, tel. 020/523-9666).

Leidseplein—Brimming with cafés, this people- and pigeon-watching square is an impromptu stage for street artists, accordionists, jugglers, and unicyclists. Sunny afternoons are liveliest. Stroll nearby Lange Leidsedwarsstraat (1 block north) for a taste-bud tour of ethnic eateries from Greece to Indonesia. The Boom Chicago theater fronts this square.

Boom Chicago—This R-rated comedy theater act was started 10 years ago by a group of Americans on a graduation tour. They have been entertaining tourists and locals alike ever since. The show is a series of rude, clever, and high-powered skits offering a raucous look at Dutch culture and local tourism (€16, nightly at 20:15, dinner seating early, Leidseplein Theater, Leidseplein 12, tel. 020/423-0101, www.boomchicago.nl). Meals are optional and a good value. Their irreverent free *Boom Chicago Amsterdam Guide* magazine is packed with practical tips and counter-cultural insights (and gives a €2.25 discount on their show).

Shopping—Amsterdam brings out the browser even in those who were not born to shop. Ten general markets, open six days a week, keep folks who brake for garage sales pulling U-ies. Shopping highlights include Waterlooplein (the flea market); the huge Albert Cuyp street market; various flower markets (such as the Singel Canal market near mint tower/ *Munttoren*, daily except Sun); diamond dealers (free cutting and polishing demos at shops behind the Rijksmuseum and on Dam Square); and Kalverstraat, Amsterdam's teeming pedestrian/shopping street (parallel to Damrak).

Tours of Amsterdam

▲▲**Canal-Boat Tour**—These long, low, tourist-laden boats leave continually from several docks around the town for a relaxing, if uninspiring, one-hour quadrilingual introduction to the city (€6.50, 2/hr, more frequent in summer). One very central company is at the corner of Spui and Rokin, about five minutes from Dam Square (daily 10:00–22:00, tel. 020/623-3810). No fishing allowed—but bring your camera. Some prefer to cruise at night, when the bridges are illuminated.

Biking Tours—The Yellow Bike Tour company offers a city tour (€16, at 09:30 and 13:00, 3 hrs) and a tour of the countryside (€21, April–Nov daily at 11:00, 6 hrs, 35 km/ 22 miles, Nieuwezijds Kolk 29, 3 blocks from train station, tel. 020/620-6940).

Wetlands Safari, Nature Canoe Tours near Amsterdam— If you'd like to "turn your back on Amsterdam" and get a dose of the *polder* country and village life along with some exercise, consider this tour. Majel Tromp, a young village woman who speaks great English, takes groups of no more than 15. The program: Meet at the VVV tourist office outside the central train station at 09:30, catch a bus, stop for coffee, take a canoe trip with several stops, munch a village picnic lunch (included), canoe and bus back into the big city by 14:30 (€30, 10 percent off with this book, May–mid-Sept Mon–Fri, reservations required, tel. 020/686-3445 or 06/53-552-669, www.wetlandssafari.nl).

Sleeping in Amsterdam
(€1.10 = about $1, country code: 31, area code: 020)
Sleep Code: **S** = Single, **D** = Double/Twin, **T** = Triple, **Q** = Quad, **b** = bathroom, **s** = shower only, **CC** = Credit Cards accepted, **no CC** = Credit Cards not accepted. Nearly everyone speaks English in the Netherlands, and prices include breakfast unless noted.

While I prefer sleeping in cozy Haarlem (see next chapter), those into more urban charms will find that Amsterdam has plenty of beds. The Queen's Birthday (April 30) and summer weekends get booked well in advance.

Sleeping near the Station
Amstel Botel, the city's only remaining "boat hotel," is a shipshape, bright, and clean floating hotel with 175 rooms (Sb/Db-€75, Tb-€84, worth the extra €5 for canalside view, breakfast-€7, €19.50/day parking pass, CC, elevator, 400 meters from train station, on your left as you leave station, you'll see the sign, Oosterdokskade 2-4, 1011 AE Amsterdam, tel. 020/626-4247, fax 020/639-1952, www.amstelbotel.com).

Ibis Amsterdam Hotel is a modern and efficient 180-room place towering over the station. It offers a central location, comfort, and good value without a hint of charm (Db-€136, family-€176, skip breakfast and save €11 per person, CC, book long in advance, air-con, smoke-free rooms on request, Stationsplein 49, tel. 020/638-3080, fax 020/620-0156, www.ibishotel.com.

Sleeping between Dam Square and the Anne Frank House
Hotel Toren is a chandeliered historic mansion in a pleasant, quiet canalside setting in downtown Amsterdam. This splurge, run by Eric and Annemika Toren, is classy yet friendly, two blocks northeast of the Anne Frank House (Sb-€95–128, Db-€110–190, Tb-€140–170, bridal suites for €205–217 make you want to get married, prices vary with view and Jacuzzi, 10 percent discount for 3 nights and cash with this book, breakfast buffet-€10, CC, air-con, Keizersgracht 164, 1015 CZ Amsterdam, tel. 020/622-6352, fax 020/626-9705, www.toren.nl).

Well-heeled readers enjoy the similar 17th-century **Canal House Hotel**, a few doors down, for its beautiful antique interiors, candlelit evenings, and soft music (Sb-€134, Db-€129–166, CC, elevator, Keizersgracht 148, 1015 CX Amsterdam, tel. 020/622-5182, fax 020/624-1317, www.canalhouse.nl).

Cheap hotels line the convenient but noisy main drag between the town hall and the Anne Frank House. Expect a long, steep, and depressing stairway, noisy front rooms, and quieter rooms in the back. **Hotel Aspen**, a good value for a budget hotel, is tidy, stark, and well maintained (S-€32, D-€41, Db-€64, Tb-€75, Qb-€87,

Amsterdam's Hotels

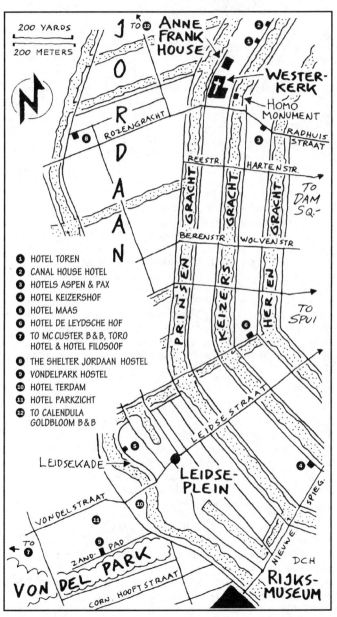

200 YARDS
200 METERS

N

JORDAAN

TO ⑫ ANNE FRANK HOUSE

②
①

WESTER-KERK

HOMO MONUMENT

RADHUIS STRAAT

③

ROZENGRACHT

⑧

REESTR.   HARTENSTR.

TO DAM SQ.

PRINSENGRACHT   KEIZERSGRACHT   HERENGRACHT

BERENSTR.   WOLVENSTR.

TO SPUI

⑥

① HOTEL TOREN
② CANAL HOUSE HOTEL
③ HOTELS ASPEN & PAX
④ HOTEL KEIZERSHOF
⑤ HOTEL MAAS
⑥ HOTEL DE LEYDSCHE HOF
⑦ TO MC CUSTER B&B, TORO HOTEL & HOTEL FILOSOOF
⑧ THE SHELTER JORDAAN HOSTEL
⑨ VONDELPARK HOSTEL
⑩ HOTEL TERDAM
⑪ HOTEL PARKZICHT
⑫ TO CALENDULA GOLDBLOOM B&B

LEIDSE STRAAT

⑤

LEIDSEKADE

④

LEIDSE-PLEIN

SPIEG.

VONDELSTRAAT

⑩

⑪

TO ⑦

⑨ ZAND PAD

NIEUWE

DCH

VON DEL PARK

CORN. HOOFT STRAAT

RIJKS-MUSEUM

no breakfast, CC, Raadhuisstraat 31, 1016 DC Amsterdam, tel. 020/626-6714, fax 020/620-0866, e-mail: hotelaspen@planet.nl, run by Esam). A few doors away, **Hotel Pax** has large, plain, but airy backpacker-type rooms (S-€25–34, D-€37–57, T-€50–68, Q-€55–77, no breakfast, prices vary with size and season, CC, 2 showers and 2 toilets for 8 rooms, Raadhuisstraat 37, tel. 020/624-9735, run by brothers Philip and Peter).

Calendula Goldbloom's B&B, run by an American couple, offers two comfortable rooms in a classy old home in a quiet Jordaan neighborhood a five-minute walk northwest of the Anne Frank House (D-€100, extra bed €34, CC, 3-night minimum, books out long in advance, good breakfasts, Goudsbloemstraat 132, tel. 020/428-3055, fax 020/ 776-0075, www.calendulas.com, e-mail: info@calendulas.com, Lynn and Dennis).

Sleeping in the Leidseplein Area

The area around Amsterdam's museum square (Museumplein) and the rip-roaring nightlife center (Leidseplein) is colorful, comfortable, convenient, and affordable. These three canalside places are a 5- to 10-minute walk from Leidseplein.

Hotel Keizershof is wonderfully Dutch, with six bright, airy rooms in a 17th-century canal house. A steep spiral staircase leads to rooms named after old-time Hollywood stars. The enthusiastic hospitality of the De Vries family has made this place a treat for 40 years (S-€45, D-€64, Ds-€68, Db-€82, T-€91, Tb-€115, 3-night minimum, CC, nonsmoking, classy breakfast, tram #16, #24, or #25 from station; Keizersgracht 618, where Keizers canal crosses Spiegelstraat, ring bell at street-level door instead of up the stairs, 1017 ER Amsterdam, tel. 020/622-2855, fax 020/624-8412, www.vdwp.nl/keizershof).

Hotel Maas is a big, well-run, elegant, quiet, and stiffly hotelesque place (S-€68, Sb-€102, one D-€91, Db-€142–157, suite-€200, prices vary with view and room size, extra person-€20, CC, hearty breakfast, air-con, elevator, Leidsekade 91, tram #1, #2, #5, or #20 from station, 1017 PN Amsterdam, tel. 020/623-3868, fax 020/ 622-2613, www.hotelmaas.nl).

Hotel De Leydsche Hof is canalside with simple, quiet rooms. Its peaceful demeanor almost helps you overlook the flimsy cots and old carpets (Ds-€60, Ts-€90, Qs-€110, no breakfast, no CC, Leidsegracht 14, near where Keizersgracht hits Leidsegracht, 10-min walk from Leidseplein, 1016 CK Amsterdam, tel. 020/ 623-2148, run by friendly Mr. Piller).

Best Western Hotel Terdam is an 89-room American-style hotel well situated on a quiet street just across the bridge from bustling Leidseplein (Db-€130–170 depending on season and air-con, CC, elevator, Tesselschadestraat 23, tel. 020/612-6876, fax 020/683-8313, www.ams.nl).

Sleeping near Vondelpark

These options connect you with the sights via an easy tram ride, a pleasant 15-minute walk, or a short bike ride through Vondelpark.

Karen McCuster, a friendly Englishwoman, rents cozy rooms in her shoes-off home. Rooms are clean, white, and bright, with red carpeting and green plants. One room has a private rooftop patio (D-€64–82 depending on room size, suite-€114, includes buffet breakfast, no CC, Zeilstraat 22, tram #2 from station to Amstelveenseweg, 3rd floor, 1075 SH Amsterdam, tel. 020/679-2753, fax 020/ 670-4578, www.bedandbreakfastamsterdam.net, e-mail: pgaldermans@chello.net).

Toro Hotel, in a peaceful residential area at the edge of Vondelpark, is your personal 19th-century hotel/mansion, with a plush lounge, elegant dining hall, and 22 rooms with TVs, safes, and phones. Rooms in the back overlook the park, canal, and garden, which is yours for relaxing (Sb-€120, Db-€147, Tb-€164, Qb-€200, CC, elevator, metered parking at door, Koningslaan 64, tram #2 from station to Koningslaan, then walk to intersection of Emmalaan and Koningslaan, 1075 AG Amsterdam, tel. 020/673-7223, fax 020/675-0031).

Hotel Filosoof greets you with Aristotle and Plato in the foyer and classical music in its lobby. Its 30 rooms are decorated with themes; the Egyptian room has a frieze of hieroglyphics. Philosophers' sayings hang on the walls, as thoughtful travelers wander down the halls or sit in the garden, rooted deep in discussion. The rooms are small (and split between two buildings), but the hotel is endearing (Sb-€39–102, Db-€93–111, Tb-€116–134, CC, elevator, Anna Vondelstraat 6, 5-min walk from tram #1 line, get off at Jan Peter Heierstraat, tel. 020/683-3013, fax 020/685-3750, www.hotelfilosoof.nl).

Hotel Parkzicht is an old-fashioned place with lots of extremely steep stairs and 13 big, plain rooms on a quiet street bordering Vondelpark (S-€34, Sb-€43, Db-€77–84, as low as €50 in winter, Tb-€109, Qb-€118, CC, Roemer Visscherstraat 33, tram #1, #2, or #5 from station, exit Leidseplein, tel. 020/618-1954, fax 020/618-0897, e-mail: hotel@parkzicht.nl). This street is in a charming neighborhood and lined with other small hotels.

Hostels

The Shelter Jordan is scruffy, friendly, well run, and in a great neighborhood. These are Amsterdam's best budget beds, in 14- to 20-bed dorms (€13–15, includes sheets and breakfast, no CC, free Internet access, maximum age 35, nonsmoking, 02:00 curfew, Bloemstraat 179, near Anne Frank House, tel. 020/624-4717, www.shelter.nl, e-mail: reservations@jordan.shelter.nl). It serves hot meals, runs a snack bar, offers lockers, leads nightly Bible studies, and closes the dorms from 10:30 to 13:00. Its sister Christian hostel, **The Shelter City**, in the Red-Light District, is similar but definitely not preaching to the choir (€13–15, includes breakfast, no CC, maximum age 35, curfew, Barndesteeg 21, tel. 020/625-3230, fax 020/623-2282, www.shelter.nl, e-mail: city@shelter.nl).

The city's two HI hostels are **Vondelpark**, Amsterdam's top hostel (€18–24 with breakfast, D-€66, nonmembers pay €2.25 extra, no CC, lots of school groups, 4–20 beds per dorm, right on the park at Zandpad 5, tel. 020/589-8996, fax 020/589-8955, www.njhc.org/vondelpark) and **Stadsdoelen** (€17 with breakfast, nonmembers pay €2.25 extra, no CC, Kloveniersburgwal 97, just past Dam Square, tel. 020/624-6832, fax 020/639-1035, www.njhc.org, e-mail: stadsdoelen@njhc.org). While generally booked long in advance, a few beds open up each day at 11:00.

Eating in Amsterdam

Dutch food is basic and hearty. *Eetcafés* are local cafés serving budget sandwiches, soup, eggs, and so on. Cafeterias, *broodje* (sandwich shops), and automatic food shops are also good bets for budget eaters. Picnics are cheap and easy. A central supermarket is **Albert Heijn**, at the corner of Koningsplein and Singel Canal near the flower market (Mon–Sat 10:00–20:00, Sun 12:00–18:00).

Of Amsterdam's thousand-plus restaurants, no one knows which are best. I'd pick an area and wander. The major action is around Leidseplein. Wander along restaurant row: Leidsedwarsstraat. For fewer crowds and more charm, find something in the Jordaan district. The best advice: your hotel's. Most keep a reliable eating list for their neighborhood and know which places keep their travelers happy. Here are a few handy places to consider:

Eating near Spui in the Center

The city university's **Atrium** is a great budget cafeteria (€4.50 meals, Mon–Fri 11:00–15:00, 17:00–19:30; from Spui, walk west down Landebrug Steeg past the canalside Café 't Gasthuys 3 blocks to Oudezijds Achterburgwal 237, go through arched doorway on the right, tel. 020/525-3999). **Café 't Gasthuys**, one of Amsterdam's many "brown" cafés (named for their smoke-stained walls), makes good sandwiches and offers indoor or canalside seating (daily 12:00–24:00, walk west down Landebrug Steeg to Grimburgwal 7, tel. 020/624-8230).

La Place, a cafeteria on the ground floor of a department store, has islands of entrées, veggies, fruits, desserts, and beverages (Mon–Sat 10:00–20:00, Thu until 21:00, Sun 12:00–20:00, near Mint Tower, corner of Rokin and Muntplein, tel. 020/620-2364).

De Jaren Café ("The Years") features eclectic energy, an upstairs restaurant, and drinks at its canalside patio (daily 10:00–24:00, Nieuwe Doelenstraat 20-22, just up from Muntplein, tel. 020/625-5771).

Eating in the Train Station
The train station has a surprisingly classy, budget, self-service **Stationsrestauratie** on platform 1 (Mon–Sat 07:00–22:00, Sun from 08:00).

Eating near the Anne Frank House
For pancakes in a family atmosphere, try the **Pancake Bakery** (€8.25 pancakes, splitting OK, offers an Indonesian pancake for those who want 2 experiences in 1, daily 12:00–21:30, Prinsengracht 191, 1 block north of Anne Frank House, tel. 020/625-1333). Across the canal, **De Bolhoed** serves serious vegetarian food (daily 12:00–22:00, Prinsengracht 60, tel. 020/626-1803). **Dimitri's** is the place for a hearty salad (€9 main-course salads, daily 08:00–22:00, Prinsenstraat 3, tel. 020/627-9393).

    Café 't Papeneiland is a classic "brown café." With Delft tiles, an evocative old stove, and a stay-awhile perch overlooking a canal, it's been the neighborhood hangout since the 17th century (overlooking the northwest end of Prinsengracht at #2).

Eating near Vondelpark
Café Vertigo offers a fun selection of French, Italian, and Spanish dishes. Grab an outdoor table and watch the world spin by (daily 11:00–24:00, beneath Film Museum, Vondelpark 3, tel. 020/612-3021).

Bars
Try a *jenever* (Dutch gin), the closest thing to an atomic bomb in a shot glass. While cheese gets harder and sharper with age, *jenever* grows smooth and soft. Old *jenever* is best.

Drugs
Amsterdam, Europe's counterculture mecca, thinks the concept of a "victimless crime" is a contradiction. While hard drugs are definitely out, marijuana causes about as much excitement as a bottle of beer. Throughout the Netherlands "coffee shops" are pubs selling marijuana. Menus dangling from strings look like the inventory of a drug bust. Display cases show various joints or baggies for sale. The Dutch roll a little tobacco into their joints. To avoid the tobacco, you need to get a baggie and papers. Baggies usually cost €11.50—smaller contents...better quality. Walk east from Dam Square on Damstraat for a few blocks and then down to Nieuwmarkt. While several Bulldog Cafés are popular with tourists, less-glitzy neighborhood places (farther from the crowds) offer a better value and a more comfortable atmosphere.

    Pot should never be bought on the street in Amsterdam. Well-established "coffee shops" are considered much safer.

Up to five grams of marijuana per person per day can be sold in "coffee shops". Minimum age for purchase: 18 years.

The tiny **Grey Area** coffee shop is a cool, welcoming, and smoky hole-in-the-wall appreciated among local aficionados as a seven-time winner of Amsterdam's Cannabis Cup award. Judging by the proud autographed photos on the wall, many of America's most famous heads have dropped in. You're welcome to just nurse a bottomless cup of coffee (open high noon to 21:00, closed Mon, between Dam Square and Anne Frank House at Oude Leliestraat 2, tel. 020/420-4301, www.greyarea.nl, Steven and John).

Near the corner of Leidsestraat and Prinsengracht, **Tops** coffee shop has Internet access. **Homegrown Fantasy**'s coffee shop and gallery, about two blocks northwest of Dam Square, has a gentle Dutch atmosphere, cosmic rest room, and a grow shop next door (daily 12:00–24:00, Nieuwe Zijds Voorburgwal 87a, tel. 020/627-5683).

▲**Marijuana and Hemp Museum**—This is a collection of dope facts, history, science, and memorabilia (€5.75, daily 11:00–22:00, Oudezijds Achterburgwal 148, tel. 020/623-5961). While small, it has a shocker finale: the high-tech grow room in which dozens of varieties of marijuana are cultivated in optimal hydroponic (among other) environments. Some plants stand five feet tall and shine under the intense grow lamps. The view is actually through glass walls into the neighboring "Sensi Seed Bank" Grow Shop, which sells carefully cultivated seeds and all the gear needed to grow them. It's an interesting neighborhood. The Cannabis College Foundation, "dedicated to ending the global war against the cannabis plant through public education," is next door at #124 (daily 11:00–22:00, tel. 020/423-4420, www.cannabiscollege .com or www.marijuananews.com). As you wander through the Foundation, ponder the 400,000 Americans serving time in jail because of U.S. marijuana laws.

Transportation Connections—Amsterdam

Amsterdam's train-information center requires a long wait. Save lots of time by getting train tickets and information in a small-town station or travel agency. For phone information, dial 0900-9292 for local trains or 0900-9296 for international trains (€0.75/min, daily 07:00–24:00, wait through recording and hold...hold...hold...).

By train to: Schiphol Airport (6/hr, 20 min, €3.25), **Haarlem** (6/hr, 15 min, €5.50 round-trip), **The Hague** (2/hr, 50 min), **Rotterdam** (4/hr, 1 hr), **Brussels** (2/hr, 3 hrs), **Ostende** (hrly, 4 hrs, change in Antwerp), **London** (2/day, 8 hrs, train to Hoek van Holland, then ferry across Channel, then train from Harwich to London; or 8/day, 6.5 hrs, with transfer to Eurostar Chunnel train in Brussels, Eurostar discounted with railpass, www.eurostar.com), **Copenhagen** (5/day, 10 hrs, transfer in Osnabrück and Hamburg; or 3-hr train to Duisberg and transfer to 11-hr night train), **Frankfurt** (8/day, 5–6 hrs, transfer in Köln or Duisburg), **Munich** (7/day, 9 hrs, transfer in Mannheim, Hanover, or Köln, one 11-hr direct night train), **Bonn** (10/day, 3 hrs, some direct but most transfer in Köln), **Bern** (5/day, 9 hrs, one direct but most transfer in Basel, Köln, or Brussels), **Paris** (5/day, 5 hrs, required fast train from Brussels with €11 supplement). If you don't have a railpass, the cheapest way to get to Paris is by bus (about $33 compared to $100 second-class by train; bus station in Amsterdam at Julianaplein 5, Amstel Station, 5 stops by Métro from Central Station, tel. 020/560-8788, www.eurolines.com).

Amsterdam's Schiphol Airport: The airport, like most of Holland, is English speaking, user-friendly, and below sea level. Its banks offer fair rates (24 hrs daily, in arrival area). Schiphol Airport has easy bus and train connections (11 km/7 miles) into Amsterdam or Haarlem. The airport also has a train station of its own. (You can validate your Eurailpass and hit the rails immediately or, to stretch your train pass, buy an inexpensive ticket into Amsterdam today and start the pass later.) Schiphol flight information (tel. 0900-0141) can give you flight times and your airline's Amsterdam number for reconfirmation before going home (€0.45/min to climb through its phone tree). To reach airlines, dial KLM at 020/649-9123 and Martainair at 020/601-1222.

HAARLEM

Cute, cozy, yet real and handy to the airport, Haarlem is a fine home base, giving you small-town, overnight warmth with easy access (15 min by train) to wild and crazy Amsterdam.

Haarlem is a busy Dutch market town buzzing with shoppers biking home with fresh bouquets. Enjoy the market on Saturday (general) and Monday (clothing), when the square bustles like a Brueghel painting with cheese, fish, flowers, and families. Make yourself at home; buy some flowers to brighten your hotel room.

The town will be more popular than ever in 2002. The **Floriade** world horticultural exhibition puts down roots in Haarlemmermeer, just five kilometers outside the city (April 6–Oct 20, 2002). Organizers expect up to 3 million visitors for the event, which is held only once every 10 years. Hotels will fill quickly and some will increase their rates dramatically. If you plan to visit Haarlem during the exhibition, book long in advance. For more information, ask at the TI or visit www.floriade.nl.

Orientation (area code: 023)

Tourist Information: Haarlem's TI (VVV), at the train station, is friendlier, more helpful, and less crowded than Amsterdam's. Ask your Amsterdam questions here (Mon–Fri 09:30–17:30, Sat 10:00–14:00, closed Sun, tel. 0900-616-1600, €0.45/min, helpful parking brochure, their €0.90 *Holidaymagazine* is not necessary).

Arrival in Haarlem: As you walk out of the train station (has lockers), the TI is on your right and the bus station is across the street. Two parallel streets flank the train station (Kruisweg and Jansweg). Head up either one, and you'll reach the town square and church within 10 minutes. If you need help, ask a local person to point you toward the *Grote Markt?* ("Main Square?")

Helpful Hints

The handy GWK **change office** at the station offers fair exchange rates (Mon–Fri 08:00–20:00, Sat 09:00–18:00, Sun 10:00–18:00). The train station rents **bikes** (€5.50/day, €45 deposit and passport number, Mon–Sat 06:00–24:00, Sun 07:30–24:00). For **Internet access**, try Hotel Amadeus (nonguests welcome, facing Market Square), High Times (if you don't mind marijuana smoke, Lange Veerstraat 47), or the Global Hemp Museum (Spaarne 94). On April 20, 2002, an all-day **Flower Parade** of floats wafts through eight towns, including Haarlem.

Sights—Haarlem

▲▲**Market Square (Grote Markt)**—Haarlem's market square is the town's delightful centerpiece. To enjoy a coffee or beer here, simmering in Dutch good living, is a quintessential European experience. In a recent study, the Dutch were found to be the most content people in Europe. And later, the people of Haarlem were found to be the most content in the Netherlands. Observe. Just a few years ago trolleys ran through the square and cars were parked everywhere. But today it's a people zone, with market stalls filling the square on Mondays and Saturdays and café tables on others. The local drunk used to hang out on the bench in front of the town hall, where he'd expose himself to newlyweds. The Dutch, rather than arrest the man, moved the bench. The big statue in the square is of Coster, the man only Haarlemers think invented printing. The little shops around the cathedral have long been church owned and rented to bring in a little cash. The fine building nearest the cathedral is the old meat hall—decorated with carved bits of early advertising.

▲**Church (Grote Kerk)**—This 15th-century Gothic church (now Protestant) is worth a look, if only for its Oz-like organ (from 1738, 30 meters/100 feet high, its 5,000 pipes impressed both Handel and Mozart). Note how the organ, which fills the west end, seems to steal the show from the altar. Pick up the English flier, which lists spots of interest, including Frans Hals' tomb (under black lantern in choir). To enter, find the small *Entrée* sign behind the church at Oude Groenmarkt 23 (€1.50, Mon–Sat 10:00–16:00). Consider attending (even part of) a concert to hear Holland's greatest pipe organ (regular free concerts Tue at 20:15 mid-May–mid-Oct, additional concerts Thu at 15:00 July–Aug, confirm schedule at TI).

▲▲**Frans Hals Museum**—Haarlem is the hometown of Frans Hals, and this refreshingly easy museum—an almshouse for old men back in 1610—displays many of his greatest paintings (€5, Mon–Sat 11:00–17:00, Sun 12:00–17:00, may be closed Mon in 2002, tel. 023/511-5775). Enjoy lots of Frans Hals group portraits (rooms 21, 25, 28) and the take-me-back paintings of old-time Haarlem. Peter Brueghel the Younger's painting *Proverbs*

Haarlem

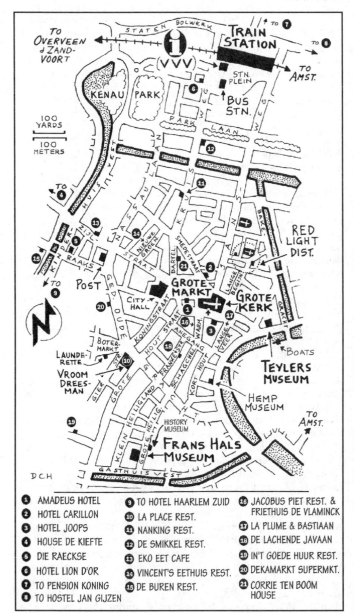

❶ AMADEUS HOTEL	❾ TO HOTEL HAARLEM ZUID	⓰ JACOBUS PIET REST. & FRIETHUIS DE VLAMINCK
❷ HOTEL CARILLON	❿ LA PLACE REST.	⓱ LA PLUME & BASTIAAN
❸ HOTEL JOOPS	⓫ NANKING REST.	⓲ DE LACHENDE JAVAAN
❹ HOUSE DE KIEFTE	⓬ DE SMIKKEL REST.	⓳ IN'T GOEDE HUUR REST.
❺ DIE RAECKSE	⓭ EKO EET CAFE	⓴ DEKAMARKT SUPERMKT.
❻ HOTEL LION D'OR	⓮ VINCENT'S EETHUIS REST.	㉑ CORRIE TEN BOOM HOUSE
❼ TO PENSION KONING	⓯ DE BUREN REST.	
❽ TO HOSTEL JAN GIJZEN		

illustrates 72 old Dutch proverbs. To peek into old Dutch ways, identify some with the help of the English-language key.

History Museum—Across the street from the Frans Hals Museum, this small museum gives a peek into old Haarlem. Request the English version of the 10-minute video. Study the large-scale model of Haarlem in 1822 before the town's fortifications were demolished, and enjoy the new "time machine" computer and video display that shows you various aspects of life in Haarlem at different points in history (€1, Tue–Sat 12:00–17:00, Sun 13:00–17:00, closed Mon, Groot Heiligland 47, tel. 020/542-2427). The adjacent architecture museum (free) may be of conceivable interest to architects.

Corrie Ten Boom House—Haarlem is home to Corrie Ten Boom, popularized by *The Hiding Place*, an inspirational book and movie about the Ten Boom family's experience hiding Jews from Nazis. The Ten Boom House is open for 60-minute English tours (donation accepted, April–Oct Tue–Sat 10:00–16:00, Nov–March Tue–Sat 11:00–15:00, closed Mon, 50 meters north of Market Square at Barteljorisstraat 19, the clock-shop people get all wound up if you go inside—wait at the door, where tour times are posted, tel. 023/531-0823). The Ten Boom family had for generations hosted a prayer meeting for peace here, for both Jews and Christians. On the 100th anniversary of the prayer meetings, the Gestapo came, tipped off that the family was harboring Jews. It's a great and inspirational story (although some may be put off by the preaching mixed in).

▲**Teylers Museum**—Famous as the oldest museum in Holland, it's interesting mainly as a look at a 200-year-old museum—fossils, minerals, and primitive electronic gadgetry. New exhibition halls (with rotating exhibits) have freshened up the place. Stop by if you enjoy mixing, say, Renaissance sketches with pickled extinct fish (€4.50, Tue–Sat 10:00–17:00, Sun 12:00–17:00, Spaarne 16, tel. 023/531-9010).

Canal Cruise—Making a scenic loop through and around Haarlem, these little trips by Woltheus Cruises are more relaxing than informative (€6, daily 10:00–17:00, 70 min, 5/day, across the canal from Teylers Museum at Spaarne 11a, tel. 023/535-7723).

Red Lights—Wander through a little red-light district as precious as a Barbie doll (2 blocks northeast of Market Square, off Lange Begijnestraat, no senior or student discounts). Don't miss the mall marked by the red neon sign reading *t'Steegje*. The nearby *t'Poortje* (office park) costs €3.40.

Global Hemp Museum—More a hemp-products store and hub of Haarlem's coffee-shop action, this friendly place runs a humble hemp museum out back (shop free, museum €2.25, Internet access-€1.35/30 min, Mon–Sat 11:00–20:00, summer Sun 12:00–20:00, down the canal from Teylers Museum at Spaarne 94, tel. 023/534-9939).

Hofjes—Haarlem is dotted with *hofjes*. These peaceful courtyards are surrounded by small row homes. Open to a quiet public, these are often accessed through an archway off the street.

Nightlife in Haarlem

Haarlem's evening scene is great. The bars around the Grote Kerk and Lange Veerstraat are colorful and lively. You'll find plenty of music.

The best show in town: the café scene on Market Square. In good weather, café tables tumble happily out of the bars.

For trendy local crowds, consider a drink at **Studio Café** (daily 12:00–24:00, on the main square, next to Hotel Carillon). Tourists gawk at the old-fashioned belt-driven ceiling fans in **Café 1900** across from the Corrie Ten Boom House (daily 09:00–00:30, live music Sun night except in July, Barteljoris-straat 10, tel. 023/531-8283).

Coffee Shops: Haarlem has 16 "coffee shops" where mari-juana is casually sold and smoked by easygoing, noncriminal types. The **Frans Hals Coffee Shop** is one of the best established (daily 09:00–24:00, in front of station at Kruisweg 46). The display case-type "menu" explains what's on sale (€2.50 joints, €11.50 baggies, space cakes—but no alcohol, only soft drinks). At **High Times**, smokers can choose from 16 varieties of joints in racks behind the bar (neatly prepacked in trademarked "Joint Packs," €2–3.50, daily 12:00–23:00, Internet access, Lange Veerstraat 47). If you don't like the smell of pot, avoid places sporting Rastafarian yellow, red, and green colors; wildly painted walls; or plants in the windows.

Crack is the wild and leathery place to go for loud music, pool, darts, and smoking (Lange Veerstraat 32). **Taverna Imper-ial** has live music Sunday through Thursday (daily 20:00–02:00, best to arrive around 00:30 on weekends, a few doors down from Crack at Korte Veerstraat 3, tel. 023/531-8283).

Sleeping in Haarlem
(€1.10 = about $1, country code: 31, area code: 023)
Sleep Code: **S** = Single, **D** = Double/Twin, **T** = Triple, **Q** = Quad, **b** = bathroom, **s** = shower only, **CC** = Credit Cards accepted, **no CC** = Credit Cards not accepted.

The helpful Haarlem TI, just outside the train station, can nearly always find you a €17 bed in a private home (for a €4.50-per-person fee plus a cut of your host's money). Avoid this if you can; it's cheaper to reserve direct.

Haarlem is most crowded in April, on Easter weekend, in May, and in July and August. Because of the once-in-a-decade Floriade festival (April 6–Oct 20, 2002), hotels are likely to fill even more quickly than usual, so it will be smart to book far in advance.

Nearly every Dutch person you'll encounter speaks English.

The listed prices include breakfast (unless otherwise noted) and usually include the €1.70-per-person-per-day tourist tax. To avoid this town's louder-than-normal street noises, forgo views for a room in the back. Hotels and the TI have a useful parking brochure.

For a **Laundromat**, try My Beautiful Launderette—handy, self-service, and cheap (€5 wash and dry, daily 08:30–20:30, bring lots of change, near Vroom Dreesman department store at Boter Markt 20).

Sleeping in the Center

Hotel Amadeus, on Market Square, has 15 small, bright, and basic rooms. Some have views of the square. This characteristic hotel, ideally located above an early 20th-century dinner café, is relatively quiet. Its lush old lounge/breakfast room, on the second floor, overlooks the square (Sb-€50, Db-€70, Tb-€87, Qb-€100, includes tax, 2-night stay and cash get you a 5 percent discount, 12-min walk from train station, CC, steep climb to lounge, then an elevator, Grote Markt 10, 2011 RD Haarlem, tel. 023/532-4530, fax 023/532-2328, www.amadeus-hotel.com, Mike and Inez take good care of their guests).

Hotel Carillon also overlooks the town square but comes with a little more traffic and bell-tower noise. Many of the 22 well-worn rooms are small, and the stairs are ste-e-e-p. The front rooms come with great town-square views and street noise (tiny loft singles-€30, Db-€70, Tb-€95, Qb-€102, includes tax, 12-min walk from train station, CC, no elevator, Grote Markt 27, 2011 RC Haarlem, tel. 023/531-0591, fax 023/531-4909, www.hotelcarillon.com, e-mail: info@hotelcarillon.com).

Hotel Joops is an innovative concept. Mr. Joops rents rooms in his own hotel, just behind the cathedral (Db-€70–90), and also administers a corral of 80 other rooms, all within a block of the church. These are a mixed bunch, ranging from cheap, well-worn, depressing rooms (S-€30, D-€55, T-€75) to modern new suites with kitchenettes (Db-€58–75 depending upon size, Tb-€20 extra, breakfast-€8.50, save about 5 percent with cash, CC, Oude Groen-markt 20, 2011 HL Haarlem, tel. 023/532-2008 or 023/512-5300, fax 023/532-9549, www.joops.hotelinformation.com).

Bed and Breakfast House de Kiefte, your get-into-a-local-home budget option, epitomizes the goodness of B&Bs. Marjet (mar-yet) and Hans, a fun-to-know Dutch couple who speak English fluently, rent four bright, cheery, nonsmoking rooms (with a good breakfast and travel advice) in their quiet, 100-year-old home (Ds-€50, T-€70, Qs-€90, Quint/s-€105, cash only, minimum 2 nights, all rooms with very steep stairs, family loft sleeps up to 5, kids over 4 welcome, Coornhertstraat 3, 2013 EV Haarlem, tel. 023/532-2980, cellular 06-5474-5272). It's a 15-minute walk or €7 taxi ride from the train station and a five-minute walk from the center. From Grote

Markt (Market Square), walk to the right of City Hall straight out Zijlstraat and over the bridge and take a left on the fourth street.

Die Raeckse Hotel is not as central as the others, with less character and more traffic noise, but its rooms are decent and comfortable (Sb-€55–70, Db-€80, Tb-€92, Qb-€100, extra bed-€25, CC, Raaks 1, 2011 VA Haarlem, tel. 023/532-6629, fax 023/531-7937).

Hotel Lion D'Or is a classy 34-room business hotel with all the professional comforts and a handy location. Don't expect a warm welcome (Sb-€104–118, Db-€136–154, extra beds-€23, prices much higher during Floriade from April–Oct, CC, elevator, some nonsmoking rooms, across the street from the station at Kruisweg 34, 2011 LC Haarlem, tel. 023/532-1750, fax 023/532-9543, www.goldentulip.nl/hotels/gtliondor).

Sleeping near Haarlem

The 300-room, very American **Hotel Haarlem Zuid** is sterile but a good value for those interested only in sleeping and eating. It sits in an industrial zone, a 20-minute walk from the center on the road to the airport (Db during Floriade-€126, otherwise €80, breakfast included or skip and save €8 each, CC, elevator, easy parking, laundry service, fitness center, inexpensive hotel restaurant, Toekanweg 2, 2035 LC Haarlem, tel. 023/536-7500, fax 023/536-7980, www.hotelhaarlemzuid.nl, e-mail: haarlemzuid@valk.com). Buses #5, #70, #71, #72, and #80 connect the hotel to the station and Market Square every 10 minutes. Bus #80 makes runs to the beach or Amsterdam. Fast buses (#236 and #362) zip to the airport.

Pension Koning, a 15-minute walk north of the station or a quick hop on bus #71, has five simple rooms in a row house in a residential area (S-€23, D-€46, T-€69, 2-night minimum, includes breakfast, no CC, Kleverlaan 179, 2023 JC Haarlem, tel. 023/526-1456).

Hostel Jan Gijzen, completely renovated and with all the youth-hostel comforts, charges €18 to €21 for beds in eight-bed dorms (€2.25 extra for nonmembers, a few D-€42–45, includes breakfast and sheets, no CC, daily 07:30–24:00, Jan Gijzenpad 3, 3 km from Haarlem station—take bus #2 from platform A1, or a 5-min walk from Santpoort Zuid train station, tel. 023/537-3793, fax 023/537-1176, www.njhc.org/haarlem, e-mail: haarlem@njhc.org).

Eating in Haarlem

Eating between Market Square (Grote Markt) and Train Station

Enjoy an Indonesian rijsttafel feast at the **Nanking Chinese-Indonesian Restaurant** (daily 16:00–22:00, Kruisstraat 16, a few blocks off Grote Markt, tel. 023/532-0706). Couples eat plenty, heartily, and cheaply by splitting a €12.50 Indonesian "rice table" for one; each eater should order a drink. Say hi to gracious Ai Ping and her daughter, Fan. Don't let them railroad you into a Chinese (their heritage) dinner. They also do cheap and tasty takeout.

Pancakes for dinner? **Pannekoekhuis "De Smikkel"** serves a selection of over 50 dinner (meat, cheese, etc.) and dessert pancakes. The pancakes (€8 each) are filling. With the €1.25-per-person cover charge, splitting is OK (daily 12:00–22:00, Sun from 16:00, closed Mon in winter, 2 blocks in front of station, Kruisweg 57, tel. 023/532-0631).

Eat well and surrounded by trains and 1908 architecture in the classy **Brasserie Haarlem Station Restaurant** (€13.75 for 3 courses, daily 09:00–21:00, between tracks #3 and #6).

Eating on or near Zijlstraat

Eko Eet Café is great for a cheery, tasty vegetarian meal (€9 *menu*, daily 17:30–21:30, Zijlstraat 39, tel. 023/532-6568). Because they serve only fresh food, the *menu* gets sparse by 21:00.

Vincent's Eethuis serves the best cheap, basic Dutch food in town. This former St. Vincent's soup kitchen now feeds more gainfully employed locals than poor (€5, free seconds on veggies, friendly staff, Mon–Fri 12:00–14:00, 17:00–19:30, Nieuwe Groenmarkt 22).

The cheery **De Buren** offers handlebar-mustache fun and traditional Dutch food (such as *draadjesvlees*, beef stew with applesauce, and *oma's kippetje*, grandmother's chicken) to happy locals (€11–16 dinners, Wed–Sun 17:00–22:00, closed Mon–Tue, outside the tourist area at Brouwersvaart 146, follow Raaks Straat west across the canal from Die Raeckse Hotel, tel. 023/534-3364). Gerard and Marjo love their work. Enjoy their creative menu, made especially for you.

Eating between the Market Square and Frans Hals Museum

Jacobus Pieck Eetlokaal is popular with locals for its fine-value "global cuisine" (€9 plate of the day, Tue–Sat 10:00–22:00, Sun–Mon 10:00–17:00, Warmoesstraat 18, tel. 023/532-6144).

For a (€1.35) cone of old-fashioned French fries, drop by **Friethuis de Vlaminck** on Warmoesstraat 3 (Tue–Sat until 18:00). Notice the old-time shop sign cobbled into Warmoesstraat's brick sidewalk.

La Plume steak house is noisy with a happy, local, and carnivorous crowd (€13.75 meals, daily from 17:30, CC, Lange Veerstraat 1, tel. 023/531-3202).

Bastiaan serves good Mediterranean cuisine in a classy atmosphere (€13.75 dinners, Tue–Sun from 18:00, closed Mon, CC, Lange Veerstraat 8, tel. 023/532-6006).

De Lachende Javaan ("The Laughing Javanese") serves

the best real Indonesian food in town. Their €17 rijsttafel is great (light eaters can split this extravaganza—€3.85 for extra plate, Tue–Sun from 17:00, closed Mon, CC, Frankestraat 25, tel. 023/532-8792).

For a candlelit dinner of cheese and wine, consider **In't Goede Uur** (Tue–Sun 17:00–24:00, Fri–Sat until 01:00, closed Mon, Korte Houtstraat 1, tel. 023/531-1174).

For a healthy budget lunch with Haarlem's best view, eat at **La Place**, on the top floor or roof garden of the Vroom Dreesman department store (Mon 11:00–17:30, Tue–Sat 09:30–17:30, Thu until 20:30, closed Sun, on the corner of Grote Houtstraat and Gedempte Oude Gracht, tel. 023/515-8700).

Picnic shoppers head to the **DekaMarkt** supermarket (Mon 11:00–20:00, Tue–Sat 08:30–20:00, Thu until 21:00, closed Sun, Gedemple Oude Gracht 54, between Vroom Dreesman depart-ment store and post office).

Transportation Connections—Haarlem
By train to: Amsterdam (6/hr, 15 min, €3.20 one-way, €5.45 same-day return, ticket not valid on "Lovers Train," a misnamed private train that runs hrly), **Delft** (2/hr, 38 min), **Hoorn** (4/hr, 1 hr), **The Hague** (4/hr, 35 min), **Alkmaar** (2/hr, 30 min), **Schip-hol Airport** (2/hr, 40 min, €4.55, transfer at Amsterdam-Sloterdijk); the direct buses #236 (use a strip card) and #362 (local cash) to the airport are faster (2/hr, 30 min, €3.20); by taxi it's €32.

Sights—Near Haarlem and Amsterdam
The Netherlands are tiny. The sights listed below are an easy day trip by bus or train from Haarlem or Amsterdam. Match your interest with the village's specialty: flower auctions, folk museums, cheese, delft porcelain, beaches, or modern art.
Floriade—This horticultural exhibition, which sounds like the world's biggest garden show, takes place every 10 years in the Netherlands. In 2002, it's coming to Haarlemmermeer, just five kilometers outside of Haarlem (April 6–Oct 20, 2002). Horticul-turalists from all over the world converge to show off their plants. The main entrance features a huge, flat "floating roof" (100 by 300 meters). The lake has been dolled up with Oriental pavilions and an open-air theater. Towering above everything is the center-piece of the park—"Big Spotters Hill." The man-made hill rises 40 meters (130 feet) above the countryside (which doesn't sound like much, but hey—it's Holland), giving you a bird's-eye view of the surrounding gardens and displays (€17, kids 4–12 €8.50, daily 09:30–19:00, ticket office open 09:00–18:00, Floriadepark 1, main entrance near town of Vijfhuizen, tel. 023/562-2002, www.floriade.nl). After this Floriade officially closes, the park will remain for people to enjoy.

Daytrips from Haarlem and Amsterdam

▲▲**Enkhuizen's Zuiderzee Museum**—This lively, open-air
folk museum in the salty old town of Enkhuizen has a "Living
on Urk" village (patterned after an old Dutch fishing town),
populated by people who do a convincing job of role-playing no-
nonsense 1905 Dutch villagers. No one said "Have a nice day"
back then. You can eat herring hot out of the old smoker and
see barrels and rope made. Children enjoy playing at the dress-up
chest, trying out old-time games, and making sailing ships out
of old wooden shoes (€10, early April–late Oct daily 10:00–17:00,
July–Aug free tours at 14:00, private guide for €40, tel. 0228/
351-111, www.zuiderzeemuseum.nl). Take the train from Amsterdam direct to Enkhuizen, where a boat shuttles you to the museum,
avoiding a pleasant 15-minute walk.

▲**Zaanse Schans**—This 17th-century Dutch village turned open-
air folk museum puts Dutch culture—from cheese making to
wooden-shoe carving—on a lazy Susan. Take an inspiring climb
to the top of a whirring windmill (gather a group and ask for a
tour). Located in the town of Zaandijk, this is your easiest one-
stop look at traditional Dutch culture and the Netherlands' best

collection of windmills (entrance to grounds free, but you must pay around €1–2 to go in windmills and other sights in the park, daily 08:30–17:30, until 17:00 in winter, parking €3.40/hr, 15/day, tel. 075/616-8218). It's 15 minutes by train north of Amsterdam; take the Alkmaar-bound train to Station Koog-Zaandijk and then walk, following the signs—past a fragrant chocolate factory—for 10 minutes.

▲▲**Aalsmeer Flower Auction**—Get a bird's-eye view of the huge Dutch flower industry. Wander on elevated walkways (through what's claimed to be the biggest commercial building on earth) over literally trainloads of freshly cut flowers. About half of all the flowers exported from Holland are auctioned off here in four huge auditoriums. Stop at one of the "listening posts" for on-the-spot information (€4, Mon–Fri 07:30–11:00, the auction wilts after 09:30 and on Thu but the warehouse swarms, gift shop, cafeteria; bus #172 from Amsterdam's station, 2/hr, 1 hr; from Haarlem take bus #140 and transfer to bus #172 or #77 in Aalsmeer, 2/hr, 1 hr; tel. 0297/392-185). Aalsmeer is close to the airport and a handy last fling before catching a morning weekday flight.

▲▲▲**Keukenhof**—This is the greatest bulb-flower garden on earth. Each spring 6 million flowers, enjoying sandy soil behind the Dutch dunes, conspire to make even a total garden hater enjoy them. This 100-acre park is packed with tour groups daily from about March 21 to May 20 for the 2002 spring show (€11, daily 08:00–19:30, last tickets sold at 18:00) and early August to mid-September for the summer exhibition (€7, daily 09:00–18:00, last ticket sold at 17:00; from Haarlem take the train to Leiden, then catch bus #54, tel. 0252/465-555, www.keukenhof.nl). Go late in the day for the best light and the fewest groups.

The 2002 Flower Parade will be held April 20. This all-day parade, featuring floats decorated with blossoms instead of crepe paper, runs through eight towns, including Lisse and Haarlem.

Zandvoort—For a quick and easy look at the windy coastline in a shell-lover's Shangri-La, visit the beach resort of Zandvoort, a breezy 45-minute bike ride or an eight-minute car or train ride west of Haarlem (from Haarlem, follow signs to Bloemendaal). South of the main beach, bathers work on all-over tans.

▲**Hoorn**—This is an elegant, quiet, and typical 17th-century Dutch town north of Amsterdam. Its TI can rent you a bike or give you a walking-tour brochure. Any TI offers the flier describing the "Historic Triangle," an all-day excursion from Amsterdam that connects Hoorn, Medemblik, and Enkhuizen by steam train and boat (€18 plus €3 for train back to Haarlem; train: 2/day in July–Aug and Sat–Sun, otherwise 1/day; boat: 1/day, Sept–June doesn't run on Mon, tel. 0229/214-862).

De Rijp—This sleepy town is worth visiting if you're driving north of Amsterdam.

Volendam, Marken, and Monnikendam—These famous towns are quaint as can be (although Volendam is very touristy).

▲**Delft**—Peaceful as a Vermeer painting (he was born here) and lovely as its porcelain, Delft is a typically Dutch town with a special soul. Enjoy it best by simply wandering around, watching people, munching local syrup waffles, or daydreaming from the canal bridges. The town bustles during its Saturday antiques market (09:00–17:00). Its colorful Thursday food-and-flower market attracts many traditional villagers (09:00–17:00). The TI on the main square has a €1.85 brochure outlining Delft's sights, including a "Historical Walk through Delft" (Mon–Sat 09:00–17:30, April–Sept also Sun 11:00–15:00, tel. 015/213-0100). The town is a museum in itself, but, if you need a turnstile, it has an impressive Army Museum (€4.30, Mon–Fri 10:00–17:00, Sat–Sun 12:00–17:00, tel. 015/215-0500). Or tour the Royal Porcelain Works to watch the famous 17th-century blue delftware turn from clay into art (€2.25, Mon–Sat 09:00–17:00, summer Sun 09:30–17:00, tel. 015/256-9214).

▲**Alkmaar**—Holland's cheese capital is especially fun (and touristy) during its weekly cheese market (Fridays April–Aug 10:00–12:30). TI tel. 072/511-4284.

▲▲**Edam**—For the ultimate in cuteness and peace, make tiny Edam your home. It's sweet but palatable and 30 minutes by bus from Amsterdam (2/hr). The Edam Museum is a small, quirky house offering a fun peek into a 400-year-old home and a floating cellar (€2, Tue–Sat 10:00–16:30, Sun 13:30–16:30, closed in winter, on main square, tel. 0299/372-644). Wednesday is the town's market day (09:00–13:00). In July and August, market day includes a traditional cheese market (10:30–12:30).

Sleeping and Eating: The TI (tel. 0299/315-125) has a list of inexpensive rooms in private homes. **Hotel De Fortuna**, an eccentric canalside mix of flowers, a cat of leisure, a pet turtle, and duck noises, offers steep stairs and low-ceilinged rooms in several ancient buildings in the old center of Edam (Db-€85–97.50, includes breakfast, CC, garden patio, attached restaurant, Spuistraat 3, 1135 AV Edam, tel. 0299/371-671, fax 0299/371-469, www.fortuna-edam.nl). The centrally located **Damhotel** (on a canal around corner from TI) has attractive, comfortable rooms with a plush feel (Sb-€52, Db-€86, Tb-€122.50, Qb-€163, includes breakfast, CC, attached restaurant, Keizersgracht 1, 1135 AZ Edam, tel. 0299/371-766, fax 0299/374-031, www .damhotel.nl). **Tai Wah** has take-out Chinese/Indonesian (eat in De Fortuna garden) and indoor seating (Mon and Wed–Sat 16:00–21:00, Sun 13:00–21:00, closed Tue, Lingerzijde 62, tel. 0299/371-088).

▲**Rotterdam**—This city, the world's largest port, bounced back after being bombed flat in World War II. See its towering Euromast, take a harbor tour, and stroll its great pedestrian zone (TI tel. 0900/403-4065, toll call-€0.45/min).

▲▲**The Hague (Den Haag)**—Locals say the money is made in Rotterdam, divided in The Hague, and spent in Amsterdam. The Hague is the Netherlands' seat of government and the home of several engaging museums. The Hague's TI is at the train station (Mon–Sat 09:00–17:30, later in summer, Sun 10:00–17:00, tel. 06/3403-505, €0.45/min).

The **Mauritshuis'** delightful, easy-to-tour art collection stars Vermeer and Rembrandt (€7, Tue–Sat 10:00–17:00, Sun 11:00–17:00, Korte Vijverberg 8, tel. 070/302-3456). Across the pond, the **Torture Museum** (Gevangenpoort) shows the medieval mind at its worst (€3.75, Tue–Fri 11:00–17:00, Sat–Sun 12:00–17:00, closed Mon, required tours on the hour, last one at 16:00, ask ticket taker if film and talk will be in English before you commit, tel. 070/346-0861). For a look at the 19th century's attempt at virtual reality, tour **Panorama Mesdag**, a 360-degree painting of nearby Scheveningen in the 1880s with a 3-D sandy-beach foreground (€4, Mon–Sat 10:00–17:00, Sun 12:00–17:00, Zeestraat 65, tel. 070/310-6665). The nearby **Peace Palace**, a gift from Andrew Carnegie, houses the International Court of Justice (€3.40, Mon–Fri, required guided tours only at 10:00, 11:00, 14:00, or 15:00, closes without warning—call ahead or check at TI, tram #7 or #8 from station, tel. 070/302-4137).

Scheveningen, the Dutch Coney Island, has a newly renovated pier and is liveliest on sunny summer afternoons (take tram #1, #8, or #9 to Gevers Deynootplein/Kurhaus and walk via Palace Promenade to the Boulevard). **Madurodam**, a mini-Holland amusement park, is a kid pleaser (€10, kids 4–11–€7, Sept–mid-March daily 09:00–18:00, mid-March–June until 20:00, July–Aug until 22:00, George Maduroplein 1, tram #1 or #9, tel. 070/355-3900, www.madurodam.nl).

Utrecht—The Museum von Speelklok tot Pierement has free and necessary guided 55-minute tours on the hour demonstrating its musical clocks, calliopes, and street organs (€6, Tue–Sat 10:00–17:00, Sun 12:00–17:00, closed Mon, last tour at 16:00, 10-min walk from station, Buurkerkhof 10, tel. 030/231-2789).

▲▲**Arnhem's Open-Air Dutch Folk Museum**—An hour east of Amsterdam, Arnhem has the Netherlands' first and biggest folk museum. You'll enjoy a huge park of windmills, old farms, traditional crafts in action, and a pleasant education-by-immersion in Dutch culture. The English guidebook (€3.85) explains each historic building (€11, Easter–Oct daily 10:00–17:00, cool new multimedia exhibit, tel. 026/357-6111, www.openluchtmuseum.nl). The park has several good budget restaurants and covered picnic areas. Its rustic Pancake House serves hearty (splittable) Dutch flapjacks.

Trains make the 70-minute trip from Amsterdam to Arnhem twice an hour (likely transfer in Utrecht). At Arnhem station, take bus #3 (direction: Alteveer) or, even better, #13 (faster, 4/hr, 15 min, runs July–Aug only) to the *Openluchtmuseum*. By car from Haarlem, skirt Amsterdam to the south on E9, follow signs to Utrecht, and take A12 east to Arnhem. Just before Arnhem, take the Arnhem Nord exit *Openluchtmuseum* (exit #26) and follow signs to the nearby museum. For the Kröller-Müller Museum, follow white signs to Hoge Veluwe.

▲▲**Kröller-Müller Museum and Hoge Veluwe National Park**—Near Arnhem, Hoge Veluwe National Park is the Netherlands' largest (13,000 acres) and is famous for its Kröller-Müller Museum. This huge, striking modern-art collection, including 55 paintings by van Gogh, is set deep in the forest. The park has hundreds of white bikes you're free to use to make your explorations more fun (€4.50 to enter park, €4.50 more for the museum, museum open Tue–Sun 10:00–17:00, closed Mon, easy parking, tel. 031/859-1041). Pick up information at the Amsterdam or Arnhem TI (tel. 026/442-6767). Bus #12 connects the Arnhem train station with the Kröller-Müller Museum (April–Oct, check ahead for times as #12 runs infrequently). A visit to the park and the open-air museum makes a great day trip from Amsterdam.

BARCELONA

Barcelona is Spain's second city and the capital of the proud and distinct region of Catalunya. With Franco's fascism now history, Catalan flags wave once again. Language and culture are on a roll in Spain's most cosmopolitan and European corner.

Barcelona bubbles with life in its narrow Gothic Quarter alleys, along the grand boulevards, and throughout the chic, grid-planned new town. While Barcelona had an illustrious past as a Roman colony, Visigothic capital, 14th-century maritime power, and, in more modern times, a top Mediterranean trading and manufacturing center, it's most enjoyable to throw out the history books and just drift through the city. If you're in the mood to surrender to a city's charms, let it be in Barcelona.

Planning Your Time
Sandwich Barcelona between flights or overnight train rides. There's little of earth-shaking importance within eight hours by train. It's as easy to fly into Barcelona as into Madrid, Lisbon, or Paris for most travelers from the United States. Those renting a car can cleverly start here, sleep on the train or fly to Madrid, see Madrid and Toledo, and pick up the car as they leave Madrid.

On the shortest visit, Barcelona is worth one night, one day, and an overnight train out. The Ramblas is two different streets by day and by night. Stroll it from top to bottom at night and again the next morning, grabbing breakfast on a stool in a market café. Wander the Gothic Quarter, see the cathedral, and have lunch in Eixample (eye-SHAM-plah). The top two sights in town, Gaudí's Sacred Family Church and the Picasso Museum, are usually open until 20:00. The illuminated fountains (on Montjuïc, near Plaça Espanya) are a good finale for your day.

Barcelona

Of course, Barcelona in a day is insane. To better appreciate the city's ample charm, spread your visit over two or three days.

Orientation

Orient yourself mentally by locating these essentials on the map: Barri Gòtic/Ramblas (old town), Eixample (fashionable modern town), Montjuïc (hill covered with sights and parks), and Sants Station (train to Madrid). The soul of Barcelona is in its compact core—the Barri Gòtic (Gothic Quarter) and the Ramblas (main boulevard). This is your strolling, shopping, and people-watching nucleus. The city's sights are widely scattered, but with a map and a willingness to figure out the sleek subway system (or a few dollars for taxis), all is manageable.

Tourist Information

There are four useful **TIs** in Barcelona: at the **airport** (daily 09:30–20:30, tel. 93-478-4704), at the **Sants train station** (daily

08:00–20:00, near track 6), on **Plaça de Catalunya** (daily 09:00–
21:00, on main square near recommended hotels, look for red
sign, Gothic Quarter walking tours in English Sat–Sun at 10:00
from TI, €6.60, 2 hrs, call to reserve, tel. 93-304-3232; fair rates
at TI exchange desk; room-finding service; half-price ticket booth
from 3 hrs before show time; www.barcelonaturisme.com), and an
all-Catalunya office at **Passeig de Gràcia** 107 (Mon–Sat 10:00–
19:00, Sun 10:00–13:00, tel. 93-238-4000). Pick up the large city
map, brochure on public transport, and the free quarterly "See
Barcelona" guide with practical information on museum hours,
restaurants, transportation, history, festivals, and so on.

Arrival in Barcelona

By Train: Although many international trains use the França Station, all domestic (and some international) trains use Sants Station.
Both França and Sants have baggage lockers and subway stations:
França's is "Barceloneta" (2 blocks away), and Sants' is "Sants
Estacio" (under the station). Sants Station has a good TI, a world
of handy shops and eateries, and a classy, quiet "Sala Euromed"
lounge for travelers with first-class reservations (TV, free drinks,
study tables, and coffee bar). Subway or taxi to your hotel. Most
trains to/from France stop at the subway station Passeig de Gràcia,
just a short walk from the center (Plaça de Catalunya, TI, hotels).

By Plane: Barcelona's El Prat de Llobregat Airport is 12 kilometers southwest of town and connected cheaply and quickly by
Aerobus (immediately in front of arrivals lobby, 4/hr until 24:00,
20 min to Plaça de Catalunya, buy €3.25 ticket from driver, tel.
93-412-0000) or by RENFE train (walk the tunnel overpass from
airport to station, 2/hr at :13 and :43, 20 min to Sants Station and
Plaça de Catalunya, €2). A taxi to or from the airport costs under
€18. The airport has a post office, pharmacy, left luggage, and
ATMs (far-left end of arrival hall as you face the street). Airport
info: tel. 93-298-3838.

Getting around Barcelona

Subway: Barcelona's Metro, among Europe's best, connects just
about every place you'll visit. It has five color-coded lines (L1 is
red, L2 is lilac, L3 is green, L4 is yellow, L5 is blue). Rides cost
€1. The new T-10 Card for €5.30 gives you 10 tickets good for
all local bus and Metro lines as well as the separate FGC line and
RENFE train lines. Pick up the TI's guide to public transport.
One-, two-, and five-day passes are available.

Hop-on hop-off bus: The handy Tourist Bus (*Bus Turistic*)
offers two multi-stop circuits in colorful double-decker buses
(red route covers north Barcelona—most Gaudí sights; blue route
covers south—Barri Gòtic, Montjuïc) with multilingual guides
(April–Dec 09:00–21:30, buses run every 10–20 min, buy tickets

on bus). Ask for a brochure at the TI. One-day (€13.25) and two-day (€16.75) tickets include discounts on the city's major sights.

Taxis: Barcelona is one of Europe's best taxi towns. Taxis are plentiful and honest (€1.90 drop charge, €0.70/km, extras posted in window). Save time by hopping a cab (Ramblas to Sants Station—€3.60, luggage—€0.60/piece).

Helpful Hints

Theft Alert: You're more likely to be pickpocketed here—especially on the Ramblas—than about anywhere else in Europe. Most of the crime is non-violent, but muggings do occur. Be on guard. Leave valuables in your hotel, and wear a money belt.

Here are a few common street scams, easy to avoid if you recognize them. Most common is the too-friendly local who tries to engage you in conversation by asking for the time, whether you speak English, and so on. If you suspect the person is more interested in your money than your time, ignore him and move on. A common street gambling scam is the pea-and-carrot game, a variation on the shell game. The people winning are all ringers and you can be sure that you'll lose if you play. Also beware of groups of women aggressively selling carnations, people offering to clean off a stain from your shirt, and people picking things up in front of you on escalators. If you stop for any commotion or show on the Ramblas, put your hands in your pockets before someone else does.

American Express: AmEx offices are at Passeig de Gràcia 101 (Mon–Fri 09:30–18:00, Sat 10:00–12:00, Metro: Diagonal, tel. 93-415-2371) and at La Ramblas 74 opposite the Liceu Metro station (daily 09:00–24:00, tel. 93-301-1166).

U.S. Consulate: Passeig Reina Elisenda 23 (tel. 93-280-2227).

Emergency Phone Numbers: Police—092, Emergency—061.

Pharmacy: At the corner of Ramblas and Carrer de la Portaferrissa (daily 09:00–22:00, 24-hour info line: tel. 010).

Local Guides: The Barcelona Guide Bureau is a co-op with plenty of excellent local guides who give personalized four-hour tours for €150 (Via Laietana 54, tel. 93-310-7778).

Internet Access: A handy choice among the many Internet cafés is Cybermundo Internet Center, a block off Plaça de Catalunya (Mon–Fri 09:00–24:00, Sat 10:00–24:00, Sun 11:00–24:00, no line likely in morning, Carrer Bergara 3, tel. 93-317-7142).

Introductory Walk: From Plaça de Catalunya down the Ramblas

A ▲▲▲ sight, Barcelona's central square and main drag exert a powerful pull as many visitors spend a major part of their time here doing laps on the Ramblas. Here's an orientation walk:

Plaça de Catalunya—This vast central square—littered with statues of Catalan heroes—divides old and new Barcelona and is the hub for the Metro, bus, airport shuttle, and both hop-on and hop-off buses (red/northern route leaves from El Corte Inglés, blue/southern route from west side of Plaça). The grass around its fountain is the best public place in town for serious necking. Overlooking the square, the huge El Corte Inglés department store offers everything from bonsai trees to a travel agency, plus one-hour photo developing, haircuts, and cheap souvenirs (Mon–Sat 10:00–22:00, closed Sun, supermarket in basement, 9th-floor terrace cafeteria with great city view—take elevator from near entrance, tel. 93-306-3800). Four great boulevards start from Plaça de Catalunya: the Ramblas, the fashionable Passeig de Gràcia, the cozier but still fashionable Rambla Catalunya, and the stubby, shop-filled, pedestrian-only Portal de L'Angel. Home-sick Americans even have a Hard Rock Café. Locals traditionally start or end a downtown rendezvous at the venerable Café Zurich (cross street from café to reach...).

Ramblas Walk Stop #1: The top of the Ramblas—Begin your ramble 20 meters down at the ornate fountain (near #129). Grab a chair—a man will collect €0.30—and observe.

More than a Champs-Élysées, this grand boulevard takes you from rich at the top to rough at the port in a 1.5-kilometer, 20-minute walk. You'll raft the river of Barcelonan life past a grand opera house, elegant cafés, plain prostitutes, pickpockets, con men, artists, street mimes, an outdoor bird market, great shopping, and people looking to charge more for a shoeshine than you paid for the shoes. When Hans Christian Andersen saw this street he wrote there's no doubt Barcelona is a great city.

Rambla means "stream" in Arabic. The Ramblas used to be a drainage ditch along the medieval wall that once defined what's now called the Gothic Quarter. The boulevard consists of five separately named segments, but address numbers treat it as a single long street.

Open up your map and read some history into it: You're about to walk right across medieval Barcelona from Plaça de Catalunya to the harbor. Notice how the higgledy-piggledy street plan of the medieval town was contained within the old town walls—now gone but traced by a series of roads named Ronda (meaning "to go around"). The five-pronged lampposts—midway down the Ramblas—mark where the gateways to the old city used to be. Find the Roman town, occupying about 10 percent of what became the medieval town—with tighter roads yet around the cathedral. The sprawling modern grid plan beyond the Ronda roads is from the 19th century. Breaks in this urban waffle show where a little town was consumed by the growing city. The popular Passeig de Gràcia boulevard was literally the road to Gràcia (once a town, now a characteristic Barcelona neighborhood).

"Las Ramblas" is plural, a succession of streets. You're at

From Plaça de Catalunya down the Ramblas

Rambla Canaletes, named for the fountain. The black-and-gold
Fountain of Canaletes is the beginning point for celebrations and
demonstrations. Legend says that one drink from the fountain
ensures that you'll return to Barcelona one day. (Take a gulp!)
All along the Ramblas you'll see newspaper stands (open 24 hours,
selling phone cards) and ONCE booths (selling lottery tickets
which support Spain's organization of the blind, a powerful advo-
cate for the needs of disabled people).

Got some change? As you wander downhill, drop coins into
the cans of the human statues (the money often kicks them into
entertaining gear). Warning: Wherever people stop to gawk, pickpockets are at work.

Walk 100 meters downhill to #115 and...

Ramblas Walk Stop #2: Rambla of the Little Birds—Traditionally kids bring their parents here to buy pets, especially on
Sundays. Apartment-dwellers find birds, turtles, and fish easier
to handle than dogs and cats. Balconies with flowers are generally
living spaces, those with air-conditioning are generally offices.
The Academy of Science's clock (at #115) marks official Barcelona
time—synchronize. The Champion supermarket (at #113) has
cheap groceries and a handy deli with cooked food to go. A newly-
discovered Roman necropolis is in a park across the street, 50
meters behind the big modern Citadines Hotel (go through the
passageway at #122). Local apartment-dwellers blew the whistle on
contractors who hoped they could finish their building before anyone noticed the antiquities they had unearthed. Imagine the tomb-
lined road leading into the Roman city of Barcino 2,000 years ago.

Another hundred meters takes you to Carrer del Carme
(at #2), and...

Ramblas Walk Stop #3: Baroque Church—The big plain
church lining the boulevard is Baroque, rare in Barcelona. While
Barcelona's Gothic age was rich (with buildings to prove it), the
Baroque age hardly left a mark (the city's importance dropped
when New World discoveries shifted lucrative trade to ports on
the Atlantic). The Bagues jewelry shop across Carrer del Carme
from the church is known for its Art Nouveau jewelry (from the
molds of Masriera, displayed in the window). At the shop's side
entrance, step on the old-fashioned scales (free, in kilos) and head
down the lane opposite (behind the church, 30 meters) to a place
expert in making you heavier. Café Granja Viader (see "Eating,"
below) has specialized in baked and dairy delights since 1870.

Stroll through the Ramblas of Flowers to the subway stop
marked by the red M (near #100), and...

Ramblas Walk Stop #4: La Boqueria—This lively produce
market is an explosion of chicken legs, bags of live snails, stiff fish,
delicious oranges, and sleeping dogs (#91, Mon–Sat 08:00–20:00,
best mornings after 09:00, closed Sun). The Conserves shop sells

25 kinds of olives (straight in, near back on right, 100-gram minimum, €0.20–0.40). Full legs of ham (*jamón serrano*) abound; *Paleta Iberica de Bellota* are best and cost about €120 each. Beware: *Huevos de toro* are bull testicles—surprisingly inexpensive... but oh so good. Drop by Mario and Alex's Café Central for an *espresso con leche* (far end of main aisle on left) or breakfast. Ask for Mario's "breakfast special" (potato omelet with whatever's fresh). For lunch and dinner options, try La Garduña, located at the back of the market (See "Eating," below).

The Museum of Erotica (€7.20, daily 10:00–24:00, shorter hours in winter, across from market at #96) is your standard European sex museum—neat if you like nudes and a chance to hear phone sex in four languages.

At #100, Gimeno sells cigars (appreciate the dying art of cigar boxes). Go ahead... buy a Cuban cigar (singles from €0.60). Tobacco shops sell stamps.

Farther down the Ramblas at #83, the Art Nouveau Escriba Café—an ornate world of pastries, little sandwiches, and fine coffee—still looks like it did on opening day in 1906 (daily 08:30–21:00, indoor/outdoor seating, tel. 93-301-6027).

A much-trod-upon mosaic created by noted abstract artist Joan Miró marks the midpoint of the Ramblas. From here, walk down to the Liceu Opera House (reopened after a 1994 fire, tickets on sale Mon–Fri 14:00–20:30, tel. 90-233-2211; tours in English Mon–Fri 09:30–11:00, reserve in advance, tel. 93-485-9900). From the Opera House, cross the Ramblas to Café de l'Opera for a beverage (#74, tel. 93-317-7585). This bustling café, with modernist decor and a historic atmosphere, boasts it's been open since 1929, even during the Spanish Civil War. Continue to #46; turn left down an arcaded lane to a square filled with palm trees...

Ramblas Walk Stop #5: Plaça Reial—This elegant neoclassical square comes complete with old-fashioned taverns, modern bars with patio seating, a Sunday coin and stamp market (10:00–14:00), Gaudí's first public works (the 2 helmeted lampposts), and characters who don't need the palm trees to be shady. Herbolari Ferran is a fine and aromatic shop of herbs, with fun souvenirs such as top-quality saffron or *safra* (Mon–Sat 09:30–14:00, 16:30–20:00, closed Sun, downstairs at Plaça Reial 18). The small streets stretching toward the water from the square are intriguing, seedy, and dangerous.

Back across the Ramblas, the **Palau Güell** offers an enjoyable look at a Gaudí interior (€2.40, usually open Mon–Sat 10:00–13:00, 16:00–19:00, Carrer Nou de la Rambla 3–5, tel. 93-317-3974). If you'll see Casa Milà, skip the climb to this rooftop.

Farther downhill, on the right-hand side, is...

Ramblas Walk Stop #6: Chinatown—This is the world's only Chinatown with nothing even remotely Chinese in or near it.

Named for the prejudiced notion that Chinese immigrants go hand in hand with poverty, prostitution, and drug dealing, the actual inhabitants are poor Spanish, Arab, and Gypsy people. At night the Barri Xines features prostitutes, many of them transvestites, who cater to sailors wandering up from the port. A nighttime visit gets you a street-corner massage—look out.

During the day, the bottom of the Ramblas is crowded with commercial artists selling their wares—look hard to find something original, or get a personal portrait. On weekends and holidays, look for the Nova Artesania arts-and-crafts market at the very bottom. This is your chance to buy jewelry and artwork directly from locals. At the bottom of the Ramblas is the Columbus Monument.

Or, from the Drassanes Metro stop, you can take a quick detour to the Fairy Forest pub (El Bosc de les Fades). To get there, cross the Ramblas on the left, walk through Pasatge de la Banca toward the Wax Museum (Museu de Cera), and turn right. This pub lives up to its name, decorated with elaborate Brothers' Grimm–style trees, elves, and waterfalls. Stop here for a drink or just a peek (Sun–Thu 10:30–24:00, Sat–Sun 10:30–24:00, Pasatge de la Banca, tel. 93-317-2649). Walk out the other end of the passageway and you'll see your next stop, the Columbus Monument.

Ramblas Sights at the Harbor

Columbus Monument (Monument a Colóm)—Marking the point where the Ramblas hits the harbor, this 50-meter-tall monument built for an 1888 exposition offers an elevator-assisted view from its top (€1.80, daily 09:00–20:30, off-season 10:00–13:30, 15:30–19:30, the harbor cable car offers a better—if less handy—view). It's interesting that Barcelona would so honor the man whose discoveries ultimately led to its downfall as a great trading power. It was here in Barcelona that Ferdinand and Isabel welcomed Columbus home after his first trip to America.

Maritime Museum (Museo Maritim)—This museum—housed in the old royal shipyards—covers the salty history of ships and navigation from the 13th to 20th centuries, showing off the Catalan role in the development of maritime technology (e.g., the first submarine is claimed to be Catalan). With fleets of seemingly unimportant replicas of old boats explained in Catalan and Spanish, landlubbers may find it dull—but the free audioguide livens it up for sailors (€5.40, daily 10:00–19:00, closed Mon off-season). For just €0.60 more, visit the old-fashioned sailing ship *Santa Eulàlia*, docked in the harbor across the street.

Golondrinas—Little tourist boats at the foot of the Columbus Monument offer 30-minute harbor tours (€3.20, daily 11:00–20:00). A glass-bottom catamaran makes longer tours up the coast (€8 for 75 min, 4/day, daily 11:30–18:30.) For a picnic place, consider one of these rides or the harbor steps.

La Rambla de Mar—This "Rambla of the Sea" is a modern extension of the boulevard into the harbor. A popular wooden pedestrian bridge—with waves like the sea—leads to Maremagnum, a soulless Spanish mall with a cinema, huge aquarium, restaurants, and piles of people out for the night.

Sights—Gothic Quarter (Barri Gòtic)

The Barri Gòtic is a bustling world of shops, bars, and nightlife packed between hard-to-be-thrilled-about 14th- and 15th-century buildings. The area around the port is seedy. But the area around the cathedral is a tangled yet inviting grab bag of undiscovered courtyards, grand squares, schoolyards, Art Nouveau storefronts, baby flea markets, musty junk shops, classy antique shops, street musicians strumming Catalan folk songs, and balconies with domestic jungles behind wrought-iron bars. Go on a cultural scavenger hunt. Write a poem.

▲**Cathedral**—As you stand in the square facing the cathedral, you're facing what was Roman Barcelona. To your right, letters spell out BARCINO—the city's Roman name. The three towers on the building to the right are mostly Roman (wander inside for good Roman Wall views).

The colossal **cathedral**, started in about 1300, took 600 years to complete. Rather than stretching toward heaven, it makes a point to be simply massive (similar to the Gothic churches of Italy). The west front, while built according to the original plan, is only 100 years old (cathedral: daily 08:00–13:30, 17:00–19:30; cloisters: daily 09:00–13:00, 17:00–19:00; tel. 93-315-1554).

The spacious interior—characteristic of Catalan Gothic— was supported by buttresses. These provided walls for 28 richly ornamented chapels. While the main part of the church is fairly plain, the chapels—sponsored by local guilds—show great wealth. Located in the community's most high-profile space, they provided a kind of advertising to illiterate worshipers. Find logos and symbols of the various trades represented. The Indians Columbus brought to town were supposedly baptized in the first chapel on the left.

The **chapels** ring a finely carved 15th-century choir (*coro*). Pay €0.90 for a close-up look (with the lights on) at the ornately carved stalls and the emblems representing the various Knights of the Golden Fleece who once sat here. The chairs were folded up, giving VIPs stools to lean on during the standing parts of the Mass. Each was creatively carved and—since you couldn't sit on sacred things—the artists were free to enjoy some secular fun here. Study the upper tier of carvings.

The **high altar** sits upon the tomb of Barcelona's patron saint, Eulàlia. She was a 13-year-old local girl tortured 13 times by Romans for her faith and finally crucified on an X-shaped cross. Her X symbol is carved on the pews.

Barcelona's Cathedral

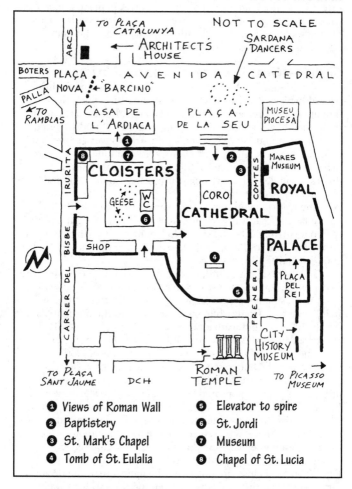

NOT TO SCALE

- ❶ Views of Roman Wall
- ❷ Baptistery
- ❸ St. Mark's Chapel
- ❹ Tomb of St. Eulalia
- ❺ Elevator to spire
- ❻ St. Jordi
- ❼ Museum
- ❽ Chapel of St. Lucia

Ride the **elevator** to the roof and climb a tight spiral staircase up the spire for a commanding view (€1.40, Mon–Fri 10:30–12:30, 16:30–18:00, start from chapel left of high altar).

Enter the **cloister** (through arch, right of high altar). In the cloister, look back at the arch, an impressive mix of Romanesque and Gothic. A tiny statue of St. George slaying the dragon stands in the garden. Jordi (George) is one of the patron saints of Catalunya and by far the most popular boy's name here. While cloisters are generally found in monasteries, this church added it to accommodate more chapels—good for business. Again, notice the symbols of the trades or guilds. Even the pavement is filled with symbols—similar to Americans getting their name on a brick for helping to pay for something.

Long ago the resident geese—there are always 13 in memory of Eulàlia—functioned as an alarm system. Any commotion would get them honking, alerting the monk in charge.

From St. Jordi, circle to the right (past a WC). The skippable little €0.60 **museum** (far corner) is one plush room with a dozen old religious paintings. In the corner the dark, barrel-vaulted Romanesque Chapel of Santa Lucia was a small church predating the cathedral and built into the cloister. The candles outside were left by people hoping for good eyesight (Santa Lucia's specialty). Farther along, the Chapel of Santa Rita (in charge of impossible causes) usually has the most candles. Complete the circle and exit at the door just before the place you entered.

Walk uphill, following the church. From the end of the apse turn right 50 meters up Carrer del Paradis to the **Roman Temple** (Temple Roma d' August). In the corner a sign above a millstone in the pavement marks "Mont Tabor, 16.9 meters." Step into the courtyard for a peek at a surviving corner of the imposing temple which once stood here on the city's highest hill, keeping a protective watch over Barcino (free, daily 10:00–14:00, 16:00–20:00).

Plaza del Rei—The Royal Palace sat on King's Square (a block from the cathedral) until Catalunya became part of Spain in the 15th century. Then it was the headquarters of the local inquisition. Columbus came here to show King Ferdinand his souvenirs from what he thought was India.

▲**City History Museum**—After a multimedia presentation on the history of the city, take an elevator down 20 meters (and 2,000 years) to walk the streets of Roman Barcelona. You'll see sewers, models of domestic life, and bits of an early Christian church. Nearly nothing remains of the Royal Palace (€4.80 includes museum, presentation, and visits to Pedralbes Monastery and Verdaguer House Museum, see museum pamphlet for details; Tue–Sat 10:00–14:00, 16:00–20:00, Sun 10:00–14:00, closed Mon, Plaça del Rei, tel. 93-315-1111).

Frederic Mares Museum—This classy collection combines medieval religious art with a quirky bundle of more modern artifacts—old pipes, pinups, toys, and so on (Tue–Sun 10:00–15:00, closed Mon, Carrer del Comtes, off Plaça de la Seu, next to cathedral).

▲**Sardana Dances**—The patriotic Sardana dances are held at the cathedral (often at 18:00 and most Sun at 12:00) and at Plaça de Sant Jaume (often on Sun at 18:00 in spring and summer, 18:30 in fall and winter). Locals of all ages seem to spontaneously appear. They gather in circles after putting their things in the center—symbolic of community and sharing (and the

Barcelona's Gothic Quarter

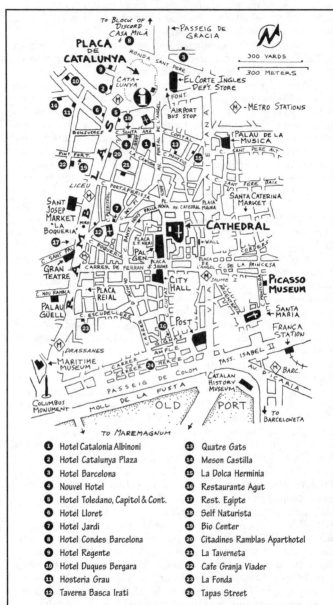

❶ Hotel Catalonia Albinoni	⓭ Quatre Gats
❷ Hotel Catalunya Plaza	⓮ Meson Castilla
❸ Hotel Barcelona	⓯ La Dolca Herminia
❹ Nouvel Hotel	⓰ Restaurante Agut
❺ Hotel Toledano, Capitol & Cont.	⓱ Rest. Egipte
❻ Hotel Lloret	⓲ Self Naturista
❼ Hotel Jardi	⓳ Bio Center
❽ Hotel Condes Barcelona	⓴ Citadines Ramblas Aparthotel
❾ Hotel Regente	㉑ La Taverneta
❿ Hotel Duques Bergara	㉒ Cafe Granja Viader
⓫ Hosteria Grau	㉓ La Fonda
⓬ Taverna Basca Irati	㉔ Tapas Street

ever-present risk of theft). Then they raise and hold hands as they hop and sway gracefully to the band. The band (*cobla*) consists of a long flute, tenor and soprano oboes, strange-looking brass instruments, and a tiny bongolike drum (*tambori*). The rest of Spain mocks this lazy circle dance, but it is a stirring display of local pride and patriotism.

Shoe Museum (Museu del Calçat)—Shoe-lovers enjoy this two-room shoe museum (with a we-try-harder attendant) on the delightful Plaça Sant Felip Neri (€1.20, Tue–Sun 11:00–14:00, closed Mon, 1 block beyond outside door of cathedral cloister, behind Plaça de G. Bachs, tel. 93-301-4533). The huge shoe at the entry is designed to fit the foot of the Columbus Monument at the bottom of the Ramblas.

Plaça de Sant Jaume—On this stately central square of the Gothic Quarter, two of the top governmental buildings in Catalunya face each other: The Barcelona city hall (Ajuntament, free Sun 10:00–13:30) and the seat of the autonomous government of Catalunya (Palau de la Generalitat). Sardana dances take place here many Sundays at 18:00 or 18:30, depending on the season (see "Sardana Dances," above).

▲▲▲**Picasso Museum**—This is the best collection of Picasso's (1881–1973) work in Spain, and the best collection of his early works anywhere. It's scattered through two Gothic palaces, six blocks from the cathedral.

Picasso's personal secretary, Sabartes, amassed a huge collection of his work and bequeathed it to the city. Picasso, happy to have a fine museum showing off his work in the city of his youth, added to the collection throughout his life. (Sadly, since Picasso vowed never to set foot in a fascist Spain, and he died 2 years before Franco, the artist never saw the museum.)

This is a great chance to see Picasso's earliest art and better understand his genius (€4.80, free on first Sun of month, Tue–Sat 10:00–20:00, Sun 10:00–15:00, closed Mon, free and required bag check, Montcada 15–19, Metro: Jaume, tel. 93-319-6310).

There's no English information inside but the art is presented chronologically. If you follow the rooms in numerical order and take this quick room-by-room tour, you can see Picasso's art evolve:

Room 4 (1895): With this earliest art, a budding genius emerges at age 12.

Room 6 (1896): Pablo moves to Barcelona and gets serious about art. The portraits (left as you enter, Padre del Artista) are of Pablo's first teacher, his father. The glass case is filled with what you do at art school. Every time Pablo starts breaking rules, he's sent back to the standard classic style.

Room 9 (1896)—reached through room 4: More school assignments. The goal: Sketch models to capture human anatomy accurately.

Room 10 (1896): On the left you see three self-portraits with a self-awareness of his genius showing in his eyes. The woman (Retrato de la Madre del Artista) is Pablo's mother. Fifteen-year-old Pablo is working on the fine details and gradients of white in her blouse. Pablo was closer to his mom than his dad. Spaniards keep both parents' surnames: Pablo Ruiz Picasso. Eventually he kept just his mom's name.

Room 11: During a short trip to Málaga, Picasso dabbles in Impressionism (unknown in Spain at the time).

Room 12: As a 15-year-old, Pablo does his first big painting for a fine-arts exhibition in Barcelona. While forced to show a religious subject (First Communion), Pablo uses it as an excuse to paint his family.

Room 13: *Science and Charity*, a prize-winning fine-arts exhibition piece, got Picasso the chance to study in Madrid. His little sister (perhaps portrayed in the arms of the nun) had just died. Here for the first time we see Picasso conveying real feeling. The doctor (Pablo's father) represents science. The nun represents charity and religion. But nothing can help and the woman is clearly dead (notice her face and lifeless hand). Pablo painted a little trick: Notice how the bed stretches and shrinks as you walk across the room. Four small studies for this painting hang in the back of the room.

Room 14: Fine-arts school in stuffy Madrid was boring. But Pablo enjoyed hanging out in the Prado Gallery and copying the masters (such as Velázquez's portrait of Phillip IV).

Room 15 (1900): Back in Barcelona, Art Nouveau is the rage. Upsetting his dad, Pablo quits art school and falls in with the avant-garde crowd. These bohemians congregate daily at the Four Cats (slang for "a few crazy people"—see "Eating," below). Picasso declares his artistic freedom by painting portraits of his new friends, and nothing more of his family.

Room 17 (1900): Picasso goes to Paris, a city bursting with life, light, and love.

Room 18: Dropping the surname Ruiz, Pablo establishes his commercial brand name: "Picasso." Here we see the explorer Picasso befriending prostitutes and painting like Toulouse-Lautrec. La Espera (Margot)—with her bold outline and strong gaze—pops out from the Impressionistic background. Painting a dwarf (*La Nana*), Picasso, like Velázquez and Toulouse-Lautrec, sees "the beauty in ugliness."

Room 19 (1902): The bleak weather and poverty Picasso experienced in Paris leads to his "Blue Period." He cranks out piles of blue art just to stay housed and fed. With blue—the coldest color—backgrounds and depressing subjects, this period was revolutionary in art history. Now the artist is painting not what he sees but what he feels.

Room 20 (1902)—across the hall, through two glass doors: Back home in Barcelona, Picasso paints his hometown at night from rooftops (*Terrats de Barcelona*). Still blue, here we see proto-cubism...five years before the first real cubist painting. The woman in pink (*Retrato de la Sra. Canals*), painted with classic "Spanish melancholy," finally lifts Picasso out of his funk, replacing the blue period with the happier pink period (of which this museum has only one painting).

Room 21 (1917): Jumping 15 years, we see Picasso is a painter of many styles. In the age of the camera, the cubist gives just the basics (a man with a bowl of fruit) and lets you finish it. We see a little post-Impressionistic Pointillism and a portrait that looks like a classical statue (inspired by a trip to Rome). The chrome-framed painting of a spool of cable (between the information sheets on the wall) is remarkably realistic. The expressionist horse symbolizes to Spaniards the innocent victim. In bull-fights, the horse—clad with blinders and who is pummeled by the bull—has nothing to do with the fight. Picasso used the horse—guts spilling out near the bull's horn—to show the suffering of war. (This shows up again in his future masterpiece, *Guernica*, which you can see in Madrid.)

Room 22 (1957): Notice the print of Velázquez's *Las Meninas* to the left of the doorway. Picasso, who had great respect for Velázquez, painted 60 interpretations of the painting many consider the greatest painting by anyone ever (it's in Madrid's Prado). In the big black-and-white canvas, Picasso plays with perspectives within the painting. The king and queen (reflected in the mirror in the back of the room) are hardly seen while the self-portrait of the painter towers above everyone. The two women of the court on the right look like they're in a tomb—but they're wearing party shoes. In this room and room 23, see the fun Picasso had playing paddleball with Velázquez's masterpiece.

Rooms 24 and 26 (1957): All his life Picasso said, "Paintings are like windows open to the world." Here we see the French Riviera. As a child, Picasso was forced to paint as an adult. Now, at age 60 (with little kids of his own and an also-childish artist Matisse for a friend), he paints like a child.

To exit, hike up the stairs through rooms 28 to 32 and lots of Picasso etchings and engravings, and out.

Textile and Garment Museum (Museu Textil i de la Indumentaria)—If fabrics from the 4th to 16th centuries leave you cold, have a *café con leche* on the museum's beautiful patio (€2.40, Tue–Sat 10:00–20:00, Sun 10:00–15:00, closed Mon, free entrance to patio, which is outside museum but within the walls, 30 meters from Picasso Museum at Montcada 12–14).

▲▲Catalana Concert Hall (Palau de la Música Catalana)—This concert hall, finished in 1908, features the best modernist interior in town. Inviting arches lead you into the 2,000-seat hall. A kaleidoscopic skylight features a choir singing around the sun while playful carvings and mosaics celebrate music and Catalan culture. Admission is by tour only and starts with a relaxing 20-minute video (€4.20, 1 hr, in English, daily on the hour 10:00–15:00, maybe later, tel. 93-268-1000). Ask about concerts (300 per year, inexpensive tickets).

Sights—Eixample

Uptown Barcelona is a unique variation on the common grid-plan city. Barcelona snipped off the building corners to create light and spacious eight-sided squares at every intersection. Wide sidewalks, hardy shade trees, chic shops, and plenty of Art Nouveau fun make the Eixample a refreshing break from the old town. For the best Eixample example, ramble Rambla Catalunya (unrelated to the more famous Ramblas) and pass through Passeig de Gràcia (described below, Metro: Passeig de Gràcia for Block of Discord or Diagonal for Casa Milà).

The 19th century was a boom time for Barcelona. By 1850 the city was busting out of its medieval walls. A new town was planned to follow a gridlike layout. The intersection of three major thoroughfares—Gran Vía, Diagonal, and Meridiana—would shift the city's focus uptown.

The Eixample, or "Expansion," was a progressive plan in which everything was made accessible to everyone. Each 20-block-square district would have its own hospital and large park, each 10-block-square area would have its own market and general services, and each five-block-square grid would house its own schools and day-care centers. The hollow space found inside each "block" of apartments would form a neighborhood park.

While much of that vision never quite panned out, the Eixample was an urban success. Rich and artsy big shots bought plots along the grid. The richest landowners built as close to the center as possible. For this reason, the best buildings are near the Passeig de Gràcia. Adhering to the height, width, and depth limitations, they built as they pleased—often in the trendy new modernist style.

Sights—Gaudí's Art and Architecture

Barcelona is an architectural scrapbook of the galloping gables and organic curves of hometown boy Antonio Gaudí. A devoted Catalan and Catholic, he immersed himself in each project, often living on-site. He called Parc Güell, La Pedrera, and the Sagrada Familia all home.

▲▲**Sagrada Familia (Sacred Family) Church**—Gaudí's most famous and persistent work is this unfinished landmark. He worked on the church from 1883 to 1926. Since then,

Gaudí & Moderniste Sights

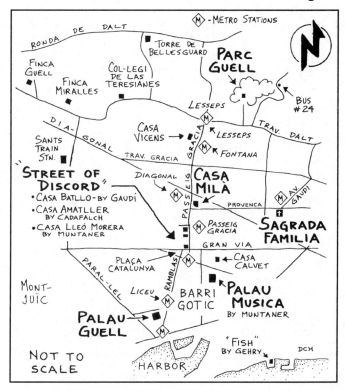

construction has moved forward in fits and starts. Even today, the half-finished church is not expected to be completed for another 20 years. One reason it's taking so long is that the temple is funded exclusively by private donations and entry fees. Your admission helps pay for the ongoing construction (€5.10, daily 09:00–20:00, Nov–March 09:00–18:00; €3 extra for tours in English: 4/day April–Oct, 2/day Nov–March; Metro: Sagrada Familia, tel. 93-207-3031. www.sagradafamilia.org).

When the church is finished, 12 100-meter spires (representing the apostles) will stand in groups of four and mark the three ends of the building. The center tower (honoring Jesus), reaching 170 meters up, will be flanked by 125-meter-tall towers of Mary and the four evangelists. A unique exterior ambulatory will circle the building like a cloister turned inside out.

The nativity facade really shows the vision of Gaudí. It was finished in 1904, before Gaudí's death, and shows scenes from

Modernisme

The Renaixensa (Catalan cultural revival) gave birth to Modernisme (Catalan Art Nouveau) at the end of the 19th century. Barcelona is its capital. Its Eixample neighborhood shimmers with the colorful, leafy, flowing, blooming shapes of Modernisme in doorways, entrances, facades, and ceilings. Meaning "a taste for what is modern," this free-flowing organic style lasted from 1888 to 1906. Breaking with tradition, artists experimented with glass, tile, iron, and brick. Decoration became structural. It comes with three influences: nature, exotic (e.g., Chinese), and a fanciful Gothic twist to celebrate Catalan's medieval glory days. It was a way of life as Barcelona burst into the 20th century.

Antoni Gaudí is the most famous modernist artist. From four generations of metalworkers, a lineage of which he was quite proud, he incorporated his ironwork into his architecture and came up with novel approaches to architectural structure and space.

The year 2002 is "International Gaudi Year," marking the 150th anniversary of Gaudí's birth. Barcelona celebrates with exhibitions, "Gaudinian" festivals, and more (tel. 93-316-1000, www.gaudi2002.bcn.es).

Two more modernist architects famous for their unique style are Lluís Domènech i Muntaner and Josep Puig i Cadafalch. You'll see their work on "The Block of Discord."

the birth and childhood of Jesus along with angels playing musical instruments. (Because of ongoing construction, you may need to access this area—opposite the entrance, viewed from outside—by walking through the museum. Don't miss it.)

The little on-site **museum** displays physical models used for the church's construction. Gaudí lived on the site for more than a decade and is buried in the crypt. When he died in 1926, only the stubs of four spires stood above the building site. Judge for yourself how the recently-completed and controversial Passion facade by Josep Maria Subirachs fits in with Gaudí's original formulation.

With the cranking cranes, rusty forests of rebar, and scaffolding requiring a powerful faith, the Sagrada Familia Church offers a fun look at a living, growing, bigger-than-life building. Take the lift on the Passion side (€1.20) or the stairs on the Nativity side (free but often miserably congested) up to the dizzy lookout bridging two spires. You'll get a great view of the city and a gargoyle's-eye perspective of the loopy church. If there's any building on earth I'd like to see, it's the Sagrada Familia... finished.

▲**Palau Güell**—This is a good chance to enjoy a Gaudí interior (see "Introductory Tour," above). Curvy.

▲▲**Casa Milà (La Pedrera)**—This Gaudí exterior laughs down on the crowds filling Passeig de Gràcia. Casa Milà, also called La Pedrera (the Quarry), has a much-photographed roller coaster of melting-ice-cream eaves. This is Barcelona's quintessential modernist building.

Visits come in three parts: apartment, attic, and rooftop. Buy the €6 ticket to see all three. Starting with the apartment, an elevator whisks you to the *Life in Barcelona 1905–1929* exhibit (well-described in English). Then you walk through a sumptuously furnished Art Nouveau apartment. Upstairs in the attic, wander under brick arches—enjoying a multimedia exhibit of models, photos, and videos of Gaudí's works. From there a stairway leads to the fanciful rooftop where chimneys play volleyball with the clouds. From here, you can see Gaudí's other principal works, the Sagrada Familia, Casa Batllo, and Parc Güell (daily 10:00–20:00; free tours in English Mon–Fri at 17:30, Sat–Sun and holidays at 11:00; Passeig de Gràcia 92, Metro: Diagonal, tel. 93-484-5995). At the ground level of Casa Milà is the original entrance courtyard for the Fundacio Caixa de Catalunya, dreamily painted in pastels (free). The first floor hosts free art exhibits. During the summer, a concert series called "Pedrera by Night" features jazz, flamenco, tango, or other classy live music, a glass of champagne, and the chance to see the rooftop illuminated (€9, July–Sept Fri–Sat at 22:00, tel. 93-484-5900).

▲**The Block of Discord**—Four blocks from Casa Milà you can survey a noisy block of competing early-19th-century facades. Several of Barcelona's top modernist mansions line Passeig de Gràcia (Metro: Passeig de Gràcia). Because the structures look as though they are trying to outdo each other in creative twists, locals nicknamed the block between Consell de Cent and Arago, "The Block of Discord." First (at #43) and most famous is Gaudí's Casa Batlló, with skull-like balconies and a tile roof that suggests a cresting dragon's back (Gaudí based the work on the popular St. Jordi-slays-the-dragon legend). By the way, if you're tempted to frame your photos from the middle of the street, be careful—Gaudí died under a streetcar.

Next door, at Casa Amatller (#41, desk sells Modernist Route combo tickets), check out architect Puig i Cadafalch's creative mix of Moorish and Gothic and iron grillwork. At the desk inside is the only place in town you can purchase Modernist Route combo tickets. For €3.60, you get a 50 percent discount to 10 of the most important modernist sights in Barcelona (valid for 1 month). Even if you only have time to see Sagrada Familia and Casa Milà, you'll save money with this ticket.

On the corner (at #35) is Casa Lleo Morera (by Lluís

Domènech i Muntaner, who did the Catalana Concert Hall—
you'll see similarities). The perfume shop halfway down the street
has a free and interesting little perfume museum in the back.
The Hostal de Rita restaurant, just around the corner on Calle
Arago, serves a fine three-course lunch for a great price at 13:00
(see "Eating," below).

Park Güell—Gaudí fans find the artist's magic in this colorful
park (free, daily 09:00–20:00) and small Gaudí Museum (€2.50,
daily 10:00–20:00, closes off-season at 18:00, Metro: Vallcarca
but easier by bus #24 from Plaça de Catalunya; €6 by taxi). Gaudí
intended this to be a planned garden city rather than a park. As a
high-income housing project, it flopped. As a park...even after
I reminded myself that Gaudí's work is a careful rhythm of color,
shapes, and space, it was disappointing. Still, some find the panoramic view of Barcelona worth the trip. Only the hill of Tibidabo
offers a better city view (see below).

More Sights—Barcelona

Tibidabo—Tibidabo comes from the Latin for "to thee I shall
give," the words the devil used when he was trying to tempt
Christ. It's still an enticing offer: At the top of Barcelona's highest
peak, you'll find the city's oldest fun-fair, the neo-Gothic Sacred
Heart Church, and—if the weather and air quality are good—
a near-limitless view of the city and the Mediterranean.

Getting there is part of the fun: Start by taking the FGC line—
similar to but separate from the Metro, also covered by the T-10
ticket—from the Plaça Catalunya station (under Café Zurich) to
the Tibidabo stop. The red Tourist Bus stops here, too. Then take
Barcelona's only remaining tram—the Tramvia Blau—from Plaça
John F. Kennedy to Plaça Dr. Andreu (€2.40, 2–4/hr). From there,
take the cable car to the top (€2.40, tel. 90-642-7017.)

Ciutadella Park (Parc de la Ciutadella)—Barcelona's biggest,
greenest park, originally the site of a much-hated military citadel,
was transformed in 1888 for a World's Fair (Universal Exhibition).
The stately Triumphal Arch at the top of the park was built as
the main entrance. Inside you'll find wide pathways, plenty of
trees and grass, the zoo, the Geology and Zoology Museums, and
the Modern Art Museum (see below). In Barcelona, which suffers
from a lack of real green space, this park is a haven. Enjoy the
ornamental fountain that the young Antoni Gaudí helped design,
and consider a spin in a rowboat on the lake in the center of the
park (€1.20/person for 30 min). Check out the tropical *Umbracle*
greenhouse and the *Hivernacle* winter garden, which has a pleasant
café-bar (daily 08:00–20:00, Metro: Arc de Triomf, east of França
train station).

Modern Art Museum (Museu d'Art Modern)—This manageable
museum in Ciutadella Park exhibits Catalan sculpture, painting,

glass, and furniture by Gaudí, Casas, Llimona, and more (€3, Tue–Sat 10:00–19:00, Thu until 21:00, Sun 10:00–14:30, closed Mon).

Barcelona's Beach—Take the trek through the charming Barceloneta neighborhood to the tip of this man-made peninsula. The beaches begin here and stretch for four kilometers up the coast to the Olympic Port and beyond. Everything you see here—palm trees, cement walkways, and tons of sand—was installed in the mid-1980s in an effort to shape up the city for the 1992 Olympic Games. The beaches are fine for sunbathing (beach chair rental—€3/day), but the water quality is questionable for swimming. Take a lazy stroll down the seafront promenade to the Olympic Port, where you'll find bars, restaurants, and at night, dance clubs.

Sights—Barcelona's Montjuïc

The Montjuïc (Mount of the Jews), overlooking Barcelona's hazy port, has always been a show-off. Ages ago it had the impressive fortress. In 1929 it hosted an international fair, from which most of today's sights originated. And in 1992 the Summer Olympics directed the world's attention to this pincushion of attractions.

There are many ways to reach Montjuïc: on the blue Tourist Bus route (see "Getting around Barcelona," above); or bus #50 from the corner of Gran Vía and Passeig de Gràcia (€0.90, every 10 min); or subway to Metro: Parallel and catch the funicular (€1.70 one-way, €2.40 round-trip, Mon–Sat 10:45–20:00, closed Sun); or taxi (about €6.60). The first three options leave you at the *teleférico* (cable car), which you can take to the Castle of Montjuïc (€2.90 one-way, €4.10 round-trip, daily 11:00–22:00, less off-season, tel. 93-443-0859). Alternatively, from the same spot, you can walk uphill 20 minutes through the pleasant park. Only a taxi gets you doorstep delivery. From the port, the fastest and most scenic way to Montjuïc is via the 1929 Trasbordador Aereo (at tower in port, ride elevator up to catch dangling gondola, €7.20 round-trip, 4/hr, daily 10:30–19:00, tel. 93-443-0859).

Castle of Montjuïc—This offers great city views and a military museum (€1.20, Tue–Sun 09:30–20:00, closed Mon). The seemingly endless museum houses a dull collection of guns, swords, and toy soldiers. An interesting section on the Spanish-American War covers Spain's valiant fight against American aggression (from its perspective). Unfortunately, there are no English descriptions. Those interested in Jewish history will find a fascinating collection of ninth-century Jewish tombstones. The castle itself has a facist past. It was built in the 18th century by the central Spanish government to keep an eye on Barcelona and stifle citizen revolt. When Franco was in power, the castle was the site of hundreds of political assassinations.

▲**Fountains (Font Magica)**—Music, colored lights, and huge amounts of water make an artistic and coordinated splash on summer nights (Fri–Sun, 20-min shows start on the half-hour, 21:30–24:00, in summer Thu eve, too, from Metro: Plaça Espanya, walk toward towering National Palace).

Spanish Village (Poble Espanyol)—This tacky five-acre model village uses fake traditional architecture from all over Spain as a shell to contain gift shops. Craftspeople do their clichéd thing only in the morning (not worth your time or €5.70). After hours it becomes a popular local nightspot.

▲▲Catalan Art Museum (Museo Nacional d'Art de Catalunya)—Often called "the Prado of Romanesque art," this is a rare, world-class collection of Romanesque art taken mostly from remote Catalunyan village churches in the Pyrenees (saved from unscrupulous art dealers—many American).

The Romanesque wing features frescoes, painted wooden altar fronts, and ornate statuary. This classic Romanesque art—with flat 2-D scenes, each saint holding his symbol, and Jesus (easy to identify by the cross in his halo)—is impressively displayed on replicas of the original church ceilings.

In the Gothic wing, fresco murals give way to vivid 14th-century paintings of Bible stories on wood. A roomful of paintings by the Catalan master Jaume Huguet (1412–1492) deserves a close look.

Before you leave, ice skate under the huge dome over to the air-conditioned cafeteria. This was the prime ceremony room and dance hall for the 1929 International Exposition (museum-€4.80, Tue–Sat 10:00–19:00, Thu until 21:00, Sun 10:00–14:30, closed Mon, tel. 93-622-0375). The museum is in the massive National Palace building above the fountains, near Plaça Espanya (Metro: Plaça Espanya, then hike up or ride the bus; the blue Tourist Bus and bus #50 stop close by).

▲Fundació Joan Miró—For something more up-to-date, this museum showcases the modern-art talents of yet another Catalan artist and is considered the best collection of Joan Miró art anywhere. You'll also see works by other modern Spanish artists; don't miss the *Mercury Fountain* by Alexander Calder. This museum leaves those who don't like abstract art scratching their heads (€4.80, July–Sept Tue–Sat 10:00–20:00, Thu until 21:30, Sun 10:00–14:30, closed Mon, Oct–June closes at 19:00 Tue–Sat).

Sleeping in Barcelona
(€1.10 = about $1, country code: 34)
Sleep Code: **S** = Single, **D** = Double/Twin, **T** = Triple, **Q** = Quad, **b** = bathroom, **s** = shower only, **CC** = Credit Cards accepted, **no CC** = Credit Cards not accepted, **SE** = Speaks English, **NSE** = No English.

Book ahead. If necessary, the TI at Plaça de Catalunya has a room-finding service. Barcelona is Spain's most expensive city.

Still, it has reasonable rooms. Cheap places are more crowded in summer; fancier business-class places fill up in winter and offer discounts on weekends and in summer. Prices listed do not include the 7 percent tax or breakfast (ranging from simple €3 spreads to €13.25 buffets) unless otherwise noted. While many recommended places are on pedestrian streets, night noise is a problem almost everywhere (especially in cheap places with single-pane windows). For a quiet night, ask for "*tranquilo*" rather than "*con vista.*"

Sleeping in Eixample

For an elegant and boulevardian neighborhood, sleep in Eixample, a 10-minute walk from the Ramblas action.

Hotel Condes de Barcelona, a four-star business hotel in a grand modernist building, rents 183 stylish and spacious rooms with all the comforts (Db-€201, extra bed-€42, CC, air con, smoke-free floor, elevator, Internet access in rooms, Gaudí-pleasing rooftop sun garden with Jacuzzi, intersection of Mallorca and Passeig de Gracia at Passeig de Gracia 73-75, 08008 Barcelona, tel. 93-467-4780, fax 93-467-4781, www.condesdebarcelona .com, e-mail: reservas@condesdebarcelona.com). Note that the hotel has two buildings. One is a 115-year-old modernist hotel (#75) and the other is new. For more charm, ask for a room in the old building when making reservations.

Hotel Regente, another big four-star place, is a notch below Condes de Barcelona but still a fine splurge (80 rooms, Db-€150, less June–Aug, CC, air con, elevator, roof terrace, Rambla Catalunya 76, 08008 Barcelona, tel. 93-487-5989, fax 93-487-3227, e-mail: regente@hoteles-centro-ciudad.es).

Hotel Gran Vía, filling a palatial mansion built in the 1870s, offers Botticelli and chandeliers in the public rooms; a sprawling, peaceful sun garden; and 54 spacious, comfy, air-conditioned rooms. It's an excellent value (Sb-€69, Db-€94 with this book through 2002—only valid with phone or faxed reservations, CC, Internet access, elevator, quiet, Gran Vía de les Corts Catalanes 642, 08007 Barcelona, tel. 93-318-1900, fax 93-318-9997, e-mail: hgranvia@nnhotels.es).

Hotel Residencia Neutral, with a classic Eixample address and 35 basic rooms, is popular with backpackers (tiny Sb-€22.80, Ds-€33, Db-€39, extra bed-€9, CC, elevator, thin walls and some street noise, elegantly located 2 blocks north of Gran Vía at Rambla Catalunya 42, 08007 Barcelona, tel. 93-487-6390, fax 93-487-6848).

Sleeping near Plaça de Catalunya and at the top of the Ramblas
(zip code: 08002 unless otherwise noted)

The first five places are on big but quiet streets within two blocks of Barcelona's exuberant central square. The next are on or near the top of the Ramblas, also just off Plaça de Catalunya. The last is buried in the Gothic Quarter. For location, see map on page 844.

Hotel Duques de Bergara boasts four stars with splashy public spaces, slick marble and hardwood floors, 150 comfortable rooms, and a garden courtyard with a pool a world away from the big-city noise (Sb-€138, Db-€168, extra bed-€18, CC, air con, elevator, a half block off Plaça de Catalunya at Bergara 11, tel. 93-301-5151, fax 93-317-3442, www.hoteles-catalonia.es, e-mail: cataloni@hoteles-catalonia.es).

Hotel Occidental Reding, a five-minute walk west of the Ramblas and Plaça de Catalunya action on a quiet street, keeps business travelers fat and happy with 44 modern rooms (Db-€114, extra bed-€32, CC, air con, elevator, near University Metro stop at Gravina 5, 08001 Barcelona, tel. 93-412-1097, fax 93-268-3482, e-mail: reding@occidental-hoteles.com).

Hotel Catalonia Albinoni (formerly Hotel Allegro) elegantly fills a renovated old palace with wide halls, hardwood floors, and modern rooms with all the comforts. It overlooks a thriving pedestrian boulevard. Front rooms have views. Balcony rooms on the back are quiet and come with sun terraces (Db-€162, extra bed-€18, CC, family rooms, air con, elevator, a block down from Plaça de Catalunya at Portal de l'Angel 17, tel. 93-318-4141, fax 93-301-2631).

Catalunya Plaza, an impersonal business hotel right on the square, has all the air-conditioning and minibar comforts (Sb-€120, Db-€144, includes breakfast, CC, elevator, ask for free nuts and a welcome glass of champagne at the desk, Plaça de Catalunya 7, tel. 93-317-7171, fax 93-317-7855, e-mail: catalunya@city-hotels.es).

Hotel Barcelona is another big, American-style hotel with bright, prefab, and comfy rooms (Sb-€114, Db-€162, Db with terrace-€204, CC, air con, elevator, a block from Plaça de Catalunya at Caspe 1–13, tel. 93-302-5858, fax 93-301-8674, e-mail: hotelbarcelona@husa.es).

Nouvel Hotel, an elegant Victorian-style building on a fine pedestrian street, has royal lounges and 71 comfy rooms (Sb-€79, Db-€120, includes breakfast, manager Gabriel promises 10 percent discount with this book, CC, air con, Carrer de Santa Ana 18, tel. 93-301-8274, fax 93-301-8370).

Hotel Toledano, overlooking the Ramblas, is suitable for backpackers and popular with dust-bunnies. Small, folksy, and borderline dumpy, it's warmly run by Juan Sanz, his son Albert, and trusty Daniel on the nightshift (Sb-€27.50, Db-€47, Tb-€60, Qb-€66, cheaper off-season, CC, not all rooms have air con—request it when you call; Rambla de Canaletas 138, tel. 93-301-0872, fax 93-412-3142, www.hoteltoledano.com, e-mail:

toledano@ibernet.com). They run **Hostal Residencia Capitol** one floor above—quiet, plain, cheaper, and also appropriate for backpackers (S-€20.50, D-€32, Ds-€36, cheap 5-bed room).

Hotel Continental has comfortable rooms, double-thick mattresses, and wildly clashing carpets and wallpaper. To celebrate 100 years in the family, José includes a free breakfast and an all-day complimentary coffee bar. Choose a Ramblas-view balcony or quiet back room (Db-€61–84, includes tax, extra bed-€12, special family room, CC, fans in rooms, elevator, Internet access, Ramblas 138, tel. 93-301-2570, fax 93-302-7360, www.hotelcontinental.com, e-mail: ramblas@hotelcontinental.com).

Hotel Lloret is a big, dark, old-world place on the Ramblas with plain neon-lit rooms (Sb-€42, Db-€66, Tb-€78, extra bed-€6, choose a noisy Ramblas balcony or *tranquilo* in the back, CC, air con in summer, elevator dominates stairwell, Rambla de Canaletas 125, tel. 93-317-3366, fax 93-301-9283).

Hosteria Grau is a homey, almost alpine place, family-run with 27 woody rooms just far enough off the Ramblas (S-€27, D-€39, Ds-€45, Db-€51, family suites with 2 bedrooms-€102, €6 extra charged July–Sept, CC, fans, 200 meters up Calle Tallers from the Ramblas at Ramelleres 27, 08001 Barcelona, tel. 93-301-8135, fax 93-317-6825, www.intercom.es/grau, e-mail: hgrau@lix.intercom.es, Monica SE).

Meson Castilla is clean, comfy, and handy, but it's also pricey, a bit sterile, and in all the American guidebooks. It's three blocks off the Ramblas in an appealing university neighborhood (56 rooms, Sb-€75, Db-€96, Tb-€129, Qb apartment-€153, includes buffet breakfast, CC, air con, elevator, Valldoncella 5, 08001 Barcelona, tel. 93-318-2182, fax 93-412-4020, e-mail: hmesoncastilla@teleline.es).

Citadines Ramblas Aparthotel is a clever concept offering apartments by the day in a bright modern building right on the Ramblas. Prices range with the seasonal demand and rooms come in three categories (studio apartment for 2 with sofa bed and kitchenette-€114–150, hotel room for 2 with real bed-€132–144, apartment with real bed and sofa bed for up to 4 people-€171–195, includes tax, CC, laundry, Ramblas 122, tel. 93-270-1111, fax 93-412-7421, e-mail: barca@citadines.com).

Hotel Jardi is a hardworking, clean, and newly-remodeled place on the happiest little square in the Gothic Quarter. Balcony rooms overlooking the peaceful leafy square are most expensive (Sb-€48, Db-€60, extra bed-€9, includes tax, 10 percent off with cash, CC if bill totals at least €90, air con, elevator, halfway between Ramblas and cathedral on Plaça Sant Josep Oriol #1, tel. 93-301-5900, fax 93-318-3664, e-mail: sgs110sa@retemail.es, Albert SE). Rooms with balconies enjoy an almost Parisian ambience and minimal noise.

Humble Places Buried in Gothic Quarter with Youth-Hostel Prices

Pensio Vitoria has loose tile floors and 12 basic rooms, each with a tiny balcony. It's more dumpy than homey, but consider the price (D-€24, Db-€33, cheaper off-season, CC, a block off daydreamy Plaça dei Pi at Carrer la Palla 8, tel. & fax 93-302-0834).

    Hostal Campi—big, quiet, and ramshackle—is a few doors off the Ramblas (D-€36, Db-€42, T-€48, no CC, Canuda 4, tel. & fax 93-301-3545). **Huéspedes Santa Ana** is plain and claustrophobic, with head-to-toe twins (S-€18, D-€36, Db-€48, T-€45, no CC, Carrer de Santa Ana 23, tel. 93-301-2246). **Hostal Residencia Lausanne**, filled with backpackers, has only its location and price going for it (S-€24, D-€36, Ds-€42-45, Db-€51, no CC, TV room, Avenida Portal de l'Angel 24, tel. & fax 93-302-1139, friendly Javier SE). **Hostal Rembrandt** keeps backpackers happy with 26 simple rooms and a good location (S-€21, Sb-€28.25, D-€33, Ds-€36, Db-€40–46, Tb-€66, no CC, Portaferrisa 23, tel. & fax 93-318-1011). **Pension Fina**, next to Hostal Rembrandt, offers more cheap sleeps (S-€24, D-€39, Db-€45, no CC, Portaferrissa 11, tel. & fax 93-317-9787).

Eating in Barcelona

Barcelona, the capital of Catalunyan cuisine, offers a tremendous variety of colorful places to eat. Many restaurants are closed in August (or sometimes July), when the owners are on vacation.

Eating near the Ramblas and in the Gothic Quarter

Taverna Basca Irati serves 25 kinds of hot and cold Basque *pintxos* for €0.90 each. These are open-faced sandwiches— like Basque sushi but on bread. Muscle in through the hungry local crowd. Get an empty plate from the waiter, then help yourself. It's a Basque honor system: You'll be charged by the number of toothpicks left on your plate when you're done. Wash it down with *sidra* (apple wine, €0.90) poured from on high to bring out the flavor (Tue–Sat 12:00–15:00, 19:00–23:00, Sun 12:00–15:00, closed Mon, a block off the Ramblas, behind arcade at Calle Cardenal Casanyes 17, near Metro: Liceu, tel. 93-302-3084). **Juicy Jones**, next door, is a tutti-frutti vegetarian place with a hip menu and a stunning array of fresh-squeezed juices (#7, lunch menu-€7, daily 10:00–24:30).

    Ria de Vigo III, a nondescript local eatery, is filled with blue-collar workers and cheap, no-nonsense food (open until 21:30, closed Sun, 3 blocks off the Ramblas at Carrer Tallers 69, tel. 93-318-4724).

    La Taverneta, an artists' bistro, brags it doesn't cater to tourists. It serves good Catalan food seasoned in the evenings with live music (lunch menu-€7.20, Mon–Sat 13:00–16:30,

19:00–24:00, closed Sun, 2 blocks off the Ramblas near Plaza Villa de Madrid at Pasatge Duque de la Victoria 3, tel. 93-302-6152).

Café Granja Viader is a quaint time trip, family-run since 1870. This feminine place—specializing in baked and dairy delights, toasted sandwiches, and light meals—is ideal for a traditional breakfast (note the "Esmorzars" specials posted). Try a glass of *orxata* (horchata—almond milk, summer only), Llet Mallorquina (Majorca-style milk with cinnamon, lemon, and sugar), or Suis (literally Switzerland, hot chocolate with a snowcap of whipped cream). It's a block off the Ramblas behind El Carme church (Mon 17:00–20:45, Tue–Sat 09:00–13:45, 17:00–20:45, closed Sun, Xucla 4, tel. 93-318-3486).

Egipte offers decent food, indifferent service, and late-19th-century ambience on the Ramblas (daily 13:00–16:00, 20:00–24:00, Ramblas 79, downhill from Boqueria, tel. 93-317-7480). **La Garduña**, located at the back of the La Boqueria market, offers tasty meat and seafood meals made with fresh ingredients bought directly from the market (€8 lunch menus include wine and bread, €10.75 dinner menus don't include wine, Mon–Sat 13:00–16:00, 20:00–24:00, closed Sun, Calle Jerusalem 18, tel. 93-302-4323).

Consider **La Poma** for a good pizza at the top of the Ramblas (Ramblas 117). For focaccia bread and good desserts, try **Buenas Migas** (Plaça Bonsuccés 6, take second right off the Ramblas and go 50 meters, tel. 93-412-1686; another location behind cathedral at Bajada Santa Clara 2, tel. 93-319-1380).

Homesick tourists flock to the **The Bagel Shop**, which offers fresh bagels, brownies, and a rare-in-Barcelona Sunday brunch of pancakes, fried eggs, and bacon (Mon–Sat 09:30–21:30, Sun 11:00–16:00, Calle Canuda 25, tel. 93-302-4161).

For **groceries**, it's El Corte Inglés (Mon–Sat 10:00–22:00, closed Sun, supermarket in basement, Plaça de Catalunya) and Champion Supermarket (Mon–Sat 09:00–22:00, closed Sun, Ramblas 113).

Restaurants in the Gothic Quarter

A chain of three bright, modern restaurants with high-quality traditional cuisine in classy bistro settings with great prices has stormed Barcelona. Each can be crowded so arrive early if you can: **La Fonda** (daily 13:00–15:30, 20:30–23:30, a block from Plaça Reial at Escudellers 10, tel. 93-301-7515), **La Dolca Herminia** (2 blocks toward the Ramblas from Catalan Concert Hall at Magdalenes 27, tel. 93-317-0676), and **Les Quinze Nits** (on trendy La Plaça Reial at #6—you'll see the line, €6.60 lunch menu, tel. 93-317-3075).

Els Quatre Gats, Picasso's hangout, still has a bohemian feel in spite of its tourist crowds. Before the place was founded in 1897, the idea of a café for artists was mocked as a place where only *quatre gats* ("four cats," meaning only crazies) would go (€27 meals, Mon–Sat 08:30–24:00, Sun 17:00–24:00, live piano Mon–Sat from 21:00, Sun from 20:00, CC, Montsio 3, tel. 93-302-4140).

Restaurante Agut, buried deep in the Gothic Quarter four blocks off the harbor, is a fine place for local-style food in a local-style setting (Tue–Sat 21:00–24:00, closed Sun, Mon, and July or Aug, Calle Gignas 16, tel. 93-315-1709).

Vegetarian near Plaça de Catalunya

Self Naturista is a quick, no-stress buffet that will make vegetarians and health-food lovers feel right at home. Others may find a few unidentifiable plates and drinks. The food seems tired—pick what you like and microwave it (Mon–Sat 11:30–22:00, closed Sun, near several recommended hotels, just off the top of Ramblas at Carrer de Santa Ana 11–17).

Bio Center, a Catalan soup-and-salad place popular with local vegetarians, is better but not as handy (Mon–Sat 13:00–17:00, closed Sun, Pintor Fortuny 25, Metro: Catalunya, tel. 93-318-0343). This street has several other good vegetarian places.

Eating in the Eixample

The people-packed boulevards of the Eixample (Passeig de Gràcia and Rambla Catalunya) are lined with appetizing places with breezy outdoor seating. Many trendy and touristic tapas bars offer a cheery welcome and slam out the appetizers.

La Bodegueta is an unbelievably atmospheric below-street-level bodega serving hearty wines and *flautas*—sandwiches made with flute-thin baguettes (Mon–Sat 07:00–24:00, Sun 19:00–24:00, Rambla Catalunya 100, at intersection with Provenza, Metro: Diagonal, tel. 93-215-4894).

El Hostal de Rita is a fresh and dressy little place serving Catalan cuisine near the street of Discord. Their three-course-with-wine lunch (€6.60, Mon–Fri at 13:00) and dinner (€12, daily from 20:30) specials are a great value (Arago 279, tel. 93-487-2376).

The classy **Quasi Queviures** serves upscale tapas, sandwiches, or the whole nine yards—classic food with modern decor (Passeig de Gràcia 24).

El Café de Internet provides an easy way to munch a sandwich while sending e-mail messages to Mom (€1.50/30 min, €2.40/hr Mon–Fri 08:00–22:00, Sat–Sun 16:00–22:00, closed Sun, Gran Vía 656, Metro: Passeig de Gràcia, tel. 93-412-1915, www.cafeinternet.es).

Sandwich Shops

Bright, clean and inexpensive sandwich shops are proudly holding the cultural line against the fast-food invasion hamburgerizing the rest of Europe. You'll find great sandwiches at **Pans & Company** and **Bocatta**, two chains with outlets all over town. Catalan sandwiches are made to order with crunchy French bread. Rather than butter, locals prefer *pa amb tomaquet* (pah ahm too-MAH-kaht), a mix of crushed tomato and olive oil. Study the instructive multilingual menu fliers to understand your options.

Eating near the Harbor in Barceloneta

Barceloneta is a charming beach suburb of the big city. A grid plan of long, narrow, laundry-strewn streets surrounds the central Plaça Poeta Boscan. For an entertaining evening, wander around this corner. Drop by the two places listed here or find your own restaurant (15-min walk or Metro: Barceloneta). During the day a lively produce market fills one end of the square. At night kids play soccer and Ping-Pong.

Cova Fumada is the neighborhood eatery. Josep Maria and his family serve famously fresh fish (Mon–Fri 17:30–20:30, closed July, Carrer del Baluarte 56, on the corner at Carrer Sant Carles, tel. 93-221-4061). Their *sardinas a la plancha* (grilled sardines, €2.10) are fresh and tasty. *Bombas* (potato croquets with pork, €0.90) are the house specialty. It's macho to have it *picante* (spicy with chili sauce); gentler taste buds prefer it *alioli*, with garlic cream. Catalunyan *bruschetta* is *pan tostado* (toast with oil and garlic, €0.80). Wash it down with *vino tinto* (house red wine, €0.50).

At **Bar Electricidad**, Arturo Jordana Barba is the neighborhood source for cheap wine. Drop in. It's €1.10 per liter; the empty plastic water bottles are for takeaway. Try a €0.50 glass of Torroja Tinto, the best local red, or Priorato Dulce, a wonderfully sweet red (Mon–Sat 08:00–13:00, 15:00–19:00, across the square from Cova Fumada, Plaça del Poeta Bosca 61, NSE).

The Olympic Port, a swanky marina district, is lined with harborside restaurants and people enjoying what locals claim is the freshest fish in town (a short taxi ride from the center past Barceloneta).

Tapas on Carrer Merce in the Gothic Quarter

Tapas aren't as popular in Catalunya as they are in the rest of Spain, but Barcelona boasts great *tascas*—colorful local tapas bars. Get small plates (for maximum sampling) by asking for "*tapas*," not "*raciones*."

While trendy uptown places are safer, better lit, and come with English menus and less grease, these places will stain your journal.

From the bottom of the Ramblas (near the Columbus Monument), hike east along Carrer Clave. Then follow the small street that runs along the right side of the church (Carrer Merce), stopping at the *tascas* that look fun.

La Jarra is known for its tender *jamón canario con patatas* (baked ham with salty potatoes). Across the street, **La Pulperia**

serves up fried fish. A block down the street, **Tasca El Corral** makes one of the neighborhood's best chorizo *al diablo* (hell sausage), which you sauté yourself. It's great with the regional specialty, *pan con tomate*. Across the street, **La Plata** keeps things wonderfully simple, serving extremely cheap plates of sardines and small glasses of keg wine. **Tascael Corral** serves northern Spain mountain favorites such as *queso de cabrales* (very moldy cheese) with *sidra* (apple wine). Have a chat with the parrot at **Bar la Choza del Sopas**. At the end of Carrer Merce, **Bar Vendimia** serves up tasty clams and mussels. Carrer Ample and Carrer Gignas, the streets paralleling Carrer Merce inland, have more refined barhopping possibilities.

Transportation Connections—Barcelona

By train to: Lisbon (1/day, 17 hrs with change in Madrid, €107), **Madrid** (7/day, 7–9 hrs, €31–41), **Paris** (3/day, 11–15 hrs, €72–102, night train, reservation required), **Sevilla** (3/day, 11 hrs, €38), **Granada** (2/day, 12 hrs, €46), **Málaga** (2/day, 14 hrs, €39), **Nice** (1/day, 12 hrs, €58, change in Cerbère), **Avignon** (5/day, 6–9 hrs, €38). Train info: tel. 90-224-0202.

By bus to: Madrid (12/day, 8 hrs, half the price of a train ticket, departs from station Barcelona Nord at Metro: Marina).

By plane: To avoid 10-hour train trips, check the reasonable flights from Barcelona to Sevilla or Madrid. Iberia Air (tel. 93-412-5667) and Air Europe (tel. 90-224-0042) offer $80 flights to Madrid. Airport info: tel. 93-298-3838.

MADRID

Today's Madrid is upbeat and vibrant, still enjoying a post-Franco renaissance. You'll feel it. Even the statue-maker beggars have a twinkle in their eyes.

Madrid is the hub of Spain. This modern capital—Europe's highest, at more than 615 meters (2,000 feet)—has a population of more than four million and is young by European standards. Only 400 years ago, King Philip II decided to move the capital of his empire from Toledo to Madrid. One hundred years ago Madrid had only 400,000 people, so 90 percent of the city is modern sprawl surrounding an intact, easy-to-navigate historic core.

Dive headlong into the grandeur and intimate charm of Madrid. The lavish Royal Palace, with its gilded rooms and frescoed ceilings, rivals Versailles. The Prado has Europe's top collection of paintings. The city's huge Retiro Park invites you for a shady siesta and a hopscotch through a mosaic of lovers, families, skateboarders, pets walking their masters, and expert bench-sitters. Make time for Madrid's elegant shops and people-friendly pedestrian zones. Enjoy the shade in an arcade. On Sundays, cheer for the bull at a bullfight or bargain like mad at a mega–flea market. Lively Madrid has enough street singing, barhopping, and people-watching vitality to give any visitor a boost of youth.

Planning Your Time

Madrid's top two sights, the Prado and the palace, are each worth a half day. On a Sunday (Easter–Oct), consider allotting extra time for a bullfight. Ideally, give Madrid two days and spend them this way:

Day 1: Breakfast of *churros* (see "Eating," below) before a brisk, good-morning-Madrid walk for 20 minutes from Puerta del Sol to the Prado; 09:00–12:00 at the Prado; afternoon siesta in Retiro

Park or modern art at Centro Reina Sofia (Picasso's moving *Guernica*) and/or Thyssen-Bornemisza Museum; then dinner at 08:00, with tapas around Plaza Santa Ana (see "Tapas: The Madrid Pub Crawl Dinner" on page 887).

Day 2: Follow this book's "Puerta del Sol to Royal Palace Walk" (see page 869); tour the Royal Palace, lunch near Plaza Mayor; afternoon free for other sights or shopping. Be out at the magic hour—before sunset—when beautifully lit people fill Madrid.

Note that Sunday is market day (El Rastro flea market; stamp and coin market on Plaza Mayor) and that the Prado and the Thyssen-Bornemisza Museum are closed on Monday. For daytrip possibilities from Madrid, see the next chapter, Toledo.

Orientation

The historic center is enjoyably covered on foot. No major sight is more than a 20-minute walk or a €3.50 taxi ride from Puerta del Sol, Madrid's central square. Divide your time between the city's two major sights—the Royal Palace and the Prado—and its barhopping, contemporary scene.

The Puerta del Sol, which marks the center of Madrid and of Spain itself, contains the "kilometer zero" marker from which all of Spain is surveyed (for its exact location, see "Introductory Walk," below). The Royal Palace to the west and the Prado Museum and Retiro Park to the east frame Madrid's historic center.

Southwest of Puerta del Sol is a 17th-century district with the slow-down-and-smell-the-cobbles Plaza Mayor and memories of pre-industrial Spain.

North of Puerta del Sol runs Gran Vía, and between the two are lively pedestrian shopping streets. Gran Vía, bubbling with expensive shops and cinemas, leads to the modern Plaza de España. North of Gran Vía is the gritty Malasana quarter, with its colorful small houses, shoemakers' shops, sleazy-looking hombres, milk vendors, bars, and hip night scene.

Tourist Information

Madrid has five TIs: **Plaza Mayor** at #3 (Mon–Sat 10:00–20:00, Sun 10:00–15:00, tel. 91-588-1636); **near the Prado Museum** (behind Palace Hotel, Mon–Fri 09:00–19:00, Sat 09:00–13:00, Duque de Medinaceli 2, tel. 91-429-4951); and smaller offices at the **Chamartin** train station (Mon–Fri 08:00–20:00, Sat 09:00–13:00, tel. 91-315-9976), **Atocha** train station (Mon–Fri 09:00–21:00, closed Sat–Sun), and at the **airport** (Mon–Fri 08:00–20:00, Sat 09:00–13:00, closed Sun, tel. 91-305-8656). The general tourist info number is tel. 902-100-107 (www.munimadrid.es). During the summer small temporary stands with yellow umbrellas and yellow-shirted student guides pop up (at places such as Puerta del Sol), happy to help out lost tourists. Confirm your sightseeing

Madrid

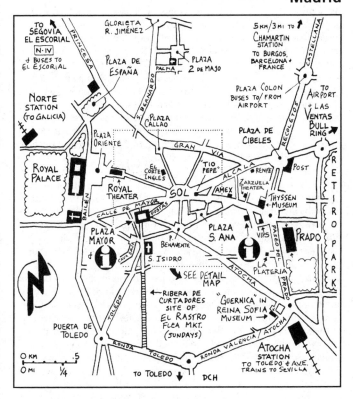

plans and pick up a city map and *Enjoy Madrid*. If interested, ask at the TI about bullfights and zarzuela (the local light opera).

For entertainment listings, the TI's free *En Madrid* is not as good as the easy-to-decipher Spanish weekly entertainment guide *Guía del Ocio* (€0.90, sold at newsstands), which lists events, restaurants, and movies ("v.o." means a movie is in its original language rather than dubbed).

If you're heading to other destinations in Spain, ask any Madrid TI for free maps and brochures (ideally in English). Since many small-town TIs keep erratic hours and run out of these pamphlets, get what you can here. You can get schedules for buses and some trains, avoiding unnecessary trips to the various stations. The TI's free and amazingly informative *Mapa de Comunicaciones España* lists all the Turismos and highway SOS numbers with a road map of Spain. (If they're out, ask for the Paradores Hotel chain–sponsored route map.)

Arrival in Madrid

By Train: Madrid's two train stations, Atocha and Chamartin, are both on subway lines with easy access to downtown Madrid. Each station has all the services. Chamartin handles most international trains. Atocha generally covers southern Spain and runs AVE trains to Sevilla. Both stations offer long-distance trains (*largo recorrido*) as well as smaller, local trains (*regionales* and *cercanías*) to nearby destinations. To travel between Chamartin and Atocha, don't hassle with the subway (which involves a transfer)—the *cercanías* trains are faster (6/hr, 12 min, €1.20, free with railpass—show it at ticket window in the middle of the turnstiles). These trains depart from Atocha's track 2. At Chamartin, it's usually track 2 or 3, but check the Salidas Immediatas board for the next departure.

Chamartin: The TI is opposite track 19. The impressively large *Centro de Viajes/Travel Center* customer-service office is in the middle of the building. You can use the Club Intercity lounge if you have a first-class railpass and first-class seat or sleeper reservations. The *cercanías* platforms cluster around track 5. The station's Metro stop is Chamartin. (If you arrive by Metro at Chamartin, follow signs to *Información* to get to the lobby rather than *Vias*, which sends you directly to the platforms.)

Atocha: Atocha is split into two halves, connected by a corridor of shops. On one side are the slick AVE trains, some Talgo trains, and a botanical garden (in the soaringly high old-station building, complete with birds, places to sit, and a cafeteria). On the other side of the station you'll find the local *cercanías*, *regionales*, some Talgos, and the Metro stop (named Atocha RENFE—not simply Atocha, which is a different Metro stop in Madrid). Each side of the station has separate schedules; this can be confusing if you're in the wrong side of the building. You'll find a tiny TI that handles tourist info only—not train info (Mon–Fri 09:00–21:00, closed Sat–Sun, 50 meters straight ahead of the Metro's turnstiles, ground floor). For train info, try the customer-service office called *Atención al Cliente* (daily 07:00–23:00); although there's one office for each half of the building, the office on the AVE side (just off the botanical garden) is more likely to speak English.

Atocha's Club AVE is a lounge reserved solely for AVE business or first-class ticket-holders or Eurailers with a reservation (daily 06:30–22:30, upstairs on AVE side of station, free drinks, newspapers, showers, and info service).

To buy tickets at Atocha for the local *cercanías* trains (e.g., to Toledo), go to the middle of the *cercanías* side and get your ticket from ticket windows in the small rectangular offices (marked *Venta de Billetes sin reserva*). You can buy AVE and other long-distance train tickets in the bigger ticket offices in either half of the building; the airier *Taquillas* office on the AVE side (next to *Atención al Cliente* off the botanical garden) is more pleasant. Station ticket offices can get really crowded (mid-morning and late afternoon are usually peaceful). It's often quicker to buy your ticket at an English-speaking travel agency (such as in El Corte Inglés) or at the downtown RENFE office, which offers train information, reservations, tickets, and minimal English (Mon–Fri 09:30–20:00, CC, go in person, 2 blocks north of the Prado at Calle Alcala 44, tel. 902-240-202, www.renfe.es).

By Bus: Madrid's three key bus stations, all connected by Metro, are: Larrea (for Segovia, Metro: Príncipe Pío), Estación Sur Autobuses (for Toledo, Ávila, and Granada, on top of Metro stop: Méndez Alvaro, tel. 91-468-4200), and Estación Intercambiador (for El Escorial, in the Metro: Moncloa).

By Plane: For information on Madrid's Barajas Airport, see "Transportation Connections" at the end of this chapter.

Getting around Madrid

By Subway: Madrid's subway is simple, speedy, and cheap (€0.90/ride, runs 06:00–01:30). The €4.60, 10-ride Metrobus ticket can be shared by several travelers and works on both the Metro and buses (purchase tickets at kiosks or tobacco shops or in the Metro). The city's broad streets can be hot and exhausting. A subway trip of even a stop or two might save time and energy. Most stations offer free maps (*navegamadrid*; www.metromadrid.es). Navigate by subway stops (shown on city maps). To transfer, follow signs to the next subway line (numbered and color-coded). End stops are used to indicate directions. Insert your ticket in the turnstile, then retrieve it as you pass through. Green *Salida* signs point to the exit. Using neighborhood maps and street signs to exit smartly can save lots of walking.

By Bus: City buses, while not as easy as the Metro, can be useful (bus maps at TI or info booth on Puerta del Sol, €0.90 tickets sold on bus, or €4.60 for a 10-ride Metrobus—see "By Subway," above; buses run 06:00–24:00).

By Taxi: Madrid's 15,000 taxis are easy to hail and reasonable (€1.10 drop, €0.60 per km; supplements for airport, train/bus stations, bags, Sunday, and night service). Threesomes travel as cheaply by taxi as by subway. A ride from the Royal Palace to the Prado costs about €3.50.

Helpful Hints

Theft Alert: Be wary of pickpockets, anywhere, anytime, but particularly on Puerta del Sol (main square), the subway, and crowded streets. Wear your money belt. The small streets north of Gran Vía are particularly dangerous, even before nightfall. Muggings occur, but are rare.

Travel Agencies and Free Maps: The grand department store, El Corte Inglés, has two travel agencies (on first and seventh floors, Mon–Sat 10:00–22:00, just off Puerta del Sol) and gives out free Madrid maps (at the information desk, immediately inside the door, just off Puerta del Sol at intersection of Preciados and Tetuan; supermarket in basement). El Corte Inglés is taking over the entire intersection; the main store is the tallest building with the biggest sign.

Books: For books in English, try the oddly-named **Fnac Callao** (Mon–Sat 10:00–21:30, Sun 12:00–21:30, second floor, Calle Preciados 8, tel. 91-595-6190), **Casa del Libro** (Mon–Sat 09:30–21:30, Sun 11:00–21:00, English on ground floor in back, Gran Vía 29, tel. 91-521-2219), and **El Cortes Inglés** (guide-books and some fiction, in its Libreria branch kitty-corner from main store, see listing within "Travel Agency," above).

American Express: The AmEx office at Plaza Cortes 2 sells train and plane tickets, and even accepts Visa and Mastercard (opposite Palace Hotel, 2 blocks from Metro: Banco de España, Mon–Fri 09:00–17:30, Sat 10:00–14:00, tel. 91-322-5445).

Embassies: The U.S. Embassy is at Serrano 75 (tel. 91-587-2200); the Canadian Embassy is at Nuñez de Balboa 35 (tel. 91-423-3250).

Laundromat: The self-service Lavamatique is the most central, just west of the Prado (Mon–Sat 09:00–20:00, closed Sun, Cervantes 1).

Internet Access: You'll find lots of computer terminals at NavegaWeb, centrally located at Gran Vía 30 (daily 09:00–24:00). Zahara's Internet café is at the corner of Gran Vía and Mesoneros (Mon–Fri 09:00–24:00, Sat–Sun 09:00–24:00).

Tours of Madrid

Hop-On Hop-Off Bus Tours—Several companies offer virtually identical 15-stop 75-minute circuits of the city with two or three buses per hour allowing you to hop on and off all day at the various sights, including the Royal Palace and Prado. The easiest place to catch any of the buses is at the south side of Puerta del Sol. Before you commit, ask if the bus has live or tape-recorded commentary; if the ticket is valid for one day or two (sometimes this is a bonus, sometimes it costs extra); and if discounts are offered for youth and seniors (about €9.50, daily 10:00–18:00, until 20:00 in summer). It's possible that in 2002 only one company, maybe Grayline, will offer these tours, depending on a ruling from the city government.

Walking Tours—British expatriate Stephen Drake-Jones gives entertaining, informative walks of historic old Madrid almost nightly (along with more specialized walks, such as "Hemingway," "Civil War," and "Bloody Madrid"). A historian with a passion for the memory of Wellington (the man who stopped Napoleon), Stephen is the founder of the Wellington Society. For €25 you become a member of the society for one year and get a free two-hour tour that includes stops at two bars for local drinks and tapas. Eccentric Stephen takes you back in time to sort out Madrid's Hapsburg and Bourbon history. Stephen likes his wine. If that's a problem, skip the tour. Tours start at the statue on Puerta del Sol (maximum 10 people, tel. 60-914-3203—a cell-phone number that will cost you €0.60—to confirm tour and reserve a spot, www.wellsoc.org, e-mail: sdrakejones@hotmail.com). Members of the Wellington Society can take advantage of Stephen's helpline (if you're in a Spanish jam, call him to translate and intervene) and assistance via e-mail (for questions on Spain, your itinerary, and so on). Stephen also does inexpensive private tours and daytrips for small groups.

Introductory Walk: From Madrid's Puerta del Sol to the Royal Palace

Connect the sights with the following walking tour. Allow an hour for this one-kilomter walk, not including your palace visit.

▲▲**Puerta del Sol**—Named for a long-gone medieval gate with the sun carved onto it, Puerta del Sol is ground zero for Madrid. It's a hub for the Metro, buses, and pickpockets.

Stand by the statue of King Charles III and survey the square. Because of his enlightened urban policies, Charles III (who ruled until 1788) is affectionately called the "best mayor of Madrid." He decorated the city squares with fine fountains, got those meddlesome Jesuits out of city government, established the public school system, made the Retiro a public park rather than a royal retreat, and generally cleaned up Madrid.

Look behind the king. The statue of the bear pawing the strawberry bush and the Madrono trees in the big planter boxes are symbols of the city. Bears used to live in the royal hunting grounds outside Madrid.

The king faces a red-and-white building with a bell tower. This was Madrid's first post office, established by Charles in the 1760s. Today it's the governor's office, though it's notorious for being Franco's police headquarters. An amazing number of those detained and interrogated by the Franco police "tried to escape" by flying out the windows to their deaths. Notice the hats of the civil guardsmen at the entry. It's said the hats have square backsides so they can lean against the wall while enjoying a cigarette.

Crowds fill the square on New Year's Eve as the rest of Madrid watches the action on TV. As Spain's "Big Ben" atop the governor's office chimes 12 times, Madrileños eat one grape for each ring to bring good luck through the coming year.

Cross Calle Mayor. Look at the curb directly in front of the entrance of the governor's office. The scuffed-up marker is the center of Spain. To the right of the entrance, the plaque on the wall

Heart of Madrid

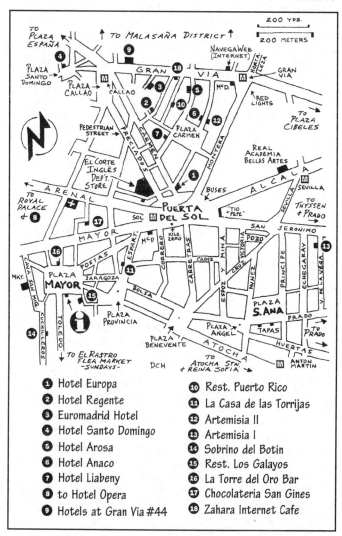

① Hotel Europa
② Hotel Regente
③ Euromadrid Hotel
④ Hotel Santo Domingo
⑤ Hotel Arosa
⑥ Hotel Anaco
⑦ Hotel Liabeny
⑧ to Hotel Opera
⑨ Hotels at Gran Via #44
⑩ Rest. Puerto Rico
⑪ La Casa de las Torrijas
⑫ Artemisia II
⑬ Artemisia I
⑭ Sobrino del Botin
⑮ Rest. Los Galayos
⑯ La Torre del Oro Bar
⑰ Chocolateria San Gines
⑱ Zahara Internet Cafe

marks the spot where the war against Napoleon started. Napoleon wanted his brother to be king of Spain. Trying to finagle this, Napoleon brought nearly the entire Spanish royal family to France for negotiations. An anxious crowd gathered outside this building awaiting word of the fate of their royal family. This was just after the French Revolution, and there was a general nervousness between France and Spain. When the French guard appeared, on May 2, 1808, the massacre took place. Goya, who worked just up the street, observed the event and captured the tragedy in his paintings *2nd of May, 1808*, and *3rd of May, 1808*, now in the Prado.

Walking from Puerta del Sol to Plaza Mayor: On the corner of Calle Mayor and Puerta del Sol, across from McDonald's, is the busy *confiteria*, Salon la Mallorquina (daily 09:00–21:15). Cross Calle Mayor to go inside. The shop is famous for its sweet Napolitana cream-filled pastry (€0.75) and savory, beef-filled *agujas* pastries (€1.20)—if you can't finish yours, the beggar at the front door would love to. See the racks with goodies hot out of the oven. Look back toward the entrance and notice the tile above the door with the 18th-century view of the Puerta del Sol. Compare this with the view out the door. This was before the square was widened, when a church stood where the Tío Pepe sign stands today. The French used this church to detain local patriots awaiting execution. (That venerable sign, advertising a famous sherry for over 100 years, is Madrid's first billboard.)

Cross busy Calle Mayor (again), round McDonald's, and veer left up the pedestrian alley called Calle de Postas. The street sign shows the post coach heading for that famous first post office. Medieval street signs came with pictures so the illiterate could "read" them. After 50 meters, take a left up Calle San Cristobal. Within two blocks, you'll pass the local feminist bookshop (Libreria Mujeres—on the left—appropriately) and reach a small square. At the square notice the big brick 17th-century Ministry of Foreign Affairs building (with the pointed spire)—originally a prison for rich prisoners who could afford the best cells. Turn right and walk down Calle de Zaragoza under the arcade into...

Plaza Mayor—This square, built in 1619, is a vast, cobbled, traffic-free chunk of 17th-century Spain. Each side of the square is uniform, as if a grand palace were turned inside out. The statue is of Philip III, who ordered the square's construction. Upon this stage, much Spanish history was played out: bullfights, fires, royal pageantry, and events of the gruesome Inquisition. Reliefs serving as seatbacks under the lampposts tell the story. During the Inquisition, many were tried here. The guilty would parade around the square (bleachers were built for bigger audiences, the wealthy rented balconies) with billboards listing their many sins. They were then burned. Some were slowly strangled with a *garrotte*; they'd hold a crucifix and hear the reassuring words of a priest as this life was squeezed out of them. The square is painted a democratic shade of burgundy—the result of a citywide vote. Since Franco's 1975 death, there's been a passion for voting here. Three different colors were painted as samples on the walls of this square, and the city voted for its favorite.

From Plaza Mayor to the Royal Palace

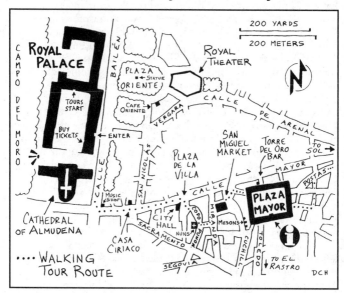

A stamp-and-coin market bustles here on Sundays from 10:00 to 14:00, and on any day it's a colorful and affordable place to enjoy a cup of coffee. Throughout Spain, lesser *plazas mayores* provide peaceful pools for the river of Spanish life. The TI is at #3, on the south side of the square. The building decorated with painted figures, on the north side of the square, is the Casa de la Panaderia, which used to house the Bakers' Guild. To the left of it is...

The Torre del Oro Bar Andalu (northwest corner of square) is a good place for a drink to finish off your Plaza Mayor visit. This bar is a temple to bullfighting. Warning: They push expensive tapas on tourists. A *caña* (small beer) shouldn't cost more than €1.20. The bar's ambience is "Andalu"...Andalusian. Look under the stuffed head of "Barbero" the bull. At eye level you'll see a *puntilla*, the knife used to put a bull out of its misery at the arena. This was the knife used to kill Barbero.

Notice the incredible action caught in the bar's many photographs. At the end of the bar in a glass case is the "suit of lights" El Cordobes wore in his ill-fated 1967 fight. With Franco in attendance, El Cordobes went on and on, long after he could have ended the fight, until finally the bull gored him. El Cordobes survived; the bull didn't. Find Franco with El Cordobes at the far end (to the left of Segador the Bull). Under the bull is a photo of El Cordobes' illegitimate son, El Cordobes, kissing a bull. Disowned by El Cordobes and using his dad's famous name after a court battle, El Cordobes is one of this generation's top fighters.

Walking from Plaza Mayor to the Royal Palace: Leave Plaza Mayor on Calle Cuidad Rodrigo (far right corner from where you entered the square, and to your right as you exit Torre del Oro). You'll pass a series of fine turn-of-the-20th-century storefronts and shops such as the recommended Casa Rua, famous for their cheap *bocadillos calamares*—fried squid-ring sandwiches.

From the archway you'll see the covered Mercado de San Miguel (green iron posts, on left). Before you enter the market, look left down the street Cava de San Miguel. If you like sangria and singing, come back tonight around 21:00 and visit one of the *mesons* (such as Guitarra, Tortilla, or Boqueron) that you'll find just down the street. These cave-like bars stretch way back and get packed with locals who—emboldened by sangria, the setting, and Spain—might suddenly just start singing. It's a fun scene, best on Fridays and Saturdays.

Wander through the newly-renovated produce market and consider buying some fruit (Mon–Fri 09:00–14:30, 17:15–20:15, Sat 09:00–14:30, closed Sun). Leave it on the opposite (downhill) side and follow the pedestrian lane left. You'll pass Taberna San Miguel, which makes good *churros* in the morning. At the first corner, turn right, and cross the small plaza to the modern brick convent. The door on the right says *venta de dulces;* to buy inexpensive sweets from cloistered nuns, buzz the *monjas* button, wait patiently for the sister to respond over the intercom, and say *dulces* (dool-thays) when she does (Mon–Sat 09:30–13:00, 16:00–18:30). When the lock buzzes, push open the door and follow the sign to *torno,* the lazy Susan which lets the sisters sell their baked goods without being seen (smallest quantities: half or *medio* kilo). Of the many choices (all good), consider *pastas de Almendra* (crumbly) or *manteados de yema* (moist and eggy).

Follow Calle del Codo (see the street sign—where those in need of bits of armor shopped) around the convent to Plaza de la Villa, the city-hall square. Ahead the flags of city, state, and nation grace the city hall. The statue in the garden is of Don Bazan—mastermind of the Christian victory over the Muslims at the naval battle of Lepanto in 1571. This pivotal battle ended the Muslim threat to Christian Europe. The mayor's office is behind Don.

From here, busy Calle Mayor leads downhill a couple more blocks to the Royal Palace. Halfway down (on the left) there's a tiny square opposite the recommended Casa Ciriaco restaurant (#84). The statue memorializes the 1906 anarchist bombing that killed 23 people as the royal couple paraded by on their wedding day. While the crowd was throwing flowers, an anarchist threw a bouquet lashed to a bomb from a balcony of #84 (which was a hotel at the time). Amazing photos of the event hang just inside the door in the back room of the restaurant.

Continue down Calle Mayor. Within a couple of blocks you'll come to a busy street, Calle de Bailen. (On the corner—to your right—is the Garrido-Bailen music store, a handy place to stock up on castanets, unusual flutes, and Galatian bagpipes.)

Across the busy street is the **Cathedral of Almudena**, Madrid's new cathedral. It's worth a look while you're here. Built between 1883 and 1993, its exterior is a contemporary mix and its interior is neo-Gothic with a colorful ceiling. Next to the cathedral is the...

▲▲**Royal Palace (Palacio Real)**—Europe's third-greatest palace (after Versailles and Vienna's Schonbrunn) is packed with tourists and royal antiques. After a fortress burned down on this site, King Phillip V commissioned this huge 18th-century palace as a replacement. How big is it? Over 2,000 rooms with tons of lavish tapestries, a king's ransom of chandeliers, priceless porcelain, paintings, and lots of clocks (Charles IV was a huge collector). While the royal family lives in a mansion a few kilometers away, the place still functions as a royal palace and is used for formal state receptions and tourist daydreams.

A simple one-floor, 24-room, one-way circuit is open to the public. You can wander on your own or join an English tour (get time of next tour and decide as you buy your ticket; tours depart about every 20 min). The tour guides, like the museum guidebook, show a passion for meaningless data (€6 without a tour, €7 with a tour, April–Sept Mon–Sat 09:00–19:00, Sun 09:00–16:00; Oct–March Mon–Sat 09:30–18:00, Sun 09:00–15:00, last tickets sold an hour before closing, palace can close without warning if needed for a royal function; cafeteria; Metro: Opera, tel. 91-559-7404 or 91-454-8800). Your ticket includes the armory and the pharmacy, both on the courtyard.

If you tour on your own, here are a few details you won't find on the little English descriptions posted in each room:

The Grand Stairs: Fancy carpets are rolled down (notice the little metal bar-holding hooks) for formal occasions. At the top of the first landing, the blue and red coat of arms is of the current—and popular—constitutional monarch, Juan Carlos. While Franco chose him to be the next dictator, J.C. knew Spain was ripe for democracy. Rather than become "Juan the Brief" (as some were nicknaming him), he turned real power over to the parliament. At the top of the stairs (before entering first room, right of door) is a bust of J.C.'s great-great-g-g-g-great-grandfather Phillip V. The grandson of France's King Louis XIV, he began the Bourbon dynasty in 1700. The dynasty survives today with Juan Carlos.

Throne Room: Red velvet walls, lions, and frescoes of

Spanish scenes symbolize the monarchy in this rococo riot. The chandeliers are the best in the house. The thrones are only from 1977. This is where ambassadors give their credentials to the king, who receives them relatively informally...standing rather than seated in the throne.

Gasparini Anteroom (2 rooms after the throne room): The paintings are of King Charles IV and his wife—all by Goya. Velázquez's masterpiece *Las Meninas* originally hung here.

Gasparini Room: This was the royal dressing room, hinting of the Asian influence popular at the time. Dressing, for a divine monarch, was a public affair. The court bigwigs would assemble here as the king, standing on a platform—notice the height of the mirrors—would pull on his leotards. In the next room, the silk wallpaper is new—notice the J.C.S. initials of the king and Sofia (the queen).

Gala Dining Room: Five or six times a year the king entertains up to 150 guests at this bowling lane–sized table. The table in the next room would be lined with an exorbitantly caloric dessert buffet. In the next room you can ogle at glass cases filled with the silver tableware used for these functions.

Stradivarius Room: The queen likes classical music and when you perform for her, do it with these precious 300-year-old violins. About 300 Antonius Stradivarius–made instruments survive. This is the only matching quartet: two violins, a viola, and a cello.

Royal Chapel: The Royal Chapel is used only for baptisms and funerals. The royal tomb sits here before making the sad trip to El Escorial to join the rest of Spain's past royalty.

Billiards and Smoking Rooms: The billiards room and the smoking room were for men only. The porcelain and silk of the smoking room imitates a Chinese opium den.

Queen's Boudoir: The next room was for the ladies, decorated just after Pompeii was excavated and therefore in fanciful ancient-Roman style. You'll exit down the same grand stairway you climbed 24 rooms ago. Near the exit is a cafeteria and bookstore, which has a variety of books on Spanish history.

The **armory**, recently renovated, displays the armor and swords of El Cid, Ferdinand, Charles V, and Phillip II.

After you finish your visit, consider walking a few minutes farther up the length of the palace to Plaza de Oriente. With your back to the palace, face the equestrian statue of Philip IV. To your far left is the Torre de Madrid skyscraper, with statues of Don Quixote and Sancho at its base (not visible from your vantage point). Behind the equestian statue of Philip IV is the Royal Theater (*Teatro Real*). Many theater-goers stop by Café de Oriente before or after the performance (using a clock as a compass, the café is at 1:00). Walk in front of the Royal Theater. Cross the square and take Calle Arenal back to Puerta del Sol.

Sights—Madrid's Museum Neighborhood

These three worthwhile museums are in east Madrid. From Prado to the Thyssen-Bornemisza Museum is a five-minute walk; Prado to Centro Reina Sofia is a 10-minute walk.

Museum Pass: If you plan to visit all three museums, you'll save 25 percent by buying the Paseo del Arte pass (€7.75, sold at each museum, valid for a year—but good for only one visit per site). Note that the Prado and Centro Reina Sofia museums are free on Saturday afternoon and Sunday (and May 18, Oct 12, Dec 6, and anytime for those under 18 and over 65); the Prado and Thyssen-Bornemisza are closed Monday; and the Reina Sofia is closed Tuesday.

▲▲▲**Prado Museum**—The Prado holds my favorite collection of paintings anywhere. With more than 3,000 canvases, including entire rooms of masterpieces by Velázquez, Goya, El Greco, and Bosch, it's overwhelming. Take a tour or buy a guidebook (or bring along the Prado chapter from *Rick Steves' Mona Winks*). Focus on the Flemish and northern (Bosch, Dürer, Rubens), the Italian (Fra Angelico, Raphael, Titian), and the Spanish art (El Greco, Velázquez, Goya).

Follow Goya through his stages, from cheery (*The Parasol*) to political (*2nd of May, 1808* and *3rd of May, 1808*) to dark ("Negras de Goya": e.g., *Saturn Devouring His Children*). In each stage, Goya asserted his independence from artistic conventions. Even the standard court portraits from his "first" stage reflect his politically liberal viewpoint, subtly showing the vanity and stupidity of his royal patrons by the looks in their goony eyes. His political stage, with paintings such as the *3rd of May, 1808*, depicting a massacre of Spaniards by Napoleon's troops, makes him one of the first artists with a social conscience. Finally, in his gloomy "dark stage," Goya probed the inner world of fears and nightmares, anticipating our modern-day preoccupation with dreams. Also, seek out Bosch's *The Garden of Earthly Delights*—a three-paneled altarpiece showing creation, the "transparency of earthly pleasures," and the resulting hell. Bosch's self-portrait looks out from hell (with the birds leading naked people around the brim of his hat) surrounded by people suffering eternal punishments appropriate for their primary earthly excesses.

The art is constantly rearranged by the Prado's management, so even the Prado's own maps and guidebooks are out of date. Regardless of the latest location, most art is grouped by painter, and better guards can point you in the right direction if you say "*¿Dónde está . . . ?*" and the painter's name as Españoled as you can (e.g., Titian is "Ticiano" and Bosch is "El Bosco"). The Murillo entrance—at the end closest to the Atocha train station—usually has shorter lines. Lunchtime, from 14:00 to 16:00, is least crowded (€3, free on Sat afternoon after 14:30, all day Sun, and to anyone

Madrid's Museum Neighborhood

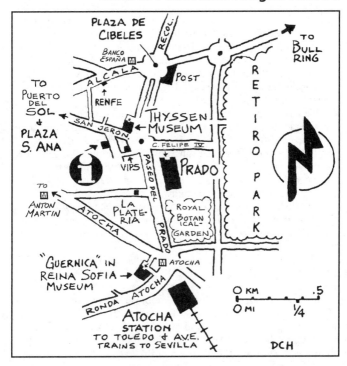

under 18 and over 65; Tue–Sat 09:00–19:00, Sun 09:00–14:00, closed Mon, last entry 30 min before closing; ticket valid for one visit—no in-and-out privileges; free, mandatory baggage check after your things are scanned just like at the airport; can't bring water bottle inside; photos are allowed without a flash; cafeteria at Murillo end; Paseo de Prado, Metro: Banco de España or Atocha—each a 15-min walk from the museum, tel. 91-330-2800, http://museoprado.mcu.es).

While you're in the neighborhood, consider a visit to the Charles III Botanical Garden (listed under "More Sights," below).

▲▲**Thyssen-Bornemisza Museum**—Locals call this stunning museum simply the Thyssen (tee-sun). It displays the impressive collection that Baron Thyssen (a wealthy German married to a former Miss Spain) sold to Spain for $350 million. It's basically minor works by major artists and major works by minor artists (the real big guns are over at the Prado). But art lovers appreciate how the good baron's art complements the Prado's collection by filling in where the Prado is weak (Impressionism). For a delightful walk through art history, ride the elevator to the top floor and do the rooms in numerical order. It's kitty-corner from the Prado at Paseo del Prado 8 in Palacio de Villahermosa (€4.75, or €6.50 to add current exhibition, free for accompanied children under 12, Tue–Sun 10:00–19:00, closed Mon, ticket office closes at 18:30, audioguide–€3, free baggage check, café, shop, no photos or videotaping allowed, Metro: Banco de España or Atocha, tel. 91-420-3944, www .museothyssen.org). If you're tired, hail a cab at the gate and zip straight to Centro Reina Sofia.

▲▲**Centro Reina Sofia**—In this exceptional modern-art museum, ride the elevator to the second floor and follow the room numbers for art from 1900 to 1950. The fourth floor continues the collection from 1950 to 1980. The museum is most famous for Picasso's *Guernica*, a massive painting showing the horror of modern war. Guernica, a village in northern Spain, was the target of the world's first saturation-bombing raid, approved by Franco and carried out by Hitler. Notice the two rooms of studies for *Guernica* filled with iron-nail tears and screaming mouths. *Guernica* was exiled in America until Franco's death, and now it reigns as Spain's national piece of art.

The museum also houses an easy-to-enjoy collection of other modern artists, including more of Picasso (3 rooms divided among his pre-civil-war work, *Guernica*, and his post-civil-war art) and a mind-bending room of Dalís. Enjoy a break in the shady courtyard before leaving (€3, free Sat afternoon after 14:30 and all day Sun, always free to the under-18 and over-65 crowd, Mon and Wed–Sat 10:00–21:00, Sun 10:00–14:30, closed Tue, good brochure, no photos or videos allowed, no tours in English—yet, free baggage check, Santa Isabel 52, Metro: Atocha, across from Atocha train station, look for exterior glass elevators, tel. 91-467-5062, http://museoreinasofia.mcu.es).

More Sights—Madrid

Chapel San Antonio de la Florida—Goya's tomb stares up at a splendid cupola filled with his own frescoes. On June 13, local ladies line up here to ask St. Anthony for a boyfriend, while outside a festival rages, with street musicians, food, and fun (€1.80, Tue–Fri 10:00–14:00, 16:00–20:00, Sat–Sun 10:00–14:00, closed Mon, July and Aug only 10:00–14:00, Glorieta de San Antonio de la Florida, Metro: Príncipe Pío, tel. 91-542-0722). This chapel is near the bus station that covers Segovia. If you're daytripping to Segovia, it's easy to stop by the chapel before or after your trip.

Next door to the chapel is Restaurante Casa Mingo, popular for its cheap chicken, chorizo, and *cabrales* cheese served with cider. Ask the waiter to pour the cider for you. For dessert, try *tarta de Santiago*—almond cake (daily 11:00–24:00, Paseo de la Florida 34, tel. 91-547-7918).

Royal Tapestry Factory (Real Fabrica de Tapices)—Have a look at the traditional making of tapestries (€1.80, some English tours, Mon–Fri 10:00–14:00, closed Aug, Calle Fuenterrabia 2, Metro: Menendez Pelayo, take Gutenberg exit, tel. 91-434-0551).

▲**Retiro Park**—Siesta in this 350-acre green and breezy escape from the city. At midday on Saturday and Sunday, the area around the lake becomes a street carnival, with jugglers, puppeteers, and lots of local color. These peaceful gardens offer great picnicking and people watching. From the Retiro Metro stop, walk to the big lake (El Estanque), where you can cheaply rent a rowboat. Past the lake, a grand boulevard of statues leads to the Prado.

Charles III's Botanical Garden (Real Jardín Botánico)—After your Prado visit, you can take a lush and fragrant break in this sculpted park wandering among trees from around the world (entry just opposite Prado's Murillo entry, €1.50, daily 10:00–20:00, until 18:00 in winter, Plaza de Murillo 2).

Moncloa Tower (Faro de Moncloa)—This tower's elevator zips you up 92 meters to the best skyscraper view in town (€1.20, Tue–Fri 10:00–14:00, 17:00–19:00, Sat–Sun 10:30–17:30, closed Mon, Metro: Moncloa, tel. 91-544-8106). If you're going to El Escorial by bus, this is a convenient sight near the bus station.

Teleferico—For a break from the big city, ride this cable car from downtown over Madrid's sprawling city park to Casa de Campo (€2.60 one-way, €3.60 round-trip, daily from 11:00, fall and winter from 12:00, departs from Paseo del Pintor Rosales, Metro: Arguelles, tel. 91-541-7450, www.teleferico.com. At Casa de Campo, you can rent a rowboat, picnic, and visit the zoo and amusement park.

Shopping

Shoppers focus on the colorful pedestrian area between Gran Vía and Puerta del Sol. The giant Spanish department store, El Corte Inglés, is a block off Puerta del Sol and a handy place to pick up just about anything you need (Mon–Sat 10:00–21:30, closed Sun, free maps at info desk, supermarket in basement).

▲**El Rastro**—Europe's biggest flea market, held on Sundays and holidays, is a field day for shoppers, people watchers, and thieves (9:00–15:00, best before 12:00). Thousands of stalls titillate more than a million browsers with mostly new junk. If you brake for garage sales, you'll pull a U-turn for El Rastro. Start at the Plaza Mayor and head south or take the subway to Tirso de Molina. Hang on to your wallet. Munch on a *pepito* (meat-filled pastry). Europe's biggest stamp market thrives simultaneously on Plaza Mayor.

Nightlife

▲▲▲**Bullfight**—Madrid's Plaza de Toros hosts Spain's top bull-fights on most Sundays and holidays from Easter through October

and nearly every day from May through early June. Top fights
sell out in advance. Fights start punctually at 19:00. Tickets range
from €3.30–102. There are no bad seats at Plaza de Toros; paying
more gets you in the shade and/or closer to the gore. To be close
to the action, choose areas 8, 9, and 10; for shade: 1, 2, 9, 10; for
shade/sun: 3, 8; for the sun and cheapest seats: 4, 5, 6, 7. Hotels
and booking offices such as the one at Plaza Carmen 3 (daily
09:30–13:30, 16:00–19:00, tel. 91-531-2732) are convenient but
they add a 20-percent service charge to your ticket and don't sell
the cheap seats. If you want to save money, stand in the bullring
ticket line. A thousand tickets are held back to be sold on the five
days leading up to a fight, including the day of the fight. The
bullring is at Calle Alcala 237 (Metro: Ventas, tel. 91-356-2200,
www.las-ventas.com).

The bullfighting **museum** (Museo Taurino) is at the back of
the bullring (free, 09:30–14:30, closed Sat and Mon and early on
fight days, Calle Alcala 237, tel. 91-725-1857).

▲▲**Zarzuela**—For a delightful look at Spanish light opera that
even English speakers can enjoy, try zarzuela. Guitar-strumming
Napoleons in red capes; buxom women with masks, fans, and
castanets; Spanish-speaking pharaohs; melodramatic spotlights;
and aficionados clapping and singing along from the cheap seats
where the acoustics are best—this is zarzuela ...the people's opera.
Originating in Madrid, zarzuela is known for its satiric humor
and surprisingly good music. The season, which runs from mid-
December through June, features a mix of zarzuela, traditional
opera, and dance. You can buy tickets at Theater Zarzuela
(€7–27, box office open 12:00–18:00 or until showtime, Jovell-
anos 4, near the Prado, Metro: Banco de España, tel. 91-524-
5400, www.teatrozarzuela.mcu.es). The TI's monthly guide has
a special zarzuela listing.

Flamenco—Taberna Casa Patas is small, intimate, smoky, and
powerful, with one drink included and no hassling after that (tickets cost around €18, shows begin at 22:00, Canizares 10, 3 blocks
south of Plaza Santa Ana, reservations tel. 91-369-0496). Café de
Chinitas, another flamenco place, is more touristy (Calle Torija 7,
just off Plaza Mayor).

Sleeping in Madrid
(€1.10 = about $1, country code: 34)
Sleep Code: **S** = Single, **D** = Double/Twin, **T** = Triple, **Q** = Quad,
b = bathroom, **s** = shower only, **CC** = Credit Cards accepted, **no
CC** = Credit Cards not accepted, **SE** = Speaks English, **NSE** =
No English. Breakfast is not included unless noted. In Madrid,
the 7 percent IVA tax is sometimes included in the price.

Madrid has plenty of centrally located budget hotels and *pen-
siónes*. You'll have no trouble finding a sleepable double for $30,

a good double for $60, and a modern air-conditioned double with all the comforts for $100. Prices are the same throughout the year, and it's almost always easy to find a place. Anticipate full hotels May 15 to May 25 (the festival of Madrid's patron Saint Isidro) and the last week in September (conventions). The accommodations I've listed are within a few minutes' walk of Puerta del Sol.

Sleeping in the Pedestrian Zone between Puerta del Sol and Gran Vía (zip code: 28013)

Predictable and away from the seediness, these are good values for those wanting to spend a little more. Their formal prices may be inflated, and some offer weekend and summer discounts whenever it's slow. Use Metro: Sol for all but the last. See map on page 870 for location.

Hotel Europa has red-carpet charm: a royal salon, plush halls with happy Muzak, polished wood floors, attentive staff, and 80 squeaky-clean rooms with balconies overlooking the pedestrian zone or an inner courtyard (Sb-€48, Db-€60, Tb-€85, Qb-€100, Quint/b-€115, tax not included, breakfast-€5, fine lounge on 2nd floor, elevator, fans, easy phone reservations with credit card, CC, Calle del Carmen 4, tel. 91-521-2900, fax 91-521-4696, www .hoteleuropa.net, e-mail: info@hoteleuropa.net, Antonio and Fernando Garaban and their helpful staff SE). The convenient Europa cafeteria/restaurant next door is a great scene and a fine value any time of day.

Hotel Regente is a big, traditional, and impersonal place with 145 plain but comfortable air-conditioned rooms and a great location (Sb-€45, Db-€78, Tb-€87, tax not included, breakfast-€3.90, CC, midway between Puerta del Sol and Plaza del Callao at Mesonero Romanos 9, tel. 91-521-2941, fax 91-532-3014, e-mail: info@hotelregente.com).

Euromadrid Hotel is like a cross between a Motel 6 and a hospital, with 43 white rooms in a modern but well-worn shell (Sb-€54, Db-€75, Tb-€84, includes buffet breakfast but not tax, CC, air con, discounted rate for parking-€8.75/day, Mesonero Romanos 7, tel. 91-521-7200, fax 91-521-4582, e-mail: clasit@infonegocio.com).

Hotel Santo Domingo is a fancy, worthwhile splurge— for its artsy paintings, inviting lounge, and 120 great rooms, each decorated differently (Sb-€114, Db-€168, pricier superior rooms are not necessary, CC, air con, elevator, Plaza de Santo Domingo 13, tel. 91-547-9800, fax 91-547-5995, www.hotelsantodomingo .com). Prices drop—and breakfast is included—on weekends (Fri, Sat, and Sun) and July through August.

Hotel Arosa charges the same for all of its 134 rooms, whether they're sleekly remodeled art-deco or just aging gracefully. Ask for a remodeled room with a terrace (Sb-€101, Db-€154, cheaper July–Aug, taxes not included, breakfast-€10.75, CC, air con, memorably tiny triangular elevator, Calle Salud 21, a block off Plaza del Carmen, tel. 91-532-1600, reservations number in Spain: tel. 90-099-3900, fax 91-531-3127).

A block away, the more basic **Hotel Anaco** has a drab color scheme, but offers 39 quiet, comfortable rooms in a central location (Sb-€69, Db-€84, tax not included, breakfast-€4.20, CC, air con, elevator, Tres Cruces 3, a few steps off Plaza del Carmen and its underground parking lot, tel. 915-22-4604, fax 91-531-6484, e-mail: info@anacohotel.com).

The huge **Hotel Liabeny** is a business-class hotel with 222 plush, spacious rooms and all the comforts (Sb-€99, Db-€132, Tb-€156, cheaper July–Aug, taxes not included, breakfast-€10.80, CC, air con, if one room is smoky ask for another, off Plaza Carmen at Salud 3, tel. 91-531-9000, fax 91-532-7421, www.apunte .es/liabeny, e-mail: liabeny@apunte.es).

Hotel Opera, a serious, modern hotel with 79 classy rooms, is located just off Plaza Isabel II, a four-block walk from Puerta del Sol toward the Royal Palace (Sb-€75, Db-€105, Db with terrace-€114, Tb-€137, tax not included, buffet breakfast-€8, CC, air con, elevator, ask for a higher floor—there are eight—to avoid street noise; consider their "singing dinners" offered nightly at 22:00—average price €42, Cuesta de Santo Domingo 2, Metro: Opera, tel. 91-541-2800, fax 91-541-6923, www.hotelopera.com, e-mail: reservas@hotelopera.com).

Sleeping at Gran Vía #44
(zip code: 28013)

The pulse (and noise) of today's Madrid is best felt along the Gran Vía. This main drag in the heart of the city stays awake all night. Despite the dreary pile of prostitutes just a block north, there's a certain urban decency about it. My choices (all at Gran Vía #44) are across from Plaza del Callao, which is four colorful blocks (of pedestrian malls) from Puerta del Sol. Although many rooms are high above the traffic noise, cooler and quieter rooms are on the back side. The Café & Te next door provides a classy way to breakfast. The Callão Metro stop is at your doorstep, and the handy Gran Vía stop (direct to Atocha) is two blocks away.

Hostal Residencia Miami is clean and quiet, with 11 well-lit rooms (3 with private bath), padded doors, and plastic-flower decor throughout. It's like staying at your eccentric aunt's in Miami Beach (Ss-€30, Ds-€36, Db-€42, T-€42, Tb-€51, Qb-€60, includes tax, CC, 8th floor, tel. & fax 91-521-1464). This *hostal* and the Alibel (see below), owned by the same family, might merge next year.

Across the hall, **Hostal Alibel,** like Miami with less sugar, rents eight big, airy, quiet rooms (D-€30, Ds-€33, Db-€36, no CC, tel. 91-521-0051, grandmotherly Terese NSE).

These next two are well-worn and suffer from street noise. **Hostal Residencia Valencia** is a tired old place with 32 big, stark rooms. The friendly manager, Antonio Ramirez, speaks English (Sb-€29.50, Ds-€39, Db-€42, Tb-€57, Qb-€63, includes tax, CC, 5th floor, tel. 91-522-1115, fax 91-522-1113, e-mail: hostalvalencia@wanadoo.es). **Hostal Residencia Continental,** with 29 older, basic but bright rooms, is downstairs and closer to the traffic (Sb-€29, Db-€42, includes tax, CC, 3rd floor, tel. 91-521-4640, fax 91-521-4649, www.hostalcontinental.com, e-mail: continental@mundivia.es, SE).

Sleeping on or near Plaza Santa Ana
(zip code: 28012 unless otherwise noted)

The Plaza Santa Ana area has small, cheap places mixed in with fancy hotels. While the neighborhood is noisy at night, it has a rough but charming ambience, with colorful bars and a central location (3 min from Puerta del Sol's "Tío Pepe" sign; walk down Calle San Jerónimo and turn right on Príncipe; Metro: Sol). To locate hotels, see map on page 888.

Cheap: Because of the following three places, I list no Madrid youth hostels. At these cheap hotels, fluent Spanish is spoken, bathrooms are down the hall, and there's no heat during winter.

Hopeless romantics might enjoy playing corkscrew around the rickety cut-glass elevator to the very simple yet homey **Pensión La Valenciana**'s seven old and funky rooms with springy beds. All rooms have balconies; three of them overlook the square (S-€13, D-€24, includes tax, no CC, Príncipe 27, lots of stairs, 4th floor, right on Plaza Santa Ana next to the theater with flags, tel. 91-429-6317, Esperanza NSE).

For super-cheap beds in a dingy time warp, consider **Hostal Lucense** (13 rooms, S-€15-18, D-€18-21, Db-€30-36, €1.20 per shower, no CC, Nuñez de Arce 15, tel. 91-522-4888, run by Sr. and Sra. Muñoz, both interesting characters, Sr. SE) and **Casa Huéspedes Poza** (14 rooms, same prices, street noise, and owners—but Sr. does the cleaning, at Nuñez de Arce 9, tel. 91-522-4871).

Moderate: Hostal R. Veracruz II, between Plaza Santa Ana and Puerta del Sol, rents 22 decent, quiet rooms (Sb-€34, Db-€46, Tb-€65, no breakfast, CC, elevator, air con, Victoria 1, 3rd floor, tel. 91-522-7635, fax 91-522-6749, NSE).

Splurges: Suite Prado, two blocks toward the Prado from Plaza Santa Ana, is a good value, offering 18 sprawling, elegant, air-conditioned suites with a modern yet homey feel (Db suite-€150, sitting rooms and refrigerators, some have kitchens, extra adult-€24, extra kid free, breakfast at café next door-€3.60, CC, elevator, Manuel Fernandez y Gonzalez 10, at intersection with

Venture de la Vega, 28014 Madrid, tel. 91-420-2318, fax 91-420-0559, www.suiteprado.com, hotel@suiteprado.com, Anna SE). Across the street, **Residencia Hostal Lisboa** is also a good value (24 rooms, Sb-€39, Db-€50, Tb-€63, CC, air con, elevator, Ventura de la Vega 17, tel. 91-429-4676, fax 91-429-9894, e-mail: hostallisboa@inves.es).

To be on Plaza Santa Ana and spend in a day what others spend in a week, luxuriate in **Hotel Reina Victoria**. This is where out-of-town bullfighters stay before a fight (201 rooms, Sb-€180, Db-€220, prices generally discounted to "weekend rate" of Db-€120 on Fri, Sat, Sun in summer, and all of July, when this becomes a fine deal, prices don't include tax, breakfast-€18, CC, Plaza Santa Ana 14, tel. 91-531-4500, fax 91-522-0307, e-mail: reinavictoria@trypnet.com). For a royal, air-conditioned breather, spit out your gum, step into its lobby, grab a sofa, and watch the bellboys push the beggars back out the revolving doors.

Sleeping Near the Prado
(zip code: 28014)

Two fine places are at #34 Cervantes (Metro: Anton Martin). **Hostal Gonzalo**—with 15 spotless, comfortable rooms, well-run by friendly and helpful Javier—is deservedly in all the guidebooks. Reserve in advance (Sb-€33, Db-€39, Tb-€51, CC, elevator, 3rd floor, tel. 91-429-2714, fax 91-420-2007). Downstairs, the nearly-as-polished **Hostal Cervantes,** also with 15 rooms, is also good (Sb-€36, Db-€48, Tb-€60, CC, 2nd floor, tel. 91-429-8365, tel. & fax 91-429-2745, www.hostal-cervantes.com).

Eating in Madrid

In Spain, only Barcelona rivals Madrid for taste-bud thrills. You have three dining choices: an atmospheric sit-down meal in a well-chosen restaurant, an unmemorable basic sit-down meal, or a stand-up meal of tapas in a bar or (more likely) in several bars. Many restaurants are closed in August (especially through the last half).

Eating near Puerta del Sol

Restaurante Puerto Rico has good meals, great prices, and few tourists (Mon–Sat 13:00–16:30, 20:30–24:00, closed Sun, Chinchilla 2, between Puerta del Sol and Gran Vía, tel. 91-532-2040).

Hotel Europa Cafeteria is a fun, high-energy scene with a mile-long bar, traditionally clad waiters, great people-watching, local cuisine, and super prices (daily 07:30–24:00, next to Hotel Europa, 50 meters off Puerta del Sol at Calle del Carmen 4, tel. 91-521-2900). **Corte Inglés'** seventh-floor cafeteria is popular with locals (Mon–Sat 10:00–11:30, 13:00–16:15, 17:30–20:00, has nonsmoking section).

La Casa de las Torrijas, looking much like it did on opening day in 1907, serves cheap home-cooked lunch specials, tapas, and good wine. Avoid the *callos* (tripe). Their dessert specialty is *torrijas*, which is like cinammon French toast, Spanish-style. Try it with *mistela* (sweet wine). Many restaurants in Madrid serve *torrijas* around Easter as a traditional treat, but you can try it here any time of year (Mon–Sat 10:00–16:00, 18:00–23:30, closed Sun and Aug, good pictures of early-20th-century Madrid, a block off Puerta del Sol at Calle Paz 4, tel. 91-532-1473).

Vegetarian: **Artemisia II** is a hit with vegetarians who like good, healthy food in a smoke-free room (great €8.50 3-course lunch menu, daily 13:30–16:00, 21:00–24:00, CC, 2 blocks north of Puerta Sol at Tres Cruces 4, a few steps off Plaza Carmen, tel. 91-521-8721). **Artemisia I** is like its sister (same hours, 4 blocks east of Puerta Sol at Ventura de la Vega 4 off San Jerónimo, tel. 91-429-5092).

Eating on or near Plaza Mayor

Many Americans are drawn to Hemingway's favorite, **Sobrino del Botín** (daily 13:00–16:00, 20:00–24:00, CC, Cuchilleros 17, a block downhill from Plaza Mayor, tel. 91-366-4217). It's touristy, pricey (€24–30 average), and the last place he'd go now, but still, people love it and the food is excellent. If phoning to make a reservation, choose between the downstairs (for dark, medieval-cellar ambience) or upstairs (for a still-traditional but airier and lighter elegance). While this restaurant boasts it's the oldest in the world (dating from 1725), a nearby restaurant brags, "Hemingway never ate here."

Restaurante Los Galayos is less touristy and plenty *tipico* with good local cuisine (daily 09:30–24:00, lunch specials, lunch from 13:00, dinner from 20:30, arrive early or make a reservation, 30 meters off Plaza Mayor at Botoneras 5, tel. 91-366-3028). For many, dinner right on the square at a sidewalk café is worth the premium (consider Cerveceria Pulpito, southwest corner of the square at #10).

La Torre del Oro Bar Andalu on Plaza Mayor has soul. Die-hard bullfight aficionados hate the gimmicky Bull Bar listed under "Tapas," below. Here the walls are lined with grisly bull-fight photos from annual photo competitions. Read the gory description above in the Introductory Walk. Have a drink but be careful not to let the aggressive staff bully you into high-priced tapas you don't want (daily 11:00–16:00, 18:00–24:00, closed Jan, Plaza Mayor 26, tel. 91-366-5016).

Plaza Mayor is famous for its *bocadillos calamares*. For a cheap and tasty squid-ring sandwich, line up at **Casa Rua** at Plaza Mayor's northwest corner, a few steps up Calle Ciudad Rodrigo (daily 09:00–23:00). Hanging up behind the bar is a photo/ad of Plaza Mayor from the 1950s, when the square contained a park.

Eating near the Sights

Near the Royal Palace: For a fine meal with no tourists and locals who appreciate good local-style cooking, try **Casa Ciriaco** (€18 meals, Thu–Tue 13:30–16:00, 20:30–24:00, closed Wed and Aug, halfway between Puerta del Sol and Royal Palace at Calle Mayor 84, tel. 91-548-0620). It was from this building in 1906 that an anarchist threw a bomb at the royal couple on their wedding day (for details, see "Introductory Walk," above). Photos of the carnage are on the wall in the dining room.

Near the Prado: Each of the big-three art museums has a decent cafeteria. The following two cafés are near the Prado. **La Plateria** is a hardworking little café/wine bar with a good menu for tapas, light meals, and hearty salads. Its tables spill onto the leafy little Plaza de Platarias de Matinez (daily 08:00–24:00, directly across busy boulevard Paseo del Prado from Atocha end of Prado, tel. 91-429-1722). Good-looking, young tour guides eat cheap and filling salads at **VIPS**, a bright, popular chain restaurant engulfed in a big bookstore (daily 09:00–24:00, across Paseo del Prado boulevard from northern end of Prado in Galeria del Prado under Palace Hotel).

Fast Food and Picnics

Fast Food: For an easy, light, cheap meal, try **Rodilla**—a popular sandwich chain on the northeast corner of Puerta del Sol at #13 (Mon–Fri 09:30–23:00, opens on Sat at 10:00, Sun at 11:00). **Pans & Company,** with shops throughout Madrid and Spain, offers healthy, tasty sandwiches and chef's salads (daily 09:00–24:00, on Puerta del Sol, Plaza Callão, Gran Vía 30, and many more).

Picnics: The department store **El Corte Inglés** has a well-stocked **deli** downstairs (Mon–Sat 10:00–22:00, closed Sun). A perfect place to assemble a cheap picnic is downtown Madrid's neighborhood market, **Mercado de San Miguel**. How about breakfast surrounded by early-morning shoppers in the market's café? (Mon–Fri 09:00–14:30, 17:15–20:15, Sat 09:00–14:30, closed Sun; to reach the market from Plaza Mayor, face the colorfully painted building and exit from the upper left-hand corner.)

Churros con Chocolate

If you like hash browns and eggs in American greasy-spoon joints, you must try the Spanish equivalent: Greasy *churros* dipped in thick, hot chocolate. **Bar Valladolid** is a good bet (daily 07:00–22:30, best in the morning, 2 blocks off Tío Pepe end of Puerta del Sol, south on Espoz y Mina, turn right on Calle de Cadiz). With luck, the *churros* machine in the back will be cooking. Notice the expressive WC signs.

The classy **Chocolatería San Ginés** is much loved by locals for its *churros* and chocolate (Tue–Sun 19:00–7:00, closed Mon). While empty before midnight, it's packed with the disco crowd in the wee hours; the popular Joy disco is next door. Dunk your *churros* into the pudding-like hot chocolate, as locals have done here for over 100 years (from Puerta del Sol, take Calle Arenal 2 blocks west, turn left on book-lined Pasadizo de San Ginés, you'll see the café—it's at #5, tel. 93-365-6546).

Tapas: The Madrid Pub-Crawl Dinner

For maximum fun, people, and atmosphere, go mobile and do the "tapa tango," a local tradition of going from one bar to the next, munching, drinking, and socializing. Tapas are the toothpick appetizers, salads, and deep-fried foods served in most bars. Madrid is Spain's tapa capital—tapas just don't get any better. Grab a toothpick and stab something strange—but establish the prices first. Some items are very pricey, and most bars push larger *raciónes* rather than smaller tapas. *Un pincho* is a bite-sized serving (not always available), *una tapa* is a snack, and *una ración* is half a meal. *Un bocadillo* is a tapa on bread. A *caña* (can-yah) is a small glass of draft beer. A *chato* is a small glass of house wine.

Prowl the area between Puerta del Sol and Plaza Santa Ana. There's no ideal route, but the little streets (in this book's map) between Puerta del Sol, San Jerónimo, and Plaza Santa Ana hold tasty surprises. Nearby, the street Jesus de Medinaceli is also lined with popular tapas bars. Below is a five-stop tapa crawl. These places are good, but don't be blind to making discoveries on your own. The action is better after 20:00.

1. From Puerta del Sol, walk east a block down Carrera de San Jerónimo to the corner of Victoria Street. Across from Museo del Jamón, you'll find **La Tourina Cervecería**, a bullfighters' Planet Hollywood (daily 08:00–24:00). Wander among trophies and historic photographs. Each stuffed bull's head is named, along with its farm, awards, and who killed him. Among the photos study the first post: It's Che Guevara, Orson Welles, and Salvador Dalí all enjoying a good fight. Around the corner, the Babe Ruth of bullfighters, El Cordobes, lies wounded in bed. The photo below shows him in action. Kick off your pub crawl with a drink here. If inspired, you could go for the *rabo de toro* (bull-tail stew, €9.60). Across the street at San Jerónimo 5 is...

2. Museo del Jamón (Museum of Ham), tastefully decorated— unless you're a pig. This frenetic, cheap, stand-up bar is an assembly line of fast and simple *bocadillos* and *raciónes*. Options are shown in photographs with prices. For a small sandwich, ask for a *chiquito* (€0.60, unadvertised). The pricey Jamón Iberico—from pigs who led stress-free lives in acorn valley—is best. Just point and eat (daily 09:00–24:00, sit-down restaurant upstairs). Next, forage halfway up Calle Victoria (passing the Irish-type pub La Fontana de Oro) to the tiny...

3. La Casa del Abuelo, for seafood-lovers who savor sizzling

Plaza Santa Ana Area

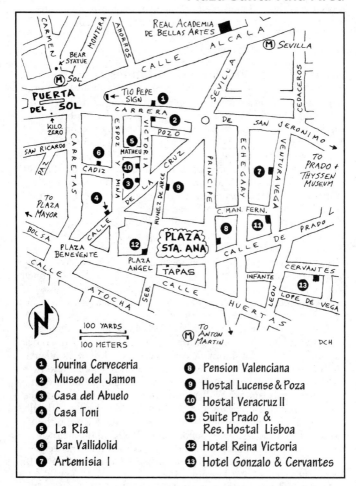

1. Tourina Cerveceria
2. Museo del Jamon
3. Casa del Abuelo
4. Casa Toni
5. La Ria
6. Bar Vallidolid
7. Artemisia I
8. Pension Valenciana
9. Hostal Lucense & Poza
10. Hostal Veracruz II
11. Suite Prado & Res. Hostal Lisboa
12. Hotel Reina Victoria
13. Hotel Gonzalo & Cervantes

plates of tasty little *gambas* (shrimp) and *langostinos* (prawns). Try *gambas a la plancha* (grilled shrimp, €3.60), *gambas al ajillo* (ahh-hheee-yoh, shrimp version of escargot, cooked in oil and garlic and ideal for bread dipping—€5), and a €1 glass of red wine (daily 11:30–15:30, 18:30–23:30, Calle Victoria 12). Continue uphill and around the corner to...

4. Casa Toni, for refreshing bowls of gazpacho—the popular cold tomato-and-garlic soup (€1.50). Their specialty is *berenjena*, deep-fried slices of eggplant (€3.60, daily 11:30–16:00, 18:00–23:30, closed July, Calle Cruz 14). Backtrack halfway down Calle Victoria and turn left, walking through an alley littered with tourist-filled dining tables to...

5. La Ria, a tapas bar that sells plates of 10 mussels (*mejillones*). Slurp out the meat, scoop the juice with the shells, and toss the shells on the floor as you smack your lips—don't look down (daily 11:30–15:30, 19:30–23:30, Pasaje Matheu 5). You can get your *mejillones* mild *con limone* or spicy—*picante* (€3). Wash them down with the crude, dry, white Ribeiro wine from Galicia—served in a ceramic bowl to disguise its lack of clarity. The place is draped in mussels. Notice the photo showing the floor filled with litter— a reminder that mussel bars, while lonely these days, have seen better times. In the 1970s they sold 14 tons a month. Now—with other, more trendy evening activities entertaining the cruising youth—it takes a year to sell 14 tons. Next door, **Las Bravas** brags that its sauce (ladled on boiled potatoes) is so good it's patented (daily 12:00–16:00, 19:30–24:00).

If you're hungry for more, head for Plaza Santa Ana. The south side of the square is lined with trendy bars that offer good tapas, drinks, and a classic setting right on the square. Consider **Naturbeer** (brews its own beers—like our microbrews), **Cervece- ria de Santa Ana** (tasty tapas with a beer-hall atmosphere), **La Moderna** (wine, pâté, and cheese plates), and others.

Transportation Connections—Madrid

By train to: Toledo (9/day, 1 hr, from Madrid's Atocha station, if daytripping there's a direct Madrid–Toledo express at 08:34 or 09:44 and a Toledo–Madrid express at 18:56), **Segovia** (9/day, 2 hrs, both Chamartin and Atocha stations), **Avila** (6/day, 90 min, from Chamartin and Atocha), **Salamanca** (4/day, 2.5 hrs, from Chamartin), **Barcelona** (7/day, 8 hrs, mostly from Chamartin, 2 overnight), **Granada** (2/day, 6–9 hrs, including an overnight train, from Chamartin), **Sevilla** (15/day, 2.5 hrs by AVE, 3.5 hrs by Talgo, from Atocha), **Córdoba** (16 AVE trains/day, 2 hrs, from Atocha), **Málaga** (5/day, 4 hrs, from Atocha), **Lisbon** (1/day, 10 hrs, pricey overnight Hotel Train from Chamartin), **Paris** (4/day, 12–16 hrs, 1 direct overnight—a pricey Hotel Train, from Cha- martin). Train info: tel. 90-224-0202.

Madrid's Barajas Airport

Sixteen kilometers east of downtown, Madrid's modern airport has three terminals. You'll likely land at Terminal 1, which has a helpful English-speaking TI (marked "Oficina de Información Turistica," Mon–Fri 08:00–20:00, Sat 09:00–13:00, closed Sun, tel. 91-305- 8656); an ATM (part of the BBVA bank) far busier than the lonely American Express window; a 24-hour exchange office (plus shorter- hour exchange offices); a flight information office (marked simply

"Information" in airport lobby, open 24 hrs/day, tel. 902-353-570); a post office window; a pharmacy; lots of phones (buy a phone card from the machine near the phones); a few scattered Internet terminals (small fee); eateries; a RENFE office (where you can get train info and buy train tickets; daily 08:00–21:00, tel. 91-305-8544); and on-the-spot car-rental agencies (see above). The three terminals are connected by long indoor walkways; it's about an eight-minute walk between terminals (the Metro is in Terminal 2).

Iberia is Spain's airline, connecting many cities in Spain as well as international destinations (Velázquez 130, phone answered 24 hrs/day, tel. 90-240-0500, www.iberia.com).

Getting between the airport and downtown: By public transport, consider an affordable, efficient **airport bus/taxi combination**. Take the airport bus (#89, usually blue) from the airport to Madrid's Plaza Colón (€2.40, 4/hr, 20–30 min, leaves Madrid 04:30–24:00, leaves airport 05:15–02:00; stops at both Terminals 1 and 2; at the airport the bus stop is outside Terminal 1's arrivals door—cross the street filled with taxis to reach stop marked "Bus" on median strip; at Plaza Colón the stop is underground). Then, to reach your hotel from Plaza Colón, you can take a taxi (insist on meter, ride to hotel should be far less than €6, to avoid supplement charge for rides from a bus station, it's a little cheaper to go upstairs and flag down a taxi). Or from Plaza Colón, you can take the subway (to get to the subway from the underground bus stop, walk up the stairs and face the blue "URBIS" sign high on a building—the subway stop, M. Serrano, is 50 meters to your right; it takes two transfers to reach Puerta del Sol).

At the airport, ignore bus #101, a holdover from the time when the airport didn't have a Metro stop (it runs to Canillejas Metro stop on Madrid's outskirts).

You can take the **Metro** all the way between the airport and downtown. The airport's futuristic Aeropuerto Metro stop in Terminal 2 provides a cheap but time-consuming way into town (€1, or get a shareable 10-pack for €4.50; takes 45 min with 2 transfers; at airport, access Metro at check-in level; from Terminal 1 arrivals level, stand with your back to baggage claim, then go to your far right, up the stairs, and follow red-and-blue diamond-shaped Metro diamond signs to Metro station, 8-minute walk; to get to Puerta del Sol from the airport, transfer at Mar de Cristal to brown line #4—direction Arguelles, then transfer at Goya to red line #3—direction Cuatro Caminos).

For a taxi to or from the airport, allow €18 (€2.40 airport supplement is legal). Cabbies routinely try to get €30—a rip-off. At the airport, get a rough idea of the price before you hop in. Approach an idle cabbie (who's not in a hurry) who is waiting farther back in the taxi lineup. Ask "*¿Cuanto cuesta a Madrid, más o menos?*" ("How much is it to Madrid, more or less?")

TOLEDO

An hour south of Madrid, Toledo teems with tourists, souvenirs, and great art by day, delicious roast suckling pig, echoes of El Greco, and medieval magic by night. Incredibly well-preserved and full of cultural wonder, the entire city has been declared a national monument.

Spain's historic capital is 2,000 years of tangled history—Roman, Visigothic, Moorish, and Christian—crowded onto a high, rocky perch protected on three sides by the Tejo River. It's so well-preserved that the Spanish government has forbidden any modern exteriors. The rich mix of Jewish, Moorish, and Christian heritages makes it one of Europe's art capitals.

Toledo was a Visigothic capital back in 554 and—after a period of Moorish rule—Spain's political capital until 1561, when it reached its natural limits of growth as defined by the Tejo River Gorge. Though the king moved to more spacious Madrid, Toledo remains the historic, artistic, and spiritual center of Spain. In spite of tremendous tourist crowds, Toledo just sits on its history and remains much as it was when Europe's most powerful king and El Greco each called it home.

Planning Your Time

To properly see Toledo's museums (great El Greco), cathedral (best in Spain), and medieval atmosphere (best after dark), you'll need two nights and a day. Note that a few sights are closed Monday.

Toledo is just 60 minutes away from Madrid by bus (2/hr), train (9/day), or taxi (about €60 one-way from Puerto del Sol—negotiate the ride without a meter). A car is useless in Toledo. See the town outside of car-rental time (pick up or drop your car here).

Toledo

200 YARDS
200 METERS

1 PLAZA ZOCODOVER

2 HOTEL SOL

3 HOSTAL DEL CARDENAL

4 HOTEL SANTA ISABEL

5 HOTEL PINTOR EL GRECO

6 TO HOSTAL GAVILANES II,
HOSTAL MADRID &
HOTEL MARIA CRISTINA

7 TO YOUTH HOSTEL
SAN SERVANDO

8 TO PARADOR

9 TO HOTEL LA ALMARAZA

10 CASA AURELIO I

11 CASA AURELIO II & III
ON SINAGOGA STREET

12 REST. - MESON PALACIOS

13 REST. LOPEZ DE TOLEDO

14 REST. LA PERDIZ

15 BAR CERVECERIA
GAMBRINUS

16 TAVERNA DE AMBOADES

17 ZAMORANO KNIVES

18 TICKETS & CATHEDRAL
ENTRY

Orientation

Lassoed into a tight tangle of streets by the sharp bend of the
Tejo River (called the Tagus where it hits the Atlantic, in Lisbon),
Toledo has Spain's most confusing medieval street plan. But it's a
small town of 65,000, major sights are well-signposted, and most
locals will politely point you in the right direction.

Look at the map and take a mental orientation walk past Toledo's main sights. Starting in the central Plaza Zocódover, go southwest along the Calle de Comércio. After passing the cathedral on your left, follow the signs to Santo Tomé and the cluster of other sights. The visitor's city lies basically along one small but central street—and most tourists never stray from this axis. Make a point to get lost. It's a small town, bounded on three sides by the river. When it's time to get somewhere, I pull out the map or ask, "*¿Dónde está Plaza Zocódover?*"

Tourist Information

Toledo has two TIs. The TI that covers Toledo as well as the region is in a small, free-standing brick building just outside the Bisagra Gate, where those arriving by train or bus enter the old town (Mon–Fri 09:00–18:00, Sat 09:00–19:00, Sun 09:00–15:00, tel. 92-522-0843). Historians: The Bisagra Gate is the last surviving gate of the 10th-century fortifications.

The second TI, which covers solely Toledo, is in front of the cathedral on Plaza Ayuntamiento (Mon 10:30–14:30, Tue–Sun 10:30–14:30, 16:30–19:00, tel. 92-525-4030). Consider the readable local guidebook, *Toledo, Its Art and Its History* (small version for €5.50, sold all over town). It explains all of the sights (which generally provide no on-site information) and gives you a photo to point at and say, "*¿Dónde está...?*"

Arrival in Toledo

"Arriving" in Toledo means getting uphill to Plaza Zocódover. From the train station, that's a 20-minute hike, taxi ride (€3), or easy bus ride (#5 or #6, €0.70, pay on bus, confirm by asking, "*Para Plaza Zocódover?*"). You can stow extra baggage in the station's lockers (buy tokens at ticket booth). Consider buying a city map at the kiosk; it's better than the free one at the TI. If you're walking, turn right as you leave the station, cross the bridge, pass the bus station, go straight through the roundabout, and continue uphill to the TI and Bisagra Gate.

If you arrive by bus, go upstairs to the station lobby. You'll find lockers and a small bus information office—near the lockers and opposite the cafeteria. Confirm your departure time (probably every half hour on the hour if you're returning to Madrid). When you buy your ticket—which you can do as late as a few minutes before you leave—specify you'd like a *directo* bus; the *ruta* trip takes longer (for Madrid, 60 vs. 75 min). From the bus station, Plaza Zocódover is a 15-minute walk (see directions from train station, above), a taxi ride (€2.40), or a short bus ride (catch #5 downstairs, underneath the lobby, €0.70, pay driver).

A new series of escalators runs near Bisagra Gate, giving you a free ride up, up, up into town. You'll end up far from Plaza

Zocódover, but just start with the synagogues, continue to the cathedral, and end at Plaza Zocódover. It's great for drivers, who can park in the lot across the street from the base of the escalator (or park in Garage Alcázar lot opposite Alcázar in old town—€1.20/hr, €12/day).

Getting around Toledo

This small city is walkable, though surprisingly hilly. For great city views, consider hopping on the cheesy Tren Imperial Tourist Tram. Crass as it feels, you get a 50-minute putt-putt through Toledo and around the Tagus River Gorge. Warning: It's a bumpy ride and the windows aren't crystal clear (€3.60, daily from 11:00, leaves Plaza Zocódover on the hour, tape-recorded English/Spanish commentary, no photo stops but goes slow; for the best views of Toledo across the gorge, sit on right side, not behind driver; tel. 925-142-274).

Sights—Toledo

▲▲▲**Cathedral**—Holy Toledo! Spain's leading Catholic city has a magnificent cathedral. Shoehorned into the old center, its exterior is hard to appreciate. But the interior is so lofty, rich, and vast that it grabs you by the vocal cords, and all you can do is whisper, "Wow."

Cost and Hours: While the basic cathedral is free, seeing the great art—located in four separate places within the cathedral (the choir, chapter house, sacristy, and treasury)—requires an €4.80 ticket (well worthwhile, sold in Tienda la Catedral shop opposite church entrance, shop open Mon–Sat 10:30–18:30, Sun 14:00–18:00; also rents audioguides for €2.70). The strict dress-code sign covers even your attitude: no shorts, no tank tops, no slouching.

The cathedral has shorter hours (daily 10:30–12:00, 16:00–18:00) than the four sights (10:30–18:00). Even though the cathedral closes from 12:00 to 16:00, if you have a ticket you can get in and tour the cathedral as well, with fewer crowds. (Note that the cloister is closed to everyone from 13:00–15:30.)

Self-guided Tour: Holy redwood forest, Batman! Wander among the pillars. Sit under one and imagine when the light bulbs were candles and the tourists were pilgrims—before the "No Photo" signs, when every window provided spiritual as well as physical light. The cathedral is primarily Gothic, but since it took more than 200 years to build (1226–1493), you'll see a mix of styles—Gothic, Renaissance, and Baroque. Enjoy the elaborate wrought-iron work, lavish wood carvings, window after colorful window of 500-year-old stained glass, and a sacristy with a collection of paintings that would put any museum on the map.

This confusing collage of great Spanish art deserves a guided

Toledo Cathedral

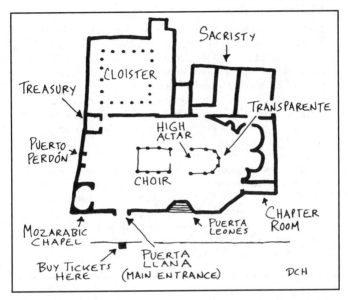

TREASURY

CLOISTER

SACRISTY

TRANSPARENTE

PUERTO PERDÓN

HIGH ALTAR

CHOIR

CHAPTER ROOM

MOZARABIC CHAPEL

PUERTA LEONES

BUY TICKETS HERE

PUERTA LLANA (MAIN ENTRANCE)

DCH

tour. Hire a private guide, freeload on a tour (they come by every few minutes during peak season), or follow this quick tour. Here's a framework for your visit:

First, walk to the high altar to marvel through the iron grill at one of the most stunning altars in Spain. Real gold on pine wood, by Flemish, French, and local artists, it's one of the country's best pieces of Gothic art. About-face...

The **choir**, facing the high altar, is famous for its fine carving and requires a piece of your four-part ticket. The lower wooden stalls are decorated with scenes from the Christian victory over the Muslims at Granada. The upper stalls feature Old Testament figures carved out of alabaster. The iron grill of the choir is notable for the dedication of the man who built it. Domingo de Cespedes, a Toledo ironworker, accepted the commission to build the grill for 6,000 ducats. The project, which took from 1541 to 1548, was far more costly than he anticipated. The medieval Church didn't accept cost overruns, so, to finish it, he sold everything he owned and went into debt. He died a poor—but honorable—man.

Face the altar and go around it to your right. The **chapter house** (*sala capitular*), which takes a chunk of your ticket, has a rich gilded ceiling, interesting Bible-storytelling frescoes, and a pictorial review of 1,900 years of Toledo archbishops. The upper row of portraits was not painted from life; the lower portraits

El Greco's Art

Born on Crete and trained in Venice, Domenikos Theoto-copoulos (tongue-tied friends just called him "The Greek") came to Spain to get a job decorating El Escorial. He failed there but succeeded in Toledo, where he spent the last 37 years of his life. He mixed all three regional influences into his palette. From his Greek homeland, he absorbed the solemn, abstract style of icons. In Venice he learned the bold use of color and dramatic style of the later Renaissance. These styles were then fused in the fires of fanatic Spanish-Catholic devotion.

Not bound by the realism so important to his 16th-century contemporaries, El Greco painted dramatic visions of striking colors and figures—bodies unnatural and elongated as though stretched between heaven and earth. He painted souls, not faces. His work is on display at nearly every sight in Toledo. Thoroughly modern in its disregard of realism, it seems as fresh as contemporary art.

were, and therefore hold more historic and artistic interest. Imagine sitting down to church business surrounded by all this tradition and theology. As you leave, notice the iron-pumping cupids carved into the panels lining the walls.

The *transparente*, behind the high altar, is a unique feature of the cathedral. In the 1700s a hole was cut into the ceiling to let a sunbeam brighten the Mass. Melding this big hole into the Gothic church presented a challenge that resulted in a Baroque masterpiece. Gape up at this riot of angels doing flip-flops, babies breathing thin air, bottoms of feet, and gilded sunbursts. I like it, as did, I guess, the long-dead cardinal whose faded red hat hangs from the edge of the hole. (A perk that only cardinals enjoy is choosing the place in the cathedral in which their hat will hang until it rots.)

The cathedral's **sacristy** has 20 El Grecos and masterpieces by Goya, Titian, Rubens, Velázquez, Caravaggio, and Bellini (there goes another part of your ticket). First, look at the fine perspective work on the ceiling. Then walk to the most important painting in the collection (end of room). El Greco's first masterpiece, from 1579, *The Spoliation* (a.k.a. *The Denuding of Christ*) hangs above the marble altar. This was one of El Greco's first Toledo commissions after arriving from Venice. Notice the parallel contrasts: Jesus' delicate hand before a flaming red tunic and Jesus' noble face among the sinister mob. On the right is a rare religious painting by Goya, the *Betrayal of Christ*, which shows

Judas preparing to kiss Jesus, identifying him to the Roman soldiers. Enjoy the many other El Grecos. Find the small but lifelike 17th-century carving of St. Francis by Pedro de Mena (to your right as you entered the door).

The **treasury** (*tesoro*) has plenty to see. The highlight is the three-meter-high, 430-pound monstrance—the tower designed to hold the Holy Communion bread (the Host) during the festival of Corpus Christi (body of Christ) as it parades through the city. Built in 1517 by a man named Arfe, it's made of 5,000 individual pieces held together by 12,500 screws. There are diamonds, emeralds, rubies, and 400 pounds of gold-plated silver. The inner part is 35 pounds of solid gold. Yeow. The base is a later addition from the Baroque period. Traditionally, it's thought that much of this gold and silver arrived on Columbus' first load home. To the right of the monstrance find the fancy sword of Franco. To the right of that is a gift from St. Louis, the king of France—a 700-year-old Bible printed and beautifully illustrated by French monks. Imagine the exquisite experience of reading this with its lavish illustrations through medieval eyes. The finely painted small crucifix on the opposite side—by the great Gothic Florentine painter Fra Angelico—depicts Jesus alive on the back and dead on the front. This was a gift from Mussolini to Franco. Hmmm. There's even a gift in this room from Toledo's sister city, Toledo, Ohio.

If you're at the cathedral between 09:30 and 09:45, you can peek into the otherwise-locked **Mozarabic Chapel** (Capilla Mozarabe). The Visigothic Mass, the oldest surviving Christian ritual in Western Europe, starts at 09:45 (not sung on Sun). You're welcome to partake in this stirring example of peaceful coexistence of faiths—but once the door closes, you're a Visigoth for 30 minutes.

▲▲**Santa Cruz Museum**—Most of this museum will be closed for renovation much of 2002. During renovation, the museum's cloister and staircase will be open and free. The building's Plateresque facade is worth seeing anytime.

This great Renaissance building was an orphanage, built from money left by the humanist and diplomat Cardinal Mendoza when he died in 1495. The cardinal, confirmed as Chancellor of Castile by Queen Isabel, was so influential he was called the third king. The building is in the form of a Greek cross under a Moorish dome. The arms of the building—formerly wards—are filled with 16th-century art, tapestries, furniture, armor, and documents. It's a stately, classical, music-filled setting with a cruel lack of English information.

Fifteen El Grecos gather in one wing upstairs, including the impressive *Assumption of Mary*—a spiritual poem on canvas (notice old Toledo on the bottom). Painted one year before El Greco's death in 1614, this is considered the culmination of his artistic development.

An enormous blue banner hangs like a long, skinny tooth opposite the entry. This flew from the flagship of Don Juan of Austria and recalls the pivotal naval victory over the Muslims at the Battle of Lepanto in 1571. Lepanto was a key victory in the centuries-long Muslim threat to Christian Europe (when museum opens, cost will be €1.20, Mon 10:00–18:30, Tue–Sat 10:00–18:30, Sun 10:00–14:00, just off Plaza Zocódover, go through arch, Cervantes 3).

▲**Alcázar**—This huge former imperial residence—built on the site of Roman, Visagothic, and Moorish fortresses—dominates the Toledo skyline. The Alcázar became a kind of right-wing Alamo during Spain's civil war when a force of Franco's Nationalists (and hundreds of hostages) were besieged for two months. Finally, after many fierce but futile Republican attacks, Franco sent in an army that took Toledo and freed the Alcázar. The place was rebuilt and glorified under Franco. Today you can see its civil war exhibits, giving you an interesting—and right-wing—look at the horrors of Spain's recent past (€1.20, Tue–Sun 09:30–14:30, closed Mon).

Sights—Southwest Toledo

▲**Santo Tomé**—A simple chapel holds El Greco's most-loved painting. *The Burial of the Count of Orgaz* couples heaven and earth in a way only The Greek could. It feels so right to see a painting left where the artist put it 400 years ago. Take this slow. Stay a while—let it perform. It's 1323. You're at the burial of the good count. After a pious and generous life, he left his estate to the Church. Saints Augustine and Steven have even come down for the burial—to usher him directly to heaven. "Such is the reward for those who serve God and his saints."

More than 250 years later, in 1586, a priest hired El Greco to make a painting of the burial to hang over the count's tomb. The painting has two halves divided by a serene—but not sad—line of noble faces. The physical world ends with the line of nobles. Above them a spiritual wind blows as colors change and shapes stretch. Notice the angel, robe caught up in that wind, "birthing" the soul of the count through the neck of a celestial womb into Heaven—the soul abandoning the physical body to join Christ the Judge. Mary and John the Baptist both intervene on behalf of the arriving soul. Each face is a detailed portrait. El Greco himself (eyeballing you, 7th figure in from the left) is the only one not involved in the burial. The boy in the foreground is El Greco's son (€1.20, daily 10:00–18:45, until 17:45 off-season, tel. 92-525-6098).

▲**Museo El Greco**—You'll see about 20 El Greco paintings, including his masterful *View of Toledo* and portraits of the Apostles (€1.20, free Sat afternoon from 14:30 and all day Sun; Tue–Sat 10:00–14:00, 16:00–17:45, Sun 10:00–13:45, closed Mon,

Samuel Levi 3). Usually this museum costs twice as much and includes a look at the interior of a traditionally furnished Renaissance home, often wrongly called El Greco's House. The house is undergoing restoration, which may be completed in 2002. Once the house is ready, you'll have to pay more, but you'll see more. Without the house, the museum is not worth it for most, because overall, you'll see better El Grecos elsewhere in Toledo.

Sinagoga del Transito (Museo Sefardi)—Built in 1366, this is the best surviving slice of Toledo's Jewish past. The museum displays Jewish artifacts, including costumes, menorahs, and books, regrettably without a word of English description (€2.40, free Sat afternoon from 14:30 and all day Sun; Tue–Sat 10:00–14:00, 16:00–17:45, Sun 10:00–13:45, closed Mon, near Museo El Greco, with same price and hours, no photos allowed, on Calle de los Reyes Católicos).

Sinagoga de Santa Maria Blanca—This synagogue-turned-church with Moorish arches is an eclectic but harmonious gem (€1.20, daily 10:00–14:00, 15:30–19:00, closes off-season at 18:00, no photos allowed, Reyes Católicos 2-4).

Museo Victorio Macho—After *mucho* El Greco, try Macho. Overlooking the gorge, this small, attractive museum—once the home and workshop of the 20th-century sculptor, Victorio Macho—offers several rooms of his work interspersed with view terraces. The highlight is *La Madre*, Macho's lifesize sculpture of a older woman sitting in a chair. But the big draw for many is the air-conditioned theater featuring a good 29-minute video on Toledo's history. You can choose a shorter nine-minute version, but why rush? (€3, Mon–Sat 10:00–19:00, Sun 10:00–15:00, cheaper for young and old, request video showing in English, Plaza de Victorio Macho 2, between the two Sinagogas listed above, tel. 92-528-4225.)

Shopping

Toledo probably sells as many souvenirs as any city in Spain. This is the place to buy medieval-looking swords, armor, maces, three-legged stools, and other nouveau antiques. It's also Spain's damascene center, where, for centuries, craftspeople have inlaid black steel with gold, silver, and copper wire.

At the workshop of English-speaking Mariano Zamorano, you can see swords and knives being made, as well as the damascene process in action. Judging by what's left of Mariano's hand, his knives are among the best (Mon–Sat 09:00–14:00, 16:00–18:00, Calle Ciudad 19, near the cathedral and Plaza Ayuntamiento, tel. 92-522-2634).

El Martes, Toledo's colorful outdoor flea market, bustles on Paseo de Marchen (near TI at Bisagra Gate) on Tuesdays from 09:00 to 14:00.

Sleeping in Toledo
(€1.10 = about $1, country code: 34)
Sleep Code: **S** = Single, **D** = Double/Twin, **T** = Triple, **Q** = Quad,
b = bathroom, **s** = shower only, **CC** = Credit Cards accepted, **no
CC** = Credit Cards not accepted, **SE** = Speaks English, **NSE** = No
English. Breakfast and the 7 percent IVA tax aren't included
unless noted. Toledo's zip code is 45001, unless otherwise noted.

Madrid daytrippers darken the sunlit cobbles, but few stay to
see Toledo's medieval moonrise. Spend the night. Spring and fall
are high season; November through March and July and August
are low. (See hotel maps on pages 892 and 901).

Sleeping near Plaza Zocódover
Hotel Residencia Imperio is well-run, offering 21 rooms with
solid air-conditioned comfort in a handy old-town location (Sb-
€26.50, Db-€39, Tb-€52, includes tax, 5 percent discount with this
book, CC, elevator, cheery café, from Calle Comercio at #38 go a
block uphill to Calle Cadenas 5, tel. 92-522-7650, fax 92-525-3183,
www.terra.es/personal/himperio, e-mail: himperio@teleline.es).

Hostal Centro rents 23 modern, clean, and comfy rooms just
around the corner (Sb-€27, Db-€39, Tb- €54, no CC, 50 meters
off Plaza Zocódover, first right off Calle Comercio at Calle Nueva
13, roof garden, tel. 92-525-7091, fax 925-257-848).

The quiet, modern **Hostal Nuevo Labrador**, with 12
clean, shiny, and spacious rooms, is a good value (Sb-€25.75,
Db-€39, Tb-€52, Qb-€60, includes tax, no breakfast, CC,
elevator, Juan Labrador 10, 45001 Toledo, tel. 92-522-2620,
fax 92-522-9399, NSE).

Hotel Maravilla is wonderfully central and convenient with
narrow halls and simple rooms (Sb-€25, Db-€40, Tb-€55, Qb-
€65, includes tax, CC, back rooms are quieter, air con, a block
behind Plaza Zocódover at Plaza de Barrio Rey 7, tel. 92-522-
8317, fax 92-522-8155, Felisa Maria SE).

Splurges: Hotel Las Conchas, a new three-star hotel,
gleams with marble and sheer pride. It's beautiful, with 35 sleek
rooms—even three ground-floor rooms for disabled travelers
(Sb-€51, Db-€69, Db with terrace-€75, breakfast-€4.50, includes tax, CC, cool elevator with phone keypad, same owners
as recommended Imperio, Juan Labrador 8, tel. 92-521-0760, fax
92-522-4271, www.lasconchas.com, e-mail: lasconchas@ctv.es).

Hotel Carlos V overlooks the cathedral midway between the
Alcázar and Plaza Zocódover. While suffering from the obligatory
stuffiness of a correct hotel, it has 69 bright, pleasant rooms (Sb-
€71, Db-€104, Tb-€140, plus tax, breakfast-€8, less off-season,
CC, air con, elevator, Plaza Horno Magdalena 3, tel. 92-522-2100,
fax 92-522-2105, SE). Ask for a room with a view of the cathedral.

Across from the Alcázar is **Hotel Alfonso VI**, a big, touristy

Toledo's Plaza Zocódover

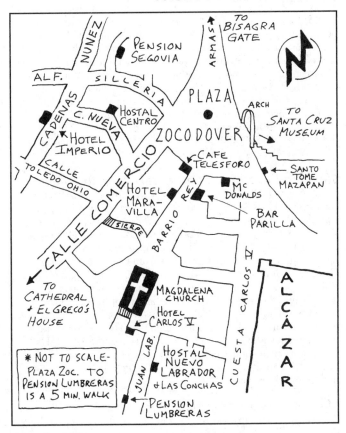

establishment with large, airy rooms, tour groups, and souvenirs for sale all over the lobby (Sb-€74, Db-€118, Tb-€157, breakfast-€8.50, plus tax, CC, air con, General Moscardo 2, 45001 Toledo, tel. 92-522-2600, fax 92-521-4458, www.hotelalfonsoVI.com, e-mail: info@hotelalfonsoVI.com). Ask for a room with a view.

Sleeping near Bisagra Gate

Hotel Sol, which has 25 plain, modern, and clean rooms, isn't exactly glamorous but is a great value on a quiet street halfway between the Bisagra Gate and Plaza Zocódover (Sb-€32.50, Db-€43.50, Tb-€56, includes tax, breakfast-€3.30, CC, air con, parking-€6.70/day, 50 meters down lane off busy main drag at Hotel Real, Azacanes 8, 45003 Toledo, tel. 92-521-3650, fax 92-521-6159, www.fedeto.et/hotelsol). Their "Hostal Sol" annex across the street is just as comfortable and a bit cheaper.

Splurge: **Hostal del Cardenal**, a 17th-century cardinal's palace built into Toledo's wall, is quiet and elegant with a cool garden and a stuffy restaurant. This poor man's parador, at the dusty old gate of Toledo, is closest to the station but below all the old-town action—however, the new escalator can levitate you into town (Sb-€45–56, Db-€72–90, Tb-€94–117, cheaper in winter, breakfast-€6.50, CC, air con, nearby parking-€11.50/day, no-fun staff likely because of the management, enter through town wall 100 meters below Puerta Bisagra, Paseo de Recaredo 24, 45004 Toledo, tel. 92-522-4900, fax 92-522-2991, www.cardenal.aser-net.es, e-mail: cardenal@asernet.es).

Sleeping beyond the Cathedral, Deep in Toledo

Hotel Santa Isabel, in a 15th-century building two blocks from the cathedral, has 23 clean, modern, and comfortable rooms and squeaky tile hallways. Avoid the few *atico* rooms that have only a skylight (Sb-€25, Db-€39, Tb-€48, includes tax, breakfast-€3.60, parking-€5.40, CC, air con, elevator; buried deep in old town so take a taxi, not the bus; drivers enter from Calle Pozo Amargo, Calle Santa Isabel 24, 45002 Toledo, tel. 92-525-3120, fax 92-525-3136, www.santa-isabel.com, e-mail: santa-isabel@arrakis.es).

Hotel Pintor El Greco, at the far end of the old town, has 33 plush and modern-feeling rooms with all the comforts, yet it's in a historic 17th-century building. A block from Santo Tomé in a Jewish Quarter garden, it's very quiet (Sb-€80, Db-€104, plus tax, includes breakfast, CC, air con, elevator, Alamillos del Transito 13, tel. 92-528-5191, fax 92-521-5819, www.hotelpintorelgreco.com).

Sleeping Cheap near Plaza Zocódover

The very central **Pensión Segovia** has eight old, rickety, and dingy rooms, with questionable beds, head-banger doorways, and memorable balconies (D-€18, T-€27, includes tax, no CC; from Plaza Zocódover go down Calle de la Sillería, take 2nd right and another right to Calle de Recoletos 2, tel. 92-521-1124).

Pensión Castilla, just around the corner, is another family-run cheapie, but has six modern and more comfortable rooms (S-€13.25, Db-€24, fans, no CC, Calle Recoletos 6, tel. 925-256-318, José SE).

Pensión Lumbreras has a tranquil courtyard and 12 simple rooms, some with views—such as room #6. Bought by the people who own the fancy Carlos V and Alfonso VI, the pension lacks the hominess and cheaper prices it used to have—the reception is now at the Carlo V around the corner. Prices may increase (S-€17.25, D-€31, Juan Labrador 9, 45001 Toledo, tel. 92-522-1571).

Sleeping Outside of Town
On the road to Madrid (near bullring): There's a conspiracy
of clean, modern, and hard-working little hotels with comfy rooms
a five-minute walk beyond Puerta Bisagra near the bullring (Plaza
de Toros, bullfights only on holidays), bus station, and TI. Drivers
will enjoy easy parking here. The downside: It's a 15-minute uphill
hike to the old-town action. Two good bets are **Hostal Gavilánes
II** (19 rooms, Sb-€33, Db-€42, Db suite-€84, Tb-€56, Qb-€69,
includes breakfast and taxes, CC, air-con, parking-€5.50/day,
Marqués de Mendigorría 14, 45003 Toledo, tel. & fax 92-521-
1628, NSE) and **Hostal Madrid** (9 rooms, Sb-€29, Db-€33,
Tb-€51, includes tax, breakfast-€2.40, CC, air-con, parking-
€6.50/day, Calle Marqués de Mendigorría 7, 45003 Toledo,
tel. 92-522-1114, fax 925-228-113, NSE). This *hostal* rents lesser
rooms from an annex across the street (Db-€36 without air-con).

Splurge: **Hotel Maria Cristina,** also next to the bullring, is
part 15th-century and all modern. This sprawling 73-room hotel
has all the comforts under a thin layer of prefab tradition (Sb-€57,
Db-€89, extra bed-€27, suites available, breakfast-€5.50, plus
tax, CC, air-con, elevator, attached restaurant, parking-€7.20/day,
Marques de Mendigorria 1, tel. 92-521-3202, fax 92-521-2650,
www.hotelesmayoral.com, SE).

Hostel: The **Albergue Juvenil San Servando** youth hostel
is lavish but cheap, with small rooms, a swimming pool, views,
and good management (€8.50 per bed if under age 26, €11 if age
26 or older, hostel membership required, no CC, in San Servando
castle 10-min walk from train station, over Puente Viejo outside
town, tel. 92-522-4554, reservations tel. 92-526-7729, NSE).

Sleeping Outside of Town with the Grand Toledo View
Toledo's **Parador Nacional Conde de Orgaz** is one of Spain's
most well-known inns, enjoying the same Toledo view El Greco
made famous from across the Tejo Canyon (76 rooms, Sb-€90,
Db-€112, Db with view-€127, breakfast-€8.50, CC, 3 windy
kilometers from town at Cerro del Emperador, 45002 Toledo,
tel. 92-522-1850, fax 92-522-5166, www.parador.es, e-mail:
toledo@parador.es, SE). Take a cab here just to see the sunset
from the terrace (€4.80 one-way).

Hotel Residencia La Almazara was the summer residence
of a 16th-century archbishop of Toledo. Fond of its classic Toledo
view, El Greco hung out here for inspiration. A lumbering old
place with cushy public rooms, 28 simple bedrooms, and a sprawling garden, it's truly in the country but just three kilometers out of
Toledo (Sb-€26, Db-€36, Db with view-€42, Tb-€48, 10 of 24
rooms have view, fans, CC, Ctra. de Piedrabuena 47, between the
3-km and 4-km markers on the Toledo-Arges road, set back off

road, marked with small sign, P.O. Box 6, Toledo 45080, tel. 92-522-3866, fax 92-525-0562, www.hotelalmazara.com, e-mail: hotelalmazara@ribernet.es).

Eating in Toledo

A day full of El Greco and the romance of Toledo after dark puts me in the mood for partridge (*perdiz*), roasted suckling pigs (*cochinillo asado*), or baby lamb (*cordero*), similarly roasted after a few weeks of mother's milk.

Toledo's three **Casa Aurelio** restaurants each offer traditional cooking, reasonable prices, and classy atmosphere (€15 menu, 13:00–16:30, 20:00–23:00, all closed Sun, each closed either Mon, Tue, or Wed, CC). All are within three blocks of the cathedral: Plaza Ayuntamiento 4 (tel. 92-522-7716), Sinagoga 6 (tel. 92-522-2097), and Sinagoga 1 (popular with Toledo's political class, has newly-opened wine cave, tel. 92-522-1392).

Restaurante-Meson Palacios serves good food at cheap prices (lunch from 13:00, dinner from 19:30, on Alfonso X, near Plaza de San Vicente). **Rincón de Eloy** is more elegant (€9 *menu*, Juan Labrador 16, near the Alcázar, tel. 92-522-9399).

Restaurante Lopez de Toledo, a fancy restaurant located in an old nobility palace, specializes in Castilian food, particularly venison and partridge (€18 meals, daily 13:30–16:00, 20:30–23:30, Calle Silleria 3, near Plaza Zocódover, tel. 92-525-4774).

For a splurge near the Santa Tomé sights, consider the classy **La Perdiz**, which offers partridge (as the restaurant's name suggests), venison, suckling pig, fish, and more (Tue–Sat 12:00–23:00, closes Sun about 16:00, closed Mon and first half of Aug, Calle Reyes Católicos 7, tel. 92-521-4658). **Bar Cerveceria Gambrinus** is a good tapas bar in the Santa Tomé area (daily 09:00–24:00, Santa Tomé 10, tel. 92-521-4440).

Restaurants Plaza and **La Parrilla** share a tiny square behind Plaza Zocódover (facing the Casa Telesforo on Plaza Zocódover, go left down alley 30 meters to Plaza de Barrio Rey). The bars and cafés on Plaza Zocódover are reasonable, seasoned with some fine people-watching.

At **Taverna de Amboades**, a wine-and-tapas bar near the Bisagra Gate, expert Miguel Angel explains the differences among Spanish wines (Tue–Sat 19:30–24:00, also Thu–Sun 12:30–16:00, Alfonso VI 5, cellular 67-848-3749).

Picnics are best assembled at the **Mercado Municipal** on Plaza Mayor (on the Alcázar side of cathedral, open until 14:00, closed Sun). This is a fun market to prowl, even if you don't need food. If you feel like munching a paper plate–size Communion wafer, one of the stalls sells crispy bags of *obleas* (a great gift for your favorite pastor).

Toledo's famous almond-fruity-sweet *mazapan* is sold all

over town. On Plaza Zocódover try the modern **Santo Tomé** (daily 09:00–22:22) or the bar-like **Casa Telesforo** (daily 09:00–23:00, go inside to the far right counter). Each has a great window display and sells single *mazapan* goodies (€0.80 each) or small mixed boxes.

For a sweet and romantic evening moment, get a pastry and head down to the cathedral. Sit on the Plaza del Ayuntamiento (on stone wall to right of TI). The fountain is on your right, Spain's best-looking city hall is behind you, and her top cathedral, built back when Toledo was Spain's capital, shines brightly against the black night sky before you.

Transportation Connections—Toledo

Far more buses than trains connect Toledo with Madrid. Consider taking the train to Madrid and the bus back.

To Madrid by bus (2/hr, 60–75 min, *directo* is faster than *ruta*, Madrid's Estación sur Autobuses, Metro: Méndez Alvaro, Continental bus company, tel. 92-522-3641), **by train** (9/day, 50–75 min, Madrid's Atocha station), **by car** (65 kilometers, 1 hr). Toledo bus info: tel. 92-521-5850; train info: tel. 90-224-0202.

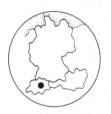

GIMMELWALD
AND THE BERNER
OBERLAND

Frolic and hike high above the stress and clouds of the real world.
Take a vacation from your busy vacation. Recharge your touristic
batteries up here in the Alps, where distant avalanches, cowbells,
the fluff of a down comforter, and the crunchy footsteps of happy
hikers are the dominant sounds. If the weather's good (and your
budget's healthy), ride a gondola from the traffic-free village of
Gimmelwald to a hearty breakfast at Schilthorn's 3,000-meter
(10,000-foot) revolving Piz Gloria restaurant. Linger among
alpine whitecaps before riding, hiking, or parasailing down
1,500 meters (5,000 feet) to Mürren and home to Gimmelwald.

Your gateway to the rugged Berner Oberland is the grand
old resort town of Interlaken. Near Interlaken is Switzerland's
open-air folk museum, Ballenberg, where you can climb through
traditional houses from every corner of this diverse country.

Ah, but the weather's fine and the Alps beckon. Head deep
into the heart of the Alps and ride the gondola to the stop just
this side of heaven—Gimmelwald.

Planning Your Time
Rather than tackling a checklist of famous Swiss mountains and
resorts, choose one region to savor—the Berner Oberland. Interlaken is the administrative headquarters and a fine transportation
hub. Use it for business (banking, post office, laundry, shopping)
and as a springboard for alpine thrills. With decent weather,
explore the two areas (south of Interlaken) that tower above either
side of the Lauterbrunnen Valley: Kleine Scheidegg/Jungfrau and
Schilthorn/Mürren. Ideally, home-base three nights in the village
of Gimmelwald and spend a day on each side of the valley. On a
speedy train trip you can overnight into and out of Interlaken.

For the fastest look, consider a night in Gimmelwald, breakfast at the Schilthorn, an afternoon doing the Männlichen-to-Wengen hike, and an evening or night train out. What? A nature lover not spending the night high in the Alps? Alpus-interruptus.

Getting around the Berner Oberland

For more than 100 years, this has been the target of nature-wor-shiping pilgrims. And Swiss engineers and visionaries have made the most exciting alpine perches accessible by lift or train. Part of the fun (and most of the expense) here is riding the many lifts. Generally, scenic trains and lifts are not covered on train passes, but a Eurail, Europass, or Eurail Selectpass get you a 25 percent discount on even the highest lifts (without the loss of a flexi-day). Ask about discounts for early (and late) trips, youths, seniors, families, groups, and those staying awhile. The Junior Card for families pays for itself on the first hour of trains and lifts: children under 16 travel free with parents (20 SF/1 child, 40 SF/2 or more children; available at Swiss train stations but not at gondola stations). Get a list of discounts and the free fare and time sched-ule at any Swiss train station. Study the "Alpine Lifts in the Berner Oberland" chart in this chapter. Lifts generally go at least twice hourly, from about 07:00 until about 20:00 (sneak pre-view: www.jungfrau.ch). Drivers can park at the gondola station in Stechelberg for the lift to Gimmelwald, Mürren, and the Schilthorn (5 SF/day), or at the train station in Lauterbrunnen (1 SF/hr, 7 SF/day) for trains to Wengen and Kleine Scheidegg.

INTERLAKEN

When the 19th-century Romantics redefined mountains as something more than cold and troublesome obstacles, Interlaken became the original alpine resort. Ever since, tourists have flocked to the Alps because they're there. Interlaken's glory days are long gone, its elegant old hotels eclipsed by the new, more jet-setty alpine resorts. Today its shops are filled with chocolate bars, Swiss Army knives, and sunburned backpackers.

Orientation

Efficient Interlaken is a good administrative and shopping center. Take care of business, give the town a quick look, and view the live TV coverage of the Jungfrau and Schilthorn weather in the window of the Schilthornbahn office on the main street (at Höheweg 2, also on TV in most hotel lobbies). Then head for the hills. Stay in Interlaken only if you suffer from alptitude sick-ness (see "Sleeping in Interlaken," at the end of this chapter).

Tourist Information: The TI has good information for the region, advice on alpine lift discounts, and a room-finding service (July–Sept Mon–Fri 08:00–18:30, Sat 08:00–17:00, Sun

Interlaken

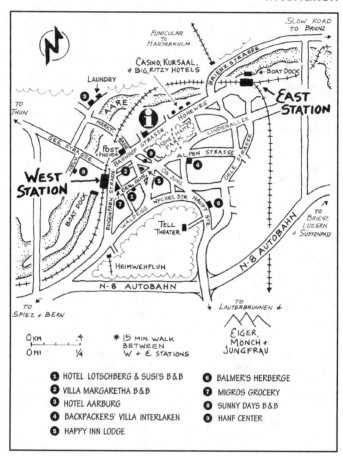

●1 HOTEL LOTSCHBERG & SUSI'S B&B
●2 VILLA MARGARETHA B&B
●3 HOTEL AARBURG
●4 BACKPACKERS' VILLA INTERLAKEN
●5 HAPPY INN LODGE
●6 BALMER'S HERBERGE
●7 MIGROS GROCERY
●8 SUNNY DAYS B&B
●9 HANF CENTER

10:00–12:00, 16:00–18:00; Oct–June Mon–Fri 08:00–12:00,
13:30–18:00, Sat 09:00–12:00, closed Sun, tel. 033-826-5300,
on the main street, 5-min walk from West station). While the
Jungfrau region map costs 1.50 SF, good mini-versions are
included in the many free Jungfrau region transportation
brochures. Pick up a Bern map if that's your next destination.

Arrival in Interlaken: Interlaken has two train stations:
East (*Ost*) and West. Most major trains stop at the Interlaken-West
station. This station's train information desk answers tourists' questions (travel center for in-depth rail questions-daily 08:00–12:00,
14:00–18:00, ticket windows-daily 06:00–20:45, tel. 033-826-4750),

and there's a fair exchange booth next to the ticket windows. Ask at the station about discount passes, special fares, railpass discounts, and schedules for the scenic mountain trains.

It's a pleasant 20-minute walk between the West and East stations, or an easy, frequent train connection. From the Interlaken-East station, private trains take you deep into the mountainous Jungfrau region (see "Transportation Connections," at the end of this chapter).

Helpful Hints

Telephone: Phone booths cluster outside the post office near the West station. For efficiency, buy a phone card from a newsstand. (Gimmelwald's only public phone—located at the gondola station—takes only cards, not coins.)

Laundry: Friendly Helen Schmocker's *Wäscherei* (laundry) has a change machine, soap, English instructions, and a pleasant riverside locale (open daily 24 hrs for self-service, for full service: Mon–Fri 08:00–12:00, 13:30–18:00, Sat 08:00–12:00, 13:30–16:00, drop off 10 pounds in the morning and pick up clean clothes that afternoon; exit left from West station and follow the main street to the post office, turn left and take Marktgasse over 2 bridges to Beatenbergstrasse; tel. 033-822-1566).

Warning: On Sundays and holidays, small-town Switzerland is quiet. Hotels are open, and lifts and trains run, but many restaurants and all groceries are closed. If this concerns you, call the Interlaken TI (they speak English) to see if a holiday (usually a religious one) falls during your visit.

Stores: A brand new **Migros supermarket** is across the street from Interlaken West train station (Mon–Thu 08:00–18:30, Fri 08:00–21:00, Sat 07:30–16:00, closed Sun). There's lots of buzz surrounding Interlaken's **Hanf Center**, a small shop selling a wide selection of products made from hemp, including clothes, paper, noodles, and beer (Jungfraustrasse 47, near end of Höhematte Park closest to West station, tel. 033-823-1552).

Sights—Interlaken

Boat Trips—*Interlaken* means "between the lakes." Lazy boat trips explore these lakes (8/day, fewer off-season, free with Eurail/Euro/Selectpass, schedules at TI). The boats on **Lake Thun** stop at the **St. Beatus Höhlen Caves** (14 SF, mid-April–mid-Oct daily 10:30–17:00, closed in winter, 30-min boat ride from Interlaken, tel. 033-841-1643, www.beatushoehlen.ch) and two visit-worthy towns: Spiez (1 hr from Interlaken) and Thun (1.75 hrs). The boats on **Lake Brienz** stop at the super-cute and quiet village of Iseltwald (45 min away) and at Brienz (1.25 hrs away, near Ballenberg Open-Air Folk Museum).

Adventure Trips—For the adventurer with money and little

concern for personal safety, several companies offer high-adren-
aline trips such as rafting, canyoning (rappelling down watery
gorges), bungee jumping, and paragliding. Most adventure trips
cost from 90 to 180 SF. Interlaken companies include: Alpin Raft
(tel. 033-823-4100, www.alpinraft.ch), Alpin Center (at Wilderswil
station and across from Balmer's youth hostel, tel. 033-823-5523,
www.alpincenter.ch), and Swiss Adventures (tel. 033-773-7373,
www.swissadventures.ch).

Recent fatal accidents have understandably hurt the adven-
ture-sport business in the Berner Oberland. In July 1999, 21
tourists died canyoning on the Saxetenbach River, 16 kilometers
(10 miles) from Interlaken (they were battered and drowned by a
flash flood filled with debris). In May 2000, an American died
bungee jumping from the Stechelberg-Mürren gondola (the operator used a 180-meter rope for a 100-meter jump). Also in 2000,
a landslide killed several hikers. Enjoying nature up close comes
with risks. Adventure sports increase those risks dramatically.
Use good judgment.

GIMMELWALD

Saved from developers by its "avalanche zone" classification,
Gimmelwald was (before tourism) one of the poorest places in
Switzerland. Its traditional economy was stuck in the hay, and its
farmers, unable to make it in their disadvantaged trade, survived
only by Swiss government subsidies (and working the ski lifts in
the winter). For some travelers there's little to see in the village.
Others enjoy a fascinating day sitting on a bench and learning why
they say, "If heaven isn't what it's cracked up to be, send me back
to Gimmelwald." If you're lucky, you might get to see the local
farmers herd a dozen cows onto the gondola to take them down
into the valley. Gimmelwald is my home base in the Berner Oberland (see "Sleeping in Gimmelwald," below; www.gimmelwald.ch).

Take a walk through the town. This place is for real. Most of
the 130 residents have the same last name: von Allmen. They are
tough and proud. Raising hay in this rugged terrain is labor inten-
sive. One family harvests enough to feed only 15 or 20 cows. But
they'd have it no other way and, unlike the absentee landlord town
of Mürren, Gimmelwald is locally owned. (When word got out
that urban planners wished to develop Gimmelwald into a town
of 1,000, locals pulled some strings to secure the town's bogus
avalanche-zone building code.)

Do not confuse obscure Gimmelwald with touristy and
commercialized Grindelwald just over the Kleine Scheidegg ridge.

A Walk through Gimmelwald

Gimmelwald, while tiny with one zigzag street, gives a fine look at a
traditional mountain Swiss community. Here's a quick walking tour:

Gimmelwald

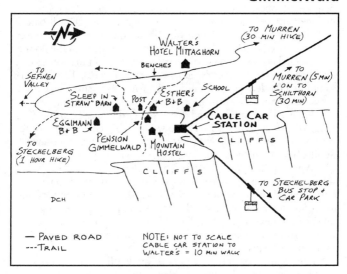

Gondola Station: When the lift came in the 1960s, this village's back end became Gimmelwald's front door. This was and still is a farm village. Stepping off the gondola you see a sweet little hut. Set on stilts to keep out mice, the hut was used for storing cheese (the rocks on the rooftop keep the shingles on through wild winter winds). Notice the yellow alpine "street sign" showing where you are, the altitude (1,363 meters/4,470 feet), and how many hours ("Std.") and minutes it takes to walk to nearby points. Behind the cheese hut stands the village schoolhouse. In Catholic-Swiss towns, the biggest building is the church. In Protestant towns, it's the school. Gimmelwald's biggest building is the school (2 teachers, 18 students, and a room that doubles as a chapel when the Protestant pastor makes his monthly visit). In the opposite direction, just beyond the little playground, is Gimmelwald's Mountain Hostel.

Walk up the lane 50 meters, past the shower in the phone booth, to Gimmelwald's...

"Times Square": From this tiny intersection, we'll follow the town's main street (away from gondola station, where most yellow arrows are pointing). Most of the buildings used to house two families and are divided vertically right down the middle. The writing on the post office building is a folksy blessing: "Summer brings green, winter brings snow. The sun greets the day, the stars greet the night. This house will keep you warm. May God give us his blessings." The date indicates when it was built or rebuilt (1911).

"Main Street": Walk up the road. Notice the town announcement board: one side tourist news, the other for local news. Cross the street and peek into the big new barn dated 1995. This is part of the "Sleep in Straw" association which rents out barn spots to travelers when the cows are in the high country. To the left of the door is a cow scratcher. Swiss cows have legal rights (e.g., in the winter they must be taken out for exercise at least 3 times a week). This big barn is built in a modern style. Traditionally, barns were small (like those on the hillside high above) and closer to the hay. But with trucks and paved roads, hay can be moved easier and farther and farms need more cows to be viable. Still, even a well-run big farm hopes just to break even. The industry survives only with government subsidies. Go just beyond the next barn and look to your right.

Water Fountain/Trough: This is the site of the town's historic water supply. Local kids love to bathe in this when the cows aren't drinking from it. From here, detour left down a lane about 50 meters (along a wooden fence and past pea-patch gardens) to the next trough and the oldest building in town, "Husmattli," from 1658. Study the log-cabin construction. Many are built without nails.

Back on the paved road, continue uphill. Gimmelwald has a strict building code. For instance, shutters can only be natural, green, or white. Notice the cute cheese hut on the right (with stones on the shingles and alpine cheese for sale). It's full of strong cheese—up to three years old. On the left (at B&B sign) is the home of Olle and Maria (the village school teachers). Gimmelwald heats with wood and, since the wood needs to age a couple of years to burn well, it's stacked everywhere. Fifty meters farther is ...

Alpenrose: At the old schoolhouse, big ceremonial cowbells hang under its uphill eave. These swing from the necks of cows during the alpine procession from the town to the high Alps (mid-June) and back down (around Sept 20). At the end of town notice the dramatic Sefinen valley. The road switches back at the ...

Gimmelwald Fire Station: Check out the notices on the fire station building. Every Swiss male does a year in the military and then a few days a year in the reserves until about age 40. The 2002 Swiss Army calendar tells the reserves when and where to go. The *Schiessubungen* poster details the shooting exercises required this year. Keeping with the William Tell heritage, each Swiss man does shooting practice annually for the military (or spends 3 days in jail).

High Road: Follow the high road to Hotel Mittaghorn. The resort of Mürren hangs high above in the distance. And high on the left, notice the hay field with terraces. These are from WWII days when Switzerland, wanting self-sufficiency, required all farmers to grow potatoes. From Hotel Mittaghorn, you can return to Gimmelwald's "Times Square" via the stepped path. (For a map and photos of this walk, visit www.gimmelwald-news.ch.)

Gimmelwald After Dark—Evening fun in Gimmelwald is found at the hostel (offering a pool table, Internet access, lots of young Alp-aholics, and a good chance to share information on the surrounding mountains) or at Pension Gimmelwald's terrace restaurant next door. Walter's bar is a local farmers' hangout. When they've made their hay, they come here to play. Although they look like what some people would call hicks, they speak some English and can be fun to get to know. Sit outside (benches just below the rails, 100 meters down the lane from Walter's) and watch the sun tuck the mountaintops into bed as the moon rises over the Jungfrau. If this isn't your idea of nightlife, stay in Interlaken.

Alpine Excursions

There are days of possible hikes from Gimmelwald. Many are a fun combination of trails, mountain trains, and gondola rides. Don't mind the fences (although wires can be solar-powered electric); a hiker has the right-of-way in Switzerland. However, as late as early June, snow can curtail your hiking plans (the Männlichen lift doesn't even open until the first week in June). Before setting out on any hike, get advice from a knowledgeable local to confirm that it is safe, accessible, and doable before dark. Clouds can roll in anytime, but skies are usually clearest in the morning. That means you need rain gear *and* sunscreen, regardless of the current weather. Don't forget a big water bottle and some munchies. Refer to maps (within this chapter) as you read about the following hikes.

▲▲▲**The Schilthorn: Hikes, Lifts, and a 3,000-Meter (10,000-Foot) Breakfast**—The Schilthornbahn carries skiers, hikers, and sightseers effortlessly to the 3,000-meter (10,000-foot) summit of the Schilthorn where the Piz Gloria station (of James Bond movie fame) awaits with a revolving restaurant, shop, and panorama terrace. Linger on top. Piz Gloria has a "touristorama" film room showing a multiscreen slide show and explosive highlights from the James Bond thriller that featured the Schilthorn (free).

Watch hang gliders set up, psych up, and take off, flying 30 minutes with the birds to distant Interlaken. Walk along the ridge out back. This is a great place for a photo of the "mountain-climber you." For another cheap thrill, ask the gondola attendant to crank down the window (easiest on the Mürren-Birg section). Then stick your head out the window . . . and you're hang gliding.

The early-bird and afternoon-special **gondola tickets** (about 56.50 SF round-trip, before 09:00 or after 15:30) take you from Gimmelwald to the Schilthorn and back at a discount (normal rate-75 SF, or 90 SF from Stechelberg car park, parking-5 SF/day). These same early-bird fares are available all day long in the shoulder season (roughly May and Oct). Ask the Schilthorn station for a gondola souvenir decal (Schilthornbahn, in Stechelberg, tel. 033-823-1444 or 033-856-2141). For breakfast at 3,000 meters,

Lauterbrunnen Valley: West Side Story

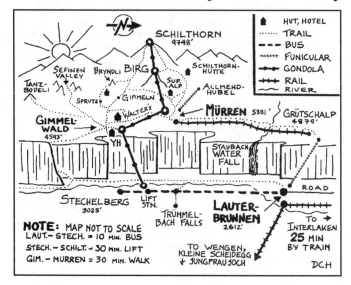

there's no à la carte, only a 15-SF and a 22.50-SF meal. Ask for more hot drinks if necessary. If you're not revolving, ask them to turn it on.

Lifts go twice hourly, and the ride (including 2 transfers) to the Schilthorn takes 30 minutes. Watch the altitude meter in the gondola. (The Gimmelwald-Schilthorn hike is free if you don't mind a 1,500-meter/5,000-foot altitude gain.) You can ride up to the Schilthorn and hike down, but it's tough (weather can change; wear good shoes). Youth hostelers scream down the ice fields on plastic-bag sleds from the Schilthorn mountaintop. (English-speaking doctor in Mürren.)

Just below Birg is **Schilthornhütte**. Drop in for soup, cocoa, or a coffee schnapps. You can spend the night in the hut's crude loft (dorm bed with breakfast-35 SF, 20 SF more for dinner, open July–Sept and Dec–April, tel. 033-855-5053, e-mail: schilthornhuette@muerren.ch).

An option for hard-core hikers is the **hike** from Birg to Gimmelwald (from Schilthorn summit, ride cable car halfway down, get off at Birg, and hike down from there; buy the round-trip excursion early-bird fare—which is cheaper than the Gimmel-wald-Schilthorn-Birg ticket—and decide at Birg if you want to hike or ride down). The most interesting trail from Birg to Gimmelwald is the high one via Grauseewli Lake and Wasenegg Ridge to Brünli, then down to Spielbodenalp and the Sprutz waterfall. Warning: this trail is quite steep and slippery in places and can take five to seven hours. From the Birg lift, hike toward the Schilthorn, taking your first left down to the little, newly made Grauseewli Lake. From the lake, a gravelly trail leads down rough switchbacks until it levels out. When you see a rock painted with arrows pointing to "Mürren" and "Rotstockhütte," follow the path to Rotstockhütte, traversing the cow-grazed mountainside. Follow Wasenegg Ridge left and down along the barbed-wire fence to Brünli. (For maximum thrills, stay on the ridge and climb all the way to the knobby little summit where you'll enjoy an incredible 360-degree view and a chance to sign your name on the register stored in the little wooden box.) A steep trail winds directly down from Brünli toward Gimmelwald and soon hits a bigger, easy trail. The trail bends right (just before the popular restaurant/mountain hut at Spielbodenalp), leading to Sprutz. Walk under the Sprutz waterfall, then follow a steep, wooded trail that will deposit you in a meadow of flowers at the top side of Gimmelwald.

▲▲**North Face Trail from Mürren**—For a pleasant two-hour hike (6 km/4 miles, 1,946 meters–1,638 meters), ride the Allmendhubel funicular up from Mürren (cheaper than Schilthorn, good restaurant at top). From there, follow the well-promoted and described route circling around to Mürren (or cut off near the end down to Gimmelwald). You'll enjoy great views, flowery meadows, mountain huts, and a dozen information boards along the way describing the climbing history of the great peaks around you.

▲▲▲**The Männlichen–Kleine Scheidegg Hike**—This is my favorite easy alpine hike. It's entertaining all the way with glorious Jungfrau, Eiger, and Mönch views. (That's the Young Maiden being protected from the Ogre by the Monk.)

If the weather's good, descend from Gimmelwald bright and early to Stechelberg. From here, get to the Lauterbrunnen train station by post bus (about 4 SF, bus is synchronized to depart with the arrival of each lift) or by car (parking at the large multistoried pay lot behind the Lauterbrunnen station, summer-9 SF/day, winter-11 SF/day). At Lauterbrunnen, buy a train ticket to Männlichen. Ride past great valley views to Wengen, where you'll walk across town (buy a picnic but don't waste time here if it's sunny) and catch the Männlichen lift (departing every 15 min, beginning the first week of June) to the top of the ridge high above you. (Trails may be snowbound into early June. Ask about conditions at the lift stations or local TI. If the Männlichen lift is closed, take the train straight from Lauterbrunnen to Kleine Scheidegg.)

From the tip of the Männlichen lift, hike 20 minutes north to the little peak for that king- or queen-of-the-mountain feeling. From Männlichen, its an easy hour's walk—facing the alpine panorama views of the north faces of the Eiger, Jungfrau, and Mönch—to Kleine Scheidegg for a picnic or restaurant lunch.

Berner Oberland

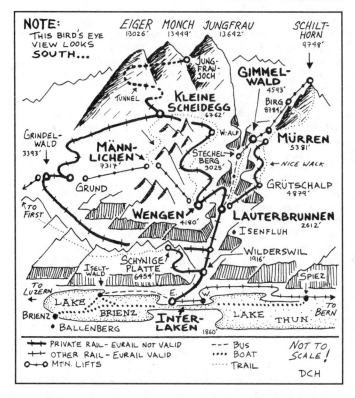

NOTE: THIS BIRD'S EYE VIEW LOOKS SOUTH...

EIGER 13026' · MONCH 13449' · JUNGFRAU 13642'

SCHILT-HORN 9748'

JUNG-FRAU-JOCH

TUNNEL

KLEINE SCHEIDEGG 6762'

GIMMEL-WALD 4593'

BIRG 8784'

W. ALP

GRINDEL-WALD 3393'

MÄNN-LICHEN 7317'

STECHEL-BERG 3025'

MÜRREN 5381'

← NICE WALK

GRUND

GRÜTSCHALP 4879'

↑ TO FIRST

WENGEN 4180'

LAUTERBRUNNEN 2612'

ISENFLUH

WILDERSWIL 1916'

SCHYNIGE PLATTE 6454'

ISELT-WALD

SPIEZ

TO LUZERN

E.

W.

TO BERN

LAKE BRIENZ

BRIENZ

BALLENBERG

INTER-LAKEN 1860'

LAKE THUN

┿┿ PRIVATE RAIL – EURAIL NOT VALID
┼┼ OTHER RAIL – EURAIL VALID
○━○ MTN. LIFTS

--- BUS
•••• BOAT
····· TRAIL

NOT TO SCALE!

DCH

From Kleine Scheidegg you can catch the train to "the top of Europe" (see "Jungfraujoch," below). Or head downhill, riding the train or hiking (30 gorgeous min to Wengeralp station; 90 more steep min from there into the town of Wengen). The alpine views might be accompanied by the valley-filling mellow sound of Alp horns and distant avalanches.

If the weather turns bad or you run out of steam, catch the train early at the little Wengeralp station along the way. After Wengeralp, the trail to Wengen is steep and, while not dangerous, requires a good set of knees. Wengen is a good shopping town. (For accommodations, see "Sleeping in Wengen," below.) The boring final descent from Wengen to Lauterbrunnen is knee-killer steep—catch the train.

▲▲▲**Jungfraujoch**—The literal high point of any trip to the Swiss Alps is a train ride through the Eiger to the Jungfraujoch. At 3,400 meters (11,333 feet), it's Europe's highest train station.

Alpine Lifts in the Berner Oberland

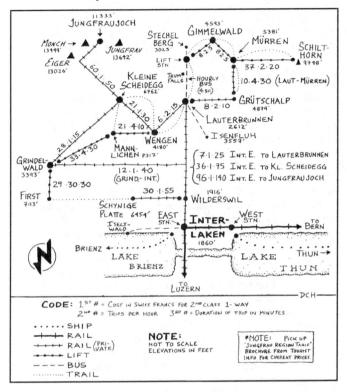

JUNGFRAUJOCH 11333'

MONCH → ▲ 13449'
JUNGFRAU 13642' ▲
EIGER 13026' ▲

STECHEL BERG 3025'
GIMMELWALD 4593'
MÜRREN 5381'
SCHILT-HORN ▲ 9748'

KLEINE SCHEIDEGG 6762'
LIFT STN
TRUM FALLS
HOURLY BUS (4 SF)
37·2·20
10·4·30 (LAUT-MÜRREN)

60·1·50
21·1·30
6·2·15
GRÜTSCHALP 4879'
8·2·10
LAUTERBRUNNEN 2612'
ISENFLUH 3557'

28·1·15
33·4·30
21·4·10
WENGEN 4180'
MANN-LICHEN 7317'

GRINDEL-WALD 3393'
12·1·40 (GRIND.- INT.)

{ 7·1·25 INT. E. TO LAUTERBRUNNEN
36·1·75 INT. E. TO KL. SCHEIDEGG
96·1·140 INT. E. TO JUNGFRAUJOCH

FIRST 7113'
29·30·30
30·1·55
WILDERSWIL 1916'

SCHYNIGE PLATTE 6454'
ISELT-WALD
EAST STN
INTER-LAKEN 1860'
WEST STN
TO BERN

BRIENZ ←
LAKE BRIENZ
LAKE THUN
THUN →

TO LUZERN

DCH

CODE: 1ST # = COST IN SWISS FRANCS FOR 2ND CLASS 1- WAY
2ND # = TRIPS PER HOUR   3RD # = DURATION OF TRIP IN MINUTES

······· SHIP
┿┿┿ RAIL
┿┿┿ RAIL (PRI-VATE)
◆◆◆ LIFT
----- BUS
·········· TRAIL

NOTE: NOT TO SCALE ELEVATIONS IN FEET

*NOTE: PICK UP "JUNGFRAU REGION TARIFF" BROCHURE FROM TOURIST INFO FOR CURRENT PRICES.

The ride from Kleine Scheidegg takes about an hour, including two five-minute stops at stations actually halfway up the notorious North Face of the Eiger. You have time to look out windows and marvel at how people could climb the Eiger and how the Swiss built this train over a hundred years ago. Once you reach the top, study the Jungfraujoch chart to see your options (many of them are weather dependent). There's a restaurant, history exhibit, ice palace (a cavern with a gallery of ice statues), and a 20-minute video (continuous). A tunnel leads outside where you can ski (30 SF for gear and lift ticket), sled (free loaner discs with a 5-SF deposit), ride in a dog sled (6 SF, mornings only), or hike 45 minutes across the ice to Mönchsjochhutte (a mountain hut with a small restaurant). An elevator leads to the Sphinx observatory for the highest viewing point from which you can see Aletsch Glacier—Europe's longest at nearly 18 kilometers (11 miles)—stretch to the south. The first trip of the day to Jungfraujoch is discounted; ask for a Good Morning Ticket and return from the top by noon (Nov–April you can get Good Morning rates for first or second train and stay after noon, train runs all year, round-trip fares to Jungfraujoch: from Kleine Scheidegg-normally about 100 SF, 62 SF for first trip of day—about 08:00 in summer; from Lauterbrunnen-about 145 SF, 110 SF for first trip—about 07:00 in summer, confirm times and prices, get leaflet on lifts at a local TI or call 033-826-7233, www.jungfrau.ch, discounts for Eurail/ Euro/Selectpass and Swiss railpass holders, trilingual weather info: tel. 033-828-7931, if it's cloudy—skip the trip).

▲▲**Hike from Schynige Platte to First**—The best day I've had hiking in the Berner Oberland was when I made the demanding six-hour ridge walk high above Lake Brienz on one side with all that Jungfrau beauty on the other. Start at Wilderswil train station (just above Interlaken) and catch the little train up to Schynige Platte (2,000 meters/6,560 feet). Walk through the flower display garden and into the wild alpine yonder. The high point is Faul-horn (2,680 meters/8,790 feet, with its famous mountaintop hotel). Hike to a small gondola called "First" (2,168 meters), then descend to Grindelwald and catch a train back to your starting point, Wilderswil. Or, if you have a regional train pass or no car but endless money, return to Gimmelwald via Lauterbrunnen from Grindelwald over Kleine Scheidegg. For an abbreviated ridge walk, consider the Panoramaweg, a short loop from Schynige Platte to Daub Peak.

▲**Mountain Biking**—Mountain biking is popular and accepted (as long as you stay on the clearly marked mountain-bike paths). A popular ride is the round-trip "Mürren Loop" that runs from Mürren to Gimmelwald, Stechelberg, Lauterbrunnen (by funicu-lar, bike costs same as person-7 SF), Grütschalp, and back to Mürren. You can rent bikes in Mürren (Salomon Station, 25 SF/ half day, 35 SF/full day, 10 SF extra for full suspension, closed May and Nov, rest of year daily 09:00–17:00, at gondola station, tel. 033-855-2330, www.staegersport.ch) or in Lauterbrunnen (Imboden Bike, same prices as Salomon, Mon–Sat 08:00–12:00, 13:30–18:30, Sun 09:00–17:30, tel. 033-855-2114).

You can also bike the Lauterbrunnen Valley from Lauter-brunnen to Interlaken. It's a gentle downhill ride via a peaceful bike path over the river from the road. Rent a bike at Lauterbrun-nen (see above), bike to Interlaken, and then return to Lauter-brunnen by train (pay 3.10 SF from East station or 4.30 SF from West station extra to take bike on train). Or rent a bike at either Interlaken station and take the train to Lauterbrunnen.

▲**More Hikes near Gimmelwald**—For a not-too-tough, three-hour walk (but there's a scary 20-minute stretch) with great Jungfrau views and some mountain farm action, ride the funicular from Mürren to Allmendhubel (1,934 meters/

6,344 feet) and walk to Marchegg, Saustal, and Grütschalp (a drop of about 500 meters), where you can catch the panorama train back to Mürren. An easier version is the lower Bergweg from Allmenhubel to Grütschalp via Winteregg. For an easy family stroll with grand views, walk from Mürren just above the train tracks to either Winteregg (40 min, restaurant, playground, train station) or Grütschalp (60 min, train station) and catch the panorama train back to Mürren. An easy, go-as-far-as-you-like trail from Gimmelwald is up the Sefinen Valley. Or you can wind from Gimmelwald down to Stechelberg (60 min).

You can get specifics at the Mürren TI. For a description of six diverse hikes on the west side of Lauterbrunnen, pick up the fine and free *Mürren-Schilthorn Hikes* brochure (at stations, hotels, and TIs). The 3-D map of the Mürren mountainside, which includes hiking trails, makes a useful and attractive souvenir (free, at TI and lift station).

Rainy-Day Options

When it rains here, locals joke that they're washing the mountains. If clouds roll in, don't despair. They can roll out just as quickly, and there are plenty of good bad-weather options.

▲▲**Cloudy-Day Lauterbrunnen Valley Walk**—There are easy trails and pleasant walks along the floor of the Lauterbrunnen Valley. For a smell-the-cows-and-flowers lowland walk—ideal for a cloudy day, weary body, or tight budget—follow the riverside trail from Stechelberg's Schilthornbahn station for five kilometers (3 miles) to Lauterbrunnen's Staubach Falls, near the town church (you can reverse the route, but it's a gradual uphill to Stechelberg). Detour to Trümmelbach Falls (below) en route. There's a fine paved car-free and riverside path all the way.

If you're staying in Gimmelwald: Take the lift down to Stechelberg (5 min), then walk to Lauterbrunnen, detouring to Trümmelbach Falls shortly after Stechelberg. To return to Gimmelwald from Lauterbrunnen, take the funicular up to Grütschalp (10 min), then either walk (60 min) or take the panorama train (15 min) to Mürren. From Mürren it's a downhill walk (30 min) to Gimmelwald. (This loop trip can be reversed.)

▲**Trümmelbach Falls**—If all the waterfalls have you intrigued, sneak a behind-the-scenes look at the valley's most powerful one, Trümmelbach Falls (10 SF, July–Aug daily 08:30–18:00, April–June and Sept–Nov daily 09:00–17:00, on Lauterbrunnen-Stechelberg road, take postal bus from Lauterbrunnen TI or Stechelberg gondola station, tel. 033-855-3232). You'll ride an elevator up through the mountain and climb through several caves—that some find claustrophobic—to see the melt from the Eiger, Mönch, and

Jungfrau grinding like God's band saw through the mountain
at the rate of up to 20,000 liters a second (5,200 gallons; nearly
double the beer consumption at Oktoberfest). The upper area is
the best; if your legs ache, skip the lower ones and ride down.

Lauterbrunnen Folk Museum—The Heimatmuseum in Lauterbrunnen shows off the local folk culture (3 SF, mid-June–Sept,
Tue, Thu, and Sat–Sun 14:00–17:30, just over bridge and below
church at the far end of town, tel. 033-855-1388).

Mürren Activities—This low-key alpine resort town offers a variety of rainy-day activities, from its shops to its slick Sportzentrum
(sports center) with pools, steam baths, squash, and a fitness center
(for details, see "Sleeping in Mürren," below).

Interlaken Boat Trips—Consider taking a boat trip from Interlaken (see "Sights—Interlaken," above).

▲▲Swiss Open-Air Folk Museum at Ballenberg—Across
Lake Brienz from Interlaken, the Swiss Open-Air Museum of
Vernacular Architecture, Country Life, and Crafts in the Bernese
Oberland is a rich collection of traditional and historic farmhouses
from every region of the country. Each house is carefully furnished, and many feature traditional craftspeople at work. The
sprawling 50-acre park, laid out roughly as a huge Swiss map,
is a natural preserve providing a wonderful setting for this culture-
on-a-lazy-Susan look at Switzerland.

   The Thurgau house (#621) has an interesting wattle-and-
daub (half-timbered construction) display, and house #331 has
a fun bread museum. Use the 2-SF map/guide. The more expensive picture book is a better souvenir than guide. (16-SF entry,
half price after 16:00, May–Oct daily 10:00–17:00, houses
close at 17:00, park stays open later, craft demonstration
schedules are listed just inside the entry, tel. 033-952-1030,
www.ballenberg.ch). A reasonable outdoor cafeteria is inside
the west entrance, and fresh bread, sausage, mountain cheese,
and other goodies are on sale in several houses. Picnic tables
and grills with free firewood are scattered throughout the
park. The little wooden village of Brienzwiler (near the east
entrance) is a museum in itself with a lovely little church.
Trains run frequently from Interlaken to Brienzwiler, an easy
walk from the museum. A "RailAway" combo ticket, available
at either Interlaken station, includes transportation to and
from Ballenberg and your admission (30 SF, add 7 SF to return
by boat instead).

Mystery Park—Opening in May of 2002, this park in Wilderswil (just south of Interlaken) explores intriguing mysteries
from the past to the future, from building Stonehenge and
the pyramids to the challenge of maintaining a space station
on Mars (for info, ask at Interlaken TI, call 033-827-5757,
or see www.mysterypark.ch).

Sleeping and Eating in the Berner Oberland
(1.70 SF = about $1, country code: 41)
Sleep Code: **S** = Single, **D** = Double/Twin, **T** = Triple, **Q** = Quad, **b** = bathroom, **s** = shower only, **CC** = Credit Cards accepted, **no CC** = Credit Cards not accepted, **SE** = Speaks English, **NSE** = No English. Unless otherwise noted, breakfast is included and credit cards are not accepted. Many places, especially in Mürren, are closed between Easter and late May.

Sleeping and Eating in Gimmelwald
(1,350 meters/4,500 feet, country code: 41, zip code: 3826)
To inhale the Alps and really hold it in, sleep high in Gimmelwald. Poor but pleasantly stuck in the past, the village has a creaky hotel, happy hostel, decent pension, a couple of B&Bs, and even a Web site (www.gimmelwald.ch). The only bad news is that the lift costs 8 SF each way to get there.

Hotel Mittaghorn, the treasure of Gimmelwald, is run by Walter Mittler, a perfect Swiss gentleman. Walter's hotel is a classic, creaky, alpine-style place with memorable beds, ancient down comforters (short and fat; wear socks and drape the blanket over your feet), and a million-dollar view of the Jungfrau Alps. The loft has a dozen real beds, several sinks, down comforters, and a fire ladder out the back window. The hotel has one shower for 10 rooms (1 SF/5 min). Walter is careful not to let his place get too hectic or big and enjoys sensitive Back Door travelers. He runs the hotel with a little help from Rosemaria from the village, and keeps things simple. This is a good place to receive mail from home (check the mail barrel in entry hall).

To some, Hotel Mittaghorn is a fire waiting to happen with a kitchen that would never pass code, lumpy beds, teeny towels, and minimal plumbing, run by an eccentric old grouch. These people enjoy Interlaken, Wengen, or Mürren, and that's where they should sleep. Be warned, you'll see more of my readers than locals here, but it's a fun crowd—an extended family (D-70–80 SF, T-100 SF, Q-125 SF, loft beds-25 SF, 3-SF surcharge per person for 1-night stays except in loft, all with breakfast, slightly cheaper if you pay in euros, no CC, closed Nov–March, CH-3826 Gimmelwald/Bern, tel. 033-855-1658, www.ricksteves.com /mittaghorn). Reserve by telephone only, then reconfirm by phone the day before your arrival. Walter usually offers his guests a simple 15-SF dinner. Hotel Mittaghorn is at the top of Gimmelwald, a five-minute climb up the steps from the village intersection.

Mountain Hostel is a beehive of activity, simple and as clean as its guests, cheap, and friendly. Phone ahead (2 days maximum) or, to secure one of its 60 dorm beds the same day, call after 09:30 and leave your name. The hostel has low ceilings, a self-service kitchen, a mini-grocery, and healthy plumbing. It's mostly a college-age crowd; families and older travelers will probably feel more comfortable elsewhere. Petra Brunner has filled the place with flowers. This relaxed hostel survives with the help of its guests. Read the signs (please clean the kitchen), respect Petra's rules, and leave it cleaner than you found it. The place is one of those rare spots where a congenial atmosphere spontaneously combusts, and spaghetti becomes communal as it cooks (20 SF per bed in 6- to 15-bed rooms, showers-1 SF, no breakfast and no sheets—bring your own, hostel membership not required, no CC, Internet access-12 SF/hour, 20 meters from lift station, tel. & fax 033-855-1704, e-mail: mountainhostel@tcnet.ch).

Pension Restaurant Gimmelwald, next door, offers 12 basic rooms under low, creaky ceilings (D-110 SF, Db-130 SF, T-150 SF, Q-180 SF, 5-SF surcharge for 1-night stays). It also has sheetless backpacker beds (25–35 SF in small dorm rooms) and a similar camaraderie. Prices include a buffet breakfast. The pension has Gimmelwald's scenic terrace overlooking the Jungfrau and the hostel, and is the village's only restaurant, offering good meals (closed late Oct–Christmas and mid-April–mid-May, CC, nonsmoking rooms but restaurant can get smoky, 50 meters from gondola station; reserve by phone, plus obligatory reconfirmation by phone 2 or 3 days in advance of arrival; tel. 033-855-1730, fax 033-855-1925, e-mail: pensiongimmelwald@tcnet.ch, run by Liesi and Männi).

Maria and Olle Eggimann rent two rooms—Gimmelwald's most comfortable—in their alpine-sleek chalet. Sixteen-year town residents, Maria and Olle, who job-share the village's only teaching position and raise three kids of their own, offer visitors a rare inside peek at this community (D-110 SF, Db with kitchenette-180 SF for 2 or 3 people, optional breakfast-18 SF, no CC, last check-in 19:30, 3-night minimum for advance reservations; from gondola continue straight for 200 meters along the town's only road, B&B on left, CH-3826 Gimmelwald, tel. 033-855-3575, e-mail: oeggimann@bluewin.ch, SE fluently).

Esther's Guesthouse, overlooking the main intersection of the village, is like an upscale, mini-hostel with five clean, basic, but comfortable rooms sharing two bathrooms and a great kitchen (S-30 SF, D-70–85 SF, T-90–110 SF, Q-140 SF, no CC, 2-night minimum, make your own breakfast or pay 12 SF and Esther will make it for you, no smoking, tel. 033-855-5488, fax 033-855-5492, e-mail: evallmen@bluewin.ch, www.esthersguesthouse.ch, some English spoken).

Schlaf im Stroh ("Sleep in Straw") offers exactly that in an actual barn. After the cows head for higher ground in the summer, the friendly von Allmen family hoses out their barn and fills it with straw and budget travelers. Blankets are free, but bring your own sheet, sleep sack, or sleeping bag. No beds, no bunks, no mattresses, no kidding (20 SF, 12 SF for kids under 12, no CC, includes breakfast and a modern bathroom, showers-2 SF, open mid-June–mid-Oct, depending on grass and snow levels, almost never full; from lift, continue straight through intersection, barn marked "1995" on right, run by Esther with same contact info as above).

Eating in Gimmelwald: **Pension Gimmelwald**, the only restaurant in town, serves a hearty breakfast buffet for 13.50 SF, fine lunches, and good dinners (10–20 SF), featuring cheese fondue, a fine *Rösti*, local organic produce, homemade pies, and spherical brownies. The hostel has a decent members' kitchen but serves no food. Hotel Mittaghorn serves dinner only to its guests (15 SF); follow dinner with a Heidi Cocoa (cocoa *mit* peppermint schnapps) or a Virgin Heidi. Consider packing in a picnic meal from the larger towns. If you need a few groceries and want to skip the hike to Mürren, you can buy the essentials—noodles, spaghetti sauce, and candy bars—at the Mountain Hostel's reception desk.

The local farmers sell their produce. Esther (at the main intersection of the village) sells cheese, sausage, bread, and Gimmelwald's best yogurt—but only until the cows go up in June.

Sleeping and Eating in Mürren
(1,650 meters/5,500 feet, country code: 41, zip code: 3825)

Mürren—pleasant as an alpine resort can be—is traffic free, filled with bakeries, cafés, souvenirs, old-timers with walking sticks, GE employees enjoying incentive trips, and Japanese making movies of each other with a Fujichrome backdrop. Its chalets are prefab-rustic. Sitting on a ledge 600 meters (2,000 feet) above the Lauterbrunnen Valley, surrounded by a fortissimo chorus of mountains, the town has all the comforts of home (for a price) without the pretentiousness of more famous resorts. With a gondola, train, and funicular, hiking options are endless from Mürren. Mürren has an ATM (by the Co-op grocery), and there are lockers at both the train and gondola stations (located a 10-min walk apart, on opposite ends of town).

Mürren's helpful **TI** can find you a room, give hiking advice, and change money (July–Sept Mon–Fri 09:00–12:00, 13:00–18:30, Thu until 20:30, Sat 13:00–18:30, Sun 13:00–17:30, less off-season, above the village, follow signs to Sportzentrum, tel. 033-856-8686, www.wengen-muerren.ch). The slick **Sportzentrum** (sports center) that houses the TI offers a world of indoor activities (13 SF to use pool and whirlpool, 8 SF for Mürren, Gimmelwald, and Interlaken hotel guests, free for guests at many Mürren hotels—

Mürren

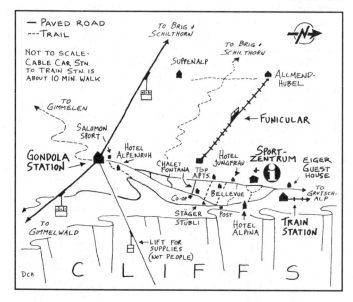

ask your hotelier for a voucher, usually open Mon–Sat 14:00–18:00, Thu until 20:00, closed Sun and in May).

Salomon Station, right at the gondola station, rents mountain bikes (25 SF/half day, 35 SF/full day, 10 SF extra for full suspension), hiking boots (12 SF/day), and is the village **Internet station** (12 SF/hr, daily 08:30–17:00, tel. 033-855-2330, www .staegersport.ch). **Top Apartments** will do your **laundry** by request (25 SF per load, 14:00–17:30, behind and across from Hotel Bellevue, look for blue triangle, please call first to drop off in morning, tel. 033-855-3706). They also have a few cheap rooms (35 SF/person first night, 25 SF/person each additional night).

Prices for accommodations are often higher during the ski season and from July 15 to August 15. Many places close in spring, roughly from Easter to late May.

Eiger Guesthouse offers good budget rooms. This is a friendly, creaky, very wooden home away from home (S-60–65 SF, Sb-80–85, D-100–110 SF, Db-130–140 SF, 39–45-SF beds in 2- and 4-bunk rooms, with sheets and breakfast, CC, closed Nov, across from train station, tel. 033-856-5460, fax 033-856-5461, www.muerren.ch/eigerguesthouse, well run by Scotsman Alan and Swiss Veronique). The restaurant serves good, reasonably priced dinners, and its poolroom (with public Internet access) is a popular local hangout.

Hotel Alpina is a simple, modern place with 24 comfortable rooms and a concrete feeling—a good thing, given its cliff-edge position (Sb-75–105 SF, Db-140–170 SF, Tb-180–210 SF, Qb-180–240 SF with awesome Jungfrau views and balconies, 4–5 person apartments-220–280 SF, CC, exit left from station, walk 2 min gradually downhill, tel. 033-855-1361, fax 033-855-1049, www.muerren.ch/alpina, Frau and Herr Taugwalder).

Chalet Fontana, run by a charming Englishwoman, Denise Fussell, is a rare budget option in Mürren with simple, crispy-clean, and comfortable rooms (35–45 SF per person in small doubles or triples with breakfast, 5 SF cheaper without breakfast, 1 apartment with kitchenette-50 SF per person, third and fourth person-10 SF each, no CC, closed Nov–April, across street from Stägerstübli restaurant in town center, tel. 033-855-2686, cellular 078-642-3485, e-mail: chaletfontana@compuserve.com). If no one's home, check at the Ed Abegglen shop next door (tel. 033-855-1245, off-season only).

Hotel Bellevue has a homey lounge, great view terrace, hunter-themed "Jäger-stübli" restaurant, and 17 good rooms at fair rates, most with balconies and views. The more expensive rooms are newly renovated and larger (Db-150–190 SF, no CC, tel. 033-855-1401, fax 033-855-1490, www.muerren.ch/bellevue, run by friendly and hardworking Ruth and Othmar Suter).

Hotel Jungfrau offers two options: a hotel with pricey, modern, and comfortable rooms and an elevator (Sb-140–150 SF, Db-260–290 SF with view, Sb-135–145 SF, Db-248–270 SF without); and a lodge in a basic, blocky, 20-room annex with well-worn but fine rooms and better Jungfrau views (Db-184–204 SF, Tb-210–225 SF, CC, near TI and Sportzentrum, tel. 033-855-4545, fax 033-855-4549, www.hoteljungfrau.ch). All rooms include the same fancy buffet breakfast; without breakfast, deduct 15 SF per person.

Hotel Alpenruh, expensive and yuppie-rustic, is about the only hotel in Mürren open year-round. The comfortable rooms come with views and some balconies (Sb-95–135 SF, Db-180–260 SF, Tb-225–270 SF depending on season, CC, elevator, attached restaurant, free sauna, tanning bed-10 SF/20 min, free vouchers for breakfast atop Schilthorn or breakfast at hotel, 10 meters from gondola station, tel. 033-856-8800, fax 033-856-8888, e-mail: alpruh@schilthorn.ch).

Eating in Mürren: For a rare bit of ruggedness, eat at the **Stägerstübli** (15–30-SF lunches and dinners). The **Kandahar Snack Bar** at the Sportzentrum has fun, creative, and inexpensive light meals, a good selection of teas and pastries, and impressive views. The **Edelweiss** self-serve restaurant is reasonable and wins the best-view award (next to Hotel Alpina). Mürren's bakery is excellent. For picnic fixings, shop at **Co-op** (normally Mon and Wed–Fri 08:00–12:00, 14:00–18:30, Tue and Sat 08:00–12:00 only, closed Sun).

Sleeping in Wengen
(1,260 meters/4,200 feet, country code: 41, zip code: 3823)

Wengen, a bigger, fancier Mürren on the other side of the valley, has mostly grand hotels, many shops, tennis courts, mini-golf, and terrific views. This traffic-free resort is an easy train ride above Lauterbrunnen and halfway up to Kleine Scheidegg and Männlichen, and offers more activities for those needing distraction from the scenery. Hiking is better from Mürren and Gimmelwald. The brand-new TI is one block from the station; turn left, go up, and look to the left, across from Central Sport (July–mid-Sept daily 09:00–18:00, mid-Sept–June Mon–Fri 09:00–12:00, 13:00–17:00, closed Sat–Sun, tel. 033-855-1414).

Several hotels offer reasonable accommodations in this otherwise upscale place. Turn left from the station along the main shopping drag to find these places: **Hot Chili Peppers** is *the* youth hangout in town, offering cheery and comfortable private rooms and dorm rooms, lockers, a common kitchen, a view deck, and a relaxed bar (45–50 SF per person in private rooms, 38 SF for dorm beds, includes breakfast, CC, tel. & fax 033-855-5020, www.wengen.com/chilis). A few doors up, the low-key **Hotel Bernerhof** is clean and a good value (S-40–60 SF, Sb-55–85 SF, D-70–110 SF, Db-100–160 SF, T-105–165 SF, dorm bed-17–23 SF, no CC, tel. 033-855-2721, fax 033-855-3358, e-mail: bernerhof@wengen.com). The same people run the pricier **Hotel Residence** across the street (Sb-70–115 SF, Db-120–190, no CC, higher prices are for view rooms, some rooms with kitchens for no extra charge, elevator, reception at Bernerhof). Prices for both hotels are without breakfast; an optional 15-SF breakfast is served at the Bernerhof.

Turn right out of the station for these places: For top views, try the tricky-to-find **Hotel Schweizerheim Garni**. It has simple but adequately comfortable rooms, a great garden terrace, and absentee management (Db-120–185 SF, buffet breakfast, CC, closed Oct–Dec and Easter–May; walk under train tracks, then down, turn right at Bären Hotel; tel. 033-855-1581, fax 033-855-2327, e-mail: schweizerheim@wengen.com). Follow the tracks uphill three minutes to **Hotel Eden**—spotless, homey, and warmly run by Kerstin Bucher (S-65 SF, D-130 SF, Db-144 SF, CC, 18 of the rooms without baths have great balcony views, breakfast-15 SF, tel. 033-855-1634, fax 033-855-3950). The same hotel runs **Eddy's Hostel**, a block away, with 26-SF dorm beds in one 20-bed room. Consider **Clare and Andy's Chalet** (one Db-74–84 SF, one Qb with 2 rooms-148–168 SF, one 4-room apartment for 4–6 people-39–44 SF/person, no CC, all rooms with balconies, breakfast-12 SF, dinner by request-28 SF, 4-night minimum preferred, tel. & fax 033-855-1712, http://home.sunrise.ch/aregez, Clare's English, Andy's Swiss).

Sleeping in Kleine Scheidegg
(2,029 meters/6,762 feet, country code: 41,
zip code: 3801)

Sleep face to face with the Eiger at Kleine Scheidegg's **Bahnhof Buffet** (dorm bed-60 SF, D-150 SF, prices include breakfast and dinner, CC, tel. 033-828-7828, fax 033-828-7830, www.bahnhof -scheidegg.ch) or at **Restaurant Grindelwaldblick** (35 SF for bed in 12-bed room, no CC, no sheets, closed Nov and May, tel. 033-855-1374, fax 033-855-4205, www.grindelwaldblick.ch). Confirm price and availability before ascending.

Sleeping near the Stechelberg Lift
(840 meters/2,800 feet, country code: 41,
zip code: 3824)

Stechelberg is a hamlet at the end of the valley. **Nelli Beer**, renting three rooms in a quiet, scenic, and folksy setting, is your best Stechelberg option (S-30 SF, D-60 SF, no CC, 2-night minimum, over river behind Stechelberg post office at big *Zimmer* sign, get off post bus at post office, tel. 033-855-3930, some English spoken).

Hotel Stechelberg, at road's end, is surrounded by waterfalls and vertical rock with 20 comfortable, spacious, and quiet rooms and a lovely garden terrace (D-76–140 SF, Db-110–140 SF, T-125 SF, Tb-150–160 SF, Qb-170–180 SF, CC, post bus stops here, tel. 033-855-2921, fax 033-855-4438, www.stechelberg.ch). **Naturfreundehaus Alpenhof** is a rugged alpine lodge for hikers (46 coed beds, 4–8 per room, 20.70 SF per bed, no CC, breakfast-8 SF, dinner-15 SF, no sheets, tel. 033-855-1202).

Here's a wild idea: **Mountain Hotel Obersteinberg** is a working alpine farm with cheese, cows, a mule shuttling up food once a day, and an American (Vickie) who fell in love with a mountain man. It's a 2.5-hour hike either from Stechelberg or from Gimmelwald. They rent 12 primitive rooms and a bunch of loft beds. There's no shower, no hot water, and only meager solar-panel electricity. Candles light up the night, and you can take a hot-water bottle to bed if necessary (S-79 SF, D-158 SF, includes linen, sheetless dorm beds-62 SF, these prices include breakfast and dinner, without meals S-35.50 SF, D-71 SF, dorm beds-18.50 SF, no CC, closed Oct–May, tel. 033-855-2033). The place is filled with locals and Germans on weekends but is all yours on weekdays. Why not hike there from Gimmelwald and leave the Alps a day later?

Sleeping in Lauterbrunnen
(780 meters/2,600 feet, country code: 41,
zip code: 3822)

Lauterbrunnen—with a train station, funicular, bank, shops, and lots of hotels—is the valley's commercial center. This is the jumping-off point for Jungfrau and Schilthorn adventures. It's idyllic in spite of the busy road and big buildings. Stop by the **TI** to check the weather forecast (June–Aug Mon–Fri 08:00–19:00, Sat–Sun 10:00–16:00, Sept–Oct Mon–Fri 08:00–12:30, 13:30–17:00, Sat–Sun 10:00–16:00, Nov–May Mon–Fri 08:00–12:30, 13:30–17:00, closed Sat–Sun, 1 block up from station, tel. 033-856-8568). You can rent a bike at **Imboden Bike** on the main street (25 SF/4 hrs, 35 SF/day, 10 SF more for full suspension, Mon–Sat 08:00–12:00, 13:30–18:30, Sun 09:00–17:30, tel. 033-855-2114). The Valley Hostel on the main street also runs an **Internet café** and a small **Laundromat** (both daily 09:00–22:00, tel. 033-855-2008).

Hotel Staubbach, a cavernous Old World place—one of the first hotels in the valley—is being lovingly restored by hardworking American Craig and his Swiss wife, Corinne. Its 30 plain, comfortable rooms are family friendly, there's a kids' play area, and the parking is free. Many rooms have great views. They keep their prices down by providing room-cleaning every third day (Db-110 SF, figure 40 SF per person in family rooms sleeping up to 6, 10 SF extra per room for one-night stays, includes buffet breakfast, CC, elevator, 4 blocks up from station on the left, tel. 033-855-5454, fax 033-855-5484, www.staubbach.ch).

Valley Hostel is practical, friendly, and comfortable, offering inexpensive beds for quieter travelers of all ages, with a pleasant garden and welcoming owners Martha and Alfred Abegglen (D-52–60 SF, beds in larger family-friendly rooms-21 SF each, new rooms with balconies, no CC, no breakfast but kitchen is available, cheese fondue on request for guests 18:00–20:00-15 SF/person, nonsmoking, Internet access, laundry, 2 blocks up from train station, tel. & fax 033-855-2008, www.valleyhostel.ch).

Chalet im Rohr, a creaky, old, woody place, has oodles of character and 26-SF beds in big one- to four-bed rooms (2 SF discount after second night, no CC, closed mid-April–mid-May, no breakfast, common kitchen, below church on main drag, tel. & fax 033-855-2182).

Masenlager Stocki is rustic and humble with the cheapest beds in town (13 SF with sheets in easygoing little 30-bed coed dorm with kitchen, no CC, closed Nov–Dec; across the river from the station, go below station to parking and take last right before garage, walk on path and then turn left over bridge, walk up and to the right 200 meters; tel. 033-855-1754).

Two campgrounds just south of town provide 15- to 25-SF beds (in dorms and 2-, 4-, and 6-bed bungalows, no sheets, kitchen facilities, no CC, big English-speaking tour groups). **Mountain Holiday Park-Camping Jungfrau**, romantically situated beyond Staubach Falls, is huge and well organized by Hans (tel. 033-856-2010, fax 033-856-2020, www.camping-jungfrau.ch). It also has fancier cabins (22 SF per person). **Schützenbach Campground**, on the left just past Lauterbrunnen toward Stechelberg, is simpler (tel. 033-855-1268, info@schuetzenbach.ch).

Sleeping in Isenfluh
(1,068 meters/3,560 feet, country code: 41, zip code: 3807)
In the tiny hamlet of Isenfluh, which is even smaller than Gimmelwald and offers better views, **Pension Waldrand** offers a restaurant and six reasonable rooms (Db-110–150 SF, Tb-210 SF, includes breakfast, no CC, hourly bus from Lauterbrunnen, tel. 033-855-1227, fax 033-855-1392).

Sleeping in Interlaken
(country code: 41, zip code: 3800)
I'd head for Gimmelwald or at least Lauterbrunnen (20 min by train or car). Interlaken is not the Alps. But if you must stay... (see map on page 908).

Hotel Lotschberg, with a sun terrace and wonderful rooms, is run by English-speaking Susi and Fritz and is the best real hotel value. Information abounds, and Fritz organizes guided adventures (Sb-100 SF, Db-145 SF, big Db-180 SF, extra bed-20–25 SF, family deals, cheaper Nov–May, CC, elevator, bar, nonsmoking, laundry 8.50 SF, bike rental, Internet access, discounted parasailing if you "Fly with Fritz"; 3-min walk from station, exit right from West station, then take a left before big Migros store, take first right and go behind the Migros, then take first left to General Guisanstrasse 31, tel. 033-822-2545, fax 033-822-2579, www.lotschberg.ch, e-mail: hotel@lotschberg.ch).

Guest House Susi's B&B is Hotel Lotschberg's no-frills, cash-only annex, run by the same people (same address and phone number as above). It has simple, cozy, cheaper rooms (Db-119 SF, apartments with kitchenettes for 2 people-100 SF; for 4–5 people-175 SF, prices drop Nov–May).

Villa Margaretha, run by perky English-speaking Frau Kunz-Joerin, offers the best cheap beds in town. It's a big Victorian house with a garden on a quiet residential street just a few minutes' walk from the West Station (D-86 SF, T-129 SF, Q-172 SF, 3 rooms share a big bathroom, 2-night minimum, apartment-156–162 SF with a 1-week minimum stay, no CC, no breakfast served but dishes and kitchenette available, lots of rules to abide by; walk up small street directly in front of the West station's parking lot entrance, go 3 blocks and look to your right for Aarmühlestrasse 13, tel. 033-822-1813).

Sunny Days B&B, run by British Dave and Swiss Brigit, is bright, colorful, cheery, and ideal for families (Sb-98–102 SF, Db-110–148 SF, each additional adult in room-45 SF, each additional child under 16-38 SF, discounts for longer stays Nov–March, CC, Internet access, laundry service; exit left out of West station and take first bridge to your left, after crossing bridges turn left on Helvetiastrasse and go 3 blocks to #29; tel. 033-822-8343, fax 033-823-8343, www.sunnydays.ch).

Hotel Aarburg offers 13 plain, peaceful rooms in a beautifully located but run-down old building five minutes' walk from the West station (Sb-70 SF, Db-110 SF, no CC, next to Laundromat at Beatenbergstrasse 1, tel. 033-822-2615, fax 033-822-6397).

Backpackers' Villa Interlaken is a creative guesthouse run by a Methodist church group. It's fun, youthful, and great for families, without the frat-party ambience of Balmer's (below). Rooms are comfortable and half come with Jungfrau-view balconies (D-82 SF, T-111 SF, Q-132 SF, dorm beds in 5- to 7-bed rooms with lockers and sheets-29 SF per person, 5 SF more per person for rooms with toilets and Jungfrau-view balconies, no CC, includes breakfast, kitchen, garden, movies, small game room, Internet access-10 SF/hr, nearby scooter rental-55 SF/half day, 85 SF/full day, no curfew, open all day, check-in from 16:00–21:00, 10-min walk from either station, across grassy field from TI, Alpenstrasse 16, tel. 033-826-7171, fax 033-826-7172, www.villa.ch).

For many, **Balmer's Herberge** is backpacker heaven. This Interlaken institution comes with movies, Ping-Pong, a Laundromat, bar, restaurant, swapping library, Internet stations, tiny grocery, bike rental, currency exchange, rafting excursions, a shuttle-bus service (which meets every arriving train), and a friendly, hardworking staff. This little Nebraska is home for those who miss their fraternity. It can be a mob scene, especially on summer weekends (dorm beds-24–26 SF, S-40 SF; D, T, or Q-28–34 SF per person, includes sheets and breakfast, CC, nonsmoking, open year-round, reservations recommended 5 days in advance, Hauptstrasse 23, in Matten, 15-min walk from either Interlaken station, tel. 033-822-1961, fax 033-823-3261, www.balmers.com, e-mail: balmers@tcnet.ch).

Happy Inn Lodge has cheap rooms above a lively, noisy restaurant a five-minute walk from the West station (S-30–40 SF, D-60–80 SF, dorm beds-20–22 SF, breakfast-7 SF, no CC, Rosenstrasse 17, tel. 033-822-3225, fax 033-822-3268, www.happy-inn.com).

Transportation Connections—Interlaken

If you plan to arrive in Switzerland at the Zurich Airport and want to head straight for Interlaken and the Alps, see "Zurich Airport," below. Train info: tel. 0900-300-300 (press 4 for English).

From Interlaken by train to: Spiez (2/hr, 20 min), **Brienz** (hrly, 20 min), **Bern** (hrly, 1 hr). While there are a few long trains from Interlaken, you'll generally connect from Bern.

By train from Bern to: Lausanne (hrly, 70 min), **Zurich**

(hrly, 70 min), **Appenzell** (hrly, 4.25, transfers in Zurich and Gossau or Bern and Gossau, or 5 hrs, change in Luzern and Herisau), **Salzburg** (4/day, 8 hrs, transfers include Zurich), **Munich** (7/day, 5.5–6.5 hrs, transfers in Zurich or Mannheim), **Frankfurt** (hrly, 4.5 hrs, some direct, some transfer in Basel or Mannheim), **Paris** (4/day, 4.5 hrs).

Interlaken to Gimmelwald: Take the train from the Interlaken East (*Ost*) Station to Lauterbrunnen, then cross the street to catch the funicular to Mürren. Ride up to Grütschalp, where a special scenic train (*Panorama Fahrt*) will roll you along the cliff into Mürren. From there, either walk an easy, paved 30 minutes downhill to Gimmelwald, or walk 10 minutes across Mürren to catch the gondola (costs 8 SF and once in Gimmelwald, you'll have a 5-min uphill hike to reach accommodations). A good bad-weather option (or vice versa) is to ride the post bus from Lauterbrunnen station (4 SF, hrly bus departure coordinated with arrival of train) to Stechelberg and the base of the Schilthornbahn gondola station (tel. 033-823-1444 or 033-856-2141), which will whisk you in five thrilling minutes up to Gimmelwald.

By car it's a 30-minute drive from Interlaken to Stechelberg. The pay parking lot (5 SF/day) at the Stechelberg gondola station is safe. Gimmelwald is the first stop above Stechelberg on the Schilthorn gondola (8 SF, 2/hr at :25 and :55, get off at first stop). Note that for a week in early May and from mid-November through early December, the Schilthornbahn is closed for servicing.

Zurich Airport

Smooth, sleek, and user friendly, the Zurich Airport is a major European transportation hub and an eye-opening introduction to Swiss efficiency. Most international flights use the B concourse. Eateries and ATMs are plentiful before and after the customs checkpoint. To reach a Suisse Bank exchange office (06:00–22:00), upscale chocolate and watch stores, and free Internet stations, bypass the immigration line and go to the back wall, behind the big staircase. The train station at the airport (with a mini-mall that includes a tidy grocery) can whisk you about anywhere you'd want to go in Europe, including downtown Zurich (5.40 SF, 10 min, leaves every 10 min—much cheaper than a 50-SF taxi ride). To reach the train station, exit the baggage claim area and ride the well-marked escalator.

Transportation Connections—Zurich Airport

By train to: Interlaken (8/day, 2.75 hrs), **Bern** (2/hrly, 1.5 hrs), **Murten** (hrly, 2.75 hrs, change in Fribourg), **Lausanne** (2/hrly, 2.75 hrs), **Munich** (4/day, 4.25 hrs), **Appenzell** (2/hrly, 2 hrs with transfer in St. Gallen or 1.5 hrs with transfer in Gossau).

APPENDIX

European National Tourist Offices in the United States

Austrian National Tourist Office: Box 1142, New York, NY 10108-1142, tel. 212/944-6880, fax 212/730-4568, www.experienceaustria.com, e-mail: info@oewnyc.com. Ask for their "Vacation Kit" with map. Fine hikes and city information.

Belgian National Tourist Office: 780 3rd Ave. #1501, New York, NY 10017, tel. 212/758-8130, fax 212/355-7675, www.visitbelgium.com, e-mail: info@visitbelgium.com. Hotel and city guides, maps, and brochures for ABC lovers—antiques, beer, and chocolates.

British Tourist Authority: 551 5th Ave., 7th floor, New York, NY 10176, tel. 800/462-2748, fax 212/986-1188, www.travelbritain.org, e-mail: travelinfo@bta.org.uk. Request the Britain Vacation Planner and free maps of London and Britain. Responsive to individual needs.

Czech Tourist Authority: 1109 Madison Ave., New York, NY 10028, tel. 212/288-0830, fax 212/288-0971, www.czechcenter.com, e-mail: travelczech@pop.net. To get a weighty information package (1-2 lbs, no advertising), send a check for $4.00 to cover postage and specify places of interest. Basic information and map are free.

Denmark (see Scandinavia)

French Government Tourist Office: For questions and brochures, call 410/286-8310. Ask for the Discovery Guide. Materials delivered in 4-6 weeks are free; there's a $4 shipping fee for information delivered in five to 10 days. Their Web site is www.franceguide.com and their offices are…

In New York: 444 Madison Ave., 16th floor, New York, NY 10022, fax 212/838-7855, e-mail: info@francetourism.com.

In Illinois: 676 N. Michigan Ave. #3360, Chicago, IL 60611-2819, fax 312/337-6339, e-mail: fgto@mcs.net.

In California: 9454 Wilshire Blvd. #715, Beverly Hills, CA 90212, fax 310/276-2835, e-mail: fgto@gte.net.

German National Tourist Office: 122 E. 42nd St., 52nd floor, New York, NY 10168, tel. 212/661-7200, fax 212/661-7174, www.visits-to-germany.com, e-mail: gntony@aol.com. Maps, Rhine schedules, events calendar, castles, winery tours, city and regional information.

Irish Tourist Board: 345 Park Ave., 17th floor, New York, NY 10154, tel. 800/223-6470 or 212/418-0800, fax 212/371-9052, www.irelandvacations.com. Useful "Ireland Magazine." Ireland map, events calendar, outdoor activities, historic sights.

Italian Government Tourist Board: Check their Web site (www.italiantourism.com) and contact the nearest office…

In New York: 630 5th Ave. #1565, New York, NY 10111, brochure hotline tel. 212/245-4822, tel. 212/245-5618, fax 212/586-9249, e-mail: enitny@italiantourism.com.

In Illinois: 500 N. Michigan Ave. #2240, Chicago, IL 60611, brochure hotline tel. 312/644-0990, tel. 312/644-0996, fax 312/644-3019, e-mail: enitch@italiantourism.com.

In California: 12400 Wilshire Blvd. #550, Los Angeles, CA 90025, brochure hotline tel 310/820-0098, tel. 310/820-1898, fax 310/820-6357, e-mail: enitla@earthlink.net.

Netherlands Board of Tourism: 355 Lexington Ave., 19th floor, New York, NY 10017, tel. 888/GO-HOLLAND, fax 212/370-9507, www.goholland.com, e-mail: info@goholland .com. Great country map, events calendar, seasonal brochures, $3 donation requested for mailing.

Scandinavian Tourism: P.O. Box 4649, Grand Central Station, New York, NY 10163, tel. 212/885-9700, fax 212/885-9710, www.goscandinavia.com, e-mail: info@goscandinavia.com. Good general booklets on all the Scandinavian countries. Be sure to also ask for specific country info and city maps.

Tourist Office of Spain: Visit the Web sites (www.okspain .org and www.tourspain.es) and contact the nearest office…

In New York: 666 5th Ave., 35th floor, New York, NY 10103, tel. 212/265-8822, fax 212/265-8864, e-mail: oetny@tourspain.es.

In Illinois: 845 N. Michigan Ave. #915E, Chicago, IL 60611, tel. 312/642-1992, fax 312/642-9817, e-mail: chicago@tourspain.es.

In Florida: 1221 Brickell Ave. #1850, Miami, FL 33131, tel. 305/358-1992, fax 305/358-8223, e-mail: oetmiami@tourspain.es.

In California: 8383 Wilshire Blvd. #960, Beverly Hills, CA 90211, tel. 323/658-7188, fax 323/658-1061, e-mail: espanalax@aol.com.

Switzerland Tourism: For questions and brochures call 877/794-8037. Comprehensive "Welcome to the Best of Switzerland" brochure, great maps and hiking material. Or contact 608 5th Ave., New York, NY 10020, fax 914/682-9093, www.myswitzerland.com, e-mail: info.usa@switzerlandtourism.ch.

Let's Talk Telephones

To make international calls, you need to break the codes: the international access codes and country codes (see below). For information on making local, long-distance, and international calls, see "Telephones" in this book's introduction.

International Access Codes

When dialing direct, first dial the international access code (011 if you're calling from the U.S.A. or Canada; 00 if you're calling from Europe). Virtually all European countries use "00" as their international access code; the only exceptions are Finland (990) and Lithuania (810).

Country Codes

After you've dialed the international access code, dial the code of the country you're calling.

Austria—43
Belgium—32
Britain—44
Canada—1
Czech Rep.—420
Denmark—45
Estonia—372
Finland—358
France—33
Germany—49
Gibraltar—350

Greece—30
Ireland—353
Italy—39
Morocco—212
Netherlands—31
Norway—47
Portugal—351
Spain—34
Sweden—46
Switzerland—41
U.S.A.—1

Calling Card Operators

Remember, it's much cheaper to dial direct than to use the following calling-card operators.

	AT&T	MCI	SPRINT
Austria	0800-200-288	0800-200-235	0800-200-236
Belgium	0800-100-10	0800-100-12	0800-100-14
Britain	0800-89-0011	0800-89-0222	0800-89-0877
Czech Rep.	00420-00101	00420-00112	00420-87187
Denmark	8001-0010	8001-0022	8001-0877
France	0800-990-011	0800-990-019	0800-990-087
Germany	0800-2255-288	0800-888-8000	0800-888-0013
Ireland	1800-550-000	1800-551-001	1800-552-001
Italy	172-1011	172-1022	172-1877
Netherlands	0800-022-9111	0800-022-9122	0800-022-9119
Spain	900-990-011	900-99-0014	900-99-0013
Switzerland	0800-89-0011	0800-89-0222	0800-89-9777

Numbers and Stumblers

- Europeans write a few of their numbers differently than we do: 1 = 1 , 4 = 4 , 7= 7. Learn the difference or miss your train.
- Europeans write dates as day/month/year (Christmas is 25/12/02).
- Commas are decimal points, and decimals are commas. A dollar and a half is 1,50. There are 5.280 feet in a mile.
- When pointing, use your whole hand, palm downward.
- When counting with fingers, start with your thumb. If you hold up your first finger to request one item, you'll probably get two.

- What we Americans call the second floor of a building is the first floor in Europe.
- Europeans keep the left "lane" open for passing on escalators and moving sidewalks. Keep to the right.

Metric Conversion (approximate)

1 inch = 25 millimeters	32 degrees F = 0 degrees C
1 foot = 0.3 meter	82 degrees F = about 28 degrees C
1 yard = 0.9 meter	1 ounce = 28 grams
1 mile = 1.6 kilometers	1 kilogram = 2.2 pounds
1 centimeter = 0.4 inch	1 quart = 0.95 liter
1 meter = 39.4 inches	1 square yard = 0.8 square meter
1 kilometer = 0.62 mile	1 acre = 0.4 hectare

Climate

Here is a list of average temperatures (first line—average daily low; second line—average daily high; third line—days of no rain). This can be helpful in planning your itinerary, but I have never found European weather to be particularly predictable, and these charts ignore humidity

	J	F	M	A	M	J	J	A	S	O	N	D

AUSTRIA • Vienna

J	F	M	A	M	J	J	A	S	O	N	D
25°	28°	30°	42°	50°	56°	60°	59°	53°	44°	37°	30°
34°	38°	47°	58°	67°	73°	76°	75°	68°	56°	45°	37°
16	17	18	17	18	16	18	18	20	18	16	16

BELGIUM • Brussels

J	F	M	A	M	J	J	A	S	O	N	D
30°	32°	36°	41°	46°	52°	54°	54°	51°	45°	38°	32°
40°	44°	51°	58°	65°	72°	73°	72°	69°	60°	48°	42°
10	11	14	12	15	15	14	13	17	14	10	12

CZECH REPUBLIC • Prague

J	F	M	A	M	J	J	A	S	O	N	D
23°	24°	30°	38°	46°	52°	55°	55°	49°	41°	33°	27°
31°	34°	44°	54°	64°	70°	73°	72°	65°	53°	42°	34°
18	17	21	19	18	18	18	19	20	18	18	18

DENMARK • Copenhagen

J	F	M	A	M	J	J	A	S	O	N	D
29°	28°	31°	37°	45°	51°	56°	56°	51°	44°	38°	33°
37°	37°	42°	51°	60°	66°	70°	69°	64°	55°	46°	41°
14	15	19	18	20	18	17	16	14	14	11	12

FRANCE • Paris

J	F	M	A	M	J	J	A	S	O	N	D
34°	34°	39°	43°	49°	55°	58°	58°	53°	46°	40°	36°
43°	45°	54°	60°	68°	73°	76°	75°	70°	60°	50°	44°
14	14	19	17	19	18	19	18	17	18	15	15

	J	F	M	A	M	J	J	A	S	O	N	D

GERMANY • Berlin

23°	23°	30°	38°	45°	51°	55°	54°	48°	40°	33°	26°
35°	38°	48°	56°	64°	70°	74°	73°	67°	56°	44°	36°
15	12	18	15	16	13	15	15	17	18	15	16

GREAT BRITAIN • London

36°	36°	38°	42°	47°	53°	56°	56°	52°	46°	42°	38°
43°	44°	50°	56°	62°	69°	71°	71°	65°	58°	50°	45°
16	15	20	18	19	19	19	20	17	18	15	16

IRELAND • Dublin

34°	35°	37°	39°	43°	48°	52°	51°	48°	43°	39°	37°
46°	47°	51°	55°	60°	65°	67°	67°	63°	57°	51°	47°
18	18	21	19	21	19	18	19	18	20	18	17

ITALY • Rome

40°	42°	45°	50°	56°	63°	67°	67°	62°	55°	49°	44°
52°	55°	59°	66°	74°	82°	87°	86°	79°	71°	61°	55°
13	19	23	24	26	26	30	29	25	23	19	21

NETHERLANDS • Amsterdam

31°	31°	34°	40°	46°	51°	55°	55°	50°	44°	38°	33°
40°	42°	49°	56°	64°	70°	72°	71°	67°	57°	48°	42°
9	9	15	14	17	16	14	13	11	11	9	10

SPAIN • Madrid

35°	36°	41°	45°	50°	58°	63°	63°	57°	49°	42°	36°
47°	52°	59°	65°	70°	80°	87°	85°	77°	65°	55°	48°
23	21	21	21	21	25	29	28	24	23	21	21

SWITZERLAND • Geneva

29°	30°	36°	42°	49°	55°	58°	58°	53°	44°	37°	31°
38°	42°	51°	59°	66°	73°	77°	76°	69°	58°	47°	40°
20	19	22	21	20	19	22	20	20	21	19	21

Road Scholar Feedback for BEST OF EUROPE 2002

We're all in the same travelers' school of hard knocks. Your feedback helps us improve this guidebook for future travelers. Please fill this out (or use the online version at www.ricksteves.com/feedback), attach more info or any tips/favorite discoveries if you like, and send it to us. As thanks for your help, we'll send you our quarterly travel newsletter free for one year. Thanks! **Rick**

Of the recommended accommodations/restaurants used, which was:

Best _____

      Why? _____

Worst _____

      Why? _____

Of the sights/experiences/destinations recommended by this book, which was:

Most overrated _____

      Why? _____

Most underrated _____

      Why? _____

Best ways to improve this book:

_____

_____

I'd like a free newsletter subscription:

_____ Yes   _____ No   _____ Already on list

_____
Name

_____
Address

_____
City, State, Zip

_____
E-mail Address

Please send to: ETBD, Box 2009, Edmonds, WA 98020

Faxing Your Hotel Reservation

Use this handy form for your fax (or find it online at
www.ricksteves.com/reservation). Photocopy and fax away.

One-Page Fax

To: _____ @ _____
                hotel   *fax*

From: _____ @ _____
                name   *fax*

Today's date: ____ /_____ /____
                day   *month* *year*

Dear Hotel _____,

Please make this reservation for me:

Name: _____

Total # of people: _____   # of rooms: _____   # of nights: _____

Arriving: ____ /_____ /____ My time of arrival (24-hr clock): _____
              day   *month* *year*   (I will telephone if I will be late)

Departing: ____ /_____ /____
              day   *month* *year*

Room(s): Single___ Double___ Twin___ Triple___ Quad___

With: Toilet___ Shower___ Bath___ Sink only___

Special needs: View___ Quiet___ Cheap___ Ground Floor___

Credit card: Visa___ MasterCard___ American Express___

Card #: _____

Expiration date:_____

Name on card: _____

You may charge me for the first night as a deposit. Please fax, e-mail, or
mail me confirmation of my reservation, along with the type of room
reserved, the price, and whether the price includes breakfast. Please also
inform me of your cancellation policy. Thank you.

_____
Signature

_____
Name

_____
Address

_____
City   **State**   **Zip Code**   **Country**

_____
E-mail Address

INDEX

AVALON
TRAVEL
publishing

How far will our travel guides take you? As far as you want.

Discover a rhumba-fueled nightspot in Old Havana, explore prehistoric tombs in Ireland, hike beneath California's centuries-old redwoods, or embark on a classic road trip along Route 66. Our guidebooks deliver solidly researched, trip-tested information—minus any generic froth—to help globetrotters or weekend warriors create an adventure uniquely their own.

And we're not just about the printed page. Public television viewers are tuning in to Rick Steves' new travel series, *Rick Steves' Europe*. On the Web, readers can cruise the virtual black top with *Road Trip USA* author Jamie Jensen and learn travel industry secrets from Edward Hasbrouck of The *Practical Nomad*.

In print. On TV. On the Internet.

We supply the information. The rest is up to you.

Avalon Travel Publishing

Something for everyone

www.travelmatters.com

Avalon Travel Publishing guides are available at your favorite book or travel store.

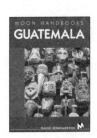

MOON HANDBOOKS

provide comprehensive coverage of a region's arts, history, land, people, and social issues in addition to detailed practical listings for accommodations, food, outdoor recreation, and entertainment. Moon Handbooks allow complete immersion in a region's culture—ideal for travelers who want to combine sight-seeing with insight for an extraordinary travel experience in destinations throughout North America, Hawaii, Latin America, the Caribbean, Asia, and the Pacific.

WWW.MOON.COM

Rick Steves shows you where to travel and how to travel—all while getting the most value for your dollar. His Back Door travel philosophy is about making friends, having fun, and avoiding tourist rip-offs.

Rick has been traveling to Europe for more than 25 years and is the author of 22 guidebooks, which have sold more than a million copies. He also hosts the award-winning public television series *Rick Steves' Europe.*

WWW.RICKSTEVES.COM

ROAD TRIP USA

Getting there is half the fun, and Road Trip USA guides are your ticket to driving adventure. Taking you off the interstates and onto less-traveled, two-lane highways, each guide is filled with fascinating trivia, historical information, photographs, facts about regional writers, and details on where to sleep and eat—all contributing to your exploration of the American road.

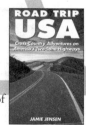

"[Books] so full of the pleasures of the American road, you can smell the upholstery."
~BBC radio

WWW.ROADTRIPUSA.COM

FOGHORN OUTDOORS guides are for campers, hikers, boaters, anglers,bikers, and golfers of all levels of daring and skill. Each guide focuses on a specific U.S. region and contains site descriptions and ratings, driving directions, facilities and fees information,and easy-to-read maps that leave only the task of deciding where to go.

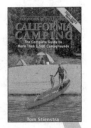

"Foghorn Outdoors has established an ecological conservation standard unmatched by any other publisher." **~Sierra Club**

WWW.FOGHORN.COM

TRAVEL SMART guidebooks are accessible, route-based driving guides focusing on regions throughout the United States and Canada. Special interest tours provide the most practical routes for family fun, outdoor activities, or regional history for a trip of anywhere from two to 22 days. Travel Smarts take the guesswork out of planning a trip by recommending only the most interesting places to eat, stay, and visit.

"One of the few travel series that rates sightseeing attractions. That's a handy feature. It helps to have some guidance so that every minute counts." **~San Diego Union-Tribune**

CITY·SMART™ guides are written by local authors with hometown perspectives who have personally selected the best places to eat, shop, sightsee, and simply hang out. The honest, lively, and opinionated advice is perfect for business travelers looking to relax with the locals or for longtime residents looking for something new to do Saturday night.

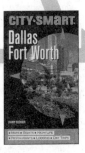

FREE-SPIRITED TOURS FROM

Rick Steves

Great Guides
Big Buses
Small Groups
No Grumps

Best of Europe ■ **Village Europe** ■ **Eastern Europe** ■ **Turkey** ■ **Italy** ■ **Britain**
Spain/Portugal ■ **Ireland** ■ **Heart of France** ■ **South of France** ■ **Village France**
Scandinavia ■ **Germany/Austria/Switzerland** ■ **London** ■ **Paris** ■ **Rome**

Looking for a one, two, or three-week tour that's run in the Rick Steves style? Check out Rick Steves' educational, experiential tours of Europe.

Rick's tours include much more in the "sticker price" than mainstream tours. Here's what you'll get with a Europe or regional Rick Steves tour...

- **Group size:** Your tour group will be no larger than 26.
- **Guides:** You'll have two guides traveling and dining with you on your fully guided Rick Steves tour.
- **Bus:** You'll travel in a full-size 48-to-52-seat bus, with plenty of empty seats for you to spread out and read, snooze, enjoy the passing scenery, get away from your spouse, or whatever.
- **Sightseeing:** Your tour price includes all group sightseeing. There are no hidden extra charges.
- **Hotels:** You'll stay in Rick's favorite small, characteristic, locally-run hotels in the center of each city, within walking distance of the sights you came to see.
- **Price and insurance:** Your tour price is guaranteed for 2002. Single travelers do *not* pay an extra supplement (we have them room with other singles). ETBD includes prorated tour cancellation/interruption protection coverage at no extra cost.
- **Tips and kickbacks:** All guide and driver tips are included in your tour price. Because your driver and guides are paid salaries by ETBD, they can focus on giving you the best European travel experience possible.

Interested? Call (425) 771-8303 or visit www.ricksteves.com for a free copy of Rick Steves' 2002 Tours booklet!

Rick Steves' Europe Through the Back Door
130 Fourth Avenue North, PO Box 2009, Edmonds, WA 98020 USA
Phone: (425) 771-8303 ■ Fax: (425) 771-0833 ■ www.ricksteves.com

FREE TRAVEL GOODIES FROM

Rick Steves

EUROPEAN TRAVEL NEWSLETTER

My *Europe Through the Back Door* travel company will help you travel better *because* you're on a budget—not in spite of it. To see how, ask for my 64-page *travel newsletter* packed full of savvy travel tips, readers' discoveries, and your best bets for railpasses, guidebooks, videos, travel accessories and free-spirited tours.

2002 GUIDE TO EUROPEAN RAILPASSES

With hundreds of railpasses to choose from in 2002, finding the right pass for your trip has never been more confusing. To cut through the complexity, ask for my 64-page *2002 Guide to European Railpasses.* Once you've narrowed down your choices, we give you unbeatable prices, including important extras with every Eurailpass, **free:** my 90-minute *Travel Skills Special* video or DVD; your choice of one of my 16 country guidebooks and phrasebooks; and answers to your "top five" travel questions.

RICK STEVES' 2002 TOURS

We offer 18 different one, two, and three-week tours (180 departures in 2002) for those who want to experience Europe in Rick Steves' Back Door style, but without the transportation and hotel hassles. If a tour with a small group, modest family-run hotels, lots of exercise, great guides, and no tips or hidden charges sounds like your idea of fun, ask for my 48-page 2002 Tours booklet.

YEAR-ROUND GUIDEBOOK UPDATES

Even though the information in my guidebooks is the freshest around, things do change in Europe between book printings. I've set aside a special section at my website (www.ricksteves.com/update) listing *up-to-the-minute changes* for every Rick Steves guidebook.

Call, fax, or visit www.ricksteves.com to get your...

☑ **FREE EUROPEAN TRAVEL NEWSLETTER**
☑ **FREE 2002 GUIDE TO EUROPEAN RAILPASSES**
☑ **FREE RICK STEVES' 2002 TOURS BOOKLET**

Rick Steves' Europe Through the Back Door

130 Fourth Avenue North, PO Box 2009, Edmonds, WA 98020 USA
Phone: (425) 771-8303 ■ Fax: (425) 771-0833 ■ www.ricksteves.com

Rick Steves' Phrase Books

Unlike other phrase books and dictionaries on the market, my well-tested phrases and key words cover every situation a traveler is likely to encounter. With these books you'll laugh with your cabby, disarm street thieves with insults, and charm new European friends.

Each book in the series is 4" x 6", with maps.

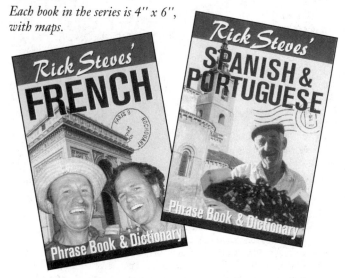

RICK STEVES' FRENCH PHRASE BOOK & DICTIONARY
U.S. $6.95/Canada $10.95

RICK STEVES' GERMAN PHRASE BOOK & DICTIONARY
U.S. $6.95/Canada $10.95

RICK STEVES' ITALIAN PHRASE BOOK & DICTIONARY
U.S. $6.95/Canada $10.95

RICK STEVES' SPANISH & PORTUGUESE PHRASE BOOK & DICTIONARY
U.S. $8.95/Canada $13.95

RICK STEVES' FRENCH, ITALIAN & GERMAN PHRASE BOOK & DICTIONARY
U.S. $8.95/Canada $13.95

Free, fresh travel tips, all year long.

Call (425) 771-8303 to get Rick's free
64-page newsletter, or visit
www.ricksteves.com for even more.